pauline frommer's

ITALY

spend less see more

2nd Edition

D0096825

by Keith Bain, Reid Bramblett, Pippa de Bruyn &
Sylvie Hogg

Series Editor: Pauline Frommer

WILEY

Wiley Publishing, Inc.

Published by:

Wiley Publishing, Inc.

111 River St.
Hoboken, NJ 07030-5774

ISBN 978-0-470-24760-0

Editor: William Travis
Production Editor: Suzanna R. Thompson
Cartographer: Andrew Murphy
Photo Editor: Richard Fox
Interior Design: Lissa Auciello-Brogan
Production by Wiley Indianapolis Composition Services
Front and back cover photo © Mark Thomas/Axiom/Getty Images
Cover photo of Pauline Frommer by Janette Beckmann

For information on our other products and services or to obtain technical support,
please contact our Customer Care Department within the U.S. at 800/762-2974,
outside the U.S. at 317/572-3993 or fax 317/572-4002.

Wiley also publishes its books in a variety of electronic formats. Some content that
appears in print may not be available in electronic formats.

Manufactured in the United States of America

5   4   3   2   1

Contents

List of Maps

An Invitation to the Reader

In researching this book, we discovered many wonderful places—hotels, restaurants, shops, and more. We're sure you'll find others. Please tell us about them, so we can share the information with your fellow travelers in upcoming editions. If you were disappointed with a recommendation, we'd love to know that, too. Please write to:

Pauline Frommer's Italy, 2nd Edition
Wiley Publishing, Inc. • 111 River St. • Hoboken, NJ 07030-5774

An Additional Note

Please be advised that travel information is subject to change at any time—and this is especially true of prices. We therefore suggest that you write or call ahead for confirmation when making your travel plans. The authors, editors, and publisher cannot be held responsible for the experiences of readers while traveling. Your safety is important to us, however, so we encourage you to stay alert and be aware of your surroundings. Keep a close eye on cameras, purses, and wallets, all favorite targets of thieves and pickpockets.

About the Authors

Keith Bain has moved around his home country of South Africa all of his life—so the travel bug is in his blood. Nevertheless, he managed to sit still long enough to get a doctoral degree in drama, and for a few years even amused himself writing and performing for the stage. He's also served his time teaching future thespians and filmmakers, but now he's quit academia to more rigorously pursue his passion for exploring the world. His assignments for Frommer's, besides recently allowing him to travel extensively in Italy, have sent him to India, Romania, Slovenia, Botswana's Okavango Delta, and even out onto the streets of Johannesburg. He's currently working on the first edition of *Pauline Frommer's Ireland*.

Reid Bramblett is the author of 10 guidebooks—7 of them to Italy, where he has lived on and off since the age of 11. He writes the weekly "The Intrepid Traveler" adventure column and is a contributing editor to *Budget Travel* magazine and Concierge.com. A Philadelphia native, he now lives in Brooklyn, New York, where he maintains the award-winning Reidsguides.com, recommended by CNN, *USA TODAY,* and *National Geographic Traveler.*

Pippa de Bruyn is an award-winning journalist, seasoned travel writer (author of *Frommer's South Africa* and *Frommer's India*), and oenophile (contributor to John Platter's *South African Wine Guide*). Her toughest assignment? Trying to fit the sybaritic pleasures of the Italian Riviera into 41 pages.

Native Californian **Sylvie Hogg** moved to Rome after graduating from Dartmouth and spent 5 fabulous years working as a tour guide and travel writer. She now lives in New York City and writes about Italy for several publications in the U.S. and the U.K. She loves rock 'n' roll, and is always planning her next trip. She is the author of *Frommer's Irreverent Guide to Rome* and *Frommer's Rome Day by Day.*

Star Ratings, Icons & Abbreviations

Every restaurant, hotel, and attraction is rated with stars ★, indicating our opinion of that facility's desirability; this relates not to price, but to the value you receive for the price you pay. The stars mean:

No stars: Good
★ Very good
★★ Great
★★★ Outstanding! A must!

Accommodations within each neighborhood are listed in ascending order of cost, starting with the cheapest and increasing to the occasional "splurge." Each hotel review is preceded by one, two, three, or four dollar signs, indicating the price range per double room. Restaurants work on a similar system, with dollar signs indicating the price range per three-course meal.

Accommodations	Dining
€ Up to 50€/night	€ Meals for 7€ or less
€€ 51€–100€	€€ 8€–14€
€€€ 101€–150€	€€€ 15€–19€
€€€€ Over 150€ per night	€€€€ 20€ and up

In addition, we've included a kids icon 🅺 to denote attractions, restaurants, and lodgings that are particularly child friendly.

Frommers.com

Now that you have this guidebook to help you plan a great trip, visit our website at **www.frommers.com** for additional travel information on more than 4,000 destinations. We update features regularly to give you instant access to the most current trip-planning information available. At Frommers.com, you'll find scoops on the best airfares, lodging rates, and car rental bargains. You can even book your travel online through our reliable travel booking partners. Other popular features include:

- Online updates of our most popular guidebooks
- Vacation sweepstakes and contest giveaways
- Newsletters highlighting the hottest travel trends
- Podcasts, interactive maps, and up-to-the-minute events listings
- Opinionated blog entries by Arthur Frommer himself
- Online travel message boards with featured travel discussions

I started traveling with my guidebook-writing parents, Arthur Frommer and Hope Arthur, when I was just four months old. To avoid lugging around a crib, they would simply swaddle me and stick me in an open drawer for the night. For half of my childhood, my home was a succession of hotels and B&Bs throughout Europe, as we dashed around every year to update *Europe on $5 a Day* (and then $10 a day, and then $20 . . .).

We always traveled on a budget, staying at the Mom-and-Pop joints Dad featured in the guide, getting around by public transportation, eating where the locals ate. And that's still the way I travel today, because I learned—from the master—that these types of vacations not only save money, but offer a richer, deeper experience of the culture. You spend time in local neighborhoods, meeting and talking with the people who live there. For me, making friends and having meaningful exchanges is always the highlight of my journeys—and the main reason I decided to become a travel writer and editor as well.

I've conceived these books as budget guides for a new generation. They have all the outspoken commentary and detailed pricing information of the Frommer's guides, but they take bargain hunting into the 21st century, with more information on using the Internet and air/hotel packages to save money. Most important, we stress "alternative accommodations"—apartment rentals, private B&Bs, religious retreat houses, and more—not simply to save you money, but to give you a more authentic experience in the places you visit.

A highlight of each guide is the chapter that deals with "The Other" side of the destinations, the one visitors rarely see. These sections will actively immerse you in the life that residents enjoy. The result, I hope, is a valuable new addition to the world of guidebooks. Please let us know how we've done! E-mail me at editor@frommers.com.

Happy traveling!

Pauline Frommer

Pauline Frommer

1 The Best of Italy

From ancient ruins to tasty cuisine, from urban verve to rural charm—how do you choose?

by Reid Bramblett

WHEN IT COMES DOWN TO IT, NEARLY EVERY REGION IN ITALY HAS QUAINT hill towns, picturesque countryside, magnificent art cities, ancient ruins, exquisite food, sublime wines, and just about any other travel cliché you want to throw in there. Italy is wonderful, it's incredible, and it's why the country remains one of the most popular destinations on the planet—but it's not going to help you plan your trip.

You probably have only 1 or 2 precious weeks of vacation time, and we suspect you have your own ideas about how to spend it. That's why we're going to cut through the brochure-speak and help you home in on the best of the best.

THE BEST OF THE BEST

While there are **ancient ruins** across the peninsula, from the Alps of the Valle d'Aosta to the very southern tip of Sicily, the real showstoppers lie in the southern half of the country. You'll find the best Roman remains in—surprise, surprise—Rome (the Colosseum, Roman Forum, Imperial Fori, and several top museums), and get the best sense of what life was like 2 millennia ago in the ancient ghost towns of Pompeii and Herculaneum, both just outside Naples, or in Ostia Antica, just a subway ride from the center of Rome.

What few folks realize is that, before the Romans, everything from Naples south was actually part of Greece (back in the 5th c. B.C., when Magna Graecia was much, much bigger), and that some of the best preserved ancient Greek ruins anywhere are actually in Sicily (Agrigento, Siracusa, Segesta, Selinunte), and on the coast south of Naples (Paestum).

When it comes to **medieval hill towns,** you have plenty of options. However, the hill-town heartland really is central Italy, particularly in Tuscany (Siena, Montepulciano, Montalcino, and especially San Gimignano, bristling with stone towers like a medieval Manhattan) and neighboring Umbria (from its capital, Perugia, to smaller cities and towns such as Gubbio, Todi, and Spoleto).

Of course, you can't swing a paintbrush in Italy without spattering it on some of the finest **Renaissance art** in the world. This is where Italy's Big Three—Rome, Venice, and Florence—really live up to their reputations. Florence (the Uffizi and Pitti Palace), Rome (the Vatican), and Venice (the Accademia) collectively have more works by old masters like Michelangelo, Donatello, Leonardo da Vinci, Raphael, Botticelli, and Titian than you could hope to see in three lifetimes. And the artwork is not limited to just the major museums. There are dozens of smaller collections, as well as countless churches where the walls (not to mention the ceilings—Sistine Chapel, anyone?) sometimes seem to be little more than grand settings on which to display masterpieces of fresco, painting, and sculpture.

LIVING *LA DOLCE VITA*

Perhaps all that's simply too much sightseeing. An endless litany of ruins, churches, and museums can make for a dull vacation. You've come to sample *la dolce vita* (the sweet life)—or even better, *la dolce far niente* (the sweetness of doing nothing). And with Italy's 8,475km (5,266 miles) of coastline, there are few better places to find that sweetness than at the **beach.** You just have to pick which kind of seaside vacation—or 2-day break from the relentless sightseeing—you want. Do you want to hang with the jet set (the Amalfi Coast), join the ever-increasing tourist hordes that hike from one fishing village to the next (the Cinque Terre), grab an umbrella and beach chair alongside vacationing Italian families (the Italian Riviera), or get off the beaten path and see what all those places looked like before they were discovered (Puglia's Gargano Peninsula)?

Or, you can opt for an **island**—no, not Sicily: the tiny islands. Now you just have to decide: Will you follow the Americans and Brits to the storied isle of Capri and its Blue Grotto; the Germans to Capri's lesser known neighbor, Ischia; or the Italians down to the string of Aeolian islands off the north coast of Sicily, where the isle of Stromboli erupts regularly like some kind of volcanic Old Faithful?

Then again, there are always the elaborate villas and sumptuous gardens of the **Lake District**—Lake Como, Lake Maggiore, Lake Garda—where the plains of Lombardy meet the Italian Alps. Speaking of which, plenty of people prefer to seek *la dolce vita* at a higher altitude. It doesn't get any higher than 3,300m (10,827 ft.) at Punta Hellbrunner atop Monte Bianco, Europe's tallest **mountain,** shared by France (which calls it Mont Blanc), and the northwestern Italian region of Valle d'Aosta. In the northeastern corner of the country, just a few hours north of Venice, rise the craggy peaks of the Dolomites, into which are tucked tony ski resorts such as Cortina d'Ampezzo.

THE BEST EATS

And, of course, there's the **food.** Don't ask us to single out just one place in Italy for its cuisine. We can't do it. That would be like choosing a favorite child. With extremely rare exceptions (usually around the biggest tourist sights and in beach resorts), it's nearly impossible to have a bad meal in Italy. These people live to eat. Their idea of an ideal evening out is not dinner, a movie, and maybe dancing; it's appetizer, main course, and dessert—preferably strung out over 3 or 4 hours. Wherever you go, you'll find regional specialties to knock out your taste buds: pizza in Naples, spaghetti carbonara in Rome, Adriatic fish in Venice, juicy steaks in Florence, swordfish in Sicily, *osso buco* in Milan, prosciutto and parmigiano in Parma, calamari in Puglia, polenta in Alpine villages, and pasta absolutely every-where you turn. Oh, and for dessert: gelato, which makes every other frozen dairy treat ashamed to call itself ice cream. (Here's a fun travel game: Race to see who can be the first to sample all three kinds of Italian gelato—the ice milk of Sicily, often delicately flavored with fresh fruits and nuts; the dense milk-and-egg-yolk-based product of Florence, which gives new meaning to the phrase "death by chocolate"; and the cream-and-custard-based gelato of northern Italy.)

To wash it all down? **Wine** from the folks who taught the French how to tend grapes. Again, every region in Italy produces phenomenal wines, from the earthy, purple-black *salice salentino* in Puglia to the light, fruity *tocai* in the Friuli, hard against the Slovenian Alps. But, if you had to pick just two regions that are constantly trying to outdo each other in the prodigious production of truly great wines, those would have to be Tuscany (the short-short list of varietals includes Chianti, Brunello di Montalcino, and Vino Nobile di Montepulciano) and the northern region of Piemonte (from which the mighty Barolo, Barbera, Barbaresco, and Nebbiolo hail—not to mention Asti spumanti, the champagne of Italian sparkling whites).

Now let's get down to specifics. You will, of course, tailor your trip to your own tastes and interest, but there are a few things no one should miss. What follow are the greatest Italian attractions and experiences—plus ways to get off the beaten path and discover the "other Italy."

THE BEST CHURCHES

ST. PETER'S (ROME)   The capital of Christendom and the pope's personal pulpit is St. Peter's Basilica, one of the most spectacular assemblages of art and architecture on the planet, and a pilgrimage point for Catholics from around the world. Michelangelo sculpted the *Pietà* as a teenager and designed the dome (great views from the top) at the height of his powers, and Bernini created the twisty-columned altar canopy. See p. 60.

THE DUOMO (FLORENCE)   Florence's cathedral is a study in the origins of the Renaissance, from the doors on the baptistery out front, which set the tone and style for all later Renaissance art, to the frescoes in the church by Paolo Uccello, one of the first masters of perspective, to Brunelleschi's ingenious dome, which revolutionized architecture. *Bonus:* You can climb up between the two layers of that dome and see Brunelleschi's genius up close, as well as the brilliant panorama of the city. See p. 122.

ST. FRANCIS'S BASILICA (ASSISI)   This massive home of the Franciscan order is a major pilgrimage destination, both for devout Catholics and art aficionados, who arrive in droves and tour buses to view the famous frescoes by Giotto—though don't miss the equally brilliant frescoes by early Sienese masters Simone Martini and the Lorenzetti brothers in the lower church of this double-decker basilica. See p. 212.

ST. MARK'S BASILICA (VENICE)   Grafted together from bits of military plunder, coated inside with golden mosaics, and sporting a quintet of vaguely Eastern-looking domes, the cathedral of Venice epitomizes this city's obsession with beauty and religious ritual, and its style reflects its ancient trading connections with the Eastern world. See p. 310.

CAPPELLA DEGLI SCROVEGNI (VENETO)   For every 100 people who visit the Giotto frescoes in Assisi, maybe one makes it to the university town of Padova, which the Gothic master painter—widely considered to be the father of

Western art—also blessed with an amazing, colorful fresco cycle in this small chapel. **Bonus:** It's an easy day trip from Venice. See p. 352.

THE DUOMO (MILAN) One of the largest churches in the world is also Italy's grandest Gothic structure, and even though it took 500-odd years to complete, the city fathers resolutely stuck by their original, medieval-looking plans. The result is stupendous: 135 marble spires, some 3,400 statues adorning the exterior, and a nave that feels like a forest of columns. Clamber up onto the roof for close-up looks at the buttresses and a lovely city panorama. See p. 403.

THE CATHEDRAL OF MONREALE (OUTSIDE PALERMO) If you thought the mosaics of Palermo's churches were something else, wait until you get to this village above the city and see the sparkling golden interior of its cathedral—not to mention the amazing Romanesque carvings and inlay work on the columns surrounding its quiet cloisters. See p. 594.

THE BEST NONECCLESIASTICAL ARCHITECTURAL SIGHTS

THE COLOSSEUM (ROME) Every modern stadium in the world is but a feeble imitation of Rome's Colosseum. Wander amid its ramparts and imagine the cheering crowds, roaring beasts, and clash of swords as gladiators battled for the amusement of Caesar and the masses alike. See p. 55.

ROMAN FORUM (ROME) Walk in the footsteps of the Caesars amid the remnants and ruins of what was once the center of the Roman world, puzzling together a picture of the ancient city from the remaining fallen pillars, corners of temples, triumphal arches, and slices of statues that fill this (free) archaeological park in the heart of Rome. See p. 52.

THE CAMPO DI MIRACOLI (PISA) Sure, it's got a famous Leaning Tower—but the brilliant green grass of Pisa's Campo di Miracoli (Field of Miracles) is also backdrop to the massive cathedral that the titling tower goes with, an amazing Gothic baptistery with perfect acoustics and a brilliant carved pulpit, a serene holy cemetery with ruinous but fascinating frescoes, and two intriguing museums. See p. 161.

PIAZZA DEL CAMPO (SIENA) The main piazza in Siena is a gorgeous sloping semicircle of brick that, on nice days, is scattered with people sunning themselves, couples sipping cappuccino at cafes, kids playing soccer, and groups strolling and chatting. The whole thing is bounded at the bottom by Siena's medieval city hall, with its amazing Gothic frescoes and 100m (328-ft.) tower. See p. 181.

THE PALLADIAN ARCHITECTURE OF VICENZA (VENETO) Vicenza's hometown hero, Andrea Palladio, is generally considered the father of High Renaissance architecture in all its geometrically precise, classically inspired glory (think Monticello in Virginia, or the marble buildings of Washington, D.C.). Vicenza has done a superb job of preserving the fine buildings of its urban fabric, including several structures designed by the master himself—though Palladio's real masterpieces are the palazzi in the hills around town. See p. 357.

POMPEII & HERCULANEUM (CAMPANIA)   The view of Mt. Vesuvius from the narrow streets of these ancient Roman ghost towns destroyed by the volcano in A.D. 79 is as eerie as it gets. You can almost smell the ashen lava, but concentrate instead on the remarkable glimpses into the daily life of those who lived—and died—here nearly 2,000 years ago. See p. 529 and 531.

THE LECCESE BAROQUE (LECCE)   Often called the Florence of the South, Lecce is overflowing with churches and palaces built of honey-colored stone along the lines of the city's unique, gorgeous take on baroque architecture— a profusion of symbolic animals, elaborate carved motifs, and complex curlicues. See p. 553.

NORMAN ARCHITECTURE (PALERMO)   Sicily was Greek, Arab, Norman, French, and Spanish long before it ever became a part of Italy. The medieval Norman rulers in particular—yes, those Normans, the ones who came from northern France and also famously conquered England in 1066—adopted a syncretic style of architecture that freely mixed Byzantine mosaics, Arabic domes, and Romanesque details, to which later rulers often added baroque flourishes and facades. See chapter 14.

ANCIENT GREEK TEMPLES (AGRIGENTO)   The 5th-century-B.C. temples on a hillside of olives and cherry trees just below the southern Sicilian city of Agrigento are among the best preserved ancient Greek ruins in the entire world— Sicily was once part of Magna Graecia, the ancient "Greater Greece." See "Touring the Ruins" on p. 613.

THE BEST MUSEUMS

THE VATICAN MUSEUMS (ROME)   The world's smallest country—Vatican City—is also home to one of the grandest museum complexes in Europe: papal apartments frescoed by Raphael; a painting gallery packed with works by Caravaggio, Michelangelo, Leonardo, and Giotto; some of the world's most famous ancient sculptures—oh, and Michelangelo's frescoes on the ceiling of the Sistine Chapel. See p. 63.

THE UFFIZI GALLERY (FLORENCE)   The 16th-century offices of the Medici family, with frescoed halls lined by ancient statuary, house their collection of some of the Renaissance's finest artworks. Don't let this museum's small size fool you: It's right up there with the Louvre, Metropolitan, and Vatican, showcasing some of the greatest artistic masterpieces in the world, including Botticelli's *Birth of Venus,* da Vinci's *Annunciation,* and Michelangelo's *Holy Family.* See p. 118.

THE ACCADEMIA (FLORENCE)   The art academy of Florence always has a long line outside. Why? Because this is where they keep Michelangelo's *David*— along with his unfinished (and far more fascinating) statues of slaves, the full-scale model for Giambologna's *Rape of the Sabines,* and a passel of fine paintings. See p. 128.

THE BYZANTINE MOSAICS OF RAVENNA (RAVENNA) On an easy day trip from Bologna you can gaze at the glittering medieval mosaics slathered on the interiors of churches and tombs in Ravenna, western Europe's last bastion of the Byzantine empire. See "Ravenna & Its Amazing Mosaics" on p. 260.

GALLERIE DELL'ACCADEMIA (VENICE) The world's most extensive collection of Venetian art is kept in a glorious Venetian palazzo on the Grand Canal. From the Byzantine-inspired technique of using gold leaf for decorative effect, to the masterful embrace of color, mood, and movement by Titian, Tintoretto, and Veronese, the Accademia provides an opportunity to penetrate beneath the surface of a vast number of superbly rendered canvases. See p. 318.

THE PEGGY GUGGENHEIM COLLECTION (VENICE) The only truly worthwhile modern-art gallery in Italy is installed in Peggy Guggenheim's former (unfinished) palazzo on the Grand Canal. It's a who's who of 20th-century artists: Max Ernst, Salvador Dalí, Joan Miró, Pablo Picasso, Constantin Brancusi, Marc Chagall, Piet Mondrian, Jackson Pollock, Alberto Giacometti, Henry Moore, Marcel Duchamp, and René Magritte. See p. 319.

THE EGYPTIAN MUSEUM (TURIN) Who would've thought that the single greatest collection of Egyptian artifacts outside of Cairo is not London's British Museum or New York's Metropolitan, but this remarkable museum in the genteel Italian industrial capital of Turin? Hey, if nothing else, it makes for a nice break from all that Italian art. See p. 445.

NATIONAL ARCHAEOLOGICAL MUSEUM (NAPLES) The artifacts housed in Naples's archaeological museum are among Western civilization's most significant, including rare finds from the ruins of Pompeii and Herculaneum, and Greek, Etruscan, and Roman artifacts that are simply unmatched in historical significance. See p. 512.

THE BEST TRAVEL EXPERIENCES

DESCEND INTO THE CATACOMBS (ROME) The web of ancient Christian burial tunnels under the Via Appia Antica park just outside Rome's city walls is an important stop for religious pilgrims and the historically curious. There are miles upon miles of these earthen corridors stacked with tombs, underground mausoleums, and marble chapels—a bit spooky, and with cheesy tour guides, but endlessly fascinating. See p. 77.

ENJOY A MARATHON DINNER (FLORENCE) We already talked about the Italian penchant for lingering over a meal for 3 or 4 hours, with all the courses—*antipasto* (appetizer), *primo* (pasta, soup, or risotto), *secondo* (meat or fish), *contorno* (side dish), *dolce* (dessert)—plenty of wine to lubricate the meal, and a grappa and espresso to finish it off. You could experience that anywhere in Italy, but if we had to pick one place to set aside the whole evening (and all plans of eating again for 24 hr.) for that marathon meal, it'd be Florence—probably at Il Latini or Cibreo Ristorante. See "Dining for All Tastes" on p. 109.

PICK A FESTIVAL, ANY FESTIVAL (TUSCANY & UMBRIA)   The heart of central Italy is a festival-happy place, hosting everything from pagan parties masquerading as Christian rites to modern music fests. Tops are Gubbio's 800-year-old race of saints' shrines; the contemporary music and arts festivals of Perugia, Spoleto, and Arezzo; and Perugia's delicious Eurochocolate Festival. See chapters 4 and 5.

TOUR THE CHIANTI VINEYARDS (TUSCANY)   These vine-covered hills between Florence and Siena have dozens of wineries you can tour, usually for free (tippling of the product included), as well as plenty of picturesque hill towns where you can pick up picnic supplies to accompany the bottles you buy directly from the source. See "Chianti Country" on p. 170.

RIDE THE VAPORETTO DOWN THE GRAND CANAL (VENICE)   For a fraction of the cost of a gondola ride, you can ply the Grand Canal on the vaporetto ① or ㉘—the motor launches that act as the public bus system in this city built on water. It's like watching a scrolling postcard of hundreds of Gothic and Byzantine palazzi, redolent of the days when Venice was a powerful maritime republic. Angle for a seat on the open-air deck up front. See p. 306.

LEARN THE SECRETS OF THE DOGES (VENICE)   The "Secret Itineraries" tour of Venice's Palazzo Ducale takes small groups of visitors into the many rooms in the palace normally locked to the public—and often hidden behind false walls, tapestries, and Renaissance paintings. This warren of secret rooms, passages, and stairways allowed the vast, often shadowy machinery of the Venetian state to continue to operate for 900 years behind the pretense of unhinged luxury that still greets visitors in the official spaces of the palace. See p. 316.

SKI THE DOLOMITES (CORTINA D'AMPEZZO)   Italy's top ski resort is a thoroughly Italian medieval village coupled with access to excellent slopes and top-notch facilities. For winter visitors, Cortina has 8 ski areas; there are another 10 within easy reach of the town. In summer, there's mountain scenery and great sports facilities to keep active types engaged. See "Cortina d'Ampezzo" on p. 383.

ATTEND THE OPERA (VENICE, MILAN, NAPLES & VERONA)   Italy is home to some of the grandest opera houses the world has ever known—and two of the greatest each emerged in 2005 from many years of restoration. Venice's Teatro La Fenice (The Phoenix) has risen from the ashes of a disastrous fire to reclaim its status as one of the world's most spectacular operatic venues. Milan's famed La Scala opera house—where Verdi was the house composer and Toscanini once waved the baton—has also finally reopened following years of restoration. Then there's the Teatro San Carlo in Naples, where the term *prima donna* (which just means "first woman"—in other words, the female lead) was born, and the magnificent 2,000-year-old Arena in Verona, the world's third-largest amphitheater, which has long since replaced gladiators with divas and become world renowned for its productions of *Aida* under the stars. See chapters 7, 8, 9, and 12.

HIKE THE CINQUE TERRE (ITALIAN RIVIERA)   While away your time on the southern end of the Italian Riviera by strolling from one lovely fishing village to another along old goat trails through terraced vineyards, gardens, and scrubby mountaintops with breathtaking views over the Mediterranean. See chapter 11.

EXPLORE THE ISLANDS OF LAKE MAGGIORE (THE LAKES)   Ferry hop your way from Isola Bella, with its ornate gardens; to Isola Madre, where peacocks stroll the exotic grounds around the Borromean palace; to Isola Superiore, a fishing village where you can dine on fresh lake trout at a table not 1.5m (5 ft.) from the water. See "Lake Maggiore" on p. 425.

HEAD TO THE TOP OF EUROPE (THE ALPS)   Ride a series of cable cars up snowy slopes and ski gondolas dangling high above glaciers to arrive at Europe's highest peak, Monte Bianco—and then continue on down the French side (call it "Mont Blanc" now) to the chichi resort of Chamonix and take a bus ride back to Italy through one of the world's longest tunnels. See p. 451.

CLIMB MT. VESUVIUS (NAPLES)   You may never again get this close to a natural disaster in waiting. Climb to the top of Mt. Vesuvius and stare down into the crater created in A.D. 79 when it destroyed Pompeii. Then turn to look out to the bay of Naples across the crusty lava fields overgrown with vineyards and dotted with houses and the Naples suburbs. All of it is smack in the path of the lava, should another major eruption occur . . . an event that's long overdue. See p. 531.

PICNIC (ANYWHERE)   Some of your most memorable meals will undoubtedly be picnics, with wonderful (and cheap!) ingredients culled from the *alimentari* (deli/grocery store), *panetteria* (bakery), *fruttivendolo* (fruit-and-veggie shop), and *vineria* (wine shop) that line the streets of every city and village. Just pick an appropriate venue—church steps, stone wall around an olive grove or vineyard, bench by the beach, even just the terrace back at your hotel room—and get ready to have a feast fit for a king on a pauper's budget. (Just don't forget the corkscrew.)

THE BEST OF THE OTHER ITALY

LEARN TO BE A GLADIATOR (ROME)   When Romans do historical reenactments, they get seriously historical, like the **Gruppo Storico Romano** group in Rome that spends its Mondays (and, in summer, Wed) dressing up as ancient gladiators and battling it out at an arena on the Appian Way. The best part: They welcome new trainees for free, 1-day lessons. See p. 82.

GET CAUGHT UP IN *CALCIO* (TUSCANY—OR ANYWHERE)   Share the locals' passion at a professional sports event—Florence and Siena have top-division Serie A (first division) soccer teams, and Siena's pro basketball team is a champion. See p. 134 and 185.

VISIT THE OLTRARNO ARTISANS (FLORENCE)   Head to the Oltrarno neighborhood to see fifth-generation craftsmen at work in ceramics, woodcarving, goldsmithing, mosaics, cobbling, and other specialties. See p. 133.

LEARN TO MAKE THE PERFECT RED SAUCE (TUSCANY, SICILY & BOLOGNA)   You could simply rave about the food in Italy when you get home—or you can learn to re-create it for your jealous friends. Try your hand at a cooking class in a Tuscan villa or restaurant in Palermo or Bologna—or stick around for a couple of weeks and attend a formal culinary school. See chapters 4, 6, and 14.

MAKE A PILGRIMAGE TO ASSISI (UMBRIA)   Though most Italians are not overtly devout, faith remains one of the cornerstones of Italian culture and society, and there are few better places to see it in action than at St. Francis's Basilica in Assisi. Masses run constantly, and are best on a Sunday—and if you can swing it to be here on Easter, you just might have a transcendent experience. See p. 212.

MASTER AN ANCIENT CRAFT (VENICE)   Tourists shell out big bucks for marbleized paper in Italy, but instead of bringing home a trinket, you can bring home a whole new skill learned from a master craftsman. And besides, how many teachers do you know who serve snacks and wine at the lessons? See p. 332.

GO BACK TO SCHOOL (ITALIAN RIVIERA)   Genoa University's annual summer school is aimed at improving foreigners' spoken Italian and grammar, and also acts as a crash course on Italian culture and history, with guest speakers from various faculties lecturing on anything from Italian cinema and art to contemporary politics. Best of all, the course, which is usually 2 weeks in September, is held at the beautiful Villa Durazzo in Santa Margherita Ligure, with gorgeous vistas of the Ligurian sea. See p. 483.

GET INTO THE UNDERBELLY OF NAPLES (NAPLES)   You need to dig deep to really understand a city's history, and Napoli Sotterranea (Underground Naples) does it better than anyone else. Take one of the winding tours through the complex of ancient underground aqueducts and cisterns that have been bomb shelters and modern-art venues. See p. 514.

SLEEP IN A *TRULLO* (PUGLIA)   Every visitor spends half the time in central Puglia snapping endless photos of its iconic whitewashed round huts with conical stone roofs. But *trulli* can be more than just a postcard sight; you can actually set up temporary housekeeping in one and feel what it's really like to live in one of these ancient structures. See p. 559.

GOING TO MARKET IN PALERMO (SICILY)   Even if you don't have the stomach for the city's exotic street food (barbecued goat intestines, anyone?), you can't go to Sicily without wandering the open-air produce, meat, and more stalls of the historic Ballarò or Vucciria markets. In these eye-popping and vibrant Palermitano institutions, you'll really begin to understand the fascinating multicultural DNA that sets Sicily apart from mainland Italy. See p. 583 and 585.

2 Rome: Where All Roads Lead

In Italy's majestic capital, the treasures of 3 millennia are yours for the taking

by Sylvie Hogg

ONCE IT RULED THE WESTERN WORLD, AND EVEN THE PARTIAL, SCATTERED ruins of that awesome empire, of which Rome was capital, are today among the most overpowering sights on earth. To walk the Roman Forum, to view the Colosseum, the Pantheon, and the Appian Way—these are among the most memorable, instructive, and chilling experiences in all of travel. To see evidence of a once-great civilization that no longer exists is a humbling experience that everyone should have.

Thrilling, too, are the sights of Christian Rome, which speak to the long and complex domination by this city of one of the world's major religions. As a visitor to Rome, you will be constantly reminded of this extraordinary history.

But it's important to remember that Rome is not just a place of the past, but also one that lives and breathes and buzzes with Vespas in the here and now. So take the time to get away from the tourist hordes to explore the intimate piazzas and lesser basilicas in the back streets of Trastevere and the *centro storico*. Indulge in oeno-gastronomic pursuits and stuff your days with cappuccinos, *trattorie*, wine bars, and gelato. Have a picnic in Villa Borghese, take a vigorous walk along the Gianicolo, or nap in the grass against a fallen granite column at the Baths of Caracalla. Rome is so compact that without even planning too much, you'll end up enjoying both its monuments and its simpler pleasures.

DON'T LEAVE ROME WITHOUT . . .

BEING AN EDUCATED TOURIST You can't come all the way to the Eternal City without visiting iconic sights like the Colosseum, the Roman Forum, the Vatican. But don't just walk by and photograph them; if you devote the time and attention they deserve—by taking a tour (see "Touring Rome—Read This Section!!" later in this chapter) or renting an audioguide—you'll pick up some fascinating knowledge that will help you make sense of the rest of Rome, too.

TAKING IN THE VIEW Rome has many majestic viewpoints where you can go to contemplate the 3,000 years of splendor below. The tree-lined Gianicolo, above the terra-cotta rooftops of Trastevere, is a classic choice for its commanding north-, east-, and south-facing panoramas. History and nostalgia buffs, however, should visit the terrace behind the Campidoglio, overlooking the ancient Forum.

11

GOING UNDERGROUND   There's about 9m (30 ft.) between modern and ancient street level, and digging down through Rome's layers, to musty archaeological grottoes and Catacombs, is one of the most atmospheric things you can do here. Venture down to the excavations below the church of San Clemente (p. 81), check out the sunken remains of the Stadium of Domitian, or head south of the center to the Via Appia Antica (p. 77) and the Catacombs (p. 77), those hand-dug labyrinths where hundreds of thousands of early Christians were buried.

VIEWING A MASTERPIECE FOR FREE   The masters of the Italian Renaissance and baroque left their life's work literally strewn about the city. Piazzas and churches don't charge admission, so you can get a museum-like dose of Michelangelo and the like just by walking around town, ducking into the right churches, and gazing at Rome's superb outdoor statuary and fountains.

WANDERING AIMLESSLY   There is perhaps no city in the world where having no agenda is more rewarding. Dive into the confusing labyrinth of streets in the district of Trastevere (p. 70) or the side streets around Piazza Navona, Campo de' Fiori, and the Jewish Ghetto, and just see where the winding maze takes you.

RIDING A SCENIC TRAM   For a mere 1€, Rome's tram lines are a great way to rest your feet and sample the various vistas and neighborhoods of the Eternal City. My favorite is the ❸, which starts at Stazione Trastevere, to Testaccio, past the Circus Maximus and the Colosseum, to San Giovanni and Porta Maggiore, through San Lorenzo and the university zone, along Viale Regina Margherita to the garden homes of the wealthy Parioli district, and back down to Villa Borghese.

HAVING A "RELIGIOUS" EXPERIENCE   The Catholic Church's busy liturgical calendar—and seemingly limitless budget for big-time productions—gives the lay visitor to Rome ample opportunities to observe Vatican pageantry at its finest. You don't even have to see the pope—you might just stumble upon a chanting procession of bishops leaving St. Peter's and feel incense fill your nostrils. Or you might happen to visit the Pantheon on Pentecost Sunday, or Santa Maria Maggiore for the Madonna della Neve ceremony (Aug 5), when rose petals shower down over the congregation.

A BRIEF HISTORY OF ROME

Well, this is Rome, so it's not going to be superbrief, but here goes:

Romulus killed Remus on the Palatine Hill on April 21, 753 B.C., and the city of Rome was off and running. Okay, so that's the simplified, mythological version of Rome's founding, but archaeologists agree: Rome began as a cluster of primitive huts atop the Palatine around the middle of the 8th century B.C. Rome was a monarchy for its first 200 years, but with the expulsion of the seventh king of Rome, Tarquinius Superbus, in 509 B.C., the Roman Republic was born. (Fast forward to 44 B.C.: The dictator Julius Caesar is assassinated because he has become too kinglike for comfort.)

During the republic, the Roman Forum was established as the center of civic life in Rome, and the first large public monuments were erected, such as the great Temple of Jupiter on the Capitoline Hill. The seven-hilled city was defended against potential invaders by fortifications built in the 5th century B.C., known as the Servian Walls (portions of which can be seen in and around Termini station). The great Roman road system began with the creation of the Via Appia in 312 B.C.

Several centuries of warfare during the republic—most notably, the defeat of Carthage in the 3rd- and 2nd-century B.C. Punic wars—brought Rome the vast influence that we associate with the Roman Empire. Technically, however, "empire" didn't begin until the first emperor, Octavian Augustus, was declared *imperator* in 27 B.C.

Excess, opulence, and peace marked the first century of Empire, when the inbred relatives of Julius Caesar, the Julio-Claudian dynasty, ruled Rome. Augustus famously said that he found Rome a city of brick and turned it into one of marble. Richly decorated temples, thermal baths, and theaters popped up all over town. Demented emperors like Caligula and Nero titillated the people with their personal lives, while Claudius, one of the great public-works emperors, brought several new aqueducts to the city. (For more on their exploits, read *The Twelve Caesars* by Suetonius—it's way racier than anything in the tabloids today!) The catastrophic fire of A.D. 64 destroyed two-thirds of the city, and Nero was blamed; when he died heirless in A.D. 68, that was the end of the Julio-Claudians.

The next 100 years in Rome were one big party (if you weren't a slave, that is). The Flavian emperors built the Colosseum and enormous public baths. At the time of Trajan's reign (A.D. 98–117), the population in the city of Rome alone was over one million. Rome was undisputed *caput mundi* (head of the world), with provinces that spread as far east as Parthia (modern Iran) and as far north as Britain. Back in Rome, there were chariot races and gladiator fights every other day, and free bread was distributed to the masses.

The heady times didn't last forever, though, and by the middle of the 3rd century A.D., barbarians caught on to the vulnerability of the city now being ruled by lame-duck emperors. Rome's second set of fortifications, the Aurelian Walls, were hastily erected in the 270s. By the 4th century, under Constantine, the vast territories of the empire had become too unwieldy to govern from Rome, so a new capital of the Roman Empire was established in Constantinople (modern-day Istanbul), closer to the geographical center of all the lands that fell under the geographical aegis of Rome.

Effectively abandoned by its strongest leaders, the city of Rome fell into a drastic period of decline in the 5th century. When barbarians sacked the city and severed most of the 13 aqueducts that gave Rome its daily water supply, public health took a nose dive, and the population dwindled. A.D. 476 is generally regarded as the year the Western Empire definitively fell, leaving only the primate of the Catholic Church in shaky control over a city constantly under barbarian attack.

In the following decades, the popes slowly adopted many of the responsibilities and the prestige once reserved for the Roman emperors. The classical city was methodically stripped of its stone and marble to build the Christian city we see today. The Middle Ages are one era of history that Rome has tried to forget—what with plagues and barbarians and having to go to church instead of the Colosseum, who can blame them? Rome has surprisingly little to show for the medieval period.

In the 14th century, Rome surged right back onto the scene in the Renaissance. Michelangelo painted the Sistine Chapel in the early 1500s, and work began on the new St. Peter's Basilica. Elsewhere in the city, the popes and noble families built grand new residences like Palazzo Farnese and restored churches with new frescoes and sculptures. Abandoned antiquities were snapped up by the Vatican Museums. It wasn't all good times, however; pope Clement VII had to hide out in Castel Sant'Angelo for 7 months when Holy Roman Emperor Charles V sacked Rome in 1527.

The following artistic era, the baroque (17th–18th c.), would really shape the look of Rome as we know it today. Such 17th-century patrons as Pope Urban VIII Barberini and artists like Bernini and Caravaggio made the city their creative playground, endowing Rome with its characteristic playful fountains, curvaceous building facades, and high-keyed sculpture and painting. St. Peter's Square, the Spanish Steps, and the Trevi Fountain all date from this ebullient period.

Italy was unified in the 19th century, and Rome became the capital of the new kingdom in 1871, after the pope surrendered to the Italian army. Almost overnight, the Church's power and influence shrank drastically. About 50 years later, the popes would have to settle for temporal power over the 44 hectares (110 acres) of Vatican City (and "spiritual power" over the Catholic world) when they signed the Lateran Treaty in 1929.

By the end of the 1800s, Rome's antiquities were seriously derelict. The Colosseum was overgrown with vegetation (a romantic sight, no doubt), and cattle were grazing in the Forum, alongside stumps of marble columns that once belonged to towering imperial temples. Scientific archaeological excavations didn't begin until the end of the 19th century, when countless monuments and works of ancient art finally emerged from beneath more than a millennium of silt and later building projects.

Mussolini made the "March on Rome" by train in 1922 and soon Rome was caught up in the fervor of Fascism. From his balcony at Palazzo Venezia, Il Duce made thundering speeches about returning Rome to its past glory. His rhetoric promised empire, virtue, and manliness, and he tried to back it up with ambitious building projects in the city center and suburbs, like Eur and the Foro Italico. Aggressive archaeological excavations continued under Mussolini, so determined was he to associate himself with the might and glory of the ancient emperors. Mussolini's own "empire" faltered, to say the least.

Rome remained the capital of the kingdom of Italy until 1946, when Italy cast off the rule of the Savoy monarchs and made Rome the capital of the new Repubblica Italiana. Rome has been the head of the continuously shifting Italian government ever since.

LAY OF THE LAND

Rome has the most compact and walkable city center of any major metropolis in Europe; however, much of the historic core of Rome does not fall under easy or distinct neighborhood classifications. Instead, most people's frame of reference when describing a location within the *centro* is the name of the nearest large monument or square, like St. Peter's or Piazza di Spagna.

CENTRO STORICO   Picturesque piazzas, fountains and masterpiece-laden churches abound in this nebulous zone that usually includes Piazza Navona and the Pantheon. It's a great area for eating and drinking, as long as you stay off the main squares. The bars of Campo de' Fiori are party central for the younger crowd.

SPANISH STEPS Sometimes called the Tridente, this toniest swath of central Rome—with ritzy lodging and retail opportunities to match—goes from Piazza di Spagna to Piazza del Popolo and back down to Piazza Augusto Imperatore. Up the hill to the east is Villa Borghese, Rome's most beloved public park.

JEWISH GHETTO The tiny pocket of medieval streets south of Via Arenula, west of Via Teatro di Marcello, and east of the Tiber is home to Europe's oldest Jewish community, though it's dwindled somewhat in recent years. The gorgeous 19th-century synagogue is the most prominent landmark in this quiet area.

TRASTEVERE Rome's bohemian "left bank"—across the river from the *centro storico* and the Jewish Ghetto, and south of the Vatican—is known for its charm and vibrant street life, and for now, it still manages to keep its authentic character intact despite a burgeoning expat population. South of Viale Trastevere is quieter and more authentic; north of Viale Trastevere is chock-a-block with merry alfresco dining and an endless stream of pedestrian people-watching.

ANCIENT ROME, MONTI & THE CELIO South and east of busy Piazza Venezia, you'll find a mix of phenomenally impressive ancient ruins, gorgeous green hills, and cozy medieval streets (in the Monti district, north of Via dei Fori Imperiali). Monti straddles either side of ugly Via Cavour and is home to some hot new shops and the best expat-frequented pubs in Rome. The Celio, directly south of the Colosseum, has lively eateries, rustic ancient churches, and the lovely "green lung" of Villa Celimontana park.

TESTACCIO & THE AVENTINE Workaday Testaccio, where the chief architectural feature is an old slaughterhouse, and the upscale Aventine, a hill with leafy residences and quiet parks, couldn't be more different, but they're next-door neighbors. Go to Testaccio for the best slice of old-school *romanitas* ("Romanness") you'll find in the modern city, and to the Aventine for tranquillity and stunning views.

THE VATICAN & PRATI North of the Vatican begins the Prati district, where many upper-middle-class Romans who can't deal with the nonsense of the historical center choose to live. Prati has wider streets and block after block of elegant 19th-century palazzi. Via Cola di Rienzo is the main commercial drag, with fashion boutiques and some of the city's best delis. Restaurants aren't the first thing that come to mind when you think of Prati (especially on the tourist- and pilgrim-soaked Vatican perimeters), but there are some good spots to be found.

TERMINI/ESQUILINO The area around the train station is a popular place to crash because it's home to (a) about 75% of the city's hotels, and (b) almost all of the budget sleeps. Trouble is, it's downright seedy (drunk vagrants far outnumber real Romans), and its grimy blocks are so far removed from the charm of Rome that, if you spend too much time here, you'll likely walk away from Rome with the wrong impression of what the city and its people are all about.

GETTING THERE & AROUND

Rome has two international airports: **Leonardo da Vinci (FCO)** in Fiumicino, 26km (16 miles) from the city center, and the smaller **GB Pastine (CIA)** in Ciampino, located 15km (9⅓ miles) from the center. Both are run by **Aeroporti di Roma** (☎ 06-65951; www.adr.it). Visitors coming from North America generally arrive in Fiumicino and those arriving via European budget carriers land at Ciampino, though bad weather and strikes have been known to divert major flights to Ciampino.

For most travelers to Rome, the most convenient way into the city from the Fiumicino airport is with the nonstop **"Leonardo Express" train** that runs from the airport terminal to Rome's central station, Roma-Termini, every 30 minutes from 6:35am to 11:35pm. The Leonardo Express takes 31 minutes and costs 11€ each way. From Termini, it's a short walk, bus ride, or 10€-to-15€ cab ride to your hotel or apartment. A second, more economical train into the city from Fiumicino is the **FR1,** a commuter train that runs every 15 to 20 minutes from 5:57am to 11:27pm and costs 5.50€ each way, regardless of where you get off. (At the airport train station, look for the double-decker train with **Fara Sabina** as its final destination.) Note that the FR1 train stops at such secondary Roman train stations as Trastevere, Ostiense (Metro ❷: Piramide), and Tiburtina (Metro ❷: Tiburtina), but it does not stop at Roma-Termini. Tickets for both trains are available from booth agents, newsstands, or at yellow self-service machines, all located

---

The Art of Crossing Streets

Traffic lights in Rome are sometimes merely a suggestion. In fact, it's a safe bet to assume that motorists and moped drivers will go through a red light rather than stop, even in the busiest parts of town. Designated pedestrian crossings mean absolutely nothing unless you are a nun or are with a group of school children in tow (so if you see either of these, cross the street with them). Despite a surprisingly low incidence of car-pedestrian accidents in Rome, there are plenty of close calls.

Some rules:

1. Never run across the street; if you trip over a cobblestone and fall, you will become a human speed bump.
2. Never, ever try to jaywalk unless you have lived here for many years. Instead, cross at the lights and zebra crossings (painted on the street). Keep in mind that these won't necessarily stop traffic.
3. When you do begin to cross, walk authoritatively and confidently, and, if you can, look the motorists in the eye.
4. If you are crossing a busy traffic square like Piazza Venezia or Piazza della Repubblica, go to the outer perimeter and cross the streets individually that lead into the piazza, even if this means you must double your distance.

—by Barbie Nadeau

Extra! Extra! Flat Taxi Fares Introduced at Rome's Airports!

In 2007, the city of Rome got rid of metered fares and random supplemental fees for cab rides between the airports and the city center. The wonderfully simple, new, all-inclusive flat fare from Fiumicino to the center of Rome, and vice versa, at any time of day, is 40€ (with a maximum of four passengers per vehicle). The flat fare from Ciampino to the center of Rome is 30€. It's standard to tip the driver 3€ for courteous service, 5€ if heavy baggage handling is involved. The new flat fares are great news for tourists—under the old fare structure, cabs used to charge about 50€ (more if an unscrupulous driver thought he could get away with it). So if your hotel offers to book you airport transfers, skip 'em, since they're likely to be more expensive than the flat taxi rate, and cabs at the airport are always plentiful.

Tip: To look at the numbers, a taxi may seem like the least economical way into town from the airport. But if you're traveling in a group, that 40€ and change to get you and your luggage delivered to the front door of where you'll be staying might be well worth it. If you do decide to take the train to Termini, just be aware that gypsies love to pick the pockets of disoriented new arrivals at the station.

within a few feet of the train platform. **Terravision** (☎ 06-65958646; www. terravision.it) offers bus service from Fiumicino into central Rome; the shuttle costs 7€ one-way and takes about an hour to reach Termini station.

To get from the Ciampino airport into the center, buses are your only public transportation option, as there's no train service here. **Cotral/Schiaffini** (☎ 800-150008; www.cotralspa.it) regional buses take you as far as Anagnina metro station; from there, it's a half-hour subway ride to Termini. Entrepreneurial Terravision has flourished thanks to the European low-cost airline boom, offering organized and comfortable coach service to the Termini area, with a schedule that usually dovetails with arrivals on budget carriers like RyanAir; a one-way ticket is 8€. Newest on the Ciampino ground transport scene is the SIT shuttle, a bus that runs from the airport to Termini station every 30 to 45 minutes; it costs 6€ each way for the 45-minute ride.

WALKING

Getting around the center of Rome is best done on foot. Sure, the Colosseum and St. Peter's are great, but the soul of Rome really lives in the little piazzas and back streets you can only see by walking. For orientation's sake, you'll find it tempting to stick to wide, straight streets like Via Nazionale, Via Cavour, and Corso Vittorio Emanuele, but it's much more rewarding to avoid these traffic-choked thoroughfares. Never mind that the doglegging alleys in the heart of Rome seem to change names every few blocks—it's actually a very easy city to navigate. Even if you're a regular walker back home, keep in mind that Rome's famous sanpietrini cobblestones will do a number on your dogs after a few hours, so wear your most broken-in, comfortable shoes (huge points if they're comfy *and* fashionable).

Rome as a Clock

An excellent central point of reference in Rome is Piazza Venezia, not the most congenial of public squares but incredibly recognizable for the giant white monument to Victor Emmanuel II (often called the wedding cake or the typewriter, but officially known as the Vittoriano) that dominates the southern side of the traffic roundabout. Imagine the Vittoriano as the center of a clock:

12 o'clock: Piazza del Popolo

1 o'clock: Trevi Fountain, the Spanish Steps, and Villa Borghese

2 o'clock: Piazza Barberini and Via Veneto

3 o'clock: Termini station

4 o'clock: The Colle Oppio and Domus Aurea

5 o'clock: The Imperial Forums and the Colosseum

6 o'clock: The Roman Forum, the Palatine, and the Circus Maximus

7 o'clock: The Aventine and Testaccio

8 o'clock: The Jewish Ghetto, Tiber Island, and Trastevere

9 o'clock: Trastevere and the Gianicolo

10 o'clock: Campo de' Fiori

11 o'clock: The Pantheon, Piazza Navona, and Vatican City

The long, straight street that extends north from the Vittoriano is Via del Corso, which slices through the historical center, ending at Piazza del Popolo and the far gate into the city. This is a noisy, smog-infested thoroughfare that you don't ever really need to walk down (the roughly parallel side streets are much more interesting), but you should always know where you are in relation to it. To get your bearings, you can always see the Vittoriano from Via del Corso.

PUBLIC TRANSPORTATION

Public transportation within the city of Rome is comprehensive, though not reliable. In general, buses in the city center should run at 10- or 15-minute intervals, but often several buses from the same line are backed up at various stops and the wait can be up to 45 minutes for others. Many bus stops in the *centro* have recently implemented electronic displays that let you know how many minutes away your bus is, and they're surprisingly accurate.

Tickets for the bus, tram, and metro are available at green self-service kiosks at Termini, Largo Argentina, and Piazza San Silvestro; they are also sold by news agents displaying the ATAC sign, as well as at all tobacco shops (look for the T sign). You can also buy tickets via your mobile phone if you have GSM capability—send a text message to 48299 with the word BIT in the body of the message; the reply you'll receive serves as your ticket (good for 75 min.). The charges will show up on your phone bill. You cannot buy tickets on the bus or tram.

Four types of tickets are available:

- **BIT** (Biglietto Integrato a Tempo): 1€ for multiple rides on any tram or bus and a one-way route on the underground metro system or the Ostia-Lido train within a 75-minute time frame.
- **BIG** (Biglietto Integrato Giornaliero): 4€ for multiple rides on all buses, trams, and the underground metro system for 24 hours.
- **BTI** (Biglietto Turistico Integrato): 11€ for all bus, tram, and metro lines, including regional trains to Ostia, for 3 days.
- **CIS** (Carta Integrata Settimanale): 16€ for all bus, tram, and metro lines, including the Ostia-Lido train, for 7 days.

Monthly passes are also available for 30€. Children under 10 or shorter than .9m (3 ft.) tall travel free on all transportation networks. You must validate your ticket in the yellow machines on each bus or tram once you get on. (Feed your ticket into the slot; the machine will wheeze and choke and then spit your ticket back out at you with a time stamp on it.) Tickets are rarely checked, though if you are caught without one, you will be fined 51€ on the spot. Validate your ticket for the underground system at turnstiles leading down to the trains.

Archeobus: Easiest Way to the Catacombs & Appian Way

At just 10€, Rome's hop-on, hop-off **Archeobus** (Piazza Venezia; ☎ 06-46954695; www.atac.roma.it; daily 9am–8pm) is the most economical way to reach the significant sights outside the city walls. You can get on at any of the stops listed below, but the best place to start is at the beginning, on Piazza Venezia near the ticket kiosk. Stops include the Bocca della Verità (p. 73), Baths of Caracalla (p. 80), Porta San Sebastiano (p. 77) and the Wall Museum, the base of the Via Appia Antica, the Catacombs (p. 77), and tombs along the Appian Way (p. 77).

Buses & Trams

Bus and tram transportation is operated by **ATAC** (☎ 800-431784; www.atac.roma.it), which has a comprehensive multilingual website to help you decipher the routes. Each bus or tram stop has an ATAC board listing relevant bus lines. Express buses are green, double-length, air-conditioned vehicles; most other buses are red and also air-conditioned. When buses are orange, they're bumpy and without A/C.

Metro

I prefer to take the bus or tram whenever possible, since they afford you a view of the city as you get around, but Rome does have two underground metro lines (see the map on p. 21), **line Ⓐ (red)** and **line Ⓑ (blue).** Lines Ⓐ and Ⓑ cross at Termini, which is the only point of transfer between the two lines. The metro system does not serve the *centro storico* or Trastevere at all (because of the multitude of protected ruins under the old city), but the metro is useful for straight shots across town, and it is generally efficient, though not nearly as encompassing as the bus network. The cars on the red line are not air-conditioned, so avoid it in summer. Pickpockets are also common, usually in the form of trendily attired Gypsy girls (who will look like regular Roman teenagers to you).

USEFUL METRO STOPS

Line Ⓐ:

Ottaviano-San Pietro for the Vatican Museums and St. Peter's (handier than the stop called Cipro-Musei Vaticani)

Flaminio for Piazza del Popolo, the Pincio and Via del Corso shopping

Spagna for the Spanish Steps, Via Condotti shopping, and Via Veneto

Barberini for Via Veneto and the Crypt of the Capuchin Monks

Termini for the main train station and only point of transfer to Metro Line B

San Giovanni for the church of St. John Lateran and the Holy Stairs

Anagnina for bus connections to Ciampino airport

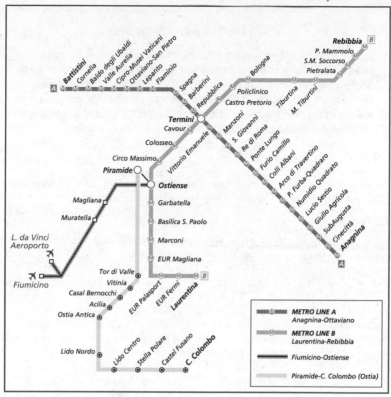

Line ⓑ:

Colosseo for the Colosseum and Roman Forum ruins
Circo Massimo for Circus Maximus, Baths of Caracalla, and Aventine Hill
Piramide for Testaccio and Ostia-Lido trains to Ostia Antica and the beaches at Ostia
EUR-Fermi for the Fascist-era monuments and museums of EUR
Ponte Mammolo for bus connections to Tivoli

Riverboat

Another recent addition to the public-transportation scene is the **Battelli di Roma** (☎ 06-6789361; www.battellidiroma.it), or **commuter** boats that glide through the muddy waters of the Tiber River. A 1-hour, multistop commuter trip is just 1€ from Tiber Island up to the northern part of Rome at Ponte Duca d'Aosta, with hourly stops at each docking point (which vary depending on the season and water levels of the river). This isn't a very efficient way of getting around Rome and don't expect anything as scenic as the Seine—the only major sight along the route is Castel Sant'Angelo. There are also seasonal options for guided tours on

---

The Eternal Acronym: SPQR

Emblazoned on ancient monuments, manhole covers, water fountains, the sides of buses, SPQR is one set of initials you'll see over and over in Rome. So, what does it mean? It stands for "Senatus Populus Que Romanus," or "The Senate and the People of Rome." It was unveiled 24 centuries ago, making it the oldest acronym still in use, and it's still used to identify all public-works projects in the modern city.

---

the river boats, starting with a 1-hour guided tour for 10€, or a 2½-hour dinner boat tour for 43€, which departs from Ponte Sant'Angelo at 8pm.

Taxis

Licensed taxis in Rome are white, with the red COMUNE DI ROMA insignia on the door, and always have a meter. Technically, cabs are only allowed to pick up new fares at taxi stands, so don't count on hailing one on any old street corner. You can also call a cab (or have your hotel or restaurant do it for you) to meet you at your exact location: Try ☎ 06-3570, 06-4994, 06-4157, or 06-6645. Expect a wait of at least 15 minutes during peak times or in the rain.

Sometimes, no cabs are available at all. However, cabs are always plentiful in the early morning, so don't worry about not finding one to take you to the train station or airport for early departures. The base fare Monday through Saturday from 7am to 10pm is 2.33€, and 4.91€ from 10pm to 7am; on Sunday and holidays it's 3.36€. For trips within the city (for example, to the train station but not to the airport), a supplement of 1.04€ is added for each large piece of luggage. For info on cab fares to the airport, see p. 17. Within the city center, tip your driver 1€ for good service. Tip courteous drivers 3€ to 5€ for airport trips.

DRIVING

Driving in Rome is not as hard as it looks; parking, on the other hand, is a nightmare. So, if your trip to Rome will be confined mostly to the city center, I'd suggest you skip the car. Getting around the city is easy on foot, and the public transportation system for both local and regional travel is comprehensive.

An additional consideration is a recent rash of vehicle arsons, which have made it necessary to either add fire protection to your car-rental policy or park in a secure garage, which costs from 10€ to 25€ a day.

If you drive in Rome, you just need to be gutsy. Do as other Roman drivers do, because you're actually more likely to have an accident if you try to follow conventional driving rules. Remember that there are no lanes on Roman city streets, and jerking left or right on the steering wheel is the preferred method of maneuvering your vehicle. Italian traffic cops—the locally reviled *vigili urbani*—will stop you (though rarely ticket you, as a tourist) for talking on a cell phone while driving, for speeding, and for driving down a one-way street the wrong way (a common mistake foreign drivers make). The most important driving law to keep in mind is that most of the city center is also closed to all but resident traffic. These restricted zones, known as ZTL, are monitored by electronic cameras that pick up signals from residents' permits. Your rental car won't have one of these electronic permits, so you risk getting a ticket if you drive into a zone that is closed.

REGIONAL TRANSPORTATION

Regional buses to neighboring towns like Tivoli (p. 88), Cerveteri (p. 91), and Viterbo (p. 91) are run by **Cotral** (☎ 800-150008; www.cotralspa.it). Cotral does not have a presence at Termini, so you generally have to travel by metro to an outlying station (Ponte Mammolo and Cornelia are the ones most tourists will use) to get on your bus. Bus tickets to such day-trip destinations as Tivoli, Cerveteri, and Viterbo are under 5€.

Train travel in and out of Rome is very easy. Information about regional, national, and international trains can be found on one handy site: www.trenitalia. com. You can buy tickets online and pick them up at self-service kiosks at any of Rome's train stations. A second-class ticket on an InterCity train from Florence to Rome (about 2½ hr.) is 28€, and from Naples to Rome (about 2 hr.) is 22€. The EuroStar (fast train) from Venice takes 4½ hours and costs 51€ for a second-class ticket.

ACCOMMODATIONS, BOTH STANDARD & NOT

Rome's standard hotels are notoriously overpriced, but I am happy to report that the city's vacation rentals (my favorite way to stay here) are *not*. Later in this section, I'll list my favorite hotel values, but I'll start with the non-traditional choices that transform tourists into travelers. In Rome, these unusual solutions—rental apartments, B&Bs, even convents and monasteries—have two great virtues: they are cheaper than standard facilities and, in almost all cases, more memorable.

SELF-CATERING APARTMENTS

Anyone looking to get into the local swing of things in Rome should stay in a short-term rental apartment. A centrally located, "economical" hotel room in Rome goes for about 120€ per night. It may be cramped and dark, with no amenities beyond a telephone. For the same price or less, you could have your own spacious one-bedroom apartment with a terrace, washing machine, A/C, and a fridge to keep your wine in! Kind of a no-brainer, isn't it? Properties of all sizes and styles, in every price range, are available for stays of 3 nights to several weeks.

More so than other major European cities, Rome has a glut of centrally located, affordable short-term rentals. Here's why: In the Jubilee Year of 2000, when Rome was inundated with religious pilgrims, many property owners renovated their large *centro storico* apartments and cut them up into small, self-catering flats for rental to tourists. As a result, the city now has a huge supply of quaint little one- and two-bedroom, even family-friendly duplex apartments all over town—and they have become an absolute godsend for budget travelers. It is very important, however, to book your apartment through a reputable agency (I've listed several below) that will be responsive should you encounter maintenance issues, and one that will make your check-in and key pickup as smooth and hassle-free as possible.

Nearly every rental apartment in Rome is owned and maintained by a third party (that is, not the rental agency). That means that the decor and flavor of the apartments, even in the same price range and neighborhood, can vary widely. Every reputable agency, however, puts multiple photos of each property they handle on its website, so that you'll have a sense of what you're getting into. The photos should be accompanied by a list of amenities, so if A/C and a washing machine are important to you, but you can live without Wi-Fi, be sure to check for those features. (In summer you'll want to opt for that A/C!) Kitchens are a major selling point for apartments, and 99% of them have one, but don't assume. Good rental agencies will also post candid descriptions of noise level, the amount of light the apartment gets, whether there's an elevator (and if there isn't, how many steps you have to climb), as well as a comprehensive breakdown of room layout and sleeping arrangements. For example, if an apartment "sleeps six," the website should tell you if that means three double beds in separate bedrooms, or one double bed in a private bedroom and two pull-out sofa beds in the living area. Always clarify details with the agency before putting down any nonrefundable deposits. That said, many great apartments have minor quirks that you'll just have to live with—chalk it up to being in Italy!

One final note: Apartments in Rome vary greatly by neighborhood. In the Vatican area, for example, rental apartments tend to go to religious pilgrims so the decor will be spartan with little decoration beyond a crucifix on the wall and serviceable (but not very comfy) furniture. It's a newer neighborhood, so white marble will replace the quaint terra cotta found in Trastevere and the historical center. On the plus side, these apartments are generally larger and you may even score air-conditioning. Apartments in Trastevere tend to have more personality, with lived-in-feeling furniture and lots of pieces of art on the walls. In the neighborhoods between these two, expect a blend of elements.

About the Money

It's standard practice for agencies to collect 30% of the total rental amount upfront to secure a booking. When you get to Rome and check in, the balance of your rental fee is normally payable in cash only, so make sure you have enough euros before you leave home. Upon booking, the agency should provide you with detailed "check-in" procedures. Normally, you're expected to call a cell or office phone when you arrive in Rome, and then the keyholder will meet you at the front door of the property at the agreed-upon time. Before the keyholder disappears, make sure you have a few numbers to call in case of an emergency. Otherwise, most apartments come with information sheets that list neighborhood shops and services. Beyond that, you're on your own, which is what makes an apartment stay such a great way to do as the Romans do!

Recommended Agencies

The companies below are especially recommended because they rely heavily on the American market, so their pricing is more sensitive (within reason) to the current weakness of the dollar.

Roman Reference (☎ 06/4890-3612; www.romanreference.com) is the best all-around apartment rental agency in Rome. Their no-surprises property descriptions (with helpful and diplomatic tags like "better for young people") even include the "eco-footprint" for each apartment (how much energy it consumes). You can expect transparency and responsiveness from the plain-dealing staff. I recently stayed in apartment no. 366 (85€–95€ per night), a cozy studio on Via del Corso, near Piazza del Popolo, and it transported me back to my full-time Roman resident days like no hotel could ever do! The kitchen was narrow and the shower ceiling was low, but I loved being able to keep prosciutto and mozzarella in the fridge, listen to Italian pop radio on the stereo, and sip wine on the tiny rear balcony, overlooking the courtyard of a trendy women's clothing boutique. Roman Reference also handles the rental units at Villa Fortuny, a wonderfully secluded complex with modern units nestled beneath the greenery of Villa Borghese, just north of the *centro storico*. The large apartments (200€) here—most sleep at least six and have outdoor living space—are a great choice for families, or Mel Gibson, who stayed here during the filming of *The Passion of the Christ*.

Rental in Rome (☎ 06/6990-5533; www.rentalinrome.com) has an alluring website—with videoclips of the apartments—and the widest selection of midrange and luxury apartments in the prime *centro storico* zone (there are less expensive ones, too). Like Roman Reference, this agency gets glowing reviews for its friendly and attentive service. Some of its picks: In an old patrician palazzo near the Pantheon, the Monthioni Palace (120€ per night for two people) apartment is lovely Roman cliché of ochre-washed walls, exposed wood ceilings, and terracotta floors. The Bevagna Garden (100€–120€ per night for two people) is a modern apartment in the Collina Fleming quarter, a well-to-do "suburb" that's conveniently connected to the *centro* by public transportation.

Rome Accom (www.rome-accom.com) has a vast selection of apartments in the most desirable central neighborhoods of Rome. This agency tends to have higher-end listings, so you should only use it as a last resort if you can't find any properties through Roman Reference or Rental in Rome. The site allows easy browsing of all properties (without first entering your dates—a nice feature), and there's a handy option for limiting your search to properties under 150€ a night. The staff will arrange for airport pickup, and drop-off as well. This agency carefully edits what properties it lists and will even act as an intermediary between you and the landlord once you are in Rome.

Bed & Breakfast Association of Rome (www.b-b.rm.it) handles both self-catering apartments and rooms for rent within private apartments, some of which charge as little as 30€. It's a difficult site to peruse, but if you can sift through the dizzying listings, there are some great accommodations options here. Pauline Frommer used this service on her last visit to Rome and reports that "our apartment was a charmer, right in the old Jewish Ghetto area on a street where tourists rarely ventured. From our balcony in the evenings, we'd look down on our neighbors feasting in the garden below, and it became a nightly ritual for them to toast us after we toasted them and wished them a good evening. We had two large rooms and a kitchen for less than 150€ a night, perfect for my husband and our two small daughters." Pauline's experience points up the hidden value of these types of accommodations: Not only will you spend less, but you'll also be much more likely to meet actual Romans and see what the life of the city is like.

MONASTERIES & CONVENTS

Staying in a convent or a monastery can be a great bargain, but remember, these are religious houses, which means that the decor is most often stark and simple, and the rules are extensive. Cohabiting is almost always frowned upon (though

Rome Accommodations & Dining

Information ⓘ
City Walls ▬▬▬▬
Metro Ⓐ ━━Ⓜ━━
Metro Ⓑ ━━Ⓜ━━
Railway ┅┅┅┅┅┅

0 ———— 1/4 mi
0 ———— 0.25 km

DINING ◆

Al Pompiere **23**
Antica Birreria Peroni **34**
Asinocotto **27**
Caffe della Pace **14**
Checchino dal 1887 **53**
Consolini all'Arco
  di San Lazzaro **46**
Da Augusto **42**
Da Bucatino **47**
Da Enzo **26**
Da Francesco **15**
Da Gino Trattoria **12**
Da Remo **48**
Dar Poeta **40**
F.I.S.H. **32**
Franchi **5**
Frontoni **45**
Gusto **3**
Il Ciak **41**
Il Mozzicone **8**
Il Seme e La Foglia **54**
L'Oasi della Birra **49**
La Montecarlo **16**
Maccheroni **17**
Margutta Ristorarte **2**
Osteria der Belli **43**
Perilli a Testaccio **50**
Roma Sparita **28**
Sora Margherita **22**
Spirito Divino **12**
Taverna Angelica **7**
Trattoria da Giggetto **24**
Volpetti **52**
Volpetti Piu **51**

ACCOMMODATIONS ■

Aprhodite **39**
Andriatic **11**
Antica Locanda **33**
Albergo del Senato **18**
Albergo Sole **20**
Beehive **38**
Bramante **9**
Colors Hotel & Hostel **6**
Daphne Inn **35**
Hotel Cisterna **44**
Hotel Domus Tiberina **18**
Hotel Forte **36**
Hotel Lancelot **31**
Hotel Mimosa **19**
Hotel San Francesco **29**
Hotel Sant'Anna **10**
Hotel Sant'Anselmo **22**
Papa Germano **37**
Pensione Panda **4**
Relais Palazzo Taverna **13**
Smeraldo **21**
Villa Laetitia **1**

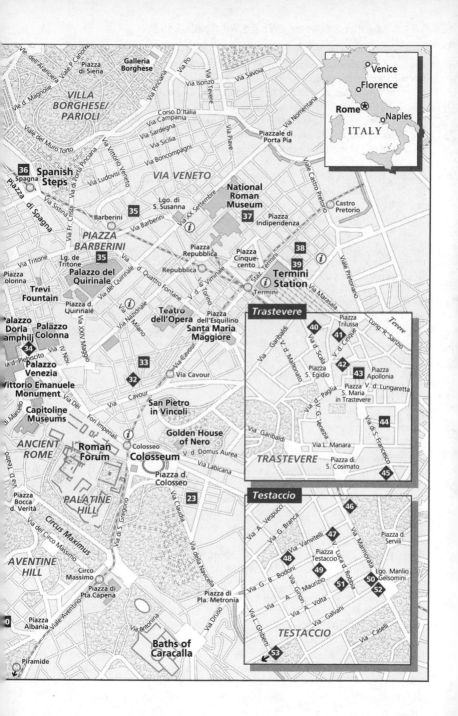

marriage licenses are rarely required), and unruly behavior is not tolerated (no staggering in after too much limoncello at dinner). Plus, there's usually a curfew. Most rooms in convents and monasteries do not have private bathrooms, but ask when making your reservation in case some are available. However, if you're planning a mellow, "contemplative" trip to Rome, and you can live with these parameters, convents and monasteries are an affordable (and fascinating) option.

Note: Prices below are per person unless otherwise noted. When booking, e-mail or call in simple English, as the sisters hail from all over the world.

Near the Vatican

€   Staying this close to Vatican City, at **Casa D'Accoglienza S. Spirito** ✖ (Borgo S. Spirito 41; ☎ 06-6861076; ssmsanpietro@libero.it; cash only) you'll be surrounded by the pomp and ceremony of the Church. The rooms are spartan, but you'll hear the bells of St. Peter's Basilica every hour, on the hour, and see Swiss Guards when you walk out the front door. It's 40€ for a double, 35€ for a triple or quadruple, 12€ children under 12, 25€ students under 25. Curfew is at 11pm in summer, 10pm in winter.

€–€€   Just across the street from the entrance to the Vatican Museums, **Suore Sacra Famiglia** (Viale Vaticano 92; ☎ 06-39091411; cash only) is perfect for exploring this area (you can be first in line when the Vatican opens!), though this convent seems a bit more stringent about the rules than others. Rooms are larger than most of the others listed here. Price per room: 30€ single, 52€ double, 70€ triple, 83€ quadruple. No breakfast, and curfew is at midnight.

On the Gianicolo

€–€€   **Suore Dorotee–Casa Fatima** ✖ (Via del Gianicolo 4A; ☎ 06-68803349; casafatima@libero.it; cash only) offers great views from the top of the Janiculum Hill, tucked in a green area perfect for those who want to appreciate Rome without the noise. The accommodations are more private and antiseptic than what you'll find in most convents, and the businesslike reception adds to the hotel-like feel. It's 77€ per person for full-board double, 67€ for half-board, and 50€ for bed and breakfast only. There's an 8€ supplement on the above prices for single occupancy. All rooms have private baths. Curfew is at 11pm.

Near Piazza Navona

€€   In terms of atmosphere and location, you definitely get your extra euros' worth at **Fraterna Domus** (Via del Monte Brianza 62, near Piazza Nicosia; ☎ 06-68802727; domusrm@tin.it; cash only). The rooms have such nice antique Roman touches as exposed wood beam ceilings and *cotto* (terra-cotta) floors, but they are "cozy" to say the least (you may have to keep your luggage closed in order to navigate around the slim double beds). The bathrooms are even smaller, and the shower is a spout hanging on the wall (no stall, so the entire bathroom gets soaked when the water is turned on—but this is a quirk you'll find in many European inns). It's 50€ for a single, 80€ for a double. All rooms have private bathrooms, and breakfast is included (additional meals on request). Curfew is at 11pm.

> ## Deal (or No Deal) Alert: Air-Hotel Packages & Internet Hotel Searches
>
> Rome is one of the top destinations in the world for travel packages, which bundle airfare, hotel, and sometimes car rental (which you probably don't need!) at one reasonable price. The cheapest of these packages generally offer well-appointed if dull hotels in areas near the train station, but there's no denying the savings: In some cases, a vacation to Italy can cost as little as $100 a day or less for airfare (not including taxes) and hotel.
>
> The following companies are particularly recommended for travelers to Rome (all have offered weeklong, off-season deals with airfares from the U.S. and accommodations from $700 per person): **Go-Today.com** (☎ 800/227-3235; www.go-today.com), **Virgin Vacations** (☎ 888/937-8474; www.virgin-vacations.com), **Gate 1 Travel** (☎ 800/682-3333; www.gate1travel.com), and **EuropeASAP** (☎ 415/750-5499; www.europeasap.com). See "Packages vs. Independent Travel" on p. 622 for more on package deals.

On the Aventine

€€   Staying at the **Villa Rosa** ✸ (Via Terme Deciane, 5; ☎ 06-5717091; villa rosa2000@libero.it; cash only) is much more like communal living with the Dominican sisters than independent accommodations. The serene location, atop the leafy Aventine Hill, is a world away from the chaos of touristy, trafficky Rome, which makes retiring here after a day of exploring such a treat. Villa Rosa's peace and relative isolation lend a real sense of belonging to those who stay here. For this reason, religious pilgrims, especially those traveling alone, flock to this lovely convent. It's 55€ for a single, 90€ for a double, including breakfast. *Warning:* The Aventine is a residential area, with very few shops and services, and public transportation connections here aren't as thorough as in other neighborhoods.

Near the Colosseum

€–€€   A supreme example of how wildly multicultural the clerical community is in Rome, **Santa Sofia** ✸ (Piazza Madonna dei Monti 3; ☎ 06-485778; santa sofia@tiscalinet.it; cash only) is run by Spanish- and Portuguese-speaking nuns from the Ukraine. (They speak English, too.) The rooms (45€ single, 70€ double, including breakfast) are very tidy and the nuns keep their distance, giving you much more privacy than many of the other convents. The location is just a few blocks from the Colosseum in an area that is brimming with ethnic restaurants and Italian favorites. Curfew is at midnight.

HOTELS IN THE HISTORICAL CENTER

Most visitors attempt to stay in this area for the simple fact that it puts them within walking distance of most of the important sights of Rome. In terms of authenticity and affordable dining options, the areas around Campo de' Fiori,

---

A Splurge with a View

€€€€   Of all the views you might wish to enjoy from your hotel room, the ancient Pantheon has got to top the list. Mere yards from the 2nd-century temple, the recently upgraded **Albergo del Senato** ★★ (Piazza della Rotonda 73; ☎ 06-6784343; www.albergodelsenato.it) has well-appointed rooms that are a relative steal, especially in low season (when the price can drop to as low as 140€; hit it wrong and you may end up paying 390€ for that same room, though). All around, this is a romantic and classy choice, with a fabulous roof terrace where you can sip wine with a bird's-eye view of the rooftops of the *centro storico*, even catching a glimpse of St. Peter's.

Piazza Navona, and the Pantheon are preferable to the Spanish Steps/Trevi Fountain area, but hotels near the Spanish Steps have the significant bonus of being near the Villa Borghese park.

Near the Spanish Steps

€€–€€€   It's no secret that **Pensione Panda** (Via della Croce 35, at Via Belsiana; ☎ 06-6780179; www.hotelpanda.it; MC, V) is the best-value hotel in the Spanish Steps area, and its 20 rooms get booked up quickly. Rooms (singles 65€–80€; doubles 75€–108€; triples 130€–140€) are spare, but not without a bit of old-fashioned charm, like characteristic Roman cotto floor tiles and exposed beam ceilings with light-colored wood. The cheaper singles and doubles don't have a private bathroom; triples are with full private bathroom only. The en-suite bathrooms tend to be cramped, however.

€€–€€€€   Okay, so its Via Veneto–area location isn't technically the historical center, but **The Daphne Inn** (Via degli Avignonesi 20 and Via di San Basilio 55; ☎ 06-87450086; www.daphne-rome.com; AE, MC, V) provides an experience that is something like staying with friends, or at least friends of friends. When you arrive, the owners sit down on the worn leather sofa in the makeshift lobby and explain the city layout; they offer suggestions and exude a sense of hospitality that is unheard of in most hotels. They offer a wide range of room choices with shared bathrooms or private bathrooms not in the room (90€–165€), or with in-room bathrooms (130€–200€). All the rooms are clean and feature new mattresses, and there's free Wi-Fi access and a lending library on-site. *One caution:* Staying here is not for those who relish privacy. There's a sense that you're part of the family and an expectation that you'll sit and talk about your day when you arrive home (which can make it a top spot for solo travelers).

€€€   Just down the street from Gregory Peck's apartment in *Roman Holiday,* the **Hotel Forte** ★ (Via Margutta 61; ☎ 06-3207625; www.hotelforte.com; AE, MC, V) is one of the better values in this area, in a classically appointed palazzo shared by antiques dealers. Doubles range from 110€–180€, depending on the season and day of the week (prices are higher on the weekends). What the hotel lacks in pizzazz it more than makes up for in its fabulous location on one of Rome's most beautiful streets. Front desk staff is polite, if not overly solicitous, and the property has Wi-Fi network and a 24-hour snack bar.

HOTELS NEAR PIAZZA NAVONA, CAMPO DE' FIORI & THE PANTHEON

€€–€€€   At first glance, the **Hotel Mimosa** ★ (Via di Santa Chiara 61; ☎ 06-68801753; www.hotelmimosa.net; MC, V) may make you wonder how it can charge so little for such a great location. The answer is that the property is owned by a noble family that doesn't need to make a profit on its hotel. Doubles (with or without bathroom) range in price from 77€ to 118€. Rooms are spacious by Rome standards, cleaner than a church, and nicely appointed, albeit hardly fancy. This is a hotel for those who need a place to sleep, without the bells and whistles and velvet curtains. The breakfast is hearty (think scrambled eggs rather than standard European continental) and the rooms are all air-conditioned. Because this hotel was converted from an army barracks, the walls between some of the 12 rooms are thin, but visitors keep coming back and noise usually isn't a problem. When booking, mention Frommer's to get a 10% discount.

€€–€€€   Beloved of student groups and budget travelers, the **Albergo Sole** ★★ (Via del Biscione 76; ☎ 06-68806873; www.solealbiscione.it; cash only) is the oldest hotel in the city and overflowing with rough-around-the-edges Roman charm. Doubles start at a mighty reasonable 95€ (without private bathroom) or 120€ (with private bathroom), and many of its rooms face the hotel's peaceful, ultra-Roman inner courtyard. Other rooms face the busy pedestrian street below, which can translate to sleepless nights when the weather is hot and you're forced to keep your windows open. (The lack of A/C in most rooms means that you'll want to think twice before booking a room here in sultry summer.) You can pay 40€ more and move up to the fifth-floor doubles, which are air-conditioned and sound-proofed. All in all, the rooms are comfortable and bright, with terrazzo floors and antique furniture, but the real perk is all the common outdoor space—sunny terraces and shaded garden areas where you can gaze out over the rooftops.

€€€–€€€€   In the tangle of cobblestoned streets south of Campo de' Fiori, the **Smeraldo** (Vicolo dei Chiodaroli 9, at Via dei Chiavari; ☎ 06-6875929; www.smeraldoroma.com; AE, MC, V) is the priciest of the "cheap" inns in this neighborhood, mostly because all rooms have a private bathroom and A/C—an important feature to keep in mind in summer. The warm and almost elegant decor (the result of a recent refurbishing) also help justify the extra euros. All rooms (doubles 120€–160€) have TV and telephone with Internet connection capability. Definitely don't be suckered into the hotel's breakfast—there's a ridiculous 8€ charge for it, and you'll find a ton of great cafes across the street from the hotel where you can get your piping hot espresso and fresh *cornetto* (croissant).

€€–€€€   A wonderful newcomer, on a quiet alley between Piazza Navona and Castel Sant'Angelo, **Relais Palazzo Taverna** ★ (Via dei Gabrielli, off Via dei Coronari; ☎ 06-20398064; www.relaispalazzotaverna.com; AE, MC, V) packs in the modern amenities and stylish furnishings—and fresh flowers in every room—at very reasonable prices for this part of town. Decor employs an elegant Roman palette of oranges, browns, and greens (and the odd splash of chic Asian-inspired wallpaper), with brand-new, top-of-the-line fixtures. Rooms (doubles from 100€–210€) are spacious, if a bit on the dark side. The 16th-century palazzo offers guest rooms only (that is, no public areas), but breakfast is served en suite, and all units are equipped with coffee and tea makers.

HOTELS NEAR THE TRAIN STATION

You stay in this area because it's cheap. Period. As in most European cities, the area around the train station is not where you want to dine or really hang out. Still, if you're looking for bargains, you'll find them at either of the places I recommend below, or at the dozens of little hotels that line the streets here (it's possible to simply go door to door and bargain during slow periods).

€–€€   Part hostel, part hotel, **The Beehive** ★★ (Via Marghera 8, near Termini; ☎ 06-44704553; www.the-beehive.com; cash only) falls squarely in the realm of the odd but wonderful. The American owners say they conceived of this lodging–cum–art show as a "kooky dream," and they've achieved it. Rooms are decorated with art pieces and flea-market treasures and are available for a variety of budgets: 20€ to 25€ for a bed in the dorm, 70€ to 80€ for a double, or 30€ to 35€ per person in large apartments off-site (on the seedier southern side of Termini).

€–€€   The warmth and gracious welcome that Gino, of **Papa Germano** ★ (Via Calatimi, 14a, 4 blocks west of the Stazione Termini; ☎ 06-486919; www.hotel papagermano.com; AE, MC, V) extends to guests is legendary in budget-travel circles. He's simply one of the nicest guys in Rome, always ready to help out a lost or confused traveler, and his modest guesthouse is spotless. It's also inexpensive, especially for those willing to share bathroomless rooms with a couple of others, dorm-style (25€ in low season, 30€ in high season). Doubles with their own bathroom and satellite TV are also available for those who require a tad more privacy (expect to pay 65€–85€). There's a small discount if you pay in cash. Call well in advance—this is a very popular hotel with the backpacker set.

€€–€€€   As you walk into the soothing reception area of **Aphrodite** (Via Marsala 90, at Via Milazzo; ☎ 06-491096; www.accommodationinrome.com; AE, MC, V), you might wonder, is this a hotel or a day spa? Opened in 2003, it's an amazing oasis of tranquillity right across the street from the grime and chaos of Termini station. Modern rooms (doubles 90€–120€; triples 90€–150€; quads 110€–160€) feature spotless wide-plank wood floors; bland furniture in light, calming tones; and boldly painted canvases above the beds. The quality of the bathrooms, considering the price, is also remarkable: Sinks have luxurious polished travertine counters, and the walls are done up in colorful mosaics. The California-style rooftop terrace, which faces the white 1930s arcades of the station, has redwood chaises, benches, tables, white canvas umbrellas, and boxes of geraniums. Unlike other accommodations in the Termini area, which are typically crammed in along with five other sketchy hotels into the same ugly palazzo, the Aphrodite is the sole occupant in its recently restored building, which helps keep the atmosphere mellow.

HOTELS IN TRASTEVERE

Akin to New York's Greenwich Village in its festive atmosphere, abundant street life, and superb restaurants, Trastevere is one of my favorite neighborhoods and highly recommended. The downsides to a stay here involve the nighttime noise, which can be problematic (especially if you're staying above a popular bar or restaurant), and the neighborhood's distance from the sights in the historical center. If you can secure a room here, however, you'll wake up to a time warp of Rome as it was 50 years ago.

€€   It's amazing to find a boutique hotel room in the heart of popular Trastevere for around 100€, but **Domus Tiberina** (Via in Piscinula 37; ☎ 06-5803033; www.domustiberina.it; AE, MC, V) doesn't come without some sacrifices. It used to be rented by the *New York Times* correspondents, until the owners realized what a tourism gold mine they were sitting on. (Former Rome bureau chief Alessandra Stanley, now a *Times* TV critic, was its last occupant before it became a hotel.) Now, as a 10-room inn with breezy Mediterranean decor, it offers a prime location in the heart of Trastevere, just 5 minutes from the Jewish Ghetto. But many of the rooms are very small and the service is marginal.

€€€   The **Cisterna** (Via della Cisterna 7–9; ☎ 06-5817212; www.cisternahotel.it; MC, V) has been a standby for many travelers returning to Rome. Rooms are modestly furnished with original beamed ceilings and low doors; room no. 57 is the largest and room no. 40 has a terrace. There is a small garden with a fountain for visitors, but the area, close to the busy Viale Trastevere, is often noisy and dusty. While the hotel could use a few refurbishments—it is not as nice as others in this list—it's still a decent value, at 140€ a night for a double.

€€€   An option that takes you to the very edge of Trastevere, closer to the Porta Portese gate than the church of Santa Maria, is the **San Francesco** ✦ (Via Jacopa de' Settesoli 7; ☎ 06-58300051; fax 06-58333413; www.hotelsanfrancesco.net; AE, MC, V), which is new to the area and will soon likely be a favorite for return visitors. The doubles, which start at 135€, are small, even by local hotel standards, but the bathrooms are downright palatial. The San Francesco oozes character; one of its best features is a top-floor garden that overlooks the other terra-cotta rooftops and church bell towers of this district.

HOTELS ON THE AVENTINE HILL

€€€   A trio of adjacent hotels under the same moniker offer very good value for the rooms: the hotel **Sant'Anselmo** (Piazza S. Anselmo 2; ☎ 06-5745174; AE, MC, V) and its cousins, the hotel **Aventino** (Via S. Domenico 10; ☎ 06-5783214; AE, MC, V) and the **Villa San Pio** (Via S. Melania 19; ☎ 06-570057; AE, MC, V). The website for all three is www.aventinohotels.com. The neighborhood is an upscale district where the residents demand quiet and decorum, which makes it a perfectly tranquil oasis in the center of the city. Here you are just minutes from the great restaurants of Testaccio and across the river from the nightlife of Trastevere. The rooms have an aristocratic touch thanks to replicated period decorations. There are very expensive rooms in the main hotel Sant'Anselmo (doubles from 180€), where celebrities and diplomats stay, but everyone comes together in the morning for breakfast in the garden. Rooms at the Aventino start at 120€. Rooms at the classy Villa San Pio start at 150€.

HOTELS NEAR THE COLOSSEUM

Staying near the Colosseum is a favorite of large tour groups, and, as a result, almost everything in this neighborhood has been diluted—from the fare at the local restaurants to the character of the area, which seems to be dwindling at an alarming speed. Still, waking up with a view of the Flavian Amphitheater is a thrill.

€€€–€€€€   **Hotel Lancelot** ★★ (Via Capo d'Africa 47; ☎ 06-70450615; www.lancelothotel.com, AE, DC, MC, V) is a mainstay for consultants to the Food and Agriculture Organization of the United Nations, down the road. It has a wonderfully homey feel, and the well-used lobby living room is a great place to meet fellow travelers. The comfortable and immaculate rooms, from 115€ for a single to 180€ for a double, aren't exactly palatial, but they all have Wi-Fi and ample room for you to unpack and spread out for a longer stay. You can relax on the rooftop bar overlooking the Colosseum after a day of touring. The on-site restaurant is a relic of old-style European pensioni, and serves family-style meals at fixed times—another great social opportunity—and can accommodate the requests of vegetarian, vegan, even celiac diners. On every level, service is well above what you normally get at a hotel of this price and classification.

€€€–€€€€   A fantastic find in medieval Monti, the **Antica Locanda** ★ (Via del Boschetto 84, at Via Panisperna; ☎ 06-484894; www.antica-locanda.com; AE, MC, V) is especially suited for couples not only because of its romantic decor, but because almost all rooms here are "matrimonial" doubles (not twin beds). Each of the 13 rooms (120€–250€) is named for a different artist or composer. The Puccini is a cozy lair with a wrought-iron bedstead, buttercream walls, exposed beam ceiling, and Oriental rugs on the handsome terra-cotta tile floor. The Rossini is homey and elegant, like the guest room in your favorite relative's house, with a blue floral coverlet, brass bedstead, and dark-wood floors. In the bohemian neighborhood, you'll find a number of excellent places to eat and drink (including Rome's bastion of Indian restaurants on Via dei Serpenti), and sights like the Roman Forum are only a 5-minute walk down the hill.

HOTELS NEAR THE VATICAN

The worst deals in town are around Vatican City, where hoteliers tend to pilfer the pilgrims' pockets. Many of the hotels here cater to large tour groups and the prices are almost always too high for what they are getting. The exceptions to this rule are the nonstandard options like monasteries and self-catering apartments, where the prices are fair. Another strike against this district: The neighborhood is not within walking distance of Rome's historical center and thus is convenient only if you plan to spend the bulk of your time at the Vatican.

€€–€€€   A longtime budget favorite near Castel Sant'Angelo, the **Adriatic** ★★ (Via Vitelleschi 25; ☎ 06/6880-8080; www.adriatichotel.com; AE, MC, V) is located in a rather unhospitable-looking 20th-century building, but once you're inside the hotel the situation improves greatly. Outgoing, courteous staff offers guests a warm welcome and will do their best to ensure you have a pleasant stay.

Staying with the Guides

€-€€   My good friends (and former bosses) Pierluigi and Fulvia opened the Enjoy Rome agency and ran it for about a decade before selling it a few years back. They decided they'd rather focus their efforts on their own, personalized accommodations, and opened **Colors Hotel & Hostel** ★★ (Via Boezio 31; ☎ 06-6874030; www.colorshotel.com; cash only), which is as delightful a place as you'll find near Vatican City. Here you can choose from dorm beds or private rooms, some with bathrooms and others with shared bathroom facilities in the hall. The most economical option is a dorm bed for 20€; doubles go for 80€–130€; the most expensive is a private triple room with bathroom for 160€. The establishment is clean, the owners are friendly and helpful, and the place has a fully equipped kitchen for cooking your own meals; there are also laundry facilities and Internet access. The folks at Colors also offer two larger self-catering apartments (called Valerio's Flat and Granny's Flat) with rates starting around 100€ a night. Enjoy Rome's excellent walking tours (p. 81) can be booked through Colors, too.

The colorful, comfortable, and carpeted rooms (doubles 90€–120€) are among the most spacious you'll find in Rome at this price. Rooms at the cheaper end of the price ranges listed below have shared bathrooms; the others have full private bathrooms. In all rooms, there's a 10€-per-day supplement for A/C. Some rooms have private terraces, but all guests have access to a communal terrace with equal parts shade and sun, and mismatched Mediterranean patio furniture. The Adriatic doesn't serve breakfast, but there's a bar/cafeteria right across the street where you can get your morning cappuccino and pastry for under 2€. With such a handy location, the Adriatic is recommended by many guidebooks and gets a lot of word-of-mouth business, so book as early as possible.

€€€   The **Bramante** (Via delle Palline 24; ☎ 06-68806426; www.hotelbramante. com; AE, MC, V) will at least make you feel as if you are getting what you pay for. The rooms, which start at 150€ for a double, are modestly furnished, but the walls are soundproofed, the beds are large, and the bathrooms are bigger than most (though none have bathtubs). Plus, the included breakfast here is spectacular, complete with eggs and toast.

€€€€   Another fairly good deal is, unfortunately, often fully booked. Why? Well, the **Hotel Sant'Anna** ★ (Borgo Pio 133–134; ☎ 06-68308717; www.hotel santanna.com; AE, DC, MC, V) has rooms that are spacious and modern with rare amenities like dataports and room service. Doubles start at 130€, though they're hard to score: The cheaper rooms tend to go to regular customers like cardinals and journalists who have long-standing agreements with the hotel. Call far, far, *far* in advance or else you'll wind up paying about 175€ a night double here.

There's a small courtyard in the back, and the location, 1 block from St. Peter's Square, is unbeatable for those who are centering their attentions on the Vatican.

€€€€   Well north of St. Peter's, but just a short walk across the river from Piazza del Popolo, the enchanting **Villa Laetitia** ★★★ (Lungotevere delle Armi 22/23; ☎ 06-3226776; www.villalaetitia.com; AE, MC, V) is the loving creation of Anna Fendi Venturini (yes, she of fashion house fame) and a worthy splurge considering the level of style and comfort this boutique hotel affords. Set back from the street inside a private garden, all 15 immaculately refurbished rooms (150€—200€) and suites (250€—350€) have a kitchen, most have a private terrace or veranda, and the furnishings are all from Fendi's own personal collection of 19th- and 20th-century antiques. This exquisite and low-key spot is one of the most amazing new hotels to open in Rome in quite a while.

DINING FOR ALL TASTES

Dining out in the evening is the preeminent social activity for Romans and they have made an art of it. That being said, Roman menus are often quite standardized, divided into *antipasti, primi, secondi, contorni,* and *dolci.* The **antipasto** is your appetizer, which may be a bruschetta with chopped tomatoes, or some prosciutto and fresh mozzarella, or a plate of mixed fried foods like *olive ascolane* (stuffed olives). The **primo** is a pasta or risotto dish. *Primi* in Rome are usually much tastier and more interesting than the **secondi** (meat or fish dish), but a good *abbacchio al forno* (roast lamb) with rosemary potatoes can't be beat on a chilly day—yummm! The **contorno** is a side dish of vegetables, like spinach or artichokes, or a small salad. You are not obliged to order every course, and many residents confine their meals to a *primo* and some wine, which at about 7€ for a liter of the house white or red, may be the cheapest part of your meal. **Dolci** are desserts but unless I am craving a particular homemade dessert, I'll usually skip the restaurant's *dolce* and just get a gelato instead somewhere out on the town. Likewise for the postdinner espresso. And often the best way to approach an Italian meal altogether is to experiment. Ask the waiter for his recommendation: *"Cosa mi consiglia?"*

   A word on pricing: I've classified selections according to the price of the *primo.* And if *primi* are cheap, *secondi* at the same restaurant also tend to be cheap. Bear in mind that you will always find better deals if you move off the main squares and try the quieter restaurants around the back corners, down the narrow alleyways, and even in neighborhoods without a single tourist site or monument.

RESTAURANTS IN THE HISTORICAL CENTER

If you're not careful, you may find that dining close to the Spanish Steps and deep inside the historical center is about style over substance, and with a high price tag at that. Restaurants here are trendy and intentionally chic in appearance but with less of the spontaneity and culinary exuberance that you find in Trastevere and Testaccio. Nonetheless, there are some very worthwhile spots in this popular area.

Near Piazza Venezia

€   Despite its location on the heavily trafficked tourist route between ancient Rome and the Trevi Fountain, **Antica Birreria Peroni** ★★ 🧒 (Via San Marcello

19, off Piazza Santi Apostoli; ☎ 06-6795310; daily Mon–Sat; AE, MC, V) remains a locals' favorite. The overriding mood is fun, rowdy, and authentically Roman. As the name suggests, beer is the drink of choice here, so ask for a pitcher as soon as you sit down. In fact, there are quotes all over the walls praising the virtues of beer. With such a loving attitude toward drinking, it should come as no surprise that the cuisine ain't fancy—the kitchen at Birreria Peroni is all about simple, time-tested, and filling regional specialties done right, like spaghetti *all'amatriciana* and rigatoni *cacio e pepe* (from 7€), a mind-boggling array of *wurstel* (from kid-friendly hot dogs on up to fancier German sausages, from 5€), and meat *secondi* like *bistecca alla fiorentina* with home fries (12€).

Near the Spanish Steps

€€ 'Gusto ★ (Piazza Augusto Imperatore 9; ☎ 06-3226273; www.gusto.it; daily 10am–2am; AE, MC, V) has succeeded in making the experience of dining en masse both enjoyable and Italian in feel. This enormous restaurant complex, which includes a wine bar (open all day), a pizzeria (open 7:45pm–1am), a drink bar with the Italian version of bar food (12:30–3pm and 7:30pm–midnight), and an upscale restaurant (7:45pm–midnight) is perhaps as trendy as Rome gets. (Reservations are only required for the restaurant.) Most dishes are around 12€. It's a popular hangout for Italians and local expats who want to escape the monotony of the quaint trattorie, and it's a magnet for Rome's glitterati, who flock here on the weekends to be seen. If you are only in Rome for a few days, give this one a skip and head to one of the more authentic Italian restaurants. But do visit the cookbook-and-gift shop.

€€ For creative vegetarian and vegan fare, **Il Margutta RistorArte** (Via Margutta 118; ☎ 06-32650577; www.ilmargutta.it; Mon–Sun 12:30–3:30pm and 7:30pm–midnight; AE, MC, V) is the city's leading spot for herbivores. What this restaurant can do with a simple zucchini flower is amazing. Established in 1979, the cosmopolitan-feeling Margutta also attracts many nonvegetarians simply because the food is so reliably scrumptious. Try the monster salads; tuck in for the famous Garfagnana soup (12€), with chestnuts, pumpkin, and mushrooms; or sample the vegetable chickpea couscous. Reservations are recommended.

Near the Pantheon

€–€€ Eating near the Pantheon is often synonymous with spending a lot of money—with two exceptions. The ever-so-rustic **Maccheroni** ★★ (Piazza delle Coppelle 44; ☎ 06-68307895; www.ristorantemaccheroni.com; daily 1–3pm and 8pm–midnight; AE, MC, V) is the first. Dinner reservations here are highly recommended as it's always packed with boisterous Italians. The waiters are flirtatious and pin-up cute, but it's the food that makes the visit worthwhile. Start your meal with the buffalo mozzarella, which comes sprinkled with bread crumbs and olive oil, and move on to the *rigatoni alla gricia* (bacon, sheep's cheese, and pepper) for just 7€. The house wine is Chianti, and the menu looks like it hasn't been updated since the 1960s—which is lucky for anyone dining here.

€–€€ Not far away is **Da Gino Trattoria** ★ (Vicolo Rosini 4, off Via della Rotonda; ☎ 06-68734341; Mon–Sat 12:30–3pm and 7:30–10:30pm; MC, V), a fave of the politicians who work in the nearby Senate. With all the ruckus in their lives, I assume that they appreciate the fact that little changes at this tried-and-true trattoria (and so do I). Ask the matron of the restaurant for advice and she'll likely suggest the specialty *coniglio al vino bianco* (rabbit cooked in white wine, 14€); if you've never had rabbit, this recipe is fab. *Primi* are 7€ to 10€.

Near Piazza Navona

€   An eternally chic spot for a midmorning cappuccino, afternoon glass of wine, or late-night cocktail, **Caffè della Pace** ★ (Via della Pace 3/7; ☎ 06-6861216; daily 9am–2am; AE, MC, V) is on one of the prettiest side streets in the *centro storico*. Grab one of the outdoor tables here (or, if it's cold, cozy up at one of the dark-wood tables inside), and watch the pageant of Rome go by. At night, it's a hot spot for jet-setters and wannabes.

€   Dirt-cheap and immensely popular with young Romans, **La Montecarlo** ★★ (Vicolo Savelli 11, off Corso Vittorio; ☎ 06-6861877; www.lamontecarlo.it; Tues–Sun 12:30–3pm and 7:30pm–midnight; AE, MC, V) feels like a party every night. Efficient, flirtatious waiters sling piping-hot, thin-crusted pies (from 6€) on metal pans, and the beer and wine flow freely. If for some bizarre reason you're not in a pizza mood, the *primi* (from 6€) and *secondi* (from 8.50€) here are also surprisingly good. As at many popular pizzerias, reservations aren't accepted, but don't be put off if the line looks long: There are a ton of tables here, inside and out, so it won't be long before you're seated—just make sure Carlo at the front door knows you're waiting. For its proximity to Piazza Navona, this place is surprisingly untouristy, and they also serve pizza at lunch (sort of unheard of in Rome).

€–€€   The indoor-only tables at the always-bustling **Da Francesco** ★ (Piazza del Fico 29; ☎ 06-6864009; Wed–Mon 7pm–midnight; cash only) are some of the coziest places to be on a chilly night in Rome (but they can be uncomfortably warm in summer). Whatever the weather, it's a place for no-nonsense, satisfying Roman fare—pastas (from 7€), meat dishes (from 10€), pizza (from 6€)—at everyman prices. The only downside? Reservations aren't accepted, so unless you come early (by around 7:30pm), expect to wait at least 15 to 20 minutes outside on a Vespa-intense patch of cobblestones.

RESTAURANTS IN TRASTEVERE

Dining in the medieval enclave of Trastevere, just across the river from the city's historical center, is always an animated affair. It has something to do with that fizzy frisson of ancient neighborhood and young (sometimes loud) patrons. Suffice it to say that dining in this district is a heckuva a lot of fun.

Most people consider the heart of Trastevere to be the area around Piazza Santa Maria, but the restaurants around Piazza di Santa Cecilia on the other side of busy Viale Trastevere are actually better. In particular, Via dei Genovesi and Via Vascellari are havens for good food.

€   If you're just looking for a picnic, head to **Frontoni** ★ (Viale Trastevere 52, corner of Via San Francesco a Ripa, Santa Maria side; ☎ 06-5812436; daily 10am–8pm; AE, MC, V), where you can order custom pizza-bread sandwiches

(3€–6€) with all kinds of gourmet fillings. Unlike most sandwich-making *alimentari* (delis), there are lots of veggies and spreads to choose from in addition to the many cheeses and meats. The jovial white-haired men who work here usually sing as they lovingly assemble your panini.

€   Later in the day, try **Dar Poeta** ★★ (Vicolo del Bologna 45, Santa Maria side; ☎ 06-5880516; daily 7:30pm–midnight; AE, MC, V) for what many agree is the best pizza (around 8€) in Rome. It's not Roman-style per se (the dough is a little thicker, a la Neapolitan pizza), but the toppings are extraordinary, and creatively combined. Kick off the carb-fest with the bruschetta mista, and get a beer, not wine, to wash it down. The lines are long to eat in, but you can also walk up to the host and order a pie for takeout. I always got the *fior di salmone* (mozzarella, zucchini flowers, and smoked salmon) or the *taglialegna* (sausage, mushrooms, and red peppers) when I lived down the street from here.

€   Of the vast array of trattorie, the most wonderful (the only word for it) is the tiny **Da Augusto** ★ (Piazza de' Renzi, Santa Maria side; ☎ 06-5896848; Tues–Sun 12:30–3pm and 7:30pm–midnight; cash only), tucked between Piazza Santa Maria in Trastevere and Via del Moro. This is one of the last original, no-frills trattorie in Rome, and no doubt someone will ruin it soon by redecorating its crumbling interior. In the meantime, enjoy the ambience. Tables here are tiny squares covered with white paper on which the waitstaff will eventually write your bill. Have what they recommend (the menu is basically for show), as whatever they've got simmering in the back is freshly made with ingredients direct from the morning market. Most plates are around 7€ and the soups here are addictive. Reservations are hard to make because no one ever seems to answer the phone, but try anyway because it fills up.

€–€€   A nifty indoor-outdoor place for pasta and seafood at very humane prices **Osteria der Belli** ★ (Piazza S. Apollonia 11, Santa Maria side; ☎ 06-5803782; Tues–Sun 12:30–3pm and 7:30–11:30pm; AE, MC, V) is right off Piazza Santa Maria in Trastevere. The Roman-inflected Sardinian menu has an excellent *spaghetti allo scoglio* (literally, "reef" spaghetti, with clams, mussels, and crustaceans, 9€) and simple entrees like *spada al forno* (baked swordfish, 12€) that put other more expensive seafood restaurants to shame. On Friday nights especially, this spot is hugely popular with boozy old-timers—that's not meant to be a warning to stay away; indeed, come for the entertainment of watching these characters at their least guarded, and expect to hear a few rousing rounds of traditional Roman odes to gluttony and sloth. Do watch your bags at the outside tables, as Gypsies frequently beg in this area. Reservations recommended.

€–€€   Back on the southern side of Viale Trastevere, **Da Enzo** ★★ (Via dei Vascellari 26, Santa Cecilia side; ☎ 06-5818355; Mon–Sat 12:30–3pm and 7:30–11pm; AE, MC, V) is a far a cry from romantic. The tables are smashed together, covered with paper runners; the shelves inside the dining room are lined with cleaning supplies; and the lighting is hospital fluorescent. But the food here is so delicious that Giuliano Brenna, the chef of the high-priced Asinocotto (see below) eats here on his days off. Portions are hefty, with specialties like *polpetti al* *limone* (meatballs in lemon sauce) costing just 8€; the simple ravioli and carbonara are even cheaper and just as savory. In summer, tables are set out on the cobblestone streets, at the base of an intersection, which means you may have to move your chair if an oversize car needs to pass by. Reservations recommended.

€€   Also in this vicinity, **Roma Sparita** ★★ (kids) (Piazza di Santa Cecilia 24, Santa Cecilia side; ☎ 06-5800757; Tues–Sat 12:30–2:30pm and 7:30–11:30pm, Sun 12:30–2:30pm; MC, V) is a rival for the title of best pizzeria in Rome (with Dar Poeta, see above). Part of it is the ambience: The owner, Ugo, makes you feel as if you're a longtime family friend, and the setting, tucked in a corner of the car-free Piazza di Santa Cecilia, is a great place for the kids to run around while you wait for your meal or linger over a limoncello. Roma Sparita is just as delightful on a cold winter day, when the fireplace inside warms the intimate lower dining room. Pizza here is made in a classic wood-burning oven. The best is the rughetta with baby tomatoes.

€€   On the northern side of Viale Trastevere, meat-lovers' dream **Il Ciak** ★ (Vicolo del Cinque 21, Santa Maria side; ☎ 06-5894774; Mon–Sat 12:30–2:30pm and 7:30pm–midnight; AE, MC, V) hasn't changed much in 40 years. It's always been frequented by movie stars and local celebrities, hence the name "Ciak" (the sound a signboard makes when clapped before filming). Don't be frightened away by the front windows, which look more like a taxidermist shop's than those of a quaint trattoria. They only trumpet the fact that this is a restaurant for carnivores, especially those who love wild game cooked, with Tuscan flair, over an open grill. There is almost no reason to have a *primo* plate here. Instead, try one of the innovative bruschetta offerings like funghi porcini paste or hot pepper paste, and sip your Chianti while Sammy, the grill chef, prepares your feast. Most second plates are around 12€, but they are generous and come with roast potatoes. ***Note:*** Even though reservations are mandatory, there's always a line of regulars who just didn't have time to call. And even if *you* did call, they will get the table first.

€€€   **Spirito Divino** ★★ (Via dei Genovesi 31 A/B, Vicolo Dell'Atleta 13–15, Santa Cecilia side; ☎ 06-5896689; www.spiritodivino.com; Mon–Sat 7:45–11pm; AE, MC, V) is not just a restaurant, it's also a tourist attraction. The name, which translates to "divine spirit" or "spirit of wine," refers to the fact that the building sits on the site of Rome's original synagogue. At the end of the meal the owner gives a guided tour of the basement excavations, which now house the restaurant's extensive wine cellar (sculptures that were found here are now in the Vatican Museums). The menu flits across the ages from such modern fare as a 12€ *bisque di crostacei e mandorle tostate* (with crustaceans and toasted almonds) to the restaurant's star dish, the succulent *maiale alla mazio* (pork in the style of Matius, 18€). The latter follows an ancient recipe that was a favorite of Julius Caesar and Augustus: The pork is marinated for 24 hours in red wine with apple slices. A truly memorable place to dine.

€€€   **Asinocotto** ★★★ (Via dei Vascellari 48, Santa Cecilia side; ☎ 06-5898985; www.asinocotto.com; Tues–Sun 8–11pm; reservations required; AE, MC, V) is somewhat of an odd duck. Its walls are slathered by ancient Broadway show posters and gay pride is a large motif here. But everyone dines here—gay, straight, and non-show-tune lovers—because it's run by local culinary celebrity Giuliano Brenna, who trained at some of the best five-star restaurants in Italy. And you'll actually meet Brenna, as it will be him who personally takes your order, explains the menu in English (and he does a good job answering questions on the subtle nuances of his innovative fare), and delivers the food to the table. This is not a cheap restaurant—most first plates are over 15€—but the food is so distinctive, I'd say it's worth it.

RESTAURANTS IN THE JEWISH GHETTO

The Jewish Ghetto is a quieter version of the quaint Trastevere, and the clientele (and overall aura of the area) is about 10 years older. No one gets very excited here about anything, except about the genuinely good food you're served.

€ It's hard to resist the sweet smell that comes out of **Il Forno del Ghetto** (Via del Portico d'Ottavia 1; no phone; Mon–Fri 8:30am–1pm and 4–7:30pm) whenever a new batch of goodies goes into the oven. This miniscule kosher bakery sells its delicious cookies by weight, and they're best enjoyed *appena sfornato* (fresh out of the oven), as they tend to turn travertine hard after a few hours.

€€ On to restaurants: The selection at **Al Pompiere** ✸ (Via Santa Maria dei Calderari 38; ☎ 06-6868377; Mon–Sat 12:30–2:30pm and 7:30–10:30pm; MC, V) is not as ample as in other parts of town, but the dishes are solid and dependable at this casual osteria, frequented by locals. And to be fair, they do the standard Roman dishes like fried zucchini flowers and batter-dipped salt cod better than most, in addition to preparing top-notch seafood pastas, which start at 10€ and are always fresh. It's a tossup between this gem and **Sora Margherita** ✸ (Piazza delle Cinque Scole 30; ☎ 06-6874216; Tues–Sun 12:30–2:30pm, Fri–Sat 7:30–10:30pm) for best hole in the wall. Sora Margherita may win, as it's strangely anonymous from the outside—there's no sign and the entrance looks like the kitchen door. But once you get inside, all is lovely, thanks to the classic Roman-Jewish cuisine, done with style and dependable grace.

€€ In the very heart of the historical Jewish Ghetto, a stone's throw away from the ruins of the Portico d'Ottavia, **Trattoria da Giggetto** ✸ (Via del Portico d'Ottavia, 21/a; ☎ 06-6861105; www.giggettoalporticodottavia.it; Tues–Sun 12:30–2:30pm and 7:30–11:30pm; AE, MC, V), is a classic Roman-Jewish restaurant. It's been run by the same family for three generations, and boy, can they cook. The fried zucchini flowers are stuffed with mouthwatering mozzarella and the seafood pastas are exquisite. First plates here start at over 12€. Another specialty of the house: hot oil–boiled (not deep-fried, mind you) artichokes.

RESTAURANTS IN TESTACCIO

In an area formerly given over to slaughterhouses (now transformed into the MACRO museum), restaurants specialize in meats from the *quinto quarto* (fifth quarter), the leftover segments of an animal after the slaughter, like sweetbreads, tripe, entrails, and other goodies you won't find on most American menus (although you also find the standard cuts). I think this neighborhood has the best meals for the price (low) in the city. It's just a short walk from the historical center and just across the river from Trastevere.

€   Rome's finest delicatessen, **Volpetti** ★★★ (Via Marmorata 47; ☎ 06-5742352; www.volpetti.com; Mon–Sat 8am–2pm and 5–8:15pm; AE, MC, V), is a massive barrage to the senses. If you even feign the slightest interest in a product, the helpful crew behind the counter will have you sampling goodies, tasting the various olive oils and vinegars until you beg for mercy. This is the place to buy vinegars and oils (in small, packable bottles that start around 5€), cheeses, or cured meats to take back home. The owners here will vacuum seal and pack everything for you, including special gift boxes with local samples. You can also buy a slice of pizza or order a custom deli sandwich to take away.

€   If you prefer to sit to eat, go around the corner to the delicious **Volpetti Più** ★ (Via Alessandro Volta 8; ☎ 06-57301439; Mon–Sat 8am–2pm and 5–8:15pm; AE, MC, V), a self-service *tavola calda* (cafe or diner) with products from the deli. They make the best potato pizza in the city, bar none, and you can walk away satisfied for under 5€. The menu here changes seasonally; other than extraordinarily tasty pizza by the slice, the specialties are lasagna and interesting cold pasta dishes, as well as rice-and-chickpea salads.

€   Another great midday meal option is **Il Seme e La Foglia** (Via Galvani 18; ☎ 06-5743008; Mon–Sat 8am–1:30am, Sun 6:30pm–1:30am; cash only), a friendly modern cafe with about five tables where you can get enormous salads (6€–8€), among other lunchy offerings (*tramezzino* sandwiches from 3€), a pint of beer, or just an espresso. It's open late at night, too, which comes in handy when you're famished after hitting the clubs around Monte Testaccio.

€   Mentioning "Testaccio" and "pizza" in the same sentence elicits only one possible response from locals: **Da Remo** ★★ (Piazza Santa Maria Liberatrice 44; ☎ 06-5746270; Mon–Sat 7:30pm–midnight; cash only) is a Roman institution. In the summer, reservations at least 2 days in advance are compulsory (imagine that at your hometown pizzeria!). The bruschetta here melts in your mouth, and every pizza is made lovingly for all to see behind the open marble counters; the most basic start at just 5€. If it's too crowded on a summer evening, order your pizza as takeout and eat it in the quaint park across the street.

€–€€   Testaccio has lately made a noble attempt to shed its grungy everyman image with some funky wine bars under track lighting. Skip 'em (the wine bars in the historical center are far more happening) and go instead to the always-interesting **L'Oasi della Birra** (Piazza Testaccio 41; ☎ 06-5746122; Mon–Sat 12:30pm–1am; cash only) which offers over 500 types of beer, including obscure Italian microbrews. The meals here are either superlight (cheese and salami plates for 6€) or beer-worthy heavy (goulash, bratwurst, and cabbage-based salads starting around 8€). And the wine list is almost as impressive as the beer offering, with many vintages served generously by the glass for 4€.

€€   On to the "real" restaurants: **Perilli a Testaccio** ★★★ (Via Marmorata 39; ☎ 06-5742145; Thurs–Tues 12:30–2:30pm and 7:30–11pm) has been doing diners right since it opened in 1911. It was a frequent haunt of Federico Fellini; even now it's not uncommon to see local celebrities at the cramped tables inside. Not that the bustling all-male waitstaff give them any special treatment; instead, all patrons in this noisy old-timer are treated like regulars. As soon as you enter, you'll notice seasonal fruits and vegetables stacked in baskets and plates on a table in the back corner by the kitchen; the chef leans out from time to time to pluck what he needs. I especially enjoy Perilli on a winter's day when the hearty cannelloni (9€) warms your insides before you get down to the serious business of devouring the superb *maialino* (roast suckling pork). Both of these second plates start at 11€ and generally include roast potatoes. There's no outdoor seating, and this restaurant is always packed for dinner, so reservations are required (you can usually snag a table at lunch, if you get there promptly at 12:30pm).

€–€€   If Perilli's is full, a good second choice is **Da Bucatino** ★★ (Via Luca della Robbia 84, off Piazza Testaccio; ☎ 06-5746886; Tues–Sun 12:30–2:30pm and 7:30–11:30pm; MC, V). It's a true home-style restaurant, with garlic garlands and dusty Chianti bottles, not to mention the head of a wild boar, on the walls. You can almost always get a table, either in the main dining room, in the basement under whitewashed arches or right on the cobblestone streets (in summer), often between parked cars. The food here is always satisfying, and the *antipasti* buffet is certainly enough for lunch. Da Bucatino offers some of the best *secondi* in the area, most starting under 12€, with such standards as juicy *pollo con peperoni* (stewed chicken with red and yellow peppers). The restaurant's namesake pasta, *bucatini all'amatriciana* (thick, hollow noodles with tomato, bacon, and grated pecorino cheese) at 7€, is so sloppy good that the gentle waiters—two married couples and their droll sons—are known to affix a napkin-bib to you if you're wearing a white shirt.

€€€   If you are looking for something more "dressed up," consider the very romantic **Consolini all'Arco di San Lazzaro** ★ (Via Marmorata 28; ☎ 06-57300145; Tues–Sun 12:30–2:30pm and 7:30–11pm), which is attached to the Aventine Hill (with an entrance on Via Marmorata). In summer, ask to sit on the flowered terraces, where you might spot a local soccer star on a date with a TV showgirl. Seafood is the specialty, and a favorite is gnocchi with lobster sauce at 14€. This is *not* a family-friendly place. Reservations required.

€€€€   For haute quinto quarto fare, **Checchino dal 1887** ★★ (Via di Monte Testaccio 30; ☎ 06-5746318; www.checchino-dal-1887.com; Tues–Sat 7:30–10:30pm; AE, DC, MC, V) is a meat-lover's paradise, set directly across from the old slaughterhouse, against the slopes of man-made Monte Testaccio. It's a more expensive choice than most of the other restaurants in this area, with prix-fixe menus starting at 31€. (There's an a la carte menu, but this is the type of place that you really make an evening of, ordering multiple courses and stuffing yourself silly.) Still, Romans from all over the city keep coming back here when they want a special, and very carnivorous, night out. Ask to visit the wine cellar, where the ancient potsherds that make up Monte Testaccio are visible.

RESTAURANTS NEAR THE VATICAN

Across the river, into the area around the Vatican, dining is a mixed bag. By day, restaurants cater to large groups that are moved through at lightning speed. By night, they're inhabited primarily by priests and cardinals, and, not surprisingly, eavesdropping Vatican journalists.

€   The cheeses and meats at deli-extraordinaire **Franchi** ★★ (Via Cola di Rienzo 204, at Via Terenzio; ☎ 06-6874651; www.franchi.it; Mon–Sat 9am–7:30pm; AE, MC, V) might be beyond your budget, but the *tavola calda* is not. Here, a well-heeled but ravenous lunch crowd jockeys for space in front of a tantalizing lineup of freshly made pastas, vegetables, roasted meats, fish plates, and fritters galore. Among Franchi's fried products, its 1.50€ *supplì*—fried rice balls, bound together by tomato sauce and mozzarella—are famous citywide. Since there's nowhere to sit at Franchi, everything is packaged to go in handy foil trays. Eat your picnic up the street in Piazza Risorgimento, amid the tourist traffic near the Vatican, or hike a little farther to Castel Sant'Angelo, where the castle's moat has been converted into a grassy park.

€   **Il Mozzicone** (Borgo Pio 180; ☎ 06-6861500; Mon–Sat 12:30–2:30pm and 7:30–10:30pm; MC, V) is a tiny little getaway just a stone's throw from the Vatican City gates. There are no surprises on the menu here, just the usual dishes like fettuccini ragù for 7€ and tripe for 9€, but considering its location, it's the best deal around. This restaurant is miniscule, so book a table to avoid a wait.

€€   **Taverna Angelica** (Piazza A. Capponi 6; ☎ 06-6874514; www.taverna angelica.it; Mon–Sat 7:30–11:30pm, Sun 12:30–2:30pm; AE, MC, V) is a standard Vatican City–area trattoria specializing in fowl-based dishes like lentil soup with pigeon breast for 10€ and duck breast with balsamic vinegar for 15€. It's a popular spot for priests with higher budgets, and it's not uncommon to overhear heated debates on church policy. If you're feeling peckish after the pope's noon Angelus blessing, the three-course, prix-fixe Sunday lunch (25€) is a deal.

A RESTAURANT NEAR THE COLOSSEUM

€€–€€€   It's possible you will not have a more stylish seafood meal in Rome than at the appropriately named **F.I.S.H.** ★ (Via dei Serpenti 16; ☎ 06-47824962; www.f-i-s-h.it; Tues–Sun 12:30–2:30pm and 7:30pm–midnight; AE, MC, V). The menu at this "Fine International Seafood House" is divided into Mediterranean, Asian, and oceanic categories, and it's about the best ethnic food you can get in the city when it comes to sushi and nasi goreng. But the Mediterranean menu is by far the most interesting, with the house dish being *volcano di riso nero*—seafood cooked in a bed of mixed rice for 12€. The atmosphere here is sleek and modern, not your grandma's fish restaurant.

WHY YOU'RE HERE:
THE TOP SIGHTS & ATTRACTIONS

You're only here for a few days, maybe a week or two, tops, right? So instead of an exhaustive discussion of every important ruin, monument, museum, church, and fountain of Rome, I've confined this chapter to a carefully edited selection of the sights—grand to humble—that most impress and instruct visitors. I've preceded those listings with recommendations on allocating your time, depending on

Touring the Vatican: Timing Is Everything

Read about people who waited 2 hours to get into the Vatican Museums? The poor souls just went at the wrong time. As a former tour guide who's spent a lot of time at the Vatican, I have some insider info that you'll thank me for later: The line is much shorter (even nonexistent) on Tuesday, Wednesday, Thursday, and Friday afternoons. Mondays and Saturdays are horrible crowds-wise, so if these are your only two possible days to do the Vatican, I would actually recommend you save it for your next trip.

I'll explain: The museum entrance (which is the only way to get to the Sistine Chapel) is open from 8:45 to 10am Monday through Saturday to reserved individuals and groups only. This time slot is cruise-ship and package-tour central, and very crowded. At 10am, the gates open up to the masses, and that's when the monster lines begin to form. However, around 1pm, something magical happens—the line dwindles to about 15 minutes or nothing at all. Once you're inside, you'll still have several hours to explore the museums and Sistine Chapel, and then head down to St. Peter's. Just remember that no matter what time you go, you'll never have the Vatican completely to yourself. Also, note that in the low season (Nov, most of Dec–Jan, and Feb), the museum entrance closes at 12:30pm (and they kick you out at 1:45pm), so you'll have to go around 11am. The upside is that low season means fewer all-around crowds. Check www.vatican.va for the full schedule, which includes those Catholic holidays on which the museums are closed.

If you decide to reserve ahead for that morning time slot at the Vatican Museums, you're required to book a 2-hour guided tour as well. The cost is 24€ (regular admission is 13€) and you can reserve by fax (06-69885100) at least 7 days and no more than 1 month before you will be visiting the museums. You'll receive a confirmation fax that you must bring with you to the exit gate of the Vatican Museums (right beside the ticket booth) 15 minutes before your reservation time.

Warning: Be wary of private companies that offer to get you these reservations; some charge as much as 75€ for the service, but you can just as easily reserve it yourself for a fraction of that.

the number of days you'll be in the Eternal City. I want you to fall in love with Rome, and if you follow at least some of my advice, you probably will.

ANCIENT ROME

Ancient Rome may look like a jumble of fallen columns and confusing ruins, but this area, which is the most historically significant in the city, is quite easy to navigate and decipher with a good map and a good imagination.

Rome Attractions

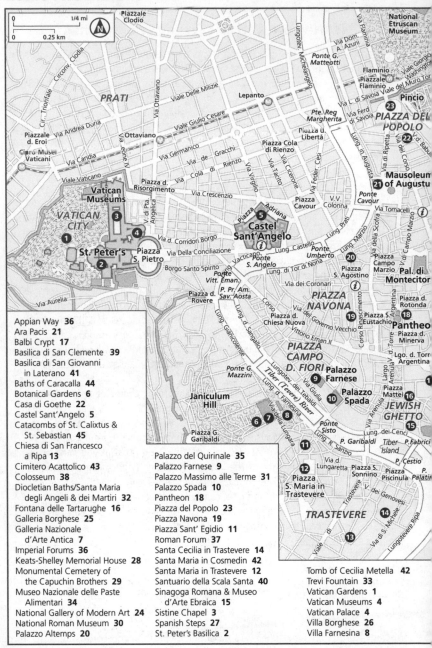

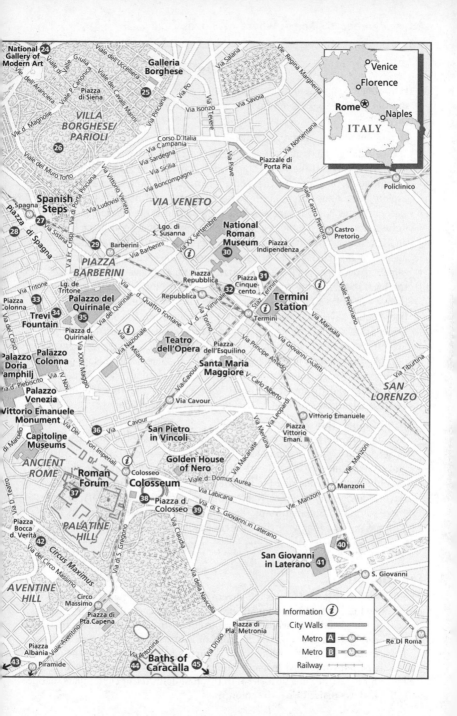

National Gallery of Modern Art 24

Galleria Borghese

Piazza di Siena 25

VILLA BORGHESE/PARIOLI 26

Venice
Florence
Rome ✱
Naples
ITALY

Piazzale di Porta Pia

Policlinico

Spanish Steps 27
Piazza di Spagna 28
Spagna

VIA VENETO

Lgo. di S. Susanna
Barberini 29
PIAZZA BARBERINI

National Roman Museum 30
Piazza Indipendenza

Castro Pretorio

Piazza Repubblica
Repubblica 32
Piazza Cinquecento 31
Termini Station
Staz. Termini
Termini

Lg. de Tritone
Piazza Colonna 33
Palazzo del Quirinale 35
Trevi Fountain 34
Piazza d. Quirinale

Palazzo Colonna
Palazzo Doria Pamphilj

Teatro dell'Opera
Piazza dell'Esquilino

Santa Maria Maggiore

Piazza Principe Amedeo

SAN LORENZO

Palazzo Venezia
Vittorio Emanuele Monument
Capitoline Museums

ANCIENT ROME
Roman Forum 37

San Pietro in Vincoli 36

Vittorio Emanuele
Piazza Vittorio Eman. II

Manzoni

Golden House of Nero
Colosseo
Colosseum 38
Piazza d. Colosseo 39

PALATINE HILL

Piazza Bocca d. Verità 42
Circus Maximus

AVENTINE HILL
Circo Massimo

Piazza di Pta.Capena

San Giovanni in Laterano 41
40

S. Giovanni

Piazza di Pla. Metronia

Re Di Roma

Piazza Albania 43
Piramide

Baths of Caracalla 44 45

Information ⓘ
City Walls
Metro A
Metro B
Railway

47

Rome Itineraries

Following are suggested itineraries for short trips that touch on all aspects of what there is to see here, from ancient Rome to holy Rome to 21st-century Rome.

If you have only 1 day in Rome

The best thing you can do is change your ticket so that you can spend more time here. Otherwise, start your day at the terraces of the **Campidoglio,** overlooking the Roman **Forum.** You won't have time to explore these ruins in full, but from here, you can see the entirety of what was once the heart of ancient Rome, set against the backdrop of the **Colosseum** and cast in the day's best light. Take an hour to visit the Forum and Colosseum, then head back to the historical center to the **Pantheon** and catch the midday light streaming through the oculus of the ancient temple. From there, walk over to **Piazza Navona** and have lunch on one of the back streets to the west of the square. After lunch, it's Vatican time. Have a cab take you to the entrance of the **Vatican Museums** (by now, the lines should have died down somewhat), and check out the Sistine Chapel. Exit via the special "tour groups only" door, which takes you directly to **St. Peter's Basilica.** After St. Peter's, you've earned a little break. Head down to **Campo de' Fiori** for a glass of wine or some gelato before going back to your hotel room to freshen up for the evening. Have dinner in **Trastevere,** and finish off the night with a trip to the **Trevi Fountain,** where you'll throw in a coin to ensure your return to Rome.

If you have only 2 days in Rome

Two days are better than one, but not by much. Start the first day the same way you would if you were in town 1 day (see above), at the **Forum** and **Colosseum.** Take a few hours to explore these sights, then head back toward **Piazza Navona** and the **Pantheon** by way of the **Circus Maximus.** Have a quick early lunch at **Maccheroni** (p. 37), then head east to the **Trevi Fountain, Spanish Steps,** and **Villa Borghese.** Stroll or sit in the park for an hour, then visit the **Galleria Borghese** (p. 75) at the 3 or 5pm

The Capitoline Hill

The **Capitoline Hill** ✮✮✮ was the government center of ancient Rome. Today, this iconic hilltop features a square designed by Michelangelo in the 1530s, flanked on either side by the glorious Capitoline Museums (p. 58). It's the ideal spot to begin your explorations of the ruins of Rome. Though it's open 24 hours, it's best to come here right before dawn. Watching the sun rise over the ancient forums is perhaps the most magical moment you'll experience in this city, and well worth the sacrifice of a little sleep. In this first light, the ancient pillars sparkle and the shadows dance below the columns.

time slot (reservations required). Rest your feet and get a drink at the **Casina Valadier,** then go back to your hotel to get ready for dinner. Eat somewhere ultra-Roman in **Testaccio** (like Perilli or Da Bucatino) and wind up your evening with a late-night view of Rome from the **Parco Savello (Orange Park)** (p. 79) on the Aventine Hill. On your second day, start the morning off with a lazy walk through the back streets of the *centro storico,* concentrating on the areas around the market square of **Campo de' Fiori.** After lunch, head across the river to the Vatican. Visit the **Vatican Museums, Sistine Chapel,** and **St. Peter's** as in the "1-day in Rome" agenda, above. After St. Peter's, recharge at your hotel for an hour or so, if possible, then go to **Trastevere** for an *aperitivo* (happy hour), dinner, and a *passeggiata* (stroll).

If you have only 3 days in Rome

Follow the itineraries above and add a half-day trip outside the walls on your third (or middle) day. Head south to the Catacombs along the **Appian Way,** or take the train to **Ostia** to see the ruins of Rome's original seaport. Or visit **Hadrian's Villa** and **Villa d'Este** (p. 88) in Tivoli (allow the best part of a day). On the third night, have dinner at a lively pizzeria like **Dar Poeta** (p. 39) or **La Montecarlo** (p. 38).

If you have 4 days or more in Rome

After following the above itineraries, fill your last few days with what you like best. For example, if antiquities are for you, spend an entire day searching for ancient Rome by visiting the church of **San Clemente,** exploring the **Domus Aurea,** and checking out the **Wall Museum.** If art is more your style, dizzy yourself with Rome's wonderful museum offerings like the **Capitoline Museums** and **National Roman Museums,** near Termini. If you are interested in the Catholic Church or religious architecture, visit the five patriarchal parish churches and duck into any basilica that looks interesting.

Once you've taken in the view, head around the back of the city hall to see the entire spread of the **Forum complex** below, which is divided broadly into four segments: the Imperial Fora (Fori Imperiali), the Roman Forum (Foro Romano), the Palatine Hill (Palatino), and the Colosseum (Colosseo). It's vital to see the outlines of these buildings, as well as the original forum layout, from up here, before delving in. From down inside the forums, you just don't get this sort of perspective; instead, you're dwarfed by the giant pillars and arches.

The modern street to the left of this vista is **Via dei Fori Imperiali,** built by Benito Mussolini in 1932 as a means to connect his famous Palazzo Venezia balcony to the Colosseum. Today, archaeologists are slowly digging out more artifacts

Cutting the Cost of Museum Admissions

For all there is to see and do in Rome, the city doesn't do a great job of making it easy or convenient. Unlike in, say, Naples and Florence, there are no all-encompassing tourist passes that integrate museum admission and public transportation. Instead, Rome's visitors have to pick and choose their deals, juggling a handful of different tickets to enjoy savings. The integrated tickets that do exist are available at any of the sites they cover, or through **APT Azienda per il Turismo Roma** (Via Parigi 5, or inside Fiumicino Airport; ☎ 06-48899200 or 06-36004399; www.romaturismo. com). It's important to note that most museums are closed on Mondays, with the exception of the Vatican Museums and the Museum of Modern Art, which makes taking advantage of a 3-day ticket purchased on a Saturday or Sunday nearly impossible.

Consider the following:

* **Capitolini Card:** Adults 8€, seniors and students 6€, 7 days: Capitoline Museums and Montemartini.
* **Museo Nazionale Romano Card:** Adults 6.50€, seniors and students 3.50€, 3 days: Palazzo Massimo alle Terme, Baths of Diocletian, Palazzo Altemps, and Balbi Crypt.
* **Appia Antica Card:** Adults 6€, no discounts, 7 days: Baths of Caracalla, Tomb of Cecilia Metella, and Villa dei Quintili.
* **Archeologia Card:** Adults 20€, seniors and students 10€, 7 days: Colosseum, Palatine Hill, Terme di Caracalla, Palazzo Altemps, Palazzo Massimo alle Terme, Baths of Diocletian, Balbi Crypt, Tomb of Cecilia Metella, and Villa dei Quintili.

and chipping away at the ruins without sacrificing the street, which would cripple the public transportation network of modern Rome. Don't let this street confuse you or be distracted by the way the forums are divided up by fences, entrance gates, sidewalks, and benches, which sit above still-unexcavated ruins. Though it doesn't appear so today, in reality these forums were part of an intricate network of small streets and alleyways—much like the present city.

You should definitely come back up here another time to explore **Piazza Venezia** and the rest of the Campidoglio, but for now take the back steps down to the Via dei Fori Imperiali.

The Imperial Forums

Almost more complicated than figuring out what you are looking at is determining in what order to visit these forums. My suggestion: Start on the left-hand side of the Via dei Fori Imperiali (facing the Colosseum) with a brief sweep through the Imperial Forums of Trajan, Caesar, Nerva, and Augustus, which were built between 42 B.C. and A.D. 112. The best preserved is the semicircular **Trajan's**

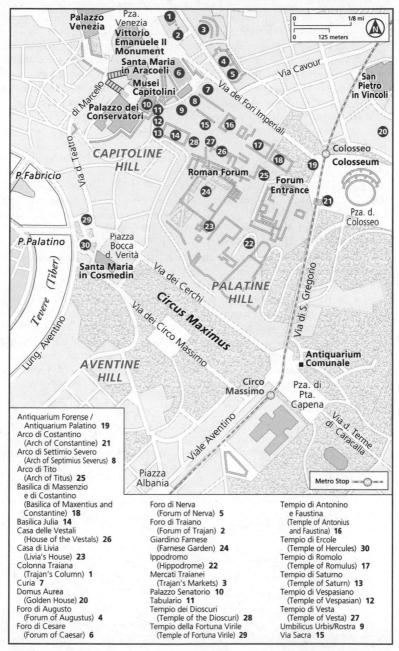

The Colosseum, the Forum & Ancient Rome Attractions

Market (entrance Via IV Novembre 94; 6.50€; Tues–Sun 9am–sunset), which gives you an idea of what an ancient 150-store Roman shopping mall looked like, though you wouldn't find Gucci and Prada here (these were primarily stores for grains, oils, spices, and other supplies). Don't enter this site unless you're an archaeology buff; you can just as easily get the idea from the perimeter. From here you will also see the intricately carved **Torre delle Milizie (Tower of the Militia)** on top of the market. Many poets have written that Nero stood here to watch Rome burn, but historians differ and say he watched from the Colle Oppio (p. 56). Farther down the street is the **Colonna Traiana (Trajan's Column),** a white column carved with war scenes from Emperor Trajan's defeat of the Dacians (who occupied what is now Romania). The statue on top is St. Peter, which fills the spot where a golden statue of Trajan was pilfered in the Middle Ages.

The forums of Augustus, Nerva, and Vespasiano are below this street joined by a walkway, which you can reach from Via dei Fori Imperiali or Piazza del Grillo. The **Forum of Augustus** was inaugurated in 2 B.C. Its main structure was the Temple of Mars, which the Emperor Augustus (known then as Octavian) built to mark the victorious battle of Philippi in 42 B.C. Next is the **Forum of Nerva,** which sits on both sides of Via Fori Imperiali. This forum held the Temple of Minerva, of which there is still a frieze depicting Minerva, the goddess of home-making and weaving. The final forum here is the **Forum of Vespasiano.** It was dedicated to the emperor in A.D. 75, but most of it burned in 192. In 193, Septimius Severus placed a giant map of Rome on the walls here. The maps you now see on the wall opposite these forums were put there by Mussolini to show the rise of his own wannabe Roman Empire in the making.

At the time of this writing, you can only visit the **Imperial Forums** (Via dei Fori Imperiali; ☎ 06-6797786; 7€; English for guided tours only at 3pm Wed and Sat–Sun) by guided tour 3 days a week. But again, it is not necessary to actually go down into the Imperial Forums to appreciate their significance. It's a much more rewarding journey to cross the street and visit the free Roman Forum.

The Roman Forum

Armed with a good guide (written or human), you can spend an entire day at the **Roman Forum** ✪✪✪ (entrances at Largo Romolo e Remo 5–6, Piazza di Santa Maria Nova 53, or Via di Monte Tarpeo; 9€ integrated ticket with Colosseum and the Roman Forum; daily 9am to 1 hr. before dusk) and still come away wanting

---

HBO's *Rome:* Scandalous—& Archaeologically Accurate

Of all the screen productions ever made about ancient Rome, by far the most faithful to academic reconstructions of the way Rome really looked back then is the HBO series *Rome.* I've studied this program and haven't found a temple, arch, or other public monument that doesn't belong there. With that in mind, consider viewing a few episodes of this engrossing show for a better understanding of now-fragmentary areas like the Forum.

Rome with Children

If you bring your children to Rome, don't expect kids' menus or highchairs. Don't get me wrong: There are few cities where children are more welcome (even at fancy restaurants), yet they are accommodated poorly. Just bring with you almost all they need or call in advance (if you make a reservation for dinner, you must also reserve the highchair, or *seggiolino*, since most restaurants have only one or two).

Children under 12 generally get in free to museums and sites in Rome. There are a handful of parks like the Villa Borghese and one in Testaccio with playground equipment, but they are laughable in comparison to what you find at home. Still, there are a few venues expressly for kids.

Rome's interactive science museum, **Explora** (kids) (Via Flaminia 82; ☎ 06-3613776; www.mdbr.it; children 3–12 7€, adults 6€; by reservation only Tues–Thurs at 9:30, 11:30am, 3, and 5pm, and Fri–Sat 10am, noon, 3, and 5pm) is specifically for children. Built in an abandoned bus depot, the museum delights kids with fun exhibits titled simply "Me," "Society," "Environment," and "Communication." All the exhibits are in Italian, but English-speaking kids don't seem to mind.

A little farther out of town is the **Museo della Memoria Giocosa (Museum of the Playful Memory)** (kids) (Via Vincenzo Coronelli 24–26; ☎ 06-24407777), a private collection of toys assembled by Fritz Bilig, an Austrian who fled Europe during Nazism. The toys are those that children growing up in Europe between 1920 and 1960 played with. It is a museum that the kids enjoy, and in which many parents feel nostalgic.

If you happen to be in Rome during the holidays, take the children to the **Befana Christmas Toy Fair** (Piazza Navona). Stuck in the past, with old-fashioned merry-go-round rides and a disturbingly thin Santa Claus (Babbo Natale), it features rows of stalls dripping with candies and Christmas goodies. Watch also for the beloved Befana witch, who brings toys to Italian children on January 6, the Feast of the Epiphany.

more. To best enjoy it, pick up a detailed map from the visitor center on the Via dei Fori Imperiali. The most central entrance is located in the middle, at Largo Romolo e Remo. Rent a 4€ audioguide here, which will save you from hearing others' often misguided explanations. *Warning:* The ruins here are among the worst labeled in the entire city, so without a detailed map, an audioguide, or a book dedicated entirely to the Forum, you'll be left with only half of the story.

From the entrance at Largo Romolo e Remo, you should first cover the area to the left heading to the Colosseum. Here you'll see the A.D. 141 **Temple of Antonino and Faustina,** which was reincarnated as a Catholic church in the 8th century. Farther down the paved road is the backside of the **Basilica of Cosmas and Damian,** which houses a Franciscan monastery with a well-placed balcony overlooking the area. If you feel adventurous, go around the front of the church and ask if you can take a peek; there are many American Franciscans here on sabbatical or assignment who will happily take you up to see the view.

Along the path in the Forum, you'll pass the barrel vaults of the ruined Basilica of Costantino, originally known as the **Basilica of Massenzio.** This was the largest structure in the entire Roman Forum and the last of the magnificent structures built before the decline of Rome. The giant vaults are said to have inspired Michelangelo, who came here often to study them before designing the dome for St. Peter's Basilica. Nearby the **Arch of Titus** tells of Titus's defeat of the Jews.

Heading back toward the entrance is the flowered courtyard of the **House of the Vestal Virgins,** where anatomically perfect, prepubescent girls tended Vesta's fire. Near here, a fragmentary, semicircular white marble wall is all that's left of the **Temple of Vesta,** where they performed their sacred task. They spent 10 years training, 10 years as dignitaries representing Vesta, and 10 years teaching the younger generation. At 40, they could finally marry, and legend says that deflowering a vestal virgin was something Roman men fought ardently to do. Vestal virgins who couldn't adhere to their vow of chastity until they reached 40 were buried alive. Not far away is what's left of the **Temple of Julius Caesar** (it's the brown tufa stone foundation with a green metal roof)—built on the site of his cremation—which is often adorned with fresh roses laid down by a Roman woman who believes she is a direct descendant.

Finally, you will come along to the **Sacred Way,** which leads in the direction of the Campidoglio. Here you'll pass by the **Basilica Aemilia,** which housed the administrative offices of ancient Rome, and the **Temple of Castor and Pollux,** whose statues flank the entrance to the Piazza del Campidoglio. The brothers are widely known as the saviors of Rome—they appeared out of nowhere to inspire the Roman military in a battle in 499 B.C. In this part of the Forum are several standing columns that mark the sites of once important buildings. Eight similar granite columns outline what was once the **Temple of Saturn,** used as the city's treasury. The three white columns, attached by a broken slab of marble on top, make up what was once a corner of the **Temple of Vespasian.** The impressive display of 12 columns (although 5 are not original) is what's left of the **Portico degli Dei Consenti,** and a tall lone column is the **Column of Phocas,** which was the very last monument erected in the Forum in A.D. 608. Near this far end of the Forum is the massive **Arch of Septimius Severus,** with its haunting reliefs on the column bases of the defeated Parthians (who occupied modern-day Iran) being led to their death in chains. See also the steps of the ruins of **Basilica Julia,** which was built by Julius Caesar to house the law courts. Note the carved squares on the remaining steps—these were board games used by those waiting for their day in court.

Also near here, look for the **Golden Milestone,** the point from which all roads leading from Rome were measured. And don't miss the **Rostrum,** where Shakespeare placed the delivery of Mark Antony's famous address, which began, "Friends, Romans, countrymen . . . ." The nearby **Curia** was the Roman Senate; it was given a new wooden roof and bronze doors in the 1930s. The original ancient bronze doors still exist—they now adorn the Basilica of San Giovanni (p. 80).

There is much, much more in the Forum than what's mentioned here, and as I said before, you could spend an entire day exploring it. But if you just want to skim the surface, as I've done here, you can see the whole thing in about 1½ hours before heading next door to the Palatine Hill.

The Palatine Hill

The Forum may be from where Rome ruled the world, but the wonderfully green grounds of the **Palatine** ✪✪ (Via di San Gregorio 30 or Piazza di Santa Maria Nova 53; 9€ integrated ticket with Colosseum and the Roman Forum; daily 9am to 1 hr. before dusk) are whence it all began. According to legend, this is where the mythical she-wolf nursed Remus and Romulus, the latter of whom is said to have founded Rome. This is also the spot where the proof of 8th-century-B.C. huts from the Iron Age can be seen, depicting the first known settlement in Rome. Emperors lived here, and you can easily see why—the views of Rome's seven hills are breathtaking.

The English word "palace" is believed to be derived from the lavish dwellings on the Palatine Hill. Most of the larger remains you see here are from the Emperor Domitian (this is another place worthy of a very detailed guide from the visitor center). The areas not to miss, though, are **Domus Augustana,** the living quarters, the **Stadio (Stadium),** and the **Baths of Septimius Severus,** which form the outer boundary of the Palatine Hill. These are the prominent, frequently photographed ruins you see from the Circus Maximus and really show the mass of these ancient dwellings.

Behind this wall of ruins, inward, are the stunning mosaic tile floors of the **Domus Flavia** and the Pompeian red frescoes of the 1st-century-B.C. **House of Livia.** The frescoes found in these ruins are on display at the National Roman Museum on Piazza della Repubblica. There are a handful of artifacts found in the excavations of the Palatine Hill in the large white Palatine Museum, which is included in your entrance ticket. Don't spend too much time here, though, because there are much better offerings at the ancient artifact museums in the city and the Vatican Museums.

From the edge of the Palatine Hill, you see the wide oval track of the **Circus Maximus,** which once held 300,000 spectators in wood and stone bleachers to watch chariots race. Rent *Ben-Hur* for a refresher of the history of this arena. Now it is a running track for Romans and a concert venue in the summer. When Italy won the World Cup in 2006, this was where the huge national party took place.

Arch of Constantine

Between the Palatine Hill and the Colosseum is the last triumphal arch, **The Arch of Constantine** ✪, that the Roman Empire was able to build, erected by Constantine in A.D. 315. The decorations on this arch were pilfered from other monuments throughout the city. If you study the battle scenes, you may notice what art historians call a decline in artisan quality and detail—just one of the many precursors to the fall of the Roman Empire. The ruins in front of the arch are those of the ancient Meta Sudans fountain, which Mussolini bulldozed in the 1930s to make way for a road that has since been removed.

The Colosseum

No matter how many pictures you've seen, the first impression you'll have of the **Colosseum** ✪✪✪ kids (Piazza del Colosseo; ☎ 06-39967700; 9€ integrated ticket with Colosseum and the Roman Forum; daily 9am to 1 hr. before sunset) is amazement at its sheer enormity. It is massive and looks as if it has been plopped down among the surrounding buildings, and not the other way around. Before you enter, you should take a long look at the Flavian Ampitheater (the Colosseum's original name) from the outside, and it's important to walk completely around its 500m (1,640-ft.) circumference. It doesn't matter where you start, but do the circle and look at the various stages of ruin before delving in. Note the different column styles on each level (if you can make them out through the black soot from the passing cars). The structure is marked with movement devices now and is carefully monitored for cracks and structural weaknesses. (The city's subway train runs nearby and it is an alarming sensation to stand at the foot of the giant theater and feel the vibrations below. There have been many attempts to reroute the subway to save the Colosseum, but so far none has been successful.)

Tip: It's a huge timesaver to buy your ticket for the inside of the Colosseum at the Palatine Hill, where lines are generally much shorter. You can then bypass the long lines here, or at least get into a shorter line to go inside. Only a few years ago, the Colosseum was free to the public, but with the addition of museum space on the second floor (complete with a shiny new elevator), visitors now have to pay. You can easily tour the whole of the Colosseum in less than an hour unless there is a particularly spectacular exhibit at the museum inside.

Once inside, walk onto the wooden platform that partially covers the center and look back at the perimeter walls. The stadium could hold as many as 87,000 spectators, by some counts, and seats were sectioned on three levels, dividing the people by social rank and gender. There were 80 entrances and historians say the massive crowds could be seated within a few minutes. Most events were free, but all spectators had to obtain a terra-cotta disc, called a *tessera,* to enter.

The Colosseum was built as a venue for gladiator contests and wild-animal fights, but when the Roman Empire fell it was abandoned and eventually overgrown with wild and exotic plants that are believed to have come from spores in the feces of the beasts that were imported from Africa for the arena spectacles. You'll notice on the top of the "good side," as locals call it, that there are a few remaining supports that once held the canvas awning that covered the stadium during rain or for the summer heat. During the Middle Ages it became a palace, and then a multihousing complex of sorts, with structures attached to its sides and top. Much of the ancient travertine that covered its outside was used for palaces like the nearby Palazzo Venezia and Palazzo Cancelleria near the Campo de' Fiori.

Now the Colosseum is one of the most visited sights in Rome, and it has lately become a concert venue, with performers like Paul McCartney and Elton John setting up giant stages on the Via dei Fori Imperiali to perform free concerts for up to a million people. It's also a holy site: The pope delivers Good Friday Mass here.

COLLE OPPIO

The gentle hill just behind the Colosseum known as the Colle Oppio holds one of Rome's most controversial treasures. Nero's **Domus Aurea (Golden House)** ✪✪ (Via della Domus Aurea; ☎ 06-39967700; Tues–Fri 10am–4pm; reservations mandatory) was built on the singed site of ruins left over after the famous fire of A.D. 64, which the eccentric emperor allegedly set himself. Originally the villa was a three-story building dripping with gold on the outside and plastered with mother-of-pearl and precious gems on the inside. That which was not bejeweled was instead frescoed by famous artists of the day. The fountains on the grounds and inside the palace courtyards flowed with perfume, and one of the rooms had an enormous revolving ceiling painted with zodiac signs and stars. There were man-made lakes and forests surrounding a 35m (116-ft.) statue (in gold, of course) of Nero himself. It was as opulent as Rome ever was—nothing before it had been so expensively decorated. But Nero was despised by the Romans and when he died in A.D. 68, the next emperor, Vespasian, set to work destroying and burying the palace. The Colosseum was built on the spot where he drained Nero's largest lake. The ruins were visited by Renaissance artists like Raphael, who were inspired by the frescoes. The site you see today officially opened in 1999, after many years of excavation. In 2005, part of the Domus Aurea collapsed and the site closed to visitors for about a year. It's currently "open for restoration," so rooms accessible to visitors may vary depending on archaeologists' work. There are still more than 30 rooms under the earth left to discover.

On the other side of the Colle Oppio is what would be an otherwise ordinary church by Roman standards, if not for its hidden masterpieces. **San Pietro in Vincoli (St. Peter in Chains)** (Piazza di San Pietro in Vincoli 4A; ☎ 06-4882865; daily 7:30am–noon and 3:30–6pm) has one of Michelangelo's most famous works, the statue of *Moses* ★. Its angry horns are a result of a mistranslation of a Hebrew text of the Old Testament in which the transcriber mistook the word for "radiant" to mean "horned." At the altar are the chains that the devoted believe were used to shackle St. Peter to his cross.

PIAZZA VENEZIA

Piazza Venezia is Rome's center square. This is where the city puts its Christmas tree, where demonstrations usually start, and where the official New Year's Eve countdown is held. It is a square rich in historical significance and it would be a wonderful place to spend time if not for the screeching, screaming, maddening traffic that whirls around the center flower beds at lightning speed.

Il Vittoriano ★ (Piazza Venezia; free; daily 9:30am–4pm), the Victor Emmanuel II monument, was built to commemorate Italy's unification under its first king in 1885, so it is a relatively new addition to this part of Rome. Many Romans consider it an eyesore. The most common complaint is that the marble is "too white" in contrast to the worn travertine and warm ochre tones of the surrounding buildings. It's often referred to as the typewriter or the wedding cake for its shape. Inside is a war museum, and on the steps in front is the tomb and eternal flame for the Unknown Soldier. The best way to appreciate this monument is to climb to the top; it's generally quiet and empty, even though it offers some of the best views, free or otherwise, of the Colosseum, forums, and expanse of ancient Rome (especially from the newly opened Terrazza delle Quadrighe, which is set at the very top of the Vittoriano; you'll pay 7€ and ride a sketchy glass elevator to get up there). Take your binoculars and look out across the rooftops for an army of statues of angels, martyrs, saints, and Romans that line the church tops and private gardens all around. They're near invisible from below, and most are long forgotten.

If you're a war buff, swing through the Risorgimento Museum, inside the Vittoriano, on your way down. It's free, and it is entirely focused on martial history, with weapons, battle plans, and uniforms used by the Italian military. There's even a bloodstained boot that Giuseppe Garibaldi wore when he was shot at Aspromonte, Sicily, during the fight for Italian unification.

CAMPIDOGLIO

Set behind the Vittoriano, the **Basilica di Santa Maria in Aracoeli** (daily 9am–5:30pm) is one of Rome's most celebrated Christmas churches when it becomes the stage for a live Nativity scene during the 12 days of Christmas. The floor is a medieval patchwork of worn marble, and the glass chandeliers provide a dim light, giving it a positively eerie feel. The foot-worn tombs in the naves are where the babies and children of Italian royalty were laid to rest. Tubby cherubs line the walls, and there is a replica of a wooden statue of the baby Jesus which was carved out of an olive tree from the Garden of Gethsemane near Jerusalem. The original was purported to have magical healing powers, especially for sick children, but was stolen from the church several years back. *Tip:* You can reach the church via Piazza del Campidoglio, a much easier climb than the steep steps of the church.

Capitoline Museums

The masterpieces in the **Capitoline Museums** ✪✪✪ (Piazza del Campidoglio 1; ☎ 06-39967800; www.museicapitolini.org; 6.50€, or 8€ for the combo ticket that includes the Centrale Montemartini; daily 9am–8pm, ticket booth closes at 7pm) are considered Rome's most valuable (remember: the Vatican Museums are *not* part of Rome's collection). They certainly were collected early: This is the old-est public museum *in the world*. Start your museum tour in the courtyard of the **Palazzo dei Conservatori** (that's the building on the right, if you enter via the Cordonata ramp, from the Piazza Venezia), a hauntingly surreal space scattered with gargantuan stone body parts (*A Nightmare on Elm Street* in marble!). They're actually the remnants of a massive 12m (39-ft.) statue of the Emperor Constantine, including his colossal head, hand, and foot, from the Basilica of Maxentius and Constantine in the Roman Forum.

The museum floor plan is straightforward, taking you through each of the rooms in a circle around the building's center courtyard. On the **first floor,** the unmissable works are in the first rooms. These include a remarkably well-pre-served 2nd-century bronze statue of Hercules; the *Spinario* (a lifelike bronze of a young boy digging a splinter out of his foot; it was widely copied during the Renaissance); and *La Lupa,* a bronze statue from 500 B.C. of the famous she-wolf that suckled Romulus and Remus, the mythical founders of Rome. The twins were not on the original Etruscan statue; they were added during the Renaissance period in the 15th century. A personal favorite is the famed *Dying Gaul,* a Roman copy of a lost ancient Greek work. Lord Byron considered the statue so lifelike and moving, he included mention of it in his poem "Childe Harold's Pilgrimage." **Room 5** has Bernini's famously pained portrait of *Medusa.* The rest of these rooms are less significant artistically, so skim them without regret until you reach the stairway to the **second-floor picture gallery** with several masterpieces, including Caravaggio's *John the Baptist,* as well as Titian's *Baptism of Christ,* Tintoretto's *Penitent Madgalene,* and Veronese's *Rape of Europa.*

At the end of the picture gallery, head down to the ground floor and the underground tunnel that will take you under the piazza to the Palazzo Nuovo.

Centrale Montemartini: Venus in the Boiler Room

Before the year 2000 Jubilee celebrations in Rome, the Culture Ministry relocated all the statues not displayed in the Capitoline Museums to an abandoned electricity warehouse outside the city gates, on Via Ostiense. Few believed the project would take off, but the **Centrale Montemartini** ★ (Via Ostiense 106; ☎ 06-5748030; www.centralemontemartini.org; 4.50€, or free with 8€ Capitoline Museum integrated ticket; bus: 23 or 769) has become one of the most provocative venues in the city. The pristine statues, many of which had never been seen, were set against shiny black machinery and spruced-up antique gasworks. The result was, and is, stunning. This museum is a favorite of Italian school groups.

The vacant **Tabularium,** built in 78 B.C. to safely house ancient Rome's city records, was later used as a salt mine, and then as a prison. The atmospheric stone gallery was opened to the public in the late 1990s as part of the Capitoline Museums.

Once inside the **Palazzo Nuovo,** start your tour in the open courtyard with the statue of Marcus Aurelius (behind bulletproof glass), which stood for decades in the center of the Piazza del Campidoglio outside. This section of the museum is dedicated to statues that were excavated from the forums below and brought in from outlying areas like Hadrian's Villa (p. 89) in Tivoli. Statues are well marked and the floor plan is very straightforward. The masterpieces here are the 1st-century *Capitoline Venus,* in **Room 3** (a modest lass covering up after a bath; Napoleon admired it so much, he took it back to Paris with him), and a chronologically arranged row of busts of Roman emperors and their families. These rooms are often filled with students of art history who study the busts for changes in sculpting techniques. I've always wondered why young stylists didn't visit, too—they're equally telling of changes in hairstyles and fashion during the Roman Empire. Staring at the vacant eyes of these real people from the past is perhaps my favorite thing to do in Rome on a winter's afternoon.

These museums can be seen in a couple of hours, if you are pressed for time. Your integrated ticket is good for multiple entrances for 3 days, so you can even revisit them.

VATICAN CITY

For many people, it is virtually impossible to separate Vatican City from Rome. The two entities seem to intertwine as one bustling metropolis, though, in reality, they are very distinct places. Vatican City, called the Holy See, has been an independent state since 1929, when Mussolini and Pope Pius XII signed the Lateran Pact giving Vatican City sovereignty and giving the pope ultimate control over this tiny parcel of land bordered by the Vatican walls. There are 800 mostly male residents in Vatican City, which has its own independent government, independent passports, embassies, and diplomatic status with nearly every country in the world. In addition, Vatican City has its own army, its own media outlets, its

The Swiss Guard

The Vatican army, or Swiss Guard, is made up of 100 Swiss men: 4 officers, 1 chaplain, 23 noncommissioned officers, 70 halberdiers (weapon carriers), and 2 drummers. In many ways they are a modern-day male version of the ancient Vestal Virgins (p. 54), though instead of the sacred flame of vestal, they are tasked with protecting the pope when he travels, and with keeping harm from the Apostolic Palace within Vatican City. Their colorful formal uniforms were designed by Michelangelo in the colors of the Medici family. They live within the walls of Vatican City and must not marry until their duty is complete—they serve between 2 and 25 years. Recruits must be under 30 and at least 1.7m (5 ft., 8 in.) tall. And, of course, they must be upstanding Roman Catholics, as witnessed by their parish priests.

own well-stocked international pharmacy, and a postal system far more efficient than the regular Italian post. Popes representing the Vatican have always had the ear of, or at least been given royal treatment by, key world leaders. In theory, the Vatican is not supposed to meddle in Italian politics; the Church's influence is, however, often obvious in policymaking in Italy, which has recently adopted fertility laws backed by the Holy See and continues to hold conservative views on gay marriage.

St. Peter's Basilica

The sensible place to start your visit to Vatican City is **St. Peter's Basilica** ✪✪✪ (Piazza San Pietro; ☎ 06-69881662; www.vatican.va; free; Oct–Mar 7am–6pm, until 7pm rest of year). Enter via metal detectors on the right-hand side of the piazza (facing the church). There's a barricade near the foot of the steps into the church where your attire will be scrutinized by the Vatican's fashion police, who enforce a strict dress code. No one wearing shorts is allowed inside. (There are dressing rooms behind the main steps into the church to change into more appropriate clothing.) At the top of the steps into the church, the queue divides again between the *chiesa*, which leads to the inside of the church, and the Cupola, which takes you to the top of the dome. Visit the church before the Cupola.

The current church took 120 years to build. It was completed in 1626 on the site of the original church that had been built 1,300 years earlier. A few remnants of the original basilica still exist, like the Giotto mosaic in the portico just opposite the main entrance door. Once inside, the natural tendency is to veer to your right to see Michelangelo's famous *Pietà* first. But you'll have a much better perspective of the sheer magnitude of this basilica if you walk down the center aisle all the way to the front (unless it is set up with chairs or otherwise closed for an event, which is common around Easter). While walking up the **middle aisle**, look for the various names of churches and brass lines inscribed into the marble floor—they identify the length of those churches compared to St. Peter's.

Head toward Bernini's baroque *baldacchino*, or canopy, over the main altar, reserved for the pope. The exquisitely detailed canopy is made from the bronze

Bronze Door **4**

Excavations office **11**

Grotto Entrance **10**

Hall of Audiences **13**

House of Pius IV **3**

Michelangelo's *Pietà* **6**

Palace of the
Governorship **8**

Sacristy & Treasury **10**

Sistine Chapel **5**

Statue of St. Peter **7**

Vatican Gardens **2**

Vatican Museums
Entrance **1**

Vatican Post Office **12**

Vatican Radio **9**

that may have once adorned the porch of the Pantheon. The design is inspired by a Mesopotamian tradition of draping woven silks made in Baghdad over a four-poster framework to mark a holy site. Bernini sculpted the face of a woman on the marble bases of each of the pillars, whose countenance is progressively contorted in childbirth pain starting with the first face on the left pillar (with your back to the entrance of the church). Circle the entire altar to see the progression until the fourth pillar, where the woman's face is replaced with a newborn's unmistakable mug.

Below the main altar in the enclave surrounded by steps is a tiny shrine with a modest 9th-century mosaic of Christ, again from the original church. Below that are what are believed by the devout to be the bones of St. Peter. From here, the top spot for pilgrims to the basilica tends to be the bronze statue of St. Peter just behind the altar. There is usually a short queue to kiss his worn foot.

From Bernini's baldacchino, head to **the right side of the church** to visit the important chapels. In the first one near the entrance is the *Pietà*, Michelangelo's first major work, completed when he was 25 years old. The crowds are thickest here, but they tend to move quickly, so it's easy to stand at the front for a few moments. From behind the baluster, it's difficult to spot Michelangelo's signature across the Virgin Mary's chest.

Other highlights include the only original painting left in this church, the *Trinity* by Pietro da Cortona, in the third chapel. The rest have been replaced with replicas made from mosaic tiles. At the very **back of the church,** pilgrims can attend Mass (check the sign at the entrance to the pews for times) under Bernini's *Throne to St. Peter.* Toward the papal altar, displayed on the pillars that support the giant dome, are several artifacts important to Catholics, including a fragment from the True Cross and a statue of St. Veronica holding a cloth she used to wipe Christ's face. All along the side aisles are chapels, shrines, altars, and monuments. These are generally not well marked, though they are worth exploring. The Vatican sells a guidebook that will give you more detail on these shrines.

The Crypt

Once you've finished exploring the inside of St. Peter's, head down to the grottoes below the current church, and above the necropolis of the ancient church. Down here are the tombs of dozens of popes from the last 5 centuries, including that of the beloved Pope John Paul II, who died in April 2005.

The Cupola

Visiting the dome of St. Peter's is an essential way to connect the various entities of Vatican City that you can see from above. Follow signs on the right-hand side of the basilica for the **Cupola** ✦ (4€, 6€ with elevator; Oct–Apr daily 8am–4:45pm, until 5:45 rest of year). The first "get-off" point is the inner rim just under Michelangelo's dome, which allows you to appreciate both the detailed mosaics of the dome's interior and the intricate marble designs on the floor of the church. The mesh fence is to deter suicides, a common problem here in the 1980s. When you leave the inner dome, follow the tiny signs for the Cupola to get to the very tip,

---

Pope Spotting

Millions of devout Catholics come to Vatican City each year to make a religious pilgrimage and, more recently, to catch a glimpse of Pope Benedict XVI, who blesses the faithful and the curious alike in St. Peter's Square every Sunday at noon when he is in Rome. Go early if you want to see him in his apartment window above Bernini's colonnade. The best place to stand is near the obelisk in the center of the square, though these spots are generally taken by locals in the know. The pope also holds a public audience each Wednesday, in St. Peter's Square on sunny days and in the Sala Nervi auditorium when the weather is grim. You must apply for the free papal audience through the **Prefettura della Casa Pontificia** (☎ 06-69883114 or 06-69883273; fax 06-69885863; Mon–Sat 9am–1:30pm), or, if you're a Catholic, through your local parish priest. Tickets must be picked up the morning of the audience at the bronze door to the left of St. Peter's Basilica on St. Peter's Square.

You can write to the pope (which often results in an autographed photo) at His Holiness Pope Benedict XVI, Apostolic Palace, Vatican City, EUROPE 00120. He also has an e-mail address: benedictxvi@vatican.va.

The Scavi Tour: Descending to Peter's Tomb ★★

Some 12m (40 ft.) beneath the behemoth that is St. Peter's Basilica are Catacomb-like excavations where most experts believe St. Peter was buried after his crucifixion in A.D. 64. With all the gravitas you might expect in such a place, hushed-voiced priests lead small groups of huddled visitors-in-the-know through the ancient tunnels of the Vatican necropolis. The taut and spiritually fraught narration about the relatively recent discovery of some actual bones (and the strong archaeological evidence that they are Peter's) is as thrilling as any Dan Brown novel. To secure a spot on one of these highly sought-after tours, write to the Ufficio degli Scavi (☎ 06-69885318; fax 06-69885518; scavi@fsp.va; 10€). Because the tour has gotten more press in recent years, it's become more exclusive: Often you can only get in with a letter of recommendation from your parish priest or from a professor if you are a student of archaeology. If you're interested, apply *well* in advance, and follow up with the office yourself because they won't track you down. English-language tours must be booked at least 25 days in advance, and children under 12 are not allowed to take the tour.

which takes about 20 minutes to reach from here. It is well worth making this trek to get a view of the Vatican's walls and Rome from the city's highest point. But do this only if you can physically manage. The passageway near the upper reaches is shoulder-width on an average person, and it is very crowded, with few options for resting, and absolutely no way to turn back until you've reached the top.

The Vatican Museums

There are many ways to visit the **Vatican Museums** ★★★ (Viale del Vaticano; ☎ 06-69883333; www.vatican.va; 13€ adults, 8€ seniors and students, 24€ reserved with guided tour; Mar–Oct Mon–Fri 10am–3:30pm, Sat 10am–1:30pm; Nov–Feb Mon–Sat 10am–12:30pm; closed Catholic holidays). If you're in Rome for only a day or two, consider the 24€ guided tour with reserved ticket (entrance before 10am). The tour takes 2 hours to cover the highlights, and you'll probably save at least that much time by avoiding lines, though you might feel rushed if you're interested in poring over certain artworks at greater length. *Note:* The Vatican's hours change on holidays and seasonally. For the most up-to-the-minute schedules, head to www.vatican.va and navigate to the current hours.

There are also four color-coded, self-guided itineraries through the massive museums, which take between 2 and 5 hours, depending on the care with which you peruse the collections. The quickest way to see the museums, if you're among the first 100 in, is to head straight for the Sistine Chapel—following the often hidden signs—when you enter the main museum, and then make your way back around to the various rooms and galleries you want to see. If you are in the middle of thousands and thousands of visitors who are allowed to enter the museums at the same time, this shortcut won't make much difference because the Sistine Chapel will be jam-packed no matter how quickly you get there.

In 2000, the Vatican Museums installed metal detectors to deter both vandalism and terrorism, so the entrance to the museums is something like boarding a commercial flight. Large monitors flash listings of closed exhibits, and there is a general sense of hasty movement, as tour leaders try to keep their groups close by and Vatican guards move the crowds quickly to let more inside. Do your best to weave through these groups and take the escalator to the mezzanine floor and the ticket booth. A separate booth rents audioguides, which are very well done and offer enlightening explanations. (Note that if you rent an audioguide, you'll have to leave ID as collateral, and you must return the audioguide at this desk, which means you can't leave the museums via the handy "secret" exit of the Sistine Chapel that leads straight to St. Peter's.)

If you can only spend a few hours here, narrow your tour to include only the **Sistine Chapel, Raphael Rooms, the Pio-Clementine ancient sculpture collections,** and the **Gallery of the Maps.**

As with most museums, your own tastes should dictate where you focus your attention, but the following highlights should help you narrow down the choices:

- **Appartamento Borgia:** The six rooms of these apartments are decorated with religious frescoes focused on biblical themes. They were originally designed for the Borgia Pope Alexander VI (1492–1503).
- **Museo Gregoriano Profano:** This small set of rooms houses sculptures found at the Baths of Caracalla (p. 80). The Greek statues are from the 4th and 5th centuries B.C.; the Roman statues are from the 1st, 2nd, and 3rd centuries A.D.
- **Galleria delle Carte Geografiche:** The 120m-long (394-ft.) Gallery of Maps was commissioned by Pope Gregory XIII. The frescoed maps were first drawn by Ignazio Danti of Perugia from 1580 to 1583 to represent each region, city, and island of Italy.
- **Pio-Clementine Museums:** Here you'll see some of the world's finest Greek and Roman sculpture, including the *Apollo Belvedere,* the *Laocoon* group, and the Belvedere torso.
- **Museo Egiziano:** The collections in these rooms represent ancient Egyptian art from 3000 to 600 B.C., including mummies, a depiction of a baboon god, and marble statues of significant leaders like *Trono di Rameses II.*
- **Pinacoteca:** The picture galleries include many masterpieces collected by various popes and cardinals over the ages, including some of the most famous works in the Vatican—Giotto's *Stefaneschi Triptych,* Raphael's *The Transfiguration* (his last work), and Caravaggio's *Entombment.*
- **Stanze di Raffaello, Loggia di Raffaello, Cappella di Niccolo V:** The Raphael Rooms are among the finest museum offerings in the world. These rooms were originally used as the Papal Suite and designed by Raphael when he was only 26 years old. If you can, see these in the order in which they were painted, starting with the Study (Stanza della Segnatura), which was completed between 1508 and 1511 on the theme of the triumph of Truth, Good, and Beauty. Most notable here is the *School of Athens,* which features portraits of famous names of the day. Leonardo da Vinci is pointing up to the heavens a la Plato; Michelangelo (who was painting the nearby Sistine Chapel when Raphael did this work) is alone in front of the steps; and even a self-portrait of Raphael is on the right-hand corner.

Almost Hell

Down the Lungotevere Prati, which borders the Tiber River from Vatican City, is Rome's smallest Gothic church, **Sacro Cuore del Suffragio (Sacred Heart of Suffrage)** (Lungotevere Prati 12; ☎ 06-68806517; Mon–Sat 7:30–11am and 4–7pm), which holds the freakish Museum of the Souls of Purgatory. A chapel inside the original church was destroyed by fire in 1897 and in the singed remains the faithful congregation could see the outline of a face they believed was a soul caught in purgatory. The singed face prompted the local priest, Father Victor Jouet from Marseilles, to seek out other signs from the souls in purgatory, which he collected over the years. These haunting relics line the corridor to the church sacristy, and include fabrics, photos, writing materials, and other items that believers attest have been somehow touched by those waiting in purgatory. A book of devotion dated 1871 with the imprint of three fingers and a photo of a deceased woman said to be asking for a holy Mass in her name are two of the relics. Followers are urged to come to this church to pray that the souls in purgatory be released.

The Sistine Chapel

Michelangelo labored for 4 years (1508–12) to paint the ceiling of the **Sistine Chapel ✪✪✪**; it is said he spent the entire time on his feet, paint dripping into his eyes. But what a result! The world's most famous fresco, thanks to a massive restoration effort in the 1990s, is as vibrantly colorful and filled with roiling life as it was in 1512. Start your visual journey at the *Separation of Light and Darkness,* and then look over to the *Creation of Sun, Moon and Planets;* the *Separation of Land and Sea;* the *Creation of Fishes and Birds;* the *Creation of Adam;* the *Creation of Eve;* the *Temptation and Expulsion from Paradise;* the *Sacrifice of Noah;* the *Flood;* and the *Drunkenness of Noah.* Once you've viewed the ceiling, turn your attention to the altar wall and Michelangelo's much later *Last Judgment* (1535–41).

At the age of 60, Michelangelo was summoned to finish the chapel decor 23 years after he finished the ceiling work. Apparently saddened by leaving Florence and by the poor, morally bankrupt state of Rome at that time, he painted these dark moods in his *Last Judgment,* where he included his own self-portrait on a sagging human hide held by St. Bartholomew (who was martyred by being flayed alive).

Along the chapel walls, starting on the left-hand side when facing the *Last Judgment,* are Perugino's *Journey of Moses,* Botticelli's *Events from the Life of Moses,* Cosimo Rosselli's *Crossing the Red Sea* and *Moses Receives the Tablets of the Law,* Luca Signorelli's *The Testament of Moses,* and Matteo da Lecce's *The Dispute over Moses' Body.* On the right-hand side facing the *Last Judgment* are Perugino's *The Baptism of Christ,* Botticelli's *The Temptations of Christ,* Ghirlandaio's *The Calling of the Apostles,* Perugino's *Handing over the Keys,* Cosimo Rosselli's *The Sermon on the Mount* and *The Last Supper,* and Hendrik van den Broeck's *The Resurrection.*

It is in this decidedly regal chapel that the conclave to elect new popes is held.

Castel Sant'Angelo

The rotund **Castel Sant'Angelo** ★ 🧒 (Lungotevere Castello 50; ☎ 06-6819111; 7€ adults, 2.50€ seniors and students; daily 9am–8pm) was built as Hadrian's family mausoleum and has been used as a fortress, papal residence, and military prison—remnants of which are still evident inside. This is a complex, multilayered site, so consider renting an audioguide at the ticket stand to help you fully understand the various entities. A wide stone ramp winds its way from the ground-floor entrance around the castle to the upper terraces, from which you can see the full facade of St. Peter's Basilica without the usual obstruction of neighboring buildings. From here, wander through passageways and Renaissance apartments used by popes. Down below the apartments are ancient dungeons once used as torture chambers. Lower terraces house replica cannons and travertine cannonballs—always fun for imaginative children. Don't miss the highest point of all, the Terrazza dell'Angelo, which is crowned by a dramatic statue of the archangel Michael shielding his sword (protecting Rome from plague). This upper rampart is where Puccini set the tragic denouement of the opera *Tosca,* where the title character takes a swan dive into the Tiber below. Castel Sant'Angelo even has a surprisingly inexpensive coffee bar with outdoor seating under the stone arches. The castle is connected to St. Peter's Basilica by **Il Passetto** (free with museum entrance; guided tours Sat 3pm). This walled escape route was used by popes who needed to make a narrow escape to the fortress.

THE PANTHEON

For many residents of Rome, the area between Piazza Navona and the Pantheon is for lingering and strolling, especially on Sundays in the fall and early spring, when everyone in the city, it seems, is here.

The **Pantheon** ★★★ (Piazza della Rotonda; free; Mon–Sat 8:30am–7:30pm, Sun 9am–6pm, holidays 9am–1pm) itself is like an enormous elephant hiding in the middle of a crowded village. The structure is the best preserved antiquity in the entire city, and holds an allure that is almost magical, especially if you happen to visit when it is raining and the drops form a cylinder from the opening in the dome to the marble drains below. Built under Hadrian's direction (many of the structure's bricks contain the emperor's seal) between A.D. 119 and 128, the Pantheon was a temple to 12 gods. It was saved from ruin only because the Catholic Church claimed it in 608, even though the Church used it primarily as a quarry for materials for other churches. (An arguable theory is that the bronze from the Pantheon's porch was removed and melted down by Bernini in 1626 to make the baldacchino, or canopy, in St. Peter's Basilica.)

The best way to appreciate the Pantheon is first from across the piazza, gazing at the sheer magnitude of the massive pillars and domed roof. Remember: The ancient street level was about 6m (20 ft.) lower than the modern cobblestones. As you walk closer to the building, the detail of the pillars (which do not match—some are pink granite, some are gray) becomes apparent. You may notice the notches on which vegetable market stalls were affixed until the 18th century.

Once inside the massive doors, look up at the 9m (30-ft.) oculus, which is believed to be there to allow worshipers direct contact with the heavens. It is the only source of light in the building, and the sunbeam acts as a spotlight on various

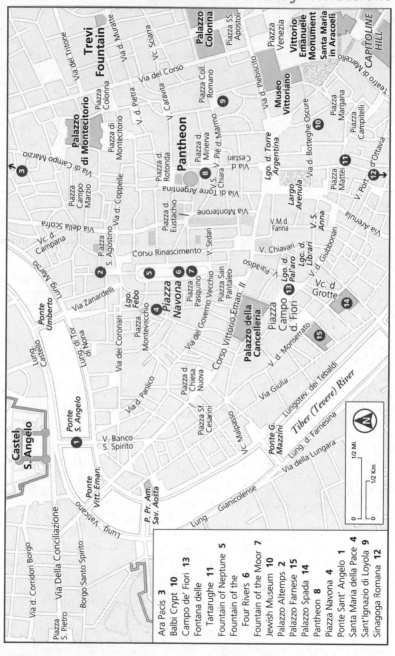

Ara Pacis **3**
Balbi Crypt **10**
Campo de' Fiori **13**
Fontana delle
    Tartarughe **11**
Fountain of Neptune **5**
Fountain of the
    Four Rivers **6**
Fountain of the Moor **7**
Jewish Museum **10**
Palazzo Altemps **2**
Palazzo Farnese **15**
Palazzo Spada **14**
Pantheon **8**
Piazza Navona **4**
Ponte Sant' Angelo **1**
Santa Maria della Pace **4**
Sant'Ignazio di Loyola **9**
Sinagoga Romana **12**

points around the building. The Emperor Hadrian would only enter the building when the sun shone on the door, around 11am, depending on the time of year.

The diameter of the dome is 44m (144 ft.), and the dome itself gets lighter and thinner toward the top, decreasing from 7m (23-ft.) thickness at the edges to a thin 1m (3¼ ft.) close to the apex. It would take a professional to notice, but the materials used to build the dome vary from a heavy concrete and travertine on the lower third of the dome, volcanic tufa in the middle section, and lightweight pumice in the upper reaches. The dome's structure was unsurpassed in terms of size and architectural accomplishment until the 1500s, when other domes were built. The seven niches, which are now tombs of kings and artists (Raphael is buried in the glass-encased tomb), once held statues of gods and goddesses.

Tip: In the summer, the Pantheon can be quite crowded during the day, but it is invariably empty when it opens at 8:30am.

Behind the Pantheon, in front of the Gothic church of **Santa Maria Sopra Minerva** ✹, sits *Il Pulcino della Minerva*—also known as Bernini's elephant—which was symbolic in the Catholic Church for its wisdom and abstinence (elephants are notoriously monogamous).

PIAZZA NAVONA

From the Pantheon it's less than a 10-minute walk west to **Piazza Navona** ✹✹, which may be Rome's favorite square. It sits above an ancient stadium built by Emperor Domitian, which you can still see below the modern city from the Piazza di Tor Sanguigna, on the northern end of the oval. In antiquity, the stadium was used for track and field competitions—like the Greek Olympics—called *agones*. In the Renaissance period, the stadium was often flooded for mock sea battles. Call ☎ 06-67103819 for guided tours of the old stadium Saturday and Sunday from 10am to 1pm.

In the center of the modern piazza above is Bernini's famous **Fontana dei Quattro Fiumi** ✹✹✹, which represents the four major rivers of the known continents: the Nile, Ganges, Plate, and Danube. There's a legend that Bernini designed one of the statues facing the church of Sant'Agnese, a project of his rival Borromini, to shield its eyes from the "horror of the church." But the legend, which is a delightful piece of trivia, is false—the fountain was built before the church. Bernini's statues, instead, are shielding their eyes from the unknown source of the rivers. In fact, if you look above the church of Sant'Agnese, you'll see the haughty statue of St. Agnes turned away from the fountain, old-timers say, in disgust. Inside the church is a reliquary containing a small skull, said to be that of St. Agnes, who was beheaded in the Stadium of Domitian in the 3rd century A.D.

At the north end of Piazza Navona is the lovely Fontana del Nettuno (Fountain of Neptune) showing Neptune fighting a sea serpent. The Fontana del Moro (Fountain of the Moor) on the opposite end depicts another sea god and a dolphin designed by Bernini.

Just north of Piazza Navona, the **Museo Nazionale Romano: Palazzo Altemps** ✹ (Piazza Sant'Apollinare 48; ☎ 06-6833566; adults 6.50€, seniors and students 3.50€; Tues–Sun 9am–7:45pm), tucked inside Palazzo Altemps, is one of Rome's most charming museums. It's rarely crowded and houses some of Rome's most famous private and public collections of art. The pieces here are not great in number, but they are individually superb. **Room 7,** in particular, has two

1st-century statues of Apollo the Lyrist, and in the south loggia do not miss the *Galatian Soldier and His Wife Committing Suicide* in **Room 26,** or the famous bust of the mother of Emperor Claudius in **Room 21.**

Duck into two area churches, if you have the time. Down the street, **Santa Maria della Pace** (Vicolo dell'Arco della Pace 5; ☎ 06-6861156; officially but rarely open Tues–Fri 10am–12:45pm) features Raphael's *Sybils*. Then pop into the Cloister of Bramante next door, which is primarily a venue for visiting art exhibits; if you only want to see the heavenly cloister, you generally don't have to pay the admission for the exhibit. These cloisters are some of the finest in Italy, and define precisely the meditative purpose these structures serve.

Back on the other side of the Pantheon is **Sant'Ignazio di Loyola** (Piazza Sant'Ignazio; ☎ 06-6794406; daily 7:30am–12:15pm and 3–7:15pm), which is the center of the Jesuit order of the Catholic Church. When it was built in 1626, those living in a nearby monastery feared that a giant dome, which was in the original plans, would block their light. Instead, the artist Andrea Pozzo just painted the ceiling to mimic the inside of a dome and it's a darn impressive illusion, even today (stand on the yellow marble disc in the nave to get the full effect).

CAMPO DE' FIORI & THE JEWISH GHETTO

The sliver of city along the Tiber River stretching from the Jewish synagogue to the busy Corso Vittorio Emanuele II is very much the lifeblood of Rome's center. The streets here are tiny alleyways and, unlike Trastevere (p. 70) on the other side of the Tiber, or the more posh Tridente close to the Spanish Steps, there's a better sense here of neighborhood and Roman culture. In the Jewish Ghetto, the matrons bring their kitchen chairs outside to sit together each evening before supper in a way more reminiscent of a tiny village than a sprawling European capital.

Campo de' Fiori ★★ is the core of this section of Rome. Starting about 6am, it offers a colorful display of regional pride as the market vendors make an art out of selling everything from rosemary plants to potatoes. It's a ridiculously expensive vegetable market, though, with prices per kilogram sometimes double those of other markets. But people don't necessarily come here for the produce—it is a piazza with energy and vibrancy, perfect for a visitor who wants to feel as if he or she is part of the community.

Midafternoon is the sketchiest time to be here; lately local police have pinpointed this area as an afternoon drug haven. But around 5pm, it becomes a mod locale to take an after-work drink, and those over 30 gather at the wine bars and beer joints around the perimeter. By midevening, the square transforms once again into an open-air mecca for the 20-something crowd. There is a sense of unnerving chaos here come midnight, especially in the summer months when the piazza is filled with drinking, smoking, moped-driving kids.

You might also consider a stroll through the **Galleria Spada** (Piazza Capo di Ferro 3; ☎ 06-6874896; www.galleriaborghese.it; adults 5€, seniors and students 2.50€; Tues–Sun 8:30am–7:30pm), the handsome palazzo that houses the private art collection of Cardinal Bernardino Spada. It's a museum for those who don't like museums. The rooms, which were built as a private home for Cardinal Girolamo Capo di Ferro in 1540, are intriguing, with original frescoes and old, uneven tile floors. The art here is literally plastered all over the walls, which makes it less assuming and somehow easier to enjoy than the showcase art at some of the more traditional museums. Its most impressive aspect is the deceptive Borromini Corridor, a 10m-long (33-ft.) gallery that looks like it's much longer (guided visits of it leave when there are enough people gathered).

Another worthwhile stop is the **Crypta Balbi** (Via delle Botteghe Oscure 31; ☎ 06-6780167; integrated ticket 6.50€ adults, 3.50€ children), which defines, in great detail, the layers of Rome and how they represent the city's evolution from the 5th to the 10th centuries. On display are tools and other objects from everyday life in ancient Rome. This museum is often empty, which is surprising because its exhibits are genuinely eye opening. Below the museum is the crypt and ruins of an old set of stores where grains were sold and distributed. This is the newest addition to Rome's National Museum and is still one of the city's best kept secrets.

The Ghetto

Between the Crypta Balbi and the Tiber River is what is known as the Ghetto, home to Europe's oldest Jewish community, which has lived in this neighborhood for 2,000 years. The jewel of this area is the synagogue, which is accessible through the **Museo d'Arte Ebraica** ★★ (Lungotevere Cenci; ☎ 06-68400661; 7.50€, includes admission to synagogue; Mon–Thurs 9am–4:30pm [until 6:30 during summer], Fri 9am–1:30pm, Sun 9am–noon). On display are a number of exquisite ceremonial items, from crowns to Torah mantles. Visitors also learn the tragic history of the persecution of Rome's Jewish citizens over the centuries. There are papal edicts that surely make the modern-day Church cringe, as well as grim artifacts from concentration camps across Europe. Nearby, on a little square called Largo XVI Ottobre, is a plaque commemorating October 16, 1943, the day that Rome's Jewish families were rounded up and deported from the Ghetto to concentration camps.

Behind the synagogue on the Via Portico d'Ottavia are the ruins of an ancient piazza and the remnants of great temples that date back to Emperor Augustus in the 1st century. You can walk behind the ruins through a small passage near the end of the street, and wind your way toward Piazza Mattei and the **Fontana delle Tartarughe (Fountain of the Turtles)** ★★ kids, one of Rome's greatest little treasures. The fountain was built in the 1580s for the Duke of Mattei in 1 night to impress his fiancée (she lived in the large palazzo, which now houses the Center for American Studies). Hers is the window now walled in, but one can easily imagine her surprise when she woke to find the fountain built just for her.

TRASTEVERE

You need to spend but 5 minutes in **Trastevere** ★★★ to appreciate its seductive allure. Decaying facades of tightly packed buildings give it an old-world feel. The buzzing energy of the 20-somethings who swarm its streets come sundown make it the most youthful spot in the city. Sometimes Trastevere does not feel like Rome at all; at other times it is the only Rome there is.

It is a mistake to explore this area with a fixed agenda. This is the place where you should wander, as aimlessly as possible, like a mouse through the dizzying maze of alleyways. The time of day you visit Trastevere will dictate what you see. Early mornings are glorious here, as the shutters are flung open and the Trasteverini start the day. You'll hear a chorus of "aoh!" and "eh!" as the locals greet each other from their windows and down in the streets. Old-timers tend to stick to their particular corner, and there are some locals who haven't been "to the other side" of the river for years. In the middle of the day, after the stores and churches close for the sacred siesta, stop and listen to the echo of footsteps and the whispers down the narrow cobblestone streets. Trastevere is like a ghost town around 2pm, an ideal time to listen to the sounds that pour out of the open windows. It is truly a voyeur's paradise.

The neighborhood is perhaps best in the late afternoons, when the children play soccer in the squares and the smell of the burning wood from the just-lit pizza ovens fills the air. At night, the restaurant scene is unimaginably vibrant, with people of every age, from tiny babies in buggies to elderly couples walking hand in hand, filling the streets. Even at midnight Trastevere is just springing to life. Because of that, don't stay in this part of town if you are fond of quiet nights.

To most people, Piazza Santa Maria in Trastevere is the proverbial heart and soul of this area. Any time of the day or night, this piazza is buzzing with the type of contagious activity that most visitors equate with life in Rome. The 17th-century fountain in the center is the meeting point for those who live here. The church on this square, **Santa Maria in Trastevere** ★★ (Piazza Santa Maria in Trastevere; ☎ 06-5814802; daily 7:30am–8pm), is famous for the 13rh-century mosaics on the facade of Mary breastfeeding Jesus alongside 10 women with crowns and lanterns (often thought to represent the parable of the wise and foolish virgins). This is one of the oldest churches in Rome and one of its most captivating (take a gander at the 12th-c. mosaics by Pietro Cavallini that cover the apse). On weekends in the spring, it's not uncommon to witness gorgeous weddings, and on Saturday evenings, you can join the faithful as they stream in for evening Mass.

Down the way from here are the lush **Botanical Gardens (Orto Botanico)** (Largo Cristina di Svezia 24; ☎ 06-49917106; adults 3€, children 2€; Nov–Mar 9:30am–5:30pm, 1 hr. later rest of the year), with over 3,500 species of plants, including a sight-and-scent garden for the visually impaired. These gardens once belonged to the controversial Queen Christina of Sweden, whose home was the adjacent Palazzo Corsini, now the **Galleria Nazionale d'Arte Antica** (Via della Lungara 10; ☎ 06-6874845; www.galleriaborghese.it; adults 4€, seniors and students 2€; guided tours Tues–Fri at 9:30, 11:30am, and 12:30pm, Sat and holidays tours at 8:30am and 1:20pm). She moved to Rome when she abdicated the Swedish throne after converting to Catholicism, but her most famous epithet is "Queen without a realm, Christian without a faith, and a woman without shame." This stemmed from her blatant bisexuality, which in the 17th century was frowned upon—at least publicly. Several other big names stayed in this beautiful palace, including Michelangelo and Napoleon's mother, Letizia. Today it houses a moderately interesting museum with mostly the runoff from Italy's national art collection. There's a Caravaggio here worth note, the *Narcissus*, but otherwise the palace history and legend are more interesting than the museum itself.

A better museum is just across the street: the **Villa Farnesina** ★ (Via della Lungara 230; ☎ 06-68027268; www.lincei.it; adults 5€, seniors and students 4€; daily 9am–1pm Mar 15–June 30, Sept 15–Oct 31, and Dec), notable for its superb collection of works by Raphael, from *The Triumph of Galatea* to *Cupid and Psyche.*

The Gianicolo: Back Street to the Vatican

Via Garibaldi in Trastevere takes you up a winding path to the Gianicolo Hill and back down to Vatican City, past residential villas, glorious fountains, and captivating views of the center of Rome from various points on the side of this panoramic ridge. It's a walk worth doing if you have solid shoes and time to enjoy it. Piazzale Giuseppe Garibaldi, in particular, is the best place to watch the sun set over Rome, as the orange hue of Trastevere below seems to wash to gray when night falls. It is ultraromantic, and you will see your fair share of public affection here. But it is also a nice diversion if you've got kids. There is a puppet theater (in Italian only) and merry-go-round and pony rides during the late afternoon. At the top of the hill, keep an eye out for the statue of Giuseppe Garibaldi; nearby is a statue of his Brazilian wife, Anita, on a feisty horse, holding their baby in one hand and a pistol in the other. When you're ready to descend, head north along the ridge until you see the peak of St. Peter's Basilica, then follow the descending roads to the Vatican City gates. *One word of warning:* The Gianicolo cannon fires a blank shot every day at noon. It's audible citywide, so if you are up here when it goes off, it'll likely scare the bejeezus out of you!

Continue your exploration of Trastevere; from the Via Lungara, make your way back to the busy Viale Trastevere, which bisects the district, and cross into the quieter side of this neighborhood. The heart of this part of the neighborhood is the charming Piazza di Santa Cecilia with its 9th-century **Basilica di Santa Cecilia** ✷ (free; daily 9: 30am–12:30pm and 3:45–6:40pm). There is much to do in this tiny church, starting with the ruins of the house where St. Cecilia once lived. She was martyred for her strong faith and vow of chastity—even to her husband—first by a failed attempt at scalding her, and then by a slow decapitation that took 3 days to finish her off. The nuns inside the church, who charge 2€ for entrance to the ruins of St. Cecilia's house below, say that she sang during the last days of her life, and so was made the patron saint of music. Her body was allegedly found intact when her tomb was opened in 1599. Artist Stefano Maderno immediately captured this image and it was later sculpted in white marble. The nuns claim the original is in the San Callisto Catacombs (though the priests at the San Callisto Catacombs say the original is here at the altar). You should also try to visit the 13th-century fresco of *The Last Judgment* by **Pietro Cavallini** (Tues and Thurs 10am–noon, Sun 11:30am–12:30pm) back in the choir, which is still used by the adjacent convent's cloistered nuns. If you're here when the frescoes are closed, you can almost certainly still see them if you pledge an offering to the sisters who tend the church. If you happen to be wandering in Trastevere in the early morning or dead of afternoon, you'll often hear the cloistered nuns of this church singing their prayers. Granted, it's no *Sound of Music*, but charming nonetheless.

From here, you can easily visit the **Chiesa di San Francesco a Ripa** (Piazza San Francesco d'Assisi 88) and its Bernini sculpture of the Beata Ludovica Albertoni, which may make you want to convert if her expression is any indication of what being a Catholic is really about. This church also has the rock that St. Francis reportedly used as a pillow, but you'll have to twist the arm of the attendant to see it; it's not usually shown to the public.

TIBER ISLAND & BOCCA DELLA VERITÀ

Between the two similarly decaying districts of the Ghetto and Trastevere lies **Tiber Island** ★ 🧒, which was said to be built on the site of a sunken ship in the 3rd century B.C. It was originally adorned with travertine in the shape of a giant ship, with an obelisk at the center for the mast. You can still see the remnants of the travertine siding on the east side of the island, below the police station, by walking down the narrow steps just below the Fate Bene Fratelli Hospital that occupies the entire northern end. The wide promenade on the bottom fills with Sunday strollers and springtime sunbathers, and is the location of Rome's annual open-air cinema for much of the summer. Kids have a lot of fun running around down here, but don't bring the really little ones, as there's no barrier between the edge of the esplanade and the river. On the southern side of the island, are the remains of the Ponte Rotto (Broken Bridge), Rome's first stone bridge, built in 142 B.C. It connected the main city with the area across the Tiber, giving birth to *tras tevere*, which means "across the Tiber."

It's a short walk from the east side of Tiber Island to the 6th-century church of **Santa Maria in Cosmedin** (Via della Bocca della Verità 18; ☎ 06-6781419; free; daily 9am–5pm winter, until 6pm in summer), home to the de rigueur photo-op **Bocca della Verità (Mouth of Truth)** ★ 🧒. Legend states that anyone who tells a lie while his hand is in the mouth will have it bitten off. Locals like to say that it was Roman wives suspicious of cheating husbands who started requiring the test. The giant mask was probably an ancient drain cover.

PIAZZA DEL POPOLO, SPANISH STEPS (TRIDENTE) & TREVI FOUNTAIN

The area immediately surrounding Piazza del Popolo, bordered on one side by the Tiber River and on the other by the Spanish Steps, is the commercial heart of historical central Rome. A balanced mix of museums, churches, antiquities, and modern amenities makes many believe they have seen all of Rome if they've spent time here. But most of the restaurants here are expensive and ultratrendy, and the stores tend to be more upmarket than those in other parts of town.

Start your exploration of this area at **Piazza del Popolo** ★, which is joined in a straight line to the Piazza Venezia by the very narrow Via del Corso. At the far end of the piazza is the Porta del Popolo, which for centuries was the main gate into the city of Rome off the Via Flaminia (which extended all the way to the Adriatic Coast near Venice). The obelisk in the center of this piazza once graced the Circus Maximus, and the two churches leading into the city center create an optical illusion—they are not actually the same size, though they look identical from under the gates on the Porta del Popolo. Next to Porta del Popolo itself is the rather gem-laden church of **Santa Maria del Popolo** ★ (Piazza del Popolo 12;

☎ 06-3610836; free; Mon–Sat 7am–noon and 4–7pm, Sun 8:30am–1:30pm and 4:30–7pm); Raphael's frescoed Chigi chapel and a pair of Caravaggio masterpieces (*The Crucifixion of St. Peter* and *The Conversion of St. Paul*, in which the focal point is the rear end of a horse) are found inside.

There isn't much to do on Piazza del Popolo but spend money in expensive cafes, so head down the Via Ripetta toward the **Mausoleum of Augustus** (Piazza Augusto Imperatore, Via Ripetta)—which is spectacular in size, but not open to the public—and the newly renovated **Ara Pacis (Altar of Peace)** ✹ (Via Ripetta, Lungotevere in Augusta; ☎ 06-82059127; www.arapacis.it; 6.50€; Tues–Sun 9am–7pm), which has become the bane of existence for most Italians who are appalled by the modernity of this renovated showcase. This museum opened in 2006 after a decade-long, multimillion-euro project. The Altar of Peace inside the boxy showcase was reconstructed from fragments found in museums across the country, and after a thorough excavation below a modern city block near Piazza San Lorenzo in Lucina. Until the 1990s the altar was housed in a rather shabby, Fascist-era enclosure. Much to his credit, the American architect Richard Meier incorporated elements from the surrounding area, but to many Italians his glassy and blindingly white box (which some critics have likened to a Texas gas station) is a far too modern addition to the area.

Next, wind your way through this charming patchwork neighborhood and across to the Via del Corso to explore the rest of the area. There are several stops you can make along the Via del Corso and close to the Spanish Steps, though most are esoteric in nature, so pick and choose as your taste dictates.

For those interested in literature, your choices range from the **Casa di Goethe** (Via del Corso 18; ☎ 06-32650412; www.casadigoethe.it; adults 4€, seniors and students 2€; Tues–Sun 10am–6pm), which has a collection of the German poet's diaries and letters, to the 18th-century **Keats-Shelley Memorial House** (Piazza di Spagna 26; ☎ 06-6784235; www.keats-shelley-house.org; 3€; Mon–Fri 9am–1pm and 3–6pm, Sat 11am–2pm and 3–6pm), which is a treasure trove for fans of the two poets. Here you'll find Keats's death mask and an urn with some of Shelley's remains, as well as many volumes of letters and handwritten diaries.

Also farther down the Via del Corso is **Palazzo Doria Pamphilj** ✹ (Piazza del Collegio Romano 2; ☎ 06-6797323; adults 8€, seniors and students 7.50€; admission includes excellent audioguide; Fri–Wed 10am–5pm), which houses one of Italy's most impressive private art collections, owned by the Pamphilj family, including Caravaggio's *Rest on the Flight into Egypt* and *Mary Magdalene*, as well as Raphael's *Double Portrait* and scores more. This gallery is tucked in a small part of a 1,000-room palazzo. At the time of this writing, the gorgeous apartments are not open to the public, which makes this museum less interesting.

From Via del Corso you can easily reach the **Spanish Steps** ✹✹ (Piazza di Spagna), an ongoing outdoor party, packed with locals—primarily 20-some-things—socializing. This graceful sweep of travertine steps, designed by De Sanctis in the 18th century on land owned by the Spanish Embassy (hence "Spanish" Steps), imparts a glamour to this district that's undeniable.

Just across the busy Via Tritone from here is the **Trevi Fountain** ✹✹✹ (Piazza di Trevi), which was built in the 1700s over the mouth of an aqueduct built in 19 B.C. to bring the famously therapeutic Acqua Vergine (Aqua Virgo in Latin) 25km

(16 miles) from the hills outside of Rome. The facade was designed by Nicola Salvi; many say he died of a virus he contracted while overseeing the project (before it was completed in 1762). The origin of the name Trevi is disputed, believed either to be for a young girl named Trivia who showed the Emperor Agrippa an original spring on the site, or from the phrase *ìregio trevii*, which may refer to the three streets surrounding the fountain. It's customary to throw a coin over your shoulder into the fountain (preferably in front of a camera) in order to ensure your return to Rome one day. The city collects these coins daily for the Red Cross.

If you've got kids in tow, or are obsessed with Italian cuisine, sample the **Museo Nazionale delle Paste Alimentari** 🖼 (Piazza Scanderbeg 117; ☎ 06-6991120; www.pastainmuseum.it; 10€ adults, 7€ children; daily 9:30am–5:30pm). Fondly called the "Spaghetti Museum," it offers much more information than you probably need about the art of making pasta by hand. Kids love it, though.

VIA VENETO & VILLA BORGHESE

Back behind the Spanish Steps and Trevi Fountain are several intriguing piazzas to savor. If you walk along Via Tritone or any of the streets parallel, you'll easily reach the bustling Piazza Barberini, with the playful Fontana del Tritone by Bernini in the center. This glorified traffic circle is at the base of Via Vittorio Veneto (pronounced "*Veh-neh-to*"), the legendary hub of *la dolce vita* (which has mostly relocated to the Tridente area below the Spanish Steps). Walking up the tree-lined slalom curve of Via Veneto now is a mixed experience. There are expensive shops near the top, as well as the standards like Harry's Bar and Le Sans Souci restaurant. But there's also touristy Hard Rock Cafe, the heavily guarded American Embassy, and a handful of staid hotels. Mostly this street is a has-been and a mere silhouette of its former glory.

There are a few stops to make, however, starting with the bizarro church of **Santa Maria della Concezione** ★★ 🖼 (Via Vittorio Veneto 27; ☎ 06-48711857; www.cappucciniviaveneto.it; donation requested; Fri–Wed 9am–noon and 3–6pm)—it's about as creepy as Rome gets. Downstairs is the Capuchin Crypt, where the bones of over 4,000 monks are used as decorative art on the walls, urns, and chandeliers in the various chapels. A sign explaining the monks' take on mortality (YOU WILL BE WHAT WE NOW ARE) hangs near the back. Your kids will either love or be totally weirded out by it—preteen boys usually lap it up.

At the top of Via Veneto lies the sprawling **Villa Borghese,** which is home to the city zoo, three magnificent museums, and the best green spot in the city complete with cultured gardens, a boating lake, and an equestrian stadium . . . not to mention its fairly new free Wi-Fi capabilities (1-hr. limit per day) through 22 hot spots across the park (www.romawireless.com).

Galleria Borghese ★★★ (Piazzale Borghese 5; ☎ 06-32810; www.galleria borghese.it; adults 8.50€, seniors and students 5.25€; entrance by appointment only every 2 hr., daily 8:30am–7pm) is the don't-miss of this area. The art here is significant, from Bernini's sexy *Apollo and Daphne* in **Room 3** to Raphael's *Deposition* on the second floor. Don't miss Canova's 1808 topless marble figure of Napoleon's sister Pauline in **Room 1,** and the collection of Roman copies of Greek original sculpture in **Room 5.** There are six Caravaggios in **Room 8,** including the much acclaimed *Boy with a Basket of Fruit* (1594) and *Sick Bacchus* (1593), which art historians believe is a self-portrait.

Events Calendar

Spring: Holy Week is the official opening of tourist season in Rome. The week preceding Easter is a religious celebration for pilgrims, but it also marks the changing to summer hours for most stores and sites. Culture Week, whose dates are found at www.beniculturali.it (☎ 800-991199), is when most of the major museums and paid exhibits like the Colosseum and Palatine Hill are free and offer extended hours.

Summer: This is the season when jazz and outdoor cinema take over. In the lush part of the **Villa Celimontana** (www.villacelimontanajazz.com) is a nightly jazz fest from July to early September with food and wine booths. Each night from late June through late August the city of Rome sponsors an **Estate Romana (Roman Summer)** (www.estateromana.it), an ongoing cultural shindig that ranges from opera in the Baths of Caracalla and chamber concerts in the churchyards to rock concerts and outdoor festivals. The banks of the Tiber become one huge party, with temporary restaurants, exhibition booths, and even a swimming pool set up for the warm months. At **Isola del Cinema** (www.isoladelcinema.com), international movies are screened on the lower esplanade of Tiber Island.

Autumn: For one Saturday in September, **La Notte Bianca** (☎ 06-0606; www.lanottebianca.it), very few people in Rome sleep. Museums, libraries, churches, stores, and restaurants stay open around the clock and the streets are filled with revelers. It's a blast.

But an added advantage to this collection, over the much larger Vatican Museums collection, is that curators insist on a limited number of people in the museum at one time. Visits are limited 2 hours, which is a perfect amount of time for sauntering through the masterpieces.

Within the Villa Borghese are two other museums. The **Museo Nazionale Etrusco di Villa Giulia** ★ (Piazzale di Villa Giulia 9; ☎ 06-3226571; 4€; daily 8:30am–7:30pm) features Etruscan artifacts ranging from cooking utensils to jewelry in the central room of the museum to a more intricate form of jewelry—astonishing granulated gold work—in the Room of the Seven Hills. These collections have been exhumed from the graves of the Etruscans found in central Italy. A reconstructed temple stands next to the coffee bar in the courtyard.

The other major museum within the boundaries of the Villa Borghese is the **Galleria Nazionale d'Arte Moderna e Contemporanea (National Gallery of Modern and Contemporary Art)** (Viale delle Belle Arti 131; ☎ 06-332981; www.gnam.arti.beniculturali.it; adults 6.50€, seniors and students 3.25€; Tues–Sun 8:30am–7:30pm). Focusing on the rarely noted 19th- and 20th-century Italian art, its collection includes massive statues like *Hercules* by Canova, and the plaster model used to make the bronze statue of *Giordano Bruno,* which stands in the center of Campo de' Fiori (p. 69). The museum is a fun departure from the Renaissance and ancient art that fill most of Rome's museums.

THE APPIAN WAY

Visiting the 312 B.C. **Appian Way (Queen of the Roads)** ★★ (bus: 118 or 660) is the closest you'll get in Rome to traveling back to ancient times. Barely a mile south of the urban chaos of central Rome, this rural landscape offers gentle and atmospheric attractions, including several Catacombs and imperial ruins, but most of all, it's the feeling of being steeped in antiquity that makes a half-day trip here so worthwhile. On either side of the ancient highway, whose original basalt flagstones are still preserved in many stretches, are fields where sheep graze and 2,000-year-old bits of brick and marble soak up the Roman sun. Resist the temptation to join one of the mass-tourism bus tours to the Catacombs—you'll want time to wander the Appia at your own pace, and public transportation down here, while not incredibly frequent, is reliable. I recommend using bus no. 118, which starts at the Piramide metro station and makes stops along the most important parts of the Via Appia Antica. To get back, take bus no. 118 or 660.

Tip: The Appian Way is closed to vehicle traffic on Sundays, so you might consider doing your touring then. Bicycles are available for rent at the visitor center (below), but the bumpy flagstones of the old road aren't the friendliest for pedaling. Instead, just bring your own two feet and some good walking shoes.

The old Appian Way officially starts outside the ancient Aurelian walls. Passing under the arched gate called Porta San Sebastiano, Via di Porta San Sebastiano changes names to Via Appia Antica. If you have plenty of time, consider getting off bus no. 118 here and visiting the **Museo delle Mura (Museum of the Walls)** (Via di San Sebastiano 18; ☎ 06-70475284; 2.60€ adults, 1.60€ seniors and students; Tues–Sun 9am–2pm), which is built inside the 3rd-century-A.D. gate and walls. The exhibits here—mostly old photos and diagrams of the wall's many gates and castles—are fine, but the museum also offers visitors the opportunity to walk atop a stretch of the ancient wall (restoration status permitting). Standing up here, surveying the green countryside south of Rome, eyes peeled for barbarian invaders, makes a great prelude to the Appian Way itself.

The first section of the Appian Way (a half-mile stretch from Porta San Sebastiano to the area of the Catacombs) is not its prettiest. Make your way down this busy first section by bus (the narrow section of road is harrowing to walk) until you reach the Appia Antica/Caffarella stop (ask the driver). Once off the bus here, it's worth stopping into the **Centro Visite Parco Appia Antica** (Via Appia Antica 42; ☎ 06-5126314; www.parcoappiaantica.org) for an excellent and colorful (and free) map of the Appian Way, and to rent bikes on the weekends (3€ for 1 hr. or 10€ for the day; Sat–Sun 9:30am–4:30pm).

Catacomb Country

Just past the visitor center, you'll enter the zone where three of Rome's most famous Catacombs are located. The Catacombs of Domitilla are package-tour central, so I recommend visiting either the Catacombs of San Callisto or San Sebastiano. To get to the Catacombs of San Callisto, either hop on bus no. 118 for one more stop, or go on foot, taking the narrow lane that rises above both the Appia Antica on the left and the Via Ardeatina on the right. (The lane is a break in the wall and looks private, but it's not.) The walk from here to the Catacombs of San Callisto entrance is a pleasant and peaceful half-mile. You can also see the Castelli foothills farther south and get a wonderful perspective on the city as you turn around and look back to the north.

The **Catacombs of San Callisto** ✸✸ (Via Appia Antica 136; ☎ 06-5130151; www.catacombe.roma.it; guided tours 5€ adults, 3€ seniors and students; Thurs–Tues 8:30am–noon and 2:30–5pm) are the largest and most impressive of the entire network of underground tombs of Christians, extending 20km (13 miles) on four levels. Nine popes and thousands of Christians are buried here, and the extraordinary height of the tunnels—some are 30 feet high and riddled with tomb openings—is thrilling and unique among Roman Catacombs.

Continuing down the lane that brought you to the Catacombs of San Callisto another 5 minutes you'll reach the basilica and **Catacombs of San Sebastiano** ✸ (Via Appia Antica 136; ☎ 06-7850350; entrance only with a guided tour, 5€ adults, 3€ seniors and students; Mon–Sat 8:30am–noon and 2:30–5pm). (This is also the last stop bus no. 118 makes on the Via Appia Antica before veering off to the left on the Via Appia Pignatelli.) The experience at the Catacombs of San Sebastiano is much more intimate than that at San Callisto; here you'll visit the site of previously pagan mausoleums that have been converted into Christian tombs. Enter the tomb of St. Sebastian, for whom these Catacombs are named. The word "catacomb" comes from this site, which means "near the quarry," or *kata kymbas* in Greek. All in all, these are more archaeologically interesting to visit than San Callisto, though not as overtly physically impressive.

After visiting the Catacombs, it's a short walk down what's left of the original Appian Way, which is lined with umbrella pines and various imperial and pagan ruins. Off to the left (east) are the brick ruins of the **Villa of Maxentius** (Via Appia Antica 153; ☎ 06-7801324; 2.60€; Tues–Sun 9am–1:30pm), a suburban retreat built by the Emperor Maxentius in the 3rd century A.D. The chariot race track *(circus)* here once sat 30,000 spectators. Another prominent feature of the Appian Way is the above-ground tombs of ancient Romans, whose pagan laws forbade the burial of their dead within the city walls. The largest and most picturesque of these is the **Tomba di Cecilia Metella** (Via Appia Antica 161; ☎ 06-7800093; 6€ adults, 3€ seniors and students; Tues–Sun 9am–4pm), which now incorporates a medieval castle built on the site of the cylindrical tomb of a wealthy 1st-century-B.C. Roman lady. The complex serves as an example of the ritual of ancient Roman burials, and many of the funerary urns which once lined the Appian Way are now housed here. From this point on, the Appia Antica gets even more parklike and romantic—there are no major monuments to visit, but you'll walk the very flag-stones that the Roman legions did, and you can peek past the gates of sumptuous villas that have been here since the Renaissance. When it's time to head back to the city, the simplest way is to hop on bus no. 660 (in front of the coffee bar near Cecilia Metella), which takes you to Largo Colli Albani (near San Giovanni), where you can then take metro Ⓐ or bus no. 87 back to the city center.

AVENTINO ✸

The Aventino is by far the quietest of the seven hills of Rome. High above the bustling local neighborhood of Testaccio, it's mostly a lush residential area and those who live here tend to frown on visitors. Ignore them . . . and take in the view. At the top of the hill on Piazza dei Cavalieri di Malta is one of Rome's most **famous keyholes** ★ at the door of the headquarters of the Priory of Malta (clearly marked). Lean close to the circular opening (which really isn't a keyhole anymore) to see a perfectly framed view of St. Peter's Basilica. Here you are also looking at three sovereign nations: Italy, Malta, and Vatican City. You can make the trek up from either the Testaccio side or from the Circus Maximus.

Next door to the famous keyhole, past the 24-hour guards, is one of Rome's best preserved original churches, the 5th-century **Church of Santa Sabina** (Piazza Pietro d'Illiria 1), which was built on the site of the original Titulus Sabinae, a private home used for worship in 442. The church has changed very little; the original wooden door (now with some replica panels) shows the life of Moses and a crucifixion scene that is believed to be one of the earliest artistic portrayals of the crucifixion of Christ.

A few meters from the church is one of this area's best kept secrets: **Parco Savello** ★★, also known as the Orange Park. In the springtime, when the grove of clementine trees is in bloom, the perfume is intoxicating. But the view from the overlook terrace is what you make this trek for; it is one you don't often see of the Roman skyline and Trastevere rooftops.

Down below the Aventino, you can't help but notice the massive and seemingly out-of-place white-marble pyramid at the edge of the **Cimitero Acattolico (Protestant Cemetery)** ★ (Via Caio Cestio 6; ☎ 06-5741900; www.protestant cemetery.it; free; Mon–Sat 8:30am–4:30pm). Stop here to see the graves of both Keats and Shelley. The pyramid is the mausoleum of a Roman family.

MUSEUMS OFF THE BEATEN TRACK

A full third of Rome's vast assortment of ancient art can be found at the **Museo Nazionale Romano: Palazzo Massimo alla Terme** ★ (Largo di Villa Peretti 1; ☎ 06-480201, bookings 06-39967700; integrated ticket 6.50€ adults, 3.50€ seniors and students; Tues–Sun 9am–7pm). Among its treasures are a major coin collection, extensive maps of trade routes (with audio and visual exhibits on the network of traders over the centuries) and busts of emperors and their families. But the real draw is on the second floor, where you can see some of the oldest of Rome's frescoes depicting scenes of ancient Roman life, dating back to the house of Livia on the Palatine Hill (p. 55). The museum is across the square from Termini station at the edge of Piazza della Repubblica.

And across the Piazza della Repubblica is an example of Roman recycling at its finest. Originally this spot held the largest of Rome's hedonistic baths (dating from 298 A.D.), but during the Renaissance both a church and a convent were plunked on top of the ruins, both designed by Michelangelo, no less. Today the entire hodgepodge is known as **Museo Nazionale Romano: Terme di Diocleziano** (Via Enrico de Nicola 79; ☎ 06-399677000; www.archeorm.arti.beniculturali.it/ sar2000/diocleziano; integrated ticket 7€ adults, 3.50€ seniors and students; Tues–Sat 9am–7:45pm) and this juxtaposition of Christianity, ancient ruins, and exhibit space make for a compelling museum stop. The collections of ancient art here make up the third part of a museum circuit consisting of the Museo Nazionale Romano, Palazzo Massimo alla Terme (see above), and Palazzo Altemps (p. 68). The church, **Santa Maria degli Angeli** (Piazza della Repubblica; ☎ 06-4880812; www.santamariadegliangeliroma.it; Mon–Sat 7am–6:30pm, Sun

7am–7:30pm) is an ingenious turn, fitted snugly inside the Baths of Diocletian. A giant 45m (148-ft.) bronze meridian runs across the main body of the church, which until 1870 was used to set Rome's clocks. On sunny days, beams of light shine through strategically placed holes in the walls, lighting up the points on the meridian and zodiac symbols. At the entrance of the church, the dome forms a prism that reflects rainbows of light on the statues below.

An even more majestic set of ruins, the **Baths of Caracalla** ★★ (Viale delle Terme di Caracalla 52; ☎ 06-5745748; 6€ adults, 3.50€ seniors and students; Mon 9am–1pm, Tues–Sun 9am–sunset) were built in A.D. 213 and used, back in the day, as a giant spa. Some 1,600 Romans could come to play in the gymnasium and swimming pool, or sack out in a series of saunas and baths with varying temperatures and humidity levels. The baths' intricate mosaic tiles are still evident in some parts of the ruins. Others are preserved in the Vatican Museums (p. 63) and the National Archaeological Museum in Naples (p. 512). Believe it or not, today the baths are a popular venue for operas during the summer.

CHURCHES OFF THE BEATEN TRACK

A number of churches off the beaten track are still worthy stops, and not just for religious pilgrims. **San Giovanni** ★ (Piazza San Giovanni 4 in Laterano; ☎ 06-69886433; metro San Giovanni or buses to Porta San Giovanni) is Rome's cathedral, making it the second-most significant church in the Catholic faith, after St. Peter's Basilica. Pilgrims visiting Rome can earn an indulgence here, as this is the spot where the pope washes the feet of ordinary (but carefully selected) people each Easter season. On the giant facade of the church are statues of Christ, John the Baptist, John the Evangelist, and the 12 Doctors of the Church. A Giotto mosaic adorns the apse, and a 13th-century cloister around the back of the church features some artifacts from the original church.

Across the street is the **Scala Santa** (Holy Stairs; Piazza di San Giovanni in Laterano; ☎ 06-7726641; daily 6:30am–noon, winter 3–6pm, summer until 6:30pm). These are said to be the stone steps from Pontius Pilate's house that Jesus climbed before his crucifixion, and were relocated to Rome in the 4th century. Now they're covered with wooden planks, but are still as significant to the thousands of religious pilgrims who climb them on their knees each year, reciting the 28 different prayers, one for each step.

Santa Maria Maggiore ★ (Piazza Santa Maria Maggiore; ☎ 06-483195; 4€; daily 7am–7pm, museum 9am–6:30pm) is one of Rome's five patriarchal basilicas. Lately it's also been the site of protests. American Cardinal Bernard Law was assigned to this church after retiring from the Boston Diocese after the 2005 pedophile scandals. This church has the best collection of mosaics in the city. Start with the 5th-century mosaic depictions of the Old Testament above the columns in the nave, and work your way through the centuries along the length of the church. Thirteenth-century mosaics of Mary being crowned queen of heaven by Christ line the apse. Rome's baroque master Gian Lorenzo Bernini is buried here, marked by a plaque on the right side of the altar. On August 5, a celebration marking the miracle of a summer snowfall, which led to the building of this church, is celebrated with the release of thousands of flower petals from the church ceiling.

Santa Maria della Vittoria (Via XX Settembre 17; ☎ 06-42740571; free; Mon–Sat 8:30am–noon, daily 3:30–6pm) is home to one of Bernini's most famous and sensual sculptures, the *Ecstasy of St. Teresa* ★★, inspired by a passage she wrote: "So intense was the pain I uttered several moans; so great was the sweetness caused by the pain that I never wanted to lose it." The statue of the angel and Teresa sits in the Cornaro chapel, which is decorated with frescoes of clouds and hidden windows that light up the room differently throughout the day.

San Clemente ★★ (Via San Giovanni in Laterano; ☎ 06-7740021; 3€ for excavations; daily 9am–12:30pm and 3–6pm, Sun opens 1 hr. later) offers one of the best examples of Rome's multilayered past. The main church, which is a relatively new 12th-century construction, is often covered with scaffolding, so skim this section and head straight to the first subterranean level for the 4th-century ruins of the original church and the chipped and faded frescoes of the life of St. Clemente, who was the fourth pope after St. Peter. Climb down another flight of dark steps to reach the pagan temple of the Persian god Mithras. Here, statues of testosterone-driven bullfighters, some actually holding testicles, indicate the types of meetings held here.

TOURING ROME—READ THIS SECTION!!

A good tour of Rome, whether it's a walk through the Forum or a survey of the Vatican Museums, can be the highlight of your trip. However, and this is a big point, you've got to be a discerning customer when it comes to choosing your tour outfit. Rome has an overabundance of melodramatic actor/guides who regurgitate hyperbolic scripts about Christians being fed to the lions, as well as disconnected old-timers who may bore you to tears (in barely intelligible English) with arcane details about electoral reform in the 5th century B.C. Luckily, there are also a number of terrific tour companies in Rome that offer a wide variety of itineraries led by engaging, factual guides.

If you're especially interested in art and architecture or want a deeper understanding of any aspect of Roman history or culture—and you can splurge a little—the in-depth tours offered by **Context Rome** (☎ 06-4820911; rome.context travel.com) are simply outstanding. Their academic, interactive approach is like the study-abroad program in Rome you never took. Context's docents are local and expatriate architects, archaeologists, art historians, and other cultural experts who take small groups on thematic tours that last from a few hours to a full day. You won't find more thoughtfully organized itineraries than these—for example, they only do the Vatican at times when the crowds are likely to be more manageable, and they always find time to stop at a coffee or wine bar, if you're interested, for post-tour discussion and camaraderie. On average, tours last about 3½ hours and cost 55€ per person or 300€ per group.

An excellent alternative for the visitor who wants to get his or her artistic and historical bearings in Rome, **Enjoy Rome** (Via Marghera 8a; ☎ 06-4451843; www. enjoyrome.com) offers a number of "greatest hits" walking tours, like 3-hour overviews of ancient Rome or the Vatican. Most tours cost 24€ per person, exclusive of entrance fees (like the Vatican Museums). They also do an early evening tour of the Jewish Ghetto and Trastevere, and a bus excursion to the Catacombs and the Appian Way (40€), with a visit to ruins of an ancient aqueduct that most Romans, let alone tourists, never see.

The self-styled "storytellers of the new millennium" at **Through Eternity** (☎ 06-7009336; www.througheternity.com) are also worth your consideration. Staffed by a group of art historians and architects, what truly sets them apart is their theatrical component, hence the dramatic scripts that many of the guides seem to follow. So, on a tour of the Forum, expect your guide to break out into a booming "Friends, Romans, Countrymen"—it can be a lot of fun, but it's not for everyone. Eternity's niche tours, like a wonderful Feast of Bacchus wine tasting and culinary extravaganza, are a culturally edifying way to party. Prices range from 30€ to 46€, but you'll get a 10% discount by booking ahead through their website.

Whenever possible, try to arrange your walking tours before you leave home, as most hotels book bus tours only, which are slow, overpriced, deadly exercises in mass tourism.

Another cost-saving idea is **to rent an audioguide** from the specific site you are interested in seeing. These are available in multiple languages, but try to find out if your narrator is a native English speaker or an Italian with a heavy accent.

THE OTHER ROME

Romans love their city for all the same reasons you will, but they certainly don't spend their days ooohing and aaahing in front of the Colosseum and St. Peter's. The rhythms and pastimes of locals in Rome are usually quite different from those of a short-term visitor. In this section, I've listed a few good ways for you to go beyond the typical tourist whirlwind, slow down a bit, get under the skin of the city, and enjoy it on the level that Romans do daily.

SOCCER

Every Italian, it seems, is born with a passion for *calcio* (soccer) in his genetic code. Romans are no exception. Going to the stadium for an A.S. Roma or S.S. Lazio game at the Stadio Olimpico is the best window on the extremes of Roman emotion you'll find in the modern city. Whether or not you're a soccer enthusiast, it's hard not to get caught up in the electricity that accompanies each match. The choruses are all stadium encompassing, more thundering than anything I've experienced at an NFL or MLB game, and the action on the field is easy to follow. But spectating is often a contact sport—when the home team scores, you can expect to be bear-hugged (or beneficently tackled) by the nearest stranger. Likewise, watch out for flying objects (like half-eaten sandwiches) from sour fans in the opponent's seating section. Between the Italian league (Serie A) and European cups, there are games at least once a week between late August and late May. To get tickets (20€–120€), go to any *tabacchi* (tobacco shop) in town that displays the LOTTOMATICA emblem. You'll see the game the best from the more expensive Tribuna Tevere and Tribuna Monte Mario seats; but the inexpensive Curva Sud and Curva Nord are where most of the physical fan action is. The midrange Laterale and Distinti seats are a good *via di mezzo* (compromise).

GLADIATOR FOR A DAY

The amazingly earnest men and women at **Gruppo Storico Romano,** a historical reenactment society whose primary function is as a "gladiatorial school," will give anyone patient enough to get past the language barrier (they speak a fair amount of Latin, but little English) a 1-day lesson in how to be a gladiator—at no charge—at their arena on the Appian Way. Club president Sergio Iacomoni (aka "Nerone," or Nero) doesn't mess around too much, so while there is room for humor as you learn this ancient fighting art, you will be expected to take your "physical and mental preparation," which involves basic stances and attack and defense techniques, seriously. Beginners train with the *rudis* (a short wooden sword), so don't worry about having to hit the emergency room after your session. Best of all, the *ludus* ("gladiatorial school" in Latin) is on the Via Appia Antica, which certainly adds appropriate nostalgia to the experience. From about April to October, training is held on Mondays and Wednesdays; in the winter, on Mondays only. For exact opening dates or for more information, visit www.gsr-roma.it, call ☎ 338-2436678 or 06-51607951 (Italian only), or just stop by—they're at Via Appia Antica 18, between Porta San Sebastiano and the Catacombs.

SHOP, COOK & EAT LIKE A ROMAN

Washington State native **Sienna Reid** operates tremendously enjoyable half-day "culinary adventures" for private groups of up to six in the Monti neighborhood near the Colosseum. After a cappuccino in a typical Roman bar, you'll start by shopping in a series of tiny mom-and-pop shops, some of which provide an eye-opening reminder of the origin of foodstuffs that we're usually accustomed to seeing already cleaned and packaged in plastic at the supermarket. Once you've completed this shopping cum local-culture tour, it's up to the kitchen, where Reid is happy to have you help prepare and cook hands on, or just relax and watch her do it. Each hearty lunch—eaten on the apartment's sunny terrace or in its 17th-century dining room, depending on the weather—includes an *antipasto*, a *primo*, a *secondo*, a vegetable *contorno*, and a dessert. Everything but the dessert will be made from what you purchased that morning. Wines accompany the meal, and are preselected to match what you're making. The big takeaway from Reid's "adventures," though (and one I heartily endorse) is "how to make simple Italian dishes with fresh seasonal ingredients that impress everyone." Four-hour tours are pricey at 400€ for two people, but if you can get a group together, the price drops considerably (each addition person pays 50€ for up to six people). Prices include all ingredients for the meal and wines. E-mail Sienna Reid at sienna@tiscali.it or visit www.italyhotline.com for more information.

Well-known food writer **Maureen Fant** offers a somewhat similar baptism into Roman cooking, except that your shopping takes place in the covered market and delis of Testaccio, known as the "belly" of Rome for its scrumptious food offerings. Then you take a short tram ride to her apartment in Monti for the prep, cooking, and eating. This walking tour/seminar/workshop, called "Roman Cuisine," lasts from 10am to 3pm and includes lecture-style information about the history of Roman food along the way. Fant's tour also takes you to the deli wonderland of Volpetti (p. 42), where you'll have the help of an English-speaking pro to help you navigate all the amazing cheeses and meats you might want to have vacuum-sealed to take home. Book Maureen Fant's culinary tours through **Context Rome** (☎ 06-4820911, or from the U.S. ☎ 888/467-1986; http://rome.contexttravel.com). Rates are 150€ per person, or 475€ for a group of three; for each additional person, add 40€.

LANGUAGE SCHOOL

Certainly, the best way to get into local life is to learn the language. I can tell you as someone who went from zero to fluent while living in Rome, learning Italian is the greatest gift I've ever given myself. The Roman branch of a well-established Florentine language school, **Scuola Leonardo** (Piazza dell'Orologio 7; ☎ 06-6889-2513; www.scuolaleonardo.com) offers a variety of Italian courses for all levels throughout the year. For example, a 2-week standard course includes 40 lessons (four 90-min. group lessons per day, Mon–Fri) and costs 300€. The school's emphasis isn't just on classroom grammar and rote vocabulary drills, but on real-world Italian and cultural literacy, a wonderful integrative approach. The Scuola Leonardo can also place you in very economical accommodations—either in a shared apartment with other students or in a Roman family residence with your own private single room (260€–310€ for a 2-week stay).

WANDERING TESTACCIO

A good bet for your first "real-Rome" indoctrination is a walk through the working-class neighborhood of Testaccio. It's one of the least pretentious spots in the city, and you never question the authenticity of what you see.

Early in the morning the locals crowd the market in the central square and haggle with vendors for their fresh produce. The fishmongers know well who caught the fish, and the vegetable sellers harvested most of the vegetables—just look at their hands. One stand is dedicated entirely to the many varieties of tomatoes in season, and the man who runs it will let you taste the difference. The stores that circle the stands sell the kinds of housewares, wines, flowers, and food that Italians buy, and you can get some of the best deals in town here. You'll find no rainbow-colored pasta in pretty packages here.

Down the street from the market you'll pass by old-fashioned candy shops and seamstresses who barely look up from their needles as you pass by.

Go for a walk around rustic Monte Testaccio. By night this is club central, but during the day, you can look up on the grassy slopes and see livestock grazing and bleating happily in their pens—mere feet from where thumping techno beats blasted hours earlier. This unexpected slice of rural life in the city center never ceases to amaze and delight me.

Testaccio is a classic Roman neighborhood. Best of all, the locals will never treat you like a tourist: If you make it to Testaccio, they'll assume you know why you came and they will treat you as one of their own.

ATTENTION, SHOPPERS!

With so much to see, who has time to shop? On the other hand, who can resist? If you do elect to do some retail damage, prepare for some serious dollar-to-euro sticker shock. Note that many stores aren't open Sunday and Monday morning and adhere to the siesta, closing between 1 and 4pm, with the exception of those around the Spanish Steps. The classic zone for high-end shopping is between Piazza del Popolo and the Spanish Steps, with a high concentration of couture boutiques on **Via Condotti.** Near here, **Via del Corso** has shops with more approachable prices (and younger fashions), but it can be a zoo on weekends. Two excellent thoroughfares for midrange fashion and accessories boutiques are **Via Cola di Rienzo,** near the Vatican, and the even lesser known (to tourists) **Viale Marconi,** southwest of Trastevere. Smaller, funkier boutiques are on **Via Giubbonari,** off Campo de' Fiori, and **Via del Governo Vecchio,** off Piazza Navona. Smoggy **Via Nazionale,** which runs from Termini to Piazza Venezia, has inexpensive leather-goods and sports-gear stores galore, but it's not the most congenial experience, and you'll need to watch out for pickpockets.

ANTIQUES

More than 40 antiques shops line the **Via dei Coronari** (which starts at the top of Piazza Navona and continues west for about a half-mile to the river), selling everything from large pieces of furniture to such small treasures as crested silverware and divine candelabras.

BOOKSTORES

Feltrinelli (Largo Argentina 11, and several locations throughout the city; ☎ 06-68663001; www.feltrinelli.it) is an American-style megabookstore complete with coffee bar. It has a large selection of music, books in English, and children's selections, in addition to stationery and calendars.

CLOTHING MARKETS

Even people who don't need to look for bargains shop at the sprawling **San Giovanni Clothing Market** (Via Sannio). The clothing here is all new and often you're better off not knowing where it came from, but the prices are exceptional. You can get very good quality leather shoes, belts, and purses at a fraction of the price you'd pay in stores. Stalls are piled high with jeans, shirts, linens, and fabrics, but you'll have to hunt through the merchandise to find your size. *One warning:* Virtually no one here speaks English, and the international size charts are a mystery. There are no changing facilities and no returns on purchases. You can also find shoes and clothes at the **Testaccio market.**

DEPARTMENT STORES

Rome's three major department stores are **Coin** (shoes, undergarments, midrange fashion, cosmetics); **La Rinascente** (sunglasses, cosmetics, mid- to upper-range fashion); and **Upim** (lower-end fashion, toys, cosmetics). Coin has locations on Via Cola di Rienzo (Vatican area) and Piazzale Appio (San Giovanni). La Rinascente is on Via del Corso at Via del Tritone. Upim has locations on Via del Tritone and Piazza Santa Maria Maggiore.

FLEA MARKETS

The best known flea market in the city, and perhaps in all of Italy, is the Sunday-morning bonanza at the gates of Porta Portese between Trastevere and Testaccio. Stalls start setting up before 5am and you can start haggling shortly thereafter. If you have ever dreamed of owning it, you can find it here. Watch out for pickpockets, and be prepared for major crowds.

GIFT SHOPS

La Chiave (Largo delle Stimmate 28; ☎ 06-68308848) sells imported crafts, interesting antique toys, and paper masks, in addition to lots of rugs, blankets, and handmade clothing. A small stationery shop in the back of the store offers journals and scrapbook albums.

If you're looking for a handmade memento, try the medieval-feeling **Polvere del Tempo** (Via del Moro 59; ☎ 06-5880704). It specializes in handmade jewelry, antique-aspect globes, candles, and time-related gifts like hourglasses made from hand-blown glass or small used Campari bottles, which are calibrated to 3 minutes or 1 hour down to the last grain of sand. The items here are priced fairly and are one of a kind.

For the inner gladiator in you, go to **Archeo Roma** (Largo del Teatro Valle 5; ☎ 06-6877590) for reproductions of statues, jewelry, and gladiator arms. You'll find costumes, capes, and realistic-looking swords—perfect for your next Halloween party.

GOURMET SHOPS

Packable, affordable gourmet foodstuffs are one of the easiest (and most appreciated) souvenirs you can bring back from Italy. Several emporia you can seek out for jars of artisanal pâté, specialty oils and vinegars, even vacuum-sealed meats and cheeses are **Roscioli** (Via dei Chiavari 34, near Campo de' Fiori; ☎ 06-6864045) or my personal favorite place in the entire world, **Volpetti** (Via Marmorata 47, Testaccio; p. 42). In the Vatican area, check out **Franchi** (Via Cola di Rienzo 204; ☎ 06-6874651), which also has a great hot-food bar during the day, and its next-door neighbor, international food market **Castroni** (Via Cola di Rienzo 196–198; ☎ 06-6874383).

SHOES

Off Campo de' Fiori, **Posto Italiano** (Via Giubbonari 37a; ☎ 06-6869373) never fails to leave me drooling for a new pair of shoes. The good news? You can actually afford their classic and fashion-forward styles for men and women. Ladies with a real shoe fetish should make their way to the Vatican area, where tiny **Martina Novelli** (Piazza Risorgimento 38; ☎ 06-39737247) consistently stocks a tantalizing area of gorgeous leather footwear (on the trendy side, but sexy and wearable) from under-the-radar Italian designers you'll never find in the shops back home. The bigger-name designers for men's and women's shoes are all well represented on and around Via Condotti.

TOILETRIES

No one sells simple soap like the Romans, and one of the oldest vendors of perfumes and other essentials is **Antica Erboristeria Romana** (Via di Torre Argentina 15; ☎ 06-6879493), a store brimming with essential oils, tinctures, and other herbal remedies, in addition to more mainstream cures. In addition, all across Rome ubiquitous *profumerie* (toiletry shops) chains like Limoni or Beauty Point peddle good-quality lotions and cosmetics. Note that OTC stuff like ibuprofen and cough medicine is only sold at *farmacie* (pharmacies), which are often your only option for sunblock and tampons, too. Go to any *ottica* (optician's—they're everywhere) for all your contact lens needs.

VINTAGE STORES

People (Piazza Teatro di Pompeo 4A; ☎ 06-6874040) is an innovative store where the designers Germana and Sara use material from vintage clothing to create updated fashions. You'll find great club wear here, as well as interesting scarves, jackets, and gloves. No two items are alike, so whatever you buy will be unique.

NIGHTLIFE

Roman nightlife goes primarily in two directions: spontaneous and fairly cheap, or organized and expensive. As you might guess, the former combination is usually the more enjoyable way to spend an evening. There are dozens upon dozens of casual wine bars and pubs to pop into as you make your way around the *centro* (on foot), but there are also circumstances when you'll want to do a bit of planning and seek out farther-flung, schedule-specific venues. Of course, for many locals and visitors alike, "nightlife" is just getting a gelato after dinner and going for a leisurely stroll through the lively piazzas and streets of Rome, admiring all the beautifully floodlit monuments—this is an absolutely valid option, too, and perfectly safe: violent crime in the city center is pretty unheard of.

The *centro storico*—especially around Piazza Navona, Campo de' Fiori, and the Pantheon—is the prime zone for the bar scene. The *aperitivo* hour begins around 6pm (see "*Aperitivo* Culture," below), when most drinking establishments offer free buffets of very good food to anyone who buys a drink. There's a break in the action at most bars when people go out (or home) to eat (around 8:30pm), but they're hopping again from about 10pm until 1 or 2am. Venues here range from old-fashioned *enotecas* (wine bars) to trendy, international-style lounges.

The area known as Monti, between the Colosseum and the train station, has the city's highest concentration of expat- and tourist-friendly Irish-style pubs, where international sports events are usually broadcast along with the local soccer games.

For proper dance clubs, just go down to Testaccio. The artificial mountain there, Monte Testaccio, is ringed with dozens of *discoteche* that are sure to have your music tastes covered. Dress sharply, and expect to pay a cover of 10€ to 20€ at any Testaccio club.

Aperitivo Culture

The mass social phenomenon of the *aperitivo* (happy hour—and so much more) can be a great way to meet, or at least observe the particular ways of, real Romans. It started in hard-working northern cities like Milan, where you'd go to a bar after leaving the office, and for the price of one drink (usually under 10€), you get access to an unlimited buffet of high-quality food—like chunks of Parmigiano-Reggiano, fresh green salad, or mushroom risotto. Luckily for Rome (a decidedly lazier city), the custom trickled down here, and now the city is filled with casual little places to drop in for a drink (from 6pm onward) and eat to your heart's content of all these tasty finger foods. Near Piazza Navona, try the bohemian-feeling **Société Lutece** (Piazza Montevecchio 17; ☎ 06-68301472), where you might find a hipster giving away puppies. Off Campo de' Fiori, you'll want to dress the part for the crowd at cosmopolitan and multilingual **Crudo** (Via degli Specchi 6; ☎ 06-6838989). In Trastevere, **Freni e Frizione** (Via del Politeama 4-6; ☎ 06-58334210) is another great *aperitivo* spot, packed with the young and young at heart in what was once a garage.

Cultural Events in Rome

Concerts at Rome's **Parco della Musica** (Via Pietro de Coubertin 15; box office ☎ 06-8082058; www.musicaperroma.it) and **Teatro dell'Opera** (Piazza B. Gigli 1; ☎ 06-48160255; www.opera.roma.it) range in price from a few euros to several hundred for big-name performers. The Italian president's office sponsors free concerts (www.quirinale.it) around the city, including a weekly Sunday-morning concert inside the Quirinale Palace. Churches cannot charge admission for concerts and, therefore, host many events sponsored through advertising. *RomaC'è* (www.romace.it) is a weekly guide, published each Wednesday, that tells what's going on in the city.

LIVE MUSIC

It might come as a surprise that Rome has some incredibly talented home-grown musicians. In addition to that, the capital pulls in a lot of acclaimed international acts throughout the year. One of my favorite venues is **Big Mama** ★★ (Vicolo San Francesco a Ripa 18, Trastevere; ☎ 06-5812551; www.bigmama.it), a down-and-dirty spot for live blues and a guaranteed good time. Booking is recommended if you want a table. Light dinner is also available, and most acts go on at 10pm. Over by the Vatican, **Alexanderplatz** ★ (Via Ostia 9; ☎ 06-58335781; www.alexanderplatz.it) is held in high esteem by jazz aficionados. The vibe here is grown-up and old-fashioned, and they also serve dinner. Check out their respective websites for up-to-date concert schedules and cover charges.

GET OUT OF TOWN

Rome's comprehensive train and bus networks make it easy to take a day or half-day trip to the Roman hinterland, which is filled with world-class sights all its own.

TIVOLI ★★★

This little hill town boasts not one but two UNESCO World Heritage Sites—the ruins of Emperor Hadrian's Villa and the Renaissance-era (and drop-dead gorgeous) Villa d'Este—making it one of the most satisfying day trips from Rome. It's also one of the easiest, as Tivoli is just 36km (22 miles) from the city center, and easily accessible by a combination of city transit and regional bus. Take metro line ❽ to Ponte Mammolo, then a blue Cotral bus up to Tivoli. Note that Villa d'Este is closed on Mondays.

Most people's first stop on a Tivoli outing is the **Villa d'Este** (☎ 0774-312070; 9€ adults, 5.75€ seniors and students; Nov–Feb 9am–5:30pm, Mar 9am–6:15pm, Apr 9am–7:30pm, May–Aug 8:30am–7:45pm, Sept 9am–7:15pm, Oct 9am–6:30pm), a Renaissance fantasyland of fountains built against a dramatic hillside. The villa is located right in the heart of Tivoli *centro*, at Piazza Trento, 1. The d'Estes were one of richest and most influential families in 16th-century Italy, and their Tivoli villa ("country home" in Roman nobility speak) was converted into a pleasure palace by Cardinal Ippolito II d'Este in 1550. You don't come to Villa d'Este to see the house;

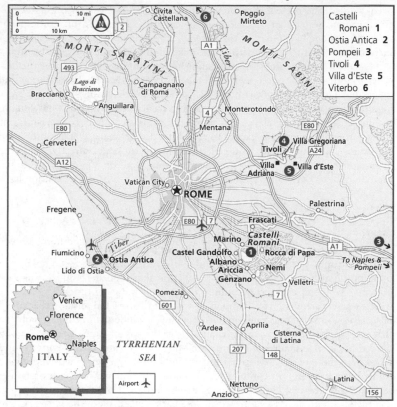

you come to see its extraordinary sloping backyard, which is adorned with thousands of gorgeous fountains and manicured gardens. There are grottoes, reflecting pools, rushing flumes, gurgling rocks, even a collection of diorama-like fountains, designed by baroque artist Gianlorenzo Bernini, that "perform," making the sounds of organs and owls, every 2 hours.

As much fun as Villa d'Este is, it's a huge mistake to come all the way out to Tivoli and not visit the fascinating archaeological site of Hadrian's Villa, too. **Hadrian's Villa** (Via di Villa Adriana; ☎ 0774-382733; adults 6.50€, seniors and students 3.50€; Nov–Jan 9am–5pm, Feb until 6pm, Mar and Oct until 6:30pm, Apr and Sept until 7pm, May–Aug until 7:30pm) is not in Tivoli proper, but about 5km (16 miles) away in the hamlet of Villa Adriana (this is also the Italian name of the site, which can be confusing), which you reach by a local orange bus from the main piazza of Tivoli. Get on a bus marked VILLA ADRIANA—if in doubt, ask the driver.

Hadrian (A.D. 117–138) was ancient Rome's most well-traveled emperor, and on this hillside plot of land east of Rome, he re-created some of the architecture—of Greece, of Egypt—that he had admired on his journeys. The result is a vast network of eye-poppingly creative structures where the emperor and his entourage lived, worked, and played when they weren't in Rome. The villa incorporates several ingenious water elements, such as the Maritime Theater, a private imperial study surrounded by a moat, or the *canopus*, an Egyptian-inspired reflecting pool surrounded by statuary, and with a grottolike dining room at one end. Hadrian's Villa merits a few hours of slow wandering and examining of details, like the delicate, 1,900-year-old stucco work in the vault of a thermal bath. Inside the museum is a miniature replica of the villa, which is worth locating first (after picking up a map at the ticket booth) so that you have a better idea of what you are looking at. The villa is splayed out along the natural contours of the land, not along perpendicular axes, so expect to get a little disoriented as you explore. Time permitting, have a meal at the excellent restaurant, Adriano, directly across the street from the ticket office. To get back to Rome, wait on Via di Villa Adriana for a blue (faster) or orange (slower) bus to Roma Centro or Ponte Mammolo.

OSTIA ANTICA ★★★

Rome's ancient seaport, **Ostia Antica** (Viale dei Romagnoli 717, Ostia Antica; ☎ 06-56358099; 6.50€; Feb–Oct Tues–Sun 9am–7pm, Nov–Jan until 5pm), is one of the most fascinating day (or half-day) trips you can make from Rome.

For centuries, Ostia's commercial and maritime functions made it a town even more bustling than Pompeii, with a population that topped 75,000 in the 2nd century A.D. (compared to one million in Rome at the same time). The ancient structures here are much like Pompeii's—without the lava and ominous backdrop of Vesuvius—and many remain intact, providing a window into Roman daily life that you won't find among the ancient sites in the city of Rome proper. Among the red-brick, pine-shaded ruins, are a well-preserved theater (where concerts and Greek tragedies are still performed during the summer), comprehensive mosaics from the floors of import companies' offices, a grain mill and bakery, a firehouse, several sets of thermal baths, a public latrine, and an ancient Roman snack bar, complete with an advertising fresco on the back wall. Explore the far reaches of the site to see how the Romans lived—from sumptuous private villas to more plebeian apartment blocks. Following the decline of the Rome, the port town was abandoned and, over the centuries, covered with river mud as the coastline receded to where it is today. Like so many ancient Roman ruins, the splendid marble that once covered the brick walls of Ostia was carted off to create some of Italy's best-known Catholic architecture, like the Leaning Tower of Pisa.

Getting Here

Metro line **B** runs to Piramide and Magliana stations, where you change for the Ostia-Lido commuter train in the direction of Ostia. Get off at Ostia Antica. You can make the whole one-way trip with a regular 1€ ATAC ticket. The excavations are a 10-minute walk from the train station. These ruins are best visited with a site map, available at the ticket booth or the site's book shop. Picnicking is not allowed at Ostia Antica, but there's a good sit-down snack bar.

If it's summer and you'd like to go for a dip in the Med, you can easily do so after your visit to Ostia Antica. Just hop back on the train to Ostia-Stella Polare or Ostia-Cristoforo Colombo, which will put you within walking distance of the beaches of Ostia Lido. From either station, it's just a few blocks to paid establishments that rent chairs and umbrellas and have showers, changing rooms, and casual beachfront restaurants. Note that Ostia is not the belle of the Italian coast, but the sand is soft and the water is refreshing.

ETRUSCAN CERVETERI & TARQUINIA ★★

Before the Romans ruled Italy, there were the Etruscans, a mysterious but sophisticated civilization that flourished in the regions of Tuscany, Umbria, and Lazio for several centuries. Two important Etruscan sites, the necropolises of Cerveteri and Tarquinia, lie within day-trip distance of Rome.

Cerveteri's **Necropoli della Banditaccia** (Piazza della Necropoli; ☎ 06/9940001; 5€, Tues–Sun 8:30am–1 hr. before sunset) is closer and all around more atmospheric than Tarquinia, with a junglelike maze of giant *tumuli,* mound-shaped tombs of volcanic tufa stone. Lax site supervision means you can climb in and all over the tombs and check out the dark interiors of the burial chambers. Bring a flashlight for the full Indiana Jones experience. To get there, take metro line Ⓐ (1€) to Cornelia, then hop on a blue Via Aurelia–bound Cotral bus (3€) to Cerveteri. From the bus stop in town, it's a pleasant 20-minute walk along rural Via della Necropoli to the entrance of the archaeological site.

Getting to Tarquinia is a bit more involved, but you're rewarded by the best-preserved tomb paintings in all of Etruscan Italy. The necropolis here, a 20-minute walk from the main town, has thousands of subterranean tombs (not raised *tumuli,* as at Cerveteri) decorated with vivid, titillating scenes of Etruscan life and rituals. You could easily spend several hours descending and emerging from the hundreds of excavated tombs here and not get bored.

Back in charming, medieval Tarquinia town is the excellent **National Museum** (Tues–Sun 8:30am–7:30pm; 4€), where the astonishing terra-cotta winged horses (found at an Etruscan temple nearby), as well as many of the artifacts found in the tombs, are now kept. The easiest way to get to Tarquinia is by car; if going by public transport, allow a full day, and take a *diretto* train (www.trenitalia.com for schedule) from Termini, Ostiense, or Trastevere station to Tarquinia (1 hr., 20 min; 6.20€ each way). The last train from Tarquinia to Rome leaves at 8:28pm.

VITERBO ★

A classic, medieval fortified town, the lure here is witnessing village culture first-hand. So while you'll want to spend some time simply ambling aimlessly, don't miss the historic highlights which include the 16th-century Palazzo Comunale (it still serves as the city's town hall). Walk in and tour the building on your own; there's no ticket booth or information desk. On the upper floors are frescoes and canvas paintings by Sebastiano del Piombo and Bartolomeo Cavarozzi. Outside the city walls, visit the Gothic chapel in the church of Santa Maria della Verità, made famous by a young boy named Lorenzo di Viterbo, whose wall scribbles are some of the most detailed frescoes in this part of Italy. You'll need a car to get to the natural sulfur springs, used by Julius Caesar for their supposed curative properties, that dot the countryside. Local Cotral buses (p. 23) from Rome to Viterbo cost just 1€. Trains (p. 23) cost 6.70€ round trip.

POMPEII ★★★

If you're not planning to visit southern Italy, you can visit the famous ruins of Pompeii on a (long) day trip from Rome. To get there, take a train from Roma

Termini to Napoli Centrale (see www.trenitalia.it for exact schedules), and then transfer at the Naples train station to the local Circumvesuviana train. Be sure to take the Circumvesuviana in the direction of **Sorrento,** and get off at **Pompeii Scavi.** Allow 3 hours each way for transportation, and at least 3 hours at the site. See p. 529 for more information.

The ABCs of Rome

American Express The main offices in Rome are at Piazza di Spagna 38 (☎ 06-67641). Travel services are open Monday to Friday 9am to 5pm, Saturday until 12:30pm. Financial and mail services operate Monday to Friday 9am to 5pm. The tour information office is open Monday to Saturday 9am to 12:30pm during summer.

Business Hours & Siesta Banks are open Monday to Friday from 8:30am to 1:30pm and 3 to 4pm; stores generally open at 9:30 or 10am until 7:30pm. Fewer and fewer stores in the center observe the siesta, but shops in quieter residential areas may be closed from about 1:30pm to 4pm. It is difficult to eat lunch before 12:30pm or dinner before 8pm unless you go to a tavola calda self-service style restaurant or pizza taglio (pizza-by-the-slice venue). Kitchens often stay open until midnight.

Car & Bike Rental Major car-rental kiosks are at both airports and in the Villa Borghese parking lot, entrance Metro Spagna, where you can also rent bicycles, three-wheel peddlers, and 50cc mopeds.

Currency Exchange Exchange bureaus are called *cambio* and are well located throughout the city. There is generally a service charge of 1½% imposed by both banks and cambio outlets.

Doctors The **U.S. Embassy** (☎ 06-46741) has a list of English-speaking doctors. For emergencies, go to a *pronto soccorso* (emergency room) at any hospital. The **Aventino Medical Group** (Via della Fonte di Fauno 22; ☎ 06-5780738; www.aventinomedicalgroup.com) is a consortium of English-speaking

specialists who cater to the large expat community in Rome.

Emergencies For an ambulance, call ☎ **118** or **113.**

Hospitals If you take a car or taxi, ask to be driven to the pronto soccorso at Policlinico Gemelli, Policlinico Umberto I, or Bambino Gesù (for kids). The ambulance will take you to the nearest hospital, which is not always the best.

Internet Cafes Internet cafes now dot the city and many hotels offer free Wi-Fi, as do some city parks, like Villa Borghese. In general, Internet cafes charge 3€ a half-hour, 5€ an hour. New anti-terrorism laws require users to provide an ID, which is photocopied.

Newspapers & Magazines The *Herald Tribune, New York Times, USA Today,* and the major American newsweeklies are all available at newsstands throughout the city. Rome does not have an English-language newspaper, but a twice monthly magazine *Wanted in Rome* has interesting English articles on local events and expat-specific classified ads.

Pharmacies There is an **international pharmacy** open 23 hours a day on Piazza Barberini 49 (☎ 06-6879098); it is closed 7 to 8pm. Most pharmacies are open Monday to Friday 8:30am to 1pm and 4 to 7:30pm and Saturday mornings. Pharmacies in each area rotate Saturday afternoon and Sunday openings; check the notice by each pharmacy for the rotation schedule.

Police For police, call ☎ **113.**

Post Office The city's main post office is at Piazza San Silvestro near the Spanish

Steps, but you can buy *francobolli* (stamps) at tobacco shops and from most hotels. Vatican City has its own postal service, run through Switzerland, with offices in Vatican City near the metal detectors at the entrance to the basilica. It is open 8:30am to 7pm Monday to Friday and 8:30am to 6pm Saturday.

Public Transportation For information on public transportation in the city, call **ATAC** (☎ **800-431784;** www.atac.roma. it); regional public transportation, **Cotral** (☎ **800-150008;** www.cotralspa.it); regional and local trains, www.tren italia.it.

Restrooms Public restrooms in Rome are frightening by most standards. The best bet is to check for facilities at coffee bars, monuments and museums, and department stores.

Safety Pickpockets remain the biggest nuisance in Rome, especially around tourist areas like the Colosseum and Trevi Fountain. Table snatching (where someone lifts your purse or valuables from a cafe table) is increasingly a problem, and there is a growing concern with nighttime arsonists setting fire to cars and mopeds, including rentals, making it vital that your car insurance cover fire.

Tourism Information Rome has an impressive website (**www.romaturismo. com**) featuring itineraries, suggestions for accommodations, and one of the best interactive maps around. You can take a virtual tour of the city before you come or use this site at computers found at the many information kiosks in the city. It has a particularly detailed list of local legends, and some great recipes for classic Roman fare.

Florence: Great City of the Renaissance

Where humankind cast off the intellectual shackles of the Middle Ages

by Reid Bramblett

THE NUMBERS JUST DON'T LIE. ONE-THIRD OF ALL UNESCO WORLD Heritage Sites are in Italy. And one-third of these are contained in the small, compact city of Florence, making it one of the most historically important cities in the world. This vaunted status is nothing new. It is exactly what most Europeans thought of Florence back in the 15th and 16th centuries, when the city's achievements in art, architecture, science, and literature were unparalleled and it was often referred to as the New Athens.

As the center of the Renaissance movement, and the hometown of its leaders—Michelangelo, Brunelleschi, da Vinci, Giotto, Galileo, and others—the city built up a store of riches that still dazzles today: the masterpiece-packed Uffizi Gallery; the ingenious domed cathedral; Michelangelo's *David;* and the city's stunningly decorated halls, palaces, and chapels. These treasures are still representative of the best mankind can achieve. And because of this, Florence remains a must-visit destination for every first-time traveler to Italy, and a must-return destination for anyone who cares about art and architecture.

DON'T LEAVE FLORENCE WITHOUT . . .

SEEING MICHELANGELO'S *DAVID* IN THE ACCADEMIA Rarely does a work of art live up to its reputation as this one does. Note that the outdoor *David,* in the city's main plaza, is a copy of the original, which is preserved in the Accademia.

TOURING THE UFFIZI Yes, everybody and their bus tour group line up for it, but for good reason: The Uffizi has one of the best art collections on earth.

GETTING INTO LEATHER Florence is a mecca for leather goods, attracting hundreds of jacket, boot, and bag makers. Tour the street stalls of San Lorenzo Market or the higher-end shops of Santa Croce for good deals and/or fine craftsmanship.

CLIMBING THE DOME Check out the Duomo, Florence's cathedral, and Brunelleschi's massive dome from the inside, the outside, and up on top.

TASTING *BISTECCA ALLA FIORENTINA*   Order the city's specialty: a thick juicy steak on the bone prepared in an open wood-fired oven. Wash it down with some Brunello and finish off with gelato.

ENJOYING THE MEALTIME THEATER AT TEATRO DEL SALE   The chef announces the upcoming entrees by screaming from a window in the kitchen. Diners jockey for spots near the huge buffet-style serving table. After dinner, sit back and enjoy the onstage entertainment at this superb new supper club run by the leading lights of Florence's culinary scene.

VISITING THE SHOPS OF OLTRARNO   See fifth-generation artisans practicing their craft in family workshops on the south side of the historic Ponte Vecchio.

CHEERING ON ACF FIORENTINA   Join the people of Florence as they root for the ACF Fiorentina, which competes for the championship of Italy's elite Serie A soccer league.

A BRIEF HISTORY OF FLORENCE

Julius Caesar founded the city of Fiorentia as an encampment by the Arno River in 59 B.C. Veterans of his Roman legions later decided that the flat plain by the river would be a good place to settle (and, notwithstanding a few thousand years of floods, it was).

Florence grew to prominence in the early Middle Ages, as various guilds (especially those involved in textiles and, later, banking) gave rise to a prosperous merchant class. In 1125 it elected a council of 100 of the richest merchants to rule the city. The most powerful families branched out to create the world's first private banking industry, amassing incredible wealth along the way. By the late Middle Ages, Florence was *the* city in Europe, supporting a population of well over 100,000. Their loans and investments financed kings and popes alike, and attracted the top artistic talent money could buy.

The same outlays brought in a huge amount of international trade, and by the mid-1300s this crowded and unsanitary medieval city was an epicenter of commerce. Shipments of spices, silks, and slaves arrived daily from the Orient via the ports of Pisa and Venice. Among these imports in 1348 was the bacillus responsible for the Black Death (buried in the bellies of fleas riding the backs of black rats). The plague swept like a tsunami through the city, the region, and all of Europe, killing nearly a third of the continent's population. In Florence and Tuscany, the Black Death wiped out half the citizens in the first year alone, flaring up again and again over the next 3 decades.

In 1401, a sculptor named Ghiberti received a commission to create low relief panels to decorate the north doors of the Baptistery outside the Duomo. The young sculptor's designs were chosen over those submitted by other, more established artists thanks in part to Ghiberti's use of naturalism, classical balance, illusion of space, and vitality of motion—all hallmarks of what historians would later dub a "rebirth" of art and philosophy that would soon sweep all of Europe. This is why many academics peg the year 1401, the city of Florence, and the humble figure of Ghiberti, as signaling the start of the Renaissance.

Not only did the city experience a reawakening following the plague's devastations, but the artists and intellectuals of the day began to take an interest in the ancient Greeks and Romans, reviving their humanistic ideals and reverence for nature. You can still see the influence of this movement in the realistic carvings on Ghiberti's doors, and in the engineering feats (some of them derived from close study of the Pantheon in Rome) that allowed Brunelleschi to create the dome on Florence's Duomo (a task he tackled, incidentally, after losing the Baptistery doors commission to Ghiberti). The late 15th and early 16th centuries saw the continued flowering of this movement in the works of Botticelli, Michelangelo, and Leonardo da Vinci—Tuscans one and all.

The history of Renaissance Florence is also the story of the powerful Medici clan, a dominant family banking conglomerate that rose eventually to become city rulers, princes, popes, and cultural leaders, men who not only created history but also often rewrote it to extol their efforts. Many of the buildings and statues—even the layout of the city—resulted from the wealth and will of this important family. Without their money, influence, and tastes, Florence simply would not have achieved the prominence and grandeur that it did.

Florence boasted military power to match its economic and artistic leadership in the Renaissance. Its armies conquered Pisa, Arezzo, Siena, and a host of other Tuscan cities. But infighting among Florence's families weakened the city, and by 1600, with the Medici fortunes having faded, Florence began its gradual transformation into a tourist town. The creation of the Uffizi Gallery, in 1581, and thus the replacement of living history with a museum, was perhaps the signal that Florence's best days were behind her.

Florence tried for another rebirth in the 1860s, following Italian unification. It was named capital of the new Republic of Italy, and, to celebrate, constructed the neoclassical Piazza della Repubblica by razing a medieval neighborhood. In 1865, the capital moved to Rome, and Florence was returned to the back burner once again.

During World War II, Florence was as divided as the rest of Italy. Nazis and Fascist collaborators fought Partisans in street battles even after the end of the war. The Germans destroyed all but one of the bridges over the Arno to slow down the Allied advance, but they left the Ponte Vecchio standing in a nod to its historical significance. Allied aerial bombers also avoided hitting monuments, using the reflection of the sun off the Duomo as a beacon.

Today Florence remains a vibrant, living city. Vespas buzz through the streets like the wasps for which they are named. Steel garage doors between old stone villas discharge Italian sports cars. The Ferragamo, akin to the Medici, rule their own mercantile empire from a fortresslike palazzo on the Arno, and important fashion fairs recall the initial rise of the city's fortunes.

LAY OF THE LAND

The first order of business is to get oriented. The **Santa Maria Novella district,** anchored by the eponymous church and the main train station, is at the far west side of the tourist's world, with the Arno River to the south. This area has spawned a tourists' ghetto of cheap lodging, Internet cafes, and souvenir stands centered on Via Faenza, Via Nazionale, and Via del Giglio. Moving toward the city center on Via Faenza, you'll pass the stall-filled streets around **Mercato Centrale and San Lorenzo Church,** claustrophobic but a good spot to shop for leather deals.

All roads lead to the **Duomo,** the site of Florence's massive domed cathedral, the Baptistery, and 10 million tourists. So it's easy to find, but hard to exit in the right direction. Remember, the Baptistery, the smaller building with the doors everyone is staring at, stands on the western end of the piazza.

Go **north from the Duomo** on Via Ricasoli, Via Cavour, or Via dei Servi to find the **Accademia** (which houses Michelangelo's *David*), **Piazza San Marco,** and **Piazza della Santissima Annunziata,** respectively. These large attractions create the northern borders of your tourist world.

The **western edge** of the historical center focuses around the cavernous **Santa Croce** church, hemmed in by leather stores. The streets are a little more residential, the feeling a bit more local than in the central part of the district.

South from the Duomo, Via Roma will lead you to the neoclassical **Piazza della Repubblica** and its huge arch. Via dei Tornabuoni, the high-end shopping street with the Ferragamo and Prada stores, is a few blocks west of Piazza della Repubblica. A couple of blocks east of Piazza della Repubblica, Via dei Calzaiuoli brings visitors from the Duomo's front steps directly through the medieval heart of town to the statue-filled medieval **Piazza della Signoria** and **Palazzo Vecchio** (the fortress with the pokey tower). Piazza della Signoria connects on the south end to the **Uffizi Gallery,** which is just east of the shop-filled Ponte Vecchio, the landmark bridge crossing the **Arno River.**

South of the Arno, across Ponte Vecchio, or Ponte S. Trinità, is the **Oltrarno** district, more of a laid-back, locals-focused part of town, with winding streets filled with artisans' workshops and small stores. But it's still tourist-friendly, with hotels, restaurants, and the massive **Pitti Palace,** along with several other interesting churches and, in the hills high above, **Piazzale Michelangelo** and **San Miniato Church** offering fantastic postcard views of the city skyline.

GETTING THERE & AROUND

Most people arrive in Florence by train, but a growing number of international and European discount airlines fly into both Florence's **Amerigo Vespucci Airport** (☎ 055-3061302; www.aeroporto.firenze.it) or Pisa's nearby **Galileo Galilei Airport.** Florence's airport is only about 4.8km (3 miles) from the city center, making it a reasonable 15€ to 20€ cab ride, or a 4€, 20-minute bus ride into town via the direct Ataf-Sita buses that leave the airport every 30 minutes. Regular city buses make the connection for about 1.50€. The Pisa airport is about an hour from Florence. Low-cost airlines have a dedicated bus service running a dozen shuttles from the airport to Florence each day for 7.50€. From other airlines, you buy a train ticket for 5.10€, and walk to the nearby airport train station. Another option I've recently employed with great success is to **fly into Bologna,** about a 90-minute drive across the mountains from Florence (or a 60- to 105-min. train ride), aboard one of EuroFly's new direct flights from New York City (see "Getting the Best Airfare to Italy" in chapter 15 for details).

All airports have a full selection of rental-car services—but you won't want a car if you're only staying in Florence. The historical center is minuscule and almost entirely pedestrian-only, street parking is nigh impossible, and garages are terribly expensive. If you plan to explore more of Tuscany, arrange to pick up a vehicle at a downtown rental office on the day you plan to leave Florence.

Florence sits on the **main rail line** between Milan (3 hr. away) and Rome (about a 2-hr. ride). **Stazione Santa Maria Novella** (often abbreviated on signage as SMN; ☎ 800-888088 in Italy, or 055-288765; www.trenitalia.it) is the main Florence station, across the street from the bus station, and a short walk from dozens of hotels and restaurants and just 10 minutes' stroll from the Duomo. A tourist information office is in the station, but it mostly operates as a hotel booking service—good enough for a basic map pamphlet, but you can get much better city info at the main office on Via Cavour, 2 long blocks north of the Duomo. Whatever you do, don't get off the train by accident at either of Florence's other two stations, **Campo di Marte** or **Refredi,** which are way out in the 'burbs.

Almost all regional and city **buses** arrive at the station right outside SMN. But since Florence is such a rail hub, there's usually no need to hassle with longer bus rides, unless you're traveling to Florentine suburbs off the rail network.

It's fairly easy to reach the outskirts of Florence **by car,** via the A1 autostrada cutting down the center of Italy. Then all hell breaks loose. Assuming you can find the historical center among the tangled collection of one-way streets, you won't be able to enter it—only cars with special permits are allowed. Even if police don't stop you, cameras can take a picture of the car's plates, and you'll get hit with a whopping fine months later. The good news is that hotels have arrangements with the city to permit guests to at least stop by to drop off luggage. But this means you need to have made arrangements with your hotel prior to arrival; don't expect to simply drive around and find a place.

For **parking,** you can make it as far as the garage under SMN for parking rates of about 2€ per hour. Most hotels offer some sort of parking arrangement with a

---

The Red & the Black: Florence Addresses

You'll notice that the street numbers on most addresses for shops, restaurants, and bars in this chapter end with an "r," while the numbers for most hotels and sights do not. That's because Florence has two overlapping street numbering systems: red for businesses and commercial addresses, black for residential ones (which, for some reason, include most hotels). The two systems do not interact, so on any given street you might pass red 1r, 3r, 5r, 7r, and 9r before you get to the black 1—which may be followed by black 3 or red 11r. And while many Florentine streets follow the common international standard of numbering one side with even numbers and numbering the other side with odd ones, on some streets the numbers just march up one side as 1, 2, 3, 4 . . ., then turn around and start with 49, 50, 51, 52 . . . back down the other. Given Florence's compact center and relatively short streets, all of this is less of an issue than it might sound, but I wanted to warn you before you got confused hunting down a given address.

Touring Florence

A number of companies offer walking tours of Florence. One of the best, which combines native English speakers with interesting stories, is **Walking Tours of Florence** (Via Sassetti 1; ☎ 055-2645033; www.italy.artviva.com). Its owners have a theater background and choose guides who are natural performers. Their spirited tours aren't just dry presentations of names and dates, and it is little wonder that everyone from Lou Reed to Michael Palin to A-Rod consider them the guides of choice. The group offers half- and full-day tours of the major sights (25€ for a 3-hr. tour of the city center; 94€ for a full-day tour, including museum admissions) and an assortment of custom tours, including out-of-town trips and a fascinating walk through the artisans' shops south of the Arno.

A less recommended way to get oriented is on a bus tour. The **City Sightseeing Firenze** (Piazza Stazione 1; ☎ 055-290451; www.city-sightseeing.it) has two lines of open-air, double-decker buses on which you can sit back and get a tan while you see the town. The 20€ ticket is pricey, but if you're jet-lagged or just don't want to deal with walking through the heat or traffic, it may make sense. The ticket is good for 24 hours, works on both lines (which take slightly different routes through the historical center; the brochure has a map), and lets you to hop off the bus, tour a sight, and catch the next coach when it comes around again.

---

nearby garage, but prices vary widely, from 10€ to more than 30€ per day. If you're far enough from the historical center, free street parking is available, but make very sure it's legal or you're going to have a nightmare of a time getting your towed car returned. The cheapest overnight parking option, at 15€ per day, is the underground **Parterre parking lot,** just north of Piazza della Libertà. On a map, this is the northernmost node in the busy ring road around the historical center. (*Florence trivia:* This ring road was built by tearing down the medieval city walls, which is why most of the little piazzas strung along the road like charms on a bracelet turn out to be traffic circles around a forlorn ancient city gate, many of which were left standing.) Again, by far the best strategy is to rent a car before and/or after your Florence stay, and not deal with any of the hassle and expense.

Despite the uneven cobblestone streets (bring comfortable shoes), the crazy high-speed Vespas, and an unnerving number of large, fast buses, the best way to get around Florence is **on foot.** The central historical district takes only about 25 minutes to cross. Avoid the city buses, which will bring you to outlying districts before you can say "there goes the Duomo!" and then you'll have to figure out how to find your way back.

ACCOMMODATIONS, BOTH STANDARD & NOT

Florence has over 1,000 registered places to stay, plus an equal number of unofficial apartment and room rentals, so there really is something for everyone. Recently, many of the semilegal private-room rentals and bed-and-breakfasts have been forced to register with authorities, creating a visible glut of rooms. Hoteliers now complain of a slow tourism market and high vacancy rates, even worse than the post-9/11 slump. Amazingly, at some hotels room rates have actually gone down, though many have stayed static and some have ventured a modest increase. Still, such market factors should give you increased bargaining power for rooms.

Christmas, Easter, and the occasional trade show (especially the Pitti Moda series of fashion expos) make for tighter times in booking rooms. A number of smaller hotels and B&Bs close for a couple of weeks in August as well, making it a little tougher to find lodging during this period.

APARTMENTS FOR RENT

As I've said, Florence currently has a glut of housing, particularly for those planning to rent an apartment, with the lowest prices going to those who rent for a week or longer. Renting an apartment can dramatically cut lodging costs, given that a decent, centrally located two-bedroom flat with kitchen and sitting room averages about 600€ to 800€ a week—much less than a similar level hotel. Plus, you can cut down on dining expenses by stocking the fridge with breakfast and snacks—though you'll certainly want to go out for many meals to sample the local cuisine. An apartment also offers a relaxing home base, and can give you a real flavor of local Italian living.

There's something for everyone, from the palatial to the monastically simple. One thing to keep in mind: A number of Internet-based companies consolidate listings from private owners, so you'll often find the same apartments on multiple sites. Research carefully before you book. In addition to the usual online rental clearinghouses—such as **Rentalo.com** and **VRBO.com**—here are a few that specialize in Florence.

Rentals Florence (☎ 055-2347206; www.rentalsflorence.com) offers a dozen apartments across the city, including one a stone's throw from the Duomo. Furnishings are basic but functional, the location is unparalleled, and you can enjoy sunset over the city from the roof patio. Rates start at 470€ per week (980€ per month) in a smaller apartment for two people, and as little as 700€ per week (1,800€ per month) in a flat that sleeps up to six. Gabriela, the rental manager, works hard to make sure people enjoy their stays and can give recommendations for rentals elsewhere in Tuscany.

For a wider selection of centrally located apartments in all price ranges, look to **Lodging in Florence** (Vicolo degli Adimari 2; ☎ 055-280007; www.lodging inflorence.com). You can trust manager Lorenzo Clemente and his team to find an apartment that matches your tastes and needs. Their cheapest rentals are tiny (but centrally located) "bedsits" going for 450€ to 640€ a week. These small studio apartments have bathroom and kitchen, and are clean and functional—but don't expect to do any entertaining. You can get up-close Duomo views starting at 920€ per week in an apartment sleeping up to five (though I think someone gets stuck with the futon). On the higher end are cushy two-bedroom, two-bathroom refurbished apartments with views across the Arno to the Uffizi for 1,450€ a week. The group also has a bed-and-breakfast option permitting you to rent a room in a local's apartment (a cheap and sometimes fun option), and can find out-of-town lodging as well.

€€€–€€€€ Because you came all the way to Florence to experience a Renaissance town, perhaps you should stay at a period apartment. **Palazzo Belfiore** ✸ (Via dei Velluti 8, Oltrarno; ☎ 055-264415 or 055-611115; www. residencebelfiore.it; AE, MC, V) offers seven unique apartments in a 15th-century palace, which you can rent by the night, week, or month. The rooms boast frescoes and antique furniture, and are restored to their original splendor, but with the addition of satellite TV, modern kitchens, and central heating or air-conditioning (the nobles never had it so good!). Rates are 800€ to 1,200€ per week (or 120€–190€ per night) for apartments sleeping up to four, 1,200€ to 1,600€ per week (or 200€–240€ per night) for apartments sleeping up to six people.

RELIGIOUS HOUSING

€–€€ While Florence doesn't have the same meditative atmosphere as, say, Assisi or a smaller town in the countryside, you can still save a bit of money, and enjoy a spiritual interlude, at a religious house in the city—both run by nuns and, as you'd expect, pretty basic. **Suore Oblate dello Spirito Santo** (Via Nazionale 8; ☎ 055-2398202; cash only), which seems a bit out of place close to the chaos of the train station, normally houses students, and therefore accepts tourists only in summer (late June to mid-Sept). It has an 11pm curfew, requires a minimum 2-night stay, and won't take unmarried couples—though these rules are easier to live with when the rates are just 56€ for a double with a private bathroom (however, Sister Maria Domencia felt it was important I warn you that they do not offer breakfast). **Suore Oblate dell'Assunzione** (Via Borgo Pinti 15; ☎ 055-2480582; cash only), between the Duomo and Santa Croce, charges 40€ per person in a room with private bathroom (in room for most, though three of the rooms each have their own private bathroom out in the hall), but is open year-round and is a bit more generous with the 11:30pm curfew—you may be able to come in as late as midnight in summer.

€ My preference is for a *semi*-religious stay. Despite the severe appearance of the **Pope Pio X Hostel** (Via dei Serragli 106, Oltrarno; ☎ 055-225044; www. hostelpiox.it; cash only), with photos of the pope and religious paraphernalia everywhere, it's really a relaxed hostel (each rooms sleeps three to six) popular with Italian students—as it should be at 17€ per person a night in a room without private bathroom, 19€ in a room with bathroom, about the cheapest option in town. Get there early to claim one of the 58 beds.

€–€€ Finally, **The Instituto Gould** ✸ 🧒 (Via dei Serragli 49, Oltrarno; ☎ 055-212576; www.istitutogould.it/foresteria; cash only) is more upscale than a regular hostel, charging 62€ for a courtyard double with private bathroom (56€ with bathroom but a street view, 52€ without bathroom), or as little as 23€ per person in a shared quad with bathroom (regardless of view), 21€ in a quad without bathroom (but on the courtyard). But the building, a palace from the mid–17th century, has been modernized to provide clean, basic dorm rooms, and boasts an attractive courtyard. A portion of your room rate goes to help the disadvantaged children whom the institute supports.

Florence Accommodations & Dining

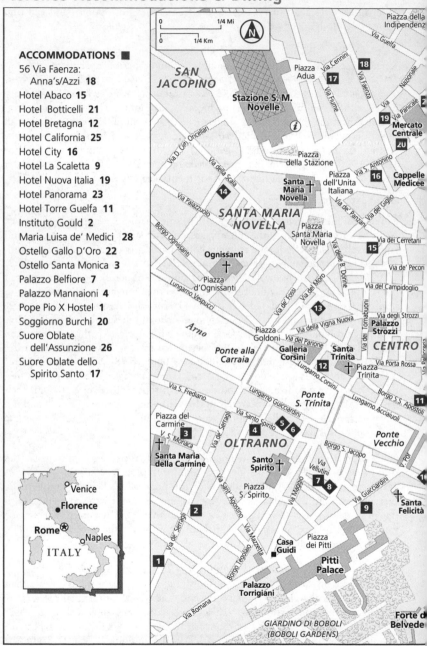

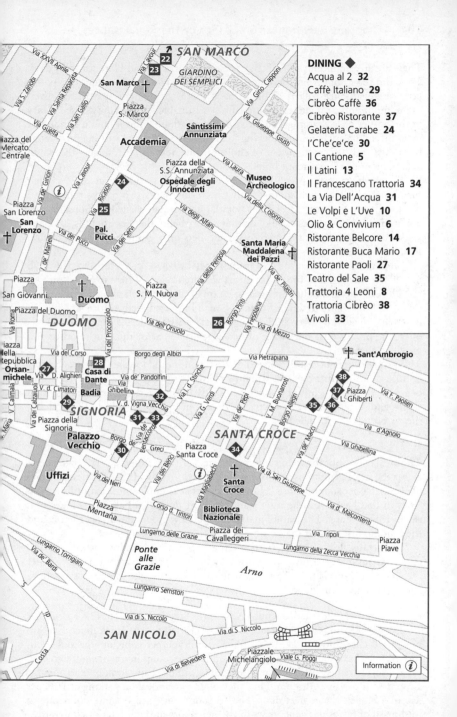

DINING ◆

Acqua al 2 **32**
Caffè Italiano **29**
Cibrèo Caffè **36**
Cibrèo Ristorante **37**
Gelateria Carabe **24**
l'Che'ce'ce **30**
Il Cantione **5**
Il Latini **13**
Il Francescano Trattoria **34**
La Via Dell'Acqua **31**
Le Volpi e L'Uve **10**
Olio & Convivium **6**
Ristorante Belcore **14**
Ristorante Buca Mario **17**
Ristorante Paoli **27**
Teatro del Sale **35**
Trattoria 4 Leoni **8**
Trattoria Cibrèo **38**
Vivoli **33**

BED & BREAKFASTS

There are an astounding 429 B&Bs operating in and around Florence these days. They run the gamut from echoing salons complete with frescoes and four-poster beds in Renaissance palazzi to bland back rooms in modern apartments. Even more importantly, the prices are incredibly reasonable. While you will see plenty of the posher pads charging 120€ to 180€ for a double room (and a handful of magnificent, palatial options clocking in as high as 360€), the vast majority range from 70€ to 120€, with dozens of choices in the 35€ to 70€ range—that's well below the price of a standard hotel.

The problem with listing B&Bs in a guidebook—aside from the fact that there's not nearly enough room—is that each only rents two to five rooms, and most only two to three. In a city as popular and heavily visited as Florence, listing individual properties would quickly overwhelm them with calls and any reader besides the lucky first two or three callers on a given day is going to find them all booked.

Good thing, then, that the **city tourism office** (www.firenzeturismo.it) lists all 429 Florentine bed-and-breakfasts on its website under "Where to Stay," providing address, phone number, website, and e-mail (if available); photos, if they have them; and the ability to send a booking e-mail inquiry directly. *Hint:* The full list is actually divided between 327 "professional" B&Bs and 102 "nonprofessional" ones; the professional ones have officially registered with the tourist office and provided their rates.

The prices are not readily apparent. What you should look at is the second row of little icons (the first row tells you how many rooms, beds, and baths); the numbers under the tiny icons of a single bed or two beds are the rates, in euros, for a single and double room, respectively. A cappuccino cup with a "C" under it means breakfast is included.

HOTELS OF THE SANTA MARIA NOVELLA DISTRICT

The area just east of the train station—where Via Faenza crosses Via Nazionale—is not the most glamorous area of town, but it does provide the greatest number of affordable accommodations. Plus, tiny Florence is unlike most major European cities in that being near the train station doesn't put you a half-hour's hike from the historical center. The leather market is just a few blocks down Via Faenza, and the Duomo just beyond that.

The area is also brimming with Internet cafes, bars, laundromats, shops, and cheap restaurants catering to the tourist trade. It's a good place for meeting other travelers, too, especially backpackers who can afford to take this baby step above basic hostel accommodations.

€   The friendly, older Italian couple who owns **Soggiorno Burchi** (Via Faenza 20; ☎ 055-268481; www.soggiornoburchi.com; AE, MC, V) doesn't speak much English, but they'll cheerfully yell at you in Italian until you get your luggage and room sorted. They have about the cheapest decent private rooms in town, at 40€ to 45€ for a clean, extremely plain but spotless double without bathroom, 50€ to 55€ for a room with private bathroom. Plus, they offer a great deal on parking at 10€ per day in a hidden garage next door. The 13 rooms on three separate floors offer a mishmash of furnishings and views of the neighbors through interior courtyards.

€€–€€€   A one-stop shop for budget lodging in this area is **56 Via Faenza.** That four-story building contains six hotels/hostels. The most surprising, perhaps, is **Hotel Anna's** ★ (Via Faenza, 56; ☎ 055-2302714; www.hotelannas.com; AE, MC, V), an extremely pleasant place tucked into the third floor of what appears from the street to be only a low-end backpacker flophouse (it's not). The newly refurbished rooms here are spotlessly clean, with the type of classy, functional furniture you'd expect to see at a three-star business hotel. It's also a friendly place with a helpful staff. Continental breakfast is served in a little frescoed alcove, or in your room upon request, adding 5€ to the 80€-to-130€ room rate. The same building's first floor is home to **Hotel Azzi** ★ (☎ 055-213806; www.hotelazzi.it; AE, MC, V), a quirky, bohemian joint comprising 16 rooms, which range in price from 80€ for a smallish double with fan to 130€ for a suite during high season. Most doubles cost between 90€ and 110€. Rooms are brightly decorated, and most feature an antique piece or colorfully painted wall to add ambience. The manager, Valentino, and his partners run a number of hotels, apartments, and B&Bs in town, offering what he calls "a total housing solution"; they'll find something for you even if the Azzi is booked.

€€–€€€   The proud motto of the service-oriented **Hotel Nuova Italia** ★★★ (Via Faenza 26; ☎ 055-287508 or 055-268430; www.hotel-nuovaitalia.com; AE, MC, V) is "Just ask!" And they mean it. Owned by Luciano Viti and his affable Canada-born wife, Eileen (they met 3 decades ago when she was a tourist, and his family's hotel was recommended in Arthur Frommer's *Europe on $5 a Day*), it's a labor of love, and the hotel has been steadily improving over the years. Recently, the couple added double-paned glass, air-conditioning, and new carpeting, and retiled the bathrooms. Luciano, Eileen, and their extended family will do anything they can to help out during your stay in Florence, with honest recommendations for sightseeing, shopping, and area travel. The official high-season rates for a double are 119€, but if that's too pricey for you, you may be able to bargain them down, especially if you're paying cash (also, Internet specials often slash the price to 85€ or even 75€). As they say, just ask!

€€–€€€€   Tucked away on a small side street, the tastefully refurbished **Hotel Botticelli** ★ (Via Taddea 8; ☎ 055-290905; www.hotelbotticelli.it; AE, MC, V) has a resort feel to it, thanks to the downright pretty rooms in a restored 16th-century villa. Many are done in the same wash of gentle colors that Botticelli himself used, and each features a nice framed print of the artist's work, along with satellite TV, air-conditioning, and minibar. It's not too far from the central market and the crowded street stalls of San Lorenzo, but enjoys the blessed quiet of being on a small side alley. The breakfast room and balcony patio are large and airy, and the buffet breakfast is good. Rooms officially go for 105€ to 240€, but you can sometimes get them as low as 86€ when business is slow. Check the website for seasonal deals.

€€–€€€€   From the outside, **Hotel City** ★ (Via Sant'Antonino 18; ☎ 055-211543; www.hotelcity.net; AE, MC, V) looks like every other undistinguished offering in this part of town. Inside, however, is another story: The rooms—98€ to 220€ for a double—are newly renovated and quiet despite the central location, and the staff is eager to please. They've recently added free Wi-Fi, serve an ample buffet breakfast, and have even installed a reserve air-conditioning system in case the primary one breaks down. With half-timbered arched rooms, whitewashed walls, and elaborate Liberty-style stained and painted glass ceilings in the public areas, this is a beautifully maintained hotel—especially when compared with others in the immediate vicinity, which seem to be operated chiefly as tax write-offs by absentee owners.

HOTELS IN THE CENTRAL DISTRICT, AROUND THE DUOMO & PIAZZA DELLA SIGNORIA

The heart of town is, of course, the ideal place to stay—especially if you can get the fabled "room with a view," allowing you to wake up each morning to the beauty of the Duomo and its nearby buildings. Consequently, lodgings here tend to be pricier than those around the train station, but if you can afford to splurge, this is one of the places in Italy where price will make a difference in the quality of your stay. Hidden among the splurges, however, are a few good budget options.

€–€€€   In a prime location overlooking the Arno, the **Hotel Bretagna** ★★ (Lungarno Corsini 6; ☎ 055-289618; www.hotelbretagna.net; AE, MC, V) has swallowed up an 1880s palace and several surrounding offices to create a warren of widely varied rooms. Some are quite nice, with a classic Victorian look; others resemble converted closets. But even the small rooms, with interior-facing windows, are a good option given the location of the hotel and the fine breakfast and common rooms. The prices are also quite fair: 45€ to 85€ for a double with shared bathroom, 55€ to 115€ for doubles with private bathroom. Renovations in 2006 created some triples (with or without private bathroom) and family rooms with frescoed ceilings, chandeliers, and balconies overlooking the river— making these rooms truly a choice pick of Florence, especially at a reasonable 100€ to 160€. Be sure to check the website for last-minute specials, which often shave 15€ off the prices.

€€   Halfway between the train station and the Duomo, the **Hotel Abaco** ★★ 🄺 (Via dei Banchi 1; ☎ 055-2381919; www.abaco-hotel.it; MC, V) is a budget charmer of nine rooms named for different artists and done up in the colors that each artist tended to use (compare the color of the drapes with the framed print by "your" artist on the wall). All rooms have air-conditioning, TV, and a nice bit of ambience thanks to the high wood ceilings and occasional stone fireplace of this 15th-century palazzo. Because some rooms share a WC (all have private showers and sinks) the prices are reasonable, especially for the toiletless rooms where doubles range from 72€ to 82€ (85€–95€ with private facilities). There are also nice triples (95€–125€) and quads (135€–155€), good for families. Breakfast is 5€ extra, but free if you pay for the room in cash.

€€   **Maria Luisa de' Medici** ★★★ (Via del Corso 1; ☎ 055-280048; cash only) is one of my favorite pensioni in all of Italy. First off, it is bang in the geographic center of the old city, on a narrow pedestrian street precisely halfway between the Duomo and the Uffizi. It also has all the creature comforts you could want—firm beds, thick walls, a hearty complimentary breakfast—in a setting that's delightfully imaginative, quirky, and, in an odd way, stylish. The decor is a mishmash of styles: rooms in a 1650s palazzo filled with funky 1960s high-design furniture, exquisite baroque paintings, and modern murals of the Medici; sculptures crowd the corridors. Most of the five rooms are oversized and terrific for families, and the Welsh-born hostess Evelyn Morris is as friendly and helpful as can be. The drawbacks? The cheaper rooms share a bathroom (these cost 80€ for a double, 110€ for a triple, and 130€ for a quad; rooms with private bathroom cost 15€ more), and to reach the pensione you'll need to walk up three flights of steps. Also, rooms do not have phones, and there's a curfew, which varies with the season (usually between 11pm and midnight). Aside from those minor quibbles, the place is a delight; it is where I usually stay when I visit Florence on my own (when I don't have, you know, 40 hotels to review).

€€–€€€€ Though it looks seedy from the outside, the **Hotel California** (Via Ricasoli 30, near the Duomo; ☎ 055-282753; www.californiaflorence.it; AE, MC, V) is actually quite nice once you make it up to the second-floor lobby. Its recently remodeled rooms are spacious and comfortable, particularly the triples and quads. Some rooms have that greatest of Florentine hotel amenities: a terrace overlooking the Duomo. All have air-conditioning, satellite TV, and positively swank bathrooms (some with Jacuzzi). The rear terrace, bedecked with flowers in spring and summer, is the perfect place to kick back with a bottle of Chianti and write postcards. Rates for a double room can vary widely by season, from 80€ to 190€—though if you tell them you found the hotel through the Pauline Frommer's guide they'll knock 5% off (this is something they offered spontaneously, not that we asked for; we figured you wouldn't mind if we accepted the discount on your behalf).

€€–€€€€ One of my favorite splurge options in any neighborhood happens to be here in the historical center, on a quiet, little-trafficked side street just off the river, 45m (150 ft.) west of Ponte Vecchio. The **Hotel Torre Guelfa** ★★ (Borgo SS. Apostoli 8, between Via dei Tornabuoni and Via Por Santa Maria; ☎ 055-2396338; www.hoteltorreguelfa.com; AE, MC, V) is one of the most atmospheric hotels in town, installed in a traditional Florentine tower-home dating back to 1380. From the canopied beds and pastel-wash walls to the soft strains of classical music or jazz echoing from the salon's vaulted ceilings, this place quietly exudes comfort and class. The real selling point is its namesake, the tallest privately owned medieval tower in Florence, offering breathtaking 360-degree views of the city around you. All that and doubles cost just 150€ to 210€ (120€–160€ for more modest room in the guesthouse down on the second floor)—though so many people request room no. 15, with a huge private terrace and a view similar to the tower's, they've had to tack an extra 60€ onto the price.

HOTELS IN OLTRARNO

More of a residential area than the one immediately surrounding the Duomo, Oltrarno has a lively mix of restaurants and bars, as well as some of the most charming shops in the city: the workplaces of jewelry makers, leather craftsmen, and woodcarvers who have toiled on the side streets of this district for decades. This is Florence's most bohemian district, though escalating rents have been driving some of the artists out. In short, it's a fun area within walking distance of all the major sights.

€€   For those who'd like the convenience of an apartment but can't commit to a full-week rental, the **Palazzo Mannaioni** (Via Maffia 9, near Piazza Santo Spirito; ☎ 055-271741; www.florenceresidence.it; AE, MC, V) offers an affordable solution. It's a 15th-century building that's been subdivided into a number of small apartments, each with its own efficiency kitchen. While these digs are nothing special decorwise, the location is terrific and the prices can't be beat for studios that can comfortably house two for as little as 70€ to 90€ a day. There are 19 little apartments, some with balcony terrace and some that can house up to eight in four double beds (120€–157€ per night for these, while apartments with two beds go for 90€–120€ per night).

€€–€€€   The views are why you want to stay at the **Hotel La Scaletta** ★★ 𝗄𝗂𝖽𝗌 (Via Guicciardini 13; ☎ 055-283028; www.lascaletta.com; MC, V). Located right next to the Pitti Palace, it has spectacular patios overlooking both the Boboli Gardens and the city. New management has extensively renovated the 13 rooms and the common areas, creating a cheery, colorful atmosphere throughout. One quadruple room is a good family choice at 105€ to 190€ a night, while doubles range from 85€ to 150€. The only downside is the small bathrooms, but those can't be helped: The hotel, like many others in this city, is set in a 15th-century palazzo with real character, thick walls, and plenty of preservation laws against knocking holes in them.

TWO HOSTEL OPTIONS

€   You know you're going into the bargain basement of budgeteering when your lodging proudly advertises that the hot showers are free and the bed linens are included in the price. Such is the case at shoestring choice **Ostello Santa Monica** ★ (Via S. Monaca 6; ☎ 055-268338; www.ostello.it; AE, MC, V). Though it is installed in a former 15th-century convent, it nonetheless manages to evince little charm and doesn't insist on too many rules. It's a good place to connect with other backpackers; there's a laundry room, shared kitchen, and Internet terminals on-site; and the bulletin boards are usually packed with budget tour options, bars, and restaurants around town. For 17€ to 19€ a night you get a bed in a shared room of 4, 6, 8, or 10 beds (the fewer beds per room, the higher the price), and a good Oltrarno location. Lockout times are 10am to 2pm and 2 to 6am; at least curfew isn't until 2am.

€€   The **Ostello Gallo D'Oro** ★ 𝗄𝗂𝖽𝗌 (Via Covour 104; ☎ 055-5522964; www.ostellogallodoro.com; AE, MC, V) is a clean, efficient hostel located a 15-minute walk north of the historical center, but the walk is worth it because you'll enjoy a friendly staff, a brand-new interior, and crisp, shiny shared rooms sleeping three to five for 32€ per person (or get a private double for 75€). The prices are a bit high for shared housing, but this is not one of your old-fashioned, rules-intensive hostels. There's no lockout or curfew, and every room has its own TV and bathroom. The lobby has two free Internet terminals (plus Wi-Fi throughout the hostel), breakfast is included in the rates, the kitchen is open to all, and the friendly manager may very well offer to cook something up for you (it's been known to happen). There are also nice private rooms—with TV, phone, and private bathroom—available at reasonable rates.

DINING FOR ALL TASTES

In general you'll find a lot of *cucina rustica* (rustic cuisine) in Florence's restaurants. This is food that's meant to stick to the ribs and leave you sated, so it's no accident that the great specialty of the city is *bistecca alla fiorentina*, a huge slab of steak on the bone, rubbed with olive oil and cracked black pepper. But this is not peasant fare by any means; there's a balance to these bold flavors that makes eating out in Florence a special occasion, even when you're just catching a quick lunch. Two other Florentine specialties that deserve singling out, as you'll encounter them on countless menus, are *ribolitta* (a thick peasant soup of cannellini white beans, tomatoes, and chardlike *cavolo nero* ladled over day-old bread) and *cantucci* (the Tuscan name for those hard little crescent almond cookies elsewhere known as biscotti) served with a tiny glass of *vin santo,* a golden sweet dessert wine.

If you need to catch a quick lunch, it's always best to arrive at a *ristorante* or *trattoria* at the beginning of the lunch hour, which is from noon to 2:30pm, and is traditionally the biggest meal of the day. Otherwise, you may have to wait for a table. Italians tend to start dinner between 7 and 9:30pm—you can assume that those are the hours of kitchen operation for the following eateries (with the exception of the gelaterie) unless indicated otherwise. For a **map of Florence's restaurants,** see p. 102.

€€   **Caffè Italiano** (Via della Condotta 56r; ☎ 055-289020; www.caffeitaliano. it; Mon–Sat 8:15am–8:15pm; MC, V), a pastry-and-sandwich bar with an early-20th-century feel, is a good spot to stop for lunch after a morning tour or shopping expedition. It serves a variety of soups, salads, and sandwiches to a full house. Morning visitors can enjoy custom coffee blends and fresh pastries made on the premises. Relax at a window table to people-watch, or dine in the large upstairs room.

€€   With its frescoed ceilings, antique fixtures, and tuxedoed waiters, **Ristorante Paoli** (Via dei Tavolini 12r; ☎ 055-216215; Wed–Mon noon–2:30pm and 7:30–10:30pm; AE, MC, V) is the type of place you'd imagine late-19th-century visitors on "the grand tour" frequented. Yes, it's a bit touristy, with a standard spaghetti-type menu, but the food is actually quite good, if expensive for what you get (pastas are 7€–14€). One highlight of the menu when it's available: the light and fresh sea bass with lemon, olive oil, and peppercorns (17€–20€).

€€   Dining at **Il Latini** ✿✿✿ (Via Dei Palchetti 6r; ☎ 055-210916; www.il latini.com; Tues–Sun 12:30–2:30pm and 7:30–10:30pm; AE, MC, V) is the closest you'll come in downtown Florence to the experience of digging into a hearty, gut-busting traditional meal at a typical Tuscan countryside osteria. It's a place where strangers and friends jam together at long communal tables under a canopy of hanging ham hocks and make like they're dining at a bucolic tavern on some saint's feast day. Though it sounds hokey, it's a chaotic, spirited experience that truly does feel Italian—even if more than half the diners are clearly foreign tourists—and the food is first rate, not to mention the wines, which come directly from the Latini family's estate in Chianti. It's doubtful that you'll get a look at the printed menu. Most patrons simply order the 35€-to-40€ family-style sampler,

Quite Simply the World's Greatest Ice Cream

Italian gelato is so rich, creamy, and dense that it doesn't seem fair to translate it into something as pedestrian as the American "ice cream." In Italy, gelato is sold by the cup or cone size, not the scoop, at prices ranging from around 2€ for the smallest cup (into which you can ask them to cram two to three flavors) up to 9€ for a bowl-sized one. Just about any gelateria in Florence can give you an excellent quick fix; just make sure they advertise *"produziona propria,"* which means homemade, and that the banana and pistachio flavors are both noticeably grayish—bright yellow or violent green means artificial colorings were used. (As at any Italian bar, pay first at the register and then take your receipt to the counter for your treat.) Two parlors stand out:

Gelateria Carabé ✪✪✪ (Via Ricasoli 60r; ☎ 055-289476; www.gelatocarabe.com; Tues–Sun 10am–midnight; closed Nov 16–Feb 14) is regarded as equal in artistic merit to Michelangelo's *David* just up the street. The caramel gelato is reason enough to immigrate to Italy, though they also do a brisk business in citrus and nut flavors made from ingredients trucked in fresh from their native Sicily.

Competing for the title of best gelato in town, **Vivoli** ✪✪✪ (Via Isole delle Stinche 7r, a block west of Piazza Santa Croce; ☎ 055-239334; www.vivoli.it; Tues–Sun 9am–1am; closed Aug and Jan to early Feb) varies its creative combinations by season, but past concoctions have included black currant and amaretto along with every variety of almond and vanilla.

a seemingly endless parade of *antipasti* nibbles, thick peasant soups, delicious pastas, and platters of grilled meats accompanied by unlimited wine, water, and espresso with a grappa at the end to top it all off. This is a fun experience, and reservations are recommended—though you'll still have to wait in the crowd at the door when it opens.

€€–€€€   Hidden on a lightly trafficked side street close to the Arno, **Ristorante Belcore** ✪ (Via dell'Albero 30r; ☎ 055-211198; www.ristorante belcore.it; Thurs–Mon noon–2:30pm, daily 6:30–11pm; AE, MC, V) features Middle Eastern–influenced Tuscan dishes in a cool minimalist white restaurant. A friendly and well-informed waitstaff will guide you through menu choices that include seared tuna with peppercorn and shallots (19€) and a soup of tortelli stuffed with goat ricotta cheese, black truffles, and porcini mushrooms (12€). Artistic presentations on Polish ceramic dishes complete the international flavor of the restaurant. Every Friday is "fish night," with a 35€ set menu featuring the catch of the day and three additional courses. Reservations are highly recommended.

€€€   It doesn't look like much from the outside, but the expansive (and expensive) **Ristorante Buca Mario** ✪ (Piazza Ottaviani 16r; ☎ 055-214179; www.bucamario.it;

Mon–Fri 7:30–10:30pm, Sat–Sun 12:30–2:30pm and 7:30–10:30pm; AE, MC, V) has been packing 'em in since 1886. A large underground warren of rooms with white walls, red-and-white tablecloths, and Italian folk art on the walls, its classic appearance is one that scores of Italian-American restaurants have tried to evoke for years. Here it's the genuine article, despite the fact that most of its clientele nowadays are tourists. Still, the food is excellent and the old-school waiters lend an air of authority (though they'll also joke with guests in perfect English). You won't go wrong if you order the *spaghetti al baccalà* tossed with salted cod (18€), or the *ribollita* (10€). The classic *bistecca alla fiorentina* is done perfectly here for 28€.

RESTAURANTS IN THE SANTA CROCE AREA

€ Chef Gino began his restaurant with only a couple of items on the menu, hence the name, **I'Che' ce' ce'** ✸ (Via Magalotti 11r; ☎ 055-216589; Tues–Sun 12:30–2:30pm and 7:30–10:30pm; AE, MC, V), which means "there is what there is." But over the years he's catered to customer requests in his intimate trattoria, and slowly expanded his offerings. Dinner begins with fried bread balls, courtesy of the house. Pastas range from 4€ to 7€, and the London-trained chef (he came home to start this restaurant) is a master of pasta: Try the *spaghetti alla brigante*— brigand-style pasta with some extra spice to it. The 11€ set menu is a good value, combining two courses (your choice from among four pastas and four main courses; the mixed grill is quite good) plus a small salad or side dish. The restaurant is a little tricky to find: Look for the alleyway sign on Borgo de Greci street en route to Santa Croce.

€€ If you have difficulty choosing just one dish, you're going to love **Acqua al 2** ✸✸ (Via della Vigna Vecchia 40r; ☎ 055-284170; www.acquaal2.it; daily 7:30pm–midnight; AE, MC, V), which has made a name for itself with its tasting plates—small dishes of lightly experimental Tuscan cuisine that give you the chance to graze through the entire menu. The best way to begin is to share the 9€ *assaggio di primi*, a selection of five different pastas and other first courses, including pasta with eggplant, broccoli, mixed veggies, and a yummy risotto with pesto. For a unique *secondo*, try the beef with the surprisingly complementary toppings of blueberry sauce and balsamic vinegar for 15€. Acqua al Due's new sister restaurant, **La Via dell'Acqua** (Via dell'Acqua 2r; ☎ 055-290748; daily noon–3pm and 6:30–11:30pm; AE, MC, V), has more of a fusion menu heavy on seafood and California cuisine (a nod, perhaps, to the fact that they run another Acqua al 2 in San Diego); a modern-jazz soundtrack and hipster artwork are part of the ambience. The 10€ spaghetti and fresh clams is particularly tasty.

€€–€€€ Don't be fooled by the graffiti on the cement walls outside, or the faded PIZZACHERIA sign above the door; this is no place for pizza. **Il Francescano Trattoria** ✸ (Largo Bargellini 16r, next to Santa Croce; ☎ 055-241605; www.ilfrancescano.com; Wed–Mon noon–2:30pm and 7–11pm, open daily in summer; AE, MC, V) serves excellent traditional Tuscan cuisine in its odd interior (marble slabs and mirrors on the walls, ornate chandeliers hung from rustic wood beamed ceilings) and on its outdoor patio set against the wall of Santa Croce church. The gnocchi with pears and Gorgonzola (10€) is outstanding, as are the grilled dishes, including *tagliata di manzo*—lightly breaded slices of beef (18€). The restaurant offers a variety of huge salads for 6€ to 10€, but save room for dessert; the crème caramel or *cantuccini* (small cookies) can top off an excellent meal.

RESTAURANTS IN OLTRARNO

€   The folks at **Le Volpi e L' Uva** (Piazza de'Rossi 1; ☎ 055-2398132; www.le volpieluva.com; Mon–Sat 11am–9pm; AE, MC, V) boast that no shop in town carries their selection of wines from small Tuscan vineyards—and they may just be right. This is an excellent place for wine lovers. Waiters will recommend cheese and meat platters (about 6€) to match any type of wine, which you can enjoy on a small outdoor patio or in a room with windows overlooking the Arno.

€–€€   Even though it has evolved over the years from a cheap student hangout specializing in giant bruschette at long picnic tables into a full restaurant of Tuscan dishes and proper tablecloths, I still love having dinner at **Il Cantione** ☆ (Via Santo Spirito 6r; ☎ 055-218898; www.ilcantinonedifirenze.it; Tues–Sun 12:30–2:30pm and 7:30–10:30pm; AE, MC, V), a charming hidden cave of a restaurant beneath busy Via Santo Spirito. It's always crowded—with both locals and visitors—and the food is always delicious. The set lunch with a pasta and grilled meat is a great deal (10€ weekdays, 12€ weekends). Besides the special, *primi* run 6€ to 8€, with *secondi* ranging from 9€ to 15€ (more for a *bistecca alla fiorentina*, at 4€ per 100g). This place prides itself on its wine list (its name means "giant wine cellar"), so ordering even just one of the house wines can easily double the price of the meal.

€–€€   For a quick bite, try **Olio & Convivium** (Piazza Santo Spirito 4r; ☎ 055-2658198; www.conviviumfirenze.it; daily noon–3pm, Tues–Sat 7:30–10:30pm; AE, MC, V), a combination shop, bakery, classroom, and restaurant—spawned by a catering company—which has a huge selection of wines, olive oils, and sandwiches to match. In fact, you can assemble a gourmet picnic here out of such ingredients as *prosciutto di cinta senese,* made from the Tuscan "belted Sienese" breed of pigs bred on chestnuts; *pecorino Toscana,* a tangy cheese created from the milk of the sheep in Italy's Maremma region; and *schiacciate con l'uva,* a scrumptious flatbread studded with juicy Sangiovese grapes. Sandwiches average about 7€, the ultratasty ravioli with meat sauce 6.50€. The restaurant also hosts cooking classes, wine seminars, and, of course, olive oil tastings (the coat of arms in the awning comes from a 14th-c. guild of oil sellers).

€–€€   There used to be statues of four lions at each corner of Piazza della Passera, but now only the restaurant, founded in 1550, bears that motif: **Trattoria 4 Leoni** ☆☆ (Via dei Vellutini 1r; ☎ 055-218562; www.4leoni.com; daily 7–11pm, Thurs–Tues noon–2:30pm; AE, MC, V). The waiters are generous with recommendations for such authentic Tuscan cuisine as *pappa al pomodoro* (tomato and bread soup, 7€), the 12€ veal *vitello tonnato,* or any of the other juicy grilled meats. For dessert, the freshly made cheesecake is excellent, and 4€ well spent. Patio seating enables you to enjoy the neighborhood feel of Oltrarno.

The Cibreo Culinary Empire

Chef Fabio Picchi, and his wife, Maria Cassi, have created a small empire of food and fun around the corners of Via Verrocchio and Via de'Macci in the Santa Croce neighborhood.

Their sniffiest venture is **Cibreo Ristorante** ✫✫ (Via A. Del Verrocchio 8r; ☎ 055-2341100; www.cibreo.com; Tues–Sat 12:30–2:30pm and 7:30–11:15pm; AE, MC, V), where there's no pasta on the menu but the fare is ultratraditional and refined (if a bit spicy). On the other side of the kitchen, **Trattoria Cibreo** ✫ (Via de'Macci 122r; ☎ 055-2341100; Tues–Sat 1–2:30pm and 7–11:15pm; AE, MC, V) has a curtailed version of the same menu at nearly half the price. Across the street from the restaurant, **Cibreo Caffè** (Via A. Del Verrocchio 5r; ☎ 055-2345853; Tues–Sat 8am–12:30am; AE, MC, V) has a small patio and a stylish interior—and it's even cheaper than the trattoria.

But the real fun starts at the couple's latest venture, the supper club **Teatro del Sale** ✫✫✫ (Via de'Macci 111r; ☎ 055-2001492; www.teatrodelsale.com; Tues–Sat 9am–3pm and 6pm–midnight; AE, MC, V). "Dinner and entertainment, 6 nights a week" doesn't really sum it up. The entertainment varies from Italian experimental theater to jazz and gospel bands to Elvis Costello, who recently played a 5-night set.

The dishes, served buffet-style, are created in a glassed-off kitchen to the side of the theater area. Chef Picchi announces each order as it emerges from the kitchen, shouting them out like a ship's captain: "Women and children, take care! The penne is powerfully hot and spicy." Diners jockey for position around the table to grab helpings from the surprise dishes as they arrive. Wine is dispensed freely from two large casks, and desserts arrive in big servings.

And Teatro del Sale really is a club. Non-Italians pay 5€ (8€ for locals) to join, and there are rules designed to preserve the spirit of the club. One command is "ethical listening"; another requirement is to share the latest cultural information with other members. "Any member discovered in the act of noncommunication" (not being chatty) can get their membership revoked.

Buffet dinners at the Teatro are 25€, including the entertainment, which comes on at 9:30pm after the plates are cleared and diners grab a seat for the show. Buffet breakfasts are available for 6€, lunches for 15€, but without the shows. The front part of the building is a store selling local olive oils, wines, and ingredients used in the cooking, as well as souvenir glasses made from recycled wine bottles.

WHY YOU'RE HERE:
THE TOP SIGHTS & ATTRACTIONS

Remember this: There is no earthly way you are going to see everything in Florence in just a few days. Even a week is not enough. I've been visiting this city for 25 years, spent months of time here, and written guidebooks on it for more than a decade, yet every time I visit I find new things to see and do.

That doesn't mean you can try your darndest to make a decent dent in Florence's overwhelming cavalcade of museums, galleries, churches, and palazzi. Just pace yourself, and try to not squeeze in too much at the expense of enjoying what you do get a chance to see. A perfectly lovely day spent lazing in the Boboli Gardens is better, in the end, than one spent dashing down the cobblestones and ticking off a dozen different churches.

The best strategy is to look over everything described here and just pick the ones that pique your interest. Don't try to do it all. The only two things I am going to insist you try to fit in are a tour of the Uffizi Gallery and a climb up Brunelleschi's dome. See: I'm not even saying you have to see the *David*.

I've organized the sights below geographically, each listed according to the nearest piazza, but know that in this open-air museum of a city you'll find delights around most every corner, making it a perfect place to spend a day of aimless wandering.

One hint: To make sure you don't waste time waiting in lines, I highly, highly, highly recommend spending the extra few euros to reserve entry tickets to the Uffizi and the Accademia ahead of time. Trust me; in summer, especially, the lines can stretch for blocks and the wait can last, quite literally, for hours.

THE SIGHTS ON & NEAR THE PIAZZA DELLA SIGNORIA

Piazza della Signoria ✪✪ is Florence's public living room, a giant space filled with massive sculptures and surrounded by cafes, palaces, and museums. This has been Florence's political center since the 1400s, when the *signoria,* a group of noblemen, ruled the city. The statues may seem like museum pieces today, but they brilliantly reveal the dynamic political nature of the square.

The immediately recognizable *David* (a copy stands where Michelangelo's original, now in the Accademia, once held court) wasn't just placed beneath Palazzo Vecchio's walls because of its beauty; it was meant as a reproof to the (temporarily) deposed Medici family in 1504. The naked youth represents the classical Greek ideal of democracy: David's slaying the giant symbolizes the stand taken by Florentines against oppressive rulers. Similarly, in 1495, city magistrates had moved Donatello's *Judith and Holofernes* (again, it's a copy out here; the original's inside the Palazzo Vecchio) from the former Medici palace to the piazza to remind all residents of the virtuous woman who slew her brutal assailant.

But the Medici eventually came back to town and proved they could play the symbolic-statue game as well. They placed Cellini's *Perseus,* done in 1545, across from *David* under the elegant portico of the Loggia de' Lanzi (this time, the original is still in place). The work, depicting a battle-clad Perseus who has just severed Medusa's head, symbolizes the military might that had defeated small, competing governments, represented by the now-dead snakes in Medusa's hair.

Florence Itineraries

If you have only 1 day in Florence

A tough break, but still enough time to do a quick highlights run from north to south: Start with Michelangelo's *David* in the **Accademia,** and then detour a few blocks west through the **outdoor leather market** around San Lorenzo on your way south to see the outside and inside of the massive **Duomo** and **Baptistery** in Piazza Duomo. Continue south to the medieval center of the city, the statue-filled **Piazza della Signoria,** and then on to the **Uffizi Gallery** for its unparalleled art collection. Cross the historic **Ponte Vecchio** to the **Oltrarno** district for a down-home dinner. This might be as far as you make it, but if you have the time make the climb to **Piazzale Michelangiolo** and **San Miniato Church** for a panoramic sunset over the town—or you could skip the walk up the hill and, instead, shop at the designer stores around **Via Tornabuoni** or spend more time in the morning haggling at the San Lorenzo market.

If you have only 2 days in Florence

Follow the above itinerary, but add visits to **Santa Maria Novella** church, at the west end of the historical district, and to **Santa Croce,** on the eastern side. Also visit the **Bargello** sculpture gallery, just northeast of Piazza della Signoria, and tour the **Palazzo Vecchio** in the central piazza. Don't forget to stop for gelato, which will fuel you for a **climb to the top of the Duomo** or **Giotto's Bell Tower.**

If you have only 3 or 4 days in Florence

You'll be able to add a leisurely tour of the shops of the **Oltrarno** district, the **Pitti Palace** and its **Boboli Gardens, Santo Spirito church** and its peaceful piazza, and the disturbing **Museo dello Specola.** In the central district, you can also visit **San Lorenzo church** and the connected **Medici chapels.** Stop by the **Central Market** to sample local produce, and escape the art world with a visit to the **Science Museum** behind the Palazzo Vecchio.

As Duke Cosimo I de' Medici consolidated power through the 16th century (eventually becoming grand duke of Tuscany), he envisioned himself as a new Roman emperor and filled the square with massive Roman-influenced statues of himself. One of them portrays him as a warrior on horseback, with reliefs at the base depicting his land-based military triumphs, while the flamboyant *Neptune Fountain* is meant to show his mastery in naval battles.

Near the fountain you'll see a small plaque commemorating the site of the original "Bonfire of the Vanities." In the 1490s, the famed rabble-rousing monk named Savonarola briefly became leader of Florence on a fire-and-brimstone platform of piety and anti-materialism. He convinced citizens (including the painter Botticelli) to bring their "vanities"—paintings, silks, jewelry, and books—to Piazza della Signoria and torch them in a huge bonfire. Eventually, Florentines

Florence Attractions

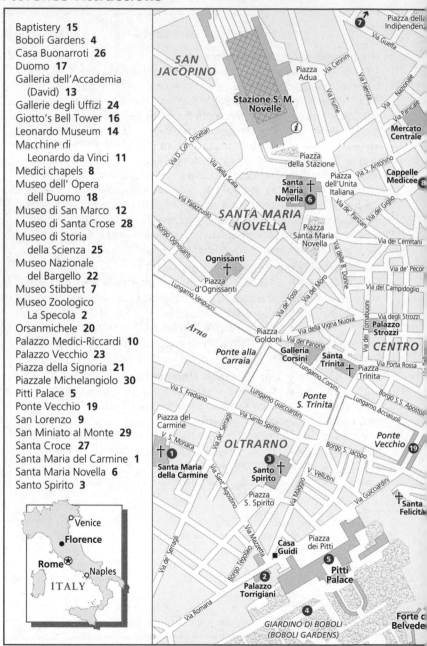

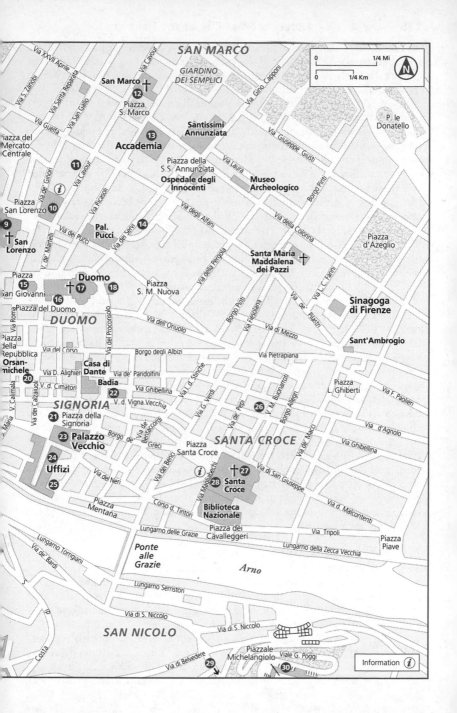

wearied of the "mad monk" preacher; by the time Savonarola had crossed the pope, was branded a heretic, and was excommunicated (along with the city), the citizens were only too happy to turn on their erstwhile theocrat and burn him at the stake—ironically, at the same spot as his original bonfires.

It's worth a visit to stroll through the beautiful central courtyard and chambers of the **Palazzo Vecchio** ★ (☎ 055-2768325; www.comune.fi.it; 6€; Fri–Wed 9am–7pm, Thurs 9am–2pm), directly on the Piazza. The Gothic building looms over the east side of the square with protruding battlements and a 94m (314-ft.) tower jutting up "like a stone hypodermic," as author Mary McCarthy described it. The multifunctional structure, built during the late 13th century and modified over the years, has been home to the city hall, a residence for the Medici, and even the chamber of deputies for the Republic of Italy before becoming city offices once again. The museum portion of the building includes the Salone dei Cinquecento (The Hall of Five Hundred), the historic gathering place for Florence's 500-man ruling congress with triumphal frescoes by Vasari, now home to a small sculpture collection including Michelangelo's *Genius of Victory.* The second floor, converted into lavish living quarters for Cosimo I de' Medici and his family during the 1540s, presents an interesting contrast.

You'll also want to head a few blocks north of the piazza on broad Via de' Calzaiuoli to stop by the **Orsanmichele** ★ (Via Arte della Lana 1; ☎ 055-284944 or 055-23885; free; Tues–Sun 10am–5pm), a 14th-century church and one of the few remaining traces of high-Gothic architecture in the city. The hours listed above are really only a rough indicator, as the church seems to open and close on a whim (call ahead), but even if it's closed you can enjoy simply touring the exterior where reproductions of saintly statues by such fabled names as Ghiberti, Donatello, and Giambologna stand in niches. To see the original statues, you'll have to visit the small museum, which is actually up on the second floor of the church but only accessible (via an enclosed bridge) from the building next door, the **Palazzo dell'Arte della Lana,** across Via dell'Arte della Lana, from the church's back entrance. Here you'll find such masterpieces as Ghiberti's *St. John the Baptist* (1413–16), which was the first life-size bronze to be cast during the Renaissance, and Donatello's marble *St. Mark* (1411–13). Its hours are even more sporadic than the church's, but officially it is open for 45 minutes at a stretch starting at 9, 10, and 11am daily (plus 1pm on Sat), but closed the first and last Monday of each month.

THE UFFIZI GALLERY

The southeast corner of Piazza dell Signoria opens into the Piazzale degli Uffizi, a long U-shaped courtyard surrounded on three sides by one of the world's greatest museums, the **Gallerie degli Uffizi (Uffizi Gallery)** ★★★ (Piazza degli Uffizi 6; ☎ 055-2388651; www.uffizi.firenze.it; 6.50€, plus 3€ booking fee—highly recommended, call ☎ 055-294883; Tues–Sun 8:15am–6:50pm, ticket office closes 6:05pm). Long lines, erratic open hours, occasionally surly staff, and galleries closed for never-revealed reasons make the Uffizi a sometimes frustrating place to visit. But these 45 rooms and marble corridors—built in the 16th century as the Medici's private office complex—are absolutely jam-packed with famous paintings, among them Giotto's *Maestà,* Botticelli's *Birth of Venus,* Leonardo da Vinci's *Annunciation,* Michelangelo's *Holy Family,* and many, many more. So for all its potential inconveniences, the Uffizi is a must-see.

Tackling the Uffizi: Planning Your Visit

Be sure to plan your visit to the Uffizi wisely or you'll waste a valuable day in Florence standing in a 2-hour line, miss the top paintings, or find the museum to be closed altogether. The first thing to do: **Make reservations.** Call ☎ 055-294883 Monday through Friday 8:30am to 6:30pm or Saturday 8:30am to 12:30pm up to a couple of weeks in advance. You can also order tickets online at www.polomuseale.firenze.it. By paying the 3€ booking fee, you'll bypass the long lines and cross the velvet rope like a Hollywood celebrity gaining entrance to a hip club. If you do come to town without a reservation, lines will be shorter toward the end of the day (which means you have to do the museum at a slow jog, but that's better than skipping it).

Start with **Room 2** for a look at the pre-Renaissance Gothic style of painting. First, compare teacher and student as you examine Cimabue's *Maestà* painted in 1285, and Giotto's *Maestà* done in 1310. The similar subject and setting for the two paintings allows the viewer to see how Giotto transformed Cimabue's iconic Byzantine style into something more real and human. Giotto's Madonna actually looks like she's sitting on a throne, her clothes emphasizing the curves of her body, whereas Cimabue's Madonna and angels float in space, looking like portraits on coins, with flattened positioning and stiff angles.

Room 7 contains the next don't-miss sight, the unflattering profiles of the Duke Montefeltro of Urbino and his Duchess, done by Piero della Francesca in 1465. The subjects are portrayed in an unflinchingly realistic way. The Duke, in particular, exposes his warts and his crooked nose, broken in a martial tournament. This focus on the earthly, rather than on the Christian, elements harkens back to the teachings of classical Greek and Roman times, and is made all the more vivid by depiction (on the back) of the couple riding chariots driven by the humanistic virtues of faith, charity, hope, and modesty (for her), and prudence, temperance, fortitude, and justice (for him).

In **Room 8,** highlights are the works of Filippo Lippi from the mid–15th century. After you examine the *Novitiate Altarpiece* (important for its use of perspective) and the brightly colored *Coronation of the Virgin,* spend some time in front of his most famous work, *Madonna with Child and Two Angels,* from 1465. The background, which frames the portrait of a woman's face with distant mountains on one side and water on the other, was shamelessly stolen by Leonardo da Vinci 40 years later for his *Mona Lisa.* Lippi's work was also a bit of a celebrity scandal at the time. The woman who modeled for Mary was said to be Filippo's lover—a would-be nun he had spirited away from her convent before she could take vows—and the child looking toward the viewer the product of their union. That son, Filippino Lippi, became an excellent painter in his own right, and some of his works hang here and in the next few rooms. However, it was Filippo's student (who would, in turn, become Filippino's teacher) who would go on to become one of the most famous artists of the 15th century. His name was Botticelli.

Rooms 10 to 14—still collectively numbered as such, even though the walls were knocked down in 1978 to make one large room—are devoted to the works of Sandro Filipepi—better known by his nickname "Little Barrels," or Botticelli. Botticelli's *Birth of Venus* (1485–88) hangs like a highway billboard you've seen a thousand times. Venus' pose is taken from classical statues, while the zephyr wind blowing her to shore, and the muse welcoming her, are from Ovid's *Metamorphosis.* On a nearby wall is Botticelli's 1478 *Primavera,* its dark, bold colors are a stark contrast to the filmy, pastel *Venus.* Be sure to seek out Botticelli's *Adoration of the Magi,* which contains a self-portrait of the artist (he's the one in yellow) on the far right side.

Leonardo da Vinci's *Annunciation* anchors **Room 15.** In this painting, though completed in the early 1470s while Leonardo was still a student in Verrocchio's workshop, Da Vinci's ability to orchestrate the viewer's focus is masterful: The line down the middle of the brick corner of the house draws your glance to Mary's delicate fingers, which themselves point along the top of a stone wall to the angel's two raised fingers. Those, in turn, draw attention to the mountain in the center of the two parallel trees dividing Mary from the angel, representing the gulf between the worldly and the spiritual.

As soon as you cross to the Uffizi's west wing—past picture windows with views of the Arno to one side and the perfect, Renaissance perspective of the Uffizi piazza to the other—you're walloped with another masterpiece. **Room 25** contains Michelangelo's 1505 *Holy Family.* The twisting shapes of Mary, Joseph, and Jesus recall those in the Sistine Chapel in Rome for their sculpted nature and the bright colors.

Room 26 has a number of Raphaels, including the often-copied *Madonna of the Goldfinch,* again with the da Vinci/Botticelli landscape in the background. The reds in the recently restored *Pope Leo X* portrait are particularly vibrant.

Titian's *Venus of Urbino* is found in **Room 28.** It's no coincidence that the edge of the curtain, the angle of her hand and leg, and the line splitting floor and bed all intersect in the forbidden part of her body. The domestic scene on the right half of the painting, with the sleeping dog, and the little girl gathering clothes, provides a contrast to the open sexuality of the left.

In stark contrast to the clean lines (and dirty mind) of Titian, seek out an El Greco masterpiece from 1600, the nearly hidden *St. John the Evangelist and St. Francis* (on the wall behind you when you walk into **Room 33** from 32). It shows the two saints stretched and blurred, with a gathering storm behind them. The miniature dragon poking its head out of St. John's goblet alludes to his miracle of turning a poison into this creature. El Greco's characteristic elongated forms and surreal landscapes provided inspiration to many 20th-century artists, including Salvador Dalí and Modigliani.

By the time most visitors reach the rooms numbered in the **40s,** they run out of gas. But do check out the Rubens and Rembrandts in this section for a feeling of Flemish versus Italian styles of painting. The detail of the hair, skin, and cloth of the Rembrandt portraits from the 1630s, in **Room 44,** are amazing—just look at the contrast between the faces of the young and old men.

On your way down from the second floor, you'll be strolling through the recently added first-floor gallery rooms—created after a bombing in 1993—one of which includes a trio of paintings by Caravaggio (*Bacchus, Medusa,* and the

Sacrifice of Isaac), and many by the 17th- to 18th-century *caravaggieschi* artists who copied his chiaroscuro (bright light and dark shadows) style of painting. Here a rare female artist in the Uffizi, Artemisia Gentileschi, has one of the more brutal paintings in the gallery, *Judith and Holofernes*.

SIGHTS NEAR THE UFFIZI

A short stroll behind the Uffizi is the **Ponte Vecchio (Old Bridge)** ✮✮✮, one of the most potent symbols of Florence. Many people cross over it before they realize they are on a bridge, since it is flanked with jewelry shops in tiny 17th century buildings. Many of the shops are owned by descendants of the original 41 artisans whom Cosimo I de' Medici invited to set up shop here (replacing butchers, who formally occupied these buildings; there's a not-so-secret enclosed corridor leading from the Uffizi, across the tops of these shops, and up to the Pitti Palace on the opposite shore, designed by Vasari for Cosimo I so he could go to and from work without having to mix with the crowds). The large metal ring at the wall was for tying up horses. Now small padlocks cover the ring—symbols left by lovers to celebrate their mutual connection.

The bridge itself has survived since 1345, despite floods, wars, and the German bombing near the end of World War II. In 1944 as the Nazis retreated, the local commander was ordered to destroy all the bridges across the Arno in order to hinder the Allied advance. He did destroy the river's other spans but, sympathetic to the Ponte Vecchio's historical importance, decided to spare it and instead blow up the buildings on the riverbanks at either end to create giant piles of rubble.

Returning to Piazza della Signoria, turn right past the palazzo Vecchio, then left up Piazza S. Firenze/Via del Proconsolo to visit one of the most important museums anywhere for Renaissance sculpture. In a far cry from its original use as the city's prison, torture chamber, and execution site, the **Museo Nazionale del Bargello** ✮✮ (Via del Proconsolo 4; ☎ 055-2388606; www.polomuseale.firenze.it; 4€; daily 8:15am–1:50pm, but closed the first, third, and fifth Mon and second and fourth Sun of each month) now stands as a peaceful sculpture garden and three-story art museum containing some of the best works of Michelangelo, Donatello, and Ghiberti.

In the ground-floor Michelangelo room, you'll witness the awesome variety of his craft, from the whimsical 1497 *Bacchus* to the severe *Brutus* of 1540. *Bacchus*, created when Michelangelo was just 22, really looks like he's drunk, leaning back a little too far, his head off kilter, with a cupid about to bump him over. Also note Giambologna's twisting *Mercury*, who looks like he's about to take off from the ground.

Be sure to cross the courtyard and climb the stairs to the enormous vaulted hall filled with, among other sculptural beauties, some of Donatello's most famous works. Notable among them is his *David*, done in 1440, the first free-standing nude sculpture since Roman times. The classical detail of these sculptures, as well as their naturalistic poses and reflective mood, is the essence of the Renaissance style.

On the right wall, note the contest entries submitted by Ghiberti and Brunelleschi for the commission to do the Baptistery doors in 1401. Both had the *Sacrifice of Isaac* as their biblical theme, and both displayed an innovative use of perspective. Ghiberti won the contest, perhaps because his scene was more thematically unified. Brunelleschi could have ended up a footnote in the art history books as a failed sculptor, but instead he gave up the chisel and turned his attentions to architecture instead, which turned out to be an incredibly wise move (see "Engineering the Duomo," below).

The second floor also has a small but elaborate chapel in which condemned prisoners prayed, and guilty magistrates atoned for their sins.

The top floor is worth a quick walk-through for the statuary of the Verrocchio Room (including yet another effeminate *David*) and the decorative helmets of the Armory; skip the many small bronzes and medals if you're short on time.

THE INCOMPARABLE DUOMO & THE PIAZZA DEL DUOMO

The undisputed, preeminent, free-standing stone dome in the world sits atop Florence's cathedral, wider than that atop the U.S. Capitol, bigger than that of the Pantheon in Rome, and a scientific marvel of its time. The **Duomo (Cathedral) of Santa Maria del Fiore** ✸✸✸ (Piazza del Duomo; ☎ 055-2302885; www. operaduomo.firenze.it; free; Mon–Wed and Fri 10am–5pm, Thurs 10am–3:30pm, Sat 10am–4:45pm, Sun 3:30–4:45pm) is the symbol of Florence and the city's biggest attraction, both in size and popularity.

Piazza del Duomo contains five sights operated by the church authorities: the central church itself, the highly recommended climb to the top of the dome, the climb up Giotto's Bell Tower, the Museum of the Duomo, and the Baptistery. In choosing which to visit, I'd say the Baptistery and a climb up the dome are mustsees; the museum is a greatly underrated sight, and worth the time; the cathedral itself doesn't take long. Giotto's Bell Tower is for die-hards whose legs haven't already turned to jelly from climbing the dome.

The **Cathedral,** like Florence, has evolved over the years. It began as a Romanesque church in the 5th century, and expanded through the 13th century before it reached its present dimensions. The top of the dome wasn't completed until Brunelleschi capped it off in 1434 (see "Engineering the Duomo," below), and it took until the late 1800s for the tricolor marble exterior to be added in honor of the new Italian Republic.

The inside of the Duomo is surprisingly empty, aside from the mobs of visitors. So like everyone else, you'll want to walk to the altar to look up at the dome soaring above you. From 1575 to 1580, Federico Zuccari—helped in part, at least in some designs, by his teacher Giorgio Vasari—painted the bulk of *The Last Judgment* fresco covering the interior of the dome. It's no Sistine Chapel, but, still, imagine the challenges involved in painting with quick-drying materials on a curved surface more than 45m (150 ft.) above the ground.

For a closer look at both the painting and the dome, take a walk up the 463 steps to the **cupola (dome)** ✸✸✸ (6€; Mon–Fri 8:30am–7pm, Sat 8:30am–5:40pm). The line for this climb can sometimes wind around the corner, but there's no better way to appreciate the engineering marvel of the dome since you actually get to climb up in between the two layers of the dome. The steps can be exhausting, crowded, smelly, and claustrophobic, but that just makes the view on top that much more appreciated. Interestingly, when seen up close, the figures painted on the dome look almost impressionistic, with vague features and skewed proportions. Vasari and Zuccari weren't lazy when they designed the figures this way; they are intended to be viewed from the perspective of people on the church floor, from which the odd proportions counterbalance the effect of the curving surface. This serves not only to make the figures appear anatomically accurate but also to aid in creating the illusion of depth.

For slightly fewer steps (414), far smaller crowds, and an actual view *of* the dome instead of *from* it, climb **Giotto's Bell Tower (Campanile di Giotto)** ★ (6€; daily 8:30am–7:30pm). This nearly became Florence's version of the Leaning Tower of Pisa because Giotto couldn't quite transfer his painting talent into architecture. He created the plans and finished the first level of the structure by his death, in 1337. When the next level was added, the tower nearly collapsed under its own weight, and had to be redesigned. Now standing a sturdy 75m (250 ft.) tall, the tower offers views over the city of Florence, and excellent photo-ops of the dome.

The **Baptistery** ★★★ (3€; Mon–Sat noon–7pm, Sun 8:30am–2pm, first Sat of month 8:30am–2pm), across from the front of the Duomo, has the doors that opened the way to the Renaissance. They are the baptistery's great bronze north doors, one of the first major works to incorporate the period's naturalism and semirealistic perspective. (Ghiberti also began the era of unreliable contractors— it took him 27 years to finish a commission that was supposed to take 5.) For an instant comparison between periods, go to the south (entry) doors and view Andrea Pisano's far less dynamic 1336 Gothic work.

The 20-year-old Ghiberti, who won the commission in a contest that included Donatello, Brunelleschi, and several other far more established Tuscan sculptors, created these north doors of New Testament scenes first. After his brilliant success with the panels, Ghiberti didn't have to compete for the right to create those on the east side of the Baptistery, and many feel that these are his real masterpieces: 10 panels of Old Testament scenes that flow splendidly one to the next, and are among the most exquisite creations of the Renaissance. When he first saw them, Michelangelo is said to have exclaimed, "These doors are fit to stand at the gates of Paradise," and ever since they've been nicknamed "the Gates of Paradise." To protect them from the elements, the original doors have been moved inside the Museum of the Duomo (see below); these shiny new ones are replicas from 1990. Amid the splendor of the doors, you may forget to enter the Baptistery, but the interior boasts some spectacular Byzantine mosaics from the 1200s.

The **Museo dell'Opera del Duomo** ★ (Piazza del Duomo 9; ☎ 055-2302885; 6€; Mon–Sat 9am–7:30pm, Sun 9am–1:45 pm) is a must for anyone who has read the best-selling *Brunelleschi's Dome* by Ross King, a highly recommended read for anyone visiting Florence. Along with many of the designs and ingenious implements used by Brunelleschi in the building of the dome (fun fact: they even have Brunelleschi's death mask) are the wooden models of proposed Duomo facades from the 16th century, when the Gothic facade was stripped off to make room for a proper Renaissance one (in the end, it would take nearly 300 years before they finally got around to slapping a front on the cathedral).

The museum is also notable for its magnificent sculptures, including four standouts. There are, of course, Ghiberti's original Gates of Paradise, cleaned and reassembled here. The disturbing but beautiful wooden sculpture of a penitent *Mary Magdalene* by Donatello depicts her torn with grief. The two *cantorie* (marble choir lofts) from the 1430s hang high on the walls just as they would have been in the church: The earlier one (its original panels at eye level; plaster copies

Engineering the Duomo

The dome crowning Florence's cathedral is impressive, but to appreciate just how amazing an accomplishment it was in the 15th century, consider that nothing even remotely its size had been constructed since the Pantheon in Rome 1,300 years before.

Because massive construction projects like the Duomo typically took more than 100 years to complete, city planners assumed somebody would figure out how to cover the church by the time they finished construction in the late 1380s. That didn't happen, though, and the church remained open to the elements for two generations.

Enter frustrated sculptor Filippo Brunelleschi. After losing to Ghiberti in the sculpture contest to design the church's Baptistery doors (p. 123) in 1401, Brunelleschi took his tools and went to Rome to study classical architecture instead. He knew of the construction challenges of the dome, so he measured, poked, and peered at the Pantheon, studying it for several years, trying to figure out the mysteries of its design.

The challenge of the dome was this: For hundreds of years, arches had been constructed by placing stones on wooden frames, and then removing the frame when the stones were able to support each other. For larger constructions (Gothic cathedrals in France, for example), flying buttresses were added for support.

The Duomo in Florence did not have the space around it to allow for buttresses. And even if that problem had been solved, nobody could imagine building a wood frame tall enough to support the dome-in-progress. The wood would have sagged under the pressure even if the heights could have been reached.

Brunelleschi came up with a three-part solution. First, he made the dome with two concentric shells that supported each other, each thinner than would have been necessary for a single dome. Second, he created a puzzle-piece set of bricks, thicker at the bottom of the dome, lighter at top, fitting them all together in a self-supporting matrix. And, finally, he added giant hoops around each level, like a barrel, to deal with the outward pressure of the bricks.

It worked, and many years after the humiliation of the Baptistery contest, Brunelleschi had his hometown victory. The pope came to consecrate the capping of the dome in 1436. To this day, nobody has built a bigger dome out of stone.

Not bad for a second-place sculptor.

on the loft itself up high) is by Luca della Robbia, who is more famous for founding the family art studio that would go on to crank out glazed terra-cotta relief panels for several generations); the slightly later choir loft by Donatello breaks tradition by having the sculpted cherubs break out of their panels to frolic around the columns diving them.

Halfway up the staircase is the final famous work, a (mostly) Michelangelo *Pietà* that nearly wasn't. Early on in the process he had told students that he wanted this *Pietà* to stand at his tomb, but when the work didn't go well, he began attacking it with a hammer. He would have destroyed the beautiful sculpture had his apprentices not intervened. The master never returned to the work, but his students later finished some of the minor characters (the figure of Nicodemus was untouched, legend has it, because this was a self-portrait of the artist).

PIAZZA SANTA CROCE & NEARBY

Basilica di Santa Croce ✸✸ (Piazza Santa Croce; ☎ 055-2466105; 5€; Mon–Sat 9:30am–5:30pm, Sun 1–5:30pm) contains the elaborate, status-symbol tombs of the brightest and the best (or at least the richest) of the Renaissance, including Michelangelo, Machiavelli, Galileo, and Rossini. Dante has a tomb, but he didn't make the trip (see "Who is Buried in Dante's Tomb?" below). Over 250 others are interred below visiting tourists. (It's said the expression "stinking rich" came from commoners holding their noses with disdain as they walked on top of these expensive graves in churches.)

The church looks large but shabby from the outside, and massive and majestic inside. Rent the comprehensive audio tour headphones from the stand outside the side doors for a nearly 2-hour explanation of over 200 locations in the church. Among the notable sights in the church is Michelangelo's grave, designed by Vasari; it's close to the front door, allegedly because Michelangelo said if he ever came to life again, he wanted to awake to see Brunelleschi's Duomo. Also walk over to Machiavelli's tomb farther along the wall to see his majestic resting place, along with his pithy epitaph: TANTO NOMINI NULLUM PAR ELOGIUM, of which a liberal translation might be, "What can you say about this guy?"

It took 90 years after his death before Galileo received the honor of having a tomb in Santa Croce because, as the audioguide delicately states, of the "complicated relationship" between the scientist and the Church (authorities originally had the heretical body unceremoniously dumped outside city walls). The grand tomb now stands near the church's front doors.

Aside from the tombs, seek out the wonderful Giotto frescoes in the two chapels to the right of the main altar. The 14th-century works have faded from their original glory, but the Tuscan Gothic master's homey, naturalistic depictions of monks in these stories from the life of St. Francis reflect the true Franciscan nature of the church much more than the self-important tombs along the aisles.

Outside the church, entered through a door to the right of the main entrance, is the **Museo di Santa Croce** (same hours and entry ticket as the church), incorporating some of the complex's cloisters and the peaceful Pazzi Chapel. Brunelleschi (of Duomo fame) designed this structure for the Pazzi family just before their unsuccessful coup/murder plot against the Medici. The Pazzi name was erased from the chapel for hundreds of years, and no Pazzi were ever buried here, but the chapel retains its simple, symmetrical Renaissance beauty.

Keep walking through the enclosed garden to reach the refectory. This quiet area contains many Renaissance artworks, including the famous Cimabue *Crucifixion,* restored after it was covered by water in the 1966 floods. The cross

Who Is Buried in Dante's Tomb?

Not Dante. Actually, Dante's tomb in Santa Croce is more properly called a "cenotaph," a memorial tribute when the body is elsewhere. Dante Alighieri, author of the sublime *Divine Comedy*, is credited with popularizing (if not creating) the modern Italian language. He was born in Florence in 1265, and from the cenotaph, the statue outside Santa Croce, and the various shrines around town, you'd think he had always been a hometown hero.

But Dante became involved in politics and chose the wrong side during one of Florence's incessant civil wars. He took the side of the pro-imperial bankers of the White Party versus the Black Party of noble families who supported the pope's financial and political interests. In 1302, the Black Party was on top, and Dante was exiled from the city for 2 years on trumped-up charges. Angered by his expulsion, he wandered the northern Italian landscape for the rest of his life, refusing all offers to return to his hometown. Instead, he wrote the *Divina Comedia (Divine Comedy)*—his three-part poetic saga of Inferno, Purgatori, and Paradiso (hell, purgatory, and heaven)—being sure to populate the lowest depths of inferno with his former opponents in Florentine politics.

Dante died in Ravenna in 1321, and the town claimed him as its own, denying Florence's continued requests for the body.

Florence had better luck with Michelangelo's corpse. Despite the fact that the artist did the bulk of his work in Rome, the Medici decided he belonged to their city. Ten years after his death, agents stole his body and brought it to Florence in 1574, ensuring only one cenotaph among the many tombs in Santa Croce.

now hangs from retractable wires so that it can be yanked up should water fill the building again.

For fans of Michelangelo (and who isn't?), the other worthy sight in the area is the small house he bought for his nephew. It's now a museum: **Casa Buonarroti** (Via Ghibellina 70; ☎ 055-241752; www.casabuonarroti.it; 6.50€; Wed–Mon 9:30am–2pm) displays some of the master's earliest works, including some bas-relief sculptures done as a teenager, as well as a number of his sketches.

PIAZZA SANTA MARIA NOVELLA, PIAZZA SAN LORENZO & PIAZZA MADONNA DEGLI ALDOBRANDINI

Just across the street from Florence's main Santa Maria Novella train station stands perhaps the most conveniently located historic site in Italy, the **Santa Maria Novella Church** ★★ (Piazza Santa Maria Novella; ☎ 055-215918; 2.50€; Mon–Thurs and Sat 9am–5pm, Fri and Sun 1–5pm). Even if you only have a 30-minute train layover in town, pop across the street to see this church, which contains some of the finest frescoes in Florence—no small feat. Construction began in the 1240s, prior to the Renaissance, and the main part was completed in 1360. The artwork inside traces this journey of pre-Renaissance styles through the dawning of the new age, and the top three treasures include Ghirlandaio's frescoes behind the altar, Giotto's *Crucifix*, and Masaccio's *Trinità* fresco.

Giotto's *Crucifix* is an early example of naturalistic depiction of the human body. Painted in 1289, Christ's body appears to hang heavily on the cross, with the twists of the limbs and curves of the torso adding to the emotional weight of the composition. Compare this piece with the church's other crucifixion scenes, done in a Byzantine, iconic style. Masaccio's *Holy Trinity* fresco, midway along the left wall of the church, is the epitome of Renaissance-style perspective. Though Gothic painters had frequently used foreshortening to denote depth, this 1428 composition was the first painting to incorporate the mathematical principles of true, one-point perspective to give the work a depth and realism heretofore unattained in art.

Domenico Ghirlandaio and his assistants (including a 16-year-old Michelangelo) created the series of frescoes behind the main altar. While formally known as *Lives of the Virgin and St. John the Baptist,* the series of religious scenes is more about Florence of the 1480s. The characters wear contemporary clothes, and random folks appearing alongside various saints are actually members of the Tornabuoni clan, the sponsors of the paintings. Before you leave be sure to stop for a moment in front of Brunelleschi's 15th-century pulpit. It was on this spot that Galileo was denounced as a heretic for declaring that the earth revolved around the sun.

If you think commercialism has only recently come to churches in Italy, look at the facade for proof otherwise. The mosaic inscription near the top has a 550-year-old advertisement that says, "This church brought to you by Giovanni Rucellai," the nobleman who funded renovation of the church in 1458. The family's symbol (Fortune's winds blowing a ship's sail) dots the frieze like so many Nike trademarks.

Now from the Rucellai to the much more important Medici, who ruled Florence and Tuscany for generations, fought popes, became popes, and wanted a church and memorial worthy of their ambitions. They had themselves entombed in great glory in their home parish, in the **Medici chapels** ✦ of San Lorenzo church (Piazza Madonna degli Aldobrandini, enter behind the Basilica di San Lorenzo; ☎ 055-2388602; www.firenzemusei.it; 6€; daily 8:15am–1:50pm, closed the first, third, and fifth Mon and the second and fourth Sun of every month). The first room is the extravagant Chapel of the Princes, displaying gaudy but entertaining marble decorations of all shapes and sizes. For a more artistic and restrained setting, continue inside to the New Sacristy. Michelangelo designed the tombs here, decorated with a famous foursome of statues, *Dawn, Dusk, Night,* and *Day.* Compare and contrast Michelangelo's figures: There's not much difference between the bulk and musculature of the massive female and male bodies, sort of a Renaissance version of the old East German swim teams.

The **Basilica di San Lorenzo** (Piazza San Lorenzo; ☎ 055-2645184; 2.50€; Mon–Sat 10am–5:30pm, Mar–Oct also Sun 1:30–5:30pm), a very short stroll west of the Medici chapels, offers a peaceful respite from the mass of vendors in the surrounding market. Brunelleschi, of Duomo fame, redesigned the interior in the 1440s. Donatello's final works, the bronze pulpits, display dramatic crucifixion scenes. For his effort (and years of service to the Medici), the artist earned a tomb in the church. Depending on your other options and interests, this church may not be worth your time or the admission charge.

Attached to the church but entered separately from a door to the left of the main entrance is the **Biblioteca Medicea-Laurenziana** (entrance via a gateway to the left of the church doors; 3€, or 5€ on a cumulative ticket with the church; Sun–Fri 9:30am–1:30pm, except when there's no exhibition on, in which case it's closed), notable not only for its historic collection of manuscripts but for the Michelangelo-designed architecture and stone staircase.

The final notable sight in this area is more of the Medici, this time at the **Palazzo Medici-Riccardi** ✸ (Via Cavour 3; ☎ 055-2760340; 4€; Thurs–Tues 9am–7pm). Once the home of Lorenzo the Magnificent (before Cosimo I moved the family to the Palazzo Vecchio), it boasts splendid **Chapel of the Magi frescoes** ✸✸ by Benozzo Gozzoli, who took as his theme the journey of the Magi and filled this lighthearted, color-rich fresco with dozens of portraits of the notables of the day.

NEAR OR ON PIAZZA SAN MARCO

Rarely does a famous piece of art live up to the hype. Michelangelo's *David*, in the **Galleria dell'Accademia (Accademia Gallery)** ✸✸✸ (Via Ricasoli 58–60; ☎ 055-2388612; www.polomuseale.firenze.it; 6.50€, plus a highly recommended 3€ booking fee—call ☎ 055-294883; Tues–Sun 8:15am–6:50pm), does. The statue is much larger than most people imagine, looming 4.8m (16 ft.) on top of a 1.8m (6-ft.) pedestal. *David* hasn't faded with time, either, and a 2004 cleaning makes the marble gleam as if it were Opening Day 1504. Viewing the statue is a pleasure in the bright and spacious room custom designed for *David* after the statue was moved here in 1873, following 300 years of pigeons perched on his head in the Piazza della Signoria. Replicas now take the abuse in the Piazza della Signoria and the Piazzale Michelangiolo.

Most people who come to see *David* are delighted to discover he is surrounded by an entire museum stuffed with other notable Renaissance works. Michelangelo's unfinished *Prisoners* statues are a superb contrast to *David*, with the rough forms struggling to free themselves from the raw stone (they also provide a unique glimpse into how Michelangelo worked a piece of stone; he famously said that he tried to free the sculpture within from the block and you can see this quite clearly here). Be sure also to visit the back room leading to the Academy part of the Accademia, where you'll see a veritable warehouse of old replica carvings, the work of hundreds of years of students. It's almost as if a Roman assembly line has just stopped for lunch. And continue through this back room, to the student section, to see some modern interpretations of the classical work.

Important tip: Along with the Uffizi, the Accademia is a sight where it's essential to make reservations. Be sure to **book ahead;** it'll be 3€ well spent.

Travelers who enjoy the serene, jewel-toned works of Fra Angelico will want to add the small **Museo di San Marco** ✸ (Piazzo San Marco 3; ☎ 055-2388608; 4€; Mon–Fri 8:30am–1:50pm, Sat–Sun 8:15am–6:50pm; closed first, third, and fifth Sun and second and fourth Mon of each month) to their itineraries. The largest collection in Florence of the master's altarpieces and painted panels reside in this former 13th-century monastery the artist-monk once called home. But perhaps the most moving and unusual work is his *Annunciation* and a fresco of the life of

The Strange Symbols of the Medici

Walk anywhere around Florence and you'll see the symbol plastered on walls and hung from the corners of palaces. A set of anywhere from 5 to 12 small circles, either as tiny balls scattered around a shield or painted red on a gold background, make up the family crest of the mighty Medici. Members would put it on any of their own buildings, or those they sponsored, renovated, or conquered over the years.

But what is the origin of these circles? Some say they represent pillboxes, symbolizing the medical derivation of the Medici name. Or, they could be coins, representing the banking foundations of the family's wealth. One story says the circles are really dents on the shield of an old knight of the family who fought and defeated a giant on behalf of Charlemagne.

Regardless of the true explanation, this coat of arms remains a recognized trademark hundreds of years after the end of the Medici clan.

Jesus painted not on one giant wall but, scene by scene, on the individual walls of small monks' cells that honeycomb the second floor. The idea was that these scenes, painted by Fra Angelico and his assistants, would aid in the monks' prayer and contemplation; the paintings are entrancing (especially in cell nos. 1, 3, and 9). The final cell on the corridor belonged to the fundamentalist firebrand preacher Savanarola, who briefly incited the populace of the most art-filled city in the world to burn their paintings, illuminated manuscripts, and anything else he felt was a worldly betrayal of Jesus' ideals. Ultimately, he ran afoul of the pope and was burned at the stake. You'll see his notebooks, rosary, and what's left of the clothes he wore that day in his cell.

THE OLTRARNO DISTRICT

Don't try to visit the **Pitti Palace** ★★ (Piazza Pitta, a few blocks south of the Ponte Vecchio; ☎ 055-2388614; www.firenzemusei.it; 12€ for a cumulative ticket valid at all its museums for 3 days, or 9€ for entry after 4pm; see below for individual museum hours) and the Uffizi on the same day. Both are astoundingly, almost exhaustively, rich collections—and the Pitti contains five major museums (including one of the best collections of paintings by Raphael in the world) plus elegant gardens.

No gallery comes closer to Mark Twain's description of "weary miles" in *Innocents Abroad* than the 26 art-crammed rooms of the Pitti's **Galleria Palatina** (8.50€, or use the cumulative ticket; Tues–Sun 8:15am–6:50pm). Paintings are displayed like cars in a parking garage, stacked on walls above each other in what the museum explains is the "Enlightenment" method of exhibition. Rooms are alternately dimly lit, or garishly bright; rugs are mildewed, restoration projects endless.

But you'll find important historical treasures amid the Palatina's haphazard collection. Some of the best efforts of Titian, Raphael, and Rubens line the walls. Raphael's *Portrait of a Young Woman* and *Madonna with Child* are a couple of favorites, along with Fra Bartolomeo's dramatically colored *Pietà,* and Caravaggio's creepy *The Tooth-Puller* and *Sleeping Cupid.* You'll also see wonderful examples of the northern European Flemish style of art, such as the intricate *Cardinal Bentivoglio* by van Dyck and Rubens' dramatic *Consequences of War.* Titian's 1536 painting of the demure *La Bella* is a good example of a proper Italian noblewoman. But if you want to see the other side of this young lady, check out the *Venus of Urbino* painting in the Uffizi, where the same model lies provocatively naked.

Included on the Galleria Palatina ticket is entry into the **Apartamenti Reali** (☎ 055-2388614; Tues–Sun 8:15am–3:50pm), where you can get an excellent feeling for the conspicuous consumption of the Medici grand dukes and their Austrian Lorena successors and see some notable paintings in their original ostentatious setting. Incidentally, they are called the Royal Apartments because Italy's first king lived here for several years during Italy's 19th-century unification movement—until Rome was finally conquered and the court was moved there.

The Pitti's **Galleria D'Arte Moderna** (☎ 055-2388601; 8.50€, or use the cumulative ticket; Tues–Sun 8:15am–1:50pm) actually has a pretty good collection, this time of 19th-century Italian paintings with a focus on Romanticism, Neoclassical works, and the Macchiaioli school of Italian Impressionists. But if you have limited time, a visit here really shouldn't take precedence over the Renaissance treasures of Florence.

Of the Pitti's cadre of lesser museums, the **Galleria Del Costume and Museo Degli Argenti** (☎ 055-2388709; 6€ each; daily 8:15am–4:30pm Nov–Feb, to 5:30pm Mar and part of Oct, to 6:30pm Apr–May and Sept to mid–Oct, to 7:30pm June–Aug, closed first and last Mon of each month)—the Costume Gallery and Museum of Silverware, respectively—combine to show that wealth and taste do not always go hand in hand. Unless you're a scholar or true aficionado of such things, they are in no way worth the admission price, but if you already have the cumulative ticket, pop in to spend some time among the Medici's over-the-top gold and jewel-encrusted household items.

The **Boboli Gardens** (☎ 055-2388786; 6€; open same hours as the Costume Museum) and the landscaped grounds steeply sloping up behind the palace to the top of a hill, with well-manicured shrubbery, statue-studded grottoes, and fine views of the city from the fortress at the peak, are quite pleasant.

And before you leave the Pitti Palace complex, be sure to stop by the grotto in the central courtyard. This covered area—with its grotesque statues, its fountain, and dripping water—suggests a Renaissance version of the grotto at the Playboy mansion.

As long as you've gone to the "other" side of the river, seek out the nontouristy **Santo Spirito** ✦ (Piazza Santo Spirito; ☎ 055-210030; free; Mon–Tues and Thurs–Fri 8:30am–noon and 4–6pm, Wed 8:30am–noon, Sat–Sun 4–6pm). Brunelleschi's last project, the simple yet elegant structure was erected in the mid-1400s (though, sadly, they never got around to putting on a real facade). Inside, it's dark and usually empty, a stark contrast to the overvisited Duomo. Many of its original works were destroyed in a 1471 fire, so most of the replacements came from the same era just afterward, creating a unified feel to the many side chapels.

One of the notable works in the left transept of the church, in the second chapel, is a severe *St. Monica and Augustine Nuns.* The 1472 painting (either by

Andrea del Verrocchio or Francesco Botticini) shows serious nuns in black and gray gathered around the saint. A couple of sisters glare at the viewer, and you almost want to apologize for interrupting them. On the right transept seek out Filippo Lippi's *Madonna and Child* for the detail of the figures, as well as for the background. Many of the other fine works throughout the church have English descriptions.

In order to visit the morgues beneath the church's hospital, Michelangelo used to sneak through the side door to the left of the main entrance. With the permission of the church director, Michelangelo studied the corpses for help in his painting and sculpting of the human form. As a thank you, Michelangelo carved a wooden crucifix and donated it to the church; pass through a door on the north wall, and you'll find it in the sacristy. The crucifix's thin, delicate body is a sharp contrast to most of Michelangelo's muscular figures, leading some to question the attribution. But written documentation seems to verify the authenticity of the piece.

The hours listed above should be more or less accurate. However, at press time, the church was temporarily closed for lack of a custodian, a situation they hope to have resolved by the time you are reading this. In short: Call ahead or ask at the tourist office for an update.

In the 18th century, a massive fire destroyed much of the nearby **Santa Maria del Carmine Church.** Miraculously, its **Brancacci Chapel** ✭✭ (Piazza Santa Maria del Carmine; ☎ 055-2382195; 4€; Wed–Sat and Mon 10am–5pm, Sun 1–5pm) survived intact, as did the masterpiece it contained within, a 1425 fresco cycle by painters Masolino, his far-more-talented pupil Masaccio, and Fra Filippo Lippi that is arguably one of the most influential of the Renaissance. Michelangelo and Leonardo da Vinci, among others, came to study and sketch the colorful biblical scenes with their contemporary Florentine background. Compare the courtly, sedate Adam and Eve in the garden on the right wall by Masolino with the vigorous, angst-filled couple being expelled from Eden by Masaccio facing it.

While I'm not pleased by the 4€ viewing fee, which was added after a highly successful 1990s restoration of the frescoes (during which they removed the prudish fig leaves painted over Adam and Eve's naughty bits), this is an important work, really a watershed in the rediscovery of perspective painting. Just try to ignore the signs that command DO NOT LINGER—you've paid, so enjoy the fresco, which is as much a testament to friendship as to anything else. After Masaccio's untimely death, at the age of 27, Fra Filippo Lippi faithfully continued to work on the piece, using his colleague's ideas and techniques.

You shouldn't leave Florence without getting a bird's-eye **view of town from Piazzale Michelangiolo** ✭. While buses and hordes of tourists don't exactly make this a reflective spot, it is quite accessible, and the vantage point over the cityscape is phenomenal, particularly at sunset. You can grab a city bus up there (no. 12 or 13; get off when you see a phalanx of parked tour buses around a bronze reproduction of the *David* on a pedestal). If you're walking, take Via del Monte alle Croci from Porta San Miniato, or the slightly less steep Via di San Salvatore al Monte to reach the piazza. For a quieter setting, climb the extra 10 minutes to the front steps of the Romanesque **San Miniato al Monte church** ✭ (Via Monte alle Croci; ☎ 055-2342731; free; winter Mon–Sat 8am–noon and 3–6pm, Sun 3–6pm, summer daily 8am–7:30pm), the second-oldest religious building in

Florence (after the Baptistery). If you make it there before 7:30pm, enter for a look at the funky 13th-century mosaic floor, with the signs of the zodiac and the spare furnishings, frescoes, and 11th-century crypt (with additional frescoes by Taddeo Gaddi, better known as the architect of the Ponte Vecchio).

FLORENCE FOR KIDS

You'll need a bus (no. 4) or a taxi to get to the site, but the kids will thank you for a visit to **Museo Stibbert** ✦ ★ (kids) (Via Stibbert 26; ☎ 055-475520; 5€; Mon–Wed 10am–2pm, Fri–Sat 10am–6pm). It's essentially the giant toy box of an eccentric Scottish-Italian arms-and-armor collector, which was made into a museum in 1906. Enter into the Hall of the Cavalcade to see a scene from King Arthur and Camelot, with gangs of life-size knight mannequins sitting fully armed and armored on horseback. Dozens of their counterparts are geared up throughout the Salone della Cupola, sort of a United Nations of medieval mayhem, with every variety of weapon, armor, and shield imaginable. Even the samurai warriors have made the trip; the museum boasts the biggest collection of Japanese armor outside of Tokyo.

The **Museo di Storia della Scienza** ✦ (kids) (Piazza dei Guidici 1; ☎ 055-265311; 6.50€; Mon–Sat 9:30am–5pm, Oct–May closes at 1pm Tues but opens the second Sun of each month 10am–1pm) actually displays a bone from Galileo's middle finger. It also has a wide collection of scientific instruments from early Arab scientists, as well as Galileo's telescopes, including the one he used to discover the moons of Jupiter. Kids (and inquisitive adults) will appreciate the old maps and globes, scary doctors' instruments, and a medieval pharmacy, all of which are a nice change from the religious art of Florence.

Another group of attractions good for young 'uns, and for those interested in engineering, are the new dueling Leonardo museums. Two independent companies have set up nearly identical exhibits of life-size versions of Leonardo's inventions based on his codex drawings. Visitors can see wooden models of everything from a medieval tank to a machine gun, parachute, glider, and hydraulic press. **The Leonardo Museum** ✦ (kids) (Il Genio di Leonardo, Via dei Servi 66r; ☎ 055-282966; www.mostredileonardo.com; 6€, 5€ for students and children; daily 10am–7pm) is the better of the two because it actually encourages visitors to touch and play with the 33 interactive models: Spin the drill and push the flying machine while you read the English description. Two blocks over, the **Macchine di Leonardo da Vinci** (kids) (Via Cavour 21; ☎ 055-295264; www.macchine dileonardo.com; 5€, 4€ for those under 25 and over 65, free for kids under 8; daily 9:30am–7:30pm) is nearly identical, but newer, with a better presentation of the models and more info on the inventor. But the spoilsports added DON'T TOUCH signs on most of the items, and since that's the most fun thing to do, I'd choose the first museum for my visit. This museum also has identical franchises in Arezzo and Lucca, while the Leonardo Museum has another exhibit in San Gimignano, so you may get another chance to see them if you've overbooked yourself with Florence sights.

A sad damsel with pale skin, half-closed eyes, and delicate lips lies on her back as if she had just fainted. Also, her torso has exploded and her intestines are spattered around her case. The wax anatomical models are one reason the **Museo Zoologico La Specola** ★✦ (kids) (Via Romana 17, follow signs to the museum entrance on second floor of Università degli Studi di Firenze; ☎ 055-2288251; www.msn.unifi.it; 4€; Sun–Tues and Thurs–Fri 9am–1pm, Sat 9am–5pm) might be the only museum in Italy where kids eagerly pull their parents from room to room. Creepy collections of threadbare stuffed-animal specimens transition into rooms filled with incredibly lifelike human bodies suffering from horrible dismemberments, flayings, and eviscerations—all in the name of science. The wax models served as illustrations for medical students studying at this scientific institute in the 1770s. But there's no real reason for the gruesome wax plague dioramas in Room 33, except that apparently the original curator liked gross stuff.

You may also like to have your kids mix with the locals at the **Museo dei Ragazzi (Museum of Children)** ★ 🎒 (Palazzo Vecchio; ☎ 055-2768224; www.museoragazzi.it; 2€ for kids, free for accompanying adults; daily 9am–6pm). The museum's courses are mainly in Italian, but highly entertaining and interactive classes on such subjects as architecture for kids (building and destroying an arch), fresco painting, clothing (an actor portrays a Renaissance noble getting dressed), and optics (assembling a replica of Galileo's telescope) can often be understood by youthful visitors. And while it can be fun to try to figure out what's going on in Italian and joining Florentine families, the museum also offers some English performances, usually on weekends. Contact them to learn about special workshops and their latest opening hours—which change often.

THE OTHER FLORENCE

Nothing says the "other Florence" like the **Oltrarno** section of town, literally the "other" side of the Arno from the main section of the city. This district has fewer tourists, and more local students and residents. While the Oltrarno has many traditional sights such as churches, museums, and hotels, it also has dozens of small artisans' shops, neighborhood stores, and neglected attractions that seem a world away from the mobbed Duomo and Signoria piazzas.

The best way to experience the Oltrarno is to allow serendipity to be your guide as you walk the narrow streets south of the river between Ponte Vecchio and Ponte Alla Carraia. Wander into small shops to see craftsmen using techniques hundreds of years old. Metalworkers, engravers, bookbinders, woodcarvers, cobblers, and jewelers operate their businesses almost clandestinely, without any sign above the shop entrances, without regular working hours, marked prices, or promotions of any sort. Don't try to drop by in August, however—that's when the artisans all go on vacation.

While some of the shop owners speak English, many don't, so you'll need a little help to learn about the various crafts. The city of Florence runs free workshop tours in the Oltrarno, during which local guides take visitors to three randomly selected shops each Monday and Thursday afternoon (3–6pm). I highly recommend these. For booking information, contact **Centro Prenotazioni** at ☎ 055-3036108 or at itinerari.turistici@siwebsrl.com.

Another good option is to book a tour through **Walking Tours of Florence** ★ (Piazzo Santo Stefano 2; ☎ 055-2645033; www.italy.artviva.com). This well-run company coordinates custom tours on which bilingual guides take visitors to meet, and learn from, a half-dozen artisans in their workshops.

For information on some of the more accessible artisans' shops south of the Arno, see p. 137.

HANG WITH THE LOCALS

To see Florentines at their most passionate, attend a local **soccer match.** The ACF Fiorentina team has arisen from both a spectacular 2002 bankruptcy and burial in the lowest division, returning to fight for the championship of the prestigious Italian Serie A league. The renovated Artemio Franchi stadium, southeast of the city center, is packed with up to 47,000 fans for weekend matches from September to May. These aren't like, say, baseball fans in the U.S.; expect singing, chanting, screaming masses of locals who live and die with each shot on goal. Tickets begin at 20€, and you need to select a "home" or "away" team section. Choose your wardrobe carefully. (*Hint:* The home team color is purple.) You can order online at www.acffiorentina.it, or buy at the stadium box office or from a variety of bars in town a few days before the match. Resellers also have tickets and can be reached at ☎ 055-503261 or 055-583300. The stadium is about 400m (a quarter-mile) from the Firenze Campo di Marte train station along Largo Gennarelli, or take bus no. 7, 17, or 20 from Santa Maria Novella station.

After Romans beheaded St. Minias in the 3rd century, he supposedly picked up his head and rushed up the hill to the spot of his future church. Visitors don't need to make such a sacrifice to join the locals for **afternoon vespers at San Miniato al Monte church** (☎ 055-2342731). Just leave your camera in the hotel, dress conservatively, and climb to the church behind Piazza Michelangiolo in time for the 5:30pm ceremonies (4:30pm in winter), which begin with Gregorian chants and half an hour of vespers followed by a Latin Mass.

If you can't make it to San Miniato, then try to attend Mass at any one of a number of other central Florence churches during those times when "tourists are forbidden." Times vary by church, but there are often daily services around 7:30 or 8am and again at 6 or 6:30pm, while on Sundays, Masses happen throughout the day. For precise hours, you can search the database (in Italian) at www.messe.firenze.it. Again, so long as you act like a parishioner, with bowed head and whispered tones, you'll be treated like one.

Florence's early fortune was built with the textile trade, and today the city is still a leader in the fashion world. There's no better way to glimpse this vibrant modern side of the Florence than to go to one of its major **fashion fairs.** This series of **Pitti Immagine** fairs—men, women, children, fragrances, living, knits, and the like—are held year-round in the Fortessa da Basso and Stazione Leopolda. Admission is around 20€ for the official events, and they're technically for "the trade" only, but you can probably fudge some info on the registration forms. For more information, go to www.pittimmagine.com. Accommodations in town can be tight during the fairs, but Florence is alive with official and unofficial events, including fashion shows, product displays, and corporate promotions. Even passing on the periphery of one of these fairs is a good way to get an insider perspective on the modern business of the Italian fashion industry.

All of the above activities are largely observational. So how about getting some hands-on experiences that'll help you get a better understanding of Florence and perhaps learn a little something along the way? I'm talking Italian lessons, cooking classes, and courses on everything from art restoration to painting your own fresco.

Learn to Read Dante in the Original

If you want to interact with the locals, a good first step would be to learn how to speak with them. When a simple *"Come stai?"* is enough to open doors of friendship, imagine what an **Italian language class** could do for you! In Florence, dozens of programs offer Italian instruction ranging from 1-week intros to multi-year degree courses. The tourist office website lists many institutes and programs, but perhaps the most respected and well-established school is the **Centro Linguistico Italiano Dante Alighieri** (Piazza della Repubblica 5; ☎ 055-210808; www.clida.it). Its 2-week Italian course combines 4-hour morning lessons with afternoon cultural seminars and field trips, starting at 440€ (one-on-one courses start at 400€ per week). They also offer 2-hour wine tasting and 3-hour cooking classes for a reasonable 35€. Speaking of which . . .

Cook La Cucina Toscana

Nothing is more valued by Fiorentini (or Tuscans, or Umbrians, or . . .) than the art and passion that goes into the preparation of their regional cuisine. And what better way to become part of this local culture than to get into the kitchen and learn how to make a meal? Florence offers a variety of options for taking a **cooking class,** ranging from the Dante Institute's half-day lessons (above) to formal courses at the **Cordon Bleu Academy** (Via di Mezzo 55r; ☎ 055-2345468; www.cordonbleu-it.com)—charging 70€ to 100€ per lesson; most courses consists of four to eight lessons, with a few one-, two-, or three-lesson courses each year on topics ranging from *cornetti* (Italian croissants) to appetizers to holiday menus (Christmas specialties in December, for example). The offerings on longer courses change weekly, but you might on any given day learn anything from how to make four kinds of gnocchi to sautéing spinach and poaching pears, or from creating cannelloni to crafting stuffed chocolates. Some courses even delve into regional specialties, perhaps teaching you a variety of *primi* ranging from Lucca's *farro* soup to the pasta rolls of Naples and the *lasagne* of Le Marche.

Another good option for a short-term tourist is the family-friendly 85€ day trip into the Chianti with **The Accidental Tourist** (☎ 055-699376; www.accidental tourist.com). Participants visit the Renaissance villa at a wine estate for a tour and tasting, followed by a hands-on lesson in making various pastas in an old monastery, and, naturally, a feast on the results.

Speaking of food, many locals do their food shopping at the **Mercato Centrale** covered market on Via dell'Ariento, near San Lorenzo (Mon–Sat 7am–2pm). Neighborhood restaurateurs come here for fresh meat, produce, and olive oils from the Tuscan-area farms. You can pick up ingredients for a picnic in the park, or just ogle the amazing colors, shapes, and sizes of the fruits and vegetables on display. Get advice from vendors about a gift bottle of olive oil or essence of truffles, or snack on some sample sausages from the butcher. There's no easier, quicker way to get into the swing of local life than just to hang around the local food market some morning, sampling the wares, striking up conversations with the stall owners, learning about the core ingredients in Italian cooking, rubbing elbows with the chefs who might be preparing them dinner that evening. Another market to hit—and one that few tourists do—is the smaller **Sant'Ambrogio Market Piazza Ghiberti** on the opposite side of town, north of Santa Croce (Mon–Sat 7am–2pm).

Festive Florence

Florence has a number of annual festivals and events, some focused on the modern business of textiles and fashion. But the more entertaining ones have history as their theme.

The games of the **Calcio Storico** are held in connection with the celebrations related to St. John the Baptist, Florence's patron saint, on his feast day of June 24.

After parading through town in 16th-century costumes, teams from each of Florence's four city quarters assemble in a dirt-filled Piazza Santa Croce. They then play a set of games said to have originated during a siege of Florence in 1530. If the Renaissance soldiers were as brutal as their modern descendants, the siege was probably broken quickly.

The games are a combination of rugby and soccer, as well as general mayhem, with teams—consisting of 26 people—beating the daylights out of each other while trying to advance from one end of the square to the other. Qualifying matches are played in the 2 weeks prior to June 24, with the final on the feast day. The winning team, assuming they have any teeth left, enjoy a roasted calf as their prize, and then they watch that night's fireworks with the rest of Florence. Tickets can be hard to come by for the bleachers in the squares (☎ 055-2616052), but the processions through town during the weeks approaching the finals are free.

The **Scoppio del Carro (Explosion of the Cart),** is Florence's Easter festival, in which the descent of the Holy Spirit to earth is celebrated by blowing up a cart filled with fireworks. This creative interpretation of heaven meeting earth is said to have begun with a burning wagon pulled around town by returning crusaders, to bring the flame of Holy Saturday to Easter Sunday. The modern buggy is hauled by six nervous bulls from Porta a Prato to the Duomo. In the piazza, a mechanical dove on a wire descends from up high to set the wagon (minus the relieved oxen) ablaze for a resulting explosion of holy spirits.

Moving to the secular, Florence's notable music festival is the **Maggio Musicale Fiorentino** (www.maggiofiorentino.com). It features opera, dance, theater, and orchestra performances at venues across town, including the Teatro Comunale, Teatro Verdi, the Palazzo dei Congressi, and several outdoor performances. The season usually runs from May to early June. Tickets begin at 15€ to 20€ for the cheap seats at ballets, 25€ to 30€ at the opera, up to 90€ for the best seats at the marquee events. A semi-related opera season runs from September through January under the auspices of the same organization.

Take Art History, Restoration, or Fresco Classes

Florence is a city of artisans, from the mightiest Renaissance artists to the humblest modern cobbler, and there's no better way to get a feel for that tradition than by **taking a course in art, art history, crafts, or fashion.** The tourist office has a list of dozens of programs, though most require a commitment of at least a month or two if not a full semester. I chose the schools below because I think they offered an intriguing variety of classes and perhaps more importantly, because they allow their students to better understand (or get involved in some aspect of) what makes Florence Florence, whether it be getting a deeper background on art history, or learning how to paint a fresco, or just what goes into the restoration work being conducted behind all that scaffolding you see everywhere you go. Here are a few of the shorter-term options (2 weeks or less) of which even a dabbling tourist might have time to partake—you can even learn to fresco in 5 days. Each offers classes in English.

Perhaps the best one-stop shopping for such an experience is **FlorenceArt.net** (Via di San Bartolo a Cintoia 15r; ☎ 055-7879097, or in the U.S. 800/420-5531; http://florenceart.net), which charges 550€ to 650€ for a variety of introductory 5-day courses. Most classes meet about 4 hours per day—leaving plenty of time for exploring—for courses in decorative painting, gilding, fresco and *graffito* (bet you didn't know we get our word "graffiti" from an Italian form of wall decoration), art restoration (you actually restore a real 19th-c. painting), metalworking (chasing and embossing/repousse), and woodcarving. The teachers are local artists and artisans who have their own studios, but enjoy teaching their skills to genuinely interested members of the public. All are members of the collective that is FlorenceArt.net.

Accademia del Giglio (Via Ghibellina 116; ☎ 055-2302467; www.adg.it; to each of the following rates add a 45€ enrollment fee) offers a half-day life drawing class for 35€, 1-week courses in various art techniques for 180€, and 1-week art history courses: on the Renaissance in Florence and Tuscany, the history of Italian fashion (both 290€), and the Italian garden and Tuscan villa (390€). If you have a full month and come equipped with some basic artistic skills, you can even take an intensive fresco workshop for 700€.

ATTENTION, SHOPPERS!

Florence built its medieval riches from the textile and clothing trade, and it continues to be a mecca for shopping as well as a center for fashion and design. Ferragamo makes its headquarters here in a riverside castle, and the high-rent Via Tournabuoni and its side streets feature showrooms of all the top **designer brands,** including Armani, Gucci, and Prada. But Florence is equally well known for its many **artisans** carrying on their family craft traditions in jewelry, furniture making, engraving, and bookbinding. Many of these small workshops can be found south of the Arno in the Oltrarno district. **Leather** is one of the major products of the city, with high-end stores selling jackets, purses, and bags in the Santa Croce district, and dozens of street-side stalls selling cheaper versions in the San Lorenzo area.

A note about hours: In general, Florence's stores are open between 4 and 7:30pm on Mondays; and from 9 or 10am to 1pm and again from 3:30 or 4pm until 7pm Tuesdays through Saturdays (though in the summer many shops also open on Mon mornings and stay open through the midday *riposo*). If you're big on shopping, you won't want to visit in August, when many shopkeepers draw their shutters and take a week or even the entire month off for vacation.

BOOKS & PAPER GOODS

Enrico Giannini does bookbinding and creates handmade artistic papers at **Giulio Giannini & Figlio** (Piazza Pitti 36–37r; ☎ 055-212621; www.giuliogiannini.it) as his family has since 1856. He speaks English well, and can be persuaded to give a near magical demonstration on how he creates the swirling colors on his book jackets and wrapping papers. He not only does custom bookbinding but also sells reasonably priced boxes, papers, and journals for unique souvenirs. Another leading Florentine shop for paper goods—more on the refined, stationery end of the business—is **Pineider** (Piazza della Signoria 13–14r; ☎ 055-284655; www.pineider. com), the oldest stationers in the city, founded in 1774 and still turning out exquisitely crafted paper and paper goods, from diaries and photo albums to engraved stationery.

There are two English-language bookstores in Florence that also serve as unofficial gathering places for expat English speakers in Florence. **BM Bookshop** (Borgo Ognissanti 4r; ☎ 055-294575) is the smaller of the two, but with a better and more rounded selection. Larger and packed with great deals on new and used books—as well as a place to trade in your own finished novels for new-used ones, and a fab new location just south of the Duomo—is the **Paperback Exchange** (Via della Oche 4r; ☎ 055-293460; www.papex.it). The largest, multistory chain booksellers in town also carry plenty of books in English (along with plenty of coffee-table souvenir photo books): **Libreria Edison** (Piazza della Repubblica 5; ☎ 055-213110; www.libreriaedison.it) and **Libreria Feltrinelli** (Via de' Cerretani 30–32r; ☎ 055-2382652; and Via Cavour 12, ☎ 055-292196; www.lafeltrinelli.it).

CHEAP NECESSITIES

A good place to stock up on **basics,** like forgotten toothbrushes, soap, paper, pens, a rubber duck, or purple tableware, is the **Nine T Nine Cent Paradise** (www.cent-shop.it), where, you guessed it, everything is .99€. Sweet! You can find its bright yellow-and-blue signs at Via Cavour 92r (☎ 055-217172), Via Nazionale 124r (☎ 055-287116), Via dei Conti 57r (☎ 055-214185), Piazza Gaetano Salvemini 22–23 (☎ 055-212153), and Via degli Orti Oricellari 16–20r (☎ 055-212153).

ENGRAVING & WOODCARVING

A cluttered cuckoo clock of a shop, packed with every variety of woodcarving and with two centrally located branches, is **Bartolucci** (Via Condotta 12r, ☎ 055-211773; and Via Borgo dei Greci 11A/r, ☎ 055-2398596; www.bartolucci.com). Since 1936, the family has been carving wood versions of everything from Tuscany's own Pinnochio to half-size motorcycles, model airplanes, picture frames, and clocks.

You can see engravers in action at **L'Ippogrifo Stampe d'Arte** (Via S. Spirito 5r; ☎ 055-213255; www.stampeippogrifo.com). Examine the cityscapes and still lifes on the walls of this Oltrarno shop, and then step back into the workshop to witness the copperplate pressing technique that has been used in Florence for 500 years. For antique engravings in an historic shop (est. 1903), stop by **Giovanni Baccani** (Via della Vigna Nuova 75r; ☎ 055-214467), which has a grand collection of prints and engravings.

FASHION

For chic Italian clothes at last season's prices (generally because you're getting last season's styles), I have two suggestions: **Stock House-Grandi Firme** (www.stockhouse-grandifirme.com), with branches at Via del Trebbio 10r, Via Lamberti 16r, and Viale De Amicis 169 (but check the website, as they seem to favor short-term leases and move locations frequently); and **Stock House Il Giglio** (Via Borgo Ognissanti 64; ☎ 055-217596). Both carry overstock clothing in perfect condition from some of the biggest names in Italian fashions—at discounts of as much as 70%.

If you need to be more *au courant* than that, you can find affordable clothes at the department store **Coin** (Via dei Calzaiuoli 56r; ☎ 055-280531; www.coin.it) or **La Rinascente** (Piazza della Repubblica 1; ☎ 055-219113; www.rinascente.it). Both are members of national chains. And for the fashionistas among you, head directly to the **Via dei Tornabuoni, Via Nuova,** or **Via degli Strozzi,** where Pucci, Gucci, and other big names in Italian fashion have their chic shops.

JEWELRY

Florence doesn't offer the same buys on jewelry that it once did. Prices tend to be high and there are some shops that will pass off inferior stones, so choose carefully. There are, however, some stores that have a reputation for both craftsmanship and honest service. For a wide variety, go to **Gioielleria Manetti** (Via dei Calzaiuoli 92r, near the Duomo; ☎ 055-214401; www.gioielleriamanetti.it), a popular family-run craft shop with jewelry, watches, and silver. For something a bit more unique, try the **Alessandro Dari Museum Shop** ★ (Via San Niccolo 115r, Oltrarno; ☎ 055-244747; www.alessandrodari.com). Goldsmith/craftsman/musician Alessandro Dari is always busy at his bench in this combination showcase, lounge, and workshop. Prices range from 120€ for a simple "love ring" to 30,000€ for what looks like an actual-size jeweled golden village for your finger.

LEATHER SHOPS & STALLS

You can find a decent leather jacket for not much more than 100€ in the stalls of the **San Lorenzo Leather Market,** stretching from San Lorenzo church up around the Mercato Centrale—but don't expect it to be an heirloom. Indeed, it's not uncommon to experience fraying stitches and broken zippers after only a few weeks' use of the cheaper leather goods, so check the craftsmanship closely before purchasing. Generally, the fewer number of pieces used for construction, the higher the quality; a jacket that looks like a quilt has a greater chance of falling apart. Both at the stalls and in the shops immediately behind them (for which the stalls are merely bait), you are supposed to haggle. You can usually get the seller to drop the initial price by half, more if you buy multiple items—wallets, purses, and other smaller leather goods make excellent gifts for the folks back home.

A less fun option, but one with a bit higher guarantee of quality, is to shop in a proper store; also, stores will usually alter a jacket at no extra cost (be sure to allow at least a day, though, if you need any work done). Top names include **Gherardini** (Via della Vigna Nuova 57r; ☎ 055-215678; www.gherardini.it) and **Beltrami** (Via della Vigna Nuova 70r; ☎ 055-287779; www.beltramifirenze.it).

Another Florentine nexus for high-quality leather goods is the Santa Croce neighborhood—and, in fact, in the church itself. The **Santa Croce Suola del Cuoio** (Piazza Santa Croce 16; ☎ 055-244533; www.leatherschool.com) initially began as a leather-crafts school for Franciscan monks, but has expanded its partnership over the years with a major Florentine trading house to develop into a well-known and full-service leather shop (with prices to match). You normally enter it through a corridor off the right transept of the church (through the sacristy and church gift shop), but now that Santa Croce has gotten greedy and begun charging admission, the leather school has opened up a back door at Via San Giuseppe 5r so you can get in without paying church admission.

A good cheaper option is **Lorenz Leather** (Piazza San Lorenzo 10r; ☎ 055-213348; www.lorenzleather.com), with a wide selection and quick turnaround on alteration. Bags and purses can be found in these same stores, and both get good reviews. The high-end Prada and Gucci stores also offer finely crafted products, but you'll be paying a lot for the name and their high-rent location. Moreover, if you've come all the way to Florence, you should probably buy something more unique than a name brand you can pick up in your hometown.

South of the Arno, **John F.** (Lungarno Corsini 2; ☎ 055-2398985; www.johnf.it) and **Anna** (Piazza Pitti, 38–41r; ☎ 055-283787; www.annapitti.it) both offer butter-soft leather goods for men and women. For more made-in-Florence accessorizing, head to **Madova Gloves** (Via Guicciardini 1r; ☎ 055-2396526; www.madova.com). Gloves are all they do in this tiny shop, and they do them well. The grandchildren of the workshop's founders do a brisk business in brightly colored, supple leather gloves lined with cashmere and silk.

NIGHTLIFE

Florence isn't especially known for its nightlife. Live-music venues are few, clubs are scattered around town, and there really isn't any particular neighborhood that lights up at night.

That being said, the influx of tourists and exchange students ensures there's always going to be an Irish pub within a couple of blocks. Additionally, the younger set has its four or five requisite dance clubs; the cultured have opera; and the too-cheap-to-buy-a-ticket can enjoy free evening concerts in historic squares during the summer. And open-container laws are lax, so if all else fails you can always kick back with a drink on the steps of a historic building and watch the evening promenade of locals and visitors (possibly the best nightlife option of all).

PERFORMING ARTS

While it's not Milan or Rome, Florence has a respectable arts scene boasting two well-regarded symphony orchestras and a large concert hall, **Teatro Comunale** (Corso Italia 16; ☎ 055-213535), which presents seasons of ballet and classical music (it's also the venue for the annual Maggio Musicale; see "Festive Florence," above). Prices can vary widely by show (up to 150€ for headliners), but in general it's possible to get a ticket here for as little as 15€ to 20€ if you're willing to accept a seat in the second gallery.

A secondary theater, the **Teatro Verdi** (Via Ghibellina 99; ☎ 055-212320; www.teatroverdifirenze.it), is where you go to see touring shows. Major international stars of opera, ballet, and classical and pop music play this venue. Ticket prices are all over the map, but it's usually possible to snag a seat for between 10€ and 30€.

Going to church might not be your idea of a night out on the town, but it often is in Florence, where the nights are filled with the sounds of Vivaldi, Bach, and Mozart, and **church concerts** are a staple. The majority of concerts take place in the autumn, but rarely does a week go by without some house of worship sponsoring one of these events. Look for signs and billboards posted at churches all over the historical center, and ask at the tourist office about any upcoming ecclesiastical concerts.

MUSIC CLUBS

For some (literally) underground live music, try **BeBop** ★ (Via dei Servi 76; ☎ 055-218799; www.bebopclub.com), a surprisingly cavernous warren of basement rooms. This is the sort of place into which local college students take their guitars, with the hopes of jamming with whoever happens to be on stage. Bands vary from awful Beatles cover groups to great funk/folk/rock combos; you just have to try your luck and see who's playing that night. On weekends the place can get quite crowded, but on a weekday it could just be you and the family of the band in the audience.

Popular with locals, the cavelike **Chiodo Fisso** (Via Dante Alighieri 16r; ☎ 055-2381290) features Italian folk singers, jazz artists, and a variety of other small acts on a tiny stage surrounded by a dozen or so tables. Performers begin around 10pm (often led off by the owner, musician Andrea Ardia), the bar gets crowded about an hour later, and visiting acts often don't start up until midnight. It's a good peek at a local scene.

Caruso Jazz Café (Via Lambertesca 15-16r; ☎ 055-281940; www.carusojazz cafe.com) is the most sophisticated choice. Its live jazz combos play most nights of the week, beginning at around 10pm. The stone arched stage area is an atmospheric setting for music. You can sit in the front section at the bar for drinks, or enjoy the tunes with your dinner. A side room has couches for relaxing and a closed-circuit TV so you don't miss any of the onstage action. They also have an expensive Internet cafe, just in case you need to look up some jazz scores.

BARS & TAVERNS

About the hippest place in town in recent summers has been **Noir** ★ (Lugarno Corsini 12r; ☎ 055-210752; www.noirfirenze.com), which changes names and decor to keep up with trends (it used to be called Capocaccia and featured beanbag chairs). The place attracts a young and beautiful crowd drawn by the buffet (which used to be free but now costs 9€ Mon–Fri and 10€ Sat) and the Tuesday menu of sushi and sashimi (still something of a novelty in Florence), the chic new look ("noir" is not only new name but also the theme of the somber new decor), and the superlative views. Really what could be cooler than sipping a mojito with a view of Ponte Vecchio on one side and the sunset on the other?

A couple of other good *aperitivo* choices in a modish setting are the minimalist-chic lounge of **Angels** (Via del Proconsolo 29-31r; ☎ 055-2398762; www.ristoranteangels.it) and the happening cafe and art gallery **Dolce Vita** (Piazza del Carmine; ☎ 055-284595; www.dolcevitaflorence.com), with live music Wednesday and Thursday from 7:30 to 9:30pm.

Among the dozen or so near-identical Irish pubs in Florence (think dark woods and lots of Celtic bric-a-brac), I've returned a number of times to the **Dublin Pub** (Via Faenza 27r; ☎ 055-293049; www.dublinpub.it) for its well-pulled pints and calm ambience—quite a contrast to the busy Via Faenza/Via Nazionale area outside.

Doubling as Firenze's favorite frat house, **The Fish Pub** (Piazza del Mercato Centrale 44r; ☎ 055-2654029) certainly can't be recommended for any cultural reason. But you can get five shots for 5€ on Thursdays, a pizza for another 5€, and between the patio and the upper floor, not to mention the main bar, there's always some sort of silliness going on.

The Joshua Tree Pub ★ (Via Della Scala 37r; ☎ 340-7353596; www.thejoshua treepub.com), a quirky neighborhood bar popular among international students, gray-haired neighborhood characters, and pink-mohawked local punks, is certainly one of the friendliest spots in town thanks to manager Max and his spirited staff. They welcome everyone equally, and offer cheap drink specials (including nine beers on tap) and amateur DJs. The neighborhood near the station gets a little sketchy, so bring a friend if you're planning a late night.

DANCE CLUBS

Central Park (Via Fosse Macinate 2, in Parco delle Cascine; ☎ 055-359942 or 055-353505; www.centralparkfi.com) attracts over a thousand partiers on a good night, including both locals and tourists. It boasts four large dance areas, with all types of high-energy music. Drinks are pricey, as is the admission (which varies by night, special events, and your gender), and it's best to go late at night; the place doesn't really get hopping until about 1am. You'll want to take a cab to and from the club, however, because the surrounding public park and neighborhood are decidedly dicey after dark.

Yab (Via Sassetti 5r; ☎ 055-215160; www.yab.it) probably qualifies as Central Park's biggest competitor (you may remember its earlier incarnation as Yab Yum), with three dance floors, house and dance music, and an enthusiastic crowd of 20-somethings. It opens nightly at 11:30pm; there is a bouncer at the front to keep out the unstylish—their logo states "Glamour Club . . . You Are Beautiful," and you better be to get in, so be sure to wear your club clothes.

Gay and lesbian nightlife centers in a neighborhood a little west of Santa Croce church, where you'll find **Crisco** (Via Sant'Egidio 43r; ☎ 055-2480580), a swinging nightspot popular with men, while **Piccolo Caffè** (Borgo Santa Croce 23r; ☎ 055-2001057) and **Flamingo Bar** (Via dei Pandolfini 26r; ☎ 055-243356) are coed. **Tabasco Bar** (Piazza di Santa Cecelia 3r; ☎ 055-213000; www.tabasco gay.it) is Italy's oldest gay disco but still going strong, and the **YAG b@r** (Via de Macci 8r; ☎ 055-2469022; www.yagbar.com) is a colorful new cafe/bar/DJ space.

The ABCs of Florence

American Express The office at Via Dante Alighieri 22r (☎ **055-50981;** Mon–Fri 9am–5:30pm) provides a currency exchange, free mail pickup, travel services, and other services for cardholders (noncardholders pay a fee).

Business Hours Shops are usually open from about 9:30am to noon or 1pm, then from 3 or 3:30 to 7:30pm—or 5pm, or 6pm, or maybe the weather's nice so they've closed for the day. In short, hours are erratic. The town comes close to shutting down in August as everyone leaves the sweltering heat for the mountains or beaches. Many museums and restaurants are closed on Mondays. It can be pretty tough to find an open restaurant any time from 3 to 6pm, though many stay open past midnight, particularly in tourist-heavy areas.

Currency Exchange Never use a *cambio* (exchange office) if there's a bank with an ATM handy, as banks invariably give you a better exchange rate and charge a lower fee. That said, if you listened to someone whose last trip to Europe was more than 10 years ago and you brought traveler's checks, exchange offices cluster around Santa Maria Novella and the Duomo.

Emergencies Dial ☎ **113** for general emergencies, **112** for police, **115** for fire, or **118** for medical emergencies.

Hospitals Italy has socialized medicine, so you can get treated without insurance or payment problems. Try **Arcispedale di Santa Maria Nuova** (☎ 055-27581) at Piazza Santa Maria Nuova 1, north of the Duomo, or for more pressing emergencies, the **Misericordia Ambulance Service** (☎ 055-212222), which is actually in Piazza del Duomo, on the south side by Giotto's Bell Tower. The **Medical Service** for foreigners is at Via Lorenzo Il Magnifico 59 (☎ 055-475411). A volunteer group, **AVO,** offers **phone translation services for medical issues** (☎ 055-2344567) from 10am to noon Tuesday and Thursday, and from 4 to 6pm Monday, Wednesday, and Friday, so it's best to get sick during these times.

Information & Tourist Offices In addition to an info desk in the Arrivals Hall at the airport (☎ 055-315874), Florence has three downtown tourist offices. One is across from the Santa Maria Novella train station at Piazza della Stazione 4 (☎ 055-212245). The "tourist office" inside the station is just a commercial hotel-booking service. The main city tourist office is at Via Cavour 1r (☎ 055-290832). It has standard city maps as well as information on hotels, restaurants, local classes, and area trips. Annoyingly, it does charge for some of the materials. There is also a newer tourist office a block south of Santa Croce (Borgo Santa Croce 29r; ☎ 055-2340444). Florence tourism's comprehensive website is **www.firenzeturismo.it.**

Internet Access Many hotels offer a free "Internet point," although sometimes it can be a hassle waiting for other guests to get off the machine. Besides a few hot spots, Wi-Fi hasn't really made it to Florence, although some high-end hotels offer Wi-Fi for a fee. Internet cafes, which usually charge about 2.50€ to 3€ per hour, are easy to find in most districts of the city. Many Internet cafes line Via Faenza, including **Caironet** at no. 49, which is open daily 9:30am to midnight, with rates starting at 2€ per hour, the same rates as their shops at Via de' Ginori 59r and Via de' Macci 90. **Internettrain** is a large chain with nine shops across Florence, including at Via dell'Oriuolo 40r, Borgo San Jacopo 30r, Via Guelfa 54-56r, Via Porta Rossa 38r, Vie de' Benci 36r, and in the shops gallery in the tunnel leading from Santa Maria Novella train station under Piazza Stazione (www.internet train.it).

Newspapers & Magazines Every major international newspaper or magazine is available at kiosks or bookstores around town. The tourist office publishes a weekly English-language newspaper, *The Florentine*, with extensive events listings, articles about tourist sites, and important headlines like "Topless in Tuscany Not Tolerated." Many advertising-driven "information" brochures are available at the tourist office and hotels, including the decent *Vivi Firenze*, targeted at foreigners living in Florence.

Police In an emergency, call ☎ 112. For filing a report, contact the Questura Centrale (Via Zara 2; ☎ 055-20391 or 055-49771); English-speaking personnel are on hand at this central police station from 9am to 2pm, as well as at the main *carabinieri* station (Borgo Ognissanti 48; ☎ 055-24811).

Post Office The main post office (Via Pellicceria, 3, by Piazza della Repubblica; ☎ 160 or 055-218156) sells *francobolli* (stamps) and sends packages—but if they're over 2 kilograms (about 4½ lb.) you must go to the package office on Via dei Sassetti 4, in Piazza Davanzati behind the regular office. You can also buy stamps at any tobacco store, and for shipping a package probably the best option is to go with DHL (Via Lamberti 39-41r, Via della Scala 63r, or in the tunnel of shops leading from Santa Maria Novella train station; www.dhl.it) or Mailboxes Etc (Via San Gallo 55r; ☎ 055-4630129; www.mbe.com), which have all the packing materials you'll need, but charge a hefty service fee.

Safety The tourist district is very safe, but it can get a little dicey around the edges (the Arno side of Santa Maria Novella station late at night, as well as some of the southern parks). The Gypsy pickpocket situation has abated somewhat in recent years, though crowds and tourists will always attract some thieves, so stay aware of your possessions.

Transit Info City **buses** (www.ataf.net) leave from the Santa Maria Novella train station on dozens of routes going across town and out to the suburbs. *You will not need one to tour the miniscule historical center.* Honestly: Countless tourists hop on a bus out of habit, only to find themselves in the suburbs within 10 minutes. For trips to the edge of town, tickets cost 1.20€ for a 70-minute ticket, 5€ for a full-day pass, with various other options available. Buy *biglietti* (tickets) at any newsstand or tabacconist (look for any store or bar with a small brown sign showing a white T). You need to validate your ticket by sticking it in a little machine once you board the bus. They rarely check tickets, but when they do, you'll pay a hefty fine if you're ticketless or unvalidated. The "I'm a tourist, I didn't know" excuse doesn't work; believe me, they've heard that one before.

Taxis are available at the train station, and line up around major piazzas. You can order one to come fetch you by calling ☎ 055-4390, 055-4242, or 055-4798—though remember, the fare begins when they get the call, not when they arrive to pick you up. Flag-fall is 2.64€ (4.48€ Sun), rising to 5.70€ between 10pm and 6pm; add .62€ for each item of luggage. Drivers expect about a 10% tip. Again, you most likely won't need one to get around town, unless you're trying to ferry luggage from the train station to your hotel.

If you like hills, you might enjoy **renting a bicycle** and riding around south of the Arno, up to San Miniato and Piazzale Michelangelo. Given the tight traffic in town, I wouldn't recommend using a bike as a way to see the city. The city now sponsors a *"Mille ed una bici"* program to encourage bicycle use by renting them for just 1.50€ per hour, 4€ for 5 hours, or 18€ per day at stands set up around the fringes of town: a Parterre parking lot, Piazza Tasso, Piazza V. Veneto, Piazza Ghiberti, Piazza Cestello, and at all three train stations. Most stands are open from around 7:30 or 8am to 7 or 8pm in summer, 6pm in winter. You might find more options and flexibility—and far cheaper daily rates—with a private bike rental, starting at 2.50€ per hour, 12€ per day, with Alinari (Via San Zanobi 38r; ☎ 055-280500; www.alinarirental.com).

Alinari also **rents motor scooters** (10€–15€ per hour, 25€–35€ for 5 hours, 30€–55€ per day) if you want to zoom around on a Vespa like a local, but you *really* need to know how to handle one. Florence is definitely not the place to learn to ride, and even experts have trouble in the traffic chaos—think bike messenger in Manhattan. That being said, it's a fun way to zip up nearby hills, pop over to Fiesole, or visit 20 sites in a single day.

It bears repeating: Florence's historical center is minuscule, the traffic impossible, and the parking fees insane. You will be miserable if you try to take a car to Florence; it is only an enormous hassle. However, **renting a car** is a great idea if you want to get out of Florence, especially if you intend to get off the beaten track in Chianti country. Remember: It's always best (and cheaper) to arrange for a rental before you leave on your trip. That said, rental agencies in town include Europcar (Borgo Ognissanti 53–55r; ☎ 055-290438; www.europcar.com), Avis (Borgo Ognissanti 128r; ☎ 055-213629; www.avis.com), and Hertz (Via Maso Finiguerra 33; ☎ 055-2398205; www.hertz.com).

4 Tuscany

On winding roads through famous wine country and in medieval hill towns, visitors lose themselves in masterworks of the past

by Reid Bramblett

THIS IS THE ITALIAN COUNTRYSIDE OF PEOPLE'S DREAMS: ROLLING HILLS covered with vineyards and castles, and fortified hill towns punctuated with medieval stone towers and Gothic church spires. In its cities are Renaissance palazzi, many now hosting charming bed-and-breakfasts, and on its vineyards and farms are houses and villas transformed into agriturismi, providing tourists the chance to stay on a working farm.

This ultrapopular part of Italy sees plenty of visitors, but the fame is deserved and the legions of tourists haven't yet diminished Tuscany's character. Pisa and Siena are historical rivals to Florence, both containing some of the most famous monuments anywhere. Little Lucca, with its massive stone walls topped by green parks, is proud of its long tradition of music, art, and architecture. San Gimignano, a "medieval Manhattan" bristling with more than a dozen stone towers, stands as a reminder of the vibrant trade centers each of these cities once were.

Take the famed Chianti road, winding like a string of spaghetti past dozens of wineries in the hills between Florence and Siena. Stop in Siena for its churches, palaces, art museums, and the lovely Piazza del Campo, site of the Palio horse races. Then head east to enjoy the architecture and festivals of Arezzo, a gateway to the north of Umbria.

In planning a Tuscan holiday, it makes sense to base yourself at one, maybe two, locations, and do day trips. It's much easier to make the commute (either by bus, train, or car) than to change hotels every day. The cities are surprisingly close to one another. For trips to Lucca, Pisa, and San Gimignano, I would either base myself in some countryside lodging or in Florence. Siena is worth several days, both as a destination and as a base to visit Chianti and nearby hill towns.

DON'T LEAVE TUSCANY WITHOUT . . .

WALKING OR BIKING ALONG THE TOP OF LUCCA'S CITY WALLS
The tree-shaded pathway along the top of these mighty 16th-century bastions is among Italy's premier *passeggiate* (promenades).

ATTENDING THE OPERA   Lucca is the home of Puccini, and the Lucchesi love to catch the latest incarnation of their hometown hero's operas in the open air during summer around Torre del Lago, or in autumn at the Teatro del Giglio.

CLIMBING THE LEANING TOWER OF PISA   Sure, it's a bit overpriced, but can you really resist the opportunity to scale the world's most famous architectural mishap?

STEPPING BACK INTO THE MIDDLE AGES IN SAN GIMIGNANO
This hill town bristles with more than a dozen of the kind of stone towers that once dominated the medieval skylines of many Italian cities, but survive only here.

TOURING SIENA'S DUOMO   This magnificent, zebra-striped Gothic cathedral is a storehouse of great works of sculpture and painting, and a work of art in itself.

RELAXING IN THE PIAZZA DEL CAMPO   Siena's central plaza is among Italy's finest. Sit with a gelato and watch mobs of tourists, street musicians, and locals enjoying the scene.

JOINING THE MOBS FOR THE PALIO   Siena hosts famous midsummer horse races. The weeks around the event are alive with many *contrada* (neighborhood) street parties.

WINE-TASTING YOUR WAY THROUGH THE CHIANTI   The vine-draped hills between Florence and Siena contain one of the world's most famous wine-producing regions, with dozens of castle-wineries offering tours, tastings, and some of the best (drinkable) souvenirs in Italy.

VIEWING FRANCESCA'S *LEGEND OF THE TRUE CROSS*   One of the greatest works of Italian art, it's in San Francesco Church in Arezzo.

LUCCA

Lucca is a bite-size city of churches, shops, and gardens, surrounded by a thick circle of walls, that's relatively free of the throngs that at times make even the most beautiful attractions of nearby Florence or Pisa feel like a chore to tour. Though no place in Tuscany could be called "undiscovered," Lucca has somehow managed to retain its historic aura.

The main attractions of Lucca are the walls themselves, arguably the best preserved Renaissance ramparts in the world. Twelve meters (40 ft.) high, 18m (60 ft.) across, and inscribing a 4km (2½ miles) circumference around the historical center, the walls, which once offered protection, are now a recreation area. Topped by trees, walking paths, parks, and playgrounds, this is where locals and visitors come to unwind; you'll see elderly women gossiping, men playing cards on benches, grandchildren picnicking in the shade, and people bicycling everywhere.

The sight from the walls is nearly as striking: a grid-patterned town, laid out by the methodical ancient Romans and characterized by the soaring bell towers and tall, arcaded facades of several Romanesque churches. Off to one side is the Anfiteatro Romano, an oval enclosure of medieval buildings built atop a Roman amphitheater. It makes a certain kind of sense that Lucca's famous son, opera legend Giacomo Puccini, grew up amid all this beauty and drama.

Tuscany & Umbria

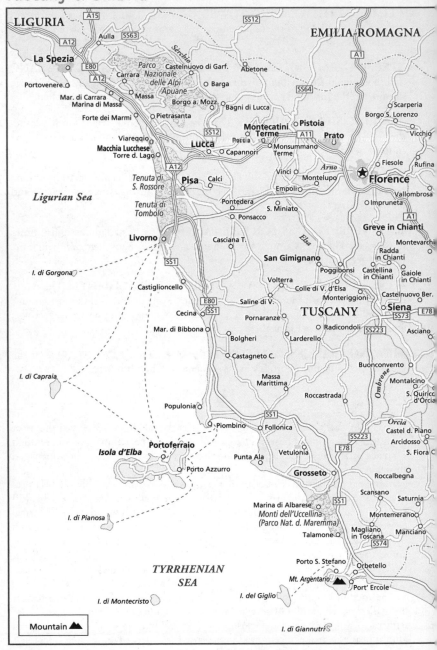

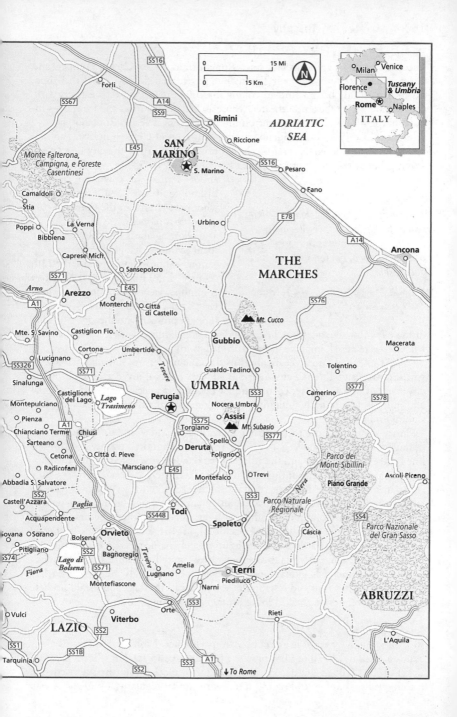

A BRIEF HISTORY OF LUCCA

Lucca has been a significant city since Roman times, when Caesar, Pompey, and Crassus met here to create their Triumvirate government in 56 B.C. At that time, Lucca had already been a Roman colony for 200 years. In the 2nd century A.D., the Romans added the amphitheater, whose arches and columns still form the supports of the medieval buildings surrounding Lucca's oval Teatro Romano piazza.

Lucca's history was also touched by the early days of Christianity. St. Paolino, one of St. Peter's deacons, is said to have brought the faith to the city in A.D. 47, making Lucca the first Tuscan city to be converted. In 588, a wandering Irish abbot settled in town to become Bishop (and later St.) Frediano, for whom the church in the northern part of Lucca is named.

> **"**Lucca . . . that compact and admirable little city, overflowing with everything that makes for ease, for plenty, for beauty, for interest and good example. **"**
>
> —Henry James, *Italian Hours,* 1909

Following the fall of Rome, Lucca spent centuries changing hands between various warlords. It wasn't until the 12th century that Lucca emerged as a free commune, erecting another set of city walls, palaces, and churches as trade brought prosperity to the city. The bulk of the city's Romanesque churches, including San Martino, San Frediano, and San Michele, were raised, improved, and expanded over the next 100 years.

The 1300s saw Lucca get involved in the Guelph versus Ghibelline civil wars wracking Tuscany. Internal city divisions allowed external invaders, including the city states of Pisa and Florence, to conquer Lucca. But Lucca reemerged as a small and independent state, maintaining its freedom over the next 430 years through skillful diplomacy.

Peace enabled Lucca to construct increasingly solid walls, until the present boundary took form between 1544 and 1645. One hundred twenty-six cannons lined these fortifications, and the adjacent parklands were cleared to give the gunners an open line of fire. But the walls never faced the test of invaders. By the time Austrian armies overran northern Italy in the 18th century, improvements in artillery technology had made such battlements irrelevant, and Lucca surrendered, along with its cannons, without a fight. When Napoleon became king of Italy in 1805, he put his sister, Elisa Baciocchi, in charge of Lucca. She freshened up the town, adding gardens and the appropriately named Piazza Napoleone.

Today, Lucca has a vibrant small-city feel amid its historical monuments, palaces, and gardens. Regional food (especially local olive oils and *farro,* a barley-like grain) fills its shops and restaurants, opera fills its theaters, and local Lucchese fill its wide avenues on their evening promenades through town.

LAY OF THE LAND

Reaching Lucca **by train** is pretty easy from Florence. More than 20 trains a day connect the cities in 70 to 90 minutes. The **Lucca train station** (Piazza Ricasoli; ticket office ☎ 0583-467013) is just a couple of blocks from the south edge of the city walls. Trains go to Pisa (30 min.) with similar regularity. While it's a snap

to walk into town (exit the station, turn left, and walk along the walls for 2 blocks to get to the city gate), if you're traveling with heavy luggage, from the train station **city bus nos. 9 and 13** head into the city walls, cut over to the eastern half of the historical center, then turn north (no. 13 continues all the way to Piazza Santa Maria and the tourist office, which in the city's infinite wisdom, they placed clear on the other side of town from the train station), while bus nos. 11 and 12 head into the city center, up to Piazza Napoleone, then cut west along Via Vittorio Emanuele and out of town. There are also plenty of taxis at the train station.

Hourly **Lazzi buses** (☎ 0583-584876; www.lazzi.it) connect Florence and the Lucca station (on Piazzale Verdi, the west end of the historical center) in 75 minutes.

It's less than an hour's drive to Lucca from Florence, about 64km (40 miles) away on the A11 expressway. The commute to Pisa is even shorter, just 24km (15 miles) to the south on SS12. Traffic and parking are restricted inside the city, though free parking can be found on city streets outside the walls.

Lucca's main **tourist office** (Piazza Santa Maria 35; ☎ 0583-919931; www.luccatourist.it and www.turismo.provincia.lucca.it) is located on the south side of the piazza, just inside Porta Santa Maria. It has the usual collection of maps and brochures, and also a bookstore selling the useful English-language *Grapevine* magazine of events and listings for 2€, as well as Internet access (3€ for 30 min.). For an entertaining and informative audio tour of the city, rent headphones from the tourist office for 6€. At a leisurely pace, the tour takes about 2 hours. Lucca has **another tourist office** with similar services in Cortile Carrara, off Palazzo Ducale, facing Piazza Napoleone (☎ 0583-919941). There's also good information on the private site www.in-lucca.it.

If you want to do as the Luchesse do, you may feel inspired to travel around the city—especially the city walls—by bike. **Bikes** are available for rent at two shops next to the main tourist office: **Antonio Poli** (Piazza Santa Maria 42; ☎ 0583-493787; www.biciclettepoli.com) and **Cicli Bizzarri** (Piazza Santa Maria 32; ☎ 0583-496031; www.ciclibizzarri.net). Just about every place in town charges the same 2.50€ per hour, or 13€ per day for basic bicycles, 3.50€ per hour and 18€ per day for mountain bikes.

ACCOMMODATIONS, BOTH STANDARD & NOT

€   The 140-bed **Ostello San Frediano** ★ kids (Via della Cavallerizza 12; ☎ 0583-469957; www.ostellolucca.it; AE, MC, V) is a choice cheap option on the north end of the historical center, a block from Piazza Anfiteatro. It was, at varying times, a convent, a library, and a school before its 2002 renovation and transformation into a clean, character-filled hostel. The wide, tiled hallways and large common rooms echo with footsteps, while the rear garden offers a nice place to relax. Rooms are institutional but ultraclean with new furnishings, and are priced from 18€ per person in an eight-bed dorm without bathroom, 19€ with bathroom, or 48€ for a double with private bathroom. They serve a decent breakfast buffet for 1.60€, and a passable lunch and dinner for 9.50€. Plus, they have beer in the vending machines.

€–€€   Because of the small number of hotels inside the city walls, Lucca is a good place to look into B&Bs, private rooms, and residences. **Casa Alba** ★ (Via Fillungo 142, just off Piazza Anfiteatro; ☎ 0583-495361; www.casa-alba.com; cash only) is a tiny but pleasant guesthouse, and one of the best lodging deals in town. Its clean and well-maintained doubles—each a hodgepodge of furnishings with TV, A/C, and one with a small fridge—cost just 50€ to 80€ per night with bathroom, or save by opting for one of the three rooms that share a bathroom on the hall for a mere 45€ to 65€. ***Bonus:*** Breakfast is included and served in your room. ***Downside:*** It's a third-floor walk-up (53 very steep steps). Note that new owners took over in 2008, so changes are afoot (credit cards may soon be accepted).

€–€€   The six rooms of the **San Frediano** ★ (Via degli Angeli 19; ☎ 0583-469630; www.sanfrediano.com; MC, V) offer much of the authentic, local flavor of a B&B and in low season can be slightly cheaper, with rates ranging from 48€ to 110€ for a double. The rooms are somewhat basic, but the building maintains the feel of its 1600 origins.

€€–€€€   Another solid alternative choice is **Residenza Centro Storico** kids (Corte Portici 16; ☎ 0583-490748; www.affittacamerecentrostorico.com; AE, MC, V), which houses six tidy rental rooms with decent beds, private baths, and minifridges just a few steps from Piazza San Michele; doubles run 50€ to 130€ depending on size, type, season, and how booked the Residenza is.

€€ The rooms are even more basic, but clean, cheap, and central, at **La Camelia** (Piazza San Francesco 35; ☎ 0583-463481; www.affittacamerelacamelia.com; AE, MC, V), where doubles go for 65€ and include breakfast in your room and free parking.

€€ Though technically a hotel, **Albergo San Martino** (Via della Dogana 9; ☎ 0583-469181; www.albergosanmartino.it; AE, MC, V) manages to exude a quaint B&B aura, with a friendly staff and doubles for 80€ to 110€, including a large buffet breakfast.

€€€–€€€€ If you'd rather stay in a more standard lodging, the **Hotel Universo** ★ (Piazza del Giglio 1; ☎ 0583-493678; www.universolucca.com; AE, MC, V) is one of the odder modern-meets-traditional hotels you'll ever see. It combines a classic 19th-century decor in some of the rooms (and the lobby) with futuristic *Jetsons*-like decorating in others. The 143€-to-183€ doubles in the "comfort" category are a little worn around the edges, and some lack air-conditioning, though the hotel says they're upgrading soon (then again, they've been saying that for a few years now). The "superior" doubles (163€–193€) truly are superior, with slick, 21st-century wood paneling and minimalist furniture. Each of the 60 rooms has a grand view either of the cathedral, the tree-lined Piazza Napoleone, or Piazza del Giglio.

€€€€ A definite step up, the **Alla Corte degli Angeli** ★★ (Via degli Angeli 23; ☎ 0583-469204; www.allacortedegliangeli.com; AE, MC, V) has flatscreen TVs to go with the stylishly decorated but still traditional rooms with wood-beam ceilings or *trompe-l'oeil* frescoes; rooms run about 155€ for a double.

DINING FOR ALL TASTES

€–€€ A prime location in front of the cathedral—a lively scene of locals and tourists—and fresh salads and appetizers make **Girovita** ★ 🄺 (Piazza Antelminelli 2; ☎ 0583-469412; summer Tues–Sun 8am–midnight, winter Fri–Sun 8am–8pm; AE, MC, V) a great spot for lunch or an evening *aperitivo* (7:30–9:30pm). Children enjoy the snack menu and frozen fruit drinks, and if they kick up a fuss, their parents can relax—it's noisy enough here to cover all but the loudest tantrums. Almost all dishes are in the 6.50€-to-8€ range, including the large seafood salad and a light veggie pasta.

€€ The one restaurant in town you can't miss is **Buca di Sant Antonio** ★★ (Via della Cervia 1/3, near Piazza S. Michele; ☎ 0583-55881; www.bucadisant antonio.com; Tues–Sat 12:30–3pm and 7:30–10:30pm, Sun 12:30–3pm; reservations highly recommended; AE, MC, V), Lucca's most popular spot for dinner since 1782. It's a homey restaurant hung with hams and pots and pans, with a fireplace in one corner and assorted antique clutter scattered around its warren of rooms. Tops on the menu of characteristic Luccan cuisine is a tummy-warming *pappardelle alla lepre* (wide noodles with wine-stewed hare) for 8.50€, and *petto di faraona all'uva moscato* (breast of guinea fowl with raisins) for 14€. On a cold evening, order the traditional dessert, *castagnaccio,* a rich combination of chestnut flour and ricotta cheese. Most *primi* cost 8€ to 9€; main courses go for between 12€ and 15€.

€€   For a change of pace, try the seafood at **Osteria del Neni** (Via Pescheria 3, between Piazza San Michele and Piazza Napoleone; ☎ 0583-492681; www. leosteriedilucca.com; daily noon–2:30pm and 7:30–11pm, closed Mon in winter; AE, MC, V). The menu varies by season, but usually offers a variety of fresh fish combined with homemade pastas. The *branzino* (sea bass) with pesto is a good combo for 12€, as is the *frutti di mare* (seafood) linguini at 9€. Pastas cost from 7€ to 8€, and *secondi* are slightly more. Summers offer the chance to dine on the restaurant's street-front patios. Even with reservations, expect to wait awhile for your meal at this very popular restaurant.

€€–€€€   The award of most original dining spot in town has to go to the **San Colombano** ★ kids (Baluardo San Colombano 10, across from the train station; ☎ 0583-464641; www.caffetteriasancolombano.it; Tues–Fri 8am–1am, Sat 8am–2am; AE, MC, V), a trendy, ultramodern bunker of an eatery installed in one of the historic bastions of the city walls. It serves as a cafeteria, restaurant, and jazz bar, its personality shifting depending on the time of day. Early on it is a snack shop/gelateria, with a 12€ set-price workmen's menu at lunch on weekdays. At dinner it's a chic restaurant serving such regional specialties as pasta with wild hare, grilled boar, and *zuppa Lucchese. Primi* run 6€ to 12€, *secondi* 9€ to 12€, and there's a traditional set-priced menu at 28€. Later in the evenings it becomes a hopping nightspot. They have, in the past, featured live jazz on Wednesday nights, and hopefully will be doing so again by the time you read this.

WHY YOU'RE HERE: THE TOP SIGHTS & ATTRACTIONS

If you go to Lucca, you are *required* to walk or bike along the **Walls of Lucca** ★★★. It's one of the highlights of a trip to Tuscany. As you saunter along the 4km-wide (2.5-mile) green pathway 12m (40 ft.) above the city, you'll become a voyeur par extraordinaire, peeking over villa walls into elaborate private gardens filled with statuary, watching as the lucky citizens of this town stroll its broad avenues. Join the locals in enjoying a picnic under plentiful shade trees, or let your kids frolic in one of the many playgrounds lining the walls.

Although the only original remaining parts are a few arches embedded in medieval walls and an empty space, the **Anfiteatro Romano (Roman Amphitheater)** ★ is another impressive site, the symmetrical oval of its shell surrounded by a crowd of medieval buildings. In 1830, city rulers cleared out the slums that stood in the middle of the piazza, creating the current scenic photo setting. The best way to see the amphitheater's outline is from the top of the **Torre Guinigi** ★ (Via S. Andrea and Via Chiave d'Oro; ☎ 0583-316846; 3.50€; daily Mar–Sept 9am–8pm, Oct 10am–6pm, Nov–Feb 10am–5:30pm), an odd 45m (150-ft.) tree-topped tower sprouting up in the middle of town. The shade trees on top were planted for the benefit of soldiers standing watch on hot summer days.

The greatest single sight in Lucca is the **Cattedrale di San Martino** ★★ (Piazza San Martino; ☎ 0583-957068 or 0583-490530; www.museocattedralelucca.it; free; summer daily 8:30am–6pm, winter 9am–noon and 3–5pm). Start with the facade, a perfect example of Pisan-Lucchese Romanesque architecture, with its repeating dwarf rows of columns. The exterior columns and atrium have intriguing bas-relief carvings, including scenes from the Bible and a labyrinth symbolic of the difficult journey to salvation. The reliefs over the doors, created in 1205, detail the life of St. Martin, a 4th-century saint famous for sharing his cloak with a beggar (as well as the usual miracles of curing lepers and raising the dead, all recounted on the panels). The interior of the church is a mishmash of styles, ranging from Gothic arches to Renaissance paintings (including a *Last Supper* by Tintoretto) and 19th-century stained glass.

The cathedral's holiest relic is the caged wooden *Volto Santo* crucifix, said to have been miraculously created by Nicodemus, an eyewitness to Jesus on the cross. The crucifix reportedly arrived in Lucca in 782 by similarly miraculous means: Set adrift on a raft to escape Muslim marauders, the statue beached near a small Italian village, where the local bishop, following a vision, put the crucifix on a cart and let oxen take it wherever God meant it to rest. Since its arrival in Lucca, the Volto Santo has been a source of pride for the city, culminating in the September 13 festival in which the crucifix is paraded through town. Art historians think the carving, with its Byzantine and Middle Eastern influences, may have been a 13th-century copy of an 11th-century copy of a Syrian statue from the 8th century (whew!).

The cathedral's other highlight is the 1407 tomb of Ilaria Carretto Guinigi, a stunning 26-year-old woman whose beauty was immortalized in an unusually naturalistic manner (note the graceful flow of her robes) by sculptor Jacopo della Quercia. The small dog at her feet symbolizes fidelity. The famous tomb has now been placed in a side room and there's a 2€ fee to see her marble figure.

Often mistaken for the cathedral, since it's larger and sits in the center of town, the church of **San Michele in Foro** ✹ (Piazza S. Michele; ☎ 0583-48459; free; daily 9am–noon and 3–6pm, to 5pm in winter) has a similar but even more spectacular exterior. Exquisitely detailed columns of every size, shape, and color bedeck the four-tiered facade in a composition that echoes that of the Duomo in Pisa. Note how the facade extends far above the church's roof, a result of ambition outstripping funding, to be topped by a statue of Michael the archangel. The interior can't quite match the outside, but does have a nice Filippino Lippi painting at the far end of the right side of the church, and a fancy organ decorated with fleur-de-lis. For two generations, the Puccini family who lived just down the street (at Corte San Lorenzo 9) served as the church's organists, and the third generation, young Giacomo Puccini, sang in the choir as a boy—quite a musical pedigree for the man who would go on to write *La Bohème, Turnadot, Tosca, Madama Butterfly,* and other immortal operas. The "Foro" part of the church's name comes from the fact that it was built on the original site of a Roman forum.

On the northern edge of the city is the **Church of San Frediano** ✹ (Piazza S. Frediano; ☎ 0583-493627; free; daily 9am–noon and 3–6pm, to 5pm in winter) with a glittering 13th-century mosaic on its facade. Among the treasures inside are an elaborate baptismal font (dismantled and hidden away in the 18th c. and only reassembled a few decades ago), and a chapel (second on the left) with magnificent fresco cycles by Amico Aspertini (1508–09) on *The Miracles of St. Frediano* and the *Arrival in Lucca of the Volto Santo.* Just beyond the baptismal font is a chapel containing the mummified body of St. Zita inside a glass case. This 13th-century maid was caught smuggling bread out of her employer's house to

Nature's Cathedral

The **Grotta del Vento (Cave of the Winds)** ★ 🎈 (Loc. Fornovolasco; ☎ 0583-722024; www.grottadelvento.com; 7.50€ for 1-hr. tour, 12€ for 2 hr., and 17€ for 3 hr., 20% discount for kids under 11; daily 1-hr. tours leave every hour 10am–noon and 2–6pm; 2-hr. tours leave at 11am, 3, 4, and 5pm; 3-hr. tours leave at 10am and 4pm; Nov 2–Mar 31 the longer itineraries are available only on Sun), an hour's drive north from Lucca, will add a nice dash of variety to any Tuscan vacation (your kids especially might enjoy this break from art and history). The stalactites and stalagmites are equal to any Gothic church spire, and the open caverns are as voluminous as the interior of a cathedral. In fact, ceilings of some rooms tower over 60m (200 ft.) above visitors, with every imaginable shape of protruding rock formations. For more wonders, there are winding underground rivers and reflective lakes and rooms with such appropriate names as "Giant's Abyss" and "The Hall of Wonders."

The caves drop about 135m (450 ft.) underground through more than 8km (5 miles) of passageways. But you don't have to be an experienced spelunker to enjoy a trip through them; the park has created tourist-friendly concrete pathways with guide rails along well-lit passages. Exploration is by guided tour only.

To get there, take the SSN12 Abetone/Brennero as far as Ponte a Moriano (8.5km/5¼ miles). Then cross the Serchio River and proceed along the main road, through the valley, as far as Gallicano (another 28km/17 miles). After passing Lake Trombacco, take the road for Fornovolasco at the 44km mark. Continuing uphill, cross another three valleys, and you've reached it.

---

feed beggars. To escape punishment for stealing, she told guards that she only had flowers hidden in her apron, and when the guards pulled her apron aside, the bread had miraculously turned into roses. The body of this patron saint of maids and ladies-in-waiting is paraded through town on her feast day of April 26. The church itself gets its name from the wandering Irish abbot who helped to develop Christianity in Lucca in the 6th century. Frediano is buried beneath the altar.

ATTENTION, SHOPPERS!

Lucca offers a wealth of shopping opportunities along Via Fillungo and Via Santa Lucia: Olive oil, jewelry, chocolates, perfumes, and wines are among the Luccan treats. A few worth mentioning:

- A branch of the historical **Officina Profumo di Santa Maria Novella** (Via Vittorio Veneto 29; ☎ 0583-490850; www.smnovella.it) sells soaps, colognes, and Vinegar of the Seven Thieves, a cure for "fainting fits."
- **Cioccolateria Caniparoli** (Via San Paolino 96; ☎ 0583-53456) offers some of the best chocolate in the region.
- **Lucca in Tavola** (Via San Paolino 130; ☎ 0583-581002) has a wide selection of famous regional olive oils.

◆ **Carli Pietro** (Via Fillungo 95; ☎ 0583-491119) is a jewelry store–cum–museum, with fresco-covered walls and jewel-filled display cases. You may not be able to afford anything here, but it offers exquisite window-shopping.

◆ The **English Bookshop** (Borgo Giannotti 493; ☎ 0583-331169) can be a good spot to buy detailed area guides, or to pick up some summer reading.

NIGHTLIFE

A city that was home to Paganini, Puccini, Boccherini, and Catalani and others obviously makes a good place to hear some classical music or attend the opera. The **Teatro Del Giglio** (Piazza del Giglio 13/15; ☎ 0583-467521; www.teatrodel giglio.it) is where Rossini premiered *William Tell* in 1831. Today it has a full opera season running from October to April. Tickets range from 20€ to 60€. Aside from opera, the theater also hosts plays and dance performances.

For more music, the University of Cincinnati College Conservatory of Music, of all places, coordinates the Opera Theater and Music Festival of Lucca in tandem with its study-abroad program. Visitors can watch rehearsals and outdoor performances around town from June to July. Check **www.ccmoperalucca.org**.

PISA

Even a lifetime of seeing images of the famous Leaning Tower of Pisa doesn't quite prepare you for your first sight of this tourist icon. Up close it looks like a giant white cylinder of a spaceship that has crash-landed at an awkward angle in a green field and discharged an army of mimes. People of all sizes, ages, and races stand in front of the tower in goofy positions. Some attempt the "Look, ma, I'm holding up the tower" pose, with outstretched arms "catching" the leaning tower in the background. Others go for the "push," the "foot save," or the "ow, it just fell on my head" pantomime.

The mob of tourists, the hot dog stands, the aggressive souvenir peddlers—these all point to the fact that Pisa is one of Italy's oldest tourist traps. But you should still go here, not only to see the Leaning Tower but also to tour the four lesser known, though equally impressive, monuments in the appropriately named Campo di Miracoli (Field of Miracles).

That being said, the city doesn't hold much beyond this central area to attract visitors. If you're pressed for time, do what 90% of tourists do and make Pisa into a day trip while staying in Florence (about 1 hr. away) or Lucca (30 min. away). But on your way out, try to stop at the Piaggio factory, birthplace of the Vespa, just for proof that Italians really can design stuff the right way.

A BRIEF HISTORY OF PISA

Pisa was once a major economic, political, cultural, and sea-faring power—before it experienced a string of disasters. Its harbor and river silted up, it lost a couple of wars, Florence conquered it, the economy tanked, and suddenly all it had left was a tower that couldn't stand straight and a few churches. In a final insult, during World War II Allied troops firebombed several of its monuments. (You really have to feel a little sorry for this faded empire.) Nowadays Pisa is a lively university town and industrial center, with an international airport and transport hubs, and a crooked bell tower that draws millions of tourists each year, but it's still just a shadow of its former self.

In its heyday in the 1100s, Pisa was the terror of Tuscany. It conquered large areas of the region, including Lucca, in a series of brutal wars. Pisa was a major naval power as well, right up there with Genova, Venice, Bari, and Amalfi, controlling Mediterranean sea lanes and expanding its empire to Corsica and Sardinia. But following a disastrous naval battle with Genoa in 1284, its sea power began to wane, and with it much of its military might.

By the time of the first wave of tourists to Italy in the 1800s, Pisa was a desolate, half-empty city teeming with beggars camped around its monuments. But the city's university, founded in 1343, remained open during all those years, and has maintained Pisa's reputation as a progressive, activist city. Native son Galileo Galilei was one of those overeducated troublemakers; at the Leaning Tower and the Duomo, he conducted experiments disproving Church-endorsed "science," and, in turn, got in trouble with the authorities.

However, Pisa's years of medieval prosperity lasted long enough to fund the construction of the major edifices in the city during the 12th and 13th centuries, including the Dumo (cathedral) and its attendant structures: the Battistero (baptistery), the Camposanto (cemetery), and the Campanile (bell tower), which was as lovely as it was, it turns out, poorly designed; it began titling before they even finished construction. The Pisan Romanesque style of architecture, with its colorful columns, striped decor, and repeating arches, permeates Tuscany, and can be seen in Lucca, Siena, and even some early structures in archrival Florence.

LAY OF THE LAND

Pisa's nearby **Galileo Galilei Airport** (☎ 050-849300; www.pisa-airport.com) receives many regional and international flights (mostly from elsewhere in Europe, though in 2007 Delta began direct flights from New York). The city center is just a 5-minute, 1.10€ train trip or a 7€ cab ride away.

Pisa is a convenient 45- to 60-minute train ride from Florence, with more than 40 high-speed trains a day. Rome is a 3-hour train journey. Lucca is a half-hour commute, with trains on that line stopping at the San Rossore station, which is closer to the Campo dei Miracoli than Pisa's Centrale station, where most of the intercity trains stop. The Centrale station is nearly a mile away from the campo, so consider a taxi (about 6€) or a bus (no. 3, 4, or A).

It's about a 90-minute drive (depending on traffic) to Pisa from Florence via the autostrada. Lucca is a half-hour trip via the ASS12. Parking in the historic district is restricted, but meters can be found just outside the walls for .50€ to 1€ per hour, or at nearby lots for the same rates. Hotels will often let visitors use (either free or for a charge) an overnight permit for street parking in the historical district.

Pisa's **main tourist office** (Piazza Arcivescovado 8; ☎ 050-560464) is on the north side of the campo, next to the Leaning Tower ticket office. It has some limited information and pamphlets, but on the whole it isn't too helpful. The lockers for the Tower (no bags are allowed during the climb) are behind the ticket counter, so the place can get pretty packed with people either waiting for their tour, or coming back to grab their stuff. Another tourist office with similar brochures is at the train station.

Pisa

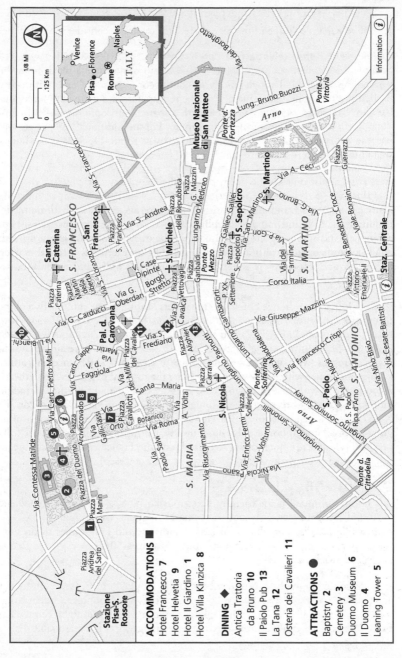

ACCOMMODATIONS ■
Hotel Francesco **7**
Hotel Helvetia **9**
Hotel Il Giardino **1**
Hotel Villa Kinzica **8**

DINING ◆
Antica Trattoria
da Bruno **10**
Il Paiolo Pub **13**
La Tana **12**
Osteria dei Cavalieri **11**

ATTRACTIONS ●
Baptistry **2**
Cemetery **3**
Duomo Museum **6**
Il Duomo **4**
Leaning Tower **5**

ACCOMMODATIONS, BOTH STANDARD & NOT

It's unlikely that you'll spend the night here, but if you do, consider the following:

€–€€   The **Hotel Helvetia** (Via Don G. Boschi 31; ☎ 050-553084; www.pisa online.it/hotelhelvetia; cash only) is a good cheap option just a block from the Campo dei Miracoli. Though utterly simple (decor begins and ends with a few framed prints, a ceiling fan, and a TV), the rooms start at a mere 62€ for a double with bathroom (45€ for a double with a shared bathroom on the hall), and 100€ for a four-person room with bathroom. For an additional 5€ per person, you can enjoy breakfast in a colorfully painted side room. Don't miss the hotel's small but lush interior garden, which has a Thai temple.

€€–€€€   Just outside the walls, behind the Baptistery, the pleasant **Hotel Il Giardino** ★ 🧒 (Via della Cavallerizza 12; ☎ 050-562101; www.pisaonline.it/ giardino; AE, MC, V) contains 16 basic but clean rooms, each with bathroom, air-conditioning, TV, and minibar (doubles 90€–110€). The furniture consists of achingly bland and aging modular units, but the owners do try to jazz it up with wildly patterned bedspreads and original artwork on the walls. "It's like staying in a small and exclusive art gallery," the owners say. Well, almost. Breakfast is included in the rate.

€€   A flurry of midrange hotels line the streets leading to the campo. Two of the nicer ones are **Hotel Francesco** ★ (Via Santa Maria 129; ☎ 050-555453; www. hotelfrancesco.com; AE, MC, V) and **Hotel Villa Kinzica** ★ (Piazza Arcivescovado 2; ☎ 050-560419; www.hotelvillakinzica.it; AE, MC, V). Both have air-conditioning in all rooms, with doubles ranging from 80€ to 110€. The Francesco features a common terrace with lovely views (including the top half of the Leaning Tower), a good lounge with free Internet access, friendly management by the Corradino family, and an airy breakfast area. Though a bit somber in mood and decor, the Kinzica has one selling point: killer views of the Leaning Tower from most of its guest rooms. Those rooms are also more upscale (furnishings with a bit more frilly personality), and the hotel offers free breakfast (the Francesco doesn't do breakfast) and free street parking (an 8€ charge at the Francesco).

DINING FOR ALL TASTES

€   Locals dominate at the friendly, boisterous **La Tana** ★ 🧒 (Via San Frediano 6; ☎ 050-580540; Mon–Sat noon–3pm and 7–10:30pm; closed Aug; AE, MC, V), with whole families crowding into large booths around long tables to dig into inexpensive but tasty *primi* averaging about 3.50€ to 4.50€, *secondi* at 5€ to 6€, and pizzas from 4€ to 8€.

€   For some late-night eats and a beer, try **Il Paiolo Pub** ★ (Via Curtatone e Montanara 9; ☎ 050-42528; daily 7:30am–2am; MC, V). A popular student hang-out, it stays open until 2am, with the kitchen serving until midnight. Simple but fresh *primi* average 5.50€; *secondi* are in the 9€ range. Beer is a reasonable 4€ for a large glass.

€–€€   The kitchen at **Osteria dei Cavalieri** (Via San Frediano 16, near Piazza dei Cavalieri; ☎ 050-580858; www.osteriacavalieri.pisa.it; Mon–Fri 12:30–2pm,

Mon–Sat 7:45–10pm; closed Aug and Dec 30–Jan 7; AE, MC, V) specializes in elegant and slightly nouveau presentations of classic Tuscan dishes. They offer a variety of set-priced menus, including three-course meals devoted variously to seafood (32€), meat dishes (30€), and even—unusual in Italy—vegetarian dishes (26€). (A la carte, *primi* cost 7€–9€, *secondi* 11€–15€.) Also available are several tasty 11€ *piatti unici* (single plates) at lunch time: steak with grilled vegetables and baked *scamorza* (smoked cheese), *osso buco* with saffron rice, or gnocchi under tomato sauce with grilled salmon. They do try to move people in and out quickly, but that means the service is fairly swift.

€€   Homey **Antica Trattoria da Bruno** ★ (Via Luigi Bianchi 12; ☎ 050-560818; www.pisaonline.it/trattoriadabruno; Wed–Mon noon–3pm, Wed–Sun 7–10:30pm; reservations recommended; AE, MC, V) is always packed for its tasty Pisan specialties and location about 270m (900 ft.) from the Leaning Tower (through the city gate and just beyond the town walls). Pots and pans hang from the ceiling, the walls are cluttered with family pictures, and the atmosphere is chaotic and friendly. Try the excellent Pisan *pasta e ceci* (with garbanzo beans) or the *baccalà con porri*, a salt cod with tomatoes and leeks, which tastes much better than it sounds. *Primi* run from 10€ to 12€, *secondi* from 15€ to 18€.

WHY YOU'RE HERE: THE TOP SIGHTS & ATTRACTIONS

The **Campo di Miracoli** is where you want to be in Pisa. This geometrically perfect, bright green "field of miracles" hugging the inside of the city walls on the north end of the historical center has the big four attractions: the Leaning Tower, the Baptistery, the Camposanto, and the Cathedral. Locals often refer to the area more prosaically as Piazza del Duomo.

Obviously, you've come here primarily to see the **Campanile (Leaning Tower)** ★★★ (☎ 050-560547 or 050-3872210; www.opapisa.it; 15€ plus 2€ reservation fee; daily Mar 21 to mid-June and Sept 5–30 8:30am–8:30pm, mid-June to Sept 4 8:30am–11pm, Oct 9am–7pm, Nov–Feb 10am–5pm, Mar 1–13 9am–6pm, Mar 14–20 9am–7pm). The experience of climbing the 300 skewed steps to the 56m-tall (185-ft.) summit is slightly claustrophobic and tiring, but not to be missed. Millions of tourists have created curved grooves in the middle of each step, making the marble stairs smooth and slippery. Walking up the stairs gives you the feeling of being on a listing ship at sea, and you almost hesitate to touch the downward-facing wall for fear of helping topple the tower.

Guards strictly enforce the 30-minute limit on visits, herding visitors up the steps and allowing them only a couple of intermediate stops on balconies for views. Once you're on top, the countdown begins: When your time is up, you'll be brought down again. To be fair, the time allotted is more than enough for everyone but die-hard engineering or architectural students.

The views from the top of the tower—taking in the old city and the mountains in the distance—are spectacular. Given the 4.5m (15-ft.) slant from the perpendicular, it's hard to believe this massive tower is secure as you peek over the edge. But it's actually more solid than ever (see "The Tipsy Tower," below).

If you want to make the climb, it's best to reserve in advance. Tickets really should be booked at least 15 days ahead of time, though it is often possible to show up and purchase a ticket on the same day (less true in summer), but arrive before 9am or else most (if not all) of the tour times will be sold out. The late closing

Buying Tickets to the Sites of the Campo di Miracoli

If you plan to enter more than two sites, you'll save money by purchasing a single ticket that covers every major tourist attraction except the biggie, the Leaning Tower. Unfortunately, the way the tickets are priced is needlessly complicated. The simple version: for entry to the Baptistery, the Camposanto, or the Museo dell'Opera alone, the price is 5€ each. For entry to two of the above sites, the charge is 6€, and for all three plus the Cathedral it's 10€. Tickets can be purchased at the office at the north end of the piazza. For more information, see **www.opapisa.it**.

Note: The Sinopie Museum (with the preparatory sketches of the Camposanto murals) closed indefinitely in 2006. When it does reopen (anybody's guess), its entry times and admission will be linked in some typically convoluted fashion to the rest of the group.

---

times in summer do allow for more tour options for last-minute planners, but obviously your views won't be as spectacular.

Bags are absolutely not allowed on the climb up the tower, and must be left in lockers at the hectic tourist office north of the tower. Children under 8 also aren't allowed up the tower (though it is not recommended to leave them in the lockers). Arrive at the ticket office an hour before your reserved tour time to pick up your ticket—and woe betide you if you've lost your receipt; it nearly takes a papal decree to get the thing reissued.

The Leaning Tower overshadows (literally) the other fine sites in the campo. But you should take time to visit the **Cathedral** ★★ (☎ 050-560547; www. opapisa.it; 2€ or as part of cumulative campo ticket; daily Mar 21–Sept 10am–8pm, Mar 1–13 10am–6pm, Mar 14–20 and Oct 10am–7pm, Nov–Feb 10am–1pm and 2–7pm), a construction (completed 1064–1275) that displays all the famous characteristics of Pisan architecture, from the multicolored, multishaped columns of the facade to the Moorish-influenced marble tiling (black and white stripes around the building). The cavernous interior is nearly 120m (400 ft.) from end to end, with more than 60 columns supporting the building's weight. Notable attractions are Giovanni Pisano's pulpit (the fire-damaged panels were restored and reassembled in the 20th-c.), Cimabue's 13th-century Christ mosaic, and large but the otherwise unassuming 16th-century lamp hanging low by the altar. This is the light that supposedly intrigued Galileo during a boring sermon one day. The lamp was bumped and began to swing side to side, and Galileo began the calculations that led to his famous formulas describing pendular motion.

The north side of the piazza has the giant **Camposanto (Cemetery)** ★★ (☎ 050-560547; www.opapisa.it; 5€ or as part of cumulative ticket; daily Mar 21–Sept 8am–8pm; Nov–Feb daily 10am–5pm, Mar 1–13 9am–6pm, Mar 14–20 and Oct 9am–7pm). Designed by Giovanni di Simone in 1278 to contain soil brought back by crusaders from Cavalry, the site of Jesus' crucifixion, it was the chic place for noble burials. To make their final resting places even more impressive, locals appropriated the sarcophagi of ancient Romans. Now the long hallways are filled with rows of these tombs, while dozens of skull-and-crossbones memorial blocks line the floors. The walls of the building were covered in extensive frescoes until 1944, when a massive fire (accidentally started by Allied bombing) torched the structure. Photos from that time are on display in a northern room. Thankfully, one set of frescoes survived, including the series *Triumph of Death, Last Judgment,* and the *Inferno.* These soaring pieces depict aerial battles between flying angels and devils, a giant Godzilla-like devil in hell, and tough angels at the Last Judgment knocking people into line. Also note the nobles on horseback holding their noses in the *Triumph of Death* as they confront three rotting corpses in the ground—the fresco was done in 1398, only months after the Black Death had run rampant through Tuscany.

The giant orange-juicer-shaped **Baptistery** ✯ (all information same as for Camposanto) is the largest of its kind in Italy (at 105m/350 ft.). Construction began in 1152, and improvements continued through the 1300s. Inside, the Baptistery is sparely decorated, with the waiflike St. John statue in the center of the room. If the pulpit looks vaguely familiar, it's because its panels were carved by Nicola Pisano from 1255 to 1260 and served as a model for those that he and his son Giovanni would produce in Siena and elsewhere, culminating 50 years later in Giovanni's masterpiece a few hundred yards away in Pisa's Duomo. The other notable quality of the Baptistery is its echoing acoustics, which you can test with an "accidental" cough or two while standing in the center of the room.

The Birthplace of Italian Scooters

Ancient Italy may have been obsessed with art and architecture, but as anyone who's driven its highways knows, modern Italians are obsessed with speed. And as anyone who's attempted to cross a street in Italy knows, they're even more obsessed with *motorini* (scooters)—most especially that most classic and curvaceous of scooters, the Vespa, which are manufactured just outside Pisa in the town of Pontedera. That yen for everything shiny, metallic, and turbo-charged is on display at **Museo Piaggio** (Viale Rinaldo Piaggio 7, Pontedera; ☎ 0587-27171; www.museo piaggio.it; free; Wed–Sat 10am–6pm), a factory museum that tells the story of Rinaldo Piaggio. Piaggio launched his engineering business in 1888, at the age of 20, and soon rose to the forefront of Italian industry, going from ship fittings to railway cars and steam ships, and finally in 1941 to that most-Italian form of transportation, the Vespa. (Be sure to check out the Vespa Alpha designed for a 1960s spy movie. In the film at least, it could be converted into a submarine and a helicopter, which are pretty good dealer options for a scooter.) Along with the many Vespas, there's an impressive collection of Gilera motorcycles and Piaggio ships and planes.

The Tipsy Tower

It seemed like a good idea at the time. Construction began on a perfectly straight tower in 1173. For a dozen years, as three levels were completed, you can imagine the conversations: "Call me crazy, but I think the thing is leaning . . .." By 1185, people had concluded that the tower was definitely tilting, and they halted construction to ponder the matter.

In 1275, after nearly a century of pondering, architects decided that rather than try to correct the tilt, they would build the next levels tilted in the opposite direction. This goofy solution now gives the tower a slight banana shape. By 1284, construction was halted again. In 1360, the belfry was added, of course leaning in yet another direction.

The 14,500-ton marble structure increased its tilt by about a millimeter a year, slowly sinking into the soft, sandy soil around it. In 1838, engineers dug a basin around the entrance because the doors had completely settled underground. They also poked around the foundations and decided to try pumping out groundwater, but that only served to accelerate the tilt.

By 1990, following the fatal collapse of a nearby church tower, authorities decided to close the Leaning Tower and deal with the issue. The top was leaning 4.5m (15 ft.) from the vertical, and with nearly a million visitors a year, they didn't want a disaster. So engineers stacked 900 tons of lead weights at the base, opposite the tilt, to even out the pressures, and wrapped huge steel hoops around the lower level to support the stressed marble. Then engineers drilled the northern grounds to remove silt and earth to counteract the tilt and solidify the earth below. Locals worried that the engineers would do too much, and fix the tilt altogether, killing their tourist industry.

Pisa reopened its tower at the end of 2001 after 11 years and over $30 million of investment. The result? The tower has reversed its lean to about 4m (14 ft.)—the same angle it had in 1838—but it should remain that way for the next 300 years.

Unknown to most visitors is the fact that most of the outdoor statues on the campo's buildings are reproductions. You can see the originals up close and personal at the **Museo dell'Opera** ★ 🎒 (all information same as for Camposanto). The museum has a kid-friendly video kiosk with interactive displays about the statues and monuments outside. You can zoom in and out, and spin the displays for 360-degree views—a cheap way to duplicate the tower-top perspective. Each room also has English descriptions of the works of art and artifacts. The items include relics and tapestries from the piazza's monuments, as well as trophies brought back from the Crusades. The building also has a good "poor man's" view of the piazza from its upper balcony.

SAN GIMIGNANO

San Gimignano once had a skyline that boasted more than 70 towers, with competing business, military, and family interests controlling trade routes through the Tuscan plains. This small town retains its unique and ancient urban character even though little more than a dozen of those towers remain. The exact number of towers is a popular debate topic in town, and the count varies from 12 to 17, depending largely upon whom you ask and what you consider constitutes a "tower"—half the houses in town are essentially the lopped-off, three- to four-story stumps of what were once tall towers.

You can easily cover the city in a day trip from Florence or Siena, and since so many tourists do so, San Gimignano has become perhaps Tuscany's greatest tourist trap after Pisa—each day hundreds of visitors are stuck for hours within the town walls waiting for the call back to their bus in a remote parking lot. The church has an electric turnstile for reading tickets, the main square hosts a tasteless torture museum, and streets are jammed with shops filled with every massproduced trinket imaginable, including an armory's worth of blunted replica medieval weapons. (Of course, I pooh-pooh that now; when I visited San Gimignano for the first time, aged 12 and deep into Tolkein, I though I had found a portal to Middle Earth and somehow convinced my parents to let me buy a pocket-sized flail.)

All that said, San Gimignano manages to keep some of its 1,000-year-old character despite the tourist influx (especially for those who overnight here and experience the city without its throngs of visitors). Many family-run restaurants in town serve traditional Tuscan specialties with San Gimignano's underrated white wines (which were the first whites in Italy to receive DOCG status). The summit of Torre Grossa offers postcard views of Tuscan farmland unchanged for centuries. The less touristed Sant'Agostino allows visitors to examine its frescoes without a prepaid ticket, and old men still assemble in the shade of the arches of Piazza del Duomo to have their breakfast and share their opinions on the state of the world.

A BRIEF HISTORY OF SAN GIMIGNANO

San Gimignano takes its name from the bishop who is said to have saved the town from Attila the Hun in the 5th century by clever diplomacy. By the 10th century, San Gimignano (the town) consisted of a fortified castle surrounded by a small village. It wasn't until the 12th and 13th centuries that the towers and town walls began to appear in great height and quantity.

As with many Italian hill towns, warring factions within San Gimignano battled each other through the 12th and 13th centuries in continuous power struggles. The towers served not only as defense fortifications but as symbols of prestige—and even as a means for drying the dyed textiles from which many of the families built their wealth. The Black Death of 1348 not only cut the town's population in half, but it also wiped out the pilgrim and merchant trade from which San Gimignano made much of its money. Florence conquered the weakened city in 1353 so easily that the conquerors didn't bother destroying the defensive towers as they did in many other cities. A couple of more visits by the Black Death, in 1464 and 1631, ensured that San Gimignano never quite got on its feet again, leaving it a backwater city of crumbling towers and poor villagers for hundreds of years.

It wasn't until the mid–20th century that tourism revitalized the town. Today, San Gimignano has leveraged its lively tourist trade into a city filled with sightseeing, dining, and festivals throughout the year. It's definitely worth at least an afternoon visit to walk the winding medieval streets under the watch of the last of the towers.

LAY OF THE LAND

Probably the easiest way to reach San Gimignano is by an organized tour from Florence or Siena. You won't have to deal with parking (which is impossible), and you can drink as much as you want with your meals. Virtually every tour operator in Florence has some kind of San Gimignano trip, and you should be able to easily book one at your hotel or a travel agency near your hotel.

If you decide to drive here for an overnight visit (highly recommended), you'll find San Gimignano just 13km (8 miles) from the Poggibonsi exit on the autostrada/SS2 between Florence and Siena, about 48km (30 miles) from Florence, 32km (20 miles) from Siena. Parking is not allowed within San Gimignano's city walls, but if you have a hotel in town, you can drive your car to the door (very carefully—the city has narrow streets) to unload your luggage. Parking is available at pay lots outside of town, or for free along the roads approaching the walls.

While San Gimignano isn't on a train line, many buses make the 10-minute trip from the station in Poggibonsi into town. Trains take from 30 to 45 minutes from Siena, and about an hour from Florence.

San Gimignano has an extremely helpful **tourist office** (Piazza Duomo 1; ☎ 0577-940008; www.sangimignano.com), which carries lists of local apartment rentals, wine tours, and events. It also offers a worthwhile audioguide city tour for 5€. The self-paced program gives visitors an extensive historical and architectural guide of the city from more than 40 viewpoints, covering everything from the usual tourist spots to deserted alleyways. The whole program takes about 2 hours.

ACCOMMODATIONS, BOTH STANDARD & NOT

If you're having trouble finding a room, try any of the following resources. The website of the **tourist office** (www.sangimignano.com) links to 19 hotels, 47 rental rooms, and 50 *agriturismi* (farm stays) in and around town. The **Association of Non-Hotel Structures in San Gimignano** (Via Cellole 81; ☎ 349-8821565; www.asangimignano.com), a title that sounds better in Italian, is the most convenient to use because, on its website, the results page for a given search shows photos and gives you the rates at 31 rental rooms and B&Bs (18 of which are in the city center; most range from 21€–35€ per person), 7 *agriturismi* (25€–45€ per person), and a couple of villas (125€ per person). The **Siena Hotels Promotion** group has a satellite office in San Gimignano (Via San Giovanni 125; ☎ 0577-940809; www.hotelsiena.com) and also represents 19 hotels, 35 rental rooms, 8 *agriturismi*, and even a nearby campground—but its online search engine, while it does provide photos, won't give you prices until you plug in dates, which makes it harder to compare options instantly (though does have the benefit of confirming availability). Also, don't forget the 55€ doubles available at Ristorante il Pino (under "Dining for All Tastes," below).

Most reliable, however, is to book a spiffy apartment managed by a local woman known simply as Carla and her English-speaking son Francesco (who is involved in the Association of Non-Hotel Structures, mentioned above). Through **Busini Rossi Carla** ★★ (Via Cellole 81; ☎ 0577-955041 or 349-4967362 or, for Francesco, 349-8821565; www.accommodation-sangimignano.it; cash only), Carla offers eight apartments, starting at 80€ to 150€ per night for two people (490€–940€ per week). My favorite is the Tortoli Palace Apartment on the upper level of a 14th-century tower with an eye-popping view of the Piazza della Cisterna. It offers a full kitchen, dining room, comfortable bedrooms (containing up to five beds), and views of the countryside and main square. They also rent nine rooms in town (55€–100€), and have a newly restored farmhouse called Podere Ponte a Nappo, just outside San Gimignano, with two apartments, three bedrooms, free parking, and a barbecue pit (prices the same as in town). Part of the fun is meeting Carla, who often treats guests to a glass of *vino* on the square after they settle into their temporary homes. Book far in advance; these apartments get many return renters.

€€   Those on a tight budget can also visit the friendly nuns at the **Foresteria del Monastero San Girolamo** ★ 🧒 (Via Folgore 32, just behind Porta San Jacopo; ☎ 0577-940573; cash only). For 30€ per person, you'll get breakfast and a bed in one of the nine basic but clean rooms. Most rooms have three to four beds, and they generally don't place random people together, so a family has a good chance of snagging an empty four-bed room (plus, kids get in for half price). Free parking is available in a dirt lot across the street. It's also handy in January and February, when most hotels in town are closed (this religious guesthouse only closes to the general public for the weeks around Easter and Christmas, when guests are limited to those seeking a prayer retreat).

€€–€€€   The choice hotel in the central Piazza della Cisterna is the **Hotel Leon Bianco** ★ (Piazza della Cisterna 8; ☎ 0577-941294; www.leonbianco.com; AE, MC, V). This crisp and clean refurbished 14th-century palazzo has 25 inviting rooms with modern fixtures combined with stone arches, wood-beamed ceilings, and terra-cotta tiles. Standard doubles run from 85€ to 115€; don't plunk down 110€ to 135€ for the Superior rooms—they're merely larger and come with a minibar. What you really want to be sure of it is that you ask for either a room with a view of the postcard-perfect piazza out front, or one on the back with a vista over terra-cotta roof tiles to the countryside beyond (rather than one overlooking the glassed-in courtyard). The hotel even has a mini–fitness center, an Internet point and Wi-Fi in the communal areas (the signal stretches to some rooms), a pleasant deck for breakfast, and a five-person Jacuzzi on a terrace.

€€–€€€   My second choice for hotel digs is the **Hotel Bel Soggiorno** (Via San Giovanni 91; ☎ 0577-940375; www.hotelbelsoggiorno.it; AE, MC, V), perched at the top of the southern walls of the city. The junior suites (120€–150€ per night) with balcony views of the countryside are the top choices, but there are also nice standard doubles with a street view for 95€, and doubles with a terrace and country view for 110€. Rooms are modern and spotless, if somewhat lacking in character. The restaurant serves dinner and boasts fine panoramic views as well.

DINING FOR ALL TASTES

€–€€€   A brasserie, set in an actual castle, complete with rib-vaulted ceilings and a terrace with great countryside view, the **Ristorante La Griglia** (Via San Matteo 34/36; ☎ 0577-940005; www.sangimignano.com/lagriglia; Fri–Wed noon–10:30pm; MC, V) is a lovely place to dine. Its lively bar is about the only thing going for nightlife in this quiet town, so dine late and then stay to socialize. If you want to avoid the *coperto* (cover) and service charges, take a table near the bar and order from the brasserie menu: Pizzas and pastas are 6€ to 8€; a half chicken, roasted, at 10€ is the most expensive item on the *secondi* menu. The interior restaurant offers more gourmet fare with wild boar and truffle covered pastas (*primi* 6€ 17€, *secondi* about 10€–18€).

€€   Very traditional Tuscan fare, in a medieval-barrel vaulted room, is paired with '80s pop music and contemporary paintings at the confused but still charming **Osteria delle Catene** ★★ (Via Mainardi 18; ☎ 0577-941966; Thurs–Tues 12:30–2pm and 7:30–9:30pm; sometimes closed Dec to mid-Mar; AE, MC, V). Try the *salsicce con fagioli all'uccelletto* (sausage with stewed tomatoes and beans) or *penne al porro* (penne covered in a cheese and cream sauce); both are delightful. Or go for one of the prix-fixe thematic menus, such as one dedicated to the *zafferano* (saffron) for which San Gimignano has been famous since the Middle Ages (21€), or one devoted entirely to *cacciagione* (game; 31€). Even the simpler, 13€ fixed-price menu will give you a good combination of flavors, accompanied by local cheeses, a light pasta, and a pastry dessert. (None of the fixed-price menus includes wine.) If you choose to go a la carte, *primi* range from 9€ to 11€, *secondi* from 12€ to 14€.

€€   Since 1929, friendly **Ristorante il Pino** ★ (Via Cellolese 6; ☎ 0577-940415; www.ristoranteilpino.it; Sat–Wed 12:15–2pm and 7:30–10pm, Fri 7:30–10pm; AE, MC, V) has served regional specialties at candlelit tables in brick-arched rooms tucked into a medieval building. *Primi* range from 12€ to 14€, *secondi* from 14€ to 18€. Try the cannelloni with goat cheese and pepper sauce or the roasted duck with truffles and potato cake. Happily, *coperto* and service charge are included in the prices. Upstairs are rooms at 55€ a night. (The rooms are actually quite nice for the price, with whitewashed walls and wood-beamed ceilings.)

WHY YOU'RE HERE: THE TOP SIGHTS & ATTRACTIONS

The main attraction is the town itself, and especially the towers poking above the winding medieval streets of this hilltop city. The Piazza della Cisterna, in particular, is a lovely place in which to linger, its central 13th-century well framed by imposing stone buildings unchanged since the Renaissance. You'll also want to walk through the gardens around the **Rocca,** the ruinous old fortress from the 1350s now turned into a (free) public park, and climb the ramparts for view of the countryside in one direction, and in the other a panorama of the town's towers worthy of printing on a postcard.

The **Torre Grossa** ★★ (Piazza del Duomo; ☎ 0577-990312; 4€ joint admission to Torre and Museo Civico; Mar–Oct 9:30am–7pm, Nov–Feb 10am–5:30pm), as the name implies, is the biggest tower left standing in San Gimignano (35m/115 ft. tall) and the only one you can climb. The view over the countryside

Pros & Cons of San Gimignano's Combination Tickets

San Gimignano also offers a 5.50€ combination ticket good for admission to the following city-managed sites:

- Torre Grosso
- Museo Civico
- Museo Archeologico (Archaeological Museum)
- Spezeria Santa Fina (a refurbished Renaissance pharmacy)
- Museo Ornitologico (museum of stuffed birds)
- Raffaele De Grada (modern art gallery)

Unless you have a specialized interest in archaeology, pharmacies, or birds, the last four museums aren't likely to excite you (though the archaeological one does have a few exquisite Etruscan pieces). Better to save the extra 1.50€ and spend your time exploring the streets, the walls, or the surrounding countryside.

is stunning, as is the bird's-eye perspective over the town—you'll see into private gardens usually hidden by compound walls, and far off into the distant countryside blanketed with vineyards. The 220 steps to the top of the tower are split at several wide landings, to allow climbers spots to rest. Connected to the tower is the city art gallery **Museo Civico/Pinacoteca** ★★, which has a small but interesting collection of artwork in its four rooms, including the emblematic 14th-century painting of San Gimignano (the saint) holding the eponymous city in his arms. The most entertaining part of the museum is the faded series of tongue-in-cheek medieval wedding frescoes on the walls of the small room off the side of the stairway; they depict a hapless husband first being ridden and whipped by his wife, then sitting naked (aside from his hat) in a bath with her, and finally in bed with her. She's turned away from him in full "I have a headache" mode while he sulks on the other edge of bed, still wearing his red hat.

You'll want to visit the splendid frescoes of **The Collegiata** ★★ (Piazza Duomo; ☎ 0577-940316; 4.50€; Mon–Sat 9:30am–7:10pm, Sun 12:30–7:10pm, Nov–Mar closes 4:40pm) as early or as late in the day as possible because the combination of surly guards, mobs of visitors, and a general carnival sideshow atmosphere can make the experience less than enjoyable if you hit it at the wrong time. The church itself (formerly a cathedral, but no bishop resides here now) was begun in the 11th century, and took its present form in the 15th century. Among the many great masters who added frescoes to its densely decorated walls were Lippo Memmi (the 22 New Testament scenes along the right wall, including the moving Crucifixion); Taddeo Di Bartolo, who added the frightening *Last Judgment;* and Bartolo di Freddi (the 26 Old Testament scenes). Pop 1€ into the AV kiosk toward the entrance to hear a decent summary of the scenes depicted on the panels. Best of all is the elaborate Cappella di Santa Fina (at the far end of the right aisle) with exquisite frescoes from Renaissance superstar Domenico

Ghirlandiao. He tells the story of Santa Fina, San Gimignano's other patron saint, a young 13th-century woman who lay for 6 years on a plank in one position to better understand the sufferings of Jesus. St. Gregory eventually came to claim her and bring her to heaven, and as she died the plank filled with flowers (a yearly festival for the saint takes place here on Mar 12, a time when the towers of San Gimignano are blooming with pansies).

The serene, undervisited church of **Sant'Agostino** ✶ (Piazza Snat'Agostino; ☎ 0577-907012; free; daily 7am–noon and 3–7pm, Oct–Apr closes 6pm), at the north edge of San Gimignano, has an elaborate interior combining over-the-top 18th-century rococo decor with a series of 15th-century frescoes. The best of the bunch is Benozzo Gozzoli's 17-panel depiction of the life of St. Augustine (1460s). Note the panel toward the lower left, which shows the 4th-century saint having a bad day at school and getting whacked by the teacher. The background in most of the scenes vividly illustrates typical daily life and city scenes in Renaissance Tuscany. Don't skip the Chapel of San Bartolo near the side door of the church. It contains the remains of this 13th-century saint. Reliefs on the altar depict the miracles of his life, including the reattaching of his toes, which had fallen off as a result of the leprosy he contracted while ministering to the poor.

CHIANTI COUNTRY

When people envision typical Italian countryside, they usually conjure visions of Chianti: vine-covered rolling hills dotted with castles and Renaissance villas, and populated by family-owned wineries, rustic *agriturismo* vacation spots, and hill tops frozen in time. Although busloads of tourists and wealthy transplants from Milan, Britain, and elsewhere have been slowly transforming—some would say destroying—the character of the region for the past few decades, the spirit of Chianti has not been entirely diluted. Smaller towns still have traditional market days, family-run restaurants continue to offer inexpensive local specialties, and not every winery has been incorporated into an international conglomerate.

You'll want to see this region sooner rather than later, though; in certain ways it's being loved to death, and you want to visit before much more changes. Also, it duels with Venice for the title of "Priciest Corner of Italy," with hotels, restaurants, and even normally inexpensive *agriturismi* and B&Bs charging a premium, a situation that only worsens with every passing year.

The 168 sq. km (65 sq. miles) of Chianti Country fill the area between Florence and Siena, sandwiched between the A1 autostrada and the SS2 highway. The famed "Chianti Road" (SP222) winds and weaves through the middle of Chianti. You can explore the region on day trips from Florence and Siena, or stay around one of the smaller Chianti towns. You can casually drop in on the smaller wineries you discover on the road, or make reservations for visits to some of the larger ones, paying upward of 30€ for a tour, tasting, and snacks.

A BRIEF HISTORY OF CHIANTI

As usual, the Etruscans got here first, and the name "Chianti"—the region came before the wine—is thought to be derived from the Etruscan *Clantes* clan. Legions of conquering Romans, Lombards, and Goths passed through the region until it stabilized under the alternating control of Florence and Siena in the 1200s.

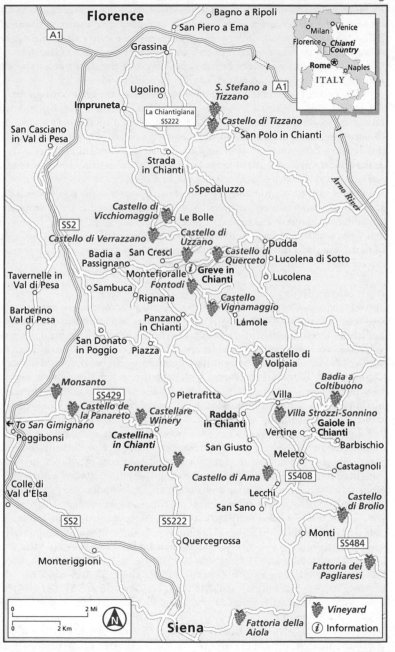

Chianti Country

Florence

Bagno a Ripoli

San Piero a Ema

A1

Grassina

Ugolino

S. Stefano a Tizzano

A1

Impruneta

La Chiantigiana
SS222

Castello di Tizzano

San Polo in Chianti

San Casciano
in Val di Pesa

Strada
in Chianti

Spedaluzzo

Arno River

Castello di
Vicchiomaggio

Le Bolle

SS2

Castello di Verrazzano

Castello di
Uzzano

San Cresci

Dudda

Badia a
Passignano

Castello di
Querceto

Lucolena di Sotto

Tavernelle in
Val di Pesa

Montefioralle

Greve in
Chianti

Lucolena

Sambuca

Fontodi

Rignana

Barberino
Val di Pesa

Panzano
in Chianti

Castello
Vignamaggio

Lámole

San Donato
in Poggio

Piazza

Castello di
Volpaia

Monsanto

Pietrafitta

Villa

Badia a
Coltibuono

Castello de
la Panareto

Castellare
Winery

Radda
in Chianti

Villa Strozzi-Sonnino

Gaiole in
Chianti

To San Gimignano

Poggibonsi

Castellina
in Chianti

SS429

San Giusto

Vertine

Barbischio

Fonterutoli

Castello di Ama

Meleto

Castagnoli

Colle di
Val d'Elsa

SS408

Lecchi

San Sano

Castello
di Brolio

SS2

SS222

Quercegrossa

Monti

SS484

Monteriggioni

Fattoria dei
Pagliaresi

0   2 Mi
0   2 Km

N

🍇 Vineyard

ⓘ Information

Siena

Fattoria della
Aiola

ITALY
Milan   Venice
Florence Chianti
Country
Rome Naples

Florence and Siena fought for dominance of the Chianti area from the 13th through the 15th centuries, each of the city-states building castles in the area to protect its interests. Under Florentine organization, the military Lega del Chianti (Chianti League) was formed in 1255 by the cities of Radda, Castellina, and Gaiole. They chose the "Gallo Nero" as their symbol, the same black rooster silhouette which serves as the symbol of Chianti Classico wine today.

Wine from the region took on the Chianti name by the early 15th century. In the early 1700s, Chianti became the first official government-designated wine area in the world. In the 1830s, Bettino Ricasoli, "The Iron Baron," brought professional processing techniques to wineries on his estates. He experimented with different combinations of grapes until he created the standard blend that served as the official, highly regulated formula for Chianti up until new national regulations loosened things up at the turn of the 21st century.

To protect the Chianti name, a group of winegrowers in the region formed the Chianti Classico Consortium in 1924. They then adopted a set of regulations regarding the blend of the wine, the production techniques, and, of course, the area from which the grapes must come. Today, nearly 104 sq. km (40 sq. miles) of Chianti are covered with over 6,800 hectares (17,000 acres) of grapevines producing some 90 million liters of wine per year.

LAY OF THE LAND

You have two choices for touring the region: Drive your own car, or join an organized tour from a nearby city. Driving obviously gives you more freedom to explore the less touristed, smaller wineries and wander back roads to your heart's content. The drawbacks are that you won't be able to sample as many wines as you'd like if you're the designated driver, and it's very easy to get lost. If you do decide on driving yourself (and I'd recommend it), take the scenic N2 highway between Florence and Siena, exiting on some of the smaller side routes to reach the central S222, turning south on it toward Siena. To see the best of Chianti in a single day, cruise the S222, and stop in Greve and Radda.

With an organized tour (widely available in Florence and Siena; ask at you hotel or the tourist office), you can sit back and let others do the work. But these tours only go to the places that can accommodate hordes of visitors, have their own fixed schedules, and eliminate some of the adventure that makes travel fun. Keep in mind that wine-tasting tours aren't the only option; you can combine them with cooking classes, biking or hiking trips, and shopping.

The Chianti area has several **tourist offices,** most of them private travel agencies that have either officially or unofficially taken over duties of promoting tourism in their respective corners of the Chianti. They are in **Greve** (a little shack by the side of the road on the way into town on the SS222 from Florence at Viale Giovanni da Verrazzano 59 and Piazza G. Matteotti 10; ☎ 055-8546287; www.comune.greve-in-chianti.fi.it), in **Castellina** (Via Ferruccio 40; ☎ 0577-741392; www.essenceoftuscany.it), in **Radda** (Piazza del Castello 6; ☎ 0577-738494; www.chiantinet.it), and in **Gaiole** (Via G. Galilei 11; ☎ 0577-749411). For general area information visit www.chianti.it/turismo and the official websites for the two provinces that between them govern the Chianti: www.firenzeturismo.it and www.terresiena.it.

Why Is a Chianti a Chianti?

To begin with, the wine is named after the region (not the other way around). As for the wine itself, there are strict rules that govern what can and cannot be called "Chianti Classico." With that designation, the grapes must come from 1 of 12 municipalities between Siena and Florence. The Sangiovese grape must compose at least 80% of the blend, and since 2006 no white grapes are allowed in the mixture (a sharp turnaround from the traditional formula in place until the 1990s, when white grapes trebbiano and malvasia had to be part of the alchemy, along with the red canaiolo nero). Also, only a certain density of vines are allowed per acre, and the end product cannot be sold until October 1 in the year following the harvest. Keep in mind that these are among the rules for Chianti Classico. Confusingly, there are other official Chianti zones in Tuscany, including Chianti Colli Senesi (from the hills around Siena that are *not* part of Chianti Classico), Chianti Colli Fiorentini (same deal but near Florence), Chianti Calli Aretini (near Arezzo), Chianti Colli Pisani (near Pisa), Chianti Montalbano, and perhaps my favorite, Chianti Rúfina (from the hills northeast of Florence—not the be confused with Ruffino, the name of one of the biggest makers and exporters of Chianti Classico and many other wines likely found at your local wine shop in the States).

ACCOMMODATIONS, BOTH STANDARD & NOT

€€   One of the best ways to experience the life of the area is to bed down at a winery for the night, and perhaps the loveliest place to do that is the **Casali Della Aiola** ✪✪ (on SP102 north of Vagliagli, a village halfway between Radda in Chianti and Siena; ☎ 0577-322797; www.aiola.net). Once a famous Sienese stronghold (the Florentines razed it in 1544, after which it was rebuilt with a moat), this estate is today a 100-hectare (250-acre) working farm operated by the extended family of Senator Giovanni Malagodi. His daughter runs the vineyards and winery, and his granddaughter, the charming Federica, and her husband, Enrico, have turned two of the farmhouses on the property into an eight-room *agriturismo,* polishing the terra-cotta floors to a shine, restoring the wood-beam ceilings, and preserving the farmhouse look. As is appropriate for this winery/lodging, the small reading room contains an honor bar where you can partake of the farm's bounty. Doubles go for 95€, including breakfast. There's also a two-roomed, family-size junior suite for 120€ for two up to 140€ for four. For those not staying here, there are cellar tours and tastings. By the way, the winery **Vicchiomaggio** (p. 176) also offers well-priced rooms for rent.

€€   The **Albergo Il Colombaio** ✪ 🧒 (Castellina in Chianti, Via Chiantigiana 29; ☎ 0577-740444; www.albergoilcolombaio.it; AE, MC, V) is right on the edge of the hill town of Castellina, with 14 rooms (doubles for 90€–100€) behind the thick stone and wood walls of a 16th-century house that once sheltered shepherds and their sheep. For a reasonably priced place, it has some very nice amenities like good-quality bed linens, fluffy towels, and a swimming pool with countryside views. Ask for an upstairs room—they're bigger with better views; downstairs was where the sheep used to sleep! Be sure to check out the Etruscan Tomb at the end of the dirt road next to the hotel. You'll see a huge green mound topped with a pair of pointy cypress. Under the mound, accessed by narrow tunnels, are the empty stone burial vaults, lit by button-operated lights. It's quite spooky to visit at night. The Albergo's sister property, the **Villa Casalta,** sits about a mile outside of Castellina, and has 13 homey rooms in the main manor house and 6 in another farmhouselike structure, with a pool between them. You can reserve a room with a kitchen, or stay B&B-style and eat in the large breakfast room. Doubles there also cost 90€ to 100€, including breakfast.

€€–€€€   The **Villa Rosa di Boscorotondo** ✪✪ (Via San Leolino 59, on the SS222 between Panzano and Radda, Loc. Panzano in Chianti; ☎ 055-852577; www.resortvillarosa.it; AE, MC, V; closed mid-Nov to Apr) is a rarity in the Chianti, offering wonderful countryside seclusion and an elegant atmosphere at perfectly modest prices (doubles 80€–140€). Giancarlo and Sabina Avuri, who co-own Florence's Hotel Torre Guelfa, opened this huge pink villa as a roadside inn in 1998, retaining the original features and roominess while modernizing with an elegance that lends it an antique rustic air. The curtained beds on wrought-iron frames rest under gorgeous beamed ceilings, and rooms along the front open onto two huge terraces that drink in views of the small valley in which the villa nestles. There are a series of small drawing rooms, a pool with a view, and a path that leads through the vineyards all the way to San Leolino church outside Panzano. Famed butcher Cecchini provides the meat for fixed-price dinners (25€, not including wine) on the terra-cotta terrace in summer.

€€€   The **Giovanni da Verrazzano** ✪ (Piazza G. Matteotti 28, Greve in Chianti; ☎ 055-853189; www.albergoverrazzano.it; AE, MC, V) overlooks Greve's triangular central piazza and its statue of the hotel/restaurant's namesake, a local explorer who first discovered and mapped New York Harbor (and is remembered in the name of the narrows between Long Island and Staten Island and the bridge that spans them). The rooms—eight with private bathrooms for 118€ double, two with shared bathroom for 103€—are a bit small but comfortable, their furnishings functional but nice: painted wrought-iron bed frames with firm mattresses, dark-wood furniture, terra-cotta floors, and a handful of wood-beamed ceilings. Rooms on the front overlook the mismatched arcades of the piazza, while those on the back have tiny terraces with late-morning sun, potted plants, and a view over lichen-spotted roof tiles to the Chianti hills. The four-sleeper in the attic is perfect for families (190€), and the restaurant serves hearty portions of highly recommendable Tuscan fare in a laid-back *trattoria* atmosphere, with summer dining on a terrace atop the piazza's arcades.

€€–€€€   **La Rignana** ✪✪ (☎ 055-852065; www.rignana.it; see the restaurant review below for driving details) is reviewed below for its excellent restaurant under separate management. But the farm complex also rents out seven country-elegant rooms in the 18th-century Fattoria B&B from April to November—85€ to 95€ for a double with a shared bathroom, 95€ to 105€ for one with private bathroom. There is also a separate villa with eight frescoed rooms on two floors. From April to November, these, too, can be rented as individual B&B rooms for 120€ to 140€ a night; year-round you can rent an entire floor as a four-room apartment (with shared living room and kitchen) for 3,500€ per week. All accommodations share a horizon pool set in an olive grove.

€€€–€€€€ **Palazzo Leopoldo** ✪ (Via Roma 33, Radda in Chianti; ☎ 0577-735605; www.palazzoleopoldo.it; AE, MC, V) in the center of Radda, has been hosting rich and famous visitors since 1434. This former nobleman's villa, with original frescoes still on the walls and ancient wooden beams holding up the ceilings, is the epitome of elegance and a worthy splurge, its rooms starting at 150€ or 190€ for a double, 190€ to 230€ for a superior room (you're paying for the view), and 240€ to 330€ for one of the huge suites. Another lure: a heated "hydromassage" pool in a hidden underground cave.

€€€€ If you've ever wanted to live in your own medieval hamlet in the heart of the Chianti, here's your chance. As its name implies, it sometimes gets windy at **Borgo Casa al Vento** (between Gaiole in Chianti and Barbischio; ☎ 0577-749068; www.borgocasaalvento.com; AE, MC, V), but the stone buildings of this converted village on the top of a ridge are as solid on the outside as they are soft on the inside, with cushy beds and couches, some canopied beds, and calming decor. They offer a number of lodging options, from apartments and bedroom suites to a huge vacation villa. Least costly are the weekly apartment rentals: 1,000€ in high season, or 250€ a night (but down to a reasonable 800€ a week when business is slow). There are also pricier suites and a high-end villa for rent.

DINING FOR ALL TASTES

€–€€ For simple, flavorful meals with little fuss, **Tre Porte** ✪ 🄺 (Via Trento e Trieste 4–8, Castellina in Chianti; ☎ 0577-741163; www.ristorantichianti.it/treporte; Wed–Mon noon–2pm and 7–10pm; closed Jan 6 to mid-Feb; AE, MC, V) is the best stop in the area, and everyone knows it—it's packed day and night with local families and large groups. The pesto linguini and the grilled pork are both particularly good, but I don't think you'll be disappointed with anything on the menu. They also fire up the pizza oven in the evening (this is the tradition in Italy; any place that offers pizza at lunch is doing so to cater to foreign tourists). *Primi* cost 7€ to 10€, *secondi* 13€ to 25€, and *pizze* 5€ to 7€.

€€ If you're looking for a genuine countryside trattoria, try **La Cantinetta di Rignana** ✪✪ (follow signs from Greve in Chianti up to Montefioralle, go around that hamlet and follow signs to Badia a Passignano, and then look for the Rignana turnoff after a few miles; ☎ 055-852601; www.lacantinettadirignana.it; Wed–Mon 12:30–2:15pm and 7:30–10:30pm, Nov and Feb Sat–Sun only; AE, MC, V). Set in a farmhouse at the end of a long dirt road, it has a folksy decor (red tablecloths and family photos, lamps on the tables, and icons and farm implements on the walls) and a lovely outdoor dining patio overlooking the vineyards from which the house wine comes. Tops here are sausage ravioli, or the *involtini di manzo* (slices of thinly pounded beef wrapped around vegetables). *Primi* range from 8€ to 10€, *secondi* from 9€ to 14€. Reservations are highly recommended for dinner.

€€–€€€   The meals aren't cheap at **Albergaccio** ✮✮✰ (Via Fiorentina 63, outside of Castellina; ☎ 0577-741042; www.albergacciocast.com; Mon–Sat 12:30–2:15pm and 7:30–9:30pm, closed Wed at lunch Apr 2–Nov 4; MC, V). Tasting menus are a whopping 52€ to 59€ (though you do get four or five courses), *primi* average 14€, and *secondi* 23€ to 25€, but it's well worth the splurge. The food is outstanding and the ambience is everything you could hope for—an outdoor dining area with views over the vines in warm weather, and on chillier nights an elegant, white-tablecloth-robed room. I still dream about their *piccione* (pigeon) stuffed with figs caramelized in Marsala wine and the ricotta gnocchi topped with thyme and truffle shavings. A top dining experience.

THE LURE OF BACCHUS—VISITS TO THE WINERIES

Consistency is a virtue when it comes to Chianti. For several thousand years, the people here have been primarily doing just one thing: lovingly tending the local grapes and producing, in vineyards that now spread across nearly 6,800 hectares (16,800 acres) of the region, one of the most prized wines in the world. Many wonderful wineries offer tours and tastings (for which it is always wise to book in advance, preferably by a day or two days if not by a full week). Here are a few favorites:

Castello Monsanto winery ✮ (Via Monsanto 8, Barberino Val D'Elsa; ☎ 055-8059000; www.castellodimonsanto.it; tours with tasting 16€), with 72 hectares (178 acres) of vineyards, produces about 400,000 bottles a year of chardonnay, Chianti Classico, and sangiovese wines. They export the bulk of their production to the U.S., so if you like what you drink, you can probably get it at home. One of the most innovative of the region's vineyards, it was one of the first to substitute steel tanks for wooden wine casks, and to play around with the number of days for maturation. You'll learn all about this fascinating history on the tour, which takes you on a stroll through the grounds, with a visit to the original 1742 cellars. It's a little tricky to find the place because it doesn't have any signs (call for directions), but it's close to the SS2, two exits north of Poggibonsi on an SS429 side route.

Just how beautiful is **Vicchiomaggio** (Via Vicchiomaggio 4, Le Bolle exit south of Strada; ☎ 055-854078; www.vicchiomaggio.it; tours 4€), a centuries-old castle? I can only assume that Leonardo da Vinci took some inspiration from its surroundings: It was here that he painted his famous *Mona Lisa,* who grew up in a nearby castle. Though the castle, which looms over the Greve Valley, was originally built in the 5th century A.D., what you see today is the Renaissance reconstruction (approximately 1450), still one of the best-preserved castles in the region. Now British owned, the vineyards here produce a number of delightful wines, particularly the Ripa Delle More, an award-winning sangiovese/cabernet. Free tastings are available at the San Jacopo shop (daily 10am–12:30pm and 2:30–6pm; on the SS222 right at the turnoff for the castle). You can arrange a tour of the cellars and castle if you reserve in advance (usually daily at 11:30am or 4:30pm; you can choose to have a light lunch with a tasting of some rarer wines after the tour for 38€ per person). If you really like it here, you can rent rooms, stay for a few days, and take one of their cooking or wine appreciation classes (rooms start at 102€ a night).

Formed from the merger of five vineyards in 1968, **Domini Castellare di Castellina** (Poderi Castellare di Castellina, about 2.4km/11/2 miles from Castellina; ☎ 0577-742903; www.castellare.it; brief tour and tastings for 9€, with a snack 13€) proudly puts out a much lower yield than neighboring wineries, eschewing the use of pesticides or herbicides and never mixing its local grapes with French or international strains. I think you'll taste the difference—these wines are quite prized and difficult to get outside the region. The direct sales outlet is open daily 9am to 1pm and 3 to 7pm (closes at 6pm Fri).

One of Italy's top vineyards for the past 300 years, **Castello di Brolio** ⭐ (☎ 0577-730220; www.ricasoli.it; 15€ to tour the bottling room with a wine tasting; daily 9am–noon and 3–6pm; reservations required; 5€ to tour the grounds, which are closed Fri in winter), a handsome 15th-century castle, was once owned by the creator of the 20th-century Chianti, the "Iron Baron" Ricasoli (see above). After a brief interlude during which the Seagrams conglomorate did its best to ruin the vineyard's reputation, in 1993 the estate returned to family hands and is now run by Francesco Ricasoli, the 32nd Barone di Brolio. The tour, while pricey, is fascinating, and the wines here are exquisite, particularly the Casalferro, which has won just about ever prize there is. The wine tastes even better with a meal at their **Osteria del Castello restaurant** (☎ 0577-747277; 18€ for an entree; generally Mar–Oct; hours to be established; AE, MC, V) on the driveway to the castle. Or just stop by for a tipple in the Enoteca Monday to Friday from 9am to 6pm (in summer also Sun 11am–7pm).

Le Cantine di Greve in Chianti ⭐ (Galleria delle Cantine 2, Greve in Chianti; ☎ 055-8546404; www.lecantine.it; daily 10am–7pm) is the region's best wine store—or at least its biggest, with more than 1,000 labels for sale—and a place where you can taste some 140 different wines at a single sitting (well, you wouldn't be able to walk if you did that, but at least you have a choice among that many wines). You can also sample 20 different olive oils and buy small samples of the oils, along with salami and sandwiches. For information on each wine, check out the computer terminals in the shop. They have tasting seminars, plus an interesting corkscrew museum (no, really, it's interesting).

SIENA

Founded by the Etruscans, and colonized by Rome, Siena rose to power in the early Middle Ages as a center of banking and the textile trade, a rival to Florence in art, commerce, culture, and military might. In 1348, however, the Black Death dealt Siena a blow from which it never fully recovered. Estimates of those who perished range as high as 75% of the town's population. Given sanitary habits at the time, and some 70,000 corpses in the city, it's a wonder that Siena wasn't completely abandoned.

With its art and architecture frozen in time, Siena today offers visitors a wealth of museums and churches. The town also supports a small university, a fair amount of shopping, a number of first-rate restaurants, and two pro sports teams, bringing just enough of a cosmopolitan breeze to freshen up the atmosphere of the medieval streets and buildings. The town is accessible but has never become as oversaturated with tourism as Florence, San Gimignano, or Pisa.

Unlike cramped and crowded Florence, Siena is a pedestrian city, its hilly streets largely free from the mopeds that menace its Tuscan rival. The Duomo and the famous campo, the wide and sloping main square guarded by the grand tower of Palazzo Pubblico, are among the notable architectural achievements of the region. Art galleries, including the Museo Civico, the Pinacoteca Nazionale, and the Museo dell'Opera Metropolitana, offer you a chance to enjoy many late Gothic and early-Renaissance masterpieces.

LAY OF THE LAND

Siena is one of the few major tourist towns where it's **more convenient to arrive by bus than by train,** as the train station is nearly 3.2km (2 miles) from the city center. If you do arrive by train (about a 2-hr. ride from Florence), most city buses will take you to Piazza Matteotti, just north of the walls. Long-haul bus lines **Tra-in** (☎ 0577-204225; www.trainspa.it) and **Sena** (that's "Sena," not "Siena;" ☎ 0577-283203; www.senabus.it) connect Florence and Siena in 75 to 95 minutes. The buses arrive on the north end of town near the stadium, either in Piazza San Domenico or just a bit farther north along Via Tozzi/Piazza Gramsci (with ticket offices in the nearby "La Lizza" underground tunnel).

Siena is a fairly simple drive from Florence (64km/40 miles via the SS2), or from Rome (193km/120 miles via the A1-326). Whatever you do, *do not attempt to drive into Siena.* Sure, as a tourist headed to your hotel, you are allowed to do so in order to drop off luggage, but the tangle of narrow one-way streets, the fact that most of the larger streets on which you are allowed to drive tend to be wall-to-wall with people (Sienese love to *passeggiata*), and the fact that, after dropping off your luggage, you'll have to navigate it all over again to get back out of town to a legal parking space—it's just not worth the hassle and stress.

> " *Siena was a flawless gift of the Middle Ages to the modern imagination. No other Italian city could have been more interesting to an observer . . .* "
>
> —Henry James, *Confidence,* 1879

Better all around if you **park** at one of public garages that encircle the historical center and either haul your luggage on foot or take the minibus into your hotel. There are eight public **parking garages** (☎ 0577-228711; www.siena parcheggi.com) ringing the historical center, most just inside or outside a city gate. Each charges 1.60€ per hour or 30€ per day—though most hotels can get you a 5€ discount. (If you'll be dumping the car for 2–3 days, take advantage of Siena's secret parking bargain: the lot down at the train station charges just 2€ for 24 hr., the one out by the Policlinico hospital 2.50€ per day; both are served frequently by buses to the center. There are also free spaces around on the northwest side of the fortress. These are unguarded, but I've never run into a problem parking there.)

Siena's **tourist office** (Piazza del Campo 56; ☎ 0577-280551; www.siena. turismo.toscana.it) hands out good free maps. The privately run **Info Casato Viaggi** office (Via Casato di Sotto 12, to the right of the palace; ☎ 0577-46091; www.sienaholiday.com), southeast of the Piazza del Campo, has better free information and a helpful staff. They can also book tours and help you find a room.

The private booking service **Siena Hotels Promotion,** on the north edge of town (Piazza Madre Teresa di Calcutta 5; ☎ 0577-288084; www.hotelsiena.com) is also helpful and good for a free map. It sponsors the Ecco Siena–guided city tour that leaves at 3pm Monday to Saturday from outside San Domenico church. The 90-minute tour is only 5€ if you have a coupon from Siena Hotels Promotion or one of the hotels in town that provide them; otherwise, it's 15€.

ACCOMMODATIONS, BOTH STANDARD & NOT

€€   Down a steep street down off Piazza San Domenico where the buses let you off sits the **Alma Domus** (Via Camporeggio 37; ☎ 0577-44177; cash only), a lodging that ranks somewhere above a hostel and below a hotel and is run by a cadre of thoroughly humorless nuns from the Sisterhood of St. Catherine. As you might imagine from a religious outfit, the rooms are fairly bland, with furnishings a mix of the modular and the old-fashioned (no TV except in the common room, and the room phones can only receive calls from the front desk), and there is a lamentable 11:30pm curfew. However, to make up for it, doubles cost just 65€, and many of the rooms have windows (and, in some, balconies) with a drop-dead gorgeous view of the striped flanks of the Duomo rising on the opposite ridge. (Unless you're really pinching pennies, if you can't get a room with that view I'd say move along and pay a bit more for one of the other options listed here.)

€€   The key word is "simple" when it comes to the central and cheap **Albergo Hotel La Perla** (Piazza Indipendenza 25; ☎ 0577-47144; www.hotellaperlasiena. com; AE, MC, V). The building (a former palace, though you wouldn't know it to look at it) is somewhat somber, and the rooms are very standard, with flowered bedspreads and tile floors. But it's only half a block from the Piazza del Campo, so the location is great and prices start at just 70€ to 80€ for a double. Expect a few minor downsides to staying here—no phones in the rooms and no elevator (meaning you've got to climb the 32 steep steps to the third floor)—but on the plus side there is free Internet access in the lobby and Wi-Fi, TV, and A/C in the rooms.

€€   One of the best values in Siena has got to be the 30-room **Cannon d'Oro** ★ (Via Montanini 28; ☎ 0577-44321; www.cannondoro.com; AE, MC, V), a converted 15th-century palazzo right on the main drag (Via Montanini is a continuation of Via Banchi di Sopra), with plenty of simple rooms—all with phones and some with stylish 19th-century furnishings—for just 60€ to 99€ per double.

€€   For rather more charm and an even better location just off Via Banchi di Sotto, just a few steps from Piazza del Campo, the **Piccola Hotel Etruria** ★ (Via delle Donzelle 3; ☎ 0577-288088; www.hoteletruria.com; AE, MC, V) is run with pride by the Fattorini family. The 13 doubles—split between the main hotel and a *dipendenza* annex across the street—cost only 86€ and all rooms have private bathroom, TV, and A/C. The killer locations and low prices mean it books up fast, so call ahead. The only big drawback: a 1am curfew (otherwise, they'd get a second star from me).

€€   One of my favorite small hotels in Tuscany, the **Hotel Bernini** ★★ (Via della Sapienza 15; ☎ 0577-289047; www.albergobernini.com; cash only; closed Dec) is a friendly family-run operation in a residential corner of town that boasts excellent views of the Duomo from the hallway and a small terrace (a great place to relax). Other pluses: new bathrooms; clean rooms with very homey, comfortable furnishings; and an extremely quiet setting above a convent. Double rooms with private bathroom go for 85€, without bathroom for 65€. Beginning around 100€ per night, you can also rent one of a couple of well-appointed apartments (with kitchens) around the corner.

€€–€€€   There are slightly more stylish digs at the **Hotel Chiusarelli** ✪ (Viale Curtatone 15; ☎ 0577-280562; www.chiusarelli.com; AE, MC, V), a colonnaded neoclassical villa just 1 block from the bus station. Rooms are light and airy, with modern decor and comfortable beds, many with good-size verandas. Double-room prices are 90€ to 125€, including breakfast. As a bonus, on weekends you get balcony views of Siena's soccer team playing in the stadium behind the hotel. The hotel has a small parking lot, a large restaurant, and an Internet terminal for guests.

€€–€€€   **Casolare la Vigna** (Strada di Fornicchiaia 20–22, near Belcaro Castle; ☎ 0577-283311 or 347-8483956; www.casolarelavigna.it; cash only) is a friendly family-run *agriturismo* just 3.5km (2 miles) southwest of town, and a good choice for those seeking a peaceful hideaway near the city. Their recently refurbished two-bedroom apartment (converted from an old stable) includes a full kitchen, antique furnishings, satellite TV, and a washer/dryer, and costs 80€ to 150€ a night— more during festival time, less in winter. Though it's not a full-service hotel, there are many extras. Your hosts will cook meals on request, and also give cooking lessons using ingredients from an organic garden behind the house. Daughter Cinzia Mariotti is a licensed guide who leads city tours and treks into the countryside. This is one of those rare *agriturismi* easily accessible even to those not traveling by car, as there is regular bus service from the house into Siena proper.

DINING FOR ALL TASTES

€–€€   One of my favorite simple trattorie in town, **La Torre** (Via Salicotto 7–9; ☎ 0577-287548; Fri–Wed noon–3pm and 7–10pm; MC, V), also happens to have one of the most convenient locations in Siena, just 50 yards off the campo down a quiet side street. Despite being near tourist central, it remains a popular local joint (reserve ahead or arrive early), with just a dozen tables crammed into a small room and an open kitchen from which arrive such homey, mouthwatering dishes as the homemade *pici* (hand-rolled spaghetti), *piccione al forno* (oven-baked pigeon), and *vitello arrosto* (roast slices of veal). *Primi* range from 6€ to 8€, *secondi* from 9€ to 10€.

€–€€   A very popular pizzeria tucked in a winding street beneath San Domenico, **Ristorante La Pizzeria di Nonno Mede** ✪ (Via Camporegio 21; ☎ 0577-247966; daily 12:30–2:30pm and 7:30pm–midnight; AE, MC, V) is a good choice for a quick but extremely pleasant meal. You may need reservations, however, because this scenic patio spot (with views of the Duomo) is packed until almost midnight. Pizzas begin at 5€, and toppings range from the usual sausages and mushrooms to seafood and artichokes. They also serve Tuscan dishes, including pasta made fresh daily in-house; *primi* go for 6.70€ to 7.80€, *secondi* from 10€ to 15€.

€–€€   You'll be spending your days among the medieval marvels of Siena, so why not dine medieval as well? At the **Gallo Nero** ★ 🆔 (Via del Porrione 65/67; ☎ 0577-284356; www.gallonero.it; daily noon–3pm and 7–11pm; AE, MC, V), the chefs have consulted with professors at the local university to create an authentic medieval menu and they don't shy away from the unusual, such as braised peacock or pork cold cuts with "aromatic lard." Kids will enjoy the Dungeons and Dragons setting (a 14th-c. palazzo of thick stone walls, stained glass, and medieval art) and costumed waitstaff, and I think you'll enjoy the food. The series of fixed-price "medieval menus" cost 30€ to 70€ and include a whopping six courses accompanied by spiced wine and such delicacies as a salted onion tart, bittersweet duck with cheese ravioli, chicken stuffed with oranges, and a pear-and-ricotta pastry for dessert. *Primi* run 5€ to 10€, while main courses are 8.50€ to 13€. It's a trip, but a colorful one and, while admittedly a bit kitschy, also a genuinely historical one.

€€€€   The high-end **Cane & Gatto** ★★★ (Via Pagliaresi 6; ☎ 0577-287545; Fri–Wed 8–10:30pm, open for lunch only upon request; reservations required; AE, MC, V) is one of Siena's finest restaurants. The interior is peaceful and intimate, with candlelit tables and modern art on the walls. Chef/owner Paolo Senni's menu changes with the seasons but if he's offering the *tagliata di fesa di vitella* (veal steak) with zucchini, be sure to order it. Simpler but still delicious is his homemade spaghetti with fresh tomato-and-basil sauce with local olive oil and greens from their garden. The typical set-price tasting menu runs 65€ to 70€ per person, wine not included (though it does cover an aperitif and a dessert wine); so it's not cheap, but if you want a night on the town, this is where to go.

WHY YOU'RE HERE: THE TOP SIGHTS & ATTRACTIONS

Siena boasts some of the finest art and architecture in Italy. Ideally, you should have 2 days to tour the sights, and even that will be a busy time. With a single day, treat yourself to the Duomo, the Duomo Museum, and the Museo Civico. On the second day, be sure to add the Ospedale di Santa Maria, the Pinacoteca, and San Domenico Church on the north edge of town.

You should start your visit, as people have been doing for centuries, at the breathtakingly beautiful **Piazza del Campo** ★★★. This large square is a logical gathering place, the site of the Palio race, and a perfect spot to sit, have a gelato, and watch mobs of tourists, street musicians, and locals enjoying the scene. Siena's ruling Council of Nine had the piazza constructed in its present form from 1290 to 1349. The council divided the area into nine segments as a tribute to themselves. The nine white dividing lines actually serve as gutters to funnel water into the grate at the bottom of the sloped area. The Fonte Gaia fountain at the peak of the piazza is topped with a goddess of the seas, and framed with the Virgin Mary flanked by the Virtues. It's a 19th-century reproduction of the 15th-century original.

The **Palazzo Pubblico (Town Hall),** at the base of the piazza, is an expression of Siena's civic power and pride, constructed in the early 14th century. The 95m (315-ft.) **Torre del Mangia** (Piazza del Campo; ☎ 0577-226230; 6€; daily Mar 16–Oct 10am–7pm, Nov–Mar 15 10am–4pm) jutting up from the structure is climbable and offers spectacular views over the city and surroundings. (Though if you're only

Siena's Confusing Cumulative Tickets

Siena's multiuse tickets—covering a shifting variety of sights, some so minor (such as the Palazzo delle Papesse's gallery of contemporary art) they're not reviewed here—can be a good deal, but only if you're planning on being in town for a few days. The tickets come from two sources (the civic museums group and the overlapping Duomo group) totaling six flavors:

- **Tower + Museo Civico:** 10€
- **"My Name is Duccio" Duomo + Museo dell'Opera:** 6€ (advanced bookings only; www.operaduomo.siena.it)
- **Duomo + Museo dell'Opera + Battistero + Cripta + S. Bernardino e Museo Diocesano:** 10€ (good for 3 days)
- **"Musei Comunali": Museo Civico + Palazzo delle Papesse + Santa Maria della Scala:** 10€ (good for 2 days)
- **"SIA Inverno": Museo Civico + Palazzo delle Papesse + Santa Maria della Scala + Museo dell'Opera + Battistero S. Giovanni + Libreria Piccolomini:** 13€ (good for 7 days)
- **"SIA Estate": Museo Civico + Palazzo delle Papesse + Santa Maria della Scala + Museo dell'Opera + Battistero S. Giovanni + Libreria Piccolomini + Oratorio di San Bernardino e Museo Diocesano:** 16€ (good for 7 days)

Here's what attractions cost if you pay separately:

	Regular	Reduced	Hours (+/- an hour by season)
Museo Civico	7€	4.50€	10am–7pm
Santa Maria della Scala	6€	3.50€	10:30am–6:30pm
Palazzo delle Papesse	5€	3.50€	noon–7pm
Duomo	3€	3€	10:30am–7:30pm
Museo dell'Opera	6€	5€	9:30am–7pm
Battistero S. Giovanni	3€	2.50€	9:30am–7pm
Oratorio di San Bernadino e Museo Diocesano	3€	2.50€	10:30am–1:30pm, 3–5:30pm
Total	33€	24.50€	

picking one place to climb, the panorama at the Museo dell'Opera is just as good, and includes admission to an art gallery.) The clunky structure sticking out from the front of the Palazzo is the Cappella di Piazza, meant as a religious offering following the end of the Black Death in the late 1300s. The city ran out of funding, and the chapel wasn't topped off for another century.

Though it's still used for government offices and functions, parts of the Palazzo Pubblico now serve as the **Museo Civico** ✦✦✦ (Piazza del Campo; ☎ 0577-226230; 7€; daily Mar 16–Oct 10am–7pm, Nov–Feb 10am–6:30pm, Nov 26–Dec 23 and Jan 7–Feb 15 10am–5:30pm), home to countless huge murals and paintings created when Siena was at the peak of her military and artistic power. In the Sala del Mappamondo is Simone Martini's first known work, his *Maestà* (1315), an extraordinary debut for any artist. Even in this early "Madonna in Majesty" you'll see Martini's mastery of color and texture in the Virgin's elaborately patterned gown. Note how Peter (with key) and other saints are on tent-post-holding duty. The knight on horseback across the room is Martini's *Guidoriccio da Fogliano,* a Sienese army captain riding by conquered Montemassi. The twin message to the town officials who would gather in the room: Govern not only with power but with justice.

The art continues to teach lessons for rulers in the Sala di Pace next door. In these allegorical works, we see the results of Good Government—people dancing, prosperous fields, and so on—and Bad Government. In the latter, a devil rules over post-plague Siena, where muggers attack villagers and thieves roam the countryside attacking travelers. The artist Ambrogio Lorenzetti himself died of plague in the epidemic 10 years after he completed the frescoes.

Siena's **Duomo** or **Cathedral of Santa Maria dell'Assunta** ✯✯✯ (Piazza del Duomo; ☎ 0577-283048; www.operaduomo.siena.it; 3€; Mar–May and Sept–Nov 1 Mon–Sat 10:30am–7:30pm, Sun 1:30pm–5:30pm; June–Aug Mon–Sat 10:30am–8pm, Sun 1:30–6pm; Nov 2–Feb Mon–Sat 10:30am–6:30pm, Sun 1:30–5:30pm) is one of the world's most handsome Gothic churches. It was begun in 1196, at a time when the Pisan proclivity for incorporating black and white marble stripes into their great church building was at its height, and these striking bands define both the exterior and interior spaces. You'll see one of the church's greatest treasures just as you enter: the 56 exquisite mosaic marble panels created by artists from the 14th to 16th centuries (a few were unfinished until the 19th c.). They're roped off, many covered with cardboard for protection (if missing these inlaid panels would spoil your visit, come in Aug when they're fully uncovered—and admission rises to 6€). The famous pulpit, carved by the father-and-son team of Nicola and Govanni Pisano in 1265, dramatizes the story of Christ's life on its panels. The northern transept has a set of tombs, including Donatello's 1415 bronze tomb of Bishop Pecci. The Piccolomini altarpiece features four statues of saints done by a young Michelangelo. He had signed on to do another 11 statues, but skipped town for a better gig—the *David* in Florence. Don't overlook the **Libreria Piccolomini,** halfway down the left nave near Michelangelo's saints, noteworthy for its beautiful frescoes by Pinturrichio. Pope Pius II (a famous humanist and scholar born Enea Silvio Piccolimini in Siena province) is the subject of 10 of the large frescoes, while Siena's St. Catherine (whom Pius II canonized in 1461) gets her own piece on the left side of the room.

Money problems plagued the construction of the Duomo and its grand plans to turn it into the largest in the world—the biggest problem of which was an actual plague, the Black Death of 1348, which wiped out two-thirds of the city's population. Under the abandoned expansion plans, the existing Duomo would have become merely the transept of a far more enormous church; as it is, they only finished one of the nave walls and the facade of the expanded church. These unfinished areas—essentially reduced to being merely tall, narrow buildings—now house the **Museo dell'Opera Metropolitana** ✯✯ (Piazza del Duomo 8; ☎ 0577-283048; www.operaduomo.siena.it; 6€; daily Mar–May and Sept–Nov 1 9:30am–7pm,

June–Aug 9:30am–8pm, Nov 2–Feb 10am–5pm), home to many of the artworks that once graced the Duomo, inside and out. If you climb the highest viewpoint in the museum (actually the top of what would have been the facade of the much larger church) you'll end up at about the same height as the Palazzo Pubblico's tower with, to my mind, an even better view. Of the many highlights in the museum, the statues in the first room by Giovanni Pisano, with their craning necks—they were taken from the exterior and meant to be viewed from below—are favorites; they look as though they're coming to life and peering around the dimly lit hall. In a room of its own, Duccio's 1311 *Maestà* was once the Duomo's altarpiece and is today the museum's star attraction. The colors, composition, and realistic (for that time) feel of the subject exhibit the characteristics of what became known as the Siena style of painting and make it one of the most famous medieval paintings in Italy.

Across from the Duomo is the **Ospedale di Santa Maria della Scala** ✪✪ (Piazza del Duomo 2; ☎ 0577-224811 or 0577-224828; http://santamaria. comune.siena.it; 6€; daily Mar 16–Oct 10:30am–6:30pm, Nov–Dec 24 and Jan 7– Mar 15 10:30am–4:30pm, Dec 25–Jan 6 10am–6pm), an erstwhile hospital, now a museum containing original sick-room frescoes, winding hallways with chapels, and recently created archaeological and contemporary art exhibits. It was a combined pilgrims' hostel and hospital that opened in the 800s and was staffed by nuns caring for the sick. The city of Siena ran it as a hospital until the 1990s, funding both patient care and the artwork now displayed within. The most notable feature is the frescoed walls of the Sala del Pellegrino, where Domenico di Bartolo (among other artists) created a telling visual history of the hospital in the 1440s, giving insights into Sienese life at the time and extolling the good works of the hospital itself. The left wall shows the founding of the hospital, with divine intervention, city officials monitoring construction, and a pope's blessing. Note the busy Siena street scenes with Middle Eastern merchants, arguing workers, and posturing politicians. The far wall's frescoes are late-16th-century additions that illustrate the role of wet nurses at the hospital—as they took in many orphans, women were needed to feed them. The right wall has a portrait of workers tending to the sick and distributing charity. Note the unappealing conditions of the hospital, with cats and dogs fighting on the floor, scary-looking instruments, and general chaos (in the next panel, don't miss the helpful baby in his mother's arms who kindly aims her breast at the beggar children). The next-to-last panel shows the hospital as a school at which the orphans were raised and educated—a somewhat grim process from the looks of the menacing teacher with a switch in his hand.

The on-site Cappella del Sacro Chiodo is worthwhile for Vecchietta's frescoes of the Last Judgment. The chapel once held a nail said to be from Jesus' crucifixion, purchased at great cost by the city of Siena in the 1300s. Hallways continue in mazelike fashion to the Fienile, which displays the original panels from the fountain in Piazza del Campo. From the Fienile level, another stairway leads to the occasionally interesting Museo Archeologico and rotating modern exhibits.

Around the back side of the Duomo (to the right, past the Museo dell'Opera, and down a steep flight of outdoor stairs) is the **Battistero San Giovanni** ✪ (Piazza San Giovanni; ☎ 0577-238048; www.operaduomo.siena.it; 3€; hours same as Museo dell'Opera), the cathedral's baptistery, which is often overlooked by tourists, but has a baptismal font worth seeing, surrounded by elaborately frescoed vaulted ceilings. The early-15th-century hexagonal font allows you to play art critic as you walk around the panels designed by competing artists. For your scorecard, Jacopo della Quercia sculpted the *Annunciation* panel facing the altar. The *Birth and Preaching of the Baptist* panels were done by Giovanni di Turino. Florence baptistery veteran Ghiberti is responsible for the panels of the *Baptism of Christ* and the *Arrest of St. John*. For my money, the best of the bunch is Donatello's *Feast of Herod*, which uses new and improved perspective techniques in a dramatic scene with naturalistic figures.

The **Pinacoteca Nazionale (National Picture Gallery)** ✶ (Via San Pietro 29; ☎ 0577-281161; 4.30€; Mon 8:30am–1:30pm, Tues–Sat 8:15am–7:15pm, Sun 8:15am–1:30pm) has nearly 40 rooms jam-packed with more than 500 paintings covering 400 years of art history. You could easily spend a full day here. The Sienese school obviously represents itself well, with rooms full of Duccio and Simone Martini on the second floor—go to this floor first if you're short on time. And be sure to check out Martini's entertaining *Il Beato Agostino Novello* in Room 5: St. Augustine appears to be the patron saint of clumsy people as he flies from scene to scene saving babies and fallen horsemen. Room 30 has large-scale charcoal-and-ink drawings made by Beccafumi as diagrams for the marble flooring in Siena's Duomo. From the Sala di Scultura (Room 26), you get a lovely view of the city. The third floor has a surprisingly good selection of Flemish works, including paintings by Dürer and a Bruegel-esque *Tower of Babel*.

It's worth the trek to see the interior of the massive **San Domenico Church** ✶ (Piazza San Domenico; free; daily Apr–Oct 7am–1pm and 3–6:30pm, Nov–Mar 9am–1pm and 3–6pm), at the northern edge of the city. The church celebrates Siena's St. Catherine with a 1414 portrait (in the raised chapel at the rear), paintings of her miracles (at the Chapel of St. Catherine midway along the right wall), and relics in the form of the poor woman's severed head and thumb. The thumb is in a case to the right of the chapel, while her head (original skull, skin redone) is in a case next to the altar. Among the paintings of the church, look for St. Catherine's three symbols, a white lily, cross, and book. St. Catherine was born in 1347 and spent her life in spiritual contemplation, in ministering to the poor in post-plague Siena, and in diplomacy. She spent many years trying to reunite papal and anti-papal factions in Europe before retiring from the world, receiving the stigmata in this very church and eventual sainthood.

THE OTHER SIENA

There's no better place to meet locals and witness the best of Sienese life than at one of the annual *contrada* parties. They are part traditional festival, part frat party, and part carnival, with everything from rock bands to weathered accordion players. Booths and local shops sell wine and food; games, gossip, and gambling on the upcoming Palio races are popular nighttime activities. These are not tourist-oriented events, but the locals are very welcoming—just don't be carrying the flag of a competing *contrada!* You can find out about these events by asking your concierge or a waiter at a restaurant, or just by hearing some noise and walking toward it. The parties take place in various neighborhoods during the month before and after the Palio races, from late June to late August.

Or go to a local game. Siena's up-and-coming **AC Siena** soccer team (Via dei Montanini 87; ☎ 0577-281084; www.acsiena.it) has risen to the top Serie A

The Palio Festival

Somehow, this 700-year-old horse race is both the most touristy and the most local event in Italy. Ten of the *contrade* of Siena have horses that compete in the three-lap race around the Piazza. If the barebacked horse finishes with the rider on top, great; if not, that's good, too. Rules are few, crashes are many, and conspiracy theories are common. In short, every July 2 and August 16 the town goes nuts. (Ten *contrade* compete in the first race; the top three compete with the remaining seven Sienese 'hoods in Aug.)

The 17 *contrade* that take part in the race on a rotating basis treat the event as a combination Super Bowl, Mardi Gras, and World War III. Parties begin weeks before the races and continue for the month after. Booster clubs spend huge amounts of money to hire the best riders and horses in Italy, and betting reaches astronomical heights. Rumors of drugged horses, mugged riders, and general thuggish behavior color the events.

But for a visitor, the races offer a glimpse into the medieval spectacles of Italy, with all of the pageantry and the generally harmless chaos. The neighborhood *contrade* parties are a welcoming blend of street fair, frat party, and Fellini movie, with free-flowing wine mixing with rock bands, gossiping elders, carnival booths, and family parties.

The grandstand, bleacher seats, and windows and balconies around the square go for hundreds of euros, are sold out months before the event, and have to be purchased directly from the shops, business, and homeowners who own them (some hotels offer Palio packages, or ask the tourist office for help if you feel you have the time, money, and negotiating skills to try on your own).

Otherwise, join the masses in the center of the square for the race. To see anything, you need to arrive hours ahead of time (by at least 4pm) and fight to hold your ground (and your bladder; you're stuck in the center of the piazza center for the full afternoon until the race itself, at 7:30pm in July and 7pm in August, and there are no port-a-johns). From the center of the square, the race doesn't make much sense. It's over in less than 2 minutes, and chances are you'll miss the whole thing, but who cares? You're part of the scene.

For more information, contact the **Consorzio per la Tutela del Palio di Siena** (Via di Città 34; ☎ 0577-43875; www.paliodisiena.biz).

division after years of barely maintaining Serie B status. Tickets begin at 20€, and can be purchased toward the sound end of the historical center at Fabbri Emanuele & C. (Via Pantaneto 154, the continuation of Via Banchi di Sotto; ☎ 0577-28435), at the north end of town at the Tra-in bus station (Piazza Gramsci; ☎ 0577-204111), and right in the center at Sogno Siena (Via dei Termini, 54, a parallel to Via Banchi di Sopra; ☎ 0577-225703). The team plays in black-and-white striped shirts in tribute to the striped Duomo and other sites in town. A spirited crowd fills the 16,000-seat Stadio Comunale on the north side of town every other Sunday from September through May.

If you're tired of soccer, choose basketball—Siena is hoops crazy. (Before you dismiss Italian b-ball, remember: Kobe Bryant grew up watching his dad—former Sixer, Clipper, and Rocket Joe Bryant—play in the Italian league.) Siena's **Montepaschi Mens Sana** pro basketball team (Via Sclavo 8; ☎ 0577-38071; www. menssanabasket.it) claims to be Italy's oldest club and won the Italian league title in the 2003–04 season. If you're there during the season (roughly Oct–Apr), check out a game—it's fun to join the raucous, singing, chanting, soccer-style crowd. You can purchase tickets (6€–48€) at most tobacco shops. Games are played at the Palazzo Dello Sport, a few miles north of town.

To check out the local English-speaking literary scene, drop by the **Book Shop** (Galleria di San Pietro, Via San Pietro 19; ☎ 0577-226594; www.bookshopsiena. com). You can attend readings or just hang out in the comfy chairs; sample English language books; and meet some British, American, and Australian expats.

ATTENTION, SHOPPERS!

Siena doesn't have nearly the depth and breath of shopping opportunities as nearby Florence, but it does offer more than most Tuscan cities. In recent summers, the city encouraged all shops to stay open until midnight; I can't say whether the experiment will be repeated, but you just may be able to get your late-night Gucci fix on in July.

Books

Libreria Senese (Via di Citta 64; ☎ 0577-280845) has a wide selection of specialty art and travel books in English, in addition to local guides, maps, and souvenirs. There's also the English-language **Book Shop** (Galleria di San Pietro, Via San Pietro 19; ☎ 0577-226594; www.bookshopsiena.com).

Clothing

For a great selection of Armani, Gucci, and all the usual suspects, stop at **Cortecci** (Via Banchi di Sopra 27, ☎ 0577-280096; also Piazza del Campo 30, ☎ 0577-280984; www.corteccisiena.it), which has a friendly staff and a large inventory.

If you're in the mood for something more unique, drop by **Tessuti a Mano** (Via San Pietro 7; ☎ 0577-282200), where the owner weaves luxurious sweaters, scarves, and shawls—you may see her hard at work on her loom.

Curios

At **Vetrate Artistiche** (Via della Galluzza 5; ☎ 0577-48033; www.glassisland. com), a glass workshop/souvenir shop, you can watch workers complete their stained-glass projects. Even if you're not building a church, you can still buy their jewelry, picture frames, and mosaic household items. They also offer apprenticeships if you're planning on sticking around for a few months.

Wine

Part museum, part wine shop, part bar, part restaurant installed in the evocative brick vaults of the Medicean Fortress, the government-run **Enoteca Italiana**

(Fortezza Medicea, Via Camollia 72; ☎ 0577-228811; www.enoteca-italiana.it; Mon–Sat noon–1am) is meant to promote Italian wines, with a focus on Tuscany. The 1,260-label, multithousand-bottle collection represents the best the region has to offer. Early evening there are snacks with the tastings.

The **Enoteca San Domenico** (Via del Paradiso 56; ☎ 0577-271181; www. enotecasandomenico.it) is a slightly more central and less intimidating place to shop for area wines as well as local gourmet products, including olive oils, dried herbs, pastas, and sweets.

NIGHTLIFE

In 1765, Scotsman James Boswell wrote of the after-hours pleasures of Siena: "I found that people lived there in a completely natural fashion, making love as their inclinations suggested . . .. Intoxicated by that sweet delirium, I gave myself up, without self-reproach and in complete serenity, to the charms of irregular love." While Siena is not the hotbed of free love that it apparently was in the 1760s, a good time can still be had at night in a variety of stylish, smaller nightspots, as well as in the requisite Irish pubs. For larger clubs, locals head down the road to Poggibonsi.

The artsy, ever-so-hip **Corte del Miracoli** (Via Roma 56; ☎ 0577-48596; www. lacortedeimiracoli.org) is a student/hippie hangout that bills itself as a "contemporary cultural center," featuring live shows, avant-garde theater, and music. The shows can be odd, but always amusing, and the crowd is quite friendly. For a more adult night on the town, catch occasional live music in the swank jazz bar, **The Tea Room** (Porta Giustizia 11; ☎ 0577-222753).

Or try what seems to be Siena's unofficial new party drink—sangria—at **Buena Vista Social Pub** (Via San Martino 31; ☎ 0577-221423) and **Antico Caffè Ortensia** (Via Pantaneto 95; ☎ 0577-40039). Both offer a Spanish/Caribbean flair with good sangria, and are popular places to hang out. Both also have limited pub grub. Indulge in Guinness and general foolishness at the pub **Barone Rosso** (Via dei Termini 9; ☎ 0577-286686; www.barone-rosso.com), which also features DJs and (Wed–Sat) live music.

AREZZO

Arezzo is most famous for its medieval square, scene of a yearly jousting festival; its massive Duomo; and Piero della Francesca's *Legend of the True Cross* fresco. But take a walk through the evocative old town and you can't help but notice you have entered the land of Vasari. Giorgio Vasari—architect, painter, sculptor, writer, and self-important cultural busybody—was born in Arezzo in 1512 and appears to have designed, built, or painted everything in town aside from the Roman amphitheater (I'm assuming he was on the renovation committee for that).

You can stand on Via Vasari in the Loggia di Vasari in Arezzo's Piazza Grande, and admire the Vasari-designed bell tower at the top of the palace. Walk uphill to the Duomo to see Vasari's *cantoria* (choir gallery), as well as his paintings in the museum there. On your way to the city museum to admire more Vasari paintings, you can stop at his self-consciously elegant house. Vasari did the altar and frescoes at the Badia church, and a work in the Santissima Annunziata. He doesn't have any frescoes in San Domenio, but, sure enough, his dad does. No matter how much you might admire Vasari, by the time you leave Arezzo, you may be feeling

like Mark Twain after an exhaustive tour of works by Vasari's personal hero, Michelangelo: "I never felt so fervently thankful, so soothed, so tranquil, so filled with a blessed peace, as I did yesterday when I learned that the man was dead."

While Vasari's achievements are worth a look, the real artistic treat in town is Piero della Francesca's fresco cycle in San Francesco. The 15th-century masterwork illustrating everything from original sin to redemption has been recently restored and is a must-see, along with the Duomo and the main square. But don't make the mistake of thinking Arezzo is as dead as Vasari: The first Sunday of every month that glorious main piazza fills with the 600+ dealers of Italy's greatest antiques fair—except for the first Sunday of September when the city holds its Giostra del Saraceno jousting competition (see "The Joys of Jousting" on p. 195)—and in late June Arezzo turns into techno paradise with the Arezzo Wave music fest.

A BRIEF HISTORY OF AREZZO

Arezzo began as an Etruscan city-state about 500 B.C., controlling trade routes through the central Apennine mountains until Roman legions colonized the area. Visitors can still see remnants of Arezzo's Roman amphitheater, built in the 1st and 2nd centuries A.D. Its 9,000 seats point to the vitality of the city at that time.

The control of trade routes enabled Arezzo to become a prosperous state in the 10th century, allowing the good times to continue until Florentine armies destroyed Arezzo forces in 1289.

While it lost its independence, Arezzo maintained its artistic vitality, giving birth to the careers of the poet Petrarch in the 1300s and Vasari in the 1500s. Music has also played a part in Arezzo's history, as can be seen in the "do-re-mi-fa . . ." plaque (at the corner of Via De Montetini and Via Desalpino) commemorating the birthplace of Guido Monaco, who created the modern diatonic musical scale.

LAY OF THE LAND

Arezzo is conveniently reached by train on the Rome-Florence line, with almost hourly departures from Rome (a 2- to 3-hr. trip) and nearly half-hour schedules from Florence (a 45- to 90-min. trip). The Arezzo train station is next to a tourist office a few blocks south of the historical center.

If you're driving, Arezzo is just off the A1 autostrada, 75km (47 miles) from Florence, 200km (124 miles) from Rome. There are free parking lots north of the city walls from which a set of escalators will take you into the city to pop out of a tunnel right next to the Duomo. Neat.

Arezzo has three different **tourist offices,** each with a wealth of pamphlet info. The main tourist office is in front of the train station in Piazza della Repubblica, 28 (☎ 0575-377678; www.apt.arezzo.it); the regional office is a couple of blocks into the city in Piazza Risorgimento, 116 (☎ 0575-23952); and a supplemental office is at the north end of the city next to Palazzo Comunale at Via Ricasoli (☎ 0575-377829).

ACCOMMODATIONS, BOTH STANDARD & NOT

€   The **Bed & Breakfast Petrarca** (Via Vittorio Veneto 101; ☎ 0575-902337 or 347-4954855; www.bebpetrarca.it; cash only), might be a few blocks south of the station (and the historical center), but on the plus side it charges a mere 40€ for a double without bathroom and 50€ for one with bathroom—and the six little rooms are actually quite nice, with frilly wrought-iron bed frames, framed pictures, and colorful rugs scattered on parquet or linoleum floors.

€€   The five rooms of **Bed & Breakfast I Due Gigli** ★ (Via Cavour 170; ☎ 338-8661934; www.iduegigli.it; cash only), in the heart of the historical center between the church of San Francesco and Vasari's House, have a kind of refined country style. Furnishings are subdued yet elegant, and there are plenty of 18th-century frescoes and decorative touches uncovered during the restoration to turn this medieval palazzo into a B&B. Rooms without private bathroom cost 70€, with bathroom 75€ (one heavily frescoed room, with bathroom, goes for 93€); breakfast is an additional 5€. Guests share two kitchens and two terraces.

€€–€€€   If you were to picture an ideal apartment in a historical Italian town, it would probably resemble a flat at **La Corte del Re** ★★ (Via Borgunto 5; ☎ 0575-401603; www.lacortedelre.com; AE, MC, V). A perfect combination of old and new, the nine apartments at La Corte have stylish and functional modern furniture and full kitchens blending coolly into the arched wood beams and stone walls of a 14th-century building. Five of the rooms look directly over Piazza Grande, the best view in town. All that and room rates are just 80€ to 150€ per night. Energetic manager Franca Gianetti will do what it takes to make sure your stay is a good one.

€€€   If you're simply seeking a normal night's lodging in a standard hotel, the **Continentale** (Piazza Guido Monaco 7; ☎ 0575-20251; www.hotelcontinentale. com; AE, MC, V) is a good call. With 73 rooms, you'll probably find space, and the rooms themselves are decent, though a little tired and noisy on the street side. Request an Old-Style room for a little more character, a Garden room for more quiet. The rooftop garden offers nice views of the city, and the lobby has a couple of free high-speed Internet terminals. The staff is professional, and the location, while not in the heart of the old town, is an easy walk from there. Prices are a reasonable 108€ to 126€ for a double.

Rural Accommodations

There's one storied *agriturismo* less than half an hour's drive from Arezzo that deserves mention:

€€   One of the first operations to put agritourism in Italy on the map, **Rendola Riding** ★ (Rendola 66, Montevarchi, about 24km/15 miles northeast from Arezzo; ☎ 055-9707045; www.rendolariding.it; cash only) is a working ranch with a dozen horses for lessons and multiday treks. Rendola Riding also raises barnyard animals and vegetables for the dinner table. Jenny Bawtree, an Englishwoman, founded Rendola in 1969, long before *agriturismo* became hip. Guests come for the riding, but are not required to be experts at the English technique used here. The place has the feel of summer camp, partially owing to the youth classes taking place in summer, but mostly from the communal dining, and the "scrape the dung off your own shoes" spirit of the place. Several detached apartments down the hill offer a good option for families, or couples looking for privacy. Double rooms and breakfast are 80€ to 90€, meals are 20€ to 25€, and riding is 18€ per hour.

€€€–€€€€   Nestled in the forested mountains flaking the west side of the broad Valdichiana valley, 17 miles southwest of Arezzo (and 22 miles east of Siena), lies a 13th-century walled hamlet—complete with a fairy-tale, crenellated castle tower—called **Castello di Gargonza** ★★★ (Loc. Gargonza, just west of Monte San Savino; ☎ 0575-847021; www.gargonza.it; AE, MC, V). Count Riccardo Guicciardini, whose family has owned the property for 300 years, decided to save the long-abandoned village from decay in the 1960s by converting the fortified village, in its entirety, into a guest "residence." This is a wonderfully evocative and isolated retreat, not a full-fledged hotel, so don't come expecting hotel amenities (no TV or A/C—though there is now Wi-Fi). The former peasant houses contain 25 self-catering apartments complete with kitchenettes and working fireplaces sleeping anywhere from two to eight people (from 735€ a week, up to 155€–175€ a night for two to three guests, if you stay a shorter amount of time), and several basic rooms with wood-beamed ceilings scattered throughout (115€ for a Classic double, 125€ for larger Comfort rooms that might be considered junior suites in a hotel). After a flirtation with 20th-century designer furniture, the complex is being refitted with simple late-17th-century pieces. The old olive-press building has been converted into a common space, with sitting/TV rooms, a bar/breakfast room, and access to the gardens. There's also a pool surrounded by wild rosemary and plenty of wooded park. The Tuscan restaurant is so good you needn't venture out for every meal. To get there, take the A1 to exit 27 (MONTE S. SAVINO), then follow the SS73 6.8 miles to the turnoff for Gargonza.

DINING FOR ALL TASTES

€   For the best food deal in town, drop by the **Martini Point** ★ (Corso Italia 285; ☎ 347-6221586; daily 5:30pm–2am; cash only) cocktail bar from about 6 to 9pm any night. For the price of a drink, you can down a buffet's worth of appetizers, and people-watch at the south gate of town. The couscous, mushrooms, and minipizzas are actually pretty good, and the olives are everything you could hope for in a bar called Martini. Light dishes cost about 5€ to 8€, but why pay when you get 'em for free during happy hour?

€   Toward the north end of town is **Trattoria Mazzoni** (Canto all Croce 1 at Via San Lorentino; ☎ 0575-26857; www.mazzoni.info; Wed–Mon noon–2:30pm and 7–10:30pm; AE, MC, V), a charming family restaurant/food shop easy to find (it's next to the sign with the pink pig face advertising its specialty: *porchetta* cooked over a wood fire). It gets crowded with locals and a few passing tourists. Of course, you'll be ordering the smoked *porchetta* for 6.50€, but those who feel sorry for the piggy out front can order an equally good pesto gnocchi for 6€. A liter of house wine goes for a reasonable 5€. *Primi* cost from 6€ to 7€, *secondi* from 6.50€ to 12€.

€–€€   As a reproof to the restaurants that achieve economy by concentrating on pizza, the **Osteria da Luchino** (Via Deccheria 3; ☎ 0575-333388; Wed–Mon noon–3pm and 7–11pm; AE, MC, V) has a sign in the window that defiantly states NO PIZZA. Instead, the osteria creates a tasty selection of homemade pastas, including tagliolini in a tomato and basil sauce for only 6€. Most other pastas range from 6€ to 8€, with grilled *secondi* in the 8€ to 12€ range. In summer, you can dine alfresco on the patio.

€€–€€€€   Or try either of two local institutions on the Piazza Grande: **Trattoria Lancia D'Oro** (Logge Vasari 18–19, on Piazza Grande; ☎ 0575-21033; www.cittadiarezzo.com/lanciadoro; Tues–Sun noon–3pm and 7:30–10:30pm, Sun noon–3pm; AE, MC, V) and **Ristorante "Logge Vasari"** ★ (Logge Vasari 19, on Piazza Grande; ☎ 0575-295894; www.loggevasari.it; Wed–Mon noon–3pm and 7:30–11pm; AE, MC, V), which are both under the same ownership, and under the same arcade at the north end of Piazza Grande. Logge Vasari is the more upscale of the two, with candelabras and antique furniture. Here, you'll sit back and enjoy a multihour Italian-style meal with perhaps an assorted prosciutto starter, followed by homemade ravioli with truffles, and a *secondi* of Chianini steak with a side of fresh vegetables. Pasta dishes cost from 11€ to 16€ (spiking up to as high as 25€ for the occasional seasonal specialty that involves white truffles), while grilled second platters are 16€ to 22€. Be sure to save room for a cheese platter or chocolate cake for dessert. The cheaper option, Lancia D'Oro, is not quite as

The *Legend of the True Cross*

Almost from the start of Christianity, the cross upon which Jesus was crucified was thought to possess mystic powers, as if sanctified by the spirit of God. Crusaders sought it out almost as fiercely as the Holy Grail, and enough alleged pieces of the True Cross appeared throughout Europe to create not only a few crosses, but Noah's ark, the tower of Babel, and a boardwalk around Jerusalem.

The legend, as detailed in della Francesca's fresco, goes like this—top to bottom, right to left:

1. Seth, the son of Adam, plants a sprig of the tree of knowledge in his dead father's mouth.
2. (diagonally from the top) Workmen for King Solomon take part of the tree to use for a bridge.
3. King Solomon constructs the bridge, which the Queen of Sheba recognizes as holy and prophesies that the wood will be used to crucify Jesus.
4. (diagonally from 3) Constantine has a vision of the cross. Constantine holds out a minicross while leading his troops in battle.
5. (across from 4) An angel tells Mary she will bear the son of God. Doesn't really have anything to do with the cross legend, but an Annunciation painting is always nice.
6. Judas is tortured by being lowered into a well until he tells where the cross is.
7. (to the left of 6) St. Helena (and her trusty dwarf) directs her people to dig up the cross, and it promptly causes the miracle of resurrecting a man.
8. (below 7) A dramatic battle scene shows Heraclius defeating the Persian king Chosroes, who stole the cross and will be beheaded on the right.
9. (above 8) Heraclius returns the cross with great acclaim to Jerusalem, where people wear clothes oddly similar to those of 15th-century Tuscany.

swank in looks but its food is darn good, especially its grilled lamb with rosemary and homemade tagliatelle with regional herbs. Their *primi* are 10€ to 15€, their *secondi* 12€ to 20€.

WHY YOU'RE HERE: THE TOP SIGHTS & ATTRACTIONS

Your first stop should be the **Basilica di San Francesco** ✹✹✹ (Piazza San Francesco; ☎ 0575-352727 or 0575-299071; www.pierodellafrancesca.it; free admission to church, 6€ for entry to chapel including obligatory 2€ booking fee; daily 9am–7pm, Nov–Mar and weekends 9am–6pm), which houses one of Italy's masterworks, Piero della Francesca's *Legend of the True Cross*. The fresco, painted on 12 panels in the 1450s, details the long story of the wood of the cross that crucified Jesus (see "The *Legend of the True Cross*," above). Its fame derives from its vivid colors, the use of perspective, and the realistic (for that time) setting of the scenes. The tourist board recommends calling the above number or using the website to make ticket reservations to view the fresco, but after the first few post-restoration years (which kicked off one of Italy's periodic minicrazes for all things Piero), the crowds seem to have abated and, at least in low season, you should be able just to show up and get a ticket for the same day. There is an official 30-minute time limit for viewing the fresco.

Arezzo's **Duomo** ★ (Piazza del Duomo; ☎ 0575-23991; free; daily 7am 12:30pm and 3–6:30pm) gets short shrift in the shadow of Francesca's mural, but it's worth a trip up for the ornate interior. It took 250 years to complete from its start in 1278, and even then residents had to wait until 1859 for the bell tower, and until the 20th century for the facade to be finished. The 16th-century stained-glass windows by Guillame de Marcillat (a French master who traveled Italy reviving the fashion for such windows) are beautiful, but they don't let in enough light to see much of the other works here, including the masterful *Santa Maria Maddalena* fresco by Piero della Francesca to the right of the tomb of Bishop Tarlati. Past the fresco is a large cantoria designed by a young Vasari in 1535.

Vasari's architecture can also be seen in the main square, the tilted **Piazza Grande** ★★ in the center of the old town. The square is used for antiques fairs the first Sunday of every month and for jousting on the first Sunday in September. It (along with the rest of town) was a setting for the Oscar-winning movie *Life Is Beautiful* in 1999. Vasari's loggia, built in 1573, is now filled with shops and restaurants on the north end of the square. In 1550, Vasari designed the bell tower, which tops off the **Palazzo della Fraternità dei Laici.** Dominicans sponsored the construction of the Gothic and early Renaissance Palazzo in the 1370s. The portal is worth a look, as is the Madonna relief above the door.

For a glimpse into the lifestyle and mind of Vasari, you can stop by his house, **Casa di Vasari** (Via XX Settembre 55; ☎ 0575-409040; 2€; Wed–Sat and Mon 9am–7pm, Sun 9am–1pm). Ring the bell outside for admission, as the door will be locked. Vasari bought the house in 1350 and decorated it as a monument to himself. You can see his wall paintings featuring his portrait enshrined among the greats of art (he places himself right next to Michelangelo), and a ceiling painting of a battle between Virtue, Envy, and Fortune, perhaps Vasari's three main concerns in life. And just to show he had some humility, there's a small bare chapel off the living room, still with some original floor tiles, and a wooden altar for his prayers.

A more serene location for prayers would be the **San Domenico church** ★ (Piazza San Domenico; ☎ 0575-23255; free; daily 9am–6:30pm) in the far northern part of town. The tree-lined piazza doesn't see many visitors, and the church interior is silent under its huge wooden arches. The church was constructed in 1275, and features an appropriately dark and somber crucifix by Cimabue, painted in 1260 and only recently restored to its original glory. Remnants of frescoes cover the walls, beyond hope of full restoration, but the fragments are compelling.

The Joys of Jousting

The most famous festival of Arezzo is the **Giostra del Saracino (Saracen Joust)** ★. Competitive jousting took place in Arezzo at least as far back as 1400, and this particular festival commemorates battles against invading Saracens. On the first Sunday in September, the Piazza Grande is filled with dirt and packed with people. Horsemen arrive in medieval garb to take their oath of combat in front of a decked-out town hall. Historical parades of flag-wavers and jugglers tour through town during the day. The event itself features horsemen competing with horse and lance to nail the metal "Saracen" figure propped up in the middle of the square. The catch is that the Saracen gets to fight back: If his shield is hit, the figure spins around, swinging the whip propped in his other arm.

THE OTHER AREZZO

About a mile outside of town is one of the world's largest gold jewelry manufacturing companies, **Uno A Erre** (Via Fiorentina 550; ☎ 0575-925403; www. unoaerre.com), which sold 41 *tons* of gold jewelry and accessories in a recent year and produces 70% of all Italian wedding rings. Arezzo has historically been a center for gold and jewelry, and Uno A Erre certainly continues that tradition in a big way. Call ahead and you can visit the fairly interesting museum to see production machinery, jewel designs, and historic collections of jewelry styles that the company has produced since its inception in 1926. Naturally, it has a factory outlet store (Mon–Fri 9am–6pm; Sat 9am–1pm), where you can sometimes get decent deals on midrange jewelry. For unique or high-end items, it's more fun, and just as expensive, to go to local artisans' shops in Arezzo or Florence.

5 Umbria

After visiting Rome, before rushing to Florence, take the time to drive the remarkable countryside and hill towns of what Italians call "The Green Heart of Italy"

by Reid Bramblett

THE SMALL BUT VITAL REGION OF UMBRIA, WHICH LIES NORTHEAST OF Rome, is made famous by St. Francis's hometown of Assisi and the Basilica there, a popular day-trip stop for tour buses. But despite that major attraction, Umbria has always played second fiddle to its western neighbor, Tuscany. And that's a darn shame because the region has much more to offer than a single side trip on the road between Rome and Florence.

Umbria has at least a half-dozen remarkable cities of unique charm and historical significance: Perugia, the capital, with a major university, jazz festival, and Umbria's best art museum; Assisi of St. Francis fame; Gubbio, a medieval town frozen in time with art-filled fortresses and churches along the slopes of a scenic mountain; Spoleto, with its own famous festival, Duomo, and shop-lined squares; Todi, a picturesque hilltop village with a maze of attractive streets; and Orvieto, with its famous wines, its underground caves, and famous cathedral.

Seeing all the major sights of Umbria in a single trip is a reasonable proposition. Umbria is a bite-size province just over half the size of Connecticut, measuring about 97km (60 miles) north to south and 64km (40 miles) east to west (though winding mountain roads can easily double distances). The ideal way to explore the area is to base yourself in an apartment or country cottage for a week, and drive a rented car on day trips to various cities. Don't waste valuable vacation time changing hotel and home city every day. Rail and bus lines connect the cities as well, but not quite as conveniently as a rental car does.

The Umbrians are a festive people whom you'll greatly enjoy mixing with, particularly in their nightly ritual, the festive "see and be seen" *passeggiata,* as they stroll up and down the streets of their historic towns.

DON'T LEAVE UMBRIA WITHOUT . . .

ATTENDING A FESTIVAL The yearly Spoleto Festival and Perugia Jazz Fest are world-class music and performance extravaganzas, not to be missed. The Race of the Ceri in Gubbio is another beaut.

POKING YOUR HEAD INTO PERUGIA'S GUILDHALLS See where the Donald Trumps of the 1400s met in the lavishly decorated and well-preserved Exchange, Merchant, and Lawyers' guildhalls.

GOING FOR AN EVENING PROMENADE The passeggiata in Perugia lets you see and be seen, culminating in a mass chill-out on the steps of the Duomo in front of the impressive Maggiore Fountain. You'll find similarly marvelous exercises in preening and socializing in Umbria's other hill towns

MAKING A PILGRIMAGE TO ASSISI'S BASILICA One of the top sites in all of Italy, the massive, two-level church is notable for its magnificent artwork (including Giotto's frescoes), and it's role as a major pilgrimage destination.

VIEWING ORVIETO'S DUOMO'S FACADE IN THE AFTERNOON LIGHT The golden-tiled mosaics shimmering in the setting sun turn the front of the church into a 46m (150-ft.) illuminated text, with Gothic spires standing as massive exclamation points. Walk closer to see the carved figures on the pillars grow even more frightening in the fading light. Then go inside to check out Signorelli's *Last Judgment* fresco, which was greatly admired (and copied) by Michelangelo himself.

TUNNELING INTO THE TUFA Visitors can experience history on guided walks through some of the 1,200 ancient caves and tunnel systems that honeycomb the rock upon which Orvieto was built.

TIPPLING SOME ORVIETO CLASSICO Orvieto is rightly famous for its Orvieto D.O.C., the white wine produced from grapes grown in the surrounding hills and valleys. They've been endorsed by everyone from ancient Romans and Gothic marauders to Signorelli himself (he insisted on some as part of his pay for the Duomo frescoes) and today's trendiest wine critics.

TAKING A STROLL ACROSS THE PONTE DELLE TORRI BRIDGE IN SPOLETO The 700-year-old stone bridge is a marvel to observe from afar, and even better to walk across.

PERUGIA

Perugia is a spirited city of 150,000 that seems at first glance to be a sprawling confusion of railroad tracks and minimarts, a spaghetti of highways, tunnels, and roundabouts. But reach the center of Perugia and you'll find one of Italy's most vibrant historical districts, with a wealth of both traditional sites and eating and entertainment options, culminating in the October Chocolate Festival and July's world-class Umbrian Jazz Fest.

Perugia, the capital, also makes a sensible headquarters from which to explore the region. Convenient highway, rail, and bus links connect it to Assisi in the east, Todi to the south, Gubbio to the north, and Cortona (in Tuscany) to the west. Once you start exploring Perugia's historical center, with the National Gallery, the Guildhalls, and its winding, stone streets linking medieval churches and museums, you won't be in any hurry to leave.

A BRIEF HISTORY OF PERUGIA

Perugia has been an Umbrian capital since Etruscan times (around 700 B.C.). Roman legions conquered the city and its trade routes in 309 B.C. Hoping to regain its former power, Perugia backed Mark Antony in his battles against soon-to-be-Emperor Octavian. Bad bet: Perugia was burned to the ground in 40 B.C. In what came across as a kind of early urban-renewal project, Octavian, after he became the Emperor Augustus, rebuilt the city and called it Augustus Perusia. Many of the city's walls, Roman aqueducts, and even Etruscan foundations are still visible.

Perugia didn't rise to eminence again until the early Middle Ages, when it became a free *comune,* then a city-state astride the same trade routes it dominated in Etruscan times. The mid–13th to late 14th century saw the construction of most of its significant landmarks, including the Duomo, the Fontana Maggiore, the central Palazzo dei Priori, and the Guildhalls. Perugia added military conquests to its economic prowess, seizing land as far north as Siena in 1358.

Perugia coupled this time of economic, military, and artistic achievement with a morally bereft ruling family, the Baglioni. The Baglioni men married their sisters, murdered their brothers, and periodically turned the city streets into bloody battlefields. As they began to spend most of their time fighting each other and other families in town, they fell prey to an outside invader. Pope Paul III's forces entered the city in 1538, destroyed the Baglioni palaces, and built a fortress above the rubble (the streets and houses the pope's forces buried to use as foundations can still be seen in tunnels beneath the city). When Paul III came to Perugia for his post-conquest victory parade, he took a page out of the Baglioni playbook and forced the nuns of the city to line up and kiss his feet.

Perugia remained subdued under papal control until citizens began to revolt during the Italian Unification campaign of the 1860s. The pope sent his Swiss Guard shock troops to Perugia, where they massacred citizens and looted the town before being forced out by Unification troops, whereupon the Perugini themselves, many using their bare hands, tore down the hated papal fortress Paul III had built.

The 20th century has seen Perugia rise again to a position of economic and cultural significance as capital of Umbria. A variety of important industries surround the town (including Italy's biggest purveyor of chocolates, Perugina), and several major universities are active within it. Today's festivals and lively food, music, and business scenes continue to keep the hills of Perugia alive with activity.

LAY OF THE LAND

Perugia is at the center of regional rail connections, an easy trip from Rome (2¼ hr.; try for the five daily direct trains, not those that transfer at Foligno) and from Florence (transferring at Cortona, taking about 2½ hr.). Trains also run almost hourly to Todi (a 45-min. trip) and twice an hour to nearby Assisi, a 20-minute ride.

Perugia's bus terminal at Piazza Partigiani also connects Perugia to Assisi, Gubbio, and Todi (about a 1-hr. ride to each); to Florence (a 2-hr. ride, once daily); and to Rome (about six times a day for the 2½-hr. trip).

The drive to Perugia is about 185km (115 miles) from Rome, 145km (90 miles) from Florence. The roads around central Perugia can be maddeningly confusing, so it may be easiest to park in the first parking garage you see and take one of the public escalators up to the historical district. Garages cost 7.75€ for a day, if you pay upfront. Free parking can be had at a lot at Piazza del Cupa, where you can walk to the series of long escalators to the center.

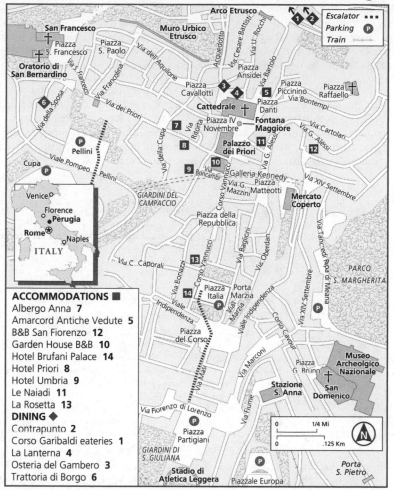

ACCOMMODATIONS ■

Albergo Anna **7**
Amarcord Antiche Vedute **5**
B&B San Fiorenzo **12**
Garden House B&B **10**
Hotel Brufani Palace **14**
Hotel Priori **8**
Hotel Umbria **9**
Le Naiadi **11**
La Rosetta **13**

DINING ◆

Contrapunto **2**
Corso Garibaldi eateries **1**
La Lanterna **4**
Osteria del Gambero **3**
Trattoria di Borgo **6**

Perugia's **tourist office** (☎ 075-5736458; http://turismo.comune.perugia.it and www.umbria2000.it), in the southwest corner of Piazza IV Novembre, has a ton of pamphlets on both the city of Perugia and the region of Umbria. The regional Umbrian tourist office located a couple of blocks away is just an administrative headquarters, so don't bother going there. Look for a copy of *Living Perugia*, a free monthly guide with restaurant, event, and activity listings.

ACCOMMODATIONS, BOTH STANDARD & NOT

Bed & Breakfasts

€€ In the realm of B&Bs—heck, of any lodgings—you simply can't get more central than **Amarcord Antiche Vedute** (Piazza Danti 28; ☎ 075-5733030 or

338-7499699; www.amarcordantichevedute.com; cash only; closed Jan 10–Mar 10) in the 15th-century Palazzo Conestabile della Staffa right on the main square. The comfy, modern 50€ to 75€ rooms come with TV, Wi-Fi, and (at the higher price) breakfast, and the B&B features a washing machine and a tower with panoramic views over the town and surrounding valleys.

€€   Nearly as central—just half a block off Piazza IV Novembre and named after the naiads on its famous fountain—**Le Naiadi** (Via Calderini 17; ☎ 333-7417408; www.beblenaiadi.com; cash only) rents two large, modern rooms with primary color themes brightened by flowers. The "Blue" room comes with a private, in-room bathroom for 70€ to 90€ per night, including breakfast; the "Red" room has its own bathroom outside the room and costs 10€ less.

€€   If you liked the feel of that buried city under the Rocca, you can live in a suite of rooms that looks just like it, only filled with contemporary furnishings, at the **B&B San Fiorenzo** ✦ (Via Alessi 45; ☎ 075-5730297 or 329-3562494, for English 320-0726001; www.bbsfiorenzo.it; cash only; closed Jan 15–Feb 15 and Nov 5–Dec 5). The rooms are in a 15th-century palazzo just below Piazza Matteotti, and each suite has its own entrance, giving you a kind of apartment-to-yourself feel (though they do provide a breakfast of pastries, yogurt, and drinks like at a hotel). The Suite Minor has a tight little sitting area with a small library, a modern bathroom, and a cozy bedroom under the arches, spandrels, and lunettes of some truly gorgeous brick vaulting; it costs 70€. The Suite Maior is worth the higher price (100€, and it sleeps four) because that evocative brick vaulting extends throughout the spacious apartment, from the cozy main bedroom to the large common room—divided by low brick archways into a main sitting area, dining room/kitchenette, and second sitting area with foldout sofa—and even in one of the bathrooms (that's right; there are two). What's more, most of the walls are of cobbled old stones to reinforce that fortress feel.

€€   The three rooms (doubles 80€–100€) at the **Garden House B&B** (Via Boncambi 29; ☎ 348-4742159, or for English 347-2361232; www.gardenhouse perugia.com; cash only; closed Jan 7–Mar 9) are cluttered with ornate furnishings to match the 18th-century setting—one room even comes complete with a frescoed ceiling of cherubs painted as if holding the chandelier. Guests also enjoy use of the building's eponymous garden. The B&B is on a crooked street leading off Corso Vannucci, less than a block from the heart of the action.

Central Hotels

€–€€   Down a steep street off the Corso, the tiny **Albergo Anna** (Via dei Priori 48; ☎ 075-5736304; www.albergoanna.it; MC, V; closed Nov and Feb) has a frilly sort of old-fashioned style, the rooms (50€–70€ doubles) rather plain but often livened up with old herringbone parquet floors, an impressive coffered wood ceiling, or an odd modern fireplace set with whimsical reliefs.

€€   Other than the great prices—55€ to 70€ for a double room (add 6€ per person for breakfast)—and killer location on a street parallel to the Corso, there's little to say about the perfectly pleasant but frankly bland standard rooms at the

Hotel Umbria (Via Boncambi 37; ☎ 075-5721203; www.hotel-umbria.com; AE, MC, V). All 18 rooms have (fairly) new bathrooms, TVs, and modular furnishings courtesy of an overhaul in 2000.

€€   For a bit more character in a similar price range, I'd book at the **Hotel Priori** (Via Vermiglioli 3, at Via dei Priori; ☎ 075-5723378; www.hotelpriori.it; MC, V), also bang in the middle of the historical center and featuring simply decorated but fairly spacious rooms with terra-cotta floors. They aren't exactly high end, but they'll do for a decent night's sleep and the prices can't be beat: 65€ to 95€ for doubles. I recommend in particular room nos. 355 and 353, which are nicely refurbished doubles with air-conditioning, though these can cost up to 115€ in high season. The hotel also has three huge suites with kitchenettes, period decor, and room for a family of four. These, however, are available only for long-term stays: 400€ to 500€ per week, 700€ to 800€ for 2 weeks. The Priori's balcony is a pleasant place for breakfast, but beware of the ravenous pigeons. Internet access is available in the basement meeting room.

€€€   An even better choice is the well-located **La Rosetta** ★ (Piazza Italia 19; ☎ 075-5720841; www.perugiaonline.com/larosetta; AE, MC, V). The hotel has refurbished its first-floor rooms to resemble those of an 18th-century palace, with frescoes, vaulted ceilings, and chandeliers in the large superior doubles. Above are less pricey digs, with lower ceilings and more modest furnishings, but all rooms come with satellite TV, minibars, safes, and air-conditioning. The hotel itself has a restaurant on-site (which provides room service) and a concierge. It's quite nice and, with 90 rooms varying in price, size, and view, most visitors will be able to find something to meet their needs and budget—so long as their budget begins at 130€, which is the starting price for a double room.

DINING FOR ALL TASTES

For the cheapest eats, follow the students. Go north of the city walls and into the smaller alleys around the Università per Stranieri for a variety of affordable dining options. **Corso Garabaldi,** due north of the Etruscan Arch, has four cheap *pizzerie,* a kabob shop, a *creperia,* and two bars in the space of 2 blocks. You can fill yourself for under 10€ at most of these spots (just don't expect health food). You'll also want to stop off at one of the city's many chocolate shops, as the city is rightly famous for its sweets (the chocolate gelato here is the best in Umbria).

€€   For a creative approach to the popular Umbrian dishes, walk behind the Duomo to **La Lanterna** ★ (Via U. Rocchi 6; ☎ 075-5726397; Thurs–Tues 12:30–2:30pm and 7:30–10:45pm; AE, MC, V), which features such novelties as *ravioli all'arancia* (orange ravioli with rose petals) and gnocchi *alla lanterna* with truffles and spinach topped by a cheese crust. Pasta dishes range from a reasonable 7.50€ to 10€ (and that includes dishes with truffles, which at many restaurants cause prices to skyrocket), *secondi* from 8€ to 12€, and a half-liter of the house wine is just 4€. The food is scrumptious, and the setting is quite charming: You'll have the choice of dining in the medieval subterranean restaurant, or in the hidden, wisteria-draped alleyway garden lunch area (both are lovely).

€€   For a true multicourse, multihour Italian feast in a traditional setting, go to **Trattoria Del Borgo** ★ ⦿kids (Via della Sposa 23/a–27; ☎ 075-5720390; Mon–Sat 7:30–10:30pm; MC, V). Both the restaurant and garden backyard dining area are packed until well past 11pm nightly, with a mostly local crowd devouring Umbrian specialties. Pastas range from 6.50€ to 10€, *secondi* from 5€ to 16€. Favorites include *tagliatelli al tartufo* (homemade pasta with truffles) for 9.50€, and the mixed meat appetizer (*misto di salumi,* 5.50€). For *secondi,* order the juicy *maialino all perugino,* a pot roast–type ensemble of suckling pig with veggies and mushrooms for 6.50€.

€€   If you're looking for a little more elegance with your meal, as well as a wide variety of local tastes, order one of the *menù degustazione* at **Osteria del Gambero** ★★ (Via Baldeschi 9; ☎ 075-5735461; www.osteriadelgambero.it; Tues–Sat 7:30–11pm, Sun 12:30–2:30pm and 7:30–11:30pm; AE, MC, V). It offers four tasting menus, each consisting of three courses and a dessert. One menu focuses on traditional Umbrian dishes (27€), the others on creative cuisine: vegetarian (27€), meat (28€), and seafood (29€). For 12€ extra you can have three glasses of wine, each one perfectly paired to each course. A la carte, *primi* cost 8.50€ to 9€, and *secondi* are 9€ to 14€. (For a strong-tasting alternative to pasta and grilled meats, try the *spigola* [sea bass] with greens, capers, and olives, for 14€.) Wine-lovers will appreciate the wide, thoughtful collection. The phenomenal food is what rates the first star (the basket of home-baked breads alone is worth the trip, and, in season, the chef goes crazy for truffles). The second star is due to the setting: on the *piano nobile* of an elegant 15th-century palazzo, with sophisticated service and lots of small rooms and nooks that make you almost feel as if you're dining alone with a personal chef and waitstaff.

WHY YOU'RE HERE: THE TOP SIGHTS & ATTRACTIONS

The recently renovated **National Gallery** ★★ (Palazzo dei Priori 4F, entrance at Corso Vannucci 19; ☎ 075-5741410 or 075-5741413; www.gallerianazionaleumbria.it; 6.50€ or as part of the Perugia museum pass; Tues–Sun 8:30am–7:30pm) contains Umbria's best collection of medieval and Renaissance art. It seems as though three-quarters of the works depict the Madonna and Child, so you'll be able to explore in depth the variations on the Madonna theme from the Byzantine style to the High Renaissance (see *"Mamma Mia,* Another Madonna & Child!" below).

The gallery culminates in **Room 23** with the greatest works by favorite son Perugino (like many artists, history remembers him by a nickname—in this case "The guy from Perugia"—rather than by his given name, Pietro Vannucci). Perugino taught painting to Raphael, collaborated with Pinturicchio, and earned consideration by art historian Vasari and others as a worthy peer to Michelangelo and da Vinci (another artist known by the name of his hometown; Leonardo came from the Tuscan village of Vinci). Look at the innovative colors, poses, and landscapes he brought to traditional themes like *The Adoration of the Magi,* the *Pietà,* and his *Madonna della Consolazione.*

For an interesting perspective (literally) on the Annunciation, go to **Room 11** to see Piero della Francesca's Madonna polyptych, and note the sci-fi look of the arches and hallway between the Angel and Mary.

The Perugia Museum Card

If you're planning to visit several of the museums in town, purchase the **Perugia Città Museo Card.** It comes in various denominations: 7€ for 1-day admission to your choice of five sites, 12€ for 3 days admission to all sites covered, 20€ for an annual pass, or 35€ for a family of four, also good for a full year. The pass covers all the sites listed here (except the science museum) along with a half-dozen other minor museums, historic palazzi, and archaeological collections and sites. Even if you're just planning on seeing the National Gallery and one or two others, the 7€ card is a good deal. You can buy the card at any of the participating attractions.

You can get a glimpse at the mercantile life of early Renaissance Perugia and a taste of the wealth and prominence of the guilds that ran its economy at **The Guildhalls** ★★, pigeonholing the flanks of the Palazzo dei Priori along Corso Vannucci **(Collegio del Cambio/Exchange Guildhall** at Corso Vanucci 25, ☎ 075-5728599; **Collegio della Mercanzia/Merchants' Guildhall** at Corso Vanucci 15, ☎ 075-5730366; **Sala dei Notari/Notaries' Hall** in the Palazzo dei Priori on Piazza IV Novembre, ☎ 075-5772339; 3.10€ combined ticket to all, or 2.60€ at the Exchange Guildhall, 1.05€ at the Merchants' Guildhall, Notaries Hall free; Tues–Sat 9am–1pm and 2:30–5:30pm, Sun 9am–1pm, Notari also Sun 3–7pm; closing hours curtailed a bit on some winter dates). Though the rooms are small—you can probably knock all three off your sightseeing list in 45 minutes—do not pass up the opportunity to see the best preserved guildhalls open to the public in Italy. In their day, the guilds had far more power and prestige than any modern business association or union. Their might is embodied by these halls, decorated by the finest artists of the era. The highlight is the **Collegio di Cambio,** with its early-16th-century frescoes by Perugino. The gods of classical antiquity along with handsome men and women personifying the various virtues are the subject, though tellingly Perugino also included a self-portrait in this pantheon (on the left-hand wall, look for the chubby fellow in the red cap up there among the great gods). Most art historians think that Perugino's protégé, Raphael, assisted with the work, possibly painting Fortitude (the figure on the cloud on the second bay of the left wall). The walls inside the nearby **Collegio della Mercanzia** are swaddled in intricately inlaid wood panels by northern European craftsmen of the 15th century. The **Sala dei Notari** was repainted in 1860, but in the spandrels of its eight large arches survive scenes from mythology and the Old Testament painted in 1297 by followers of medieval Roman master Pietro Cavallini.

Spend some time in **Piazza IV Novembre** ★ (named for Italy's National Unity day), a picturesque medieval square built directly atop of a Roman reservoir. Life in the square revolves around the **Fontana Maggiore,** a massive fountain designed by a local monk named Bevignate in 1278. Peek through the protective iron fence to see the carved marble scenes from daily life of the Middle Ages, plus figures from Aesop's Fables, signs of the zodiac, and portraits of local government

Mamma Mia, Another Madonna & Child!

Spend even a few hours in any Italian city, and you'll see dozens of Madonna and Child pictures, paintings, and statues on restaurant walls, car windows, street corner shrines, and church entrances. Enter a cathedral and museum, and you'll see dozens more, with Mary and Jesus in every possible pose and period of life, paired with saints, angels, and local patrons. After a day or two, you may have Madonna overload, and give them no more than a passing glance.

But look closer. As Perugia's Madonna-heavy National Gallery demonstrates, the dominant Mary-and-baby-Jesus theme in Italian art is a window through which you can understand Italian culture and history. The closer you look, the more will be revealed about the time and place of the art, and the people who made it.

A few things to look for:

1. **What are they wearing?** You can see a Madonna and Child in every type of garment, from royal robes to contemporary regional fashions to richly decorated Byzantine costumes. Mary usually wears a blue robe atop a red dress, the blue symbolizing fidelity and purity, the red standing for the blood of Christ. Jesus is either naked, or wearing a regional costume of the time. The nudity suggests the vulnerability of the sacrificed son, while contemporary robes link Jesus closer to contemporary life.

   If you find the standard blue robe and red dress next to a haloed naked baby, the artist or the original owner of the work may have had a strict interpretation of the Bible and the role of the Church. If Jesus has a Florentine robe and Mary a stylish belt, then you can guess that the painter or patron wanted to more directly address the spirituality of contemporary life, and make the teachings more "modern" and accessible.

2. **What are their expressions? Their gestures?** The Baby Jesus may be pointing to the heavens, or to an unfurled banner. A bent thumb and two small fingers signify the trinity of the Father, Son, and Holy Ghost, with the first two fingers extended in benediction. Jesus could be holding an apple, pear, or grape, the seeds symbolizing rebirth. Mary and child can look at each other with love and caring, or directly at the viewer with a "God is watching you" type message. A sad or downcast Mary communicates her awareness that her child is doomed for crucifixion.

3. **And what's this? A pelican?** On many crucifixion scenes of the suffering Jesus and the weeping Mary, you'll see what seems to be a random seabird hanging out at the top of the cross. The pelican, in times of need, will cut its own throat with its beak in order to feed its children with its blood. This natural symbol parallels Christ allowing his own blood to be spilled to atone for the sins of mankind.

officials. On the far side of the square is the **Duomo**—skip it. For Italy—where cathedrals are routinely swathed in frescoes by the greatest artists of all time—the Duomo of Perugia is a rather modest affair, with little more than a few second-rate baroque canvases (and a nice *Madonna* by Renaissance master Luca Signorelli) to relieve the dark, baroque interior. The massive **Palazzo dei Priori** on the other side of the square, built from about 1300 to 1450, still houses government offices along with the National Gallery and all those guildhalls.

To appreciate the ingenuity of the Etruscans who founded Perugia, climb down into the **Pozzo Etrusco (Etruscan Well)** ✦ 🚸 (Piazza Danti 18; ☎ 075-5733669; 2.50€; May–July and Sept–Oct Wed–Mon 10am–1:30pm and 2:30–6:30pm, Nov–Mar to 5pm, Apr and Aug daily 10am–1:30pm and 2:30–6:30pm). More than 2,200 years ago, Etruscans dug this 38m-deep (125-ft.), 5.4m-wide (18-ft.) well to provide water for the city. Nowadays, visitors can walk down the slippery steps and cross a walkway at the bottom. The ticket includes admission to the nearby **Cappella di San Severo** (Piazza Raffaello; ☎ 075-5733864; same hours), which features frescoes by a young Raphael.

A good spot for weekend visits with the kids is the **POST (Perugia Officina per la Scienza e la Tecnologia)** 🚸 (Via del Melo 34; ☎ 075-5736501; www.perugia post.it; 3€; Sat 3:30–7:30pm, Sun 10:30am–1pm and 3:30–7:30pm) science museum. It's a hands-on museum of the button-pushing, interactive-display type, although most of the explanations are in Italian only. Regardless, parents and kids can figure out what's going on together, and it makes a nice break from all the art and ancient ruins.

THE OTHER PERUGIA

For insight into the people of Perugia, you'll want to delve more deeply into their daily pleasures: chocolate, chocolate, and leisurely strolls in the evenings.

In particular, you simply must take part in the daily **passeggiata** ✦✦, an evening promenade along Corso Vanucci that lasts late into the night as Perugini stroll from Piazza Italia to Piazza IV Novembre. Along the way, do some window-shopping, stop at a bar or café, and just be part of the scene. Finish up by gazing over the countryside from the balcony at Piazza Italia, or sit with half the town at the steps in the medieval Piazza IV Novembre. It sounds like a simple activity, but it is truly at the heart of the life of this city.

Continue your walk underneath Piazza Italia through the refurbished exhibit spaces and streets of **Underground Perugia.** In the 1530s, the pope's forces razed the southern part of rebellious Perugia and built the Rocca on top of it. Many of the streets and stone houses remained forgotten under the fortress for hundreds of years. Now, escalators lead people through the area on the way to parking garages. Get off the escalator and tour the hidden streets, some with art galleries.

You'll also want to visit that mecca for chocoholics, the **Perugina Chocolate Factory** 🚸 (E45 Hwy. Madonna Alta exit, end of San Sito Rd.; ☎ 075-5276796; www.perugina.it; free; Mon–Fri 9am–1pm and 2–5:30pm), about 20 minutes outside of Perugia. Perugina celebrated its 100th anniversary on November 30, 2007, and visiting its headquarters is a Willy Wonka–like experience as you take a guided tour around a huge plant processing tons of chocolate in every size and shape. (The only downer: The pretour instructional video in English is a long corporate advertisement; watch the animated presentation for kids in Italian—it's much

The Foreign University

The oldest and largest university in Italy for foreigners is the **Università per Stranieri di Perugia** (Piazza Forteraccio 4; ☎ 075-57461; www.unistrapg.it/english). Since 1921 it has been teaching the language, culture, and arts of Italy. The school offers 3-month intensive language courses for all levels of students, as well as monthlong cultural classes for non-Italian speakers. Fees run 250€ to 300€ per month, and classes are taught year-round. Also of note is the university's free Wednesday lecture series, which sometimes features English-speaking guest speakers on all aspects of Italian art, culture, and history. Finally, the University hosts music, sports, and performing groups for foreigners—hang around the lobby and you may be able to sneak into a few.

more entertaining.) The factory museum boasts a hollow replica of the world's largest piece of chocolate (2.1m/7 ft. tall, weighing 6 tons) wrapped in foil. It also has photos of famous Perugina spokespeople, from Joe DiMaggio to Frank Sinatra, and an odd picture of Mussolini visiting the factory about a year before it was bombed to the ground in World War II. The tour is free (and so are the samples!) but phone ahead for reservations, especially as the workforce is prone to 1-day strikes. *Note:* The staff gets quite testy if you take pictures during the tour. Perugina also has a shop at Corso Vannucci 101 in town.

If you'd really like to dip into the world of chocolate (sadly, I mean that only as a metaphor), **The Eurochocolate Festival** (Viale Centova 6; ☎ 075-5025880; www.eurochocolate.com) is an annual mid-October bacchanalia devoted to all things brown and sugary. Organizers say they attracted a mind-boggling 900,000 visitors to a recent 10-day festival. The event has featured more than 100 booths of international chocolate makers, exhibits on "crucial periods in chocolate history," a ChocoCircus, and a "choco-reality" show (I swear I'm not making any of this up). Naturally, local producer Perugina plays a big role in the happenings.

A DAY TRIP FROM PERUGIA: IN SEARCH OF CERAMICS

If you've been admiring the colorful ceramics in Italy, hold off on making any purchases and make a special side trip to **Deruta** (20 km/13 miles south of Perugia by car; you can also take a 30-min, 3€ bus ride from Perugia). Since the 12th century it has served as a center for the creation of glazed terra cotta. Today there are more than 300 ceramic manufacturers in town whose bowls, plates, ladles, and other goods are shaped and glazed here and then shipped to all parts of Italy (in fact, there's a pretty good chance that that bowl you admired in Venice, Milan, or Rome was actually thrown and painted here). Consequently, you'll find a greater variety in Deruta than anywhere else in Italy, at a much lower cost. You can simply walk from store to store along Via Tiberina or Via Umberto I. Among my favorites (where I've purchased plates off of which my family still eats almost nightly) include traditionalists **Deruta Placens** (Via B. Michelotti 25, ☎ 075-972277; also at Via Umberto I 16, ☎ 075-9724027) and the more inventive modern designs of Marcella Favaroni at **Miriam** (Via Umberto I 16; ☎ 075-9711452).

NIGHTLIFE

With its large university population and a world-famous jazz festival, Perugia has the critical mass to support a lively entertainment scene of pubs, discos, and live music venues for people of all tastes. Check out www.perugiabynight.com for a good listing of current entertainment options.

Contrapunto ★ (Via Scortici 4; ☎ 075-5733667) not only features regular live entertainment (jazz on Tues; rock, funk, or reggae on Wed) but also boasts an outstanding view of the countryside north of Perugia. The terraced patios are a good place to grab a beer at the end of a day, or to gather with friends to hear some music. The club is located across Piazza Fortebraccio and around the corner from the Foreigner's University, so it attracts an international crowd.

If you're just looking for a beer, check out one of Perugia's Irish pubs: **Rob Roy** (Via Fabretti 95; ☎ 075-5724682), **Shamrock Pub** (Piazza Danti 18; ☎ 075-5736625), or **Sullivan's Pub** (Via del Bovaro 2; ☎ 075-5724381). Rob Roy is often jammed with students (especially during happy hours), because the university is just around the corner; Sullivan's turns into a live jazz club Tuesday nights with a variety of live music Thursday to Sunday.

Kadinsky (Via dal Pozzo 22; ☎ 075-5728130; www.kandinskypub.it) is a more sophisticated scene, with local art showings, parties, and music events. It has some good drink specials, and you can order pub grub from its always-open kitchen. Kadinsky's is usually open daily 9pm to 2am.

ASSISI

Assisi is a typical Umbrian village that also happens to be the hometown of St. Francis. Don't be put off by the busloads of visitors, though. St. Francis's Basilica isn't a standard tourist attraction; it's home to some of the finest art in Italy, and remains a deeply spiritual pilgrimage site. Beyond the Basilica and the souvenir stands lies a peaceful medieval town full of natural retreats in stark contrast to the flag-waving group tours. Every visitor should explore it: from the peaceful Ermeo delle Carceri in the woods outside town, to the panoramic views from the ruined fortress standing above Assisi.

A BRIEF HISTORY OF ASSISI

Assisi had the usual history of an Umbrian hill town: Umbrian tribal origins, Etruscan influence, Roman colonization, barbarian invasions, a sacking by Barbarossa. The usual history, that is, until St. Francis and his female counterpart St. Clare were born at the end of the 12th century (see "The Life & Times of St. Francis" on p. 214). Then Assisi took off, becoming one of Italy's major centers for religious pilgrimages. Following papal approval of Francis's new sect in 1210, and the increasing popularity of his preaching, Assisi began to attract its first hordes of followers. After Francis died in 1226, the massive Basilica project began. Contrary to Francis's teachings of poverty and simplicity, the pope and some of Francis's followers directed the construction of the epic structure over the next 20 years. The Basilica has been a steady pilgrim and tourist attraction ever since.

After the time of Francis, Assisi suffered from continuous attacks—as much from within as without. For nearly 200 years, Assisi's Parte de Sotto (lower part) fought the Parte de Sopra (upper part) in almost continuous factional battles for control of the city, which then left Assisi open to be sacked and looted by invading forces no fewer than four times. It is no wonder that in 1578, the writer Cipriano Piccolpasso found Assisi to be "a poorly arranged city where one sees many abandoned and ruined houses . . . they are unpleasant people, not very courteous to foreigners nor even to each other." For good measure, Napoleonic troops invaded and looted the city (was there anything left?) in 1808.

Times have changed. The city is now quite prosperous and well maintained, owing to the continuous tourist and pilgrim trade. The many religious seminaries, workshops, and festivals create an atmosphere of spirituality, while the now-courteous residents make a good living serving an army of visitors. The only danger comes from the earthquakes that continue to shake the city. The most recent major quake, in 1997, resulted in five deaths and damage to many of the buildings and even some frescoes, from which they are only just now recovering.

LAY OF THE LAND

Assisi isn't the simplest town to reach by train, but it's definitely doable. Assisi's station is 4.8km (3 miles) from town, requiring you to wait for the half-hourly bus, or take a 12€ (or more) cab ride. A walk to town up the steep roads amid heavy bus traffic isn't recommended.

Trains from Rome connect through Foligno, a journey of close to 3 hours. It takes about the same time from Florence, transferring at Cortona. Perugia is only a 30-minute train ride from Assisi's station. Buses also connect Assisi to Perugia and Gubbio and parts beyond via the bus terminal at Piazza Matteotti.

The drive to Assisi is about 193km (120 miles) from Rome, 177km (110 miles) from Florence. Take SS3 from Perugia, then the SS75 in the direction of Foligno. The Assisi exit drops you in the modern lower town (Santa Maria degli Angeli), where you have to keep your eyes open for signposts to Assisi up on its hillside.

Parking is pretty much impossible in town, but it's available in a variety of pay lots at the edges for about 11€ per day, 1.50€ per hour (ask your hotel when you call to book and they'll direct you to the closest lot where they offer a discount). If you're willing to walk a few extra blocks, free parking can be had below the pay lots at Porta Nuova, along the road, or in the dirt lot across from the hospital. The Porta Nuova lot has a covered escalator reaching town level. You can also drive up and around the city to reach free street parking on the approach to the Rocca, thus avoiding the steep hike up there.

Assisi's **tourist office** (☎ 075-812534) is on the main Piazza del Comune. It has the usual maps of the city, as well as a good collection of "Franciscan Itinerary" hiking and site guides for the area around Assisi. The official website (www.assisi.umbria2000.it) is weak; try the independent **www.assisionline.com** for better information in English.

ACCOMMODATIONS, BOTH STANDARD & NOT

It is vitally important to reserve well ahead when you're visiting Assisi—rooms fill up, particularly during Easter and other religious holidays. Good thing, then, that the tourist office (**www.assisi.umbria2000.it**) lists 78 **rental rooms** and 34 **B&Bs** scattered around town, most costing an eminently reasonable 35€ to 60€ for a double room (though a few B&Bs charge as much as 75€–100€ in busy months). Just as the prices vary, so will the looks of these places and the amenities offered. Some are absolutely delicious with exposed ceiling rafters, country antiques, stone archways, and terrazzo floors, while others have bland but comfortable modern modular furnishings on linoleum. Most are a hodgepodge of those elements, mixing the functional with old-world charming.

Key tip: Be sure when perusing the list you only consider ones listed as being in "Assisi," not in "Santa Maria degli Angeli," the modern town around the train station in the valley below, or some other satellite location (the name of the town appears, in all uppercase, immediately after the street address).

€–€€ For a one-stop shop for lodging, go a quarter-mile east of Porta Cappuccini to the **Complesso Turistico Fontemaggio** (Via Eremo delle Carceri 7; ☎ 075-812317; www.fontemaggio.it; cash only), which consists of a 15-room hotel in a 17th-century farmhouse, a youth hostel, campgrounds, bungalows, and a house for rent. There are endless lodging options, but a **camping** spot is 6€ per person (plus 5€ per tent and 3€ per car; bungalows sleeping four to eight start at 8€ per person), a bed in the **youth hostel** is 20€, a double in the **hotel** is 52€, and the first-floor apartment of **Papi House** is 120€ to 140€ for two suites and a kitchen. (No matter where you stay, breakfast costs 5€ extra.) There's also a phenomenal restaurant (see La Stalla on p. 211) and a convenience store. This turns into quite the community, especially at holiday times, when the 250-site campground gets rowdy with late-night guitar-led hymns.

Assisi is also the place to try a stay at a **monastery, convent, or religious retreat.** There are more than a dozen in town and an equal number scattered in the general area (all listed on the official tourism website). Not only do they tend to be much cheaper than a hotel (with rates as low as 16€ per person per night), they also offer you the chance to absorb more of the religious spirit of Assisi. Here are four of the best:

€ Catholic-school flashbacks aside, there's no reason whatsoever to be intimidated by the French nuns at the **Monastery of St. Colette** ★ (Borgo San Pietro 3; ☎ 075-812345; Apr–Oct; cash only). They're a friendly bunch (just take a peek at the bulletin-board photos of them partying on their retreats) who love welcoming travelers to Assisi. The sisters offer 19 basic but recently refurbished rooms with one to three beds for 22€ to 27€ per person. Even better, they throw in free parking, impose no curfews, and offer great suggestions for low-cost places to eat in the neighborhood. There's also a lovely garden and several lounges where guests can relax.

€ Just down the block sits the **Monastery of San Giuseppe** (Via S. Apollinare 1; ☎ 075-812332; www.msgiuseppe.it; cash only), a Benedictine monastery that, as ordained by the saint himself, must "welcome guests as if Christ Himself were knocking at the door of the monastery." Apparently, they would provide the Son of God with a simple, cell-like room of chunky wood furnishings for the bargain price of 29€ to 35€ per person. Other amenities include free parking, meals (13€–16€), and a quite lovely garden and panoramic terrace.

€€ Prices are marginally higher, but the rooms are a bit nicer, at **St. Anthony's Guesthouse** (Via G. Alessi 10; ☎ 075-812542; atoneassisi@tiscalinet.it; cash only), run by the Franciscan Sisters of Atonement, an American order of nuns. Each of their 20 comfortable hotel-like rooms comes with a bathroom, and some even have views over the city rooftops, and rates—including breakfast—run 35€ to 42€ per person in a single, or 28€ to 31€ per person in a double. It's open from March through October, requires a minimum stay of 2 nights, and usually asks for a deposit by mail.

€€   If those are all booked up, turn to **La Cittadella** (Via Ancajani 3; ☎ 075-813231; www.cittadella.org; MC, V), a huge religious institution housed in an extended complex of buildings. On-site are 70 guest rooms, a dining hall for 500, a conference center, a library, an art gallery, and a church. Not surprisingly, the place has a rather bureaucratic flavor, and it can be a hike to reach the rooms spread around the campus. On the positive side, with so much activity in the area, you'll feel part of the pilgrim community. Lodging is of the college-dorm-room variety, but with private bathrooms. Rooms with breakfast range from 42€ for a single, 33€ per person double, and 28€ per person in a room with four people (bring all four—they don't mix and match). This is a popular group destination, so reserve in advance.

€€   The **Hotel Sole** ★ (Corso Mazzini 35; ☎ 075-812373; www.assisihotelsole.com; AE, MC, V) is one of the loveliest family-run hotels in Umbria for the price (65€). It has an excellent location between Piazza del Comune and Santa Chiara and recently redone rooms with furnishings that range from contemporary decor to antique (and antiques-inspired) wrought-iron painted beds. Angle for a spot in the main building, where the rooms are more spacious and charming than those in the annex. The family's restaurant, the Hostaria Ceppo della Catena, is set in theatrically stone-vaulted rooms in a 15th-century palazzo above the hotel; half-board costs 50€ per person.

€€–€€€   Two quite decent and centrally located hotels under the same ownership are the **Priori** (Corso Mazzini 15; ☎ 075-812237; AE, MC, V) and the **Alexander** 🄺🄸🄳🅂 (Piazza Chiesa Nuova 6; ☎ 075-816190; both at www.assisi-hotel.com; AE, MC, V). The Priori fills three floors of a 16th-century palazzo with 34 rooms and antique furniture, frescoed ceilings, and small but modern bathrooms. A double is 140€ in high season, but can drop to 115€ the rest of the year. The Alexander lacks air-conditioning, elevators, and meal service, but has a nice roof terrace, and most rooms have extra beds, which make it a good spot for families. It's also nearly half the price of the Priori, at 60€ to 80€ for a double.

€€–€€€   Three generations of a local family have proudly run the **Hotel Umbra** ★★ (Via degli Archi 6, just off Piazza del Comune; ☎ 075-812240; www.hotelumbra.it; AE, MC, V) just 15 paces off the main square but a world removed from the pilgrimage jostle. The bulk of the structure dates from the 15th century, but the basement's laundry and kitchen area boast ancient Roman foundations. Most rooms (96€–125€) are highlighted with well-worn 18th- and 19th-century antiques; ask for one overlooking the Umbrian Valley. The Umbra is also known for its well-respected alfresco restaurant (fixed price 25€; closed all day Sun, and Wed at lunch), a shaded garden patio where lunchtime bird song easily reminds you that St. Francis was born just blocks away. The lamp-lit dinners are no less romantic.

Rural Accommodations

€€–€€€ For an out-of-town treat, make your Assisi-area headquarters **Le Silve Hotel** ★★ (Loc. Armenzano; ☎ 075-8019000; www.lesilve.it; AE, MC, V), a remote hideaway in the hills beyond Assisi (about 20 min. east). Rooms in the main old converted farmhouse have a rustic elegance, while those in the detached building have patios with panoramic views for a reasonable 100€. Le Silve has a swimming pool, tennis court, and even miniature golf. Apartments and villas are also available for rent on the extensive property. The apartments have fireplaces, kitchenettes, an outdoor barbecue, and their own swimming pools, and rent for about 600€ per week during summer. (There's also a four-star "Romantik" hotel on the property, where doubles start at 160€–180€.)

DINING FOR ALL TASTES

€ For cheap eats, you can first try **Foro Romano** [kids] (Via Portica 23; ☎ 075-815370), a very popular postmodern cafeteria-style eatery in the historical center, between the Basilica of San Francesco and Piazza del Comune. Dishes such as *lasagne,* asparagus risotto, penne, faro soup, roast chicken, pork chops, and sausages each go for a mere 5€ to 6€, with various cheese and meat platters for 2€ to 3.50€. Foro Romano claims to serve over 60,000 dishes a year, so they must be doing something right.

€ Connected with the Fontemaggio campground/hostel complex a mile outside of town, **La Stalla** ★★ [kids] (Via Eremo delle Carceri 8; ☎ 075-812317; Tues–Sun 12:15–2:30pm and 7:15–10pm; cash only) is about as genuine a country *trattoria* as you're ever going to find. When they say the place is a "refurbished" barn, they mean they moved the sheep out of the stalls and put in tables. The walls are blackened with decades of smoke from the open fire near one end where the staff cooks sizzling sausages and local game dishes on grills and foil-wrapped potatoes among the coals. Long benches encourage fun communal dining with extended families taking a leisurely Sunday lunch together and mobs from the campground.

€€ While it's close to Piazza del Comune, **Restaurant Pallotta** ★ (Via San Rufino 4; ☎ 075-812649; www.assisionline.com/trattoriapallotta and www.pallottaassisi.it; Wed–Mon 12:15–2:30pm and 7:15–9:30pm; AE, MC, V) isn't your typical tourist trap. Through an arch and at the end of an alleyway off the piazza, it features traditional Umbrian specialties such as *strangozzi* with mushroom sauce, homemade tagliatelle, gnocchi of potatoes, and cacciatore-style rabbit. Dishes range from 5€ to 18€, though most *primi* hover around 8.50€. The tasting menu (without wine) is 25€, and offers a great selection of local delicacies. You get less selection, but a very filling meal, with the 16€ *menù turistico,* which includes a *primo, secondo,* side dish, dessert, water, and wine.

WHY YOU'RE HERE: THE TOP SIGHTS & ATTRACTIONS

La Basilica di San Francesco (St. Francis's Basilica) ★★★ (Piazza San Francesco; ☎ 075-819001; www.sanfrancescoassisi.org; free; upper church Mon–Sat 8:30am–5:45pm, Sun 8:30am–6:45pm, though note that Sun morning the entire church is reserved for worship; lower church Mon–Sat 6am–6:45pm, Sun 6am–7:15pm; Nov–Mar both close at 5:45 Mon–Fri) is among the must-see sights of Europe, not only because of its magnificent Giotto frescoes but also because it is still the second most important pilgrimage site in Italy (after Rome), and third in the world (after Bethlehem). Unlike many of Italy's churches, which have more snapshot-taking tourists than worshippers, the Basilica and Francis's teachings attract devout pilgrims. Busloads of religious groups fill the Basilica, celebrating Mass in side chapels, kneeling at Franciscan relics, and praying silently at altars around the church. And if there's too much talking, be prepared to hear a voice from the heavens as *"Silenzio!"* booms from the security guards' PA system.

To be sure, there are plenty of people visiting just for art, and this, too, is a worthwhile pilgrimage. Seeing these frescoes, paintings, and altars in the context of the Basilica is a much more rewarding experience than seeing dozens of Madonna and Childs stacked side by side and out of context in a museum.

The massive Basilica is split between an upper and a lower church. To first appreciate the artistic then the religious nature of the structure, I'd recommend going in reverse chronological order, from the top down. Start with Giotto's frescoes and the traditional upper church, then descend to the darker, meditative lower church, and finally enter the almost mystical crypt of St. Francis.

Begin with the 28 panels lining the nave walls of the upper church, **Giotto's Life of St. Francis frescoes,** which will give you the perfect overview of the life of the saint, as well as the story of medieval Italian art as it breaks away from Byzantine tradition. Giotto's work, done about 1296, is significant not only for its accessible cartoon-strip method of communicating the life of St. Francis but for its "form follows function" philosophy. Traditional Byzantine art, which dominated church decoration for a thousand years, outlined stiff figures, draped in gold, a symbolic representation of the glory of God. Giotto chose to paint the life of St. Francis with the simplicity and attention to nature that Francis himself espoused. Although the perspective is askew and detail rudimentary, the robes flow; the expressions of surprise, pain, and fear seem genuine; and St. Francis seems humble, even as he ascends to the heavens on a big pink cloud (panel 12).

From the front of the right aisle of the church, going clockwise, you'll follow Francis as he renounces his worldly goods in the fifth panel, expels demons from multicolored Arezzo in panel 10, gives his sermon to the birds in panel 15, and receives the stigmata in panel 19, about a quarter of the way down the left wall.

Don't leave the upper church until you take a look at Cimabue's *Crucifixion,* which, though damaged in the quakes (and faded by time), still retains some of its former radiance.

Exit the airy Gothic upper church for the **lower church** to see another series of astonishing frescoes. You'll see Sienese Gothic works lining the walls of the chapels, including masterpieces like the Simone Martini frescoes in the Cappella di San Martino, and Cimabue's famous *Madonna with St. Francis,* the portrait that is reproduced all over town, on the right wall.

Take the stairs in the middle of the lower church to visit St. Francis's **crypt.** This formerly secret room contains the body of St. Francis in a humble stone tomb, more fitting to his wishes than the huge church above it. Pilgrims kneel, touch the stone, pray, and radiate joy as they come close to the object of their worship.

On your way out, check out the side Chapter Hall to see the **relics of St. Francis,** such as his robe, sandals, prayer book, and other personal items.

As you leave the Basilica you'll pass dozens of souvenir stands selling every imaginable item emblazoned with the saint's name or the image of him preaching to the birds. The rampant commercialism is a stark contrast to St. Francis's teachings of poverty, personal reflection, and God's message communicated through the purity of nature. You can almost hear the whirring as St. Francis spins in his grave below.

For a more serene experience, head to **San Pietro** (Piazza San Pietro at end of Borgo San Pietro; ☎ 075-8155204; www.museiecclesiastici.it; 2.50€ admission to crypt; daily 10am–1pm and 3–7pm; closed Mon in winter), a neglected church on the southwest edge of town, reopened after years of earthquake retrofitting. The plaza outside offers lovely views of the countryside, and a peaceful rest away from the tourist hordes. Head down into the crypt for the best Franciscan diorama in all Christendom: A miniature electric fisherman casts his reel and the wood chopper chops in a 7.5m-long (25-ft.) medieval town filled with plastic sheep. Other rooms in the crypt museum include a random assortment of rotating modern-art exhibits, Roman artifacts, and a Salvador Dalí lithograph.

Towering above the town is **Rocca Maggiore** ★★ (☎ 075-812033 or 075-812534; 3.50€; daily 10am–sunset), the fortress built by Cardinal Albornaz to extend his control over Umbrian towns in the 1360s. While most of the Rocca remains shut due to earthquake damage, you can enter and climb two of its towers. Between the thick stone walls in a hallway lit only by narrow slits, try imagining how terrifying it must have been to defend the castle during a siege from these claustrophobic quarters. Then ascend to the roof at the end of the corridor for an unmatched 360-degree view of the Umbrian countryside and Assisi.

When the famed German writer Goethe visited Assisi in the 1780s, he passed up the Basilica "with great distaste" and focused instead on the **Temple of Minerva** ★ (daily 7:15am–noon and 2–7pm) in the main Piazza del Comune. The well-preserved facade of this 1st-century-A.D. Roman temple with its Corinthian columns and original paving stones provides a window into Assisi's ancient past. Don't

Free Tours with the Brothers

The Franciscans affiliated with the Basilica offer free English-language tours every Monday through Saturday. Though the tours don't go into the Basilica itself, they discuss the church in detail and visit a number of other sites associated with St. Francis and his teachings. Meet at the visitor center (the office just to the left of the lower church entrance) between 9am and noon, or from 2:30 to 5:30pm. You may wish to call in advance (☎ **075-8190084**) for more information.

The Life & Times of St. Francis

Francis of Assisi was born in 1182, the son of a wealthy cloth merchant. As a teen, he enjoyed all the passing pleasures of life—drinking, partying with other rich kids—and then joined a military expedition to Perugia, probably for the glory of it. He was taken prisoner, and, following his release, became more spiritual, committing himself to a life of poverty and self-sacrifice. After extended meditation he began to have visions. In 1209, the crucifix of St. Damiano is said to have spoken to him and told him to "rebuild the church." Francis first took this literally to mean that he should find some stones to support the building's walls. (In Giotto's Basilica frescoes, St. Francis can be seen lifting the church, superhero-style.)

Francis's father criticized him for squandering his company's profits on church stones, and for preferring the company of lepers to nobles. In protest, Francis stripped naked in the main square in Assisi, and gave away all his material possessions. In Giotto's fresco, Assisi's father is being restrained from smacking his son.

It would seem that Francis's philosophy of poverty was in direct conflict with the jewel-encrusted, power-hungry, institutional Church of the day. But his humility and obedience to Church rule (per the scene of the monks kneeling in front of the pope) made his order more attractive to Rome than other splinter sects. So Rome approved the Franciscan Order in 1211.

Francis spent the remaining 17 years of his life ministering to the poor and communing with nature and all of God's creatures, which helped earn him the title of "patron saint of animals." He also converted thousands, including a close friend and neighbor who would go on to found the sisterhood of the Poor Clares and be canonized herself as St. Clare (see "The 'Poor Clares' & the Patron Saint of TV," below).

In 1224, Francis was said to have received the stigmata of Christ, when bleeding wounds appeared on his hands, feet, and sides. He was canonized in 1228, only 2 years after his death.

The Roman church, and some of Francis's followers, promptly co-opted the Franciscan Order by funding the building of the ornate Basilica in the 1230s, in part by selling indulgences to visitors, pardoning their sins on behalf of St. Francis for a few gold coins. Nevertheless, the Franciscan Order has kept its philosophy intact, as can be seen by the many Franciscan brothers still walking the streets of Assisi dressed in their brown sackcloth robes tied with a simple rope belt.

bother going in; the interior was transformed into a lackluster baroque church in the 17th century.

Three kilometers (2 miles) outside of town and well worth the journey, the **Ermeo delle Carceri** ★ (☎ 075-812301; free; daily 6:30am–7:30pm, Oct–Mar closes at 5pm), is the hermitage where St. Francis retreated to pray, meditate, and

The "Poor Clares" & the Patron Saint of TV

In a life that paralleled that of St. Francis, Clare was born in Assisi in 1194, and walked away from her family fortune to preach a life of poverty. From age 17, she was a close follower of Francis, cutting off her long blond hair as a symbol of her rejection of the material world. Locks of her hair are said to be on display at Assisi's **Church of St. Chiara** (Piazza Santa Chiara; free; daily 7am–noon and 2–6:45pm), alongside other relics in the Oratorio del Crocifisso room, including the crucifix that talked to St. Francis. The church also houses her body in its garishly decorated crypt. The upper church is decorated sparingly, not so much at the behest of Clare but because a later bishop erased most of the frescoes to keep tourists away.

St. Clare founded the order of the Poor Clares for women whose lives were to be occupied with work and prayer, penance, and contemplation. The pope, in 1215, approved the right of the Poor Clares to live solely on alms, without any personal property.

Despite Clare's rejection of the material world, and her commitment to a life of spiritual contemplation, Pope Pius XII declared her the patron saint of television in 1958. Apparently when St. Clare was on her death bed, too sick to attend Mass, she nonethless miraculously saw and heard the services being performed miles away. Thus, every August 11, St. Clare's feast day, TV writers, workers, and watchers send a prayer her way.

preach to his disciples. A ramshackle collection of rooms cut into the stones many centuries before Francis lived, this rustic friary seems much more in line with St. Francis's teachings than the massive Basilica that looms over the town. You can visit the cell where Francis prayed, and follow the path outside to the woods where he must have experienced a close connection with nature. At the door is a 1,000-year-old oak, where, according to legend, Francis blessed birds that then flew off in four directions—a symbol of how Francis's teachings would eventually reach all four corners of the globe. Along the path is an amusing statue of St. Francis lying on the ground with his sandals off, hands behind his head, peacefully pondering the clouds in the sky. Friars still live in these simple caves and will guide you, though be sure to give a donation as the monks live entirely on alms. The hermitage is a tough uphill walk from Porta Cappuccini, but it's on the main road, so it's easy to drive and pay a couple of euros for parking, or to take a cab.

THE OTHER ASSISI

Tourists are not permitted to visit St. Francis's Basilica during Mass on Sundays, and gawkers are discouraged from entering chapels during a daily Mass. But if you want to experience the spiritual and ceremonial side of the Basilica, leave your camera in the hotel, dress conservatively, keep silent, and join local and international pilgrims as they **celebrate Mass.** For the faithful who flock to Assisi, Mass is generally held in the Basilica's lower church. Monday to Saturday there are matins at 6:35am followed by a 7am service, with a second service on Saturday at 5pm (and a priest on hand to minister to the faithful daily from 11am to 5pm in the Cappella Santa Caterina). Masses are held Sunday at 7:30, 9, 10:30am, noon, 5, and 6:30pm, with vespers at 6pm.

ORVIETO

To the average traveler, Orvieto is a wine. To the connoisseur of art, it's the site of Signorelli's *Last Judgment,* the fresco cycle that helped inspire Michelangelo's work in the Sistine Chapel. To anyone who makes the wise decision to hop off the train and take a peek (it's on the main line from Rome to Florence), Orvieto tends to become one of their favorite Italian discoveries, an almost perfectly preserved medieval hilltop town with amazing frescoes, fantastic wine, and a delightfully spooky warren of underground tunnels the Orvietani have been carving into the soft tufa beneath the city since Etruscan times.

Even your arrival in the city is something special. Orvieto sprouts from the top of a squat volcanic plug rising a thousand feet from the surrounding plains, and to get there you ride a steep funicular (cog railway) from the train station. You spend much of your visit yo-yoing between exploring underground Orvieto—either as part of a guided tour of historic tunnels or to tipple the wine in a vaulted vintner's cellar—and climbing the heights of the Torre del Moro bell tower for a panorama that stretches across all of southern Umbria and northern Lazio.

After going up and down all day, you'll be ready to join the citizens of the town for the evening see-and-be-seen promenade along the mercifully flat street of Via Cavour. Then its time to descend again, into a cavernlike restaurant carved into the tufa to dig into a hearty plate of *umbrichelli* (hand-rolled spaghetti) and roasted meats and wash it down with that fine Orvieto wine.

A BRIEF HISTORY OF ORVIETO

Orvieto (*urbs vetus,* or "old city") sits on a plateau of tufa and clay left from a volcano rising from a seabed millions of years ago. The Etruscans were the first to build a major settlement here, about 600 B.C., choosing the location for its seemingly perfect defensive position. The Romans flattened the city in 254 B.C., and there followed an equally devastating series of conquests by Byzantine, Lombard, and papal invaders (so perhaps the plateau method of defense had some kinks to work out).

Most of the towers, churches, and buildings you'll see were constructed in a period of prosperity from the 12th century right up until 1348, when the smallest invaders had the most lasting impact on the city. Fleas carrying the bubonic plague killed over half the population of Orvieto in 5 months—including six of the Council of Seven leaders of the town. The labor force was decimated, commerce crumbled, and construction of new buildings ground to a halt, leaving the same medieval tourist town you see today. Beginning in the 1400s, a number of popes used this now backwater fortress as a hideout whenever things got too dangerous in Rome. The papal connection sponsored the creation of several more tourist favorites, including the magnificent Signorelli frescoes in the Duomo.

Present-day Orvieto has had a rebirth of sorts, hosting the Umbria winter jazz festival, as well as a quorum of ceramic makers, wine producers, and fine-dining chefs. Seasonal dance, theater, and academic conferences breathe life into a city that has seen its share of both figurative and literal ups and downs.

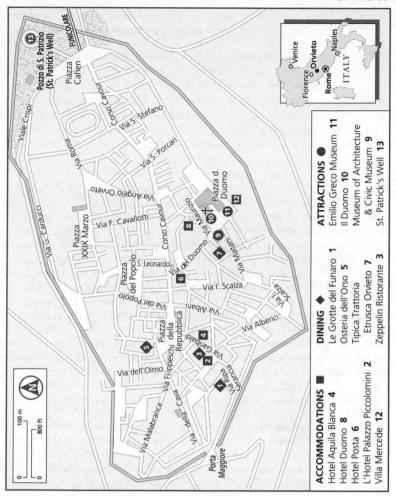

ATTRACTIONS ●
Emilio Greco Museum **11**
Il Duomo **10**
Museum of Architecture
& Civic Museum **9**
St. Patrick's Well **13**

DINING ◆
Le Grotte del Funaro **1**
Osteria dell'Orso **5**
Tipica Trattoria
Etrusca Orvieto **7**
Zeppelin Ristorante **3**

ACCOMMODATIONS ■
Hotel Aquila Blanca **4**
Hotel Duomo **8**
Hotel Posta **6**
L'Hotel Palazzo Piccolomini **2**
Villa Mercede **12**

LAY OF THE LAND

Orvieto is 150km (90 miles) south of Florence, 120km (75 miles) north of Rome on the A1 autostrada. You can park in pay lots near the town center, in underground lots connected to the city center by escalator and elevator, or park for free by the train station.

Trains stop almost hourly on the Florence-Rome line, and take 1¾ hours from Florence, or 80 minutes from Rome. From the train station, cross the street to grab the funicular (short cable car) that will take you up to Piazza Cahen and the medieval heart of the city. From there, the minibus no. A can whisk to you the Piazza Duomo and the **tourist office** (Piazza Duomo 24; ☎ 0763-341772; www.orvieto.umbria2000.it, www.comune.orvieto.tr.it, or www.orvietonet.it).

A Helpful Museum Card

If you're planning on seeing most of Orvieto's central sights, save some cash by purchasing the **Carta Unica.** The tourist office and participating museums sell this comprehensive ticket for 13€. It covers admission to the Cappella di San Brizio, Torre Del Moro, the Museo Claudio Faina, the Orvieto Underground tour, and a few other, minor sites (the other archaeological museum, several privately held Etruscan tunnels and tombs, and some others) and a round-trip funicular ride. It also gives small discounts at some restaurants and shops. The museums alone cost 17€.

ACCOMMODATIONS, BOTH STANDARD & NOT

For a vacation home or apartment rental, contact local real-estate agency **Galli Immobiliare** (Via del Duomo 19; ☎ 0763-343933; www.galliimmobiliare.com; AE, MC, V). The staff knows the area and local properties inside and out. Apartments begin at 80€ per night for a small room, while out-of-town villas begin at 1,100€ a week. Most rentals are either by the week, month, or season, whether its a basic one-bedroom apartment in the heart of Orvieto or a five-bedroom villa with swimming pool, barbecue, and modern kitchen out in the countryside. The rental office (and the website) has photos of the rentals with details of features, and they tend to be fairly accurate. I'd be wary, however, of renting an apartment that only has an exterior shot accompanying the listing. Note that the **tourist office** in town also has an extensive rotating list of local and regional apartment properties, though these are probably not as carefully vetted as those at Galli Immobiliare. Also don't overlook the lovely little apartment right on Piazza del Duomo that is rented out for 75€ by the **Museo Claudio Faina** (under sightseeing section below).

€–€€ The cheapest standard option in town is the **Hotel Posta** (Via Luca Signorelli 18; ☎ 0763-341909; cash only), which offers small but decent rooms with new beds, thick walls, and a friendly but frantic staff (they're overworked). The shared bathrooms are clean; those connected to rooms are small but workable. Rates range from 40€ to 43€ for a double without a bathroom to 51€ to 56€ for a double with bathroom. The old building is a little decrepit, but in a personable sort of way. The central "garden" doubles as a storage area, contributing to the "squatting in a nobleman's villa" feeling of the place. There's no air-conditioning, but the thick walls keep the rooms pretty cool in summer.

€€ Orvieto also offers a monastery stay option, but one with a twist—a monastery with its own tennis courts, soccer field, private parking spaces, rooms with private facilities, and none of the elaborate curfews and rules that usually accompany these types of accommodations. All that and the **Villa Mercede "Religious Guest House"** ★ (Via Soliana 2; ☎ 0763-341766; www.argoweb.it/casa religiosa_villamercede/villamercede.uk.html; MC, V) lies just around the corner from the Duomo. If you've ever wanted to do this type of stay and get a small peek into monastic life, but have been worried about all the sacrifices you'd have to make, this is the place to try. As usual, rooms are spartan, whitewashed, and filled with religious paraphernalia, but the prices are incredibly low: 12 rooms, all with bathroom, at 60€ for a double, which includes breakfast and parking. Book far in advance; it tends to fill with student and religious groups.

€€–€€€ Rates are refreshingly reasonable at the high-class **Hotel Aquila Blanca** ★ (Via Garibaldi 13; ☎ 0763-341246; www.hotelaquilabianca.it; AE, MC, V), a 250-year-old palace that has served as a hotel for more than a century. A royal-looking lobby stuffed with antiques (and a random rickshaw) gives it an imperial feel. Rooms are bright and cheerful, with a surprisingly homey flowered bed-and-breakfast ambience. Double rooms range from 80€ to 105€.

€€–€€€ The pick of the three-star hotels in Orvieto is the **Hotel Duomo** ★★ (Vicolo di Maurizio 7; ☎ 0763-341887; www.orvietohotelduomo.com; AE, MC, V). Completely renovated in 2001, the family-run Hotel Duomo has a bright, fresh decor, with modern art, new furniture, spacious bathrooms, and a street front garden. It's also perfectly located just around the corner from the Duomo. In an odd move, one Internet point is set up for guest use at the front desk—but there is no chair (the manager, Giovanni, likes to keep things moving). Doubles run from 100€ to 130€, and five suites range from 120€ to 160€ for up to five people (although five would be cramped).

€€–€€€€ Orvieto is also a good place to indulge in a mild splurge, since the luxe hotel choice in town—**L'Hotel Palazzo Piccolomini** ★★ (Piazza Ranieri, 36; ☎ 0763-341743; www.hotelpiccolomini.it; AE, MC, V), set in a 16th-century family palazzo—doesn't actually cost that much more than the other inns at 108€ to 154€ for a double. It's also a beaut, with whitewashed walls and exposed stone masonry in the rooms, tasteful furniture, and terrific views over the rooftops of the city (though the windows do tend to be on the small side, as do the showers, which are coffin-cramped). A helpful, friendly staff and free valet parking add to the appeal, as does the vaulted basement breakfast room—a cool place to eat, both architecturally and temperature-wise. In the lobby is a free Internet point for guest use.

Farm Stays

€€€ It's worth lodging outside the city to stay at the lovely and terrifically family-friendly **Villa Ciconia** ★ 🟨 (Via dei Tigli 69, Loc. Orvieto Scalo; ☎ 0763-305582; www.hotelvillaciconia.com; AE, MC, V). Kids will enjoy the swimming pool, and the twisting hallways, hidden alcoves, and old-fortress feel of this 16th-century villa surrounded by a 2-hectare (5-acre) park. Parents will like the secluded peace of the gardens and the wood-beamed ambience, with colorful tiled floors and elaborate tapestries on some of the walls. The Standard rooms (100€–150€) are large, with iron fixtures, whitewashed walls, and a combination of antique and more modern furniture. The Superior rooms (150€–180€) are even bigger, with canopied beds and the best garden views. Both varieties have space to add a cot for children. The villa's restaurant is open to the public, and features a truffle-oriented pasta and grill menu, with *primi* ranging from 6.50€ to 10€, and main dishes going for 10€ to 14€ (closed Mon).

DINING FOR ALL TASTES

€€   Two stars for ambience go to **Le Grotte del Funaro** ★★ 🧒 (Via Ripa Serancia 41; ☎ 0763-343276; www.grottedelfunaro.it; Tues–Sun noon–3pm and 7pm–midnight; AE, MC, V), where you'll descend a long stairway into this "cave of the rope maker," walking under stone arches through the extensive wine storage/tasting area and past the open wood-fire stoves to several long rooms containing a dozen dining tables each. Kids will like the hidden bat-cave feel of the place (I know I did when I was 12), as well as the pizzas, which cost around 6€ to 8.50€. Adults can dig the *ombrichelli del funaro* (hand-rolled spaghetti in a rich sauce of tomatoes, sausage, artichokes, and mushrooms) followed by a mixed grill of suckling pig, lamb, sausages, and yellow bell peppers. Pastas range from 9€ to 14€, and secondi from 9€ to 18€. Service is on the borderline between relaxed and just plain slow, but the food and setting are worth it.

€€   For a friendly restaurant popular with both locals and tourists, you may want to try **Osteria dell'Orso** (Via della Misericordia 16–18; ☎ 0763-341642; Wed–Sun 12:30–2:30pm and 7:30–10pm; closed Feb, July, and Nov; AE, MC, V), where chef Gabriele di Giandomenico serves fresh country-style meals, including a delicious vegetable-and-mushroom tagliatelle with local truffles and a mouthwatering game hen on a bed of polenta. *Primi* run 7€ to 11€, *secondi* 10€ to 15€.

€€   An interesting (but slightly pricey) Art Deco take on an Umbrian restaurant is the **Zeppelin Ristorante** (Via Garibaldi 28; ☎ 0763-341447; www.cookinginitaly.it; daily 12:30–2:30pm and 7:30–10:30pm; AE, MC, V). The name comes from the fact that this converted warehouse is long and narrow with a rounded ceiling and windows on the side, in proportions vaguely like a zeppelin. The grilled wild boar with sage and tomatoes is delicious, as is the spaghetti *alla norcina,* with truffles, garlic, and anchovies. A first course will run you from 8€ to 12€, grilled second dishes from 12€ to 18€ (up to 21€ for a steak with truffles). For info on their cooking classes, see "The Other Orvieto," below.

€€–€€€   My favorite place to splash out is **Tipica Trattoria Etrusca Orvieto** ★ (Via Lorenzo Maitani 10; ☎ 0763-344016; www.argoweb.it/trattoria_etrusca; daily noon–3:30pm and 7–11pm; AE, MC, V). Dishes in this crisp, clean restaurant focus on local specialties that include handmade *umbrichelli* pasta, rabbit dishes, fresh bread with olives and rosemary, and an outstanding minestrone soup with fennel. *Primi* average 8€ to 15€, *secondi* 10€ to 15€. Salads are mixed at the table, and the desert cart features the *torta estruscana,* a sweet cake of lemon and almond. Also try their local Passito sweet wine. The manager greets diners at their tables, and will show off the medieval well and the old cellars, which are 20m (66 ft.) underground, complete with a long dining table (which can be reserved for tastings), dusty bottles of wine, hanging bananas, and a general feel of a secret gastronomical cult hideaway.

WHY YOU'RE HERE: THE TOP SIGHTS & ATTRACTIONS

Orvieto's **Duomo** ★★★ (Piazza del Duomo; ☎ 0763-341167; www.opsm.it; free, 1€ for brief history recording; daily 7:30am–12:45pm and 2:30–7:15pm, Mar and Oct closes at 6:15pm, Nov–Feb closes 5:15pm) deserves its status as one of the indispensable attractions of Italy. Even from miles outside the city, you can see its

Dueling Underground Tours: Which Is Better?

Every visitor to Orvieto should take the opportunity to descend into the depths and explore some of the caves hidden beneath the city.

The Etruscans were the first to burrow into the soft stone for building materials and wells more than 2,500 years ago. Now there are over 1,200 caves underneath Orvieto, essentially turning the plateau into a huge black chunk of Swiss cheese.

During extended sieges of this fortified city, townspeople discovered that pigeons were an almost magical source of food. Hundreds of pigeon coops were dug into the cave walls, creating a kind of giant shoe rack. Pigeons nested in the holes, and flew out gaps in the walls to the countryside to feed themselves. As pigeons reproduce every 20 days, Orvietans could alternate between feasting on eggs and on birds without jeopardizing their food source.

Though many restaurants and shops (and, of course, private homes) sit atop caves and tunnels—and a few offer to let you pop down for a peek for a euro or two—for a more holistic and interesting view take one of two competing underground tours.

For more of an archaeological perspective, join the city-organized **Orvieto Underground** (begins at tourist office; ☎ 0763-344891 or 339-7332764; www.orvietounderground.it; 5.50€ or on Carta Unica; tours daily at 11am, 12:15pm, 4pm, and 5:15pm, in Feb weekends only). Coordinated by the Speleological Society, this tour has a feature-rich bent. You get plenty of historical background on the various caves and rooms you visit: an Etruscan well, an olive press, an underground stable, olive-oil workshop, World War II bomb shelter, and those pigeon farms. You visit a few more rooms, and the spaces are larger and better lit than on the other tour.

However, if you're looking for the personal touch, try the tour with the same name but that's actually quite different. This other **Orvieto Underground** (Via della Pace 36; ☎ 335-1806205; www.orvietosotterranea.it; 6€; daily tours hourly from 10:30am) starts at a stairway underneath a restaurant. It has more of an "exploration feel." Caves are a little cramped, and one passageway is quite claustrophobic (you can opt out of cistern viewing). Another bonus: As these private caves are under a restaurant, you get to sample some of the owner's wines with tasty snacks.

glittering facade, massive bulk, and spires reaching above the plateau like the control tower of a massive ship. Up close, the square can hardly contain the structure (and unless your camera has a wide-angle lens, your photos won't either).

The front of the Duomo is awe inspiring. The afternoon sun reflects off a dozen golden mosaics as if a holy light were shining down on you. Beneath them are amazing marble panels carved in the early 14th century by Lorenzo Maitani and his assistants with psychologically intense scenes from Genesis and the Last Judgment. The latter are a preamble for the star attraction inside.

The Duomo is world renowned for its **Cappella di San Brizio** ★★★ (☎ 0763-342477 or 0763-343592; www.opsm.it; 5€ or free with Carta Unica; hours same as Duomo except it opens at 9am and is off limits Sun mornings), which Luca Signorelli frescoed in 1499 to 1504 with scenes from the Last Judgment. What is most memorable about Signorelli's work is his ability to vividly transfer the feeling of contorted bodies, like those in the Maitani carvings outside, to the two-dimensional world of painting. Even Michelangelo came here to study how it was done, applying the lessons learned to his work on the Sistine Chapel. If the overly stretched bodies and surreal landscape in the *Resurrection of the Dead* (the segment on the right upon entering) seem familiar, check some paintings by Salvador Dalí, another great artist inspired by Signorelli.

Signorelli left a signature in the form of a self-portrait: the man dressed in black, at the left edge of the wall to the left of the entry. He looks annoyed, perhaps because his mistress dumped him while he was painting the fresco. She is now forever immortalized (1) as the blonde prostitute in the blue skirt, standing nearly in front of him, taking money for her services; (2) riding naked on the back of a devil, about to be plunged into hell (top center of the right front fresco); and (3) in the pits of hell, being groped by a blue devil whose face looks suspiciously like Signorelli's.

The chapel across from Cappella di San Brizio is almost forgotten by today's tourists, but it's worth a glance to see the religious relic for which this church was originally constructed in 1290: a cloth said to be stained with the blood of Christ that dripped from the raised host during a Mass being celebrated in 1263 on the shores of nearby Lake Bolsena. The jeweled case containing the relic and the surrounding paintings illustrate this "Miracle of Bolsena."

The **Museo Claudio Faina e Museo Civico** (Piazza del Duomo 29; ☎ 0763-341216; www.museofaina.it; 4.50€ or on Carta Unica; Apr–Sept daily 9:30am–6pm, Oct daily 10am–5pm, Nov–Mar Tues–Sun 10am–5pm) houses an extensive and eclectic collection of Etruscan and Roman artifacts, coins, art—basically anything spoiled rich kid/grave robber Claudio and his father could seize in the 1800s. Museum management has tried to liven up the displays with interactive signs, as well as buttons to rotate the coin trays. Note the three-legged candleholder from 300 B.C. on the third floor, in Room 16—and if you don't think pottery can be lively, check out the pornographic penis procession on the urn in the upper-right case in Room 7. As a bonus, the museum's second- and third-story windows offer the city's best views of the Duomo's facade directly across the piazza. Also, in what I do believe is a first in Italy, the museum has begun renting out a nice little B&B apartment—with a modest but nice bedroom, living room, and dining room—for 75€ per night, which, for being bang on the Piazza Duomo, you can't really beat.

You can follow your descent into underground Orvieto (see "Dueling Underground Tours: Which Is Better?" above) with an ascent toward heaven at the 13th-century **Torre Del Moro** (at the corner of Via Duomo and Via Cavour; ☎ 0763-344567; 2€ or on Carta Unica; daily 10:30am–1pm and 2:30–5pm; often stays open until 8pm in summer). Climb 162 steps on a wide, well-lit stairway to the top of this 45m-tall (150-ft.) tower. You'll feel like you're on top of the mast

Who Are the Etruscans & Why Are They Following Me?

Across Tuscany and Umbria the signs are always the same: THIS BUILDING IS THE RECENTLY REFURBISHED VILLA OF A RENAISSANCE NOBLEMAN WHO EXPANDED A MEDIEVAL HOME BUILT FROM A ROMAN WATCHTOWER BASED ON AN ETRUSCAN FOUNDATION. NOTE THE ORIGINAL ETRUSCAN WALLS IN ROOM Y. Or, THE TOWN WELL WAS DEVELOPED IN THE 14TH CENTURY FROM THE ETRUSCAN ORIGINAL.

Who were these people whose apparent mission in life was to bake pottery, stack stones, and bury their dead all over Tuscany and Umbria?

It is known that the Etruscans settled widely across northern and central Italy in the 9th century B.C., and reached the peak of their power and influence across the western Mediterranean between 700 and 600 B.C. Their presence was felt in trade, war, culture, and shipping, until they were defeated in the Greek naval wars in the 4th century B.C. Later, they were absorbed into the Roman Empire, providing several of its early, pre-Republican kings (the Tarquins). Beyond all that, things get fuzzy. Even as far back as 500 B.C., the Greek historian Herodotus was trying to figure out where the Etruscans came from. Were they indigenous peoples of Italy? Had they emigrated from Asia Minor?

Secondhand Greek and Roman histories, combined with archaeological evidence gleaned from Etruscan ruins and tombs, suggest that the Etruscans developed a unique culture native to Tuscany and Umbria. They consolidated local tribal groups into a collection of city-states centered on 12 cities, including those than have since become Orvieto, Perugia, and Arezzo. The Etruscans are credited with the creation of much of the art, language, and architecture commonly associated with the Roman Empire, including arches, aqueducts, Rome's famous and innovative urban plumbing and rural irrigation systems, and, yes, the first paving of an ancient autostrada. Their downfall came after they developed the art of internecine warfare.

What is exciting today is to stare at stacked 2-ton stones, a 90m (300-ft.) well shaft, or a thousand symmetrical, decorated urns and think, "How in the world did they *do* that?" Imagine the effort, the ingenuity, and the communal spirit that was necessary not to re-create, not to improve upon, but to build all these major structures with little more than tools of bone and bronze, and brute strength. On the other hand, there's plenty of evidence that the Etruscans themselves built on top of the even more mysterious Villanovan culture, who were influenced by the early Phoenicians, who studied the . . .

—*by William Fink*

of the USS *Orvieto,* gliding through a sea of farms, watching waves of wine fields undulating on the horizon. It has particularly nice sunset views during the extended summer hours.

THE OTHER ORVIETO

Lorenzo Polegri, who owns the Art Deco Zeppelin Ristorante, offers a very popular series of **cooking courses** (Via Garibaldi 28; ☎ 0763-341447, www.cooking initaly.it). These range from tourist-perfect, single-day courses (four hours of cooking for 135€, including the wine served with the resulting meal) to the more serious weeklong classes. The latter cost from 1,450€ and are thematic, focusing on local, seasonal, medieval, or countryside cuisines. They also offer weeklong courses that mix cooking classes with lessons in painting or jewelry making.

TODI

Todi is a classic Umbrian hilltop village with winding cobblestone streets, stone towers, and spectacular views of the countryside. Although much of the city has been refurbished and taken over by Rome weekenders, it maintains its medieval charm. It doesn't boast enough sights to merit an extended stay, but is worth at least a day trip if you're based in nearby Assisi, Perugia, or Spoleto—though you could also make the argument that quiet little Todi would make a nice regional base, away from the tourist machine of Assisi and the (relatively) more crowded towns of Perugia and Orvieto.

The best experiences in Todi come from merely wandering the streets and enjoying the views of the countryside, and from the buildings themselves. Four churches in town merit a visit. The **Duomo** on the town square has colorful stained glass, a fresco modeled after the Sistine Chapel, and an odd "pope in a boat" modern bronze statue jutting from one wall. You can climb the tower of **San Fortunato,** at the top of town, for impressive views. The interior, unlike the crumbling facade with its weathered but still brilliant carved reliefs by Lorenzo Maitani (same guy who did the facade of Orvieto's Duomo), has a cool whitewashed solidity that is worth a peek.

On a side street, as you come back down to the road, is **Santa Maria in Camuccia,** housing a curious (and twice-stolen) 12th-century wood Madonna and Child statue in a protective plastic box. Just off the main road out of town is a masterpiece of High Renaissance architecture, the **Temple of Santa Maria della Consolazione** ★, which is scenically framed with the countryside behind it, and is far more impressive outside than within. You can get maps and information from the **tourist office** (Piazza del Popolo; ☎ 075-8942526 or 075-8943395; www.todi.umbria2000.it).

ACCOMMODATIONS, BOTH STANDARD & NOT

If you decide to spend a night in town, you have four good options.

€€–€€€   You need to cut down a side street from the main square, and then climb three flights of dark stairs to find **San Lorenzo Tre** ★ (Via San Lorenzo 3; ☎ 075-8944555; www.todi.net/lorenzo), a "Residenza d'Epoca" consisting of six villa apartments in a 17th-century palazzo turned into charming lodgings cluttered with old-fashioned furnishings and blessed with spectacular views of distant plains. Double rooms are 65€ to 78€ without private bathroom, 95€ to 110€ with bathroom. In the back streets of town, **Dimora Ada** (Via Mercato Vecchio 10;

☎ 075-8942444 or 338-3856001; www.dimoraada.com; cash only) rents out two homey, double rooms with a shared bathroom, shared kitchen, and panoramic terrace for 50€ to 90€.

€€   The **Crispotti Holiday House** (Via di Santa Prassede 36; ☎ 075-8944827; www.crispoltiholidayhouse.com; MC, V) offers bland modern rooms (doubles 70€–90€) in a lovely setting with views either over the wide Tiber valley or into the evocative 13th-century courtyard of this converted Agostinian convent. It's designed for groups, so while the rooms lack soul, the hotel doesn't lack for amenities, which in Italy means, in addition to parking, an Internet point and a panoramic dining terrace (meals cost 15€ for two courses, a side dish, fruit, wine, and water); there's also an on-site artificial-turf soccer field.

€€€–€€€€   You can get far more class and style—but at twice the price—at the **Hotel Fonte Cesia** ★ (Via Lorenzo Leonj 3; ☎ 075-8943737; www.fonte cesia.it; AE, MC, V), a visual stunner of a hotel combining the architectural elements of a 600-year-old building—lots of wood accents and low brick arches— with post-modern glass construction, stunning views, a high-end restaurant, and modern, comfortable rooms. The balconied, thematic junior suites ("Novecento" with 19th-c. antiques, "Jacopone" with Wassily chairs and a claw-foot tub, "Venturini" with a canopy bed) are particularly nice and worth the splurge. Doubles are 140€ to 164€ a night; a junior suite is 192€ to 208€.

€€€–€€€€   Near Todi on the road to Orvieto is the **Tenuta di Canonica** ★★ (Loc. Canonica 75–76; ☎ 075-8947545; www.tenutadicanonica.com; MC, V; closed Dec–Feb), a great base from which to explore central Umbria. The complex, with a swimming pool and stellar views, includes three handsome stone structures—one medieval, one Victorian, and one that actually boasts ancient Roman foundations. The buildings are plush and comfortable, filled with antique furniture and offering dozens of nooks and crannies filled with Italian art and history books hoarded by co-manager Maria Fano, a former art-history teacher. She and her husband, Daniele, can help arrange local activities, including horseback riding, language classes, and hikes. A superlative chef trained at the Cordon Bleu Perugia, Daniele also offers cooking classes on-site. If you prefer to let him do all the work, you can simply enjoy a set-priced dinner for 35€, not including wine (Tues–Sun around 8pm, with reservations only). The rooms, each with oversize modern bathrooms, rich fabrics, and comfortable beds, cost 135€ to 170€, breakfast included.

DINING FOR ALL TASTES

€–€€   Todi offers the usual tourist fare of pizza and set-menu tourist specials. One better option is the **Il Donatello** ★ (Via della Storta 29; ☎ 075-8942444; Mon–Sat noon–2pm and 7–9pm; AE, MC, V), run by a former apprentice to one of Italy's top chefs. The small alley restaurant has a country charm, with bright colors livening up its stone interior. The menu features only a handful of items, but it changes every few weeks to feature the best seasonal dishes. Try the *piccola torre di pomodoro e mozzarella* (little tower of tomatoes and mozzarella), excellent mixed bruschetta, and an herbed lamb steak. *Primi* average 6€ to 8€, *secondi* 7.50€ to 11€.

€–€€   The **Umbria** ★★ (Via S. Bonaventura 13, though the archway under the Palazzo del Popolo; ☎ 075-8942737; Wed–Mon 12:30–2:30pm and 7:30–10:30pm; AE, MC, V) is justly famous for its 15th-century interior and the views from the patio over the countryside. The food is special, with steak, boar, and other meats grilled over the roaring open fire on one wall, and rich spaghetti dishes, including the *spaghetti alla boscaiola,* which I still make at home to impress guests (it's basically a carbonara sauce—pancetta bacon, black pepper, eggs, and loads of parmigiano cheese—but studded with fresh asparagus). Given its popularity, the place can be packed, and the staff sometimes indifferent, but the meal is worth it. Pasta dishes range from 7€ to 13€, *secondi* from a smaller mixed grill for 9€ to a big steak for over 15€.

SPOLETO

Spoleto is famous for its summer music festival—and is then unfairly ignored during the rest of the year. That's a shame, since this southern Umbrian city deserves to be just as well known for its ancient bridge, its glowering fortress, its fabulous Duomo, and (in the fall) its status as one of the few places in the world where both white and black truffles are found. It's also a town where the ancient and the modern mingle well and to wonderful effect.

Walking through the medieval streets of the old town, you can see a Roman amphitheater converted into a jazz stage, and a medieval monastery refurbished into a hotel and restaurant. The Duomo rose from the rubble of a Spoleto destroyed in 1155, using scavenged stones, the foundation of an early Christian temple, and the marble flooring of a previous church. The mighty Rocca fortress above town has been recycled many times; it began as a Roman watchtower, was converted into a papal castle, then into a garrison headquarters, and finally into a modern high-security prison. It's now a combination gallery, museum, performance space, and civic office building. Walk around the back side of the fortress and you'll see a deep, verdant gorge spanned by the towering, narrow Ponte delle Torri bridge built on top of a Roman aqueduct using stones recycled from Roman ruins, Etruscan walls, and wrecked town towers.

The greatest example of recycling in Spoleto has been the city itself. This once-proud town became a central Italian nonentity for 500 years, before leaping back into the spotlight with the Festival of Two Worlds (now the Spoleto Festival) in 1958, which has grown to become one of the world's premier music fests. Spoleto has become home to year-round schools for world-class opera, music, and theater performance, highlighted by the annual summer event. But any time of year, the medieval streets and connected series of squares provide a colorful setting in which to experience the best of Umbrian food, wine, and entertainment.

> ❝ We came to Spoleto . . . I never saw a more impressive picture; in which the shapes of nature are of the grandest order, but over which the creations of man, sublime from their antiquity and greatness, seem to predominate. ❞
>
> —Percy Bysshe Shelley,
> *Letters from Italy,* 1840

Spoleto

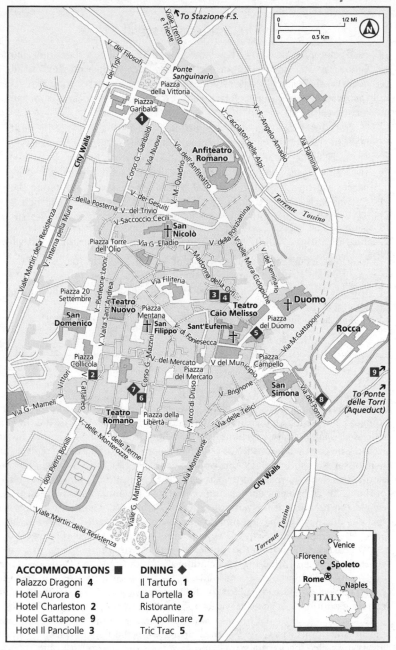

To Stazione F.S.

V. Trento e Trieste

V. dei Filosofi

L. dei Tigli

Ponte Sanguinario

Piazza della Vittoria

Piazza Garibaldi

City Walls

Corso G. Garibaldi

Via Nuova

Via dell'Anfiteatro

V. M. Quadrio

Anfiteatro Romano

V. F. Angelo Amadio

V. Cacciatori delle Alpi

Via Flaminia

Torrente Tossino

V. della Posterna

V. dei Gesuiti

V. del Trivio

V. Saccoccio Cecili

San Nicolò

Via G. Elladio

V. della Ponzianina

V. delle Mura Ciclopiche

V. del Seminario

Piazza Torre dell'Olio

Via Filiteria

Via Madonna della Oli

Viale Martiri della Resistenza

V. Interna della Mura

Piazza 20 Settembre

Teatro Nuovo

V. Vaita Sant'Andrea

V. Pierleone Leoni

Piazza Mentana

San Filippo

di Fonsesecca

Teatro Caio Melisso

Sant'Eufemia

Duomo

Piazza del Duomo

Rocca

San Domenico

Piazza Collicola

Corso G. Mazzini

V. del Mercato

Piazza del Mercato

V del Municipio

Piazza Campello

Via M. Gattaponi

V. Cattaneo

V. Vittori

Teatro Romano

Piazza della Libertà

V. Arco di Druso

V. Brignone

V. delle Telici

San Simona

Via del Ponte

To Ponte delle Torri (Aqueduct)

Via G. Mameli

V. delle Monterozze

V. delle Terme

Via G. Matteotti

V. don Pietro Bonilli

City Walls

Viale Martiri della Resistenza

Torrente Tossino

ACCOMMODATIONS ■

Palazzo Dragoni **4**
Hotel Aurora **6**
Hotel Charleston **2**
Hotel Gattapone **9**
Hotel Il Panciolle **3**

DINING ◆

Il Tartufo **1**
La Portella **8**
Ristorante
   Apollinare **7**
Tric Trac **5**

Venice
Florence
Spoleto
Rome
Naples

ITALY

The Spoleto Festival

For Spoleto, the dawn of a new age came in 1958. It was then that Gian Carlo Menotti, an Italian-American composer, settled on this small medieval town after an extensive search for the perfect spot for a festival that would, in his words, "match and exchange American and European artistic cultures."

From the very beginning, he recruited top names in the arts, both mainstream artists and experimental: Louis Armstrong, Al Pacino, Twyla Tharp, Pablo Neruda, Franco Zeffirelli, and Andy Warhol, to name but a few. The festival was (and is) a powerhouse in the worlds of opera, music, dance, and theater. Today, over 200 official events take place during the festival each summer (usually the last couple of days of June and first 2 weeks of July), and just as many side activities are sponsored by restaurants, hotels, and shops.

Menotti chose Spoleto to take advantage of its superb historical performance venues, including the ancient Roman amphitheater, the 17th-century Caio Melisso theater, and the Duomo square, where over 15,000 fest-goers jam for the yearly finale. The town, restaurants, and hotels are absolutely packed for the duration, so plan ahead.

For more information, call ☎ 0743-220320, or check out **www.spoletofestival.it**.

A BRIEF HISTORY OF SPOLETO

Like many Umbrian cities, Spoleto's history cycles through Etruscan origins, Roman colonization, Italian infighting, and papal misrule. In 217 B.C., a well-defended Spoleto stopped Hannibal's invading armies from marching toward Rome. The city then flourished as a Roman colony, and to this day is replete with remains of Roman buildings and walls. Thanks in part to its strategic position astride the Rome-Ravenna route, the city developed into the powerful city-state of the duchy of Spoleto, dominating central Italian politics and commerce. This caught the attention of the warlord Emperor Barbarossa, who didn't like the fact that the duchy wasn't paying him tribute. Barbarossa invaded Spoleto in 1155, and literally flattened the city, destroying every one of its famed 100 towers.

Spoleto was rebuilt from the rubble. Most of the city's current landmarks were constructed in the 13th century, including the Duomo and the Ponte delle Torri bridge. As Pope Innocent VI consolidated his rule over central Italy in the 14th century, papal armies constructed the Rocca fortress, which still occupies a commanding position over the city. Vatican forces kept the city subjugated under the intimidating watch of the fortress, and Spoleto faded from significance—until Italian-American Gian Carlo Menotti dreamed up the festival (picking Spoleto for its unspoiled, backwater status) and gave the city a new burst of life.

LAY OF THE LAND

More than a dozen trains reach Spoleto daily from Rome (1½ hr.) and Perugia (45 min.). The Spoleto train station is about a mile outside the old town, so you'll probably want to catch the C bus to the historical center or take a cab.

If you're driving, Spoleto is easy to reach, directly on the SS3, about 130km (80 miles) from Rome, 193km (120 miles) from Florence. Parking in the old town is nearly impossible, but you can park for free on the streets just outside the old city walls, on Viale Martiri Della Resistenza or Via Don Bonilli, next to the soccer stadium.

Spoleto's **tourist office** (Piazza della Libertà 7; ☎ 0743-238911; www.spoleto. umbria2000.it) has a good selection of fliers about events in town, and brochures on dozens of farmhouse stays outside town.

Note: The **Spoleto Festival** usually extends over 3 weeks from the end of June to mid-July. For this period, accommodations need to be booked far in advance. After the festival concludes, most of the city takes a 2-week holiday, so expect to see many restaurants, shops, and hotels closed at that time.

ACCOMMODATIONS, BOTH STANDARD & NOT

Except during the time of its world-renowned festival, Spoleto's hotel rates are reasonable.

€€   The centrally located **Hotel Aurora** (Via Apollinare 3; ☎ 0743-220315; www.hotelauroraspoleto.it; AE, MC, V) is a steal, with pleasant rooms for 70€ to 100€ in summer, and only 55€ in low season. Bathrooms are a little on the small side but functional; rooms are clean, with hardwood floors and air-conditioning. The breakfast room is especially cheery, with tiled floor and wood-beamed ceiling. And guests get a 10% discount at the Ristorante Apollinare (reviewed below), with which the hotel shares its original Roman walls.

€€   Tiny **Hotel Il Panciolle** (Via del Duomo 3–5; ☎ 0743-45677; cash only) is an even cheaper but satisfactory and centrally located option. It costs 55€ to 65€ for a double, though only two of the seven sizeable rooms have air-conditioning. The friendly manager doesn't speak much English, but can wrangle his grandkids to help with local recommendations.

€€–€€€   On a hilltop near Spoleto (right off the highway, call for directions) **Il Castello di Poreta** ★ (Loc. Poreta; ☎ 0743-275810; www.ilcastellodiporeta.it or www.seeumbria.com; AE, MC, V) boasts a primo historical setting in a fortified 14th-century keep and 18th-century church, with a high-end restaurant on the premises, but basic rooms. In a crazy arrangement typical of Italy, the province owns the site, the walls are owned by the state of Italy, the olive groves are privately owned, and the Vatican still has the deed to the church. The restaurant has been rated one of the top 50 in Italy. The eight rooms are serviceable, but nothing special, aside from the old priest's quarters called Corbezzolo, which are decorated in a traditional style. However, only two (Cotogno and Agrifolgio) do not come with sweeping countryside views. Doubles run 100€ to 115€ a night.

€€–€€€   **Hotel Charleston** ★ (Piazza Collicola 10; ☎ 0743-220052; www.hotelcharleston.it; AE, MC, V) is tucked away in a square next to the modern-art museum. Like the museum, the hotel is an interesting combination of old and new, with the original tiled floors and wood beams of the 17th-century villa filled with contemporary art and furniture, the walls often painted in deep, rich colors. The junior suites (110€–135€) are very nice, and the double rooms a decent deal at 52€ to 135€; Wi-Fi, a private garage, a sauna, and breakfast on the quiet little piazza out front are all perks. The Charleston also rents out lovely stone-walled apartments in an adjacent building for 350€ to 450€ per week (depending on season), plus 50€ to 75€ for utilities (light, gas, and such).

€€€   Prices at the **Palazzo Dragoni** ★ (Via del Duomo 13; ☎ 0743-222220; www.palazzodragoni.it; MC, V) are a bit higher, but come with a lot of class. Most rooms have views over the valley and a great period feel with antique furniture and a light, cheery decor. Some public spaces date back to the 12th century, including an old Dark Ages street that got incorporated as a hallway into the palazzo when it was built in the early 1500s. The superior rooms at 150€ are *really* superior, with canopy beds and super views, while the standard rooms are still quite nice at 125€. As a special bonus the Dragoni has free Wi-Fi access in all rooms.

DINING FOR ALL TASTES

€   Bar/gelateria **La Portella** 🧒 (Via del Ponte, after Piazza B. Campello and before Hotel Gattapone; no phone; closed Tues) is a nice place to hang out, grab a small meal (gelato and snacks for less than 5€) or beer, and look over the bridge and the gorge. Walk up the stairway to the left of the entrance to reach a terrace half hidden by greenery.

€€   In the same building as Hotel Aurora, tucked behind the walls of a 12th-century Franciscan convent and St. Apollinare's Church, is **Ristorante Apollinare** ★ (Via Sant'Agata 14; ☎ 0743-223256; www.ristoranteapollinare.it; daily noon–2:30pm and 7–10 pm; closed Tues in winter; AE, MC, V). It's long on atmosphere, installed amid timbered ceilings and stone walls, with an outdoor gazebo for summer dining. The food is tasty and rather creative: pumpkin gnocchi with pigeon, tortelli of saffron and rosemary stuffed with ricotta and spiced pork, and oven-roasted suckling pig in a sauce of pecorino and pears cooked in red wine. Let the chef run nuts and order the *menù à sorpresa*, a "chef's surprise" meal of three (25€) to five courses (35€) with a glass of wine included. A la carte, *primi* run 8€ to 14€ (up to 22€ for something with truffles), and *secondi* cost 12€ to 25€—but that includes the side dish (which in most Italian restaurants costs another 5€–8€).

€€–€€€   Named for a card game and right in front of the cathedral, the **Tric Trac** ★ (Piazza Duomo; ☎ 0743-44592; www.trictrac.it; Thurs–Tues noon–3:30pm and 6:30–10pm; AE, MC, V) is an old artists' hangout that is jam-packed at festival time. The menu changes weekly, but you can usually find a grilled guinea hen or a kitchen salad piled with the freshest ingredients, or in winter, a thick lamb stew. Primi cost 8€ to 13€ (up to 19€ with truffles), though to keep prices in check you might want to steer clear of the *secondi*, which range from 19€ to 29€.

€€–€€€€   Known as *the* place to go for truffles, **Il Tartufo** ✦ (Piazza Garibaldi 24; ☎ 0743-40236; Tues–Sat 12:30–3pm and 7–10:30pm, Sun 12:30–3pm; AE, MC, V; reservations required) is considered by many to be the finest restaurant in town. Even if you're not a truffle connoisseur, once you try an Umbrian pasta or risotto with fresh grated local truffle, you're likely to be converted. *Primi* run 8€–12€, up to 20€ for something with truffles; *secondi* go for 14€ to 18€ (25€ with truffles). The location in the lower town is a bit inconvenient for those staying in the historical center, but if you want to try the best, it's worth the trip.

WHY YOU'RE HERE: THE TOP SIGHTS & ATTRACTIONS

The three main attractions of Spoleto's **Duomo** ✦✦ (Piazza del Duomo; ☎ 0743-44307; free; daily 8:30am–12:30pm and 3:30–7pm) are (1) the eight intricately carved rose windows and glowing mosaics on the facade, (2) Filippo Lippi's *Life of the Virgin* apse fresco, and (3) the original inlaid marble floors. The Duomo is a reconstruction of the original structure destroyed in 1155 by Barbarossa. The facade features late-12th-century Romanesque stained-glass windows and mosaics that glow in the late-afternoon sun. The portico was a late-Renaissance add-on meant to bring the church into the "modern age."

Filippo Lippi painted the *Life of the Virgin* fresco filling the apse in the late 1460s. It was recently restored, and today the colors and vivid figures practically leap off the walls, especially the circular rainbow and the bright gold sun in the *Coronation of the Virgin* in the center of the work, which give the fresco a New Age feel. Take a close look at the scene of the *Virgin's Dormition* (not her death; doctrine holds that, at the end of her life, Mary merely fell asleep and was taken bodily up to Heaven). The monk in that panel wearing a white robe and black hat facing the viewer is a self-portrait of the painter, who died in 1469 just before finishing the work (it was completed by his assistants). Filippo did, however, have enough time to include, as the candle-holding angel in front, a portrait of his 11-year-old son, Filippino Lippi, who would go on to become a great artist in his own right, trained by Filippo's famed student Botticelli.

Be sure also to look down at the intricate geometric designs of the inlaid marble floor, said to be the original of the Christian temple built in the 7th century. Then walk to the chapel at the left of the altar to see one of only two known genuine St. Francis autographs (the other is in Assisi), his signature at the bottom of a letter he wrote to one of his followers, now preserved behind glass in an ornate frame. On the right side of the altar is a chapel containing a spooky black-and-silver Virgin Mary icon. Barbarossa stole the icon from Constantinople, and then donated it to the newly constructed Duomo in a "sorry I destroyed your town" gesture.

At the back of the Rocca fortress is Spoleto's famous **Ponte delle Torri bridge** ✦✦ 🧒. This awe-inspiring arched stone structure towers 76m (249 ft.) above the Tessino gorge and 230m (754 ft.) across the river, from Spoleto to the forested mountain of Monteluco. The architect Gattapone designed the bridge in the 14th century on top of an ancient Roman aqueduct's lithe arches. A number of shaded mountain paths begin at the far side of the bridge. Maps are available in the tourist office.

Viewed from the bridge, or from anywhere else in town, the **Rocca fortress** (Piazza Campello 1; ☎ 0743-43707; 6.50€; Mon–Fri 2:30–5pm, Sat–Sun

10am–5pm) stands in intimidating watch over Spoleto, and was designed to look that way. Pope Innocent VI had his "pit bull," the Cardinal Albornoz, supervise construction of this castle in the 1360s, and populated it with troops to keep Spoleto under Vatican control. As the need to subjugate the city faded, the fortress served as a prison for hundreds of years. It went through renovations the reverse of those seen in many Italian hotels: medieval walls stripped bare of frescoes, rooms made *less* hospitable, windows bricked shut. It has housed enemies of the state, including Slavic political prisoners, Red Brigade terrorists, and the man who tried to assassinate Pope John Paul II.

Nowadays, the Rocca has been converted once again, this time into an art gallery, performance space, and medieval museum, showing off restored frescoes and original gardens. Admission is only by guided tour, and English-language tours are offered only twice daily, at 11am and 3pm. But because the guides don't really add much beyond the info pamphlet, consider joining one of the hourly Italian tours and simply admiring the views. Tickets can be bought at the wood shed at the gate of the castle drive at the end of Via Saffi, where a minibus will take you to the fortress. Tours (in Italian) run from 10am to 5pm in summer, but are more limited in winter months. To gain an appreciation of ancient Spoletium, visit the **Teatro Romano** ★ and the connected **Museo Archeologico** (Via San Agata 18, just below Piazza della Libertà; ☎ 0743-223277; www.archeopg.arti.beniculturali.it; 4€; daily 8:30am–7:30pm). The theater, constructed in the 1st century A.D., sank into the ground and immediately had to be rebuilt, sort of an ancient Leaning Tower of Pisa. It lay buried over the years, and was only excavated and restored in the 1950s. Today it's used as part of the Spoleto Festival. The museum has some noteworthy artifacts, including a set of stone tablets outlining local Roman laws, and a shield and weapons recovered from a Bronze Age tomb.

Another view into the distant past can be seen in the crypt of the usually ignored **Sant'Ansano Church** (next to Piazza del Mercato; free; daily 7:30am–noon and 3–6:30pm, Nov–Mar closes 5:30pm). Stairs to the left of the altar lead to the underground chambers of the crypt. The rough Byzantine fresco fragments on the walls (possibly dating to the 8th c. or earlier), the darkened room, and the funereal nature of the altar all open a window into the early days of the Church.

THE OTHER SPOLETO

Sure, the Spoleto Festival is the town's big draw, but culture doesn't begin and end there. If you arrive before the festival in June you can visit a number of competitions in which aspiring artists studying in the city strut their stuff, hoping to earn a spot in the main festival. The European Community Competition for Young Opera Singers is in March, the International Dance Competition is in April, and a biannual Competition for New Chamber Opera debuts its winner in the off season. For information about specific show times and locations, pick up a copy of the bilingual *Nuovo Spoleto,* a free monthly magazine, or stop by the tourist office, which will have listings of upcoming performances.

After the festival, both novices and near-professionals can join a course at the **Spoleto Arts Symposia** (☎ in the U.S. 212/665-3544; www.spoletoarts.com) that takes place in late July to early August. They offer workshops in music, cooking, and writing. Wondering what to do with the kids? No problem, the arts group also offers the **Spoleto Kids Camp** 🧒 with arts and crafts, drama, music, sports, and field trips. Enrollment can be from 5 days to 3 weeks. Many attendees stay together at the Istituto Bambin' Gesù convent.

GUBBIO

Geography saved Gubbio. Because it's so far off the beaten path, and so difficult to get to by any means other than private car, this classic medieval hill town survived the 20th century with much of its historic soul intact. At night, when the streets are largely deserted, the medieval stone walls loom in the darkness and eerie lights illuminate the ruins of the amphitheater in a field outside the town walls. You'd almost expect to see toga-clad Romans rushing to catch the latest entertainments. Walking around a corner and gazing at the ethereal silhouette of the ruined medieval watchtower, you wouldn't be surprised to have to dodge a 10th-century horseman, or the contents of a chamber pot tossed from a window above. Instead, the next day, screaming kids kick soccer balls around the same squares and locals gather for lively discussions over thimbles of espresso at street-front bars.

A BRIEF HISTORY OF GUBBIO

The Romans declared an alliance with the city of Iguvium at present-day Gubbio in the 1st century B.C. The empire's print can be seen in the still-extant amphitheater, and in the relics in the local museums. With the fall of Rome, the citizens of Gubbio retreated up the hill to a more fortified city to fend off barbarian attacks, but this didn't stop the marauding armies. Not until the 12th century did Gubbio develop into a stable city, with walls and leadership strong enough to fend off invaders. In 1155, Bishop (later to be St.) Ubaldo negotiated peace with the warlord Barbarossa, preserving the city from destruction.

By the 13th century, Gubbio had developed into a prosperous city-state, enjoying its important commercial location on the road from Rome to Ravenna. Peace and prosperity through the mid-1300s fueled the construction of most of the palaces, walls, and churches still standing today. But then Gubbio succumbed to the 1348 plague, to generations of mismanagement by the dukes of Urbino, and to 100 years of neglect by the papal states. Discarded as an unimportant backwater, Gubbio was able to preserve its medieval traditions, architecture, and spirit.

Gubbio's spirit was particularly evident during World War II, when it hosted a number of anti-Nazi Partisan groups. The Germans retaliated with a massacre in 1944, memorialized in the Mausoleum of 40 Martyrs below town. Post-war Gubbio has seen a rebirth of artisans' workshops, traditional festivals, and an epically ugly cement factory north of town.

LAY OF THE LAND

Reaching Gubbio can be a bit of a challenge because it's not on any of the main highways or rail lines. Probably the best option is by car, taking the winding SS298 north about 39km (25 miles) from Perugia or the No. 3 to the 219 coming south 90km (60km) from Arezzo. Free parking is available at the lot next to the Roman amphitheater.

If you're train-bound, stop at Fossato di Vico, about a half-hour bus-shuttle away from town on the Rome-Ancona line, itself about a 2¼ hour ride from Rome. Buses also go from Perugia to Gubbio 11 times daily, taking just over an hour.

The Gubbio **tourist office** (Via della Repubblica 15; ☎ 075-9220693; www. umbria2000.it or www.comune.gubbio.pg.it) distributes tons of maps and brochures.

ACCOMMODATIONS & DINING

€€   For the feel of a hidden apartment in the medieval city, try the **Residenza Le Logge** ✸ (Via Piccardi 7–9; ☎ 075-9277574; www.paginegialle.it/residenza-lelogge; AE, MC, V). This small building on a side street off Via Baldassini offers six smallish but homey rooms (doubles 65€–80€), and a quiet backyard garden area where guests can enjoy morning coffee or a picnic lunch while they gaze at the palaces above.

€€–€€€€   Rodolfo Mencarelli and his family have built a bit of an empire in the region with four restaurants and three hotels—the Gattapone, the Bosone Palace, and the Relais Ducale (for more information on that pricey last one, go to www.mencarelligroup.com)—which happen to be the best in town. The **Gattapone** (Via Ansidei 6; ☎ 075-9272489; AE, MC, V) is the best deal of the bunch (doubles around 90€–110€), but with its generic refurbishing in 1999, lacks the charming ambience of its sister hotels. It's on a quiet street (the church bells notwithstanding) and has perfectly decent rooms, albeit with small bathrooms.

The **Bosone Palace** ✸ (Via XX Settembre 22; ☎ 075-9220688; AE, MC, V) has a real claim to fame: Dante himself stayed here as a guest of the Rafaelli family in the 14th century soon after the palace was built. The rooms are a little weathered compared to the Relais Ducale, but still comfortable; the hotel decor gives you the feel of coming to the Continent on a grand tour. Doubles cost 110€ to 140€ a night. The **Relais Ducale** ✸✸ (Via Galeotti 19; ☎ 075-9220157; AE, MC, V), as the name implies, is built from a duke's palace, and even has its own secret tunnel. Each of the 30 rooms is unique, ranging from the smaller, cheaper, but still atmospheric stone-walled, wooden-arched rooms on the lower level, to larger rooms with citywide views above. The smaller cheaper doubles can often be had for 155€ (larger rooms are quite pricey).

€€   A good out-of-town base is the **Cinciallegre Agriturismo** ✸ (Fraz. Pisciano; ☎ 075-9255957 or 347-0866889; www.lecinciallegre.it; AE, MC, V). About a 20-minute drive northwest of Gubbio, this secluded hideaway consists of seven converted farm buildings perched on top of a ridge overlooking dense Umbrian forests. Each room has the characteristics of the bird for which it's named: Depending on your preferences, you can choose the Robin room, with its bright spring theme; the Titmouse, with its small windows; or the Sparrow, a small single. Price per person is 48€ for bed and breakfast, 70€ including dinner. Maria Cristina, co-owner and chef, prepares excellent meals using ingredients from her organic gardens; the rabbits, geese, and ducks are also raised on the property. Her husband, Fabrizio, can give tips for peaceful hiking treks on local trails, and the two even rent ATVs. Cinciallegre can be reached on SS219, signposted from Mocaiana, on tricky winding gravel mountain roads, so try arriving during the day.

€   While it looks like a small bar from the Piazza Boscone, the **Osteria de Re** ✸ (Via Cavour 15/B; ☎ 075-9222504; Thurs–Tues 12:30–2:30pm and 7:30–9:30pm; MC, V) has two large underground vaulted chambers full of happy diners munching away on the restaurant's specialty, a sampler platter of fried breads, olives, bruschetta, veggies, and baked cheeses—a good feast for two at 12€ per person. In summer, you can sit at tables in the piazza while locals shout from windows above and kids play soccer. Simple *primi*, sandwiches, and soups cost 3.50€ to 5€, *secondi* (with a side dish) go for around 7.50€, and nothing costs more than 9€ (for a platter of particularly rare cheese).

€€–€€€€ The Mencarelli empire stretches to restaurants, featuring the excellent (but pricey) **Taverna Del Lupo** ★ (Via Ansidei 21, under the Bosone Palace; ☎ 075-9274368; Tues–Sun 12:15–3pm and 7pm–midnight; AE, MC, V), a medieval restaurant of five rooms with stone arches giving it the feeling of a nobleman's banquet hall. Older waiters in bow ties and tuxedoes lend the restaurant a feeling of upscale propriety, as does the book-length wine list. Its set menus run from 20€ to 24€ (not including wine), change by the season, and feature excellent local pastas, including *Srangozzi all'ortolana*, with fresh vegetables, and a grilled meat assortment with mouthwatering boar, rabbit, and chicken morsels. You can also order a la carte (*primi* or *secondi* 10€–30€).

€€–€€€€ The Rosati group competes with the Mencarelli for control of the Gubbio hospitality industry, with three hotels, a residence, two restaurants, and an *enoteca* (wine bar). Most worthwhile of the lot is their **La Fornace di Mastro Giorgio** (Via Mastro Giorgio 2, just off of Via XX Settembre; ☎ 075-9221836; www.rosatihotels.com; Thurs–Mon noon–2:30 and 7:30–10:30pm, Wed 7:30–10:30pm; AE, MC, V), slightly less expensive and stuffy than the Lupo (above) and with atmosphere to spare in a converted 15th-century ceramics workshop. The restaurant features characteristic Umbrian cuisine with a creative twist, including *filetto alle prugne* (steak with prune sauce), and roasted duck with oranges. *Primi* pasta dishes cost 10€ to 25€, while *secondi* range from 12€ to 30€.

WHY YOU'RE HERE: THE TOP SIGHTS & ATTRACTIONS

Every visit to Gubbio should include some time spent just hanging around the lively **Piazza Grande** ★★. This wide, stone-covered plaza spans the open space from a medieval city hall on one end to another medieval hall on the other, and while backed by the long neoclassical Palazzo Ranghiasci on one side, the other is completely open to a panoramic view of the lower city and the Umbrian countryside beyond.

To learn about the city, walk to the right of the plaza and up the fanned steps to enter the **Palazzo dei Consoli (Palace of Consuls)** ★ (☎ 075-9274298; 5€; daily Apr–Oct 10am–1pm and 3–6pm, Nov–Mar 10am–1pm and 2–5pm). The same ticket offers entry to all exhibits in the Civic Museum, which is inside the palace. Originally constructed in the 1330s as the headquarters for the city assembly, the Palace now serves as a multilevel museum exhibiting art and history of the region. The archaeological exhibit features the famed Eugubian tablets, discovered in the 15th century, upon which are carved some of the world's oldest and most detailed descriptions of religious rites, from at least 200 B.C.

The upper floors of the palace contain an art museum with works by local son Giorgio Andreoli, who developed innovative ceramic techniques in the early 1500s that helped put Gubbio firmly on the map as a top town for fine pottery. His *Circe* and *Fall of the Phaeton* can be seen in the Sala della Loggetta. Walking

Gubbio's Festivals ★★★

While Gubbio's art and architecture remain locked in medieval times, the festivals live vividly in the modern age and are tremendous fun:

- **Procession of the Dead Christ:** Good Friday.
- **Corsa dei Ceri (Race of the Ceri):** May 15. Most important of the yearly events, the town becomes feet-can't-touch-the-ground crowded, with people watching three teams race around town carrying a trio of giant "candles" (6.6m/22-ft. carved wooden logs on platforms) representing three saints: Ubaldo, Anthony, and George. They then sprint with them 300m (1,000 ft.) up Mt. Ingino. *Hint:* Bet on Ubaldo—he's the patron saint of Gubbio, and his team hasn't lost in about 700 years.
- **Palio della Balestra (Crossbow Festival):** Last Sunday in May.
- **Spettacoli Classici (Classicals Spectacular):** July to August. Classical concerts in the ruins of the Roman Theater just outside town.
- **Palio dei Quartieri (Tournament of the Neighborhoods):** August 14.
- **Gubbio Italian Jazz Festival:** August.
- **Mostra Mercato Nazionale del Tartufo Bianco (White Truffle Fair):** End of October/early November.
- **The World's Biggest Christmas Tree:** December 7 to January 10. The city attaches lights in the shape of a giant Christmas tree in the forest on the slopes of Mt. Ingino. Guinness has declared that this is indeed the world's biggest Christmas tree at 800m (2,624 ft.) tall and 400m (1,312 ft.) wide. It is also, unofficially, the gaudiest.

from the Piazza Grande, take one of the city's public elevators (!) off Via XX Settembre to reach the street outside the 13th-century **Duomo** ✚ (Via Ducale and Via della Cattedrale; ☎ 075-9220904; free; daily 9am–6pm), with a wagon vault of arches supporting the roof inside. The bent, curved beams are meant to represent praying hands but look more like a vast, upturned boat keel. The cool, silent interior has pleasant stained-glass windows and frescoes, which are overshadowed by the gaudy baroque chapels.

Around the corner from the Duomo is the **Museo Diocesano** ✚ (Via Federico da Montefeltro; ☎ 075-9220904; www.museogubbio.it; 5€; daily Apr–Oct 10am–7pm, Nov–Mar 10am–6pm), a well-presented collection of art and antique relics in three stories of vaulted stone rooms of a 12th-century palace. If you want to save the 5€ admission fee, at least walk into the lower-level bookshop entrance and poke your head into the side room to see a must-have for any decent medieval party: a 19,760-liter, 3.6m-tall (12-ft.) wine barrel from the 15th century.

No visit to Gubbio is complete without a trip to the top of **Mt. Ingino,** towering 750m (2,500 ft.) above the town. The peak boasts 360-degree views over Gubbio and Umbria to the west, and the wilderness of the Marches to the east. You can reach the top via a quad-burning hike up the path from Porta Sant'Ubaldo, east of the Duomo, or by driving the dizzying road up the mountain.

But the most fun way to ascend Mt. Ingino is to take the **cable car** ★ (☎ 075-9273881; 5€ round-trip) from the south edge of town. You'll ride in a rickety coffin-size metal basket hanging from a cable slung 45m (150 ft.) or so over the ground. It's definitely not for those scared of heights, but it's a cool way to fly up a mountain. The cars run daily from roughly 10am to around 5pm (winter) to 7:30pm (summer), but times vary widely by season, and note the occasional lunch closing times or you may be spending an extra hour on top.

Once up Mt. Ingino, go to the **Basilica di Sant'Ubaldo** (daily 8am–6pm) to see the mummified remains of St. Ubaldo himself (minus a few fingers snipped off by one of his servants eager to sell saintly remains) in a glass box on top of an altar. You can also see the three pagoda-like "candles" carried in the Corsa dei Ceri race from the city to this church.

Walk up the road across the street from the Basilica to reach the remains of the **Rocca** ★ on the mountain peak. The 12th-century fortress and tower is in ruins, and unremarkable, but the views are spectacular, broken only by the spectacularly ugly framework used for the famed Christmas lighting (see "Gubbio's Festivals," above).

THE OTHER GUBBIO

To get the very best feel for Gubbio, don't just walk by and look at the ceramics—take a class and make some! The city of Gubbio, in cooperation with **In Umbria da Nord Est** (☎ 075-9222027 or 075-9220066; www.inumbria.net), runs a dozen **single-day classes,** including ceramics, mosaic- and fresco-making, cooking, and, for the adventurous, truffle-hunting, hang-gliding, and mountain biking. Costs range from 10€ to 55€ for a 2- to 4-hour crafts course, to 65€ for a 15-minute hang-gliding ride. Reservations are required at least a day in advance. *Hint:* They sort of hide this information on their website; once on the English language homepage, mouse over "Tourist Facilities" at the top of the screen, then on the drop-down menu click on "Things to do and information," or try this deep link: www.inumbria.net/eng_fr_servizi.htm.

ATTENTION, SHOPPERS!

Gubbio became famous in the 14th century for its ceramics, and keeps up the tradition today with dozens of shops around town. One shop I recommend is **Rampini** (Via dei Consoli 52; 075-9274408; www.rampiniceramiche.com), which also has a workshop on Via Leonardo da Vinci 92, where you can stop by to watch the craftspeople at work. The second-generation family owner spent years in Brazil, and now gives a bit of a tropical spin to traditional works.

6

Bologna & Emilia-Romagna

You'll find plenty of great art and architecture here—but not many tourists

by Reid Bramblett

MANY TRAVELERS WHIZ THROUGH THE EMILIA-ROMAGNA REGION, OF which Bologna is the capital, en route to and from Florence, Milan, Venice, or Rome. This is a terrible shame because they are not only bypassing some of Italy's finest art and architecture, but also missing the opportunity to experience a way of life that has been largely unaffected by the mass tourism and massive industrialization that so altered many regions of Italy in the 20th century.

Those ills are largely absent in Emilia-Romagna, a region comprising two ancient lands: Emilia, named for the Via Emilia, the ancient Roman road that bisects its plains and art cities; and Romagna, named for its prominence in the Roman Empire. History has left its mark here on some of Italy's most beautiful, yet lesser known, cities—Ravenna, last capital of the empire and later the stronghold of the Byzantines and the Visigoths (the former leaving behind spectacular mosaics); Ferrara, a center of art and culture during the Renaissance; and Parma, one of the most powerful duchies in Europe under the Farnese family and still world renowned for its cheese (parmigiano, or Parmesan) and cured ham *(prosciutto di Parma)*.

Bologna, the regional capital, is home not only to great pasta (spaghetti bolognese, anyone?) and cured meats, but also to the oldest university in Europe. This venerable institution accounts for much of Bologna's great sights—from frescoed and sculpture-adorned churches to rich museum collections—and for the liveliness and active cultural scene of this student-filled city.

DON'T LEAVE BOLOGNA WITHOUT . . .

SEEING A TEENAGED MICHELANGELO'S SCULPTURES They adorn the revered tomb of San Domenico.

STUFFING YOURSELF ON SOME OF THE BEST FOOD IN ITALY Even the non-Bolognese agree: Emilia-Romagna is the culinary heart of the country.

CLIMBING TO THE TOP OF TORRE DEGLI ASINELLI You'll be rewarded with a panoramic view of the city.

HANGING OUT WITH THE COLLEGE KIDS Why not? You're on vacation. You'll find them in the wine bars, pubs, and osterias lining Via del Pratello and Via Zamboni.

ACCOMMODATIONS ■

Accademia **15**
B&B Miramonte **22**
Beatrice Bed & Breakfast **13**
Bologna nel Cuore **3**
Casa Ilaria **18**
Centrale Byron **9**
Collegio Erasmus **20**
Dei Commercianti **7**
Hotel Touring **21**
Novecento **5**
Orologio **8**
Panorama **4**
Roma **6**
Rossini **19**

DINING ◆

Anna Maria **17**
Enoteca Italiana **12**
L'Osteria del
  Montesino **2**
Olindo Faccioli **11**
Ristorante al Montegrappa
  da Nello **10**
Trattoria Belfiore **14**
Trattoria Da Danio **1**
Trattoria Fantoni **2**
Trattoria-Pizzeria
  Belle Arte **16**

A BRIEF HISTORY OF BOLOGNA

Since the opening of its university (the oldest in Europe) in 1088, scholars began descending upon Bologna in droves, and the growing city took shape to accommodate them. The burgeoning community built palazzi and churches, and artists came from throughout Italy to decorate them.

These treasures remain amid a handsome cityscape of ocher-colored buildings, red-tile rooftops, and the occasional tower constructed by powerful medieval families to display their wealth and power. Bologna's famous 40km (25 miles) of *loggie* have turned it into a city of covered sidewalks, allowing students and locals alike to stroll and discourse even in bad weather. The students remain a vibrant presence in Bologna, giving the city a youthful exuberance.

LAY OF THE LAND

Bologna is 105km (65 miles) north of Florence and 210km (130 miles) both south of Venice and southeast of Milan.

Flights, including **Eurofly**'s (www.euroflyusa.com) new direct flights from New York, land at **Aeroporto G. Marconi** (☎ 051-6479615; www.bologna-airport.it), 8km (5 miles) north of the city. The bus to the **train station** (☎ 051-290290; www.atc.bo.it), a 15-minute ride, runs daily about every quarter-hour from 6:05am to 11:45pm.

Trains arrive from and depart for the following major Italian cities almost hourly. Florence (60–90 min.), Rome (3–4 hr.), Milan (1½–2½ hr.), and Venice (1¾–2¼ hr.).

The **center** of Bologna is Piazza Maggiore, about a 15-minute walk down Via dell'Indipendenza from the train station (or take bus no. 25 or 30). Since old Bologna is densely concentrated within the ring roads that follow the lines of its old walls, most everything of interest lies within a 10- to 15-minute walk from this central square.

Following Via Rizzoli, which skirts the north end of the piazza, you come to Bologna's famous leaning towers, and from there Via Zamboni leads northeast toward the university and the Pinacoteca Nazionale; Via Ugo Bassi runs west from the piazza to Via del Pratello and its antiques shops and osterias; and Via degli Orefici takes you southeast into the midst of Bologna's colorful food markets and toward the San Stefano church complex.

The **main tourist office** (Piazza Maggiore 1, in the Palazzo Comunale; ☎ 051-239660 or 051-251947; www.bolognaturismo.info; daily 9:30am–7:30pm) has a hotel-booking service (www.cst.bo.it) in addition to the typical information. The branch office in the train station is open Monday through Saturday 9am to 7pm, Sunday 9am to 3pm; the airport office is open daily 8am to 8pm. For tourism information on the region, visit www.emiliaromagnaturismo.it and www.provincia.bologna.it/cultura.

ACCOMMODATIONS, BOTH STANDARD & NOT

In a city devoted to students and their needs, you can be sure that there are many nonstandard accommodations. I'll give three cheers to the **tourist office,** which has posted on **www.bolognaturismo.info** the complete database of hotels, B&Bs, residences, *affittacamere* (rooms for rent), and religious hostelries in Bologna—as well as *agriturismi* (farm stays) in the surrounding area. Unlike most local websites, this one includes all the details you need to make an informed decision: phone numbers, number of rooms, amenities, prices, and websites.

And what will you find here? Everything from modest folk charging 20€ to 40€ per person, to hosts who feel their accommodation's size, beauty, or location is good enough to charge 100€ per person. In a very, very general sense, I'd say rental rooms and B&Bs tend to go for 30€ to 50€ per person in this region, though, again, it depends on the place. Regarding style, there is no norm. I've stayed in B&Bs and rental rooms that were just the spare bedroom in a modern apartment, others that were a cluster of bedrooms in an old-world apartment full of creaky antiques and doilies (like staying with your Italian great-aunt Maria), and still others that were like having my own little loft.

As for apartments, there also is no formula. Price varies depending on size, location, number of bedrooms, number of guests, length of stay, type of apartment, time of year, and mood of the owner. Honestly, you could spend 500€ per week or 500€ per night. So study the site carefully because you could find a gem.

€–€€€ Bologna boasts more than 270 B&Bs and rental rooms. Because winnowing that list will take a while, here are some surefire choices in the historical center. Perhaps the best option is Maria Ketty's boutique-ish **Bologna nel Cuore** (Via Cesare Battisti 29, west of Piazza Maggiore; ☎ 051-269442 or 329-2193354; www.bolognanelcuore.it; cash only), in which you can rent two stylish rooms with a pleasingly odd assemblage of designer furnishings and antique touches—bang in the center of town—for 80€ to 180€, depending on period and length of stay. **Casa Ilaria** (Largo Respighi 8, just off Via Zamboni in the university district; ☎ 051-270512 or 335-5336613; www.casailaria.com; cash only) rents a pair of rooms with frilly curtains, Wi-Fi, and Jacuzzi tubs or showers for 90€ for two people, or for 150€ during trade fairs. They can also arrange 4-hour cooking classes for 50€ per person.

€ Halfway between the train station and Piazza Maggiore, **Beatrice Bed & Breakfast** (Via dell'Indipendenza 56, near Piazza dell'VIII Agosto; ☎ 051-246016 or 338-9203407; www.bb-beatrice.com; cash only) offers three rooms—elegant "Beatrice," plain "Elizabetta," and "Patrizia," which can sleep up to four—with a shared bathroom. Rooms cost 75€ to 85€ per night for two, up to 130€ on weekends, holidays, or trade fairs. Internet access is available in the fifth-floor apartment of a young couple and Cip, their cat.

€–€€ At the southern edge of the historical center, **B&B Miramonte** (Via Miramonte 11; ☎ 339-5697513; www.miramonte-bologna.it; MC, V) is nice because it's made up of a pair of modern two-room apartments—the one on the second floor has wood ceilings—and you can choose whether to rent just one of the rooms (with private bathroom, TV, and Internet for 80€) and share the living room/kitchenette with the other room on that floor, or you can rent the entire

Beware the Trade Fairs & Watch the Seasons

Bologna is a city of *fiere* (trade fairs) that frequently leave the city booked solid—and cause every hotel to jack up rates to the maximum allowed by law. You can get more information on them (and a calendar of when they'll occur) at www.bolognafiere.it.

Count on having to book far in advance for the heaviest trade fair periods, which vary from year to year but tend to cluster in the middle 2 weeks of February, the second half of April, mid-December, and (in general) 4 or 5 days in the second week and the fourth week of May, September, and October.

You'll find the cheapest hotel rates in summer, especially in August, when the Bolognese flee the city for cooler climes.

two-room apartment on either floor for 150€. They also rent three small stand-alone modern apartments starting at 70€ to 91€ per night. The contemporary **B&B Anna** (Via Orfeo 24; ☎ 349-9011981; www.bebanna.it; cash only), in the southeast corner of the historical center, offers a single (39€–50€) and a double (72€–80€), as well as optional shiatsu massages.

The tourist office also has a list of 29 local **religious institutions that provide housing** for students during the academic year, and will often rent the rooms to tourists during the summer.

€   There's also a university-run student dorm in which you can snag a room—which includes a bathroom, telephone, and Internet connection for 45€ per single, 50€ per double—from the end of the school year (which varies) to July 19: **Collegio Erasmus** (Via de' Chiari 8; ☎ 051-276711; www.ceur.it/collegio-erasmus; cash only).

ACCOMMODATIONS NEAR PIAZZA MAGGIORE

€   I'm delighted whenever I discover another charming, old-fashioned pensione like the **Panorama** ✦ (kids) (Via Livraghi 1, off Via Ugo Bassi, 3 blocks west of Piazza Maggiore; ☎ 051-221802; www.hotelpanoramabologna.it; cash only) still in business. In fact, if you don't mind rooms without bathrooms and a lack of breakfast service, you may want to consider staying in one of these 75€ doubles even if your budget allows for more luxurious accommodations. The location near Piazza Maggiore is excellent, and the women who own/manage the hotel, which occupies the top floor of an old apartment house, make guests feel like family. The rooms are very large and high ceilinged, with creaky old parquet floors in a herringbone pattern, and most look through large windows over a pleasant courtyard to the hills above the city (avoid room nos. 6–10, whose double-paned windows can't keep out the traffic noise). The furnishings are functional but modern and include enough wooden armoires and other homey touches to make them cozy. Some rooms even sleep four (95€) or five (105€) people.

€–€€   The attractive **Centrale** ✦ (kids) (Via delle Zecca 2, off Via Ugo Bassi, 2 blocks west of Piazza Maggiore; ☎ 05l-225114; www.albergocentralebologna.it; AE, MC, V) offers one of Bologna's best values: It's cheap, central, and clean, and has all the amenities you need plus the occasional touch of class in the form of a chandelier hanging from decorative ceiling moldings. An ancient cage elevator deposits you at the door on the third floor of an old apartment house in the amiable company of an interesting mix of travelers from all over the world. The rooms—80€ for a double without bathroom, 86€ to 98€ with; skip the overpriced 7€ extra for breakfast—have been redone with crisp modern furnishings and either pleasant pastel or brocaded deep blue fabrics. The bathrooms can be small but come with large sinks and showers. Most rooms are unusually spacious for Italy, and several have three and four beds or futon-chairs, making this an especially affordable stopover for families. (I like room no. 18, with a big window overlooking a brick tower and church dome.)

€€€   If you prefer your hotels a bit less creaky and more modern, the gracious **Roma** ✦ (Via d'Azeglio 9, just a few steps south of Piazza Maggiore; ☎ 051-226322; www.hotelroma.biz; AE, MC, V) offers many of the amenities you'd expect in larger hotels. Those include a cozy lobby bar, an adequate though not outstanding in-house restaurant, efficient English-speaking staff, porters to carry your bags, and a garage—all for 150€ per double. What really makes this hotel worth seeking out, though, are its unusually comfortable rooms. They're large and bright (albeit dominated by overwrought floral patterns), with brass beds that are often king-size, roomy armchairs, and long tables; most rooms also have a dressing-room foyer between the bathroom and bedroom. The green-tiled bathrooms were redone several years ago and tend to be huge, with bidets and luxuriously deep tubs—though you'll have to hold the shower nozzle yourself, and there's rarely a curtain. Ask for one of the top-floor rooms with terrace (room nos. 301–303, 306–309, 422–425, and 428–429).

ACCOMMODATIONS NEAR THE UNIVERISTY

€–€€ The plain but comfortable **Rossini** (Via Bibiena 11, off Piazza G. Verdi, between Via Zamboni and Via San Vitale; ☎ 051-237716; www.albergorossini.com; AE, MC, V) will fill the bill, if not thrill, for basic comfort at a good price. Its location in the heart of the university district is what draws many guests and visiting academics. The rooms aren't much more than functional, right down to the no-nonsense small bathrooms, but at least they're large, with very firm beds, and cheap: Doubles without bathroom cost 55€ to 68€, with bathroom 80€ to 100€; breakfast is an extra 3€. Regular renovations have kept the place up-to-date, with TVs in all but one room and air-conditioning in the eight top-floor rooms. The lobby bar is a fun place to listen to intellectual chatter.

€–€€ If you're looking for a high level of comfort and service (or a pleasant staff), don't even consider the **Accademia** (Via delle Belle Arti 6; ☎ 051-232318; www.hotelaccademia.com; cash only). On the other hand, it's cheap—65€ to 110€ for a double without a bathroom, 70€ to 160€ with bathroom—the location on a lively street near the university is superb, and the centuries-old palazzo is full of character. The lobby and staircase, with well-worn stone flooring and vaulted ceilings, are deceivingly grand; the bright, no-frills, functional rooms are far simpler. The bathrooms don't seem to have been updated for a couple of decades, so the worn fixtures and half-size bathtubs can pose a bit of a challenge. On the plus side: free Internet and Wi-Fi.

ACCOMMODATIONS NEAR SAN DOMENICO

€–€€€ Quiet **Hotel Touring** ★ (Via de' Mattuiani 1–2, off Via Garibaldi; ☎ 051-584305; www.hoteltouring.it; AE, MC, V) lies on the edge of the *centro storico* near San Domenico. The stylish rooms are nicely fitted out with shiny hardwood or faux-marble ceramic floors, sleek contemporary furnishings, rich upholstery, and (in almost all) air-conditioning (a few have ceiling fans). Most bathrooms are striking, many with gilt-framed mirrors on the white-tile walls, deep sinks (double sinks in a few units), and roomy showers. Some rooms are quite large indeed, and many on the third and fourth floors have big balconies. The eight nonsmoking rooms come with minibars. The roof terrace, complete with Jacuzzi, affords wonderful 360-degree views. The hotel also offers plenty of freebies: bicycles, Wi-Fi, a guided walking tour on the weekend, and a pass for entering the city's communal museums. Double rooms start around 119€ (jumping up to 260€ during trade fairs).

ACCOMMODATIONS WORTH THE SPLURGE

Bologna Art Hotels (☎ 051-7457335; www.bolognaarthotels.it; AE, MC, V) is a small local hotel empire of ultrarefined inns with a premium placed on service: free bikes, Internet access, and city walking tours every Sunday—all of which make the slightly high prices more reasonable than they first appear.

€€€€   Rates for a standard double at other Art Hotels properties start at 200€ to 240€ (up to 370€ during trade fairs), so I won't waste too much space on them. The **Dei Commercianti** ★★ (Via Pignattari 11; ☎ 051-7457511) has an enviable location and history—facing the flank of San Petronius and built in the 12th century as the city's first seat of government—with bits of original beams, flooring, and the occasional fresco fragment adding to the antiques, Oriental carpets, canopy beds, and polished woodwork. From the outside, the **Novecento** ★ (Piazza Galileo 4; ☎ 051-7457311) looks like a turn-of-the-20th-century theater; inside it's a sleek boutique hotel done in a repro Secession style (the Viennese version of Art Nouveau—very modernist, with lots of straight lines, simple curves, and a restrained color palette).

€€€–€€€€   A loyal cadre of travelers have come to love the 34-room **Orologio** ★ (Via IV Novembre 10; ☎ 051-7457411), which overlooks a small pedestrian street off Piazza Maggiore on the clock-tower side of the town hall (*orologio* means "clock"—hence the name). Aside from this wonderful location, two of the attractions are the lounge, with its comfy couches, free snacks, and free Internet terminal; and the adjacent breakfast room with its generous morning buffet. The rooms—doubles for 140€ to 270€ (up to 340€ during trade fairs)—are often small but nicely done, with patterned silk walls and old photos of Bologna, wrought-iron bed frames or inlaid wood headboards, handsome contemporary furnishings, and well-equipped marble-clad modern bathrooms.

DINING FOR ALL TASTES

There's a good reason it's called "Bologna the Fat." Chubby tortellini are filled with cheese and meat and topped with cream sauces. Heaping platters of grilled meats are served without a care for cholesterol. Yes, you can eat very well in Bologna—what is surprising is that you need not spend a fortune doing so.

RESTAURANTS NEAR THE UNIVERSITY

€   At the **Enoteca Italiana** ★★ (Via Marsala 2b; ☎ 051-235989; www.enoteca italiana.it; daily 10:30am–3pm and 6–9:30pm; AE, MC, V), an inviting and award-winning shop–cum–wine bar on a side street just north of Piazza Maggiore, you can stand at the bar and sip on a local wine while enjoying a sandwich or platter of cheese and mortadella. Simple, family-run **Trattoria Da Danio** (Via San Felice 50; ☎ 051-555202; daily noon–3pm and 7–11:30pm; AE, MC, V) consists of one brightly lit tiled room, usually filled with the clamor of families who live in this old neighborhood just east of Piazza Maggiore (follow Via Ugo Bassi its length to Via San Felice). The kitchen sends out good, substantial servings of traditional bolognese fare: heaping bowls of tortellini topped with Bolognese sauce, delicious gnocchi stuffed with spinach and ricotta, homey chicken and pork dishes, and the like. The weekday 7.50€ *menu turistico* (single course with wine and water) and 12€ *menu prezzo fisso* (pasta, main course, side dish, wine, water, and cover) are great deals—though they warn that, after 4 years without raising prices, those menus might soon go up by 1€.

€–€€ **Trattoria Belfiore** (Via Marsala 11a; ☎ 051-226641; Wed–Mon 12:30–2:30pm and 7:30–11:30pm; AE, MC, V) is a series of narrow, high-ceilinged rooms on one of the old streets between Via dell'Indipendenza and the university area, and as a result it attracts an incongruous group of students and businesspeople who chatter noisily as friendly waiters run to and from the kitchen. This is not the place for a romantic conversation or a foray into haute cuisine—simple is the rule. Dishes don't get much more elaborate than tortellini or a platter of *salsiccia ai ferri* (grilled sausages). But like much of the fare, including the pizzas, they're prepared over an open fire and are delicious and very fairly priced—I don't think a dish has topped 7€ or 8€ in several years.

€–€€ Why do theatergoers flock to the **Trattoria-Pizzeria Belle Arti** (Via delle Belle Arti 14; ☎ 051-225581; www.belleartitrattoriapizzeria.com; Thurs–Tues noon–3pm and 7–11:30pm; AE, MC, V) after performances at the nearby Teatro Comunale? Because the food is excellent and the kitchen keeps later hours than most in Bologna. Even on weeknights you may have to wait to get a table in the handsome brick-and-panel dining room, but once the *tortellini neri tartufati* (homemade tortellini in a truffle sauce, 9.50€) or *tagliatelli con funghi porcini* (flat noodles with porcini mushrooms, 9.50€) starts arriving at the table, you'll be glad you waited. You can also choose from a stupendous selection of pizzas (4.50€–9€) that emerge from a wood-burning oven.

€€–€€€ At the animated **Trattoria Anna Maria** ✪ (Via delle Belle Arti 17a; ☎ 051-266894; Wed–Sun 12:30–3pm and 7:30pm–midnight; AE, MC, V), the lady herself always seems to be on hand, serving some of the finest food in Bologna in a big room wallpapered with the head shots of hundreds of actors and opera stars who've dined here following performances at the nearby Teatro Comunale. All the pasta is freshly made and appears in some unusual variations, including wonderful tortellini, prepared in a soup, *al ragù, al Gorgonzola, al pomodoro* (tomato sauce), or *al burro e salvia* (butter and sage) for 9€ to 12€. While any of these pasta dishes is a meal in itself, you may be tempted to try one of the substantial second courses, most of which are simple, deliciously prepared dishes from the region: *trippa con fagioli* (tripe and beans; 11€), *fegato alla Veneta* (liver and onions; 11€), or roasted rabbit, guinea fowl, or duck (9€–11€).

RESTAURANTS AROUND VIA PRATELLO

€€ Of the many osterias lining Via del Pratello, the tavern **L'Osteria del Montesino** ✪ (Via del Pratello 74b; ☎ 051-523426; daily 8am–1:15am; MC, V) would be my choice for a light meal. It has a huge selection of *crostini* (toasted bread with a variety of toppings), and you can get a heaping sampler platter of *crostini misti* (6.20€). A daily trio of pastas costs 6€ for one, 6.50€ to sample two, or 7€ for all three (or for the ricotta-and-spinach *tortellacci,* available weekends only). These *primi*—along with most wines and the mixed meat-and-cheese platters—ignore the famed local cuisine and are proudly Sardegnan.

€–€€   The down-to-earth **Trattoria Fantoni** ✯ (Via del Pratello 11a; ☎ 051-236358; Tues–Sat noon–2:30pm and 8–10pm, Mon noon–2:30pm; cash only), on the other hand, is my fave for a full meal. The two simple dining rooms are almost always jammed with people who work in the neighborhood, and the menu reflects their culinary tastes. You can sample horse meat, which appears on many traditional Bolognese menus, prepared here several ways, including *bistecca cavallo* and *cavallo alla tartara* (horse steak and horse-meat tartare, respectively; 8€–9€). Or you can opt for nicely prepared versions of more familiar fare, such as *salsiccia* (grilled sausage, 5€) or *tacchino* (grilled turkey breast, 9€). The food is so good and the prices so low—especially at lunch—that you can expect to wait for a table just about any evening.

RESTAURANTS NEAR PIAZZA MAGGIORE

€€   Wander into inconspicuous **Olindo Faccioli** ✯✯ (Via Altabella 15b; ☎ 051-223171; Mon–Sat 6pm–2am; MC, V) for a glass of wine and you may end up spending the entire evening. Just a few tables are wedged into two tiny rooms behind a bar lined with the more than 400 vintages and manned by Carlo Faccioli (grandson of founder Olindo). There's no menu, but the daily fare is posted on a chalkboard—or, when Carlo forgets to do that, recited orally. A carpaccio of tuna or a selection of bruschetta or crostini misti is a perfect opener, followed by zucchini flowers stuffed with mozzarella, *tagliatelle al ragù* (8€), and the almost-too-rich *involtini di melanzane alla mortadella* (a cheesy mess of eggplant and bologna, 12€). While 1am is the official closing time, Carlo often stays open later.

RESTAURANTS WORTH A SPLURGE

€€–€€€€   Just watching the whirl in the clamorous, cavernous dining rooms of **Ristorante al Montegrappa da Nello** ✯✯ (Via Montegrappa 2; ☎ 051-236331; Tues–Sun noon–3pm and 7–11:30pm; AE, MC, V) is part of the experience at this venerable Bologna institution. You can get by with a simple and relatively inexpensive meal here, but you'll probably want to splurge on a full meal. Truffles and porcini, the hallmarks of the house, appear in salads, atop rich pastas, and accompanying grilled meats, which range into wild boar and venison in season. There's a menu, but because the chef only prepares what's fresh at the market that day, it's best just to let the waiters tell you what they're serving.

WHY YOU'RE HERE:
THE TOP SIGHTS & ATTRACTIONS

AROUND PIAZZA MAGGIORE

The central **Piazza Maggiore** is the heart of Bologna, and it's flanked by the city's finest buildings: the medieval **Palazzo di Rei Enzo,** named for Enzo, king of Sardinia, who died here in 1272 after languishing in captivity for 23 years; the Romanesque **Palazzo del Podestà;** and the **Palazzo Comunale,** seat of the local government. The square is dominated, though, by a relative newcomer: an immodestly virile 16th-century bronze state of Neptune, who presides over the ornate **Fontana del Nettuno** ✯✯, inhabited by sensual sirens.

Bologna Itinerary

If you have only 1 day in Bologna

Start in the heart of the action—the lovely **Piazza Maggiore**—with an early (around 8:30am) peek inside the **Basilica di San Petronio.** Head east on Via Orefici to plunge into the city's lively **morning street market** (see "The Other Bologna" on p. 251), making your way back to Piazza Maggiore and down Via dell'Archiginnasio to pop in and see the fascinatingly gruesome **Teatro Anatomico.**

Continue south to pay your respects to St. Dominic (and some early Michelangelos) at **San Domenico,** and then make your way back north into the university district. Lunch at **Trattoria Anna Maria,** and then work it off by wandering the galleries of old masters at the **Pinacoteca Nazionale.** Next, climb the **Torre degli Asinelli** before popping into the frescoed oratory of **Santa Cecilia** and its attached church of **San Giacomo Maggiore.** Finally, spend some time at **San Stefano** making sense of the seven churchlets, built willy-nilly against one another, from the 5th through 13th centuries.

For dinner and late-night gallivanting, head to hopping Via del Pratello.

Massive as the **Basilica di San Petronio** ★★ (Piazza Maggiore; ☎ 051-225442; www.bologna.chiesacattolica.it/cattedrale; free; daily 8am–noon and 4–6:15pm) is, it's not nearly as big as its 14th-century architects intended it to be. Rome got wind of the Bolognese scheme to build a church bigger than St. Peter's and cut off funding. Even so, the structure that was erected over the next 3 centuries is impressively grand. Its facade is partially striped in white and red (the city's heraldic colors) and punctuated by one of the great works of the Italian Renaissance: a marble doorway surrounded by bas-reliefs depicting the Madonna and Child and other biblical scenes carved by Jacopo della Quercia, which are now sadly weather-worn.

Several of the chapels in the cavernous interior, where Charles V was crowned Holy Roman Emperor in 1530, are richly decorated with frescoes, the best of which are in the chapels to the left as you enter. One contains Lorenzo Costa's *Madonna and Child with Saints,* and the other (fourth on the left) is enlivened with colorful depictions of heaven and hell, the life of St. Petronius, and *Stories of the Magi* by Giovanni da Modena (who also did the frescoes in and around the left aisle's first chapel).

Embedded in the floor of the left aisle is an enchanting curiosity—Italy's largest **sundial,** a 66m (216-ft.) astronomical clock installed by the astronomer Cassini in 1655. The two-room **treasury museum** (free; Mon–Sat 9:30am–noon and 4–5:30pm, Sun 2:30–5:30pm) at the end of the left aisle contains drawings and wooden models of the church; some fine illuminated choir books; and the usual gilt and silver reliquaries, robes, and chalices.

THE LEANING TOWERS OF BOLOGNA?

Only a few of the more than 200 towers that once rose above Bologna, built by noble families as symbols of their wealth and prestige, are still standing—and just barely. The two most famous lean alarmingly toward one another on Piazza di Porta Ravegna, where the seven main streets of medieval Bologna converge. The 50m (165-ft.) Torre Garisenda tilts a precarious 3m (10 ft.) off the perpendicular, while Torre degli Asinelli, which is nearly twice as tall, is 2.3m (7½ ft.) out of plumb. Best of all, you can climb the **Torre degli Asinelli** ✪ (Piazza di Porta Ravegna; 3€; daily May–Sept 9am–6pm, Oct–Apr 9am–5pm), 500 steps to the reward of a stunning view over Bologna's red-tile rooftops and the surrounding hills.

TOP MUSEUMS

Though a Roman wall runs through the courtyard of the **Museo Civico Medioevale** ✪ (Via Manzoni 4; ☎ 051-2193916; www.comune.bologna.it/iperbole/MuseiCivici; free; Tues–Fri 9am–3pm, Sat–Sun 10am–6:30pm), the collection itself is devoted to depicting life in medieval Bologna. During the Middle Ages, the city revolved around its university, and the most enchanting treasures are the sepulchers of professors, surrounded for eternity by carvings of dozing and mocking students. Also on view are fascinating cooking utensils from daily life in medieval Bologna, illuminated manuscripts, and a sizable collection of arms and armor. It also has a healthy handful of medieval objects from cultures around the world (collections left over from previous incarnations of the museum), and the museum's name hasn't kept it from squirreling away a few small Renaissance and baroque bronzes by the likes of Giambologna, Bernini, and Algardi.

Europe's First University

Bologna's university is Europe's oldest, rooted in a Roman law school from A.D. 425 and officially founded in the 10th century. By the 13th century, more than 10,000 students from all over Europe were descending on this center of learning. Their scholarly numbers have included Thomas à Becket, Copernicus, Dante, Petrarch, and, much more recently, Federico Fellini. Always forward-thinking—even in the unenlightened Middle Ages the university employed female professors—the political leanings of today's student body are displayed in leftist slogans that emblazon the 15th- to 19th-century buildings.

While most of the university is now housed up Via Zamboni, the most interesting bit to visit is in one of its oldest buildings just south of Piazza Maggiore: the Teatro Anatomico inside the baroque **Palazzo di Archiginnasio** ✪ (Piazza Galvani 1; ☎ 051-276811; www.archiginnasio.it; free; Mon–Fri 9am–6:45pm, Sat 9am–1:45pm). In this quite theatrical anatomical theater, ancient wooden benches surround a marble slab used for the continent's first (legal) gross anatomy classes, and carved skinless human pillars support the lectern.

Many of the galleries at the **Pinacoteca Nazionale** ✯ (Via delle Belle Arti 56; ☎ 051-4209411; www.pinacotecabologna.it; 4€; Tues–Sun 9am–9pm) are devoted to either Bolognese painters or painters from elsewhere who worked in Bologna, including Italy's largest collection by the city's most illustrious artist, Guido Reni (1575–1642). Perhaps his best known work is the *Ritratto della Madre*, a portrait of his mother, hanging in a Reni room that also includes *Samson the Victorious*. More striking, however, is the *St. George and the Dragon,* an early work (1335) by one of Emilia-Romagna's first great masters, Vitale da Bologna. The contorted figures and sense of movement evoked by George's fluttering cloak and wind-whipped hair show an expressive side to early Gothic painting every bit as impressive as that being practiced by the followers of Giotto south of the Apennines. The museum's most sought-out work is not by a native son but by Raphael, whose *Ecstasy of St. Cecilia* is one of the great achievements of Renaissance painting.

The Etruscan and Roman finds from the surrounding region and many fine Egyptian antiquities make Bologna's **Museo Civico Archeologico** ✯ (Via dell'Archiginnasio 2; ☎ 051-2757211; www.comune.bologna.it/museo archeologico; free; Tues–Fri 9am–3pm, Sat–Sun 10am–6:30pm) one of Italy's most well-rounded collections of antiquities. The Egyptian holdings include a portion of the Book of the Dead and bas-reliefs from the tomb of Horemheb, followed by replicas of well-known Greek and Roman statues, plus a peaceful central court-yard littered with ancient milestones from Via Emilia. The next floor is filled with the museum's impressive Etruscan collection (crowded into glass cases, a la the 19th c.), including remnants from Bologna's own beginnings as the Etruscan out-post Felsina. Among the burial items and other artifacts is a bronze urn from the 5th century B.C., the Situla di Certosa, decorated with a depiction of a ceremo-nial procession.

MORE CHURCHES

The remarkable assemblage of hallowed buildings known as **Basilica di Santo Stefano** ✯✯ (Via Santo Stefano 24; ☎ 051-223256; www.abbaziasantostefano.it; free; daily 9am–noon and 3:30–6pm) actually incorporates seven separate churches and chapels dating variously from the 5th to the 13th centuries. A walk through the complex provides a remarkable overview of the history of Bologna. The first church you enter is the Crocifisso, begun in the 11th century (as you enter, notice the pulpit built into the facade). San Petronio, Bologna's patron saint, lies in the church to the left—the most charming in the group—the 12th-century San Sepolcro, a polygon modeled after the church of the Holy Sepulcher in Jerusalem. According to legend, the basin in the courtyard is the one in which Pontius Pilate absolved himself after condemning Christ to death (in truth, it's an 8th-c. Lombard piece). The oldest church is the 5th-century Santi Vitale e Agricola, incorporating fragments of a Roman temple to Isis; Charlemagne allegedly wor-shiped here in the 8th century. Just beyond is the 13th-century Trinità and the complex's 11th-century cloisters, where plaques honor Bologna's war dead. A small museum/gift shop opens off the back, containing some unmemorable paintings and frescoes spanning the 13th to the 18th centuries. And out here you'll find yet another church: the tiny Cappella della Benda.

In the sixth chapel on the right inside **San Domenico** ✖ (Piazza San Domenico 13; ☎ 051-6400411; free; Mon–Sat 9:30am–12:30pm and 3:30–6:30pm, Sun 3–5:30pm) is one of the great treasures of Bologna, the beautifully crafted **tomb of San Domenico** ✖✖. St. Dominic, founder of the teaching order that bears his name, died in Bologna in 1221, and his venerated modern X-ray decorates the chapel wall (it's an actual X-ray of his bones; I've seen pilgrims kiss their fingers and touch it before turning to pray at the tomb). These saints and angels are a joint effort of Michelangelo, Pisano, and, most notably, Nicolo di Bari, who was so proud of his work on the cover of the tomb *(arca)* that he dropped his last name and is better known as Nicolo dell'Arca. Postcards near the entrance to the chapel show you who carved what. A 20-year-old Michelangelo did the candle-bearing angel at the lower right as well as the statue of San Petronius bearing a tiny model of Bologna up on the tomb toward the left. He also carved San Proculus—his cloak slung over one shoulder—on the tomb's backside. The chapel's apse fresco is by Guido Reni, who's buried in the baroque chapel across the nave. The two striking stilt-tombs on the piazza out front date from 1298 and 1300.

The masterpiece of the 13th-century **San Giacomo Maggiore** (Piazza Rossini; ☎ 051-225970; free; daily 7am–noon and 3:30–6:30pm) is the chapel/burial chamber of the Bentivoglio family, who ruled Bologna through the 15th century. Among the masterpieces here are a *Madonna and Child* by Francesco Francia, along with the frescoes the Bentivoglios commissioned from Ferrarese master Lorenzo Costa to depict life in a Renaissance court—an apt decoration for Bologna's most influential (and tyrannical) clan.

Guided Walks & Bike Tours

Looking for a guided intro to Bologna? Take a 13€, **2-hour walking tour**, in Italian or English, that hits most of the sights around Piazza Castello and the Two Towers, plus the creepy Teatro Anatomico in the Palazzo Archiginnasio and the septet of churches making up San Stefano.

Reservations are not necessary, but because the virtually identical tours are run by different companies on different days, where you meet changes slightly. Those on Wednesday, Saturday, or Sunday at 10:30am (☎ 051-246541), and on Saturday and Sunday at 3pm (☎ 051-2750254; www.guidedarte.com) all meet at the tourist office on Piazza Maggiore. The tours on Monday and Friday at 11am and on Tuesday and Thursday at 3pm (4pm July–Aug) meet nearby at the Fontana del Nettuno (☎ 051-524274 or 340-2207699).

If wheels are more your style, you can take a 18€, **2-hour guided bike tour** (☎ 340-2207699 or 051-6814920) on one of several itineraries, given Wednesdays at 10am, weather permitting; call for details and to book.

Toward the back of the left flank of the church, with a separate entrance, is the **Oratorio di Santa Cecilia** ✦ (Via Zamboni 15; ☎ 051-225970; free; daily 10am–1pm and 2–6pm). This oratory was frescoed with scenes from the lives of St. Cecilia and her husband, St. Valerian, by the best artists working in Bologna in the 16th century. These included Il Francia (who painted the best of the bunch: the *Marriage of St. Cecilia* to the left of the altar and the *Burial of St. Cecilia* to the altar's right), Lorenzo Costa (the two panels abutting Il Francia's), and Amico Aspertini (the two scenes closest to the entry door on either side; he may have had a hand in the four middle panels as well).

THE OTHER BOLOGNA

The Bolognese people just love to eat—and eat well. Life in Bologna revolves around the kitchen, so to get under the skin of this city, forget the museums and monuments. Take a morning to explore the gastronomic side of Bologna. Start early, around 8am, to mingle with the market workers, professional *trattoria* chefs, and home-kitchen master chefs out doing their morning shopping.

Bologna's **main-street market** lines Via Drapperie and Via delle Pescherie Vecchie with fishmongers and fourth-generation grocers. **A. F. Tamburini** ✦ (Via Caprarie 1, at Via Drapperie; ☎ 051-234726; www.tamburini.com) has stacks of salami, pendulums of prosciutto, and cheap cafeteria-like *tavola calda* (pasta and simple meat dishes, 3.50€–6€) in the back. **Drogheria Gilberto** (Via Drapperie 5; ☎ 051-223925), maintains shelves stacked to the ceiling with chocolates, candies, liqueurs, marmalades, and preserves, and always offers free samples (I scored brownies on my last visit). Also nip down Via Caprarie to **Paolo Atti & Figli** ✦✦ (Via Caprarie 7; ☎ 051-220425; www.paoloatti.com), purveyors of Bologna's finest baked goods since 1880 under high frescoed ceilings.

My favorite stands along here, though, are the numerous **fruit-and-vegetable stalls** groaning under the weight of purple-fringed artichokes, crinkly bunches of arugula, sleek indigo eggplant, pink pomegranates, orange zucchini flowers, pungent mushrooms, tiny *susine* plums, pointy San Marzano tomatoes, mounds of grapes, trays of chestnuts, garlands of fiery red pepperoncini, and ropes of garlic.

In a city this devoted to food, there are also two **covered markets**—though the **Mercato Clavature,** in the midst of that street market, has definitely seen better days (word is that the owners are trying to run out the few remaining traditional stall owners with high rent and dilapidated conditions in order to turn the place into a more upscale cafe-and-shops joint).

Far more of a going concern is bustling **Mercato delle Erbe** ✦ with a blink-and-you'll-miss-it entrance on Via Ugo Bassi, 2 blocks west of its intersection with Via G. Marconi. This covered market houses 36 specialty food shops and 72 fruit and vegetable stands; make sure you get here before they close up shop for the lunch break around 1pm.

Exit the market from the back onto Via Belvedere, where you can still see the market's original 1910 facade in all its orange-and-yellow neoclassical grandeur. Across the street is **Le Sflogline** (Via Belvedere 7B), a traditional *sfoglini* shop run by a trio of smiling ladies who spend their days making fresh pasta and pastries, as well as lasagna in tiny takeout foil containers. (*Sfoglini* are Bolognese pasta

Ragù Straight from the Source

Don't just describe those fantastic meals to your friends back home; learn to make them at a Bologna cooking school. There are several in town that offer short classes (in English on request) designed for the passing tourist. **Gli Amici di Babette** (Via San Felice 116, scala G; ☎ 051-6493627 or 339-7011003; www.lacucinadibabette.com) offers more than a dozen 3-hour courses on breads, pastas, pastries, and desserts for all skill levels for 60€ to 80€ per lesson so long as at least five people sign up; fewer than that and it's 130€ per person.

La Vecchia Scuola Bolognese (Via Malvasia 49; ☎ 051-6491576; www.lavecchiascuola.com) gives 4-hour courses on making fresh pastas at 70€ a pop (or 5-day courses from 200€). **Cookitaly** (☎ 051-6448612; www.cookitaly.com) costs more: 300€ for one person or 200€ per person for up to four gets you a half-day class with market tour; for 400€ a person or 250€ a person for up to four, you get a full-day lesson and learn to cook a three-course meal—*primo, secondo,* and dessert.

makers who roll out fresh pasta in great sheets, and then cut it into strips using rolling pins set with rows of plastic discs.) There's another such shop, **La Braseria Sfoglia,** at Via A. Tostoni 9A.

End your gastronomic journey with a pilgrimage to **Majani** ✹✹ (Via Carbonesi 5; ☎ 051-6562209; www.majani.com), chocolatiers extraordinaire since 1796. About 4.50€ will buy you a sampler baggie filled with their greatest hits—one each of the chocolate "tortellini" (in milk, dark, and white, each filled with a chocolate cream), a selection of the famous *cremini Fiat* (chocolate napoleons), and a few *scroza* (thin sheets of dark chocolate, roughly accordioned into a bar).

NIGHTLIFE

A good way to keep up with performances in Bologna—whether a poetry reading in the back of a bar or a pop concert at the Stadio Comunale—is to scan the posters plastered on walls around the university. Just troll Via Zamboni, and ignore all the notices looking for roommates or selling "slightly used" couches and TVs.

The **Teatro Comunale** (Largo Respighi 1; ☎ 051-6174299; www.tcbo.it) hosts Bologna's lively opera, orchestra, and ballet seasons, as well as intriguing shows, such as homages to Frank Zappa or Charlie Chaplin. The box office (☎ 051-529995; www.comunalebologna.it or www.charta.it) is open Tuesday to Friday 3 to 7pm, and Saturday 10am to 12:30pm and 3 to 7pm.

If you're in Bologna April to October, you can spend your evenings at the classical and jazz concerts and other events that are part of the **Bologna Festival** (Via delle Lame 58; ☎ 051-6493397; www.bolognafestival.it; many tickets start around 10€–20€ but can start as high as 80€ for headliners). The performances are held in church cloisters and other scenic settings throughout the city center. Performances can range from Mozart to the Academy of St. Martin in the Fields, from Dee Dee Bridgewater to the Tokyo Quartet.

BARS & PUBS

Because of its young and restless student population, Bologna stays up later than most Italian cities. The main night-owl haunts are Via del Pratello and, near the university, Via Zamboni and Via delle Belle Arti. You can usually find a place for a drink, a shot of espresso, or a light meal as late as 2am.

There's Guinness and Harp on tap and an attendant Anglophone following at the **Irish Times Pub** (Via Paradiso 1; ☎ 051-261648), though a well-dressed, but not always so well-behaved, young Italian crowd predominates in the noisy, smoky, publike rooms; happy hour lasts until 9pm (10:30pm Tues). More popular these days is the **Cluricaune Irish Pub** (Via Zamboni 18b; ☎ 051-263419), a raucous joint near the university with quite good live music some nights (no cover), and where the party spills out under the street's arcade. Happy hour lasts until 8:30pm (10:30pm on Wed).

The **Osteria de Poeti** (Via Poeti 1; ☎ 051-236166; www.osteriadepoeti.com) is Bologna's oldest osteria and has been in operation since the 16th century—the brick-vaulted ceilings, stone walls, and ancient wine barrels provide just the sort of ambience you'd expect in such a historic establishment. Stop in to enjoy the live jazz and folk music. (It's also open for light lunches Tues–Fri.)

You'll want to retire at 10:30pm to the cellars of a 16th-century palazzo near the university at **Cantina Bentivoglio** (Via Mascarella 4b; ☎ 051-265416; www.cantinabentivoglio.it). That's when you'll hear some of the best jazz in Bologna. It's also a popular spot for filmgoers, who stop in for some food (most dishes 7€–16€) and tunes after catching one of the first-run movies at the Odeon 2 across the street.

Bologna's Thriving Gay Scene

Bologna is the seat of Italy's Arcigay movement, and that plus the large student population make it rather more open to same-sex couples than most Italian cities.

Cassero/Salara (Via Don Minzoni 18; ☎ 051-6494416, "phone friend" help line 051-555661; www.cassero.it; Mon–Fri 10am–1pm, 2–7pm, and 8–11pm) is a combination of the main gay/lesbian organization's offices, help center, and meeting point that happens to turn into the hottest gay/lesbian disco Saturday nights. The downstairs disco also hosts a variety of shows, cabaret, movies, and concerts throughout the week, especially Friday and Saturday. They offer gay-friendly services, including a library and a help line. Though Italians need to be members of Arcigay to use the facilities, the bar is more than happy to welcome foreign tourists free of charge.

SIDE TRIPS FROM BOLOGNA

I recommend taking at least one of these three side trips from Bologna.

FERRARA

One family, the Estes, accounts for much of what you'll find in Ferrara, an enchanting city on the plains of Romagna. From 1200 to 1600, the Estes ruled from their imposing castle that's still the centerpiece of Ferrara. They endowed the city with palaces, gardens, and avenues, as well as intrigues, including those of their most famous duchess, Lucrezia Borgia.

After the Estes left (when Rome refused to recognize the last heir of the clan as duke), Ferrara fell victim to neglect and finally, during World War II, to bombs. Despite the bombing, much of the Renaissance town remains and has been restored. In fact, this city of rose-colored brick is one of the most beautiful in Italy and, shrouded in a gentle mist from the surrounding plains as it often is, one of the most romantic.

Lay of the Land

Ferrara is 45km (27 miles) north of Bologna. Trains arrive from and depart for Bologna (25–60 min.) and Venice (1¼–2 hr.) every half-hour. There are one to two trains per hour to Ravenna (1–1¼ hr.) and Padua (45–85 min.).

The train station is a 15-minute walk from the center (or take bus no. 1 or 9); just follow Viale Costituzione through the small park in front of the station to Viale Cavour, which leads directly into the center of town.

The **tourist office** (in the Castello Estense; ☎ 0532-299303; www.arte cultura.fe.it) is extremely helpful. Also useful is the city's website, www.comune.fe.it.

Accommodations, Both Standard & Not

€–€€   For basic budget lodgings, choose **Pensione Artisti** (Via Vittoria 66; ☎ 0532-761038; cash only), in the atmospheric medieval Jewish quarter a few blocks from the Duomo. It's utterly utilitarian, but excellently priced at 48€ for

---

Bike Like a Ferrarese

To get around like a true Ferrarese—especially for that Sunday tool along the park that rings the city atop its massive walls—you need a bike. Several of the recommended hotels provide free bikes (Borgonuovo, San Paolo, Europa) or cheap rentals (San Paolo). Otherwise, you can **rent a set of wheels.** The rental stand **Pirani e Bagni** (Piazzale Stazione 2; ☎ 0532-772190) is located just outside the train station to the left. In the center, just west of Piazza Castello, you can rent from **Romanelli** (Via Aldighieri 28/A, at Via Garibaldi; ☎ 0532-206017; www.ferraracicli.it). At the town's main southern gate, Porta Paula, east of the bus station, are two outfits: **Ceragioli** (Piazza Travaglio 4; ☎ 339-4056853) and **Itinerando** (Via Kennedy 2; ☎ 0532-202003; www.itinerando.it), on the right as you exit the *centro storico* parking garage. Rates tend to be the same at all: 2€ to 2.50€ per hour, 5€ to 6€ for 3 hours, and 10€ to 11€ per day.

---

a double without bathroom, 60€ with. The simple rooms are big, bright, and clean; the heavy 1950s-era furnishings are a nice change from the banal furnishings in most cheap hotels; and the shared bathroom facilities are plentiful and clean. Rooms have orthopedic mattresses, sinks, and bidets. Plus, there are some pleasant and unusual amenities here—a few rooms have vine-covered balconies, guests have use of kitchen facilities on each floor, and there's a shared roof terrace.

€€ A step up in amenities and price, the **San Paolo** (Via Baluardi 9; ☎ 0532-762040; www.hotelsanpaolo.it; AE, MC, V) faces the old city walls at the southern edge of the Jewish ghetto with its warren of lanes and small shops. Add to this atmospheric location the attentive service of the proprietors, who rent bikes, dispense advice on sightseeing and restaurants, and serve coffee from the little lobby bar. The 95€ doubles are pretty bland but comfortable, with inoffensive contemporary blond furnishings and small but functional bathrooms. They're always taking small steps to invigorate the place. In 2004, they added air-conditioning to roughly half the rooms, and by 2008 will have installed it in all, along with wider beds in the singles. They will also start serving a buffet breakfast and stop charging to lend out bikes to clients.

€€–€€€ The elegant **Borgonuovo Bed & Breakfast** ★★★ (Via Cairoli 29; ☎ 0532-211100 or 0532-248000; www.borgonuovo.com; AE, MC, V) is the most charming hostelry in Ferrara. The gracious owner, Signora Adele Orlandini, has spruced up an apartment that once housed her father's engineering offices in a medieval palazzo on a pedestrian street around the corner from the *castello*. The four large, stylish rooms are a tasteful mix of rustic and Art Deco antiques with posh new bathrooms (one large double also has a kitchenette), and rent for 90€ to 110€. She serves a hearty breakfast (in the lovely garden, weather permitting), and offers bicycles, discount coupons for museums and nearby shops, and plenty of advice on how to enjoy her native city. Book well in advance—the Signora's rooms and hospitality are much in demand.

Fortunately, she has recently added three elegant new apartments with antique furnishings in the building next door. Two are mansard apartments with rooftop views, the other has higher ceilings and a large living room. All come with two double bedrooms and a kitchenette, and can comfortably sleep up to five (but cost no more than a regular double for two). Services in the apartments are the same as in the main *locanda* itself (you take your breakfast there), but get your own key to a separate entrance. The Signora also offers an 8-day Italian language course for adults (in conjunction with a nearby language school), consisting of 3-hour lessons each day in the hotel garden.

€€€ Built in 1700, the elegant **Europa** (Corso Giovecca 49, between Via Palestro and Via Teatini; ☎ 0532-205456; www.hoteleuropaferrara.com; AE, MC, V), 1 block from the Castello Estense, has served as a hotel since 1880. Multiple renovations have left it with a somewhat contemporary look, though enough of the original architecture remains to render the premises atmospheric. Several of the enormous guest rooms—including most along the main street—were converted from grand salons and have frescoed ceilings, the original checkerboard terra-cotta tile floors, Art Nouveau furnishings, and Murano chandeliers. Unfortunately, you pay the same price (90€–115€) even if you end up in one of the less grand rooms—though even those are gracious and large, with a nice mix of contemporary furnishings and reproduction Venetian antiques. There's a free Internet terminal, and free bikes for guest use.

Dining for All Tastes

The walls and Ferrara's other green spaces are ideal for a **picnic.** Buy what you need on narrow brick Via Cortevecchia, near the cathedral, lined with cheese shops and bakeries. The nearby **Mercato Comunale,** at the corner of Via Santo Stefano and Via del Mercato, is crowded with food stalls open Monday to Saturday 7:30am to 1pm (Fri also 3:30–7:30pm). At Negozio Moccia, Via degli Spadari 9, you can indulge in a chunk of *panpeteto,* Ferrara's hallmark chocolate-covered fruitcake.

€–€€   **Al Brindisi** ★★ (Via Adelardi 11; ☎ 0532-209142; www.albrindisi.com; Tues–Sun 9am–1am; closed July 10–Aug 10; MC, V) claims to be the oldest wine bar in the world (established 1435), with a roster of famous artists (Titian, Cellini) and poets (Tasso, Ariosto) who used to get sloshed here. It serves a staggering selection of wines by the glass (from 2.50€) and a wonderful selection of *affettati misti* (mixed cured meats and salamis) for 8€. The *cappellaci di zucca* (pumpkin ravioli, 8€) is also sublime. When the weather is nice, you can sit at boothlike tables on a little lane facing a flank of the Duomo.

€–€€   Dozens of beers and an extensive selection of local wines are available at the cozy **Antica Osteria Al Postiglione** ★ (Vicolo Chiuso del Teatro 4; ☎ 0532-241509; daily 9:30am–3:30pm and 5pm–1am; AE, MC, V) wine bar/osteria on a narrow lane off Piazza Castello. You can also eat very well. The family members who cook and wait tables make the pastas fresh each day, and pride themselves on such simple home-cooked dishes as grilled *salsiccia* (sweet sausages), *mozzarella al forno* (baked mozzarella), and *pasta e fagioli* (a substantial soup of beans and pasta)—all for 6€ to 8€. Come here for lunch for a bargain bonanza of fixed-price menus ranging from 8.50€ (*primo* or *secondo*, side dish, and drink) to 20€ (two courses, side dish, dessert, drinks, coffee).

€€   Just south of the city walls, a block from the traditional market square, **Antica Trattoria Volano** ★★ (Viale Volano 20; ☎ 0532-761421; Fri–Wed noon–2:30pm and 7–10pm; AE, MC, V) is a roadside trattoria that has been satisfying hungry travelers since the 1700s. The decor is unassuming (and a tad staid), and the traffic noise detracts, but the cooking is superb. The menu is a veritable study in traditional Ferrara specialties. To sample the best of them all, order a 10€ *tris di primi:* a trio of *cappellaci di zucca* (squash-stuffed ravioli), *taglioline al prosciutto,* and *tortelloni di ricotta.* Or warm yourself up with their delicious *cappelletti in brodo* (pasta soup; 8€). Stay in the sampler category with the *misto di bolliti* (a selection of hand-carved boiled meats; 15€), or try the ultratraditional *salama da sugo* (salty salami diced, cooked in red wine and cognac, and dolloped over mashed potatoes; 11€).

€€–€€€   One of the pleasures of dining at **La Provvidenza** ★ (Corso Ercole I d'Este 92, at Vicolo Parchetto; ☎ 0532-205187; Tues–Sat noon–2:30pm and 8–10:30pm, Sun noon–2:30pm; AE, MC, V) is the walk here along a stone-paved road leading past the Palazzo dei Diamanti and many of the city's most lovely old mansions and brick-walled gardens. Once inside the dining room, with its cream-colored walls and attractively rustic furnishings, you'll feel you're in the country; there's even an arbor-shaded, partially enclosed garden for dining in good weather. The pastas are excellent and include *cappellaci* (pasta pillows stuffed with squash in a butter-and-sage sauce, 8€) and tortellini stuffed with Gorgonzola and wal-nuts (8€). The *salama da sugo* (giant sausage stewed in tomato sauce, 14€) comes with mashed potatoes. They make their own pastries; try the Ferrarese specialty *torta di tagliatelle* (5€).

Why You're Here: The Top Sights & Attractions

The imposing, moat-encircled **Castello Estense** ★ (Via Cavour and Corso Ercole I d'Este; ☎ 0532-299233; www.castelloestense.it; 7€, more when there's a tempo-rary exhibit; Tues–Sun 9:30am–5:30pm) dominates the city center as it did much of Ferrara's Renaissance history. It was built in 1385, and it was here in 1435 that Nicolo III d'Este, with a contrivance of window mirrors, caught his young wife, Parisina Maletesta, *in flagrante delicto* with his son Ugo and had them beheaded in the dank dungeons below. Robert Browning recounted the deed in his poem "My Last Duchess," and today's visitors can clamber down a dark staircase to visit the damp cells where the lovers, and others who fell out of favor with the Este clan, once languished. Not to be overlooked is the fact that the Estes also made Ferrara a center of art and learning, and the infamous (and unjustly maligned) Lucrezia Borgia entertained poets and artists beneath the fragrant bowers of the *orangerie*.

Most of the palace is now used as offices for the province, but you can still catch a glimpse of the Estes' enlightenment in what remains of their grand salons—the **Sala dell'Aurora** and **Sala dei Giochi (Game Room),** both ornately festooned with frescoes. Another remnant of court life is the marble **chapel** built for Renata di Francia, the daughter of Louis XII. Those fond of views and stout of heart can climb the 122 steps to the top of the **Torre dei Leoni** (which predates the castle) Tuesday through Sunday from 9:30am to 4:45pm; admission is an extra 1€.

With its pink-marble facade highlighted by layers of arches, Ferrara's hand-some 12th-century **Cattedrale (Cathedral)** ★★ (Corso Libertà and Piazza Cattedrale; ☎ 0532-207449; free; Mon–Sat 7:30am–noon and 3–6:30pm, Sun 7:30am–12:30pm and 3:30–7:30pm) reflects a heady mix of the Gothic and the Romanesque. The glory of the otherwise austere structure is its marble portal, where carvings by an unknown artist depict a fearsome *Last Judgment*.

An 18th-century renovation relegated many of the paintings, sculptures, and other works that noble families commissioned for the cathedral over the centuries to the **Museo della Cattedrale** (☎ 0532-244949; 5€; Tues–Sun 9am–1pm and 3–6pm), installed in the former Church of San Romano around the right side of the Duomo, at the corner with Via San Romano. The pride of the collection is a painting depicting St. George slaying the dragon by Cosmè Tura, Ferrara's 15th-century master. Another masterpiece here is Jacopo della Quercia's *Madonna of the Pomegranate*, in which Mary seems to balance the fruit in one hand and the Christ Child in the other. A nearby relief showing the 12 months of the year once graced the cathedral's exterior, where it served prosaically as a calendar for the largely illiterate citizenry.

The **Loggia dei Mercanti (Loggia of the Merchants),** a line of shops flanking one side of the church, is still the scene of active secular trade, as it has been since the 18th century, and the surrounding streets and piazzas are filled with lively cafes.

Ferrara is loaded with elaborate old palazzi, many containing one or several small museums, while others are simply frescoed and elaborately bedecked monuments to the grandeur of centuries past.

Borso d'Este, who made Ferrara one of the Renaissance's leading centers of art, commissioned the Salone dei Mesi frescoes in the **Palazzo Schifanoia** ✸ (Via Scandiana 23; ☎ 0532-244949; 5€; Tues–Sun 10am–8pm). It's a fascinating cycle of the months that's both a Renaissance wall calendar and a rich portrayal of life and leisure in the 15th-century Este court. Each of the 12 sections shows Ferrara's aristocrats going about their daily business; looming above them, though, are gods from classical mythology. The work is a composite of the geniuses of Ferrara's heyday—Francesco del Cossa painted the March, April, and May scenes; Ercole de'Roberti and other court painters executed the rest; and Cosmè Tura, the official painter of the Este court, oversaw the project. The palazzo also houses the **Museo Civico d'Arte Antica,** a small collection of coins, bronzes, and other artifacts unearthed from the plains around Ferrara, 14th- and 15th-century ivories, and some medieval and Renaissance ceramics (including a pair of Andrea della Robbia saints).

A recent restoration has returned the 16th-century **Palazzina Marfisa d'Este** (Corso Giovecca 170; ☎ 0532-244949; 3€; Tues–Sun 9am–1pm and 3–6pm) to its former splendor. Marfisa was an ardent patron of the arts, and period furniture and ceiling frescoes (most retouched in the early 1900s) bespeak the glory of the Este dynasty. The little theater in the garden is a reminder that drama, onstage as well as off, was one of the family's great passions.

You'll have no problem figuring out where the **Palazzo dei Diamanti (Palace of Diamonds)** (Corso Ercole I d'Este 21; ☎ 0532-205844; www.palazzodiamanti.it; 4€; daily 9am–7pm) gets its name: the 9,000 pointed marble blocks covering the facade. Less interesting are the collections in the museums clustered within. The most deserving of a visit is the **Pinacoteca Nazionale,** containing some notable works by Cosmè Tura, Il Garofalo, and other painters of the Ferrara school, as well as Carpaccio's *Death of the Virgin.* By and large, though, the holdings aren't spectacular. The ground-floor galleries often house temporary exhibits and charge

A So-So Cumulative Ticket

Ferrara's 14€ **Card Musei (Museums Card)** is only a good deal if you plan to visit most all the museums listed here. It does get you into all the communal museums for free, plus a 2€ reduction on tickets to the Palazzo dei Diamanti. The communal museums covered include those in the Palazzo Schifanoia, Palazzina Marfisa, and Palazzo Massari, plus the Cathedral Museum. Still, if you skip the Palazzo Massari's little collections but do all the others listed here, your savings only come to 1€. You can purchase the card at the ticket office of any of the participating museums.

In the Garden of the Finzi-Continis

Ferrara's **Jewish Cemetery** ✦ (Via della Vigna, near the walls off Corso Porta Mare; ☎ 0532-299303; Sun–Fri 9am–6pm, in winter to 4:30pm), with its ancient tumble of overgrown tombstones, is the most haunting place in Ferrara. A monument to the Ferrarese murdered at Auschwitz, it's a reminder of the fate of the city's once sizeable Jewish community, whose last days are recounted in the book (and film) *The Garden of the Finzi-Continis*, evocatively set in the gardens and palaces of Ferrara and required viewing for anyone planning to visit the city. The book is semiautobiographical, and its author, Gorgio Bassani, died in 2000. He is buried here, in a tomb designed by famed modern sculptor—and Romagna native—Arnaldo Pomodoro. Nearby, the gorgeous **Cimitero di Certosa** (Via Borso 1; ☎ 0532-230175; daily 7:30am–7:30pm) is centered on the long, graceful loggie sweeping out from the church of San Cristoforo, designed by Biagio Rossetti.

To learn more about Jewish Ferrara, book a guided tour—in Italian only—at the **Museo Ebraico** (Via Mazzini 95; ☎ 0532-210228; 4€; Sun–Thurs tours at 10, 11am, or noon; www.comune.fe.it/museoebraico).

separate admission; check with the ticket office here or with the tourist office to see what's on view.

Ludovico il Moro, famed duke of Milan who married Beatrice d'Este, commissioned the lovely little **Palazzo Costabili** (Via XX Settembre 124; ☎ 0532-66299; www.archeobo.arti.beniculturali.it/Ferrara; 4€; Tues–Sun 9am–2pm) as a place to retire from his courtly duties. Unfortunately, Beatrice died young, and the duke spent his last years as a prisoner of the French. The couple's 15th-century palace, built around a lovely rose garden, contains their furniture and paintings, and provides a lovely view of life in Ferrara during its Renaissance heyday. Part of the palazzo houses the small but fascinating collections of the **Museo Archeologico.** The bulk of the treasures are Etruscan and Greek finds unearthed near Ferrara at Spina.

The quartet of museums housed in the exquisite late-15th-century **Palazzo Massari** (Corso Porto Mare 9; ☎ 0532-244949; see below for individual admissions; Tues–Sun 9am–1pm and 3–6pm) contain Ferrara's modern-art holdings. The Museo Giovanni Boldini (5€) has works by the 19th-century Italian painter; its ticket also gets you into the palazzo's skippable Museo dell'Ottocento of frankly less interesting 19th-century art. The palazzo's Museo d'Arte Moderna e Contemporanea (3€) is largely devoted to the output of Filippo de Pisis—who studied the *metafisica* school of Giorgio de Chirico—plus works by contemporary regional artists. There's also a Padiglione d'Arte Contemporanea in the former stables, open only for special exhibits.

RAVENNA & ITS AMAZING MOSAICS

Few cities in Europe are so firmly entrenched in such a distant past. This flat little city on the edge of the marshes that creep inland from the Adriatic was witness to the last days of ancient Western Civilization. Strong connections with the Eastern Byzantine empire kept the ideals of ancient Rome alive a bit longer while the rest of the west fell to barbarian hordes and dissolved into 1,000 bickering feudal fiefdoms. Ravenna is where the final emperors of the west ended their reign, gilding churches and tombs with glittering mosaics.

Though Ravenna has been an off-the-beaten-track backwater since the 6th century, it continues to dazzle visitors with its mosaics and other artistic vestiges of the Romans, the Byzantines, and the Visigoths. Aside from its horde of treasures, Ravenna is a fine place to pass the time in sun-drenched piazzas and pleasant cafes.

Lay of the Land

Ravenna is 75km (47 miles) east of Bologna, with hourly trains (70–90 min. trip), and 75km (47 miles) southeast of Ferrara, from which there are 12 trains daily (1–1¼ hr. trip). Ravenna's train station is only about a 15-minute walk down Viale Farini (which becomes Via Diaz) from the central Piazza del Popolo.

The **tourist office** (just off Piazza del Popolo at Via Salara 8; ☎ 0544-35404; www.turismo.ravenna.it) now gives visitors free bikes to use for the day. You might also want to check out the private website www.ravennablu.it for info on the city.

Accommodations, Mostly Standard

With the notable exception of Cappello (see below), the lodging scene in Ravenna is pretty dismal. Few of its largely bland hotels are in the historical center. The tourist office has a general lodging booklet listing 44 tiny (two- and three-room) **B&Bs** scattered throughout the city, a list also available on their website. Double rooms go for 45€ to 90€—though, again, only a handful are in the center.

€–€€   Among the cheapest options, **A Casa di Pino** (Via Baccarini 37; ☎ 0544-38524; www.acasadipino.it; cash only) offers a comfy double (49€–54€) and a single (29€–34€) just inside the city's southern walls. **Casadelena** (Via Don Minzoni; ☎ 0544-454790; www.casadelena.it; cash only) has three contemporary-country rooms, including one that opens right onto the garden, for 45€ to 60€, and is located on the road running along the outside of the city's northwest walls, just 180m (600 ft.) from the mosaics of San Vitale. **Bondi B&B** (Viale Pallavicini 7; 347-542-9541; www.bondibandb.it; cash only) may be in a bland location—a block south of the train station—but its three rooms have a homey touch, and cost just 55€ to 70€.

A Summertime Music Festival

The **Ravenna Festival International** (☎ 0544-249211; www.ravennafestival.org)— 6 or 7 weeks between June and August—has become world renowned, drawing a top list of classical musicians and opera stars in concert in palazzi and on piazzas.

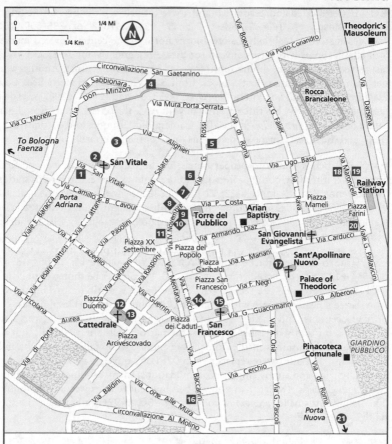

ATTRACTIONS ●

Basilica di San Vitale **2**
Basilica di Sant'Apollinare
  Nuovo **17**
Battistero Neoniano **12**
Dante's Tomb/
  Museo Dantesco **15**
Mausoleum of Galla Placidia **3**
Museo Arcivescovile &
  Cappella di San Andrea **13**
Sant'Apollinare in Classe **21**

ACCOMMODATIONS ■

A Casa di Pino **16**
B&B Galla Placidia **1**
Bondi B&B **20**
Cappello **9**
Casa Masoli **6**
Casadelena **4**
Centrale Byron **11**
Diana **5**
Minerva **19**
Ravenna **18**

DINING ◆

Ca de Ven **14**
Cantina Cappello **10**
La Gardela **7**
Mercato Coperto **8**

€€   Better located and decorated (and a wee bit pricier), the best of the bunch is **Casa Masoli** ★ (Via G. Rossi 22; ☎ 0544-217682 or 335-609-9471; www.casamasoli.it; cash only), a few blocks north of the central covered market: four stylish rooms with Art Nouveau touches, A/C, and TV for 70€, and breakfast served in an elegant dining room frescoed in the 18th century. Another winner with a great location half a block from San Vitale, the modern **B&B Galla Placidia** (Via Mura di San Vitale 12; ☎ 0544-33287 or 339-444-6396; www.galla placidia.it; cash only) has three rooms, all with A/C: the 65€ Camera Rosa (giant mural of Disney's *Jungle Book*), the 70€ Camera Blu (antiques and decorative textiles), and the 80€ Camera Verde (opens onto a private terrace)

€–€€   When it comes to proper hotels, in the bargain bin are two perfectly serviceable, if terribly boring, joints just to the right as you exit the train station. The **Ravenna** (Viale Maroncelli 12; ☎ 0544-212204; www.hotelravenna.ra.it; MC, V) charges 60€ to 90€ for a double room, while the slightly nicer **Minerva** (Viale Maroncelli 1; ☎ 0544-213711; www.minerva-hotel.com; MC, V) sells bland but nicely standardized doubles for 55€ to 90€.

€€   True to its name, the **Centrale Byron** (Via IV Novembre 14; ☎ 0544-33479 or 0544-212225; www.hotelbyron.com; AE, MC, V) couldn't be more central: right off Piazza del Popolo. The second part of the name is a tribute to Lord Byron, who shared a nearby palazzo with his mistress and her husband. Despite these colorful associations (and an elegant marble lobby and chandeliered bar), this hotel is no nonsense and serviceable. Upstairs, the narrow halls are harshly lit, but the modern-style furnishings in the immaculate rooms, while fairly run-of-the-mill, are pleasant, and most were replaced in 2002. Lone travelers make out well with unusually large and sunny single accommodations, many of which are equipped with "French beds" (wider than a single bed but a little narrower than a double). The handful of smaller *economica* rooms cost 80€ to 92€ rather than the standard 95€ to 110€.

€€–€€€   Though the stylish **Diana** ★ (Via G. Rossi 47; ☎ 0544-39164; www.hoteldiana.ra.it; AE, MC, V) occupies an old palazzo just north of the city center, it has the feel of a pleasant country hotel. The surrounding streets are residential and quiet, and the bright lobby and bar open onto a lovely garden. The rooms, no two of which are the same, are handsomely decorated with an innovative flair—with pretty striped wallpaper and mahogany headboards and armories. Those on the top floor are the most charming, with sloped ceilings and large skylights. Rates depend on the room category: 83€ standard (slightly smaller with blander, but new, furnishings), 110€ superior (larger, with nicer stuff and minibars), 125€ deluxe (superior plus ADSL Internet), and 135€ executive (deluxe with a canopy bed).

€€€   Now about that one exciting option: The boutique inn **Cappello** ★★ (Via IV Novembre 41; ☎ 0544-219813; www.albergocappello.it; AE, MC, V) has been a hotel since 1885—though the current, seven-room version only opened in 1998—occupying a beautifully restored, 14th-century palazzo in the city center. The four suite-category rooms (200€–230€) have been carved out of the grand salons and are enormous, while smaller doubles (150€) occupy less grand, but no less stylish, quarters of the old palazzo. Fifteenth-century frescoes grace the corridor, lounge, sitting room, and two junior suites (no. 106, "Towards Blue," and no. 103, "Amaranthine Dream"), while throughout the rest of the hotel, terracotta floors, painted beamed ceilings, and other architectural features have been restored when possible. The furnishings are either reproduction or contemporary design. Because the Cappello is operated as an annex of the Diana (see above), services are minimal—the front desk is staffed only during the day—but there are two restaurants on the premises (for the cheaper, cozier osteria, see Cantina Cappello, below). The hotel is up two short flights of stairs from a hallway often used to exhibit work by a local artist. Reserve well in advance.

Whatever you do, stay away from the nearby Al Giaciglio, recommended in some guides—unless, of course, you don't mind sharing your room with bedbugs.

Dining for All Tastes

For picnic pickings, take a stroll through Ravenna's lively **food market,** the Mercato Coperto, near the center on Piazza Andrea Costa, open Monday to Saturday 7am to 2pm.

€   The most atmospheric osteria in Ravenna, **Ca de Ven** ★★ (Via Corrado Ricci 24; ☎ 0544-30163; www.columbiaracing.it/cadeven; Tues–Sat 11am–2pm and 5:30–10:15pm; AE, MC, V) is tucked away under massive brick vaults on the ground floor of a 16th-century building next to Dante's tomb. In fact, Dante is said to have lived here when the premises served as a lodging house. The ornate shelves that line most of the walls come from a later reincarnation and were installed to outfit a 19th-century spice shop; they now display hundreds of Emilia-Romagna wines, many of which are available by the glass (from 1.50€). *Piadine,* the delicious local flatbread, is a specialty here, topped with cheeses, meat, or vegetables—or served plain as a perfect accompaniment to cheese and assorted salamis (3.50€–6€). The osteria offers three to four pasta courses (6€–8€) and an equal number of meat courses (8.50€–14€) daily. If there are two of you, you can share a *bis di primi* (pick any two pastas) for 8€ each, or a *tris di primi* (sample three) for 9€.

€€   The high-shuttered windows, timbered ceiling, and ocher-colored walls render **Cantina Cappello** ★★ (Via IV Novembre 41; ☎ 0544-219876; Tues–Sat 12:30–2:30pm and 7:20–10:30pm, Sun 12:30–2:30pm; AE, MC, V) as chic and inviting as the hotel (above). Add friendly service, excellent grub, garden courtyard seating at lunch, and a handy location, just off Piazza del Popolo, and this becomes my first choice for a full meal in Ravenna. You can order just about any wine from Emilia-Romagna; half-liter carafes cost 8€. Accompany it with a *tavolozza* (mixed platter of cheeses, crostini, salami, and salad) or choose from the daily pasta (11€) or seafood (17€–18€) specials.

€€€   The plain but elegant **La Gardela** (Via Ponte Marino 3; ☎ 0544-217147; www.ristorantelagardela.com; Fri–Wed noon–2:30pm and 7–10pm; AE, MC, V) is a good place to satisfy your appetite after wandering through the food stalls of the Mercato Coperto across the street—if you don't mind glacially slow (albeit friendly) service. Daily specials often include seafood from the nearby Adriatic, and there's a killer "piccolo menu" that includes a pasta (tortelli stuffed with pumpkin and spinach in a butter-and-sage sauce), meat (grilled shish kabob with rosemary potatoes), mineral water, glass of wine, and coffee, all for 15€.

Why You're Here: The Top Sights & Attractions

Ravenna's most dazzling display of mosaics adorns the dome of the 6th-century octagonal and exotically Byzantine **Basilica di San Vitale** ✹✹ (Via San Vitale 17; for all details, see "Ravenna's Cumulative Ticket & Open Hours," below) commissioned by Emperor Justinian. The emperor and his court appear in splendidly detailed mosaics of deep greens and golds on one side of the church. Theodora, his empress (a courtesan born into the circus whose ambition, intelligence, and beauty brought her to these lofty heights), and her ladies-in-waiting appear on the other; and above and between them looms Christ, clean-shaven in this early representation.

Perhaps the most striking of Ravenna's monuments lies on a lawn behind the Basilica: the small and simple **Mausoleum of Galla Placidia** ✹✹, lit only by small alabaster windows. This early Christian was the sister of Honorius, last emperor of Rome, and wife of Ataulf, king of the Visigoths. Upon his death, she became regent to her 6-year-old son, Valentinian III—meaning she was, in effect, ruler of the Western world. The three sarcophagi beneath a canopy of blue-and-gold mosaics—a firmament of deep blue lit by hundreds of bright gold stars—are meant to contain Galla Placidia's remains and those of her son and husband, but it is more likely that she lies unadorned in Rome, where she died in A.D. 450.

The enchanting 4th-century octagonal **Battistero Neoniano** (Via Battistero; for all details, see "Ravenna's Cumulative Ticket & Open Hours," below) was built as the baptistery of a cathedral that no longer stands; it's now behind Ravenna's banal present-day Duomo, built in the 19th century. Fittingly for the structure's purpose, the blue and gold mosaics on the dome depict the baptism of Christ by St. John the Baptist, surrounded by the Twelve Apostles.

Nearby is the tiny **Museo Arcivescovile & Cappella di San Andrea** (Piazza Arcivescovado; for all details, see "Ravenna's Cumulative Ticket & Open Hours,"

Ravenna's Cumulative Ticket & Open Hours

They keep changing the way this works, but currently a single 7.50€ cumulative ticket, valid for 7 days, covers admission to the Basilica di San Vitale, the Mausoleum of Galla Placidia, the Battistero Neoniano, the Cappella di San Andrea/Museo Arcivescovile, and the Basilica di Sant'Apollinare Nuovo. From March 1 to June 15, the Mausoleum of Galla Placidia tacks on a 2€ supplement.

All sights are open daily as follows: November to February 10am to 5:30pm; March and October 9:30am to 5:30pm; and April to September 9am to 7pm (exception: Mar–Oct, San Vitale and Galla Placidia open a half-hour earlier). For more information, call ☎ 0544-541611 or 0544-541-688, or visit www.ravennamosaici.it.

Et Tu, Dante?

Exiled from his native Florence on trumped-up political charges, the poet Dante Alighieri ended up making Ravenna his home. It is here that he finished his epic *Divine Comedy*, of which the famed *Inferno* is but the first third. It is here that he died in 1321. And—despite efforts by the Florentines to reclaim their famous son—it is here that he resides for eternity, in an elaborate **tomb** behind the Basilica di San Francesco. The tomb's inscription reads: HERE IN THIS CORNER LIES DANTE, EXILED FROM HIS NATIVE LAND, BORN TO FLORENCE, AN UNLOVING MOTHER. There's a small collection of Dante memorabilia in the adjoining **Museo Dantesco** (Via Dante Alighieri 4; ☎ 0544-30252; www.centrodantesco.it; closed as of this writing, but in the past it charged 2€; daily 9am–noon, Apr–Sept also 3–6pm).

above), housed in the 6th-century Archbishop's Palace. The highlight of the one-room collection is the stupefyingly intricate ivory throne of Emperor Maximilian. Adjoining the museum is a small chapel built in the shape of a cross and dedicated to St. Andrea, every inch of which is emblazoned with dazzling mosaics. Sadly, this is currently closed for renovations and may remain so for years.

The famous mosaics in the 6th-century **Basilica di Sant'Apollinare Nuovo** ★ (Via di Roma; for all details, see "Ravenna's Cumulative Ticket & Open Hours," above), punctuated by Greek columns taken from a temple, are clearly delineated by gender. On one side of the church, the side traditionally reserved for women, a procession of 22 crown-carrying virgins makes its way toward the Madonna; on the other, 26 male martyrs march toward Christ. The mosaics near the door provide a fascinating look at the 6th-century city and its environs—one on the right shows the monuments of the city, including Emperor Theodoric's royal palace, and one on the left shows the port city of Classe.

Silt covered that ancient port long ago, but Ravenna's final grand 6th-century sight remains there, a 15-minute bus ride south of town, looming above farm fields and pine woods: the early-Christian basilica and campanile of **Sant'Apollinare in Classe** ★★ (Via Romeo Sud 224, Classe; ☎ 0544-473569; 3€; Tues–Sat 8:30am–7:30pm, Sun 1–7:30pm; bus: 4 or 44 from Piazza Farini in front of the train station, every 20 min.). The plain exterior belies a splendor within, a long sparse nave punctuated by Greek columns, capped by an apse dome slathered with lustrous gold mosaics. Imagine how transporting the effect was when the floor, too, was tiled in gold mosaic. The dominating figure depicted here, flanked by 12 lambs representing the apostles, is St. Apollinare, bishop of Ravenna.

PARMA

Its prosciutto di Parma hams and Parmigiano-Reggiano cheeses are justly famous, as they have been since Roman times, but the pleasures of this exquisite little city extend far beyond the gastronomic. The Farnese, who made their duchy one of the art centers of the Renaissance, were succeeded by Marie-Louise, a Hapsburg and the wife of Emperor Napoleon. Her interest in everything cultural ensured that Parma never languished as a once-glorious backwater, as was the case with nearby Ferrara and Ravenna. As a result, today's residents of Parma live in one of Italy's most prosperous cities and are surrounded by palaces, churches, and artwork.

Parma is also a city of music, a favorite of Verdi's and the hometown of the great 20th-century conductor Arturo Toscanini. If you're here for the concert (late Oct/early Nov through Apr) or opera (mid-Dec to mid-Apr) seasons, be sure to catch a performance at the glorious Teatro Regio (see "A Night at the Theater," below).

Lay of the Land

Parma is 95km (59 miles) northwest of Bologna and 122km (76 miles) southeast of Milan. Because it lies on the busy north-south rail lines, connections are excellent. There are two to four trains per hour to and from Bologna (50–77 min.), many of which continue all the way to Milan (1½–1¾ hr.). About six high-speed trains a day connect with Florence (1¾–2¼ hr.).

The train station is about a 20-minute walk from the city center; from the front of the station, follow Viale Bottego east for 1 block to Via Garibaldi, which leads past the grassy lawns of Piazza della Pace, backed by the massive and museum-filled Palazzo della Pilotta, and then continue on to the central Piazza Garibaldi.

The **tourist office** (Via Melloni 1A; ☎ 0521-218889; turismo.comune.parma.it) is closed Sunday afternoons.

Accommodations in the Heart of Town

You can download from the tourist office's website a document listing about two dozen small **B&Bs** in Parma, which run from 65€ to 120€ for a double room.

€€   Most Parma B&Bs are outside town or across the river, but there are two gems in the historical center—though each only rents one room. My favorite is **Bed & Breakfast Armonia di Marco Farris** (Borgo del Naviglio 16; 0521-230385 or 348-2250069; cash only), a gorgeous and huge studio apartment on the quiet streets at the north end of the historical center. It comes complete with wood-beamed ceilings, kitchenette, two double beds with a fold-out sofa, an entertainment center featuring a flatscreen TV with satellite channels, and even a washing machine in the large bathroom. It costs just 70€ for two people (50€ for one, 90€ for three) and since the owner, who lives upstairs, operates it as a B&B rather than a rental apartment, she brings you a breakfast tray in the morning. A 10-minute walk south of Piazza Garibaldi, **Il Giardino Nascosto** (Borgo Felino 17; ☎ 0521-236886 or 329-8867718; http://xoomer.virgilio.it/ilgiardinonascosto; cash only) is a slice of countryside style in the city, and the 85€ room with wood floors, beamed ceiling, TV, kitchenette, and solid country-style wooden furniture opens directly onto a lovely garden with a fountain.

€€–€€€   The charming **Hotel Torino** ★★ (Via A. Mazza 7, just off Strada Garibaldi; ☎ 0521-281046; www.hotel-torino.it; AE, MC, V) is my top choice for moderately priced accommodations in Parma, with doubles going for 105€ to 130€. The location—in the pedestrian zone between the Teatro Reggio and the

Duomo—is only half the allure. The elegant proprietor has fitted out her modern hotel with a careful eye to style and comfort. There are fresh-cut flowers and a collection of antique porcelains in the pretty lobby, with Liberty-style accents like a chandelier and lots of curves, and antiques gracing the breakfast room and bar. Breakfast, by the way, is something of an occasion, served on china and including fresh pastries, excellent coffee, and a selection of teas and juices; in summer, you can take it in the pretty little terra-cotta courtyard. The tile-floored rooms are comfortably modern with modular furnishings but natty grace notes, including in some dramatic headboards emblazoned with reproductions of Correggio frescoes. The bathrooms are clean, if cramped, and fitted with box showers.

€€   Tucked into the quiet warren of little streets and squares just off the southeast corner of Piazza Garibaldi, the pleasant **Button** ★ (Borgo Salina 7; ☎ 0521-208039; www.hotelbutton.it; AE, MC, V) is usually filled with European tourists. The rooms cost 97€ (breakfast is an extra 9€) and are large and serviceable, though a little somber, with dark floral wallpaper and spartan modern furnishings. The bathrooms are nicely tiled and have stall showers. Single travelers enjoy quarters much larger than the ones to which they are usually relegated, with French beds that are quite a bit wider than standard single beds. A few of the doubles have small balconies overlooking a *piazzetta* behind the hotel. The Cortesi, who run the place, are most accommodating, and you're always welcome to join them in the lobby lounge to watch a soccer match.

€€€€   One of the best deals in Parma has to be the seven elegant suites of the 13th-century **Palazzo dalla Rosa Prati** ★★ (Strada al Duomo 7; ☎ 0521-386429 or 335-5622089; www.palazzodallarosaprati.it; AE, MC, V), right on the cathedral square with 18th-century styling, gorgeous antiques, kitchenettes, and herringbone wood floors. The rates for two people start at 160€ per night—as high as 190€ for those rooms that have killer views past Parma's famed baptistery to the facade of the Duomo—or 220€ for the four-person *violetta* apartment. The nice owners also arrange for cooking courses in a farmhouse outside town, and (if they're not using them) can make available their box seats at the Teatro Regio concert hall and opera house. Pretty spiffy.

Accommodations near the Station

€€   The **Brenta** (Via G. B. Borghesi 12; ☎ 0521-208093; www.hotelbrenta.it; AE, MC, V) is a perfectly decent fallback if the more atmospheric places in town are full. The lobby is a little drab, but don't let that put you off. The English-speaking management is very helpful and eager to point visitors to sights and nearby restaurants. Surroundings brighten considerably as you go upstairs. Guest rooms—85€ per double, plus 5€ for breakfast—are large and quite up-to-date, with functional modern furniture and new bathrooms with stall showers. Most face side streets and are extremely quiet.

€€€€   No nonsense and businesslike are the terms that come to mind to describe the **Astoria Executive** (Via Trento 9; ☎ 0521-272717; www. piuhotels.com; AE, MC, V), down the street to the left as you exit the station. The facade is sheeted in blue-tinted glass, and everything inside sports a contemporary decor. This doesn't mean the Astoria isn't welcoming—if you don't mind the complete absence of old-world charm. It's an excellent choice for wood-veneer cabinetry, firm low-slung beds, and efficient bathrooms. Double sets of double-glazed windows ensure a good night's sleep, even on the side facing the railroad tracks (honest, there's barely a whisper when a train passes). Doubles officially go for 130€ to 180€, but Internet specials and weekend packages can bring rates as low as 65€.

Dining for All Tastes

If there's one thing that has brought the name of Parma to the attention of the wider world, it's the food. This is, after all, where they cure that **prosciutto di Parma** ham that costs twice as much as the domestic kind in your local deli, not to mention that aged "cheese of Parma" (in Italian: **parmigiano**) that people from Boise to Bangkok grate over pasta.

Speaking of pasta, the favored *primi* in Parma are tagliatelle noodles and tortellini (look for the kind stuffed with *zucca,* or pumpkin), which come to the table with some wonderfully creative sauces—from simple butter and sage to *arrabiata,* a "hopping mad" mix of tomatoes, onions, bits of meat, and spicy pepperoncino. Main courses lean heavily toward meat, including the *filetto di cavallo* (filet of horse meat), which is a staple on most menus. Parma's hallmark wine is **Lambrusco,** a rich, sparking red that goes great with pizza.

For picnics, stop by the **food market** on Piazza Ghiaia, near the Palazzo della Pilotta, open Monday to Saturday 8am to 1pm and 3 to 7pm.

€   Parma is blessed with many excellent wine bars, but the best just may be **Enoteca Fontana** ✦ (Via Farina 24/a; ☎ 0521-286037; Tues–Sat 9am–3pm and 4:30–9pm; cash only). Belly up to the ancient bar, take a seat at one of the long communal tables, or snag one of the crowded little tables out on the flagstones of the street and settle in for an evening of sampling any of hundreds of wines from Emilia-Romagna and beyond. There are a couple of dozen available by the glass (1.20€–3€), though even a whole bottle won't break the bank, as they start at 6.50€, and there are more than 50 choices that cost 10€ or less. For a truly special experience, though, flip to the back of the wine list and the hand-scrawled page devoted to *ottimo rapporto prezzo-qualità* (excellent value): 15 bottles of amazing quality that ring in under 16€. To accompany your tasting, pick from among a dizzying 55 varieties of panini (2.50€–6€) or a platter of local salamis and prosciutto or of cheeses (from 7€). At lunch you can also get a simple plate of pasta (6€–7€) such as *farfalle piccanti* (bowties in a spicy tomato sauce).

Parma Violets

Pasticceria Torino, with branches at Via Garibaldi 61 (☎ 0521-235689) and Via Farini 60 (☎ 0521-282796), is an elegant, century-old shop-cum-coffeehouse, where you can enjoy Parma violets: a prissy delicacy of violets coated in sugar that you've probably encountered affixed to wedding cakes. Here, they come plain or topping an assortment of cakes and tarts (and they make a great gift for pastry-chef friends back home).

Splurge on a Memorable Feast

€€€–€€€€   One of Parma's true temples of gastronomy, **La Greppia** ★★ (Strada Garibaldi 39A, at Via Bodoni; ☎ 0521-233686; reservations recommended; Wed–Sun; closed July) manages to be unpretentious while at the same time making you feel as though you're experiencing the meal of a lifetime. This is because the wife-and-husband team of Paola Cavazzini and Maurizio Rossi preside over the plain dining room with grace and ease. While you can enjoy many traditional Parmigiana favorites—their *stracotto* (braised beef) is the city's best—the menu also offers dozens of exciting dishes that rely on Parma's famous hams and cheeses as well as fresh vegetables. Parmigiano-dusted tortelli stuffed with fresh herbs is a perfect starter. My favorite main course is veal kidneys with truffle shavings, though a very close second is the veal scaloppini with lemon and a light sauce of white wine and herbs. Or you can splurge on a steak (beef this time) *filetto* for 24€—the only thing on the menu that costs more than 16€ (most *primi* go for 12€). The dessert chef prepares many kinds of fruit tarts, including one made with green tomatoes (6€), and the chocolate cake with zabaglione cream (6€) will convince you that you have indeed enjoyed the meal of a lifetime.

€   **Pizzeria La Duchessa** (Piazza Garibaldi 1b; ☎ 0521-235962; Tues–Sun noon–2:45pm and 7:30pm–midnight; MC, V) is the most popular pizzeria in Parma—open late and almost always crowded. You'll probably have to wait for a table, especially if you want one outdoors, but there's a lot of activity to watch in the piazza while you're waiting. Although you can eat a full meal here, you're best off with the exquisite pizzas (4.50€–7€) and meals-in-themselves plates of pasta (6€–8€), washed down with a carafe of the house Sangiovese or a bottle of Lambrusco, Italy's best pizza wine.

€€   Diners are wedged in among an odd assortment of antique toys, movie posters, and casks of the wonderful house Lambrusco in the maze of rooms inside **Gallo d'Oro** ★ (Borgo Salina 3A; ☎ 0521-208846; www.gallodororistorante.it; Mon–Sat noon–2:30pm and 7:30–11pm, Sun noon–2:30pm; AE, MC, V), a lively trattoria 1 block south of Piazza Garibaldi. The huge *antipasto* platters of prosciutto di Parma and assorted salamis (8€) make a satisfying late-night supper. The sublime *tris di tortelli* (8€) is a sampler platter of homemade tortellini stuffed variously with cheese, herbs, or pumpkin. The lamb with artichokes (8€) is nice, or take your cue from the Parmigiani in the room and dig into a delectable *stracotto di asinina* (tender, braised donkey served with sticky polenta, 7.50€)—though I'd steer clear of the *pesto di cavallo* (basically, horse hamburger patties served raw and cold, 6.50€).

€€–€€€   The lunchtime crowd at boisterous **Trattoria Lazzaro** (Borgo XX Marzo 14; ☎ 0521-208944; Fri–Wed noon–2:15pm and 7:30–10:30pm, Sun noon–2:15pm; AE, MC, V) is mostly neighborhood businessmen, replaced at dinner by neighborhood families out for a night of fun and good food. The largely carnivorous menu begins with a tray of prosciutto and other cured meats (8.50€), followed by succulent lamb chops (12€)—though the locals really come for a traditional *filleto di cavallo* (horse-meat steak; 13€) like grandma used to make. The homemade pastas (7€–8.50€) are wonderful, served in copious portions and vary month to month; you might get lucky and happen upon their *strozzapreti* (pasta so rich it'd "strangle a priest") with zucchini and saffron.

Why You're Here: The Top Sights & Attractions

When the abbess of the convent containing the **Camera di San Paolo** ★ (Via Melloni 3, just off Piazza Pilotta, down a little gated, shade-lined street; ☎ 0521-233309; www.gallerianazionaleparma.it; 2€; Tues–Sun 8:30am–1:45pm) sought to commission an artist to fresco her dining room, she went to Correggio, a High Renaissance master who lived and worked in Parma in the early 16th century. He rose to the occasion by turning the room's late-Gothic umbrella vaulting into a magnificent deep-green pergola framing colorful, muscular *putti* (cherubs). His portrait of the abbess as Diana, goddess of the hunt—and, more to the point in a convent, of chastity—is painted above the fireplace. These intimate rooms are an excellent place to begin a tour of Parma—you'll encounter Correggio again in the city's churches and its museum, but nowhere else are you able to observe his work so closely. The ceiling of the adjacent room (which you actually pass through first) was frescoed in 1514 by Alessandro Araldi.

Parma's **Duomo** ★ (Piazza del Duomo; ☎ 0521-235886; free; daily 9am–12:30pm and 3–7pm), made of soft pink marble and embellished with three rows of loggie and flanked by a graceful campanile, was built in the 12th century; it's one of the great achievements of Italian Romanesque architecture. Once inside, all eyes are lifted to celestial realms, as every inch of the nave walls and ceilings is slathered in mid-16th-century frescoes. They culminate in Correggio's great masterpiece, his dramatic *Assumption of the Virgin,* swirling up inside the octagonal cupola. The Virgin and her entourage of putti seem to be floating right through the roof into a golden heaven. Correggio captured them in what seems to be three-dimensional depth—long before this technique became prominent during the baroque period. Even before Correggio added his crowning embellishment, between 1522 and 1534, the Duomo shone with another masterpiece—a bas-relief of *The Deposition* by 12th-century sculptor Antelami. It's in the right transept.

In front of the Duomo stands the pink-and-white marble octagon of the 1196 **Battistero (Baptistery)** ★★ (Piazza del Duomo; ☎ 0521-235886; 4€; daily 9am–12:30pm and 3–6:30pm), a tribute to the work of Benedetto Antelami, one

---

A Hidden Fresco

For an added treat, exit the Camera di San Paolo gate and take two rights to get onto Borgo Giordani, which runs along the back side of the convent's garden. Enter those gardens to peek through the window of the hutlike Cella di Santa Caterina, named for its marvelous Araldi fresco of *The Mystical Marriage of St. Catherine.*

A Night at the Theater

Parma's opera house, the **Teatro di Regio** (Via Garibaldi 16A; ☎ 0521-039399; www.teatroregioparma.org), is not too far down the scale of high regard from Milan's La Scala. After all, Verdi was born nearby and Arturo Toscanini, who often conducted at the theater, is a native son. Tickets (from 20€ for decent seats, 8€ for nosebleeds and standing-room-only/SRO) can be hard to come by because they're swallowed up for the entire October-to-March season well in advance by opera buffs from across the region. However, the tourist office sometimes sells SRO tickets. You should also check the box office for last-minute cancellations.

of the most important sculptors of the Italian Romanesque. His friezes of allegorical animals encircle the base of the structure, which rises in five graceful tiers. Inside is his famous 14-statue cycle depicting the 12 months as well as winter and spring, now stuck way up in the lower colonnade above the tall niches that once held them. Those niches and the ceiling are covered in 13th-century frescoes (by an unknown artist) that portray the lives of the apostles, Jesus, and other biblical figures in a stunning display of visual storytelling and color.

Behind the baroque facade of **San Giovanni Evangelista** (Piazzale San Giovanni, just behind the Duomo; ☎ 0521-235311; free; daily 8am–noon and 3–7:45pm) are works by the two masters of Parma, Correggio and Il Parmigianino. Il Parmigianino frescoed the first two chapels on the left aisle, as well as the fourth one. Drop 1€ in the box at the end of the left aisle to light up, in sequence, Correggio's fresco of *St. John the Evangelist* writing down his vision (accompanied by his iconic eagle, preening its feathers) in the lunette above the sacristy door in the left transept, followed by the artist's *Transfiguration of St. John* in the dome, infused with golden light and widely considered to be one of the great achievements of the High Renaissance. (After that light snaps off, the apse fresco of the *Incarnation of the Virgin* lights up, if for no other reason than to show how much better an artist Correggio was than the hack who slapped that one on the walls.) Correggio also did the narrow frieze surrounding the nave of prophets, sibyls, putti, and pagan altars. Off the cloisters in the adjoining monastery (entrance just left of the church doors; the cloisters close at 6pm) is a *biblioteca* (library) frescoed with grotesques, maps, and battle scenes.

Around the corner is the entrance to the **Spezeria** (Borgo Pipa 1; ☎ 0521-233309; 2€; Tues–Sun 8:30am–1:45pm), the pharmacy from which the good monks have supplied Parma with potions and poultices (today, honeys, *ptisans*—an herbal tea infusion—and beauty products at the cloister entrance) for nearly 700 years. An array of medieval-looking mortars and jars continues to line the shelves.

The grim-looking massive fortress, which the Farnese put up near the banks of the river Parma in 1603, would be an empty shell if it weren't for Marie-Louise, the Hapsburg wife of Emperor Napoleon and niece of Marie Antoinette, who ruled the duchy in the early 19th century. Marie-Louise shared her aunt's passion for art, and under her guidance, paintings from throughout her domain were brought here to fill the rooms the Farnese had left empty when Isabella Farnese assumed the throne of Spain in the 18th century and the clan left Parma for good. Though Allied bombings came close to flattening the palace in May 1944, much of it has been rebuilt and continues to house Parma's **Galleria Nazionale** ★★ (Palazzo della Pilotta, Piazzale Marconi; ☎ 0521-233309 or 0521-133617; www.galleria nazionaleparma.it; 6€, or 2€ for just the theater; Tues–Sun 8:30am–1:45pm).

You enter the museum through the Teatro Farnese, a wooden jewel box of a theater that Giambattista Aleotti, a student of Palladio, built for the Farnese in 1618, modeling it after the master's Palladian theater in Vicenza. This was the first theater in Europe to accommodate moving scenery. Its elegant proportions provide a warm, intimate atmosphere, and the stage floor slopes, er, dramatically up and away from the audience. That's to help achieve the illusion of great depth, helping the set builders force a sense of long perspectives and the actors seem to bestride the distances like giants. If it looks in too good a shape to be that old, it is. American bombs destroyed it in 1944, and the current version is a faithful, painstaking reconstruction carried out from 1956 to 1965.

Though one of the prizes of the museum's outstanding collections is a Leonardo da Vinci sketch, *La Scapigliata,* the real stars are the works by Parma's great masters, including Correggio's *Madonna of St. Jerome* and *Rest on the Flight from Egypt,* and Il Parmigianino's pink-cheeked *Schiava Turca,* along with good stuff from lesser known local talents Il Temperelli, Filippo Mazzola, Josaphat and Alessandro Araldi, Del Grano, and Michelangelo Anselmi, who moved to Parma from Siena and worked alongside Correggio and fellow Mannerist Parmigianino.

Every room has little signs, translated into English, that do a great job explaining and contextualizing the works and artists, so I can just list some of the other great names you'll run into: Fra Angelico, Spinello Aretino, Sebastiano del Piombo, Tintoretto, Il Guercino, El Greco, Tiepolo, Canaletto, and several members of the Carracci clan (Agostino even contrived to die here in Parma). Maria-Luisa's tastes were worldly, and she collected works from north of the Alps as well, including one of Hans Holbein the Younger's most famous portraits, *Erasmus,* along with a small collection of canvases by Jan and Pieter Brueghel the Younger, Paul Brill, and van Dyck. There's also a long hallway at the end that helps contextualize Parma itself, with 19th-century street scenes and lots of reproductions of old maps and portraits of the Farnese dukes.

The Other Parma

For a true taste of Parma, in addition to visiting the **outdoor food market** at Piazza Ghiaia, you should also sniff out **Salumeria Specialità di Parma** (Via Farini 9C; ☎ 0521-233591) for a huge selection of prosciutto and other meats.

Cheese aficionados can visit the official body in charge of regulating Parmesan producers, the **Consorzio del Parmigiano Reggiano** (Via Gramsci 26C; ☎ 0521-292700; www.parmigiano-reggiano.it), with free 2-hour tours Monday through Friday at 8am (book ahead at least 3 weeks). If you don't have time for the tour, at least visit the website for a series of surprisingly interesting movies detailing how parmigiano is made. If you call ahead you can also arrange to visit the consortium in charge of Parma's other great contribution to world cuisine: the **Consorzio del Prosciutto di Parma** (Via Marco dell'Arpa 8b; ☎ 0521-246211 243987; www.prosciuttodiparma.it).

7 Venice

Though threatened by the ravages of time and tourism, Venezia continues to enthrall its visitors

by Keith Bain

VENICE WAS ONCE THE RULER OF A GIANT MARITIME AREA, A VIRTUAL empire whose army and navy dominated what is today Turkey, the Greek Isles, and Crete (as well as the inland areas of Italy that immediately surround the city). And as befits that position, it created palazzi and churches as grand and impressive as any in the world. The military, commercial, and political of Venice have long since vanished, but its artistic impact is undiminished. Its monuments, its facades, its paintings and sculpture, its graceful docks and mooring poles, its fanciful gondolas—all reach across the ages and never fail to enchant.

The city is a testament to human creativity. As you wander the streets that no motor vehicle has ever seen, you encounter genius at every turn. Titian, Tiepolo, Tintoretto, and Bellini are among the painters whose frescoes and canvases fill churches and museum galleries. Vivaldi's *Four Seasons* stirs hearts at church recitals and in hotel lobbies. The designs of Palladio and Longhena grace the waterfronts. Even the contemporary, mostly foreign art collection assembled by Peggy Guggenheim seems perfectly at home here.

Sadly, the city faces many dangers. Its squares flood nearly every year, and its buildings are deteriorating under the weight of time. The city's very uniqueness makes it an expensive, difficult place to live. Everything takes longer to get done, and even the simplest items—like bread—seem overpriced. The city's population has dropped to about 62,000, and the average resident is on the brink of retirement.

Venice is sinking into the sea, but Italy, and the world, will never permit Venice to disappear. People have always written about it, painted it, photographed it. For as long as Venice remains afloat, people will continue to be seduced by *La Serenissima*.

DON'T LEAVE VENICE WITHOUT . . .

GETTING LOST   Venture deeper into the maze of streets and canals. So sublime is Venice's lineup of architectural eye candy that the city simply forces one to venture forth. And believe me, if you stick to the areas thick with tourists, you'll never discover the real Venice.

SAILING THE WATERS OF THE GRAND CANAL   If snuggling up with your beloved in the hull of a lacquer-black gondola is in your list of fantasies, don't pass up the costly opportunity, and be sure to budget accordingly. Even if you're taking a more modest approach to holiday expenditures, you'll have no excuse for passing up at least one complete circuit of the Canal Grande by water bus. Hop aboard vaporetto **❶** for a complete lap of Venice's main highway, adorned with views of the city's most jewel-like palazzi.

BEING OVERWHELMED BY THE DRAMA OF PIAZZA SAN MARCO (ST. MARK'S SQUARE)   In the city's pigeon-covered main piazza, it's free and fun simply to spend a part of a day watching other tourists at play in the square. On it, the Basilica is one of the greatest examples of architectural overkill, but is no less worthy because of that.

SNACKING ON *CICCHETTI* (APPETIZERS) AT A *BACARO*   Tapas-style snacking is all the rage in Venice; order your late-morning spritz along with reasonably priced *tramazzini* or panini, or order a plate of pickled sardines. And the smorgasbord of potential bite-size treats doesn't end there.

EXPERIENCING ART, ART & MORE ART!   The Accademia Gallery has the greatest collection of classic Venetian art on earth, while the nearby Peggy Guggenheim Collection displays some of the best of Western Modernism. All around the city are churches and *scuole* (schools) stuffed with compelling masterpieces, while every 2 years the International Biennale fills the city with cutting-edge contemporary art from around the globe.

A BRIEF HISTORY OF VENICE

Over the centuries, Venice thumbed its nose at those who tried to undermine its independence, and survived against the odds. Once a group of muddy islands set in a lagoon on the Adriatic Sea, Venice was settled by farmers retreating from the onslaught of the Huns and other violent conquerors. The city later became a part of the Byzantine Empire, but over time asserted its independence and became a self-sustaining republic and a major world power. The city's central monument—the Basilica di San Marco (St. Mark's Basilica)—is devoted to another act of defiance; in 828, a group of merchants stole the body of St. Mark from Alexandria, so that he could be installed as Venice's patron saint. You'll spot St. Mark's symbol—the winged lion—everywhere, a constant reminder of the city's sovereign past. In later years, the bodies of St. Nicholas and St. Isidore were also snatched and reinterred here, as spiritual protectors of Venice.

The Venetian city-state next established dominance over the Adriatic and its eastern shores. Not only was its naval and merchant might secured with the construction of the famous Arsenale (or naval dockyard) at the start of the 12th century, but it controlled the Brenner Pass and several mainland territories. Motivated primarily by commercial prospects, Venice continued to grow as an imperial power, contributing to the defeat of Constantinople during the Fourth Crusade and once again, Venice got its fair share of the spoils of war.

The aristocrats of Venice elected their first doge (the Venetian word for "duke") back in 697, taking power away from the tribunes who had represented the various lagoon settlements, and putting it in the hands of a single authority. Over time, Venice developed a complicated governmental structure combining Byzantine and Islamic elements. The system included all manner of checks and balances, mostly in the form of councils and noble bodies, like the much-feared

Council of Ten, which had the power to try and convict anyone in the state. While there was much bureaucratic wheeling and dealing, the system contributed to a thriving economy, boosting the city's position as a trade center, and creating a lucrative taxation system. With its port abuzz, and with Venice the principal connection between the East and West, the government worked industriously to sustain the economic might of the city-state; international trade and diplomacy were prioritized and Venice functioned much like a well-oiled corporation.

Venice was much esteemed by other major powers, drawing diplomats and travelers from around the world. It was here that East truly met West. As fortunes grew, Venetian life developed a reputation for licentiousness—so much so that the author Thomas Coryate (1577–1617) compared Venice to Sodom and Gomorrah, and feared a downpouring of fire and brimstone. Venice became Europe's playground, attracting yearlong revelers smitten with its beauty and the voluptuous pleasures offered by its libertine citizenry. This is, after all, the city that spawned Casanova and the world's first casino.

With the focus on play rather than work, Venice eventually went into decline, its foreign influence undermined by the opening of new trade routes by competing powers, and the rise of newer monopolies of markets that Venice had begun to take for granted. By the 18th century, the empire was waning. Napoleon Bonaparte arrived in 1797, at the end of Venice's final fling; the doge and his administration quickly conceded to his military power. Venice was given to the Austrians in 1798, only to become part of Napoleon's Kingdom of Italy between 1805 and 1814, after which it again became an Austrian territory. Finally, in 1866, Venice became part of Italy. Its popularity as a destination for foreign visitors has never abated.

LAY OF THE LAND

Venice is a collection of 118 islands, most of them separated from each other by narrow canals but linked by hundreds of small bridges. Cutting an S through that checkerboard is the relatively wide Canal Grande. Venice is located in a shallow lagoon, protected from the Adriatic by a narrow strip of land known as the Lido.

In modern times, Venice has grown a tail, a man-made causeway linking the historic city to the urban sprawl of mainland Mestre. The railway linking Venice to the mainland was built in the 19th century, the motor causeway in the 20th. Europe's largest parking garage stands at the Venetian end of this causeway, and a major bus terminal—the Piazzale Roma—is just steps away from the Grand Canal.

Generally, walking will be your principal mode of transportation, and certainly your only means of getting to many hotels, sights, and restaurants that lie any distance from the water-bus stops or taxi landings. Maps can be difficult and confusing, and take some getting used to; don't get impatient—rather, enjoy the experience of learning to navigate this city of bridges, alleyways, and dead ends. If you're carrying heavy luggage, be aware that every bridge means two sets of steps.

Venice consists of six *sestiere*—districts—which gives some structure (at least for address purposes) to the tangle in which you'll find yourself.

San Marco is always the busiest area, and many visitors never venture far beyond its souvenir-infested epicenter (which is a great pity, since it is the area least likely to expose you to authentic Venetian culture).

Acqua Alta & Sirocco

The pessimists will claim that Venice is drowning. Much of the lagoon is a shallow, muddy area that is susceptible to oceanic tides, and in certain seasons, the water level rises to flood parts of Venice. When *acqua alta* (high water) hits—generally late September through April—it is usually the result of a combination of a very high tide, low atmospheric pressure, and the onset of the sultry sirocco, a wind that blows from the Adriatic, forcing water into the lagoon. (To get a haunting sense of the sirocco, watch Luchino Visconti's film version of Thomas Mann's *Death in Venice* [1971], shot principally in the Lido's famous Hotel Des Bains.)

Freak acqua alta floods leave their mark. On October 31, 2004, the water rose 135 centimeters (53 in.) to put 80% of the city under water. Areas in the low-lying historical center are more susceptible to flooding, and elevated boardwalks are set in place here for foot traffic (you'll find route maps at some of the vaporetto stops). Rubber boots are never in short supply. A siren will begin to sound several hours before the arrival of any particularly high tide, but there's no real need to panic. The high water has long been a part of Venetian culture and there are numerous tales of pleasure-loving locals refusing to leave parties even as the floor beneath them begins to flood. There has been increasing cause for concern, however; whereas tidal flooding occurred roughly 8 times a year a century ago, that figure rose to 108 in 2002.

The Italian government has already taken action. A system of 79 hinged flood barriers is currently being installed at the edge of the lagoon; these will function with compressed air, rising from the seabed during acqua alta to form a wall against the threat of floods. Despite warnings from some environmental agencies that the plans will turn the lagoon into a dank swamp, it seems that the city, at least for a while, will remain afloat.

East of San Marco is traditional, working-class **Castello,** still inhabited by the old-time Venetians. Venture far enough east, possibly strolling along the broad lagoon-side promenade of Riva degli Schiavoni, and you'll come upon Castello's hushed, tree-shaded public parks and gardens, largely undiscovered by the visiting masses. Castello is also where Venice's world-renowned maritime dockyard, the Arsenale, is situated. To the extreme east are the islands of Sant'Elena (home to the soccer stadium) and San Pietro.

To the north of Castello is **Cannaregio,** another residential neighborhood that stretches eastward from the train station. This is a wonderfully varied part of Venice, with busy markets and forgotten corners; it's also home to the world's first Jewish ghetto. From the Fondamente Nuove promenade along Cannaregio's northern shore, you can see the cemetery island of San Michele. **San Polo** is

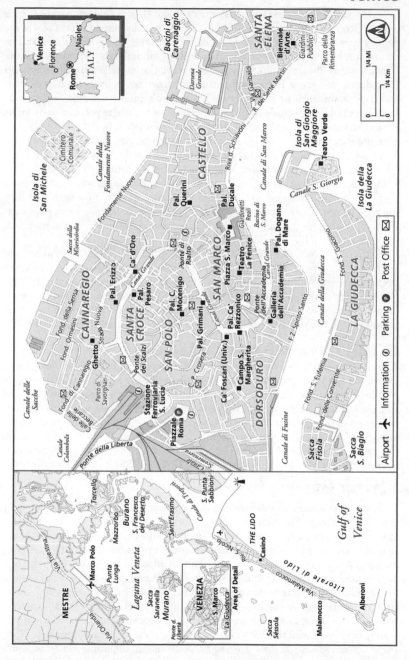

Venice

ITALY
Venice
Florence
Rome
Naples

Bacini di
Carenaggio

Darsena
Grande

SANTA
ELENA

Biennale
d'Arte ☒

Giardini
Pubblici

Parco della
Rimembranza

1/4 Mi
1/4 Km
0   0

Cimitero
Comunale

Isola di
San Michele

Canale della
Fondamente Nuove

Via Garibaldi

R. de Sette Martiri

Riva d. Schiavoni

Isola di
San Giorgio
Maggiore

Teatro Verde

Isola della
La Giudecca

Sacca della
Misericordia

Fondamente Nuove

CASTELLO

Pal.
Querini ☒

Pal.
Ducale ☒

Canale di San Marco

Canale S. Giorgio

Fond. della Sensa

CANNAREGIO

Pal. Erizzo

Ca' d'Oro ☒

Ponte di
Rialto

SAN MARCO

Giardinetti
Reali

Bacino di
S. Marco

Fond. Ormesini

Strada Nuova

Pal.
Pesaro

Canal Grande

Piazza S. Marco

Teatro
La Fenice ☒

Pal. Dogana
di Mare

Canale della Giudecca

Ghetto ☒

SANTA
CROCE

Pal. C.
Mocenigo

Pal.
Grimani

Canal Grande

Pal. Ca'
Rezzonico

Ponte
dell'Accademia

Canal Grande

LA GIUDECCA

Parco di
Savorgnan

SAN POLO

Galleria
dell'Accademia

F.Z. Spirito Santo

Fond. S. Giacomo

Ponte
dei Scalzi

Ca' Foscari (Univ.) ☒

Campo S.
Margherita

☒

Fond. S. Eufemia

Calle delle
Beccarie

Stazione
Ferroviaria ☁
S. Lucia

C. P. Crosera

DORSODURO

Fond. delle Convertite

Canale di Cannaregio

Piazzale
Roma ☁ Ⓟ

Scomenzera

Canale di Fusine

Sacca
Fisola

Sacca
S. Biagio

Canale delle
Sacche

Fond. di Cannaregio

Canale
Colombola

Ponte della Libertà

Torcello

Burano

Mazzorbo

S. Francesco
del Deserto

Sant'Erasmo

Canale di Treporti

S. Punta
Sabbioni

Gulf of
Venice

Via Triestina

MESTRE

Marco Polo

Punta
Lunga

Laguna Veneta

Sacca
Saranella

Murano

Ponte d.
Libertà

Sacca
Séssola

Rio di S. Nicolò

THE LIDO

Casinò ■

Via Malamocco

Litorale di Lido

Alberoni

Via Olanda

VENEZIA
S. Marco
La Giudecca
Area of Detail

Malamocco

Airport ✈   Information ⓘ   Parking Ⓟ   Post Office ☒

277

linked to San Marco by the famous Ponte di Rialto (Rialto Bridge), named for the islands (Riva Altus) upon which Venice was originally settled. San Polo is the densest part of Venice, home to some of its narrowest streets and alleys, and of course the ancient Rialto markets that still are abuzz today. Bordering **Santa Croce** and San Polo, and linked to San Marco by the lovely Ponte dell'Accademia (Accademia Bridge), is **Dorsoduro,** an area defined by its lively student culture, and a predominance of art galleries. Dorsoduro's southern border is lined by another popular promenade, the Fondamenta Zattere, where you can enjoy views across the Giudecca Canal toward the island of Giudecca.

Giudecca was once a refuge for victims of the plague; today it's a refuge for locals wanting to escape the endless stream of tourists in Venice proper; it's also where VIPs like Elton John and Madonna have their little piece of Venice. The island near the eastern tip of Giudecca is **San Giorgio Maggiore.**

Elsewhere in the lagoon are a number of smaller islands, most with tiny fishing populations. The most popular of these are **Murano,** famous for its glassware; **Burano,** famous for its lace; and **Torcello,** increasingly famous for its almost total loss of population (down to under 30).

Sheltering Venice and the lagoon from the Adriatic is a long, narrow strip of land known as the **Lido,** one of the world's most famous beach resorts, which began attracting well-to-do Europeans during the 19th century; today it's also home to one of the great international film festivals, and a good place to escape crowded Venice on a bicycle. Certainly, it's where locals go in summer to bronze themselves on the very beaches that made a global institution of sunbathing.

GETTING TO & FROM THE AIRPORT

The cheapest way to get from Marco Polo Airport to Venice is by bus (as little as 2€ on the no. 5, which stops outside the arrivals door and takes you all the way to Venice's Piazzale Roma), but this will rob you of one of the biggest thrills for the first-time visitor—coming upon Venice by water. For 12€, you can catch the half-hourly water shuttle from the airport (there's a free bus that will take you from the airport building to the departure point) to one of several important vaporetto (water-bus) stops around Venice. The transfer between the airport and the city is operated by **Alilaguna** (San Marco 4267/A; ☎ 041-5235775; www.alilaguna.it).

GETTING AROUND

If, like me, you have a penchant for getting lost, you're best off navigating by prominent landmarks, such as a (large) bridge, a particularly striking palace (palazzo), or one of the many public squares, known as campi. The latter are meeting points for locals because many are lined with cafes, bars, and restaurants, and are home to the obligatory church with an attached bell tower. Pay attention to the peculiarities of these squares and you'll help ease the trauma of navigation.

There are signs posted—in yellow—with arrows indicating the (general) direction of major sights, important areas, Grand Canal bridges, and vaporetto launches, but using these signs as a means of navigation is an art unto itself; you simply have to go with the direction of the arrow as far as humanly possible. Don't be confused when you find two signs pointing in opposite directions, both marked RIALTO; there will always be numerous routes to wherever you need to go.

Warning: Venetian addresses do not make any sense; each building is numbered according to a difficult-to-fathom system, supplying it with a seemingly arbitrary three- or four-digit code. You'll need to use this number (in addresses, it appears after the name of the *sestiere* in which the building is located) in conjunction with the name of the "road" (although many Venetians insist that Venice does not have roads) which forms the first part of the address. Now, as convoluted and confusing as Venice's footpath network is, the city planners have provided names for the plethora of streets *(calli),* be they canal-side boulevards *(fondamenta);* major streets *(salizzada);* larger streets *(lista);* wide lagoon-side streets *(riva);* streets formed by filling in canals *(rio terrà);* or streets lined with shops *(ruga),* canals *(rio),* courtyards *(corte),* or passageways *(sotoportego).* Be aware that there may be more than one *calle* with the same name. To increase the muddle, at the intersection of certain bridges and streets are a number of seemingly conflicting signs painted on the buildings; there was a time when I would stand on a bridge for ages trying to figure out which of the signs refers to the calle I'm looking for. Don't panic: The confusion eventually turns to smugness as you find yourself zipping along the back alleys. Remember: Venice has only one *piazza*—St. Mark's—all other squares are called campi (singular campo).

There are now four bridges traversing the Grand Canal. The Rialto Bridge is considered to be the geographical center of the city, and sees an almost endless stream of tourists passing over it, often on their way to or from the popular Rialto markets. Also important is the Accademia Bridge, linking San Marco with Dorsoduro (and providing spectacular views).

There are several **tourist offices** scattered around Venice, though none of these is overwhelmingly helpful; they are best at dishing out maps and advertising materials, and selling dated guidebooks and tickets for certain city events. For a full list of contacts, see "The ABCs of Venice," at the end of this chapter, or visit www.turismovenezia.it.

PUBLIC TRANSPORTATION

As I've already mentioned, you'll be relying chiefly on your feet to get around; there are no cars, buses, rickshaws, bicycles, carts, or horses. The only public transport is waterborne.

Venice's public water buses are known as vaporetti, which run through the Grand Canal and also circle the entire city, stopping at strategic points. There is, as well, water transport to some of the islands of the lagoon. As with any metro transport service, vaporetto services follow a number of lines (color-coded on maps), and run in both directions; lines are numbered, but nevertheless require some analytical skill if you don't want to find yourself heading off to some island when you're simply trying to get back to your hotel. The lines running along the Grand Canal are ❶ and ❽❷, the latter being the faster as it does not stop at every landing stage; both lines continue on to the Lido (where there are buses and bicycles). Many other vaporetto lines circle the city (known as a Giracittà route), also connecting various islands around the lagoon.

The vaporetti are operated by the **ACTV** (☎ 041-5287886; www.actv.it). You can purchase a variety of tickets at the booths found at most vaporetto stops. A journey along the Grand Canal is a hefty 6€ (valid for just 1 hr.). If you're planning to make fairly regular use of the water buses, it's a far better idea to buy a

The Great Gondola Splurge: *O Sole Mio,* Indeed!

Should you, the visitor, ever hire a gondola? If romance is what you're after, and given that it really is considered one of those once-in-a-lifetime travel experiences, throw budgetary caution to the wind and cough up for this enchanting experience. Technically, there are fixed prices in place, but most gondoliers will make at least some attempt to "take you for a ride" when negotiating the price; it's a good idea to know how much you're meant to be paying. In 2007, the official rate was 80€ for 40 min. (although when I last spoke to a gondolier based near Piazza San Marco he told me that it's more likely to be 35 min.), with each additional 20 min. costing another 40€. Night fares (100€ for 40 min.) start from 7pm and apply until 8am. I suggest you ask for the going rate at one of the tourist offices, or contact the **Gondola and Gondolier Institute** (☎ 041-5285075) to avoid being ripped off. Bear in mind that you're paying for up to six passengers, so it may be worth sharing your fare with fellow hotel guests (although it's worth getting to know them before you hop on a gondola with just anyone); also consider that the farther away from Piazza San Marco you go, the more chance you'll have of bargaining for a cheaper ride. Of course, there are other add-on factors you can consider, such as a private serenade from a bellowing soloist, or an onboard accordionist. Much of this might sound like a scene from a far-fetched romantic movie. But in Venice, such romance earns the muscled oarsmen and larger-than-life crooners a substantial living.

The cheapest gondola ride you'll get in Venice is aboard a *traghetto,* a ferry that transports passengers across the Grand Canal between two fixed points; you'll pay a "mere" .50€ for the short trip, but at least you'll be able to say you tried a gondola if the real thing is too expensive—and you'll cut down on a considerable amount of walking and getting lost trying to find one of the four bridges across the Canal.

travel card. The cheapest costs 13€ and allows unlimited public transport for a 12-hour period, but a far more useful deal is the 15€ version which allows 24-hour access. These cards, which also come in 36-hour and 72-hour versions, are good for bus services on the Lido and to the airport.

The fine for being caught traveling without a valid ticket is 30€ (plus the price of the ticket); during my last visit in October 2007, ticket inspections were carried out fairly randomly and infrequently and usually only at the busier stops. I'm told that there are imminent plans to introduce electronic ticket inspecting that—like at most metro rail systems around the world—will only allow you on board if you have a valid ticket. Until the new system is in place, try to make sure you get your ticket before boarding, and ensure that it is validated at one of the time-stamp machines at the stops. If you happen to get on board without a ticket (many stops don't have ticket booths), ask the conductor for one immediately.

ACCOMMODATIONS, BOTH STANDARD & NOT

Finding the right lodging in Venice can be daunting, not only because there is so much choice, but high demand regularly fills out virtually every bed in town. Don't take your chances by arriving without a booking. In a city this compact, with real estate at a premium and so many travelers looking for a bed, prices peak and even expensive rooms may be much smaller than you'd expect. Sadly, life in Venice is expensive; it takes more time and much more moolah to get anything done here (and that includes building, repairs, and even bread deliveries), so take that into account before assuming that high prices are a con. Sure, a room rate that might afford you superlative luxury in some other cities may not get you quite so far in Venice, but try to focus on the sheer privilege of having a bed in a city whose very existence often seems miraculous. And fear not: I've found some amazing deals, so you're sure to find something to your liking among the choices below.

If you'd rather avoid the hotel scene, I've included a number of apartment rentals, hostels, and other alternatives. Venice's smaller B&Bs are a really good option—not only will you save cash but get to schmooze with locals, taking advantage of their insider tips.

In general, all hotel rooms have air-conditioning, a TV (usually tiny and mostly Italian-only, but who watches TV in Venice?), and bathrooms that range in size from tiny to small. If you find yourself in a room that feels like the smallest space on earth, well . . . that's pretty much the norm in Venice, and even some of the city's most gracious, upmarket, and expensive glamour pads include some lilliputian rooms. Unless I've noted otherwise, breakfast is included in the rate.

Finally, **a word on location.** It may sound logical to want to stay near the tourist epicenter of Piazza San Marco, but I think it's preferable to escape the constant bustle and soaring inflation of this densely crowded area. Remember that no matter where you are in Venice, you're never too far from the rest of the city, and each neighborhood has something unique and memorable to offer.

LIVING LIKE A VENETIAN: FINDING A SELF-CATERING APARTMENT

The best way to get a sense of Venetian life is to stay in an apartment where you can prepare your own meals and occasionally share an elevator or stairway with "locals" rather than with other foreign guests. Start out by contacting **Venetian Apartments** ★★★ (☎ 041-5226441; www.venice-rentals.com). This well-established operation has around 85 very different apartments on its books. Operated by a London office (☎ 020-31784180), it provides a relatively hassle-free method of finding a place that's right for you. The price? You're looking at paying anything upwards of 995€ per week for a fairly lovely one-bedroom first-floor place that sleeps three and has a little garden, while an attractive midrange flat with a view and a terrace will cost around 1,495€. If you're into designer chic, there are superbly modernized spaces, while plenty of old, romantic homes grace their large inventory. There are even apartments on the Grand Canal (one pied-a-terre is right next to the Peggy Guggenheim Museum, 1,595€ per week for two people), and if you ever wanted to boast about returning to your very own palazzo, they have more dizzying options to satisfy your decadent side.

Venice Accommodations & Dining

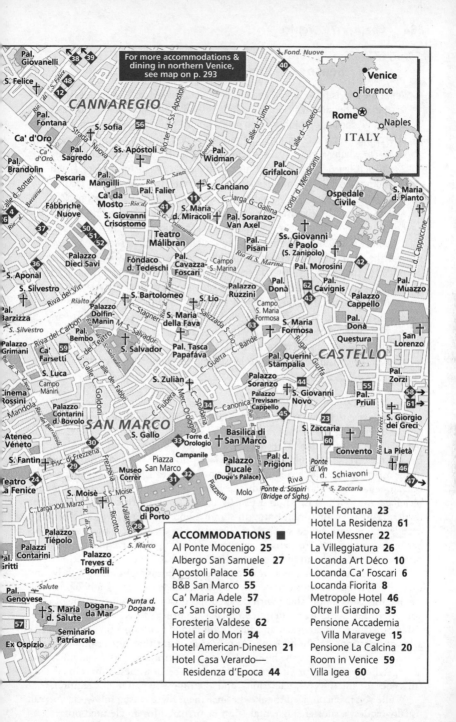

For more accommodations & dining in northern Venice, see map on p. 293

ACCOMMODATIONS ■

Al Ponte Mocenigo **25**
Albergo San Samuele **27**
Apostoli Palace **56**
B&B San Marco **55**
Ca' Maria Adele **57**
Ca' San Giorgio **5**
Foresteria Valdese **62**
Hotel ai do Mori **34**
Hotel American-Dinesen **21**
Hotel Casa Verardo—
   Residenza d'Epoca **44**

Hotel Fontana **23**
Hotel La Residenza **61**
Hotel Messner **22**
La Villeggiatura **26**
Locanda Art Déco **10**
Locanda Ca' Foscari **6**
Locanda Fiorita **8**
Metropole Hotel **46**
Oltre Il Giardino **35**
Pensione Accademia
   Villa Maravege **15**
Pensione La Calcina **20**
Room in Venice **59**
Villa Igea **60**

Seasonal Fluctuations & Discounts

Venetian hotels have one of the most convoluted seasonal pricing systems in the world, all because of the nearly endless popularity of the city. Generally speaking, high season runs for as long as business permits, stretching over the Christmas-to-New Year's period, then from February 13 to 24 (or whenever Carnevale is scheduled), April 1 to July 21, and August 28 to October 31. Low season runs from January 4 to the end of March, excluding the busy Carnevale period, and again from November through Christmas. There's a quiet "middle season" when many Venetians pack up and go on holiday themselves, usually from late July through late August, but this period may not remain all that much quieter for much longer.

Venice's low seasons are generally coupled with soggy, chilly weather and the inconvenience of the acqua alta (see "Acqua Alta & Sirocco" on p. 276). These are also the times when tourist numbers are down, meaning you'll be paying less to have more of the city to yourself.

Note that price ranges given in this chapter typically reflect the low season rate and, at the top end, the prolonged high season rate. Nearly every Venetian hotel operates a Web-based discount system enabling last-minute reservations at more affordable prices; at budget hotels, you can also usually ensure a better rate by staying for more than 1 night.

The really good news is that, if you think it sounds like they're charging a lot, bear in mind that the weekly rate could break down to as little as 142€ a night per apartment (often for more than two people)—not bad in a city this pricey. Besides the level of cleanliness and the obvious pride that has gone into the styling of the apartments, what has impressed me over the years is the discerning eye the operators have for offering places that feel comfortable and homey. Even the simpler flats are well furnished, and usually reflect some stylistic preference of the owner; most have air-conditioning in summer and heating in winter. You could even land one with a view of St. Mark's, and as I've mentioned, there are a number of very prestigious (expensive) homes—including exclusive palazzi, with all-original artwork and antique pieces—which can be arranged. At a price!

While Venetian Apartments features excellent photographs on its website and each property comes with detailed descriptions, the key to using a booking service like this is to supply them with detailed specifications about the type of place you're seeking. Some are modern, complete with brushed steel and designer trim, while others are more relaxed and filled with family heirlooms (or cast-offs). Ask a lot of questions before booking. Also bear in mind that, for example, not all Venetians have a kettle in the home (they're not tea drinkers), so if you must have any specific appliances or kitchenware, be sure to request these things in advance (this goes for microwaves, televisions, and anything else you might require).

While you're encouraged to take the apartment for at least a full week, you can usually request a shorter stay rental—but be prepared for an elevated price.

Convenient if you're not able to stay in Venice for a full week is **Flats in Venice** (☎ 041-2413875; www.flatsinvenice.net), a smaller operation that rents out six different apartments; its daily rentals for two people start at 90€ in low season, and hit 150€ during busy periods. Most of these are very basic spaces (with one or two bedrooms, a kitchen, and a bathroom with shower); they are, however, characterized by their convenient locations, mostly right near Piazza San Marco. While they may not be my first choice for a comfortable self-catering stay, they're clean, offer reasonable value, and certainly have everything you need (including a washing machine if you request one in advance). Note that the cost of these apartments goes up with each additional person in your party.

I've also found a few individually owned and rented apartments that offer tremendous value, as you won't be paying an agency markup. First up is either of two self-catering apartments owned by Jonathan Hollow and Alasdair Wight; they only do Saturday-to-Saturday rentals, but offer an excellent deal if you're traveling as a family or in a group. Both **Casa Tre Archi** ✪✪ and **Casa Battello** ✪ (www.visitvenice.co.uk) are in Cannaregio (one of my favorite *sestiere,* where you get to rub shoulders with real Venetians), close to the fresh produce markets of Rio Terà San Leonardo. Battello is the smaller of the two; although it doesn't have a major canal view, it's more affordable at 790€ per week in low season (Jan 7–Feb 18 and Nov 4–Dec 23) and 1,090€ a week during peak periods (Feb 18–Mar 4, Apr 1–Sept 30, and Dec 23–30). Built in the early 19th century, the house occupies two floors off a narrow *sottoportego* (side street); it has one bedroom and two living rooms, each with a double sofa bed (meaning that you can squeeze five people in here at a stretch). Situated on the top floor of a 17th-century merchant's building, the larger and wonderfully renovated Tre Archi has a superb view of Cannaregio Canal; it's a little more expensive (990€ in low season; 1,360€ in peak periods), but still a good value. The apartment has two air-conditioned bedrooms (one double, one twin), and a living room with sofa bed; the kitchen is well equipped. There's plenty of wardrobe space, and I also like that you can hang your washing across the courtyard the way most Venetian households do. Unlike Battello, Tre Archi has a dishwasher and telephone. The owners provide guests with information and tips that will improve their stay in Venice, and there are always a handful of useful recipe books to help spice things up in the kitchen.

A little pricier, but oh so perfect, is a gorgeous apartment in the Salute area (near the Guggenheim and La Salute church) rented by Mariana Marina and called **Ca' Foscarina** (☎ 347-2521901; marianimarina@yahoo.it). An attractive and very spacious third-floor pad, it has two double bedrooms and a third single room (suitable for a child), plus bathroom (with shower), full kitchen, and wonderful living room. The apartment has been beautifully renovated (light-filled with wood beam ceilings) and it's graciously decorated (individual furniture, rugs on wooden floors), with none of that faux-antique styling that's so ubiquitous in Venice. For all this, you pay just 1,300€ per week (do the math, and that's 186€ a day for up to five people!), plus a 50€ end-of-stay clean-up fee. Minimum stay is 2 days.

For a further apartment rental recommendations, see my reviews of B&B San Marco (p. 291) and La Calcina (p. 289).

If you're looking for a one-stop website where you can search for a reliable—and cost-effective—lodging option among local B&Bs, www.venere.com does bookings for almost 50 such accommodations in Venice. Each property is described on their website. These range in price from 58€ to 140€ per room (which is excellent value for Venice), and each property is listed clearly and extensively, together with a photo gallery (with exterior and interior pictures) and a map to help get a sense of exactly what to expect.

ACCOMMODATIONS IN SAN MARCO

San Marco has some of the most expensive of the city's hotels; Venice's grande dames are mostly along the Grand Canal or on the Riva degli Schiavoni, which marks the start of the neighboring *sestiere* of Castello. Packed into the alleyways and in ramshackle buildings near Piazza San Marco are many average hotels charging exorbitant rates on account of their location and trumped up star rating. But there are some worthy options even in this overexploited area.

€–€€   Not far from the Rialto Bridge is the extremely well-priced B&B **Room in Venice** ★★ (Calle San Antonio, San Marco 4114/a; ☎ 041-5229510; www.roominvenice.com; cash only). Claudette and Andrea rent out three bedrooms in their apartment situated in a lovely neighborhood taken up mainly by municipal offices (meaning it's *very* quiet). Rooms are big, light-filled, and spotlessly clean, with antique furniture that you'll appreciate coming back to at night. There are no televisions or telephones, so it's the ideal place if you've come for a real break, and the great value rates (from 50€ a night with shared bathroom, up to 100€ a night with private bathroom in high season; ask about discounts for several-day stays) will allow you to see that much more of what Venice has to offer. Claudette prepares breakfast, and this is served in your room. She and her husband are also a wonderful source for advice and you might want to ask about the beautiful ladies' shoes that Claudette makes. Note that the apartment is reached via several sets of marble stairs, so it may be impractical for some.

€–€€€   If you're determined to sleep as close to Piazza San Marco as is humanly possible, then look no further than **Hotel ai do Mori** ★ (Calle Larga San Marco, San Marco 658; ☎ 041-5204817; www.hotelaidomori.com; MC, V), an excellent budget option that is 10m (33 ft.) from all the heaving, pulsating tourist action. And while there's some heavy aerobics up the steep stairway to get to your room (which may feel quite cramped), you'll be in a bright, clean space with modern decor, wooden floors, and a comfortable bed (60€–140€ for an en suite double). Some upper level rooms have views of the Basilica. When you book, see if you can coax Antonella, the lovely proprietress, into giving you room no. 6 (for a particularly spectacular view that includes the campanile and the top of the clock tower), or—better still—the impossibly popular no. 11, where you can lounge on your private rooftop terrace (for the sake of her sanity, Antonella doesn't charge differently for this very special room). There's one room without a private bathroom that starts at 50€ and never costs more than 95€. If you'd rather forgo the views in favor of more spacious accommodations (and far fewer stairs), opt for one of three rooms in the annex, just a few feet from the main hotel (where it's also noticeably quieter). Pay with cash for a 10€ discount.

€€–€€€€   Wonderful, wide-open Campo San Stefano is strategically located within easy walking distance of both Piazza San Marco and the Accademia. This is where you'll find **Locanda Art Déco** ✸ (Calle delle Botteghe, San Marco 2966; ☎ 041-2770558; www.locandaartdeco.com; AE, DC, MC, V), with rooms that stand out from the copycat crowd thanks to their complete lack of faux-antique styling so typical elsewhere. Instead, decor is minimalist and furniture consists of individually chosen pieces complemented by spectacularly comfortable orthopedic mattresses, as insisted on by the hotel's charming French proprietor, Judith. While bathrooms are quite small, they're immaculate, much like the well-priced rooms which start at 90€, and cost 175€ during peak periods. Check the hotel's website for a discounted rate, there are often deals for stays of 2 nights or more. If, you're looking for bargain basement rates and don't mind turning a blind eye to aesthetic considerations, Judith also runs the recently spruced up **Albergo San Samuele** (Salizzada San Samuele, San Marco 3358; ☎ 041-5205165; www.albergo sansamuele.it), where the emphasis is on no-frills affordability (60€–120€ en suite double). There's no air-conditioning or breakfast, and you can even share a bathroom for a lower rate (50€–90€ double). But rooms in this simple hotel (which noticeably slants to one side) are clean and larger than expected. Guests at either of these hotels can also get a package that includes a unique gondola ride with Venice's only female gondolier.

€€–€€€€   Also near Campo San Stefano, on a quiet campiello, **Locanda Fiorita** (Campiello Novo, San Marco 3457; ☎ 041-5234754; www.locandafiorita.com; MC, V) occupies a lopsided salmon-colored building topped by a profusion of chimneys. White garden chairs cluster around the entrance, easily mistaken for someone's private home. Things are very low-key—a small, neat lobby with timbered ceilings and mountains of brochures, and just 10 rooms, all following the city's ubiquitous antique styling regime; mattresses are firm, bathrooms small. Room nos. 1 and 10 have tiny private terraces overlooking the square, so you know where to put your money. Doubles start at 80€, even in busy February, and you'll seldom pay much more than 150€ in choc-a-block September; there are also great deals on rooms with shared bathrooms.

ACCOMMODATIONS IN CANNAREGIO

Occupying the northernmost swath of Venice, Cannaregio stretches from the train station, an area I find devoid of appeal. The rest of Cannaregio—particularly east of Canale di Cannaregio—is lovely; this is the preferred stamping ground of the many Venetians who go about their routine, nontouristy lives here. Behind many of those weathered facades, there's a great deal of restoration going on, testament to people's commitment to maintaining Venice's historic charm.

Hotels near the Train Station

€–€€€   If being near the station is a priority, and you don't mind a slightly grungy atmosphere (payphone and kitschy posters in the lobby), the **Hotel Adua** (Lista di Spagna, Cannaregio 233/A; ☎ 041-716184; www.aduahotel.com; cash only) offers a reasonable deal (and staff are try-hard friendly); the clean, air-conditioned rooms have tiled floors and so-so mattresses, and those with shared bathroom facilities go for between 55€ and 90€ double. There's an even cheaper annex (the *dependence*) in the adjacent building, where rooms are usually 70€ double. Adua's en suite units aren't worth the high season rate of 140€, though—rather read further to see a number of better deals. Breakfast (5€–7.50€) is not included—much better to get a fresh croissant and espresso elsewhere, and pick up fresh fruit at the market near the Guglie Bridge.

€€–€€€   In a completely different league, and still just 270m (900 ft.) from the station, is the good-value **Hotel San Geremia** ★ (Campo San Geremia, Cannaregio 290/A; ☎ 041-716245 or 800-391992; www.sangeremiahotel.com; AE, DC, MC, V). Guest rooms are cheerfully painted and get enough light, and those on the top floors have terraces (management is mulling over whether or not to add air-conditioning). If you get one overlooking the square for which the hotel is named, you'll be able to keep track of the artists who come here to sketch or paint the multidomed St. Geremia Church. En suite rooms cost between 95€ and 125€ on weekends in high season—or shave off 15€ by visiting during the week. It's also 30€ cheaper if you opt for a room with shared bathroom facilities. Either way, the San Geremia is a sound deal, and you won't get lost if arriving by train; just turn left as you exit the station and keep going till you reach the square.

Hotels in the Heart of Cannaregio

€–€€   Two people who always make me feel right at home are Leonardo and Maria Teresa Pepoli, the outgoing couple who have run **Hotel Bernardi Semenzato** ★★★ (Calle dell'Oca, Cannaregio 4363–4366; ☎ 041-5227257; www.hotelbernardi.com; AE, DC, MC, V) for nearly 30 years. The good value offered here is combined with a relaxed, friendly atmosphere that has made regulars of many guests; most recently, the *Simpsons* voice artists stayed here and sang its praises. The magic spark is the presence of people who go out of their way to make guests happy; whether you need enthusiastic dining recommendations or a babysitter, there's always a solution. Also impressive are the genuine antiques and artwork scattered throughout the main hotel and—even more so—its nearby annex, where rooms are much larger and more attractive, and feature newer amenities. Maria Teresa (a dead ringer for Giulietta Masina, the star of films by hubbie Federico Fellini) is a seasoned purveyor of antiques and shamelessly worships art and places of architectural beauty; her enthusiasm for Venice is intoxicating. Ask her to point you toward a special church or to the place serving the best spritz in town, and she'll put you on to a good thing. The Pepolis offer the best lodging deal in Cannaregio (and arguably the best in the city); you'll pay between 75€ and 100€ for a room, with off-season specials at ridiculously low prices. If you don't mind sharing bathroom facilities, you can score a deal from just 50€ for a double.

€€–€€€€   Situated in the historic Jewish ghetto quarter with its functioning synagogues and faintly tragic atmosphere, **Locanda del Ghetto** ★ (Campo del Ghetto Nuovo, Cannaregio 2892; ☎ 041-2759292; www.locandadelghetto.net; AE, DC, MC, V) may not look like much if you go by the crumbling 15th-century facade, but step inside and you'll feel your spirit lift. In fact, it's a rather smart renovation of a former synagogue, and accommodations (100€–185€ double) hint at genuine style: parquet floors, modern furnishings offset by antiques, and soothing, neutral fabrics make for a comfortable stay; the two junior suites have small terraces (yes, these are the ones you want, just 15€ extra). Breakfast is served in a smart little room with views onto the canal at the back of the hotel.

€€–€€€€   When it comes to getting your luggage to your hotel, **Locanda Cà San Marcuola** ★ (Campo San Marcuola, Cannaregio 1763; ☎ 041-716048; www.casanmarcuola.com; AE, DC, MC, V) is a smart choice. Its lion-flanked entrance is just a few steps from the San Marcuola vaporetto stop on the Grand Canal; this seriously cuts down the time you spend getting lost while dragging your luggage along every possible wrong alley. Guest rooms are fairly spacious for Venice, with quaint, comfortable design. Remarkably, you can get a standard double for 140€ during high season (80€ in the off-season).

€€–€€€€   An unexpected gem hidden down an inconspicuous lane far from the crowds, **Apostoli Palace** ★ (Calle del Padiglion, Cannaregio 4702; ☎ 041-5203177; www.apostolipalace.com; AE, DC, MC, V) offers eight handsome guest rooms at the top of a narrow, steep stairway. If you don't mind being some way off the beaten track, head here. After the tiny reception area, the bedrooms are fabulously spacious (exceptional by Venetian standards), with handmade Venetian floors, timbered ceilings, and antique-styled furniture; bathrooms, too, are particularly bright. Two rooms have balconies, while the San Andrea unit has its own terrace. Double rooms range from 85€ in November to 250€ in summer.

ACCOMMODATIONS IN DORSODURO

Dorsoduro is a vibrant neighborhood with a number of lively student hangouts and affordable restaurants; wherever you stay you'll never be far from an art gallery or a social event. In the early evening, residents come to Dorsoduro's Zattere, a long strip of south-facing promenade, to relax, jog, or walk their dogs.

€€–€€€   Dorsoduro's last word in standard budget hotels has got to be **Locanda Ca' Foscari** (Calle della Frescada, Dorsoduro 3887/B; ☎ 041-710401; www.locandacafoscari.com; AE, MC, V), where a double with private bathroom costs just 100€ in high season (15€ cheaper if you share a bathroom). Be warned, however: While the rooms (reached via a steep, carpeted stairway) are adequate, they're also very plain, with bland floral bedspreads and beds that need replacing. Sure, this is a viable option when other plans fall apart (and the hosts are a cheerful family who've been at it for decades), but you'll probably sleep more comfortably if you fork out a bit extra for a night at **Hotel Messner** (Fondamenta Ca' Balà, Dorsoduro 216–217; ☎ 041-5227443; www.hotelmessner.it; AE, DC, MC, V), which has proper hotel facilities (including a restaurant and bar), and offers three tiers of accommodations: The cheapest are the standard rooms in an annex 20m (66 ft.) from the main lobby; these are heavy on linoleum but clean, and cost a reasonable 90€ to 115€ per double without air-conditioning or television; their midrange superior rooms, meanwhile, border on budget-plush (30€ more gets you the air-conditioning and TV).

€€–€€€€   Call me sentimental, but there's something of the aura of writer John Ruskin that still hangs in the air at the ever-popular **Pensione La Calcina** ★★

(Zattere, Dorsoduro 780; ☎ 041-5206466; www.lacalcina.com; AE, DC, MC, V), a classic Venetian hotel owned and run by Debora and Alesandro Szemere. A typewriter displayed on the stairway is a reminder that Ruskin wrote most of his novel, *The Stones of Venice,* in room no. 2, a lovely corner unit looking onto the Giudecca Canal; spacious, with parquet flooring, 19th-century antiques, Murano chandelier, and a good-size bathroom, it's certainly the room I covet most. These days, most of the rooms (refurbished, but retaining a sense of tradition) have something special to offer, but those with views toward Giudecca's Redentore church are the most advantageous (and popular, so book well ahead; 130€–225€ double); a room without a view is substantially more affordable (99€–158€ double), but nevertheless light-years ahead of Ca' Foscari and Messner (reviewed above) when it comes to ambience and style. There are also singles (with or without en suite bathroom) for 90€–110€ in high season; the more expensive option includes a tiny balcony. There's a lovely rooftop terrace, and the restaurant, **La Piscina** ★★, which floats on the Giudecca Canal, is a very special breakfast spot, where you'll probably want to return for dinner.

€€–€€€€   Although it's a standard hotel (and its position not quite so privileged as at La Calcina), returning to **Hotel American-Dinesen** ★★ (San Vio, Accademia 628; ☎ 041-5204733; www.hotelamerican.com; AE, DC, MC, V) always feels like coming home. The faces are friendly and welcoming, and the service sweet. From helpful porters to useful recommendations made by the desk clerk, everybody here makes a concerted effort. Occupying two adjoining buildings facing a small canal, it's ideal for art lovers; not only is it close to Venice's two best galleries, but the walls are crammed with paintings and photographs, making the public spaces feel like someone's rambling, cared-for home. Rooms (90€–260€ double) are neat and functional, with patterned silk-covered walls, reproduction antiques, and gold-lacquered fittings; the automatic blinds over the windows ensure complete blackout and are good for noise control, although the neighborhood is pretty quiet anyway. Bathrooms are cramped.

€€€–€€€€   Hotel gardens are scarce in Venice, and few are as pretty as the leafy grounds at **Pensione Accademia Villa Maravege** ★ (Fondamenta Bollani, Dorsoduro 1058; ☎ 041-5210188; www.pensioneaccademia.it; AE, DC, MC, V). This 17th-century villa was formerly occupied by the Russian Embassy and retains a distinctive, elegant feel, enhanced by Victorian relics and pretty antique styling. Operating since the 1950s (but thoroughly refurbished a few years back), you'll quickly pick up on the try-hard sophistication as staff members maintain a purse-lipped composure for a posh clientele, but a social and congenial breakfast in the garden overcomes any such pretensions, and you'll feel right at home. Last-minute deals are regularly offered on the website, lowering the price to as little as 60€ single, 100€ double; without them, standard doubles are 140€ to 225€.

ACCOMMODATIONS IN CASTELLO

Castello can be a fine place to stay in Venice; many of its hotels are close to St. Mark's and yet feel miles away from the crowds. Rates are also considerably better than in neighboring San Marco.

€€–€€€   Word of mouth has made **B&B San Marco** ★★★ (Fondamenta San Giorgio degli Schiavoni, Castello 3385/L; ☎ 041-5227589 or 335-7566555; www.realvenice.it; MC, V) a favorite with smart travelers keen to avoid the banality and inflated prices of hotel living. And why not? Here you enjoy the pleasure of large, individually styled accommodations, while getting to know life lived as a local and spending time with your engaging hosts, Marco Scurati and his wife. Guest rooms are in Marco's family home, on the third floor of a century-old apartment building; the location is superb, close to the San Zaccaria vaporetto launch and an easy 6-minute walk to Piazza San Marco. All three rooms are spacious, but fork out a little extra to have the largest room, with its terrace and views toward the Greek Orthodox San Giorgio church and its leaning bell tower. Rooms are lovingly appointed (wooden floors, rugs, desks, antique chairs, and wrought-iron beds), but the real charm lies in the fact that one room is styled just the way it was when Marco's grandparents lived there, while another echoes his parents' taste; expect to pay between 70€ and 110€ per night, according to season. Bathroom facilities are shared, but unless you keep precisely the same schedule as your fellow guests, this shouldn't be a huge problem. A basic breakfast (tea, coffee, croissants, and toast) is served in the homey kitchen; there's also an extra fridge for your own drinks and snacks.

Marco also rents a fully furnished **self-catering apartment** 🧒 ideal for families as it has two bedrooms, a living room, a bathroom, a dining nook, a kitchen, and its own balcony (daily rate 100€–180€; weekly 600€–950€). Decor is faintly 1970s, but you do have your own television, DVD player, and useful library. The apartment shares a main entrance with the B&B.

€€–€€€   Anna, the owner of **Ca' del Dose** (Calle del Dose, Castello 3801; ☎ 041-5209887; www.cadeldose.com; MC, V), is so full of good cheer, great advice, and enthusiasm (for her little hotel, for Venice, for life) that seeing her smiling face in the morning makes you feel that much more prepared for a day of solid sightseeing. And no wonder she's so perky: her guesthouse (in a restored and refurbished early-20th-c. building) is not only ideally located (just a few bridges from St. Mark's and close to main vaporetto stops), but marvelously neat and well managed. Rooms are spruce and comfortable, and are provided with kettles and packaged breakfast items (biscuits, toast, jam, tea, and instant coffee). Doubles are 95€ in low season and 150€ in high season—excellent value for this area; a room with a balcony is 15€ more. A word of warning to light sleepers who like to lie in: You're in the midst of an early-rising neighborhood, so rooms overlooking the calle are noisy in the morning.

€€–€€€€   On bustling, lively Campo San Provolo is one of Castello's family-run pearls: **Hotel Fontana** ★ 🧒 (Castello 4701; ☎ 041-5220579; www.hotel fontana.it; AE, DC, MC, V). Owned and operated by the Austro-Italian Stainer family since 1968, it's planning a major 40th anniversary upgrade in its rooms and later installing an elevator and inevitable three-star rates. Until that's happened (2009), take advantage of its continuing good value. The best rooms in the main hotel are on the third floor; these are spacious but spartan (Art Deco pieces against stark white walls); they may seem a little dark, but open the windows, and light streams in while affording lovely views of the street below. Double rooms cost 85€ to 180€—a range reflecting both the varying sizes and seasonal fluctuations; you'll pay a higher rate for a private terrace. Most rooms also have a fold-out bed, useful for families. Downstairs, there's a bar, lounge, and dining area. Diego, who operates the business, also offers five rooms in a palace across the campo; rates are lower simply because you're not in the main building.

€€–€€€€   And if you're looking for something really special, try the **Hotel Casa Verardo—Residenza d'Epoca** ★★ (Calle della Sacrestia, Castello 4765; ☎ 041-5286138; www.casaverardo.it; AE, DC, MC, V), which occupies a restored 16th-century palazzo just 3 minutes from Piazza San Marco. A proud combination of good taste and tranquillity, it's a relative value (a classic double goes for 90€–250€; deluxe units are much more but only marginally larger). Owners Daniela and Francesco acquired the palazzo in 2000, and have been hard at work ever since transforming it into a haven of understated luxury. Each room is unique, with unusual and individual period furniture, Murano chandeliers, and stucco wall detail. Some ceilings feature bits of original frescoes. There's also a gorgeous courtyard where long, casual breakfasts are served in summer. Last-minute deals are common the hotel's website, so check there before booking.

ACCOMMODATIONS IN SAN POLO & SANTA CROCE

Santa Croce and San Polo are both seeing an explosion of development as far as accommodations are concerned; in particular, entrepreneurs are fashioning beautiful and stylish guest accommodations from old family homes and apartments, and—as you'll see from my discussion below—they're considerably better value than you'll find in San Marco, which is really just a short traghetto ride, or bridge walk, away.

€–€€   Absolute bottom-of-the-barrel pricing is the lure at the functional **Albergo Casa Peron** (Salizzada San Pantalon, Santa Croce 85; ☎ 045-710021; www.casaperon.com; MC, V). Clean, spartan bedrooms with private bathrooms go for just 80€ in peak season. The main problem here may be the quality of the mattress, but a backache won't hurt your budget. The hotel has a ramshackle feel, with some tawdry decor, and you'll probably find the owners' parrot sleeping in the lobby, but such oddities—surprisingly—add character.

€€–€€€€   Neat, simple, unassuming **Hotel Locanda Salieri** (Fondamenta Minotto, Santa Croce 160; ☎ 041-710035; www.hotelsalieri.com; AE, MC, V) is a refurbished one-star proffering relative comfort at very comfortable rates. Situated on a lively canal-side promenade, the hotel offers a choice of views from smallish, modern, spick-and-span rooms: They either overlook the Gaffaro Canal (125€ double), or look onto the garden at the back (115€ double) where, invariably, the cheaper rooms are considerably quieter. In low season you can bag a room for 70€; also keep an eye out for website specials. The hotel's next-door neighbor is **Ristorante Ribò,** a classy but pricey Michelin-rated eatery with a garden, which is where Salieri's guests take breakfast.

€€–€€€€   My hands-down favorite accommodation in Santa Croce is the unassuming but exceptionally welcoming **Al Ponte Mocenigo** ★★★

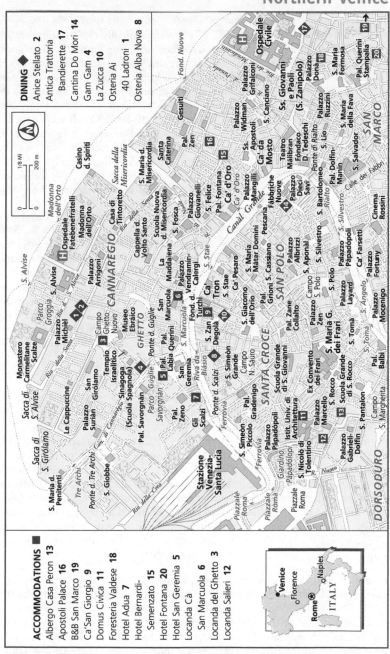

Northern Venice

(Fondamenta Rimpetto Mocenigo, Santa Croce 2063; ☎ 041-5244797; www.alpontemocenigo.com; AE, DC, MC, V)—conveniently close to the San Stae Grand Canal vaporetto stop as well as a traghetto mooring for quick, cheap access to Cannaregio. With a magical garden courtyard and beautiful, spacious rooms, Mocenigo offers the Venetian equivalent of budget rates for a measure of genuine luxury and elegance. White-marble stairways carpeted in red velvet lead up to the high-ceilinged first-floor accommodations—each individually styled (remodeled from different rooms of the original palazzo; even the former kitchen is now a red-hued guest room) and each with unique design advantages: canopied beds in some, exposed wood beams in others, and a few have terraces. Doubles are under 100€ in low season (up to 165€ in busy periods). And the Mocenigo offers the distinct advantage of hands-on management, combined with feel-good service that includes helpful dining advice and a genuinely warm welcome. I'll be back.

€€–€€€€   Tucked into one of those few parts of the city that feel undiscovered by the crowds, **Ca' San Giorgio** ★★ (Salizzada del Fontego dei Turchi, Santa Croce 1725; ☎ 041-2759177; www.casangiorgio.com; AE, DC, MC, V) is a real find in a pleasantly restored 18th-century building. Although it's way off the beaten track, it's just short steps from the Grand Canal, and within easy reach of the Riva de Biasio vaporetto stop. Guest rooms here are luxurious, spacious, and special, benefiting from a contemporary collaboration between classic Venetian styling and such thoughtful modern conveniences as flatscreen TVs, Wi-Fi, and hi-fi systems. The look is fresh and inspired, with bathrooms to match. Expect to pay anywhere between 80€ and 180€ for a double room. Search the website for specials during quieter months, particularly April.

HOSTELS

€–€€   It may sound overbearingly institutional, but the **Domus Civica** ★ (Campiello Chiovere, San Polo 3082; ☎ 041-5227139; www.domuscivica.com; MC, V) is not a bad option at all; it's a great value, and just 10 minutes' walk from both the train and bus stations. Near the Frari church, this hostel operates June through September in a centuries-old building with a spiral staircase and an ancient elevator. You can get a single room (31€), or a bed in a shared double or triple room (27€ per person); these all have metal cots, a desk, bookshelf, and cupboard, with shuttered windows overlooking the campiello below; some rooms have small balconies. Bathroom facilities are shared but clean, with individual shower cubicles. There's no lockout during the day (but you'll have to observe a 12:30am curfew), and there's free Internet access, a TV lounge, and a luggage store. Card-carrying students get discounts of 20%.

€–€€   Occupying the renovated 16th-century Palazzo Cavagnis in Castello is Protestant-run **Foresteria Valdese** ★ (Calle Lunga Santa Maria Formosa, Castello 5170; ☎ 041-5286797; www.foresteriavenezia.it; MC, V), another cheap place to park your backpack, particularly if you don't mind making your own bed or sharing with church pilgrims. Accommodations include en suite doubles with canal views (84€), and rooms with a kitchenette (86€ double). There are also family-size rooms (122€ for four people with a private bathroom), or beds in eight-person dorms (from 22€). All rates include bedding, towels, and a simple breakfast.

The welcoming atmosphere, canal-side balconies, and excellent rates more than make up for any lack of sophistication; there's a TV room, library, and even a fridge so you can stock up on fresh goods and save on meals. One serious downside: You can only check in between 10am and 1pm, or between 6 and 8pm. On Sundays, reception closes at 1pm.

€   You can also stay cheaply on the island of Guidecca. **Ostello di Venezia** (Giudecca 86; ☎ 041-5238211; www.hihostel.com), right near the Zitelle vaporetto launch, benefits from its shore-front location, affording great views back toward Dorsoduro. Breakfast is included in the 20€ you'll pay for a bed in a unisex dorm, and while this hostel isn't church-operated, management believes that cleanliness is next to godliness, so things are particularly sanitary, perhaps even *too* clinical (the staff are also a bit stripped of good humor). Book online, and coordinate your arrival to coincide with reception times (7–9:30am and 1:30–11:30pm). Dorm access is restricted during the day, and there's an 11:30pm curfew. If you don't already have one, you can purchase your HI (Hostelling International) card upon arrival.

DINING FOR ALL TASTES

Venice has absorbed a remarkable variety of culinary influences, resulting from centuries of occupation, borrowing, and assimilation. Naturally, the ocean is responsible for many of the more expensive dishes on the city's menus; fish and a range of exotic-sounding shellfish are taken from nearby waters and sold at the *pescheria* (fish market) in Rialto. You'll be able to order everything from *granseola* (spider crab) to *caparozzolli* (carpet-shell clams) to the very unusual *cappelunghe,* a long, pencil-shaped shell creature. One Venetian delicacy you have got to try is *sarde in saor,* a cold sour-sweet dish of sardines in vinegar and onions, which is a great starter or bar snack.

Sarde in saor is one of the many varieties of cicchetti, Venice's version of tapas-style snacking, which usually takes place at any of the myriad wine bars, or bacari, and tends to be dominated by a smorgasbord of panini and *tramazzini.* Other local specialties are *baccalà montecato* (dried, salted stockfish whipped into a mousse), cuttlefish prepared in its own ink, *fegato* (calf's liver with onions), and—less regularly—*anquilla* (eel). *Bigoli* is a variety of large Venetian pasta you'll see on most menus.

Don't Let Them Eat Cake

Venice has long had a love affair with fine dining, so much so that in times gone by, the city fathers passed laws to curb the tide of conspicuous overconsumption of decadent, expensive foods. In 1514, a body of "Luxury Commissioners" known as *Provveditori alle Pompe* was set up to tone down the reportedly depraved tastes of the citizenry. It became illegal to serve oysters at large dinner parties, and there were serious limitations on the type of confection that could be served for dessert.

Venice's range of influences makes it an excellent place to experiment with new tastes, but if you do have a conservative palate, there's always pizza, pasta, and even steak to fall back on. Every menu in town has something for vegetarians. Don't expect to get away with anything too cheap, because for the most part Venetian restaurants are aimed squarely at the tourist buck. I've met a number of waiters who've worked in reputable establishments that operate three pricing systems: one for Venetians, one for Italian tourists, and one (the highest) for foreign tourists. Unfortunately, there's not much you can do about this economic discrimination, but eating where locals tend to congregate, and avoiding the most markedly "tourist-hungry" places, will make a big difference; another general rule is to avoid most restaurants directly around Piazza San Marco, those near the Rialto lining the Grand Canal, and places advertising *menu turistico* (tourist menus). You needn't be quite so suspicious of *menu fisso* (fixed menus), however, which are often offered by places catering to locals at lunch times. For maps of Venice's restaurants, see p. 282 and 293; for more places to consider for casual dining, see "Nightlife," later this chapter.

RESTAURANTS IN SAN MARCO

€–€€€   My recommendation for San Marco's warmest service and good-value food is **Osteria Al Bacareto** ✹ (Calle delle Botteghe, San Marco 3447; ☎ 041-5289336; Mon–Fri 7:30am–4:30pm and 6:30–11pm, Sat 6:30–11pm; AE, MC, V), a family-run restaurant, just out of reach of the tourist chaos (close to Campo San Stefano, and easy to find). Decorated with black-and-white photographs of Venice, it's has a simple, agreeable charm, and is the type of place where you can trust your waiter to make a selection for you. For dinner, the handful of tables outside are very pleasant, but during the day you can always stand at the counter and order a filled panino (from 2.50€), or choose from various Venetian specialties (ask about the price first). Sit-down meals will cost quite a bit more (*primi* dishes will run you anywhere from 7.50€–19€; add to this a 1.60€ *coperto*, plus 12% service charge). Local dishes include *pasta e fagioli* (pasta-and-bean soup), *bigoli in salsa* (spaghetti with anchovies and onion), and Venetian fish soup. With the bill, you may receive a nip of sherry.

€€   During intermission at La Fenice (p. 318), I like to race back to **Vino Vino** ✹ (Calle del Cafetier, Calle delle Vesta, San Marco 2007/A; ☎ 041-2417688; www. vinovino.co.it; Wed–Mon 11:30am–11:30pm) for a glass of wine (there are over 350 bottles to choose from); it's a good time to peruse the menu which changes daily, and plan for a late after-show dinner. This small bacaro is owned by Emilio Baldi, the proprietor of next-door **Antico Martini,** one of Venice's classiest—and priciest—restaurants, so you can look forward to comparable quality at far better value and amid a more down-to-earth clientele. As the name suggests, there's also a formidable selection of local wines. For food, expect to choose from such diverse options as sautééd calf's kidneys, quail served with polenta, baked guinea-fowl, braised beef in Barolo wine, and loin of pork prepared in milk sauce. Pastas run 8€ to 12€; mains start at 11€; *coperto* is 1€.

€–€€€   At **Trattoria Da Fiore** (Calle delle Botteghe, San Marco 3461; ☎ 041-5235310; www.dafiore.it; Wed–Mon 9am–10pm; MC, V) you have a choice of either

Ultimate Gelati

The last word in Venetian ice cream has got to be the mind-boggling assortment of flavors available at **Alaska** ★★★ (Calle Larga dei Bari, San Polo 1159; ☎ 041-715211), where gelati maestro Carlo Pistacchio (yes, his real name) surprises first-time customers with exotic seasonal plant and vegetable flavors like artichoke, asparagus, fennel, mint, and celery. He's been concocting the city's most delicious ice cream for over 20 years, and is something of a local legend: Step into his tiny gelateria and you'll notice an endless stream of Venetians stopping off for their regular indulgence. Carlo doesn't ever seem to stop scooping, and at just 1€ per scoop, or 2.10€ for three, you can't afford to not indulge. The secret to Carlo's success isn't just his love of using unusual flavors (like ginger, cinnamon, cardomon, or *atzuki,* an exotic Japanese bean), but his near-religious belief in natural ingredients; he only uses organic sugar from South America, insists on pure organic chocolate, and his fruit and veg ingredients are market fresh, of course. Speak to Carlo about his philosophy on flavor, and you'll leave Alaska not only with a new addiction, but some delicious, gastronomical insights.

---

traditional bacaro-style snacking (which is far easier on the wallet) or a real Venetian seafood feast in the sit-down restaurant. Either way, you'll be under the careful watch of Sergio Boschian, who has been satisfying locals and tourists for over 20 years. What makes the bacaro special is that you can have calamari as a snack rather than the usual ham-and-cheese panino you'll find everywhere else in the city; and while you're snacking, try the delcious sardine fritters. In the restaurant (where you'll have to fork out 3€ for *coperto* plus 12% service), your best bet is to ask Sergio (or his son David) about the day's specials, or order "fish in a bag," his famous mixed seafood spaghetti. Sit-down *primi* dishes are all in the 10€ to 19€ range, and consist mostly of fish or seafood pastas.

€€€   It may be pricey, but in the vicinity of Piazza San Marco you won't find a classier, more quality-conscious restaurant than the chic **Osteria Enoteca San Marco** ★★ (Frezzeria, San Marco 1610; ☎ 041-5285242; Mon–Sat 12:30–11pm; MC, V). Serving updated versions of local specialties as well as international dishes, it's part of a wave of young businesses in Venice operated by locals who want to move away from the tourist exploitation that preoccupies so much of the service industry. Quality control begins with above-average prices (*coperto* alone is 3€), but the sexy, contemporary wine-cellar ambience; the above-average wine selection; and innovative dishes make this one of Venice's worthy splurges. Expect to pay from 16€ for a starter, from 14€ for a *primo* dish, and double that for a *secondo.* The menu regularly changes, but here's a recent selection that had me salivating: A light salad of goose, pear, walnut, and celery, followed up with tagolioni pasta with prawns and ginger. Other innovative offerings: steak with coffee sauce, or pork with chocolate!

RESTAURANTS IN SAN POLO & SANTA CROCE

€   **Cantina Do Mori** ★ (San Polo 429; ☎ 041-5225401; Mon–Sat 8:30am–8pm), near the Rialto markets, is a Venetian institution. A dark tavernlike wine bar, it offers not only tasty cicchetti—such as chunks of pecorino cheese, or fishy *baccalà*, spread thickly over slices of wholesome bread—but also gallons of wine, most of it on tap. If the standard cicchetti don't look like they're going to fill the gap, the helpful mensch behind the bar will also whip up a freshly made panino with ham sliced from a huge leg stashed behind the counter. You come in from either of two entrances (one is on Calle Galiazza, another on Calle Do Mori), and immediately feel working-class tradition hanging in the air, just like the copper pots dangling from the ceiling; there's plenty of history here, including original 17th-century bar licenses. Be aware that just despite the fact that you're only snacking, you can still rack up a hefty bill; I once had seven or eight little cicchetti items (I really couldn't help myself), and at 1.30€ to 1.80€ a piece, I could just as easily have enjoyed a large plate of pasta at a sit-down *trattoria*.

€–€€   Having run a restaurant in her native Paris for 15 years, Maria Lacombe came to Venice several years ago to be in the city she adores and established **Osteria Alba Nova** ★ (Lista Vecchia dei Bari, Santa Croce 1252; ☎ 041-5241353; Mon–Sat noon–3pm and 7–10:30pm; AE, MC, V), a small, family-run eatery that caters first and foremost to local working-class people. It's all very unassuming; dishes are chalked up on the board, and there's always something to suit a lighter wallet. At lunchtime Alba Nova hums with locals who've come for a glass of *vino* (from 1€) and pasta (her four-herb, tomato-based sauce flavored with mint is excellent). Maria also prepares extravagant-sounding dishes from ancient recipes you won't find anywhere else; in winter try her pasta with crab and strawberry sauce, or—even more decadent—pasta with chocolate and mixed seafood sauce. Portions are generous and filling, and well worth the detour. Most *primi* are around 9€.

€–€€€   Owners Annalisa and Renato arrive at **Osteria al Garanghelo** ★★ (Calle dei Botteri; San Polo 1570; ☎ 041-721721; www.algaranghelo.it; Mon–Sat 11:30am–9pm; MC, V) at the crack of dawn to transform fresh ingredients (from the nearby Rialto market) into some of the most authentic and reasonably priced food in Venice. I'm talking sautéed clams, sweet-and-sour marinated octopus, and traditional *sarde in saor*. There's a complete lack of pretence here, and the crowd is decidedly local. A big selection of *primi* dishes (most are 9€–12€) is complemented by excellent meat and fish options. Specialties of the house include *seppie in nero* (sliced cuttlefish in ink, 10€), *baccalà montecato* (14€), and straightforward but delicious lasagna (9€). Note that this restaurant closes earlier than most . . . maybe because the owners were up so early cooking!

€€   Laid-back jazz and equally laid-back service set the pace at popular **La Zucca** ★ (kids) (Santa Croce 1762; ☎ 041-5241570; www.lazucca.it; Mon–Sat 12:30–2:30pm and 7–10:30pm), a place where you can find healthful options that fly in the face of typical Italian standard dishes. The menu adapts to the whims of the kitchen, delivering decidedly un-Venetian alternatives such as English roast beef with guacamole, or pumpkin flan. New dishes appear every day, but there's a careful nod to the health-conscious, and vegetarians are particularly well looked after. In summer, you probably won't get a seat outside (or anywhere for that matter) unless you've reserved a table. Pasta dishes will run you 8€ to 14€; meat and chicken options are a bit pricier. Add 1.50€ *coperto*.

€–€€€ The trick to dining at **Il Réfolo** ★★ (Campiello del Piovan, Santa Croce 1459; ☎ 041-5240016; www.dafiore.net; Wed–Sun 12:15–2:30pm and 7–10:30pm, Tues 7–10:30pm; MC, V), is to come in single-minded pursuit of pizza (6€–12€). Yes, it's that good. My friendly waitress insisted I try the *nocina* (mozzarella, rucola, Gorgonzola crème, walnuts, and olive oil, at 8€), and she was dead on, although I suspect it would be hard to go wrong with any of the toppings. Other dishes include unusual-for-Venice options like chicken curry. Seating is most popular out on the square, or you can squirrel away in a small wood-beam room with slow-turning overhead fans and a frenzy of Mark Rothko prints. If you're on a budget, forgo the 2€ cover plus 10% service charge by getting your pizza to go; it's among the tastiest takeout in town.

€€–€€€ Most restaurants near the Rialto Bridge and fronting the Grand Canal are shameless tourist traps with snappy service and soulless cuisine. However, despite their fantastic location (near the Rialto and with tables near the Grand Canal), the kitchens at both **Bancogiro** (Campo San Giacomo di Rialto, San Polo 122; ☎ 041-5232061; Tues–Sun 10:30am–11:45pm or later; cash only) and **Naranzaria** ★★ (San Polo 130; ☎ 041-7241035; www.naranzaria.it; Tues–Sun noon–2am) make a habit of thinking up interesting dishes to accompany their impressive wine lists. Bancogiro has a daily-changing fish selection, healthful salads (like gamberoni and avocado, 15€), and generous cheese platters (12€); dishes average out at 15€. Unfortunately, service is unsufferable, thanks to a grumpy owner, so I can't in good conscious give it any stars (it gets a mention thanks to its locale and the quality of the food). Naranzaria is a much friendlier place and its food selection is small but varied, with Venetian and exotic specialties to accompany an impressive wine list.

RESTAURANTS IN CASTELLO

€–€€ For a truly "local" night out, and the cheapest pizzas in town, here's a discovery I made while strolling through Castello one Sunday evening. Drawn by the roar of garrulous diners, I ventured into **Trattoria dai Tosi** ★ (kids) (Secco Marina, Castello 738; ☎ 041-5237102; Thurs–Tues 11am–4:30pm and 5:30–11:30pm; cash only). Outside, most of the tables had merged into one big fiesta, while inside, pizza after pizza was being thrust into the two-door oven behind the busy serving counter. On return visits I found it just as raucous; it's a great place to try if you prefer the cackling of Venetian gossips to the restrained ambience of recorded versions of Vivaldi's *Four Seasons*. Operated by a husband-and-wife team (he's local, she's from Cornwall in the south of England), this down-home eatery has been packing 'em in for well over a decade. Start with one of the house aperitifs (a deadly combination of vodka and fruit juice). Pizza is always top-notch (and splendidly priced at 3.50€–11€); on my most recent visit, nearly everything had sold out, but Paolo managed to prepare his favorite (and namesake) pizza for me, topped with spicy salami, black olives, and anchovies. Pasta dishes and seafood items are only served on weekends.

€€   The name means "little anchovy," but popular **Aciugheta** (Campo SS. Filippo e Giacomo, Castello 4357/4359; ☎ 041-5224292; www.aciugheta-hotelrio.it; daily 8am–midnight, Nov–Mar closed Wed; AE, MC, V) has evolved into quite a big fish in the sea of Venetian restaurants. The original wine bar is still a smart space where you can pore over an abundance of freshly prepared cicchetti. (Sample the meat-balls or the marinated anchovies that gave this place its name; you can try a range of different tastes from as little as 1€ per item). If you grab a table (service is 12%), either indoors (where you might dine alongside gondoliers or groups of gossiping women) or outside on the square (where it's more touristy), you can choose from fine, affordable pizza (7.50€–14€) or a full menu, with *primi* in the 10€ to 14€ range. Service can be a bit dronelike.

€€   Not far from the church of SS. Giovanni e Paolo, **Antica Trattoria Bandierette** (Barbaria delle Tole, Castello 6671; ☎ 041-5220619; Wed–Sun noon–2pm and 7–10pm, Mon noon–2pm; MC, V), doesn't look like much, but its seafood is wonderful. And the lack of ambience sure keeps prices low: most dishes cost 10€, *coperto* is 2.50€, and wine starts at just 5€ a bottle. Start with *schie con polenta* (shrimp served with creamed polenta, 8€), and, if available, get a serving of baked scallops for the table—prepared either in garlic or a variety of sauces, they're delicious. Although it sounds like a mouthful, I'm crazy about the *filetti di branzino con crema di carciofi* (12€), a filet of fish with a fragrant artichoke sauce. Give dessert a skip, and move straight on to grappa; there's a fine selection of top-grade stuff that will ensure a good night's sleep.

€€–€€€   **Enoteca Mascareta** ★ (Calle Lunga Santa Maria Formosa, Castello 5183; ☎ 041-5230744; Fri–Tues 7pm–2am) is, strictly speaking, a wine bar, and has grown famous for the cozy atmosphere that makes people want to settle in for a long night (so famous, in fact, that even Microsoft's Paul Allen has been spot-ted here). It's owned by bow tie–wearing wine expert Mauro Lorenzon; he is so fond of wine and so keen to see his customers enjoying his vast selection of vin-tages, that he'll gladly open any bottle, even to let you try a single glass. His cheer-ful, cantina-style eatery has a limited menu, but the freshly prepared dishes include excellent snack platters, such as seafood morsels or deli cuts with a vari-ety of cheeses and cured meats (18€ per plate). There are also individual dishes such as soup, vegetable ravioli, homemade meat lasagna, roast duck, traditional Venetian cuttlefish in black-ink sauce, and *baccalà*. Food is only served after 8pm, and a *primo* dish is 15€.

RESTAURANTS IN CANNAREGIO

€   An exceptionally lovely bacaro, **Un Mondo diVino** ★★ (Salizzada San Canciano, Cannaregio 5984/A; ☎ 041-5211093; Tues–Sun 1pm–3pm and 5–10pm), resounds with a near-nonstop chorus of "Ciao, Sabina!" and "Ciao, Ambra!" followed by hearty replies as regulars stream in and out if this tiny space offering the best-looking cicchetti in Venice. The numerous clay jugs dangling from the ceiling bear the names of regulars aged 60-plus who've earned a personal drinking vessel. At lunchtime it's pleasantly crowded, but smiling Sabina will gladly dish you a selection of delicious, three-bite-size, filled panini (1.50€ per piece), or something more substantial, like a plate of lasagna, *sarde in saor,* or *bac-calà montecato* (for under 7€); and do try a chunk of goat's cheese rolled in herbs.

Prices for wine by the glass are chalked up, and it's one of my favorite stops for a spritz, any time of day.

€–€€ Cannaregio is steadily becoming the place to seek out great dining deals, and you can start by hovering at the bar counter of **Osteria Antica Adelaide** (Calle Priuli Racchetta, Cannaregio 3728; ☎ 041-5232629; daily 12:30–10:30pm; MC, V) where cicchetti costing as little as .50€ are available in the late afternoon and early evening. Sit-down meals are also a good deal, thanks to the 10€ prix-fixe lunch. There's a new menu every day, and selections depend on what looks best at market. Expect a strong seafood focus (fish lasagna, spaghetti with anchovies, and risotto with monkfish), and wonderfully friendly service.

€–€€ The lunch crowd at **Trattoria Storica** ★ (Ponte dei Gesuiti, Cannaregio 4858; ☎ 041-5285266; Mon–Sat noon–2:30pm and 7–10:30pm; MC, V) is quite mixed, with tables of smartly dressed office workers bumping shoulders with the blue-collar crowd. They're drawn by the 12€ (and 2€ *coperto*) deal here: a big plate of pasta plus a choice of meat *secondi* served with vegetables. It's nothing out of the ordinary, but neither your wallet nor your tummy will feel empty after you've feasted here. Dinner is an upgraded affair featuring a medley of different seafood *antipasta* to share, and then a pasta dish (Antonio, the trattoria's hands-on proprietor, will recommend what's best).

€€ It's pronounced *quaranta ladroni,* and the name means "40 thieves," but you'll never feel robbed at **Osteria Ai 40 Ladroni** (Fondamenta della Sensa, Cannaregio 3253; ☎ 041-715736; Tues–Sun noon–2:30pm and 7–10:30pm; MC, V), where the food surpasses expectations even if service (2€) is ho-hum and you're relying on the buzz of other patrons (or the radio) for atmosphere. Book a canal-side table if you can. Selections are traditional, but solidly well done such as *sarde in saor* (9€) and simple down-to-earth pasta *primi*, like *bigoli in salsa* (10€), a typical Venetian spaghetti with anchovies and plenty of flavor. *Secondi* include grilled jumbo shrimps (13€), and fish sold by weight.

€€ Practically next door to 40 Ladroni is another favorite spot, **Anice Stellato** ★ (Fondamenta della Sensa, Cannaregio 3272; ☎ 041-720744; Wed–Sun 12:30–2pm and 7:30–10pm; MC, V), which is nearly always full, so if it's a sit-down meal you're after, reservations are essential. If you can't get a table along the canal, you'll find cozy booths inside, and there's always bar-counter snacking. Here, it's the clever use of spices—recalling Venice's ancient links with Eastern trade—that adds flavor to traditional Venetian dishes. The menu is small and changes weekly; there's usually a cicchetti platter with various fish items, including eel marinated in two different ways (a small platter costs about 8€). If, like me, you're a fan of Japanese *sashimi*, sample the *carpacci di pesci*—thin slices of raw fish (including swordfish).

€€ If you keep kosher, you may become a regular at **Gam Gam** (Canal di Cannaregio, Cannaregio 1122; ☎ 041-715284; Sun–Thurs noon–10pm, Fri noon–3pm; MC, V), which serves some unique additions to the usual Venetian lineup; falafel as part of an appetizer platter (9.80€), homemade potato latkes with apple sauce (5.50€), several couscous dishes, and Red Sea spaghetti (9.50€). Every meal should be followed by a stiff shot of Israeli grappa. On Friday

Make Mine a Double

If, like me, you need a stiff espresso to get you going in the morning, you'll be interested to know that in 1763, Venice already had over 200 coffee shops. Coffee became known in Venice in the 1600s, when it was served as a type of medicine. The first "cafe," where coffee was served recreationally, opened in 1683, somewhere in the vicinity of the famous Caffè Florian, and it seems that the popularity of sipping the bitter liquid has never quite diminished. In the 19th century, Adolphus Trollope noted that the caffè played a greater part in Venetian life than in any other city. He further remarked that this was the only city in Italy where female aristocrats frequented the **caffè**. Originally called "Venice Triumphant," Florian was opened in 1720 by Floriano Francesconi, and immediately earned a powerful reputation that has kept it at the center of fashionable Venetian life ever since.

Getting your caffeine fix at either **Caffè Florian** or its archrival, **Gran Caffè Quadri**, will be outrageously expensive; you're looking at paying around 8.50€ for a cappuccino, or much more if you happen to be sitting down when the band starts playing music in the evening. If it's simply a pick-me-up you're after, follow my lead and head to **Caffè Aurora** (right next door to Florian), being sure to stand at the bar counter while you order and drink your beverage (a shot of espresso is an acceptable .90€). I've stood at that counter with gondoliers and local policemen who've popped into the piazza to see what the tourists are up to, but certainly aren't keen on courting bankruptcy.

Another favorite stop-off is **Caffè Costa Rica** (Rio Terrà San Leonardo, Cannaregio 1337; ☎ 041-716371); here the air is fragrant with coffee that's been brewing at this spot since 1930, and most of the clientele is from the neighborhood. You'll find the small outlet facing Cannaregio's fruit-and-vegetable market near the Guglie Bridge: The sign above the entrance reads ANTICA TORREFAZIONE DI CAFFE (1930). Stand at the orange linoleum counter where rows of cups on saucers let you know that your hosts mean business; you sip (or down) your espresso (.80€) surrounded by sacks of beans imported from (among other bean-growing nations) Costa Rica. All the while, locals drift in to adjust their own caffeine levels, stopping for a spirited conversation with the staff.

evenings, a Shabbat service is held, followed by a special meal; if you want to join in, make arrangements in advance for a unique opportunity to mingle with members of the local Jewish community.

€€   Lolo, the animated owner of **Al Fontego dei Pescatori** ✭✭✭ (Calle Priuli, Cannaregio 3726; ☎ 041-5200538; Tues–Sun 12:30–2pm and 7:30–10pm; AE, MC, V) has his own fish stall at Rialto's market, but he brings his best, freshest selection directly to his restaurant. In fact, before spoiling me with his remarkable raw seafood *antipasto* ("The Clock," 28€), he told me that I could stab him with a fork if anything on my plate required sauce. I think he was being serious! I also love his *spaghetti al nero di sepia* (pasta made with cuttlefish ink, so it's black; 13€), although the chef's personal faves are risotto (28€ for two people) and his scrumptious tuna steak with sesame seeds (19€). I'd go so far as to say this is my favorite seafood restaurant in Italy, all the more perfect for the good value; cover and service charges are all included.

RESTAURANTS IN DORSODURO

€–€€   At large, lively, and hugely reliable **Ristorante San Trovaso** ★ 🄺🄸🄳🅂 (Fondamenta Priuli, Dorsoduro 967; ☎ 041-5230835; Fri–Wed noon–2:30pm and 7–9:50pm; AE, DC, MC, V), a bevy of young waiters scurry this way and that, carrying platefuls of fish and liters of wine to a festive clientele. And that's the main draw here: large portions of fresh, simply prepared seafood (10€–20€). I like to start with a mountain of *cozze e vongole* (a mussel and clam *antipasta*, 9€), and then see if I can still manage a *primi* pasta (7€–13€). All vegetarian options are 4.50€. *Coperto* is 2€. On summer nights, sit outside, where you'll be rewarded with a cool breeze.

€–€€   Those two supple, naked, Barbarella-type temptresses on the place mats at **Casin dei Nobili** ★★ (Dorsoduro 2765; ☎ 041-2411841; Tues–Sun noon–11pm, may close occasionally for late afternoon) allude to the myth that the neighborhood you're in was once awash with bordellos. Who knows if it's true, but there's still bohemian drama aplenty at the packed tables here as waiters in burgundy aprons prance about, delivering armloads of pizzas (usually with an armada of toppings) as well as more exotic fare to a clientele of all ages and incomes. Despite the good value, tables are set with high-quality olive oil and balsamic vinegar into which you can dunk the fresh bread that's served here (*coperto* 1.50€). The menu regularly includes special recommendations by the chef, such as oven-baked rabbit with rosemary, gnocchi with Gorgonzola cheese, and filleted turbot prepared with saffron and zucchini flowers; *primi* are all in the 10€–13€ range. When it's busy—which it usually is—be prepared to wait up to 30 minutes or more for your pizza (all just 4.50€–8.50€, and served only after 7pm). But it'll be worth it; I last ordered a "Zola" (8€), which was easily the cheesiest pizza in Venice, brimming with salami and Gorgonzola. *Word to the wise:* Don't ignore the chocolate soufflé (5.50€)–it's criminally good.

WHY YOU'RE HERE:
THE TOP SIGHTS & ATTRACTIONS

The major problem on a visit to Venice is running out of time. Even longtime residents will claim that there is always something more to see that they have somehow missed. See "Venice Itineraries" (below) for the indispensable sights for a visit of varying lengths. If you have the inclination, also visit www.meetingvenice.it, a fabulous site with itineraries, news of events, and great ideas for what to do when you're in town (many of them not your common or garden activities).

Venice Attractions

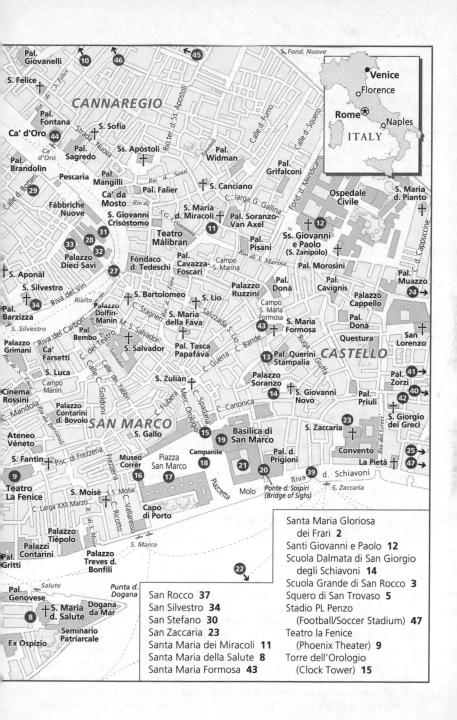

CANNAREGIO

Pal. Giovanelli 10 46 45 Fond. Nuove

S. Felice

Rio d. S. Felice

S. Sofia

Pal. Fontana

Ca' d'Oro 44

Ca' d'Oro

Pal. Sagredo

Strada Nuova

Ss. Apóstoli

Calle d. fumo

Calle d. Squero

Pal. Brandolin

Pal. Mangilli

Pescaria

Rio d. Santi

Pal. Widman

Venice
Florence
Rome
Naples
ITALY

Fábbriche Nuove

Ca' da Mosto

Pal. Falier

Rio d.

S.G. Crisostomo

S. Maria d. Miracoli 11

Pal. Grifalconi

Fond. d. Mendicanti

Ospedale Civile

S. Maria d. Pianto

C. larga G. Gallina

S. Canciano

Pal. Soranzo-Van Axel

C.d. Cappuccine

Calle d. Botteri

S. Giovanni Crisostomo

Teatro Málibran

Ss. Giovanni e Paolo (S. Zanipolo) 12

33 28 31

Palazzo Dieci Savi 32 27

Fóndaco d. Tedeschi

Pal. Cavazza-Foscari

Campo S. Marina

Pal. Pisani

Rio di S. Marina

Pal. Morosini

S. Aponàl

S. Silvestro 34

Riva del Vin

Rialto

Palazzo Dolfin-Manin

S. Bartolomeo

S. Lio

Palazzo Ruzzini

Pal. Donà

Pal. Cavignis

Pal. Muazzo 74

Pal. Barzizza

C. Stagneri

S. Maria della Fava

Salizzada S. Lio

Campo S. Maria Formosa

Palazzo Cappello

S. Silvestro

Riva del Carbon

Pal. Bembo

M. S. Salvador

43 S. Maria Formosa

Pal. Donà

Ruga Giuffa

San Lorenzo

Palazzo Grimani

Ca' Farsetti

S. Salvador

Pal. Tasca Papafáva

C. Guerra

C. Bande

13 Pal. Querini Stampalia

Questura

CASTELLO

Cinema Rossini

S. Luca

Campo Manin

C. del Teatro

C. del Fabbri

S. Zulián

Merc. Orologio

C. Fiubera

C. Spadaria

Palazzo Soranzo

S. Giovanni Novo

Pal. Zorzi 41

42 40

Palazzo Contarini d. Bovolo

SAN MARCO

14 S. Giovanni Novo

Pal. Priuli

S. Giorgio dei Greci

Ateneo Véneto

S. Gallo

15 Torre dell'Orologio

19 Basilica di San Marco

S. Zaccaria 23

Convento 25

S. Fantin

Pisc. di Frezzeria

Frezzeria

Museo Corrèr 16

Piazza San Marco 17

Campanile 18

21 20 Pal. d. Prigioni

39 La Pietà 47

9 Teatro La Fenice

S. Moisè

C. Vallaresso

Piazzetta

Riva d. Schiavoni

S. Zaccaria

C. Larga XXII Marzo

Molo

Ponte d. Sospiri (Bridge of Sighs)

Palazzo Tiépolo

Palazzi Contarini

Pal. Gritti

Palazzo Treves d. Bonfili

Capo di Porto

Punta d. Dogana

22

Salute

Pal. Genovese 8

S. Maria d. Salute

Dogana da Mar

Ex Ospizio

Seminario Patriarcale

San Rocco **37**
San Silvestro **34**
San Stefano **30**
San Zaccaria **23**
Santa Maria dei Miracoli **11**
Santa Maria della Salute **8**
Santa Maria Formosa **43**

Santa Maria Gloriosa
  dei Frari **2**
Santi Giovanni e Paolo **12**
Scuola Dalmata di San Giorgio
  degli Schiavoni **14**
Scuola Grande di San Rocco **3**
Squero di San Trovaso **5**
Stadio PL Penzo
  (Football/Soccer Stadium) **47**
Teatro la Fenice
  (Phoenix Theater) **9**
Torre dell'Orologio
  (Clock Tower) **15**

Venice Itineraries

If you have only 1 day in Venice

The quickest, cheapest, and most convenient way to see a lot of Venice is to hop on a vaporetto and do the entire stretch of the Grand Canal; you'll see most of the city's finest palazzi and get a sense of life along the arterial highway. Start your day by boarding the boat at the train or bus station and heading in the direction of Piazza San Marco. Jump off at Rialto, and cross the bridge to visit the early-morning fish markets. You should still have enough time on your ticket to continue with the vaporetto as far as **Piazza San Marco.** Take the elevator to the top of the **campanile** to scan the city, before heading back to terra firma and taking in the **Basilica** and the **Palazzo Ducale.** If possible, you should book in advance one of the **Secret Itineraries tours,** which is the best way to see the **Doge's Palace** and learn a great deal about the city (see "The Secret Life of the Doges" on p. 316). Then venture over to **Dorsoduro,** picking your way past the **Teatro La Fenice** and heading over the **Accademia Bridge.** Explore the **Accademia Gallery** for an overview of Venetian art. If you have enough time, head back to Piazza San Marco and wander along **Riva degli Schiavoni,** stopping to admire the **Bridge of Sighs,** and enjoying the non-stop activity on the lagoon.

If you have only 2 days in Venice

If you don't have to rush through the city in a single day, try to schedule a performance at **Teatro La Fenice** on your first night in town, and save the Accademia for a combined tour to the nearby **Peggy Guggenheim Collection** on the second day. Then pop into the **Salute church.** From here you can catch a vaporetto to the San Tomà stop, getting off to visit the **Scuole Grand San Rocco** and nearby **Santa Maria Gloriosa dei Frari.** Try to leave time for simply wandering through the streets and idling in the campi; Santa Margherita Square is particularly lively, often busy with antiques markets and impromptu street performances.

EXPLORING THE GRAND CANAL

In 1498, a French envoy to Venice declared the canal to be "the most beautiful street . . . that exists in all the world." His observation remains valid despite the addition of motor-propelled boats, overburdened vaporetti, speeding water taxis, tourist-laden gondolas, floating fruit stalls, police boats, and ambulances zipping up and down. It is without doubt the world's most privileged highway. And it's also a grand, watery, moving auditorium from which to observe the ceaseless activities of a floating city. Like an endlessly changing film reel, a trip along the canal provides nonstop views of the most spectacular facades, on magnificent buildings carved from marble and stone. Some are frescoed and some are simply

If you have only 3 days in Venice

Cannaregio and **Castello** are refreshingly laid-back, once you get away from the main areas. Use your third day to see beautiful Carpaccios in Castello's **Scuola Dalmata di San Giorgio degli Schiavoni** and wander through its relaxed public gardens **(Giardini Pubblici)** for a completely different sense of the city; then head toward Cannaregio's ancient **Jewish Ghetto**. En route, explore the massive church of **SS. Giovanni e Paolo** and the comparatively miniscule **Santa Maria dei Miracoli**. While venturing along Cannaregio's Strada Nuova, visit Venice's Golden Palace, **the Ca' d'Oro**, with its important art collection, and try to time your visit for a meal along the Fondamente Nuove.

If you have only 4 days in Venice

Use one of your days to experience lagoon island life; there are regular vaporetti to **Murano, Burano,** and **Tortello.** You'll notice the tourist numbers dropping off as you get farther away from Venice. Alternatively, if you're a fan of contemporary art and you happen to be in town during the Biennale (happening again in 2009), you should consider devoting a day to the myriad pavilions celebrating some of the world's current most-happening or up-and-coming artists.

If you have 1 week in Venice

Rather than cram all the major sights into a shorter time, divide them up, and take time to walk through the different neighborhoods, perhaps venturing into the occasional church or low-key museum along the way. Being in Venice with enough time to savor just a fraction of its sweet, melancholic charms is a unique privilege; the trick is not to feel the constant need to rush from attraction to attraction. Explore the **Giudecca,** and visit less touristy museums and galleries like the **Querini Stampalia, Ca' Pesaro, Ca' Rezzonica, Palazzo Mocenigo,** and the **Correr Museum** at one end of Piazza San Marco.

extraordinary in their designs; much of the architecture you'll witness today is the same that greeted that French envoy 5 centuries ago. I never cease to be impressed by the sinking, crumbling palaces made of brick and mortar but fashioned by hands that seem to have stitched lace and floating tapestries from the hard, rough materials of the building trade.

The canal curves its way between the train and bus stations in the northwest and spills into the Bacino di San Marco (St. Mark's Basin) right in front of Piazza San Marco. There are regular vaporetto stops all along it, many of them close to important palaces, museums, and other attractions; look especially for the facade of Ca' d'Oro, once the most opulent canal-side palazzo, and the

Carnevale!

Venice may not be throbbing with nightclubs and discothèques, but it has festivals and special events galore. Most famous of these is Carnival (Carnevale di Venezia), which in its very earliest days earned Venice a reputation as a city of outrageous hedonism. In a pagan-style inversion of social order, the Carnevale was a period of nonstop partying leading up to Lent (today it runs for the 7 days leading to Shrove Tuesday, the day before Ash Wednesday). Technically, Carnevale is derived from the Latin term for "Farewell, meat!" referring to the need to clear the pantry before the start of the Christian fast. Celebrations were first held in 1162, when a military ritual ended with the slaying of a bull and 12 pigs in Piazza San Marco. Annual festivities caught on, and the revelries soon grew into full-on bacchanalia.

Carnevale has long been associated with the wearing of masks, first documented in 1268. By the 14th century, laws were being decreed to prevent licentious behavior associated with those concealments, as gangs of masqueraders were going around town at night performing all manner of undesirable acts. In 1458, a law had to be passed to prevent men from dressing up as women in order to gain access to convents. By 1608, the Council of Ten so feared the moral decline of the republic that it banned mask wearing, with the exception of the days of Carnevale. It was also the only time when dancing was permitted.

Carnevale was a time of fancy-dress balls and excessive parties. In its heyday, so called Forze d'Ercole (Feats of Hercules) were enacted in Piazza San Marco, and a bullfight culminated in the beast's decapitation before the doge and his dogaressa. During the "Volo," an acrobat would slide along a rope strung from the top of the bell tower to the Palazzo Ducale's Scala dei Giganti, and present the doge with a bouquet.

squat, single-story palazzo that houses the Peggy Guggenheim Collection. The famous Rialto Bridge lies approximately halfway along the canal, and is probably the most distinguishable feature along its length.

PIAZZA SAN MARCO ✹✹✹, AT THE HEART OF IT ALL

Piazza San Marco is Venice's photographic hot spot, permanently mobbed by camera-clicking visitors drawn by the city's most celebrated attractions: the whimsical Basilica di San Marco and the urbane Palazzo Ducale, which stand side by side like some testament to the yin and yang of Venice.

I'll assume you've arrived here by boat and thus approached Piazza San Marco the way foreign dignitaries would have done during the heyday of the Venetian Republic. Once you climb off the vessel (at San Marco's Vallaresso stop), turn right and walk through the souvenir stands until you are standing between the two statue-capped columns that once represented the entrance to the city. These

During the 18th century, Carnevale reached its pinnacle, and was deeply entrenched in the city's spirit of decadence and moral decline; the world's wealthy revelers came here to taste its infamous pleasures. Part of the allure was the sense of anonymity granted by the masks. Whether you were dressed as a character from the *commedia dell'arte* or something far more extravagant, no one could identify you or assess your social status; wanton flirtation and open debauchery became permissible. You can get a sense of what the streets were like during Carnevale in the film version of Henry James's *The Wings of the Dove*.

The popularity of Carnevale waned until the 1930s, when it was banned outright by Mussolini. Only in 1979 did the annual event start up again. Certainly, Carnevale is not the same as it was in the 1700s; today, there's a great deal of sponsorship and marketing and expensive parties and events, not to mention hordes of perplexed tourists afraid to participate. If you want to get the best out of the experience, you'd do well to actually don a costume and mask and get out in the streets. (Be warned that for many, Carnevale is just an excuse to get drunk and misbehave—usually in and around Piazza San Marco.) Get your mask and costume from **Nicolao Atelier** (Calle del Magazin, Cannaregio 5590/a; ☎ 041-5209749), the city's largest costume supplier. If you make a prior appointment, you can also visit the workshop, where you can see costumes being sewn. Another option is the historical costumes for sale and rent at **Atelier Pietro Longhi** (San Polo 2580; ☎ 041-714478; www.pietrolonghi.com), close to the Frari church. If you're not up for getting into full drag, you can always settle for a *corno dogale,* one of the princely skullcaplike hats that Venice's doges wore; and there are wigs too.

are the **Column of San Marco** (topped by a creature suspiciously resembling the winged lion of St. Mark in bronze) and the **Column of San Teodoro** (topped by a marble statue of the city's original patron saint standing on the sacred crocodile of Egypt). In less civilized times (when capital punishment still prevailed in Europe; it has since been abolished throughout), open-air executions were carried out between these two columns. Public humiliations and other extreme punishments were also meted out here; even today, locals superstitiously refuse to walk between the two columns.

As you stand between these columns with your back to the lagoon, you'll be looking along the length of the **Piazzetta San Marco,** with the **Palazzo Ducale (Doge's Palace)** on its right, and the **Biblioteca Marciana (Libreria Sansoviniana)**—capped by a series of statues of gods from antiquity—on its left. Head straight through the *piazzetta,* toward the Basilica until you pass the tall, rather ordinary-looking (brick-face) bell tower, or **campanile;** Piazza San Marco is the pigeon-and-tourist-covered concourse that stretches out behind the tower.

To best appreciate the Basilica, head for the middle of the square, which is actually trapezoidal and enclosed on three sides by arcaded wings. As you stand and face the Basilica, you will have the **Procuratie Vecchie** on your left, the **Procuratie Nuove** on your right. Behind you is the **Ala Napoleonica,** built by Bonaparte to house a ballroom; today it forms part of the Museo Correr, which includes an impressive picture gallery. The ground floors of these buildings are mostly occupied by shops and expensive cafes.

During the occupation of Venice, Austrian officers gathered at **Grand Caffè Quadri** in the Vecchie, while Venetians favored **Caffè Florian** across the way; today, such political rivalry has been replaced by a more melodic battle in which the quartets and quintets of the rival cafes play competing renditions of stirring classics and Andrew Lloyd Webber favorites.

At one end of the Procuratie Vecchie (toward the Basilica) is the 15th-century **Torre dell'Orologio (Clock Tower),** which marks the entrance to the **Mercerie,** a back-alley tangle of shops that is always clogged with tourists.

Basilica di San Marco (St. Mark's Basilica) ★★★ (☎ 041-5225205; go to www.alata.it for preferential entrance through St. Peter's Door; free; Mon–Sat 9:45am–5pm, Sun 2–4pm) has a history infused with pirate-style adventure. In 828, the remains of St. Mark the Evangelist were smuggled out of Egypt in a cask—some say it was filled with pickled pork, others wine, but whatever the substance, it was enough to deter Muslim guards from searching the cask, paving the way for one of the greatest heists in the history of Christianity. All this chicanery is actually recorded in one of the 17th-century mosaics above the entrance (see if you can spot it on the right). Fanciful as the story sounds, St.

> **"** Venice is like eating an entire box of chocolate liqueurs in one go. **"**
>
> —Truman Capote

Mark—who had foreseen Venice as his final resting place in a vision—became the city's patron saint; if you cast your eyes to the very top of the central arch above the facade, you'll see a 15th-century statue of him, attended by angels. Also above the entrance are four horses, which are actually replicas of another stolen treasure, the Quadriga gilded bronze horses stowed today inside the Basilica.

The first church on this site burned down in the 9th century. The second version was torn down so that, during the 11th century, a far more flamboyant church could be built in direct imitation of Constantinople's Basilica of the Apostles. The main structure was built according to a Greek cross plan; the Oriental additions—perhaps most evident to the untrained eye in the five bulbous, onion-capped domes of the roof—remind me of Venice's connection with Byzantium. It grew and grew over the years, to be aptly nicknamed the "Golden Church," largely thanks to the endless plunder brought back from the Orient by Venice's thrifty marine fleet. Everything from columns to capitals to friezes were filched and used for the steady upgrade of the church. Of course, the building didn't exactly suffer from local neglect, and the ongoing attempts of various wealthy nobles to outdonate each other also contributed to the immense wealth of the Basilica.

For real gilt-edged sensory overload, join the queue and step inside. The visual decadence within the most riveting and spectacularly confusing church in the

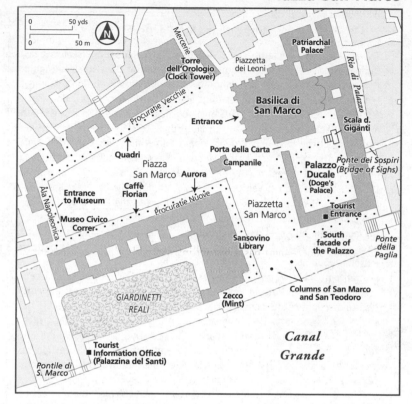

world is a must-see. The queue for the Basilica may be long, but it usually moves at a steady pace; be prepared by keeping shoulders and knees covered—this is a house of worship, after all, and you'll be scanned, briefly, for modesty, as you enter. **Note:** If you have brought large bags (particularly backpacks) with you, follow the signs to the left-luggage facility.

Once you're allowed inside, study the **mosaics on the ceiling** of the atrium to the right of the entrance; scenes from the Creation cover the cupola. In the **Zen Chapel,** the life of St. Mark is depicted in a series of 13th-century mosaics.

Just beyond the main entrance, on your immediate right as you enter the atrium, look for the steep stairway marked **Loggia dei Cavalli;** note that you'll be charged 3€ when you get to the top. This fee is for admission to the **Galleria della Basilica,** from which you can enjoy a quite enchanting bird's-eye view of the Basilica's interior, and get a closer look at some of the ceiling mosaics; in more prudish times these high-up, out-of-the-way vantage points would have served as the women's gallery.

Adjoining the gallery is the **Museo Marciano** (daily 10am–4pm), where the real Quadriga **bronze horses** are kept. Although their origin is believed to predate Byzantium, the statues were stolen from Constantinople's Hippodrome in 1204 when Venice took part in the Fourth Crusade. Also adjoining the gallery is the balcony above the entrance to the church; from here you can look across the

What's in the Cards?

The city has two **museum cards.** The **San Marco Museum** ticket is a no-brainer good buy, since it's required for entry to the Doge's Palace (again: this is the most important paying attraction in Venice, so don't miss it), but includes all the museums around Piazza San Marco (12€, Nov–Mar). *Note:* From April to October the San Marco Museum ticket becomes the **San Marco Museum Plus** ticket; for an additional 1€ (so 13€ in total), you can visit all the museums around Piazza San Marco *plus* one other civic museum. The second ticket, the **Museum Pass** (18€ adult), additionally gets you into Ca' Pesaro (the city's modern-art museum), Ca' Rezzonica (the museum of 17th-c. Venice), Palazzo Mocenigo (the costume museum), the Museo del Vetro (Murano's glass museum), and the Museo del Merletto (Burano's lace museum). The pass is only recommended if you're in town for more than 2 days—the chances of getting to the lesser museums if you have only 2 days are slim; and, as you know, there is more to Venice than museum hopping.

Neither card is worthwhile for people under 30, who pay less and benefit more from the **Rolling Venice Card.** For a mere 4€, holders are entitled to discounts at numerous attractions, restaurants, hotels, events, and shops across the city. They're even able to buy 3-day public boat tickets for just 18€. The card is valid for an entire year, and can be bought at any tourist office, as well as at certain ACTV Ve.La offices and ticket kiosks; pick one up at the ACTV office at Piazzale Roma upon arrival in the city (☎ 041-2747650; daily 7am–8pm).

Finally, for visitors planning an intensive look at Venice, there's a series of comprehensive discount cards called **VENICEcard** (☎ 041-2424; www.venicecard.it)—at its most basic (Blue) level it gets you free public transport and public toilet access (usually 1€) for varying periods of time, while the heftier (Orange) version includes entrance to civic museums and 16 chargeable churches. I'm not entirely convinced that you can make either work all that well for your pocket unless you're absolutely bingeing on museums and churches; and, quite frankly, if you turn you Venice trip into a sightseeing marathon you'll rob yourself of the chance to truly savor being in Venice. So, make careful calculation before ordering the card, which you can do online. The organizers of the discount card advertise that you can save up to 30€ per day, with the card, but you'll have to use it for accommodations, all restaurants, theater performances, and every sight in town to achieve that level of savings.

piazza and experience the crowds the way Venetian doges once did as they presided over important events that took place in the piazza below.

Returning downstairs via the same narrow stairway, turn right to go into the bosom of the Basilica, an enchanting, cavernous space lit by candles and decorated to every last inch with mosaics, frescoes, statuary, marble, and religious artifacts. Beneath you, the lavish mosaic floor is warped with age, spilling out as a dramatic tapestry of patterns and scenes; meanwhile, far above, the domed ceiling glistens with gold leaf, particularly when the midday sun penetrates what few windows there are. Over the center of the church is the Ascension Dome, decorated by a 13th-century mosaic of Christ in Glory.

Deeper into the church, toward the right, is the **Tesoro (Treasury;** 2€), with its small (though priceless) exhibition of the Basilica's most important treasures; a difficult-to-follow audioguide is included in the admission. This is also where the actual bones, teeth, and other relics of various doges and saints are kept, so some of it's a little grisly.

More worthwhile is a visit to the **Sanctuary** (1.50€), where the main altar is believed to be built over the remains of St. Mark. Alabaster columns, carved with **New Testament scenes,** support the green-marble *baldacchino* (canopy) raised high above the altar. But the main reason to visit the Sanctuary is to have access to the 10th-century **Pala D'Oro;** perhaps the greatest treasure in the Basilica, it's a spectacular screen featuring 255 panels painted on gold foil and framed by silver gilt. The screen is further embellished with precious stones and pearls, but is incomplete thanks to some petty theft by Napoleon.

Before leaving the Basilica—which you should visit more than once—take time to meditate in the **Cappella della Madonna di Nicopeia,** on the far left side of the church. Here, the pews face the Altar of the Virgin with its valuable Madonna of Nicopeia icon. That image of the Madonna is believed to have protected Venice in times of war. The icon itself was pillaged from Constantinople, where it had long served as protection for the Byzantine army.

The other great sight off Piazza San Marco is the magnificent **Palazzo Ducale (Doge's Palace)** ✪✪✪ (Piazza San Marco; ☎ 041-5209070; www. museicivicivenezian.it; 13€; daily Apr–Oct 9am–7pm, Nov–Mar 9am–5pm). Passing through the vast array of rooms and halls here is like being transported to another age; unfortunately, you may have to struggle against large groups of people to really get into the spirit of things. Your best bet is to try to get inside the monument the moment it opens and avoid the crowds simply by staying ahead of them.

The Architecture of Venice

Venice's buildings rest on flexible but immensely sturdy foundations made of pine and oak piles, driven into the layers of sand and clay at the bottom of the lagoon. These wooden piles are packed closely together in order to form a solid enough base on which the brick or stone buildings can rest. While the water of Venice served as a natural defense against invaders, making the construction of genuine fortresses unnecessary, it also meant that the structures were always damp inside. This is why there is seldom much happening on the ground floor of canal-side buildings; not only was this a place to load and offload boatfuls of people and supplies, but the open arcades served as "breathing room" for the entire building.

Once you've gotten through the ticket turnstiles (and I repeat: do this early), turn right and head directly for **The Golden Staircase,** which will take you into the heart of the place (you can return to study the courtyard later). Gilt-painted, this ceremonial stairway (1559) leads to the myriad government chambers and the Doge's Apartments.

Bear in mind that the palace was constructed to serve several functions; not only was it the seat of government and the place where Venice's exhausting bureaucracy—er, administration—was carried out, but it was also the home of the doge and a ceremonial palace for receiving foreign dignitaries. The flamboyant, over-the-top decoration of the staircase and numerous official rooms was really a form of frivolous-yet-functional showing off, whereby the glory and might of the Venetian Republic was rubbed solidly in the eyes of all visitors. It's up this staircase that ambassadors and emissaries would be led en route to meet with the doge and his officials.

Other architectural details serve as compensation for size (Venice, in anyone's terms, was tiny, but had a gigantic image to project, so had to find ways of compensating); when you look at the upper levels of the palace from the courtyard, for example, note how clever design and large shuttered windows create the impression of regal, high-ceilinged floors, while in actual fact, they are a disguise for two floors of cramped offices.

The first landing off the Golden Staircase leads to the Doge's Apartments; including the **Scarlet Chamber**—restored in 2005, with a rediscovered painting by Carpaccio. Beyond this is the **Sala delle Mappe (Hall of Maps),** housing off-kilter cartographic murals of the 16th-century world, with Venice at its center, of course. This section of the palace gives some idea of the doges' domestic environment; the **Erizzo Room**—with its patterned silk-covered walls—is not unlike the styling of many of Venice's three-star hotel rooms. The adjacent **Grimani Room** features **paintings of the city's iconic winged lion,** including Carpaccio's *The Lion of St. Mark* (1516); note how the lion's front legs rest on land while the hind legs are on the sea, signaling Venetian dominion over both. While on this floor, find the **Philosopher's Room** and ask for directions to Titian's *St. Christopher,* a fresco completed in just 3 days (it's hidden above a doorway).

Glorious **works of art** decorate the official spaces upstairs, as well; here the city's masters—including **Veronese, Tintoretto,** and **Titian**—are spectacularly represented. In the official waiting room, or **Anticollegio,** foreign emissaries would gaze on Paolo Veronese's *Rape of Europa* while waiting to meet their hosts. Veronese's allegorical paintings glorifying Venice adorn the **Chamber of the Full Council.** In the adjoining **Sala del Senato (Senate Chamber)**—where 300 members would meet to listen to reports and debate major issues (and no doubt gossip)—different renditions of Christ by Tintoretto, create the impression that the singular role of the Lord was to protect the doge, and—by inference—Venice itself. On the ceiling is Tintoretto's *Triumph of Venice* (1587–97), a beautiful exercise in forced perspective, with earth in the distance, beyond the heavenly scene. For the best view of this ceiling fresco, stand near the doorway leading into the **Sala della Quatro Ponte.** From here you can pass through quickly into the **Chambers of the Council of Ten,** where judgments were once uttered against an accused, and which features more work by Veronese. In the adjoining **Sala della**

Venice's Great Lover

The most famous convict ever to cross the Bridge of Sighs into Venice's state prisons was Giacomo Girolamo Casanova, he of bodice-ripping world renown. Casanova, who earned universal recognition as an erotic hero who made love to incomparable numbers of women (122 of these adventures are recounted in his feisty, and undoubtedly exaggerated, autobiography), was actually busy with a great many activities other than satisfying his libidinal desires. Born in 1725 to theatrical parents, he was a sickly child who demonstrated considerable intellectual prowess. Between womanizing and boozing, he managed to earn a doctorate from the University of Padua but dropped plans he once had to join the priesthood.

Frequently afflicted with all manner of sexually transmitted diseases, he built a prominent public image, traveling through Europe and consorting with nobles, royals, and noteworthies—despite attempts by the Inquisition to challenge his moral virtue. After the love of his life, a Frenchwoman named Henriette, abandoned him, the heartbroken stud took up a career as a writer, which was cut short when he was convicted as a magician and placed in the prisons of the Palazzo Ducale. Apparently, Casanova managed to escape the supposedly impenetrable prisons, and later claimed to have slept with the chief of police's wife on the very same night that her husband was out searching for him!

After fleeing to Paris, Casanova's celebrity was much increased; he introduced the lottery to the French capital and made himself a millionaire through gambling and cheating. Always pursued by creditors, Casanova turned to spying in his later years, and eventually ended up as a librarian in Bohemia, where he set about putting his memoirs on paper. Venice practically ignored one of its most famous sons for years until finally, in the 1990s, the city hosted a Casanova exhibition, with only the smallest attention given to his most celebrated talent—as the world's original Casanova, the ultimate "Italian stallion."

Bussola, a secret wooden stairway entrance leads to every floor in the palace. The room itself is dedicated to justice, and it was here that Venice's version of the CIA met to discuss matters of state security.

An extensive **armory** fills the next few rooms followed by the L-shaped *liagò* (raised platform), where you'll find a pair of marble sculptures of Adam and Eve by Antonio Rizzo. From the liagò, enter the **Sala del Maggior Consiglio (Hall of the Great Council),** which houses the largest oil painting on earth, Tintoretto's 23m (75-ft.) *Paradiso,* above the seat occupied by the doge during sessions of the council. And above you, on the ceiling, is Veronese again, his *Triumph of Venice.*

At the far end of the hall, you'll next see a long frieze of portraits of the Republic's first 76 doges. Look carefully, and you'll spot one faceless portrait—a

The Secret Life of the Doges

If there's one Venetian encounter worthy of a splurge, it's the Palazzo Ducale **Secret Itineraries tour** ✫✫✫ (bookings by phone ☎ 041-5209070 or at the ticket office; 16€). Led by an expert on Venetian history and culture, the tour takes a small group of visitors to some of the many rooms in the palace that are kept locked to the general public; these are the secret chambers, passages, and stairways that allowed the machinery of the Venetian state to keep working independent of the luxury show that greeted official visitors to the palace. The tour reveals how the doge was always under scrutiny and supervised by an all-powerful Council of Ten, despite being personally responsible for the upkeep of the palace. You'll also discover how Venice thrived on secrets, how spies and diplomats gathered valuable information from rival states, and how documents recording this information were kept—in triplicate—in the offices and halls of the palace.

For many, the highlight of the tour is learning more about Casanova, who escaped from the prisons here after blackmailing his guard and enlisting the aid of a priest who had been imprisoned for fathering a string of children. The tour also introduces you to clever psychological tortures: Prisoners were strategically jailed where they could see and hear terrible violence being done to another accused offender—this ensured that those next in line for the same punishment would confess more readily. You'll not only explore those secret rooms where the state machinery was operated by an army of bookkeepers and administrators, but—in the roof over the largest room in the palace—you'll get a sense of the complex architectural solutions keeping it all together.

black veil covers the face of Doge Marin Falier, who was executed for treason against the state and consequently dishonored by having his image defaced. The portraits, which continue in the adjoining **Sala dello Scrutinio,** are also by Domenico Tintoretto.

Make your way next to the **Chamber of the Magistrato alle Leggi** (follow signs for the prison), where legal regulations were considered and decided by a special council. Here you'll see Hieronymus Bosch's particularly spooky depiction of *Hell,* as well as his idea of *Heaven*—a tunnel of white light much like that reported by people who claim to have died and returned to life. Having thus had a sense of the spaces in which Venice's government authorities operated, you can now try to imagine yourself a condemned prisoner by crossing the **Ponte dei Sospiri (Bridge of Sighs).** This is where convicts on their way to the prisons said farewell to freedom and headed to lengthy internment or execution. At some point, you may feel lost in a tangle of cells and passages (it's almost worryingly mazelike), but just follow the arrows and you'll eventually reach the **Sala dei Censori (Chamber of Censors),** where the city's small council of moral consultants met. Also worth visiting around Piazza San Marco: Rooms of the **Museo Civico Correr** ★ (Sottoportego San Geminian, in the Procuratie Nuove's Ala Napoleonica, Piazza San Marco; ☎ 041-2405211; included in San Marco Museum ticket; Apr–Oct 9am–7pm, Nov–Mar 10am–5pm) display a broad array of art and memorabilia related to the culture of Venice. Starting with the androgynous angels of the neoclassical sculptor Antonia Canova, the tour goes into 20 rooms of historical items like coins, rare manuscripts, furniture, busts, paintings, and early maps of the city (just in case you thought getting around Venice is difficult today), always highlighting the line of doges as key figures in the city's proud history.

A highlight of the tour is the air-conditioned **Quadreria picture gallery** ★★ on the second floor. Though not in the same league as the Accademia (p. 318), it provides a useful understanding of how Venetian painting developed through Byzantine, Gothic, and Renaissance periods. Among the standout artworks is Cosmé Tura's *Pietà,* a Mannerist painting (from around 1460), in which Christ is represented as an old man. Mannerism emerged as a counterreaction to the careful balance and proportion of the High Renaissance; artists sought to deliberately distort physical proportions and use irrational space to generate an emotional effect. Although the movement is more directly associated with Rome, Florence, and Mantua, the artists of Venice also pursued their own Mannerist course, and this is evidenced in the distinctive styles of Titian, Jacopo, Tintoretto, and visiting Greek artist Domenikos Theotokopoulos, known as El Greco (their works are in Room 41).

The magnificent **Torre dell'Orologio (Clock Tower)** ★★ is once again in action and on view, consistently pulling focus from the Basilica after being hidden behind renovators' scaffolding for a number of years. Terribly photogenic, with its Renaissance clock face displaying the signs of the zodiac and indicating the phases of the sun and the moon, the central part of the tower was designed by Mauro Coducci in 1496, and is topped by a pair of bronze Moors that strike the giant bell hourly. It's more than enough simply to gaze at the clock from the outside, but if you want to literally get inside the mechanics of the thing, you can arrange for a guided tour, but only by prior arrangement (☎ 041-5209070; 12€). Back across the square, many more tourists will be queuing up all day long to catch the elevator to the top of the rather humble-looking **Campanile di San Marco (St. Mark's Bell Tower)** ★, which affords a 360-degree view of the city. Visitors travel up almost 100m (328 ft.) to the bell stage, where you can squeeze your way into position for a unique look at the city in splendid panorama. Originally built in the 12th century, the bell tower functioned as a beacon for passing ships; in 1609, Galileo used it to demonstrate his telescope to a group of local politicians. In 1902 it actually collapsed and was rebuilt exactly as it had been a decade later. On May 9, 1997, eight armed men claiming to be "soldiers of the serenissima Venetian government" used a truck to break down the campanile gates so they could climb the stairs to the top and hoist the flag of St. Mark, claiming that they wished to revive the republic, some 200 years after its demise. Needless to say, their attempt failed and they were less than popular with local authorities.

If the line at the campanile is daunting, skip it and hop aboard vaporetto ⑧② to San Giorgio instead, an island just one stop from San Marco, where you can visit the **Church of San Giorgio Maggiore** ★★★ (☎ 041-5227827; free; Mon–Sat

It's Not Over Till the Fat Lady Sings

Venice was home to Italy's very first opera house, the Teatro di San Cassiano (1637), which gave way to the glorious **Teatro La Fenice (Phoenix Theater)** ★★★ (Campo San Fantin; ☎ 041-786575; www.teatrolafenice.it; 7€ includes audioguide; daily 10am–6pm) in the 18th century. Celebrated as one of the world's great indoor opera spaces, the lavish arena had an unfortunate history of burning to the ground; in 1996—160 years after the last such disaster—the world mourned when the Phoenix was once again gutted by fire; courts found two lackadaisical electricians guilty of arson (although mafia links have not been ruled out; read John Berendt's *The City of Falling Angels* for the whole intriguing saga). Those two are now sitting in prison, while—after years of painstaking redesigning, hard labor, and attention to decorative and fire-safety details—La Fenice is once again staging world-class performances. Reconstruction was based on plans by architect Aldo Rossi, who died before the project was complete, but who added a massive basement with water tanks designed to prevent future pyrotechnic disasters.

Much of the finer detailing of the theater's interior was re-created using close analysis of Visconti's first color film, *Senso* (1953); the first 10 minutes were shot inside La Fenice. Enter the 1,076-seat auditorium, and you're immediately struck by the glint of 24-karat gold leaf; around 1,672 sq. m (18,000 sq. ft.) of it was used throughout the building, most of it in the auditorium, where it sets off the frescoed floating cherubs and mermaidlike busts protruding from just beneath the ceiling. Above the velveteen Molteni seats, a massive chandelier hangs as if in homage to that famous scene in *Phantom of the Opera*. The reconstruction cost in excess of 50 million euros. If you're at all attracted to theater, dance, and opera, attend a performance here (see "Nightlife," later in this chapter).

9:30am–12:30pm and 2:30–6pm, Sun 2–6:30pm). The top of its **bell tower** (3€) is far less crowded than St. Mark's and it affords views of the *entire city* as well as the lagoon; on clear days you can see the white tips of the Dolomites in the far distance. The church itself has a rich collection of paintings by Jacopo Tintoretto, including several collaborations with Domenico. My favorite is his *Martyrdom of Saints Cosma and Damiano* (1592), because of its unusual composition; amid the near jumble of flesh-bound humanity, notice how the saints' glowing haloes draw your eye to the heroes in the piece.

ATTRACTIONS IN DORSODURO

The **Gallerie dell'Accademia (Accademia Gallery)** ★★★ (Campo della Carità, Dorsoduro 1050; ☎ 041-5222247; 6.50€; Tues–Sun 8:15am–7:15pm, Mon 8:15am–2pm) holds the world's most important collection of Venetian art.

Ironically, the world has Napoleon to thank for this splendid collection; the impressive display was moved here in 1807, when Bonaparte closed down the church and took over the oldest of the city's six Scuole Grande (confraternity halls), packing the building with a formidable inventory of artistic plunder from churches around the city. A detailed study of the works—displayed more or less in chronological order—gives great insight into those qualities that distinguish the different stylistic epochs, from the 13th through 18th centuries.

Among the many masterworks you'll view are early-Renaissance masters Jacopo Bellini and his sons, Giovanni and Gentile (**Room 2** primarily) and Vittore Carpaccio, whose *Crucifixion and Apotheosis of the Ten Thousand Martyrs of Mount Ararat* (1515) is a standout favorite (you'll swear the artist tried to include all 10,000 willing victims).

In addition, there are Giorgione's stirring studies of humanity, *La Tempesta* and *La Vecchia,* which broke ground in their use of landscape to amplify atmosphere. For many, however, the highlights of the Accademia are the works by Titian, who is not much represented in other galleries or museums in Venice; you'll encounter his work in **rooms 6, 10, and 13,** alongside paintings by Tintoretto and Veronese (Titian's *Pietà* is especially noteworthy for its almost Impressionistic quality). Be sure to carefully scan Paolo Veronese's *Feast in the House of Levi* (1573, **Room 10**), which was commissioned as *The Last Supper,* but was considered so defamatory that the artist was hauled before the Inquisition and ordered to remove details that were thought to corrupt the biblical event; clearly, he didn't comply. Baroque paintings (often by non-native Venetians) occupy **Room 11.**

Size matters in **Room 20,** where massive canvases by Carpaccio, Mansueti, and Gentile Bellini depict some of the major religious-historic events that have affected Venice. The work of Vittore Carpaccio (1460–1526) fills **Room 21;** the nine remarkable studies are from a series depicting the legend of St. Ursula transposed into 15th-century Venice. Your tour of the Accademia ends in the **Sala dell'Albergo.** Titian's *Presentation of the Virgin at the Temple* is the masterpiece beneath the gilded ceiling.

To get the most out of the gallery, join one of the **guided tours** (Tues–Sun 11am–noon; 3€ per person, 4€ for two people, 1€ children 6–14).

Directions: You can take a vaporetto, getting off at the second-to-last stop before the Grand Canal spills out into the lagoon. Alternatively, if you're walking from any point in San Marco, you'll see plenty of signs indicating the way to Accademia. Take the bridge spanning the Grand Canal and linking San Marco to Dorsduro; on the other side, you'll walk almost directly into the gallery. *Photo op:* Don't forget to get up on top of the Accademia bridge, from where you'll drink in some of the most iconic images of Venice, the Grand Canal, and the lagoon.

Dorsoduro is filled with art galleries where you can buy originals and prints by contemporary artists, but for lovers of modern art, there's nothing to beat a visit to the world-class **Collezione Peggy Guggenheim** ★★★ (Calle San Cristoforo, Dorsoduro 701; ☎ 041-2405411; www.guggenheim-venice.it; 10€; Wed–Mon 10am–6pm). One of the world's finest private art collections, it is housed in the unfinished one-story Palazzo Venier dei Leoni, which Guggenheim purchased in 1948. You enter Peggy's home by way of the **Nasher Sculpture Garden,** which includes works by Ernst, Giacometti, Henry Moore, and Jean Arp. It's here that the patron's ashes are interred along with the many dogs she owned. Her museum surveys the major art movements of the 20th century; there are over 300 pieces in the permanent collection alone.

Introduced to modern art by Marcel Duchamp (whose work is on display here), Ms. Guggenheim at one stage set out to buy one artwork every day. Determined to protect and nurture the work of her contemporaries, she gathered a major collection. She poured energy (and money) into artists she believed in, collecting some of them as lovers, or even—in the case of Max Ernst—as a husband.

The collection includes groundbreaking works by international superstars: In the Surrealist Room, Dalí's contemplation of his own sexual awakening, evidently out of his anxiety resulting from fear of castration by his father *(Birth of Liquid Desires)* hangs next to Joan Miró's somber, hallucinatory *Seated Woman II*. René Magritte's famous simultaneous evocation of night and day in *Empire of Light* also shares the space. And so it goes . . . a house full of Ernst, Dalí, Miró, Picasso, Constantin Brancusi, Marc Chagall, Piet Mondrian, Jackson Pollock, and other innovators of modern art, laid out with a deep respect for the effect the different styles tend to have on the viewer. There are also several rooms dedicated to Italian innovators, like the futurist Gino Severini and little-known Mario Sironi.

An excellent **audioguide** (5€) is available; it's narrated by the gallery's director and forcefully presents details that bring the works and their relationship to Ms. Guggenheim to life. Better still, try to join one of the **free guided tours** (☎ 041-2405440) presented from time to time.

There's an attractive art and gift shop attached to the Guggenheim, well worth a visit (see "Attention, Shoppers!" later in this chapter).

For a peek into the lavish home environments of 18th-century Venetian nobility, visit **Ca' Rezzonico** (Fondamenta Rezzonico, Dorsoduro 3136; ☎ 041-2410100; 6.50€; Apr–Oct Wed–Mon 10am–6pm, Nov–Mar 10am–5pm), a gorgeous palazzo that now serves as the Museo del Settecento Veneziano (Museum of 18th-Century Venice). Palazzo Rezzonica was co-designed by Baldassare Longhena, who cut his architectural teeth on La Salute church (below). In later years it was home to the poet Robert Browning, who lived here until his death in 1889. The museum gives visitors some idea of the material and artistic beauty that Venetian

The Cursed Palace

Next door to Palazzo Vernier dei Leoni is one of Venice's most gossiped-about buildings, the Palazzo Dario. Believed to be cursed, it's also considered the city's most haunted abode. Gabriele D'Annunzio, who lived across the Grand Canal, described it as "a decrepit courtesan, bowed beneath the pomp of her baubles." Ca' Dario was built in 1486 by Giovanni Dario; it supposedly brings outrageously bad luck to anyone who lives there, tragedy often spilling over into murder and suicide. As recently as 1992, the curse apparently moved the owner to shoot himself. Woody Allen was considering purchasing the empty-standing property until he heard of its mysterious reputation and abandoned his plan.

Church Hopping

Avid church enthusiasts should purchase a **Chorus Pass** (☎ 041-2750462; www.chorusvenezia.org) admitting them to a large number of Venetian churches for 8€ per adult (16€ per family). This brings about significant savings when you consider that each church usually charges 2.50€ for entry. *Note:* A few important churches do not participate, so consider carefully before buying a pass; the 16 churches covered by the pass are Santa Maria del Giglio, Sant Stefano, Santa Maria Formosa, Santa Maria dei Miracoli, San Giovanni Elemosinario, San Polo, Santa Maria Gloriosa dei Frari, San Giacomo dall'Orio, San Stae, Sant'Alvise, Madonna dell'Orto, San Pietro di Castello, Santissimo Redentore, Santa Maria del Rosario (Gesuati), San Sebastiano, and San Giobbe.

---

aristocrats lavished upon themselves. The baroque ballroom certainly conjures up images of all-night debauchery under a magnificent frescoed ceiling by the artist Crosato; there are more ceiling frescoes by Tiepolo in the salons, along with a portrait gallery. Amid the Tiepolos, Vivarinis, Longhis, and Tintorettos are amusing renderings of daily life that provide insight into the very different worldviews of noble and working-class Venetians.

Toward the tip of Dorsoduro, where the Grand Canal flows into the lagoon, directly across the waters from Piazza San Marco, there's almost always a group of tourists relaxing on the steps of the imposing **Santa Maria della Salute** ★ (Campo della Salute, Dorsoduro; ☎ 041-2743928; www.marcianum.it; free; daily 9am–noon and 3:30–6pm). La Salute, as it's known, has its own vaporetto launch, so it's easy to visit. The 17th-century baroque church—built on an octagonal plan—commemorates the city's deliverance from the plague, and honors La Salute, the Virgin Mary of Good Health.

At the other end of Dorsoduro, along the border with San Polo, is Campo San Pantalon, site of unfairly overlooked **San Pantaleone Church** (☎ 041-5235893; free; Mon–Sat 8–10am and 4–6pm), which has what I regard as one of the most beautifully frescoed ceilings in Venice, depicting the martyrdom of San Pantaleone. The saint was a court doctor who was beheaded; ironically, the artist responsible for the ceiling is said to have fallen from the scaffolding where he spent some 24 years completing it, and died.

ACROSS THE GUIDECCA CANAL

Giudecca has often been associated with isolation and banishment; it's where problematic citizens have been sent to cool off, where the sick have been quarantined to prevent the spread of plague, and where Michelangelo spent time in exile from Florence. Despite a somewhat run-down appearance (many of its factories have long stood abandoned), its north-facing promenade offers superb views back toward Venice, and its ghostly quiet neighborhoods make for sublime exploration—largely because they've long been fairly devoid of tourists.

But things are changing thanks to the hotels and hostels popping up here. The island's most worthwhile architectural visit, Palladio's **Santissimo Redentore** (☎ 041-2750642; 2.50€, free with Chorus Pass; Mon–Sat 10am–5pm, Sun 1–5pm) was commissioned to celebrate the end of the plague that struck Venice in 1575. The church, with its massive dome and classical facade topped by statuary figures that seem always to be giving thanks, is the most prominent building on the island; inside are paintings by Tintoretto and Veronese. Farther east is another church by Palladio, the comparatively miniscule **La Zitelle;** I'm told that Elton John owns the "small" yellow house right next door.

ATTRACTIONS IN SAN POLO & SANTA CROCE: THE RIALTO & BEYOND

Legend has it that the **Rialto** is where the very idea of Venice began; it was on this high bank *(rivo alto)* that some of the first settlers sought a new life. Today, the **Ponte di Rialto (Rialto Bridge),** which delivers tourists and locals to the city's famous markets, is geographically more or less in the very center of the city. Linking the *sestieri* (districts) of San Marco with San Polo, it's one of only four bridges spanning the Grand Canal. Lined with shops and practically always flooded with tourists, the existing bridge was constructed of stone after the original wooden bridge repeatedly collapsed.

The **Rialto Markets** have stood at Venice's economic center for nearly 1,000 years, and they remain an interesting early-morning outing for those interested in watching the daily jostle for fish and other fresh produce. Frankly, once the crowds arrive and clog up the area around the souvenir stands, the Rialto can become a nightmare experience. Instead head straight for the fascinating *pescaria* **(fish market),** open early (when all the action happens) and catering to the city's myriad seafood eateries; it's a great place to ogle freakishly unusual sea creatures.

Also around the Rialto are a few **churches worth investigating.** Closest to the Rialto Bridge is **San Giacomo di Rialto** (Campo San Giacomo; ☎ 041-5224745; free; Mon–Sat 9:30am–noon and 4–6pm), purportedly the city's oldest church, founded on March 25, A.D. 421—the same day as Venice itself. Of course, what you see today is a far more recent construction. Not too far from the Rialto, and surprisingly little visited, is **San Silvestro** ★ (Campo San Silvestro; ☎ 041-5238090; free; Mon–Sat 7:30–11:30am and 4–6pm), mostly interesting for two wonderfully juxtaposed paintings: Tintoretto's *Baptism of Christ* and Girolamo di Santacroce's earlier *St. Thomas à Beckett Enthroned* (1520). Notice how the latter suggests the artist's overt obsession with creating depth through forced perspective techniques (the checkerboard floor, the diminished landscape background), while Tintoretto's interest is almost purely in conveying emotion through his treatment of the human form.

While in San Polo, another church worthy of your time is **San Cassiano** (Campo San Cassiano; ☎ 041-721408; free; Mon–Sat 9:45–11:30am and 4:30–7pm), reached by heading northwest out of the Rialto market area (back toward the fish market). Inside is Tintoretto's magnificent rendition of *The Crucifixion.* Campo San Cassiano was once the center of Venice's red-light district, and many of the buildings around this part of the Rialto area were once brothels; women for hire would lean from windows and beckon lasciviously to potential clients passing below. Some joke that the nearby Ponte delle Tette (which literally means "Bridge of the Roofs," but sounds a little crude in English) is named after that display.

Just north of San Cassiano, large signs hand-painted on the walls will let you know where San Polo ends and Santa Croce begins; there are two attractions in the latter area that will appeal to the museum-goer. First up, fronted by the Grand Canal, is **Ca' Pésaro, the International Gallery of Modern Art** ★★ (Fondamenta Ca' Pesaro, Santa Croce 2070; ☎ 041-5241173; 5.50€; Tues–Sun Apr–Oct 10am–6pm, Nov–Mar 10am–5pm), with an enjoyable selection of modern and contemporary art principally by relatively unknown Italians. It offers a handsome overview of the range of developments in Italian painting and sculpture in the modern age. If you're only interested in big names, you'll find a few of those here, too, with mostly unheralded works from international masters, including the likes of Klimt, Kandinsky, Klee, Miró, Matisse, Jean Arp, Marc Chagall, and Max Ernst. But it's a better place to concentrate on the lesser Italian artists: the unfathomable sculptures of Medardo Rosso; the strange, ghostlike nudes of Cesare Laurenti; and Felice Casorati's humorous depiction of the banal.

Right around the corner from Cà Pesaro, and almost never visited (the ticket officer has assured me of this), is **Palazzo Mocenigo** ★ (Salizzada San Stae, Santa Croce 1992; ☎ 041-721798; 4€; Tues–Sun Apr–Oct 10am–5pm, Nov–Mar 10am–4pm), where you're forced to ask yourself where kitsch begins and ends in a city with so much rococo and baroque. Here's another opportunity to get a sense of the decadent Venetian home interiors of the 18th century. Formerly the residence of a family that bred seven doges, it was left to the city by Count Alvise Nicolò Mocenigo, who died a half century ago, the last in his family line; today it's a costume and textile museum (which explains the general lack of public interest) that's worth a look if only for its opulent rooms.

Western San Polo: The Frari & Environs

Scuola Grande di San Rocco (Confraternity of St. Roch) ★★★ (Campo San Rocco, San Polo; ☎ 041-5234864; www.scuolagrandesanrocco.it; 5.50€; Mar 28–Nov 2 daily 9am–5:30pm, Nov 3–Mar 27 daily 10am–4pm), is Venice's most important guild hall, and home to some extraordinary works by Jacopo Tintoretto. The **lower gallery** features paintings dedicated to the Virgin Mary; here, in the dramatic *Slaughter of the Innocents,* notice how the bravery of the women gives a feminist edge to Tintoretto's work. Executed at a time when he was grieving the loss of one of his children, the painting seems to capture the personal torment and anxiety of the artist. Upstairs, in the Sala Grande (Great Hall), the work that's commonly referred to as "Tintoretto's Sistine Chapel" impresses. Vivid scenes from the Old Testament grace the ceiling, while New Testament images cover the walls; the hall is dominated by the central ceiling image of *The Miracle of the Bronze Serpent,* which suggests parallels between the afflicted, snake-bitten Israelites and the victims of Venice's plague (1575–76), when the city called upon St. Roch for aid. In contrast with other Venetians artists of the time, Tintoretto opted for darker tones, downplaying the use of color in order to evoke an atmosphere of somber spiritual contemplation. John Ruskin probably said it best when he called Tintoretto's *La Crocifissione (Crucifixion)* "above all praise"; seek it out in the **Sala dell'Albergo,** a side chamber off the Great Hall, which is also where you'll find *San Rocco in Glory* (it's on the ceiling). The latter is the painting which Tintoretto used to win the commission to supply the guild with all its canvases; a compulsive overachiever, he boldly outbid his peers by donating the completed canvas to the guild instead of turning in some basic sketches.

Once you've absorbed as much Tintoretto as you can, set aside some time to do a comparative study of works by Titian, Bellini, and Donatello at the nearby **Basilica di Santa Maria Gloriosa dei Frari** ★★ (Campo dei Frari, San Polo 3072; ☎ 041-2728618; www.basilicadeifrari.it; 2.50€, or free with Chorus Pass; Mon–Sat 10am–5pm, Sun 1–5pm). Built by the Franciscan friars *(frari)* from around 1236 and completed in 1338 (although some accounts make it a century later), this vast Gothic pile is one of those "Where do I begin?" ecclesiastical attractions, generally considered the next most important after The Basilica di San Marco; a studied visit should give you some sense of the stylistic and creative developments within Venetian art, from the late Middle Ages through to the neo-classical period. Titian's *Assumption of the Virgin* over the main altar, completed in 1518, makes such revolutionary use of color and style that the church initially rejected it; now it is said to signal Venice's first brush with the High Renaissance. Ironically, it was Titian's innovative use of brilliant, dramatic colors (in contrast to Tintoretto's more somber tones) that made him the city's darling, and the Frari now houses an immense neoclassical monument in his honor; you'll find it in the nave, across from the bizarre pyramidal monument honoring the sculptor Antonio Canova. Titian was buried in the Frari in 1576.

Completely upstaged by the Frari is the undervisited **San Polo Church** (☎ 041-2750462; 2.50€, free with Chorus Pass; Mon–Sat 10am–5pm, Sun 1–5pm) on the campo of the same name. It may be smaller and less famous, but it includes two paintings by Tintoretto, *The Virgin and the Saints* and *The Last Supper.* The church hearkens back to the 9th century, but was heavily reworked in the Gothic style during the 14th and 15th centuries.

ATTRACTIONS IN CASTELLO

After pushing through the tourist throngs of Piazza San Marco, I love setting off along Castello's long, uninterrupted waterside promenade. It begins just after you've gotten over the exasperating **Ponte della Paglia (Bridge of Straw),** where everyone halts to pose for photographs backed by the **Ponte dei Sospiri (Bridge of Sighs),** which connects the Palazzo Ducale with the prisons. Once over the bridge, you're in Castello, on the **Riva degli Schiavoni** ★★, remarkable for its ribbon of palazzi, now mostly transformed into expensive hotels; most famed among these is the **Danieli,** which has been a hotel since 1822, and hosted such luminaries as Dickens, Proust, and Balzac. Today, it's a shamelessly snooty place, but I dare you to wander inside, if only to admire the sumptuous old-world lobby lounge and bar. If you continue far enough along the promenade you'll reach the **Giardini Pubblici,** where Venetians go to relax on the grass. It's here that one of the world's premiere art events, **the Biennale** ★★★, erects the bulk of its exhibitions, in pavilions designed and built specifically for individual contributing nations.

About midway between the Danieli and the public gardens (near the Arsenale vaporetto stop) you'll notice a building marked by two black anchors. This is the city's naval and shipbuilding museum, or **Museo Storico Navale** (Campo San

Biago; ☎ 041-5200276; 1.55€; Mon-Fri 8:45am–1:45pm, Sat 8:45am–1pm), which is also where you can turn off to get a closer look at the entrance to Venice's renowned shipyard, the **Arsenale** (Campo dell'Arsenale), where the city's powerful mercantile and military fleets were assembled and repaired. The shipyard is a veritable city-within-a-city; in its heyday, over 15,000 men would toil here on a seemingly endless supply of ships, often for military expeditions that demanded serious armadas. According to local lore, in its busiest times the dockyard could complete an entire ship in 24 hours, or produce 100 warships in 2 months. At the 15th-century gateway, four stone lions—the spoils of war—stand guard; one of them, dating back over 2 millennia, is believed to have been taken from ancient Athens. But since the Arsenale is now administered by the Italian Navy, visitors generally don't get to tour it. For a bare glimpse inside the Arsenale, you need to be in Venice during the Biennale (see "Festival City," later in this chapter), when buildings within the dockyard open up as massive exhibition spaces (there are a few other events as well that will afford you a peek inside).

Most of Castello's more popular churches and historic attractions lie back toward San Marco. First up is **San Zaccaria** ★★ (Campo San Zaccaria; ☎ 041-5221257; Mon–Sat 10am–noon, daily 4–6pm), a Gothic church dating to the 9th century but dominated by Coducci's 15th-century Renaissance facade; it's closely associated with an infamous nunnery whose cloistered ladies were renowned for allegedly shirking their vows. St. Zacchary's bodily remains are on display, but it's Bellini's *Sacra Conversazione* that deserves your attention: Notice how the architectural details within the painting echo the detailing in the marble columns and arches around the painting, causing the painting and church walls to form a synthesized whole. That's what you see free of charge, but get a ticket (1€) to see the small, remarkable collection inside the **Chapel of the Choir.** Beside paintings by Tintoretto and Tiepolo, as well as a simple and moving *Crucifixion* attributed to Anthony van Dyke, you can also visit the so-called **Golden Chapel,** which is above the **crypt** where the tombs of eight early Venetian doges lie almost permanently underwater.

As far as compact art collections go, **Scuola Dalmata di San Giorgio degli Schiavoni** ★★ (Calle dei Furlani, Castello 3259A; ☎ 041-5228828; 3€; Tues–Sat 9:15am–1pm and 2:45–6pm, Sun 9:15am–1pm) is among my favorites, mainly for its works by Vittore Carpaccio. The magnificent ground-floor interior is mainly covered with Carpaccio's early-16th-century paintings of the patron saints of Dalmatia, George, Jerome, and Tryphone (the Scuola was founded by Venice's Slavic population).

It may be difficult to imagine today, but there was a time when horses were permitted on Venice's cobblestone walkways; evidence of this is the bronze equestrian statue of Bartolomeo Colleoni on **Campo Santi Giovanni e Paolo.** The Renaissance statue is by Andrea Verrocchio, a Florentine who taught da Vinci. The canal-side campo is worth visiting (even if it's not on most itineraries) for a look at the sumptuous 15th-century facade of the city's main hospital, Ospedale Civile.

After the showstopping hospital facade, you may be a little put off by the beguilingly simple (as well as incomplete) exterior of its neighbor, an enormous Gothic church, **Santi Giovanni e Paolo** ★★ (Campo SS. Giovanni e Paolo, Castello 6363; ☎ 041-2416014 or 041-5235913; 2.50€; Mon–Sat 7am–12:30pm and 3:30–7pm, Sun 3–7pm), which many claim stands next in line after The Basilica di San Marco in terms of importance to Venice. Dedicated to St. John and St. Paul, it was built by the Dominicans between the 13th and 15th centuries; it's the final resting place of numerous venerable Venetians, among them 25 doges and Titian, the city's favorite artist. Inside, brilliantly colored patterns are cast by the sun shining through the stained-glass side window, and you'll be wowed by the lineup of artistic treasures and their special significance as markers of Venetian history. Here are excellent canvases by Veronese and Giovanni Bellini; the latter created the altarpiece near the mortal remains of the military hero Mercantonio Bragadin. Bragadin's fate was to be skinned alive by the Turks in the late 16th century, after a noble attempt to defend Cyprus—all this is pictured in the fresco below his urn. In fact, much of the commemorative effect of the church is linked with military heroism and victory; the lovely **Cappella del Rosario (Rosary Chapel)** was built to celebrate and remember the defeat of the Turks at Lepanto in 1571, a major victory for the republic. The chapel you see today is not the original 16th-century version, because that was gutted by fire in the 19th century, but the paintings on the ceiling are Veronese masterpieces, and well worth a look.

Campo SS. Giovanni e Paolo is one bridge away from neighboring Cannaregio, but it's also near the site of **Santa Maria Formosa** (☎ 041-5234645; 2.50€, free with Chorus Pass; Mon–Sat 10am–5pm, Sun 1–5pm), Venice's first Renaissance-style church, built in 1492 and considered the architectural pinnacle of Mauro Codussi's career. It was founded (legend has it) after St. Magnus was instructed to do so by a particularly alluring vision of the Virgin. You'll find an allegorical representation of the church's mythical origins behind the main altar; uniquely, the painting is by an 18th-century woman artist, Giulia Lama.

Around the corner is the **Querini Stampalia Foundation** ★ (Santa Maria Formosa, Castello 5252; ☎ 041-2711411; www.querinistampalia.it; 8€; Tues–Thurs and Sun 10am–6pm, Fri–Sat 10am–10pm), another important cultural institution occupying a 15th-century palazzo, and established as a center for the preservation and restoration of Venetian culture and art. The museum is crammed with period furniture and paintings by the likes of Bellini, Tiepolo, and Jacopo Negretti (seek out his superb rendition of *The Deposition*), offering a peek inside the home world of Venetian nobility; there are paintings of major city events, giving you documentary-style images of Venetian social life in times gone by. The foundation presents occasional exhibitions of more contemporary art, which may spice up your tour, but I encourage you to time your visit with one of the early evening **weekend music recitals** ★★ held in the museum (Fri–Sat at 5 and 8:30pm). Unlike the touristy performances by musicians in period costume that are held all over Venice, these recitals focus on the authentic reproduction of musical and vocal qualities directly from the Renaissance and baroque periods. When I last attended a performance, a female vocalist, accompanied by an *arciliuto* (lute), transported me several centuries back in time; museum tickets includes the recital.

ATTRACTIONS IN CANNAREGIO

The compact island of Cannaregio's **Jewish Ghetto** ★ has the distinction of being the world's first ghetto neighborhood, founded in 1516. Before that time, the Jews, who had settled in Venice in the early 10th century, were scattered across the city. Many worked as moneylenders or pawnbrokers after being forced out of their

Venice's Cemeteries

Many people visit Venice's brick-walled, cypress-sporting **island cemetery of San Michele** (daily Apr–Sept 7:30am–6pm, Oct–Mar 7:30am–4pm) to see the final resting place of Ezra Pound, Igor Stravinsky, and other such luminaries. It's easy to get there; just hop on vaporetto ❹ (headed for Murano). While you're here, spare a moment for **San Michele in Isola**, Venice's earliest Renaissance church; inside you can get a map of the cemetery, helping you seek out the more notable graves.

Then, if you're tying together various pieces of Venice's Jewish history and culture, you may want to visit the ancient Jewish cemetery at San Nicolò, on the Lido. The grounds were granted to Venice's Jewish community in 1386, but the cemetery was closed down in the late 18th century, and remained shut for some 300 years. Contemporary restoration has meant that the cemetery is now open to the public and can be visited with 1-hour guided tours on Sundays in spring and summer (8.50€); for visits on other days you must reserve a guide in advance. Contact the **Jewish Museum** (☎ 041-715359) for information and bookings.

other professions during the early Middle Ages. The authorities chose Cannaregio because it was far from the city's centers of power. The term "ghetto" is derived from the fact that there were once two foundries—or *geto,* in Venetian dialect—in this district. Here, inhabitants had an enforced lock-in from midnight until dawn (and were forced to pay the Christian guards who barred the two access points on and off the island), while during the day they were required to wear a yellow hat. Because the community rapidly grew—from just 700 in the 16th century up to nearly 5,000 a century later—the area became known for its unique, multistoried buildings (to deal with the overcrowding). The Jewish community was a diverse one with Jews from all over the known world gathering here, each community founding its own synagogue. You'll see today the profound contrasts between the German synagogue (the oldest of the group) and the Turkish or Spanish synagogue.

During World War II, Jewish residents again suffered abhorrent treatment; having been declared enemies of the state, 104 people were rounded up and incarcerated on the night of December 6, 1943, and subsequently nearly 250 Jews were deported from Venice to concentration camps, where most of them perished. Sadly, only eight of the deportees have returned to their home city.

In contrast with its bleak history, the open square at the heart of this Jewish quarter, Campo del Ghetto Nuovo, is now a very pleasant place to watch all manner of daily life—including tour groups getting a very thorough look at some of the leaning nine-story apartment blocks; look especially for the two Holocaust monuments by Arbit Blatas.

There are five synagogues in the ghetto. Two of these—the Scuola Grande Tedesca and the Scuola Canton—were built in the early 16th century on the top floors of adjacent buildings, which have now become the **Museo Ebraico di Venezia (Jewish Museum)** (Campo del Ghetto Nuovo, Cannaregio 2902/b; ☎ 041-715359;

Catching Rays on the Lido

The Lido of Venice is one of the places where the modern seaside vacation first became popular. In the late 1800s, wealthy Europeans came here on the advice of their doctors to enjoy the sultry air and restorative effects of ocean saltwater. The famous beaches of the Lido were lined with cabanas where aristocrats and well-to-do's could strip down to their cover-all bathing suits to maintain a sense of public dignity. It was along these salubrious shores that Thomas Mann set his study in morbidity, *Death in Venice*, which Visconti refashioned as a film set in the Hotel des Bains, the ultimate turn-of-the-20th-century resort.

Today Hotel des Bains continues to attract privileged summer vacationers intent on taking a dip in the warm and—some would say—polluted waters of the Adriatic. Unfortunately, catching rays on the Lido can be a pricey business; locals and seasonal visitors fork out hefty sums to occupy a beach cabana for a day or the entire season, the cost dependent chiefly on proximity to the water's edge. Prices are outrageous and there is little—besides the promise of swimming alongside some Italian celebrity—to make them particularly worth your own attention.

A far better idea is to catch a bus—or hire a bicycle from **Bruno Lazzari** (21B Gran Viale Santa Maria Elisabetta; ☎ 041-5268019)—and head for Alberoni, at the far end of the Lido, and acquire a tan where the locals come to play. The bathing establishments here, built under Mussolini, are a popular hangout for families and also attract a sizable gay beach culture. And you won't have to rent a cabana to enjoy the sand, sea, and sexy sunbathers.

www.museoebraico.it; 3€; Oct–May Sun–Fri 10am–5:45pm, June–Sept Sun–Fri 10am–6:45pm). The exhibits within are of mostly 17th- and 18th-century Jewish artifacts. Of special interest are the tempera-painted marriage contracts, or *ketubah*. Look also for the lavishly decorated 17th-century Torah ark—next to it is a ketubah dating back to 1775. To learn more about the ghetto and to actually see its synagogues, join the hourly tours departing from the museum from 10:30am until 5:30pm (June–Sept) or until 3:30pm (Oct–May); a combined 8€ ticket will get you into the museum and onto one of the tours.

With its entrance hidden down a side alley off Cannaregio's main drag, you need to look for signs pointing toward **Ca' d'Oro** ★ (Calle Ca' d'Oro, Cannaregio 3933; ☎ 041-5222349; 5€; Tues–Sun 8:15am–7:15pm, Mon 8:15am–2pm), an early-15th-century palace, that's considered the single **best example of Venetian Gothic** architecture (and which is really best witnessed from the Grand Canal). It was commissioned by Marino Contarini, of one of the city's wealthiest families, whose talents lay in creating matchless opulence, rather than in cohering to any single, recognizable architectural style. Accordingly, there was no end to the fussy

Festival City

Revelries inspired by spiritual events are significant in the calendars of Venetians. Chief among these is the **Festa del Redentore,** held during the third week in July in celebration of the end of the tragic plague that crept through the city during the 16th century, killing upwards of 50,000 Venetians. Besides watching the fireworks (best seen from a boat on the lagoon), you can join in the celebrations by crossing the temporary bridge set up for the festival between Zattere and the island of Giudecca, where the Redentore church serves as a reminder of the city's salvation. During the original years of the celebration, the procession would have been led by the doge himself, and the 311m (1,020-ft.) bridge would have been built on gondolas; today, there is no doge, and heavier, more manageable barges are used for the construction of the bridge. The all-night event is usually accompanied by picnics and much drinking of wine. At sunrise, many of the younger revelers row out to the Lido.

The **Venice Film Festival** (☎ 041-5218711; www.labiennale.org) is second only to Cannes as a center for European glamour, attended by movie stars and other celebrities from all over the world. Continuing for 12 days, the festival gets underway in late August and is centered on the Lido's Palazzo del Cinema. You can get in on some of the action by attending one of the public screenings.

Venice's **International Contemporary Art Biennale** ★★★ (☎ 041-5218828; www.labiennale.org) is a highlight on the world's art calendar (held June–Nov in odd-numbered years), offering visitors the chance to see some of the most unusual and experimental art on the international scene. Some of the exhibits are spread across the city in dozens of palazzi that are usually closed to the public (and entry to these "pavilions" is free), but the two main centers are at the Giardini della Biennale, where various nations have permanent exhibition spaces designed by native architects, and at the Arsenale; one ticket (15€) gets you into both venues, and you'll need a full day to do them justice.

Su e Zo per i Ponti, held on the second Sunday in March, is Venice's very own city marathon, made extra grueling by the fact that runners have to cope with all those bridges; I'd say it's one of the most interesting ways to tour the city without having to put up with crowds of tourists blocking your way all the time!

detailing he brought about through the marriage of marble and expensive ultramarine, which kept master craftsmen busy for over a decade. The "House of Gold" gets its name because of the gold trim that once adorned the richly ornamented facade; although its bold coloring has long faded, and the gold has disappeared, the landmark house received a second lease on life when it became the **Galleria Giorgio Franchetti,** named in honor of the baron who went to great efforts to restore the building to its original glory, and then filled it with an eclectic collection of artworks from across the ages; some of it is worthwhile, but some may find the view of the Grand Canal even more inspiring than the art.

At least three churches in Cannaregio demand your attention. The first is **I Gesuiti** ★★ (Campo dei Gesuiti; ☎ 041-5286579; daily 10am–noon and 4–6pm), just a stone's throw (or a right and then a left turn) from Fondamente Nuove vaporetto stop. Since it was recently freed from the renovators' scoffolding, this Jesuit church (built 1714–29) has become one of my favorite ecclesiastical visits. Venture in and you'll feel the giddy excitement of a kid in a candy store: Try to imagine how the illusion of dramatically flowing fabric was created from rock solid marble. Everywhere, sculpted surfaces have been made to look like material that's light as silk. If the flamboyant overkill and excess architectural detailing leaves you cold, go in search of Tintoretto's *Assumption of the Virgin,* and Titian's sobering nocturne depicting St. Lawrence being roasted alive while spectral figures seem to haunt the darker areas of the canvas.

Venetians dig pretty little **Santa Maria dei Miracoli** ★ (Rio dei Miracoli; 2.50€, free with Chorus Pass; Mon–Sat 10am–5pm, Sun 1–5pm) so much that many of them choose to tie the knot here. Built in the 1480s to a design by Pietro Lombardo, it typifies Venetian Renaissance architecture. Miracoli's exterior beauty lies in the superb treatment of multihued marble—lovely pinks, grays, and whites—to create a patterned finish. You'll enter a beguilingly simple space worthy of closer attention; look up at the vaulted ceiling and observe the 17th-century paintings of the prophets by Pier Maria Pennacchi and his students (it wouldn't hurt to have a pair of opera glasses or small binoculars with you, since making out the detail, or even where each of the 50 panels begins and ends, is tough work), while a search around the church will reveal some sublime carvings. The church takes its name from a precious icon of the Virgin (you'll see it above the altar) said to have been responsible for a series of miracles in the 1470s.

Finally, **Madonna dell'Orto** (Campo Madonna dell'Orto; ☎ 041-2750462; 2.50€, free with Chorus Pass; Mon–Sat 10am–5pm, Sun 1–5pm) is an essential visit for Tintoretto fans; not only does the artist lie buried here, but a number of his works keep his mortal remains company. The present version of the church, with its impressive Gothic facade, was completed in 1473.

THE OTHER VENICE

In a city almost wholly devoted to the tourist trade, is it possible for the visitor to get beneath the surface, spend time with locals in a nontouristy environment, or get to grips with the culture without merely being an onlooker? Hallelujah! Yes! Below are a number of experiences that will throw an alternate—and alternative—light on a city that many residents fear has become too much like a museum.

BEFORE YOU LEAVE FOR ITALY   For real, unabashed insight into the special way of life experienced (and endured) by Venetians, pick up a copy of John Berendt's *The City of Falling Angels,* an absorbing read (by the author of *Midnight in the Garden of Good and Evil*) that digs deep into the psyche and the heart of the contemporary Venetian. It's the perfect primer for an alternative look at the city.

TAKING TO THE WATER

To really get a feel for the Venetian Zeitgeist, you need to understand the significance of the city's situation right in the heart of a watery lagoon, and how its canals play such an indelible role in the day-to-day functioning of the city. They are the lifeblood of Venice and just about every true-blooded native Venetian has some sort of craft for navigating the waterways. Little wonder, then, that I'd recommend getting involved in one of the many **boating regattas** staged during the rowing season as one of the best ways of meeting and fitting in (well, almost) with the locals. The noncompetitive **Vogalonga Regatta** (☎ 041-5210544; www.vogalonga.it) is held in May and has been one of the highlights of the Venetian calendar for over 3 decades. Just imagine being on one of the 1,500 man-powered boats that race out of the Bacino di San Marco to remind Venetians—and the world—of the environmental dangers caused by the increasing number of engines operating in Venice's canals. Boats of every conceivable variety, shape, and size (as long as the only horsepower is human) gather in the waters opposite the entrance to the Doge's Palace; they then set off on a course that's roughly 30km (19 miles), winding between the lagoon islands and back to Punta della Dogana via Rio di Cannaregio. Most competitors belong to local rowing clubs, but there are many foreign participants; the regatta is a chance to see Venice differently, while enjoying the spirited excitement of racing (but not really competing) against rowers and fun lovers who include gondoliers, hard-training sportsmen, and locals up for a laugh. To register, visit the website, where there are pictures suggesting what a hoot it all is; you'll find links to rowing clubs that can help you find a vessel.

Whether or not you end up competing in a regatta, you can build up those forearms (and meet some fun-loving locals) by signing up for Venetian **rowing lessons.** At Venice's oldest **rowing club, Reale Società Canottieri Bucintoro** (Dorsoduro 15, Zattere; ☎ 041-5205630; www.bucintoro.org) you can take a full-on 2-week course in Venetian rowing, which may not enable you to join the ranks of club members who've rowed their way to Olympic glory, but will certainly put you in their company. Lessons are available Tuesday through Saturday 9am to 5pm and Sunday 9am to 1pm, and you'll pay about 100€ for a set of eight; you can also do a *voga al terzo* (sailing course) here. For information about courses call ☎ 335-6673851, or write to elmar@bucintoro.org.

You can also let someone else do the rowing—**Venice's only woman gondolier,** Alexandra Hai, who came to Venice and fell in love with the city and it's gondolas. For years, Alex studied and practiced the art of the gondoleering, and finally qualified for the strict exams that protect the integrity of the Venetian tradition. But Alex's status as a foreigner and a woman threw a spanner in her plans. While the rules don't officially discriminate against women, it's clearly a fiercely guarded tradition, and macho-heavy, so the men on the examining body made sure Alex failed repeatedly by backpedaling the rules—a brutish move by the powerful gondolier union that, quite frankly, hoped to ensure that no woman ever again dare covet the life of a gondolier. But Alex persisted, and her determination paid off, at least to some extent.

The good news is that Alex has achieved her dream, and is now a practicing gondolier. But she's still battling for legitimate acceptance—you won't find her on any of the mainstream gondola circuits or stationed at any of the traditional stops;

instead, you'll need to contact her directly, through her association, **Incantesimo Veneziano** (☎ 348-3029067; www.incantesimoveneziano.com). The upshot is that you'll see canals and parts of Venice that average tourists don't; far better than being rowed around by a bored stranger for 40 minutes, and you'll be able to get the inside scoop on the secret politics of the gondola trade. Alex offers a truly romantic gondola experience, and she'll take you to unexpected corners of the city, venturing through seldom-visited canals, while sharing some of the history and intrigue of the age-old gondola tradition. If you're keen, Alex will let you try your hand at steering, so you too can grasp the difficulty of handling something that looks so marvelously simple. Or if Alex's tale has ignited a flame and you too dream of being a gondolier, sign up for a **private gondoleering lesson;** an hour on the Grand Canal will probably let you know if you've got what it takes, or should rather stick to your day job. And, for kids ages 6 to 13, Incantesimo offers a special hour-long **children's boat ride** 🧒 on the Grand Canal. The lessons and the kids boat ride are just 20€ each.

If your fascination with gondolas runs to voyeurism, you can always head over to the **Squero di San Trovaso** (Rio di San Trovaso, Fondamenta Nani Dorsoduro), which is essentially a **gondola workshop** where the black-lacquered craft are built, repaired, and given touch-ups. It's closed to the public, but you can usually see workers busy in the open air any time of the day, so no need to make any official arrangements to watch, stare, or ogle.

ARTS & CRAFTS

There are many artisans working in Venice, many of them still applying centuries-old techniques that have been handed down through the generations. Unfortunately, much of their trade is now related to tourism, and many of the stores you pass or venture into are pretty much focused on getting your credit card out of your wallet. One way of getting to meet the artisans and seeing them engaged in their craft without feeling obligated to make a purchase is to join a **Venetian handicraft tour** offered by **Venice Shopping** (☎ 340-7771185; www.veniceshopping.net). You'll visit the workshops and studios of mask makers, ceramicists, paper makers, and glass blowers (just about any other type of artisan you're keen to watch work); you'll have a little demonstration, a brief explanation, and—naturally—an opportunity to purchase some of the goods. It's always nicer to buy something when you know who created it, although there's no pressure to buy anything. The tour lasts 2 hours and is 33€ per person (maximum of six people on a tour); they happen Monday through Saturday in the morning or afternoon and Sunday by arrangement.

Away from the tourist hordes, Giudecca is where a number of artists and artisans have banded together to establish a Venetian craft laboratory, **Cosma e Damiano** (Giudecca 621/B-17), based in a restored 15th-century convent. Here, you can see blacksmiths, glass blowers, and paper and mask makers in action, and possibly negotiate a good deal directly from the artist. For information, you can visit www.cosmaedamiano.it, but to make arrangements to visit, contact Ljupka Deleva, one of the resident artists (☎ 348-0105823).

But rather than just watch the masters absorbed in their craft, you might want to get your fingers dirty and creative juices flowing by **learning one of Venice's traditional crafts;** who knows, you may even pick up a skill you can put to use when you get home. Venetian mask makers—or *mascareri*—have been practicing their craft since 1436, and masks have enjoyed an important place in the city's social life (even being banned at some point because they allowed the citizenry to get away with all sorts of debauched behavior). Gualtiero Dall'Osto has been making masks for 25 years; his **Tragicomica** 🧒 (Calle dei Nombolli, San Polo 2800; ☎ 041-721102; www.tragicomica.it) is one of the city's top-rated mask outlets with a powerhouse workshop just round the corner. Rather than browsing haplessly through the myriad designs on offer, he'll teach you to paint your own mask or even create one from scratch. Tragicomica offers two kinds of **mask-making workshops.** There's a 2½-hour session which includes a brief historical presentation, after which you're guided through painting and decorating a premolded mask (this costs 65€–75€, depending on the type of mask you select), and you can go for something as simple or complicated as your imagination allows. While there's some serious skill (not to mention time, patience, and concentration) involved in creating the more intricate and detailed masks, you really don't have to be a trained artist to have a go at the less complicated designs, and children are well looked after, too. If you're really keen on going at it in a more serious manner, there's a 20-hour course run over 5 days; you'll follow every step in the process, from modeling, to making the positive and the negative, to creating the papier-mâché mask and then painting and embellishing it (this costs 100€–200€ per day, depending on how elaborate your chosen design is, and what you choose to decorate it with). Book by first e-mailing info@tragicomica.com.

Paper marbling is a technique that came to Venice from Persia via Turkey over 400 years ago; it involves creating elaborate, colorful motifs that imitate the veins in marble or stone in order to create a decorative effect on paper. At **Ebrù** (Campo Santo Stefano, San Marco 3471; ☎ 041-5238830; www.albertovalese-ebru.com), you can attend a **paper-marbling class** presented by the shop's owner, Alberto Valese. Valese has been practicing this craft for decades and has exhibited around the world; classes take place at his home in Castello, accompanied by snacks and wine. A 3-hour introductory session costs 100€; the full-day (6-hr.) course is 170€; a 3-day intensive course is 440€ (18 hr.); a special weeklong intensive course is 350€ (for 15 hr.).

COOKING CLASSES

Venice is home to many unique and unforgettable dishes, many of which you won't come across anywhere else on earth. You could buy yourself a local cookbook, of course, but what's the fun in that? Especially when there are fabulous locals, like Roberta Molani, who love nothing better than imparting their culinary skills. Roberta's homegrown cooking school is called **Peccati di Gola** (Via Felisati 68b; ☎ 041-977866 or 339-5251493; www.peccatidigola.info), and has been contributing to the gastronomic education of visitors to Venice for 2 decades now. Roberta and her team conduct classes in her private kitchen in a 16th-century palazzo not far from the Rialto Bridge, and experience has taught her patience and good humor. She holds 3-hour, single-menu **gastronomic classes** for those with limited time. You prelude your lesson with visit to the Rialto markets, where you'll take a gander at the fish and vegetable sections, and select the ingredients for the day ahead. Then it's off to the kitchen, where you'll prepare a full-on Venetian lunch—I'd go for the fish menu option, which includes *sarde in saor,* Venetian-style tagliolini, and fresh sea bass. You'll get a pack of recipes, a certificate, and get to savor the fruits of your labor. Roberta's good, but not exactly cheap: Classes start at 280€ (for a one on one), but if there are three pupils you pay 150€ each (or 100€ if there are 10 of you).

Da Fiore (Calle del Scaleter, San Polo 2202; ☎ 041-721308; www.dafiore cooking.com) is widely touted as one of Venice's top (most expensive) restaurants, and hosts some of its most spectacular **cooking classes,** run by Michelin-rated chef Mara Martin. These weeklong courses start Monday, but the experiential, getting-to-know-one-another tone means that the first kitchen class is not until Wednesday. Here your "training" includes market visits, glass factory tours, and wine bar excursions. You'll learn to make different kinds of pasta, including Venetian whole-wheat *bigoli,* breads, risotto, vegetable dishes, and desserts. You'll also discover the proper way to clean seafood, and meet some crazy crustaceans (like spider crab and mantis shrimp) in the process. Lunch, with wine, is included, and at the end of the course you get a certificate, and you take home a wad of printed recipes.

FOR SOCIAL SUBVERSIVES, INTELLECTUALS & VOLUNTEERS

So many people come to Venice and invariably—unwittingly—contribute to its decline. Not only must the city be maintained and (little by little) restored, but there are also constantly new discoveries being made—many of them beneath the observable surface. Much of this work is in the hands of specialists, of course, but if you're the **volunteering** sort, and inclined to explore history with your hands as much as your eyes and mind, it may be worth your while contacting **UNESCO World Heritage** (http://whc.unesco.org/en/71) to find out if there are any Venice-based projects that you can contribute to. During my last visit to Venice, in late 2007, one series of ongoing ventures linked to UNESCO was being coordinated by the French organization Rempart. They're working to excavate and protect the island of Lazaretto Nuovo. Volunteers contribute to building restoration, take part in actual archaeological digs, help with the conservation of valuable ceramic discoveries, and assist with on-site tourism. You even get taught to use archaeological tools and learn about stratigraphy (artefact dating) and how to classify certain objects. Volunteers should apply well in advance (up to a year), but I'd say you can probably work your way into the system faster if you're insistent and prepared to demonstrate just how keen (and worthy) you are. The organization will assist (a little) with food and lodging, but you'll be expected to shoulder of the majority of the costs involved with your own upkeep (so you'll pay a portion of your rent), and you'll be responsible for all travel arrangements. Most stints last just 2 weeks, but you'll come away with romantic-sounding memories of having worked as an archaeologist, even if only for a while.

Nighttime entertainment in Venice often feels as though it's limited to wining, dining, and listening to Vivaldi recitals. However, there's one place that dares to be different and hankers after a more rigorous sloughing off of the mundanities of conformist tourism. It's a place where more socially adventurous visitors like yourself can rub shoulders with local artists and self-proclaimed intellectuals in an environment that's fun, upbeat, and cool. And it all happens right in the center of the tourist precinct, at my favorite daytime espresso haunt, Caffè Aurora. At night the transition from genteel coffee shop is daringly radical: while the bands at Caffè Florian and Gran Caffè Quadri are celebrating Vivaldi, Aurora's nearly always has a sublime and wonderful gathering underway—the waiter's station becomes a DJ booth, and house or electro tracks attract a hip crowd. It's because Aurora is "head-quarters" of a band of social reformer-entrepreneurs—calling themselves the **Aurora Street Cultural Association** (☎ 041-5286405; www.aurora.st)—who argue that Venice has become a museum with a conveyor belt mentality. They rebel against this sad, slow "death" by organizing events involving artists, DJs, photographers, multimedia designers, and other cultural practitioners. Basically, they've theorized a really good excuse to kick back and party. According to their manifesto, "we at Aurora take off our masks and 18th century carnival costumes and take a risky chance at revealing our true and rebellious identities." Wow! Not that you have to be a hippie or subversive to be excited by what they're doing, but you should make every effort to attend one of their functions; the evening runs from 8pm to 2am, and most events are free so long as you buy at least one drink. Expect young, high-energy DJs and innovative multimedia talents to provide cutting-edge entertainment, while the drinks flow fast and furious.

If your desire for intellectual stimulation goes beyond late-night carousing with bohemian subversives, there's a rather more traditional and institutional organization that will help you get deeper under the skin of the city and take home new knowledge. **Fondazione Giorgio Cini** (☎ 041-5289900; www.cini.it), based on the island of San Giorgio Maggiore, runs regular lectures, seminars, and cultural events that should satisfy the quest to delve deeper and explore the city's cultural affinities in a more meaningful way. While there are enriching-yet-entertaining events (like weekend presentations of rare and uncommon music recordings), the foundation's work is not to be taken lightly and you should know that some of their seminars are strictly for specialists (prepare for a barrage of sophisticated-sounding academic jargon), and not all are presented in English.

ATTENTION, SHOPPERS!

An old Venetian proverb boasts, "Money is our second blood." Another warns, "A man without money is a corpse that walks." These should both alert you to the fact of the bottom line in Venice: Its shops are overpriced. Everywhere you turn, some delightful item is up for grabs, and nine times out of ten, the price tag will be well out of your reach. Retain your sanity by seeking out those items that can't be found elsewhere. When it comes to classic, quality goods like one-of-a-kind Murano glassware or a custom-made leather-bound book, then and only then should you open your wallet or purse. There's spectacular craftsmanship worth investing in, but be on your toes.

If you can find an off-the-beaten-track shop in this city, the chances are you'll strike a bargain. But, bear in mind that the majority of shopkeepers have *only* tourists in mind, so the real trick becomes finding stores away from the hordes. Go to quiet corners of Venice where you can engage an artisan or artist in conversation about his or her work. Stay away from shops around Piazza San Marco and leave the tacky kitsch of the Rialto's souvenir stalls exactly where it is—these places thrive on conveyor loads of tourists who'll buy anything for the sake of having a souvenir or gift to take home. The good buys in Venice are unique, special pieces, and—like all good investments—worth taking time and effort over.

Note: Numerous Venetian shops are prevented from carrying any sort of signage advertising their name, so you will need to take heed of addresses and check if you're indeed in the right place once you're there.

ART, ANTIQUES & COLLECTIBLE ODDITIES

If there's one piece of kitsch that's worth considering, it has to be the striking **Calendario dei Gondolieri (Calendar of the Gondoliers)** (8€), available at just about every souvenir cart in town since 2002. The calendars are the brainchild of Piero Pazzi, and while they may not be Pirelli standard, the black-and-white images of 12 (mostly) studly oarsmen will certainly remind you of your stay. Try the stands on the Dorsoduro side of the Accademia Bridge.

Dorsoduro is also popping with art galleries and showrooms; at **BAC Art Studio** (S. Vio, Dorsoduro 862; ☎ 041-5228171; www.bacart.com) posters are manufactured on the in-store press. Among the many lovely prints, lithographs, and original paintings of Venetian themes (notably Carnevale scenes), you'll find etchings of homoerotic angels by the artist Paolo Baruffaldi, and surreal images of the bespectacled bald man repeatedly painted by David Dalla, whose work is exhibited internationally.

I'm usually suspicious of gallery stores, but the **Museum Shop** (☎ 041-2405410; shop@guggenheim-venice.it) attached to the Peggy Guggenheim Collection (and directly managed by it) stocks some unique items. Besides the expected spate of arty reproductions, clever souvenirs, and elegant books (including an excellent children's guide to Venice), this is the place to pick up a pair of Peggy Guggenheim sunglasses (147€), manufactured by Sàfilo, and for real Peggy G. fans, copies of the millionaire's memoirs, *Out of This Century—Confessions of an Art Addict.* There's also useful kitschy souvenir stuff, like an umbrella bespeckled with vaporetto route numbers (12€).

If you are after more serious, collectible works, **Venezia, le stampe** (Calle Teatro Goldoni, San Marco 4606/B; ☎ 041-5234318) stocks a formidable range of antique prints, including original historic maps of Venice, etchings of palazzi, and architectural motifs. One of the more unusual stores in Venice is Enzo Giacomazzo's **Forma** (Campo San Rocco, San Polo 3044; ☎ 041-5231794)—although the sign outside reads JURASSIC SHOP. Forma stocks fossils, precious rocks, and geological finds, and also such bizarrely ornamental collectibles as crocodile skulls, mounted butterflies, horned beetles, and even a few dragonlike flying lizards.

BOOKS

Libreria Mondadori (San Marco 1345; ☎ 041-5222193) is the largest bookstore in Venice, and can easily keep you browsing for hours; there's an excellent selection of English tomes on the city, its history, and its art. Cultural events and book talks are occasionally held in the store's events area. Come browsing here first for huge savings.

Purveyors of one-of-a-kind first editions and vintage publications should head for Cannaregio's ghetto to discover real treasures at **Old World Books** (Al Ponte del Ghetto Vecchi, Cannaregio 1190; ☎ 041-2759456). The selection of rare books with a connection to Venice is particularly excellent; you'll even dig out a good number of English books. The shop is at the bridge connecting the new and old ghetto squares.

Marco Polo International Bookshop (Calle del Teatro Malibran, Cannaregio 5886/A; ☎ 348-5691125) sells and trades old and new books, including popular English literature.

CLOTHING & ACCESSORIES

You'll find plenty of big-name clothing boutiques where you can blow your budget quite spectacularly in the vicinity of Piazza San Marco; browse here if you must, but think carefully before reaching for your wallet since you'll inevitably find the same garment for less in another city. One that's a bit more unique—in fact, it reminds me of those fun, funky shops found around Miami's South Beach—is **Penny Lane** (Salizzada S. Pantalon, Santa Croce; ☎ 041-5244134), which features new, vintage, and secondhand clothing stocked by the young owners, Luisa and Piero, who have a deep-seated aversion to what they call Italian fashion's obsession with Dolce & Gabbana. Although the space is small, you can browse for ages, while listening to old-flavored rock 'n' roll, searching for jewelry, bongs, cushions, and Dragonfly shirts with bright purple images of Jimi Hendrix—all very un-Venetian!

Custom-made and one-of-a-kind shoes and original hats are what Venetian cobbler **Giovanna Zanella** ★ (Campo San Lio, Castello 5641; ☎ 041-5235500) makes in her shop near the Rialto; take a look if you don't mind paying upwards of 250€ for top-quality apparel. Speak to Giovanna about those strange-looking slippers you'll see in shop windows; they're called *furlanes,* and are traditional gondoliers' shoes of velvet and brocade, available in marvelous colors, with soles made from recycled bicycle tires.

Rosario Soprano hails from Naples, and she's brought not only her warm personality, but also her magical handbag designs to Venice, where she's set up shop. Rosario makes unique, gorgeous designer bags using real Italian leather made from calf skin; you'll find her always hard at work in her small leather workshop-cum-store, **Soprano Handbags** ★★ in Castello (Salizzada dei Greci; ☎ 041-5212768).

GLASSWARE & HANDICRAFTS

Sensibly upmarket **Marina e Susanna Sent** ★★ (Campo San Vio, Dorsoduro 669; ☎ 041-5200205) is a boutique with classy, contemporary Murano glass sculptures, vases, and unique jewelry. There's more jewelry and artfully crafted glassware at **Genninger Studio** ★ (Calle del Traghetto, Dorsoduro 2793/A; ☎ 041-5225565; www.genningerstudio.com) with its entrance on the Grand Canal, at the Ca'Rezzonica vaporetto stop. The studio is operated by Leslie Ann Genninger, an American expat.

Crossing the Rialto Bridge can drive you crazy if you encounter slow-moving hordes of tourists, but there's one good reason to stop here: a visit to **Rivoaltus Legatoria** ★ (Ponte di Rialto 11; ☎ 041-5236195). This is Venice's original hand-bound leather-journal and book emporium, which owes its success as much to superior craftsmanship as it does to Wanda and Giorgio Scarpa, a husband-and-wife team who've been here since the 1970s. Pick up a ready-made notebook or photo album, or have that extra-special journal made to order. Another good outlet for beautiful bound books, journals, diaries, and picture frames made with attractive handmade designer paper is **Legatoria Polliero** (Campo dei Frari, San Polo 2995; ☎ 041-5285130); a small notebook costs just 8€ to 12€, while a large album could be as much as 310€. Also available are sheets of handsome wrapping paper.

MASKS & COSTUMES

Right near Campo dei Santi Giovanni e Paolo is **Laboratorio Artigiano Maschere** (Calle Barbaria delle Tole, Castello 6657; ☎ 041-5223110); working here is Giorgio Clanetti, one of several major figures responsible for reviving the Venetian art of mask making.

Guerrino Lovato set up his gallery workshop, **Mondonovo Maschere** (Rio Tera Canal, Dorsoduro 3063; ☎ 041-5287344; www.mondonovomaschere.it) in 1978, and he's probably the most renowned practitioner of his craft, having produced masks for Stanley Kubrick's *Eyes Wide Shut* and Kenneth Branagh's *Much Ado About Nothing*. Stop in here not only to browse, but potentially for a chance to see the man in action.

SWEETS

Move over, Willy Wonka. **VizioVirtù Cioccolateria** (San Polo 2898A; ☎ 041-2750149; www.viziovirtu.com) is a miniature wonderland of all things cocoa. Chocolate is made while you watch (and fantasize), and the lineup of treats is almost too much to bear. Some unusual ingredients—like saffron and ginger—go to making this store a standout, and there are such weird treats as tobacco-flavored chocs named after Sigmund Freud. Boxes in different sizes are on standby so you can mix and match gifts, and Mariangela will gladly explain her sugary assortment while you sip hot chocolate at the counter.

NIGHTLIFE

The first source for all entertainment and nightlife needs is **HelloVenezia** (☎ 041-2424; www.hellovenezia.it; daily 7:30am–8pm), a hot-line service that deals with ticketing and provides information about most cultural events, including the Biennale and shows at the various theaters.

FOR THE CULTURALLY INCLINED

No indoor experience can take your breath away quite like an evening at one of the world's great opera houses; my favorite night out in Venice invariably involves a presentation at **Teatro La Fenice** ★★★ (Campo San Fantin, San Marco 1965; ☎ 041-786575; www.teatrolafenice.it); there's a full program most of the year, and the main theater attracts some of the world's biggest names. Check out the program online in advance of your visit, and don't dally in making reservations. Affordable tickets for the bigger events sell fast.

Italian dramas and musicals are performed at **Teatro Goldoni** (Calle Goldoni, San Marco 4650/B; ☎ 041-2402011; www.teatrostabileveneto.it). Programs typically include works by Luigi Pirandello and, of course, Venice's own comic genius, Carlo Goldoni. Italian versions of such international names as Goethe, Neil Simon, and Edward Albee ensure a varied lineup; productions are often quite innovative and visual, so the language needn't be an issue. **Teatro Malibran** (Calle dei

Milion, Cannaregio 5013; ☎ 041-786603) has been operating since 1678 and shares the theatrical program of La Fenice; details can be found on the main website.

Venice's popular (if, in my opinion, cheesy and touristy) Vivaldi performances keep many musicians from going hungry; you'll frequently come across costume-clad students handing out brochures for these nightly events, most of which include some allusion to the *Four Seasons* and other recognizable-to-the-novice classical music numbers. Arguably the city's best performing group is **Interpreti Veneziani,** a string ensemble that regularly tours the globe, and that has been active in Venice since 1987. Concerts, which center on Vivaldi, but are not entirely limited to his oeuvre, take place in **Chiesa San Vidal** (San Marco 2862/B; ☎ 041-2770561; www.interpretiveneziani.com). One of the many costume-wearing concert groups is **I Musici Veneziani** (☎ 041-5210294; www.imusici veneziani.com), performing every day during summer (excluding Aug). Patrons can expect either Vivaldi's *Four Seasons* or an evening of "Baroque and Opera"; performances (8:30pm) usually take place in the Main Hall of the Scuola Grande di San Teodoro (Campo San Salvador) near the Ponte di Rialto. You can purchase **tickets** (25€–35€) for any of these events (and hear about a whole lot more) at Cristiano Nalesso's famous **Vivaldi Store** (Campo San Bartolomeo; ☎ 041-5221343; www.musicinvenice.com). Cristiano is a prolific producer of Venetian music albums, and he also sells a wide selection of CDs here.

DRINKING & RELAXING

Venetians aren't particular about the time they choose to gather at their favorite watering holes for a drink. Whether it's midmorning or early evening, you're likely to encounter locals engaged in passionate conversation with a glass in hand. Daytime get-togethers are usually aided by a glass of wine, while evenings are brought to life with that uniquely Venetian concoction known as "spritz," a mix of prosecco (or white wine and soda water) and Campari (or Aperol, if you prefer it sweet); the famous aperitif—which you simply have to try—was originally brought here by the Austrians during the occupation, and now it's an absolute institution. Of course, if that sounds too much like bad news in the morning, you could settle for a flute of straight prosecco, Italy's delicious sparkling wine. You certainly won't want for choice when it comes to finding a drinking spot: There are classy wine bars, publike student hangouts, and extremely posh hotel and restaurant bars where prices are so outlandish I won't bother to mention them. Significantly, in Venice, there's often little distinction between places for drinking and for finding a light bite to eat; where alcohol is served, you'll almost always find a selection of appetizers to stave off the hunger. So, step up to the bar, order, and relax; but do ask before sitting down, since table occupancy might push up the price quite considerably.

Early evenings, I like to head for Dorsoduro's Zattere, which is where many Venetians head for a stroll or to walk their dogs; I think it's a sterling spot to join locals for an evening spritz. Famous for its wonderful ice cream, the popular **Gelati Nico** ★ (Zattere, Dorsoduro 922; ☎ 041-5225293), has a very friendly bar counter as well as a few tables outside, where you'll be served (at a reasonable markup in price) by handsome waiters. You'll quickly get caught up in the good humor of the staff members who seem to be having a tremendous amount of fun pouring potent drinks for their regular customers. Nearby, you can also enjoy a (slightly pricier) drink at **Al Chioschetto** (Fondamenta della Zattere; ☎ 348-3968466), the green kiosk right near the water's edge; students gather at the lagoon-side tables to enjoy their drinks accompanied by live music or a DJ session.

Over in Castello, just off Campo Santa Maria Formosa, a similar atmosphere can be enjoyed at **Zanzibar** ✭ (Castello 5840; ☎ 339-2006831), a tiny canal-side bar and *paninoteca*, with a handful of outside tables. You can start your day here with an espresso and croissant, and then join the cool evening crowd that gathers for spritz, cocktails, and upbeat lounge tunes. Cannaregio recently became home to the final word in spritz; on the menu at **Profondo Rosso Spritz Bar** (Fondamenta Ormesini, Cannaregio 2839; ☎ 333-3037205) are at least 10 varieties (although Venetians will argue most are deviations from the real thing), including a mind-blowing house specialty which will have you bopping at the friendly little bar where locals shoot the breeze. All spritz just 1.20€ during happy hour, 7 to 8pm.

Then there are two particularly popular campos, where you'll usually find a student crowd. The first is Dorsoduro's **Campo Santa Margherita** ✭✭, a verita-ble hotbed for youthful hormones. Santa Margherita's best resto-pubs also offer agreeable, fairly affordable dining, so if you decide to spend the evening, ask to see a menu. Billing itself as a "restaurant and champagne lounge," **Orange** ✭ (Campo Santa Margherita, Dorsoduro 3054/A; ☎ 041-5234740; www.orangebar.it) is good for generous cocktails and glasses of vino: You can choose from 60 differ-ent Italian wines, and another 20 imported varieties. Opposite Orange is **Margaret Duchamp** ✭✭ (Campo Santa Margherita, Dorsoduro 3019; ☎ 041-5286255), which may not be quite so wannabe-chic, but attracts a wonderfully mixed crowd; I'm also happy to report that drinks here (notably some of the best spritz in town) are being poured more generously than ever before. Another friendly drinking spot with an affordable dining menu is **Imagina Caffè** (Ponte dei Pugni, Dorsoduro 3126; ☎ 041-2410625), around the corner from Santa Margherita. Park at a table outside and sip your drinks while watching the ebb and flow of crowds heading in and out of the square.

The other choice is in San Polo, close to the Rialto. Vegetable market by day, but swinging party district by night, **Campo San Giocometti** ✭✭ packs out with fine young things drinking the night away. Two recommended restaurants are here: **Bancogiro** (p. 299) and **Naranzaria** (p. 299) both offer an excellent selec-tion of wines. Kick off by grabbing an outdoor table at either of these venues; you'll be seated right near the Grand Canal (around the corner from the Campo), perfectly poised to toast the setting sun with a great vintage from the Veneto region.

Another top spot after wandering through the Rialto markets is **Muro Vino e Cucina** ✭ (Campo Cesare Battisti, San Polo 222; ☎ 041-5237495), a slightly trendy wine bar where the drinking crowd usually spills out onto the square, while the chic upstairs restaurant serves innovative but pricey dishes to a discerning clientele. If you're feeling peckish, do as I do and order one of the scrumptious, olive oil–infused cicchetti (an attractive alternative to a sit-down meal): you've more chance of meeting locals who've popped in to do the same. Live music out on the square often ensures that the party continues till relatively late.

A more sedate contemporary-style drinking venue is the shimmering oval counter of the **Bacaro Lounge Bar** ✭ (Salizzada San Moisè, San Marco 1348;

☎ 041-2960687), behind the Libreria Mondadori bookstore. Don't confuse Bacaro Lounge Bar with inexplicably popular **Bàcaro Jazz** (San Marco 5546; ☎ 041-5285249), a heaving Venetian favorite—it's not just for fans of recorded jazz, but also with countless tourists who find themselves completely caught up in the goings on at the cocktail bar, polished by the elbows of numerous late-night patrons. It's one of the few places in Venice where you can actually order a Bellini—that other blue-blood Venetian landmark, **Harry's Bar** (Calle Vallaresso, San Marco 1323; ☎ 041-5285777), where the peach juice–and–prosecco cocktail was invented, is outrageously expensive.

But if you'd prefer to get more bang for your buck, a far better bet would be to strut your way over to Dorsoduro and into **Impronta Café** ★ (Calle dei Preti, Dorsoduro 3815; ☎ 041-2750386), where Paduan-born owner Massimo serves wine by the glass from 2€ or by the bottle; you can order from a selection of panini, salads, and *primi*. The vibe here is modern and funky—lounge tunes, stylish contemporary furniture, and blackboards with chalked-up wine lists.

DANCE CLUBS, DJ EVENTS & LIVE MUSIC

If jazz is your thing, you can book a table at **Venice Jazz Club** (Fondamenta del Squero, Ponte dei Pugni, Santa Margherita 3102; ☎ 041-5232056; www.venice jazzclub.com), which has a mixed and varied lineup on Fridays, and the in-house quartet on Mondays, Wednesdays, and Saturdays.

Opportunities are fewer if you want to hit the dance floor; the real clubs are on the mainland. In the heart of the student district, between Campo Santa Margherita and Campo San Barnaba, **'Round Midnight** (Calle del Squero, Dorsoduro 3102; ☎ 041-5232056) advertises itself as a "DiscoClub," but that's really just another term for a bar where some punters occasionally do some DJ-inspired toe tapping and booty wiggling on a matchbox dance floor. It usually operates on Friday, Saturday, and some Thursday nights; doors open at midnight and "dancing" continues until 4am, making it a popular meeting point for late-night revelers when the other bars close.

One of Venice's classiest flirtations with contemporary chic is **Centrale Restaurant Lounge** ★★ (Piscina Frezzaria, San Marco 1659; ☎ 041-2960664; www.centrale-lounge.com), predictably all the rage with the trendy crowd. Combining glass and brushed metal in a cavernous room of exposed brick and ambient lighting, Centrale is a restaurant serving Mediterranean and contemporary Venetian cuisine, but it's also a good place to hang with the beautiful people,

---

Romance in the Piazza

Night falls, and there's life on Piazza San Marco. The sextet at Caffè Florian has progressed from Vivaldi's *Four Seasons* to Ravel's *Bolero* and the assembled crowd—none of them paying customers—is delighted. The music pelting out of Florian, or Quadri across the way, is available absolutely free of charge to anyone not sitting down. Grab your partner and dance the night away right in the heart of St. Mark's, under the stars, in one of the world's most romantic cities.

an experience that will be enhanced if you dress the part. The kitchen stays open later than most, and live music or DJ sets often accompany the classy, laid-back ambience; check the website for upcoming events, which include occasional gay evenings.

Also see "The Other Venice," earlier in this chapter, for interesting DJ-driven happenings at **Aurora** (☎ 041-5286405), including regular gay nights (usually on Wed).

ISLAND HOPPING TO MURANO, BURANO & TORCELLO

Getting to the islands of the lagoon is simple, especially if you have a vaporetto pass for 24 or 72 hours, which will allow you to go to each of the three most-visited islands in a single day without having to worry about paying for each leg of the journey. I strongly urge you to avoid the agency-operated tours that are touted in major tourist areas.

Murano ★ is celebrated almost exclusively for its glassware; this is where many innovations were developed to give the world better qualities and types of glass and mirrors. Today, there are two levels of glassmaking: ultradesigner chic for those with hard-wearing credit cards, and cheap trinkets that usually come from China. You can take time to admire the craftsmanship of some of the better glass factories (which are more like art studios), but you should know that you'll be the object of a sales pitch immediately following the demonstration. Some of the showrooms are enjoyable, but there is only so much colored and textured glass you can appreciate in a day.

One of the finest producers of high-end glassware is **Vivarini** (Fondamenta Vetrai 138; ☎ 041-739285; www.formiaglass.it or www.vivariniglass.it), where the furnace of the Mian family has produced some of the most coveted glass pieces to come off the island. But if you wish to purchase a really beautiful—*and affordable*—creation, visit **Rossana & Rossana** (Riva Longa 11; ☎ 041-5274076; www.ro-e-ro.com), where two friends sell exquisite glass jewelry (there are earrings from 6€) and traditional wine glasses (from 25€). Do go inside to admire the fabulous color combinations (the yellow-and-black pieces are particularly striking); even the wine goblets with handles shaped like seahorses and dragons, which are a bit too over the top for my taste, are strangely beautiful. Nearby, at **Galleria Regina** (Riva Longa 25/a; ☎ 041-739202; www.galleriaregina.com), Giovanni Regina curates and sells a fantastic collection of glassware sculptures, which he'll ship home for you. Even if you're not able to make a purchase, Giovanni has a gift for the gab, so spend some time chatting.

Only visit the **Museo Vetrario (Museum of Glass Art)** (Fondamenta Giustinian 8; ☎ 041-739586; 5.50€ or free with Museum Pass; Thurs–Tues 10am–6pm, Nov–Mar till 5pm) if you have a serious interest in the history of glass production; while there are a few unusual and eccentric pieces here, it is otherwise a very dull exhibit of lifeless glassware.

A far better reason to hang around Murano is to try one of two worthwhile restaurants. **Ristorante Ai Pianta Leoni** (Riva Longa 25; ☎ 041-736794; Tues–Sun 8am–5:30pm; MC, V) is next door to Galleria Regina, with a terrace on the water. The cuisine is Venetian, with delicious fish and meat dishes. **Trattoria**

"Busa alla Torre" da Lele (Campo S. Stefano 3, Murano; ☎ 041-739662; Tues-Sun 9am–5pm; AE, MC, V) is tremendously popular, possibly because of the large personality of its charitable owner. Lele developed a close relationship with New York in the wake of the 9/11 terrorist attacks by setting up a trust fund for the orphaned son of one of the victims. Now he brings New York City firefighters to Venice to take part in rowing regattas.

Vaporetti leave Murano every half-hour, headed for the fishing-village island of **Burano** ✦✦. Dominated by lace shops, Burano is one of the most colorful places on earth. Not much happens here, but just about every house is painted a different color, creating an immensely picturesque visual palette. And it really is a quiet, restful place with real village charm. Across the way from the Scuola dei Merletti—the lace museum where the art of lace making is also taught—is **San Martino** church, with a *Crucifixion* by Tiepolo.

To really escape humanity, catch vaporetto ❶ from Burano to the island of **Torcello** ✦✦, where a once-substantial population (over 20,000 some 600 years ago) has dwindled to around 20; in fact, when a baby was born here in 2007, it made headline news in Venice. Nevertheless, traces of a prosperous past (this was also where Venice's first settlers came) still exist in its churches, particularly 7th-century **Santa Maria Assunta** (☎ 041-730119; 3€, audioguide 1€; Nov–Feb daily 10am–5pm), celebrated for its excellent Byzantine mosaics of sinners being tortured in vivid scenes from the Last Judgment. Next door, Mass is still held at 11th-century **Santa Fosca** (free; daily), while the **Campanile di Torcello** (☎ 041-730119; 3€; daily)—great for panoramic views of the island and the lagoon—has recently been closed for major work to save it from falling over.

The ABCs of Venice

American Express Located at Salizzada San Moisè, in San Marco (☎ **041-5200844**).

Banks ATMs (known here as Bancomat) are the most convenient way of accessing funds; there are ATMs at the airport and many all over the city. Most banks are along San Marco's Calle Larga XXII Marzo, and also near Campo Manin; try to get your banking done in the morning (8:30am–1:30pm) on a weekday.

Emergencies Dial ☎ **113** for any emergency. In case of fire, dial ☎ **115.** For an ambulance or other medical emergency, dial ☎ **118.**

Hospital Venice's **Ospedale Civile** (Campo SS. Giovanni e Paolo; ☎ **041-5294111)**, is in Castello, and has a **24-hour emergency room** (☎ 041-5294517). A **waterborne ambulance (**☎ **118)** can be dispatched from here and will transfer patients directly in an emergency.

Internet If your hotel doesn't have Internet facilities, inquire about the Telecom communication center, where there's free Internet for 30 minutes. Otherwise you'll be paying around 8€ to 10€ per hour and dealing with paperwork. San Marco's **Internet Point San Stefano** on Campo San Stefano (☎ **041-8946122**) and is open daily from 10:15am until 11pm; look for the large "@" sign above the door. A popular place to log on is **Casanova** (Lista di Spagna, Cannaregio 158/A; (☎ **041-2750199;** 9am–1:30pm).

Police Call ☎ **113** in case of emergency; or alert the officers at the **Pronto Intervento Stranieri** (Fondamenta S. Lorenzo; ☎ **041-5284666**) in cases of theft and petty crime.

Post Office Venice's central post office (on Salizzada del Fontego dei Tedeschi;

☎ 041-5285813; Mon–Sat 8:30am–6:30pm) is near the Rialto Bridge.

Restrooms In a city where you'll easily spend the entire day away from your hotel, it's good to know that there are public restrooms, particularly near the major tourist areas; these cost 1€ per entry.

Telephones To place an **overseas call**, dial ☎ 170 for assistance from an operator; for **general assistance**, dial ☎ **4176**. While there are many payphones around the city, don't expect them to work; coin-operated machines are particularly pphonecards that you buy from *tabacchi* or from the post offices.

Tourist Offices **Venice Pavilion** (☎ **041-5225150;** www.turismovenezia.it) is the main tourist office, located in a lagoon-side building (Palazzini Santi) near the Giardinetti Reale, around the corner from Piazza San Marco. Other offices are in strategic positions: at the train station (Cannaregio; ☎ **041-5298727**); across from the entrance to the Museo Correr; in Piazza San Marco's Procuratie Nuove (☎ **041-5298740**); at the Garage Comunale, in Piazzale Roma (☎ **041-5298711**); and on the Lido (Santa Maria Elisabetta 6/a; ☎ **041-5265721**). There's also one in the airport arrivals hall (☎ **041-5415887**).

8 Padua, Verona & the Dolomites

See why the Veneto's art treasures are strong competitors to the attractions of more heavily visited areas, and then ski or hike the heavenly Dolomites

by Keith Bain

A WINGED LION—THE SYMBOL OF ST. MARK AND THE ONCE POWERFUL Venetian Republic—will be your constant companion as you tour the Veneto, the region that lies just inland of Venice, and was once its proud vassal. "Leo" is everywhere, a reminder of how and why the region became as rich as it now is in great works of art and architecture. Back in the days when the Venetians ruled trade and the seas, such Veneto cities as Padua and Verona were carefully nurtured as centers of art. Their Venetian overlords made a heavy investment to glorify their powers by employing only the top "interior decorators" and architects—Giotto, Veronese, Titian, Tintoretto, Tiepolo, Palladio, and many more—to build, gild, and prettify the palazzi, villas, churches, and government buildings of the region.

Of course, this region was important well before the Venetians took over. Verona, in particular, has the nickname "Little Rome" for its abundance of classical ruins and fortifications that hearken back to an age when gladiators were superstars and Christians were fed to the lions.

Enhancing the appeal of the great cities of the Veneto is the nearby mountainous area of the Dolomites. Along Italy's border with Mitteleuropa, these peaks inhabit a landscape so dramatically different from the flat Veneto that they might as well be a million miles apart instead of just a few hours away by bus or train. These mountains, separating the Veneto from the Germanic Tyrol, are a playground for outdoor thrill seekers and nature lovers. Here, in and around towns like Cortina d'Ampezzo, skiing and mountaineering is offered in one of the finest Alpine environments on the Continent.

It's the combination of these elements—classical, Venetian, and Alpine—that makes the region such a worthy destination for those who have already experienced Italy's major tourism triumvirate of Rome, Florence, and Venice. If you only have time for one or two of the sights in the region—perhaps in a day trip from Venice—Padua should be your pick, for its lively college-town atmosphere and exquisite frescoes by Giotto (it's also a quick 30-min. train ride from Venice). Those who have more time should include Verona, one of the prettiest medieval cities in Italy (and that's no small claim), which boasts the best collection of Roman ruins north of Rome itself.

DON'T LEAVE THE VENETO & DOLOMITES REGION WITHOUT . . .

TAKING IN THE FABULOUS FRESCOES BY THE FATHER OF WESTERN ART   Giotto's magical take on the drama and pathos of biblical narratives makes for Padua's finest 15 minutes. Unfortunately, that's as much time as you'll be allowed inside the Scrovegni Chapel (p. 352), which is decorated with beautifully rendered episodes from the Gospels.

RELIVING YOUR COLLEGE DAYS, THE PADUAN WAY   When students at the University of Padua celebrate graduation, festivities take on a raucous, heady edge: The lively *goliardia* celebration is a blend of academic upheaval and pagan ritual that takes place in the vicinity of the Palazzo del Bò (p. 354). If you're not around at graduation time, you can always join the pub-crawling students as they meander through the watering holes of the atmospheric Ghetto quarter.

PAYING YOUR RESPECTS TO ST. ANTHONY   Join the pilgrims who throng to the **Basilica di Sant'Antonio** (p. 355) in Padua to pay homage to the remains of the patron saint who is said to help bring back that which has gone missing or gotten lost. While visiting with spiritual devotees from around the world, you can take in the work of the great sculptor Donatello.

ACTING OUT YOUR OWN VERSION OF ROMEO & JULIET   Romantic strolls through the cobblestone streets and squares of Verona will evoke Shakespeare's star-crossed lovers. Head for the Piazza delle Erbe (p. 372) and wend your way through, around, and under the remarkable buildings, statues, and archways left by the powerful Scaligeri clan who once ruled here.

TAKING IN 1,000 YEARS' WORTH OF ART   The **Museo di Castelvecchio** (p. 371) is housed in a castle on the banks of the River Adige in Verona and is stuffed full of artwork from across the ages. How better to discover the who and how of Bellini, Carpaccio, Tintoretto, and Veronese—without the hassle of the crowds that heave through Venice's brilliant museums?

RIDING THE ARROW IN THE SKY   The Freccia nel Cielo (p. 388) is one of Italy's great funicular experiences, taking you from Cortina's Olympic Ice Skating Stadium to the lofty heights of the incredible Dolomites. Views from the top—3,244m (10,640 ft.) above sea level—are unforgettable.

PADUA

With Venice—one-time ruler and superstar neighbor—casting such a powerful shadow, Padua is easily ignored as a destination, often cited as suffering an inferiority complex. Shakespeare relegated Padua to a rather grim background role in *Romeo and Juliet,* while in *The Taming of the Shrew* it's the setting for some radically dodgy gender politics. Little wonder that before I made my first visit here, I assumed it would be an old-fashioned, backwater of a town. And knowing it to be home to the country's second-oldest university, I pictured it populated by a fraternity of academics, draped in ancient robes, paying eternal homage to Galileo Galilei, the city's most famous scholar, who taught here some 400 years ago.

Veneto

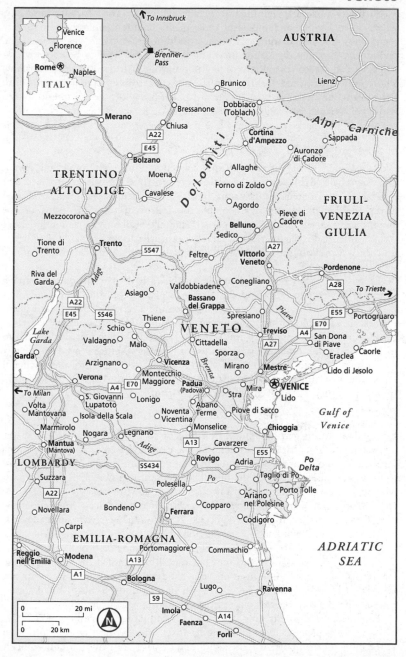

Such silly quixotic imaginings are quickly shattered in this hip, happening city, where ancient ruins and medieval monuments collide seamlessly with trendy nightspots, chic restaurants, and hubs of bustling student life. It's far from the boondocks. Literally thousands of young people come here to be educated. In addition, Padua receives millions of pilgrims, paying their respects to St. Anthony, whose holy remains are enshrined in the city's incredibly popular superbasilica. For tourists the city's most sublime crowd-puller has got to be the interior of the Scrovegni Chapel, covered with Giotto's fantastic legacy: a fresco cycle that—7 centuries ago—marked a shift in Western art.

A BRIEF HISTORY OF PADUA

Padua has had plenty of time to build a reputation as an important center. Historians believe the Veneti tribe settled here as early as the 6th century B.C., and in 45 B.C., the Romans set up camp. In 602 A.D., when the Lombards marched across the Veneto, Padua was completely destroyed; only the ruins of the amphitheater, a few bridges, and parts of the city wall survive as reminders of Roman rule. Padua slowly rebuilt, taking 5 centuries to recover. By the time the university was established, in 1221, Padua had achieved political and economic stability.

Padua once again became desirable; in the early 14th century, the warring counts of the Carrara clan stepped in with new plans to put the city on the international map. A thriving city-state, Padua became a center of artistic and scientific excellence, able to lure preeminent artists like Giotto. Soon, the Carraras' expansionist passions inflamed the Venetian Republic, which was also seeking to make inland gains. So at the start of the 15th century, Venice moved on the city and absorbed it into the empire, of which it remained a part until the decline of La Serenissima, under Napoleon. After a short spell as an Austrian possession in the 19th century, Padua eventually became part of Italy in 1866.

LAY OF THE LAND

Of the daily **trains** leaving Venice, over 80 stop in Padua, just 37km (23 miles) away; the half-hour trip costs under 5€. There are also trains connecting Verona (around 60 min.; from 2.50€) and Milan (up to 3 hr.; from 12€). You'll alight to find local buses waiting in the busy Piazzale Stazione; nos. 3, 4, 8, 12, 18, A, M, and T (weekdays), or 8 and 32 (weekends) go downtown.

Pick up a free map of the city—along with friendly advice—from either the central **tourist office** (Galleria Pedrocchi; ☎ 049-8767927; www.apt.padova.it; Mon–Sat 9am–12:30pm and 3–7pm), the booth on Piazza del Santo, or the office at the train station (turn right when you exit the station; ☎ 049-8752077).

Padua's attractions are spread out, but can all be handled on foot if you can read a map and have some time on your hands. Bus transport is free with the PadovaCard (p. 353); otherwise, it's 1€ per ticket (valid 75 min.). You'll almost certainly need a bus (or taxi) to get from the station to your lodgings.

For hassle-free sightseeing, popular **CitySightseeing Padova** (☎ 049-8704933; www.padova.city-sightseeing.it; 15€) offers a "hop on, hop off" tour of the city's most important sights, and is an easy way of getting around quickly and efficiently if you don't mind feeling like a shuttled tourist. The tour makes 10 stops, including the train station (perfect if you're on a day trip) and almost all the attractions I've discussed below. A few of their stops are of dubious significance, and at one point you're encouraged to join a "Bus 'n' Boat" itinerary which may, irritatingly, add to the cost.

ACCOMMODATIONS, BOTH STANDARD & NOT

If you're only in town for a short while, stay in the center; you'll be close to most of the attractions, and will easily find a good deal. Padua also has a number of bed-and-breakfast options, and there's a hostel if you're on a very tight budget.

€€   I'll start with those B&B options, which in the 1990s distinguished this city from its neighbors. In fact, a Padua resident, a math teacher named Lucia Cherlotti, was one of the first people in all of Italy to set up a small, home-based B&B and then a network of such B&Bs. Named **Koko Nor Association** (Via Selva 5; ☎ 049-8643394; www.bandb-veneto.it/kokonor; cash only), for a lake in Tibet, it currently represents eight homey, affordable B&Bs in Padua itself and a handful elsewhere in Italy. The great benefit of staying at these B&Bs—beyond the fact that you'll see life in a residential neighborhood, and get the inside scoop on the city—is that guests have kitchen privileges, which can mean big savings on food. On the downside, five of the eight lodgings are quite a distance from the center of Padua, so get ready for a commute. Through this agency, I've stayed at **Tibetan House,** a large suburban apartment with Buddhist ornaments and a mellow 1970s atmosphere; each of the three large bedrooms here has a private bathroom, while the fully equipped kitchen, lounge–cum–dining room, and small terrace are shared. The digs are a good value (rooms within the network go for 60€–100€ for a double), but those seeking daily maid service should look elsewhere. And unlike the B&Bs of the U.K., breakfast here is a disappointing, help-yourself affair.

Hotels near the Center

€€   If you'd rather stay in a hotel, you can enjoy excellent value at **Hotel al Fagiano** ★ (Via Locatelli 45; ☎ 049-8750073; www.alfagiano.com; AE, DC, MC, V). It has the ambience of a funky bohemian inn—albeit one conveniently located in the midst of the city—thanks to Rosella Faggian's arty makeover. Her flamboyant paintings, sculptures, and collages have transformed the interior of this 40-something-year-old hotel into a place that feels personally cared for. At just 74€ to 81€ for a double, guest rooms are superbly neat and spacious (even the singles have room enough for a small desk; 54€–58€), but it's the artful, individual touches (creating some surprisingly beautiful accommodations) and quality mattresses that make the Fagiano a standout. Upstairs rooms have timber-beam ceilings and views of either the back garden or Sant'Antonio square (these rooms are particularly lovely in summer). Service is perhaps less personable, and the family owners can seem a little distant, although if you make the effort to get chatting, you'll reap the rewards. Breakfast is charged separately, and parking costs 10€.

€€–€€€   A great surprise, also near Il Santo, is **Belludi 37, Hotel in Padova** ★★ (Via Luca Belludi 37; ☎ 049-665633; www.belludi37.it; AE, DC, MC, V), which is actually a very flattering reincarnation of the old (and ugly) Buenos Aires hotel. The designers seem to have gotten hold of a smart contemporary style catalogue and remodeled the entire place (bathrooms less so), filling it with chic, no-nonsense furniture and several layers of soothing neutral-toned paint. Sleek design give the best rooms (110€ double with private bathroom) an extra dollop of usable space. They earn my enthusiasm, too, for their dark-hardwood floors and great big back-supporting beds. There are also smaller rooms with bathrooms (90€), as well as singles with and without baths (50€–70€). But just in case you don't get the message that this really is a trendy, modern little hotel, there's a flatscreen TV, DVD player, cordless phone, and Internet access in all 17 rooms. Breakfast is included, but there's only the tiniest between-floor dining area, so ask to be served in-room (no extra charge). Bicycles are available for free; parking is 10€.

€€€–€€€€   If you're up for a minor splurge, there's no better place for it than in the heart of Padua's Ghetto, where a night at the **Majestic Toscanelli** ★★ (Via dell'Arco 2; ☎ 049-663244; www.toscanelli.com; AE, DC, MC, V) feels like authentic luxury. Majestic wears its formal (but unstuffy) elegance well, and it's a sumptuous retreat after a day's sightseeing on foot. It's a small hotel, but lots of hard work in recent years has ensured that guest rooms are smart and comfortable; reproduction furniture, pretty fabrics, and unusually textured designer wallpapers hint at an old-world pedigree, and add up to just the right amount historic ambience in a city that's pushing for a complete contemporary makeover. Doubles typically go for 175€, but last-minute specials and low-season rates regularly lower the rate to as little as 130€.

A Hostel Option

€   Padua's cheapest beds are in its coed hostel, **Ostello Citta di Padova** (Via Aleardi 30; ☎ 049-654210; www.ctgveneto.it/ostello), situated far from the train station, right across town. Beds in a large dorm are under 20€, but be warned that you'll inevitably find yourself sharing with nontravelers (including pilgrims, for example), who may have unusual ideas about dorm etiquette. If you'd rather not take your chance bunking with strangers, get a double room (about 40€). A shower and very basic breakfast are included in the rate, but, and here's the real rub, all-day lockout runs from 9:30am to 4pm, and a strict 11pm curfew will curb social possibilities in this late-night student town.

DINING FOR ALL TASTES

€–€€   For reliable pizza, served directly from a wood-fired oven amid a rowdy crowd of students, locals, and tourists, head to **Al Borgo** (Via Belludi 56; ☎ 049-8758857; Wed–Mon noon–2:30pm and 7pm–midnight; MC, V). Unpretentious (despite the inexplicable 2.50€ *coperto* charge) and conveniently located just off Piazza del Santo, Al Borgo offers good value and darn good food (pizzas 4€–9€).

€–€€   On the edge of the Prato square, **Zairo** ★ (Prato della Valle 51; ☎ 049-663803; Tues–Sun 11:30am–3:30pm and 6:30pm–2am; AE, DC, MC, V) has a frescoed indoor section dotted with faux-classical sculptures, but it's more relaxed outdoor terrace is ideal in summer. Waistcoated, charmless waiters are quick to pinpoint just how much you're willing to spend: *"Ristorante? Pizzeria?"* they'll inquire while looking you up and down, and seat you according to what you intend to eat. Both menus are impressive, but if you're counting euros, order one of their excellent pizzas (4€–8.30€)—a perfect base heaped with toppings—and dine at your leisure, enjoying the fabulous parade of well-to-do locals striding toward the fancy indoor tables. If you opt for the ristorante, there's a selection of homemade pastas (*primi* run 5.70€–14€), grilled fish, and a great filet topped with juicy boletus mushrooms. *Coperto* is 1.50€.

€€   Also near Il Santo is the fairly elegant **Antica Trattoria dei Paccagnella** ★ (Via del Santo 113; ☎ 049-8750549; daily 8am–4pm and 6:30pm–midnight; AE, DC, MC, V), where I once asked the owner to recommend his most typically Padovani dishes. After a rigorous interrogation of the menu, he suggested the *baccalà mantecato* (dried codfish, boiled, skinned, and whipped up with olive oil, and then served with polenta), which makes a decent (though pricey) starter. Far better is Padua's traditional chicken dish, *bigoli con sugo di gallina imbriaga,* made with extra-thick spaghetti; it's wickedly good, although portions—like all the *primi* (7€–11€)—are small.

€€–€€€   In the center of town, **Ristorante Pizzeria PePen** (Piazza Cavour 15; ☎ 049-8759483; Mon–Sat 10:30am–3:30pm and 6:30pm–2am; AE, DC, MC, V) has indoor and outdoor seating, and a vast menu of (very yummy) pizzas and more substantial dishes that hasn't really changed in 25 years. Sulky, serious waiters—all sporting designer five o'clock shadow—carry out their business as though it were the most serious endeavor on earth; yet when PePen fills up with families, lovers, and other assorted locals, it can actually be quite a bit of fun. If you're tired of pizza (around 7.50€), try the *gnocchi Verdi,* potato pasta stuffed with spinach and ricotta, and made with calamari, tomato, moscardini, and virgin olive oil (9€). *Coperto* is 2€.

€€–€€€   **Donna Irene Ristorante Enoteca** ★★★ (Vicolo Pontecorvo 1; ☎ 049-656852; Tues–Sun 10:30am–3:30pm and 6pm–1am; www.donnairene.com; AE, MC, V) is the one place in town worth reserving for. A labor of love for Sicilian owner Ubaldo Ingrassia, it's the prettiest, best located, and most romantic restaurant in town, situated at the edge of a stream, with a gorgeous shaded garden. Each of the *primi* (8.50€–16€) is a fresh, imaginative pasta dish (the *linguine tonno*—flat pasta with tuna lemon, pecorino, capers, and olives, at 9€—is to die for), but the real value here are the varied tasting menus (from 15€, including water and coffee). Wine aficionados be warned—there are 450 labels on offer, and the list reads like a biblical tome (young sommelier, Frederico, conducts tastings in winter).

WHY YOU'RE HERE: THE TOP ATTRACTIONS

Padua's attractions are varied; it's not just Renaissance art and museums stuffed full of Roman rocks, although there's that, too. Venture through the narrow streets and alleyways of the atmospheric Ghetto, and you'll get a vivid sense of history and an equally strong impression of student life. The university itself is something of an event, and its main building makes for an interesting visit; if you hit town at the right time, the students' boozy graduation rituals can keep curious visitors entertained for hours. South of the center, the huge Il Santo basilica draws millions of pilgrims, who come to ask the city's patron saint for a blessing.

Besides the top attractions I've discussed below, you may want to inquire about the status of Padua's medieval **castle** (www.castellodipadova.it)—money is now pouring in for its restoration (after spending much of its modern life as a prison); it's situated on Piazza Castello, near the **Astronomical Observatory,** which is a rather disappointing museum.

Giotto's Sublime Frescoes & a Nearby Museum

If time allows for only one attraction in Padua, make it the **Cappella degli Scrovegni (Scrovegni Chapel)** ★★★ (Piazza Eremitani 8, off Corso Garibaldi; ☎ 049-8204550 for information; see below for admission fees, hours, and reservation details), which is decorated with Giotto's remarkable frescoes (he's widely considered the father of Renaissance art, and this chapel will show you why).

The chapel was built by Enrico Scrovegni in 1303 as a bid to try and atone for the sins of his father, a moneylender so despised that he was denied a Christian burial. (Dante features him by name in his *Inferno* in the seventh circle of hell, all rivers of boiling blood and minotaurs, reserved for usurers, sodomites, and suicides.) Enrico enlisted Giotto to cover the chapel walls in visual biblical narrative of the lives of Mary and Jesus, which he did between 1303 and 1306, bringing an experimental edge to the 38 panels here. His compositions are determinedly focused on storytelling; notice how the treatment of the space to create perspective, and the placement of the characters within that space, brings a laser-sharp focus to the central drama within each frame. Consistently, your eyes are drawn to the main action through the rhythms, lines, and character details within each picture.

From the visitor entrance, turn right and head toward the western entrance, which the Scrovegnis would have used. Interestingly, this is where Giotto chose to put his frightening fresco of *The Last Judgment,* no doubt intended as a warning to the living. In the fresco, as fiendishly imaginative and detailed as later Bosch scenes of hell, you'll witness horrendous tortures administered by hairy demonic figures, including one large monster that eats and excretes sinners. Throughout the church, notice Giotto's use of fine coloring—cobalt blues, rich reds—often in elaborate, exotic combinations. Notice also how, in nearly every fresco panel, Giotto stages an architectural device that pushes the illusion of perspective, and sets off the human figures, which have been endowed with realistic, detailed facial expressions (an innovation at the time). Pay careful attention to the panel depicting the Last Supper and you'll notice how Judas's halo is rendered black, a symbolic pointer to the betrayal (today, it is harder to perceive, as all the disciples' halos have darkened with time).

As a precautionary measure to prevent atmospheric contamination of the frescoes, visits to the chapel are scientifically controlled, and last only 15 minutes per person. After prebooking your visit, you'll wait in a video-viewing room for a quarter-hour air-purification process before being allowed inside.

In the same grounds as the Scrovegni Chapel, the ancient monastic cloisters of the Eremitani have become the **Musei Civici Eremitani,** which has a prestigious archaeological collection on the ground floor and a gallery of works by the Venetian masters upstairs; Titian, Tiepolo, and Tintoretto are all featured, as are Bellini and Giorgione. Downstairs, a multimedia room highlights Giotto's career and his work in the Scrovegni Chapel.

Saving with the PadovaCard ★★

I highly recommend purchasing the PadovaCard, which covers admission to a wide range of attractions and also includes unlimited bus fare. Valid for 48 hours, or for the entire weekend if you buy it on a Friday, the card costs 14€ (an absolute bargain considering that the Scrovegni Chapel alone costs 12€) and is good for one adult and one child under 12. In addition to saving on entry at most museums, the card attracts discounts at some shops and restaurants, on certain guided tours, bed-and-breakfasts, and boat trips along the Brenta. It's a good idea to ask about discounts wherever you go, just in case; if you're driving, it even allows free parking in certain lots. The easiest place to purchase it is at the ticket office in the Musei Civici Eremitani (see above), when you should immediately book your visit to the Scrovegni Chapel. You can also book at www.turismo padova.it.

The Eremitani friars were responsible for services at the nearby **Eremitani Church,** which you can visit to see lively frescoes by Guariento and Giusto de' Menabuoi (14th c.), as well as works by a young Andrea Mantegna (15th c.).

Entrance to the **ticket office** in the **Musei Civici Eremitani complex** is well signposted; buy the money-saving PadovaCard here (see above). Alternatively, you'll pay 12€ for joint admission to the chapel and the museums, plus a mandatory 1€ reservation fee. When purchasing your ticket, you must book a specific time for your chapel visit—be on time or you'll lose your spot. The chapel is open 9am to 7pm year-round (excluding Jan 1, Dec 25–26, and May 1). From Mar 1 through Jan 6, visits continue until 10pm; visits from 7 to 10pm cost 8€ and there are rumors that you're more likely to get an extra few minutes at night. At night there's also a "Double Turn" promotional ticket (12€ plus 1€), valid 7 to 9:40pm, affording you half an hour in the chapel. Scrovegni admissions are free March 25. When it gets busy, you may need to reserve a day in advance, but I've had no problem turning up in summer and getting an immediate chapel visit. The ticket office is open daily 9am to 7pm February to October and 9am to 6pm November to January; advance bookings are also available through the **Telerete Nordest call center** (☎ 049-2010020; Mon–Fri 9am–7pm, Sat 9am–1pm), or online at www.cappelladegliscrovegni.it.

The University, Historic Squares & Jewish Ghetto Quarter

A top activity in Padua is simply wandering from one lively square to the next; this will give you a strong sense of the very public lives led by the people who have populated Padua over the centuries. The piazzas are where students gather between lectures, or to plot their evening on the town, which often starts out at one of the many bars or cafes.

One cafe where you probably won't find any students is also one of the most famous and historically significant in Italy. Local tradition dictates that it's bad luck for students to frequent **Caffè Pedrocchi** ✦ (Via VIII Febbraio 15; ☎ 049-8781231; www.caffepedrocchi.it) until after graduation; high prices probably also keep them away. Recognizable by its neoclassical entranceway guarded by two stoic stone lions, and looking more like an ancient temple than a venue for drinking and dining, the cafe was commissioned in 1831 by Antonio Pedrocchi. Once a favored haunt of intellectuals, it was here that students launched an uprising against Austrian rule in 1848. Today, the Pedrocchi generally attracts an upmarket crowd, but no visit to Padua is complete without grabbing a table on the open-air terrace and raising an eyebrow at passing pedestrians.

On Pedrocchi's upper floor, the **Piano Nobile** (☎ 049-8205007) is a museum of sorts to 19th-century refinement; the various rooms are decorated in different styles, kitschily drawing on Egyptian, Roman, and Greek influences. Today, parties and dinners are still hosted in the ballroom. Also in the Piano Nobile is the **Museum of the Risorgimento and of Contemporary Art** (☎ 049-8781231; 4€; Tues–Sun 9:30am–12:30pm and 3:30–6pm), which will only be of interest to staunch history buffs with a particular bent for war stories. The exhibit covers the history of Padua from the fall of the Venetian Republic in 1797 until the Constitution of the Republic in 1948, with particular emphasis on the world wars and, perhaps more interestingly, the impact of Mussolini.

The sheer historical weight of the centuries of learning that have gone on at the University of Padua makes a visit to its main building—the **Palazzo del Bò** ✦ (Via VIII Febbraio; ☎ 049-8273044; free)—worthwhile. The university opened in 1221, making it the second oldest in Italy. Hidden up a stairway off the main courtyard is a statue of the world's first female university graduate, Elena Lucrezia Corner Piscopia, who earned her philosophy degree in 1678; her feat represented a major leap in women's rights (if you can't find the statue, ask for directions at the university souvenir shop).

Bò is also home to the first permanent anatomy theater, set up in 1594; you can visit this claustrophobic auditorium (where medical students would witness cadavers being sliced up) by joining a tour of the Bò's most significant rooms. These run Monday through Saturday, three times a day (Mon, Wed, and Fri at 3:15, 4:15, and 5:15pm; Tues, Thurs, and Sat at 9:15, 10:15, and 11:15am), and cost 5€; organize your ticket (in the Bò or through the tourist office) a few hours in advance so you can ask what language the tour will be conducted in—I once found myself with a UN-affiliated guide who spoke everything but English. The tour includes the university's senate room, where velvet-upholstered seats are reserved for the institution's intellectual elite; you also get to see the massive lectern built especially for Galileo, whose lectures were so popular they required a specially built room.

Not far from the Bò, pretty much slap-bang in the center of town, between Padua's markets on **Piazza delle Erbe** and **Piazza della Frutta,** is the **Palazzo della Ragione** ✦, built in 1218 and expanded in 1306 by one of the Eremitani monks. The vast single-room upper floor—or **Il Salone** (☎ 049-8205006; 8€; Feb–Oct Tues–Sun 9am–7pm, Nov–Jan 9am–6pm)—once constituted the largest upstairs hall on earth. With its enormous wooden ceiling and eye-catching 15th-century fresco cycle of more than 300 astrological and religious scenes by Nicola Miretto, the hall housed Padua's law court until the late 1700s, but is now an exhibition space, often hosting notable Italian artists. On permanent display is a massive wooden horse with overlarge testicles, and if that's not excitement enough, head for one of the balconies from where you can watch the scene on one of the piazzas below; it's a wonderfully lively part of town.

On Il Salone's ground floor is one of Padua's most atmospheric spaces, an 800-year-old covered **market;** between the butchers and fishmongers, you'll find coffee shops and wine merchants, where locals gather to gossip.

Nearby, **Piazza dei Signori** is another expansive, pretty square lined with cafes and marked by a gorgeous astrological clock; just short of the clock is one of the Venetian empire's winged lions high up on a column.

From Piazza delle Erbe it's a short walk along Via del Manin to Padua's barren and gloomy **Duomo** (Piazza del Duomo; ☎ 049-662814), supposedly built according to a plan by Michelangelo. What is worth a look here (besides the menagerie of students sipping drinks at the tables at the edge of the square), is the small 12th-century Romanesque-style **Baptistery** ★★★ (☎ 049-656914; 2.50€, free with PadovaCard; daily 10am–6pm); it features a mesmerizing fresco cycle by Giusto de'Menabuoi, a Florentine painter who worked here from 1375 to 1378.

From the Duomo, you are ideally poised to plunge into the back alley tangle of Padua's ancient **Jewish Ghetto** ★★, now rejuvenated and well stocked with fab little stores; it's also a good area to discover bars and cafes, many of them swarming with keen-to-party students.

The Basilica & Beyond

Padua's principal pilgrimage destination is the **Basilica di Sant'Antonio** ★★, a veritable spiritual Disneyland, known to most simply as **Il Santo** (Piazza del Santo; ☎ 049-8789722; free; daily 6:20am–7:45pm). St. Anthony was a Portuguese missionary heading for Africa. When a storm blew his ship off course he ended up in Italy under the discipleship of St. Francis; his popularity earned him sainthood after he died just outside Padua in 1231. Completed in 1307, Il Santo's massive domes and heaven-reaching spires cast a fantastic shadow over the square below and suggest something of the region's Byzantine architectural roots. Inside, the vast, cavernous brick-walled space is filled with the buzz created by a nonstop parade of pilgrims, some of whom have journeyed from as far as South America to pay homage to Anthony and seek his blessing. If you're lucky, one of the nuns or monks on duty will be able to explain the significance of the various devotional acts happening around the church; alternatively, ask for the audio tour available at the front desk.

Under a massive marble archway is **Anthony's tomb;** join the queue of devotees who silently pray to Il Santo for aid. As you move around the tomb, do as they do, and touch your hand to the wall; like me, you may just feel a surge of energy. Besides being a patron of childbirth and the poor, Anthony is also the saint responsible for the recovery of things gone missing (including, it would seem fortunes, love ones, and good health); sadly, the walls are lined with photos of missing children and absent loved ones, so emotions are piqued. Whatever your beliefs, being here is no ordinary experience.

Among the most important artworks in the church are the **relief carvings** and **bronze sculptures** in the high altar; these are **by Donatello,** and are said to have signaled Padua's first brush with the Renaissance in the mid-1400s. Behind the main altar is the **Cappella del Tesoro,** where more bits of the saint are preserved, including his tongue. St. Anthony's big day comes on June 13, when his feast is celebrated with a procession through the streets of Padua. An army of pilgrims follows his relics from the Cappella del Tesoro through town in a spectacular display of religious fervor and devotion. For a more mundane look at the saint's life, study the bronze scenes around the tomb, or join one of the free screenings of the short film about Anthony.

Outside the church, the **bronze equestrian statue** is another early-Renaissance monument by Donatello; it depicts the heroic mercenary soldier known as Gattamelata, who died in Padua in 1443. The work effectively altered the history of sculptural casting, not least because of its immense proportions.

Adjacent to Il Santo is the **Museo Antoniano** (2.50€) a small ecclesiastical museum, that you can happily skip. Around the corner from this, is part of Padua's **civic museum,** occupying a pretty palazzo that periodically hosts fabulous exhibitions, usually free of charge. Even if the exhibits don't interest you, pop inside for a gander at the frescoed walls.

From the Basilica, make your way along Via Luca Belludi, and you'll come upon the **Prato della Valle,** a large square famous more for its size than for anything else (until Russia joined Europe, it was the largest square on the Continent, an honor that now belongs to Moscow's Red Square). Now a recreational park, this elliptical expanse of paved tracks, pathways, a fountain, and grassy areas was originally a Roman theater. On weekends, this is a prime spot to watch the city at play. It's also the setting for small concerts, markets, and fairs.

If you've made it this far, do spend a few minutes visiting one of the largest churches in Europe, the **Basilica di Santa Giustina** (☎ 049-8220445; Mon–Sat 7:30am–noon and 3:30–6:45pm, Sun 7:30am–12:30pm and 3:45–7:45pm), unmistakable thanks to its splendid domes.

THE OTHER PADUA

My favorite Padua activity is watching the students celebrate upon receiving their hard-earned degrees in a spontaneous street performance called *goliardie.* Despite the earnestness of the institution they attend, the graduation party is nothing short of medieval debauchery. The poor graduate's friends create massive posters depicting the "victim" of the ritual as a caricature surrounded by an uncensored history of his or her university adventures; judging from the lurid pictures, much of this revolves around sexual experimentation. Dressed in a hideously unfetching outfit (perhaps a pair of underpants and rubber gloves), the candidate undergoes a variety of humiliating tortures, all the while being fed deadly alcoholic concoctions, much to the glee of the assembled crowd. It's a far cry from togas and mortar boards, and it says a great deal about the local sense of fun. You can catch sight of these ritualistically unceremonious ceremonies around the Palazzo Bò, usually in July and September; to see who's earned their degrees, look for the semisleazy caricature posters tacked up on the wall around the Bò entrance.

Or you could become a student yourself by signing up for a **language course** at one of Padua's rather serious language institutes: The **Bertrand Russell Language School** (Via E. Filiberto 6; ☎ 049-654051; www.bertrand-russell.it) is a highly respected no-nonsense institution offering four tiers of study, from Beginners up to Diploma level. Each full course consists of 80 hours spread over a month (600€); classes run Monday through Friday 9am to 1pm. Maximum class size is 10, and there are film screenings, discussion groups, and guided weekend tours to other Veneto towns to enhance your language acquisition and cultural immersion. The school will also arrange accommodations (400€ for a month in a home with a local family, or 1,000€ in a single room with half-board). Foreigners can also take an Italian course at **Istituto Dante Alighieri** (Riviera Tito Livio 43; ☎ 049-8751151; www.istitutodantealighieri.it); write lingue@istituto dantealighieri.it for details.

NIGHTLIFE

The bars and cafes of the Ghetto are where you'll rub shoulders with the students of Padua University; however, if you cruise around the neighborhood you will find other types of nightlife as well. Gearing itself to trendy adults, **Lounge Aperitif Miracle** (Via San Francesco 15; Tues–Sun 4pm–1am), lays claim to "probably the best barman in the world"; ask for Mauro Lotti by name, and then ask him to whip you up a superb martini. Alternatively, join the grown-ups at **Godenda** ★★ (Via Squarcione 4/6; ☎ 049-8774192; Mon–Sat 10am–3pm and 6pm–midnight; MC, V), a fabulous wine bar in the Ghetto. Besides excellent and unusual vintages, you can order snacks and meals.

I'm a sucker for any venue that offers good people-watching, and one place I usually can't tear myself away from is small, friendly **Paparazzi Fashion Café** ★ (Via Marsilio da Padova 17; ☎ 049-8759306; Tues–Sun 6pm–1am), where cool, funky types sip equally cool cocktails before heading for the clubs. Stand at the red marble bar, or grab a seat under the rows of paparazzi pics, while the DJ plays selections from his very own compilation album. Panini and fresh salads are available, but you'd be forgiven for getting hung up on the cocktails and the human eye candy. Things only start heating up after 10pm, and if you're up for a night of clubbing, this is the best place to ask where the late-night action is.

The city's principal indoor theater is **Teatro Verdi** (Via dei Livello 32; ☎ 049-8777011), which hosts classical music as well as professional comedies and dramas; the season runs from September through April or May. During summer, events at the **Roman Amphitheater** are particularly varied; expect Spanish salsa dancers, film screenings, and rock bands to fill a program that changes daily.

SIDE TRIPS FROM PADUA

Padua is an ideal setting-out point for day outings to the small-but-exquisite cities of Vicenza and Treviso, or for languid river cruises along the Riviera del Brenta to scope a selection of beautiful villas. Vicenza, in particular, should be a high priority for anyone even remotely interested in architecture; the heart of the city is an eye-popping maze of venerable palazzo, many designed by the maestro of Western architecture, Andrea Palladio.

Vicenza ★★★

The splendor of Vicenza is world renowned, and is principally associated with Andrea Palladio, the father of Renaissance architecture, who began his career here when he moved from Padua at age 16 to start his trade as an apprentice stone mason. Palladio's work in this small city brought about a design revolution that profoundly impacted the development of architecture across Europe and worldwide; in America, Australia, and India, Palladio's monumental style became synonymous with architecture associated with civil power. Today, thanks to Palladio (real name: Andrea di Pietro della Gondola), Vicenza is a UNESCO World Heritage Site, and a prosperous one at that; besides tourism, the city's business folk count textiles, gold, and silicon chips among the enterprises that have upheld the entrepreneurial spirit of this lofty town.

Palladio's impact on global architecture will be celebrated with extra-special intensity in 2008, when his 500th anniversary becomes a good excuse to spotlight the city's splendor and encourage visitors to get to know more about its art, architecture, and local culture; find out what's on the program when you're in town by visiting www.andreapalladio500.it, or www.palladio2008.info.

Vicenza is a 20-minute train ride from Padua (from 2.70€), and at least one connection every hour.

Walking Tour: Palladio's City

Start: Train station (Piazza Stazione; ☎ 0444-325046)
Finish: Piazza dei Signori

With its glamorous architecture and exuberant atmosphere, Vicenza feels like the set for a big-budget period film. Walking through the cobblestone streets, you'll find yourself constantly forced to crane your neck backwards to take in the imposing palazzi and looming monuments that stand side by side, as testament to Palladio's stylistic impact. In the town center alone, he had his hand in around 10 different projects, but his influence—evident in the myriad designs by his students, devotees, and rivals—is everywhere.

From the train station, walk directly along broad Viale Roma (lined with cheap stalls and often pulsating with students) until you reach the Giardini Salvi, a relaxed urban park. Don't enter the gardens, but instead turn right, passing under the archways of the Torrione di Porta Castello into Piazza del Castello. Pause here for a moment, and look to your right to catch a glimpse of:

❶ Palazzo Porto Graganze

This rather slender sliver of Palladian architecture is wonderfully photogenic (and one of the few facades that you can actually get up on to in order to have your picture taken).

From Piazza del Castello, your tour gets properly underway as you follow the city's main road to:

❷ Corso Andrea Palladio

This palazzo-lined street sweeps northeast through the heart of Vicenza like an arterial spine, practically dividing the city in two. Don't blink: Virtually every step reveals another architectural marvel, and the road is an excellent primer for the look and feel of the entire city. As you stroll past the boutiques and banks, and watch the self-satisfied locals hiding behind sunglasses and sipping espresso at enticing cafes, the most imposing building along this strip will come up on your right: The

Palazzo del Comunale is Vicenza's Town Hall (1592) and is considered the finest work of Palladio's finest student, Scamozzi (1552–1616).

Farther along, your attention will also be grabbed by the **Ca d'Oro,** or Golden Palace. Although rebuilt in 1950 after being bombed in 1944, the facade was once detailed with gold leaf, which must have been quite a sight. Palladio lived on this street, at no. 163.

At the end of Corso Palladio, you'll reach the helpful **tourist information office** (Piazza Matteotti 12; ☎ 0444-320854; www.vicenzae.org; daily 9am–1pm and 2–6pm, mid-Oct to mid-Mar closes at 5:30pm), where staff will provide a map and tell how to purchase the cumulative admission ticket known as the Vicenza Card (8€), which gets you into six city museums.

Conveniently, the tourist office is right near two important Palladian monuments. Start by visiting the one right next door:

❸ Teatro Olimpico ★★

This theater (Piazza Matteotti; ☎ 0444-222101; admission with Vicenza Card; Sept–June Tues–Sun 9am–5pm, July–Aug 9am–6pm) is arguably Palladio's finest urban project, and one which he did not see completed (it was begun the same year that he died, and took 5 years to finish). Its historical importance is grounded in the fact that this was Europe's first indoor, covered theater although the half-moon auditorium is strongly influenced by ancient arena-style design. It was so expensive that the city had to get financial aid from the Venetian Republic.

There are various historical exhibits in the theater building, but the main draw is the interior of the auditorium itself. Once inside, go up to the top row (just mind not to walk on the seats),

from where you'll get a proper idea of the grandeur of the space; it looks small, but the steep, raked auditorium seats as many as 1,000 patrons. The theater was inaugurated in 1585 with a performance of *Oedipus the Tyrant.* Resembling the classical Greek city of Thebes, the stage was designed by Palladio's student, Vincenzo Scamozzi, to force the illusion of depth.

Once you've toured the theater, walk back past the tourist office and across Corso Palladio to the:

❹ Museo Civico ★

This art gallery (Piazza Matteotti; ☎ 0444-321348; admission with Vicenza Card; Sept–June Tues–Sun 9am–5pm) occupies Palladio's Palazzo Chiericati. Inside is an extensive collection of artwork by local masters (notably Bartolomeo Montagna, founder of the Vicenza school of painting), as well as paintings by more recognizable stars like Tintoretto (his *St. Augustine Healing the Cripples* is a favorite), Veronese, and Tiepolo.

Having explored the Museo Civico, double back along Contrà Palladio, and take the second street to the right: Contrà Santa Corona. On your right-hand side, you soon come upon:

❺ Santa Corona

This church (Contrà Santa Corona 2; ☎ 0444-321924; Tues–Sun 8:30am–noon and 3–6pm) was built by the Dominicans in about 1261, apparently as a place to keep one of the thorns from Christ's crown, sent here by way of France. More visibly impressive (the church itself is nothing to write home about) are two exquisite paintings: Giovanni Bellini's *Baptism of Christ* (1502), and *The Adoration of the Magi* (1573) by Paolo Veronese.

From Santa Corona, wander past some of Vicenza's most impressive urban palazzi, a significant number of them now UNESCO World Heritage monuments.

The first is on your left-hand side as you continue along Contrà Santa Corona after exiting the church:

6 Palazzo Leoni Montanari

This baroque palazzo (☎ 800-578875; www.palazzomontanari.net; included in Vicenza Card; Tues–Sun 10am–6pm) was commissioned by a wealthy cloth merchant named Giovanni Leoni Montanari and completed in the first part of the 18th century. Today, the palazzo doubles as an art gallery featuring notable Venetian paintings (the best of which are by Pietro Longhi), and also exhibits an impressive collection of Russian icons.

Turning left when you exit Leoni Montanari, it's a short walk to the end of Santa Corona; turn left and follow the road until—again, on your left—you come to:

7 Contrà Porti

This pedestrianized road features some of the city's most impressive palazzi, including many of Gothic design (look out for elaborate balconies and decorative windows). Here, Palladio alone churned out designs for three equally pretty, but all perceptibly unique, buildings: First up is **Palazzo Iseppo da Porto** (1552), on your right at no. 21. Next to this is the 14th-century **Palazzo Colleoni Porto** (not Palladio's work, but impressive nonetheless). A few steps along, you'll reach the intersection of Contrà Porti and Contrà Riale. On your left, at no. 12, is Palladio's **Palazzo Thiene** (1545–50; now a bank), and, on your right, his **Palazzo Barbaran da Porto** (1570;

now an international center for Palladian studies, open to the public during temporary exhibitions; www. cisapalladio.org) at no. 11. You may want to go up to inspect the surface of Palazzo Thiene, which should reveal one of Palladio's clever building secrets. Although the exterior is designed to look like masonry, it is in fact ordinary, low-cost brick modified to make it look like expensive stonework. Also on the right, at no. 17, is 15th-century **Palazzo Porto-Braganze,** the interior courtyard of which you can usually sneak a peek of by quickly popping through the ornamental archway entrance.

Continue to the end of Contrà Porti, and then double back and turn left into Contrà Riale. It's a short walk along this road to Corso Fogazzaro; turn right and you'll soon hit:

8 San Lorenzo ★★

This church (daily 7am–noon and 3:30-7:15pm) is arguably Vicenza's most impressive, featuring an impressive Gothic facade, pretty fountain, and exquisite interior (with frescoes that are now badly damaged).

After visiting the church, double back along Corso Fogazzaro, keeping a look out on your left for Palladio's most peculiar design, **Palazzo Valamarana Braga Rosa** (at no. 16, built 1566), which looks like it's in need of a good scrub.

Continue along Corso Fogazzaro (which becomes Contrà Battisti) until you reach the:

9 Duomo

Dating from the 9th century and finished with a Palladian dome in 1574, this cathedral has been extensively restored after being pummeled during World War II.

As you exit the Duomo, turn left and cut diagonally across the Piazza del Duomo to reach Contrà Sant'Antonio. Turn left into this road and follow it until it becomes Contrà Antonio Pigafetta, where—on your right—you'll spot:

⑩ Casa Pigafetta

This house, with its arched doorway, was where Antonio Pigafetta was born. His esteem stems from having accompanied Magellan on his round-the-world sailing expedition in 1519 (Pigafetta was one of the few survivors of that voyage). The house was built in 1481 in the Spanish Gothic style; note the Moorish influence of the windows.

Having admired Pagafetta's house, it's a few more steps before Contrà Antonio Pigafetta intersects Contrà Pescaria. Turn left into this road and you'll soon find yourself on the edge of:

⑪ Piazza dell'Erbe

This is Vicenza's fresh produce market square. The tower diagonally across the square from you is the 13th-century **Torre del Tormento,** once the city's torture chamber. The large building directly in front of you is one of Palladio's early commissions, popularly known as the **Basilica Palladiana** (Piazza dei Signori; ☎ 444-323681). Palladio's contribution to this monument (which is not a church, but a basilica in the Roman sense of the word, meaning that it housed public administration rooms) was actually an architectural solution rather than a building conceptualized from scratch. Authorities asked Palladio to convert the existing (and collapsing) Palazzo della Ragione (with the Law Courts and Assembly Hall) into something more fashionable (and stable). His

revolutionary solution gave the basilica its splendid two-tiered loggia. Destroyed during World War II, the copper-covered roof has been rebuilt; a menagerie of classical gods is featured along the balustrade. Note that in late 2007, the Palladiana was undergoing extensive renovation, meaning that its roof may or may not be back on in time for the 2008 Palladio celebrations. If renovations are complete, you'll also be able to explore the shops and cafe within the Basilica itself.

The Basilica is surrounded on all sides by squares. To reach the most important of these, you need to get to the other side of the Basilica. You can walk around the Basilica clockwise or counterclockwise to get there. If you go counterclockwise, you'll pass more market stalls as well as a statue of a very elegant-looking Andrea Palladio, before reaching:

⑫ Piazza dei Signori

The tallest structure here is the **Torre di Piazza** (or Torre Bissara), a 82m (269-ft.) high bell tower. Nearby, you'll spot two columns, one topped by the Venetian winged lion (with which you should be quite familiar by now), and the other sporting a statue of the Redeemer *(Redentore).* The square separates the Basilica from Palladio's incomplete **Loggia del Capitaniato,** built for the Venetian military; the reliefs decorating it commemorate Venice's victory over the Turks at Lepanto.

A lovely spot from which to take in the visual drama of the Basilica and the Piazza is the terrace of historic **Gran Caffè Garibaldi** (☎ 0444-544147; closed Wed), where a freshly made panino won't hurt your wallet too badly.

ATTRACTIONS ON THE CITY OUTSKIRTS

La Rotonda ★★★ (☎ 0444-321793; Mar 15–Nov 4 Tues–Sun 10am–noon and 3–6pm), is the stuff of architectural legend and widely considered Palladio's finest work; some architects consider it the closest humans have come to creating a "perfect" building. Built on a square plan, and capped by a dome, it was inspired by ancient Greek and Roman designs, and begun in 1567. Palladio's star student, Scamozzi, was responsible for seeing the project to its completion in 1592. The easiest way to get to the villa (properly known as **Villa Capra Valmarana**) is on bus no. 8, but cycling or walking is also manageable (it's 3km/2 miles from the station). There are two viewing alternatives: either observe from the gate, or—from March through November only—pay to get into the grounds (3€; Tues–Sun 10am–noon and 3–6pm) for a closer look. On Wednesday, you can also see the interior (6€; same hours).

From Villa Rotonda, you can walk to **Villa Valmarana "ai Nani"** ★ (☎ 0444-321803; 6€; Mar–Nov Tues–Sun 10am–noon and 3–6pm), built by Antonio Muttoni, an admirer of Palladio, in 1688; the real reason to visit is for the splendid Tiepolo frescoes which cover the interior walls with sublime epic scenes. The nickname—"ai Nani"—refers to the sculpted dwarves atop the building.

Overlooking Vicenza, a 10-minute walk from Valmarana, is the baroque basilica and sanctuary, **Monte Bérico** ★ (☎ 0444-320999; Mon–Sat 6am–12:30pm and 2:30–7:30pm, Sun 6am–7pm), a popular destination for pilgrims who believe that this was the very spot where the Virgin herself made two appearances to announce that Vicenza would escape the grip of bubonic plague which struck in 1426. Inside, a *Pietà* by Vicenza's Bartolomeo Montagna is particularly stirring. In front of the Basilica, there's a relaxed cafe with a garden terrace; stay awhile and enjoy the handsome city panorama.

A RELIABLE DINING VALUE

€ All that walking through the streets of Palladio's city will build up quite an appetite; to find an affordable, atmospheric *taverna,* turn off Corso Palladio into Contrà della Morette (a pedestrian alleyway that links with Piazza dei Signori), where **Antica Casa della Malvasia** ★ (☎ 0444-543704; Tues–Sun; *coperto* 1.30€) attracts a devoted local following (many loyal primarily to the bar). The cuisine is typical of the region, unpretentious and usually very good. On weekdays, you can take advantage of a special, with a choice of *primi* (like *fettuccine ai finfarli* or *tagliolini al tartufo*) for 3€, and *secondi* for 4.50€.

Treviso

Off-the-beaten-track Treviso is easily overlooked by time-constrained tourists (many think of this merely as a point of arrival for low-priced flights from the U.K. to Venice), but that's a shame, because the medieval town makes for an attractive outing. Although much of the Treviso you see today resulted from extensive postwar restoration, within the historical center, fortified by 16th-century walls, an ancient system of canals quaintly sets off the cityscape of houses with pretty, frescoed facades.

Treviso is small enough to get around easily on foot; pick up a map at the **tourist office** (Piazzetta Monte di Pietà 8; ☎ 0422-547632; http://tourism.provincia.treviso.it; daily 9am–12:30pm, Tues–Fri 2–6pm) right in the center of the town; to get there from the train station, head along Via Roma and continue as it becomes Corso dei Popolo, until you reach the Piazza dei Signori, at one end of the city's main street, Calmaggiore. Here stands the **Palazzo dei Trecento,** Treviso's 13th-century town hall (much rebuilt after destructive bombing raids on Good Friday 1944), and the more recent **Palazzo del Podestà** (19th c.). Nearby, two churches well worth a visit are **San Vito** and **Santa Lucia** (free; daily 9am–noon), around the other side of the block. The chapel in the latter church showcases works by Tomaso da Modena (1325–79), Treviso's most celebrated artist, who came to prominence after Giotto.

The city's 12th-century **San Pietro Cathedral** (free; closed noon–3:30pm) is farther along Calmaggiore; Titian's *Annunciation* (1570) is usually considered the highlight, although I find the remains of the frescoed *Adoration of the Magi,* by the relative unknown Pordenone (1520), far more compelling.

Near the city wall to the south, is the Dominican church, **San Nicolò** (Via San Nicolò; free), with more examples of work by Tomaso da Modena; the best of his legacy, however, is in the **Sala del Capitolo** (enter via the Seminario Vescovile; free; Mon–Fri 8am–12:30pm and 3–5:30pm, in summer until 6pm) of the attached monastery. Here, you must check out the portraits of 40 monks of the Dominican Order, rendered in Tomaso's entertainingly droll style.

The former church and convent of **Santa Caterina** (Via Santa Caterina; ☎ 0422-591337) is home to Tomaso's impressive fresco cycle depicting *The Life of St. Ursula.* Other works that have been transferred here include Titian's *Portrait of Sperone Speroni* and Bessano's *Crucifixion.* Problem is, it's been intermittently closed due to restoration work, so ask at the tourist office before heading off to see it.

A DINING SPLURGE   €€–€€€   One of my favorite restaurants in all of the Veneto is expensive-but-worth-it **Don Fernando** ★★★ (Via delle Absidi 8/10; ☎ 0422-543354; closed Tues lunch and Wed lunch; AE, DC, MC, V) near San Nicolò church. Local vocalists and musicians regularly get up from their tables to serenade the other diners. It's a classy place where you can expect Fernando himself to come and introduce the dishes to your table (the menu changes with the whims of the kitchen, but on average you'll pay 30€ for a full-blown meal, before wine). Highlights include Fernando's *carrello dei bolliti,* a meat stew, which has made a loyal following of Treviso's in-the-know foodies, and delicious *mari e monti,* or "sea and land," a shellfish dish prepared with porcini mushrooms and *granchio* sauce, and served with polenta. Veneto wines start at 12€ per bottle.

The Riviera del Brenta

Palladian-inspired villas, built in the heyday of Venetian aristocracy, line the Brenta Canal, which stretches between Padua and Venice, providing a marketable venture for tour operators who've clung to Riviera del Brenta as the romantic term to lure visitors on expensive boats chugging up and down the waterways. A Brenta boat cruise isn't my favorite outing—they're expensive and crammed with boatfuls of package-deal groups. Nevertheless, the trip does allow you to observe around three dozen villas from the deck of the boat, stopping at three for a close-up inspection and tour. The inconsistent operating hours of these villas means that a boat cruise greatly eases the fuss you'll need to go through trying to plan your trip; there's not much emphasis on customer satisfaction, however, and some of the villa stops feel a bit truncated.

Popular cruises include **I Batelli del Brenta** (☎ 049-8760233; www.antoniana. it) and **Il Burchiello** (☎ 049-8206910; www.ilburchiello.it), both of which are pricey (you'll pay around 60€ or 71€ for the cruise and three villas; the optional fish lunch is 26€; the cheaper rate applies July–Aug). Needless to say, you'll save a fortune by seeing the Pisani and Fóscari villas by public transport; hourly ACTV buses (1.50€; 90-min. trip) go past both villas en route from Padua to Venice.

First stop on the full-day boat tour is **Villa Pisani** (Strà; ☎ 049-502074; 5€ garden and museum; Oct–Mar Tues–Sun 9am–4pm, Apr–Sept 9am–7pm), built in the 18th century for Doge Alvise Pisani and known chiefly for the Tiepolo fresco on the ballroom ceiling, as well as its famous garden hedge maze (garden only, 2.50€). Napoleon bought it for his stepson in 1807; later, it became the site of the first meeting between Hitler and Mussolini in 1934.

The only Brenta villa designed by Palladio is **Villa Fóscari** ★★★ (Via dei Turisti 9; Mira; ☎ 041-5203966; www.lamalcontenta.com; 7€–8€; May–Oct Tues and Sat 9am–noon, Wed–Fri and Sun by appointment only), so this is usually included on every cruise. Also called La Malcontenta (The Unhappy Woman), the villa was built in 1558 for two brothers descended from a Venetian doge; after the fall of the Venetian Republic in 1797, the house remained abandoned for an entire century, spawning a legend of a woman existing there in absolute, unhappy seclusion for many years. If you arrive under your own steam, you need to pre-book a guided tour; book it online.

Near Fóscari is **Barchessa Valmarana** (Mira; ☎ 041-4266387 or 041-5609350; 6€; usually Apr–Oct Tues–Sun 9:30am–noon and 2:30–6pm), where visitors are led on a half-hourly guided tour. Some cruises include a visit to **Villa Widmann** instead of Valmarana.

VERONA

Centuries ago, Shakespeare set a play about dizzying pubescent romance in a town he referred to as "Fair Verona." Today, Verona is far more dazzlingly romantic than the Bard's brutal tragedy about star-crossed lovers ever let on. Self-confident and stylish, Verona has the exuberant air of a city that knows it's beautiful enough to entertain visitors simply by being there.

Verona's visual drama and postcard-perfect feel have much to do with its medieval architecture pounded together from a generous supply of rose-colored limestone, quarried from the surrounding hills and known as *rosso di Verona.* Flower-filled balconies, like the one immortalized in *Romeo and Juliet,* protrude from noble houses, daintily overlooking the maze of cobblestone streets and lovely open squares; some of the buildings date back to the reconstruction that followed a catastrophic earthquake in 1117. Along with the historic houses are a number of elegant high-end boutiques, where visitors enjoy the pleasures of conspicuous consumption against the refined, historic backdrop of the city center. After Venice, this is the most visited city in the region, and once you spend a lazy day wandering its streets and seeing the sights, I think you'll understand why Verona has stolen so many hearts, including my own.

A BRIEF HISTORY OF VERONA

As suggested by the city's vast public Arena and superb collection of excavated ruins, Verona was a Roman stronghold, first occupied in 89 B.C. Its favorable position at the mouth of the Adige River made it a popular conquest, and it drew consistent attention from various Italian and Mitteleuropa invaders once the Roman Empire fell. Verona's very own Della Scala (or Scaligeri) family put an end to the invasions when it came to power in the 13th century, holding considerable sway in northern Italy. Much like the Medicis in Florence, this despotic family ruled Verona harshly, but at the same time beautified it immensely. They also forced the citizenry to pay taxes for expanding their miniature empire, and imported some of the region's best artists and architects. The Scaligeris were important patrons of the poet Dante.

The Della Scalas remained in power until 1387, when Milan's Viscontis took over briefly. In 1404, Verona fell into the welcome embrace of *La Serenissima;* Venice was developing its inland empire, and Verona happily remained under Venetian rule until 1797, when Napoleon got his claws into much of Europe. Later, in 1814, Verona—along with the whole of the Veneto—became part of Austria and only shook off foreign rulers when it joined the Kingdom of Italy in 1866. Today, she is a large, prosperous city, although the expanse of industrialization beyond the historical center is almost unnoticeable.

LAY OF THE LAND

Verona's **Stazione FS Porta Nuova** (☎ 8488-88088) is served by direct rail connections from most major destinations, including Rome, Milan, and Bologna. There are over 40 trains per day from Venice (around 90 min.), and there are regular departures to and from the nearby towns. (In fact, Verona's charms are complemented by her usefulness as a base from which to explore several other not-too-distant towns: Trent in the north, Mantua in the neighboring province of Lombardy, and Treviso, are all within easy reach of the city.)

Orange **AMT Buses** (☎ 045-8871111; www.amt.it) and **taxis** (for around-the-clock assistance, call **RadioTaxi** at ☎ 045-532666) constantly arrive in the adjacent Piazzale XXV Aprile concourse; from here, all buses head along Corso Porta Nuova in the direction of the city's historical center, about a kilometer northeast of the station; look for bus 11, 12, 13, 72, or 73 or—on the weekend—91, 92, or 93. Tickets cost 1€; purchase them from the *tabacchi* before exiting the station

You can also fly directly to **Aeroporto di Verona Valerio Catullo** (☎ 045-8095666; www.aeroportoverona.it), 12km (7½ miles) from the center; there are regular shuttle buses to town (3.60€; purchase directly from the driver).

Verona's historical center can be explored on foot, but if you require **public transportation,** there is a reliable, regular bus network; for all city transport routes go to www.atv.verona.it (Italian only), or call ☎ 045-8057811. If you're self-driving, be warned that access to the historical center is limited to certain times, and parking can be expensive; you'll need to purchase a prepaid **Verona Park card** (1€–1.50€ per hour) from tabacchi or authorized bars. Hotel parking rates range from 10€ to 20€ per night, depending on the season.

The **tourist information office** (Via degli Alpini 9; ☎ 045-8068680; www.tourism.verona.it; Mon–Sat 8:30am–7pm, Sun 9am–1pm and 2–5pm) is near the Arena, and works hard to supply maps and information about the city and surrounding area. There's also one at the **train station** (☎ 045-8000861), so you can grab a map upon arrival.

ACCOMMODATIONS, BOTH STANDARD & NOT

At most of Verona's hotels, rates are seasonal, soaring by around 50% during the Arena's summer opera season (June to early Oct); this is also when it's difficult to find a vacant room. Plan well ahead for this period.

€€   The cheapest decent digs in the city (at least for those not willing to camp or bed down in a hostel) are offered by **Al Quadrifoglio Bed & Breakfast** ✪✪ (Via XXIV Maggio 6; ☎ 338-2253681; www.alquadrifoglio.it; cash only). A reasonably easy walk from Verona's historical center, Al Quadrifoglio benefits from the hands-on efforts of David and Giusy. This personable couple will go so far as to pick you up from the station if you make arrangements, and they'll indulge you with conversation (in English) and good suggestions for dining and exploring the city (and the region, if you like). The B&B offers three sizeable rooms (60€–80€ double); one is en suite, while the other two share a bathroom (not too much of an inconvenience). All are clean, air-conditioned, and Wi-Fi-enabled. Breakfast is hearty, with homemade preserves and great coffee. You'll pay the lower rates on weekdays or if you stay for more than 1 night.

€€–€€€   If you insist on being in the immediate vicinity of the Arena, **Hotel Torcolo** ✪ (Vicolo Listone 3; ☎ 045-8007512; www.hoteltorcolo.it; AE, DC, MC, V) is the ideal choice. Childhood friends Silvia and Diana have fashioned a homey, comfortable, and professional little hotel that's earned a near-legendary reputation with frequent travelers (many of whom return annually during opera season). Besides my key ingredient—firm, comfortable mattresses—all 19 guest rooms are soberly tasteful, most with wooden floors and shuttered windows looking out over Verona's back streets. Rooms on the third floor have low ceilings, so indicate if this is likely to bother you. Rates are seasonal, reaching a peak of 116€ in the popular opera season (which is still very reasonable) but costing about 70€ otherwise. Breakfast is usually extra (8€–13€); parking is 12€ to 18€.

€€–€€€   Verona's other top value is **Hotel Aurora** ✪✪ (Piazzetta Novembre 2; ☎ 045-594717; www.hotelaurora.biz; cash, MC, or V preferred), offering everything a discerning traveler wants—a good location in the heart of the ancient city, helpful staff, and little details that make you forget you're in budget digs. Exceptionally neat rooms are bolstered by antique wardrobes, the odd lithograph or painting, and a flower and chocolate on your pillow at day's end. Even the tiny bathrooms are easily forgiven. Be quick to reserve room no. 18; best in terms of size, it also has delightful views. Kick-start your day with breakfast (included) on the terrace where you feel like you're part of the neighborhood, often with free entertainment provided by musicians busking on Piazza dell Erbe below. Doubles start at 100€, and go to 145€ during opera season; there are also singles with shared (58€–70€) or private (90€–125€) bathrooms.

€€€–€€€€   Named for the romantic tale that has put Verona on the tourist map, **Hotel Giulietta e Romeo** ✬ (Vicolo Tre Marchetti 3; ☎ 045-8003554; www.giuliettaeromeo.com; AE, DC, MC, V) is a popular option in the historical heart of town. There's nothing glamorous or special about the place, but the pink- ish facade conceals neat, soothing public spaces and pleasant enough guest rooms with cherrywood furnishings and floral-patterned wallpaper. Doubles start at 105€, which is excellent value, but are 230€ when opera comes to town (not sur- prising, given the prime location, right near the Arena), and I wouldn't dream of paying that here. Parking is 18€ per night. Bicycles are loaned free of charge.

Hostels & Campgrounds

€   Many budget-savvy Italians combine their love of the opera with their taste for the outdoors by forgoing the city's concrete hotels and heading instead for **Campeggio Castel San Pietro** (Via Castel San Pietro 2; ☎ 045-592037; www. campingcastelsanpietro.com), a seasonal camping site (mid-May until mid-Oct) on a hillside overlooking the city. Sheltered by trees and nestled in tranquillity, this laid-back spot offers a great opportunity to meet down-to-earth Italians; there are terraced areas for dining, kicking back, or soaking up the sun. Rates are very reasonable: 6.50€ to 8.50€ per tent; 6.50€ per person (4.50€ for children under 8); 3.50€ per car. You can even rent a tent. The only real drawback, besides need- ing your own sleeping bag, is the 5-minute walk up a rather steep hill from the bus stop if you're using public transport (bus: 41 or 95 to the first stop on Via Marsala).

€   I wouldn't recommend Verona's coed hostel, **Ostello della Gioventù Villa** Francescatti (Salita Fontana del Ferro, 15; ☎ 045-590360) if you're on a tight schedule; it involves a steep uphill climb along the road behind the Teatro Romano. Nevertheless, if you're here for several days and would prefer to keep a lid on that budget, bring your Hostelling International card and follow the yel- low signs. Dorms (16€ per bed, with breakfast) are spartan, but there are slightly more expensive family rooms (19€ per person), which you can book in advance. Despite the hike, the hillside neighborhood is rather quaint, and there's a lovely garden (something you won't find at most hotels in town). The major drawback is the daylong lockout, and there's also an 11:30pm curfew, which is only relaxed for ticket holders during the opera season.

DINING FOR ALL TASTES

Cafes abound throughout the center, and the area around the Arena is constantly abuzz with people-watching coffee drinkers. But it's really worth getting away from the most obvious spots to find charming *trattorie* hidden down quieter back streets; the selection below caters to most tastes, and allows you to get some idea of the peculiarities of local cuisine—especially the affection for horse and donkey meat.

€   A spot that's great for light lunches—and an almost essential stop for vegetar- ians—is **Caffè Coloniale** (Piazza Viviani 14C; ☎ 045-8012647; daily 8am–mid- night; MC, V), where you can grab a table on the roadside courtyard just around the corner from Juliet's tourist-mobbed house, and miraculously feel as though you've completely escaped the crowds. At lunch, this is *the* place for a healthful salad (5.80€–8€) or a light *primi* of the day (usually 6€), which invariably tides me over until dinner. Warm vegetarian dishes (like aubergine baked with Parmesan; 5.80€) and tasty pizzas are also available.

€   For an introduction to authentic regional cuisine head for **Osteria al Duca** ⭐ (Via Arche Scaligeri 2; ☎ 045-594474; Mon–Sat noon–2pm and 6:30–10:30pm; AE, MC, V), a bustling family restaurant near the Scaligeri tombs, supposedly in part of Romeo's family home, a 13th-century palace originally owned by the Della Scalas. You're waited on by the family women; decked out in black, they squabble among themselves while clutching their notepads and explaining the menu in well-enunciated Italian. The homey vibe is maintained by the casual layout—diners share tables, and the family Labrador cruises about looking for a spot to nap. Get here before 7:30pm, after which it fills up quickly. Alessandro, whose family runs this lively eatery, explains that the food's authenticity results from the firm matriarchal grip in the kitchen where local delicacies—horse-meat steak, horse tartar, horse prepared with Parmesan and arugala, and spaghetti served with donkey meat—are prepared. You're encouraged to order the good-value fixed menu, so you'll be able to taste one of the rich pastas, plus a *secondo*, for just 14€. Finish off with a decadent portion of homemade tiramisu (3.50€).

€–€€   Whether you simply want to sample from the interesting wine selection, or really want to better understand Verona's unusual gastronomical bent, locals' fave **Alcova del Frate** ⭐ (Via Ponte Pietra 19/A; ☎ 045-8000653; Mon–Fri 5pm–1am, Sat–Sun 10am–3:30pm and 6pm–1am; MC, V), should fit the bill. Here, you'll find lovely snack platters featuring assorted *tartina* (bite-size nibbles; 1€ per piece) to stave off your appetite while you sip Custoza San Michelin by the glass (1.80€). Most pasta dishes are 7.50€, but ask your friendly barman-cum-waiter to guide you through the menu, and he'll point out which dishes include horse or donkey meat, making this as much an education as a well-priced dinner spot.

€–€€   Disguised as a house of worship, **San Matteo Church** (Vicolo del Guasto 4; ☎ 045-8004538; Mon–Sat noon–2:30pm and 6:30pm–12:30am; AE, DC, MC, V) has been converted into a very affordable pizzeria where a basic marinara costs just 4€. Situated down a quiet alleyway off Corsà Porta Borsari, it's perfect if you favor low prices over atmosphere, although the cheeky waiters do try to impress. For a rather more decorous dining experience, head over to **Le Cantine de L'Arena** ⭐ (Piazzetta Scalette Rubiani 1; ☎ 045-8032849; www.lecantine-arena.com; AE, MC, V), just meters from the Arena, with lively outdoor seating. Whatever goes into that big brick pizza oven, comes out tasting delicious. Just make sure you study the list of toppings before placing your order; among the many options is a pizza with horse meat, arugula, and Parmesan. My favorite is the lip-smacking "Baito," piled full of Veronese cheese, fleshy boletus mushrooms, and mozzarella. Pasta specials (around 8€) are chalked up on the board, and winter dining tends to focus on grilled meat.

€€   Off a small courtyard square shared with trendy shops, another favorite is family-run **Ristorante Greppia** ⭐⭐ (Vicolo Samaritana 3; ☎ 045-8004577;

Vino Amore

A must-visit for wine lovers is Oreste dal Zovo's wonderfully overstocked liquor store, **Enoteca dal Zovo** (Vicolo San Marco in Foro 7; ☎ 045-8034369; www.enotecadalzovo.it; cash only), operating in the former archbishop's chapel since the 1950s. Its walls are packed tight with booze, and the selection of wines is overwhelming, stacked between pictures of bare-breasted women competing for space with caricatures and images of Christ. If it's a special bottle of wine you're after, Valpolicella Amarone is one of the region's standouts. Oreste and his American-born wife, Beverly, will also help you find rare vintages, or introduce you to some exotic-sounding liqueurs such as the fabled herb concoction, Elisir del Pozzo dell'Amore, which is said to have magical properties, particularly as a prelude to romance! Oreste doesn't speak English, but Beverly once gave me a tour of the neighborhood; if you want to get her chatting, ask to be shown the nearby Pozzo dell'Amore (Well of Love). Enoteca dal Zovo is open Tuesday through Sunday 8am to 1pm and 2 to 8pm, and until 9pm over weekends; pop in around 5pm for a glass of wine (from 1.50€).

---

www.ristorantegreppia.com; Tues–Sun noon–2:30pm and 7–10:30pm; AE, DC, MC, V), specializing in Veronese cuisine for 30 years and still a top contender. Apparently, the secret's in the homemade pasta created by the family matriarchs. In winter, spring, and fall you can order *bollito misto con salse* ("trolley meat"), which is cut for you at your table and then prepared to suit your tastes. Among the selection of steaks, the *osso buco* is particularly wonderful, prepared in a local vegetable sauce and served with polenta. The downside here? A 3€ *coperto*.

€€   Mention **Osteria Sgarzarie** ✪✪✪ (Corte Sgarzarie 14/A; ☎ 045-8000312; Wed–Mon 12:30–2:30pm and 7:30–10:30pm, daily in summer; AE, DC, MC, V) in the company of Verona's sharpest foodies, and their faces light up. This remains a spectacularly well-kept secret despite its proximity to Piazza della Erbe, where the bulk of tourists end up dining at average, overpriced venues. A jazzy atmosphere is complemented by professional waitstaff, and the kitchen is ruled by Mamma, who combines much-loved local dishes with imaginative innovations. The menu changes quarterly, introducing variants such as lasagna with artichoke and truffles, black ravioli stuffed with sea bass, or octopus salad with sprouts and wild lettuce (*primi* are all 10€–12€). Sgarzarie's single most legendary dish has got to be *risotto del cuoco,* or "the chef's risotto," prepared with that glorious local red wine, Amarone. Local dishes with a loyal following include *pastisada* (horse-meat stew, 13€), served with polenta, and *baccalà* (dry codfish prepared with milk and olive oil, 13€). In summer, you can sample homemade gelato. A bottle of Valpolicella Classico is 10€, a glass of prosecco 3€, and *coperto* 2€.

€€–€€€   Wine philosophers and connoisseurs should immediately book an evening at award-winning **Antica Bottega del Vino** ✪✪ (Via Scudo di Francia 3;

☎ 045-8004535; www.bottegavini.it; Wed–Mon 10:30am–3pm and 6pm–midnight)—even if it means going hungry for the next few days! You may be familiar with the New York branch; well, here's the original, operated by the Barzan family for 2 decades. Ultimately, it's the ambience and selection of over 3,400 varieties of wine that draw the regular clientele (and regular awards); recommended bottles are chalked up on the board behind the bar counter. The menu reflects local and international tastes, but you might want to splurge on a juicy steak (the Florentine sirloin is served by weight and is arguably the best meat you'll eat in the Veneto). One thing you won't find on the NYC menu is *pastissada di cavallo* (20€), delicious as locals claim their favorite horse meat delicacy to be; this version is prepared with lemon and oil, and served with polenta, as tradition dictates. If you're looking to buy wine to take home with you, you can also visit the bottle store right next door, La Bottega della Bottega.

WHY YOU'RE HERE: THE TOP SIGHTS & ATTRACTIONS

Verona's cobblestone streets, ancient Roman monuments, medieval urban architecture, and palpably romantic air make it ideal for relaxed exploration. Specific sights are spread out, but the strolls between them—most are located around the Piazza delle Erbe, across the Adige River, or close to the mighty Arena amphitheater—are tremendously rewarding; just try to avoid colliding with cars, bicycles, or people as you drift from one delightful scene to the next.

If you'd like to be guided around the city, you can join one of the walking tours starting at the equestrian statue of Vittorio Emanuele II, in the Arena Square, every evening at 5:30pm (Apr–Sept). Contact **Juliet & Co.** (☎ 045-8103173; www.julietandco.com) for information; tickets are 10€, free for kids.

The Roman Arena

The 2,000-year-old **Arena di Verona** ✮✮✮ (☎ 045-8003204; 4€; Tues–Sun 8:30am–7:15pm, Mon 1:30-7:30pm; hours vary during opera season; ticket sales end 6:30pm), on the edge of Piazza Brà, is arguably the most important Roman structure in northern Italy, and certainly the best preserved Roman amphitheater anywhere. Once located outside the walls of the city, the Arena was a massive entertainment stadium seating nearly 30,000 citizens who would flock here regularly to watch gladiatorial combat, mock battles, and thrilling naval displays for which the Arena was flooded. It also hosted public executions and bullfights, but such bloodfests have now given way to opera and music concerts that draw equally spirited—if more civilized—crowds. Facing the central performance space are 44 tiers of stone seats, reached via a thorough system of well-preserved stairways and passages.

Frankly, the best way to see and experience the Arena is to pick up a ticket for one of the performances during the world-renowned opera season; if you're in town for Verdi's *Aida,* do not pass on the opportunity to see it. The spectacle of witnessing the world's third-largest amphitheater fill up with excited spectators (many of whom would never consider going to the opera) is one of those "before-you-die" experiences, and you're allowed to take a picnic in with you, if you can't imagine sitting still for 3 or 4 hours.

Don't Pass on the Pass

If you plan on swinging by a whole bunch of the city's museums and churches, it's worth investing in a **VeronaCard** ✦ (www.veronacard.it), a handy money-saving tool for tourists. You'll get free bus trips, and access to 17 different attractions (including all those I've recommended); it's probably one of the best multi-entry tickets in the country, since Verona is compact enough to enable you to actually cover everything that's on offer. It's valid for 1 day (8€) or 3 days (12€), and is available from all participating attractions, tabacchi, and tourist offices.

If for some strange reason you're only planning on visiting churches (all covered by the VeronaCard), there's a 5€ **combined church ticket,** which will get you into the Duomo complex as well as the Santa Anastasia, San Zeno, San Fermo, and San Lorenzo churches, which usually charge 2.50€ each. It's available from any participating church.

The Castle & the Basilica

Verona's main art museum, **Museo di Castelvecchio** ✦ (Corso Castelvecchio 2; ☎ 0495-8062611; 4€; Tues–Sun 8:30am–7:30pm, Mon 1:30–7:30pm), is less than 10 minutes by foot from the Arena, at the end of Via Roma. Built on a bank of the River Adige between 1355 and 1375, Castelvecchio looks very much the ancient castle; it served as both a military fortress (to ward against foreign invasion and popular uprisings) and a residence for the various rulers of Verona before being transformed into a museum in the 1920s. Attacked by the Nazis during World War II, the structure you see today is a meticulous restoration by acclaimed Venetian architect Carlos Scarpa, who not only repaired the damage done by bombs but also by the 1920s restoration—when ugly Gothic and Romanesque features were added.

I'd proceed briskly through the first few rooms of the museum, which feature fairly prosaic Roman and early Christian art, glasswork, and jewelry. It's the fierce attempts at realism of the early Renaissance painters that are the glories of this museum, notably in the works of Tintoretto, Tiepolo, Veronese, and Bellini, which you'll see throughout. As well, give some time to the Venetian painters featured in the **Pisanello Room (Room 10),** many of them combining a sense of Gothic refinement with Byzantine embellishments. Note in particular how the background of Gothic rocks in Jacopo Bellini's *St. Jerome in the Desert* heavily suggests the appearance of the Dolomite mountain ranges. Upstairs, the picture galleries continue, and although I feel that there's way too much to take in, there are some wonderful works worth seeking out. Among them are Francesco Bonsignori's *Madonna and Child,* done when he was just 20 years old; and Girolamo dai Libri's colorful *Madonna of the Umbrella* (with clues that pooch parlors were already in vogue during the 16th c.). In **Room 22** you'll find works by Venice's great masters, Tintoretto and Veronese. If you want more thorough explanations of the works on display, you can pick up an **audioguide** (3.60€) at the ticket counter.

From Castelvecchio, it's a 15-minute walk—mostly along the River Adige (and then a sharp left when the riverside promenade ends)—to get to the remarkable **Basilica di San Zeno Maggiore** ✪✪ (Piazza San Zeno 2; ☎ 045-592813; 2.50€; Mar–Oct Mon–Sat 8:30am–6pm, Sun 1–6pm; Nov–Feb Tues–Sat 8:30am–1pm and 1:30–4pm, Sun 1–5pm), a mammoth 12th-century church featuring quintessential Romanesque striped brickwork, and dedicated to Verona's patron saint, San Zeno, whose remains are preserved inside in a downstairs crypt. San Zeno came from Africa and became the city's bishop in the 4th century. Before entering, spend some time giving your attention to the lovely facade, with its large *Wheel of Fortune* rose window above the entrance. Above the doorway is a relief sculpture in which Zeno is seen overcoming Satan. On either side of the doorway are ornate relief carvings, helping to make this one of the most celebrated Romanesque churches in Italy. The main doors are perhaps the church's greatest treasure, but they cannot be seen from the outside.

To see them, enter the church via the small side entrance on the left. Made of wood, the doors are plated with 48 bronze panels featuring biblical scenes and important moments from San Zeno's life. Thrown into the mix are more bizarre images of dubious origin and meaning; see if you can figure out what that woman is doing with those two crocodiles attached to her breasts!

There's plenty more to explore in the church; start by noticing how the nave resembles the keel of a ship, and the walls are covered with early frescoes and later prayers to the patron saint, graffitied on the walls by troubled believers during desperate times. Andrea Mantegna's 15th-century *Madonna and Child* triptych—usually on view at the altar—is currently on long loan, following much-needed restoration work. Don't miss the polychromatic statue of the sublimely smiling San Zeno, carved out of marble in the 12th century, and fondly referred to as "San Zeno Laughing." Attached to the church is a cloister enclosing a lawn courtyard, and there's a 72m (236-ft.) campanile (bell tower), the construction of which began in 1045. An antiques market held in Piazza San Zeno on the third Saturday of every month is definitely worth a visit.

In the Crook of River Adige: Squares, Tombs & Churches

The original, fortified Verona was centered on its ancient Roman forum, which became the site of the city's medieval market, popular for its sale of exotic herbs, spices, and other lifestyle goods imported through Venice's bustling trade port. Today it is still known as the **Piazza delle Erbe,** and vendors still man the stalls at what is an irresistibly lively and eclectic market. Besides fresh goods from nearby farms, many of the umbrella-canopied stalls hawk VERONA-emblazoned junk. At the northwestern end of the square is the baroque-style **Palazzo Maffei,** built in the 17th century, and worth a close-up look for the classical statuary atop the balustrade—gods and goddesses from the ancient pantheon. In the square, the **Colonna di San Marco** (right in front of the palace) is topped by the winged lion of St. Mark, symbolizing Venetian rule. Nearby, the beautiful 14th-century fountain is capped by a Roman statue inappropriately known as the **Madonna of Verona.**

To the east of the fountain, you'll find the **Arco della Costa** or "arch of the rib"; pass under the whale rib bone which hangs from the archway and you'll find yourself in **Piazza dei Signori** ✪✪✪ (also called Piazza Dante), a large square that's a feast for the eyes, although frequently mobbed by tour groups (try to see it early or at the end of the day). The square is centered on a **statue of Dante,** the great poet, who found refuge in Verona (1301–04) under the patronage of the Scaligeris after he fled Florence for political reasons.

But it's the sublime architecture all around the square that's really worth your attention. Directly across from the Arco della Costa is the 13th-century home of the Scaligeri family. Dante stands facing the **Palazzo della Ragione (Palace of Reason),** built in the 12th century in the Romanesque style; visit the courtyard behind the imposing facade, and note the Gothic-style stairway, built in the mid–15th century. If you've bought a VeronaCard, you should use it now to climb **Torre dei Lamberti** (☎ 045-9273027; Mon–Thurs 9:30am–8:30pm, Fri–Sun 8:30am–10pm, in summer till midnight on weekends), a clock tower affording some of the best views within the historical center.

Back in the square, notice the **Loggia del Consiglio,** a Renaissance-style council chamber, behind Dante; statues of several important Romans who were born in Verona are featured here. Then continue through the Piazza Dante, exiting under the archway directly opposite the arch of the rib. Immediately on your right you'll see some rather fantastical Gothic funerary sculpture—the elaborately decorated 14th-century **Scaligeri Tombs** ✚✚, with spiking turrets issuing toward the heavens. The level of detail hints at the perceived importance of these rulers, now guarded by stone warrior saints. The raised outdoor tombs all but completely conceal a 7th-century church, **Santa Maria Antica** (free), which served as the private chapel of the Scaligeris; above the side entrance to the church is the tomb of Cangrande I, and above that is a copy of his equestrian statue (the original is at the Castelvecchio Museum).

Two blocks from the tombs is the **Chiesa di Santa Anastasia** ✚ (Piazza Santa Anastasia; ☎ 045-592813; 2.50€; Mar–Oct Mon–Sat 9am–6pm, Sun 1–6pm; Nov–Feb Tues–Sat 10am–4pm, Sun 1–5pm) with its incomplete facade. Begun in 1290 for the hard-line Dominicans, the church took over 200 years to build, and serves as an excellent example of Italian Gothic architecture. Erected on a near-perfect cross plan, it features a vast Romanesque interior of soaring arches supported by massive pillars; there are 16 chapels scattered along the sides of the church. Among the standout Gothic elements of the interior are the *gobbi,* carved hunchback beggars who are permanently buckled under the weight of the holy water fonts at the entrance. Do look for Claudio Ridolfi's *Christ Being Scourged at the Pillar in the Rosary Chapel,* which reminds me of a scene from Mel Gibson's *Passion of the Christ;* and then look up to inspect the damaged but incredible 15th-century fresco over the dome. In the Giusti Chapel, which is intended only for legitimate worshiping visitors, see if you can spot the tourists on their knees pretending to pray so that they can check out the paintings, and then join them. In the Pellegrini Chapel, the 24 terra-cotta tableaux tell the story of the life of Christ; while above the chapel is Pisanello's famous fresco of *St. George Freeing the Princess of Trebisonda,* considered the most important work in the church.

From Sant'Anastasia, head to the **Duomo** ✚ (Via Duomo; ☎ 045-592813; 2.50€; Mar–Oct Mon–Sat 10am–5:30pm, Sun 1:30–5:30pm; Nov–Feb Mon–Sat 10am–4pm, Sun 1:30–5pm), the city's imposing 12th-century cathedral complex, recognizable by its red and white stripes. The Romanesque facade features a double-level porch around the main doorway, which is guarded by two bellicose stone

Empty Romance: Giulietta's Home & Tomb

Call me a cynic, but the only thing I find romantic about the famous **Casa di Giulietta** (Via Cappello 23; ☎ 045-8034303; 4€ or 5€ including Juliet's tomb; Tues–Sun 8:30am–7:30pm, Mon 1:30–7:30pm, last admission at 6:45pm)—Verona's most popular attraction—is the suspended disbelief of the thousands of couples who crowd in here each day and give themselves over to the highly dubious notion that this was ever the home of anyone even remotely connected to the love-struck Juliet, or the Capulet clan. (In fact, rumor has it that this building was a brothel in a former incarnation.) However, authorities are doing their best to simulate something resembling a medieval house museum, and I've never seen so many teenagers take so much interest in anything even closely associated with Shakespeare. You enter Juliet's courtyard via a small arcade, usually covered with graffitied messages of love. To keep the hopefuls amused, there's a bronze statue of Juliet in the small courtyard below; visitors queue up to have their picture taken, usually while grabbing her left breast—an odd tradition that has left it buffed to a high gloss. Meanwhile, the interior of the **palazzo** has a rather cheap pseudo-museum atmosphere, packed full of assorted portraits of the young lovers who made the city so famous. You'll also have to get into the **palazzo** if you feel the need to be photographed on Juliet's balcony.

Those who decide to visit **Tomba di Giulietta** (same hours) have to walk across town (about 20 min.) to the Capuchin Monastery of San Francesco al Corso, where her empty tomb is found in a lovely medieval cloister; her body was removed by nuns many years ago when they grew irritated by pilgrims turning up to pay homage to the Juliet's mortal remains as though she were a saint.

griffins; you can't get in through there, however, as the tourist entrance is around the side of the building. Inside, magnificent detailing abounds, accompanied by the droning of recorded, chanting monks creating an atmosphere of religious melancholy. You really need to spend time looking at each of the chapels around the church. As you enter, the first one on your left features Titian's *Assumption* (1530); take the time to find Liberale da Verona's surprising, sublime *Adoration of the Magi*. In the **Chapel of the Madonna,** note how—in the spirit of baroque overkill—devotees with their offerings have transformed the Virgin into something more reminiscent of a Versace or D&G advertisement than a religious icon. In the half dome of the main chapel, pay some attention to those delightfully cheerful frescoed figures by Francesco Torbido, rendered in 1534.

Attached to the main church is **Sant Elena** (Verona's first cathedral) and the baptistery; en route to these, you'll pass through an area of excavation, where the archaeological remnants of an ancient church have attracted the attention of coin-tossing believers. The baptistery—known as San Giovanni in Fonte (St. John of the Spring)—is an especially solemn space enclosed by walls of exposed pale brickwork, creating a ghostly atmosphere, which I love for the large baroque crucifix that hangs like a giant mobile from the wooden beams of the ceiling.

Modern art lovers will appreciate the sophisticated collection at Verona's **Galleria d'Arte Moderna** ✪✪ (Via A. Forti 1; ☎ 045-8001903; www.palazzo forti.it; 5€; Tues–Fri 9am–7pm and Sat–Sun 10:30am–7pm); four distinct permanent collections explore key themes in art from the modern era spanning the work of earlier names like De Pisis, Guidi, Nardi, and Francesco Hayez (be sure to look for his *Meditazione,* 1851), to more recent notables like Rosai, Roig, and Cindy Sherman. The gallery occupies the 13th-century **Palazzo Forti,** where Napoleon once stayed but where little of the original architecture remains.

Across the River Adige: The Teatro Romano

Over the River Adige, across the **Ponte Pietra,** you'll come to a lovely hillside neighborhood around the Castel San Pietro complex. At its base, excavated from beneath a labyrinth of medieval structures, is the ancient **Teatro Romano (Roman Theater)** ✪ (Rigaste Redentore 2; ☎ 045-8000360; 3€; Tues–Sun 8:30am–7:30pm, Mon 1:30–7:30pm), probably dating back to the 1st century B.C. Around the theater, with its original stone semicircular seating plan, a cluster of ancient buildings vividly recalls the city's original Roman occupation. Archaeologists think that the hillside location of the outdoor theater was the site of the very first human settlements in Verona. Today the theater offers postcard-worthy views of the city, and it's possible to catch a show here; while the program content has certainly been modernized, attending a show here is a wonderful way of transporting yourself back to the days when theatrical performances and spectacles were the primary entertainment (but be aware that the open-air theater offers an experience entirely different from that of the spectacular Roman Arena down in the city center, where the emphasis has always been on spectacle). A visit to Teatro Romano can be combined with a tour of the town's small on-site **archaeological museum.**

THE OTHER VERONA

Today, Verona's most spectacular battles take place not in the Arena but at the Marc'Antonio Bentegodi Stadium, where the city's population turns out en masse to witness magnificent **football (soccer) matches.** Verona boasts two significant

---

It's a Dog's Life

The name Scaligeri comes from the Latin word for ladder *(scala),* a feature on the family crest of Verona's most famous rulers. But it was from the domestic animal on the coat of arms that the Scaligeri patriarchs took their names: Mastino I (Mastiff the First) was the first in the line, while others in the dynasty included Cangrande I (Big Dog the First) and Cansignorio (Head Dog). Look carefully for the dogs supporting a ladder on Big Dog's tomb.

European clubs; the relative importance of each will depend on who you talk to. Locals who take football less seriously will tell you both teams are fighting to maintain what little dignity they have left. Just a few years ago, **Chievo Verona** (www.chievoverona.it) was considered one of the country's finest teams, but is once again fighting it out in the B-league; **Hellas Verona** (www.hellasverona.it) meanwhile is treading water in the C-league. The stadium, which has hosted the World Cup, has a capacity of 39,000 and is home to both the city's teams, which enjoy a consistently hard-core fan base, despite their be*league*red situation. The stadium is about 1.5km (1 mile) west of the city center, and is a great place to rub shoulders with real locals whose physical displays of emotion are likely to outstrip anything demonstrated by the opera crowd. It's easy enough to walk to, but even easier to get there by bus. Nos. 11, 12, and 13 all run from the historical center to the stadium. The ticket offices are outside the stadium, or purchase tickets from either the **Verona Box Office** (Via Pallone 12/A; ☎ 045-8011154) or online from Chievo's website. Cheap seats start at just 10€.

Heading to the opera and feeling a little perplexed at the thought of sitting through 3 hours of foreign-language singing? Fear not. The **Arena Foundation's Artists** (☎ 045-8009461; www.anteprimaopera.it) offer a fun and informative "**Introduction to Opera**" evening prior to every performance of the official opera season, designed to make people like yourself feel more comfortable with a musical form that can admittedly be rather intimidating. And, it's an opportunity to meet some of the stars of the show. Presented in the Gran Guardia Palace, at the piano, by singers and maestros who know the show backwards, participants are given a thorough overview (in Italian and English) of that evening's performance, so at the very least, you'll understand the story and the context of the opera. They also talk a bit about the specific production being staged later that night. For many, the best part of the evening is the wine tasting which follows, when you get to sample top-rated D.O.C. wines from around Verona. For 85€, there's a gala dinner (with more wine) thrown in. The event starts at 5:15pm and the dinner ends in time for the evening's opera at the Arena.

Without the invention of the printing press, humankind might still be stuck in the Dark Ages. But with the way printing technology and electronic have evolved, the original presses with hand-carved letters slotted into place by meticulous typographers are largely obsolete relics relegated to museums. Rossana Conte comes from a family of typographers—her father started practicing in 1834—and she still operates out of one of the oldest printing houses in Italy, in operation since 1750. Rossana not only dotes upon the historic **art of printing**, but runs an international laboratory, giving visitors the opportunity to learn about the history of printing in Italy; you can even try your hand at operating the old-fashioned printing presses. The session lasts 2 hours and costs 6€ (or 10€ with a take-home printed souvenir). For more information, visit the **Conte Museum and Cultural Laboratory** (Via Santa Maria 3/C, Chiavica; ☎ 045-8003392), or contact Rossana ahead of your trip (www.tipoarche.com). Keeping it in the family, if you want to do something more hands on, Rossana's mother runs an etching course—you'll do an engraving on a copper plate and then learn how to print your design to paper; the course lasts 10 hours and costs 300€.

Each September, Verona hosts **The International Festival of Street Games,** known as **Tocatì** (www.tocati.it), a unique event that sees cardboard cut-out figures going up all over town to forewarn of 3 days of pedestrian-only streets where ancient and modern games—Italian and international—are played in and around the medieval heart of the city. Besides showcasing a variety of activities that range from popular board games to ancient sports and even modern-day distractions like BMX-riding, the festival provides an opportunity to sample local cuisine and listen to folk music. But if you're in town for the event, don't just stand around watching; step up and take part. The active—and interactive—nature of the games compels you to meet local people.

Looking for an excuse to hole up in romantic Verona for a few weeks? Fair Verona make a great base to **learn Italian and get a grasp on local culture.** A vibrant atmosphere, coupled with proximity to many essential northern Italy getaways, means you'll never be bored or without exciting weekend prospects. There're a multitude of language schools—most include programs and outings to enrich your appreciation of Italian culture. You'll be spoiled for choice at **Lingua.It** (Via Anfiteatro 10; ☎ 045-597975; www.linguait.it), its mind-boggling array of language programs starts with 12-hour weekend courses (250€) or 20 hours in a week (200€). Then there are **guided opera evenings** where an expert helps you understand that night's Arena performance; **wine and cooking classes,** which can be combined with language classes; **art history courses** that will finally bring the differences between Romanesque, Gothic, Renaissance, and baroque art and architecture into focus for you; and even **guided tours** with local professors of Italian history and fine art. **Idea Verona** (Via Provolo 16; ☎ 045-8015352; www.ideaverona.com) prefers students to sign up for 4 consecutive weeks of **Italian classes,** with grammar, vocab, and syntax studies in the morning, and afternoons devoted to conversation and culture studies—but you can take shorter or longer courses, as you prefer. They also offer **cooking and wine classes,** and arty creative types can take **specialized art classes** which teach the *Affresco* painting technique (covering the canvas with lime before drawing in charcoal and then adding color).

NIGHTLIFE

If you're lucky, you may catch a performance of *Romeo and Juliet* at the outdoor **Teatro Romano,** where a **Shakespeare Festival** ★★ is held annually from June through early September. I've seen a thoroughly entertaining Italian version of the tragic romance here, with such visually dynamic staging that I didn't need to understand a word that was being said. The Teatro Romano also hosts summer musical performances, as well as contemporary dance shows and ballet; unlike operas at the Arena, here you can actually make out the faces of the people on stage. The Verona Jazz program usually draws an impressive international lineup. **Theater tickets** are available at the **box office** (Piazza Brà; ☎ 045-8077500 or 045-8066485; www.estateteatraleveronese.it); in purchasing them, note that it's more expensive to sit on reserved plastic chairs nearer the stage, but that you have a more authentic experience by paying less and taking a cushion for a place with the plebes on the original stone seats a little farther back.

Drinking & Relaxing

Verona has a vibrant cafe culture and is filled with all-day schmoozing venues. Although it's expensive, my favorite venue for pre-opera drinks is **Via Roma 33 Café** ★★ (Via Roma 33; ☎ 045-591917; daily 7am–2am), where contemporary

Rock Opera

When **opera season** ✮✮✮ rolls around, the unassuming town of Verona raises its head and prepares for an influx of cultured nobility; suitably attired and ready to be escorted to their 150€ seats, this refined set— who turn up to give standing ovations to some of the finest voices on earth—make one forget that the Arena was initially intended for Roman spectacles of violence and bloodshed.

The season traditionally runs from mid-June until the end of August, the highlight usually being performances of Verdi's *Aida;* the version I saw in 2005 featured mind-boggling scenery and staging by Franco Zeffirelli (known for directing a big-screen, men-in-tights version of *Romeo and Juliet* back in 1968), with colossal gold pyramids and sphinxes filling the stage. Even those of us sitting far away could appreciate the spectacle. *Aida* is probably the one show you must consider booking for in advance; tour leaders practically insist that their groups attend this show, and the midrange reserved seats are often sold out (particularly on weekends).

The opera season had its 85th season in 2007, when some surprising innovations were put in place, effectively stretching the season out to include a disastrously rained-out concert by The Who; a brand-new operatic *Romeo and Juliet* written by a former Italian pop star (in mid-Sept); and plans for many more popular music concerts. It's no secret that the Arena is gearing up to host more and more popular entertainment spectaculars.

You can purchase tickets for the opera at the box office beneath the Arena itself (Via Dietro Anfiteatro 6/B); credit cards are accepted, although the phone line is frequently down, so it's a good idea to take cash just in case. You can also phone in your booking (☎ 045-8005151) or go to www.arena.it, where you can also get program details. Opera season 2008 kicks off with Aida on June 20. Bear in mind that while the rock-bottom tickets being sold for 15€ to 20€ may sound like a bargain, there's a good chance that there will be some obstruction of your view because you'll be watching the show from the side of the stage.

Note: If you're attending a performance at the Arena, bring a cushion, or rent one on your way in. If you fail to heed this warning, you'll be using your backside to polish some of the same hard rock as Roman spectators did nearly 2,000 years ago, and you'll regret it deeply. Binoculars are handy, too!

Interpreti Italiani (Chiostro S. Luca, Corso Porta Nuova 12; ☎ 349-0901700; www.interpreti-italiani.it) isn't exactly competing with the opera at the Arena, but it offers alternative classical music performances on a much smaller scale between late June and early September. The lineup includes a very mixed bag of concerts, aimed at the more serious music lover.

stylishness draws Verona's definitive "in" crowd, who are, in turn, served by beautiful waitstaff brandishing dazzling smiles. You can sit under umbrellas outside, or enjoy the chilled, cosmopolitan ambience of the all-white interior. Although a cocktail here will set you back a whopping 8€, it's likely to be the best mixed drink you'll enjoy anywhere in the Veneto—and early evenings there's usually an aperitif buffet to stave your appetite.

For a more smoldering atmosphere at the edge of the River Adige, head over to **Cappa Café** (Piazzette Brà Molinari 1/A; ☎ 045-8004516; www.cappacafe.it; daily 7:30am–2am), which stands out not only for its terrace with views of the Ponte Pietra, Verona's most romantic bridge, but also for the striking bohemian-elegant interior and extensive drinks menu; some nights, DJ-spun tunes push the tempo up a notch or two. Food is also served, but I implore you not to treat this as a dining venue (the food is dire). A half-liter of the house Volipolicella is 4.50€.

SIDE TRIPS FROM VERONA

You can take two worthwhile side trips from Verona, both offering very different experiences. If you choose to visit the Alpine town of Trent, 100km (62 miles) away, consider spending the night, even if only for a chance to get a taste of Italo-Germanic nightlife at a local brewery-cum-restaurant. You could also choose Trent as an overnight stopover before moving on the Dolomite ski resort town of Cortina d'Ampezzo (discussed later in this chapter).

Mantua ✿

Mantua's historical center is all cobblestone streets, Roman ruins, and classical monuments, and its interlocking squares in the heart of the city easily evoke a sense of Middle Ages bonhomie. Fashioned out of muddy marshland, this small Lombardy city, called Mantova in Italian, was the home of Virgil and is believed to be where the blood of Christ is kept in a crypt, having been brought here by the soldier who pierced his side while he hung upon the cross. Mantua was also a creative center for a number of remarkable Renaissance artists, many of whom were sponsored and subsidized by the city's powerful Gonzaga clan.

Although they started out as peasants (originally named Corradi), the Gonzagas emerged as one of Europe's most prosperous and powerful dynasties, ruling here with an iron fist for almost 4 centuries and improving their political interests through a series of tactical marriages that expanded their power and improved their bloodlines. The spirit of acquisition that drove the Gonzagas has all the elements of a good melodrama, which you can get a feel for by visiting their vast palace complex, still rich with artistic treasures. Thankfully, the wealthy Gonzagas also fostered a period of intense cultural development, centered on their patronage of architects and artists. Whatever your feelings are regarding factual and mythical history, Mantua is hugely romantic and well worth a visit; unencumbered by tourist hordes, it's a most convenient side trip from Verona.

Get up early to catch the 9:33am **train** from Verona (2.30€), which will allow you to spend a full day enjoying the many sights. *Warning:* Don't visit Mantua on a Monday, when nearly every attraction in town is closed.

From the train station, you can take **bus no. 1** directly into the historical center, which you can also reach on foot (count on about 10 min.). Here, with its entrance on **Piazza delle Erbe,** you'll find an extremely thorough **Tourist**

Information Office (Piazza Montegna 6; ☎ 0376-328253; www.turismo.mantova. it; Mon–Sat 8:30am–12:30pm and 3–6pm, Sun 9:30am–12:30pm), with reams of ideas for how you can spend your day, and maps that will help you find your way.

The tourist office has its entrance directly opposite the small round **Rotonda di San Lorenzo** (free; daily 10am–1pm and 2–6pm), the city's oldest church, originally built in the 11th century. Although it has been partially demolished and rebuilt, there are still some 800-year-old frescoes on display.

Around the corner, the imposing facade of the Renaissance-era **Basilica of St. Andrea** ✪ (Piazza Mantegna; ☎ 0376-328504; free; daily 8am–noon and 3–7pm) looms gracefully over Piazza Mantegna. Commissioned by Lodovico II Gonzaga and designed in monumental style by Leon Battista Alberti, this church centers on a holy crypt in which soil soaked with the blood of Christ is kept. The sacred relic was supposedly brought to Mantua by Longinus, the Roman soldier who pierced Christ's side while he was on the cross, and its authenticity was demonstrated when a visiting pope claimed that it cured his gout. You can visit the crypt with permission for 1€; those in town on Good Friday witness a procession in which the relic is paraded through the city streets. Above the altar of the crypt is the Octagon, and above this is the church's main dome, decorated with a fresco featuring a frenzy of activity. The first chapel on the left is also the final resting place of Andrea Mantegna, the much-sought-after court painter employed by the Gonzagas during the 15th century.

Mantegna is celebrated as the most important investment the Gonzagas made in a long and sensitive relationship with the arts. Sure, they mostly relished having themselves immortalized, but they also supported artists like Titian and Pisanello, thus inadvertently making a valuable contribution to museums around the world. To see Mantegna's famous rendition of the Gonzagas, visit the fascinating **Palazzo Ducale** ✪ (Piazza Sordello; ☎ 0367-224832; www.mantovaducale.it; museum 6€, *castello* 8€, combined ticket 10€; Tues–Sun 8:45am–7:15pm), a city-within-a-city that was the Gonzaga family home, a palace that expanded along with their wealth and means. Among these inclusions is the **Castello di San Giorgio,** where the most interesting rooms are found. Pressed for time, I'd single out the **Camera degli Sposi** (1€ advanced booking required by calling ☎ 041-2411897), one of the apartments of Isabelle d'Este, who married Francesco Gonzaga at the end of the 15th century; here, Mantegna spent 9 years capturing life at court in his famous fresco cycle—a marvel of Renaissance painting.

Amid the palace's maze of architectural styles, you'll encounter hundreds of treasures of the Renaissance and Roman eras, although it remains a sore point that many of Mantegna's canvases have been removed to other museums across the globe. Pisanello's frescoes decorate the **Sala del Pisanello;** his 15th-century celebration of the Arthurian legends remained under plaster until rediscovery in 1969. Also worth a look is the **Appartemento dei Nani (Apartment of the Dwarves)** with its miniature version of the Vatican's holy staircase, built to amuse the "little people" who were members of Isabella's court.

Hedonism and frivolity are the principal qualities that defined the design and decoration of the **Palazzo Te** ✪✪ (Viale Te; ☎ 0376-323266; www.itis.mn.it/palazzote; 8€; Tues–Sun 9am–6pm, Mon 1–6pm), my favorite attraction in Mantua, about 20 minutes south by foot from the center. It was here that Isabella's fun-loving son Frederico Gonzago sought refuge from the rigors of court life. He commissioned Giulio Romano to build this beautiful Mannerist suburban villa as an unabashed tribute to worldly pleasures; throughout the palace, frescoes depict horses, cherubs, and classical myths with an overtly erotic edge. In the splendid **Sala** the dramatic perspective of the ceiling fresco forces the spectator to share the experience of imminent collapse as the crumbling slopes of Mt. Olympus bring about the defeat of the Giants at the hands of Jupiter and the gods.

Sampling the Taste of Mantua

Even more than Verona, Mantua is horse-meat country. To sample this classic Roman delicacy, visit the 250-year-old **Antica Hosteria Leoncino Rosso** (Via Giustiziati 33; ☎ 0376-323277; Mon–Sat noon–3:30pm and 7–10:30pm, Sun noon–3:30pm; closed for half of Aug; AE, DC, MC, V), in the historical center. There's plenty to choose from the menu of Mantuan, Italian, and Roman dishes; why not expand your options by getting a variety of dishes—starting with Mantuan *salame mantovano* (garlic salami, particularly good with the house tap wine)—and sharing with the table? Some of the more exotic dishes include risotto with Mantua sausage or *maccheroni con stracotto* (macaroni with stewed horse meat), or you can go for plain horse stew. If you're not into equine meat, try the roasted guinea fowl, or rabbit stuffed with olives. Most dishes are under 12€.

Trent ★★

The Adige River links Verona with the dazzling Alpine town of Trent, 101km (63 miles) to the north. Here, betwixt soaring mountains and lush scenery, a pretty sun-drenched valley town of painted medieval buildings stands atop an ancient Roman city once known as Tridentum. Known as a place of prosperity in the days of Emperor Augustus, Trento reemerged in the 15th century to become a cultural center, benefiting from its strategic position and robust political administration. Today, with its well-preserved Romanesque, Gothic, Renaissance, and baroque architecture and restful, tranquil atmosphere, Trent is a great respite from the crowds of more touristed destinations, made all the more pleasant by its extensive pedestrian-only areas and a setting that encourages you to discover the outlying countryside. Trent has a great many attractions that are worth seeing, but you can just as easily spend your time wandering its lovely streets, setting off on a hike, or skiing the white powdered slopes.

Of course, the laid-back atmosphere you'll experience today is in stark contrast to the town's history as the seat of powerful Church overlords: Trent was ruled by dynastic bishops from the 10th century until the 1700s. It was here that furiously militant Christianity exercised a fierce grip during the 16th century, when the Catholic Church staged its Council of Trent in response to Martin Luther's Reformation on the other side of the Alps. Stern meetings, held over 18 years, were designed to halt the spread of the Protestant gospel before it oozed into Italy; it was during these sessions that a blueprint for the coming Inquisition was established. Many of the town's attractions remain suffused with the legacy of the council's proceedings.

Frequent **trains** from Verona to Trent take just 70 minutes and cost around 5€ (or 58 min. for 3€ more); visit www.trenitalia.com for full schedules. From the train station, ask for directions to the helpful **tourist office** (Via Manci 2;

☎ 0461-216000; www.apt.trento.it; daily 9am–7pm); pick up a map and the euro-saving 24-hr. **Trento Card** (10€; valid for one adult plus one child under 12), which allows free entrance to all museums (there are more besides those I've recommended), and saves on public transport. The card also allows free bicycle rentals, discounted meals at some restaurants, and the possibility of guided tours and wine tastings. There's also a 48-hour version with added benefits for 15€.

From the tourist office, head along Via Belenzani—lined with the beautifully frescoed facades of Renaissance palazzo—to the expansive **Piazza del Duomo,** a gorgeous urban hub centered on a baroque Neptune fountain statue (1767) and fringed by more buildings, most imposingly the magnificent San Vigilio Cathedral (Duomo). Construction of the **Duomo** (☎ 0461-234419; free to church, 1€ for the crypt; Mon–Sat 9:30am–12:30pm and 2:30–6pm) began in the 13th century in honor of the martyred third bishop of Trento, Vigilio. Built largely in the Romanesque-Lombard style, there are also Gothic touches, and the onion dome atop the bell tower suggests altogether different influences. It was here that the Council of Trent announced many of its decisions, particularly after its most important meetings were held here in the Chapel of the Crucifix, recognizable by its massive cross. Beneath the altar are foundations of the 6th-century Basilica Paleocristiana where Trent's early prince-bishops are buried.

Adjacent the Duomo is the 13th-century **Palazzo Pretorio,** where the prince-bishops once lived like nobility; now it's the surprisingly good **Diocesan Museum** ★★ (☎ 0461-234419; www.museodiocesanotridentino.it; 4€; Wed–Mon 9:30am–12:30pm and 2–5:30pm, till 6pm in summer), with a superbly curated display of paintings and other treasures (including valuable relics, reliquaries, and religious vestments) from the church's rich collection. What might have been a dull lineup of familiar religious images is in fact a telling mix of modern and classical works, intelligently juxtaposed to stirring effect. Also on display are pictorial accounts of the proceedings of the Council of Trent (not unlike modern "artist's renditions" of courtroom proceedings).

If you want a better sense of Trent's ancient roots, you can go into the belly of the city with a visit to the **S.A.S.S. Roman ruins** (Piazza Cesare Battisti; www.provincia.tn.it; 2€; June–Sept Tues–Sun 9:30am–1pm and 2–6pm, Oct–May 9am–1pm and 2–5:30pm), now a stylishly excavated underground "museum" where you walk along and over some of the original Roman streets and ruins. Discovered by archaeologists during the 1990s, the ruins date back to 1000 B.C., and include paved roadways, sewage systems, and mosaics.

A visit to the formidable **Castello del Buonconsiglio** ★★ (Via B. Clesio; ☎ 0461-233770; www.buonconsiglio.it; 6€; Tues–Sun 10am–6pm), is rewarding not only for the richness of some of the painted decoration within, but also for the variety of architectural elements that were clearly added over the centuries, commencing with the early-13th-century keep, the castle's secure, circular watchtower. A repository for the city's art treasures collected by Bernardo Cles (a powerful ruler of Trent), this was also another venue for the Council of Trent, but there are also prisons, a breezy *loggia,* and a lovely garden. Comprising two castles in a single complex, the original medieval **Castelvecchio** (a temporary exhibition venue) was extended in the 16th century with the addition of the **Magno Palazzo;** this Renaissance residential wing features superb frescoes of biblical, mythical, and historical scenes. Particularly outstanding is the **Torre dell'Aquila**

(Eagle Tower), renowned for its exquisite International Gothic fresco cycle depicting Middle Ages court life; it's the single most impressive part of the castle, but you need to reserve in advance to see it (1€ extra).

For a bird's-eye view of Trent, ride the **Funivia Trento** (☎ 0461-822075), a cable car departing every 15 to 30 minutes from Ponte di San Lorenzo (southwest of the train station) to Sardagna, a village on the lofty slopes of Monte Bondone.

A farther (somewhat out-of-the-way) attraction is Italy's largest modern and contemporary art museum, **MART** (Corso Bettini 43; ☎ 0464-438887; www. mart.trento.it; 8€; Tues–Thurs 10am–6pm, Fri–Sun 10am–10:30pm), in Rovereto, some 25km (16 miles) south of Trent. Over and above the permanent collection of almost 10,000 paintings, sculptures, and other works, there's a lineup of temporary exhibitions. It's a good place to learn more about 20th-century avant-garde art and the Futurist movement, dominated here by Italian works. If you purchase the 48-hour version of the Trento Ticket, admission is free; otherwise you pay full price. If you're feeling active, you can cycle there using the track along the Adige River, or catch bus no. 301 from the station. Part of MART's collection is in Trent's **Palazzo delle Albere** (5€); but it rather pales in comparison with the real thing in Rovereto, so don't waste your money.

ACCOMMODATIONS & DINING

€   Trent's youth hostel, **Giovane Europa** (Torre Vanga 9; ☎ 0461-263484; MC, V) is close to the station and one of the best deals in the country for a cheap sleep. Same-sex dorm beds (mostly bunks) are just 14€ to 16€, and twin-bedded double rooms work out to less than 50€; each dorm has its own bathroom. You can do laundry here, and a canteen dispenses low-priced food (and a sad inclusive breakfast). There's no lockout or curfew, but don't forget to bring earplugs.

€€€   When I was last in town, stalwart budget hotel **Aquila d'Oro** (Via Belenzani 76; ☎ 0461-986282; www.aquiladoro.it) was being completely over-hauled, but should come back to life looking fabulous in late 2008. Until then, a reasonable deal is **Hotel America** (Via Torre Verde 52; ☎ 0461-983010; www. hotelamerica.it; AE, DC, MC, V), where some of the smart, comfortable rooms have views of the castello, and breakfast is included in the price (102€ double).

€–€€   Although Trento's square-side cafes are wonderful for people-watching, I can spend hours immersed in the authentic loud 'n' down-home atmosphere stirred up by the combination of Tyrolean food, homebrewed beer, and hungry locals who gather en masse at **Birreria Pedavena** ★★ (Piazza Fiera 13; ☎ 0461-986255; www.birreriapedavena.com; Wed–Mon 9am–12:30am; AE, MC, V) to feast on traditional specialties like *wurstel* sausages, or—my personal favorite—*stinco con patate* (8.80€), a juicy leg of pork, served with fried potatoes and sauerkraut. And to wash it all down, mug after mug of Lag's Bier, which is produced on-site, and is the principal aesthetic value at this rustic, festive hall.

CORTINA D'AMPEZZO

The craggy, soaring peaks of Italy's Alpine Dolomite range are unmistakable; like a massive coral reef ripped from the sea, strung with conifers and laced with snow, these mountains have a look distinct from any other major range in the world (they also have some of the most exotic-sounding names: Cristallo, Tofane, and Sorapiss). Picturesque Cortina d'Ampezzo, at the center of it all, has been drawing skiers for over a century, its reputation cemented when the Olympics were held here in 1956. Today it's prime schussing ground for the designer set, the place to ski side by side with European jet-setters and celebrities who, during the season, multiply by fivefold the 7,000-strong population of this village. When it's not a bustling ski resort, it becomes a center for hard-core hikers and climbers, who are challenged by the endless selection of routes on offer.

LAY OF THE LAND

There is no direct rail service to Cortina; the nearest railway is in **Dobbiacco,** 27km (17 miles) away, and is the point of arrival if you're coming from Verona via Trent; if you're traveling here from Padua or Venice, the closest station is **Calalzo di Cadore,** 35km (22 miles) south. Routes to either of these towns can be fairly convoluted, so consult the schedules on www.trenitalia.it to determine the most direct approach. From both Dobbiacco and Calalzo, there are regular bus services to Cortina; these depart from right outside the train stations, but you may have a fairly substantial wait for some services. The entire journey from Venice to Cortina should take around 3½ hours. If you're traveling from Rome, Eurostar Italia has daytime services to Mestre (mainland Venice), from where shuttle buses can transfer you directly to Cortina; these shuttles are scheduled to coincide with your train times—contact **Servizi Ampezzo** (☎ 0436-867921). You can also catch a direct bus from Venice to Cortina; it takes the entire morning (departing 7:50am), but the scenic journey makes it worthwhile.

During peak season—the so-called "white weeks" of winter—buses deliver hotel guests directly from Venice and Treviso airports to their hotels, but only on Saturday and Sunday. An excellent source of information regarding shuttle services into Cortina is www.dolomiti.org.

Cortina's **Dolomiti Bus** (☎ 0436-867921; Mon–Fri 8:15am–12:30pm and 2:30–6pm, Sat 8:15am–12:30pm) is useful for getting to out-of-town cable cars and hotels. Tickets are available from tabacchi and bars near the bus stops; books of tickets (5€ for 6, or 9.50€ for 12) are also available. For round-the-clock taxi service, call **RadioTaxi** (☎ 0436-860888).

ACCOMMODATIONS, BOTH STANDARD & NOT

Cortina's hotels aren't cheap, and the popularity of the resort means that you can struggle to find a bed in peak periods when skiers are in full force; plan your high-season trip well in advance. Out of season, Cortina is quiet and low-key, and hotel prices ease up; some even close down during the slowest periods. But when the snow falls and demand skyrockets, so does the cost of a bed in even the simplest of hotels. *Note:* Many hotels will ask you to stay for a full week during high season; at best they might offer discounted rates for extended stays. Cortina's great boom happened in the 1950s when the town prepared for the crowds attending the Olympic Games; ideas about hotel style have not exactly moved on since then so accommodations remain simple (or "homey") and a trifle "cottagey," with plenty of wood paneling and floral bedspreads.

€–€€   The best way to save on lodging, without settling for a camping site (see below), is to stay in a **private home** or **bed-and-breakfast;** visit the **tourist office**

(Piazzetta San Francesco 8; ☎ 0436-3231) to see what's on offer. Its website (www.infodolomiti.it) carries extensive listings of these and other alternative lodging options, including **farm stays.** If you're the genuinely outdoorsy type, you can forgo town life completely, and head out (on a mapped hike) with your camping equipment, making use of one of the many **refuges** dotted around the d'Ampezzo area; these are basically mountain cabins (some with a large inventory of beds) offering shelter and basic facilities in the mountains. Most operate in the summer period from late June until late September; the tourist office and website has extensive information.

€€–€€€ Slap-bang in the town center, facing the church and campanile, **Hotel Montana** ★ (Corso Italia 94; ☎ 0436-862126; www.cortina-hotel.com; AE, DC, MC, V) is one of the town's great values, affording excellent rates, comfort, and public spaces packed with modern artworks. The best deals here—as elsewhere in Cortina—are for stays of 7 days or longer (in popular Feb, you'll pay 450€ on average per person for a 1-week stay, while the Jan rate is closer to 300€). Surf online for excellent specials (for example, rates were 155€ per person for 5 days in Sept–Oct 2007). Guest rooms are mostly spacious and sparse, with wooden floors and old-fashioned draperies and simple furniture; but ask for one with a balcony (shared), and you'll enjoy first-class views of the Dolomites. It's breakfast only, but all the rooms (and their balconies) have tables where, like me, you can sit down to a homemade picnic cheaply put together with supplies from one of nearby supermarkets.

€€–€€€€ Another well-priced option is **Hotel Villa Gaia** (Via Guide Alpine 96; ☎ 0436-2974; www.hotelvillagaia.it; MC, V), which has benefited from a refreshing makeover. It may not be the most fabulous hotel in town, but there's a quaintness about the place that is greatly helped by the low prices. The rate for a double with breakfast generally ranges from 80€ to 120€, and goes to 160€ during the ultrapeak Christmas to New Year's period, including breakfast. There are a multitude of discounts for weeklong stays during the popular "white weeks." Guest rooms are simple, with wood-paneled walls and the usual, basic styling; some of the rooms have spectacular views from tiny terraces.

€€–€€€€ If want to be near the center and are arriving by bus but don't fancy dragging your luggage too far, there are more than enough options right near the bus terminal. Unpretentious and unassuming, **Hotel Cornelio** (Via Cantore 1; ☎ 0436-2232 or 0436-2535; www.hotelcornelio.com; DC, MC, V) is a good-value option run by the welcoming Vecchiato family. Rooms (95€–180€ double, including breakfast) are snug, and almost entirely done in wood, so there is some creaking and groaning, and you have a good idea of when your neighbor is flushing the loo or moving around the room, but that's pretty much standard for Cortina's quaint, though aging, three-star hotels. Even my tiny single room (60€–100€) had a small terrace with a Dolomite panorama (insist on one when booking), and given the dearth of affordable dining options in the town, you could do worse than to use the in-house ristorante, **La Taverna Di Cornelio** (daily noon–2:30pm and 7–9:30pm), where regional dishes are served. *Primi* dishes on the classic menu cost 7€ to 8€, and there are daily specials.

€€–€€€€   A bit of a distance beyond the town center, stalwart **Hotel Menardi** ★ 🧒 (Via Majon 110; ☎ 0436-2400; www.hotelmenardi.it; DC, MC, V) feels just the way an Alpine retreat should. It's been a family concern since the early 20th century, when the Menardis swapped farming for hospitality; in 2007, the original 1836 farmstead was extensively renovated. Rooms are generally spacious, defined by an abundance of pine—in the floors, walls, cupboards, and furniture—and eclectic, fussy fabrics, all underscoring the old-fashioned, homey atmosphere. Rooms in the newer annex are larger and carpeted (and a touch more modern); I'd ask for a first-floor corner room, where you can enjoy breakfast on your wooden balcony while drinking in sweeping mountain views. There's a wellness center where you can defrost in the Jacuzzi, sauna, or steam bath, or enjoy a deep-tissue massage. Quaint touches include a lobby filled with statues of the Virgin; a cozy bar, fire-warmed in winter; and a downstairs nook for wine tastings. Pricing—as at all of Cortina's hotels—is complicated and subject to myriad seasonal fluctuations; in summer a double room with breakfast costs 100€ to 220€, while in winter half-board is mandatory and costs 190€ to 260€ double.

€€€–€€€€   While Menardi's charms draw heavily on its rambling garden that's dotted with wooden barrows of colorful flowers, if you're after a more urbane experience, you might prefer **Hotel Ambra** ★ (Via XXIX Maggia 28; ☎ 0436-867344; www.hotelambracortina.it; AE, DC, MC, V), situated in the center. It's the smarter, more refined hotel, and offers similar rates (150€–260€ double) during most of the winter season (although it's pricier in summer—130€–220€ double—when Menardi's gardens are more useful). There may not be as much space at Ambra (it's quite compact, and rooms are snug), but a sense of modest luxury makes up for that. Ambra will finally have a much-needed terrace in 2008.

A Camping Option

€   In Località Fiames, 5km (3 miles) north of Cortina, but still on the urban bus route (take bus no. 1 to the access road), is **International Camping Olympia** (☎ 0436-5057; www.campingolympiacortina.it; cash only), which has good facilities (including a restaurant, bar, swimming pool, and sauna) and is open year-round. Adults pay 4.50€ (7.50€ Dec 20–Jan 10), and there's a tent-and-car charge of 9€. Bunk beds in dorms are 20€. *Warning:* You'll have to put up with a plethora of rules, including nighttime and *siesta* silence.

DINING FOR ALL TASTES

If you're looking to make up a **picnic basket,** the best pastries and breads in town are available from **Panificio Alvera Pasticceria** (Corso Italia 191; Thurs–Tues 6:30am–1pm and 3:30–7:30pm). Then head farther along Corso Italia, toward the town center, just beyond the church, and stock up on the remaining ingredients at the food section of Cortina's department store, **La Cooperativa** (☎ 0436-861245; www.coopcortina.com; Mon–Sat 8:30am–12:30pm and 3:30–7:30pm; MC, V). You'll also be able to pick up a corkscrew and other essential dining accessories here. There's even more variety (and some cheaper items) to be found at **Kanguro** (Via B. Franchetti 1; Mon–Sat 8:30am–12:30pm and 3:30–7:30pm; MC, V), tucked away on a street just off Corso Italia.

Cortina's restaurants offer the opportunity to try both authentic Tyrolean cuisine and Italian food with a Germanic edge. Expect to find plenty of meat, including sausage, veal, and venison, on the menu. Asparagus, wild mushrooms, and radicchio are widely used, often in hot, creamy sauces, while ravioli stuffed with beetroot is another specialty. Besides the recommendations below, I've also enjoyed the fare at Hotel Cornelio's traditional ristorante (see above).

€–€€   You'll find plenty of choice at **Pizzeria Ristorante Ghedina al Passetto** (Via Marconi 8; ☎ 0436-2254; www.alpassettoghedina.it; MC, V), right across from the bus depot. Usually packed with skiers, this well-priced, wood-paneled restaurant is filled with the aroma of hearty food. There's pizza (4.50€–8€) and pasta galore, but it's the regional specialties that deserve attention: Tyrolean balls with melted butter and Parmesan, and especially Tyrolean dumpling soup (all *primi* dishes are 6€–8€). A profusion of meat and sausage dishes help stave off the cold in winter—beef filet in a vodka sauce, or sausage in cabernet sauce, served with polenta, are the more elaborate offerings (meat *secondi* are 9.50€–17€). Wine is served by the glass, bottle, or carafe, and the tiramisu here is famous.

€€   A 10-minute walk east of town is popular, rustic **Al Camin** (Via Alvera 99; ☎ 0436-862010; Tues–Sun noon–3pm and 7–11:30pm; MC, V), where you'll find the kind of authentic fare usually only served in local homes. Try local specialties—like *kenederli* (liver-flavored dumplings), Alpine hare, or any of the other game dishes, best accompanied by wild mushrooms. *Primi* average around 8€ to 9€ and are served up in a rustic dining hall, centered on an old stone fireplace.

WHY YOU'RE HERE: THE TOP SIGHTS & ATTRACTIONS

The best sights in and around town are natural ones; come here any time of year and you'll view spectacular mountain scenery. Stony peaks rise from valleys that are carpeted by lush forest and meadows, and that are dotted with pretty Alpine houses. On those days when the weather doesn't cooperate, you can cruise through the center of town, exploring picturesque Corso Italia or browsing boutiques aimed at high-end spenders. There are a couple of churches (most notably **Santi Filippo e Giacomo** in the town center), expensive art galleries, and—adjacent to the town church—the **Regole d'Ampezzo Museums** (Corsa Italia 69; ☎ 0436-2206; www.musei.regole.it; 5€; Jun–Sept Tues–Sun 10am–12:30pm and 4–7:30pm, daily July–Aug), which cover enthnography, paleontology, and modern art.

For all sorts of skiing and hiking information, you can start by dropping in at the **tourist office** (Piazzetta San Francesco 8; ☎ 0436-3231; www.infodolomiti. it; daily 9am–12:30pm and 3:30-6:30pm, closed Sun afternoon in low season). Another excellent source of information is **Cortina Turismo** (Via Marconi 15/B; ☎ 0436-866252; www.dolomiti.org), which supplies an outstanding map of footpaths in the mountains around town.

Of course, you don't have to be a skier or rock climber to appreciate the high-altitude Alpine peaks; simply hop on a funicular to enjoy a steady, no-hassle climb through achingly beautiful mountain scenery. **Funiculars** generally run from mid-July to early September and from mid-December until May 1; summer

Skiing the Dolomites ★★★

Not only is Cortina's reputation as Italy's leading ski resort justified, but as a candidate to host the 2013 World Alpine Ski Championships, there's likely to be some major improvements to slopes and facilities which are already top-notch. With many fine ski routes, all easily accessible thanks to the system of funiculars, Cortina has 8 distinct ski areas and another 10 within easy reach; all fall under the scheme covered by the Dolomiti Superski pass, which allows unlimited skiing and ski-related travel (on shuttle buses, funiculars, and chairlifts) for a predetermined period; you'll have access to 1,220km (756 miles) of ski runs and 450 chairlifts. Prices vary according to the number of days you choose, starting with a 1-day pass at 42€ during high season (discounted for children and seniors); by comparison, a 7-day pass costs 222€ for the same period. High season generally runs from around December 23 to January 5 and February 3 through March 24; there are slight savings during the lower season (mid-Jan and mid-Mar). To get your pass, or for more information, go to **Dolomiti Superski** (Via di Castello 33; ☎ 0436-862171; www.dolomiti superski.com), where you can also explore a number of savings schemes.

departures start at 9am and run every 15 minutes until 5pm. The aptly named **Freccia nel Cielo (Arrow in the Sky)** ★★★ (☎ 0436-5052 for information), provides the most breathtaking ascent in the region; departures are from the ground station not far from Olympic Ice Skating Stadium. You can travel as far as the second stop—Ra Valles (altitude 2,470m/8,102 ft.)—for 20€ round-trip (high season); once there, you can sit back and take in the ragged Dolomitic peaks while enjoying a drink on the terrace of the bar. For 24€ you can head all the way to the top and back—the final station, Tofana, is a magnificent 3,244m (10,640 ft.) above sea level.

Operating from a station nearer the town center and bus depot, on the other side of town is the popular, slightly cheaper **Funivia Faloria** ★★ (☎ 0436-2517); the trip all the way to the top and back costs about 16€, and you can spend the money you've saved at the bar of the **Faloria Refuge** (2,123m/6,963 ft.), high up in the Cristallo range, where you can enjoy a beer on the terrace, taking in panoramas of the Dolomites and eagle-eye views of Cortina town. Faloria has longer operating months than Arrow in the Sky, closing late September and reopening in November. The Faloria funicular station is also where you'll find the headquarters of **Scuola di Sci Azzurra,** should you wish to learn how to ski or need a few brush-up lessons. There are also **ski-rental** facilities (www.skimanservice.com).

If you see a mountain as something in need of physical conquest and chairlifts for the not-so-brave, you'll probably want to start by contacting **Gruppo Guide Alpine** (Corso Italia 69/4; ☎ 0436-868505; www.guidecortina.com), which offers a range of **mountain-based activities** for beginners and experts. Many of the adventures are snow-related, and the guides here can help you discover many active pursuits, including fairly danger-free snowshoeing and more daring ice climbing. In the snow-free seasons, they provide experts in hiking, rock climbing, and mountain biking. There are specialized programs for children and also for older adventurers. With nearly 60 years in the business, and around 30 guides aged 27 to 65, the company has a sterling reputation; if you're an adrenaline junkie, its outings may well be the highlight of your visit to Italy.

Snowboarding is offered by several outfits, one of which is **Boarderline** (Via XXIX Maggio 13/b; ☎ 0436-878261; www.boarderline.it); a 1-hour session—or advanced lesson—costs 41€ to 46€. Beginners should try slightly cheaper **Scuola Sci e Snowboard Dolomiti Cortina** (Via Roma 91; ☎ 0436-862264; www.dolomiti scuolasci.com) at 35€ to 42€ per hour.

Even if you're not a climber, you might consider challenging yourself with one of the hiking routes along the **Via Ferrata (Iron Way)** ★★★, which even offers novices a chance to experience the thrill of high-altitude climbing thanks to an extensive infrastructure of ladders, already-secured cables, and bridge mechanisms that help take the sting out of any rational fear of heights or even a naturally clumsy predisposition. Hiking the Via Ferrata is one of the world's unforgettable mountaineering experiences, and there are a few hundred different routes in the Dolomites open for action from the middle of June until mid-September; once again, Gruppo Guide Alpine is your best bet for advice, equipment, and a guide who will make you feel secure.

For children, especially, there's thrilling fun to be had at the **Cortina Adrenaline Center** (kids) (☎ 0436-860808; www.adrenalincenter.it), based at the Pista Olimpica di Bob (Olympic bobsled arena). You can take on canyoning, rafting, hydrospeeding, kayaking, mountain biking, and—if you're truly brave— try "Taxi Bob Wheel," a thrilling, 110kmph (68 mph) simulation of the bobsledding experience, only with tires and a brake system! A further activity for kids wishing to test their mettle (or burn off excess energy) is the army-training-course-type Adventure Park, where, armed with climbing gear and pulley attachments, you swing on vines, pull yourself along ropes, and traverse mountain bridges. There's a junior version for younger kids, too.

For those who prefer independent adventures, the terrain around Cortina draws hard-core cyclists keen to develop their **mountain-biking** stamina. There are some easier routes out of town, or you can stick to the roads (although you should be wary of heavy traffic during certain periods); you can **rent bikes** from **2ue & 2ue** (Via Roma 70; ☎ 0436-4121; www.dueduecortina.com), which offers special deals on family rentals, and which can give you advice on where to peddle. If you'd prefer to go on a mountain-biking tour with someone who knows the area and the terrain, these are also available and cost 20€ for a half-day or 35€ for a full day; visit www.freeridecortina.com for details.

If you want a break from the vastness of the great outdoors, head for the Olympic ice-skating arena, **Stadio Olimpico del Ghiaccio** (kids) (Via del Stadio; ☎ 0436-881811; daily 9am–7pm), which has two ice-skating rinks open to the public. Admission and skate rental is generally 10€, although in peak ski season, high demand may push this up dramatically. Stadio Olimpico is also where national and international ice hockey events are held.

Milan & the Lake District

The wealthy region of Lombardy combines commerce with high living

by Reid Bramblett

MILAN IS THE GLITZY CAPITAL OF LOMBARDY (LOMBARDIA), ITALY'S MOST prosperous region. Its factories largely fuel the Italian economy, and its attractions—high fashion, fine dining, hopping dance clubs, and da Vinci's *Last Supper*—have much to offer the visitor. But there's much more than a sophisticated city to Lombardy. To the north, the region bumps up against craggy mountains in a romantic lake district, and to the south it spreads out in fertile farmlands fed by the mighty Po and other rivers.

Lombardy has a different feel from the rest of Italy. The Lombardi, who descended from one of the Germanic tribes that overran the Roman Empire and who have over the centuries been ruled by feudal dynasties from Spain, Austria, and France, are a little more continental than their neighbors to the south; indeed, the Lombardi are faster talking, faster paced, and more business oriented. They even dine differently, tending to eschew olive oil for butter and often forgoing pasta for polenta and risotto.

The Italian lakes have entranced writers from Catullus to Ernest Hemingway. Backed by the Alps and ringed by lush gardens and verdant forests, each lake has its own charms and, accordingly, its own enthusiasts. Not least among these charms is their easy accessibility from many Italian cities, making them ideal for short retreats: Lake Maggiore and Lake Como are both less than an hour from Milan, and Lake Garda is tantalizingly close to Venice and Verona. Each of these world-renowned resorts—Como (the choicest), Maggiore (speckled with elegant islands), and Garda (a windsurfing hot spot and microcosm of Italy, with the Mediterranean lemon groves and vineyards of the south gradually shading to Teutonic schnitzel and beer on the north end)—can make for a great 1- or 2-day break from Italy's sightseeing carnival.

DON'T LEAVE MILAN & THE LAKE DISTRICT WITHOUT . . .

PAYING HOMAGE TO DA VINCI & MICHELANGELO   You'll find *The Last Supper* in Milan's Santa Maria delle Grazie and the *Pietà*, Michelangelo's last work, inside the medieval Castello Sforzesco.

CLIMBING TO THE ROOF OF THE MILAN DUOMO   Wander amid the Gothic buttresses and statue-topped spires for a citywide panorama.

SEEING THE BRERA & AMBROSIANA PICTURE GALLERIES Tour these Milan museums packed with stunning works by such old masters as Raphael, Caravaggio, and Leonardo da Vinci.

TAKING A WINDOW-SHOPPING SPIN Walk past the high-end boutiques in Milan's Golden Rectangle, and then go on a budget shopping spree through the stock shops and outlets of Corso Buenos Aires.

INDULGING IN THE NIGHTLIFE The converted warehouses along Milan's Navigli canals are always hopping after dark.

FERRYING BETWEEN LAKE MAGGIORE'S BORROMEAN ISLANDS You can tour the palaces of one of Lombardy's last remaining Renaissance-era noble families and watch the peacocks wander their exotic gardens.

MILAN

Milan (Milano) is Italy's financial center, business hub, and fashion capital, as well as one of its most industrialized major cities. That also means it's crowded, noisy, and hot in summer; damp and foggy in winter; and distinctly less easygoing (and more expensive) than most Italian cities.

Milan reveals its long history in monuments, museums, and churches—its cathedral is one of Europe's great Gothic structures, and another church contains Leonardo da Vinci's *Last Supper*. This sophisticated city also supports a thriving cultural scene embracing La Scala (one of the world's top opera houses), high-fashion boutiques and shows, and a throbbing nightlife.

LAY OF THE LAND

Think of Milan as a series of concentric circles radiating from the central **Piazza del Duomo,** the Cathedral Square. Within the inner circle, once enclosed by the city walls, are many of the churches, museums, and shops that'll consume your visiting hours. For a general overview, obtain one of the serviceable maps with a street index that the tourist offices provide for free.

The city's major neighborhoods encircle the hub that is Piazza del Duomo. Looking east from the Duomo, you can see the imposing **Castello Sforzesco,** at one end of the well-heeled **Magenta neighborhood.** You can walk to the Castello in about 15 minutes by following Via Orefici to **Piazza Cordusio** and from there Via Dante. The other major draw in Magenta is the major draw in all of Milan: the church of **Santa Maria delle Grazie** housing **Leonardo da Vinci's** *The Last Supper;* to reach it, leave Via Dante at Via Meravigli, which becomes Via

Tip for Departing Passengers

If you're going to the airport to leave on a flight, make sure you call the airline beforehand to find out which terminal you need, as Malpensa's Terminal 1 and Terminal 2 are actually several kilometers apart.

Milan

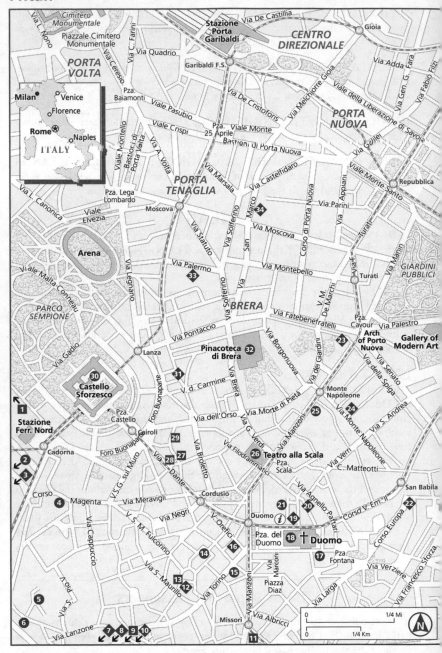

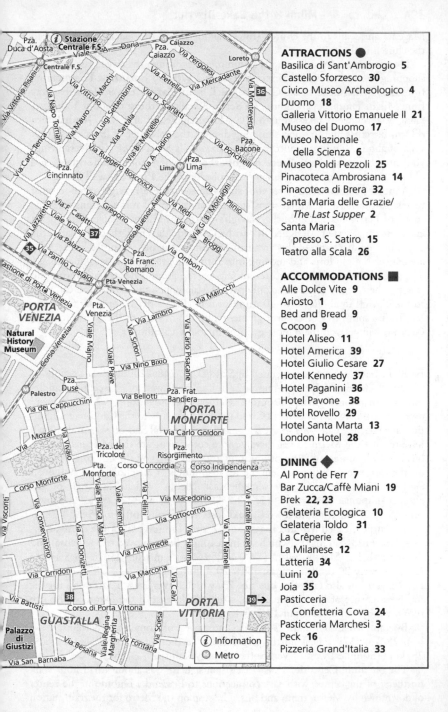

ATTRACTIONS ●

Basilica di Sant'Ambrogio **5**
Castello Sforzesco **30**
Civico Museo Archeologico **4**
Duomo **18**
Galleria Vittorio Emanuele II **21**
Museo del Duomo **17**
Museo Nazionale
 della Scienza **6**
Museo Poldi Pezzoli **25**
Pinacoteca Ambrosiana **14**
Pinacoteca di Brera **32**
Santa Maria delle Grazie/
 The Last Supper **2**
Santa Maria
 presso S. Satiro **15**
Teatro alla Scala **26**

ACCOMMODATIONS ■

Alle Dolce Vite **9**
Ariosto **1**
Bed and Bread **9**
Cocoon **9**
Hotel Aliseo **11**
Hotel America **39**
Hotel Giulio Cesare **27**
Hotel Kennedy **37**
Hotel Paganini **36**
Hotel Pavone **38**
Hotel Rovello **29**
Hotel Santa Marta **13**
London Hotel **28**

DINING ◆

Al Pont de Ferr **7**
Bar Zucca/Caffè Miani **19**
Brek **22, 23**
Gelateria Ecologica **10**
Gelateria Toldo **31**
La Crêperie **8**
La Milanese **12**
Latteria **34**
Luini **20**
Joia **35**
Pasticceria
 Confetteria Cova **24**
Pasticceria Marchesi **3**
Peck **16**
Pizzeria Grand'Italia **33**

Magenta and leads to the church (total walking time from Piazza del Duomo to the church is about 20 min.).

Heading north from Piazza del Duomo, walk through the city's glass-enclosed shopping center (the world's first), the **Galleria Vittorio Emanuele II.** Emerging from the northern end of the Galleria, you'll be in **Piazza della Scala,** steps away from Milan's famous opera house, **La Scala.** A walk northeast of about 5 minutes along Via Manzoni takes you to Via Montenapoleone and the **Quadrilatero d'Oro,** the city's high-fashion shopping district, the epicenter of Italian design. A walk of about 10 minutes northwest of Piazza della Scala along **Via Brera** brings you into the atmospheric **Brera neighborhood,** where cobblestone streets and old palazzi surround the city's major art collection, the **Pinacoteca di Brera.**

Another neighborhood to set your sights on is **Ticinese/Navigli,** often referred to just as the Navigli, which translates as "canals." A 15-minute tram ride due south of Piazza del Duomo, the Navigli's old quays follow what remains of an elaborate canal system, designed in part by Leonardo da Vinci, that once laced the city. The moody charm of this area isn't lost on prosperous young Milanese, who are converting old lofts and moving into former quarters of the working classes. The attendant bars, shops, and restaurants on the ground floors have sprung up to serve their needs. It's also the only part of Milan open in August. You can walk to the Navigli in about 30 to 40 minutes from Piazza del Duomo by following Via Torino south to Corso Porta Ticinese, but a tram ride (or the Metro to Porta Genova) will get you there more quickly, in about 15 minutes.

GETTING THERE

Both of Milan's airports are operated by **SEA** (☎ 02-74852200; www.sea-aeroporti milano.it). **Milan Malpensa,** 45km (27 miles) northwest of the center, handles most international flights. A 40-minute **Malpensa Express train** (☎ 199-151152; www.malpensaexpress.it) costs 11€ and heads half-hourly to the Cadorna train station in western Milan—*not* to the larger and more central Stazione Centrale (you'll have to take the Metro to get there). More convenient are the Malpensa shuttle buses, which run every 20 to 30 minutes and will take you directly to a bus stop on the east side of Stazione Centrale in 50 minutes. Your choices are **Malpensa Shuttle** (☎ 0331-258411; www.malpensashuttle.it), which costs 6€, or the cheaper **Malpensa Bus Express** (☎ 02-33910794)—same exact service at a lower price: 5.50€. The trip into town by **taxi** costs a whopping 60€ to 75€.

The airport called **Milan Linate,** only 7 km (4 miles) east of the center, handles some European flights (which are increasingly being moved to Malpensa) and domestic flights. **Starfly buses** (☎ 02-58587237) run from Linate to Stazione Centrale every 20 to 30 minutes; allow 20 minutes for the trip, which costs 4€. For 1€ you can also take **city bus no. 73,** which leaves every 10 minutes for the southeast corner of Piazza San Babila, a few blocks east of the Duomo. The trip into town by taxi costs about 12€ to 18€.

By train, Milan is 552km (342 miles) northwest of Rome (hourly trains; 4½–6 hr.), 288km (179 miles) northwest of Florence (hourly trains; 2¾–4 hr.), and 257km (160 miles) west of Venice (half-hourly trains; 2½–3½ hr.).

The **Stazione Centrale,** a vast Fascist-era structure, is about a half-hour walk northeast of the center, with easy connections to Piazza del Duomo in the center of downtown by Metro, tram, and bus. The stop on the Metro for the train station is Centrale F.S. To get downtown, the Metro is fastest (10 min.), but if you want to see something of the city en route, take bus no. 60 from the station to Piazza del Duomo. If you decide to walk, follow Via Pisani through the district of high-rise office buildings around the station to the equally cheerless Piazza della Repubblica, and from there continue south on Via Turati and Via Manzoni to Piazza del Duomo.

Chances are you'll arrive at Stazione Centrale, but some trains serve Milan's other train stations: Stazione Nord (with service to/from Como, among other cities), Porta Genova (with service to/from Alessandria and Asti), and Porta Garibaldi (with service to/from Lecco).

GETTING AROUND

An extensive and efficient **Metro** (subway system), **trams,** and **buses** make it very easy to move around Milan. The Metro closes at midnight, though some buses and trams run all night. Tickets good for one Metro ride (or 75 min. worth of surface transportation) cost 1€. You can also get a *carnet* of 10 tickets for 9.20€, or purchase unlimited-ride tickets good for 1 day (3€) or 2 days (5.50€). Tickets are available at Metro stations and at newsstands. You must stamp your ticket when you board a bus or tram—you can be slapped with a hefty fine if you don't. For info about Milan public transportation, visit the information office in the **Duomo metro stop** (☎ 02-72524301 or 800-808181; www.atm-mi.it).

The main Azienda di Promozione Turistica del Milanese (APT) **tourist office** has recently moved into the charmingly Deco former premises of an old "day hotel," in the undercrofting of the palazzo on the north side of Piazza del Duomo—look for the stairs leading down and around a column with a burnished brass plaque reading ALBERGO DIURNO (Piazza del Duomo 19A; ☎ 02-77404343 or 02-72524301; www.milanoinfo.eu). There is also an extremely well-hidden office in the **Stazione Centrale train station** (☎ 02-72524360). To find it, as you exit the train platform into the main commercial hall—before taking the escalators downstairs to the ticketing areas—head to your left and look for the side corridor on the right whose entrance is lined in flashing neon lights. The tourist office is down that corridor, just past the rock shops flanking either side.

These offices issue maps, museum guides, hotel and restaurant listings, and other useful information, but because they're now privately run, they charge nominal fees for the majority of the more useful materials. The **tourism section of the city's website** (www.turismo.comune.milano.it) is also helpful, as is www.musei delcentro.mi.it, which covers several of the minor, special-interest museums in the historical center. The private www.hellomilano.it is particularly good for events. They publish a monthly events newspaper, free at the tourist offices; online, click "What's On" for the events calendar.

ACCOMMODATIONS, BOTH STANDARD & NOT

Most Milan hotels are oriented toward business types, with precious few left over for the relatively few tourists who don't arrive in Milan, see *The Last Supper,* and then immediately high-tail it for more popular cities such as Venice or Florence.

It's difficult to find rooms in *any* price category when **fashion shows** and **trade fairs** are in full swing (dates vary from year to year, but these tend to cluster in groups of 3 days to 1 week, Oct–Mar). Many hotels nearly double their prices at these times, too, which is why you'll often see official rates listing some ludicrous range like "60€ to 220€," in which case it's a good bet that, outside trade fairs, the highest rates charged are roughly half the listed top price. I'll try to indicate the "true" highest rates, generally applied Easter to October (except Aug) and not during trade fairs, and use that figure (and the low-season rates) to determine the appropriate price category of each hotel below. **August** is low season, and hotels are often willing to bring prices down considerably (though you really don't want to be in Milan then anyway, as much of the city is shut down), as they will sometimes do on slow weekends. Always ask for the lowest possible rate when booking and be prepared to bargain.

Though they won't book a room for you, the tourist office (see "Getting Around," above) will help you track down hotels within your budget (and, if you go to the main office in person, will even call around for you).

Bed & Breakfasts in Milan

Milan doesn't go in much for alternative accommodations. There are only about two dozen registered B&Bs in the entire city, and few of them are anywhere near the historical center, nor do they offer particularly good savings over hotels.

€€–€€€   There is, however, a clutch of them in the residential district just north of the Navigli, packed with locals' restaurants and low-key bars, and within about a 10-minute walk from a Metro stop. Closest to the Navigli is **Cocoon** (Via Voghera 7; ☎ 02-8322769 or 349-8606014; www.cocoonbb.com; Metro: Porta Genova), with three 75€-to-100€ rooms done in a stylish modern decor—Rossa, opening onto a garden, has wood floors and a Balinese four-poster bed; cozy Bianca has a double bed dramatically against a curtained window; and Grigia has twin beds with modern lamps and the legends "SLEEP" above one and "WELL" above the other. A few blocks farther north you'll find **Alle Dolce Vite** (Via Cola di Rienzo 39; ☎ 347-3773044 or 02-48952808; www.ladolcevite.net; Metro: S. Agostino), named for the "sweet grapevines" decorating the arbor of its lovely garden; its three 120€ to 130€ rooms are in the refinished attic, so think sloping, wood-beamed ceilings and a modern look. Between Piazza Vesuvio and Piazza Po, **Bed and Bread** (Via Vetta d'Italia 14; ☎ 02-468267 or 333-8396441; www.bedandbread.it) offers three small, simple, but nice and colorful rooms for 100€ to 110€ and a denlike shared living room with a DVD player and low vaulted brick ceiling. You can always find a handful of other B&Bs, as well as apartments for short-term let, at the official tourist office site **www.milanoinfo.eu,** and at the private broker **www.friendly-home.org**.

Hotels near the Duomo

€€   A 15-minute walk south of the Duomo, the **Hotel Aliseo** (Corso Italia 6; ☎ 02-86450156 or 02-804535; AE, MC, V; Metro: Missori) offers a lot of comfort in addition to its good location and great rates: 60€ to 75€ for a double room without bathroom, 80€ to 100€ for one with. The management is friendly, and rooms are furnished with pleasant modern pieces and decent beds (no phones, though). Rooms without a bathroom come with a tiny washroom with sink and a bidet, just no toilet or shower (large, spanking-clean bathrooms are in the hallway). Rooms on the street side open to small balconies, but are noisier than those overlooking the *cortile* (courtyard). The Aliseo—which used to be called the Ullrich—books up quickly, so be sure to call ahead.

€€€ The narrow Via Santa Marta is a slice of old Milan, cobblestoned and lined with charming old buildings, one of which houses the **Hotel Santa Marta** ★ (Via Santa Marta 4; ☎ 02-804567; www.hotel-santamarta.it; AE, MC, V; Metro: Cordusio or Duomo). Recent modernizations have preserved the old-fashioned ambience while adding such modern comforts as air-conditioning, but rates for a double have stayed around 130€ (spiking to 210€ during trade fairs). It's also across the street from one of the city's most atmospheric restaurants (La Milanese, p. 400), and a short walk from the Duomo and other sights. The tile-floored guest rooms are comfortable and decorated with a matter-of-fact fashion sense; some are cramped and others are quite large. If they're full, they'll send you to their sister hotel, the Rovello (see below).

The Magnificent Midrange Hotels of Via Rovello

Halfway between the Duomo and the Castello, just above Piazza Cordusio, a quiet side street angles off the wide, cafe-and-shop-lined artery of Via Dante. It's called Via Rovello, and it's home to a trio of wonderful midpriced hotels that put you in the heart of the action—no more than a 10-minute stroll from the castle, Duomo, Brera museum, and La Scala opera house—yet tucked away from the busy streets.

€€–€€€ Unlike its neighbors, the **London Hotel** ★ (Via Rovello 3; ☎ 02-72020166; www.hotellondonmilano.com; MC, V; Metro: Cordusio) sticks to its old-fashioned ways—and lower prices. Doubles without bathroom go for 100€ to 130€, with bathroom go for 120€ to 150€. The big fireplace and cozy green-velvet furniture in the lobby say a lot about the comfort level and friendly atmosphere that bring many guests back time after time. Just beyond the lobby, there's a bar where beverages are available almost around the clock; guests can purchase a continental breakfast in the morning. Upstairs, the rooms look as if they haven't been redecorated in a number of decades, but they're roomy and bright, and the heavy old furnishings lend a charm very much in keeping with the ambience of the hotel. Rooms on the first floor tend to be the largest, and they get smaller as you go up.

€€€ Like its sister hotel the Santa Marta (above), the 10-room **Hotel Rovello** ★ (Via Rovello 18; ☎ 02-86464654; www.hotel-rovello.it; AE, MC, V; Metro: Cordusio) normally charges 120€ for a double room, through the price jumps to 210€ during trade fairs. The unusually large guest rooms occupy the first and second floors of a centuries-old building and incorporate many of the original architectural details, including exposed timbers and wood-beam ceilings. Handsome contemporary Italian furnishings are set off by gleaming hardwood floors, the tall casement windows are covered with attractive fabrics, and walls are painted in soothing green and gold tones. The orthopedic mattresses are covered with thick quilts for a homey feel. Many of the rooms have dressing areas in addition to the large new bathrooms. A breakfast of rolls and coffee is served in a sunny room off the lobby.

€€–€€€€   A recent renovation has brought **Hotel Giulio Cesare** ★ (Via Rovello 10; ☎ 02-72003915; www.giuliocesarehotel.it; AE, MC, V; Metro: Cordusio) thoroughly up-to-date, with a grandiose marble lobby and a handsome lounge and bar area with deep couches—though management can be a bit brusque. The rooms are contemporary chic, with starkly modern minimalist furnishings, but do reflect the building's centuries-old heritage with their tall windows and high ceilings. Some are quirkily shaped, and a few singles are cramped. Doubles go for 153€, though Internet specials often bring it down below 100€.

Cheap Hotels Far East of the Duomo

€€–€€€   Though tiny **Hotel America** (Corso XXII Marzo 32, in the block east of Piazza Emilia; ☎ 02-7381865; www.milanohotelamerica.com; Metro: Porta Vittoria, though it's more convenient by tram/bus: 12, 27, 45, 60, 66, 73, or 92) is a bit off the beaten track, in a middle-class neighborhood a 10-minute tram ride east of Piazza del Duomo, the young owner and his family work overtime to make this pensione one of the best lower-priced lodgings in Milan. The rooms occupy the fourth floor of an apartment house, with streamlined, wood-veneer modern furnishings. Thank goodness they replaced the old thematic stars-and-stripes decor with a more sedate red-and-dusty-rose motif during a spring 2007 complete renovation. However, the upgrade came with a price: Rates have shot up more than 25% to 60€ to 90€ for a double (up to 150€ and even 200€ during trade fairs). Guests are welcome to join the resident innkeepers in the living room and watch TV. The Rolling Stone music club, a venerable fixture on the Milan nightlife scene, is on the ground floor of the building, a good reason to ask for a room facing the quieter giardino courtyard (room no. 10 even has a balcony).

€€–€€€   The family-run **Hotel Pavone** ★ 🦘 (Via Dandolo 2, off Corso di Porta Vittoria; ☎ 02-55192133; www.hotelpavone.com; AE, MC, V; tram: 12, 23, 27, 60, or 73) is around the corner from the Palace of Justice, about a 15-minute walk east of the Duomo in a neighborhood more geared to business than to the tourist trade. Double rooms run 60€ to 120€ (during trade fairs up to 220€) and tend to be a bit sparse, with gray-tile floors and no-nonsense Scandinavian-style furniture, but they were spruced up in 2003 with new linens and decor. Most are unusually large and cloaked in a silence, uncommon for big-city Milan (room nos. 12, 14, 16, and 18, all of which overlook a garden, are the quietest of the bunch). Many rooms are outfitted as triples and are large enough to accommodate an extra bed, making this a fine choice for families.

Cheap Hotels near Stazione Centrale & Corso Buenos Aires

€–€€   Occupying an old house on a quiet residential street off the north end of Corso Buenos Aires, the **Hotel Paganini** ★ (Via Paganini 6; ☎ 02-2047443; AE, MC, V; Metro: Loreto) has minimal public areas (except for a reception area with a self-serve espresso machine), but the guest rooms are large, bright, and embellished with tile floors, high ceilings with elaborate moldings, solid beds, and banal modular furnishings—all for just 50€ for a double. The one room with a private bathroom is just inside the entrance, with wood floors, a ceiling decorated with molded stuccoes, and plenty of elbow room for 60€. The shared bathrooms are modern enough and kept spanking clean by the owners, who are happy to point their guests to restaurants and sights. The best rooms are in the rear, overlooking a huge private garden. There is much to be said for this location: The Stazione Centrale is only a 10-minute walk way, and if shopping is on your agenda, the nearby Corso Buenos Aires is one of the city's bargain fashion meccas.

€€–€€€ The Bianchi family is genuinely welcoming to the many English speakers who find their way to their **Hotel Kennedy** (Viale Tunisia 6; ☎ 02-29400934; www.kennedyhotel.it; AE, MC, V; Metro: Porta Venezia), a block from the southern end of Corso Buenos Aires. Their homey establishment on the sixth floor of an office-and-apartment building (there's an elevator) is sparkling clean and offers basic accommodations in large, tile-floored rooms that cost 52€ to 80€ for a double without private bathroom, 65€ to 120€ for one with bathroom. Room no. 13 has a terrace, while room no. 15 has a small balcony that even glimpses the spires of the Duomo in the distance. Amenities include a bar in the reception area, where coffee and soft drinks are available, as is a light breakfast of brioche and coffee that doesn't cost much more than it would in a cafe.

A Hotel near *The Last Supper*

€€–€€€€ Tucked away in a residential neighborhood of apartment houses and old villas, the **Ariosto** ★★ (Via Ariosto 22; ☎ 02-4817844; www.hotel ariosto.com; AE, MC, V; Metro: Conciliazione) is a refreshingly quiet retreat—all the more so because many of the newly refurbished rooms face a private garden, and some open onto balconies overlooking it. All the rooms are decorated with wood-and-wicker furnishings, shiny parquet floors, and hand-painted wallpaper, and while most are decently sized, singles tend to be skinny. Many of the doubles have separate dressing areas off the tile or stone bathrooms, which are equipped with hair dryers (and a few with Jacuzzis). The rack rate for doubles is 240€, but that's only applied during trade fairs; at all other times, doubles run a far more reasonable 99€ to 120€ (check the website's calendar).

DINING FOR ALL TASTES

The Milanese are more willing than Italians elsewhere to break the sit-down-meal tradition and grab a sandwich or other light fare on the run. And with so many students and young professionals, Milan has no shortage of *pizzerie* and other low-cost eateries.

Restaurants near the Duomo

€ **Luini** ★★ (Via S. Radegonda 16, 2 blocks east of the Galleria Vittorio Emanuele II; ☎ 02-86461917; www.luini.it; cash only; Tues–Sat 10am–8pm, Mon 10am–3pm; closed Aug; Metro: Duomo) has been a Milan institution since 1948, and it's so good they've even opened a branch in London. You'll have to elbow your way through a throng of well-dressed patrons at this stand-up counter in order to plunk down 2.30€ to 2.50€ for the house specialty: *panzerotto*, a pocket of pizza crust stuffed with all sorts of ingredients, including the basic cheese and tomato.

€ Busy **La Crêperie** (Via C. Correnti 21, an extension of Via Torino, about a 10-min. walk southeast of Piazza del Duomo; ☎ 02-8395913; www.la-creperie.it;

cash only; Mon–Fri noon–3pm and 4pm–midnight, Sat noon–3pm and 4pm–1am, Sun 4pm–midnight; closed July 15–Aug 25; Metro: Sant'Ambrogio) is an ideal stop for a light lunch or a snack while visiting the nearby church of Sant'Ambrogio or Museo Nazionale di Scienza. Crepes come in both the meal-like *salata* variety ("salty" ones stuffed with prosciutto, cheese, and so on) and the dolce ("sweet") dessert variety (I recommend the Nutella, with its creamy hazelnut-chocolate spread). During weekdays, they offer a lunch menu of two crepes (one salty, one sweet) plus a drink for 6.50€; otherwise, salty crepes run 3€, sweet ones 2.50€ to 3€. They've recently expanded beyond crepes to serve other foreign and exotic foods, such as *hot dogs americani* and waffles.

€   If you're looking for an excellent, cheap, and quick meal, head to any branch of the national chain **Brek** (closest to the Duomo is at Piazzetta U. Giordano 1, near Santa Babila; ☎ 02-76023379; www.brek.com; Mon–Sat 11:30am–3pm, daily 6:30–10:30pm; AE, MC, V; Metro: Babila), one of the world's best food chains. Even when the Italians do something as low concept as a cafeteria, they can't help but make it fashionable and pour their hearts into the quality of the food. At the various food-prep stations, the friendly and helpful staff makes pasta and risotto dishes on the spot, and roast pork, veal, and chicken to order. The large selection of cheeses would put many a formal restaurant to shame, and you can even get excellent wines in tiny bottles. Best of all: Almost every dish goes for just 3€ to 8€. There's another branch at Via dell'Annunciata 2 (☎ 02-653619), just off Piazza Cavour, a 5-minute walk from the Brera museum, the shops of the Quadrilatero d'Oro, and the Giardini Pubblici park.

€–€€   **Peck** ★★ (Via Spadari 9; ☎ 02-8023161; www.peck.it; Mon 3–7:30pm; Tues–Sat 8:45am–7:30pm; closed Jan 1–10 and July 1–20; AE, MC, V; Metro: Duomo) is Milan's most famous food emporium, its glittering cases filled with a wonderful selection of roast veal, risottos, *porchetta,* salads, aspics, cheeses, pastries, and other fare from its exquisite larder for 3€ to 12€. You can eat at the stand-up bar where, especially around lunchtime, it can be hard to find elbow room, or you can put together a gourmet picnic to go.

€€–€€€   For a sit-down meal, head to Milan's most classic restaurant since 1933, **La Milanese** ★★★ (Via Santa Marta 11; ☎ 02-86451991; Wed–Mon noon–3pm and 7pm–1am; closed Dec 25–Jan 10 and mid-July to Aug; AE, MC, V; Metro: Cordusio; reservations recommended), tucked into a narrow lane in one of the oldest sections of Milan just west of the Duomo. In the three-beamed dining room, Milanese families and other patrons share the long, crowded tables. Giuseppe prepares traditional Milanese fare, and you can even try their twin specialties—without pigging out: *risotto e osso buco,* a half portion each of *risotto alla milanese* (rice cooked with saffron and beef marrow) and perfect *osso buco* (tender veal shanks on the bone), for 24€.

Restaurants in Magenta & Brera

€   Any time my Milanese friends say, "Hey, let's go get pizza!" they invariably take me to **Pizzeria Grand'Italia** ★★ (Via Palermo 5; ☎ 02-877759; daily noon–2:45pm and 7pm–1am; AE, MC, V; Metro: Moscova). It serves up a huge assortment of salads (7.50€), pizzas (from 5€), homemade pastas (5.50€–7€), and *focacce farcite* (focaccia bread stuffed with cheese, mushrooms, and other fillings; 7.50€) along with wine and oil from the Furfaro family's farm in Tuscany. Unusually for Italy, rather than a whole pie you get one thick-crusted mega-slice (what, in America, might be called "Sicilian style," only twice as big) topped however you like it and diced into bite-sized pieces to be eaten with a fork. The late hours make this a prime nightspot, and part of the fun is watching the chic young Milanese stopping buy for a snack as they make the rounds of the nearby Brera district bars and clubs.

€€   The main business at **Latteria** ★★ (Via San Marco 24; ☎ 02-6597653; cash only; Mon–Fri 12:30–2:30pm and 7:30–10pm; closed Aug; Metro: Moscova) was once dispensing milk and eggs to a press of neighborhood shoppers, but now the emphasis is on serving the La Brera neighborhood delicious homemade fare in a room decorated with paintings and photographs of roses. The minestrone and other vegetable soups are delicious, but I can't really share with you specifics since the menu changes daily with whatever they find at the market. I can tell you that *primi* generally run about 9.50€ (a bit more for pasta with fish). Don't worry; the friendly staff, including owners Arturo and Maria, won't mind explaining the different dishes. The place is tiny, doesn't take reservations, and is immensely popular; so arrive right when it opens at 7:30pm—or wait until 9pm or later, when a few tables will free up as the early-dining tourist clientele clears out and the locals take over.

A Vegetarian Splurge near Stazione Centrale

€€€–€€€€   A few blocks from the southern end of Corso Buenos Aires is the decidedly upscale worthy splurge of **Joia** ★★ (Via P. Castaldi 18; ☎ 02-2049244; www.joia.it; Mon–Fri 12:30–2:30pm and 7:30–11pm, Sat 7:30–11pm; closed Aug; AE, MC, V; Metro: Repubblica; reservations recommended), once called by Michelin the best vegetarian restaurant in Europe. (Translation: Book ahead, and bring your credit card.) The innovative vegetarian creations of Swiss chef Pietro Leemann—a welcome respite from northern Italy's orientation to red meat—incorporate the freshest vegetables and herbs in a seasonally changing menu. You can even fiddle around with the traditional Italian menu, ordering *primi* as *secondi*, and many of the *secondi* can be served as *antipasti*. The one drawback is the price: 18€ or 20€ for *primi*—whew!

Restaurants in the Navigli

You can't swing a salami without smacking some place in which to eat or drink along the quays of Milan's defunct canal system. The former warehouses are now packed with bars, pubs, *pizzerie, trattorie,* and restaurants. Here are my faves.

€   The most popular pizzeria in the Navigli, **Premiata Pizzeria** ★ (Via Alzaia Naviglio Grande 2; ☎ 02-89400648; Wed–Mon noon–2:30pm, daily 7:30–11:30pm; AE, MC, V; tram: ❸, ⑮, ㉙, ㉚, or ㊽) stays packed from early dinnertime until the barhopping crowd stops by for late-night munchies. The restaurant rambles back forever, exposed copper pipes tracing across the ceilings of rooms wrapped around shaded outdoor terraces set with long, raucous tables. Seating is communal and

Cafes & Gelaterie

€   **Bar Zucca/Caffè Miani** (at the Duomo end of the Galleria Vittorio Emanuele II; ☎ 02-86464435; www.caffemiani.it; Metro: Duomo) is best known by its original name, Il Camparino. It's the most attractive and popular of the Galleria's many bars and introduced Italy to Campari, the country's ubiquitous red cordial. You can linger at the tables set up in the Galleria for views of the Duomo's facade, or in one of the Art Nouveau rooms inside.

€   You can find organic gelato at the **Gelateria Ecologica** (Corso di Porta Ticinese 40; ☎ 02-58101872; Metro: Sant'Ambrogio or Missori), in the Ticinese/Navigli neighborhood. It's so popular, there's no need for a sign out front. Strollers in the atmospheric Brera neighborhood sooner or later stumble upon the **Gelateria Toldo** (Via Ponte Vetero 9; ☎ 02-86460863; Metro: Cordusio or Lanza), where the gelato is wonderfully creamy and many of the *sorbetto* selections are so fruity and fresh they seem healthy.

€   The **Pasticceria Confetteria Cova** (Via Montenapoleone 8; ☎ 02-76000578; Metro: Montenapoleone) is approaching its 200th year in refined surroundings near the similarly atmospheric Museo Poldi-Pezzoli. It's usually filled with shoppers making the rounds in this high-fashion district. You can enjoy a quick coffee and a brioche at the long bar, or take a seat in one of the elegant adjoining rooms.

€   The **Pasticceria Marchesi** (Via Santa Maria alla Porta 13; ☎ 02-862770; Metro: Cordusio) is a distinguished pastry shop, with an adjoining wood-panel tearoom. Because it's only steps from Santa Maria delle Grazie, you can enjoy the old-world ambience and a cup of excellent coffee (or one of the many teas and herbal infusions) as you dash off postcards of *The Last Supper*. Of course, you'll want to accompany your beverage with one of the elegant pastries, perhaps a slice of the *panettone* (cake laden with raisins and candied citron) that's a hallmark of Milan. No one prepares it better than they do at Marchesi.

service hurried, but the wood-oven pizzas are excellent (6€–12€). If you're hungrier, there's a long menu of pastas and meat courses, while those with lighter appetites can enjoy a selection of salads (5€–9€) or cheese or salami platters made for two (14€).

€€–€€€   **Al Pont de Ferr** ★★ (Ripa di Porta Ticinese 55, on the Naviglio Grande; ☎ 02-89406277; daily 12:30–2:30pm and 8pm–1am; MC, V; tram: ❸, ⓯, ㉙, ㉚, or ㉟) has long been one of the more respectable of the Navigli joints, with tables set out on the flagstones overlooking the canal (regulars know to bring bug spray to battle the mosquitoes in summer). The menu changes constantly, so I can only give you an indication of prices (*primi* cost 12€–15€, *secondi* run 18€–22€), and describe some of the delectable dishes I've enjoyed here, including risotto with a guinea fowl *ragù*, Camembert, and milk, and the oven-baked rosette of fresh pasta, which is inventively stuffed with Prague ham, cheese, and walnuts. There's a surprisingly good selection of half bottles of wine, but most full bottles start at 15€ and go senselessly higher. On the whole, portions could be a lot larger at these prices, but you gotta love a place whose menu opens with the quip, "Good cooking is the friend of living well and the enemy of a hurried life."

€€–€€€ **Ponte Rosso** ★ (Ripa di Porta Ticinese 23, on the Naviglio Grande; ☎ 02-8373132; Mon–Sat noon–3pm and 7–11pm; AE, MC, V; tram: ❸, ⓯, ㉙, ㉚, or ㊲) is an old-fashioned trattoria on the canal, a long railroad room crowded with tiny tables and a short, simple menu of hearty home cooking. The owner hails from Trieste (which explains the old Triestino photos on the walls), so kick a meal off with a 10€ *antipasto di salami misti,* a mixed platter of cured meats from the Friuli region, famous for producing San Daniele, the most delicate prosciutto in Italy. In fact, dishes on the always-changing menu hail from all corners of Italy, from Milanese risotto with saffron (10€), to *sartu di riso napoletano* (rice stuffed with tiny meatballs, mozzarella, and prosciutto, 12€), to Sardinian spaghetti *con la bottarga* (dried fish roe) with crumbled sheep's cheese (12€). In the realm of *secondi,* they do a gangbuster business with the ever-popular *costoletto di vitello alla Milanese* (veal chop, 18€,) and the mixed vegetarian fry (14€).

WHY YOU'RE HERE: THE TOP SIGHTS & ATTRACTIONS

Despite hosting some major sights—Leonardo da Vinci's *Last Supper;* the gargantuan Gothic Duomo bristling with statues, spires, and pinnacles; the old masters in the Brera and Ambrosiana picture galleries; the fashion boutiques; and La Scala opera house—Milan is not a place that rewards folks who linger too long.

Sure, it's a nice enough town, with great restaurants and a hopping nightlife. But when you compare this gray, work-oriented city with beauty queens like Venice, Florence, and Rome, or with the charms of Tuscan hill towns, Sicilian villages, or the resorts of the coast or nearby lake district, Milan just doesn't hold a candle. For that reason, give Milan a day or two, hit the highlights, then move on.

Luckily, Milan's airport is second only to Rome in international arrivals, so it's easy to route yourself through here, spending the first or final night of your holiday in the city in order to knock off that *Last Supper* and maybe catch an opera at world-renowned La Scala.

Il Duomo (The Cathedral)

When Milanesi think something is taking too long, they refer to it as being like *la fabbrica del Duomo* (the making of the cathedral). It took 5 centuries to complete Milan's magnificent Gothic **Duomo** ★★★ (Piazza del Duomo; ☎ 02-72022656; www.duomomilano.it; daily 7am–7pm; Metro: Duomo), which was begun by the ruling Visconti family in 1386. The last of Italy's great Gothic structures is the fourth-largest Catholic church in the world (after St. Peter's in Rome, Seville's cathedral, and a new one in Côte d'Ivoire), with 135 marble spires, a stunning triangular facade (currently under restoration wraps), and 3,400-some statues flanking the massive but airy, almost fanciful exterior.

Milan Itineraries

If you have only 1 day in Milan

Book ahead—at least 2 weeks in advance if possible—for the very first entry time of the day (8:15am) to see **Leonardo da Vinci's** *Last Supper.* Head east to Milan's gargantuan **Castello Sforzesco** for Michelangelo's final *Pietà* and a clutch of fine Renaissance paintings. Stroll down the largely pedestrianized Via Dante, pausing for a cappuccino break in one of its many cafes, to Piazza del Duomo and Milan's enormous Gothic **Duomo.** Be sure you make it up onto the roof—my favorite Milan experience—to duck under buttresses and wend your way between the statue-topped spires for thrilling citywide panoramas that, on the few winter days when industrial smog doesn't interfere, stretch all the way to the Alps. Join the throngs of locals and businessmen on break and grab a panzerotto from **Luini** for a typical Milan lunch on the go, and then wash it down with a view of the Duomo facade and Italy's prototypical aperitif, a Campari-soda, in the very bar that invented it, **Caffè della Zucca.**

Amble through the glass atrium of the historic **Galleria Vittorio Emanuele II,** ending up in front of **La Scala** opera house, where you can visit the operatic collections in its **Museo Teatrale** and check into last-minute tickets for that night's performance. While you window-shop the world-famous boutiques of **Quadrilatero d'Oro,** pop into the private collections of the **Museo Poldi Pezzoli** for 30 minutes, whetting your appetite for the artistic giants in the **Pinacoteca di Brera,** where you can peruse the paintings until they kick you out at 7:30pm. Hop on a tram down to the **Navigli,** Milan's trendiest restaurant district and nightlife scene, strung out along the remnants of the city's old canals.

The cavernous interior, lit by brilliant stained-glass windows, seats 40,000 but is unusually spartan and serene, divided into five aisles by a forest of 52 columns. The poet Shelley used to sit and read Dante amid monuments that include a gruesomely graphic statue of *St. Bartholomew Flayed* ✦ and the tombs of Giacomo de Medici, two Visconti, and many cardinals and archbishops. Another British visitor, Alfred, Lord Tennyson, rhapsodized about the view of the Alps from the **roof** ✦✦✦ 🦵 (elevators on the church's exterior northeast corner for 6€; stairs on the exterior north side for 4€; daily Nov 2–Feb 2 9am–4:45pm, Feb 3–Nov 1 9am–5:45pm), where you get to wander amid the Gothic pinnacles, saintly statues, and flying buttresses. You are joined high above Milan by the spire-top gold statue of *Madonnina* (the little Madonna), the city's beloved protectress.

Back on terra firma, the cathedral's **crypt** (1.50€; hours same as roof) contains the remains of San Carlo Borromeo, one of the early cardinals of Milan and a member of the noble family that still owns much of the prime real estate around Lake Maggiore (later in this chapter). A far more interesting descent is the one down the staircase to the right of the main entrance, to the **Battistero**

If you have only 2 days in Milan

On Day 1, start off at the **Pinacoteca Ambrosiana** when it opens (10am) for 90 minutes of old masters (Raphael, Caravaggio, da Vinci) before moving on to see Bramante's illusory architectural masterpiece inside the tiny church of **Santa Maria Presso Santo Satiro,** and then plunge right into the sights around Piazza del Duomo: the **Cathedral** itself (don't forget the roof!), a light lunch at **Caffè della Zucca,** and a stroll through **Galleria Vittorio Emanuele II** to La Scala opera house. Give its **Museo Teatrale** 30 minutes of your time, and check into buying tickets for tonight's (or tomorrow's) performance. End the day as above, window-shopping the **Quadrilatero d'Oro,** visiting the **Museo Poldi Pezzoli,** and touring the **Pinacoteca di Brera** until it closes—but instead of heading to the Navigli tonight, stick around the Brera neighborhood, which is also chock-a-block with bars and pubs and great restaurants.

Start Day 2 at the medieval **Castello Sforzesco.** On your way to see **da Vinci's** *Last Supper* (book tickets for noon), stop into the **Museo Archeologico** to see how the Roman town of Mediolanum grew to become the metropolis of Milan. Take lunch at the bistrolike Art Nouveau **Bar Magenta,** and head south to the gorgeous 4th-century church of S. Ambrogio and the nearby **Museo Nazionale della Scienza,** filled with scale models of Leonardo's inventions. Make your way east to the ancient church of **San Lorenzo Maggiore,** and then stroll south a few blocks to jump into the pub, jazz club, and restaurant scene of the Navigli.

Paleocristiano S. Giovanni alle Fonti (1.50€; hours same as roof), the ruins of a 4th-century baptistery believed to be where St. Ambrose baptized St. Augustine.

The Duomo houses many of its treasures across the piazza from the right transept in a wing of the Palazzo Reale devoted to **Museo del Duomo** (Piazza del Duomo 14; ☎ 02-860358; 6€; daily 10am–1:15pm and 3–6pm). Among the legions of statuary saints are a significant painting, Tintoretto's *Christ at the Temple,* and some intriguing displays chronicling the construction of the cathedral.

The best place from which to admire the Duomo facade is an outdoor table at Caffè della Zucca, the bar that invented Italy's consummate aperitif, Camparisoda. This genteel cafe lies at the entrance to the elegant **Galleria Vittorio Emanuele II** ✹✹, Milan's late-19th-century version of a mall. This wonderful steel-and-glass-covered, cross-shaped arcade is the prototype of the enclosed shopping malls that were to become the hallmark of 20th-century consumerism—though it's safe to say that none of the imitators have come close to matching the Galleria for style and flair. The designer of this urban marvel, Giuseppe Mengoni, didn't live to see the Milanese embrace his creation: He tripped and fell from a

A Duomo Combo

Catch the elevator to the Duomo's roof and see the cathedral museum together with a 8€ Combination Ticket.

girder a few days before the Galleria opened in 1878. His shopping mall par excellence provides a lovely route between the Duomo and Piazza della Scala and is a fine locale for watching the flocks of well-dressed Milanese.

The Last Supper

What draws so many visitors to Milan is the *Cenacolo Vinciano,* better known to English speakers as **Leonardo da Vinci's *The Last Supper* ★★** (Piazza Santa Maria delle Grazie 2, a wide spot along Corso Magenta; ☎ 02-89421146; www.cenacolo vinciano.org; 6.50€ plus a required booking fee of 1.50€; Tues–Sun 8:15am–7pm; Metro: Cardona or Conciliazione). From 1495 to 1497, Leonardo da Vinci painted this poignant portrayal of confusion and betrayal for the wall of the refectory in the Dominican convent attached to the church of Santa Maria delle Grazie. Aldous Huxley called this fresco the "saddest work of art in the world," a comment in part on the deterioration that set in even before the paint had dried on the moisture-ridden walls. The fresco got a lot of well-intentioned but poorly executed "touching up" in the 18th and 19th centuries, though a recent lengthy restoration has done away with all that overpainting, as well as tried to undo the damage wrought by the clumsy patching and damage inflicted when Napoleon's troops used the wall for target practice, and from when Allied bombing during World War II tore off the room's roof, leaving the fresco exposed to the elements for 3 years.

In short, *The Last Supper* is a mere shadow of the work the artist intended it to be, but the scene, which captures the moment when Christ told his apostles that one of them would betray him, remains amazingly powerful and emotional nonetheless. Only 25 people are allowed to view the fresco at a time, with a 15-minute limit, and you must pass through a series of devices that remove pollutants from clothing. Accordingly, lines are long and tickets are usually sold out days in advance. I'm serious: If you don't book ahead—preferably a week or two in advance—you'll most likely be turned away at the door, even in the dead of winter when you'd expect the place to be empty (tour bus groups swallow up inordinately large batches of tickets, leaving precious few for do-it-yourself travelers).

Often overlooked are the other great treasures of the late-15th-century **Church of Santa Maria delle Grazie** (☎ 02-48014248; www.grazieop.it; Mon–Sat 7am–noon and 3–7pm, Sun 7:30am–12:15pm and 3:30–9pm, may close earlier in winter; Metro: Cardona or Conciliazione), foremost among them the fine dome and other architectural innovations by one of the great architects of the high Renaissance, Bramante (one of the architects of St. Peter's in Rome). To one side of the apse, decorated in marble and terra cotta, is a lovely cloister.

Other Outstanding Sights

The **Brera** ★★★ (Via Brera 28; ☎ 02-722631; www.brera.beniculturali.it; 5€; Tues–Sun 8:30am–7:15pm; Metro: Lanza or Montenapoleone) is one of Italy's top museums of medieval, Renaissance, and 20th-century paintings, including the world's finest collection of northern Italian works. The concentration of so many masterpieces in this 17th-century palace is the work of Napoleon, who used the palazzo as a repository for the art he confiscated from public and private holdings throughout northern Italy; fittingly, a bronze likeness of the emperor greets you as you enter the courtyard.

Just to give you a sampling of what you'll encounter in these 40 or so rooms, three of Italy's greatest masterpieces hang here: Andrea Mantegna's amazingly foreshortened *Dead Christ* ★★★, Raphael's *Betrothal of the Virgin* ★★, and Piero della Francesca's *Madonna with Saints* ★★ (the Montefeltro altarpiece). It is an indication of this museum's ability to overwhelm visitors that the last two absolute masterpieces hang near each other in a single room dedicated to late–15th century works by Tuscan and Umbrian masters.

Among the other important works are Jacopo Tintoretto's *Finding of the Body of St. Mark* ★, in which the dead saint eerily confronts appropriately startled grave robbers who come upon his corpse, and several by Caravaggio, including the masterful *Supper at Emmaus* ★★. Just beyond is a room devoted to works by foreigners, among them Rembrandt's *Portrait of a Young Woman.* Given Napoleon's fondness for the Venetian schools, it is only just that the final rooms are again filled with works from that city, including Canaletto's *View of the Grand Canal.*

Sights Between the Duomo & the Brera

The stunning treasure trove of antiques and Bellinis, Botticellis, and Tiepolos in the private **Museo Poldi Pezzoli** ★★ (Via Manzoni 12; ☎ 02-794889; www.museo poldipezzoli.it; 8€; Tues–Sun 10am–6pm; Metro: Duomo or Montenapoleone) leans a bit toward Venetian painters (such as Francesco Guardi's elegantly moody *Grey Lagoon*), but also ventures widely throughout Italian painting—Antonio Pollaiuolo's *Portrait of a Young Woman* is often likened to the *Mona Lisa*—and into the Flemish school. It was amassed by 19th-century collector Giacomo Poldi-Pezzoli, who donated his town house and its treasures to the city in 1881. CD-ROM terminals let you explore bits of the collections not currently on display, especially arms and armor, the best of which is housed in an elaborate *pietra serena* room designed by Pomodoro. Pick up a free audioguide in English at the ticket desk.

Milan's renowned opera house, **Teatro alla Scala** ★★ (Piazza della Scala; ☎ 02-88791 or 02-860775 for the box office; www.teatroallascala.org; Metro: Duomo or Montenapoleone), was built in the late 18th century on the site of a church of the same name. La Scala is hallowed ground to lovers of Giuseppe Verdi (who was the house composer for decades), Maria Callas, Arturo Toscanini (conductor for much of the 20th c.), and legions of other composers and singers who have hit the high notes of fame in the world's most revered opera house. La Scala emerged from a multiyear restoration on December 7, 2005—the traditional gala opening night—and between opera, ballet, and orchestral performances, the theater now maintains a year-round schedule. Treat yourself to an evening performance; the cheap seats start at just 10€.

With restoration now complete, the **Museo Teatrale alla Scala** (☎ 02-88792473; 5€; daily 9am–12:30pm and 1:30–5:30pm; Metro: Duomo or Montenapoleone) has also moved back into its permanent home just to the left of the main entrance. The operatic nostalgia includes such mementos as Toscanini's batons, a strand of Mozart's hair, a fine array of Callas postcards, original Verdi scores, a whole mess of historic gramophones and record players, and costumes designed by some of Milan's top fashion gurus and worn by the likes of Callas and Rudolf Nureyev on La Scala's stage.

Sights Between the Duomo & *The Last Supper*

The collection of the **Pinacoteca Ambrosiana** ★★ (Piazza Pio XI 2; ☎ 02-806921; www.ambrosiana.it; 8€; Tues–Sun 10am–5:30pm; Metro: Cordusio or Duomo) focuses on treasures from the 15th through the 17th centuries: An *Adoration* by Titian, Raphael's cartoon for his *School of Athens* in the Vatican, Botticelli's *Madonna and Angels,* Caravaggio's *Basket of Fruit* (his only still life), and other stunning works hang in a series of intimate rooms. Notable (or infamous) among the paintings is *Portrait of a Musician,* attributed to Leonardo da Vinci but, according to many scholars, of dubious provenance; if it is indeed a da Vinci, the haunting painting is the only portrait of his to hang in an Italian museum. The adjoining Biblioteca Ambrosiana, open to scholars only except for special exhibitions, houses a wealth of Renaissance *literaria,* including the letters of Lucrezia Borgia and a strand of her hair. The most notable holdings, though, are da Vinci's *Codice Atlantico,* 1,750 drawings and jottings the master did between 1478 and 1519. These and the library's other volumes, including a rich collection of medieval manuscripts, are frequently put on view to the public; at these times, an admission fee of 10€ allows entrance to both the library and the art gallery.

Though it's been clumsily restored many times, most recently at the end of the 19th century, the fortresslike **Castello Sforzesco** ★★ (Piazza Castello; ☎ 02-88463703; www.milanocastello.it; 3€; Tues–Sun 9am–5:30pm; Metro: Cairoli, Cadorna, or Lanza) continues to evoke Milan's two most powerful medieval and Renaissance families, the Visconti and the Sforza. The Visconti built the castle in the 14th century and the Sforza, who married into the Visconti clan and eclipsed them in power, reconstructed it in 1450. The most influential residents were Ludovico il Moro and Beatrice d'Este (he of the Sforza and she of the famous Este family of Ferrara), who commissioned the works by Bramante and Leonardo da Vinci in the kilometers of rooms that surround the Castello's enormous courtyard.

The castle's salons house a series of small city-administered museums known collectively as the Civici Musei Castello Sforzesco—which were, up until the city got greedy in 2005, always free. Ah, well. They're still worth the relatively small admission charge for the *pinacoteca,* with its minor works by Bellini, Correggio, and Magenta, and the extensive holdings of the Museo d'Arte Antica, filled with Egyptian funerary objects, prehistoric finds from Lombardy, and several giant tapestries in a room containing historical musical instruments. The biggest draw is the final work of an 89-year-old Michelangelo, his unfinished *Rondanini Pietà* ★★, a work so intense and abstract it almost seems to prefigure 20th-century art. Apparently, the master was dissatisfied partway through—or there was a flaw in the material—and he started reworking the piece, but died before he could finish; look for an extraneous arm from the earlier version.

The most fascinating finds in the **Civico Museo Archeologico** ★ (Corso Magenta 15; ☎ 02-86450011; 2€; Tues–Sun 9–1pm and 2–5:30pm; Metro: Cadorna) are the everyday items from Milan's Roman era—tools, eating utensils, jewelry, and some exquisite and remarkably well-preserved glassware. The exhibits fill a 16th-century monastery with Greek, Etruscan, and Roman pieces from throughout Italy; there's also a section devoted to ancient remains from Ghandara, India. You can get a glimpse of Roman architecture in the garden: two Roman towers and a section of a road, part of the walls enclosing the settlement of Mediolanum, once capital of the Western Roman Empire.

If you didn't get enough of Leonardo da Vinci with *The Last Supper*—or just want to see another side of his genius—check out the scale wooden models of many of his most amazing inventions at the **Museo Nazionale della Scienza e della Tecnologia Leonardo da Vinci** ★ 🅺 (Via San Vittore 21; ☎ 02-48555331; www.museoscienza.org; 8€, though families pay 6€ per adult plus 3€ per child under 18; Tues–Fri 9:30am–5pm, Sat–Sun 9:30am–6:30pm; Metro: Sant'Ambrogio), including submarines, helicopters, and other engineering feats that, for the most part, the master only ever invented on paper. This former Benedictine monastery and its beautiful cloisters are also filled with planes, trains, carriages, sewing machines, typewriters, optical devices, and other exhibits, including enchanting re-creations of workshops, that make up one of the world's leading collections of mechanical and scientific wizardry.

From here, you're just 2 blocks from one of the most underrated sights in Milan, the Basilica di Sant'Ambrogio (see below), which lies in the neighborhood south of the Duomo.

A Trio of Top Churches South of the Duomo

In the 4th century A.D., Milan was (briefly) the capital of the Western Roman Empire—and the capital of Western Christendom. Long before the bishop of Rome turned the papacy into the most powerful center for the church, it was the bishop of Milan who called the shots, and the greatest bishop of 4th-century Milan was St. Ambrose.

Little remains of the first **Basilica di Sant'Ambrogio** ★ (Piazza Sant'Ambrogio 15; ☎ 02-86450895; www.santambrogio-basilica.it; free; Mon–Sat 7am–noon and 2:30–7pm, Sun 7am–1pm and 2–8pm; Metro: Sant'Ambrogio), constructed by the saint on this site, but the 11th-century structure built in its place (and renovated many times since) is remarkable. It has a striking atrium, lined with columned porticos, and a brick facade with two ranks of *loggie* flanked by bell towers. Look carefully at the door on the left, where you'll see a relief of St. Ambrose. Note the overall effect of this architectural assemblage, because the church of Sant'Ambrogio set a standard for Lombard Romanesque architecture that you'll see imitated many times throughout Lombardy. On your wanderings through the three-aisled nave you'll come upon a gold altar from Charlemagne's days in Milan, and, in the right aisle, the all-too-scant remains of a Tiepolo fresco cycle, most of it blown into oblivion by World War II bombs. The little that remains of the original church is the Sacello di San Vittore in Ciel d'Oro, a little chapel in which the cupola glows with 5th-century mosaics of saints (2€; enter from the right aisle).

The skeletal remains of Ambrose himself are on view in the crypt. As you leave the main church from the left aisle you'll see one of the "later" additions, by the great architect Bramante—his Portico dell Canonica, lined with elegant columns, some of which are sculpted to resemble tree trunks.

What makes the beautiful church of **Santa Maria presso Santo Satiro** (entered down a short alley on the east side of Via Torino, just south of Via Speronari and Piazza del Duomo; ☎ 02-874683; free; Mon–Fri 7:30–11:30am, Sat 9:30am–noon, Sun 8:30am–12:30pm, daily 3–7pm; Metro: Duomo or Missori) so exquisite is what it doesn't have—space. Stymied by not being able to expand the T-shaped apse to classical Renaissance, cross-shaped proportions, the architect Bramante designed a marvelous relief behind the high altar that creates the illusion of a fourth arm. The effect of the *trompe l'oeil* columns and arches is not entirely convincing but is nonetheless magical. Another gem lies to the rear of the left transept: the Cappella della Pietà, so called for the 15th-century terra-cotta *Pietà* it now houses, but built in the 9th century to honor St. Satiro, the brother of St. Ambrose, and covered in lovely Byzantine frescoes and Romanesque columns.

Set back from the road beyond a free-standing row of 16 ancient Roman columns (probably from the 2nd c. A.D.), the **Chiesa di San Lorenzo Maggiore** ★ (Corso di Porta Ticinese 39; ☎ 02-89404129; www.sanlorenzomaggiore.com; free; daily 7:30am–12:30pm and 2:30–6:45pm; Metro: Missori) is further testament to the days when the city was the capital of the Western Roman Empire. The 4th-century early-Christian structure has been rebuilt and altered many times over the centuries (its dome, the highest in Milan, is a 16th-c. embellishment), but retains the flavor of its roots in its octagonal floor plan and a few surviving remnants. These include 5th-century mosaics—one depicting a beardless Christ—in the Cappella di Sant'Aquilino, which you enter from the atrium (2€; opens at 9:30am). A sarcophagus in the chapel is said to enshrine the remains of Galla Placidia, sister of Honorius, last emperor of Rome, and wife of Ataulf, king of the Visigoths. Just where Ms. Placidia ended up is a point of contention. Her official mausoleum is one of the mosaic masterworks of Ravenna, but she is most likely buried in Rome, where she died. You'll be rewarded with a glimpse of even earlier history if you follow the stairs from behind the altar to a cryptlike room that contains what remains of a Roman amphitheater.

THE OTHER MILAN

Unlike other Italian cities, Milan doesn't give much thought to tourism beyond its major sights. Sure, it has a vibrant cultural scene; a busy schedule of events, exhibitions, and trade fairs; and a fashion industry that, outside of the boutiques, keeps itself behind closed doors and invitation-only parties. But because most of Milan's cultural events are conducted in Italian only, they're a bit inaccessible to the visitor who doesn't speak the language. Which brings me to the first way to break out of the tourist mold in Milan.

Parla Italiano?

Lots of foreigners come to Milan for business reasons, many on frequent visits or for stints of a few months or longer, so the city is better equipped than most with language schools—especially the kinds devoted to getting you up to speed quickly, teaching you how to get by in everyday conversation rather than mucking about for weeks with obscure verb conjugations. All of these institutions offer lengthy courses spread over many weeks or months; I'll just mention the courses they offer that last a week or two and are thus better suited to tourists.

The **Società Dante Alighieri** (Via Napo Torrani 10; ☎ 02-6692816; www. societadantealighieri.org) has the benefit of the longest pedigree—it's been around since 1889—and offers one-on-one lessons from 35€ per hour (40€ per hour for two people). The **Scuola Leonardo da Vinci** (Via Darwin 20; ☎ 02-83241002; www.scuolaleonardo.com) has been teaching Italian to foreigners since 1977; 2 weeks of 40 lessons in small classes (12 people max) cost 300€. The **International House Milano** (Piazza Erculea 9; ☎ 02-8057825; www.ihmilano.it) offers two levels of courses: standard (20 lessons per week) for 1 week (198€), 2 weeks (349€), or 3 weeks (517€), or intensive (28 lessons per week) for 1 week (261€), 2 weeks (458€), or 3 weeks (689€).

Attend Mass in a Historic Church

The Milanese may worship the almighty euro Monday to Friday, and pray for bargains on haute couture during Saturday-morning shopping sprees, but come Sunday they remember that they're Italian—and Catholic—and show up for Mass. As so much of Milan's urban fabric is made up of gray, utilitarian architecture lining broad boulevards strung with tram lines and teeming with traffic, it comes as a bit of a shock to realize that the city is also home to some stupendous churches— a heritage from its 4th-century role as a capital of Western Christianity.

On Sundays, dress to the nines (this *is* Milan, after all) and you can have your pick of churches for Mass, from the huge, echoing nave of the Gothic **Duomo** (Sun at 7, 8, 9:30, 10, 11am, 12:30, and 5:30pm—plus lauds at 10:30am and vespers at 4pm) to that hidden jewel box of Renaissance architecture, **Santa Maria Presso Santo Spirito** (Sun at 10am or 6pm). Perhaps the most evocative spaces, though, are those 4th-century churches just south of the center: the elegant Romanesque interior of **Sant'Ambrogio** (a popular place, with Sun Masses scheduled at 8, 10, and 11am—that one's in Latin—and at 12:15, 6, and 7pm) or the ancient octagon of **San Lorenzo Maggiore** (Sun at 9:30, 11:30am, and 6pm—or, for an odd experience, pop into the 4pm Mass in Tagalog; this church serves as a cultural center for Milan's sizeable Filipino community).

CHIC SHOPPING

For the best discounts, you want to "Shop with the Locals" (see below). But bargains be damned, the best spot for fashion gazing and supermodel spotting is along four streets north of the Duomo that form a box around the **Quadrilatero d'Oro (Golden Quadrilateral):** Via Montenapoleone, Via Spiga, Via Borgospesso, and Via Sant'Andrea, lined with Milan's most expensive high-fashion emporia. (To enter this hallowed precinct, follow Via Manzoni a few blocks north from Piazza della Scala; San Babila is the closest Metro stop.)

The main artery of this shopping heartland is Via Montenapoleone, lined with chichi boutiques and the most elegant fashion outlets, with parallel Via della Spiga running a close second.

If your fashion sense is greater than your credit line, you may want to limit your Milan shopping excursions to the periods of citywide *saldi* (sales): from early January into early February, and again in late June through July.

Shop with the Locals

So many people come to Milan for the shopping, but so very few can afford the prices in the Quadrilatero d'Oro boutiques. That's why the real Milanesi don't bother buying there; they just window-shop and pause for see-and-be-seen drinks at Cova. When it actually comes time to break out the credit cards, most Milanesi head instead for two neighborhoods where prices are cheap, stock shops abound, and midpriced middle-class goods take precedence over Prada and Armani designs.

To the northwest of the historical center lies *the* neighborhood for true bargain hunters, the grid of streets southeast of the train station surrounding the broad **Corso Buenos Aires** (follow Via Vitruvio from Piazza Duca d'Aosta in front of the station; Metro stops Lima and Loreto are the gateways to this bargain stretch). This wide boulevard is home to a little bit of everything, from shops that hand-sew men's dress shirts to CD megastores. As it crosses Piazza Oberdan/Piazza Venezia heading south, it becomes Corso Venezia and the stores start moving up the scale. It is lined with hundreds of shops, bars, and boutiques. You can take a virtual tour of many of its shops, complete with loads of photographs, at www.milanomia.com/via/corsobuenosaires/corsobuenosaires.htm.

There are loads of stock shops and discounters in the neighborhood from here to the central train station. For designer shoes at a discount, look no further than **Rufus** (Via Vitruvio 35; ☎ 02-2049648; Metro: Centrale F.S. or Lima), which carries men's and women's styles from lots of labels for under 100€. **Fashion Outlet** (Via Vittor Pisani 12/A; ☎ 02-67380150; www.fashionoutlet-italia.com; Metro: Centrale F.S. or Piazza delle Repubblica) offers 40% to 80% off men's and women's fashions from such labels as Fendi, Prada, D&G, Armani, Gucci, and Roberto Cavalli.

Spacci Bassetti (Via Procaccini 32; ☎ 02-3450125; www.bassetti.it; Metro: Garibaldi F.S., but closer on tram ㉝ or ㉞) is a discount outlet of the august Bassetti line of high-quality linen, and the huge space offers luxurious towels and sheets at excellent prices. They also have regular (nondiscount) stores at Corso Buenos Aires 52 (☎ 02-29400048; Metro: Lima) and Corso Genova 20 (☎ 02-58104149; Metro: Porta Romana), near the Navigli.

The other hunting ground for discount fashions is south of the historical center in the **Navigli district** (starting at the south end of Corso di Porta Ticinese; Metro: Porta Genova; trams to Piazza XXIV Maggio). Shops in this trendy and developing district have a tendency to open and close on a monthly basis, making it tough to single many out, but it's well worth wandering the streets, especially those along either of the two main canals. One stalwart that seems here to stay, **Biffi** (Corso Genova 6; ☎ 02-83116052; Metro: S. Agostino), attracts fashion-conscious hordes of both sexes in search of designer labels and the store's own designs at a discount.

Even if your wallet can't afford it, stop by to browse the new flagship **Armani megastore** (Via Manzoni 31; ☎ 02-72318630; www.armani.com; Metro: Montenapoleone). To celebrate 25 years in business in the summer of 2000, Giorgio opened this new flagship store/offices covering 743 sq. m (8,000 sq. ft.) with outlets for his high-fashion creations, the Emporio Armani and Armani Jeans lines, plus the new Armani Casa selection of home furnishings; flower, book, and art shops; a high-tech Sony electronics boutique/play center in the basement; and an Emporio Café and branch of New York's Nobu sushi bar.

Books

Milan has two English-language bookshops. **The American Bookstore** (Via Camperio 16, at the corner with Via Dante; ☎ 02-878920; Metro: Cordusio) and **The English Bookshop** (Via Ariosto, at Via Mascheroni 12; ☎ 02-4694468; www.englishbookshop.it; Metro: Conciliazione).

The glamorous outlet of one of Italy's leading publishers, **Rizzoli** (in the Galleria Vittorio Emanuele II; ☎ 02-8052277; www.libreriarizzoli.it; Metro: Duomo), also has a good selection of English-language titles (in the basement), as well as a sumptuous collection of art and photo books.

High Fashion at Low Prices

Inspired by the window displays in the Quadrilatero, you can scour the racks of shops elsewhere for designer seconds, last year's fashions, imitations, and other bargains. The best place to begin is **Il Salvagente** (Via Fratelli Bronzetti 16, off Corso XXII Marzo; ☎ 02-76110328; Metro: San Babila), where you can browse through an enormous collection of designer clothing for men, women, and children (mostly smaller sizes) at wholesale prices. **Dmagazine** (Via Montenapoleone 26; ☎ 02-76006027; Metro: Montenapoleone) may sit on the boutique-lined main shopping drag, but its merchandise is pure discount overstock from big labels such as Armani (I saw slacks for 99€), Prada (how about a sweater for 72€?), and Fendi (designer scarves for 44€, anyone?).

Italian Design

The top name in Italian homeware design since 1921 has been **Alessi** (Corso Matteotti 9; ☎ 02-795726; www.alessi.com; Metro: San Babila), which since the late 1980s has hired the likes of Michael Graves, Philippe Starck, Frank Gehry, and Ettore Sottsass to design the latest in teakettles, bottle openers, and other housewares.

The 1980s was really part of a renaissance of Italian industrial design. This is the era when design team **Memphis** (Via della Moscova 27; ☎ 02-6554731; www.memphis-milano.it; Metro: Turati), led by Ettore Sottsass, virtually reinvented the art form, recruiting the best and brightest architects and designers to turn their talents to lighting fixtures, kitchen appliances, office supplies, and even furnishings. Italian style has stayed at the very top of the designer homewares market (well, sharing popularity space with Scandinavian furniture) ever since. Part of the Memphis credo was to create the new modern, and then bow out before they became establishment, so they self-destructed in 1988, though you can still find their influential designs in many homeware shops, and in the main showroom.

NIGHTLIFE

On Wednesdays and Thursdays, Milan's newspapers tend to devote a lot of ink to club schedules and cultural events. If you don't trust your command of Italian to plan your nightlife, check out the tourist office on Piazza del Duomo—there are usually piles of flyers announcing upcoming events. The tourist office also keeps visitors up-to-date with the *Hello Milano* (www.hellomilano.it) free newspaper and *Milano Mese,* the official events, exhibitions, and trade fairs monthly.

The Performing Arts

For the lowdown on Milan's premier opera house, **Teatro alla Scala** ★★★, see p. 407.

Milan's **Giuseppe Verdi Symphony Orchestra** plays at the Auditorium di Milano, a renovated 1930s movie house (Via S. Gottardo 42/Largo Gustav Mahler; ☎ 02-83389401; www.auditoriumdimilano.org; Metro: Duomo, then tram ❸ or ⑮). Concerts run from mid-September to late April, usually on Thursdays at 8:30pm, Fridays at 8pm, and Sundays at 4pm.

Bars

A publike atmosphere, induced in part by Guinness on tap, prevails at Liberty-style **Bar Magenta** (Via Carducci 13, at Corso Magenta; ☎ 02-8053808; Tues–Sun; Metro: Cadorna), in the neighborhood for which it takes its name. One of the more popular La Brera hangouts, with a young following, is **El Tombon de San Marc** (Via San Marco 20, at Via Montebello; ☎ 02-6599507; Mon–Sat; Metro: Moscova), which despite its name is an English pub–style bar and restaurant.

Among the Navigli nightspots (growing in number all the time) is **El Brellin** (Vicolo della Lavandaia, off Alzaia Naviglio Grande 14; ☎ 02-58101351; Mon–Sat; Metro: Genova F.S.), an intimate, canal-side piano bar with its own minicanal. **Birreria La Fontanella** (Alzaia Naviglio Pavese 6; ☎ 02-8372391; Tues–Sun; Metro: Genova F.S.) has canal-side tables outside in summer and the oddest-shaped beer glasses around—that half-a-barbell kind everyone seems to order is called the "Cavalliere."

A Jazz Club

Since Capolinea got ousted (*warning:* the club's name is still there at Via Ludovico il Moro 119, but it is *not* the old jazz club where the greats came to play; rather, it's some pathetic mimic of it slapped together by the next-door neighbors who forced the true Le Scimmie owners out of the original space), the best venue on the jazz-club scene is the Navigli's **Le Scimmie** (Via Ascanio Sforza 49; ☎ 02-89402874; www.scimmie.it; Wed–Mon; Metro: Porta Genova). Shows start around 10pm, the cover ranges from free to 8€ (up to 15€ on some Sun and for big acts)—plus it has its own bar-boat moored in the canal.

Nightlife Tip

The Navigli/Ticinese neighborhood is currently on the rise as Milan's prime night turf, though the Brera retains its pull with night owls as well.

Discothèques

The dance scene changes all the time in Milan, but at whatever club is popular (or in business) at the moment, expect to pay a cover of 5€ to 20€, depending on how good-looking and/or female you are. Models, actors, sports stars, and the attendant fashion set favor **Hollywood** (Corso Como 15; ☎ 02-6598996; www. discotecahollywood.com; might be closed July 23–Sept 7, though lately has been staying open in summer; Metro: Moscova), which is small, chic, and centrally located in La Brera.

Grand Café Fashion (Corso di Porta Ticinese 60, at Via Vetere; ☎ 02-89400709 or 02-89402997; Metro: Porta Genova) is a multipurpose nightspot (restaurant open from 9pm; disco nightly from 11:30pm) with a kitschy neo-baroque decor, halfway to the Navigli. It's owned by a modeling agency, hence both the name and the beautiful crowd it draws to the Ticinese neighborhood, where they dance the night away, sometimes to thematic evenings like Latino Mondays and, er, lap-dance Sundays.

Milan's most venerable disco/live music club is **Rolling Stone** (Corso XXII Marzo 32, just east of Piazza Emilia; ☎ 02-733172; www.rollingstone.it; closed Sun–Mon; tram: ⑫, ㉗, ㊺, ㉚, ㉞, ㉝, or ㉒), in business since 1981. Most of the performers these days are of a rock bent, and the club is as popular as ever.

The ABCs of Milan

Consulates The **U.S. Consulate** at Via Principe Amadeo 2/10 (☎ 02-290351; milan.usconsulate.gov; Metro: Turati) is open Monday to Friday 8:30am to noon. **Canadians** should contact their consulate in Rome (see chapter 2). The **British Consulate** at Via San Paolo 7 (☎ 02-723001; www.britain.it; Metro: Duomo), is open Monday to Friday 9:15am to 12:15pm and 2:15 to 3:45pm. The **Australian Consulate** at Via Borgogna 2 (☎ 02-777041; www.italy.embassy.gov.au; Metro: San Babila) is open Monday to Thursday 9am to 5pm, Friday 9am to 4:15pm. The **New Zealand Consulate** at Via Guido d'Arezzo 6 (☎ 02-4990201; www.nz embassy.com; Metro: Pagano), is open Monday to Friday 8:30am to 5pm.

Crime For police emergencies dial ☎ **113.** There is a police station in Stazione Centrale. The main **Questura (police station)** is just west of the Giardini Pubblici (Via Fatebenefratelli 11; ☎ **02-62261;** Metro: Turati), though the entrance for the office for foreigners and passport problems is at Via Montebello 26 (☎ **02-62265777;**

Metro: Turati). Milan is generally safe, with some notable exceptions, especially at night—the public gardens, Parco Sempione, and the area to the west of Stazione Centrale. The train station is notorious for pickpockets, whose favorite victims are distracted passengers lining up for the airport buses at the east side of the building. You should likewise be vigilant for pickpockets on all public transportation and in street markets.

Drugstores Pharmacies rotate 24-hour shifts; look for signs posted in most pharmacies announcing which shops are open all night on any given day. The **Farmacia Stazione Centrale** (☎ 02-6690935), in the main train station, is open 24 hours daily and some of the staff members speak English. There are also night pharmacies at Piazza del Duomo 21 (☎ **02-878668**), Corso Buenos Aires 4 (☎ **02-29513320**), Via Boccaccio 26 (☎ **02-4695281**), Viale Lucania 10 (☎ **02-57404805**), Piazza Cinque Giornate 6 (☎ **02-55194867**), and Via Stradivari 1 (☎ **02-29526966**).

Emergencies The general number for emergencies is ☎ **113**. For the *carabinieri* police, call ☎ **112**. For first aid or an ambulance, dial ☎ **118**. For a fire, call ☎ **115**.

Hospitals For an ambulance, call ☎ **118**. The **Ospedale Maggiore Policlinico** (Via Francesco Sforza 35; ☎ **02-55031** or 02-55033255 for emergencies; www.policlinico.mi.it; Metro: Crocetta and S. Babila are closest, Missori and Duomo also work; tram: ⑫, ⑯, ㉔, ㉗, ㉓; bus: 60, 73, 77, 94) is centrally located, a 5-minute walk southeast of the Duomo, between Corso di Porta Romana and Corso di Porta Vittoria.

Lost Property The city-run *ufficio oggetti rinvenuti* (lost-and-found office)—where you check for items lost on the street or public transportation—is just south of Piazza del Duomo (Via Friuli 30; ☎ **02-88453907**; Metro: Duomo or Missori) and is open Monday to Friday 8:30am to 4pm. The *oggetti smarriti* (lost objects) at Stazione Centrale (☎ **02-63712667**) is located in the same office as the luggage storage and is open daily from 6am to 1am.

Post Office The main post office, Poste e Telecommunicazioni, is just west of Piazza del Duomo, at Via Cordusio 4; (☎ **02-72482126**; www.poste.it; Metro: Cordusio). Windows are open Monday to Friday 8am to 7pm, Saturday 8:30am to noon. Most branch offices are open Monday to Friday 8am to 2pm, Saturday 9:30am to 1pm.

Taxis You don't hail a cab in Italy; they rarely stop (it's not that they're rude; it's just not their custom). Instead, walk to the nearest taxi stand, usually located near major piazzas and major Metro stops. In the center, there are taxi stands at Piazza del Duomo and Piazza della Scala. Or call a **radio taxi** at ☎ 02-4040, 02-8585, 02-4000, or 02-6969 (the desk staff at many hotels will be happy to do this for you, even if you are not a guest). Cab meters start at 3.10€, and add a surcharge of 3.10€ at night, 1.55€ on Sundays.

THE LAKE DISTRICT

Poets, composers, and mere mortals have been rhapsodizing about the Italian lakes for centuries—most vocally since the 18th century, when it became de rigueur for travelers on the Grand Tour to descend through the Alps and enjoy their first days on Italian soil on the shores of the lakes.

LAKE COMO ★★★

If you have time for only one lake, make it Como. The first sight of the dramatic expanse of azure Lake Como, ringed by gardens and forests and backed by the snowcapped Alps, has a history of evoking strong emotions. Over the centuries, the lake has inspired poets (Lord Byron), novelists (Stendhal), composers (Verdi and Rossini), and plenty of less famous visitors.

The lake has drawn everyone from deposed queens (George IV of England exiled Caroline of Brunswick here for her adulterous ways) to well-heeled travelers, and is still sought after by the rich and überfamous. George Clooney moved into the neighborhood a few years back, buying a villa from Teresa Heinz and her hubby, Senator John Kerry—it featured as the bad guy's home in *Ocean's Twelve*.

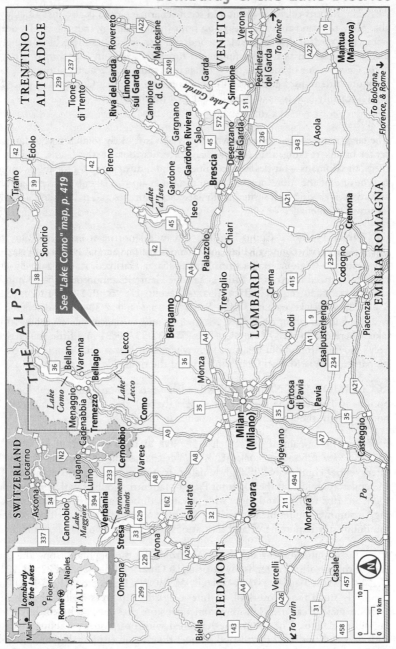

See "Lake Como" map, p. 419

Aside from its celebrity status and scenic charms, Como is also just an enjoyable place to spend time. Less than an hour from Milan by train or car, its deep waters and verdant shores provide a wonderful respite from modern life. Tellingly, Lake Como served as a backdrop for the romantic scenes in *Star Wars II: Attack of the Clones*—one of the very few settings in the film *not* created entirely by CGI computer programs. I guess even George Lucas realized that Como was a place of such unearthly beauty as to need little digital touching up.

Como

The largest and southernmost town on the lake isn't likely to charm you. Long a center of silk making, this city—which traces its roots to the Gauls, and after them, the Romans—bustles with commerce and industry. You'll probably want to stay in one of the more peaceful settings farther up the lake, but Como amply rewards a day's visit with some fine Renaissance churches and palaces and a lovely lakefront promenade.

GETTING THERE   Como is 78km (48 miles) northeast of Milan. One to three trains hourly connect Milan and Como's Stazione San Giovanni on Piazzale San Gottardo (regional trains from Milan's Piazza Garibaldi station take 55–65 min.; high-speed trains from Milan's Stazione Centrale station take 35–40 min.).

The **regional tourist office** (Piazza Cavour 17; ☎ 031-269712 or 031-3300128; www.lakecomo.org; Mon–Sat 9am–1pm and 2:30–6pm) dispenses a wealth of information on hotels, restaurants, and campgrounds all around the lake. There is also a **city tourist office** (☎ 031-3371063) in a little trailer that keeps moving around but is always somewhere near Piazza del Duomo; currently it's parked on Via Maestri Comacini, around the right side of the cathedral.

ACCOMMODATIONS & DINING   For years Como had no real lodging options in between the bare-bones Sociale (below) and a gaggle of higher-end hotels. Finally, though, a few B&Bs opened in the historical center.

€–€€   The bargain of the bunch is **In Riva al Lago** (Via Crespi 4; ☎ 031-302333; www.inrivaallago.com; AE, MC, V for charges of 100€ or more), which offers several comfortable, if slightly dated, rooms and apartments above the El Merendero pub just off the lakefront Piazza Matteotti. Doubles with shared bathroom are 40€ to 47€, and those with private bathroom are 55€ to 63€ (including, in summer, buffet breakfast). The apartments sleep from 2 to 10 people (no minimum-stay requirement) and start at 65€ to 70€ for two people per night.

€€   Just around the corner on Via Manzoni, the thoroughfare along the east edge of the historical center, is my favorite, **La Canarina** (Via Manzoni 22; ☎ 031-301913; www.bed-and-breakfast-como.it; AE, MC, V). Prices are higher (90€) but the lovely small rooms overlook an interior garden, its trees fluttering with the B&Bs namesake canaries, leftovers from a pet store that once occupied the building's ground floor. The rooms are furnished with postmodern minimalist flair, with iron bedsteads and dark-wood parquet flooring all fashioned from materials recovered during the building's recent restoration, and the shared bathroom is cocooned in smooth poured cement.

€–€€ If you're really pinching pennies, you could do worse (not much worse, mind you) than the seven bare-bones rooms above the **Ristorante Sociale** (Via Maestri Comacini 8; ☎ 031-264042; AE, MC, V), tucked under an arcade next to the Duomo's right flank. Its big selling points: a prime location next door to the Duomo and double rooms that go for just 43€ without private bathroom, 53€ with. The **restaurant** ★ (Tues–Sun noon–2pm and 7:30–10:30pm)—which features simple dishes at low prices—far outshines the rooms. This is where locals go to dine after a play at the Teatro Sociale (the restaurant's walls are plastered with playbills and signed actor photos), where the local soccer team celebrates its victories, and where the local equivalent of the ladies' auxiliary meets to have long, voluble conversations while enjoying one of the best fixed-price menus on the lake. For 17€ you get a choice from four *primi,* then one of four *secondi,* plus a side dish and water or wine—though they usually give you both at no extra charge. Just steer clear of the fish—it's frozen . . . rather scandalous for a place located just 2 blocks from the fishing boats bobbing in the harbor.

€   I'd take dinner at the Sociale, above. But the best lunch spot is **Pasticceria Monti** (Piazza Cavour 21; ☎ 031-301165; Wed–Mon 7am–2am), a busy cafe on the main lakefront piazza and one of Como's favorite places to gather and watch passersby. They make excellent sandwiches and other light fare from 2.50€, including daily pasta dishes, not to mention sublime coffee, pastries (from 1.50€), and gelato (from 1€).

WHY YOU'RE HERE: TOP SIGHTS & ATTRACTIONS   Part Gothic and part Renaissance, Como's **Duomo** ✹✹ (Piazza del Duomo, in the center of town just off the lake; ☎ 031-265244; daily 7:30am–noon and 3–7pm) is festooned with exuberant masonry and sculpture. Statues of two of the town's famous native sons, Pliny the Elder and Pliny the Younger, flank the main entrance. Inside, beneath an 18th-century dome by Juvarra—the architect who designed much of Turin—is a lavish interior hung with mostly 16th-century paintings and tapestries, with helpful leaflets in English to explain the artwork.

The black-and-white-striped 13th-century **Broletto (Town Hall)** abuts the Duomo's left flank, and adjoining it is the **Torre del Comune.** As a study in contrasts, the starkly modernist and aptly named **Casa del Fascio,** built in 1936 as the seat of the region's Fascist government, rises just behind the Duomo.

Como's main drag, **Corso Vittorio Emanuele II,** cuts through the medieval quarter, where wood-beamed houses line narrow streets. Two blocks south of the Duomo, the five-sided **San Fedele** (Piazza S. Fedele; daily 8am–noon and 3:30–7pm) sits on a charming square. Though largely 12th century, parts of the church, including the altar, date from the 6th century.

To see **Como's most alluring church,** though, you've got to venture into the dull outlying neighborhood southwest of the center where, just off Viale Roosevelt, you'll come to the five-aisle, heavily frescoed **Basilica of Sant'Abbondio** ✹✹ (☎ 631-3388111; daily 8am–6pm, except during weddings, which are hugely popular here), a Romanesque masterpiece from the 11th century lined with great 14th-century frescoes.

Lakeside life revolves around **Piazza Cavour** and the adjoining **Giardini Pubblici,** where the circular **Tempio Voltano** (☎ 031-574705; 3€; Tues–Sun 10am–noon and 3–6pm, Oct–Mar Tues–Sun 10am–noon and 2–4pm) houses memorabilia that'll enlighten you about the life and experiments of native son and electricity pioneer Alessandro Volta.

For a quick retreat and some stunning views, take the **Brunate funicular** (Lungo Lario Trieste; ☎ 031-303608; www.funicolarecomo.it; 4.25€ round-trip; every 15 to 30 min.) for a 7-minute ride up to the top of the forested hill above the town. The tourist office has maps that detail several trail hikes from the top.

Bellagio

Bellagio is often called one of the most beautiful towns in Italy. Nestled amid cypress groves and verdant gardens, its earth-toned old buildings climb from the lakefront promenade along stepped cobblestone lanes. It has become a popular retreat for everyone from Milanese out for a day of relaxation to Brits and Americans who come to relax for a week or two.

It also occupies by far the loveliest spot on the lake, the section known as the Centro Lago where the three legs of Lake Como meet. Bellagio is at the tip of the peninsula at this fork with frequent ferry service, making this a great base for exploring Varenna (see below) and other spots on the nearby shores of the Centro Lago.

GETTING THERE There are one to three **SPT buses** (☎ 031-247111; www. sptlinea.it) per hour from Como (70-min. trip), where you can get train connections. **Ferries** (☎ 800-551801 or 031-579211; www.navigazionelaghi.it) from Como take 2 hours, hydrofoils 35 to 45 minutes. Schedules vary with season, but from Easter to September a ferry or hydrofoil makes the trip from Como to Bellagio and other towns along the lake at least hourly; in winter, there are four or five per day. The picturesque lakeshore **road** from Como, the SS583, can be very crowded in summer, so allow at least an hour of traveling time by car.

Bellagio's **tourist office** is at Piazza della Chiesa 14; (☎ 031-951555; www. bellagiolakecomo.com), a steep 1½ blocks up from the port, with a smaller info desk at the dock on Piazza Mazzini (☎ 031-950204).

ACCOMMODATIONS & DINING Note that you can find a wider selection of moderately priced hotels across the lake from Bellagio in Varenna (see below). If you're traveling on a budget, your best bets are either to lodge in Varenna and make Bellagio a day trip, or to take a rental room over one of three restaurants:

€€ **La Barchetta** (restaurant reviewed below; call ☎ 031-951030), a block up from the port on one of those classic stair-stepped streets, rents four rooms above the restaurant for 80€ each, including breakfast. Half a block farther up the same street, the **Antico Pozzo** (Salita Mella 26; ☎ 339-8736188; www.bellagioantico pozzo.it; AE, MC, V) rents six small apartments, each sleeping up to four people (flip for which two get the sofa bed) for 80€ to 100€. They're pretty bland and functional, but come with A/C, satellite TV, and kitchenettes (though no phones or breakfast). Those on the second floor are a bit better as they feature nice sloping modern beamed ceilings and views of the lake beyond the rooftops below. Two of the rooms on each floor can be linked by shutting a common door, and you can get a great deal on these "two-room" apartments at just 80€ to 120€. Another bonus in seasonal Bellagio: The Antico Pozzo is open year-round. About a mile outside town, in a century-old summer villa, the restaurant-pizzeria **Alla Torretta** (Via Nuova 3; ☎ 031-951272; www.allatorretta.com; MC, V) rents three double rooms for 70€ to 80€ (add 5€ for breakfast). The owner is a bit of a sportsman and can arrange for you to go paragliding or horseback riding with one of his clubs.

€€ The best deal on a proper hotel is the little family-run **Giardinetto** (Via Roncati 12, just off Piazza del Chiesa; ☎ 031-950168; cash only; closed Nov–Mar), at the top of town. Rooms are basic, but quite large and bright, with solid old armoires, big windows, and—in the better rooms—box-spring-and-mattress beds rather than the standard cots. The best part: Doubles cost a mere 60€ (on the first floor) to 65€ (on the second floor with a bit of lake view);

breakfast tacks on another 6€ per person. Most rooms overlook a grapevine-covered terrace, where you're welcome to bring your own food for an alfresco meal, and those on the upper floors even catch a glimpse of the lake from their balconies (especially room nos. 18–20). Some, though (particularly singles), are on the airshaft or even come with no window whatsoever, so be sure to check out the room first.

€€–€€€   The 10 simple rooms at the **Suisse** ★ (Piazza Mazzini 23; ☎ 031-950335; www.bellagio.co.nz/suisse; AE, MC, V; Oct–Feb closed Wed), a 15th-century lakeside villa right on the main harbor square, have a pleasant but budget decor: parquet floors, stylish solid-wood furnishings with lovely inlaid or carved details, and plain bathrooms. Not only do you get water views, but the 92€ to 170€ for a double room includes half-pension at the restaurant, so it's like getting breakfast and another meal each day for free. What's more, the restaurant is pretty good—Italian fare year-round, with an inventive fusion flair in summer—served either alfresco under the arcades, in a plain ground-floor room, or in the understatedly elegant upstairs dining room, with a decorated ceiling and a lake-view terrace.

€€€€   Spend a bit more to splurge on Suisse's neighbor, the 150-year-old **Hotel Du Lac** ★★ (Piazza Mazzini 32; ☎ 031-950320; www.bellagiohoteldulac. com; MC, V; closed early Nov to Easter), run with an air of graciousness and old-fashioned comfort by the Leoni family. Downstairs, a bar opens onto the arcaded sidewalk, there is a series of pleasant sitting rooms, and meals are served in a nicely appointed dining room with panoramic views of the lake (half-board is an extra 20€ per person). Each of the smallish guest rooms is unique, though they tend toward cushy armchairs and a nice smattering of antiques and reproductions. Standard doubles cost from 175€ to 190€ (the latter for a lake view); Superior doubles with a balcony or small terrace run 220€. There's a rooftop sun terrace with sweeping lake views, and free access to the Leoni's nearby sports center with a pool, tennis courts, and a children's center.

€   **Bar Café Rossi** ★ (Piazza Mazzini 22/24; ☎ 031-950196; Fri–Wed 7:30am–10pm, Oct–Mar closed Thurs; AE, MC, V) is one of the nicest of Bellagio's pleasant lakefront cafes, tucked under the arcades of the town's main square. You can dine at one of the few outside tables or in the delightful Art Nouveau dining room with its intricate tilework, carved wood cabinets, and stuccoed ceilings. Wine and the excellent house coffee are available all day, and a nice selection of pastries and sandwiches (2.50€–4€) makes this a good stop for breakfast or lunch.

€–€€   **La Grotta** (Salita Cernaia 14; ☎ 031-951152; July–Oct daily noon–2:30pm and 7pm–1am, Sept–Nov 14 and Dec 18–June Tues–Sun noon–2:30pm and 7pm–1am, closed early Nov–Dec 28; AE, MC, V accepted only for bills total-ing more than 25€) is tucked away on a stepped street just off lakefront Piazza Mazzini, and has a cozy, informal series of vaulted-ceiling dining rooms with extremely friendly service, not to mention a wide-ranging menu. Most of the regulars come for the fish specials, including lake trout (12€), or the delectable pizzas (5.50€–11€) that are the best for miles around (I've made sure of this by sampling them six or seven times).

€€–€€€   **Barchetta** ★★ (Salita Mella 13; ☎ 031-951389; www.ristorante barchetta.com; Wed–Mon noon–2:30pm and 7–10:30pm; closed late Oct–Mar; AE, MC, V; reservations recommended) is one of Bellagio's best restaurants, specializing in fresh lake fish (try the perch or angler fish). In all but the coldest weather, food is served on a bamboo-enclosed heated terrace. The menu changes frequently based on seasonal ingredients and the whims of the chef, but as an indication, most *primi* run 12€ to 16€. And the chef can be whimsical indeed; most of the pastas and rice dishes are innovative variations on traditional recipes. I've sampled *ravioli caprino* (with goat's cheese, topped with pear sauce) and a savory risotto with hazelnuts and pistachios.

BELLAGIO'S GARDENS   One of Bellagio's famed gardens surrounds the **Villa Melzi** (☎ 031-950204 or 031-950318; 6€; late Mar to early Nov daily 9am–6pm), built in 1808 by Francesco Melzi, a friend of Napoleon and an official of his Italian Republic. The villa was later the retreat of Franz Liszt and is now the home of Count Gallarati Scotti, who allows the public to stroll through his acres of manicured lawns and fountains and visit a pavilion displaying a collection of Egyptian sculpture.

Bellagio's other famous gardens are those of the **Villa Serbelloni** ★ (☎ 031-950204 or 031-951555; 7€; Apr to early Nov, tours Tues–Sun at 11am and 3:30pm), occupying land once owned by Pliny the Younger and now in the hands of the Rockefeller Foundation. You can visit the gardens and villa on twice-daily guided tours (reserve ahead), about 1½ hours long, in Italian and English (tours require at least six people to depart). You meet at the little tower on the backside of Piazza della Chiesa.

Varenna

You can happily spend some time clambering up and down the steep steps that substitute for streets in this charming fishing village on the eastern shore of the lake, just 10 minutes by ferry (5 min. by hydrofoil) from Bellagio. The tiny **tourist office** is at Piazza S. Giorgio/Via IV Novembre (☎ 0341-830367; www.aptlecco.com).

The hilltop ruins of the **Castello di Vezio** (☎ 335-465186; www.castellodivezio.it; 4€; Apr–Oct daily 10am to sunset, Feb–Mar and Nov Sat–Sun only, Dec Sun only, closed Jan) lie a 20-minute hike above the town. The main reason for a visit is to enjoy the stunning views of the lake, its shoreline villages, and the backdrop of mountains at the northern end.

The gardens of the **Villa Monastero** ★ (☎ 0341-830129; www.villamonastero.org; 2€; Mar–Oct daily 9am–7pm) are more easily accessible at the southern edge of town along Via IV Novembre, and you can reach them by following the series of lakeside promenades through the old town from the ferry landing. This villa and the terraced gardens that rise from the lakeshore were once a not-so-spartan monastery—until it was dissolved in the late 17th century, when the nuns in residence began bearing living proof that they were on too friendly terms with the priests across the way. If you find it hard to tear yourself from the bowers of citrus trees and rhododendrons clinging to terraces, you'll find equally enchanting surroundings in the adjoining gardens of the **Villa Cipressi** (☎ 0341-830113; www.hotelvillacipressi.it; 2€; Mar–Oct daily 9am–7pm).

ACCOMMODATIONS & DINING   As I said before, a stay in Varenna is one of the best options for value-conscious travelers (and the village is also quite lovely in its own right). Two B&Bs have recently opened up in Varenna. The nicer, **Orange House** (Via Venini 156; ☎ 347-9187940; www.orangehouse.org; AE, MC, V), has two brightly lit rooms with chunky, rustic wooden furnishings near the edge of town for 69€ to 73€. Cheaper, simpler, and right on the main square is **Villa Elena** (Piazza San Giorgio 9; 0341-830575; cash only), its three antiques-filled rooms renting for 46€—try for room no. 1 with a private bathroom and terrace.

€€€€   You'd have to look hard to find a more pleasant retreat by the lake than the **Milano** ★★ (Via XX Settembre 29; ☎ 0341-830298; www.varenna.net; MC, V; closed late Nov to Feb), an old lakefront house renovated into a boutique hotel by Bettina and Egidio Mallone, a friendly young Italian-Swiss couple. The modern common area now has a TV with satellite channels and computer with free Internet. The rooms feature new beds and antique-style furnishings, and spanking new bathrooms as of 2004. All rooms have balconies. Room nos. 1 and 2 (which open onto a wide terrace) and room nos. 5 and 6 have full-on lake vistas (doubles 135€–150€); the others overlook the neighbor's pretty garden with askance lake views (doubles 125€–135€). In summer, breakfast is served on the outdoor terrace, as are the 27€ three-course dinners, available upon request Monday and Wednesday through Saturday. They also have an apartment nearby (no views, though) that they'll rent out—preferably to families or groups of four—starting at 53€ per person, including breakfast back at the hotel.

€€€–€€€€   If you enjoyed your tour of Varenna's lush gardens (see above), there's no need to leave. The 16th-century **Villa Cipressi** ★★ (Via IV Novembre 18; ☎ 0341-830113; www.hotelvillacipressi.it; AE, MC, V; usually closed late Oct to Mar, but some years open for periods in winter, frequently Dec 6–Jan 6) was converted to a hotel nearly 2 centuries ago, and though it's geared toward hosting conferences, other guests can book, space permitting. The rooms have been renovated without any attempt to retain historic character, but they remain extremely large and attractive. Not every room gets a lake view (doubles 140€–160€; during winter openings, 110€), but all save a few small ones on the roadside enjoy marvelous views over those famous gardens (and they cost less: 125€–140€). Deluxe rooms (150€–170€) take advantage of the high ceilings and contain loft bedrooms, with sitting areas below that can easily fit a couple of single beds (45€ extra) for families.

€€–€€€   One of your most memorable experiences in this region could be a meal at the romantic **Vecchia Varenna** ★★ (Via Scoscesa 10; ☎ 031-830793; www.vecchiavarenna.it; Tues–Sun; closed Jan; MC, V; reservations required), on a terrace over the water or in a beautiful stone-floored room with white stone walls. The kitchen makes the most of local ingredients—try the 11€ pasta strips with chestnuts, white beans whipped into a cream, and *guanciale* (a kind of bacon)—and, of course, the bounty of the lake—one of the best of the many risottos combines fontina cheese (for a creamy consistency) with *pesce persico* (a white fish from the lake; 12€). The grilled lake trout stuffed either with mountain herbs or a radicchio rice is sublime (15€).

LAKE MAGGIORE

Anyone who reads Hemingway's *A Farewell to Arms* will recognize this lake and its forested shores. That's just the sort of place Lake Maggiore (Lago Maggiore) is: a pleasure ground steeped in associations with famous figures—Flaubert, Wagner, Goethe, and Europe's other great minds seem to have been inspired by the deep, moody waters backed by the Alps—and not-so-famous wealthy visitors. Fortunately, you need be neither famous nor wealthy to enjoy Maggiore, which is on the border between Lombardy and Piemonte (and nosing toward Switzerland to the north) just a short dash east and north of Milan.

Stresa & the Borromean Islands

Strolling and relaxing seem to be the main activities in Stresa, a pretty little place with a long lakefront promenade, a lively center, and a bevy of restaurants and hotels that range from the expensive and splendid to the affordable but comfortable. Sooner or later, though, most visitors climb onto a ferry for the short ride to the most rewarding sight on the lake, a trio of famed islands just off Stresa's shore called the Isole Borromee.

GETTING THERE   Stresa is 80km (48 miles) northwest of Milan, linked by 20 **trains** daily (58–84 min.). The **tourist office** is at the ferry dock (Piazza Marconi 16; ☎ 0323-31308; www.comune.stresa.vb.it; closed Sun Nov–Apr). Various regional tourism sites are also useful: www.distrettolaghi.it, www.illago maggiore.com, and www.stresa.it.

EXPLORING THE ISLANDS   Since the 12th century, the Borromeo family has owned these three islets, which seem to float in the misty waters off Stresa and entice visitors with their stunning beauty. Isola Bella and especially Isola Superiore have villages you can hang out in for free, but Isola Madre consists solely of its admission-charging gardens.

    Isola Bella ★★ (☎ 0323-30556; www.borromeoturismo.it; 11€; late Mar to late Oct daily 9:30am–5:30pm) remains true to its name, with splendid 17th-century gardens that ascend from the shore in 10 luxuriantly planted terraces. The Borromeo palazzo includes a room in which Napoleon and Josephine once slept.

    The largest and most peaceful of the islands is **Isola Madre** ★★ (☎ 0323-30556; www.borromeoturismo.it; 9€; late Mar to late Oct daily 9am–5:30pm), all 3.2 hectares (8 acres) of which are covered by the Orto Botanico, teeming with exquisite flora and exotic, colorful birds. The villa in the center of it all was built from 1518 to 1585 and is still filled with Borromeo family memorabilia and some interesting old puppet-show stages.

    Most of Isola Superiore, also known as Isola dei Pescatori (Fishermen's Island), is occupied by a not-so-quaint old fishing village—every one of the tall houses on this tiny strip of land seems to harbor a souvenir shop or pizza stand, and there are hordes of visitors to keep them busy. Even so, lakeside lunch at the Verbano (p. 428) makes for a lovely afternoon.

Public **ferries** (☎ 800-551801 or 0322-233200; www.navigazionelaghi.it) leave for the islands every half-hour from the big building with triple arches on Stresa's Piazza Marconi. Round-trip tickets to any one island cost 6.40€ (Isola Bella or Isola Superiore) to 8.20€ (Isola Madre), so it's far more economical to get a 12€ day pass allowing you to ride as much as you'd like around this part of the lake. *Warning:* You'll see other, private ticket kiosks and touts dressed as sailors who will try to lure you aboard; avoid these overpriced hucksters and stick with the public ferry service.

ACCOMMODATIONS   This is one of the few places in the region where the options include both standard hotels and more interesting B&B accommodations.

€€   Of those B&B options, only two are in the heart of Stresa. Less of a looker but a better deal, **Il Viaggiatore** (Corso Italia 38; ☎ 0323-934674; www.bb-il viaggiatore.it; closed Jan–Feb) offers two large, homey rooms (70€–80€) with a shared kitchen and killer views of the lake right across the street. Owner Rosanna is an avid outdoorswoman and rock climber who helps run a guide service for hiking and climbing in nearby Piemonte parkland.

€€   **La Stellina** (Via Molinari 10; ☎ 0323-32443; www.lastellina.com; closed Jan 1–16, July 20–Aug 17, Nov 12–Dec 31) is in a century-old palazzo in the heart of town, slightly twee—floral wallpaper, oriental rugs on hardwood floors—but charging just 75€ to 90€ for its three doubles ("Le Rose" has a lofted sleeping area).

€€–€€€   For much of the spring and summer, the street in front of **Hotel Primavera** ★★ (Via Cavour 30; ☎ 0323-31286; www.stresa.it; AE, MC, V; closed Dec 20, and some years Jan–Feb) is closed to traffic and filled with flowering plants and cafe tables. The relaxed air prevails throughout this bright little hotel a block off the lake in the town center. The tile-floored rooms are furnished in functional walnut veneer and go for 70€ to 105€. Many rooms have balconies just wide enough to accommodate a pair of chairs; a few on the fourth floor even get a sliver of lake view around the apse and bell tower of the Duomo.

€€–€€€   The same family runs the more modern, though equally priced, **Hotel Meeting** ★ (Via Bonghi 9; ☎ 0323-32741; www.stresa.it; AE, MC, V; closed Dec some years, Jan–Feb others), named for its proximity to a conference center. It's a 5-minute walk from the lakefront in a quiet and leafy setting—though light

---

Cumulative Ticket

You can get a cumulative ticket covering both Isola Bella and Isola Madre for 16€. Audio tours help make sense of it all for 3.50€ each or 5€ to rent two sets of headphones.

Making the Most of Your Time Here

To squeeze as much of Stresa's sights in as you can in a day, note that the ferry back from the Isole Borromee stops first at the Mottarone Funivia area before chugging down the coast to the center of Stresa and the main docks. You can hop off here either for either of two relaxing activities. You can simply walk back into Stresa itself along a pretty lakeside promenade, past crumbling villas and impromptu sculpture gardens, in about 20 minutes. Those with more time can ride the scenic, 20-minute cable car from here up to an Alpine botanical garden (Mar–Oct), 1,475m (4,920 ft.) above the town (☎ 0323-30295; www.stresa-mottarone.it; 15€/12€ in winter round-trip or 8.50€/7€ in winter one-way, then walk back down). Even better, get a one-way ticket up plus a mountain bike to coast back down for 10€ (9€ in winter)—or keep the bike for a few hours to explore the high Alpine plain before biking back down at 16€ for a half-day rental, 22€ for a full day.

sleepers on the back may notice the trains passing in the distance. The Scandinavian rooms are big and bright, and all come with balconies.

€€ Just uphill from the train station—and an unfortunate 10-minute walk from the center of town and the lakeside—the family-run **Mon Toc** ✸ (Via Duchessa di Genova 69; ☎ 0323-30282; www.hotelmontoc.com; AE, MC, V; closed Jan or Nov) is surrounded by a private garden for an almost countrylike atmosphere. The functional 80€ doubles are unusually pleasant for a hotel this cheap (though a few of the tidy bathrooms are of the miniscule, molded, airplane variety). The friendly owner refuses, out of honesty, to call the sliver of lake visible over the rooftops from the second-floor rooms a "lake view."

€€€€ For a truly unique lake experience, stay on the Isola Superiore itself. From March to October, the dusty rose–colored **Verbano** ✸ (see "Dining in Stresa," below) rents some beautiful lakeview rooms in the villa upstairs filled with big old wood furnishings and wrought-iron bedsteads for 150€ to 180€ per double. Book well ahead of time if you want to request room no. 2, on the corner with a balcony on one side and a terrace on the other—great views of Isola Bella—that it shares with room no. 1 (both also enjoy working fireplaces). Rooms on the first floor share a large terrace overlooking the lake toward Isola Madre and the eastern, Lombard shores.

   If you don't luck out with those, there are always the bland rooms at the **Fiorentino** (see below).

DINING   As befits the select nature of the area, the restaurants of Stresa are also quite special.

€–€€   It's hard to find friendlier service or homier trattoria-type food in Stresa than at the **Hotel Ristorante Fiorentino** (Via A. M. Bolongaro 9–11; ☎ 0323-30254; www.hotelfiorentino.com; daily 11am–3pm and 6–10pm; closed Nov–Feb; AE, MC, V), especially at these prices—the three-course 15€ *menu turistico* is a steal, even if it doesn't include wine. Everything that comes out of the family-run kitchen is made fresh daily, including cannelloni (6€) and other pastas. You can dine in a big cozy room or on a patio out back in good weather. As you might have guessed from the name, they also rent rooms—quite nice, if boring, ones, too, at just 75€ to 85€ per double.

€–€€   Most of Stresa seems to congregate in the **Taverna del Pappagallo** (Via Principessa Margherita 46; ☎ 0323-30411; www.tavernapappagallo.com; Thurs–Tues 11:30am–2:30pm and 6:30–10:30pm; AE, MC, V; closed Dec–Jan) for the most popular pizza in town (4.50€–10€). But just about all the fare that comes out of the family-run kitchen is delicious, including delectable homemade gnocchi and such dishes as grilled sausage with beans. Weather permitting, try to dine at one of the tables in the pleasant garden. *Primi* go for 6.50€ to 8€, *secondi* from 9€ to 14€.

€€   **Verbano** ★★ (Via Ugo Ara 2 on Isola Superiore dei Pescatori; ☎ 0323-30408 or 0323-32534; www.hotelverbano.it; daily noon–2:30pm and 7–10pm; closed Nov 4–Mar 10; AE, MC, V; reservations recommended) has a fairy-tale location on the point of Fisherman's Isle, taking up the jasmine-fringed gravelly terrace next to the hotel. The waters lap right up to the wall and the views are over the back of Isola Bella and the lake around you on three sides. The cooking needn't be anything special given its location in a prime tourist spot, but surprisingly it's almost as lovely as the setting. *Primi* cost just 8€ to 12€ and include such delectables as a *zuppa di verdure* (vegetable soup) hearty with barley and grains, and a *paglia e fieno* ("hay and straw") mix of regular (yellow) and spinach (green) tagliatelle noodles in a *ragù* made of scorpion fish, carrots, and zucchini. Definitely leave room for a grilled lake trout accompanied by rice stained black with squid ink. March to October, they also rent some beautiful rooms in the villa upstairs for 150€ to 180€ per double.

LAKE GARDA

Lake Garda (Lago di Garda), the largest and easternmost of the lakes, laps against the flat plains of Lombardy and the Veneto at its southern extremes, and in the north, where it juts into the Trentino–Alto Adige region, becomes fiordlike and moody, its deep waters backed by Alpine peaks. All around the lake, Garda's shores are green and fragrant with flowery gardens, groves of olives and lemons, and forests of pines and cypress.

This pleasing, vaguely exotic landscape has attracted everyone from the poet Gabriele D'Annunzio to the dictator Benito Mussolini who, retreating with his Nazi minders, founded the short-lived Republic of Salò on the lake's western shores (where he ultimately was captured and killed by Partisans).

Long before them, the Romans discovered the hot springs that still gush forth at Sirmione, the famed resort on a spit of land at the lake's southern reaches.

Today's visitors come to swim (Garda is the cleanest of the major lakes), windsurf (Riva del Garda, at the northern end of the lake, is Europe's windsurfing capital), and enjoy the easygoing ambience of Garda's many pleasant lakeside resorts.

Sirmione

Garda's most popular resort sits on the tip of a narrow peninsula of cypress and olive groves that juts due north from the center of the lake's southern shore. Despite an onslaught of visitors, Sirmione manages to retain its charm (though just barely in the heaviest months of July–Aug). Vehicular traffic on the narrow, marble-slab streets is kept to a minimum; only by booking a hotel within the old city can you get your name on the list of cars allowed past the guard at the lone city gate. The emphasis here is on strolling, swimming in waters that are warmed in places by underwater hot springs, and relaxing on the sunny terraces of pleasant lakeside hotels.

GETTING THERE Sirmione lies just off the A4 **autostrada** between Milan, 127km (79 miles) to the west, and Venice, 149km (92 miles) to the east. **Train** connections are via nearby Desenzano (20 min. from Sirmione by half-hourly bus), which is on the Milan-Venice trunk line. There are trains almost every half-hour in either direction, stopping in Verona (25 min.), Venice (1½–2½ hr.), and Milan (1–1½ hr.).

Hydrofoils and **ferries** operated by **Navigazione Lago di Garda** (☎ 800-551801 or 030-9149511; www.navigazionelaghi.it) ply the waters of the lake. One or two hourly ferries and four daily hydrofoils connect Sirmione with Desenzano (20 min. by ferry; 10 min. by hydrofoil). Two daily ferries and three daily hydrofoils connect Sirmione with Riva (almost 4 hr. by ferry; 2 hr. 10 min. by hydrofoil). Service is curtailed from October to April.

The **tourist office** is just outside the old town near the castle (Viale Marconi 2; ☎ 030-916245 or 030-916114; www.bresciaholiday.com; Nov–Mar closed Sat afternoon and Sun).

ACCOMMODATIONS & DINING Sirmione's gaggle of moderately priced hotels book up quickly in July and August, which is when they charge the higher rates quoted below. The tourist office will help you find a room in your price range on the day you arrive, but they won't book ahead of time.

€–€€ One of Sirmione's best-value lodgings also is also one of its most romantic. The **Grifone** ✭✭ (Via Bocchio 4; ☎ 030-916014; www.sirmionehotel.com; cash only; closed late Oct to Easter) is a vine-clad stone building with fantastic views of the neighboring castle and lake from its simple, plain, pleasant, and remarkably cheap (42€–62€ per double) rooms. Top-floor rooms (nos. 36–42) even have small balconies. There's also a shady patio off the lobby and a small pebble beach. Brother and sister Nicola and Cristina Marcolini oversee the hotel and adjoining restaurant with a great deal of graciousness, carrying on several generations of a family business.

€€ The family-run **Corte Regina** ✭ (Via Antiche Mura 11; ☎ 030-916147; www.corteregina.it; AE, MC, V; closed Nov–Mar) doesn't enjoy the lake views of the

Grifone, but this attractive hotel—housed in a stone building fronted by a vine-shaded terrace on a narrow side street—has nicer rooms and just as friendly a welcome for 70€ to 100€ for a double. The large tile-floored rooms have been recently renovated, with contemporary furnishings under modern, wood-beam ceilings and bathrooms.

€€€–€€€€   Ezra Pound once lived in the pink-stucco **Hotel Eden** ★ (Piazza Carducci 17/18; ☎ 030-916481; www.hoteledenonline.it; AE, MC, V; closed Nov–Easter) on a quiet side street leading to the lake in the center of town. The Eden has been modernized with taste and an eye to comfort, and the management is exceedingly friendly and helpful. You can see the lake from most of the attractive, contemporary rooms (doubles 129€–180€; breakfast 10€), whose mirrored walls enhance the light and lake views. The marble lobby opens to a delightful shaded terrace and a swimming pier that juts into the lake.

€€€–€€€€   If you're looking for more of a resort hotel (or just something open through much of the off season), the modern **Olivi** ★★ (Via San Pietro 5; ☎ 030-9905365; www.hotelolivi.info; AE, MC, V; closed Jan) offers a taste of the high life at fairly reasonable rates: 136€ to 208€ for two. It's not directly on the lake—which you can see from most rooms and the sunny terrace—but instead commands a hilltop position near the Roman ruins amid pines and olive groves. The rooms are decorated in varying schemes of bold pastels and earth tones, with dressing areas off the bathrooms, and balconies. There's a large pool in the garden and, to bring a lakeside feeling to the grounds, an artificial river that streams past the terrace and glass windows of the lobby and breakfast room.

€–€€   You can get a quick pizza (7€–11€) with a view of the lake from the terrace at **L'Arcimboldo** (Via Vittorio Emanuele II 71; ☎ 030-916409; www.ristorantearcimboldo.com; Wed–Mon 11:45am–2:45pm and 7–10:45pm; closed Nov; AE, MC, V). They also offer massive set-price meals including a sampler of two *primi* (often one risotto and one pasta dish), a main course, and dessert for 30€ to 35€ (up to 40€ for fish).

€–€€   For better pizza—but no view—head to **La Roccia** (Via Piana 2; ☎ 030-916392; Fri–Wed 12:30–3pm and 7–10:30pm, daily in Aug; closed Nov–Mar; AE, MC, V), serving excellent food in pleasant surroundings, especially if you sit in the large garden. The menu features more than 20 wood-oven pizzas (4.50€–9€), plus plenty of traditional pastas, including lasagna and excellent cheese tortellini in a cream-and-prosciutto sauce (8€).

€€   You'd think that a location smack in the heart of the main drag's boutiques and gelaterie would turn any restaurant into a pricey and awful tourist trap. That, normally, is too true—but not in the case of Sirmione's **Ristorante Al Progresso** ★ (Via Vittorio Emanuele II 18–20; ☎ 030-916108; Fri–Wed noon–2:30pm and 6:30–10:30pm, daily in summer; closed either Nov–Dec or Dec–Jan, depending on flow of tourism; AE, MC, V), an appealingly plain spot with a touch of style, low prices, and quite excellent home cooking. Fresh lake trout (9.50€) is often on the menu—simply grilled or served *al sirmionese* (boiled with a house sauce of garlic, oil, capers, and anchovies)—as is a tangy 9€ *scaloppine al limone,* veal in a sauce made from fresh lemons grown on the lakeshore.

EXPLORING SIRMIONE In addition to its attractive though tourist shop–ridden old town, Sirmione has many lakeside promenades, pleasant beaches, and even some open countryside where olive trees sway in the breeze. Anything you'll want to see can be reached easily on foot, though an open-air tram makes the short run out to the Roman ruins from the northern edge of the old town (except 12:30–2:30pm).

The moated and turreted **Castello Scaligero** ✫ (☎ 030-916468; 4€; Tues–Sun 8:30am–7pm) still guards the only land-side entrance to the old town. Built in the 13th century by the Della Scala family who ruled Verona and many of the lands surrounding the lake, the castle warrants a visit mainly for the views from its towers.

From the castle, Via Vittorio Emanuele leads through the center of the town and emerges after a few blocks into the greener, garden-lined lanes that wind through the tip of the peninsula to the **Grotte di Catullo** ✫ (☎ 030-916157; 4€; Mar–Oct Tues–Sun 8:30am–7pm, Nov–Feb Tues–Sun 8:30am–5pm). Whether these extensive ruins at the northern tip of the peninsula were actually once the villa and baths of the pleasure-loving Roman poet (and Sirmione native) Catullus is open to debate. But their presence here, on a hilltop fragrant with wild rosemary and pines, demonstrates that Sirmione has been a deservedly popular retreat for millennia, and you can wander through the evocative remains while taking in wonderful lake views.

If you want to enjoy the lake's clean waters, head to the small **Lido delle Bionde beach,** near the castle off Via Dante. In summer, the beach concession rents lounge chairs with umbrellas for 5€ per day, as well as kayaks and pedal boats (8€ per hr.).

Riva del Garda

Riva del Garda is not just a resort but also a real town (the northernmost on the lake), with medieval towers, a nice smattering of Renaissance churches and palazzi, and narrow cobblestone streets where the everyday business of a prosperous Italian town proceeds on its alluring way.

GETTING THERE Riva del Garda is roughly 2 hours by **bus** from a number of nearby cities and lake towns, including Trent (24 buses daily), Verona (16 buses daily), Brescia (5 buses daily), the busy train station at Desenzano (6 trains daily; see "Sirmione" for details), and Sirmione (although from there only the 4:30pm run is direct; for all others, you must transfer at Peschiera).

It's far more genteel—if slower—to arrive by **boat** (☎ 800-551801; www. navigazionelaghi.it). Schedules vary with the season, with very limited service in the winter, but in summer you can opt for one of three daily hydrofoils (80 min. from Gardone, 2 hr. 10 min. from Sirmione), or the two daily ferries (2¾ hr. from Gardone, almost 4 hr. from Sirmione).

Get Physical in Riva

Riva is a magnet for active vacationers of all stripes, offering everything from bocce and fishing to base jumping and free climbing—though most people come here for the excellent windsurfing.

You can rent a **windsurf** board for 18€ to 24€ for an hour, 37€ to 45€ for a half-day, 42€ to 60€ all day (assorted extras—wetsuit, harness, life jacket, insurance—may each add 3€–4€ to the price) at any of the following, listed roughly in ascending order of cost: **Sailing Du Lac** (in the Hotel Du Lac, Viale Rovereto 44; ☎ 0464-552453; www.sailingdulac.com); **Surf Segana**, Porfina Beach (at Camping Bavaria, Lungolago dei Pini 19; ☎ 0464-505963; www.surfsegnana.it), which also rents catamarans and kayaks; **Conca d'Oro Windsurfing Center Torbole** (Lungolago Verona 6; ☎ 0464-548192; www.windsurfconca.com); or **Pier Windsurf** (in the Hotel Pier, Località Gola 2; ☎ 0464-550928; www.pierwindsurf.it). All also offer multiday packages as well as lessons, which start around 68€ to 79€ per day, or 47€ to 59€ per hour for private lessons.

For a more sedate outing on the lake, at the beach next to the castle you can **rent rowboats or pedal boats** for about 6€ to 7€ per hour (buy 2 hr., get a third free) from March to October daily 8am to 8pm.

Prefer wheels to water? Rent a **mountain bike** (around 4€–5€ per hour, 10€–13€ per day) from **Superbike Girelli** (Viale Damiano Chiesa 15; ☎ 0464-556602) or **Cicli Pederzolli** (Viale dei Tigli 24; ☎ 0464-551830; www.pederzolli.it).

The fastest way to Riva by car is the A22, which shoots up the east side of the lake (exit at Mori, 13km/9 miles east of Riva). It's far more scenic to drive along the western shore, past Gardone, and along the beautiful corniche between Riva and Salò that hugs cliffs and passes through kilometer after kilometer of tunnels.

The Riva del Garda **tourist office**, which supplies information on hotels, restaurants, and activities in the area, is near the lakefront (Giardini di Porta Orientale 8; ☎ 0464-554444; www.gardatrentinonline.it and www.trentino.to). It's closed Sundays April to June 15 and September 16 to October, and closed weekends November to March.

ACCOMMODATIONS & DINING   Perhaps the least pretentious of the major lake towns, Riva del Garda has a handful of affordable options for travelers.

€   **La Montanara** (Via Montanara 18–20; ☎ 0464-554857; MC, V; closed Nov–Easter), for example, ain't fancy, but it's cheap. The exceedingly basic, mid-size rooms (doubles 48€) are squirreled away above an equally inexpensive trattoria in an old palazzo in a quiet part of the *centro storico*. It's all a bit down at the heels, but immaculately kept, with a picture or two framed on the whitewashed walls to relieve some of the spartan-ness. The two units on the top floor are the best for their general brightness and high ceilings.

€€–€€€ The management at **Hotel Portici** (Piazza III Novembre 19; ☎ 0464-555400; www.hotelportici.it; MC, V; closed early Nov to late Mar) pays much more attention to their ground-floor restaurant/bar under a portico of the main square than they do to the hotel, but perhaps that's because their rooms are mainly booked by tour groups—keeping this central and surprisingly reasonable choice off the radar of more independent travelers. Sadly, its location in the upper leg of the piazza's L-shape deprives almost all rooms of a lake view—and the functional units are boringly modern to boot, done up in a monotonous blue tone. Still, for these low prices—doubles from 56€ to 112€, depending on the season—you can easily cross the piazza to a cafe to get a view.

€€–€€€€ For a bit more scratch you can move across the piazza to **Hotel Sole** ✪✪ (Piazza III Novembre 35; ☎ 0464-552686; www.hotelsole.net; AE, MC, V; closed Nov to mid-Mar except at Christmastime and during frequent trade fairs), one of the finest hotels in town with a wonderful location right on the lake. The management charges a fair price yet still lavishes attention on the hotel's rooms and guests, with amenities from a casual cafe with lakeside terrace, to a rooftop solarium with sauna, to free bikes for guest use. This place screams class: a lobby filled with rare Persian carpets and abstract art, a sweeping circular staircase, and warm and luxurious rooms fitted with tasteful furnishings and marble-trimmed bathrooms. The best rooms are outfitted in antique style with balconies and lake views costing 112€ to 200€ for a double. Penny pinchers can get a modern-functional room overlooking the square and town for 96€ to 160€. Half-board in the formal restaurant is a steal at only 8€ extra per person; full-board costs 15€, but then you couldn't dine out.

€€–€€€ If the restaurants attached to the hotels above don't satisfy, indulge in the Teutonic side of this Trentino town at the noisy indoor beer garden of **Birreria Spaten** ✪ (Via Maffei 7; ☎ 0464-553670; www.hotelbenini.com; Thurs–Tues 11:30am–2:30pm and 6pm–midnight; closed Nov–Feb; MC, V), occupying the ground floor of an old palazzo. Many of the German and Austrian visitors who favor Riva opt for the schnitzel-and-sauerbraten side of the menu, but you can also enjoy a pasta like *strangolapreti* (spinach-and-ricotta dumplings in a butter sauce; 8€), one of 30 pizzas (5€–9€), or a simply grilled lake trout (15€). If you can't decide, the 14€ Piatto Spaten is an ample sampler of Tirolean specialties: *cotechino* (spicy sausage), *wurstel, canederli* (a giant bread dumpling), a ham steak, and sauerkraut.

EXPLORING RIVA DEL GARDA Riva's old town is pleasant enough, though the only historic attractions of note are the 13th-century **Torre d'Apponale** and, nearby, the moated lake-side castle, **La Rocca.** Part of the castle interior now houses an unassuming **museum of local art and crafts** (Piazza C. Battisti 3; ☎ 0464-573869; www.comune.rivadelgarda.tn.it/museo; 3€; Mar 19–June 12 and Oct Tues–Sun 10am–6pm).

Most years, the tourist office runs a few **free guided tours** in English—weekends around the town itself, Tuesdays and Fridays to sights in the surrounding area. You must book in advance, by 5pm the previous day, at ☎ 0464-554444.

The main attraction is the lake itself, which Riva takes advantage of with a waterside promenade stretching for several kilometers past parks and pebbly **beaches.** The water is warm enough for swimming from May to October, and air currents fanned by the mountains make Garda popular for **windsurfing** year-round (see "Get Physical in Riva," above).

10 Turin & the Alps

Olympic glory is only part of the story

by Reid Bramblett

IT'S OFTEN SAID THAT TURIN IS EITHER THE MOST FRENCH CITY IN ITALY or the most Italian city in France. And it makes sense: From the 13th century until Italy's 1861 unification (when the city served briefly as the new country's capital), Turin was home to the House of Savoy, whose last three monarchs—Vittorio Emanuele II, Umberto, and Vittorio Emanuele III—became the first kings of Italy. The Savoys were as French as they were Italian, with holdings that extended well into the present-day French regions of Savoy and the Côte d'Azur. The city's Francophile 17th- and 18th-century architects laid out broad avenues and airy piazzas and lined them with low-slung neoclassical buildings.

Turin is also called the Italian Detroit, but that's largely because Fiat and tire manufacturer Pirelli are based here. In every other respect, the comparison is unfair. Turin is, in fact, the most genteel and elegant city in all of northern Italy next to Venice, and may finally have earned its place on the world tourism map by hosting the 2006 Winter Olympics.

Turin is capital of the Piemonte (Piedmont) region, wedged into Italy's northwest corner. Piemonte means "at the foot of the mountains," which are, in this case, the Alps. Dramatic peaks are visible throughout Piemonte, most of which rise and roll over the fertile foothills that produce a rich bounty of cheeses, truffles, and, of course, wines—among them some of Italy's most delicious reds: Barbaresco, Barbera, and Barolo (the last considered one of Italy's top beefy, yet structured, wines).

North of Piemonte, the tiny but dramatic region of Valle d'Aosta is hemmed in by high mountains on all sides, a wide valley scattered with Roman ruins and postcard castles and ending at the mighty Monte Bianco, Europe's highest peak.

DON'T LEAVE PIEMONTE WITHOUT . . .

TOURING THE EGYPTIAN MUSEUM   Turin is home to the largest collections of Egyptian antiquities outside of Cairo; the painting gallery upstairs has one of Italy's richest collections of Flemish old masters—bonus!

MUNCHING YOUR WAY FROM CAFE TO CAFE   Torinesi spend their early evenings strolling from cafe to cafe, sipping coffee and red wine and nibbling on vast (usually free) buffets of canapés and finger food.

RIDING TO THE TOP OF MONTE BLANC   A series of cable cars and gondolas, each more dramatically scenic than the last, carries you from the Italian ski resort of Courmayeur to the top of Europe's highest peak.

TURIN

Most visitors come to Turin with business in mind, but those who take the time to look around the historical center will find fine museums, excellent restaurants, and a sophisticated city with scads of old-fashioned class.

LAY OF THE LAND

Turin lies 669km (415 miles) northwest of Rome, and 140km (87 miles) east of Milan. For now, the city's main train station is Stazione Porta Nuova, just south of the center on Piazza Carlo Felice, at the intersection of Turin's two major thoroughfares, Corso Vittorio Emanuele and Via Roma. There are, on average, one to two trains per hour to and from Milan (2 hr.), Venice (5–6 hr.), and Genoa (2 hr.), and nine trains daily to and from Rome (7–9 hr.).

There are long-term plans to move all rail service from the Porta Nuova station to the Porta Susa station, west of the center on Piazza XVIII Dicembre, which currently merely connects Turin with outlying Piemonte towns. However, work on preparing the city for the Olympics put all that on hold, and now it probably won't happen until 2011 (though some preliminary work might be going on during the shelf life of this book, so I wanted to fill you in).

Domestic and international flights land at the **Caselle International Airport** (☎ 011-5676361; www.turin-airport.com), 16km (10 miles) north of Turin. **SADEM Buses** (☎ 011-3000611; www.sadem.it) run between the airport and the Porto Nuova train station every half-hour to 45 minutes; the trip takes 40 minutes and costs 5.50€ (6€ if bought on the bus).

Turin's refined air becomes apparent as soon as you step off the train into the mannerly 19th-century Stazione Porta Nuova. The stately arcaded Via Roma, lined with shops and cafes, proceeds from the front of the station through a series of piazzas toward the Piazza Castello and the center of the city, about a 15-minute walk.

The circular Piazza Carlo Felice, directly in front of the station, is built around a garden and surrounded by outdoor cafes that invite even business-minded Torinese to linger. A few steps farther, Via Roma opens into the Piazza San Carlo, which is flanked by the twin churches of San Carlo and Santa Christina. The Palazzo Madama, at the end of Via Roma, dominates the main Piazza Castello. Flanking the north side of the piazza is the Palazzo Reale, residence of the Savoys from 1646 to 1865, whose gardens provide a pleasant respite from traffic.

From here, a walk east toward the Po River along Via Po takes you through Turin's university district to one of Italy's largest squares, the much-elongated Piazza Vittorio Veneto. At the end of this elegant expanse runs the Po.

City Bus & Tram Tickets

It's easy to get around central Turin on foot, but there's also a vast network of **GTT (Gruppi Torinese Trasporti)** (☎ 011-57641 or 800-019152; www.comune.torino.it/gtt) trams and buses. Tickets are sold at newsstands: 1€ for a single 70-minute ride, 3.50€ for 24 hours. The Torino+Piemonte Card (p. 449) gets you free travel for the duration of the card's validity.

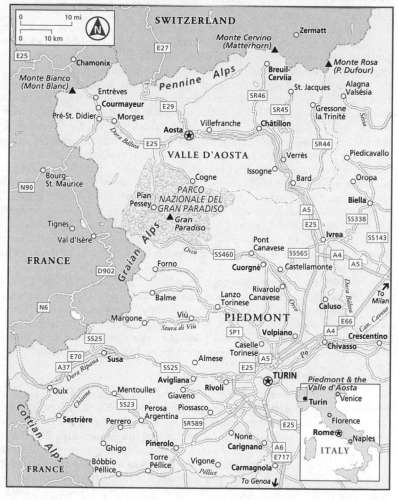

For the past few years the **main tourist office** (☎ 011-535181; www.turismo torino.org or www.comune.torino.it; daily 9:30am–7pm) occupied a pavilion in the middle of Piazza Solferino, but that was a temporary structure put in place for the 2006 Olympics. Around the time when this book hits the shelves, the information office will move—the only problem is, they still had no idea where by press time. Check their website for updates. There's also an office in the airport, and another at the Porta Nuova train station.

For arts calendars, cultural events, sports, and nightlife—plus, under the "Torino Grand Tour" section, **free downloadable mp3s of self-guided city walking tours**—check out www.comune.torino.it/torinoplus. You'll find more **information on the surrounding region** at www.regione.piemonte.it.

ACCOMMODATIONS, BOTH STANDARD & NOT

The **tourist office** (☎ 011-535181; www.turismotorino.org) will book hotel rooms for free, but only 48 hours in advance of your arrival (for B&Bs, a week in advance). Frustratingly, the city's tourist office doesn't list *affittacamere* (rental rooms), which range in price from 20€ to 80€ for a double, though most are in the 30€-to-40€ bracket. While you can get a list of the 46 rental rooms in Turin from the **Piemonte Region's official site** (www.regione.piemonte.it), you have to use the Italian-language version of the site; the stripped-down English version doesn't include lodging info. As a shortcut—though, given how websites are sometimes reorganized, a deep link such as this might eventually go out of date— try typing in www.regione.piemonte.it/turismo/ricettivita.htm to go directly to the lodgings search-engine page. Just click "Affittacamere" on the left. On the next page, select "Torino" in the Provincia column, and a list of towns will pop up in the Comune column to the right. Scroll down to select "Torino" again, then click "Cerca." Follow the same steps from that main lodging page to search for *campeggi* (campgrounds), *agriturismi* (farm stays), *ostelli* (hostels), *case vacanze* (residence hotels and vacation rentals), and other options. There are a number of good, affordable options that are fairly represented on the site, for those willing to surf a bit.

If you want to rent an apartment, contact **The Salt Way** (☎ 0183-930244; www.saltway.it), which has 18 places scattered about town, sleeping anywhere from two to six people, for a minimum of 3 nights. They come in a wide range of looks from vaguely rustic to blandly functional to chicly postmodern, so ask a lot of questions before you book if particular amenities are important to you. Prices start at 45€ to 70€ for two people, 60€ to 95€ for three to four.

Bargains in the Historical Center

€€   I just love it when a hotel with one of the best locations in town also happens to be one of the cheapest. Tiny **Albergo San Carlo** ★ (Piazza San Carlo 197; ☎ 011-5627846; www.albergosancarlo.it; AE, MC, V) isn't fancy, with knocked-about-but-nice antiques mixed with the functional furnishings, little Persian rugs by the beds, and quirky touches like the crystal chandelier in room no. 12, or the marble-topped dresser and carved headboard of room no. 7. But the price—60€ for a room without private bathroom, 78€ for one with—can't be beat, and the location is phenomenal: It occupies the fourth floor of the 17th-century Palazzo Isnardi di Caraglio, flanking the east side of elegant Piazza San Carlo. Ask to see several rooms, as they differ dramatically in space and atmosphere (but all have free Wi-Fi). The five rooms on the piazza side have sloping mansard ceilings with dormer windows, and tend to be larger (if a tad noisier) than rooms nos. 1 to 7 in the back.

€€–€€€   A few blocks west, just south of Piazza Solferino, are the twin hotels **Artuà & Solferino** ★ 🔘 (Via Brofferio 3, off Corso Re Umberto; ☎ 011-5175301; www.artua.it; AE, MC, V)—20 rooms evenly split between the fourth floors of neighboring buildings (you check in at the reception for the "Solferino" half). This is a real family-run joint; the owner's kids leave toys scattered and hang around the breakfast room/lounge to watch cartoons or videos on the communal

Turin

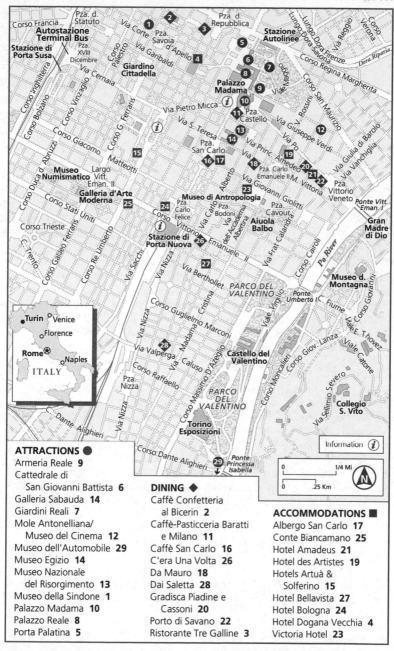

large-screen TV. The rooms are simple—creamy wood floors, beat-up white lacquer modular furnishings, and small, but nice, new bathrooms—but the place is full of thoughtful extras, like high-speed Internet access for 3€ a hour, and a sauna/hydromassage unit in Solferino. You can even save a few bucks by opting for a 90€-to-100€ standard room (smaller or noisier, with sloping roofs, older furnishings, no satellite TV channels, and no breakfast) instead of a 110€-to-120€ "comfort" double.

€€–€€€　The best value for your money in the center—110€ for a double, falling to 85€ Friday to Sunday nights—is the **Hotel Dogana Vecchia** ★ (Via Corte d'Appello 4, at Via Milano; ☎ 011-4366752; www.hoteldoganavecchia.com; AE, MC, V), installed in the old 18th-century customhouse, just a few blocks west of Piazza Castello (and a few blocks east of the wine bars and *trattorie* around Piazza Em. Filiberto). The hotel's an odd marriage of fading old-fashioned style and bland modernity, the bright and friendly reception giving way to dimly lit corridors with frilly moldings decorating the vaulted high ceilings. If you don't care to splash out 130€ on the "Camera Mozart" where the great composer himself once slept (other illustrious clientele have included Napoleon, Giuseppe Verdi, and a local saint who performed his first miracle cure in a room here), try to snag one of the "Antiche" rooms, which have been left with a splash of style—stucco decorations, crystal chandeliers, herringbone wood floors, and Art Nouveau bed frames and wardrobes. The standard rooms have lower ceilings and modern terrazzo flooring. Want to save even more? They don't advertise this fact, but the hotel retains two older rooms without private bathroom, which sell for around 50€, breakfast not included.

Hotels near Piazza Vittorio Veneto

€€–€€€　There are a pair of pleasant and moderately priced, if slightly dull, hotels along one of Torino's arcaded boulevards leading from the city center east toward Piazza Vittorio Veneto and the river. **Hotel Amadeus** ★ (Via Principe Amadeo 41 bis; ☎ 011-8174951; www.hotelamadeustorino.it; AE, MC, V) has the slight edge of affordability—90€ per double on the weekends, 85€ to 120€ during the week—and a bit more of a swank feel, with coffered edges to the ceilings, textured wallpaper, colorful fabrics and carpets, and well-lit marble bathrooms. Rooms ending in -03 are the largest—though none are really that spacious—but for optimum quiet pick a room ending in -04 or -05, facing the back courtyard.

€€€　Solo travelers take note: Both the Amadeus and its neighbor, **Hotel des Artistes** (Via Principe Amadeo 21, at Via Accademia; ☎ 011-8124416; www.desartisteshotel.it; AE, MC, V), feature extra-wide *francesina* beds in their single rooms. Otherwise, the 95€ to 127€ doubles at the Hotel des Artistes are bland but comfy. The hotel received a functional overhaul 5 years ago, with bathrooms jammed into room corners as an afterthought and heavy drapes over the double-paned windows.

Hotels near the Train Station

Unlike the areas around train stations in most large cities, the Porta Nuova neighborhood is semistylish and perfectly safe, and many of the city's hotels are here, just a 10-minute stroll south of the central sights.

€€ Step off the elevator at the simple, sixth-floor **Hotel Bellavista** (Via Galliari 15, between Via S. Anselmo and Via Principe Tomasso; ☎ 011-6698139; AE, MC, V), on a quiet street in the residential neighborhood between the station and Parco del Valentino, and you'll find a sun-filled corridor brimming with houseplants and opening onto a wide terrace. The 18 rooms are airy and comfortable but uninspired, with functional modern furnishings. Most, though, afford pleasant views over the surrounding rooftops—the best stretching across the river toward the hills. What most rooms don't have is a private bathroom, though the several communal facilities are well placed, only steps away from most rooms. The seven doubles with bathroom go for 70€, the two without for 50€, breakfast included.

€€ In fact, for 75€ to 80€ per double (including breakfast), you can have a room in a gracious 18th-century apartment house directly across the street from the station at the family-run **Hotel Bologna** ✦ (Corso Vittorio Emanuele II 60; ☎ 011-5620193 or 011-5620290; AE, MC, V). Some rooms are quite grand, incorporating frescoes and fireplaces. Others have been renovated in sleek modern style with laminated, built-in cabinetry and glossy wood floors. Still others fall in between, with well-maintained 1970s style furnishings and linoleum flooring. Whatever the vintage, all of the rooms are spotlessly clean and nicely maintained, and were overhauled in the fall of 2005.

€€€ Costing a bit more than its neighbors (95€–125€ for a double)—but with oodles more class—is the fading glory of the **Conte Biancamano** (Corso Vittorio Emanuele II 73, at Corso Umberto 5 blocks west of the station; ☎ 011-5623281; www.hotelcontebiancamano.it; AE, MC, V). Admittedly, most of that class is limited to the grand public rooms—all frescoed ceilings and fancy stuccowork. The guest rooms are rather plain, suffering from a kind of mod furniture that must have looked oh-so-stylish in 1984—though on the plus side, they now have Wi-Fi. Rooms on the back courtyard are considerably quieter than those on the front, which overlook one of the busiest boulevards in Turin.

DINING FOR ALL TASTES

The Piemonte region stretches from the Po plains through the Langhe and Roero wine hills, to the mountain villages of the Alps. This vast geographic diversity—not to mention a heavy influence from neighboring France—informs the local cuisines you'll find in city restaurants. Piemontese cooking is big on meats stewed in red wine, the most favored being *brasato al barolo* (beef or veal braised in Barolo). The best dish with which to kick off a meal is usually only available in winter: *bagna cauda*, literally translated as "hot bath," a plate of raw vegetables that are dipped into a steaming sauce of olive oil, garlic, and anchovies.

Two local pastas dishes you will encounter are *agnolotti* (a thick pasta tube often stuffed with an infusion of cheese and meat) and *tajarin* (a flat egg noodle that may be topped with porcini mushrooms, sauce made with walnuts, or the local delicacy that is perhaps the region's greatest contribution to Italian cuisine: the white truffles of Alba). Italian Alpine cuisine leans toward polenta (a cornmeal mush varying from soupy and sticky to almost cakelike), and stews thick with beef and red wine (the best of which is a typical dish from neighboring Valle d'Aosta: *carbonada*).

A Worthy Splurge

€€€€   Pass through the doors of a plain-looking building between the Via Roma and the river, and you'll think you're in an English country house. That's the idea at the **Victoria Hotel** ✪✪ (Via Nino Costa 4, a tiny street, unlabeled on most maps, at the corner of Via Giuseppe Pomba between Via Giolitti and Via Cavour; ☎ 011-5611909; www.hotelvictoria-torino.com; AE, MC, V), and the Anglophile decor works splendidly. The lobby resembles a drawing room, with floral sofas, deep armchairs, and a view onto a garden. The glass-enclosed breakfast room feels like a conservatory. Standard guest rooms—210€ per double—are handsomely furnished in a chic style that soothingly combines contemporary and traditional styles, with mahogany bedsteads and writing desks, and rich fabric wallcoverings and draperies. Deluxe accommodations (240€ double), each with a distinctive look, are oversize rooms furnished with carefully chosen antiques and such flourishes as canopied beds and richly upholstered divans. The prices are a bit high, but can fall on weekends and with special packages, so call ahead.

€   For picnic pickings—or merely a look at the bounty of the surrounding farmlands—wander through the extensive outdoor food market at Porta Palazzo, Monday through Saturday from 6:30am to 1:30pm (also Sat 3:30–7:30pm). If all you want is a quick sandwich, head to **Gradisca Piadine e Cassoni** (Via Principe Amadeo 41A; ☎ 011-8159331; Mon–Fri, Sat until 3pm), where Carmela or Alessandro will knead and cook a flatbread while you wait, and then stuff it with your choice of fillings for 2.50€ to 5€.

€€   One of the few kitchens in Turin that remains open until 10pm, **Dai Saletta** ✪ (Via Belfiore 37, just south of Via Oddino Morgari; ☎ 011-6687867; Mon–Sat 12:30–2:30pm and 8–10:30pm; AE, MC, V) turns out a nice selection of homey trattoria fare in a cramped dining room several long blocks south of the train station. Homemade pasta dishes are delicious and cost just 9€. Try the hearty *tortelloni alla salsiccia* (a large pasta shell stuffed with sausage) or *peposelle* (a thick pasta tossed with Gorgonzola and walnuts).

€€   **Da Mauro** (Via Maria Vittoria 21, between Via Bogino and Via San Francesco da Paola; ☎ 011-8170604; Tues–Sun 12:30–3pm and 7–10pm; no credit cards) is more relaxed than many Torinese restaurants, and if the informal ambience and the menu remind you of regions farther south, your instincts are right. The family who owns the restaurant emphasizes Tuscan dishes, though the menu seems to run the gamut of Italian cooking. There are several spicy pasta dishes, including deftly prepared cannelloni for 6€, and the meat courses are similar to those you would find in Tuscany—simply grilled or roasted steak, pork chops, and game birds for just 7€ to 8.50€.

€€   **Porto di Savano** ✫✫ (Piazza Vittorio Veneto 2; ☎ 011-8173500; www. portodisavona.com; daily 12:30–2:30pm and 7:30–10:30pm; MC, V) is probably the most popular trattoria in Turin. Seating is family style, at long tables that crowd a series of rooms beneath old photos and mementos, and the typically Piemontese fare never fails to please (all the more so on Sun, when many other restaurants in central Turin are closed). Several variations of gnocchi are usually made fresh daily, as is the Piemontese flat noodle *tajarin* (7.50€), and *agnolotti al sugo d'arrosto* (cheese-stuffed pasta in a roast pork *ragù,* 8€). They also honor an old working man's tradition: At lunchtime, Monday through Saturday only, you can order a *monopiatto,* which consists of a plate of hearty pasta (8.70€) or a meat dish (12€) with a dessert, coffee, and either water or wine included in the price—one of Turin's great bargains.

Worth a Splurge

€€€€   Arriving at **C'era Una Volta** ✫✫✫ (Corso Vittorio Emanuele II 41, next to Libreria Zanaboni at Via Goito; ☎ 011-655498; www.ristoranteceraunavolta.it; Mon–Sat 7–10:30pm; AE, MC, V)—which translates as "Once Upon a Time"—you'll feel as if you've entered a bit of a time warp: a large, old-fashioned second-floor dining room filled with heavy old tables and credenzas, and a highly professional waitstaff that seems to have been in place, unchanged, since the 1950s. Until a few years ago, the restaurant only offered a set-price tasting menu (26€–28€) of authentically Torinese dishes that never stopped coming; if you choose this option, don't bother making plans to eat for the next 24 hours. But due to popular demand the restaurant has introduced a la carte choices as well. The menu changes daily, but might include crepes with ham and cheese, risotto with artichokes, a carrot flan, rabbit stew, or a slice of beef with polenta. A meal like this deserves a fine Barolo—and almost always requires that you book ahead.

Weekend Hotel Bargains

Turin is such a business-oriented city that rooms are actually cheaper on the weekends, when hotels have to scramble to fill beds. Some 38 Turin hotels (most in the three- to five-star category) offer a "Torino Weekend" promotion; 25 of these hotels charge between 59€ and 99€ per person for a package that includes a room for 2 nights (Fri–Sat), breakfast, a 48-hour Torino Card (which is an 18€ value), and a little extra something that varies from hotel to hotel—could be free parking, a box of chocolates, or a CD of classical music.

Of the hotels recommended in this book, those participating include the **Hotel Amadeus** (98€ per person; includes a free guided tour of the city or Egyptian Museum and "typical Torinese gift"), the **Artuà** (125€ per person; free parking), and the **Hotel des Artistes** (99€; breakfast in bed and a bottle of local wine). The city tourism office (www.turismotorino. org) has a full list of participating hotels.

€€€€   Another Torino classic, **Ristorante Tre Galline** ✪✪ (Via Bellezia 37; ☎ 011-4366553; Tues–Sat 12:30–2:30pm and 7:30–10:30pm, Mon 7:30–10:30pm; AE, MC, V) has been one of the city's most popular eateries for more than 3 centuries, a bright wood-paneled room with friendly, professional service and a seasonal tasting menu that's a steal at 38€. The salami are hand-carved at your table for an appetizer, and the daily changing menu mixes Torinese and Piemontese specialties with slightly creative dishes using local ingredients. You might run across such delectables as *agnolotti* (meat-filled pasta ringlets) in a pink *ragù*, risotto with basil and truffles, *carré d'agnello in crosta di erbette* (lamb cooked with herbs), and rabbit cooked in apple vinegar. If you don't book ahead, don't expect to get in. *Primi* tend to run around 12€ to 15€, *secondi* 14€ to 20€.

WHY YOU'RE HERE: THE TOP SIGHTS & ATTRACTIONS

Though best known for its famed shroud, Turin has a number of worthy sights and attractions, from world-class museums to art-filled churches. Allow a full 2 days to explore the town fully.

Around Piazza Castello

Don't be misled by the baroque facade on the **Palazzo Madama** ✪ (Piazza Castello; ☎ 011-4433501; www.palazzomadamatorino.it; 7.50€; Tues–Fri 10am–6pm, Sat 10am–8pm), which was added by architect Filippo Juvarra in the 18th century. If you walk around the exterior of the palazzo—named for its most popular resident, Madama Reale, aka Marie Christine of France—you'll discover that the massive structure incorporates a medieval castle, a Roman gate, and several Renaissance additions. Juvarra also added a monumental marble staircase to the interior, most of which has been given over to the far-reaching collections of the Museo Civico di Arte Antica. The holdings focus on the medieval and Renaissance periods, shown off against the castle's unaltered, stony medieval interior. One of Italy's largest collections of ceramics is here, as well as some stunning canvases, including Antonello da Messina's 1476 *Portrait of a Man.*

The **Palazzo Reale (Royal Palace)** ✪ (Piazzetta Reale/Piazza Castello; ☎ 011-4361455; www.artito.arti.beniculturali.it; 6.50€; Tues–Sun 8:30am–7:30pm) is the former royal residence of the House of Savoy. Begun in 1645 and designed by the Francophile count of Castellamonte, it reflects the ornately baroque tastes of European ruling families of the time—a fact that will not be lost on you as you pass from one opulently decorated, heavily gilded room to the next. (The Savoys had a keener eye for painting than for decor, and most of the canvases they collected are in the nearby Galleria Sabauda.)

What's most notable here are some of the tapestries, including those depicting the life of Don Quixote in the Sala delle Virtu (Hall of Virtues) by the finest workshop in baroque-era Europe, the royal French manufacturer Gobelins; and the collection of Chinese and Japanese vases in the Sala dell'Alcova. One of the quirkier architectural innovations, an antidote to several monumental staircases, is a manually driven elevator from the 18th century.

One wing houses the **Armeria Reale** ✪ (Piazza Castello 191; ☎ 011-543889; www.artito.arti.beniculturali.it; 4€; Tues–Fri 9–2pm, Sat–Sun 1–7pm), one of the most important arms and armor collections in Europe, especially of weapons from the 16th and 17th centuries.

Musical September

September is the month to enjoy classical music in Turin. More than 60 classical concerts are held on stages around the city during the monthlong **Settembre Musica festival** (☎ 011-4424777; www.settembremusica.it).

Behind the palace, and offering a refreshing change from its frippery, are the **Giardini Reali (Royal Gardens),** laid out by Le Nôtre, more famous for the Tuileries and the gardens at Versailles.

Just north of the Piazza Castello and the Royal Palace sits the bland facade of the **Cattedrale di San Giovanni Battista** ★ (Piazza San Giovanni; ☎ 011-5661540 or 011-4361540; free; daily 8am–12:30pm and 3–7pm). Far more interesting is the single chapel inside the cathedral's pompous, 15th-century interior—the baroque **Cappella della Santa Sindone,** occasional home to the controversial **Santissima Sindone (Shroud of Turin;** see below). Even without the presence of one of Christendom's most precious relics—only rarely on view in a silver casket elevated on the altar in the center of the room—the chapel is still well worth a visit. Restored after a 1997 fire (one of many the shroud has miraculously survived, with occasional singeing, over the centuries), the chapel is somberly clad in black marble. But, as if to suggest that better things await us in the heavens, it ascends to an airy, light-flooded, six-tiered dome, one of the masterpieces of Italian baroque architecture.

In front of the cathedral stand two landmarks of ancient Turin—the remains of a Roman theater and the Roman-era city gate **Porta Palatina,** flanked by twin 16-sided towers.

The Top Museums

Turin's magnificent **Museo Egizio** ★★★ 🅺 (Via Accademia delle Scienze 6; ☎ 011-5617776; www.museoegizio.org; 6.50€; Tues–Sun mid-Sept to May 8:30am–7:30pm, early June to early Sept 9:30am–8:30pm) is the world's largest Egyptian collection outside of Cairo. This was, in fact, the world's first Egyptian museum, thanks to the Savoys' habit of ardently amassing artifacts throughout their reign, and the museum continued to mount collecting expeditions throughout the early 20th century. Of the 30,000 pieces on display, some of the more captivating exhibits are in the first rooms you enter on the ground floor. These include the 15th-century-B.C. Rock Temple of Ellessiya, which the Egyptian government donated in gratitude for Italian efforts to save monuments threatened by the Aswan Dam. The two nearby statuary rooms are staggering, both in the size and drama of the objects they house; notable among the objects are two sphinxes and a massive, richly painted statue of Ramses II. Smaller objects—mummies, funerary objects, and a papyrus Book of the Dead—fill the galleries on the next floor. The most enchanting exhibit here is the collection of everyday paraphernalia, including eating utensils and shriveled foodstuffs, from the tomb of the 14th-century-B.C. architect Khaie and his wife.

The Savoys' other treasure trove, a magnificent collection of European paintings, fills the salons of the **Galleria Sabauda** ★★ (Via Accademia delle Scienze 6; ☎ 011-547440; www.museitorino.it/galleriasabauda; 4€; Tues and Fri–Sun 8:30am–2pm, Wed–Thurs 2–7:30pm), upstairs in the same building as the Egyptian collection. The Savoy's royal taste ran heavily to painters of the Flemish and Dutch schools, and the works by van Dyck, van Eyck, Rembrandt, and van der Weyden, among others, make up one of Italy's largest collections of northern European paintings. In fact, two of Europe's most prized Flemish masterpieces are here: Jan van Eyck's *Stigmata of St. Francis* and Hans Memling's *Passion of Christ*. Italian artists, including those from the Piemonte, are also well represented; one of the first canvases you see upon entering the galleries is the work of a Tuscan, Fra Angelico's sublime *Virgin and Child*.

The **Mole Antonelliana** ★★ (Via Montebello 20; ☎ 011-8138560; www.museonazionaledelcinema.org; Tues–Fri and Sun 9am–8pm, Sat 9am–11pm) is by a long shot Turin's most peculiar building; in fact, it's one of the strangest structures anywhere. It consists of a squat brick base, a steep conelike roof supporting several layers of Greek temples piled one atop the other, and a needlelike spire, all of it rising 166m (544 ft.) above the rooftops of the city center—a height that, at one time, made the Mole the world's tallest building. Begun in 1863 and designed as a synagogue, the Mole is now a monument to Italian unification and architectural hubris and, as of 2000, home to the thoroughly fascinating **Museo Nazionale del Cinema (National Film Museum)** 🧒 (6.50€ for just the museum, 8€ for the museum plus an elevator ride).

The museum's first section tracks the development of moving pictures from shadow puppets to kinescopes. The rest is more a tribute to film than a true museum, offering clips and stills to illustrate some of the major aspects of movie production, from *The Empire Strikes Back* storyboards to the creepy steady-cam work in *The Shining*. Of memorabilia, masks from *Planet of the Apes, Satyricon,* and *Star Wars* hang together near *Lawrence of Arabia*'s robe, Chaplin's bowler, and *What Ever Happened to Baby Jane?*'s dress. Curiously, most of the clips (all in Italian-dubbed versions), as well as posters and other memorabilia, are heavily weighted toward American movies, with exceptions mainly for the major players of European/international cinema like Fellini, Bertolucci, Truffaut, and Wim Wenders.

Even if you skip the museum, you can ride the dramatic glass elevator (4.50€ for the ride) to an observation platform at the top of the spire, an experience that affords two advantages: The view of Turin and the surrounding countryside, backed by the Alps, is stunning; and, as Guy de Maupassant once said of the Eiffel Tower, it's the only place in Turin where you won't have to look at the damned thing.

Tours

The **tourist office** (☎ 011-535181; www.turismotorino.org) runs a number of well-thought-out tours, including a basic 90-minute **Saturday morning "Giro Torino" tour around town** at 10am, followed by a tour of the Egyptian museum at 11:30am (8€ for either tour alone, 10€ for both). On the first, third, and fifth Saturdays of each month, these tours are in Italian and English, on the second and

Turin's Renowned Cafes

Cafe-sitting is a centuries-old tradition in sophisticated Turin. Via Roma, and the piazzas that open off of it, is lined with gracious salons that have been serving coffee, and the world's first aperitif—that Turin invention called vermouth—for decades. Espresso and pastries are the mainstays of every cafe's menu, but most also serve chocolates—including the mix of chocolate and hazelnuts known as *gianduiotti*—that are among the city's major contributions to culinary culture. Around 5 or 6pm, many central bars and *caffè* lay out a sumptuous buffet of finger foods and other delectables—usually for free, occasionally charging a token 5€ or so.

€ **Caffè Confetteria al Bicerin** ✹ (Piazza della Consolata 5; ☎ 011-4369325; www.bicerin.it; Thurs–Tues) claims to be Turin's oldest continuously operating cafe (since 1763). It is famous for the illustrious clientele, which has included Nietzsche, Dumas, and Puccini, as well as for its signature drink, the *bicerin* (local dialect for "something delicious"), a heady combination of coffee, hot chocolate, and cream. The house pastries are exquisite.

€ Part of the pleasure at stylish **Caffè-Pasticceria Baratti e Milano** (Piazza Castello 27; ☎ 011-4407138; Tues–Sun), opened in 1875, is watching a diverse clientele sipping espressos and munching on the delicious house pastries—the crowd ranges from auto executives to students from the nearby university, and from elegantly clad shoppers to visitors to the nearby museums.

€ The classic **Caffè San Carlo** ✹ (Piazza San Carlo 156; ☎ 011-5617748; www.caffesancarlo.it) opened its doors in 1837, and ever since has been an essential stop on any tour of Turin, accommodating patrons beneath a huge chandelier of Murano glass in a salon that houses a remarkable assemblage of gilt, mirrors, and marble. An adjoining frescoed tearoom is quieter and only a little less grand.

fourth Saturdays in Italian and French. The office also runs intriguing **themed walking tours on Saturday evenings** for 8€ each. The themes change, but may include film locales (among others, the original *Italian Job* was filmed here), contemporary art installations, a "Tasty Turin" tour of historic cafes, or "Literary Turin" tours of places where Nietzsche, De Amicis, and Alfieri lived. The language schedule on these is reversed: in Italian and English the second and fourth Saturdays of the month, Italian and French on the first, third, and fifth Saturdays. All of these tours depart from the Atrium info pavilion on Piazza Solferino. Holders of the Torino+Piemonte Card get 20% to 25% off.

Somewhere (☎ 011-6680580; www.somewhere.it), a private tour agency, offers another series of guided tours. Get the dirt on the city's secret side with either the 2-hour "Magic Turin" tour, which traces the city's traditions of black and white magic (meet at Piazza Statuto; 20€; Thurs and Sat at 9pm), or on the 3-hour "Underground Turin" tour, which takes you under the baroque palazzi to cellars, air-raid shelters, and other spaces laced with stories of mystery, intrigue, and murder (meet at Piazza Vittorio Veneto; 25€; Fri 8:30pm). Gourmands in a hurry might prefer the 2-hour "Delitram," a gourmet meal with a guide and a sax player, aboard a trolley car converted into a roving restaurant (meet at Piazza Carlo Emanuele II; 45€; Sat 9pm). There's also a 2-hour shopping and culture tour of the historical center (meet at Piazza Savoia; 25€; Sat 10am).

THE OTHER TURIN

Most tourists in Italy stick to the major sights and museums that tend to be focused on great art and ancient sights. Few take the time to learn more about the country's recent history and current culture and industry, which can make for a far more interesting and rewarding vacation.

To understand Italy—or at the very least to learn the stories behind Cavour, Garibaldi, Mazzini, Vittorio Emanuele II, Massimo d'Azeglio, and other people after whom most of the major streets and piazzas in Italy are named—you need to brush up on the Risorgimento, the late-19th-century movement that launched Italian unification. While any self-respecting town in Italy has a museum dedicated to it, Turin's **Museo Nazionale del Risorgimento** (Via Accademia delle Scienze 5; ☎ 011-5621147; www.regione.piemonte.it/cultura/risorgimento; 5€; Tues-Sun 9am-7pm) is the best of the bunch. After all, much of the history of Italy's unification played out in this Turin palazzo, which was home to unified Italy's first king, Vittorio Emanuele II, and later became, in 1861, the seat of its first parliament. Documents, paintings, and other paraphernalia recount the heady days when Vittorio Emanuele II banded with General Garibaldi and his Red Shirts to oust the Bourbons from Sicily and the Austrians from the north to create a unified Italy. The plaques describing the contents of each room are in English, and the last rooms house a fascinating collection that chronicles Italian fascism and the resistance against it, which evolved into the Partisan movement during World War II. Note that the museum will be closed for renovations, probably until sometime in late 2008.

As befits a city responsible for 80% of Italian car manufacturing, the **Museo dell Automobile (Automobile Museum)** (Corso Unita d'Italia 40; ☎ 011-677666; www.museoauto.it; 5.50€; Tues-Sun 10am-6:30pm) is a shiny collection of most of the cars that have done Italy proud over the years, including Lancias, Isotta Frashinis, and the Itala that came in first in the 1907 Peking-to-Paris rally. Among the oddities is a roadster emblazoned with the initials ND, which Gloria Swanson drove in her role as faded movie queen Norma Desmond in *Sunset Boulevard*. The museum lies well south of the center; take bus no. 34 or 35, or tram ❶ or ⑱. However, it, too, will remain closed for renovations until sometime in late 2008—in this case, a complete overhaul courtesy of the same folks who created the avant-garde Museum of Cinema in Mole Antonelliana, turning this car showcase into a much more sprightly and interactive modern museum.

But to really delve into the other Turin, you need to go beyond a museum displaying a century's worth of Fiats and see where today's Fiats are rolling off the

The Torino+Piemonte Card

A Torino+Piemonte Card (sold at the tourist office) will grant you (plus one child under 12) discounts on concerts and the like, free admission to 150 museums (including all those mentioned here) throughout the province, free public transport within Turin, and a whole host of discounts on everything from cultural events and car rentals to concert and guided tours to ski rentals and lift tickets at neighboring resorts. The 2-day card costs 18€, the 3-day card 20€, the 5-day card 30€, and the 7-day card 35€.

assembly line. The Torinesi pride themselves on their city's booming industrial economy, and to get a sense of the real lifeblood of this city and this defining aspect of its culture, you need to head out to the factories that ring the town and inform its identity. Luckily, the tourist office has made that easy with a series of 3- to 4-hour **Turismo Industriale tours** (☎ 011-535181; www.turismotorino.org; 10€; Mar–Dec 2, four times a month). On a rotating schedule, these bus tours visit one of Turin's top industrial and design firms. The most frequent tours are, naturally, to *il grande* Fiat itself (usually once a month), but there are plenty of other trips to such notable local firms as Martini & Rossi, producers of the vermouth that lent (half) its name to James Bond's cocktail of choice, and Lavazza, which roasts $1.38 million worth of coffee each year, supplying 48% of the coffee drunk in cappuccino-crazed Italy (not to mention the famed cafes of Turin). Some tours are to one of a quartet of fine pen makers (from Aurora's classy engraved fountain pens to Lecce Pen's famous biodegradable ballpoint) or to a trio of top-notch design firms. These include Bertoni (designing Fiats and Lancias since the 1920s—not to mention cars for MG, Maserati, Aston Martin, BMW, Volvo, Ferrari, and the incomparable Lamborghini Countach), Giugiaro (a firm that helped assemble the winning Olympic bid), and Pinin Farina (their 1947 Cisalpino high-bullet train was the first vehicle ever honored by New York's MoMA as one of the "eight wonders of our time").

A SIDE TRIP FROM TURIN

The little town of Cogne (29km/18 miles south of Aosta; seven buses daily, 50 min.) is the most convenient gateway to the **Parco Nazionale del Gran Paradiso,** one of Europe's finest parcels of unspoiled nature—a third of it lies on the Piemonte side of the regional boundaries, accessible from Turin.

The former hunting grounds of King Vittorio Emanuele II are now a vast (3,626 sq. km/1,400 sq. miles) and lovely national park. In five valleys of forests and pastureland, many Alpine beasts roam wild—including the ibex (a long-horned goat) and the chamois (a small antelope), both of which have hovered near extinction in recent years. Cogne also offers some downhill skiing, but it is better regarded for cross-country.

Humans can roam these wilds via a vast network of well-marked trails. Among the few places where the hand of man intrudes ever so gently on nature are in a

The Shroud of Turin

The Shroud of Turin is said to be the piece of fabric in which the body of Christ was wrapped when he was taken down from the cross—and to which his image was miraculously affixed. The image on the fabric is of a man 5 feet 7 inches tall, with bloodstains consistent with a crown of thorns, a cut in the rib cage, cuts in the wrists and ankles, and scourge marks on the back from flagellation.

Recent carbon dating suggests that the shroud was manufactured sometime around the 13th or 14th centuries. But the mystery remains, at least in part because no one can explain how the haunting image appeared on the cloth. Debunkers constantly attempt to create replicas using lemon juice and the sun, mineral pigments, even aloe and myrrh (the last because, according to funerary traditions at the time, Jesus' body would likely have been treated with these oils before being wrapped in the shroud). Every few years, a new crop of naysayers publishes the results of their adventures in fakery, and a competing crop of faithful apologists points out how the success of newly made facsimiles doesn't necessarily negate the authenticity of the Turin shroud itself. Additional radio carbon dating has suggested that, because the shroud has been exposed to fire (thus affecting the carbon readings), it could indeed date from around the time of Christ's death. In the end, faith and science are unlikely to reach agreement (unless, of course, science suddenly decides the shroud is genuine). Despite scientific skepticism, the shroud continues to entice hordes of the faithful.

The shroud was last on display during Italy's Jubilee celebrations in 2000. Technically, it shouldn't be on display again until the next Jubilee, in 2025, but it pops up every 5 to 15 years for special occasions. (Rumor has it that the shroud may go on permanent exhibit, either in the cathedral or in its own space.)

Until such a display exists, to see the shroud you'll have to content yourself with three alternatives: a series of dramatically backlit photos near the entrance to the Cappella della Santa Sindone; a replica on display in the church, and a museum devoted to the relic, the **Museo della Sindone** (Via San Domenico 28; ☎ 011-4365832; www.sindone.org; 5.50€; daily 9am–noon and 3–7pm).

---

few scattered hamlets within the park borders and in the **Giardino Alpino Paradisia** (☎ 0165-74147; 2.50€; daily July–Aug 10am–6:30pm, June and Sept 10am–5:30pm), a stunning collection of rare Alpine fauna near the village of Valnontey, 1.6km (1 mile) south of Cogne.

The park actually has five entrances (three on the Valle d'Aosta side, two on the Piemonte), and seven info centers, but the main information center is in the

Piemonte village of **Noasca** (Via Umberto I; ☎ 0124-901070). There are also offices in **Turin** (Via Della Rocca 47; ☎ 011-8606211) and **Aosta** (Via Losanna 5; ☎ 0165-44126), but perhaps the best stop is the tourist office at the park entrance in **Cogne** (Via Bourgeois 34; ☎ 0165-74040; www.cogne.org), providing a wealth of information on hiking and skiing trails and other outdoor activities in the park and elsewhere in the region. You can also get info at **www.pngp.it** and **www.parks.it**.

COURMAYEUR & MONT BLANC

The one-time mountain hamlet of Courmayeur is now the Valle d'Aosta's resort extraordinaire, a collection of traditional stone buildings, pseudo-Alpine chalets, and large hotels catering to a well-heeled international crowd of skiers. Even if you don't ski, you can happily while away your time sipping mulled wine while regarding the craggy bulk of Mont Blanc (called Monte Bianco on this side of the border), which looms over this end of the Valle d'Aosta and forms the snowy barrier between Italy and France. The Mont Blanc tunnel, through which you can zip into France in just 20 minutes, reopened in 2002, 3 years after a devastating fire.

The cable-car system up Monte Bianco actually begins not in Courmayeur, but in La Palud, outside the village of Entrèves, 3km (2 miles) to the north, a pleasant collection of stone houses and farm buildings surrounded by pastureland. Quaint as the village is in appearance, at its soul Entrèves is a worldly enclave with hotels and restaurants that cater to skiers and outdoor enthusiasts who prefer to spend time in surroundings quieter than Courmayeur.

LAY OF THE LAND

The Valle d'Aosta is a region best explored by car, but if you're coming by public transportation, first you have to get to the regional capital of Aosta, 113km (70 miles) northwest of Turin and about 35km (22 miles) east of Courmayeur-Entrèves. Aosta is served by 12 trains a day to and from Turin (2–3 hr.), and 10 trains daily to and from Milan (3–4 hr., with a change in Chivasso).

Thirteen daily buses (☎ 0165-262027) connect Aosta with Courmayeur (1 hr.). Buses also run between Courmayeur's Piazzale Monte Bianco and Entrèves and La Palud (10 min.), at least every hour, more often in summer (☎ 0165-841305).

By car, the A5 autostrada is the fastest way from Aosta to Courmayeur (less than 30 min.)—but you spend much of that time in tunnels. For more scenery, hop on the parallel SS26, which winds through villages and suburbs but takes a good hour.

Drinking with the Best of Them

€ **Caffè della Posta** (Via Roma 51; ☎ 0165-842272; www.caffedellaposta.it) is Courmayeur's most popular spot for an après-ski grog. Since it opened more than 100 years ago, it has been welcoming the famous and not so famous into its series of cozy rooms with a fire roaring in the open hearth.

The villages themselves are tiny and walkable.

The **tourist office** in Courmayeur (Piazzale Monte Bianco 8; ☎ 0165-842060 or 0165-842072; www.regione.vda.it/turismo), provides information on hiking, skiing, and other outdoor activities in the region, as well as hotel and restaurant listings (though note that in the off-season periods of Dec 1–24 and Jan 7 to late Apr, it's open only Sat–Sun).

ACCOMMODATIONS AROUND MONTE BIANCO

€€–€€€   **La Grange** ★★ (C.P. 75, 11013 Courmayeur-Entrèves; ☎ 0165-869733, off season ☎ 335-6463533; www.lagrange-it.com; AE, MC, V; closed May–June and Oct–Nov) may well be the most charming hotel in the Valle d'Aosta. This converted barn in the bucolic village of Entrèves is ably managed by Bruna Berthold. None of the rooms are the same, though all are decorated with pleasing antique and rustic furnishings; some have balconies overlooking Mont Blanc,

---

Schussing the Slopes

Recreation draws many people to the Valle d'Aosta—hiking in summer, sure, but especially the skiing. You'll find some of the best downhill skiing and facilities at Courmayeur, Breuil-Cervínia (the Italian side of the Matterhorn, here called Monte Cervino), and in the Valle di Cogne/Gran Paradiso. Ski season starts in late November/early December and runs through April, if the snow holds out, reaching its height mid-January through mid-March.

At Courmayeur/Monte Bianco expect to pay 35€ to 41€ for daily lift passes, depending on the season. Breuil-Cervínia is slightly less expensive, at 24€ to 33€ per day. Cogne is the bargain at 20€ per day. Multiday passes, providing access to lifts and slopes of the entire valley, run 106€ for 3 days, 138€ for 4 days, and so on, with per-day rates on a sliding scale that end up at 14 days for 375€.

One money-saving option is to take one of the Settimane Bianche (White Week) packages—room and board and unlimited skiing—available at resorts throughout the Valle d'Aosta; such packages cost around 300€ to 600€ at a midrange hotel. You can find lists of them at www.regione.vda. it/turismo (though, frankly, the Italian-language version is easier to use for this; just click on "L'inverno" on the left menu to get to the winter section, then "Settimane Bianche" and you'll get a clickable map; the rest is easy).

Cross-country skiing is superb around Cogne in the Parco Nazionale del Gran Paradiso, where there are more than 48km (30 miles) of trails.

For more skiing info, call ☎ 0165-238871 or go to www.skivallee.it. For more on all sorts of outdoor activities in the region, contact the tourist boards of **Aosta** (☎ 0165-236627; www.regione.vda.it/turismo), **Breuil-Cervínia** (☎ 0166-949136; www.montecervino.it or www.cervinia. it), and **Cogne** (☎ 0165-74040; www.cogne.org).

Mont Blanc Hours & Prices

Hours for the Monte Bianco/Mont Blanc cable cars vary wildly, and service can be affected by weather conditions (winds often close the gondola between Helbronner and Aiguille du Midi). In theory, the cable cars run roughly every 20 minutes. For a report of weather at the top and on the other side, dial ☎ 0165-89961 or go to www.fondazionemontagnasicura.org or www.ohm-chamonix.com.

Now for the hours (deep breath): June 1 to 29 and August 27 to November 4, the cable car's first run up is at 8:30am, last run down is at 4:30pm; June 30 to July 13 and August 20 to 26, hours are 8am to 5pm; July 14 to August 19 it's 7:30am to 5pm; November 5 to May 31 hours are 8:30am to 12:40pm and 2 to 4:30pm. That's just from the base station at La Plaud up to Punto Helbronner. The Hellbronner–Aiguille du Midi gondola is only open June through late September.

When it comes to prices, there are infinite variations depending on time of year and whether you alight at intermediate stations to walk part of the way, but I'll focus on the basic trip: La Palud–Punta Helbronner–Aiguille du Midi.

The ride from La Palud to Punta Helbronner costs 33€ round-trip, or 91€ for the family pass (two adults and two kids ages 4–15). In high season (approx. June 23–Sept 4; precise dates vary each year), the family ticket rises to 100€. From Helbronner to Aiguille du Midi, you must buy tickets at Helbronner for an additional 17€.

To continue all the way from Helbronner to Chamonix in France costs 45€ *each way*—which is why it makes more sense to buy the 87€ "Trans Mont Blanc" tickets at La Palud, which includes all five cable car rides, from La Palud up over the top and back down to Chamonix, then a bus ride through the Mont Blanc tunnel back to Italy. Since the Punta Hellbronner–Aiguille du Midi stretch is closed in winter, this service only runs June through late September.

The system of discounts is also confusing. In summer, kids 5 to 11 get 50% off, kids 12 to 15 get 25% off, and adults over 60 get a 10% discount. In winter, kids 5 to 11 still get 50% off, but older kids pay full price, and for some reason the age for seniors rises to 65 (but the discount also rises, to 20% off).

---

which hovers over the property. The stucco-walled, stone-floored lobby is a fine place to relax, with couches around a corner hearth, a small bar area, and a prettily paneled room where the lavish buffet breakfast is laid out. There is an exercise room and a much-used sauna. The highest rates of 150€ for a double are only charged December 23 to January 6, January 27 to February 24, and March 16 to 23; otherwise doubles go for 100€ to 120€.

€€–€€€   In winter, the pine-paneled salons and cozy rooms of the chalet-style **Edelweiss** ★ (Via Marconi 42; ☎ 0165-841590; www.albergoedelweiss.it; AE, MC, V; closed at least May–June and Oct–Nov, sometimes a bit longer) attract a friendly international set of skiers. In summer, many Italian families spend a month or two at a time at this hotel, near the center of Courmayeur. The Roveyaz family extends a hearty welcome to all and provides modern mountain-style accommodations and free bikes (just a few; first come, first served). Many rooms—which range from 80€ to 140€, depending on the season—open onto terraces overlooking the mountains, and the nicest rooms are those on the top floor, tucked under the eaves. Note that, during ski season, they may fill up with guests staying for weeklong ski vacations, so the management may be less willing to rent you a room for just a night or two.

DINING FOR ALL TASTES

€€   I never expected to find fresh fish at the foot of Mont Blanc, but that's just what you can enjoy at a table in front of the hearth of cozy **Ristorante La Palud** (Strada la Palud 17; ☎ 0165-89169; Thurs–Tues noon–3:30pm and 7:30–10:30pm; AE, MC, V), in the little cable-car settlement just outside Entrèves. Seafood isn't the only option here at 1,290m (4,230 ft.), however. Plenty of Valdaostana specialties are on hand, and *primi* rarely cost more than 10€: mountain hams, creamy *polenta concia* (cooked with fontina cheese and butter) and, in season, *cervo* (venison). The best dessert is a selection of mountain cheeses. The wine list borrows heavily from neighboring Piemonte, but includes some local vintages.

Worth a Splurge

€€€€   It's expensive, but I consider the **Maison de Filippo** ★★ (Loc. Entrèves; ☎ 0165-869797; www.lamaison.com; Wed–Mon 12:30–2:30pm and 7:30–10:30pm; MC, V; closed June and Oct to early Dec), in Entrèves, to be among the top 10 restaurants in all of Italy. Yes, it's "just" rib-sticking mountain food created from traditional local recipes and not some fancy-schmancy nouveau fusion menu, but the true gourmand will value these perfectly executed classics more highly than even the best modern flights of culinary fantasy. Dinner, an endless parade of Valdaostana dishes, is so generous you may not be able to eat again for a week—which more than makes up for the steep 45€ price tag. Daily menus vary but often include an *antipasto* of mountain hams and salamis, a selection of pastas filled with wild mushrooms and topped with fontina and other local cheeses, and a sampling of fresh trout and game in season. Service is casual and friendly. In summer you can choose between a table in the delightfully converted barnlike structure or on the flowery terrace. Reserve far, far in advance.

ACROSS MONT BLANC BY CABLE CAR

One of the Valle d'Aosta's best experiences is to ride the series of **cable cars** (☎ 0165-89925; www.montebianco.com; see "Monte Bianco Hours & Prices," for the ridiculously complicated practical details) from La Palud, just above Entrèves (10 min. from Courmayeur on hourly buses), across Mont Blanc to several ski stations in Italy and France, and finally down into Chamonix, France.

You make the trip in stages—first past two intermediate stops to the last aerie on Italian soil, Punta Helbronner (20 min. each way). At 3,300m (11,000 ft.), this ice-clad lookout provides stunning views of the Mont Blanc glaciers, the Matterhorn, and other peaks looming in the distance. (In summer, you may want to hop off at Pavillion Frety, before you get to Punta Helbronner, and tour a pleasant botanic garden, **Giardino Alpino Saussurea;** daily June 24–Sept 30.)

For sheer drama, continue from Punta Helbronner to Aiguille du Midi in France dangling in a tiny gondola more than 2,300m (7,544 ft.) above the Géant Glacier and the Vallée Blanche (30 min.). From Aiguille du Midi you can descend over more glaciers and dramatic valleys on the French flank of Mont Blanc to the resort town of Chamonix (50 min.).

11 The Cinque Terre, the Portofino Promontory & Genoa

The impossibly romantic northwest of Italy

by Pippa de Bruyn

MOTHER NATURE WAS KIND TO ITALY, BUT IN LIGURIA HER GENEROSITY knew no bounds. The coastline forms a graceful arc, rising sharply into the foothills of the Appenines, affording dizzying views of the sea that laps its shores. West, toward the French Riviera, is the Riviera di Ponente, its crescent-shaped bays and sandy beaches spawning a seemingly endless string of resort towns, including the grand old dowager San Remo. East, toward the Tuscan coast, lies the Riviera di Levante, home to the glamorous Portofino promontory and the medieval villages that cling to the jagged cliffs and terraced vineyards of the famous Cinque Terre.

It is this eastern stretch of shore, a mere 2- to 3-hour drive from Florence and Milan, that is the Ligurian coastline at its finest, its precipitous slopes punctuated by hidden inlets and rocky coves, where boats bob and ancient abbeys cluster. It's grand hiking country, but even the sedentary can enjoy the rural scenes come harvest time, when weather-beaten old-timers bent double under sacks of grapes trudge down to their timeless *garagiste* cellars, and fishing boats come in with fresh fish destined for seaview restaurants that epitomize the lazy, languid idea of romantic Italy.

Of course, the Cinque Terre is no well-kept secret. During the summer and early fall the five medieval villages and their stunning cliff paths swarm with tourists, and you need to plan your time and location quite carefully. Nor does this region offer the type of really important art and architecture that abounds in the hill towns of Tuscany, or Rome and Venice. But these are small quibbles when you're there, hiking the hills with their jaw-dropping views, or walking the cobblestone streets, stopping for fresh focaccia slices, washed down with the local wine. There's good reason why this ancient land has become one of the top honeymoon destinations in all of Italy: So much of what you experience here is impossibly romantic, with exquisite vistas around nearly every corner.

And if the tourist crowds get too much, there is (a brief train trip away from the Cinque Terre and Portofino) that oft-forgotten seafaring giant, Genoa: Among Italy's most tangibly atmospheric cities, this is where you go to get lost in an endless theater of intriguing local characters—trendy go-getters alongside modern-day pirates—playing out their daily dramas against a sublime backdrop of stunning architecture in a mysterious maze of eerie alleyways and sumptuous boulevards.

DON'T LEAVE THE LIGURIAN COAST WITHOUT . . .

TOASTING THE SETTING SUN WITH GOLD   The Riviera di Levante is famous for its sunsets, and justifiably so. Not only do its sheer cliffs afford huge, humbling views of this blazing show but they also produce one of Italy's most delicious wines—the much-vaunted golden Sciacchetrà—a perfect match to toast the sinking sun.

GETTING LOST IN GENOA   It's been 160 years since Charles Dickens enthused on the wonders of losing yourself in the labyrinth of Europe's largest preserved medieval city, but it is still enthralling. Set aside a day to explore this fascinating honeycomb of narrow lanes, and simply wander at will.

PICNICKING IN THE PARKS   Among my most memorable meals are Ligurian picnics, with fresh (and cheap!) ingredients culled from the delis and *focaccerie* that line the main street of every village. In Portofino, you can picnic on stone benches in the shadow of a church; in Santa Margherita Ligure, in the gardens of a 17th-century villa overlooking the sea; and in the Cinque Terre, on the private terrace of your rented apartment or hotel.

HAVING YOUR SEAFOOD ON THE ROCKS   There's something deeply satisfying about eating seafood while gazing into the azure depths of the sea—especially when you're so close you can hear the breakers. Many Riviera restaurants offer this pleasure, but three personal favorites are Trattoria dö Spadin (Punta Chiappa; p. 479), La Camogliese (Camogli; p. 478) and Santa Chiara (Genoa; p. 490).

THE CINQUE TERRE NATIONAL PARK

The Cinque Terre has a long history—an amphora bearing its ancient name was discovered in the ruins of Pompeii—but this sleepy land of gravity-defying vineyards and intact medieval villages catapulted into the global spotlight only after it was declared a UNESCO World Heritage Site in 1997. The past decade has brought an unprecedented growth in tourism, and the Cinque Terre (pronounced "*Chink*-weh *Teh*-reh," literally meaning "Five Lands") is today one of northern Italy's top draws, with September bringing hordes of hikers flourishing walking poles, while June and August find the villages jam-packed with Italian families.

Even if this is your first visit here, it's not hard to discover the reasons for its popularity. Walk along a cliff pathway and the stupendous view of clear blue waters will stop you in your tracks. Above and below are the terraced vineyards that cascade like hooped petticoats down the mountains, supported

> **There is nothing in Italy more beautiful to me than the coast between Genoa and La Spezia.**
> —Charles Dickens, 1845

by mile upon mile of dry stone walling—a backbreaking feat that took over a millennia to create.

Across the bay, tiny villages cling to jagged cliffs like medieval building blocks. And when evening falls, there is still one more impressive show—the sinking sun turns the sea into a cauldron of gold.

The principal activity in the Cinque Terre is hiking, but the evening is my favorite part of the day: settling down to a hearty meal in town and, later, having the tangle of romantically lit medieval *caruggi* (alleyways) at my disposal.

LAY OF THE LAND

The Cinque Terre was founded in the early Middle Ages, after the ever-present threat of Saracen pirates had finally dwindled, and each village still retains a distinctive character, even though now it's only a few minutes by train from one village to another. You'll want to settle on one before leaving home (not least because, having dragged your luggage up steep hills and then lugged it up six flights of stairs, you're unlikely to want to move again). Ask any group of travelers which of the five villages makes the best base and you're likely to get five different answers. To me, the village you choose is less important than whether you can bag a room with a terrace or balcony, preferably with a table and chairs overlooking the sea. Of course, in peak season you may have to take whatever you can get.

Given the torturous roads and lack of adequate parking facilities (a privilege for which you also have to pay around 12€ per day), the Cinque Terre is best accessed by train. Trains run the length of the coast from dawn to around midnight once or twice an hour. Genoa, home to the closest international airport, lies 70 to 90 minutes west by train; La Spezia, the eastern gateway, can be reached in a mere 10 to 20 minutes. (Incidentally, Florence lies about 2 hr. away via La Spezia—and a midmorning intercity connection costs as little as 7.50€.) A fun way to get here is by boat—ferries ply the waters from as far afield as the Tuscan Archipelago in peak season (July–Aug), but there are regular trips running from Portovenere and the Portofino promontory from Easter to the end of October (for contact details, see "Getting Around," below).

Travel between the villages is also easiest and quickest by train (it takes about 5 min. to go from one village to another); a ticket costs 1.10€ (weekdays) or 1.20€ (weekends), and is valid for 6 hours, so you can use it more than once to get between the villages during this time (don't forget to validate it before travel at the yellow machines posted at stations).

But because most of the journey is through the mountains, this is not the most scenic way to travel, so plan to incorporate at least one **boat** trip into your itinerary (it takes 25–120 min. to walk between villages; see below). Boats working the water on this stretch of coast include those of the **Consorzio Marittimo Turistico "5 Terre Golfo dei Poeti"** (☎ 0187-732987 or 0187-818440; www. navigazionegolfodeipoeti.it); in summer they usually run from Riomaggiore from 9:25am (from Monterosso at 10:30am) till 5:45pm; there is no service from November to March. You can purchase a ticket from Monterosso to Riomaggiore (or Manarola) for 8€; round-trip is 12€. The cheapest run is between Monterosso and Vernazza, at 3.50€ (6€ round-trip). You can also purchase a daily ticket, good for any and all trips linking Riomaggiore, Manarola, Vernazza,

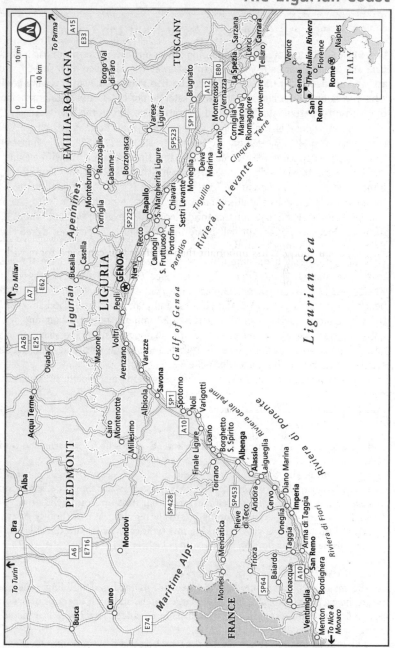

Peace & Quiet . . . Away from the Crowds

Levanto and **Bonnasola** are neighboring towns on the western outskirts of the park and a smart option if you want to get away from it all in high season; both are well connected by train and boat to the five villages. **Levanto** is larger, with a hard-working tourist bureau and a wide selection of hotels and restaurants, most of which offer better value than nearby Monterosso. But in the beauty stakes the hands-down winner is the tranquil seaside village of **Bonnasola**, where **Villa Belvedere** ★★★ (Via Ammiraglio Serra 33; ☎ 018-813622; www.bonnasola hotelvillabelvedere.com; AE, DC, MC, V) is a real find. Set on a hill with expansive views over the town's wide, gorgeous sandy beach (you won't find anything this tranquil near water in the Cinque Terre), the hotel is a haven of good taste, featuring sensible antiques and all-round good comfort. A double suite with balcony and sea view (ask for one on the third floor; no elevator) will run you 115€ including breakfast, 154€ for half-board during August. Arrange for a free shuttle to pick you up from the train station. The Villa owners, Barbara and Vincenzo (who are effortlessly goodhearted in their professionalism), also have the best-located restaurant in the Cinque Terre, **L'Antica Guetta** ★★★ (Via Marconi 1; ☎ 0187-813797; Thurs–Tues 12:30–2pm and 7:30–9:30pm), which is right on the beach. Wear a swimsuit under your clothes, and plan a lazy afternoon soaking up the sun. L'Antica Guetta is worth the 10- to 20-minute train trip from any of the villages; start with the mixed *antipasto* seafood platter (steamed scampi, anchovies in a zesty lemon sauce, swordfish and salmon carpaccio, and octopus salad; 14€), and you'll be back for more.

A mild warning: Bonnasola is on the verge of being discovered, so get in there now.

---

and Monterosso, and costing 13€; there's a 1€ discount for an afternoon-only ticket.

Travel within the villages is only possible on foot—easy enough, given their tiny size. Almost all tourist services—ATMs, grocers, wine shops, delis, and various eateries—are strung along the main street that runs up from each harbor. The park also has methane buses running relatively regular services (hourly or twice hourly) from the villages via the parking lots (you can't drive into the villages) up to the hillside hamlets dotting the coastline. Tickets range from 1.50€ to 2.50€.

ACCOMMODATIONS & DINING

As the majority of accommodations listed are in medieval buildings, there are (with the exception of Monterosso) no large hotels, and each operator offers only a handful of rooms—often booked months in advance. That's why I've included a fairly numerous selection.

The following discussion includes the very best available accommodations village by village, and the top dining choices in each. Given the tiny size of the villages, there are an amazing number of restaurants to choose from, but with few

exceptions, all share almost identical menus (as do almost all restaurants on the Ligurian coast). Pesto is featured without fail, as is every conceivable combination of seafood. It is virtually impossible to have a truly bad meal here, so stroll around the village and survey all the options before making a choice. While dining in the Cinque Terre is by no means prohibitively expensive, it's not cheap, either; be prepared for 8€ to 16€ for a *primo* course, plus a 2€ to 3€ *coperto,* or cover charge. If you're willing to shell out a little more on a top meal, dine at the costlier of my recommendations and make up the difference with plenty of picnics (see "Delicious. Cheap. Local. Making Meals from the Village Deli," on p. 471).

Riomaggiore

The prolonged, and I would argue, unchecked, incursion of tourists has impacted quite strongly on this village, which is also the principal headquarters of the Park authorities, and the main point of arrival for many (and I mean *many*) visitors who traipse in annually to walk the trails and plunder the souvenir shops for ridiculous memorabilia. It also seems to appeal to a younger crowd, probably because it also has the best-value accommodations in the Cinque Terre, with a handful of very good agents managing privately owned holiday apartments. This

Before You Book

Before the tourist explosion that hit the Cinque Terre at the end of the '90s, most visitors would plan only an overnight stay and then very much regret that decision. Since 2000, though, the average stay has increased to 3 nights. You'll likely want that much time, too—it's only after sundown that the villages empty of day-trippers and you can wander the fascinating caruggi alone, or sit in the shadows beside the old-timers as they gossip about the day. Three nights also gives you the opportunity to tackle two different hikes, and time to relax along the way. Some questions to ask before booking:

What type of lodging should I seek?   You'll come across three types of accommodations in this region: hotels, B&Bs, and *affittacamere* (rooms for rent). The truth is that there's no difference between the three in price (in fact, these towns are so small that when one lodging raises or lowers a rate, all of its neighbors tend to follow suit). And there's very little difference in terms of visitor experience. Outside of Monterosso, many of the places that bill themselves as hotels are actually more like well-run B&Bs—sometimes without the breakfast. Family operated, they are perfectly comfortable (despite their tiny rooms) and scrupulously clean, but with absolutely no facilities. You'll rarely have air-conditioning, a television, or a bathtub, not to mention much space or soundproofing. Most B&Bs are as efficiently run as these so-called hotels, but have perhaps one or two fewer rooms. Affittacamere have much the same look, but may give you a smidgen more privacy—they tend to be self-contained units, with no other guest rooms in the building. Another advantage of affittacamere is that some come with kitchenettes for no additional cost.

Standards are high at all three, but for peace of mind, always look for the park's "Mark of Quality," a gray stone plaque placed prominently outside the building. All rooms that have earned this designation are also listed in the "Ospitalità nel Parco" booklet, found at any park outlet. Or

---

is the best village in which to find a small self-catering apartment, with a *terrazzo* from which to watch the passing parade, or a sea view to toast the sunset. It's also the place where you'll most likely hear the sounds of inebriated tourists roaming the main street at awkward hours of the morning.

The pickings for the budget-conscious traveler in Riomaggiore are rich indeed, with a broad selection of apartments and private rooms, well managed for their absentee landlords by the holiday-letting agents whose offices line Via Colombo. You can take a virtual tour of these rental agents by visiting www.emmeti.it; click on "Hotels-Accommodation," then "Liguria," then "Residences-Flats," and you'll see a list of options for Riomaggiore listed under "La Spezia and environs"; click on any of the five individual choices for details, rates, and photographs of what's on offer.

stick to the recommendations listed here. (Note that if breakfast is not included, every village has plenty of bar/cafes serving good cappuccino and fresh pastries every morning, and this can entail quite a savings.)

How do I go about making reservations? If a hotel won't respond to your e-mails or faxes, you should phone. Sometimes proprietors have a minimal understanding of English or—especially in the case of affitta-camere—are unwilling to hold a room too far in advance (too many bad experiences with people who don't turn up). If you don't mind traipsing around a bit, you might want to wait till you get here: You'll ultimately find a bed, but not the best room.

Must my room have a view? Given the popularity of the region in high season, it's worth booking well in advance if you want to bag a room with a terrace and/or a sea view—and given the beauty of the sunsets and the tiny size of most rooms, believe me, you do. Rooms with views usually cost the same as those without so, when reserving, always ask for a room with a balcony and sea view, and then double-check whether this is what you'll be getting before you hand over the cash (note also that many hoteliers won't guarantee a sea view for, say, 1 night, in case they get a longer booking for that particular room).

How far is it from the rail track? Because trains run all night, light sleepers should pick accommodations as far away from the rail tracks as possible. Many travelers don't realize how thin the walls can be, so pack earplugs if you're a light sleeper.

Are there discounts for paying in cash? If you are prepared to wait till you get here before finding a room, it's worth knowing that most people are happy to give a cash discount of 5% to 10% (for rentals longer than 1 night, of course).

€–€€€ Of these, the most efficient and helpful outfit by far is **Mar-Mar** ★ (Via Malborghetto 4; ☎ 0187-920932; www.5terre-marmar.com; cash only; closed Nov), not least because there's a good chance of getting a very helpful English voice on the other end of the line (California-born Amy is usually in the office, which is open daily 9am–5pm). E-mail your requirements (sea view and/or balcony, one or two bedrooms, equipped kitchen or kitchenette, dining room, and so on) and the response—often accompanied by photographs—comes with clear, truthful descriptions of what's available; 75€ will get you a sea-facing double with a terrace, while for 60€ you'll forgo the sea view, but still be in the historical center. Fancier apartments that sleep up to six go for as little as 120€. Besides its 35 unique flats, Mar-Mar has **dorm rooms** (20€ per person) with 24-hour access and well-equipped kitchens; these are actually large multibedded apartments, so lack the horrid institutional feel of most hostels (notably Manarola's rule-obsessed one). Mar-Mar also acts as an informal tourist bureau, putting guests in contact with organizers of wine-tasting events, kayak-rental agencies, scuba-diving outfits and the like, although you may find such assistance sluggish as their small office gets terribly crowded.

€€–€€€   If you'd prefer to have more hotel-like facilities, with breakfast thrown in, I have two recommendations. Both properties are situated a little way above the village center (out of earshot from the train but a bit of a schlep if you're burdened with heavy luggage and arriving by train). A stone's throw from the parking areas above the entrance to the town is the stalwart **Villa Argentina** ★ (Via A De Gasperi 170; ☎ 0187-920213; www.villargentina.com; cash only), a small hotel dressed up with artworks by one of the Cinque Terre's most respected artists (you'll see his murals all over Riomaggiore, in fact). Like most hotels in the Cinque Terre, the rooms (94€–130€ double), though nothing to write home about, are functional—book one with a sea-facing terrace and the view will more than make up for the dull decor.

€€€   Nearby **Residence Cinque Terre** ★★ (Via de Batté 67F; ☎ 0187-760538; www.cinqueterreresidence.it; MC, V) is the more modern complex (a rather good reinterpretation of the slim historic buildings in the heart of Riomaggiore). It is well maintained (with slate stone floors and relatively spacious bathrooms) and outfitted with modern conveniences; some units open onto private or semi-private terraces, and you can also get one with a kitchenette. It doesn't have the views of Villa Argentina (above), but offers excellent value (110€–120€ double; 140€ suite) and a more personal feel, with hands-on owners at your beck and call.

€€€   You'll find the main drag of this overtouristed town littered with over-priced fast-food dens hawking focaccia slices and sad-looking pizza squares. But don't despair. If you'd prefer something more akin to a memorable feast, and if seafood's your bent, there's only one place to be: right on Riomaggiore's harbor, at **La Lanterna** ★★ (☎ 0187-920589; daily noon–3pm and 7–10:30pm; AE, MC, V), where even the pickiest seafood lover will not find fault. *Primi* range between 7€ and 9€ (no *coperto;* tips are welcome) but splurge on the seafood *antipasto* (small 9.50€; large 12€). With eight or nine varieties of fish, each prepared differently, this is a great introduction to the coast's bounty. This place is tiny, so make reservations—particularly for a seat on the outdoor terrace (the tavernlike interior is claustrophobic).

€€   Both of the hotel choices above are within easy walking distance of Riomaggiore's best restaurant (and one of the best in the Cinque Terre): **Ripa del Sole** ★★★ (Via de Gasperi 282; ☎ 0187-920143; www.ripadelsole.it; Tues–Sun noon–2pm and 6:30–9:30pm; AE, DC, MC, V). It has lovely views from its terrace, service is unpretentious, and the food is superb. *Primi* dishes are typical of Ligurian kitchens; all cost 9.50€, while other fresh pasta dishes are 11€ (*coperto* 2.50€). With such decent value, this is probably the place to try fresh tagliatelle with lobster, or the gnocchi with scampi and white truffles. *Secondi* here are an especially good value—sea bass filet oven-cooked with potatoes and the region's famous Taggiasche olives (irritatingly, unpitted) is a mere 8€.

Manarola

Clinging to the stark gray crags above crashing breakers, Manarola is the village most exposed to the elements. It's also more isolated than neighboring Riomaggiore, a mere 20-minute stroll away but more than double that by car. With no natural harbor, fishing boats clutter the narrow streets, hoisted safely away from the frothy fingers of the sea by a crane. Behind the boats are convivial *trattorie* and *ristoranti* (friendlier than in smug Vernazza), packed to the brim with as many domestic as foreign tourists. Stroll to Punto Bonfiglio, the headland across the harbor, for lovely views of the village, or take the bus up to Volastra, the tiny rural hamlet set high above its seaside counterparts, and arguably the most tranquil place to base yourself in the entire Cinque Terre.

€–€€€   Located higher up than those recommended below, with great village and sea views, is Manarola's justifiably popular B&B, **La Toretta** ★★★ (Via Rollandi 58; ☎ 0187-920327; www.torrettas.com; AE, DC, MC, V). This is perhaps the place in the Cinque Terre with the most acute sense of taste and style, no doubt thanks to the efficient management of affable Gabriele Baldini, who ensures that guests enjoy a great breakfast on the terrace in the morning and organizes wine tastings in the evening. All rooms (50€–120€ for a standard double) open onto the requisite small terrace with sea views, and are outfitted with such niceties as CD players. He also has a student room with two single beds and private bathroom (from 35€ for two people), as well as more expensive suites, and apartments (50€–130€ double).

€€   Of Manarola's few designated hotels, the peaceful, family-run **Ca' D'Andrean** (Via Discovolo 10; ☎ 0187-920040; www.cadandrean.it; cash only), located in the heart of the old village in an old winery, offers the best service. Bright, comfortable, spartan double rooms, some with terraces, go for 70€ to 94€; breakfast is 6€ per person.

€€–€€€   Closer to the harbor, **Marina Piccola** ★ (Via Birolli 120; ☎ 0187-920103; www.hotelmarinapiccola.com; AE, DC, MC, V) enjoys a better location (albeit one that includes the noise of passing trains and hikers heading for the trail), with some rooms overlooking the sea—request a sea view and/or terrace or balcony; rooms vary considerably, but no. 10 is a particularly good choice. Doubles go for 115€. Next door, Marina Piccola is also the **best restaurant** in the village (Wed–Mon noon–3:30pm and 6:45–10:30pm; average *primo* 9€, *coperto* 2.50€), with tables right on the harbor; you'd do well to order the chalked-up fish of the day—particularly if it's *orata branzino,* which Corrada, the manager, believes is close to heaven. Reserve ahead. (Budget hunters may want to investigate the en suite room with private entrance just a little farther up from the Piccola's restaurant—you'll get the same sea view for around 65€. Contact Nella Capellini—who speaks limited English—at ☎ 0187-920135 or 3201-964550.)

€€   But for the best views in the entire Cinque Terre, head up to **Volastra** (buses run from Manarola almost every hour, 7am–9:30pm). Running to the east along Volastra's ridge are a few B&Bs worth looking into: **Ca'del Michelè** (Via Pasubio 58; ☎ 0187-760552; www.cadelmichele.com; MC, V) has four rooms, two with sea view; or ask for Patrizia at **Il Vigneto** (Via Pasubio 64; ☎ 0187-762053; www.ilvigneto5terre.com; MC, V) and request a sea view. Doubles at both properties run 60€ to 85€.

€€–€€€   Room no. 8 at **Albergo Luna Di Marzo** ★★ (Via Montello 387/c; ☎ 0187-920530; www.albergolunadimarzo.com; DC, MC, V) has the absolute best view in the park—book this top-floor corner unit with large terrace immediately (110€ double). A custom-built hotel, Luna Di Marzo enjoys an extraordinary position on the edge of the village, with distant views of tiny Manarola and Corniglia, and a horizon so big it curves at the edges. Accommodations, outfitted with the usual bland, mass-produced furniture and fittings, are the most spacious in the region, and most cost 95€ (but if it's available don't think twice before spending the mere 15€ extra required for room no. 8 and plan to have at least one romantic candle-lit picnic on your private terrace; room nos. 5, 6, and 9 share the same stupendous views but with windows at waist height).

Corniglia ★

Perched some 100m (328 ft.) above the sea, with no harbor, Corniglia is the oldest of the five villages, and has spectacular views. For most visitors the main drawback is its location. But while it's a schlep to get up here if you've missed the (more or less) half-hourly shuttle from the station, once you arrive you'll enjoy the most splendid views in the region. After Volastra, Corniglia is the most peaceful of the villages, with the sound of passing trains muffled by tunnels way below. Corniglia also lays claim to the region's best beach, the nudist Guvano (reached by following the signs from the north side of the railway station; 3.50€).

€€   Corniglia has only one hotel, and it's among the most authentic (in the sense that your hosts have a real salt of the earth sensibility) and inexpensive options in the region: Pronounced "*Cheech*-io," the **Cecio** ★★ (Via Serra 58; ☎ 0187-812043; www.cecio5terre.com; MC, V, but cash preferred) lords it over gorgeous views of the sea and the village. It's small (only eight rooms), family-owned, and very laid-back—when you book, ask to speak to the manager (and self-proclaimed tiramisu maestro), Giacinto; he's the only one with a reasonable command of English (you can also call him on his cellphone at ☎ 3343-506637). For the best views, book room no. 3 (a great corner room), 2, 4, or 5; these will run you a mere 65€ for two people. You can picnic on the rooftop, enjoying almost 360-degree views. Cecio now also has a handful of rooms (half with sea views) in a building in the historical center.

€€   **La Terrazze Bed & Breakfast** ★ (Via Fieschi 102; ☎ 3498-459684; www.eterasse.it; cash only) is the classiest lodging in the village, not least because the two en suite rooms (double 95€) open onto the most delightful terraced garden (shared with an upstairs two-bedroom apartment), shaded with lemon and olive trees bedecked in candles and colored baubles. Oddly for a B&B, breakfast is 10€ extra.

€€–€€€ But, still the best restaurant in the heart of the village is quirky **Mananan** ★ (Via Fieschi 117; ☎ 0187-821166; Wed–Mon 12:45–2:30pm and 7:45–9:15pm; cash only). Owned by Agostino Galletti (who makes a most sublime ricotta-and-herb ravioli, topped with a walnut sauce), this authentic trattoria is housed in a cozy-and-cluttered 18th-century wine cellar. It's best to call ahead because Agostino doesn't open unless he's feeling up to it, and his menu changes according to daily whims. Prices vary greatly, but there's usually nothing on the messily chalked-up menu for over 15€; *coperto* is 2€.

Vernazza ★★

With a long harbor affording picture-perfect views of its bobbing boats, ruined 12th-century castle, Gothic church, and dinky town square, Vernazza is the most popular of the five villages, and understandably so although it's best at night and in the early morning, before the day-trippers arrive. It's almost as pretty as Portofino, and has seen little change in over a century. The only village with a natural harbor, it enjoyed a dominant position in regional trade and a natural sense of superiority; climb up to the top of the **Castle Tower** (1.50€) for spectacular views of it all. Vernazza's prominence is evident in the handsome detailing you'll see throughout the village, and in the high degree of civic pride. Its houses are immaculately kept, and carefully spaced trees line the main drag and pretty harbor piazza. However, it's totally insufferable in peak season—at least after 10:30am, when the ferry disgorges its first full load of visitors, topped off every hour by the train; the little sandy beach gets crowded quickly, with more sunbathers clinging to the rocks along the harbor walls. Thankfully things do settle down at night: The village's day-trippers leave, and you can wander its romantically lit alleyways and find a table at its harbor piazza. Some of the best dining is to be had in Vernazza, and it's worth eating here one evening, even if you're staying elsewhere (trains run well into the night). Accommodations consist of a large selection of mostly tiny rooms.

Vernazza has only three hotels, but these are not really different from the affittacamere (rooms for rent) lodgings everywhere, and a trained service culture is almost entirely lacking.

Be Aware of the Seasons

Peak season runs from mid-June to August, when the villages are packed with Italian families taking their annual holiday, and continues full steam into September, when hikers arrive in droves and the harvesting of grapes begins. Crowds are particularly evident on weekends, when day-trippers arrive from the landlocked hinterland. Easter and May are also busy times, but you're more likely to negotiate a discount then—at the very least, hoteliers are refreshed and ready to face the season with a friendlier face than at the tail end of an exhausting September. Many businesses close from November to March; others offer up to a 50% discount on lodgings and the like.

€–€€   An exception to the norm is **Albergo Barbara** ✦✦ (Albergo Barbara, Piazza Marconi 30; ☎ 0187-812398; www.albergobarbara.it; MC, V), which boasts friendly, professional service from husband-and-wife team Giuseppe and Patricia (whose excellent English and helpful advice are a bonus). It offers nine simple rooms, located on the top floors (there's no elevator) of a building right on Piazza Marconi, the main harbor square. The two en suite rooms with the most fantastic sea and harbor view (100€ double) are the best (and certainly worth the splurge), but the two double rooms in the attic (reached via a tiny twirling stairwell), which share a bathroom (each with in-room basin, and one with a gorgeous sea view), are an exceptional value at 50€ (of these, I stayed in room no. 3, with its low-pitched ceiling and the cutest little view of the harbor, and the dramatic Cinque Terre rock face plunging into the sea). In between, there are other affordable rooms with private bathrooms for 60€ to 65€.

€€–€€€   The longest-running hotelier is **Gianni Franzi** (Piazza G. Marconi 5; ☎ 0187-821003; www.giannifranzi.it; AE, DC, MC, V), with a range of rooms in two separate buildings a short but steep haul from his trattoria. Choose between the slightly larger rooms—with private bathrooms but no views (100€)—or the prettier rooms with sea views from the small Juliet-style balconies, but dank, shared bathrooms (80€). With some double rooms going for 65€ (shared bathroom, and no balcony), this is well-pitched value indeed, although in peak season you may need a minimum 2-night stay. Gianni also manages a few independently owned rooms scattered across town (if you can book "Stalin," you'll be perched on a seaside cliff and have the most stupendous view in Vernazza). Decor is generally a blend of hand-me-downs and antiques—a welcome break from the mass-produced chip and pine found elsewhere—but in 2008, several new, costlier rooms will be added to the inventory, and these will include air-conditioning and a few other "upscale" modern conveniences. Gianni's is a very efficient family-run organization with wife, Marisa, controlling the room inventory.

€–€€€   Of the myriad affittacamere available, look into the four studio-type apartments overlooking the harbor square (from the same block as Albergo Barbara) offered by **FrancaMaria** (☎ 0187-812002); during high season, these cost 75€ to 100€. One even has a small dining room and a kitchenette (110€ double); son Giovanni also has three rooms but these are poky. Make sure you're booking a room overlooking the Piazza Marconi. Alternatively, there are the four rooms (most overlooking Piazza Marconi) offered by **Martina Callo** (☎ 0187-812365 or 329-4355344; roomartina@supereva.it) for 50€ to 90€ (room no. 3, which has a terrace, is the one to go for here). There are also five rooms available from **Affitta Camera da Annamaria** (☎ 0187-821082) for 60€ to 90€; it's located on Via Carattino—again, ask for a room with a terrace. **Maria Taddei** (☎ 3474-977748; mflorisa@hotmail.com) has a small apartment overlooking Piazza Marconi for around 70€. Or contact **Tilde** (☎ 3392-989323); they have a studio with lovely sea view for a similar price.

€–€€   Need a break from the crowds and hankering for a taste of the Cinque Terre's finest pizza? Between Vernazza's harbor and train station, you find **Pizzeria da Ercole** ✦ (Via Visconti 34; ☎ 0187-812545; Thurs–Tues 10:30am–10:30pm;

cash only), where young, friendly guys serve up take-away pizza (available from noon), and robustly topped focaccia breads. If you have nowhere to picnic (or want to escape the tourists), step farther inside and onto their quiet, shaded terrace, where you'll be served with real vigor and a smile. Big bottles of chilled Moretti beer are 3€, and the wood-fired pizzas, made from scratch and dripping with delicious toppings, start at 6.50€. I feasted on a humungous wafer-light base smothered with Gorgonzola and mozzarella, and packed with flavorful shaved ham (*proscuitto crudo*) for a mere 7.50€; at dinner I was back for a similar pizza, this time with dollops of creamy mascarpone. Locals also tell me this is the perfect place for inexpensive roast meat dishes, and there's house wine available for 10€.

€–€€   In a town generally believed to have the region's best restaurants, Vernazza's oldest trattoria (almost 45 years now), owned by main man **Gianni Franzi** ★ (☎ 0187-821003; Thurs–Tues noon–3pm and 7–9pm; AE, DC, MC, V), is arguably the best place to test the theory—it's certainly the most attractive dining option in the village. And if you're tiring of the usual variations of seafood pasta (black spaghetti with prawn sauce is 13€), Gianni does a mean veal roast for a mere 8€. Then again, the maestro himself proclaims, "Our pesto is the best." Served with *trofie* pasta, it's 10€. *Coperto* is 2.50€; guests staying in one of Gianni's rooms get a 7% discount.

€–€€   You might want to climb the stairs to **Al Castello** ★ (☎ 0187-812296; Thurs–Tues noon–3pm and 7–10pm; cash only). Named after the castle (whose entrance is a few steps higher) where guards kept a look out for marauding pirates, this is a great luncheon refuge from the crowded harbor square, and at dinnertime, when the lights start to twinkle below, you'll feel as if you're floating. It's the same menu you'll see everywhere—with *primi* ranging between 5€ and 10€, and *coperto* coming in at 2€—but the seafood is good and fresh, and the view is certainly worth the climb.

Monterosso Al Mare

Monterosso is more resort than village, with two crowded sandy beaches and a plethora of accommodations options (it has the only real hotels in the Cinque Terre). In short, Monterosso has been entirely given over to tourism. It has facilities typical of the Riviera's resorts—beachfront bars and rows of umbrellas and beach chairs for hire. (Incidentally, there's free access to the beach only where you see no umbrellas.) Not surprisingly, there are fewer stairs and hills to negotiate here than in the rest of the Cinque Terre. In a region lacking "to-do" sites, it also has one of the few listed attractions: the 17th-century **Chiesa del Convento del Cappuccini,** perched on a hillock in the center of town. It's also worth taking a look in the adjacent **Church of San Francesco** to view the 17th-century van Dyck painting of the Crucifixion, as well as work by the prolific Ligurian artist Luca Cambiaso. The biggest drawback here is that, even when night falls, the voices you hear all around you are unlikely to be Italian, and the "new" residential part of town, west of the railway station, is ugly; make sure you book in the more charming historical center, accessed through a large tunnel (though to be sure, walking through here on a weekend feels like you're being processed through a sausage factory). Perhaps it's obvious, but I'd be remiss if I didn't say that Monterosso al Mare is my least favorite village in the Cinque Terre.

With Monterosso awash in three-star accommodations falling in the 100€-to-150€ category, and most of the one- and two-star hotel options offering very poor value, this is not a good base for budget hunters. So choose this "village" only if you really do want more hotel-like facilities, or if you're after a beach holiday (albeit one where you'll be sandwiched between many like-minded sardines).

€€   Well situated on the beachfront, but with no frills whatsoever (no breakfast, either), is the one-star **Agavi** (Via Fegina 30; ☎ 0187-817171; www.paginegialle.it/hotelagavi), a stone's throw east of the station (toward the historical center). What you do get is your key handed over by the sparkling owner, Hilary, who asks you to pay cash and to check in before noon, or risk losing your reservation. A sea-facing room costs 100€.

€€–€€€   The **Locanda Il Maestrale** ★ (Via Roma 37; ☎ 0187-817013; www.locandamaestrale.net; MC, V) is as close as Cinque Terre gets to a boutique hotel. On offer are only six rooms (100€–140€ for doubles; 130€–170€ for split-level junior suites) with some with lovely frescoed ceilings and stylish public rooms. It's run by a perky husband-and-wife team.

€€€   Two pricier beachfront options in the "new" (read: unattractive) part of town are **Hotel Baia** (Via Lungomare Fegina 88; ☎ 0187-817512; www.baiahotel.it; MC, V) and neighboring **La Spiaggia** (☎ 0187-817567; www.laspiaggiahotel.com; cash only), both on the beachfront road linking the station with the tunnel that leads to the old town. If you get a sea-facing room at Baia (where decor is a tad better; 110€–150€ double with breakfast), you'll more than likely tout Monterosso as the best of the Cinque Terre's villages (you will be wrong, of course). But don't stay if there are no seaview rooms left.

€€€   If there are no sea-facing rooms available in the beach hotels, your best bet in Monterosso is **Villa Steno** ★ (Via Roma 109; ☎ 0187-817354; www.pasini.com; MC, V). It's a modern building in a tranquil location above the old town; most rooms come with a private seaview balcony furnished with table and chairs, ready for the evening sundowner and picnic (the local supermarket is not too far away). While a double goes for 150€, there are also triples with a little garden, sea views, and loungers for 170€.

€€€   Down-to-earth **Albergo Marina** ★ (Via Buranco 40; ☎ 0187-817613; www.hotelmarinacinqueterre.it; MC, V) has bright rooms (all made over in recent years) with hardwood floors and furnishings done up with antique effects; rooms are almost pretty, but you should insist on a sea view (and preferably also opt for a superior unit, which gives you more space). There's a great personal atmosphere here, with the entire family (three generations) very hands-on (Marina herself was pawing over the 2007 winter renovation plans when I last visited), and the dinner—sometimes served in the roof garden—is a very good value if you go for the half-board option. Less personal is Marina's neighbor, **Albergo Amici** (Via Buranco 36; ☎ 0187-817544; www.hotelamici.it; MC, V), where the rooms are comparatively insipid (105€–132€ double, no breakfast), but the lemon-tree roof garden enjoys a magical view, over the historical center's rooftops; you can watch the church bells clanging in the foreground of the idyllic sea.

Delicious. Cheap. Local. Making Meals from the Village Deli

Invariably, one of the best meals that I have in the Cinque Terre is a picnic lunch composed of a few slices of *coppa di parma*, a small bunch of arugula, a plum tomato, a wedge of olive-studded focaccia, and a bottle of chilled Vermentino—all enjoyed on my private terrace overlooking the main street in Riomaggiore. Every village has at least two superb delis and/or *enotece* (wine bars), as well as tiny *focaccerie*, where wood-burning ovens churn out large squares of fresh focaccia. For best value in providing picnic fixings, head straight for one of the **Coop 5 Terre** shops located on the main streets of Riomaggiore, Manarola, and Vernazza.

For a picnic in Corniglia, you'll find the delightful **A Bütiega** at 142 Via Fieschi (the main lane). And Monterosso has plenty of shops, a few good bakeries, and a rather pricey supermarket.

€€€–€€€€   From the station and through the tunnel, immediately on your left, you'll find the only beachfront option in the historical part of town, located on what is often referred to as "fishermen's beach." All the rooms at **Hotel Pasquale** ✮✮ (Via Fegina 4; ☎ 0187-817550; www.pasini.com; AE, MC, V) have brilliant views, and although there are no balconies, you'll enjoy a sense of privilege opening your shuttered windows and gazing down over the beaches and nonstop pedestrian traffic. The hotel is ingeniously built right into the rock (with exposed boulders bulging through the walls of the stairway, here and there), and while furnishings are unspectacular and bathrooms miniscule, there's a high level of service that comes with a family's pride in a venture well done. At 150€ to 180€, it's still a rather good value, given that it's both beachfront and old town. My only qualm: When that train passes (which it does, often), you'll know all about it.

€   Possibly my favorite wining and dining spot in Monterosso is the village's oldest wine cellar, **Enoteca Internazionale** ✮ (Via Roma 62; ☎ 0187-817278; www.enotecainternazionale.com; daily 8:30am–11pm; DC, MC, V). The selection on its shelves is almost overwhelming (over 1,000 labels), so take a seat at one of the rustic timber tables outside and sample a few (2.50€–5€ per glass). But first line your stomach with fresh bruschetta (3€–6€); toppings range from the simple (slices of fresh tomato with whole basil leaves and olive oil) to the sublime (fresh anchovies marinated in lemon juice and topped with tomato, mozzarella, capers, and oregano). This is also the ideal place to sample a good Sciacchetrà (Cinque Terre's famed dessert wine; 7€)—order it with a side of bruschetta topped with Gorgonzola and candied fruit. Your quick lunch may just turn into an afternoon affair, but be sure to call hands-on owner-sommelier Susanna Barbieri over to your table; she's a font of information on wines from the region and across the country, and can help you select vintages to take home (also see

"The Other Cinque Terre," later in this chapter). This is a good place to pick up cheeses, attractively packaged jars of pesto, and Liguria's specialty pasta, *trofie.*

€€   Given its small size, Monterosso has a remarkable selection of traditional restaurants, but the hands-down winner is **Ciak La Lanterna** ★★ (Piazza Don Minzoni 6; ☎ 0187-817014; Thurs–Tues noon–2pm and 7:30–9:30pm, sometimes later; MC, V). Ciak excels not only with food (a bit of a splurge, with *coperto* at 3€ and *primi* around 13€) but also atmosphere. Pick a table inside and you'll be sandwiched among loud Italian families, around which waiters scurry like soldier ants to serve the hungry masses. The owners have made a point of warning me that reservations are essential. You're also required to book for a table at **Porto Roco** (☎ 0187-817502; 12:30–1:30pm and 7:30–9pm; MC, V), where you'll be treated to superb sea views from your table up on the headland jutting out above the path that leads to Vernazza. Of course, it's the seafood spread that's meant to be the big draw here, but I'm rather more impressed by the spectacular views, and the fact that the crowds are relatively far away. *Primi* dishes cost 9€ to 13€, but you could go wild at the seafood buffet, which starts at 17€.

WHY YOU'RE HERE: EXPLORING THE NATIONAL PARK

The Cinque Terre is crisscrossed with a network of well-marked trails (around 60). Some pass within leaping distance of the crystal-clear waters of the sea, some through cultivated terraces and the fragrant vegetation of the Mediterranean flora. All hikes are listed, together with the estimated times to complete each segment, in "The Park By Foot," which is available at the park offices. (Though not always in English, paths are clearly marked/numbered and can be used in conjunction with the advice set forth below.) **Park office headquarters** are in Riomaggiore (Via Telemaco Signorini 118; ☎ 0187-760000; www.parconazionale5terre.it).

By far the most popular trail is the **coastal "blue" path** (referred to as *sentiero azzuro,* or simply "no. 2") that links the five villages, and recognizable by the fact that it always seems to have people on it. To walk any stretch of the coastal blue path you have to purchase a Hiking Pass which costs a minimum of 5€ for a single day's worth of hiking (for details, variations, and combination tickets, see "The Cinque Terre Cards & Passes: A Stacked Deck?" below). If you wish to complete the full coastal walk (Riomaggiore to Monterosso), set aside an entire day (if you're reasonably fit it should take about 5 hr. without stops), and bear in mind that it's easier to walk from east to west—that is, to set off from Riomaggiore and end in Monterosso.

A less arduous plan is to **walk from Riomaggiore to Vernazza.** It's a 3-hour hike, which includes a 20-minute amble between Riomaggiore and Manarola, called the **dell Amore** (a name that is more evocative than the actual walk, considering the crush of hikers seemingly oblivious to the spatial constraints of some parts of the concrete footpath, sections of tunnel covered in unflattering graffiti, and even a cafe blaring lurid music along the way); a much more satisfying 45-minute stride between Manarola and Corniglia; and the final tiring but very rewarding 2-hour stretch from Corniglia to Vernazza. (The latter is the most attractive part, so if you have time for only one good walk, make it this leg.) From Vernazza, I suggest you catch the ferry to Monterosso (3.50€; one almost every hour), and then take the train back to your home base. But if you're fit and up for

The Cinque Terre Cards & Passes: A Stacked Deck?

In this heavily touristed region, not even walking comes free. In order to hike between the Cinque Terre towns on the most popular "blue" path, you'll be required to fork over a park entry fee; this **Hiking Pass** costs 5€ for a single day, 8€ for 2 days, 10€ for 3 days, or 20€ for an entire week; only kids under 4 get in free. You can buy the pass at any of the trail heads or park offices (and usually at train stations).

If you're planning a tremendous amount of backwardsing and forwardsing within the park, you might save a few euros by investing in a 1-, 2-, 3-, or 7-day **Cinque Terre Card** (8€, 14€, 19€, and 34€ respectively); this entitles you to unlimited train trips between La Spezia and Levanto, unlimited bus trips within the park, and unrestricted hiking access. Family passes are also available (20€ covers two adults and two children for a day, for example), while kids 4 to 12 pay half price. While this is a convenient way to get around (no standing in lines to purchase train tickets), it does not represent a real savings unless you're packing in a very full day with more than two train trips and additional activities, such as mountain biking (free for card holders), and plan to make use of Corniglia's shuttle bus (taking you from the station to the town and back; usually 1.50€ one-way or 2.50€ round-trip) and the elevator at Riomaggiore's train station. So, while you might need to work really hard to make the card translate into any meaningful savings, do take the time to make some calculations before purchasing one.

Cards can be purchased from any of the park offices (located at all the five village train stations as well as at La Spezia and Levanto, and must be validated at one of the yellow machines inside the stations.

---

it, do tackle the final stretch between Vernazza and Monterosso, generally considered to be the most challenging, with the undulating path taking another 2 hours. It's almost as rewarding as the Corniglia-Vernazza leg.

Walks That Include a Visit to the Sanctuaries

Like most of Liguria's coastal towns, the five villages all have sanctuaries built high up on the hillsides; it was to these that villagers would beat a hasty retreat when sighting the masts of pirates on the horizon. Time allowing, incorporate at least one of the Cinque Terre sanctuaries (also known as shrines) into your hiking program, of which the following two are especially recommended:

The **Sanctuary of Soviore,** located above Monterosso, is possibly the oldest place of worship in Liguria, with ruins and early records dating pilgrimages to this place way back in A.D. 740. Today the principal reason to make the 90-minute pilgrimage to the "new" 18th-century sanctuary is the view: On a clear day, you can see as far as Corsica and the Tuscan archipelago. To get here, either catch the bus that runs from Monterosso, or head up path no. 9 and then east along path no. 1. Descend back to the coast to visit the **Sanctuary of Reggio,** surrounded by century-old ilexes, before passing through vineyards and olive groves into Vernazza.

For even more awesome views, plan a trip up to the **Montenero Sanctuary.** A number of attractive paths lead there, but if your knees have seen better days, simply catch one of the buses that run from Riomaggiore to Biassa and ask to be dropped off at the closest point to the sanctuary; from here it is about 20 minutes up a footpath. As a place of refuge, the Montenero Sanctuary dates back to 1335, but today it is particularly popular with wedding parties, not least because the park authorities have opened a rather good *ristorante* in the vaulted 14th-century refectory; it also offers 15 (very spartan) cottages on the grounds, but with the mandatory 20-minute walk uphill with luggage, this is only for diehard hikers and solitude seekers. For restaurant or cottage bookings, call ☎ 0187-760528, or visit www.manario.it.

Alternatives for Exploring the Park

Another good way to get off the overburdened coastal track is to explore the higher routes on **mountain bike** (at press time, horseback riding in the park had been suspended, but do ask, just in case). There are also four well-marked **mountain-bike trails,** most of which start from the **Montenero Sanctuary** (☎ 0187-760528), where you can also rent the cycles and any other gear you may need (6€ for a full day; free with Cinque Terre Card).

Better still, get out your swimsuit and explore the translucent waters of this beautiful coastline. A dinghy should cost in the region of 70€ for 4 hours (fuel extra), or you can **rent a kayak** for 7€ to 12€ an hour (look for the rental signs at Riomaggiore harbor or at the sandy cove at Vernazza's harbor). Alternatively, **hire a boat** from **5 Terre Natura** (Via Magenta 1, Monterosso; ☎ 328-0155008; www.5terrenatura.com) and head out to explore the coastline and its hidden coves—perfect for **snorkeling** or remote sunbathing opportunities; you can get an affordable Zodiak, which you operate yourself, for 50€ per hour (or 150€ per day; one full tank of fuel included), or a 7m (24-ft.) boat with captain included for 100€ per hour (or 450€ for a maximum of 6 hr.). In either case, up to six passengers are allowed. It's also possible to dive in these parts. **Diving 5 Terre**

Tips to Avoid the Crush

Whatever hiking trail you choose, be prepared for columns of fellow walkers winding their way along the coast if you're here during September (or May, to a lesser extent), when the weather is optimal.

The only way to avoid the frustrating crush is to **start early**—sunrise if possible—and have breakfast in a village along the way. If you're not an early riser, **opt for one of the less popular paths;** generally, the higher up you go, the less traffic you'll come across, with the highest path (no. 1) virtually free of any hikers. Paths that lead east of Riomaggiore are also practically empty. Note that you needn't climb all the way to these higher routes; conserve your energy by catching a bus to one of the hillside hamlets—for example, from Manarola to Volastra, and then walk through vineyards along path no. 6d to the small settlement of Porciana before descending into Corniglia via path no. 7.

Eating on the Hoof: The National Park Restaurants

The Cinque Terre Park authorities run a number of restaurants and refreshment points situated on the hiking routes—you can reach these on foot, or simply catch one of the park buses in hillside hamlets. Most feature great views and offer simple fare typical of the region; for good value, try the fixed-price "hiker's meal," comprising a two-course meal—usually with fish—as well as dessert, a glass of red or white wine, water, and coffee). It's an excellent value given that the price (around 17€) includes the iniquitous *coperto* (if you order any items from the a la carte menu, however, the 2€ *coperto* will be charged). Note that if you book your lunch or dinner through one of the official park offices in advance, you'll get a 10% discount on your meal, so long as you have at least two courses; always call ahead if you're planning a serious meal, as opening times vary with the seasons and with the whims of the park authorities.

The following four refreshment points can be utilized as pit stops while hiking: The (least recommended) **Dell'Amore** (☎ 0187-921026; daily 8am–8pm; closed Jan–Feb; MC, V), located on Lovers Lane between Riomaggiore and Manarola. Second, located in the hills almost halfway between Corniglia and Vernazza, **San Bernardino** (☎ 0187-812548; daily 10am–10pm; MC, V) makes a perfect halfway break, with lovely views back to Corniglia. Third, **Montenero** (☎ 0187-760528; daily 10am–10pm; closed Dec–Feb; MC, V), the starting point to most mountain-bike trails and a number of walks, serves traditional meals in a vaulted, whitewashed 14th-century refectory. Finally, although not a hiking route stop-off, **Monesteroli** (☎ 0187-758214; opened on request only and reached by Biassa bus from Riomaggiore; MC, V) is one of the most attractive venues, with warm golden hues offset by avocado-green lampshades, and where you can enjoy a splendid *vista con mare* from the terrace in the evening.

(☎ 0187-920011; www.5terrediving.com), which operates out of Riomaggiore (they're based in the underbridge subway that takes you down to the harbor), rents out **snorkeling gear** (10€ per day), and will take you **scuba diving** for 60€, including equipment hire (35€ without equipment), and your second dive will be slightly cheaper.

THE OTHER CINQUE TERRE

One of the greatest challenges facing the Cinque Terre is the decline in full-time residents, and with an aging population, the Cinque Terre is in danger of losing its cultural traditions. Attending 11am **Sunday Mass with the villagers** in one of their Gothic-style churches (each sporting a beautifully carved marble rose window, proof that the villagers were turning a reasonable profit in the Middle Ages) is one of the best ways to experience an authentic slice of village life. Other times for Mass are as follows: 4pm on Saturday and Sunday (Riomaggiore and Vernazza); 5pm on Saturday (Manarola); 5:30pm on Saturday and Sunday, and 9am on Sunday (Monterosso).

Cinque Terre's park authorities run a series of guided tours showcasing **traditional activities** that will get you deeper into the spirit of the local culture. If you're interested in winemaking, consider going on the "Nature and Cultivated Terraces" tour; after visiting Manarola, you are taken for a walk through the nearby vineyards, introduced to one of the young local vintners who gives a short lesson on local grape cultivation, and finally, taken for a traditional lunch at Via dell'Amore restaurant. The guided tour costs 118€ per person for two people, but if there are six in the group, the price drops to 62€. Even better, if you'd like to return home with a local culinary skill, opt for "Cookery Lesson in Montenero," which begins with a walk up to the Montenero's Nostra Signora Sanctuary, where you are given a demonstration on **the traditional way to make pesto** (Liguria's most famous culinary export), and then enjoy the results in Montenero's 14th-century refectory, where its ristorante is located. The cost is 125€ per person (less if the group is larger), including lunch. All park tours (including those of guided hiking trails) run once a week on specified days only, and only July through October. The downside is that the chef delivering the cooking lesson only speaks Italian, so you'll need to factor in the cost of a translator, who will be organized by the park authorities. To learn more, contact David or Margaret at ☎ 0187-258690 or agenziaviaggi@parconazionale5terre.it.

Informal, fun, and likely to elate your taste buds, sommelier Susanna Barbieri—the owner of Monterosso's **Enoteca Internazionale** (p. 471), partially hidden behind the tallest trees on Via Roma—will conduct a **private wine tasting** for you at her wine bar at just about any time (daily 8:30am–11pm). She'll talk you through a selection of four (10€) or six (15€) wines and probably convince you that, if you've come to walk the Cinque Terre, you've come for the wrong reason!

THE PORTOFINO PROMONTORY

This pristine piece of coast, a jutting triangle that divides the Golfo Paradiso from the Golfo Tigullio, was a favored haunt of Hollywood stars and jet-set moguls in the 1950s, and its villages and towns still ooze the kind of sophisticated charm their cousins south of Genoa have long since sacrificed to mass-market tourism.

Portofino is glamorous. Its chichi boutiques hawk everything from Pucci to Picasso and socialites teeter along its cobblestone lanes in high heels. Neighboring **Santa Margherita Ligure,** on the other hand, is larger and less pedestrian-friendly, but has the slightly faded elegance of an aging Hollywood star—great bone structure and still beautiful. East of Santa Margherita, where the promontory joins the mainland, is the bustling harbor town of **Rapallo,** which has its fair share of Liberty-style (Art Nouveau) buildings and palm-lined promenades. But the encroachment of bland, modern structures now detracts from what must once have been the equal of Santa Margherita Ligure.

Of all the harbor-side settlements, my favorite is **Camogli,** a tiny fishing village that lies west of Santa Margherita, on the western flank of the promontory. Once mother to the legendary Mille Bianchi Velier (Thousand White Ships) that set sail from here, it's an unpretentious beauty with a pedestrian promenade that follows a pebble beach. Tall, narrow houses—decorated with restrained *trompe l'oeil* detailing and green shuttering—stand near the shore. It's a relatively undiscovered gem, with an excellent selection of good-value restaurants and hotels. Even the ferry trips (☎ 0185-772091; www.golfoparadiso.it) are significantly cheaper if taken from here. Come as a day-tripper, but if you regret not basing yourself here, you'll find suggested accommodations below.

LAY OF THE LAND

Like everywhere else on this stretch of coast, getting to **Camogli** and **Santa Margherita Ligure by train** is easy (and cheap): It takes about an hour to get here from Monterosso (3.90€–6.50€; 20–26 trains daily), and half that from Genoa (from 1.90€). Traveling by car can be tedious, with parking anywhere carrying a price tag that pushes up your daily hotel budget by as much as 30%. And that's if parking is available at all (don't make the mistake of parking illegally, a misdemeanor for which you'll pay 100€ in Portofino). If you want independence from public transport, it's better by far to hire a **scooter;** call **GM Motor Center Rent** (☎ 329-4066274; 40€–50€ per day).

From **Santa Margherita,** there is only one (narrow) road **into Portofino** (the southern tip of the triangle); the **bus** journey between the two takes about 15 minutes and costs 1.30€. You can also get there **by boat** (6€). Buses run with equal regularity for the same price between Santa Margherita and Rapallo.

Portofino can only be reached **by foot** (around 5 hr.) or **by boat** from Camogli (a very pleasurable journey with two possible stops along the way—the first at Punta Chiappa where there is a truly great trattoria, the second at the San Fruttuoso Abbey; see top sights below). To get between Camogli and Santa Margherita, you can either take the 10-minute train journey (runs hourly or twice hourly; 1.10€) or the more scenic 25-minute bus journey.

ACCOMMODATIONS & DINING

In addition to the hotels reviewed below, you can also stay at **Da Giovanni** (☎ 0185-770047; AE, MC, V) at the little beach hamlet of San Fruttuoso. While this is okay for an unspoiled experience of the Abbey, which is flooded with daytrippers until nightfall, you may have to pinch pennies elsewhere—accommodations (180€ double) are rather steep given that rooms (small) share bathrooms; bear in mind, however, that all meals are included.

Camogli

€–€€ For a most peaceful stay on the Ligurian coast, and for an array of good-value dining options, the pretty fishing village of Camogli can't be beat. If you don't mind a 5-minute walk to the beach, **Da Roberto** (Via S. Bartolomeo 27; ☎ 0185-774094 or 338-4533042; www.camogliroberto.it; cash only) offers two independent studios (50€–90€ double)—each with kitchen and washing machine—located in the olive groves behind town. Surrounded by trees, they offer a rural ambience (good for families), yet are minutes from the promenade action.

€€ On the other side of the harbor, is **Locanda Il Faro** (Via P. Schiaffino 116–118; ☎ 0185-771400; www.locandailfaro.it; MC, V), which is really a handful of rooms (some of them en suite) attached to a rather good **restaurant** (Wed–Mon 12:30–2pm and 7:30–10pm; *primi* 5€–7.50€; MC, V) run by the

Amendola family. Lodgings are exceptionally basic, and only to be considered if you can't get in elsewhere. Although it's not on the seafront, you can see the water from many of the rooms, so specifically request a sea view. Be prepared to fight off mosquitoes in summer, and breakfast doesn't get more bland than this (despite the credentials of the restaurant). En suite rooms cost between 70€ and 95€; others with private bathrooms (but down the hall) go for 60€ to 85€.

€€   Bargain hunters looking for a fantastic deal right near the beach should look no further than **La Camogliese** ★★ (Via Garibaldi 55; ☎ 0185-771402; www.lacamogliese.it; AE, MC, V), where rooms (87€–97€ double) are bright, exceptionally neat, and relatively spacious (there's even a small writing desk!), and someone is always on hand at reception to assist with queries. During a recent stay in one of the corner rooms (try for the one on the second floor, which has the best views), I was blessed with a view of the sea and the nearby beach; at night the sound of the pounding waves lulled me to sleep, while a wonderful breeze floated through the windows which I couldn't bring myself to close. Staff provided towels for the beach, and when I returned from sunbathing on the beach (just 1 min. away), I could hang my wet swimming gear beneath the window, just the way the locals do. The hotel also has five rooms with small balconies overlooking the stream that runs into the ocean. At breakfast—a fine little spread—guests who've been coming back for years greet one another like old friends.

€€–€€€€   If you have a little more money to burn, **Hotel Casmona** (Salita Pineto 13; ☎ 0185-7700156; www.casmona.com; AE, DC, MC, V), in a 19th-century seafront villa, enjoys the best location, right on Via Garibaldi, the seafront promenade. Almost all rooms boast idyllic sea views, with ordinary doubles running 85€ to 145€, and Superior units—with seaview terraces—for a rather reasonable upgrade price of 105€ to 165€.

€–€€   Setting foot in a restaurant in Camogli can be pricey; not only are *coperto* charges rather chilling, but somewhere there's a stupid rule saying that fresh seafood must be overpriced. But if you're saving up for that boat to San Fruttuoso, why not consider a take-away from tacky-looking **Ristorante la Moreia** (Via Garibaldi 103; ☎ 0185-776056; www.lamoreia.com; MC, V)—limited takeout deals include a choice of pizzas (6€–8€) and a memorable *tuffie al pesto* (just 5€), which can be combined with a salad to create a virtual feast for under 10€.

€–€€   Another money-saving option is an intimate (and seemingly always-packed) eatery tucked away at one end of Via Garibaldi, at the arch leading to the harbor; **Il Portico Spaghetteria** (☎ 0185-770254; www.ilporticodicamogli.it; MC, V) is a viable option with a wide range of sensibly priced pastas (*primi* dishes 6.50€–9€), freshly prepared by an honest, hardworking local lady.

€€–€€€€   But if you're up for a splurge, make it at lunchtime, when you must head for Via Garibaldi (the seafront promenade), where you'll find the most wonderful seafood restaurant in a tiny timber Swiss-style chalet cantilevered over Camogli's pebble beach. With great sea views, old-fashioned decor, and personal service (I once drank the proprietor's Vermentino wine choice, Il Monticello, for my entire trip), **La Camogliese** ★★ (Via Garibaldi 55; ☎ 0185-771086;

Waiter, Could You Order My Boat?

There is something wonderfully romantic about having to catch a boat to get to your restaurant table, something which **Trattoria La Cantina** (☎ 0185-772626) and **Da Giovanni** (☎ 0185-770047) have certainly capitalized on over the years. Both are fortunate enough to be located in the tiny village of San Fruttuoso, the latter enjoying the greater fame, but both play to packed houses. Lesser known, and even more stunningly situated, is **Trattoria dö Spadin** ★★★ (Punta Chiappa, you can't miss the sign as you approach; ☎ 0185-770624; Tues–Sun 12:30–3:30 pm and 7:30–10:30pm; MC, V). Though a meal here is pricey (*primi* around 15€; *coperto* 3€), it is classic *cucina povera*—simple, fresh, light, and delicious—but the cost undoubtedly has as much to do with the glorious location as it does with the fare (after all, a simple, flavorless panino on the beach at San Fruttuoso could cost you an exorbitant 6€). The restaurant faces Camogli and the entire Golfo Paradiso, and it's sandwiched between the startling blue sea, which crashes below your seat, and a tiny kitchen that looks like it's been styled for a cookbook on Riviera cuisine. Pack your swim gear, and, after coffee, wander down to the harbor and wade in the ocean. My idea of heaven. *Note:* Call ahead to reserve a table and check on opening times; credit cards are usually accepted, but take cash along just in case the machine or phone line goes on the fritz.

Thurs–Tues 12:30–2:30pm and 7:30–10:30pm; AE, DC, MC, V) is a lunch experience that evokes a Riviera holiday: a dreamy afternoon spent slurping up the most memorable seafood pasta. *Primi* dishes range from 8€ to 18€; *coperto* is 2.10€.

€€–€€€   Other top (not exactly inexpensive) Camogli picks are **Ristorante Rosa** ★★ (☎ 0185-773411; closed Tues, and Wed lunch) for superb sea bass and great sea views, tiny **Da Paolo** ★★★ (☎ 0185-773595; closed Mon) for seafood so fresh it's almost still moving (the owners have their own boat), and **La Cucina di Nonna Nina** ★★ (☎ 0185-773835) for traditional Ligurian cuisine. The latter is the place for pesto and very popular with the locals—make sure you book early or you'll end up in the plastic tent behind the actual restaurant. Count on spending upwards of 20€ at all three.

Santa Margherita Ligure

With a bustling, jet-set atmosphere, its bars and cafes buzzing with people (and the streets with cars and scooters), Santa Margherita Ligure is more glam-town than laid-back village. And it attracts the lion's share of tourists. You should definitely plan your reservations well in advance. For an additional dining option, see **à Crêuza du Giò** (p. 483).

€€–€€€   Run by one of Liguria's many eccentric and gruff hoteliers, the Liberty-style **Hotel Villa Anita** ★ 🧒 (Viale Minerva 25; ☎ 0185-286543;

www.hotelvillaanita.com; V) is my first choice in this price category, and with a small playground and outdoor table tennis, it's ideal for families. Tucked away in a tranquil neighborhood a few minutes' stroll from the seaside action (and town center), nothing much has changed since the Tarellas opened their doors 50 years ago—but that is precisely its charm. Ask for a room with a terrace or a balcony (room no. 4 is a good choice). Doubles range from 75€ to 105€.

€€–€€€ **Albergo Fasce** ✹ (Via Luigi Bozzo 3; ☎ 0185-286435; www.hotelfasce.it; AE, DC, MC, V) is clearly a labor of love for Aristede Fasce and his English wife, Jane, who've fashioned an exceptional little hotel with a relaxed ambience. Set in a busy residential neighborhood, you'll hear schoolchildren playing and housewives sorting out their families for the day. Besides the spruce, light-filled accommodations—all spotlessly white with red trim, good bathrooms (with plenty of hot water and powerful showers), flatscreen TVs, and even tea- and coffeemakers—the Fasces offer great breakfasts (Aristede prepares your bacon and eggs), bicycles, and a laundry service. You can even sunbathe on the rooftop terrace, or try for one of the rooms with its own balcony. But, aside from welcome amenities, it's the old-fashioned welcoming attitude of the Fasces that will make this a memorable base from which to explore the Portofino Promontory. In the off season, prices often drop here to less than 100€ a night; expect to pay 115€ otherwise (though the owners have promised to give a rate of 111€ to anyone who flashes this guidebook).

€€–€€€€ Also recommended—largely for its close proximity to both the station and the seafront (100m/328 ft.)—is the ever-popular **Hotel Conte Verde** (Via Roma 9; ☎ 0185-287139; www.hotelconteverde.it; AE, MC, V). Every room is different in size (some are small) and individually decorated (although not necessarily design-conscious); if you are staying for more than 1 night, request a room with a terrace. You can borrow bicycles, and there are comfy public areas to catch your breath. Alessandro's rates start at 80€ (low season) and go up to 160€ for a double (reduced for 3-day stays).

€€€ The centrally located **Hotel Jolanda** ✹✹✹ (Via Luisito Costa 6; ☎ 0185-287512; www.hoteljolanda.it; AE, DC, MC, V) is a wonderful over-the-top creation of glamorous Miriam Pastine. Given the atmosphere of decadence and old-fashioned luxury (there's plenty of wood paneling and gilt mirrors), it's a very good value; opt for the Superior category, which are well priced from just 112€ for two (including breakfast taken on the peaceful terrace)—that's a mere 12€ more than you'll pay for a rather tiny standard unit (100€–138€ in high season). You might well splurge and add 20€ to 30€ more for a suite, where you'll feel like you've fallen into the lap of luxury.

€€–€€€ There are few surprises at **Il Faro** ✹ (Via Maragliano 24a; ☎ 0185-286867; Wed–Mon 12:15–3pm and 7:15–11pm; AE, DC, MC, V), with all the usual suspects typical of Ligurian fare, and plenty of seafood. But locals regularly remind me that this is *the* place to come for down-to-earth traditional dining, and the three-course menu at 25€ is a real bargain; there's also no *coperto* charged here, and you won't feel constantly compelled to order more and more courses. Also good for a reasonably priced lunch menu is **Ristorante Antonio** (Piazza San

Bernardo 6; ☎ 0185-289047; Tues–Sun noon–2:30pm and 7–10:30pm; MC, V); for 16€ you get a choice of pasta *primi*, followed by veal escalopes, baked fish, or fried calamari; usually you'll also need to spend 2€ *coperto* and pay 10% service. **Trattoria Cesarina** (Via Mameli 2/C; ☎ 0185-286059; Wed–Mon 12:30–2:30pm and 7:30–11pm; MC, V) is another regularly lauded restaurant—Fabrizio changes his small menu almost daily, depending on his mood and what's available at the market; *primi* here usually range between 12€ and 15€.

€€€ Santa Margherita is also where the most creative cooking is happening: Head for stalwart **Piccolo Ristorante Ardiciocca** ✦✦ (Via Maragliano 17; ☎ 0185-281312; www.ardiciocca.it; Tues–Sun noon–2:30pm and 8pm–late; AE, DC, MC, V), and you'll be stumped with a choice of intriguing combinations (a recent menu featured red mullet ravioli with wild fennel, lemon risotto with *provola* cheese, and spaghetti with sea urchins) as well as more predictably delicious selections—salt-cooked sea bass cooked with lemon leaves. Count on spending at least 14€ at the Artichoke, before a sip of wine.

Portofino

This postcard-perfect village is *the* place for people-watching, and while you could settle for just doing dinner here (a far more convivial affair than lunch), it's rather marvelous to wander from the gorgeous harbor (where most restaurants are) to your own bed without having to worry about bus or ferry schedules. Portofino isn't cheap, but this is your chance to overnight in one of the prettiest places on earth, along with the privileged few bobbing in the bay. If you want to picnic in Portofino, head up to **Chiesa di San Giorgio** and settle on the stone benches that line the church wall facing the Golfo Paradiso—there's a little fresh-produce shop on the staircase that leads up to the church (or you can take your pick from the deli in Via Roma).

€€€–€€€€ Your best bet—particularly if you avoid the high season—is to book yourself into **Hotel Eden** (Via Dritto 18; ☎ 0185-269091; www.hoteleden portofino.com; AE, MC, V), which has doubles starting at 150€ (going all the way up to 280€ during high-demand periods), and which is a few strides from the harbor.

€ You can avoid paying for a seat in one of Portofino's wallet-stinging eateries by popping in to **Canale Panificio Pasticceria** (Via Roma 30; ☎ 0185-269248; daily 8am–7:30pm; cash only), which has long been serving up slices of focaccia (plain, salted, or infused with olives or other herbs and flavors), salted breads, and a range of gleaming pastries; you pay for most of these by weight. There are also small pizzas for a mere 3€. Then venture over to the harbor (just meters away) and plunk yourself down on one of the benches where you can spend hours watching befuddled and enraptured pedestrians trying to decide where next to point their cameras.

€–€€ Given the astronomical prices featured on menus all around this billion-aire's playground, it'll surprise you to know that I once had one of my cheapest Italian meals in Portofino—a most delicious Stracchino cheese pizza for a mere 7€. **Pizzeria El Portico** ✦✦ (Via Roma 21; ☎ 0185-269239; Wed–Mon noon–3pm and 7:30–11pm; cash only) is a few steps away from the harbor where the billionaires park their yachts, and yet everyone seems to know that this is where you can still get a really good deal (all pizzas 6€–8€, *primi* range from 8€–13€). *Coperto* is 2.50€, but that gives you a ringside seat right opposite the Pucci shop, so you can watch (as I did) middle-aged socialites parade in Pucci cat-suits for their bored husbands while the butler waits outside.

WHY YOU'RE HERE: THE TOP SIGHTS & ATTRACTIONS

The **Abbey of San Fruttuoso** (☎ 0185-772703; www.fondoambiente.it; 4.50€ no exhibition, 6€ with exhibition; May–Aug daily 10am–6pm, Mar and Oct Tues–Sun 10am–4pm, Apr and Sept Tues–Sun 10am–5pm, Dec–Feb only for holidays; closed Nov) is the oldest remnant of the Benedictine empire that flourished along this coast between the 13th and 18th centuries. Tucked away in a beautiful cove between Portofino and Camogli, this modest complex—built with money from the once-powerful Doria clan—was the heart of the Benedictine Order, with jurisdiction over some 10 churches, a few as far afield as Sardinia. But the real treasure lies in San Fruttuoso's bay. Seventeen meters (56 ft.) below the surface of the translucent water is *Il Cristo degli Abissi (Christ of the Abyss)* ★★★, his arms outstretched and eyes ever-imploring since being submerged here in 1954. On the last Saturday in July, garlands of flowers float down in memory of all those who have lost their lives at sea. You'd have to be made of stone not to be moved. You can either swim or dive out to the statue (**B&B Diving Centre;** ☎ 0185-772751; www.bbdiving.it), or hire the services of a fisherman and his boat (around 4€); it's 200m (656 ft.) from the shore.

Today San Fruttuoso is still only accessible by boat or on foot; sadly, that does not mean it isn't crowded with day-trippers who come in by the boatload. For the most atmospheric visit, try to get here early (9€ return from Camogli, with Golfo Paradiso); you can either join the hordes who rush in by boat and hang for a while before dashing off again, or, alternatively, you can settle into one of the seven rooms on offer at **Da Giovanni** (p. 477) and you can have it all to yourself in the evenings when the day-trippers finally leave.

Less visited but equally worthwhile is the Abbey of San Girolamo at **La Cervara** (Via Cervara 10; ☎ 0185-293139; www.cervara.it), situated high up on a headland east of Portofino village. It has beautiful sea views from the Belvedere Terrace, but the gardens are the real delight here, particularly the immaculately maintained Renaissance-style **Monumental Garden,** with box hedges pruned in rigid geometrical shapes. It's open only on the first and third Sunday of the month, and only with prebooked **guided tours** (☎ 800-652110; visite@cervara.it) commencing 10am, 11am, and noon.

If gardens are your thing, head for Santa Margherita's **Villa Durazzo** (☎ 0185-293135; free; daily summer 9am–7 or 8pm, winter 9am–5 or 6pm), clearly visible on the hill around which the town spreads. As romantic as it is salubrious, this is where Rod Stewart married model Penny Lancaster in June 2007, and while it's not essential that you enter the 17th-century villa (worthwhile only if you're not planning to see the palazzi in Genoa), the elevated and shady gardens, with their classical statues and pruned hedges, are a great place to enjoy a little peace and quiet, and an ideal spot for a picnic (although, technically, this is not allowed!). The views of the bay are lovely, and there are plenty of strategically placed park benches. Next to the gardens is the lovely **Chiesa San Giacomo;** it's worth checking out the baroque interior and the frescoed ceiling dripping with chandeliers, proof of Santa Margherita's time-tested relationship with wealthy patrons. *A tip for the peckish:* On the staircase alley that leads up to Villa Durazzo from Piazza Martiri della Libertà, you'll find **à Crêuza du Giò** (Salita S. Giacomo 4; ☎ 0185-280438), where the bearded Gio takes his ingredients very seriously and serves up focaccia slices (.80€–2.50€ for a piece sprinkled with Gorgonzola) and great pizza; he also stocks ice-cold beers (3€–5€).

A Few Good Walks

Having arrived in Portofino and finding very little to do, most people feel compelled to walk up to the 16th-century **Fortezza di San Giorgio,** or **Castello Brown** (named after Montague Yeats Brown, the 19th-c. British consul in Genoa who briefly owned it), and beyond to the **faro** (lighthouse) that marks the promontory tip. If it's a busy day, ditch this and head up one of the Portofino Park's trails.

Perhaps it's because most people in Portofino walk only when there's a luxury shop beckoning at the end, but the park trails are usually a great deal less congested than the Cinque Terre's, even in peak hiking season. All are well marked, and big intersections have maps showing the trail network. Park authorities have printed up a small guide detailing the different walks called "In the Promontory of Portofino Between Sea and Land," which gives some idea of the lay of the land, relative distances, and information about what you'll see or encounter along the way.

For a highly recommended, brisk 90-minute walk, follow **the trail from Portofino to San Fruttuoso** ✸✸; take the route via Pietre Strette (which has picnic tables), but be sure to take the less direct path (for more expansive views) via Base Zero. Another recommended route from Pietre Strette is to follow the level trail (marked with red triangles) to Semaforo Nuovo—the coastal views here are splendid. Double back to the intersection where a map shows you the descent to San Rocco and Punta Chiappa, where you can catch a well-deserved ferry home.

If you're the more rugged, adventurous hiker (and don't have a problem using chain ropes for part of your "walk"), consider the difficult but richly rewarding **walk from Camogli to San Fruttuoso by way of San Rocco** ✸✸✸; the route (marked by two solid red circles) hugs the coast almost all the way, affording frequent panoramic views of enchanting coves and the gorgeous coastline. You'll need decent hiking shoes and a steady constitution (no fear of heights); there are a few points where you feel like you're on the edge of a plunging cliff face. Allow 3 hours, and consider taking a boat back to Camogli (6.50€ one-way), or—if you've the strength left—continue on to Portofino, and then either grab a bus home, or use the ferry boat (9€).

THE OTHER PORTOFINO PROMONTORY

If you're frustrated by how few Ligurians speak English (and you will be), it's time to learn Italian. The focus of Genoa University's annual **summer school** (aimed predominantly at descendants of Ligurian immigrants) is designed to improve spoken Italian, with grammar courses pitched at four different proficiency levels, from beginner to advanced. It is also a crash course on Italian culture and history, with guest speakers from various faculties speaking on anything from Italian cinema and art to contemporary politics (in Italian, of course). While there is an entry exam, it is not necessary to be fluent in Italian (one woman I met could not speak a word when she first arrived, and was receiving one-on-one tutorials as a result). The course is usually scheduled for 5 weeks from mid-August until late-September at Villa Durazzo in Santa Margherita Ligure and costs 400€ (tuition and lunch included); basic lodgings can be arranged for 13€ to 15€ per night. For an application form, write to the **Segreteria del Centro Internazionale di Studi Italiani** (Palazzo dell'Università, Via Balbi 5, 16126 Genova; centrint@unige.it); for more information on the course, visit www.unige.it/centrint, or contact Patrizia Burley, one of the language teachers, at pburley@libero.it. In 2008, the course celebrates its 50th anniversary, so should entail an extra bit of fanfare.

GENOA

"Ever been to Marseilles? Well, Genoa is worse." This was a pretty standard response from the few people I knew who had actually been to Genoa before I made my first visit to the city. Which is why I was shocked to find myself wandering the narrow winding alleyways of its ancient heart—the largest preserved medieval center in Europe—totally enraptured. I marveled at the myriad tiny bustling shops, their shopkeepers seemingly unaware of the magnificence of their vaulted ceilings, frescoed alcoves, and marble pillars. How misinformed its detractors were! This was like stepping into a massive film set, an urban labyrinth designed for a scene from the Middle Ages, yet bizarrely with all the actors in 21st-century fashions.

The contrasts everywhere are extreme: Right next to the cafe, which looks just as it did when Verdi took his coffee here 150 years ago, a small furniture boutique showcases the best in modern Italian design; glamorous middle-age women, wearing chunky jewelry and dark shades, stride past veiled Muslim shopkeepers; and a few steps past gloomy lanes where prostitutes eye potential customers, a white-aproned fishmonger digs his fingers into a silver mountain of perfect *acciughe* (anchovies), the contents of his stall so fresh it smells of the sea. It's exotic, and best of all, this "secret, inward-looking casbah city" (as Renzo Piano, Genoa's celebrated architect, fondly describes it) is relatively undiscovered. All around you are the lilting sounds of Italian, with barely another tourist in sight. Given that its urban regeneration dates back a mere decade, it's simply a matter of time before this "Venice without water" joins the list of must-see destinations in Italy.

Beyond the labyrinthine *centro storico,* which abuts the Porto Antico (home to the largest aquarium in Europe), Genoa is not a conventionally attractive city. It has a large industrial sector leading to massive urban degeneration, and many of its hillsides are blighted by ugly apartment blocks dating from the 1960s. To get the most out of your stay (and, yes, Genoa definitely warrants a few nights), base yourself in the *centro storico* and confine yourself to exploring the many attractions that lie within this seductive medieval village—a virtual island within a city that sprawls 34km (21 miles) along the coast.

A BRIEF HISTORY OF GENOA

Genoa has always been a mercantile city. By A.D. 1000, Genoa was already minting its own money. Its power lay in its ability to dominate the Mediterranean, with superior boat-building skills and a ready army of mariners. The end of the medieval period saw a gradual waning in Genoa's maritime dominance, but the ruling oligarchy, made up of a few powerful families—headed in the mid–16th century by Admiral Andrea Doria, a naval genius—had by now diversified into banking and financing, and thrived on exploiting the political intrigues of the times. By loaning money to the various monarchs embroiled in imperialist wars, and charging a whopping 10% to 40% interest for the favor, Genoa, already impossibly wealthy, became the most glamorous city in Europe, so much so that the period between 1550 and 1650 became known as the "century of the Genoese," and the city as "La Superb" (The Proud).

> ❝ *Gold is born in the Americas, dies in Seville, and is buried in Genoa.* ❞
>
> —A popular 16th-century saying, referring to the power of the Genoese bankers of the time

But fortunes declined as emerging nations aggressively moved into the shrinking Mediterranean trade arena (sapped, ironically enough, by the discovery of Atlantic trade routes by Columbus, now one of Genoa's most famous sons, but forced at the time to turn to Spain to fund his ambitious journey). By the beginning of the 19th century, Genoa found itself stagnating economically, but politically it remained a hotbed of plot and intrigue. Stirred by the speeches of Giuseppe Mazzini (born here in 1805), the fiercely determined Giuseppe Garibaldi sailed from Genoa to Sicily with his "thousand Red Shirts" in 1860, and so set in motion the force that would flatten all resistance to the unification of Italy.

The 1900s saw the maritime city turn into a major industrial center, much of it state-controlled, and huge urban construction projects that led to the visual decay of the city. Many middle-class Genoese fled to the outlying green hills. It was only in 1992, when the 5th centenary of the voyage of Christopher Columbus appeared on the events calendar, that the city fathers awoke from their long slumber and kick-started various urban renewal projects. The process was further stimulated by the city's hosting the G8 summit in 2001, and being designated Cultural Capital of Europe in 2004. With record numbers of visitors in recent years, it would seem that "Genoa the Proud" is on the rise once again, proof of which is evident in the sprucing up of monuments around the city, the expansion of the underground metro system, and in the vitality of its welcoming people.

LAY OF THE LAND

Aeroporto Cristoforo Colombo (www.airport.genova.it) is 20 to 30 minutes from the old city center. A **taxi** ride costs 7€–8€ per person (minimum three people); the VolaBus 100 only 4€ (it departs hourly 6am–11:20pm, depositing you outside Stazione Principe). You can also get to Genoa **by boat** from Sardinia and Sicily, or from various points along the Ligurian coast. Based in Camogli, **Golfo Paradiso ferries** (www.golfoparadiso.it) serve the east coast, including Cinque Terre (17€ one-way, 25€ round-trip) and Portofino (10€, or 15€ return). **Consorzia Liguria ViaMare** (☎ 010-265712; www.liguriaviamare.it) covers the same area as well, offering harbor tours, whale-watching trips, special night trips, and a few stops along the west coast; both depart from the Porto Antico.

Your energies should be focused on Genoa's medieval heart, the *centro storico*, and the best (and usually only) way to get around this pedestrian area is on foot. If you're arriving **by train,** alight at **Stazione Principe** (home to a small but excellent tourist bureau; pick up a copy of the detailed city map, which has every street in the medieval city marked). Walk down Via Balbi to Via Garibaldi (the northern borders of the historical area), stopping off to view a few museums, and then lose yourself in the *centro storico*, which bleeds out into the Porto Antico, home to the aquarium (a 10-min. direct walk from the station).

If you're overnighting in the "modern" side of town, get off one stop earlier, at **Stazione Brignole.** From here catch a bus (1€, valid 90 min.) to Piazza Ferrarri (the eastern boundary of the old town) and head west.

If you'd like to get a better sense of the city, including its hillside neighborhoods, the 3-hour **Girocittà bus tour** (☎ 010-5582414; 14€) gives an insight into the extraordinary variety of Genoa, and includes a short walking tour of the historical center. More satisfying and focused **walking tours** (in the historical center or through the interiors of the palazzi that line Via Garibaldi) are offered once weekly from June to mid-September; both are fascinating. To find out when these are running this year, call ☎ 010-2359331.

Genova Bus and Boat (☎ 010-2759318; 10€) operates a six-language open-top bus tour that circulates through some of the city's more important tourist spots, and also runs a harbor tour; both tours depart from the aquarium. Tours run daily during summer, but are limited to weekends October through March.

Note: The one time you don't want to be in Genoa is during the Salone Nautico Internazionale (International Boat Show) held every year in October (see www.fiera.ge.it for exact dates). Prices skyrocket and you'll be lucky to find a bed.

ACCOMMODATIONS, BOTH STANDARD & NOT

The following suggestions (with the exception of Villa Pagoda and the youth hostel) are all conveniently located in the medieval heart of the city:

€€   In the historical center (off Via Balbi, and very close to Stazione Principe), **Agnello D'Oro** ★★ (Via Monachette 6; ☎ 010-2462084; www.hotelagnellodoro.it; AE, DC, MC V) is an old-fashioned *albergo*, where hands-on owner Concetta (and her English-fluent daughter) ensure that guests are well informed and well looked after. Rooms (averaging 80€ double) have little balconies—ask for a top-floor garret room for the best view (no. 56 is my favorite). Two big pluses here are the better-than-average breakfast (Concetta personally serves your first *cafè* of the day), and the later-than-usual checkout.

€€   Loredana Galante's aptly named **Art B&B** ★★ (Via San Luca 12/49; ☎ 338-8834826; www.loredanagalante.it; cash only), near the Porto Antico, is not just a place to bed down, but also a great social hub. With an infectious laugh and delicious sense of humor, Loredana is one of Genoa's top artists (specializing in conceptual and performance art); meeting her is like finding your long-lost cousin in Italy. Loredana's stylishly renovated apartment (maximum 90€ double) is full of her quirky artwork, and she hosts regular themed parties with performance moments aimed at loosening everyone up. Coincide your visit with one of these *feste* and you'll meet some of Genoa's most interesting (and eccentric) citizens. But don't expect to get to bed early. *Note:* You may need to e-mail Loredana (loredanagalante@fastwebnet.it) as her site goes down from time to time.

€€–€€€ **Hotel Colombo** ✦ (Via Porta Soprana 27/59R; ☎ 010-2513643; www.hotelcolombo.it; AE, DC, MC, V), a two-star hotel in the historical center (within spitting distance of the 12th-c. Porta Soprana), is one of the most popular budget accommodations in the city, frequented by a truly mixed clientele. Rooms are small (average size for historical Genoa, though) with really quirky decor (upturned turn-of-the-20th-c. trunk as TV table, ostrich-feather cushions on wrought-iron chairs, secondhand Corbusier classics—you get the picture), and when you open your windows you get a real sense of what living in the historical center is all about. Doubles go for 95€, and prices only really change during the Boat Expo. Patrizia, a delightful bohemian, keeps upgrading as the money comes in—she's even finally bought the building and now promises to transform the seventh-floor roof terrace, with commanding city views (and plenty of fresh breeze), into the seasonal breakfast room (breakfast has always been a bit of a finger meal here).

€€–€€€ Although it's a family business, the award-winning **Hotel Cairoli** ✦✦ (Via Cairoli 14/4; ☎ 010-2461454; www.hotelcairoli.com; AE, DC, MC, V) is proudly professional, and they've gotten it right to maintain clean, attractive rooms that are infused with plenty of light and brightened up with eye-catching modern murals. Situated in a historic apartment building (with an ancient elevator), guest rooms (75€–150€ double) are varied in size and character (I like the ones overlooking the street scenes below), but the location—on an attractive pedestrian-only street that spills onto Via Garibaldi—means that you won't be hanging around your bedroom. There's a reading room and terrace, and the infectious pleasantries at breakfast will surely kick-start your day in the right way.

€€–€€€ For a more old-school hotel experience, renovated **Hotel Helvetia** ✦✦ (Piazza Nunziata 1; ☎ 010-2465468; www.hotelhelvetiagenova.it; AE, DC, MC, V) offers top value in its price bracket (75€–150€ double); ask the manager, Nedo (a source of great restaurant recommendations), for a room on the second floor with a terrace facing the piazza (one of the city's open-air hubs); but do it now—there are only three. You'll feel like you're still in the old city, but without the claustrophobia of its narrow lanes.

A Hostel Option

€ Genoa's upscale **youth hostel** (Passo Costanzi 120n; ☎ 010-2422457; www.ostellionline.org; MC, V), rated as one of the best in Europe, is large, clean, and functional, with great views of the port, and at 16€ a night offers the cheapest bed in town (24€ for a single room). Its biggest drawback (besides the institutional atmosphere) is that it's a 20-minute bus trip from town, and another 5 to 10 minutes into the medieval center (bus no. 40 from Brignole station; from Principe station you need to change from no. 35 to no. 40). Stay there only if you're on the strictest of budgets.

DINING FOR ALL TASTES

€   Genoa is perfect for money- and time-saving eating; rather than paying for a seat in a restaurant and dealing with a menu, simply stand at a counter and point at the filled panino you fancy. For as little as 2.30€, you can get a large sandwich stuffed with brie and speck or mozzarella and spicy salami, always freshly prepared at hundreds of *paninoteca* (sandwich bars) or bars throughout the city. To rub shoulders with a broad spectrum of Genovese, I like to grab a sandwich (toasted on request) at **Panini e Dintorni** (Via Sottoripa 2/4R; ☎ 010-2467327; till very late every night except Sun; MC, V), where the beer and wine by the glass is also dirt cheap. Don't be put off by some of the less savory-looking sandwich choices (or the suspicious location not too far from the waterfront): This is where the locals hang (no need to feel like a cheapskate—folks around here just don't seem to bother with pretense).

€–€€   **Sopranis** (Piazza Valoria 1R; ☎ 010-2473030; www.sopranis.com; Tues–Sat 12:30–3pm and 7:30pm–midnight, Mon 12:30–3pm; MC, V) is another of Genoa's best-value restaurants (*coperto* 1€). Service is a real joy and the food (predominantly pizzas, 6€–9€) is good. Set in a small and cozy cross-vaulted room dating back to 1594, Sopranis has an atmosphere more toney than similarly priced venues.

€€   But there's also atmosphere to spare at **Squarciafico** (Piazza Invrea 3r; ☎ 010-2470823; www.squarciafico.it; Mon–Sat 12:30–2:30pm and 7:30–11pm; AE, MC, V), a vaulted cellar in a 15th-century palazzo near San Lorenzo Cathedral. *Primi* run around 10€ to 13€, but there isn't that wide a choice; the real draw here seems to be the delicious, healthful variety of salads (8€)—a swell change from all the carbo loading you'll be doing in Italy. While this cantina is renowned for its simple but innovative approach to traditional recipes, do give chef Maurizio's market-fresh seafood paella a try. *Coperto* is 2€.

€€   Located in a walled harborside neighborhood (just moments from the aquarium, but far away from the touristy hub) is another extremely popular restaurant with locals: **Antica Osteria di Vico Palla** ★★ (Vico Palla 15/R; ☎ 010-2466575; Tues–Sun 12:15–3pm and 7:30–11pm; AE, MC, V), the perfect place to discover authentic Ligurian cuisine. The atmosphere is fantastic: The tiny space buzzes with large Italian families and their friends, as well as with loud waiters laden with plates of traditional fare. Don't even hesitate before ordering the *mandilu* silk-handkerchief pesto lasagna (which is sheer heaven), and since this won't fill you up (in fact, it will have you pining for more), consider following it up with any of their traditional Genovese seafood dishes (the octopus is recommended). Note also that staff here are justifiably proud of their homemade *trofie* (slim, twirled dumplings served with a variety of sauces for 10€), and the ravioli stuffed with fish, prawns, and mushrooms (11€) is also wonderful. On a visit in late 2007, there was no *coperto* and service gave new meaning to the term "laid-back."

Ligurian Cuisine

Ligurians are proud of their traditional dishes, which is no doubt why most menus are virtually identical, with the presence of the coast exerting an indomitable influence. Seafood aside, Liguria's most famous export is pesto—that fragrant blend of fresh basil, garlic, pine nuts, pecorino and Parmesan cheeses, and olive oil (because of its low acidity, Ligurian olive oil is said to be among the finest in Europe). It's often served with green beans and potatoes, and is best sampled with the local pasta, *trenette* or *trofie*. Both are slightly more robust than your average pasta, being thickened with potato; *trofie*—short, slim, twirled dumplings—are truly unique, and considered the ideal partner for pesto.

Liguria is also the birthplace of focaccia, a thick bread made with olive oil, usually salted or topped with softened onions or olives, but also made with a variety of other toppings. Be warned that some can be incredibly oily—always ask for a tiny sliver (you're charged by weight) before committing to a large slice. *Focaccia con formaggio* is another must-try—two layers of pastry oozing with Stracchino cheese. Ligurians also have a way with *acciughe*—fresh anchovies—which you should definitely try (select *acciughe* marinated in lemon and olive oil, and buy a small tub at a deli, where it costs a quarter of the price charged by restaurants, then eat it with a slice of plain focaccia).

Other dishes to look for include *pansotti,* pasta parcels sometimes stuffed with *preboggion* (a paste of wild herbs that grow on the coast, including the fragrant borage) and cheese, and served with a walnut sauce or with olive oil and sage; *cima ripiena* (stuffed cold veal); *pesce al sale* (fish coated in rock salt and oven baked); *polpo in umido con potate* (octopus stew with potatoes and olives); *torta verde* or *pasqualina* (layers of thin pastry filled with vegetables, often spinach); *capponata* (bread soaked in vinegar with a mix of anchovies, tuna, eggs, basil, tomatoes, and beans); and the ubiquitous *fritto misto alla ligure* (mixed selection of fried shellfish and calamari).

The region is not generally known for fine wines, but there are a few exceptions, notably Rossesse, a delicious red from a small region of which Dolceaqua (near San Remo) is the center. The Cinque Terre is better known for its whites, of which Vermentino is serviceable (Pope John Paul II was apparently a fan and regularly requested cases to be sent to the Vatican), but don't leave without sampling a really good Sciacchetrà, the dessert wine from the Cinque Terre, where 10 kilograms (22 lb.) of "raisins" produce only 1.5 liters (50 oz.).

€€–€€€   If you're looking for a taste of the Italian Riviera in an untouched medieval fishing village, catch the bus to Boccadasse, and take a table at **Santa Chiara** ✹✹ (Via Capo Santa Chiara 69r; ☎ 010-3770081; Mon–Sat; closed Aug 5–25 and Dec 20–Jan 7; AE, MC, V), where Luisa and her husband, Luigi, serve wonderful seafood on rocks beaten by the sea. And the restaurant has stunning views that stretch all the way east to Mt. Portofino, which is why you won't even wince at the 4€ *coperto* and all-round upscale prices; rather, make a day of it and prepare to splurge. You can sit in the cool whitewashed rooms, with excellent art on the walls and perfectly framed views through the windows; however, I would opt for a table on the edge of the terrace, where you can take in the variegated blues and greens of the coastline.

WHY YOU'RE HERE: THE TOP SIGHTS & ATTRACTIONS

With some 30 museums clamoring for your attention, Genoa offers that typical Italian dilemma—so much to see, so little time. That said, my top picks are all within walking distance of each other on pleasant streets from which vehicular traffic is banned. Your stroll will include the following:

- The **Strada Nuova,** the city's famous Renaissance streets. These include Via Garibaldi, created in the mid–16th century and known as Rue des Rois (Street of Kings), and Via Balbi, created in the early 17th century. Both are living proof of the city's historical high point, when its wealthiest flexed gilded financial muscles by creating semiprivate streets wide enough for new carriages, from which they would enter mansions that were the envy of Europe.

- The *centro storico.* This is the city's ancient heart, dating between the 12th and 16th century, where space constraints forced its inhabitants to build ever upwards, resulting in a sort of medieval Manhattan. The converging buildings create narrow, twisting lanes, which every now and then open onto "breathing spaces": tiny squares, often lined with cafes or bars. You might want to ignore the stops I advise below and just lose yourself here.

- The **Porto Antico,** home to Europe's largest aquarium. Besides offering that structure, the harbor affords a pleasant albeit touristy stroll (particularly at night, when the views of the terraced city are splendid), and is a must-see for anyone traveling with kids.

Via Garibaldi (Strada Nuova) ✹✹

"I'm overwhelmed, struck, in rapture; my eyes are full of gold, marble, crystal," wrote Charles Dupathy, declaring: "If you want to see the world's most beautiful street, go to Strada Nuova in Genoa." Strada Nuova, now known as Via Garibaldi, must have been a real eye-opener when it was built 500 years ago as an elite new street to house Genoa's five wealthiest families. From the filthy, tangled web of the city's medieval center, you would have suddenly stepped into a wide street lined with Renaissance mansions, each covered in *trompe l'oeil* paintings, with chandeliers dominating the frescoed and gilded entry halls.

Today most of the palaces on this pedestrians-only street are home (aptly enough) to large banks and financial institutions. If you have to change money, do so at the **Bancho di Chiavari,** where you can admire the still magnificent remnants of its frescoes and marble columns. Then walk across to Palazzo Podestà to admire the grotto and fountain in its small courtyard.

But if you have only limited time, make **Via Garibaldi 12 ★★★** (☎ 010-2530365; www.viagaribaldi12.com; Tues–Sat 10am–2pm and 3:30–7pm), your chief port of call; it's the most glamorous shop in Genoa, and residents joke that people get married just so they can post their wedding registry here. You'll be bowled over by the contrast of seeing a large selection of the world's modern-design classics set within rooms that boast 16th-century pillars and ceiling frescoes. In the dining hall, with its 18th-century gilded ceiling and mirrored walls, you'll find a Zahar Hadid sofa that's curved like a snake.

At the opposite end from the Bancho is the **Musei di Strada Nuova complex ★★** (☎ 010-8787452; 7€, or purchase a 16€ museum card here for free entry to all the top museums; Tues–Fri 9am–7pm and Sat–Sun 10am–7pm). The complex consists of **Palazzo Rosso** and **Palazzo Bianco**—housing what is billed as **Genoa's finest art collection**—and the grand **Palazzo Tursi,** which has an eclectic group of exhibits, including a Guarneri-designed violin belonging to Paganini (the great virtuoso who played the violin so seductively that his straight-laced listeners likened him to the devil), letters written by Columbus, and a fascinating coin collection that charts Genoa's mercantile history. Viewing the art collections is not essential (though there are a few Caravaggios as well as some works by the Flemish masters Rubens and van Dyck, who were very popular with the Genoese fat cats of the time), but it's worth entering the palazzi just to marvel at the lavish decoration and fine proportions that inspired Rubens to publish a book of his drawings of the Strada Nuova.

Built in the style of Via Garibaldi by the Balbi and Durazzi families in the early 1600s, **Via Balbi** is Genoa's equally famous street. However, its traffic makes it less pleasant than the pedestrians-only Via Garibaldi, and there is only one stop really worth making: the **Palazzo Reale ★** (Via Balbi 10; ☎ 010-2710211; 4€; Tues–Wed 9am–1:30pm, Thurs–Sun 9am–7pm). This is by far the most beautiful and luxurious of Genoa's palaces, not least because it was home to the Savoyard royals, who spared no expense in outdoing every other home in the city. They covered every inch with gold and created a hall of mirrors that challenged the supremacy of the Palace at Versailles as the royal residence in Europe. You'll be required to wait for the half-hourly chaperoned "tour" (you'll mainly be using the brief historical descriptions provided in each of the rooms to make sense of it all, but you can ask questions in English), after which time your neck will be aching (not for nothing did Gustave Flaubert wax lyrical about "the beautiful ceilings of the palaces of Genoa, under which it would be such a delight to love").

Centro Storico ★★★

From Via Garibaldi, you can plunge directly into the labyrinthine *centro storico* and get thoroughly lost—even armed with a map, you'll be tempted to take a short cut only to find yourself a few steps from where you started. If you'd like to see a house museum, with a smaller but more focused art collection, stop at **Palazzo Spinola ★★** (Piazza Pellicceria 1; ☎ 010-2705300; free with museum card; Tues–Sat 8:30am–7:30pm, Sun 1–8pm). It displays a smaller but better selection of artworks than those in the Musei di Strada Nuova (including a particularly haunting *Ecce homo* by Antonello da Messina, and fine portraits of Genoese patrons by Rubens and van Dyck). Artworks have detailed descriptions in English, and the attic (take a look at the rooftop to see where the Genoese servants would come up for air) has textiles and ceramics that provide insight into the life and times of one of Genoa's wealthiest families, who donated the house to the city after extensive bomb damage in World War II.

From here you should head in the general direction of Palazzo Ducale and San Lorenzo Cathedral, cut through **Campetto**—one of the old city's most charming "breathers"—and pass **Piazza Matteo,** the Dorias' old stamping grounds (before Admiral Andrea, Genoa's uncrowned king, moved up and out, building his **Palazzo del Principe Doria Pamphilj** just beyond the Stazione Principe).

A hodgepodge of Romanesque, Gothic, and baroque styles, **San Lorenzo Cathedral,** the city's religious heart, is nevertheless an interesting stop, particularly if you set aside the time to visit the cathedral's **Museo del Tesoro** (☎ 010-2471831; 5.50€; Mon–Sat 9am–noon and 3–6pm). Worth visiting for Franco Albini's 1950s interior design alone, the Treasury claims to house the ashes of St. John the Baptist—a claim dating back to 1099, when the Genoese soldiers who played a crucial role in liberating the Holy Land during the First Crusade returned triumphant, bearing the saint's remains. Besides the purported ashes, the Treasury houses a number of fascinating relics (including a green glass bowl said to be the Holy Grail, and the platter upon which the martyr's head was presented to Salome).

Behind the cathedral, alongside the 16th-century **Palazzo Ducale** (now an important exhibition space featuring the city's best temporary exhibits; to find out what's showing, visit www.palazzoducale.genova.it), is **Del Gesù** ★★, built by the Jesuits between the 16th and 19th centuries. This is Genoa's finest baroque church, with a wealth of marble and gilded plaster covering every crevice (so much so that some of the city's more puritanical citizens have suggested that God is offended by such vulgarity).

From Del Gesù you can slip through to **Piazza Ferrari,** which seems to be the city's central meeting point, great for a breather around the massive, soothing fountain, or you could wander up to the twin-towered A.D. 1155 **Porta Soprana,**

The Sightseeing Dash: 48-Hour Museum Marathon

In this city of many sights, a genuine bargain is the **Genoa Card Musei,** which costs 16€ and provides 48-hour free entry to 22 museums (including all those recommended here), as well as reduced fare at other top attractions, including the pricey aquarium, a ride on the Bigo, and Villa Durazzo in Santa Margherita Ligure; pay 20€ and the card includes free public transport for the same 48-hour period. Be warned that just about every museum (with the exception of the cathedral's Tesoro) is closed Mondays, so avoid activating your card on a Sunday. Cards can be purchased from the bookshop adjacent to the Strada Nuova museum complex in **Via Garibaldi** (☎ 010-2759185), as well as any of the museums covered by the scheme.

which is worth admiring from the ground but is not worth the 4€ admission fee to climb the "medieval tower" (touted as **Torri di Porta**) for a view of the city. Also avoid the nearby house museum purporting to be where Columbus grew up; it's a total rip-off, with nothing of interest inside. Personally I'd plunge back into the mysterious honeycomb, heading farther south to the oldest part of the city to view the Genoese church that tops my list: the restrained, serenely beautiful Romanesque **San Donato,** a million miles from the baroque style of Del Gesù, yet only a short stroll away, down Via Pollaiuoli. Surrounded by 11th-century city walls, it was untarnished by the baroque fever that gripped the city some 600 years later; its simple interior is a touching ode to a millennium of faithful worship. Holy Mass begins at 6pm Monday to Saturday; 10:45am on Sunday.

From here you can either take a look at the impressive **Faculty of Architecture,** located in the nearby Convent of San Silvestro (there are great views of the city from here), or head downhill along Via dei Giustiniani or Via Canneto il Lungo, passing Muslim butchers, bars, and the **Bottega di Barbiere** (Vicolo Caprettari 14), a gorgeous barbershop and one of Genoa's many Art Nouveau treasures, to the Porto Antico.

Porto Antico ✪

Genoa's ancient **port** has indeed been transformed into a very touristy waterfront area, but it's also a balm for beleaguered parents, who come here in droves to visit Europe's largest aquarium, **Acquario di Genova** ✪ (☎ 010-2345678; www.acquariodigenova.it; 15€ adults, children 4–12 9€; daily 9:30am–7:30pm). Designed by Genoa's most famous architect, Renzo Piano, it looks appropriately enough like a container ship filled with watery exhibits, and has certainly put the wind back into Genoa's tourism industry, attracting an annual average of 1.2 million visitors. All in all, 4 million liters of fish-filled waters are on view, with tanks containing full Caribbean coral reefs, dozens of sharks, dolphins, and more. Most children who visit—even those who have seen it before—are awestruck. Exploring is very straightforward: A walkway takes you past 71 tanks hosting some 600 species. Set aside around 2 hours to cover it all.

From here, families with kids should walk over to the nearby **Città dei Bambini** (☎ 010-2475702; www.cittadeibambini.net; 5€ adults and 2-year-olds, 7€ children aged 3–14; Tues–Sun Oct–June 10am–6pm, July–Sept 11:30am–7:30pm, visits must be reserved in advance), Italy's first center of science—and probably the last place you want to be while exploring this enigmatic city—but it's designed to raise the IQ of kids aged 2 to 14. Activities are divided by age, and though much is in Italian, even children who only speak English find it fascinating.

Renzo Piano also designed the Porto Antico's **Bolla biosphere,** a large sci-fi ball housing tree ferns and birds, and—supposedly evoking the harbor-side cranes, but more like tentacles of a giant submerged arthropod—the **Bigo** (3€; daily 10am–6pm). The latter hoists a **glass elevator** ascending 60m (197 ft.), where you can enjoy a panoramic view of Genoa; equally impressive is to simply take a stroll along this busy waterfront at night (when it's bustling with party spirit, especially on weekends) and look back at Genoa, its undulating hills glittering with pinprick jewels of light.

For a rather less commercial introduction of Genoa's longtime relationship with the sea, maritime buffs should make a beeline for **Galata Museo del Mare**

(☎ 010-2345655; www.galatamuseodelmare.it; 10€, 5€ children 4–12; Tues–Fri 10am–6pm, Sat–Sun 10am–7:30pm, extended hours Mar–Oct), where model boats, simulated sea voyages, and multifangled accounts of Genoa's seafaring prowess may hold your attention for a while, but I found myself distracted by the views of the city from the expansive windows.

THE OTHER GENOA

If you're traveling on your own, or want the inside track on what's happening in Genoa—especially in the world of art—try to make sure you stay as the paying guest of **Loredana Galante** at her homey little B&B. Loredana is a leading social figure in Genoa and a highly rated artist whose soirees are also quite legendary. It's quite likely—particularly if you're able to stay for several nights—that you'll soon be rubbing shoulders with many of Genoa's most luminous citizens, and you'll have the wherewithal to seek out the most happening joints in town. Even if you can't stay at **Art B&B** (p. 486), it's always worth contacting Loredana to find out about her latest art project; you must get an invite to one of her get-togethers.

She steps out of the Mercedes in a swirl of lace and satin, resplendent with joy as only a bride can be. The waiting groom holds her in delight; when he kisses her, the glamorous guests (no one out-glams the Italians) raise a small cheer. This is a typical scene outside the **Municipio offices** in **Palazzo Tursi** on Via Garibaldi, a public ritual repeated throughout the day until the flagstones are pale with confetti and rice. September is usually the best month for **weddings,** but who knows when the spirit of romance will blossom for Genoese lovers? Get here on a Saturday morning in summer and you'll likely be part of the genial crowd that wishes the bride and groom well.

Tipping the other end of the emotional scale is a visit to **Cimitero Monumentale di Staglieno** ✿✿✿ (bus: 31 from Stazione Brignole). The Genoese have been burying their dead in this lush, parklike cemetery since 1844, and it is both graveyard and museum, featuring the work of some of Italy's most talented stonemasons (incomparably better than the city's truly dead masonry museum, **Museo di Sant'Agostino**). Filled with mossy tombs and imploring angels, grieving maidens and Gothic spires, it's a deeply moving, atmospheric place, and it's still used daily by the Genoese who honor their dead.

Then, if you've decided you'd rather fit in than stand out like a tourist, challenge yourself to learn the language while getting a firmer grasp on local culture. **A Door to Italy** (Via Caffaro 4/7; ☎ 010-2465870) is an Italian language school focused on foreign students; 1-week language courses start at 195€, but rather maximize your efforts by combining the language classes with lessons on culture (270€ for the combo) hooking into aspects of La Dolce Vita such as cinema, literature, wine, and theater. Other add-ons include cooking classes and diving courses. The school can set you up with a wide range of accommodations; you can even stay with a local family (from 155€ per week), or in a private studio for 300€ per week.

ATTENTION, WINDOW-SHOPPERS!

The city is not really a shopping destination, but it's still a great place to check out **atmospheric** *caruggi*—hardware shops, picture framers, and the like—which cater primarily to residents rather than to tourists.

Of course, **Via Garibaldi 12** (p. 491), is a destination in its own right, and just the place to pick up a Renzo Piano cutlery set. And do pop into **Upim,** a department store, and the antiques shop **Galleria Imperiale,** both on the **campetto,** a small square in the heart of the historical center; these two stores are worth a visit just to see the interiors.

The campetto leads into **Via degli Orefici (Street of Goldsmiths)** and Piazza Soziglia, where you will find the sweet shop **Pietro Romanengo** (no. 71r). Nothing has changed here since it first opened its doors in 1814, including the recipe for its "rosolio drops." Those are the rose oils in which Catherine de Medici is said to have bathed. Mixed with lemon, peach, anise, lime, and orange, they make a sublime combination.

A SIDE TRIP FROM GENOA

Stretching west of Genoa, the coastline known as the Riviera di Ponente must once have been a paradise. Large bays backed by lush vegetation and shimmering mountains create ideal conditions. But as is so often the case, its beauty has been marred by the crush to exploit its charms, from a lengthy sprawl of seaside resorts and ugly apartment blocks swamping the medieval centers to the acres of plastic tunneling that produce the cut flowers of the Riviera dei Fiori. It has little to recommend it to the time-pressed traveler, with the exception perhaps of **San Remo,** a 2- to 3-hour train trip from Genoa (8€–13€).

This grand old resort town took shape in the 1860s, when a Piemontese, Pietro Bogge, built the first Grand Hotel des Londres (still operational). A decade later, the ailing Russian Empress Maria Alexandrovna arrived, fleeing the humiliation of her husband's infidelity. She proceeded to find solace in her brief sojourn here and brought along the origins of a sizable Russian community. The spires of its Russian Orthodox church are now as much a part of San Remo's character as its Art Nouveau casino, built in 1905. After Maria Alexandrovna's departure, San Remo's exotic glamour was sustained by an interesting array of entrepreneurs, artists, and aristocrats (including the composer Tchaikovsky and Swedish scientist Nobel), and 190 villas and 25 hotels were built between 1874 and 1906 to accommodate them.

Nowadays the town has no real identity beyond tourism, so the experience is a little hollow, not least because a few town-planning catastrophes have all but ruined her once beautiful visage. Besides trying your luck at the pretty **Casinò of San Remo** (☎ 0184-534001; www.casinosanremo.it; 7.50€ Fri–Sun, free Mon–Thurs; men must wear jacket and tie), there isn't that much to see or do in town itself, so your hotel choice is rather crucial here.

€€ Personally, rather than staying in posh-but-touristy San Remo, I'd opt to base myself in nearby **Dolceaqua,** an inland medieval village that is one of Italy's most beautiful towns (Monet was inspired to paint it) and where the Rossesse, Liguria's best red wine, is produced. Dolceaqua is gorgeous and feels relatively undiscovered, yet has a sophisticated **tourism office** (www.dolceaqua.it), excellent wine-tasting venues, and a number of charming, inexpensive B&Bs charging between 70€ and 90€ for a double. The pick of these B&Bs are **Dei Doria** (Via Barberis Colombo 40/44; ☎ 0184-206343; www.deidoria.it; cash only), with great views; and the classy **Talking Stones** ✪ (Via San Bernardo 5; ☎ 0184-206393; www.talkingstones.it; cash only), with three en suite rooms for 70€.

€€–€€€   But, if you find yourself in pricey San Remo, the best value among the hotels along the Corso dell'Imperatrice is **Lolli Palace** (☎ 0184-531496; www.lollihotel.it; AE, MC, V). Doubles range from 83€ to 150€, with a small supplement (5.50€) for a balcony.

€€€€   Among the upscale choices, the grand **Royal Hotel** (Corso dell'Imperatrice 80; ☎ 0184-5391; www.royalhotelsanremo.com; AE, DC, MC, V) is pricey at 232€ to 466€ (check the Internet for deals), but still a relatively good value given its high standards, grand rooms, and old-fashioned luxury.

12 Naples, Pompeii & the Amalfi Coast

Meet the uniquely passionate Neapolitans & then tour one of the most awesome coastlines on earth

by Keith Bain

IT'S A PLACE WHERE PEOPLE WEAR THEIR EMOTIONS ON THEIR SLEEVES. It's a boisterous, pulsating city, with a flavor and cuisine all its own. It's fun and unforgettable. And yet legions of people are terrified at the thought of making a visit to Naples because this big metropolis of just over a million people has the dubious honor of being Italy's crime capital and home base to the Camorra, the country's largest organized-crime outfit. Even though the Camorra hasn't killed a tourist in years, not even accidentally, the perception that thugs roam the Neapolitan streets is enough to sway many would-be visitors from including Naples in their plans.

But to skip Naples out of fear of its reputation is the real crime. Naples is a city so vibrant it seems to be writhing with energy and passion Whether you're pondering an ancient relic at a world-class museum or dodging mopeds on the narrow cobblestone streets of the historical center, spending time here is like getting a shot of adrenalin.

Naple's day-trip opportunities are just as impressive: Hop on a bus and in less than an hour, you'll be strolling the ruins of Pompeii or Herculaneum, two entire ancient cities that have been unearthed from the debris spat out by Mt. Vesuvius nearly 2 millennia ago. Or take a short boat trip to the legendary Isle of Capri or a heart-jolting bus trip along the scintillating Amalfi Drive, where—amid the abysses and coves and spectacular dropaway cliffs that plummet into cobalt blue below—you'll find the dreamy little towns of Positano, Amalfi, and Ravello, each perfectly poised for lazy, intimate exploration.

Again, I don't want to whitewash Naples' faults. Its traffic is deadly, and the winding streets are crowded with helmetless prepubescent kids careering around pedestrians and trinket peddlers. Pollution is a genuine problem, too, from pungent litter to toxic emissions from vehicles that have likely never been street legal. And there's a good chance that someone will take advantage of you somehow, whether by merely pilfering a couple of extra euros for a taxi ride or double-charging you for bread at a *trattoria*. But, I promise, if you can concentrate on the city's strengths and take advantage of the wonderful side trips in this region, Naples will win you over.

DON'T LEAVE NAPLES WITHOUT . . .

STEPPING LIVELY DOWN THE SPACCANAPOLI   Quaint and quiet it is not, but walking down the long strip known as the Spaccanapoli (so called for the way it "splits" the city in two) is exhilarating. Shop owners, selling everything from handmade Nativity ornaments to Pulcinella, a classic Neapolitan mask with the nose in the shape of a beak, haggle with both locals and *stranieri* (foreigners). It's here that Neapolitan culture is most fully revealed, and most accessible.

GETTING UNDER THE SKIN OF THE ANCIENT CITY   Naples has an incredibly well-preserved underground network of tunnels and caves, which have housed everything from graves and clandestine worshipers to cisterns of drinking water. Take one of the guided tours offered by Napoli Sotterranea (p. 514), and experience the haunting and sometimes claustrophobic sensation of being under the surface of a city that's been around for millennia.

SCANNING THE COAST FOR INCREDIBLE VIEWS   The best place to gaze out over the Bay of Naples is from the lip of Mt. Vesuvius (p. 531); on a clear day, as they say, you can see forever. In Naples, too, there are some fine spots: the terrace of the glorious Certosa di San Martino monastery (p. 522) or nearby Castel Sant'Elmo (p. 523). Better still—if you don't mind a short hike—is the perspective from the top of Monte Echia (p. 520).

TUCKING INTO THE FINEST PIZZA ON EARTH   Neapolitans truly believe that they invented pizza and that Neapolitan pie is second to none. One of the best places to decide for yourself is at Di Matteo (p. 508), beloved by Neopolitans and uncompromisingly simple, the pizza is nothing short of amazing. If you're in town in September, stay on the lookout for the annual pizza festival, the Olympics of pizza making, drawing *pizzaioli* from around the globe.

ENJOYING A HAIR-RAISING JAUNT ON AMALFI DRIVE   Forget blind faith! The skillful bus drivers who ply the narrow world-famous cliff-hugging Amalfi Drive between Sorrento and Salerno could probably navigate the route blind-folded. But that doesn't make the journey along this succession of eye-popping bends and curves high above the water's edge any less heart-stopping. Or any less thrilling. Grab a window seat and prepare for the ride of your life as you start up one love affair after the other, each with a more beautiful vista—craggy mountains thrusting heavenwards from cobalt waters and paradisiacal coves below.

SWIMMING IN THE BLUE GROTTO   There are rewards aplenty on the fabled Isle of Capri, a verdant, hilly landscape set within the watery perfection of a gorgeous coastline. Chief among the heavily touristed activities here is a boat ride to the Grotto Azzurra (p. 535), after which visitors are rowed inside to experience the luminescent aquamarine glow of the submerged cave. But you'll save the price of your ferry trip and have a more pleasurable experience by taking a bus to the cave and then swimming inside (absolutely free in early evening).

A BRIEF HISTORY OF NAPLES

Naples is one of the most precariously situated cities on the planet. The historical center sits at the base of one of the world's most dangerous volcanoes, Mt. Vesuvius. From atop the volcano, it looks as if the city slid down the mountainside, stopping just short of the Tyrrhenian Sea and leaving a scattering of villages along its flanks. But, in fact, the region around Naples was settled from the sea inward and upward, with the Greeks likely the first to have arrived, in the 8th century B.C.

Naples was first called Neapolis, meaning "new city." Together with nearby Cuma, the ancient region was a powerful trade center and a force to be reckoned with, not to mention an attractive acquisition for invading tribes like the Etruscans and Romans, lured by its climate and the beauty of the coastline. It was the Romans who finally captured Neapolis from the Greeks around 326 B.C., and quickly connected the new city to the eternal city by the Appian Way, literally paving the way for its destiny as a cultural center.

From the beginning, life has never been particularly easy for the Neapolitans. Mt. Vesuvius erupteded, pushing the villages back down toward the sea; wars and conflicts diminished much of its former glory. The scars of World War II, for example, are evident in the pocked churches and quiet plaques that mark the sites of destroyed treasures. More recently, decades of crime, high unemployment, and corruption have taken a toll on all but the city's unique spirit.

As you visit Naples, you'll easily spot the evidence of its rich and varied past. The historical center, a UNESCO World Heritage Site, still follows the same street pattern the Greeks used. In the area of Santa Lucia, along the waterfront to the north, you'll see where the Normans left their statues and castles. Palaces along the entire waterfront, like the Palazzo Reale, were shaped by numerous occupations. The palace, built by the Spanish viceroys in the 17th century, was expanded by the Bourbon monarchs in the 18th century and decorated in its present neoclassical design by the French in the 19th century. Back from the water in the grid-work section known as the Spanish Quarter, the influence of Spain's rule still rings in the local dialect and most of the surnames of the locals.

Directly above these areas are the Vomero and Capodimonte hills, where the monastery of San Martino and the remains of catacombs testify to later Christian influences. Contemporary Naples has been built snugly around the monuments of its past. Ancient churches and convents sit among the modern buildings in more recently developed areas of the city, like the main industrial port to the south. And all along the northern shoreline, especially near the Mergellina port and the Posillipo, modern apartment blocks are perched above ancient caves and ruins.

LAY OF THE LAND

Naples is serviced by the relatively small **Capodichino International Airport** (Via Umberto Maddalena 192; ☎ 081-7896259), with regular direct flights from major European cities. There are no direct flights to Naples from North America; **British Airways** (www.ba.com) and **EasyJet** (www.easyjet.com) offer good rates (even on one-way flights) from London's Gatwick Airport. The airport is only 7km (4½ miles) north of the city, so getting in is fast and relatively easy. The half-hourly **AliBus** goes directly to Stazione Centrale (Piazza Garibaldi), the primary train and bus terminus in the city center; a 3€ ticket valid for the journey from the airport to the city plus any onward bus or metro travel is valid for 90 minutes. However, unless you have precise details on which bus to take to get to your hotel, you're probably best off using a taxi from the station. A taxi into the center direct from the airport will cost between 13€ and 25€, subject to the disposition of the driver—and your observable level of gullibility. Watch that meter!

One of the easiest ways to visit Naples from other cities in Europe is by train. Tickets within Italy can be booked online at www.trenitalia.com, but tickets still have to be collected at self-service kiosks in the train station. A one-way ticket from Florence to Naples is around 50€, from Milan to Naples (6–10 hr.) around 67€, and from Rome to Naples (90–120 min.) anything between 21€ and 36€. Get off at Stazione Centrale, which is well connected (by bus or metro) to the city center and the port, and also—by means of the Ferrovia Circumvesuviana terminus (signs will show you the way)—to Pompeii and Sorrento (check schedules with www.vesuviana.it).

GETTING AROUND

The best way to get around central Naples is as a very alert, quick-footed pedestrian. **City buses** (☎ 081-5513109; www.unicocampania.it) are almost always packed and do get stuck in traffic—it's faster to walk. Most hoteliers will happily help you find the right buses for trips into the hills; you certainly won't want to walk up to Capidimonte. But for trips to far-flung suburbs like Pozzuoli or to get to the football stadium, the metro rail system, **Metronapoli** (www.metro.na.it), is very useful. Extensive additions are being made to the inner city's underground portion of the system, with new subway stops still under construction at many of the city's major piazzas; aside from traditional bureaucratic problems, work came to a halt for a year due to the discovery of two ancient warring sea vessels beneath the ground during excavations work for the new subways. There are now plans to incorporate the archaeological finds into the underground station at Castel Nuovo where they were discovered, creating a subterranean museum that will inevitably make metro fares to this stations slightly pricier (but certainly worthwhile). The **funicular system** (☎ 800-568866), also run by Metronapoli, is essential to get to the top of the Vomero. A 90-minute travel card costs 1€, and there's a 24-hour version for 3€.

Transportation to outlying side-trip destinations, including Pompeii, Ercolano (for Herculaneum), and Sorrento (at the head of the Amalfi Coast), is abundant; there are buses for Pompeii (**SITA:** ☎ 199-730749) and Herculaneum (**ANM:** ☎ 800-639525; www.anm.it), as well as trains (run by **Circumvesuviana;** ☎ 800-053939; www.vesuviana.it). You can catch ferries or faster hydrofoils to get to the island of Capri, or any of the highlighted towns along the coast. Whatever you do, do not consider driving in Naples (you'll battle to find a vehicle that hasn't been battered), and be warned that a certain skill is required to negotiate the famously narrow and notoriously clogged Amalfi Highway.

From Naples, it's easy to get to Sicily (8–10 hr., usually overnight), to the main villages and towns along the Amalfi Coast (Sorrento, Positano, and Amalfi), and even to coastal towns in northern Italy by boat: try **Tirrenia** (☎ 081-8449297; www.tirrenia.it), **SNAV** (www.snav.it), **Caremar** (www.caremar.it), or **AliLauro** (www.alilauro.it), which have regular, reliable ferry services. A ferry trip to Amalfi is just under 2 hours, with stops at Positano and Sorrento. It takes just over half an hour to get to Capri by hydrofoil, and only 45 minutes for Ischia; if you go by slower ferry, you'll save money but lose a bit of time.

In Naples, there is no shortage of boat companies that will ferry you from the coast to the islands. Simply go to the ferry dock at Molo Beverello (the port of Naples, across from the gloomy fortress), where you'll find ticket stands for all the major companies at a fixed kiosk. You can browse the signs posted above each company's name, listing the next departure and destinations. There's no need to book ahead but you should be wary of anyone selling a service without tickets; scam artists are always ready to prey on the unsuspecting.

You can generally buy your tickets the same day you're traveling, but be sure to check whether the boats are delayed by choppy seas or other unforeseen problems. The most efficient of the lines is **Metro del Mare** (☎ 199-600700; www. metrodelmare.com), which operates huge no-nonsense hydrofoils, but you could simply choose your operator according to the next available ride if you simply turn up with your luggage—or save time and effort by joining the shortest queue (just check the signs up on the cashier windows to make sure you're about to buy for the right destination). What they offer is more like a bus service on the water than a Mediterranean cruise, but they're generally on time and will almost always get you where you're going.

To help plan all your travel (train or otherwise) in this region, consult **Campania Transport** (www.campaniatrasporti.it), which covers all local networks.

ACCOMMODATIONS, BOTH STANDARD & NOT

Anyone who has fallen for the chaotic charms of Naples knows that an overnight stay in the city core is a must. Whether you choose a funky hotel around the Scappanapoli or a waterfront room with a view, sleeping in the city is a far better choice than in the suburbs. Especially avoid the all-inclusive tourist hotels on the outskirts. Also steer clear of accommodations in the Spanish Quarter. There are a few reputable hotels there, but safety is not guaranteed—and if you can't leave your room for dinner, why bother?

APARTMENT RENTALS

Two useful and reliable Web-based services are available for finding self-catering and otherwise out-of-the-ordinary accommodations in Naples and along the entire Amalfi Coast. My first choice is **My Home Your Home** ★★★ kids (Via Duomo 196; ☎ 081-19565835; www.myhomeyourhome.it), a well-stocked service offering choice apartments, as well as converted attics and walled-off sections of larger apartments; but there are also fairly formidable spaces situated in historic palazzo (some even have terraces and a view of some sort), and for a bump up in price you could score an entire villa. Fortunately, you won't get too big a surprise, since the website listings includes photographs and quite detailed inventories of what you can expect. Most run between 90€ and 150€ a night for a bedroom, bathroom, kitchen, and living area; the price you pay will invariably be based on the amount of space you have at your disposal and your location. You'll save a bit if you rent the place for an entire week (a few are only available on a weekly basis). This is a particularly suitable option if you have children because most of the owners will provide extra beds or fold-out sofas to accommodate everyone for only a small extra fee. An example is the spacious, if eclectically furnished, Via delle Cartiere apartment, on the fourth floor of a block equipped with an elevator and expansive terraces. A week will cost as little as 750€ (double), and the package includes two bedrooms, two bathrooms, a living room, and a kitchen. If you are traveling with family, 1,000€ secures a place for four guests. Most apartments come standard with A/C and TV, while some will have stereo systems and Internet access.

The best source for finding rooms in occupied private apartments, farmhouses, and even docked boats in Naples and along the Amalfi Coast is **Rent A Bed** ★ (Vico Serqente Maqqiore 16; ☎ 081-417721; www.rentabed.com). It represents these types of accommodations along with plenty of cushy, well-priced private pads with living rooms and equipped kitchens—just like the excellent-value Casa Chiai, a fourth-floor apartment in the lovely centrally located, yet upmarket, neighborhood of Chiai (great for shopping, dining, and nightlife). It's neat, clean, and tidy, and comes with such modern-day conveniences as air-conditioning, a stereo system, and a washing machine. And there's a small, but fully equipped, kitchen. Because you'll be in a block with other Neapolitans (rather than tourists), you'll have a sense of living in the community, and pay just 70€ (July–Aug) or 96€ to 106€ (Sept–June) for two. Of the many other apartments I've inspected, not one was a disappointment, whether it was a sun-drenched, chic, Scandinavian-modern place in the historical center (around 100€) or a very simple but white-glove-clean apartment in the residential hill zone (under 50€). The website gives full details and photos (even noting the amount of light and number of windows you can expect), and includes flats on the Amalfi Coast and the islands.

B&Bs & HOTELS

You have several good choices for safe, affordable, and comfortable accommodations in the historical center, which is a great place to be based if you want to experience the full-on effect of the unique Neapolitan inner-city ambience. However, if you'd like forgo the slightly claustrophobic intimacy of the center, there are very affordable options near the waterfront and even in upmarket Chiaia; there's something to suit every budget. High season in Naples and the Amalfi Coast begins at Easter and runs through September; many smaller hotels are actually closed (especially on the islands) for the rest of the year, with a handful opening at Christmas time.

€–€€   Beds in Naples fill up extraordinarily quickly, so book well in advance for one of the spick 'n' span en suite rooms at **Bella Capri** ★ (Via Melisurgo 4; ☎ 081-5529494; www.bellacapri.it; AE, DC, MC, V), a tidy, homegrown little hotel on the sixth floor of an office block. Don't let the location put you off: Alfredo, the fun-loving, soccer-worshipping owner is a great host, and has worked hard to create a comfortable base. When booking, ask for a unit overlooking the port (doubles are 60€–80€, or 50€–60€ for a shared bathroom); from your little balcony, you'll be able to watch the city come to life from early in the morning as hundreds of boat passengers lug their luggage toward the docks for trips to Capri and the Amalfi Coast. Needless to say, you'll be perfectly poised when you want

Naples Accommodations & Dining

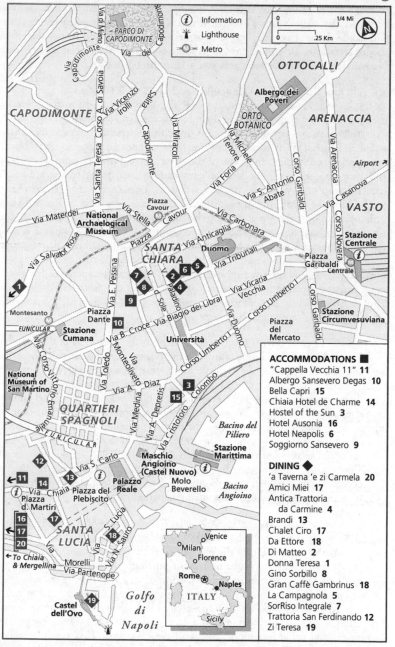

Legend:
- (i) Information
- Lighthouse
- (M) Metro

0 — 1/4 Mi
0 — .25 Km

ACCOMMODATIONS ■
- "Cappella Vecchia 11" **11**
- Albergo Sansevero Degas **10**
- Bella Capri **15**
- Chiaia Hotel de Charme **14**
- Hostel of the Sun **3**
- Hotel Ausonia **16**
- Hotel Neapolis **6**
- Soggiorno Sansevero **9**

DINING ◆
- 'a Taverna 'e zi Carmela **20**
- Amici Miei **17**
- Antica Trattoria da Carmine **4**
- Brandi **13**
- Chalet Ciro **17**
- Da Ettore **18**
- Di Matteo **2**
- Donna Teresa **1**
- Gino Sorbillo **8**
- Gran Caffè Gambrinus **18**
- La Campagnola **5**
- SorRiso Integrale **7**
- Trattoria San Ferdinando **12**
- Zi Teresa **19**

to make the same journey. Breakfast is simple, and taken just downstairs, in the common area of Bella Capri's hostel, which is another great money-saving option with some dorms having as few as four beds (18€–21€) and in-room showers; they're ultraclean, air-conditioned, and some even have Bay of Naples and Castel Nuovo views. This guidebook gets you a 10% discount.

€€   In hip, affluent Chiaia, **Cappella Vecchia 11** ★★ (Via Cappella Vecchia 11; ☎ 081-2405117; www.bednaples.com; AE, MC, V) is a find—an inviting B&B on the first floor of a chunky palazzo. Run by gracious entrepreneur Stefano and his wife, this small and personable place is quite the Neapolitan trendsetter: smartly styled and within reach of just about everything you might hope to see in Naples. It's especially convenient for some of the city's best nightlife options, restaurants, and shopping. Echoing the lounge–cum–dining area, guest rooms are bright, cheerful, and contemporary: parquet wooden floors combine with snatches of local tradition—a painting or two and colorful glass light fittings. Room D has a little balcony over the street and the loveliest bathroom (gorgeous mosaic tiles, nice big basins, and powerful hot showers); unit E is the largest, while F is a big-gish corner room, also with a balcony. After a great night's sleep in firm beds, my only cautionary flag is to be prepared for a neighborhood that rises early (you'll invariably find Naples noisy in the early hours). A breakfast spread of fresh crois-sants and real espresso had me bopping through the day. Standard doubles cost 75€ to 100€, while the marginally larger "comfort" units (which can serve as triples) are never more than 20€ extra.

€€–€€€   A great way to live the atmosphere of the historical center is to base yourself in a hotel tucked inside one of the city center's gracious old palazzi. Located on Piazza del Gesù Nuovo, one of the very best is the **Albergo Sansevero Degas** ★★ (Calata Trinità Maggiore 53; ☎ 081-7901000; www.albergosansevero.it; AE, DC, MC, V), where, as the name implies, the apartments once belonged to French Impres-sionist painter Edgar Degas. Rooms are enormous, appointed with smart cane fur-niture and generally modern touches; the biggish in-room bathrooms are a bonus. Ask for a room overlooking the square (60€–110€ double with breakfast). A fine alternative if Degas is full is the **Soggiorno Sansevero** ★★ (Piazza San Domenico Maggiore 9; same contact details), which once belonged to the Prince of Sansevero (an eccentric 18th-c. noble); guest rooms—in the same price range—are defined by evocative architectural detailing and attractive period furniture.

€€€   Stay at **Hotel Neapolis** ★★ (Via Francesco del Giudice 13; ☎ 081-4420815; www.hotelneapolis.com; AE, MC, V), and you really will be in the heart of it all—perfect for exploring the old part of the city. The street entrance to the hotel is somewhere between quaint and off-putting; you have to walk through a courtyard shared by the entire palazzo, so you may trip over a tricycle or get dripped on by the wet laundry hanging overhead. An elevator transports you up to the third and fourth floors of an inner-city block, where the rooms are border-line smart, with shuttered windows and decent appointments (including personal computers and cable television). Standard doubles cost 125€ (with breakfast), and for an extra 20€ you score a Superior room with a bathroom (although, for the most, bathrooms are cramped). Ask for one of the rooms with a tiny balcony facing the Via Tribunali for a bird's-eye view of the lively Neapolitan scene below.

€€€   The farthest from the city center that you might want to stay is near the Mergellina port. Here, **Hotel Ausonia** (Via Francesco Caracciolo 11; ☎ 081-682278; www.hotelausonianapoli.com; AE, MC, V) occupies the second and third floors of a slightly run-down-looking palazzo, right across the road from the waterfront. Rooms start at 120€ (includes breakfast and air-conditioning) although discounts of 15% crop up regularly, particularly if you're here for a couple of days. The entire hotel has an intense nautical atmosphere (in fact, it's dressed up like a ship, with portholes, lots of knots, and navigation maps; in tiny bathrooms, the loo gets wet when you shower), but it's long been a favorite with returning clientele. Two rooms have balconies. The owners are personable and accessible (but only Daniele really understands English).

€€€–€€€€   Farther down toward the very expensive hotels on the waterfront is the best find in downtown Naples: **Chiaia Hotel de Charme** ✮✮✮ (Via Chiaia 216; ☎ 081-415555; www.hotelchiaia.it; AE, DC, MC, V). It wasn't so long ago that a lively brothel next door serviced many of the city's politicians and bankers, but in 2003, the hotel bought it to add to its eclectic collection of individually designed rooms—those in the old brothel are named for the girl who once worked inside (Mimi do Vesuvio, for example, is a large corner unit with two balconies), and are quaintly wallpapered, retaining a slightly edgy yet upmarket vibe. This place overflows with character. Furnishings are all original antiques, most of which belonged to the former owner, the Marquis Nicola Lecaldano Sasso III, who clearly had great taste in furniture. Double rooms (125€–165€ Standard; 145€–185€ Superior) have high ceilings and enormous beds, and come with Jacuzzi tubs and tiny balconies. At 5:30, the Chiaia hosts Neapolitan Hour, when local pastries are served along with an informative chat on aspects of "hidden Naples." Be sure to investigate the website for occasional specials.

A HOSTEL OPTION

€–€€   MTV Italy's latest hits erupt from a wide flatscreen TV above a library of DVDs in the cozy lounge of bright, funky **Hostel of the Sun** ✮✮ (Via Melisurgo 15; ☎ 081-4206393; www.hostelnapoli.com; MC, V), where the buzz is almost electric. This is easily the best place for the young to be based for a warm introduction to the city; it owes its success to zestful hands-on owner, Luca Coda, who—along with an upbeat team—goes the extra mile to ensure guests find their feet in Naples, experience the most authentic it has to offer, and have fun. The four dorms (20€) are clean and colorful (bright primaries, framed pop-art prints), and almost always full. If you prefer privacy, there are also double rooms (70€ with private bathroom, 55€ without), triples, and quads; these have wardrobes, TVs and DVD players, fans, potted plants, and a desk. The hostel occupies two floors of a seedy-looking apartment block right near the port. Hospitality is matchless: free pasta-and-wine nights, pizzeria excursions, and legendary tours exploring wilder, after-dark Naples. There's free Internet, Skype telephone, inexpensive laundry, and a host of other reasons to let your hair down here. Fear not: There's no curfew, no age limits, and breakfast (real coffee, OJ, cereal, fresh croissants, and enormous jars of Nutella) is included. Pay 10% less in low season and with this book.

DINING FOR ALL TASTES

The food in Naples is virtually always fresh, recipes are original, and the production of the common pizza is widely considered a venerable art form in this, the city that is generally considered the progenitor of the world's favorite fast food. Not only is the pizza to die for, but you'll need to try real hard to have a meal here that isn't excellent. That said, some of the more down-home Neapolitan restaurants and pizzerias may take a little getting used to, with the focus on tasty, belly-filling food that often flies out the pizza oven and onto your table with little more than a sneer by way of service. Don't be too put off by this unaffected approach; it may even come as a welcome antidote to the smarminess of so many places where you know your budget is about to be blown to smithereens.

Besides ubiquitous (and deservedly famous) pizzas, sun-ripened tomatoes and buffalo mozzarella (made from water-buffalo milk), capers, and unique pastas like cavatelli (made with only durum wheat and water) are popular on most menus. In Naples, a classic dish is *spaghettini alla puttanesca,* made with fresh tomatoes, garlic, anchovies, capers, and olives. Grilled swordfish and shellfish are also standard fare, and grilled cheeses and a wide variety of vegetables, from eggplant to wild chicory, round out most menus. Desserts tend to focus on candied fruits and nuts, or on the old standby: gelato. In the summer months, you might feel a little left out is you don't have an ice-cream cone in your hand.

Note that nearly every restaurant recommended here—particularly those not reliant on tourist business—closes for around 2 weeks in second half of August. Reservations are rarely required in Naples mostly because no one ever seems to answer the phone to take them. I've marked below the restaurants you should attempt to call first to secure a place. For a map of Naples's restaurants, see p. 503.

RESTAURANTS IN THE HISTORICAL CENTER

€   Vegan-friendly, but not at all foodie-unfriendly, **SorRiso Integrale** ★ (Vico San Pietro a Maiella 6, Piazza Bellini; ☎ 081-445026; www.sorrisointegrale.com; Mon–Sat 10am–midnight; AE, MC, V) is that rarest of heath-food restaurants in that it coaxes sinfully delicious flavors out of all those good-for-you foods. Menu offerings vary daily, but the emphasis is on healthful organic dishes that might help you out of that guilty slump following too many delicious, decadent pizzas. At press time, a *primi* portion of pasta with zucchini and ricotta cost just 4.50€, while all *secondi* dishes were 5.50€. A *piatto unico* (mixed plate), brimming with superb vegetarian concoctions, is a good deal (9€) if you want to savor different tastes, and you can easily split it between two. Organic wine and beer are also available. Definitely try for a table outside, where you'll dine under monstrous rubber trees (inside, the atmosphere is less appealing). Besides dining in, you can stock up on healthy organic goods available from the restaurant's deli.

€–€€   For a simple, affordable lunch in the historical center, without any airs or pretences, waltz determinedly into **La Campagnola** (Via dei Tribunali 47; ☎ 081-459034; daily noon–4pm; AE, DC, MC, V), marked by a near-invisible sign above the entrance. I'll never forget coming here for a quick pasta (in a very basic tomato sauce for just 4€), only to have a photo album filled with pictures of the menu items shoved in my face; the photographs are far from appealing, but the food certainly fills the gap. While listening to classical Italian music and a

Caffè, Café, Caffettiera

Neapolitan espresso is famously super-extra-strong, and provides a stellar jolt that will keep you on your toes throughout the day. A favorite spot to experience the full-on rush of Neapolitan java is **Chalet Ciro** (Via Francesco Caracciolo, Mergellina; ☎ 081-669928; www.chaletciro.it; daily 6:45am–2am; cash only), where locals form a spirited crowd all day long. I like to stop off here for an early-morning espresso (a mere .80€)—you pay for your shot of syrupy-sweet black sludge (you need to make a special request if you want it without sugar) and then join the heaving mass at the counter—and then return late at night to witness what looks like a diner scene from *Grease,* with hundreds of young and old punters, many on motorcycles, joining the crush for Ciro's famous ice cream.

At the other end of the scale—where snootiness and a high snob-quotient is all part of the deal—is **Gran Caffè Gambrinus** (Via Chiaia 1–2; ☎ 081-417582; www.caffegambrinus.it; daily 8am–1:30am; AE, MC, V), where you'll quickly part with a whole wad of 10€ notes if you don't keep your wits about you. Remember, it's the view and the distinguished company you're paying for. May as well order that pricey cocktail, and sip very, very slowly. This is the best place to people-watch in Naples, and maybe even in all of Italy. The waitstaff must have trained hard to be this unfriendly, but that somehow adds to the appeal. Neapolitans doll up to saunter by the outdoor tables in what is a cross between a fashion show and a vaudeville act. The Gambrinus has been graced by everyone from Oscar Wilde to Bill Clinton.

sing-song chorus of locals discussing family business, try to figure out what has put the grouchy, gum-chewing waiter in such a foul mood—I've certainly never seen him even attempt a smile. But so what? None of the *primi* dishes is over 6€.

€–€€   If your idea of a typical Neapolitan trattoria is a tiny restaurant with small tables piled high with good food, **Antica Trattoria da Carmine** ★★ (Via dei Tribunali 330; ☎ 081-294383; Mon–Sat noon–2:30pm, Wed–Sat 7–11pm; AE, DC, MC, V) should be your first stop. Come for lunch and you won't need more than a sliver of pizza for dinner. The restaurant will serve only what's in season, and then only if it's fresh—which means that the menu is usually pretty slim. That being said, portions are hefty, and the tabs are low, with *primi* going for 4€ to 12€. The chef has been known to come out of the kitchen after you've ordered to explain that he's run short of an ingredient or is unhappy with a piece of fish, and to tell you what you should order instead. Take his advice: This is exactly the type of experience you came to Naples for.

€–€€   For a taste of authentic home-style cooking, coupled with the atmospheric buzz of a very local crowd, head for **Da Ettore** ★★ (Via Santa Lucia 56; ☎ 081-7640498; Sept–June Tues–Sat 1–3pm and 8–11:30pm, Sun 1–3pm;

Devouring Pizza in the City That Thinks It Invented It

In Naples, the mark of guaranteed quality when it comes to the city's favorite export is VERA PIZZA—if you see this sign hanging outside a restaurant, you know that you'll be getting the real deal. Nevertheless, there are a few favorite pizzerias that demand your attention.

The three generations of *pizzaiole* at **Gino Sorbillo** ✦ (Via dei Tribunali 32; ☎ 081-446643; Mon–Sat noon–3:30pm and 7–11:30pm; AE, V) may convince you that this is the place to come to discover the last word in Neapolitan pizza (3€–6€). The diner-style venue (where silverware arrives in a wicker boat wrapped in a napkin) has more rave reviews than Taillevant in Paris (or at least that's the way it looks from the wall of self-acclaim at the front, where Sorbillo displays every article ever written about the restaurant—and there are many); beware the namesake upmarket venue on the same road. But Neapolitans will probably send you down the road to **Di Matteo** ✦✦ (Via Tribunali 94; ☎ 081-455262; www.pizzeria dimatteo.it; Mon–Sat 9am–midnight; cash only), where you have to squeeze through the heaving pizza oven–dominated kitchen area to get to one of the less-than-cheerful looking tables. Don't panic! You're not here to soak up the atmosphere, and you may wait awhile before anyone helps you; they're not being rude, they're simply enormously busy, servicing customers with arguably perfect pizza (there's more variety here than at Gino Sorbillo). Try to get a table that affords a view into the pizza-producing heart of the operation; you may imagine yourself witnessing the confluence of art and science. While you're here, look for clues letting you know which former U.S. president once supposedly ate here.

I'm also a fan of the ultra-laid-back, family-run 'a **Taverna 'e zi Carmela** ✦ (Via Nicolò Tommaseo 11-12, Chiaia; ☎ 081-7643581; Tues–Sun 9am–3pm and 6pm–midnight; AE, DC, MC, V), where a Neapolitan friend first took me for fabulously good pizza (4€–10€) and beer. No need for the menu here: If it's pizza you want, ask for *Margherita al filetto di Pomodoro,* a deliciously simple version of the classic tomato and mozzarella pizza with split cherry tomatoes grown in the volcanic soil of Mt. Vesuvius. Fish dishes are also highly recommended, and cost around 10€—again, don't bother with the menu; simply ask the chef to guide you to a selection. *Primi* dishes range from 3.50€ to 12€; *coperto* is 1.10€, and there's 15% service.

AE, DC, MC, V), an easy walk from Piazza del Plebiscito in a swank part of Naples (utterly out of place thanks to its no-frills decor). You'll find all the classic Neapolitan dishes here, with most pastas for just 7€. They're good (particularly the house favorite, made with Gorgonzola and aubergine), and it's a boon for vegetable lovers (try the perfect eggplant Parmesan), but meat dishes are also highly recommended.

€€   Up on the Vomero, the best choice you can make is the cozy **Donna Teresa** ★★ (Via Michele Kerbaker 58; ☎ 081-5567070; Mon–Sat 1–3pm and 8–11pm; reservations recommended; cash only), a terrifically popular restaurant with locals, especially at lunchtime, so you really must book ahead; this is when you can order a bargain-priced fixed menu. Once you've eaten here, you will understand the appeal—the food is marvelous, hearty, and unique. A favorite on the menu is the *pasta patata e provala*, a casserole of pasta, potatoes, and smoked cheese (just 12€).

€€   Do not even dream of coming to **Amici Miei** ★★ (Via Monte di Dio 78; ☎ 081-7644981; Tues–Sat 1–3pm and 8–11:30pm, Sun 1–3pm; reservations recommended; AE, DC, MC, V) without an appetite. Unmissable is the house pasta—*paccheri Amici Miei* (8€), made with eggplant and ultracreamy Gorgonzola sauce. Grilled meats are the other specialty. In a similar vein, **Trattoria San Ferdinando** ★★ (Via Nardones 117; ☎ 081-421964; Mon–Sat 12:30–3:30pm, Wed–Fri 8–11:30pm; AE, DC, MC, V), specializes in fish plucked right from the waves; the menu changes frequently, but standards like *pasta e fagioli* (8€) and pasta with calamari (9€) are always good. Grilled squid is also a perennial on the menu (and highly recommended). These are both classic Neapolitan restaurants—copious helpings, service with a twinkle in the eye—and you'll talk about them long after your trip.

A ROMANTIC WATERFRONT SPLURGE

In the shadow of the Castel dell'Ovo is a small restaurant mecca known as the Borgo Marinaro—basically a tiny fishing village stuck onto the edge of the city. Hands held across the table, romantic conversations, couples practically ravaging one another with their dreamy stares, surprise proposals: These are common sights at the restaurants of the Borgo Marino, where romance isn't just in the air, it's on the menu and playing footsie under the table. All of this loving is inspired by the lovely waterside views from each terraced restaurant (when the weather is chilly, they bring out heaters rather than close these money-making terraces). Many of the restaurants are carbon copies, romantic all the same, offering only slight variations of classic Neapolitan seafood dishes, but one stands out among the rest, largely thanks to its great legacy of survival: **Zi Teresa** ★★ (Borgo Marinaro 1; ☎ 081-7642565; reservations recommended; Tues–Sat 1–3:30pm and 8–11pm, Sun 1–3:30pm; AE, DC, MC, V) was a famous eatery after World War II— Norman Lewis wrote about the debauched goings on there in *Naples '44* (a keen account of the Neapolitan mind-set during the war). The former dive, named for a favorite aunt, is now a swank restaurant on an expansive terrace. But even though it's pricier than the trattorie in the center, it's still a very good value—for fresh seafood and fresh pasta, in particular—especially compared to what you get in cities like Rome for these prices. If you watch what you order, you can easily get a filling and delicious plate of pasta, a salad, and a carafe of the house white for around 30€, including service.

WHY YOU'RE HERE:
THE TOP SIGHTS & ATTRACTIONS

Naples is tremendously underrated as a place for great art and monumental architecture. As you walk its streets, you'll get a sense of history that is very much lived and breathed by its inhabitants who really don't seem to notice that they're amid so much that is genuinely eye-catching. In fact, I find it rather startling that so little has been done to curb the graffiti that clings to just about every building in the historical center, or to put an end to the street litter. But, then again, what may be off-putting to some visitors is actually a very clear indication of the authentic, down-to-earth, inner-city destination you're visiting.

Discussed below are the top attractions in a city that is brimming over with undiscovered delights; for extensive listings of events and other sights in and around Naples, pick up "Qui Napoli," a booklet published by the tourist authority every 2 months; or visit www.inaples.it for more information. Another excellent sightseeing tool are the audioguides available at the **MuseoAperto Napoli (Naples Open Museum)** (Via Pietro Colletta 89-95; ☎ 081-5636062; www.museoapertonapoli.com; Thurs–Tues 10am–6pm). The Museo's recorded tours cover 81 attractions throughout the city; you can also glean the latest tourist information here, and even leave your luggage (if you've checked out of your hotel or have yet to find one).

Note: If you're 18 to 25 you'll usually pay just half price for most attractions, while kids under 18 and persons over 65 get in free; however, you may be asked to produce EU identification to qualify (depending on who's selling the tickets).

SIGHTSEEING IN THE HISTORICAL CENTER

It is in Naples' *centro storico* that the raw Neapolitan energy is most evident. The performance begins with the early-morning buzz of mopeds and roar of tiny delivery trucks zipping through the crowds. In the late afternoons in the winter, these streets are filled with smocked school children playing soccer. In the summer, you'll see the Neapolitan elders—in windows and on street corners—catching up on neighborhood gossip. It's common to witness heated marital spats, passionate romantic trysts, near-fatal car accidents, and Neapolitan road rage, often in the same moment, and sometimes in the same family. This unbridled passion is what makes Naples so off-putting—and so captivating.

This part of town also has some of the city's best museums and most venerable churches. But it would be a shame not to stop and take time to really absorb the local color. Window-shop along the Spaccanapoli (comprising Via Benedetto Croce, Via San Biagio dei Librai, and Via Vicaria Vecchia) and Decumano Maggiore (now called Via dei Tribunali). Sit at an outdoor table at Café Diaz (Piazza Santa Maria Maggiore della Pietrasanta) or down farther at Lontano da Dove (Via Bellini 3). There are very few tourists here, so you won't pay an exorbitant table charge as you would on touristy Piazza Trieste e Tridente.

Alternatively, cross Via dei Tribunali into lovely Piazza Bellini, which is home to great restaurants and a magnet for Naples' more bohemian crowds. There are even cordoned-off ruins here, as if to remind you that Naples' history began long

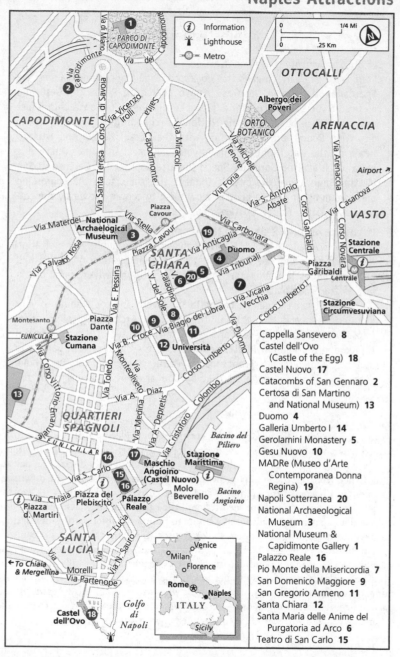

Naples Attractions

Cappella Sansevero **8**
Castel dell'Ovo
(Castle of the Egg) **18**
Castel Nuovo **17**
Catacombs of San Gennaro **2**
Certosa di San Martino
and National Museum) **13**
Duomo **4**
Galleria Umberto I **14**
Gerolamini Monastery **5**
Gesu Nuovo **10**
MADRe (Museo d'Arte
Contemporanea Donna
Regina) **19**
Napoli Sotterranea **20**
National Archaeological
Museum **3**
National Museum &
Capidimonte Gallery **1**
Palazzo Reale **16**
Pio Monte della Misericordia **7**
San Domenico Maggiore **9**
San Gregorio Armeno **11**
Santa Chiara **12**
Santa Maria delle Anime del
Purgatoria ad Arco **6**
Teatro di San Carlo **15**

Naples Itineraries

If you have only 1 day in Naples
Start with an early breakfast (*sfogliatella* and cappuccino) along the **Spaccanapoli.** Take in the **Gesù Nuovo** church on Piazza del Gesù and make sure you see the cloister adjacent to the church of **Santa Chiara** just next door. Then head up to the **National Archaeological Museum** in the city core. Round out the morning with the **Castel Nuovo** and **Palazzo Reale** on the waterfront. If this is your only meal in Naples, make it a pizza lunch at **Gino Sorbillo.** Spend the afternoon at the **Certosa di San Martino** high above the city. If there is still time, take the engrossing underground tour 40m (131 ft.) below the city center offered by the cultural association **Napoli Sotterranea.**

If you have only 2 days in Naples
Buy a 13€ ArteCard (p. 515), which gives you free public transportation (land and sea) and free admission to two paying attractions (plus half price on the rest). Again, start the first day with an early-morning breakfast on the Spaccanapoli.

On the first day, add the **Cappella Sansevero** and the **Duomo** to your morning walk, and then take in the **National Archaeological Museum** (closed Tues). Spend the rest of the day in the center, visiting the **Castel Nuovo** and the **Palazzo Reale,** and add to them the **Teatro di San Carlo** and the gorgeous **San Francesco di Paola** church on the Piazza del Plebiscito. If you've done all that by late afternoon, take a boat tour

before the trendy cafes occupied this spot. Keep wandering until you get to Via Toledo (aka Via Roma), the city's main shopping street and one of its most congested footpaths. Cross over to the Spanish Quarter, but only during the day and only when you see the streets crowded. This is the seediest part of downtown Naples, and home to the Camorra and other thriving crime gangs. It's worth a quick exploration, though, to see firsthand the *casa bassa,* the classic ground-floor Neapolitan apartment, traditionally home to poorer inhabitants. Residents' doors and windows are invariably open, so you'll discover the neighborhood's deep sense of community. Here, too, you'll see religious demonstrations in the form of neon shrines to the Madonna and ornate crucifixes against a sea of billowing laundry. But be careful here—it's easy to get lost in the maze of streets, and you may feel uneasy as conversations almost always halt when strangers pass by. Again, the area is best avoided late at night, and—as everywhere in Naples—don't carry valuables that might make you seem like an obvious target for petty thieves.

Ancient & Modern Art

The crown jewel of the Neapolitan museum scene is the **National Archaeological Museum** ★★ (Piazza Museo 19; ☎ 081-4422111; www.archeona.arti.beniculturali.it; 9€; Wed–Mon 9am–7:30pm), Europe's oldest and, experts agree, most around the Bay of Naples to the **Posillipo.** Finish up the evening by either splurging for a romantic dinner down on the waterfront at **Borgo Marino** under the shadow of the Castel dell'Ovo, or enjoying a cheap and authentic Neapolitan pizza at **Gino Sorbillo** on Via Tribunali.

On your second day, head up to the **Certosa di San Martino** (closed Wed) as early as you can and catch the views from the terrace or the old monastery windows. Then take in even better views from the rooftop terrace of nearby **Castel Sant' Elmo.** Also up on the hills above the city center, don't miss the **National Museum of Capodimonte** (closed Wed) and the **Catacombs of San Gennaro** (plan your arrival to fit in with one of the scheduled tours). After you've done the upper reaches, head back down and catch an underground tour by **Napoli Sotterranea.** Follow that up with some shopping on the **Via Toledo** and treat yourself to a cold drink at the **Gambrinus** on Piazza del Plebiscito before heading out of town.

If you have only 3 days in Naples

Immediately buy a 25€ ArteCard, and start out by visiting **Pompeii** or **Herculaneum,** starting out as early as possible, and then catch the bus to **Mt. Vesuvius.** Round off the day with an evening tour of **MADRe,** Naples' impressive modern art gallery where you can enjoy a drink in the bar at the end of your tour. Then follow the same 2-day itinerary above, making sure to adjust your schedule to account for museum closings on Tuesdays and Wednesdays.

comprehensive archaeological museum. Disappointingly, it's poorly managed, to the extent that your experience will be greatly hampered if you don't plan ahead—some of the most provocative exhibition rooms (like the Gabinetto Segreto, see below) open only for short periods at unpredictable times, so you need to call in advance to time your visit accordingly. On the **lower floor** surrounding an open courtyard, you'll wander through a massive collection of statues and bronze works; you can't help but be wowed by the graceful statues of muscled men towering over you (even if many are embarrassingly emasculated). Most of these pieces were excavated from digs in the Roman Forum and along the coast of Campania, between Naples and Sorrento. The ground floor also has masterpieces from the Farnese collections, notably, the exemplary Farnese Bull, and colossal statues of Hercules and Tiberius; notice how so much of the collection stresses the body's beauty—not unlike much fashionable photography today.

If you're pressed for time, head straight up the original open stairway to the **mezzanine floor,** and feast your eyes on some extraordinary mosaics, interesting as much for their delicacy as for their frequently mundane subject matter. The best of these is the large *Alexander the Great Defeating Darius,* brought here from the House of Faun, one of the finest examples of private architecture found in Pompeii. There are 1.5 million tiny tiles in this 3×6m (10×20-ft.) mosaic masterpiece, which was dug out from under the crusted lava and reconstructed here at the museum.

The mezzanine is where you'll see the best of the artifacts and relics carefully removed from the lava-encrusted ruins of nearby Pompeii, Herculaneum, and Stabiae. Check out the ancient coins and the unbroken pottery—the latter seems impossible when you consider that all of these pieces were covered by 2.7m (9 ft.) of smoldering ash and pumice moments after Mt. Vesuvius's A.D. 79 eruption.

To get an idea of just what kind of people the ancient Pompeians were, don't miss the seriously erotic art that is kept in the **Gabinetto Segreto (Secret Room)** on the mezzanine; the collection includes overtly humorous works, as well as an overview of the Pompeians curious interest in the wanton behaviors of "exotic" peoples—notably of Africa's mythically well-endowed Pygmies. Strangely, although it's probably the most popular room in the entire museum, it's only periodically opened, so coordinate your visit by calling ahead to check these times.

While the museum houses a priceless and important collection, not all of it will appeal to everybody; if you're pressed for time, you'll quickly get an idea of which rooms to scoot through, or enrich your experience of the old-fashioned museum by renting an audioguide (4€).

Nearby is Naples' excellent new art museum, **MADRe (Museo d'Arte Contemporanea Donna Regina)** ★★★ (Via Settembrini 79; ☎ 081-292833; www.museomadre.it; 7€, free on Mon; Wed–Mon 10am–9pm, Fri–Sat 10am–midnight), with a well-curated collection by international superstars (and lesser knowns) of the modern and contemporary schools—including Jeff Koons, Warhol, and Lichtenstein. Some standouts worth your attention (or your scorn) are local boy Piero Manzoni, a mid-20th-century conceptual artist (who notoriously gave us cans of his own excrement in the early 1960s); and Robert Rauschenberg, whose aesthetically vapid *Pompei Gourmet Kitchen Glut (Neapolitan)* (1987) seems to upend the cheerfulness of pop art. One of Damien Hirst's formaldehyde-preserved sheep (*Away from the Flock*, 1994) is here, too, occupying the same room as Gilbert & George's pithy *Shitty World* (also 1994). And, by the time you arrive at a few of Robert Mapplethorpe's photo-images of idealized naked, muscled men, you've only just reached the end of the permanent exhibition. Upstairs, there's even more weird and wacky and edifying work in top-rated temporary exhibitions; Rauschenberg will be taking over from Piero Manzoni in spring of 2008.

Inside the Ancient City

The best way to get a sense of Naples' intriguing history is to get down, right inside of it. One of my favorite experiences in the historical center, and a definite must-do for anyone with an interest in architecture, city planning, or human survival, is a tour given by **Napoli Sotterranea** ★★★ (Piazza San Gaetano 68; ☎ 081-296944; www.napolisotterranea.org; 9.30€; tours Mon–Fri at noon, 2, and 4pm; Sat–Sun 10am, noon, 2, 4, and 6pm). These private, guided tours (90 min.) in English, Italian, or German take you some 40m (131 ft.) under the city center to explore the labyrinth of tunnels that have served as aqueducts, catacombs, clandestine worship space, and, most recently, a garbage dump. Pro-Mussolini graffiti line the walls of the ancient cisterns; nevertheless, the atmosphere down there is akin to some arcane subterranean cathedral. All in all there are 170km (105 miles) of aqueducts (serving about 6,000 wells) beneath the

Naples' Attractions at a Fraction of the Price

Thumb your nose at scandalous museum prices by purchasing the excellent-value integrated ticket **ArteCard** (☎ 800-600601; www.campaniartecard.it), a smart investment if you plan to go to at least two museums or archaeological sites, like Pompeii and Caserta. Here's how to make the most of it.

The 13€ entry-level card—valid only for sites within the city of Naples (your first two attractions free and you pay half price for all subsequent sites) and free public transport for 3 days—is useful for city slickers who aren't keen on ancient ruined cities. Fair enough. But if you are planning a romp among the ruins of Pompeii or Herculaneum (or both), then don't think twice about getting the 25€ card, covering attractions farther afield. To play the system to the max, make sure your first two visits are the most expensive (I'd see Pompeii and Herculaneum first), ensuring that you save the most on entry fees. You can then relax your way through the rest of your chosen attractions, where you'll pay half the normal ticket price for the 3 days it's valid.

Even if you are only in town for 2 days, play your cards right (no dawdling) and you'll score. If you're 18 to 25, you qualify for a cheaper version of the card and get free admission to all sites. You can buy the card at any of the sights, at the airport, and at train stations, hotels, and some tobacco shops. In theory the card is also supposed to allow you to cut long lines at ticket stands, but in most cases, you still have to go to the ticket agent to validate the card.

city. They were decommissioned as late as 1885 due to a cholera outbreak; for around 60 years they became a dumping ground, until their usefulness as air-raid shelters was realized during World War II. Stirringly, many Neapolitans who lost their homes during air raids simply continued living here, beneath the surface. A favorite part of the tour is when everyone is given a candle for the evocative walk through some very skinny passages (if you're claustrophobic or stocky, you're allowed to skip this part), when you get an unnerving idea what life might have been like for the children who once worked down here as water cleaners.

The other part of the tour explores the initial excavation of a massive ancient Greek-Roman theater, which is said to be where Nero made his artistic debut (he notoriously paid 5,000 spectators to witness his agonizing performance). The entrance alone is an eye-opener, as your animated guide takes you into a tiny street-level apartment—*bassi*—and pushes a bed out of the way to reveal a hidden stairway. It's simply fascinating to note that the modern-looking "box" almost directly in the middle of the underground excavation is the floor and sewer piping of someone's modern kitchen in the apartment block above; it's an excellent way to discover firsthand how Naples has grown upward over the centuries, with new constructions simply plopped on top of older buildings and foundations. This is one of the most fascinating tours in Naples today; make it a priority.

Churches in the Historical Center

The archaeological museum is at the edge of the historical core of the city, an easy launching point for visiting Naples' most venerable churches, including its main basilica, **Il Duomo** ✸✸✸ (Via Duomo 147; ☎ 081-449097; free; audioguide 4€ for chapel and cathedral combined; daily 8am–12:30pm and 4:30–7pm, public holidays 8am–1:30pm and 5–7:30pm). If you're coming from other Italian cities like Rome or Venice, you may be disappointed by its drab neo-Gothic facade. But venture in and you'll be justly rewarded by the stunning interior built between the 1200s and 1300s. It holds many remnants of the two previous churches that occupied this site, including much of Naples' oldest church, the 4th-century Basilica di Santa Restituta, which now serves as the chapel on the right-hand side. The left-hand nave leads to the archaeological area (3€; Mon–Sat 9am–noon and 4:30–7pm, Sun 9am–noon) and to more remains of the Basilica di Santa Restituta. These excavations are worth exploring to see the ancient Greek and Roman columns that remain. Remnants of an old Greek road will give you an idea of the level of ancient Neapolis.

Back inside the church, most of the relics have to do with San Gennaro, Naples' patron saint. There are frescoes of the saint's life, statues of his contemporaries, and a bust with his skull bones inside. Beside the main altar are two vials said to contain his congealed blood. In May, September, and December, the Neapolitan faithful (and curious tourists lucky enough to be in town for the spectacle; see "The Other Naples," on p. 524) crowd into the tiny Chapel of the Treasury to witness a miracle, as a vial of St. Gennaro's blood liquefies. Legend has it that this miracle will save Naples from disaster. It's hard not to get caught up in the moment and even to believe the legend because the last time the blood failed to liquefy was in 1944, when Mt. Vesuvius last erupted.

To learn more about San Gennaro—or least see more of the worldly treasures associated with him—peek into the **Museo del Tesoro di San Gennaro** (☎ 081-294980; www.museosangennaro.com; 5.50€; Tues–Sat 9:30am–5pm, Sun 9:30am–2:30pm), attached to the Duomo, and packed with shiny, precious objects of devotion and fascination; an audioguide is included in the steep admission fee.

The area between the Spaccanapoli and Via dei Tribunali is rich with churches, cloisters, and monasteries. Each has its own story to tell, though unfortunately, not many offer any sort of explanation. If you see a nun or priest lingering around the naves, don't be shy about asking questions. More often than not, they will speak some English and many are happy to help if they know the answers. You might even be lucky enough to get a quick private tour. On the other hand, there is just as good a chance that you'll be greeted with an annoyed shrug.

You can wander in and out of the tiny churches and chapels in this area at your leisure, but definitely save time for the area's two most famous churches that border the Piazza del Gesù (see below). Right on the piazza is **Gesù Nuovo** ✸✸ (☎ 081-5518613; daily 7am–12:30pm and 4–7:30pm), a former 15th-century palazzo, but now a church with a baroque interior full of fabulous art, from the Cosimo Fanzago sculptures of David and Jeremiah to the enormous 1725 fresco *Expulsion of Heliodorus from the Temple* by Francesco Solimena. Off to the left is a room of relics dedicated to the popular local saint Giuseppe Moscati, who tended medically to the poor. The walls are lined with a bizarre collection of golden syringes and notes of thanks offered up by the faithful who came here to ask the saint for health. There's even a handwritten note on the left-hand side announcing when the local vicar will let the devoted into a private sanctuary to kiss the saint's relics.

Adjacent to the piazza, through a decaying 14th-century arch, is the austere **Santa Chiara** ★ (Via Benedetto Croce; ☎ 081-5526280). Most of the church was destroyed by World War II bombing in 1943, so the interior is largely unembellished. The fire that followed the bombing took 6 days to put out, and destroyed all the original Gothic and baroque features and frescoes by masters like Giotto. Local children play soccer in front of the main entrance in the summer, and a slew of Gypsy women line the steps asking for a little *spicci*, or small change. The main draw here is its **14th-century cloister** ★★★ (4€ for cloister and museum; Mon–Sat 9:30am–1pm and 2:30–5:30pm, Sun 9:30am–1pm) around the back on the left. It's hard to believe you're still in the center of Naples when you step into this peaceful haven. And it's no surprise that these serene gardens are a frequent meeting point for Neapolitan elders, who sit on the always-cool stone benches along the perimeter. If you follow these old-timers in, watch how the ticket seller casually walks away to let them pass by without paying. But stay away from the maze of colorful benches in the center; these are strictly off-limits, and if you try to sit here, a SWAT team of church officials will intervene. Nevertheless, look closely at the details of the tiles, which range from floral landscapes to happy village scenes from the 18th century. Adjacent, the bitty museum is unimpressive except for a few salvaged archaeological treasures.

There are two fascinating smaller churches in this quarter. First is the Gothic **San Domenico Maggiore** ★ (daily 8:30am–noon and 4:30–7pm) on the piazza of the same name, which was built right on top of the church of Sant'Angelo a Morfisa. Small chapels on each side are named for those who took solace here, like Giordano Bruno, who was burned at the stake in Rome's Campo de' Fiori; and St. Thomas Aquinas, who stayed here in the 13th century and whose chapel features an icon that is said to have spoken to him. You're sure to be deeply moved by the beautiful frescoes by Pietro Cavallini. The second of these smaller churches is the **Cappella Sansevero** ★★★ (Via Francesco de Sanctis; ☎ 081-5518470; www.museosansevero.it; 6€; Mon–Sat 10am–5pm, Sun 10am–1:10pm), with an astonishing *Veiled Christ* by Giuseppe Sanmartino, a sculpture which will make you rethink any preconceptions you had about the limitations of marble. The frescoed ceiling (*Glory of the Holy Spirit*, 1749) is also rather mind-boggling—the vivid colors, spatial arrangement, and illusion of 3D depth is extraordinary, especially after the bleakness of the streets outside.

Also worth a look is the 17th-century **Pio Monte della Misericordia** ★★ (Via Tribunali 253; ☎ 081-446944; www.piomontedellamisericordia.it), if only for its stunning Caravaggio masterpiece, *The Seven Acts of Mercy* (1606–07), said to have been inspired by the alleyways of Naples. Study the picture close up to appreciate Caravaggio's immense understanding of the power of light and shade, as well as his ability to encapsulate tension and movement; then step to the back of the little church for a near-filmic view of the same painting. Make sure you also see Luca Giordano's moving *Deposizione*.

Closer to Via dei Tribunali, don't miss the Renaissance **Gerolamini Monastery** (Via Duomo 142; ☎ 081-449139; Mon–Sat 9:30am–12:50pm), with its 60,000-volume library of ancient books and documents (generally off limits). It's not the

Never on a Sunday

Unless you're prepared to attend Mass, don't even think about visiting Naples' churches on Sunday mornings. You'll be hushed and rushed out of the nave before you can make the sign of the cross. Churches open as early as 6:30am; almost all are open by 8am. They close again around noon, some as late as 1pm. (The churches tend to open again at 4pm and close by 9pm). Stay away from churches during unannounced services like funerals and weddings, no matter how tempting it may be to steal a peek at a gorgeous bride. In time, she'll be out on the church steps for all to see.

books you come to see but the inner garden of the cloisters, filled with lemon trees. You pass through the garden on your way to the library and its adjacent gallery, with fascinating works by Luca Giordano, like his *Mourning the Death of Christ* (studied for its grotesque style). Also worth a look is the baroque **Santa Maria delle Anime del Purgatoria ad Arco** ✪ (Via Tribunali 39; daily 9am–1pm), which was once the site for a Christian cult—now supposedly banned—that focused on the dead. You'll easily spot this church by the funerary decorations on its facade, including skulls and bones on the columns. Inside, take a quick peek at the sculpted skull with wings and crossbones of the church's designer Cosimo Fanzago, the region's king of baroque architecture. Next, if you've a weak spot for the truly outlandish, you can arrange a visit to the **hypogeum (underground chamber)** (2.60€; open by arrangement or Sat 10am–1pm), where there are still piles of bones and skulls that were said to have been "adopted" by women married to soldiers during the war. These women would care for the skulls and even sleep next to them in the absence of their husbands.

SIGHTS IN & AROUND ROYAL NAPLES

The grime and edginess of the *centro storico* and Spanish Quarter seem to melt away when you enter Santa Lucia and the waterfront area. Whether you're having a glass of wine and people-watching on Piazza Trieste e Trento or at the nearby Piazza del Plebiscito, or discovering art and history at the Palazzo Reale or Castel Nuovo, there's plenty in what is referred to as Royal Naples to tempt your imagination.

Castel Nuovo ✪ (Largo Castello, entrance from Piazza Municipio; ☎ 081-7952003; 5€; Mon–Sat 9am–7pm) is probably the first thing you see, after Mt. Vesuvius, if you arrive in Naples by boat. Its stoic exterior is a mainstay in the waterfront skyline, with its five towers and stark Renaissance doorway. Enter from the back, off the Piazza Municipio, and head straight to the top for the view of the harbor and city. Don't miss the bronze doors by Guglielmo Monaco, complete with an embedded cannonball. Unfortunately, the museum, meant to specialize in Neapolitan artists is poorly curated and confusingly laid out. Only a few works are outstanding, including 19th-century Vincenzo Caprile's *Vecchia Napoli,* which shows the famous Zizze fountain in its original glory; Camillo Miola's near-camp flour mill scene, *Plauto mugnaio* (1864); and Gerolamo Starace *Franchis' Baptism* *of Christ*. More captivating than the museum is the Cappella delle Anime del Purgatorio, which has vivid, if unnerving, frescoes of the tortures meted out in purgatory. The Sala dei Baroni is where the modern-day Neapolitan City Council meets—feel free to snoop if they're not in session.

A few minutes away is **Palazzo Reale** ★ (Piazza del Plebiscito, entrance near Piazza Trieste e Trento; ☎ 081-400547; 7.50€; Thurs–Tues 9am–7pm), which is not to be confused with the Palazzo Reale on Capodimonte Hill. This one is a natural accompaniment to the nearby Castel Nuovo. Its main courtyard and charming gardens are free, and Neapolitan nannies bring the city's wealthy children here to play. Once inside, you'll tour the glorious living quarters, built for the Spanish royalty in 1600; later the Bourbon kings and queens ordered their expansion. It's easy to imagine the extravagant goings-on under the ornate frescoes. The best rooms are the Court Theatre, with its ornate ceiling; the Ambassadors' Hall; the Palatine Chapel; and the library, with its million-plus volumes.

Adjacent to the Palazzo Reale is the extraordinary **Teatro di San Carlo** ★★ (Via San Carlo 101–103; ☎ 081-7972412; daily 9am–7pm). Europe's oldest working theater it was built in 1737 by Charles of Bourbon, but rebuilt after being destroyed by fire in 1816. If you can't make it for a performance, prebook a guided tour with **Itinera** (☎ 081-664545; www.itineranapoli.com; 5€; Mon–Sat 9am–5:30pm). Also see "Nightlife," p. 528.

EXPLORING BEYOND PIAZZA TRIESTE E TRENTO

Just across the street from Teatro di San Carlo are the adjoining squares of Piazza Trieste e Trento, with its hectic traffic circle and buzzing cafes, and Piazza del Plebiscito. From the Bar del Professore on Piazza Trieste e Trento, you can access a slightly hidden underpass leading to the **Napoli nella Raccolta de Mura** (☎ 081-7957736; free; Mon–Sat 9am–6pm), a funky underground museum celebrating the golden age of Neapolitan music. It's worth a peek, if just for a few minutes. The adjacent Piazza del Plebiscito is one of Naples' most recognizable squares; its Roman Pantheon knock-off church of San Francesco di Paola is embraced by two colonnades of Doric columns. Built in 1817 by King Ferdinand to celebrate Naples' escape from French rule, this neoclassical church lacks the warmth of other city-center churches; it's also much more impressive from the outside, so if you're pressed for time, skip the inside.

The piazza, a major hub for Neapolitan celebrations, outdoor concerts, and political rallies, is another matter. It's hard to imagine now, but this square used to be nothing more than a giant parking lot until the city closed it to traffic in 1994 to welcome the G8 conference. From this square, you can head down to the main ferry port or cross over to the museums of Castel Nuovo and Palazzo Reale.

The other streets around this area make up Naples' main shopping district, centered on Via Toledo (officially Via Roma). But better than shopping here, is the early evening "street theater," when, starting around 5pm, it seems that every Neapolitan is out for a *passeggiata*—a parade of color and emotion. Also great for a slow amble is gracious Via Chiaia, a pedestrian zone that attracts as many street performers as window-shoppers. Via Chiaia feeds into the designer shops around Piazza dei Martiri (see "Attention, Shoppers!" on p. 527), from where you can safely wander the vibrant, upmarket Chiaia district.

If you're more interested in actually *seeing* Naples than in being seen, head up to the summit of the **Monte Echia** ✦✦, which was originally settled in the 7th century B.C. as the city of Parthenope. Getting here is a short but grueling hike up the hill from the Piazza Carolina, just behind the north end of Piazza del Plebiscito. When you reach Via Egiziaca a Pizzofalcone, just keep climbing until you reach the top and are presented with spectacular views.

BORGO MARINARO & THE WATERFRONT

Castel dell'Ovo (Borgo Marinari; ☎ 081-2400055; free; Mon–Sat 8am–6pm, Sun 8am–2pm), the oldest castle in Naples, almost always seems to be in some sort of transition, whether it's a new excavation or a general shoring up of the ancient walls. Most of the interior is closed to the public and used as office space, so unless there's a special exhibit of note, there's little reason, beyond the view, to visit. Do take in the view while you're here. More interesting in this area is the **Borgo Marinaro** ✦✦, a tiny fishing village that's attached like a barnacle onto the side of the city center. There are some apartments, but the dock area is mostly sidewalk cafes and seafood restaurants overlooking the expensive yachts and fishing boats moored here. It's a vibrant spot in the summer, but can be blistering in winter.

PIAZZA GARIBALDI, CORSO UMBERTO I & THE PORTA NOLANA MARKET

The area around Piazza Garibaldi is among the more chaotic in the city, its sleazy reputation centered on the down-at-heel district of Forcella, where poverty and crime are endemic. But this part of town also has its charm. It's here that the city's many immigrants set up stalls and shops, giving the city an almost Middle Eastern feel. Here, too, is Chinatown.

The two most noteworthy churches in this area are **Santa Maria del Carmine** (Piazza del Carmine; ☎ 081-201196), which is known for a swath of miracles including an incident in which—during a 15th-century siege—a crucifixion effigy of Christ is said to have ducked and blinked to avoid being struck by a cannonball; and **San Pietro ad Aram** (Corso Umberto I 292; ☎ 081-286411).

Surviving the Neapolitan Market

No description can do justice to the sensory overload of Naples most famous market, the **Mercato di Porta Nolana** ✦✦✦ (mornings along the Via Cesare Carmignano and Via Sporamuro). Not even a camera can capture the experience—there's simply too much going on. The chaos reaches its apogee as you approach the fishmongers, whose yelps and howls can be downright unnerving. Don't back away; instead, start up a conversation with them. Many know some English and will be glad to share seafood recipes with you (if there is an open jar of home-canned sardines nearby, you'll be obliged to take a taste). If you have the kids along, don't be surprised if they're soon holding squid and starfish. These burly men are possibly the most gentle Neapolitans around, so don't be shy.

Both are uniquely Neapolitan and steeped in religious tradition. At San Pietro ad Aram, for example, the crypt (currently undergoing restoration) of the unknown martyrs is supposedly buried behind the white walls; the souls of these martyrs are still worshipped by the local faithful. Buy a red votive candle, and listen as they hum Gregorian chants and reach out toward the wall—it's a magical experience and a very good introduction to the religious fervor of the Neapolitans.

The university buildings on and around the southwestern end of Corso Umberto I are worth investigating for their magisterial architecture; if they're open, you can even venture inside. The nearby **State Archives** (Piazzetta Grande Archivo 5; ☎ 081-204491; www.archivi.beniculturali.it/sitoenglish.html; free; Mon–Fri 9am–6pm, Sat 9am–1pm) are set in a former 9th-century monastery comprising four unique cloisters, each with entrancing artwork.

CAPODIMONTE & LA SANITÀ

The hill and valley of Capodimonte and La Sanità are as contradictory as Naples gets. La Sanità's residential streets are congested and dirty, and there don't seem to be any businesses other than motorcycle repair shops. But up above, on the Capodimonte, are some of Naples' best attractions, starting with the exquisite **Museo di Capodimonte** ★★★ (Parco di Capodimonte, Via Miano 2; ☎ 081-7499111; http://capodimonte.spmn.remuna.org; 7.50€, 6.50€ after 2pm; Thurs–Tues 8:30am–7:30pm). A massive palazzo, it was intended as a hunting lodge for the Bourbon king Charles VII in 1738, but during its construction it evolved and became what it is today: a palace housing the art collections of Charles and his mother, Elisabetta Farnese. In 1860, the museum expanded to house Naples' Gallery of Modern Art. In 1957 it evolved again to become the Museo Nazionale di Capodimonte and Farnese Collection. It is widely considered one of the world's best Renaissance and post-Renaissance art collections, with some 160 rooms spread out over three floors (invest in an audioguide for 4€!).

Don't try to do the whole museum in one visit—there is simply no way you can survive that much art in one dose. Instead, dedicate a couple of hours to the highlights, kicking off with a number of paintings of morbid-looking Catholic cardinals (notably Raphael's portrait of a beady-eyed future Pope Paul III, in **Room 2**); the *Crucifixion* (1426) by Masaccio, in **Room 3;** Botticelli's *Madonna with Baby and Angels,* in **Room 6;** Titian's stand-out *Danäe*—featuring a woman reclining on a white sheet (she's Argos's daughter, and is being seduced by Jupiter, who has craftily turned up in the guise of gold raindrops), with darkness looming ominously in the background—in **Room 11.** Once you've seen those, snoop around the Gallery of Rare Objects to view such treasures as the gold-embossed dining table of Cardinal Alessandro Farnese. There are also porcelain collections in the Royal Apartments that are spread through rooms **31 to 60,** and intricately woven Belgian tapestries on the second floor. **Room 78** is dedicated entirely to Caravaggio's *Flagellation* (1607–10). Along the way, catch exceptional works by Bellini (1432–1516) in the Farnese collection. Among the surprises of the collection are modernist works by the likes of Domenica Spinosa, Gianni Pisani, and Guido Tatafiore, and an incredibly violent feminist revenge work by female baroque artist Artemesia Gentileschi, depicting two women killing a man.

The museum is set inside the former 130-hectare (321-acre) hunting reserve called the Parco di Capodimonte (free; daily 8am to 1 hr. before sunset). It boasts five lakes, several villas, and an old porcelain factory, but unless you're in Naples for an extended stay, this park is probably not worth your time.

Instead, head down to the **Catacombs of San Gennaro** ★★ (Via Capodimonte 16; ☎ 081-7411071; 5€; Tues–Sun, hourly guided tours only 9am–noon and 2–3pm). The entrance is hidden back behind the church (Madre di Buon Consiglio), on the left side. These are Naples' oldest and most intriguing catacombs, dating back to the 2nd century. There are two levels of catacombs, complete with frescoed ceilings, pillars, and arches holding up the passageways among the tombs. Naples' patron saint, San Gennaro, was moved here in the 5th century when the site became a must-see for religious pilgrims.

When you're exploring this part of Naples, it's impossible not to notice the beautifully tiled dome of the **Santa Maria della Sanità** (Via della Sanità 124; ☎ 081-5441305; free; daily 9:30am–12:30pm); below that church are the **Catacombs of San Gaudioso** ★ (5€; guided tours daily at 9:30, 10:15, 11, 11:45am, and 12:30pm), named after St. Gaudiosus, an African bishop who died in Naples in the 5th century and was buried here. Some remnants of mosaics and weathered frescoes date as far back as the 5th and 6th centuries. You'll learn much about burial rites here including the fact that corpses of the middle class and the poor were left in the fetal position, symbolizing that human beings should leave the world as they entered it. Wealthy families apparently stuck the skulls and assorted bones of their dead into walls, and had frescoes of skeletons painted around them. You'll see the stone chairs where corpses were placed to decompose for this macabre wall art. Starting from the basilica, the catacomb tour takes about an hour and is as grisly as it is engrossing.

VOMERO

Until the 1800s, this area was nothing more than a grassy field, accessible only by the winding steps of the Pedamentina a San Martino. These steps are still intact, and I highly recommend them as a way to get back down to center city in about 15 minutes. But going *up* these steps is grueling—take the funicular or bus instead.

Present-day Vomero is mostly a swank residential area but it's worth visiting, if only for its glorious **Certosa-Museo di San Martino** ★★ (Largo San Martino 5; ☎ 081-7499580 or 848-800288; 6€; Thurs–Tues 8:30am–7:30pm; metro to Vanvitelli, funicular Montesanto to Morghen, Centrale to Fuga), the large monastery that dominates the hill above the city. Built as a Carthusian monastery in the 14th century, San Martino now consists of an exquisite baroque church and an art museum as well as the bizarre Sezione Presepiale—an extensive display of 4 centuries' worth of super-kitschy hand-carved Nativity scenes, like those sold today in Naples. Carry on through this part of the museum and out into the Great Cloister, a serene oasis . . . except for the odd display of skulls along the railings. On the far side of the cloister is a tiny waiting room where you may be able to engage one of the experts to take you through the locked portion of the museum. It holds a fascinating collection of old maps and scenes of Naples, along with ebony boxes and intricate clocks. Most people come here to see the famous Pietro Bernini sculpture, *Madonna and Child with the Infant John the Baptist,* but note that you may be disappointed to find the art gallery, Museo dell'Opera, closed—so call ahead to ensure that staff can open it for you. An audioguide (4€; 2.50€ with ArteCard) can help you gather more intelligence on the history, luminous frescoes, and other artworks; irritatingly, several important rooms are closed except at certain strategic times (usually 9:30, 11am, and 1pm).

Tip: The view is as awe inspiring as the church/museum. To take it in, pass the ticket stand and bookstore in the courtyard, and then head left through the first set of arches, past the ornate carriages, and out onto the tiled overlook: Terraced gardens seem to cascade down the hill, and the whole of historical Naples stretches out before you.

Your ticket for San Martino scores you free entry to the odd **Castel Sant'Elmo** (Via Tito Angelini 20; ☎ 081-5784030; 3€; Thurs–Tues 9am–6:30pm), just down the road. Originally built in 1329 over the site of a 10th-century church, it's notorious for the plethora of prisoners (many of them Neapolitan heroes) who have been held in the dungeons here. The rooftop (or Piazza d'Armi) affords untainted panoramas over the Bay of Naples, Mt. Vesuvius, and the entire city.

MERGELLINA & POSILLIPO

The port of Mergellina is brimming with trendy cafes, wine bars, and restaurants making it a lively place to spend a summer or fall evening (but on a cold winter day, you'll be positively miserable here). Along the promenade from Castel dell'Ovo (p. 520) to Mergellina is **Villa Comunale** (Mon–Sat 7am–10pm, Sun 7am–midnight), a pleasant park tucked inside of which is the uninspiring Acquario, the first aquarium in Europe open to the public (founded 1872).

The highlight of this part of town is the Posillipo, one of the most romantic spots in Naples, judging by the many couples who visit. The modest will turn their eyes from the activity in the cars that line the streets on the main Via Petrarca. For others, it will be voyeur's paradise. In summer, this is the best place in Naples to sunbathe, if you don't mind paying for beach space. These beaches are not suitable for children, though, because the water is deep and the shoreline is unpredictable and hard to navigate. It's an enchanting area to explore if you have time (and good shoes), with highlights like the **Grotta di Seiano**, ★ (Discesa la Gaiola 36, or Discesa Coroglio; ☎ 081-7952003; guided tours Mon–Sat 9:30, 10:30, and 11:15am only; bus: 140), a 720m (2,361-ft.) tunnel with many galleries and stunning views of the sea right off the Posillipo cape.

Monumental Merrymaking in the Merry Month of May

The best cultural event this side of Rome is Naples' **Maggio dei Monumenti (Monument of May)** (☎ 081-2471123), when the city is alive with activity. Owners of impressive palazzi, which are generally closed to the public, open their doors for a peek inside. The city sponsors open-air concerts, exhibits, and street fairs in nonconventional places and out-of-the-way piazzas. You could wander around Naples every day of the month without repeating your steps. It's a cultural bonanza well worth catching.

THE OTHER NAPLES

Sure, there's history and art and architecture galore in this ancient city. So much so that at times it feels like a swooping sensory freefall—intoxicating, overwhelming, even dangerous. But what really turns me on about this unique city is the sheer, unbridled passion of its people. It's evident in the way religion is celebrated, the way soccer teams are supported, the way motorcycles are raced (often dangerously and illegally), and the way people embrace life. Share a beer or a bottle of wine with a Neapolitan, and you'll soon have the inside scoop on family, social, and political intrigues as if you've been lifelong compatriots. This is a place where melodrama is synonymous with engagement, and emotive sharing is a way of life. You've read about some of the many attractions that unlock some of the secrets of the past; now here are some ways in which you can access the Neapolitan spirit that's very much alive and kicking today.

Naples is often called the "city of blood," not because of Mafia activity, but because of the religious rites associated with the so-called **Miracle of San Gennaro.** In this and other Neapolitan blood liquefaction ceremonies, a celebration of pure spectacle and blind, astonishing faith draws thousands of parishioners who gather to witness the liquefaction of the congealed blood of the city's heroic saints and protectors. Naples' patron, San Gennaro—who was notoriously stripped of his sainthood in the 1960s, only to be readmitted in 1980—was beheaded in 305; it was with considerable foresight that a devoted woman collected some of his blood, and accounts of the first liquefaction miracle are diverse and unreliable. Nevertheless, history places the first official blood miracle in the late 1300s, and it's become a barometer of the likelihood of any major disasters befalling the city in its immediate future. When the blood takes too long to liquefy—or, heaven forbid, not liquefy at all—the worst imaginable punishments are said to be in store for the city and its people. When the blood failed to liquefy in 1944, Vesuvius erupted, and Naples suffered an earthquake in 1980 when the miracle didn't proceed as expected. So, it's easy to imagine the city's collective religious zeal around such an all-important event. But why just imagine, when—with enough planning—you can witness the miracle for yourself, amid the flurry of expectant, excitable, chanting crowds that flock to the Duomo on the first Saturday in May, and also on September 19 and December 16. Whatever you make of the phenomenon (and even some of the most hardened Neapolitan "believers" will tell you that they know it's not real), witnessing the ritual makes for a unique and stirring experience; and an opportunity to be among people who submit themselves to belief in a centuries-old faith-based miracle, even in this hitech age when faith often takes a back seat.

The blood ritual is not restricted to San Gennaro; if you're looking for more opportunities to see the strange phenomenon, try the church of **San Gregorio Armeno,** where St. Patrizia's blood is said to liquefy every Tuesday, on August 25, and on request! At the church of San Gregorio Armeno, San Giovanni Battista's blood has one chance only—on August 29.

Another emotional roller-coaster ride in Naples is being part of the surging crowd at the 80,000-seater **Stadio San Paolo football stadium** (in Fuorigrotta; ☎ 081-5933223; accessible by metro), as I was for the first game of the 2007 Serie A championship. Having climbed back from B league obscurity, the young

Neapolitan team had so much to prove and so much to fight for as virtually every male citizen turned up in support; in other words, to pray, scream, sing, and cry. With religious intensity, banners were unfurled, war cries chanted, and a palpable charge of pure faith surged through the stadium long before the game had begun. Striking in their pale blue jerseys, the home side was worshipped with chants echoing heroic salutes from gladiatorial days. Even if you're not that into sport (I'm not), Neapolitan football will keep you plenty entertained; there's soap-operatic drama (on and off the field), a cool-without-trying spectators' fashion show (fat sunglasses, exposed designer underwear), and a semireligious ritual of furious faith.

While I bought a last-minute ticket from a scalper outside the stadium (20€–25€), you'd do best to go the route of purchasing yours in advance from a legitimate source (scalped tickets are illegal, and all tickets bear the name of the holder, so you can get stopped and questioned at the gate). It doesn't really matter where you sit (expensive numbered seats are around 40€), but the cheaper seats (14€) will inevitably let you in on the raw drama of the most energetic fans. Tickets can be purchased—up to 1 hour before games—from **Azzurro Service** (☎ 081-5934001; www.azzurroservice.it); alternatively, try any city *tabacchi*, or wherever Lotto tickets are sold. Whatever you do, be prepared with sunblock, a hat, binoculars if possible, and something to quench your thirst.

If you really want to experience the fiery determination of the Neapolitan community, why not get involved with a crowd that seeks to change the way the city is run and hopefully contribute to a better world? **Attending a protest rally** in heady Naples may sound a bit rough, but it's a quick fix introduction to the spirit of the local population, its problems, deep-felt concerns, and belief in acting rather than sitting around complaining. And given the enormity of the environment question in Campania (see below), Naples is probably the most exciting place to join a crowd of protesters. Keen or curious? Then contact Luca Coda (info@hostelnapoli.com), the passionate young owner of Hostel of the Sun (p. 505), whom I've often told should go into politics. He thinks I'm joking, but you should hear him address the environmental crisis facing Naples—a result of political corruption and the Commora's stranglehold over key businesses like garbage collection, Luca says. Luca will tell you that the problem is a simple yet complicated one: One of the Commora's big money-making initiatives involves buying up cheap lands and forcing garbage men to strike. Only when the problem explodes out of all proportion and the streets become unbearably strewn with garbage, does public protest—or a media initiative—provoke local government to take action. So what happens? Well, the Camorra kindly steps up to the plate and offers to sell prime dumping land to the government—legitimate, but at extortionate rates, of course. Vast tracts of land are soon covered with mountains of garbage. Apparently, even if proper recycling and waste management projects were to be put in place, it would take at least another 20 years to make a dent in existing waste "farms." So, if—like Luca—you believe we can all make a difference, consider joining one of the peaceful-but-serious demonstrations that he attends (and organizes) from time to time. Luca will also let you know about other protests against the government's well-publicized corruption and incompetence—in 2007, for example, Vaffanculo (or "F-Off!") Day was celebrated in cities all around Italy on September 8.

The Virgin, Her Cave & a Street Orgy. Well, Almost . . .

What do ancient Bacchanalian orgies, apparitions of the Virgin Mary, and Naples' greatest street festival all have in common? No, it's not a joke. And it's quite safe for kids, too—not even PG-13, actually.

It's called **Piedigrotta** (☎ 081-4107211; www.festadipiedigrotta.it), and it's Naples' latest revival of an ancient religious celebration, and was said to be quite the party back in the 17th century. This latest incarnation (and there have been a few)—organized for the first time in September 2007—doesn't involve quite the same erotic lasciviousness or unabashed singing of obscene lyrics that apparently accompanied the original "festivals" when worshippers would dance around the shrine of Priapo, an ancient pagan god with immense carnal power. That cult was eventually Christianized and sanitized, and a statue of the Virgin Mary replaced the pagan symbols inside the Neapolitan Crypt—Piedigrotta's sanctuary cave. The statue resurfaced in 1353 when the Virgin appeared to three different people on the same night with instructions to each about how to find her statue. And so the cult of Santa Maria di Piedigrotta evolved and grew into something immense, with multitudes of pilgrims arriving on the anniversary of the Virgin's apparition (Sept 8). Many were women seeking husbands or pregnancy.

The parties officially started up in the 17th century—they were full-blown carnivals of prayer, feasting, singing, and dancing. In 1835, the Piedigrotta Song Festival evolved out of the annual celebrations, giving the world two well-known Neapolitan favorites: "Funiculi funicula" (in 1880) and "O Sole Mio" (1898). After the First World War, and under Mussolini, the festival started to lose momentum, and the lack of interest grew with the appearance of television, yet it dragged on into the 1980s before finally gasping its final breath. So 2007 was something of an historic revival, driven by a renewed vigor that's largely based in tourism and what that can mean for the city. With street lights, allegorical street floats, music concerts, stage shows, kids' workshops, public Mass, and lots of free guided visits to the Neapolitan Crypt, it's intended to be a blend of funky extravaganza and traditional fervor. Whatever the outcome, it's sure to be an eye-opener for anyone visiting the city during the **first 2 weeks of September,** and certainly an entertaining way of meeting Neapolitans, who are always at their best when they're having a good time.

Of course, while Neapolitan body language—alive with juicy, infectious gesticulations (including some hearty finger signs)—may help you get the gist of the emotional tone of what's going on, you'll go a lot further if you have a basic grip on the language. At **Centro Italiano** (Vico Santa Maria dell'Aiuto 17; ☎ 081-5524331; www.centroitaliano.it), you can take classes covering Italian and aspects of local culture that will greatly enhance your experience here; 4 weeks of intensive lessons cost 580€, and include enlightening lectures on Italian music, theater, art, and cinema. There are other levels of intensity and duration to consider. You can also combine your language lessons with some serious kitchen schooling—I can't imagine a better place to learn about preparing great food than in a Neapolitan kitchen. The school can arrange accommodation for you, too, either in a well-priced hotel or in a shared apartment. If you're keen to take a cooking course and don't really want the intensive language component, you should consider basing yourself in nearby Sorrento, where the region's best value-for-money classes are given at Mami Camilla (p. 539), which has on-site accommodations.

Finally, if the hectic overload of Neapolitan energy gets too much for you, why not sign up for a relaxing yoga class and meet some of the other health-conscious types who must deal with the chaos every day of their lives? Call ☎ 333-4438199, or make enquiries at SorRiso Integrale vegetarian restaurant (p. 506), which occupies the same block as the yoga studio.

ATTENTION, SHOPPERS!

Even though there are designer stores along Via Calabritto toward Piazza dei Martiri, and some very elegant boutiques in Chiaia, shopping here is just not the same as it is in Rome, Milan, or Florence. In Naples, you should hunt and peck for bargains and one-of-a-kind objects like handmade jewelry and Nativity ornaments. *Note:* Don't plan to spend a single euro in the middle of the day: Most shops close from around 1 to 4pm for the still-observed *siesta*.

BOOKS & MAPS

There is a great selection of stores selling rare and used books along the Via Port'Alba. Many of the books are English translations of European titles. Many more are Italian translations of English titles. Some of the most intriguing titles are shelved in the stands in front of the stores.

Feltrinelli is the usual choice for maps, books, music, and stationery. In Naples, **Libreria Feltrinelli** ★ (Piazza dei Martiri/Via Santa Caterina a Chiaia 23; ☎ 081-2405411) is a three-story structure with lots of books in English.

You'll also find some wonderful old books and maps at the **Colonnese** ★ (Via San a Maiella 33; ☎ 081-459858; www.colonnese.it), down in the historical center. They also carry famous Neapolitan tarot cards, some books on witchcraft, and a stunning collection of medical texts. It's the best place in town for reprint lithographs and maps.

FASHION

High-fashion shops like Ferragamo, Armani, Gucci, Versace, and Valentino all have boutiques around Piazza dei Martiri. For one-stop designer-label shopping, the Neapolitan favorite is **Maxi Ho** (Via Nisco 20, Chiaia; ☎ 081-414721; bus: C25), but you may want to prevent early bankruptcy by making your visit a people-watching exercise only. For more moderate prices, you can't go wrong at **Carla G** ★ (Via Vittoria Colonna 15, Chiaia; ☎ 081-400005; bus: C25), which offers very up-to-date fashion options (though not with the impressive labels). Another bargain-hunters paradise is **Chi Cerca Trova** ★ (Via G. Fiorelli 3, Chiaia; ☎ 081-7647592; bus: C25) where you may wonder if the clothes fell off the back of a truck destined for far smarter outlets. Prices are excellent here, and the fashions are cutting edge.

MUSICAL INSTRUMENTS

Neapolitan music is world renowned, and there are more musical-instrument sellers per capita here than in any other Italian city. Most dealers are in the historical center on Via San Sebastiano, which connects the Spaccanapoli to Via dei Tribunali. You'll find stores selling music and musical instruments, some so unique you'll just have to stop to ask for a demonstration; if you're a collector, the one you'll want to buy is undoubtedly the traditional Neapolitan mandolin. There are also two music schools on nearby Via Tribunali. In the morning, you can often hear students of classical piano through the open windows, and it's not uncommon to witness recitals and practice sessions.

WINE & CHOCOLATE

One of the few chains in Naples is the line of sweets shops called **Gay-Odin** ★★★ (Via Toledo 214; ☎ 081-5513491), named after founder Isidore Odin, who legendarily fell in love with his beguiling assistant Onorina Gay. Five locations sell scrumptious handmade chocolates and ice cream. You may also want to ask if it's possible to visit their old-fashioned chocolate factory. Another great spot for handmade treats is award-winning **Dolce Idea** ★ (Via Solitaria 7/8; ☎ 081-7642832), which has three branches in the city. Famous for the chocolate sculptures, they also do a great job with packaging for the trip home.

To buy wines from all over southern Italy, look no further than **Enoteca Vinorum Historia** ★ (Via Tribunali 33; ☎ 081-2110079; www.professionevino.it), tucked between the two Gino Sorbillo restaurants. The friendly shopkeeper will help you pick from the overwhelming assortment of vintages, and you can also conduct a mini-tasting for as little as 1.70€. Looking for a good, inexpensive red? Try the Falerno del Massico 2004 Moio (8.35€), a superlative primitive vintage. The Fiano di Avellino is a highly recommended dry white (10€).

NIGHTLIFE

The funny thing about Naples is that despite its incredibly vibrant energy during the day, there is very little that goes on late at night. You'll find a handful of nightclubs and discos, but the Neapolitans seem to prefer lingering over a long meal to going out and dancing; but that doesn't mean there won't be something to hold your attention.

Generally, if you're looking for a club or bar, your best bet is the historical center. Piazza Bellini is a popular hangout, where you can sip cocktails and beer at quaint outdoor tables at any of the bars. A favorite is the **Intra Moenia** (Piazza Bellini 70; ☎ 081-290720; www.intramoenia.it; daily 10am–2am), traditionally an intellectual hangout (that's also a bookstore) which serves light snacks and late-night munchies. It's also a popular place for a smart gay crowd.

Or head to the seaside along the Chiaia and Mergellina, where the same places that gave you a morning cappuccino will serve you a glass of wine by the water's edge. One of the sexiest venues in this part of town (or anywhere in Naples), **S'move Light Bar** (Vico dei Sospiri 10/A; ☎ 081-7645831; www.smove-lab.net; Mon–Sat 11am–3am, Sun 7pm–3am; closed Aug) draws a glamorous and youthful crowd. A DJ spins music of all genres.

LIVE MUSIC

It's often joked that virtually no big-name performers are brave enough to come to Naples, but that's a bit mean, and the city's image and profile is changing rapidly. Ask the proprietor at your hotel or B&B about current events, or check the schedules at **Palapartenope** (☎ 081-5700008; www.palapartenope.it) on the chance something is going on in town during your stay. For live jazz, which is oddly popular here in the land of the Neapolitan love song, try **Bourbon Street** (Via Bellini 2; ☎ 328-0687221; closed Jun–Aug). Someone plays Tuesday through Sunday, but listen closely before you pay your cover charge.

For classical events, check out the **Teatro di San Carlo** (Via San Carlo 101–103; ☎ 081-7972111; www.teatrosancarlo.it) and the Festival Musicale di Villa Rufolo (www.ravelloarts.org) along the Amalfi Coast in Ravello.

DAY TRIPS FROM NAPLES

I probably don't need to encourage you to visit popular Pompeii. But the ruins at Herculaneum and Mount Vesuvius itself are often overlooked by travelers and really shouldn't be. It's possible to see all three in one very long day (see below).

POMPEII

Among the most famous ruins on earth, the **Scavi di Pompeii** ★★★ (Via Villa dei Misteri 2; ☎ 081-5365154; www.pompeiisites.org; 11€ or 20€ combined 3-day ticket with Herculaneum and three other sites; daily Apr–Oct 8:30am–7:30pm, last entrance 6pm, Nov–Mar until 5pm, last entrance 3:30pm) is where most tourists go to see the damage caused by Vesuvius when it erupted on August 24, A.D. 79. For 18 hours, according to archaeologists and historians, hot ash and pumice rained on the city of Pompeii, collapsing roofs and filling in every conceivable gap with a soft powder that solidified to a thickness of 9m (30 ft.) in some places. Lava eventually ran over the top of the ash-covered wasteland, and Pompeii, a prosperous Roman colony was forgotten until waterworks excavations found it by accident in 1594. In 1748, excavations began to reveal what was underneath.

While traipsing through Pompeii and seeing the legendary city with your own eyes is undeniably one of those must-see travel experiences, visiting can be daunting unless you're an archaeologist or historian specializing in the ancient world. The site is, frankly, overexploited and overcommercialized—its entrances done up like those of a theme park, rather than the gateway to another time—and tourist traffic may ultimately ruin your adventure amid the ruins. The sheer size of Pompeii also makes it fairly hard work; the biggest mistake you can make here is to wander aimlessly. It's an easy place to get lost; without a map, the sites are hard to identify, and in all honesty, everything may start looking the same after an hour or so. So consider selecting a few top attractions within that city and getting a grasp of those sites in order to better understand the world inhabited by the 20,000 Pompeians who lived here 2,000 years ago. To really enjoy and appreciate Pompeii, you should consider renting one of the **audioguides** (6.50€; 10€ for two) at the entrance (there's even a special version designed for kids). On a practical level, be prepared with protection against the sun, decent footwear for walking on uneven surfaces, and plenty to drink and eat (the on-site eating options are overpriced, so consider packing a picnic lunch). Be aware, also, that Pompeii is not really a very good place for children to spend too many hours.

Head straight for the **Forum,** which was the economic, commercial, political and legal nerve center of the city and the location of its most significant public buildings. Adjacent to the Forum is the **Temple of Apollo,** one of the oldest temples in a city that was clearly inclined toward religion, evidenced not only in the quantity of sacred buildings, but also in the prevalence of religious decoration within private homes. Another keen interest was hygiene, and there are a number of spas and public baths—including the **Forum Baths**—around the city where people would give themselves over to the rituals of cleansing, and also take massages and other beauty treatments. Besides the social event of communal bathtime (supposedly in the early afternoon), Pompeians also socialized at any of three significant theater spaces: the covered **Odeon** (a little theater for mime and smaller musical shows), the **Teatro Grande** (a 5,000-seater for classical comedies and tragedies), and the **Amphitheater** (which is the oldest on earth), where most popular and spectacular entertainments (typically gladiatorial combats) were held. The latter, in particular, is worth visiting, if only to behold its grand-scale dimensions. Don't miss the mosaics in the **House of the Tragic Poet** (named for a mosaic found here—but now in Naples Archaeological Museum—depicting a theater rehearsal); it's especially famous because of the black-and-white mosaic of a dog accompanied by a Latin inscription meaning "BEWARE OF THE DOG." Many tourists hover around the **House of the Faun** (Pompeii's largest house, dating back to the early 2nd c. B.C.); the main point of interest is the exuberant little bronze statue of the faun in question (although the one here is a copy; the original is in Naples), but there are also several excellent mosaics around the property. For an experience akin to visiting to an art gallery, make a point of seeing the **House of the Vetti,** where friezes depict cherubs busy with various artisan trades; the use of Pompeii red in several wall panels is quite striking. Of course, most visitors just love the erotic art, which includes Priapus, the god of fertility, resting his giant member on one side of a scale—on the other end is a sack of money. Outside the main walls of the city, don't neglect to visit the **Villa dei Misteri (Villa of Mysteries)**—included in your Pompeii ticket—which might have originally been an out-of-town retreat (although just 5 min. from the city) for the wealthy owner, although some say it may have been an agricultural property. Frescoes depict mysterious rituals believed to have been a Dionysian initiation ceremony for women preparing for marriage. On the walk back out you'll pass the ancient tombs of Pompeii, which stood outside the city walls, as was the custom of the time. The casts of victims from the **Garden of Fugitives** have been placed inside movable display cases; the curators relocate them based on the season and weather. Ask where they are when you buy your tickets.

Tip: If your exploration of Pompeii has you ravenous, consider late lunch at **Zi Caterina** ★★ (Via Roma 20; ☎ 081-8507447; Wed–Mon noon–11pm; AE, DC, MC, V), the most reasonable and authentic restaurant in town (albeit a 12-min. walk from the ruins). Abundant pizza and freshly caught fish is served amid a riot of activity—loud families, screaming waiters, and a busking soloist resonating off the walls, all add to the atmosphere.

HERCULANEUM

Far more manageable than Pompeii—and intriguing despite the lack of hype—are the comparatively unknown ruins of **Herculaneum** ★★★ 🧒 (Corso Resina 6; ☎ 081-7390963; 11€, or 20€ for 3-day ticket including Scavi di Pompeii; daily Apr–Oct 8:30am–7:30pm, last entrance 6pm, the rest of the year until 5pm daily, last entrance 3:30pm), in the town of Ercolano, more or less midway between Naples and Pompeii, and easily reached on the same train line. Actually, I find Herculaneum a more entertaining romp than Pompeii because, though smaller, it's better preserved and less crowded with tourists. Herculaneum has many more intact structures than Pompeii, with rooftops and multistory houses, because this town was buried quickly in volcanic mud while Pompeii was covered slowly with the ashen rain. Sure, this was basically a seaside holiday resort for wealthy Romans, so you don't see that wide a range of houses, but it doesn't take an archaeology degree to imagine this site in pre-eruption glory. Besides well-preserved houses, spas, and other public buildings, you'll see preserved, carbonized furniture (exactly where it was 2,000 years ago) and some beautiful mosaics. If you go down to the old shoreline, you can see many of the 250 skeletons that were unearthed in the 1980s, and the layers of volcanic deposits that stopped at the sea. These excavations are a fraction of the size of Pompeii's and both sites can be explored on the same day. Give yourself a couple of hours here; besides the good map and booklet you receive with your ticket, you can rent an audioguide (6.50€, or 10€ for two).

MT. VESUVIUS

Looming ominously over Pompeii and Ercolano, Mt. Vesuvius is a natural disaster waiting to happen. Over three million people live on its flanks and down the crusty lava path to the Bay of Naples. It smolders constantly, drawing warnings from volcanologists, who consider it one of the most dangerous volcanoes in the world.

That really should not deter you from seeing it, however; the experts at the **Osservatorio Vesuviano** ★★ (Via Osservatorio; ☎ 081-6108483; www.ov.ingv.it; free; Sat–Sun 10am–2pm) monitor this giant so closely that even the slightest earth tremor sets off a buzz of activity. This observational center has survived seven eruptions and has an interesting museum with models and movies.

Vesuvius National Park (☎ 081-7710939; www.parconazionaledelvesuvio.it/grancono; 6.50€; daily Nov–Mar 9am–3pm, Apr–May 9am–5:30pm, June–Aug 9am–6:30pm, Sept–Oct 9am–5pm), is a fertile agricultural zone, and a UNESCO Biosphere Reserve. You can get there from either Ercolano (with the Vesuvio Express shuttle bus; ☎ 081-7393666; www.vesuvioexpress.it; 10€ round-trip) or Pompeii. The latter involves catching the Circumvesuvia bus from right outside the Pompeii ruins; tickets cost 8.50€ round-trip and are sold at the Pompeii Scavi train station. Buses depart regularly (at least one per hour) between 8:05am and 3:25pm daily, with the final return bus departing Vesuvio at 5:40pm (be sure to check up-to-date departure times before setting off). Buses arrive at a parking lot at altitude 1,000m (3,280 ft.), and from here you hike for around 15 to 20 minutes to peer into the 200m (656 ft.) cone and its fumaroles, which emit a thick steam. This is the only place from which you can truly get a sense of the havoc Vesuvius caused to the towns below during its A.D. 79 eruption. From this vantage point on top, you can easily make out the lava fields, overgrown with lush vegetation. From here it's also easy to see how much of Pompeii, Herculaneum, and other villages are still unexcavated. But do try to visit on a clear day so that you can enjoy the phenomenal views of the Bay of Naples, too.

THE PHLEGREAN FIELDS & THE CASERTA PALACE

The coastline west of Naples is dotted with spectacular ruins tucked amid the badly planned suburbs of the city. The best are **Cuma** (☎ 081-8543060), with its Cave of the Sibyl, and **Baia** (Via Fusaro 75, Baia; ☎ 081-5233797), with its ruined baths and mosaics. You can visit both of these sites with a combined ticket for 4€. To reach them, take the local train line from Naples, toward Pozzuoli (20-min. trip).

Don't discount Caserta either, particularly if you have an abiding interest in the Neopolitan baroque architecture and the luxury of time; 19km (12 miles) north of Naples, it's where you'll find one of Italy's largest palaces, **Reggia di Caserta** (Via Douet 2; ☎ 0823-277111; www.reggiadicaserta.org; 8€; Wed–Mon 8:30am–7:30pm), which has a magnificent 120 rooms built around four inner courtyards.

THE ISLE OF CAPRI & THE AMALFI COAST

If you make it as far south as Naples, you've simply got to check out at least one of the nearby islands and explore the Amalfi Coast—one of the most dramatic stretches of coastline in Europe, with a head-spinning cliff-edge highway to match. World-famous (and infamous, when the traffic gets backed up) Amalfi Drive runs from Punta della Campanella, on the Sorrento peninsula, to Salerno, some 50km (31 miles) away. Along the way, are three beautiful historic towns: posh and pretty Positano, quaint Amalfi, and—high above the sea—suave Ravello. Each is unimaginably lovely, and along the way, you'll be dazzled by rugged, vertical-plunging cliffs, sandy coves, and some seriously precariously dangling terraced towns. It's worth every effort to see.

In what should be considered nothing short of miraculous, the tiny islands of Capri (*Ca*-pree), Ischia (*Isk*-ee-ah), and Procida (*Pro*-shee-da) manage to remain enticing in spite of the hordes of summer invaders who storm the shores every day from about April through October. Overcrowded boats stream from the mainland to these islands like ants to cupcakes, but the masses are absorbed and the islands rarely seem crowded, except in town centers.

Weaving down the treacherous stretch of coast-hugging highway in a local bus is no longer the favored way to get to the coastal towns (although it's certainly the cheapest). Now there are myriad ferries and hydrofoils to choose from, all offering exquisite views of the coast—and of those big blue buses often stuck on hairpin curves. To go by water from Naples to the towns along the Amalfi Coast, or to the island of Capri (or Ischia), you have two choices. You can go from the main ferry and hydrofoil port at Molo Beverello (you'll have many more options here), or from the smaller marina of Mergellina. But before you just get in line at the ticket counter for the next boat out of Naples, it's well worth walking down to the dock to see exactly what kind of boat you're booking a seat on. Some are open-topped cruisers that are driven with the same reckless abandon as a Neapolitan

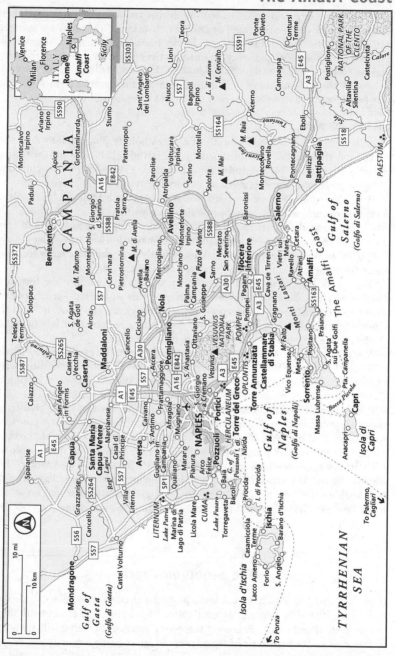

taxi. Others are large, no-nonsense hydrofoils that are basically aquabuses. These things matter if you have luggage or children, as many of the boats are jammed with little or no room for big suitcases. Ferries from Naples to Capri should cost 8€, and hydrofoils 16€ (one-way); compare prices online by exploring the websites of **Snav** (www.snav.it), **NLG Linea Jet** (www.navlib.it), and **Caremar** (www.caremar.it). Operational only during peak summer months is the **Metro del Mar** (www.metrodelmare.com) service, which links Naples and Capri.

CAPRI ★★★

Capri is idyllic—a near perfect swath of nature's bounty plopped into the azure waters and then coiffed and primped by her island inhabitants into what has becomes a jet-setter's playground. From shimmering coves to terraced cliffs and plunging rock faces, Capri is every bit as dazzling as you might expect.

And it's not only a place for blue bloods to hang with their ilk. You too can surround yourself with the glamour of the place without feeling too much of a pinch in your wallet. Certainly, given the cost of getting to the island, and considering all there is to see (specially in terms of natural vistas), spending a night or two on the island is almost essential, particularly since the place really feels like home when the thousands of day-trippers have scooted off.

The Isle of Capri has two distinct towns, Capri and Anacapri; the former is where most chichi boutiques and ultraluxurious hotels are located—it's also where most of the crowds end up. Anacapri is comparatively calm and down-home, with a more provincial atmosphere. The two towns are connected by bus (a rather exhilarating drive; always make sure you're near a window).

You'll arrive at the Marina Grande, where it's easy to be overwhelmed by the crush of day-tripping tour groups queuing up for various boat trips. You'll want to make the connection to your hotel as quickly as possible. If you're staying in Capri town, take the funicular (1.70€); if you're based in Anacapri, you can either wait for a direct bus (infrequent) or take a bus to Capri town and then transfer to one of the more frequent buses that stops in the center of Anacapri. Of course, if you're in a devil-may-care kinda mood, there are plenty of convertible taxis, in which you can imagine yourself living the life of the rich and famous if only for a few breezy moments (expect to pay around 18€ for the trip to Anacapri, but always ask first). If you're on a day trip and feeling incredibly energetic, you could even walk up to Capri town via the steep, zigzagged urban steps that go all the way to the top. Stop often and gaze at the coastline below and the turquoise sea beyond.

The Scoop on Capri

If you're looking to structure your visit, pick up a seasonal magazine called *Capri Press Guide Magazine*, available at most coffee bars, hotels, and stores, with maps of nature walks and events. Following these very detailed itineraries will allow you to check off all the highlights of the island, though roaming aimlessly will do you no harm.

The most crowded spot you'll encounter on the entire island is Capri's *piazzetta,* the main square, where visitors sit at restaurants under a ring of colorful umbrellas. These places charge a hefty price for even a glass of water, but they're the ultimate for people-watching. Unfortunately, there's nowhere to sit but at one of the four restaurants, and loitering in front of any of them isn't tolerated. Customers are paying for the view, after all.

For the best views of the cliffs, follow along to the **Arco Naturale** ★★. The expensive boutiques and hotels are all along Via Camarelle. Be sure to visit the old monastery of **Certosa di San Giacomo** (established 1371) on the far end of Via Matteotti, which has been restored in recent years (call ahead to find out if it's open; ☎ 081-8376218). It was here in 1656 that the Carthusian brotherhood of San Giacomo, facing a plague, literally sealed themselves inside instead of tending to the sick, as they were expected to do. The Capresi people, angry at being abandoned, threw the corpses of the plague victims over the monastery walls.

> **❝** The island of Capri is a miracle. Yes, a miracle! I have been to Capri three times, for long periods, and I tell you: the impression will remain with me until death. **❞**
>
> Ivan Turgenev, 1871

You can't go wrong stopping by the **Giardini di Augusto** (open dawn to dusk) to relax in the cultivated gardens, or visiting the lookout point indicated on the signs as the **Belvedere di Tragara** ★★★. From here you can see the famous Faraglioni rocks protruding from the sea.

Anacapri ★★, on the other side of the island, is like the country cousin of the posh town of Capri. More rural than its swank counterpart, it has a slight bohemian vibe. It is often said that until the mid–18th century, most of the people in Anacapri had never been to the town of Capri—and vice versa.

The highlights of Anacapri are the detailed majolica tiles on the floor of the church of **San Michele Arcangelo** (Piazza San Nicola; 1€; daily July–Oct 9:30am–7pm, Nov–Dec and Feb–May 9:30am–4:30pm, Jan 10am–2pm), in the main piazza; and the **Villa San Michele** (Viale A. Munthe; ☎ 081-8371401; 5€; daily Nov–Feb 10:30am–3:30pm, Mar 9:30am–4:30pm, Apr and Oct 9:30am–5pm, May-Sept 9am–6pm), once home of the Swedish author Axel Munthe. The appeal here is the tranquil gardens and songbirds. And, of course, you're welcome to join the hordes who clamber for the funicular trip up **Monte Solaro** (Via Caposcuro 10; ☎ 081-8371428; www.seggioviamontesolaro.it; 7€ round-trip; Mar–Oct 9:30am–4:30pm, Nov–Feb 9:30am–3pm), which is really a soft option for getting to some of the most fantastic views on the island—walking to the English fort at the top takes an hour and isn't all that difficult; although the chairlift will shave 50 minutes off the ascent.

One of the most enchanting adventures you can have on Capri is a visit to the **Grotta Azzurra (Blue Grotto)** ★★★ (9am to 1 hr. before sunset), a stunning miracle of nature and curious optics—geologists believe that this is a cave that actually sank into the water, accounting for its magical light effects. Most visitors are duped into believing that you can only see this awesome, impossible sunken cave by taking a motorboat from the **Marina Grande** (around 12€ per person), and then paying an entrance fee (4€) on top of forking out a mandatory 4.50€ for a rowboat to take them into the cavern; here they get a disappointing 5 minutes to take in the sublime azure glow created by the sunlight penetrating through the water inside the cave. And, if you're only on Capri for the day, by all means, get your wallet ready, and prepare for a throng of like-minded people (usually herded off the same chartered boat together). But few people know that after 5pm, when the rowboats stop operating, entrance to the grotto is free, and you can enjoy a far more captivating, and refreshing, experience of the cave by swimming into it. To get there, you can take the bus (15 min.) from Anacapri, or even walk down (1 hr.) along Via Grotto Azzura; there are plenty of signs and your hotelier (or someone at a tourist info point) will be able to guide you. A swim into the grotto to savor the jewel-like glow from inside the water itself is the hands-down highlight of visiting Capri.

Accommodations

Yes, you can fork over a bundle for a chichi hotel in Capri, but you don't have to. The Capresi have been at it long enough to have come up with excellent value options for those travelers who aren't famous, or more important, rich. Generally, there's far better value in and around Anacapri, and this is also where you'll be certain to escape the crowds—particularly the scores of tour groups that manage to block every imaginable doorway and sidewalk. If you stay in Anacapri, phone your hotel in advance to ask about transportation options; they might send a vehicle to pick you up.

€€–€€€   If you're staying on Capri, and want to be near the main beat of Capri town, the hands-down best deal is **La Tosca** ★★★ (Via Birago 5; ☎ 081-8370989; www.latoscahotel.com; MC, V), an unbelievable good value that's coupled with style (each room is immaculately white, simple, and contemporary–and perfect for enjoying relaxing views, either toward the sea, or into a quiet back garden). Best of all, your hosts, Ettore (whose grandmother built this place) and his Connecticut-born wife will treat you like an old friend. This is absolutely the best deal on the island, with rooms ranging from 71€ to 135€, but the 11 rooms are popular so need to be reserved well in advance (sea views especially).

€€–€€€   While Bussola di Hermes (below) has a more organized hotel feel, a few hundred meters farther from Anacapri, **Villa Eva** ★★ 🧒 (Via La Fabbrica 8; ☎ 081-8371549; www.villaeva.com; AE, MC, V) is set in a vast, splendidly wild garden. It feels almost like a miniature resort, where the holiday vibe hangs heavily in the air and seems to scream: "Grab a cocktail and put your feet up!" Which is precisely what you can do—either around the pool, or in the lovely partially open-to-the-elements bar-lounge. Bedrooms (90€–120€ double) are a mixed bag—not particularly lavish, but homey with restored furniture and antiques that feel like they've been in Eva's possession for decades. In-room frills are few (no air-conditioning), but the superb breakfast buffet and sultry romance of the place somehow justify the absence of such modern conveniences.

€€–€€€   Extensively whitewashed, **Bussola di Hermes** ★ (Trav. La Vigna 14, Anacapri; ☎ 081-8382010; www.bussolahermes.com; AE, MC, V) has a decidedly Mediterranean ambience; add to this a profusion of fluted columns, colorful paintings (recalling the legend of the sirens, for example), kitschy classical-style statues, and sculpted lion heads poking from the walls ready to spout water into a trough of white pebbles, and you have a characterful place that—even more importantly—benefits from the active attentions (and imaginative design details) of hands-on owners. What I love most about Ciro and Rita is the insider information they provide (whether about restaurants, or a swimming spot nobody knows about). Rooms are pleasant, with blue majolica-tile floors, firm beds, and flatscreen TVs; standard units are 70€ to 130€, but do consider paying an extra 10€ for a private terrace with sea view—it just opens up the space beautifully.

Dining

Dining on the island of Capri can be expensive, but there are good deals to be found—particularly if you steer clear of what are overt tourist traps. Capri is home of the famous mozzarella and tomato Caprese salad—and still better here than anywhere else on earth—and ravioli Capresi (fat ravioli stuffed with herbed ricotta cheese). Besides my favorites, reviewed below, other reliable budget-friendly options are **La Pergola** (Via Traversa Lo Palazzo 2; ☎ 081-8377412), whose owner/chef grows his own lemons to make superbly zesty green ravioli with lemon and cream, and **La Cisterna** (Via Serafina 5; ☎ 081-8375620), a classic Caprese trattoria just behind Capri's *piazzeta*, but light years away in terms of affordability.

€–€€ To find out where locals go to chill out with their entire family, make a dinner (or bar) stop at **Aumm Aumm** ★ (kids) (Via Caprile 18; ☎ 081-8373000; daily noon–3pm and 7pm–late; AE, DC, MC, V), which is nothing sophisticated, but makes me feel like I'm one of Capri's privileged permanent inhabitants. The soundtrack is local radio plus the buzz of big families (there are even hot dogs and burgers for the kids), and a constant chorus of "ciao," as locals pop in and out to pick up takeaways, and have a quick drink at the bar. The whopping Caprese salad (6€) is a meal in itself, with humungous chunks of mozzarella. And the fabulous pizzas run just 5€ to 8€; when I was last there, my waitress—with big, fluttering eyes and constant good humor—recommended a delicious parmigiana pizza, topped with eggplant and *scamorza* cheese. You can also try traditional *ravioli all Caprese* here (all pastas are 7€–9€), and there's some delicious wine by the glass (3€).

€€–€€€€ **Il Cucciolo** ★★ (Via La Fabbrica 52; ☎ 081-8371917; daily noon–3pm and 7–11:30pm; AE, DC, MC, V), a wonderfully situated seafood restaurant—high above the Blue Grotto, with a terrace affording an enchanting panorama of the sea—attracts a stellar clientele (according to the owner, George W. Bush's brother had visited the month before I did). But that doesn't mean it's expensive or pretentious (despite the dazzling ambience). I'd opt for a lunch of light starters—Caprese salad (9€), fresh oysters (14€ for five), or garlicky octopus salad (14€)—followed by a pasta (try *tagliolini al limone,* thin tagliatelle with lemon sauce, 10€), or simply grilled or oven-baked fish (7€ per 100g) with potatoes and basil. Free transportation is provided; just call ahead.

€€€ Down near the Arco Naturale there's a wonderful dining experience to be had in **Le Grottelle** ★★ (Via Arco Naturale 13; ☎ 081-8375719; July–Aug daily noon–3pm and 7pm–midnight; Oct Fri–Wed noon–3pm; Mar–June and Sept

Fri–Wed noon–2:30pm and 7pm–midnight; MC, V), which specializes in grilled fish, rabbit, and chicken, and does some excellent seafood pastas. But the real draw here is the atmosphere—the restaurant is tucked inside two natural caves, and the ambience, especially at night, could not be more romantic.

OTHER ISLANDS IN THE BAY OF NAPLES

Capri isn't the only island here but it's the most picturesque and certainly the most romantic. If you're looking to explore other islands, and perhaps make a deft escape from the crowds consider a day trip to **Ischia,** easily accessible by boat from Naples, Capri, or the coast. You can tour the island on the cheap with the local bus. You'll also want to leave time for a dip in its therapeutic thermal waters, which are popular with many German tourists. Go to www.ischiaonline.it for general information; www.venere.it has the best hotel deals, but if you're looking for something extraordinary, reserve a seaview room at **Il Monastero** (☎ 081-992435; www.albergoilmonastero.it), where a standard double goes for 100€ to 120€. The hotel is located within Castello Aragonese, Ischia's fortified citadel, with a history stretching back 2,500 years.

Tiny **Procida**—used as a movie set for *The Talented Mr. Ripley*—is a peaceful island where you can escape the modern world. Explore walled villages, watch fisherman bringing in their catch, wander from church to church, take a diving course, or simply get caught up in a rhapsody of peace and quiet (although this is rapidly disappearing). Accommodation options remain slim, so book very early to get a room at **Casa Giovanni da Procida** (☎ 081-8960358; www.casagiovanni daprocida.it), a neat little B&B where doubles cost 65€ to 110€. For more information, check out www.procida.net.

THE AMALFI COAST

Deciding between boat or bus to reach the Amalfi Coast from Naples is a matter of taste and budget. For trains from Naples to Sorrento or Salerno, use **Circumvesuviana** (☎ 081-8780862; www.vesuviana.it). Trains do not stop at the towns along the Amalfi Coast. If you value your dignity (and sanity), don't even consider renting a car; traffic is completely out of hand and the roads can be harrowing. Anyway, once you've got the darn thing where you want to be, you'll have to cough up for parking.

By Bus   The most economical option is the bus, but it's also the most time-consuming. **SITA buses** (☎ 081-6106711; www.sitabus.it) leave hourly but take a solid 2½ hours, longer when traffic is bad at the height of the summer. Frankly, if you get a window seat and sit back and enjoy the (okay, hair-raising) ride, you'll probably enjoy the time anyway (just make sure you're following the coastal route). Tickets for travel between Naples and Amalfi (5€–7€) are valid 24 hours, so you can get off at any of the stops along the way. You can purchase tickets at the kiosks in the bus terminus at Naples' Central Station or at any tabacchi along the perimeter of the square. Bus tickets for return trips from Sorrento, Positano, and Amalfi are also available at self-service kiosks or at the tabacchi at each terminus.

By Boat   The average cost of a straight 85-minute run between Naples and Amalfi by boat is 12€ one-way; price-wise heftier than a bus ride—comfier, too, but without the built-in fun-ride thrill of the Amalfi Drive hairpins. This can be a good option for scenery (although the hydrofoil windows are almost opaque from mist and water spray) and ease—the boats are generally covered and you usually have concessions on board. The seas in the summer are rarely choppy, but winter timetables can be iffy due to rough seas.

SORRENTO ✦

Larger than the villages farther along the Amalfi Coast, and with a fairly developed infrastructure, Sorrento—a pretty town that's as good for aimless wondering as it is for enchanting sea views—makes a convenient base for explorations farther south (to Positano, Amalfi, and Ravello), for trips to the islands in the Bay of Naples, and even to see Naples, Pompeii, and Herculaneum. The town sits high on a bluff above the sea, and affords gorgeous cliff-top views; it has a biggish fishing harbor, beaches suitable for sunbathing, and a nightlife that (relative to the rest of the Amalfi Coast) positively rocks (albeit largely with the evening parade of pedestrians up and down the main street). There's an energy here that may overwhelm you if you're after a peaceful getaway, but thrill you if you're looking to live it up just a little.

Much of the activity in Sorrento revolves around boat trips; it's a good place from which to set out for Capri, and you'll see opportunities advertised everywhere (or just ask your host). A great way to discover the magnificence of this stretch of coastline is by getting under the surface of the water and checking out the pristine coral reefs within the Marine Reserve; visibility is excellent. At the **Sorrento Diving Center** (Marina Piccola 63, Porto di Sorrento; ☎ 081-8774812), you can sign up for a half-day of diving (two dives plus equipment, 95€). If you haven't dived before, you can take a PADI-affiliated half-day course (90€) which culminates in your first dive; and what a place to enjoy that experience!

Accommodations & Dining

Sorrento is conspicuously beholden to tourists, and it's hard to find anyone here who isn't sustained by the tourism industry. This explains why the town has numerous comfortable and often expensive hotels and restaurants. The old town sprawls out from the main square, Piazza Tasso, and most of the expensive hotels are around Via Capo, the busy coastal road. In the summer months, booking ahead is mandatory.

€–€€ Whether you're traveling with a backpack and looking for a cheap bed; or would simply prefer a quiet, very affordable private room a little way out of Sorrento's main center; or are looking for a dining experience that's out of the ordinary, a little experimental, and involves meeting other people (both like-minded travelers and locals), consider staying (or reserving for dinner) at **Mami Camilla** ✦✦ (Via Cocumella 4, S. Agnello di Sorrento; ☎ 081-8782067; www. mamicamilla.com; cash only, except for long-stay guests), a cooking school–cum-guesthouse where a different four-course set meal is served every night (dinner starts at 8pm and costs 15€, including water; reserve ahead), and there's a choice of lodgings, ranging from dorm beds (16€–20€) to immaculate and comfortable private double rooms with en suite bathrooms (50€–100€). Family-run, the guesthouse is set in a large garden with a homey atmosphere and real comfort; amenities include a bar, and access to a private boat. This is one of Sorrento's best-kept secrets; for cooking course details, see p. 546.

€€   **Casa Astarita** ★★★ (Corso Italia 67; ☎ 081-8774906; www.casastarita.com; AE, DC, MC, V) is not only the best deal in town, but what started as a summer business out of their home for the Astarita sisters has turned into one of the loveliest bed-and-breakfasts you'll find in southern Italy. While the rooms (85€–95€ double) are quite handsome—colorful majolica-tile floors, family antiques, large flatscreen TVs, smart and sensible bathrooms, and delightful little balconies (behind shuttered, double-glazed glass doors) overlooking the scene along Sorrento's main drag—it's the warm atmosphere of the common parlor, where the friendly hostesses often socialize with guests over glasses of house-made limoncello, that makes this such a great choice.

€€   Ten minutes on foot from the city center, along an avenue of some of Sorrento's most privileged accommodations, **Hotel Désirée** (Via Capo 31/B; ☎ 081-8781563; www.desireehotelsorrento.com; cash only) perches precariously at the edge of a high cliff overlooking the sea, giving it the best views in this price range. Be certain, however, to reserve well ahead and get a corner room, which has a window toward the sea and a biggish balcony overlooking both the water and the deep-slice valley that cuts into the landscape right next to the hotel. Rooms are adequate, despite the all-round obsession with linoleum. Considering that you have access to a gorgeous little private beach far below (reached by private elevator), and you can catch a breeze and a cocktail on the panoramic terrace above, the room rates are a real bargain—standard doubles cost 75€ to 95€, with smaller units (not recommended) for 66€ to 83€. Breakfast is 3€ per person.

€€–€€€€   Close to the harbor, **Hotel Il Faro** (Via Marina Piccola 5; ☎ 081-8781390; www.hotelilfaro.com; AE, DC, MC, V) is another good value, with rates starting at 90€ if you score a low-season deal on the website (add 20€ for a sea view)—definitely on the economical end along this coast. Room decor is stuck in the 1970s, and the breakfast is mediocre, but with the money you save, you can go out for a morning meal in the old town.

€–€€   Since laid-back Mami Camilla (above) only serves dinner, the best deal for a hearty lunch of seafood or pasta is **Sant'Anna Da Emilia** (Via Marina Grande 62; ☎ 081-8072720; July–Aug daily 12:30–3pm and 7:30–11pm; closed Tues Apr–June and Sept; call ahead for other times; cash only), a seaside venue with friendly service. Try to get a seat outside.

Lick Your Way to Heaven

Ice cream is serious business in Sorrento, and the main outlets are locked in battle to out-impress the public. Don't leave town without at least one visit to **Prima Vera** (Corso Italia; ☎ 081-8073252; www.primavera sorrento.it; daily 10am–2am), where the zany staff will do just about anything to generate hype around their heavenly, creamy gelato.

€–€€   Tops for old-world romance, **O'Parrucchiano** ★★ (Corso Italia 71–73; ☎ 081-8781321; www.parrucchiano.com; daily noon–3:30pm and 7–11pm, closed Wed Nov 15–Mar 15; MC, V) continues to draw a loyal local following, as it's done since opening in 1868. Its first owner left the seminary to found the original trattoria, and when his friends came to visit, they taunted him that he hadn't become a parish priest, or *parrucchiano* (hence the name). Dressed up not unlike a greenhouse, the voluminous space is set on different levels linked by elegant marble stairways. Cannelloni tops the list of specialties—apparently it was invented here in the early 1900s; try the "Favorita" (7.50€) if you want to put the legend to the test, although I wouldn't miss the *tonnetto alla brace* (grilled tuna with balsamic vinegar; 12€). *Coperto* is 1.80€ and there's a 15% service fee.

€€€   If you're looking more for character than for cuisine, and don't mind coughing up that little bit extra, try **Ristorante il Buco** ★★ (Rampa Marina Piccola 6; ☎ 081-8782354; www.ilbucoristorante.it; Feb–Dec Thurs–Tues noon–3pm and 7–11pm; AE, MC, V), just outside Sorrento's old town. Built inside an old convent wine cellar with curved ceilings and ancient stone, its carefully prepared dishes lean toward seafood, accompanied by a superb wine list. It's a favorite among well-to-do locals who don't mind spending around 18€ to 22€ for a *primi* dish.

POSITANO ★★

Positano is still widely considered the jewel of this stretch of coastline, probably as much for its unshakeable good looks as for the list of impressive personalities who've sashayed through here. Fashionable since the 1950s, when arty celebrities were attracted by Positano's perceived bohemian atmosphere, Elizabeth Taylor (in her glam days), Pablo Picasso, and John Steinbeck helped make this an irresistible destination for the rich and famous, so much so that a night or two here is virtually beyond the reach of most humble travelers.

But then again, Positano is beautiful enough to be humbling; so if you want to be among the distinguished crowd that roams between the pretty pastel-colored houses magically clinging to near-vertical slopes, make the effort and come see what all the fuss is about. Fortunately, Positano is easy enough to visit from any of the more affordable Amalfi Coast towns. The reason you come here is to explore the stepped streets, window-shop, and take in the views from along the cliffs. Aside from wandering (aimlessly if you like) the only real sight, other than the obvious views of the sea and coastline, is the gorgeous Byzantine church, **Santa Maria Assunta** (Piazza Flavio Gioia; free; 8am–noon and 3:30–7pm). Stick to the northern side of town if you want to avoid the crowds. The best way to explore is just to wander, climb, turn the corners, and follow your instincts. You cannot get lost here—in this town of *scalinatelle* (small stairways) you either go up or down.

And certainly, if you've just gotta buy something, might as well pick up a pair of famous Positano sandals; they're decorated with seashells and are very conspicuous.

Accommodations & Dining

In catering to an ever more affluent and prestigious set of guests, this little village of under 4,000 people (and most of them of retirement age) has all but outpriced itself to the average tourist. If you'd like to stay here, it's really worth investigating well in advance, and focusing your energies on renting an apartment or private room (see "Apartment Rentals," on p. 501); while even these tend to cater to the fatter wallets in Positano, at least you'll be able to cook for yourself (make sure it has an equipped kitchen), thereby saving on expensive restaurants.

€€   A great value for Positano is the tiny, well-situated **Pensione Maria Luisa** ★★ (Via Fornillo 42; ☎ 089-875023; www.pensionemarialuisa.com; cash only). Rooms are very compact and without air-conditioning, but rates are the best in town; in the summer you get a double with terrace for just 85€. Be sure to book many months in advance. Similarly priced **La Tavolozza** ★★ (Via Colombo 10; ☎ 089-875040; celeste.dileva@tiscalinet.it; cash only) is a small, peaceful, family-run hotel where you're assured of a view from a private balcony (95€ double).

€€€   If you don't mind being on the edge of town, you won't completely break the bank at my favorite Positano hideaway: **La Fenice** ★★★ (Via Marconi 4; ☎ 089-875513; cash only). Constantino Mandara's lush, terraced estate consists of the family villa and a number of scattered cottages. The best lodgings (130€ double) are in peaceful rooms near the pool, and also close to the pathway leading to a semiprivate beach. There's an overwhelming sense of tranquillity here, supported by the perpetually magnificent views—which may help you overlook the 3-night minimum stay policy.

€€–€€€€   After major renovations in 2007, **La Bougainville** ★★ (Via Cristoforo Colombo 25; ☎ 089-875047; www.bougainville.it; AE, DC, MC, V) is still just about the last word in the pricey Positano budget hotel scene; a hillside location means some of the rooms have sea views (150€–170€ double), but pack lightly in anticipation of the stiff climb up to your bright, clean room. If you even consider one of the cheaper rooms without a view (95€–115€) then you might as well stay in another town.

€€–€€€   Grab a plastic chair on the terrace at **Lo Guarracino** ★★ (Via Positanesi d'America 12; ☎ 089-875794; Apr–Dec daily noon–3pm and 7:30–11pm; AE, DC, MC, V) and you'll find yourself drifting into the most satisfying reverie as you drink in the magnificent view that spreads beneath you and beyond. The food's not half bad either, delicious and satisfying cuisine inspired by the seemingly limitless range of creatures that are fished from the sea. The superb location will have you back for more (the service and decor probably won't), and when you tire of seafood, there's reliable pizza for 9€ to 12€.

AMALFI ★★★

Amalfi is possibly my favorite little town along the Amalfi Coast, and certainly a lot more peaceful that Sorrento or Positano. It also has a far more interesting history than any other village on the coast, and was not only once a thriving fishing port with a population of 70,000 along either side of the river that divides it, but considered a formidable power along this coast; some of the local people still allude to the ancient might of this tiniest of kingdoms with a strong degree of pride. The major trade route between Tunis, Constantinople, and Beirut went through the town, and much of the local architecture reflects these influences. But what makes Amalfi a better choice than the others is that there's still a sense of community that doesn't revolve around tourism. Sometimes, especially in the off season, you actually get the feeling that the locals could live without you—and that, oddly enough, is a welcome change.

Amalfi has a very impressive Cathedral of St. Andrew, also known as **Duomo di Amalfi** ✸✸ (Piazza Duomo; ☎ 089-871059; free; daily 7am–7pm, later on Sun), on the main square. Up the stairs and around the back is the **Chiostro del Paradiso** (2.50€; 10am–5pm), or "Cloister of Paradise," in which the head and other bones of St. Andrew (Christ's first disciple) are interred. There are few better places to sit at sunset than the stairs leading up to this magnificent church. From down below in the piazza, if you're lucky, you may even get to watch a bride perform the accomplished art of stair-climbing in stiletto heels and a long dress.

Amalfi also has a couple of fascinating museums, including the **Museo della Carta** ✸ (Palazzo Pagliara, Via delle Cartiere 23; ☎ 089-8304561; www.museodella carta.it; 3.50€; Apr–Oct daily 10am–6:30pm, Nov–Mar Tues–Sun 10am–3:30pm), which received European Union funding to refurbish its original paper presses dating back to the 14th century. Amalfi is believed to be the first European city to produce paper rather than import it. Consider buying the lovely handmade paper as a gift or souvenir. The guided tours are worthwhile.

A 15-minute walk from Amalfi's harbor is **Atrani** ✸✸, a tiny town with a good beach and bizarrely lively nightlife in its town square. Nowhere near as tourist-heavy as Amalfi, it qualifies as the smallest municipality in Europe; little boats bob in the water and the fishermen still sell their catch on the rocks. If you want to swim in the sea or soak up some rays, this is the place to unfurl your towel.

Accommodations & Dining

For private apartments and rooms, which is a great way to spend an extended stay here, my top choice is **Amalfi Accommodation** (www.amalfiaccommodation.com). They seem to have the cream of the crop, and if what you're looking for is not listed on their website, the proprietors of this agency will find it for you. You may have to pay cash, as you often do when you rent an apartment along the coast, but this also gives you a little room to haggle. Sometimes owners will knock off half a day's board if you do pay in cash, and if they don't suggest this, don't be shy about asking. Private apartments are rarely licensed and fees are therefore up to the owner's discretion. The above website also handles *agriturismo* (farm-stay) options on the coast, but these aren't recommended here because most are far from the sea view.

€€–€€€ **Albergo Lido Mare** ✸✸ (Vico dei Pastai 3; ☎ 089-872440; www.hamalfi.it; AE, DC, MC, V), provides the kind of cheerful family welcome that makes you feel like you're coming home every time you walk through the door. Accommodations occupy a big home filled with antiques in such naïve arrangements that you instantly take a shine to the genuine people (including Grandma, who's usually stationed in the lounge, minding her own business) who've created this warm, hospitable, and increasingly professional little hotel. Decently sized rooms (90€–130€ double) are air-conditioned, have pretty floor tiles, and beds with carved headboards. Look around the hotel for traditional Nativity scenes, old maps, and bookcases filled with antique volumes.

€€–€€€   Down on the waterfront inside an old pasta factory, **La Bussola** (Lungomare dei Cavalieri 16; ☎ 089-871533; www.labussolahotel.it; AE, DC, MC, V) is one of the few "modern" buildings in town, built as recently as 1905. A hotel for 65 years, the owner also owned a tile factory and consequently each room has a uniquely designed set of floor tiles. Rooms here vary from very affordable (94€–126€) with few frills (including A/C), to marginally bigger Type A (104€–136€) and Superior (114€–158€) units, a number of which have sea views, and the best of which have balconies right on the waterfront. The hotel has a private lido on the rocks below. As at Hotel Residence (below), the waterfront setting means you're right near the ferry and bus terminals, so no struggling with luggage up and down all those steps.

€€€   While La Bussola is one of the few relatively modern buildings along Amalfi's shore, what I love about **Hotel Residence** ★ (Via della Repubbliche Marinare 9; ☎ 089-871183; www.residencehotel-amalfi.it; AE, MC, V) is the sense of history that hangs about the place; from the near-crumbling facade to the frescoes and other decorative gems scattered throughout the cavernous public spaces, this place exudes its pedigree, yet is completely without pretense. In fact, it's pretty laid-back, with helpful staff who make choice restaurant recommendations that will steer you clear of the tourist hubs. All rooms have balconies, but while a standard unit costs 125€ to 140€ (with no air-conditioning), you'll need to fork over a little more for a direct sea view.

€–€€   Catering to locals and giving hardly a thought to tourists (although the menu's in English), family-run **Il Mulino** ★ 🄺 (Via delle Cartiere 3; ☎ 089-872223; Tues–Sun noon–3:30pm and 7pm–midnight; AE, DC, MC, V) is a thoroughly good value where you can happily indulge in a multicourse meal—with wine and beer—without watching your wallet too closely (*coperto* is 1.50€). It's a 10-minute walk inland from Amalfi's center, and while not high on looks or formalities, is the perfect place to dine if you have kids. Pizza (6€–7€) is only served at night, but it's the homemade pasta and the fresh, home-style fish dishes that make this place truly worthwhile.

€€–€€€   Amalfi's most contemporary take on dining is to be had at **Maccus** ★★★ (Largo S. Maria Maggiore 1-3; ☎ 089-8736385; www.maccusamalfi.it; Tues–Sun noon–3pm and 7–11:30pm; MC, V), a rather trendy eatery hidden away on the piazza at the entrances of the church of Santa Maria Maggiore and the Chiesa dell'Addolorata. Finding the venue is half the fun, but you'll discover the menu just as inviting as the young staff, who all look like they stepped out of a fashion catalogue. The kitchen likes to experiment with simple, classic ingredients, always fresh and of the finest quality. It's also a festive place for occasional wine and food tastings.

€€–€€€   Arguably the best seafood restaurant along the entire Amalfi Coast is **Trattoria da Ciccio** ★★★ (Via Nazional per Sorrento; ☎ 089-831265; Wed–Mon 12:30–3pm and 7:30–11pm, daily in Aug; closed Nov 8–Dec 1; AE, DC, MC, V), which is famous for its so-called *spaghetti al cartocch*—easily the best clam-based pasta I've ever had, cooked in a paper bag, and served with a hint of drama at your table, where the bag is stabbed with a knife and torn open. It's also famous for its proximity to Sophia Loren's house. The brightly lit restaurant (perched on the edge of the cliff over the sea) is 3km (2 miles) north of Amalf—you can ask to be picked up when you reserve; I was chauffeured by Guiseppe, the owner's son, who also waiters there, so by the time I got to my table I'd had a complete rundown of the menu. You could end up spending a small fortune here, but be firm about sticking to a starter and a *primi* and you won't blow your budget (*coperto* 3€). Kick off with the Fantasy of Seafood (10€), then opt for pasta or more fish. When I insisted that I couldn't afford dessert, I was bought a portion anyway ("because you must try it"), along with assorted liqueurs (including limoncello), on the house. The Ravello house wine is highly quaffable.

€€–€€€   In town, the favorite restaurant for locals and visitors alike since 1872 has been **Da Gemma** ✦✦ (Via Fra' Gerardo Sasso 10; ☎ 089-871345; Thurs–Tues 12:30–2:30pm and 7:30–10:30pm; AE, DC, MC, V). But high demand means it's become increasingly expensive. The rooftop terrace overlooking the main square is the payoff, but still it's pricey (*coperto* 3€). Gemma was the current owner's mother, and her *zuppa di pesce* (14€) remains excellent. There are Middle Eastern desserts like eggplant dipped in chocolate, and wonderful local wines.

RAVELLO ✦✦

Ravello—"the City of Music"—is a sophisticated, cultured, and exquisite village of just 2,500 permanent residents, perched high above the cluttered coast. The views from up here are truly majestic and drinking them in constitutes the central activity here, besides exploring the immaculate gardens and wandering through the tranquil streets. Ravello is a haven for relaxed contemplation. But the rich have long ago figured that out too, so Ravello is an expensive place to stay. Still, for just 1€, and without staying over, you can take the 15-minute bus from the waterfront in Amalfi to the heart of this paradise; even the bus ride is scintillating.

Start by visiting **Villa Cimbrone** (5€; daily 9am–8pm), which is about a 20-minute walk from the last bus stop through some of the quaint neighborhoods that cling to the cliffs. As you wind through the narrow, stepped streets, look below to terraced hills overgrown with lemon trees and vineyards, which cascade down to the turquoise sea below. Designed by Lord Grimthorpe (who also designed Big Ben in London), this 20th-century villa is nothing short of heavenly. The gardens are perfectly cultivated, with the smell of lavender and chamomile wafting through the air. But what makes the hefty entrance fee worthwhile are the views from the Belvedere Cimbrone, a lookout point affording unmatchable vistas up and down the coastline.

Once you've finished here, head back down toward the main square and the Duomo, which was founded in 1086 and has undergone countless renovations and reincarnations; the blood of St. Pantaleone is kept in a reliquary here. The attached **Museo del Duomo** (free; daily 9am–7pm) includes a hard-to-find collection of imperial and medieval artifacts, but keep searching, following the corridors until you get there.

Next head to nearby **Villa Rufolo** (5€), where the famous Ravello Music Festival (www.ravelloarts.org) is held each summer—it's worth whatever effort you can make to attend at least one concert. The stage juts out from the edge of the garden cliff, suspending the performers over the sea. Villa Rufolo was founded

Other Towns Along the Amalfi Coast

Several other villages along the Amalfi Coast are worth exploring, at least for an afternoon. **Scala** and **Minori,** toward Salerno, are both enchanting and largely undiscovered. Inland from the coast are great options as well. Paestum, which was originally known as Poseidonia, has a wonderful excavation of Greek ruins and what archaeologists label the best Doric temples on earth, better even than the Parthenon.

in the 11th century. Richard Wagner composed an act of *Parsifal* here, and Boccaccio was so moved by the spot that he included it in one of his tales.

Accommodations & Dining

€€€   If you'd like to spend the night (and really, it's beautiful enough to consider staying just to savor the views as they adapt to the subtle changes in the light), look no further than small, good-value **Garden** ★ (Via Boccaccio 4; ☎ 089-857226; www.hotelgardenravello.it; AE, DC, MC, V), which is right at the bus stop and enjoys an exquisite setting overlooking the bay; you could spend your entire stay perched at the terrace restaurant. Rooms are quaint, air-conditioned, tile-floored, and— importantly—firm-bedded. Book one with a balcony, pick up a bottle of the local *vino* (Gran Caruso) in the village, organize a corkscrew and a couple of glasses, and stare at the sea while the sun goes down. Doubles are just 105€ to 120€. A bargain!

€–€€   A good choice for lunch is **Cumpá Cosimo** (Via Roma 46; ☎ 089-857156; daily noon–3:30pm and 6–11pm, closed Mon Nov–Feb; AE, DC, MC, V), where the menu focuses on a range of homemade pastas and exotic-sounding meat dishes. And while it ain't "budget" by cheapskate standards, it's certainly fair for Ravello, with most *primi* in the 6€ to 13€ range, a Caprese salad for 10€, and meat dishes convincing enough at 10€ to 15€.

THE OTHER AMALFI COAST

Just when you thought Sorrento was all about endless parades of tourists, here's a great opportunity to combine your vacation with an unforgettable immersion in southern Italian culture, learn to cook, and get a grasp on the basics of the language. Sign up for a culinary arts course (groups of no more than nine) at **Mami Camilla** ★★★ (Via Cocumella 4, S. Agnello di Sorrento; ☎ 081-8782067; www.mamicamilla.com) and you'll engage with locals and learn the secrets of great Italian cooking. Add to that affordable accommodations to suit different budgets (p. 539), excursions, and the chance to hop aboard a private yacht and sail to Capri, and you have all the makings of a dreamy guilt-free holiday opportunity. Under the tutelage of head honcho Chef Biago, Mami Camilla offers minimum 1-week courses, but those with more time on their hands can participate for up to 7 weeks; there are also specialty baking and pizza courses. And, if you thought this might be an opportunity to slack off, think again: You'll earn your certificate with 4 hours of kitchen work each day, preparing the fixed four-course menu that will be served to paying guests that night. Each day you'll toil over one new *antipasto, primo* (you'll even learn how to make your own pasta from scratch), *secondo,* and pastry dessert; when I ate at Mami Camilla in 2007, we feasted on such spectacular (and complex) fare as stuffed rabbit and a delicious risotto. At the end of a hard day in the kitchen, you can look forward to simple but lovely air-conditioned accommodations—neat, moderately spacious, and light-filled, with white linens under bright bedcovers (50€–100€ private en suite double). For younger euro-counters there are dorm beds (16€–20€); set amid lemon groves, with a homey garden strung with hammocks, there's a relaxed open-to-the-elements bar, and breakfast is taken on an al fresco terrace. And, if all that isn't enough, your hosts also offer the unique opportunity to hop aboard a 10m (33-ft.) traditional boat (50€ per person) for a full day outing that includes a tour of the bay and goes to Capri (where you'll swim in the marvelous Blue Grotto, and have a few hours to wander around the island before returning home). After just a few days here, you really will feel as if this was home.

If you fantasize about being based in a beautiful town by the sea while you take your time learning a new language, consider signing up for a tailor-made Italian course with **Sorrento Lingue** (Via San Francesco 8; ☎ 081-8075599; www.sorrento lingue.it); program organizers also put together outings and sightseeing trips (with an eye on further enhancing your language efficacy), and can also find accommodation to suit your budget.

Further along the coast, near Positano, you'll have a fabulous time in the company of Chef Salvatore Barba, who runs a cooking school at his restaurant **Il Ritrovo** ✹✹ (Via Montepertuso 77; ☎ 089-812005; www.ilritrovo.com) in the little cliff-top village of Montepertuso. Once you've spent the day working in the kitchen, you get to feast on the rewards, accompanied by selected wines and an evening serenade by the restaurant staff. Daylong cooking classes are held October through April and cost 200€ (this includes transfers from Positano, materials, and the services of an interpreter); weeklong courses are 950€.

The ABCs of Naples & the Amalfi Coast

Business Hours Banks and public offices are officially open 8:30am to 1:20pm and 2:45 to 3:45pm, though nothing really gets going until around 9am. Churches are open 8 or 9am to 1 pm, and then again from 4 to 6 or 7pm. Coffee bars open around sunrise and many close late in the evening. Restaurants generally do not open until 12:30pm for lunch and 7:30pm for dinner.

Currency Exchange A great many *cambio* centers are found around Naples and the Amalfi Coast, but make sure their rates are up-to-date. Use **Banco di Napoli** (Via Toledo 177–178; ☎ 081-7924567) for money transfers. Main post offices also have exchange counters. It's always less time and hassle (and often cheaper) to use ATMs to extract local currency.

Doctors For medical advice by telephone, call ☎ **081-2542424** in central Naples.

Emergencies For police, call ☎ **112;** for the fire department, **115.** For an ambulance, call ☎ **118** or rush to a *pronto soccorso* (below).

Hospital An emergency room in Italy is called pronto soccorso. Those in Naples with 24-hour service are **Cardarelli** (Via Cardarelli 9, Vomero; ☎ 081-7471111) and, for children, **Santobono** (Via M. Fiore

6, Vomero; ☎ 081-2205111). On Capri: **Ospedale Capilupi** (Via Provinciale Anacapri, Due Golfi; ☎ 081-8381205). In Sorrento: **Ospedale Civico** (Corso Italia; ☎ 081-5331111).

Internet Access In Naples, virtually every hostel and hotel I've recommended comes with free Internet or Wi-Fi, usually both. Internet access on Capri and in towns along the Amalfi Coast is available at Internet cafes and also some bars with dated computers; try to avoid these as you'll waste your precious time in a place best experienced outdoors.

Newspapers & Magazines Major national Italian news dailies *Corriere della Sera* and *La Repubblica* have special *cronaca* sections for individual cities with local listings of events. *Qui Napoli*, a free magazine issued by the Naples Tourist board, has the most comprehensive listings in both English and Italian. *Le Pagine dell'Ozio* is a monthly guide to events and a comprehensive listing of bars, restaurants, and nightlife options.

Post Office Naples' main post office is at Palazzo Centrale della Posta, Piazza Matteotti (Toledo; ☎ **081-5511456**),

open weekdays until 7pm, Saturday in the morning only.

Safety Despite its notoriety, Naples is a relatively safe city. Pickpockets around the tourist sights are standard, as in most Italian cities, only here they seem a little less obvious. There aren't blatant groups of Gypsies, but there are skilled moped drivers who can grab a purse strap before you know what happened. Don't wander through the Spanish Quarter at night. Don't flash your diamond necklace around Piazza Garibaldi. Don't pull out a wad of money in a clip anywhere. Don't go out with anything you can't afford to lose; most hotels have wall safes where your passport and valuables are safer than on your person.

Transit Info The main website for transportation in and around Campania is www.ctpn.it. Each entity of the public transportation network has its own contact information. For bus service in Naples, contact **ANM** (☎ **800-639525** toll-free; www.anm.it). Boat timetables are published daily in the Neapolitan newspaper *Il Mattino*. **Water-taxi services** (☎ **800-547500** or 081-8773600; www.taxidelmare.it) are astronomically expensive.

13 Lecce & the Bucolic Charms of Puglia

Moderately priced villages, a fascinating history & an enchanting countryside—why discerning travelers try to keep Puglia to themselves

by Keith Bain

WHAT'S THE "NEXT TUSCANY"? MANY SAY IT'S PUGLIA—PRONOUNCED "*Pu*-lia"—the region that stretches from Tremiti to the very bottom of Italy's boot heel. So much of what makes Tuscany captivating—expansive views of vineyards and olive groves, as well as a very distinct cuisine and wine—is mirrored in Puglia (minus the heavy influx of foreign tourists and high prices, at least for now).

Puglia, which in English is sometimes called Apulia, is largely rural, its country roads flanked with stone fences, its hills dotted with elfin *trulli* houses. In its countryside magnificent natural wonders await—rare limestone caverns, underground rivers, soaring sea cliffs, and brilliant coastal coves. And, just across the border in the oft-forgotten region of Basilicata, the surreal spectacle of the rock-carved city of Matera is so ancient that for 50 years it's been making appearances in biblical epics. Many age-old customs, long since disappeared from other parts of Italy, live on here. Wander through the back alley of a coastal town like Gallipoli, and you may come upon wizened matriarchs, hand-rolling pasta and conversing with passersby. At the eastern tip of the peninsula, it's not uncommon to hear locals using a Greek dialect, heard nowhere else on the Boot.

But it's not all wide-open space, quaint fishing villages, and natural vistas. Puglia's man-made creations are boastfully varied, thanks to scores of foreign invaders over the centuries—Roman, Norman, Arab, Greek, you name it. Their influences can be traced through the art and architecture, which runs the gamut from monumental castles (built by the great Swabian king, Frederick II) to ancient fortresses, whitewashed cities, and—in the gorgeous student town of Lecce—possibly the most beautifully over-the-top church facades you ever did see.

But despite its charms, it's wise to remember that Puglia is not Tuscany—nor can it be. Its museums are not on par with those in Rome, Naples, Venice, and Florence. Much of what's on display is best appreciated by those with a keen understanding of Italy's history. While tourists are welcome, you never feel particularly catered to here. Of course, that makes Puglia a great place to meet locals. So go, savor, and shhh!

DON'T LEAVE ITALY'S HEEL WITHOUT . . .

GETTING LOST IN A FANTASY OF LECCESE BAROQUE   There is something quite otherworldly in the lush, abundant designs found on the facades of Lecce's exuberant churches (see "Why You're Here: Top Sights & Attractions," on p. 555).

EXPERIENCING THE *TRULLI*   Almost everyone associates Puglia with the strange upside-down ice-cream-cone-shaped structures called *trulli,* but nothing really prepares you for the sight of these elfin houses (p. 559). You can even spend the night in one of these unique structures.

CATCHING RAYS ON THE GARGANO PROMONTORY   The lush green Foresta Umbra of the Gargano Promontory in northern Puglia (p. 570) literally sprouts from the surrounding farmlands that make up the spur of Italy's boot. This nature lover's dream boasts some of the most spectacular coastal cliffs and coves and sandy stretches in all Italy. Don't forget your beach gear.

GOING SPELUNKING   What's below ground is as interesting as what's above in Puglia, particularly if you take the time to explore the Grotte di Castellana (p. 561) with its profusion of stalactites and stalagmites.

STAYING IN MATERA'S CAVELIKE *SASSI*   Amble around the ruins of this eerie city of caves carved into the ravines, and you'll feel as though you've been sent 2,000 years back in time. The experience is even more haunting at night, and you can sleep in one of the cave houses—called sassi—some of which are now carefully restored as hotels (p. 565).

A BRIEF HISTORY OF PUGLIA

Puglia is basically the heel of Italy's boot, surrounded by the Adriatic and Ionian seas. Because it's the first piece of land jutting out to the east, it served as the point of entry for most invasions into Italy. In fact, Puglia has been conquered, claimed, or rebuilt by the Greeks, Byzantines, Romans, Normans, and Spanish.

The most obvious influence in Puglia's history was that of Frederick II of Hohenstaufen, who reigned as Holy Roman Emperor until he died in 1250. His interests were nature and geometry, and the architecture he inspired is stunning. You won't see much in Puglia that he didn't build or otherwise influence.

Today, Puglia is a vital agricultural and fishing center, with its low, rolling hills producing more grain, tomatoes, lemons, and olives than any other Italian province. Eighty percent of the durum wheat for Europe's pasta industry is grown here, as are almost all of Italy's olives for oil, as well as some of the country's most legendary grape vintages like Primitivo red and Salento whites. Puglia alone produces more wine than Germany does. The fishermen along the Adriatic coast are the county's most prolific. Across the peninsula along the Ionian coast, the mussels and clams are highly sought after.

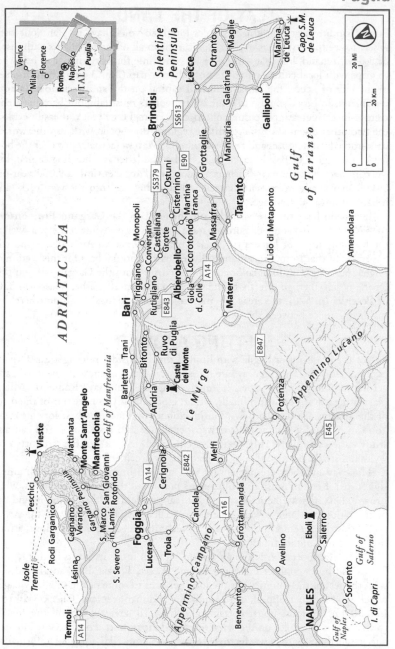

LAY OF THE LAND

Puglia is quite large (400km/248 miles long), so you'll have to plan your time wisely to see the best it has to offer. You can fit in all of the highlights with just 4 or 5 days in hand, but that won't give you any time for side trips or to really get to grips with local culture. If you're on a shorter trip (2 or 3 days), base yourself in the city of Lecce, the vibrant cultural capital on the **southernmost Salento peninsula.** In Lecce you'll find some of the world's most fabulous baroque architecture in an increasingly cosmopolitan city. From Lecce you can easily explore the two other essential must-sees in the region, Alberobello with its otherworldy cone-roofed trulli houses and ravine straddling **Matera** (actually just over the border in the region of Basilicata; p. 563). Today the latter is a bustling capital, but the commercial modern city shelters a place out of another time, a 9,000-year-old city of man-made caves, with homes and churches cut into the very rock, and inhabited until 50 years ago.

If you do have time to visit **the north,** head to the **Gargano Promontory** (p. 570), which has some of Europe's most impressive coastline scenery, as well as the medieval town of **Lucera** (p. 567), which was once an Arab village and still has traces of that former incarnation. Lucera is an optimal base for this section of Puglia, bursting with local color and an easy drive from the Gargano. If you prefer the beach, then go directly to the Gargano coast itself. Either **Vieste** (p. 570) or **Peschici** (p. 570), the area's two picturesque seaside locals, will do (there's no major difference between the two).

GETTING AROUND

To get the most out of Puglia with limited time, consider renting a car. Driving here is a pleasure. The highways are not as traffic-laden as those in the north, and getting around Puglia's cities is much simpler than, say, Rome or Milan. Navigating the region isn't difficult, either; especially if you have one of the maps of the Touring Club Italia (www.touringclub.it) in hand (the best for this area). You can pick up a map at most newspaper stands and bookstores. You can also study the complete highway system and check traffic reports on www.autostrade.it—a good tool for planning your itinerary.

Highway numbers are not always well marked but the towns are all amply signposted. Keep in mind that **blue signs** point you to towns and villages, while **brown signs** indicate heritage sites. Your real problem will be getting in and out of the cities and large towns; generally, you'll be navigating toward the *centro storico* (historical center), where nearly all recommended accommodations, attractions, and restaurants are located.

Public transportation is also an option, though it has its limits in this region. Trains and buses connect the major towns—Lecce, Foggia, Bari, and Brindisi—with the rest of the country, but the local services to some of the smaller villages, which hold so much appeal, can be sporadic and inconvenient. Check **www.tren italia.it** for the most updated train schedules. To navigate around the smaller towns, check schedules on the **www.ferroviedellostato.it**. For the Gargano area, check schedules with **www.ferroviedelgargano.com**. For updated information on bus timetables, consult **www.sitabus.it** or call ☎ 0881-773117.

The Regional Gateways

Britain's low-priced airlines (see the "Essentials of Planning" chapter) have now have regular flights from London directly to Puglia's main port cities. No one, however, *really* wants to visit either Bari or Brindisi, the cities one flies or ferries into. They hold little allure and neither is nearly as rewarding or relaxing as the rest of the region; in fact, they both have problems with petty crime (sometimes directed at tourists). So, arrange your transportation into these places and then get out of town ASAP.

If you do find yourself in Bari or Brindisi before a ferry connection and need to kill time, don't panic. There are suspicious characters lurking around the ferry port and a concentration of Gypsy kids in the center, but if you're aware of their presence and vigilant, they likely won't bother you.

LECCE ★★★

Lecce's reputation is gaining ground—not only as Puglia's most cosmopolitan hub, but as a premiere Italian travel destination, particularly worthwhile for architecture buffs. Lecce (pronounced "*Letch*-eh") is known for its honey-colored baroque monuments—dozens of late-Renaissance churches, palazzi, and gateways heavily embellished with all manner of fanciful designs. Cherubs, saints, cornucopias, oceanic waves, and pagan figures adorn the many eye-catching facades, while interiors are ornamented with mosaics and carvings that recount the often-violent history of the region. Lecce also bears reminders of Roman influence—including its partially excavated 1st-century-B.C. amphitheater—and there are ancient underground tombs going back to prehistoric times.

What elevates Lecce's charms even further is its laid-back manageability. Its compact, easy-to-explore walled *centro storico* is packed with wide-open piazzas and the cobbled streets are lined with handsome palazzi, meaning that there's always something to see (even if you don't seek out museums and formal galleries). Virtually all of its attractions are concentrated here, so you never feel the need to rush around or figure out local public transport. The historical center boasts a heady student scene, plentiful shops and boutiques, and a decent lineup of restaurants where you can sample traditional Pugliese and Salentine cuisine. And, inundated with pubs and bars, the vibrant scene continues well into the night. You can easily wander from one hot spot to the next, looking for your ideal poison, or discover a summer concert or impromptu performance often staged on the squares in front of the finest monuments.

Pick up a map (1€) and gather useful tips for exploring Lecce at the **Tourist Info Point** (☎ 0832-246517; Mon–Fri 9am–9pm, Sat–Sun 9:30am–9pm) in the entrance of **Castello Carlo V,** Lecce's 16th-century fortress right outside the walls of the old city. It's staffed by keen, young, English-speaking staff. You'll be able to explore the entire historical center on foot, so there's no need to worry about transport. If you do drive here, however, be sure to organize parking details with your host in advance—alternatively, you'll need to park outside the *centro storico* (various parking meter fees apply).

ACCOMMODATIONS, BOTH STANDARD & NOT

€–€€   Raffaele Bitetti's **Salento in Casa B&B** ★★ (Corte San Blasio 1; ☎ 0832-242960; www.salentoincasa.it; AE, DC, MC, V) handles bookings for several different B&Bs—either in the historical center, around Lecce, or anywhere in Salento province—all priced from just 50€ to 80€ double. Some examples of what you might snag include **B&B Piazza San'Oronzo,** which boasts oversized bedrooms (50€–80€ double) in a five-room apartment on the fourth floor (reached by elevator) of a block near the amphitheater; they have such cushy amenities as mosaic marble floors, electronic blinds, air-conditioning, a small fridge, and decent bathrooms. **Il Castello** ★★ kids is a larger (10-unit) option located right on the corner as you enter the historical center from the Castle; the three-floor building was entirely renovated in 2006 and offers atmospheric lodgings with vaulted ceilings, great bathrooms, and colorful decor. My favorite double is no. 8, which is huge and has a great shower (80€ double; 10€–15€ for an extra bed). If you're traveling with children (and don't mind dealing with all the stairs), take the top-floor suite (100€–150€ for four people); it has a kitchen, dining area, lounge, and a massive terrace; there's even a stereo, so you can really make yourself at home.

Beyond simply booking the rooms, Raffaele acts as a one-man travel agency, helpfully arranging airport transfers (15€), convenient parking (10€), and affordable Smart car rentals. He can also pair you with knowledgeable guides, if you wish, and has been known to arrange more unusual experiences, like horse-riding tours around Salento.

€€   If you prefer booking a B&B on your own, that's doable, too. Lecce has over a hundred tidy little B&Bs, perfect for discerning budgeters. The very first was **Centro Storico** kids (Via Vignes 2/b; ☎ 0832-242727; www.bedandbreakfast.lecce.it; AE, DC, MC, V), on the second floor of a 16th-century palazzo. It's a comfortable come-and-go-as-you-please affair with a few attractively restored suites (90€–100€) and one Standard double, with private balcony but shared bathroom (just 57€). All rooms have wrought-iron beds and antique furniture. Best of all is the roof terrace where you can recline on a sun bed; the rooftop is also where the nicest suite (Duomo) is found. The massive Imperial suite is ideal for those traveling with kids as it offers an extra upstairs bed and basic kitchenette along with a piano and small private balcony. There's Wi-Fi and free parking within the walled old city.

€€–€€€   But my favorite lodgings and Lecce's best value are the superb, pretty suites at Marcello Apollonio's **Chiesa Greca B&B Suites** ★★★ kids (Piazzette Chiesa Greca 11; ☎ 0832-302330 or 335-5344644; www.chiesagreca.it; AE, DC, MC, V), where you stay in a palazzo dating back around 700 years, built above 3,000-year-old underground tombs. Each generous, individually decorated suite (60€–120€ double) is filled with eclectic artworks and furnished with period pieces. The overall impact is akin to staying in a historical monument, albeit with modern comforts like air-conditioning, kitchenettes, and homey living-room areas. A few have their own terrace; you can even barbecue while looking over the *piazzetta* below. One—a former chapel of the adjacent 18th-century church—boasts original frescoes, vaulted stone ceilings, and wooden floors. Some suites have more stairs to negotiate than others.

DINING FOR ALL TASTES

€ I like to start the day with espresso at **Caffè dell'Anfiteatro** (daily 6:30am–2:30am; cash only); right next to the amphitheater, it's popular throughout the day. Return later for a tasty midday panino (1.50€), or enjoy a sunset beer with the lads.

€ A sweet place to mix with an up-for-it crowd is **Trumpet** ★ (Via P. di Sarora; ☎ 339-6059889; Tues–Sun noon–3pm and 7:30pm–2:30am; MC, V), which is as much a place people come to watch football on TV as it is a wine bar. Ask for Charles, the hipper-than-thou manager who loves engaging with English-speaking visitors. You can order excellent sandwiches, salads, or remarkably big meat-and-cheese platters along with an affordable glass of wine (Charles will have a recommendation). More substantial hot dishes are also served, and the value is astounding; you probably won't spend over 10€ even after two glasses of wine.

€–€€ **Trattoria Cucina Casareccia** ★★ (Via Colonnello Costadura; ☎ 0832-245178; daily 12:30–2pm and 8–11pm; MC, V) is actually the living room of a private home that has been converted over time into a family restaurant. What's on the menu is basically whatever Grandma decides to cook, which means you'll be getting an opportunity to sample real traditional homemade fare. You should know that this place is the perennial favorite for anyone and everyone visiting Lecce, so book early. The good news is that you'll eat very well for around 14€ including wine; the bad news is that it closes down for a few weeks in August and September.

€–€€ As smart as it looks, vibey little **Boccon Divino** ★ (Via Libertini, 17; ☎ 0832-309583; daily 10:30am–2pm and 6pm–1am; MC, V) is thoroughly unpretentious—although you may have to wait to get one of the few popular tables outside. Pizzas are just 3€–8€, but this is a great place to try out some typical Salento specialties (all 6.50€): *parmigiana* (fried aubergine baked with tomato sauce, ham, mozzarella, and other cheeses); *polpo in pignata* (octopus soup with potatoes and spices); *pezzetti di cavallo al sugo* (chunks of horse meat in spiced tomato sauce). For an interesting pasta, try *tagliolini boccon divino,* made with pine seeds, almonds, anchovies, olives, and herbs, all pounded to a delicious pulp (7.50€). Be prepared to wait as dishes are prepared fresh and take awhile; there are some interesting beers to hold your attention like the double malt Moretti (3€).

WHY YOU'RE HERE: TOP SIGHTS & ATTRACTIONS

Lecce is often referred to as the "Florence of the south," and is special not only for its cultural energy but also for its architecture—the exquisite style of "Leccese baroque." For a number of reasons, the architecture of Lecce evolved directly from the Romanesque to the high baroque, skipping the Gothic stage. That is emphasized here by the extensive use of the quirky, fanciful symbols that were popular in the Middle Ages, but rarely used elsewhere on baroque churches: snarling dragons, griffins, placid mermaids, pelicans, and a menagerie of other pagan symbols. These fantastic beasts are carved in exquisite detail, thanks to the use of a local sandstone that's particularly soft and malleable when first quarried, hardening after long exposure to the air. The plasticity of this stone allowed the carvers here to give free rein to their imaginations, giving birth to wonderful flights of fancy and fantasy, greatly enhanced by the golden hues of the stone that seem to radiate the sun's light.

The obvious starting point for a tour of Lecce's old walled city is the **Roman Amphitheater.** Only a quarter of it is visible today, the rest buried under the large adjacent square, **Piazza Sant'Oronzo.** Legend has it the ampitheater once held 25,000 spectators, this despite the fact that the city's population was only 4,000. The rest of the audience was drawn here from far and wide; Lecce has long been the centerpiece of the region. Today the square is named for St. Oronzo—the bishop of Lecce in the 1st century—who was fed to the lions during the reign of Nero. The tall column topped by a bronze statue of the saint was sent here from Brindisi in 1666 as a gesture of gratitude after the saint was said to have rescued the town from a plague a few years earlier.

Next, head to the marquee attraction among Lecce's many churches: the 17th-century **Basilica della Santa Croce (Church of the Holy Cross)** ★★★ (on the Piazza della Santa Croce; free; daily 9am–noon and 5–8pm). Designed, in part, by local superstar Giuseppe Zimbalo (fondly referred to as "Zingarello," or Gypsy), it took 150 years to complete, and epitomizes the flamboyant, detail-rich Zimbalo style. The facade is divided into two orders: Along the lower order are symbols of evil (dragon, griffin, ogres, and giants, some of which seem almost like cartoon villains), which are actually being crushed, or overcome, by the obvious forces of good seen in the second order above. Above the entrance, the exquisite rose window symbolizes the perfection of God, who encircles all. Inside, local history—and a long-held grudge—takes center stage in the **Chapel of St. Francis of Assisi** at the front of the church; the 12 finely carved panels—six on either side of the painting of St. Francis—depict the Venetians' betrayal of the people of this peninsula. The execution of the women of Otranto is depicted in some of the carved panels, so detailed that they have been compared to tapestries.

Next in importance is Lecce's other main square, **Piazza Duomo,** and Lecce's main cathedral, also designed by Zimbalo (by now you should be able to recognize his "signature"—the carved fantasy elements in the corners of the rectangular sections of his facades, which symbolize the lower part of the skirts worn by the wealthy women back in the day). You'll notice that the **Duomo** ★★★ (free; daily 7am–noon and 5–7:30pm) has two facades—the original is the one adjacent the **Bishop's Palace.** The bell tower is another Zimbalo design.

Other churches worthy of a visit include the **Basilica of San Giovanni Battista** ("del Rosario")—another Zimbalo masterwork—and **Santa Chiara, Santa Irena, San Matteo,** and **Santa Teresa,** all marked on the map provided by the local tourist bureau. You may find that you'll enjoy this church hopping most if you can book a tour with the erudite and entertaining **Fabio Leo** ★★★ (☎ 380-7056501; fabioleo74@jumpy.it); a translator and art history graduate, his passion for the city is almost combustible. He'll bring the Leccese baroque alive for you in ways you never imagined possible, infusing your experience with wonderful anecdotes and tidbits that will help you fall even more in love with the city. Fabio charges 90€ per half-day in Lecce, but will also accompany your visits to other highlights of the Salentine peninsula (such as Gallipoli and Otranto) for 100€ (these prices are irrespective of the number of people in your party). His tours will include a visit to a papier-mâché store and a local product tasting, if you want. Fabio also conducts seasonal walking tours of the city for **Cooperative Theutra** (enquiries at Castello Carlo V; ☎ 0832-279195; 7€ for 2 hr.), a local cultural initiative; English tours are infrequent, but I once accompanied one of Fabio's Italian tours and between stops he gave me the lowdown in English.

THE OTHER LECCE

Puglia's distinctive cuisine draws on a variety of influences, absorbed over the centuries as foreigners have invaded and ruled here. The Greeks left behind a tradition of preparing roasted lamb, while the Romans no doubt left a legacy of eating horse meat. You'll note a Spanish influence in the paella-like *taiedda*. Fish dishes abound, as do those based around a wide variety of fresh produce as this is a vital agricultural center, and the capacity of the earth and sea to provide so abundantly has enabled a rich and varied regional cuisine to develop.

The point is that Puglia is a fascinating place to learn all kinds of culinary skills you might never have thought existed. Consequently, the region is positively bursting with quality **cooking schools,** many of which are, unfortunately, quite expensive. A wonderful exception are the **cooking classes** offered by **Scuola Porta d'Oriente** (☎ 0836-804431 or 338-4562722; www.porta-doriente.com), situated 50km (31 miles) from Lecce, in the pretty seaside town of Otranto. Here, culinary skills are combined with dedicated language and Italian culture classes. Courses are run virtually every week, and there's a flexible schedule, which means you can take a one-on-one class to learn the secrets of a specific dish (perhaps learning how to make one that's typically Apulian), or fall in for a longer period, adding an antipasta, the local orecchiette pasta, fish dishes, sweets, and bruschette to your kitchen repertoire. If cooking isn't your thing, the school also offers classes in all sorts of local arts and crafts, so you could sign up for a **painting and drawing** course, **mosaic** course, or even a **ceramics** course, which is run in Lecce and—aside from getting your hands dirty—includes a visit to a traditional ceramics factory. You could also learn to **sculpt** using the famous Pietra Leccesse soft stone that enabled the Lecce baroque to evolve the way it did. Most of these courses involve about 10 hours worth of workshop time, spread over a week or two; costs range from 340€ to 370€, not including housing. If you simply want to **learn Italian,** there's a language course for around 225€ per week (20 lessons), or 36€ for a 1-hour private session; and Otranto is a great place for meeting Italians—90% of the tourism here is domestic, and the locals are the kind who will stop in the streets and chat. Parents, note that while most students here are in their 30s and 40s, there are also special courses run just for kids.

Lecce has a proud tradition of artisanship, and is especially famous for its papier-mâché sculptures (in some of the churches, in fact, entire ceilings that look like they're made of beautifully crafted wood are actually finely carved and cleverly painted papier-mâché). It can be fascinating to witness the local artists in action, seeing how they create elaborate figurines from such humble material as paper pulp. A tour of artisan workshops is another way of meeting local people. To get in on the action, contact **Salento Luau** (Vico del Theutra 5; ☎ 0832-303633), which organizes—among other activities—a tour of artisan workshops, observing artists and craftsmen involved in the papier-mâché, terra-cotta, leather, and other industries. While it's possible to simply wander into shops around town and observe some of these crafters in action, a guided tour will enable you to get past the language barrier, since few of Lecce's artisans speak English. The people at Salento Luau have identified the most rewarding workshop experiences and will translate any questions you may have for the people you meet (such tours cost 15€–80€ per person, depending on the number of participants). For information in English, contact **Brenda Beatty** (☎ 328-5391622).

ATTENTION, SHOPPERS!

You'll no doubt want to get your hands (and taste buds) on some of the standout food and wine of Puglia. Locals favor **Panetteria Valentina** ✰✰ (Via Petronelli 3; ☎ 0832-300549), which specializes in regional delicacies like pasta, cookies, and fig paste. The owner is a delightful elderly man who all but hand-feeds you his goods, so don't be shy—it's great fun to sample. For sweet gifts, try the local handmade chocolate from **Maglio Arte Dolciaria** (Via Templari 16; ☎ 0832-243816); the chocolate-covered figs are indescribable and the staff members will package your sweets to make up great little gifts.

Lecce has been known since the 17th century for the *cartepesta* (papier-mâché) and ceramic figurines that its artisans produce for churches around the globe. I find them a little kitschy, but many disagree with me and it's possible to purchase a smaller figure for approximately 25€ to take home. One of the more popular outlets, where you might see the molding, torching, and painting that goes into making the statuary, is **La Casa Dell'Artigianato Leccese** (Via Matteotti 20; ☎ 0832-306604; www.artigianatoleccese.com).

SIDE TRIPS FROM LECCE

From Lecce, you can easily explore the entire Salento region, including the island town of **Gallipoli** (about an hour's drive from Lecce), which attracts local Italian tourists who come to relax in the village square or along the sandy beaches. The main industry is small-time fishing, and it's mesmerizing to stand on the promenade above the port and watch the fishermen untangle their nets by hand at the end of the day. A sweet, whitewashed city, it was a famous seaport in ancient times and a hub for the export of olive oil. It now thrives principally on domestic tourism. Along these streets is everything from tomatoes sun-drying on the walls to town elders playing cards outside their kitchen doors. There aren't many true attractions, but do stop inside the **Duomo,** and consider making use of the string of free beaches sprawling out on either side of the city.

Another easy and recommended trip out of Lecce is **Otranto** (an hour by train), one of Italy's prettiest little towns. Once a bustling port that saw a great deal of traffic during the Crusades, it was pretty much decimated in 1480 when the Turks sacked the place, killing just about everyone before beheading the 800 survivors because they refused to convert to Islam. Mention Otranto to anyone in the Salentine Peninsula and they'll insist you visit it's famous Romanesque **Cathedral** (daily 8am–noon and 3–6pm), primarily to see the floor mosaic that is the town's pride and joy. Writhing with an extraordinary range of images, legendary characters, animals, and mythical creatures, it's likely to be unlike anything you've seen before. For something more grisly, take a peek inside the **crypt** where skulls of the martyrs are displayed. While you're here, try and visit the hulking mass of the nearby **Castello,** and the Byzantine chapel of the **Basilica,** where you'll see frescoes created a thousand years ago.

ALBEROBELLO ★★ & TRULLI COUNTRY

The rural highways through the Itria Valley are lined with vineyards, ancient olive trees, almond groves, and peach and cherry orchards, which makes a leisurely drive through the back roads one of the great pleasures of exploring this part of southern Puglia. This is also where you begin to see the conical houses called trulli, which are whitewashed stone huts with stacked gray slate-tile roofs. Many trulli rooftops are painted with astrological signs and almost all of them in this area are inhabited.

Few people know why these structures exist, but the most credible local legend states that they were originally built as a way to avoid housing taxes (because they had only stacked rocks and no mortar, they theoretically weren't houses). There is, after all, an old Italian proverb, *"Fatta la legge, trovato l'inganno"* ("As the law is made, the deception is found"), which still holds true today. Another believable piece of trulli trivia is that when a baby was about to be born, the man of the trulli would build another room with its own cone, so anyone passing by could easily see how many children each family had, and thus how fortunate they were.

The capital of the trulli area is the Disney-esque town of Alberobello, which has 1,500 of these dwellings, now mostly housing trinket peddlers, wine bars, and clothing shops. You should definitely stop here, but the best part of Alberobello is across the Largo Martellotta, away from the tourist mecca into the residential zone around the Piazza M. Pagano. These trulli are still primarily private houses, and a quiet walk-through will give you a better idea of how the population lives. The houses are so tiny that it is common to see residents either dining at a table outside the kitchen doors or visiting with friends on chairs in the alleyways. You can visit the **Trullo Sovrano** (1.50€; daily 10am–7pm), which is the only trullo with an upstairs floor; capped by a 14m (46-ft.) comic dome, it's served as a court, a monastery, a grocer's, and a family home. This latest incarnation is how it's been preserved as a cute little UNESCO-protected museum. Meanwhile, the biggest organized diversion in town is the **Museo de Territorio** (3€; July–Sept daily 10am–7pm, Oct–June Tues–Sun 10am–1pm and 3:30–7pm), which links 15 different trulli homes, and includes an arts and crafts section and a wine museum.

ACCOMMODATIONS & DINING IN & AROUND ALBEROBELLO

€€–€€€ Sleeping in a trullo can be a real eye-opener into the simpler way of life of ordinary "peasant" folk who traditionally lived in these small, economical houses. These were people with limited means and few needs, so be prepared for a rather basic living experience. The easiest way to spend a night in a trullo is through **Trullidea Resort** ★ (Via Monte San Marco 25; ☎ 080-4323860; www.trullidea.it; AE, MC, V), an experienced agency in Alberobello which has a wide inventory of places both in town and in the surrounding countryside. For the most authentic experience, go for one of the more economic standard units (86€–102€ double)—a bed in an alcove off a single-room space (with table, two chairs, kitchenette, and wardrobe); there's a tiny attached bathroom, and a fireplace for chillier months (it's a myth that trullo are miraculously warm in winter). As you'd expect by checking these elfin cottages from the outside, there ain't too many windows, and you need to mind your head all the time (I bumped mine even while reminding myself to warn you). More luxurious superior trulli (102€–125€) are also on offer; check out the different options on the website, but be sure to take the descriptions with a grain of salt.

€€   If you'd prefer to combine your trulli experience with an honest-to-good-ness country sojourn, I recommend a night or two at the disarmingly tranquil **Masseria Cappuccini** ★★ (Corsa da Cappuccini, Ostuni; ☎ 333-4120241; www.masseriacappuccini.it; cash only). Gianfranco Nardelli and his family have converted the trulli behind their honey-colored farmhouse to create a beautiful, bucolic retreat. Its white surfaces are dazzling under the Puglian sun, while packed stone walls divide horse paddocks from olive groves, and the most gorgeous pool I've ever laid eyes on begs you to come on in for a dip. Inside the cone-roofed, thick-walled trulli houses, things are a little simpler (though not as rudimentary as you'll find in the standard trulli offered by Trullidea Resort in Alberobello). Walls are starkly white, the ceilings seem to disappear to infinity, and (a typical trulli feature) there are almost no windows. Decor is old-fashioned, yet unclut-tered; think monastic chic with a few of Grandma's foibles thrown in. They're far more spacious than expected; I stayed in a two-room unit, where the large sofa in the sitting room becomes a bed for children. Breakfast is served in another trulli. Ostuni is just 16km (10 miles) away. And the big surprise: A night costs just 50€ per person.

€–€€   My absolute favorite Alberobello restaurant is **La Locanda di Don Antonio** ★★★ (Via Giové 8; ☎ 080-4326084; Thurs–Tues; AE, DC, MC, V), run by two brothers; Massimo cooks up a storm, bringing clever innovation to tradi-tional Pugliese cuisine, while tattooed, sweet-faced Roberto makes theatrical displays of serving great vintages. Roberto also talked me into ordering *risottaccio*—rice with primitive wine and smoked cheese (6.50€)—and while I'm not usually a fan of rice, this was really good. So good, in fact, that I promptly "splurged" on a plate of perfectly grilled Murgia lamb, or *agnello murgese alla brace* (7€)—again, Roberto's choice. Truly, a top-notch place, with many worthy menu options. Expect a mixed local crowd to start filling up the tables from around 9pm. *Primi* are 5€–8€.

ATTENTION, SHOPPERS!

Artisan shops occupying trulli houses are dime a dozen, some flogging obscenely touristy junk. Offering a smattering of legitimacy is the little outlet at **Trullo Siamese** (Via Monte Nero 50; ☎ 080-4322702), built in the 15th century but per-manently divided into two in the 1700s when the pair of brothers who lived here fell in love with the same girl, causing an unshakeable rift between them. Anyway, now it's a family outlet for traditional *fischietti*—colorful terra-cotta figurines that make upbeat ornaments (bizarrely, they have a decidedly Mexican look). Each design has a different symbolic meaning: a bell flower represents trust and love, a peacock is long life and health. You can pick up a traditional terra-cotta whistle, shaped like a *cola* (cock) for 2.50€. Traditional handloom linens made with nat-ural dyes are also sold.

If you are looking for **gifts to take home,** duck into **Tholos Wine Bar di Luigi Minerva** (Via Monte S. Michele 20; ☎ 080-4321699; www.trullodelgusto.it),

Journey to the Center of the Earth . . . Well, Nearly

From central Puglia's eastern coastline, a 150×50km (93×31-mile) lime-stone plateau called **Le Murge** reaches inland from the sea. The terrain here is marked by caves and ravines and dotted with little villages. An intriguing cave outing—just a short drive from Alberobello—is the **Grotte di Castellana** ★★ 🧒 🔊 (☎ 081-4998211; www.grottedicastellana.it; 8€ short tour, 13€ for longer tour; daily Oct–Mar 8:30am–12:30pm, year-round 2:30–6:30pm), which is a visually stunning labyrinth of stalactites and stalagmites twisting from the cavern floors and ceilings. There are two options for joining the guided tours of the caves: a standard 1km (²/₃-mile) tour lasts 50 minutes and costs 8€ (English tours are at 9:30am and 1pm in high season only, although you can join the hourly Italian tours 9:30am–12:30pm and 2:30–5:30pm). A far more enticing tour is the extended 3-hour version, which culminates with the so-called **Grotto Bianca (White Cave)**, which is a large opening in the deepest part of the cave network that is lined with glassy, shimmering stalactites. This 2-hour option costs 13€; English tours are at 11am and 3pm, while the Italian version runs hourly between 9am and noon and 3 and 5pm. Note that low-season tours are only between 9:30am and 12:30pm and only in Italian. Times changes regularly, so always call first. These caves were used prima-rily as a landfill for the area's trash until 1938, when they were explored fully and now are one of the most educational stops in the province. Bring a long-sleeve shirt—it's always 60°F (16°C) inside the caves.

where you can sample some wonderful local wines, salami and cheese, and local confections. They will package and ship gifts for you.

The classiest Alberobello memorabilia is from **Click Art Gallery** (Via Monte Nero 23, Rione Monte; ☎ 3494236481; www.clickartgallery.com), much of it fea-turing stylish photographs by Luigi Minerva.

A SIDE TRIP TO OSTUNI ★★★

Ostuni—also known as *la città bianca* (the white city)—is a dramatic sight visi-ble from miles around thanks to the brilliant whitewashed surfaces of its histori-cal center, set upon a hilltop, seemingly gazing toward the sea. Founded in the 9th century, Ostuni oozes character and, in recent years, has made itself into a fash-ionable little destination, spawning top-rated restaurants and myriad boutiques, many of them worked by local artisans. Head into the center of Ostuni, and you'll discover a metropolis reminiscent of the stepped towns along the Amalfi Coast, though you've got a distinctively North African feel here with arched stairways, tight passages, and rambling alleys connecting houses and restaurants.

Just keep climbing up the maze of winding streets from the main square, Piazza della Libertà, until you reach the pinnacle of Ostuni, on which stands a completely out-of-place 15th-century **Gothic church** with a red-brown exterior and a green-and-yellow-tiled cupola. It's like a peacock among doves in this white-washed town. Stand back as far as you can to take in the detailed Gothic facade, which is divided into three sections with pilaster strips. Above each door is a carved rose window with 24 external arcades representing the 24 hours of the day. The interior is standard issue for Puglia, with its requisite marble floors and ornate ceiling, and in keeping with the calendar theme, the 12 arched internal arcades represent the months of the year, and the seven angel heads represent the days of the week. Outside the church, you'll enjoy a panoramic view across the olive groves to the sea. If you want to head off to the beach, it's a mere 7km (4½ miles) away, and the sandy shore has some lovely swimmable spots.

You can explore Ostuni in an hour or two, so see it as a side trip from either Lecce, Alberobello, or—better still—from your base at nearby Masseria Cappuccini (see above).

€–€€   Ostuni is a favorite tourist town, and the upshot of this is the profusion of little **restaurants** you'll find tucked away in the historical center; even if you're just here on a day trip, try to factor lunch or dinner into your schedule. Older establishments such as **Spessite** (Via Clemente Brancasi 43; ☎ 0831-302866; Thurs–Tues 1–2:30pm and 7:30–11pm; AE, MC, V), set in a vaulted cellar down a series of stepped streets from the main cathedral, and **Porta Nova** (Via Petrarolo 38; ☎ 0831-331472; Thurs–Tues 1–3pm and 8pm–midnight; AE, DC, MC, V), with it's panoramic views from the terrace, are both time-tested favorites—the latter is popular for seafood. **Tempo Perso** (☎ 0831-303320; Tues–Sun 7:30–11pm; AE, MC, V) looks like a white cave, and serves excellent orechiette pasta with clams; *primi* are 8€ to 12€. But there's emerging talent (and a touch of class, too) at

---

Town Spotting Between Alberobello & Ostuni

The towns between Alberobello and Ostuni lie along one of the most picturesque highways in all of Puglia. Try the following route (see the map on p. 551):

* Leave Alberobello, on Hwy. 604, and drive for 8km (5 miles) to reach **Locorotondo,** often referred to as the "balcony" for the way the highway overlooks the valley below. This is one of the best areas in which to pick up some local wines like Primitivo.
* From Locorotondo, set off on Hwy. 172, traveling 9km (5½ miles) to reach **Martina Franca** to take in some of the area's best baroque architecture outside of Lecce, particularly evident on the facade of **Chiesa di San Martino.**
* Now head 9km (5½ miles) down the highway to **Cisternino,** one of Italy's most beautiful villages.
* From Cisternino, it's a pleasant 14km (8¾-mile) drive to Ostuni on Hwy. 604.

Back to Nature

The coastal towns between Puglia's two commercial hubs, Bari and Brindisi, are mostly busy fishing ports and strange beach-club enclaves. There isn't much appeal on this stretch of coast beyond the towns of **Torre a Mare,** which is perched above a set of coastal caves; **Polignano a Mare,** with its medieval old center; and **Monopoli,** which is a bustling seaport almost halfway between Bari and Brindisi.

Also occupying this coastal stretch is **Torre Guaceto** 🅺🅸🅳🆂 (Via Piazzetta A/32, Serranova di Carovigno; ☎ 0831-989885; www.riservaditorreguaceto. it), a nature reserve with both marine and terrestrial zones where landlubbers can take **bicycle treks** or go on a **guided hike.** Walks last about 3 hours and will take you all around the "humid zone," a natural habitat for cranes, egrets, and red herons, primarily comprising small lakes, reed thickets, and wild grasses. The beaches here are free and lightly populated, even at the height of summer. If you want to go face to face with creatures beneath the surface of the Adriatic, there are also snorkeling adventures.

bright young **Trattoria del Frantoio** (Via Bixio Continelli 54/64; ☎ 0831-301402; www.trattoriadelfrantoio.com; Tues–Sun 1–3pm and 7:30pm–midnight; AE, DC, MC, V), which offers a refreshing take on the vaulted cellar theme: diners can take a between-course tour of the underground excavations downstairs.

MATERA ★★★

Like a surreal trip back in time—not to the Renaissance, or even the medieval period, but to biblical times—Matera's otherworldly sassi ruins make for a absorbing visit, unlike anything you're likely to see anywhere in Europe (though bits of Turkey's Cappadocia bear some resemblance). Matera is a few kilometers over Puglia's border in neighboring Basilicata, and well worth the little effort it'll take to get here (2 hr. from either Lecce or Lucera). While the haunting ruins of the sassi cityscape have featured in numerous period films—most notably in Mel Gibson's *The Passion of the Christ*—they remain far off the beaten tourist trail, making a visit all the more evocative of a forgotten time. But things are changing fast, and there's a fervent spirit of revival (and mass renovation), so you'll want to visit before it loses its unique luster.

Matera is believed to be 9,000 years old, first inhabited by prehistoric man who settled around the deep canyon along which numerous grottoes were found. The cleft in the earth formed a natural defense against the elements and against would-be enemies, so the settlement prospered. It was also a place where mystics, from as far as the Orient, came to meditate in the caves upon the hill. As the need for more dwellings arose, many more caves were simply hewn out of the soft, workable rock. Brick frontages were added to the man-made caves, giving the cityscape its geometric appearance, but behind these facades, people were living deep within the bowels of the rock, often is surprisingly large spaces. Numerous churches (over 150, in fact) were also carved into the rock.

During the Middle Ages, the town prospered, and soon rock surfaces suitable for excavation had run out, and overcrowding became a problem, exacerbated by water shortages, sewage crises, and the obvious lack of ventilation. Such problems only came to light after World War II, when Carlo Levi's book, *Christ Stopped at Eboli,* scandalized the country with its news that Italians of the 1950s were essentially troglodytes, living in woefully uncivilized conditions. The cavelike houses were windowless, often holding an entire family and its animals. Malaria was rampant and poverty killed many of the children. Most famously, Levi's book described children with the "wizened faces of old men" reduced to skeletal frames from starvation, heads crawling with lice. His words prompted the government to pour money into the poorer areas in the south to eradicate malaria.

In 1960, a new town was built above the ancient city, and Matera's 20,000 sassi inhabitants were forcibly removed and relocated there. The ancient district was left deserted and derelict until it became a UNESCO World Heritage Site in the mid-1990s. Now, a decade on, Matera's sassi district is being thoroughly revitalized, largely thanks to a burgeoning tourism market. The opening of hotels, guesthouses, restaurants, and art galleries in the ancient city has enabled entrepreneurs to pour financing into the restoration (some very beautiful) of the cave dwellings; filmmaker Francis Ford Coppola is opening a boutique hotel in Bernalda, not too far from Matera (www.blancaneaux.com).

Pick up a map of the area at the **tourist office** (Via Lucana 238; ☎ 0835-319458; www.sassitourism.it); someone will mark out the highlights, and even if they don't speak a word of English you'll get a good idea of what's being pointed out. Besides, there's absolutely no way of getting lost, and nearly everything is well signposted. You may want to use an audioguide to tour the sassi area (and it also segues into the historical center, just above the sassi zone); you can rent one from **La Casa di Lucio** (www.viaggilionetti.com) for 8€. You can also engage the services of a **guide** through **PUBLItourist** (Via Lucana 184 F/G; ☎ 0835-344116), for 10€ per person; the tour includes an introduction to local artisan crafts and food tastings.

Although, you'll find just wandering around and exploring fascinating enough, it's worth getting inside some of the more monumental caves. There's a clutch of six **rock-cut cave churches** ✫✫ (daily summer 9am–1pm and 3–7pm, winter 9:30am–1:30pm and 2:30–4:30pm; 2.50€ per church or 6€ for all six) scattered about town, which are worth seeing. If you just want to get an idea of what these churches are like, head up to the rocky outcrop that sticks out like a sore thumb; it's where you'll find **San Maria Idris,** but actually features two churches (you pay one entry). You'll have a sense of an authentic cave interior—including the damp humidity—generally well preserved and well excavated, although with frescoes in an understandably miserable state.

Beyond the churches you'll want to get a gander at how the people of Matera actually lived. There are currently two competing "open cave homes," dressed up to look just the way they would have when people were living in them (sans animals and real people, of course), which you can visit; I recommend **Casa Grotta del Casanuovo** ✫ (1.50€; daily Nov–Mar 10am–5pm, Apr–Oct 9:30am–7:30pm), a four-room cave dwelling that is indeed an eye-opener. A CD-recorded running commentary in English talks you through the layout of the home and explains how it impacted on the lives of the family (and its livestock, which all lived in there together—the hens and chickens were usually under the bed). A visit takes just a few minutes, but is terribly humbling—these people only got running water in the 1920s, and this particular home was inhabited until 1958.

Finally, for art enthusiasts, a visit to the phenomenal gallery that has been fashioned out of the rock-hewn cathedral, **Madonna della Virtù e San Nicola dei Greci** ✪✪ (☎ 0835-319825; www.lascaletta.net or www.materacultura.it; 6€; Tues–Sun 10am–8pm), is very worthwhile. What was once a series of caves and rocky passages has become an extraordinary exhibition space for contemporary sculpture; the juxtaposition of old and new makes for an exciting visit and I can't imagine a better way to show off the cave's sublime spaces, which incidentally still feature original early Christian frescoes. This ranks among the most interesting galleries I've seen anywhere. In a similar vein is **MUSMA (Museum of Contemporary Sculpture)** (Via San Giacomo, Sasso Caveoso; ☎ 320-5350910; www.zetema.org; 8€; Tues–Sun 10am–2pm, Apr–Oct also 4–8pm) with permanent exhibits in a combination of cave galleries and more formal excavated spaces. Then, if you've got a little more time, consider seeing the **Crypt of Original Sin** (by appointment only; ☎ 320-5350910; 8€), set in a naturally occurring cave outside the city, overlooking a ravine; it is regularly referred to as the Sistine Chapel of rock-hewn wall painting, with an impressive fresco cycle that predates Giotto by 500 years. Arranging to get to the cave will take some forward planning—especially in terms of your time. There's little need to prioritize this with so much else to see in Matera proper (unless, of course, cave art is close to your heart).

You'll need at least a half-day or more to do Matera justice; there's a lot to explore, and at night it transforms into an eerie and mystical place, the experience often heightened by the effects of a solitary drummer who pounds out a heart-stopping beat that echoes through the enchanted, cobbled streets.

ACCOMMODATIONS & DINING

€–€€€ People have been staying at **Le Monacelle** ✪ (Via Riscatto 9/10; ☎ 0835-344097; www.lemonacelle.it; AE, DC, MC, V) since 1594, when it was founded by a Capuchin friar, and functioned through the centuries as a convent, nursery, and orphanage. Now it's a big, airy, extraordinarily restored and renovated hotel-cum-hostel with good facilities and wonderful grounds; there's also a huge terrace overlooking the ravine. A dorm bed is 18€, while private doubles (en suite, spacious, very comfortable) are 86€; breakfast is included.

€€–€€€€ Bless the ingenuity of the clever designers who converted a mini-neighborhood of abandoned sassi dwellings into what is now the chic, stylish **Locanda di San Martino** ✪✪✪ (Via San Martino, Sasso Barisano; ☎ 0835-256600; www.locandadisanmartino.it; AE, DC, MC, V). Each of the 28 conversions is a bright, low-key, semiluxurious pad combining straightforward style, with simple comfort and a sense of the fascinating history that makes these accommodations so utterly unique. Rooms are scattered and varied, keeping the original shape, size, and natural stone coloring, incorporating ancient archways and

A Castle in the Middle of Nowhere

Much vaunted for the perfection of its design, a favorite attraction slap-bang in the middle of Puglia is the 13th-century UNESCO World Heritage Site, **Castel del Monte** ✪✪✪ (west of Andria on Hwy. S170; ☎ 088-3569997; www.castellipuglia.org/en/monte.html; 3€; daily Apr–Sept 9am–7pm, Oct–Mar 9am–6pm), the most famous of the Swabian castles.

Built by Puglia's celebrated and visible ruler, Frederick II, the purpose of the fortress is a source of fierce debate; while the building—austere and beautifully simple—lacks any military or defensive features (like a moat) that would have been mandatory at the time, it is also certainly not a hunting lodge as so many "experts" will try to convince you. Rather, there is a profound air of mystery surrounding the existence and design of the massive octagonal castle, built between 1229 and 1249. In particular, the mix of mathematical and astronomical precision in the dimensions of the structure afford some peculiar optical illusions as you wander through the eight 25m-high (82-ft.) octagonal towers. From every point you see octagonal glimpses of the sky, and the shadows within the castle's court-yard form more octagons. The number eight is symbolic in astronomy and religion, and many believe this castle is the perfect symbol of the union of the infinite and finite; mathematicians and conspiracy theorists will thrill at the notion that the proportions of the castle correspond to the so-called golden number (1,618), which was apparently full of symbolic significance

exposed rock (interestingly, it gives the place a rather contemporary look and feel). For the best experience, ask for a unit with a view, and—as I did during my recent stay—marvel at the changing hues of the honey-colored stone of the rock-hewn Sasso Barisano across the way. Rates (89€–109€ for a Standard double; there are also Luxury units and family-size suites that work out to 40€–50€ per person) include a cheese-heavy breakfast with fresh croissants, delicious savories, and great coffee, as well as access to attractive public spaces (a fusion of modern, antique, and bits of archaeological excavation). Service here is pretty sharp, too.

€ I include **Osteria Al Vicinata** ✪ (Via Fiorentini 58; Sasso Barisano; ☎ 0835-344180; lunch from 11:30am, dinner from 7:30pm; AE, DC, MC, V) among my most memorable meals in southern Italy, thanks in no small part to the enormous personality of the ultra-eccentric chef-cum-owner-cum-waiter-cum-cashier who looks like a Breughel character and talks to himself between shouting at his poor assistant, a waitress who simply grins and bears it. She obviously knows that her boss is on to a good thing—he prepares great, affordable, and very authentic local dishes. He also makes sure that you eat everything that's brought to your table, including unexpected appetizers (pickled olives, a small platter of cheese and figs, bruschetta topped with a tasty eggplant paste). There are three *primi* options, each in medieval architecture and extensively studied by the great Swabian court mathematician, Leonardo Fibonacci!

The rest of us can appreciate how the design of the castle combines elements from classic antiquity, Islamic architecture, and northern European influences, giving it a unique cultural pedigree. Each room has floors originally laid with hexagon-patterned marble and adorned with Muslim influences like double-painted arches, some of which remain in the eighth room from the stairway. From the fifth room you explore what used to be an aviary for falcons. From the terrace, note the double-slanted roof, which diverted rainwater to both a holding tank and into the castle's bathrooms, which for modern visitors are possibly the most significant Muslim influence, occurring at a time when only Islamic architecture included indoor ablutions.

The castle sits high above the plains and although history books claim it has never been inhabited, you'll no doubt marvel at the ancient architecture, despite the fact that there's relatively little to see. Be sure to pack a picnic lunch; once you've driven some distance to get here, exploring the castle won't take up too much time, and the on-site sandwich bars are pricey.

Upon arrival, you must park 2km (1¼ miles) below the castle, in the public lot, which has a handful of sandwich bars, picnic areas, and public toilets; 4€ covers all-day parking and the ride on the shuttle bus to the entrance, which leaves every 15 minutes.

with an obscure symbolic name; I tried the "Two Rocks" pasta, which turned out to be a delicious fusion of two different varieties of pasta, and sipped the full-bodied house red (2€ for a half-liter carafe) while the couple at the adjacent table shouted *"Fantastico!"* as they shared their bowl of pasta. The scrawled (slightly inaccurate) bill was presented with homemade oatmeal cookies, although they'd run out of espresso.

LUCERA ✦✦

Based in Lucera, you'll quickly get to grips with the unique character of Pugliese town culture—it's life lived at a gentle, unhurried pace. You'll also experience one of Puglia's premier examples of a **reincarnated Arab village.** In the early 13th century, the entire Saracen population was removed from Sicily and relocated within Lucera's city walls. But far from being persecuted as they were in so many other parts of the province, the Arab community was allowed to worship and live according to their customs, in exchange for providing security for the kingdom.

Much of what the Saracens built was destroyed by the French after the reign of Frederick II, when Charles of Anjou—under the banner of the Catholic Church—decimated the Islamic population. But hints of the past can still be found: Look for Arabic carvings on the cornerstones of buildings; and the local museum (hopefully reopening in 2008, after years of renovation) is filled with exhibits of Arabic-scripted pottery and depictions of the original city. If you're able to get high enough up for a bird's-eye view of the city (you can do this from the little terrace of my favorite B&B, reviewed below), you'll spot Saracenic onion-shaped domes. Many of the city's palazzi still feature courtyard gardens, harkening back to Islamic building plans.

While there's really not all that much going on in this small provincial town—which is part of its great charm—Lucera is the cultural capital of northern Puglia, and has more wine bars and restaurants per capita than anywhere else in the region. On August weekends, the local wine club turns a section of the historical center into a giant candlelit wine-tasting venue, where you can wander from one piazza to the next sampling the best of the local vintages. It's also exceedingly friendly with a marked sense of community pride and spirit. Rather than being turned off by a constant barrage of *stranieri* (foreigners), the Pugliese of Lucera are genuinely interested in sharing their town with visitors; tourism is a relatively new phenomenon here. It's not uncommon to strike up a conversation with someone at a coffee bar or *trattoria.*

The heart of Lucera is its central square, the **Piazza del Duomo;** in summer, locals from Lucera and surrounding towns gather for an evening stroll or to take part in one of the town's many events (see listings at **www.luceraweb.net**). The square is flanked by the 14th-century **Duomo** ✯ (daily 7:30am–12:30pm and 4:30–8pm), one of the few remaining examples of Angevin architecture in the country. It was built after the death of Frederick II on the site of a mosque, after the Angevins defeated the Arabs here; rumor has it that the altar was actually Frederick's dining table. Seek out the rather unique carving of Christ on the cross, unusual because it is so expressive of both the emotional and symbolic significance of the Crucifixion. If you're here on a Sunday, visit the piazza's laid-back antiques market—you can pick up interesting prints, lithographs, and vintage memorabilia from as little as .25€. Across the piazza, a small donation gets you a guided tour of the **Diocesan Museum,** an extensive ecclesiastical exhibit with a varied schedule.

Nearby, the Gothic-Byzantine **Chiesa di San Francesco** ✯✯ is an even more dramatic 4th-century church, with original frescoes and a display of vestments worn by the local saint, Francesco Antonio Pasani, known as Padre Maestro. Lucera's other attraction is the **Castello** (follow signs from Via Bovio and Via Federico II to Piazza Matteotti; free; Tues–Sun 8am–2pm and 4–8pm, closed winter afternoons), built by Frederick II in 1233 on the highest hill at the edge of town. The pentagon fortress walls around the castle were once topped with 24 towers, and extensive renovations in recent years uncovered the last of these towers after an earthquake in 1980 had all but destroyed the structure. While it looks promising from the outside, inside there's precious little to see other than disorganized archaeological mounds. There are limited areas that you can climb for elevated views of the surrounding landscape, though.

Whatever you do, don't miss the nightly *passeggiata,* an immense early-evening street theater experience when just about everyone wanders up, down, and all around the most public walkways in town; the event is known here in the south as the *struscio,* a mildly ironic historic reference to the elegant sound of ladies' dresses scraping over the ground as they move, often very slowly.

ACCOMMODATIONS & DINING

€€ Time at **Le foglie di acanto** ✪✪ (Via Frattarolo 3; ☎ 349-4514937 or 340-3652912; www.lefogliediacanto.it; MC, V) is like a visit with long-lost relatives. Each bright, breezy room (from just 85€ for a double) has patterned tile flooring and antique furniture (my room had an old piano and frescoed ceiling), complemented by large bathrooms (some are the size of city hotel bedrooms) with plenty of big light-reflecting mirrors. Tall doors open on little balconies, or—in the case of the suite—onto a private rooftop terrace. In the heart of the ancient walled city, the house itself is an early-19th-century palazzo, with Gothic archways, hidden nooks, a gorgeous walled garden, and panoramic rooftop views. The hard-working people who restored, converted, and now run this memorable place are keen to share their passion for the region, and make Lucera feel like a second home; the whole family comes up with design ideas and Dad prepares breakfast. Get chatting with savvy Antonio about anything from art history to Italian politics to his passion for the region, and you'll come away with a deeply satisfying impression of Lucera.

€ When it comes to food, I'm very fond of quaint little **Trattoria L'Isola che non c'e** ✪ (Via Scassa 36; ☎ 0881-530438; dinner usually from 7pm; cash only), which is warm and inviting, despite the naive decor and ambience (a brightly lit fake palm tree, postcards tacked up on a mirror, and local radio for background buzz). Here, a kind elderly husband-and-wife team use whatever is freshest at market to prepare their daily offering of authentic home-style dishes based on uncomplicated handed-down recipes. There's no need to understand the menu (and there's no one here to translate)—you'll communicate with smiles and hand gestures. Indicate that you'd like *"pasta fresca"* and let your hosts make a selection for you (these two seem to *know* what you're in the mood for). All the *primi* dishes cost 6.50€, and 4€ gets you a liter of house wine. Note that the laid-back, down-home atmosphere extends to business hours—you can expect it to open for dinner around 7pm, but closing times will vary according to whim.

€€ Can you say *"Buono!"*? Some of the most memorable pasta I've tasted is being prepared by masterful chef Paolo Giuseppe di Laskavj at his smart-but-low-key restaurant **Il Cortiletto** ✪✪✪ (Via de Nicastri 26; ☎ 0881-542554; www.ristoranteilcortiletto.it; Tues–Sat 12:30–4pm and 6pm–midnight, Sun 12:30–4pm; AE, DC, MC, V). Meals here are innovative and always exceptionally tasty. The menu, usually limited to three dishes per course, changes daily and consists of wonderful culinary experiments, courtesy of Paolo's imagination (and his time abroad). Nevertheless, while adding his special brand of magic to every dish, he also pays homage to tradition, so ask for something local. My recent 10€ *primi* consisted of *oriechette* (ear-shaped pasta) smothered with a rich, tangy, creamy cheesy sauce of parmigiano and pecorino. Count on spending around 20€ before wine.

THE GARGANO PROMONTORY ✮✮✮

The unrivaled other draw of northern Puglia is this broad knob of lush forest and stepped cliffs plunging into the sea. The Gargano Promontory juts into the Adriatic, forming a peninsular dominated by spectacular coastlines and almost entirely covered by Italy's last original forest, the **Foresta Umbra.** It tends to be a haven for Italians in RVs in the summer months, making travel through winding park highways slow and cumbersome (unless you can manage the drive midweek, or midmorning, when the campers are mainly all in place)—but the slow pace is probably what you've come here for. An altogether more serious problem is with devastation by fire; when I visited in late 2007, vast swaths of forest were still black from an appalling blaze which swept across the Promontory the previous year. It's still not certain if the fire was accidental or—conspiratorially—started by would-be land developers, or, worse still, by local firemen who only get paid when they're called to work.

This lush **national park** (www.parks.it/parco.nazionale.gargano/eindex.html) is made up of ancient beech trees and giant oaks. There are outstanding walking trails here—to get the most out of these, stop at the main visitor center for the most current maps. The open trails vary depending on seasons, and are also affected by wildlife migrations. North of the promontory, the **Tremiti Islands** archipelago is another popular getaway, particularly if you want to get in and under the water to snorkel or scuba among the fish and colorful coral beds.

If you're in search of a beach holiday, consider either **Vieste** ✮✮ or **Peschici** ✮, the two main seaside villages perched on and above the coast. Of the two, Vieste probably has the edge; it has a more interesting cathedral (in the heart of the old quarter) and a castle built by Frederick II, now a military base and closed to the public. Peschici, which has traditionally been more isolated, is less developed than Vieste, but the real drawback, if you're coming to spend time on the beach, is its location high above the coastline—getting to the sea means traversing many steps.

Then again, some of the best beaches are *between* Vieste and Peschici, and the main road is dotted with hotels and more affordable camping spots. Be aware that you'll be required to pay at most beaches, usually for the facilities (parking or otherwise) offered by the camping resorts that hold claim to the beaches. Arguably the loveliest little beach of all is at **Vignanotica** along the road between Manfredonia and Vieste; it's well signposted, so be on the lookout.

ACCOMMODATIONS & DINING

€€–€€€€   There is certainly no shortage of places to stay in Vieste, although in peak season, rooms sell out quickly. Because it's in the historical center, close to the sea and very modestly priced, I think **Hotel del Seggio** (Via Veste 7; ☎ 0884-708123; www.hotelseggio.it; AE, DC, MC, V) is one of the best values on this coast (so book early). Bear in mind that the former town hall building (17th-c.) wasn't custom built, so not all units make for good bedrooms (nor do they all have a view); but you can get a large double room with a balcony and view of the Adriatic Sea (when booking, specify balcony and sea view and make sure you get confirmation of this). Doubles are 75€ to 95€ most of the year, but go for 115€ to 140€ in busy August (avoid!). The hotel benefits from a private beach and a small pool. Staff may not always speak English, but you'll manage.

€€ At **Madonna Incoronata Farm Holiday Centre** 🧒 (Mattinata; ☎ 0884-582317 or 336-285648; www.agriturismogargano.it; cash only) a variety of outbuildings on an old farm now serve as comfortable bungalows with full kitchens. The smallest one-room apartments are 72€ (most of the year) or 92€ (July 15–Aug 31), and the largest three-bedrooms (usually for four people) are 105€ or 148€. This is a great option if you really want to be away from the crowds, and particularly if you've got children. Bear in mind, of course, that amenities (such as fresh daily linen and dining facilities) are not part of the deal. And there's a minimum stay of 2 nights.

€–€€ Vieste's top dining spot is **Al Dragone** ★★ (Via Duomo 8; ☎ 0884-701212; www.aldragone.it; daily noon–2pm and 7pm–late; AE, DC, MC, V), a well-priced option (despite the near grandeur of the interior, carved right into the rock face). Personally, I'd go straight for the highly recommended sea bass, baked with slices of potato (13€), but there are some interesting starter options: carpaccio of octopus with arugula; courgettes of cuttlefish and shrimp; or tagliolini pasta with a shellfish *ragú* and arugula pesto (all *primi* 6€–10€; *coperto* is 2€).

THE OTHER GARGANO

The Gargano isn't just for nature lovers, it's also the site of an ancient **religious pilgrim trail,** which still draws masses of Catholic devotees. The trail follows the narrow road connecting the towns of Monte Sant' Angelo (an attractive destination in its own right) and San Giovanni Rotondo and is a magnet for religious visitors, additionally offering sweeping views and interesting architecture. Anyone can join the religious pilgrimage—you don't even have to be Catholic, and it's a fascinating way to get a glimpse inside this ancient tradition (meeting the pilgrims is another high point).

Christendom's second-most-visited pilgrimage site (by some accounts the most visited) is the little village of **San Giovanni Rotondo** ★★, not only an important destination for many Catholics, but also the headquarters of one of the most significant cults of the modern age. As the burial site of a beloved local priest, Padre Pio—a Capuchin friar who was a religious superstar thanks to his ability to heal by touch, to be in two places at the same time, and to give off a floral smell—the town swarms with believers. Pio, who came to prominence after receiving the stigmata, died 40 years ago, and was canonized in 2002. You'll recognize his picture (the kindly, bearded monk with a frayed frock and fingerless glove) pinned up in venues across the country. But nowhere else is he as venerated and celebrated as he is here in his hometown, where millions of religious pilgrims visit each year. Some devotees arrive in traditional garb, and in summer the place becomes a hotbed of Catholic ritual where people come from across the country to ask a favor, give thanks for blessings received, or simply pay their respects (if you really want to get caught up in the thick of things, arrive for the religious feast days on Sept 8 and June 29).

In addition to paying homage at the tomb of Padre Pio in the sanctuary below the church, you can visit the 14th-century church of **Sant'Onofrio,** with a baptistery, and a 16th-century church of **Santa Maria delle Grazie.** And, as if all that weren't enough, there's also the crowd-pulling massive modern church dedicated to Pio, designed by Renzo Piano (the architect responsible for the Pompidou as well as Osaka's airport), which opened in 2004.

In more salubrious **Monte Sant'Angelo** ✫✫✫, 25km (16 miles) along winding roads, the big draw is the **Basilica San Michele Arcangelo** (☎ 0884-561150; free; daily July–Sept 7:30am–7:30pm, Oct–June 7:30am–12:30pm and 2:30–5pm), and more specifically, the **Shrine of St. Michael the Archangel** ✫✫✫, built inside a cavern beneath the church. Legend has it that the archangel first appeared here in A.D. 490 and his footprint is enclosed behind glass just behind the altar. Religious "fashion police" will stop you at the entrance to the grotto and give you a blue or yellow cape to cover up any offensive skin you may be showing.

Outside the church, climb the hill to the **Castello** (1.80€; same hours as the Shrine); while children will get a kick out of the ghostly, festering dungeons, you should go directly to the top to catch the view of the terra-cotta rooftops of the cascading town of Monte Sant'Angelo. On clear days you'll see the Gulf of Manfredonia, populated with trolling fishing boats and naval ships scouting for terrorists and traffickers.

Having spent time kneeling and praying with the pilgrims, you can bed down among them at the local *foresteria,* **Casa del Pellegrino** (Via Carlo d'Angiò; ☎ 0884-562396; casadelpellegrino@santuariosanmichele.it), a comfortable three-star run by a religious order; doubles range from 42€ to 55€.

14 Sicily

Fiery, friendly & utterly unlike any other region of Italy

by Sylvie Hogg

AS ITALIAN REGIONS GO, SICILY ISN'T AS EASY TO SUM UP FOR TRAVELERS as, say, Tuscany, which is rather homogeneous and predictably pleasant. It's a formidable, otherworldly, sun- and sea-washed patchwork of influences—Greek, Arabic, Norman, Spanish, and Italian—the aggregate of which is something totally apart from the culture of mainland Italy. Head to Sicily and you'll encounter cacophonous city markets that feel like the Third World and sleepy hill-town piazzas that seem drawn from a fairy tale, busy seaports and idyllic beaches, and a landscape that ranges from the charcoal and desolate summit of Mt. Etna to dense green forests that look as if they were lifted from somewhere in Bavaria.

Then, take the Sicilians themselves: Sure, plenty of the men look like extras from a mob movie, but just as many look like Olympic swimmers, with blond hair, blue eyes, and tall frames, proof that the Norman occupation left not only important works of architecture but a significant impact on the gene pool.

As for Sicilian cuisine, there are parts of the island where couscous is more common than pasta—a result of Muslim influences—and street markets in Palermo that have more in common with Marrakesh than Milan. Even with these contrasts, there are times when Sicily fully lives up to your folksy "Italian" expectations. Shout "Salvatore" in a crowded marketplace, and half the male population there will turn around. Visit a church at the end of Mass, and watch how many black-clad widows file out. Stuff yourself with cannoli from bakeries on every corner.

Sicily's multifaceted delights have yet to break into the "big time" of international tourism, but over the past several years, I've watched Sicily's infrastructure steadily rise as a function of its growing popularity. That means better transportation to and on the island, more varied accommodations options, and a veritable deluge of enthusiastic websites to help you plan it all. Given the manageable distances and extraordinary variety of attractions, Sicily is one of the most user-friendly and satisfying regions in Italy for travelers. Still, with the exception of resort-y Taormina, I hardly ever run into other Americans when I'm down here—and after the throngs you'll encounter in Venice, Florence, and Rome, this is quite a refreshing change. (Americans are quite welcome in Sicily, however, if only because almost everyone here has at least a distant cousin who emigrated to the United States in the past 100 years.) Sicily is varied enough to keep anyone interested for weeks, but not so vast as to be overwhelming if you only have a short amount of time to travel here. So no matter what type of travel you're looking for, whether it's ancient ruins, beaches and water, or culinary exploration, Sicily really does have it all, and at a lower price than most of the rest of Italy.

DON'T LEAVE SICILY WITHOUT . . .

TEMPTING FATE ON AN ACTIVE VOLCANO   Massive Mt. Etna (p. 604) dominates Sicily's eastern coast and still rumbles and spews quite frequently, sometimes erupting in spectacular fashion. A trek to its 3,326m (10,910-ft.) summit is a thrilling must-do. Off the northern coast of Sicily, the extremely active volcanic island of Stromboli (p. 598) never stops emitting a tall column of smoke, and nighttime excursions to see lava spurts at the crater (only offered when conditions are safe) are also an unforgettable experience.

DOING JUSTICE TO PALERMO   The sensory overload in Sicily's capital can be overwhelming. It's the ultimate city of contrasts—where Norman palaces stand triumphant around the corner from apartment buildings still heavily scarred by World War II bombing—and it reveals its delights slowly, like a morphine drip.

GOING GREEK   Sicily has the finest ancient Greek ruins outside of Greece, and they make a satisfying contrast to all the Roman ruins you'll be seeing in the rest of Italy. Agrigento's Valley of the Temples (p. 612), on the island's southern flank, is a world-class archaeological site, where the skeletons of seven Doric temples stand along an atmospheric ridge with almond trees. The Greco-Roman Theater in Taormina may have the most stunning natural setting of all ancient playhouses. Siracusa's lush archaeological park is a delight to explore, from the Greek theater to the "Ear of Dionysius" cave. Several other important 2,500-year-old sites, like the temples at Segesta and Selinunte, round out the mix.

GETTING OUT ON THE WATER   The seas that surround Sicily are today among the most unspoiled that Italy has to offer. From the sandy beaches at Cefalù and Fontane Bianche (Siracusa) or the dramatic coves near Taormina, don't miss a chance to go for a dip in these sparkling waters.

SPIKING YOUR BLOOD SUGAR   Throw that diet out the window because Sicily has some otherworldly *dolci* (sweets) that are nearly impossible to find done properly anywhere else. Number one on the list is the *cannolo* (you may know it better by the plural form, cannoli), whose name means "little tube." It's a fried pastry shell filled with sweet and creamy mascarpone, vanilla, and bits of chocolate and sometimes pistachio. Sicily's other sweet par excellence, *cassata*—sponge cake with ricotta filling and marzipan or chocolate frosting—goes back 1,000 years to when the Arabs ruled Sicily. Most Sicilian towns and provinces have their own specialties, so stop into the local *pasticceria* (pastry shop) to sample the local treats.

A BRIEF HISTORY OF SICILY

Sicily's tenuous position—strung between North Africa and the European mainland, just 160km (100 miles) from Cap Bon in Tunisia on one side and 3km (2 miles) from Calabria in Italy on the other—has made it a natural stepping stone

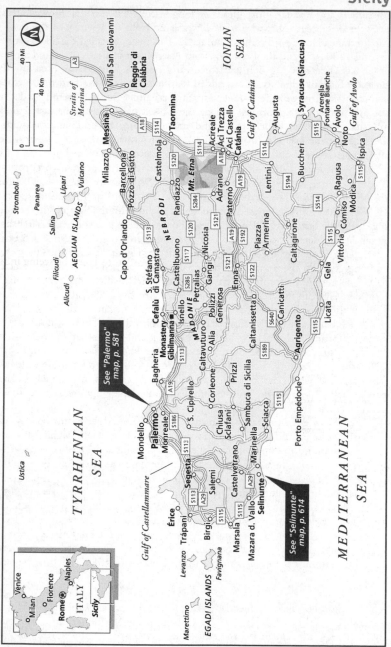

for settlers and invaders throughout its long history. The earliest-known inhabitants were the Sicanians, who most likely came from somewhere in the eastern Mediterranean in the 3rd millennium B.C. A Latin people called the Sikels arrived around 1200 B.C., and the Elymians from Asia Minor came to the island around 1100 B.C. The merging of these three early peoples formed the basis for the uniquely Sicilian ethnicity; it was added to, of course, over the next 3,000 years.

Sicily's Hellenistic cities—Siracusa, Catania, and Messina—were founded in the 6th through 8th centuries B.C. by the Greeks, who later built vast temples all over the island, which still stand at Agrigento, Segesta, and Selinunte. Throughout the 4th and 5th centuries B.C., the Carthaginians of North Africa fought the Greeks—and later the Romans—for control and turned the island into a bloody battlefield. After the fall of Rome, Sicily underwent many occupations before returning to the Arabs, or Saracens, in the 9th century, when Islam became the official religion. The Arab rulers tolerated Christianity and Judaism on Sicily.

When the Normans wrested control of the island from the Saracens in the 11th century, Sicily began its golden age, throughout which its ancient Greek, Arab, and Byzantine influences would blend together and eventually define so much of its character. Sicily fell to the French in the 13th century and was repeatedly sacked and oppressed for the next several hundred years. The Sicilians eventually reacted to this oppression by forming their own secret society, which they called Mafia, a term derived from the Arabic word for "refuge." In the 1700s, this secret society, by then also known as the Cosa Nostra ("our thing"), began distributing a picture of a black hand as a formal request for protection money. Those who didn't pay faced misfortune—or worse. (The Cosa Nostra is still very much a force in Sicily, though it's unlikely you'll be aware of its presence. They do not target tourists.)

By the 19th century, Sicily and Naples formed a sovereign kingdom called the "Two Sicilies," which unified with Italy in 1861. After unification, Sicily became part of Italy's "poor south," and its problems were largely ignored by the Italian government.

Today Sicily exists primarily as an agricultural region, its economy heavily subsidized by tourism and profits manipulated by an ever-efficient Mafia. Efforts to turn the region into a mini–Silicon Valley are beginning to see results, and a growing premier wine industry is starting to get international attention. Five million people live on Sicily; 1,300,000 of them are in Palermo.

One delight in visiting Sicily is viewing its many pasts, one layer upon the other. Phoenician ruins on the western coast (now anchored by modern-day Palermo) sit below Norman-Arab castles. In Siracusa, a splendid baroque cathedral lies directly on top of a Greek temple. And in Corleone, the hill town and real-life Mafia stronghold that inspired the name of the famous "Godfather" character, the main bus terminus is on Piazza delle Vittime della Mafia (Mafia Victims' Square).

LAY OF THE LAND

The Greeks called Sicily "Trinacria," which means three apexes, for the isosceles triangle shape of the island. It's the largest island in the Mediterranean, surrounded by three seas, the Ionian (to the east), the Tyrrhenian (to the north), and the Mediterranean (to the south), each of which gives the island a different character. Sicily also has several smaller islands off its shores: The Aeolians are to the northeast, the Egadi are to the west, and exotic Pantelleria is to the southwest.

For your first visit to Sicily, traveling around the coast is more rewarding than attempting the mountainous and largely rural interior. The towns or attractions I encourage you not to miss are Palermo (p. 580) and Cefalù (p. 595), to the north; Taormina (p. 600), Mt. Etna (p. 604), and Siracusa (p. 604), to the east; and the temples in Agrigento (p. 612), to the south.

GETTING ON & OFF THE ISLAND

No matter how you get here, the approach to Sicily is the most thrilling in the Mediterranean.

BY AIR

Palermo's **Falcone e Borsellino** (PMO) (www.gesap.it) and Catania's **Fontanarossa** (CTA) (www.aeroporto.catania.it) airports have frequent nonstop connections with mainland Italy (it's a 1-hr. flight from Rome and Milan), and some of the European low-cost carriers offer nonstop service from London. From May to October, there's even a nonstop flight from New York's JFK airport to Palermo a few times a week on newcomer Eurofly (average rate $634). Palermo's dramatic topography makes for a wonderful approach onto this passionate island, so be sure to get a window seat. Flying into Catania, at the foot of Mt. Etna, can also be an unforgettable experience, especially if the volcano is acting up.

For travel in winter 2007, nonstop round-trip airfares to Sicily from other European cities were available on such carriers as AirOne (www.flyairone.it), Alitalia (www.alitalia.com), Blu-express (www.blu-express.com), easyJet (www.easyjet.com), Meridiana (www.meridiana.it), Wind Jet (www.volawindjet.it), and Ryanair (www.ryanair.com). Lowest rates, believe it or not, were from London (as low as $80 round-trip on easyJet), followed by Rome ($105 round-trip to Catania on Blu-express).

To reach Palermo's city center from Falcone e Borsellino Airport, just hop on a **Prestia e Comandè** coach (☎ 091-586351) right outside the terminal. These buses (4.50€) leave every half-hour from 6:30am to midnight and take about 35 to 50 minutes to reach downtown (they make stops at the Teatro Politeama, the port, and Piazza Giulio Cesare, in front of the train station). In the reverse direction, Prestia e Comande buses run every half-hour from Palermo to the airport from 5am to 11pm. There's also the Trinacria Express train, which runs every half-hour 5:30am to 10pm and costs 5€ for the 50-minute ride between the airport and Palermo Centrale station. Taxis from the airport to downtown Palermo (and vice versa) are pricey at 50€, though, depending on traffic, you may get where you're going faster this way—and they're the only option for very early-morning flights.

From Catania's Fontanarossa airport, there are several daily bus connections to all the main cities and towns in central and eastern Sicily, even Palermo. To name a few, **Etna Trasporti** (☎ 095-532716; www.etnatrasporti.it) handles the Taormina run; **Interbus** (☎ 095-565111; www.interbus.it) goes to Siracusa; and in high season **Giuntabus** (☎ 090-673782; www.giuntabus.com) shuttles travelers to the port of Milazzo, where boats depart for the Aeolian islands.

All Italian and international rental-car companies are represented at both Palermo and Catania airports, making vehicle pickup very convenient.

BY SEA

If you're coming from anywhere near Rome or Naples, the most romantic way to arrive in Sicily is by sea. It's also an economical way to go, since the ferries sail overnight, saving you the price of a hotel. Palermo is accessible by ferry from Civitavecchia (the port of Rome, about 1 hr. from the city, where all the cruise ships dock) or Naples (the most popular port for the Sicily route). The trip takes about 10 to 12 hours, so you can get a decent night's sleep (if you choose to book a private cabin), and then head out on deck to watch the sun rise over the stunning terrain as you approach Palermo. Some bigger and newer ferries (like those run by Grandi Navi Veloci from Civitavecchia) even have casinos, dance clubs, pools, and gyms. You can also bring cars on these ships, for a supplement of about 80€.

Hydrofoils (faster, only in high season, and only when seas are calm enough) and ferries (slower, year-round, any weather) also sail from Naples to the Aeolian islands. You cannot bring cars on hydrofoils, and the streamlined nature of the boats means there's no space for hanging out on deck.

The website www.traghettionline.com does a decent job of summarizing information about sea transport to Sicily, but here are some sample routes:

- **Naples to Palermo:** Tirrenia (www.tirrenia.it) and SNAV (www.snav.it) operate ferries, 50€ to 80€ per person in a double-occupancy cabin, 30€ to 40€ per person for a reserved seat. Ferries depart Beverello port in Naples at 8pm and arrive at the port of Palermo at 6:30am daily.
- **Civitavecchia (Rome) to Palermo:** Grandi Navi Veloci (www.gnv.it) and SNAV (www.snav.it) run ferries, 80€ to 120€ per person in a double-occupancy cabin, or 45€ to 70€ per person for a reserved seat. GNV is the nicer of the two and even has spacious "family suites" from 100€ per person. The ships leave Civitavecchia at 8pm and arrive in Palermo at 8am.

BY TRAIN

Another option is to take the train from Rome (9–13 hr.) or Naples (7–11 hr.) to Messina, Taormina, or Palermo. Trains from all over Europe arrive at the port of Villa San Giovanni (which is sort of the "bunion" on the toe of the boot of Italy), where they roll onto enormous barges for the 1-hour trip across the Strait of Messina to Sicily (you don't have to change trains). Regular fares for any Rome-to-Sicily train run from 36€ to 44€; couchettes and sleepers cost an extra 18€ to 35€ and must be booked at least 24 hours in advance. These overnight trains are one of the great old-fashioned travel experiences. For more information about schedules and pricing, visit www.trenitalia.com.

BY CAR

A car is a major asset for travelers in Sicily, so if you're already planning a major auto tour as far as southern Italy, you might also consider driving right on to Sicily (via ferry, of course). The car ferry across the Strait of Messina (from Villa San Giovanni in Calabria) offers departures every 20 minutes or so throughout the day. Tickets can be purchased at a little ticket booth in Villa San Giovanni in Calabria (you'll have to jump out of your car and run to the little house with your car-rental form and license-plate number) and cost from 17€ per car, or just 1€ for foot passengers. Ferry information can be had from **Tourist Ferry Boat s.p.a.**

(☎ 090-3718510 in Messina, or 090-361292 in Villa San Giovanni). Do keep in mind that Villa San Giovanni is *waaaay* down there—allow at least 7 hours from Naples and 9 hours from Rome in good weather conditions.

GETTING AROUND THE ISLAND

If you can swing it, I recommend renting a car while on Sicily (see below), but if not, it's still a snap to hop from one town to another, thanks to efficient rail and bus lines. Local trains are run by **Trenitalia** (☎ 892021; www.trenitalia.com), which has a very helpful and easy-to-use website in English. Bus service on the

---

Sicily Itineraries

The suggestions below touch on Sicily's "greatest hits," which won't disappoint, but as with travel anywhere, some of the most memorable experiences come when you venture off the beaten path.

If you have only a few days in Sicily

Spend your time in Palermo. As the island's capital, Palermo serves as its cultural and financial hub, and enjoys a broad range of well-priced hotels and restaurants, as well as ample public transportation. Palermo also offers an intimate glimpse of Sicily's distinct brand of chaotic charm—from its eclectic multicultural architecture to its many museums with their comprehensive collections of Greek, Etruscan, and Roman artifacts. Based in Palermo, you can make day trips, with or without your own transportation, to the fishing village of Cefalù (p. 595) or the Valley of the Temples (p. 612) near Agrigento.

If you have 1 week in Sicily

Spend a few nights in Palermo (coming or going), and then divide the rest of your time between Siracusa (try to stay in the city's charming old center, Ortygia island) and Taormina, and plan on a half-day excursion to Mt. Etna in there somewhere. If you're traveling by air, you can also leave the island from Catania (some airlines will allow open-flight tickets to and from Sicily at little or no extra charge).

If you have more than 1 week in Sicily

Divide your time between Palermo and the eastern coast of Sicily, as above, and add a day or two on the Aeolian islands (p. 596), the volcanic archipelago just off the northern coast of Sicily, and one of Italy's best-kept secrets—for now—offering everything from watersports to beach-combing to volcano tours. Anyone visiting Sicily for more than a week should also try to fit in the Roman mosaics at Piazza Armerina (central Sicily) and the Greek ruins at the Valley of the Temples (Agrigento, southern Sicily). If you've got 2 weeks, you can either add in western Sicily (Erice and the Greek sites of Segesta and Selinunte), or give the sightseeing warpath a rest and just relax in a smaller, more rural part of the island.

island is even more comprehensive and can be faster than train connections (though schedules are a bit more, ahem, *flexible* than those of trains). For public transportation, try www.palermotourism.com, which has a searchable interactive map for Sicilian bus, train, and sea routes, or ask for tickets and information at *tabacchi* in individual towns.

Driving in Sicily is an immense pleasure and my personal recommendation for getting around. The distances are never great, the island is easy to navigate, traffic is light outside Palermo, and parking is rarely a problem. What's more, you'll be cruising some of the country's best highways, thanks to the organized-crime syndicates that reportedly dominate public works contracts. Say what you will, they keep the roads in top-notch shape.

You'll save big bucks on car rentals by bypassing international chains like Avis and Hertz and renting from such Italian companies as **Maggiore** (www.maggiore. it) or **Sicily by Car** (www.sbc.it). Sicily by Car consistently has the best weekly rates for a compact vehicle, at around 200€ for a 7-day, unlimited mileage rental. (Maggiore charges around 250€ per week; other car companies charge 50%–100% more). Note that Sicily by Car will charge a hefty security deposit (upward of 1,000€, to be refunded when you return the car) on your credit card at the time of pickup, so make sure you have plenty of funds available.

PALERMO

Decadent, indulgent, sultry Palermo is the ultimate city of contrasts. With a fabulous natural setting, surrounded by rugged mountains and the sea, it's a place that combines tarnished gems like the Kalsa district—its buildings still pocked from World War II and years of neglect—with dazzling jewels like the Norman Palazzo Reale and city cathedral. Chances are this cacophonous and imperfectly maintained city won't win you over at first glance, but it's also the kind of place where just a few impressions—someone you meet on the street, or a breathtaking cloister where you're the only visitor—can leave you cackling with delight and striving to make sense of it all: the good, the bad, and the ugly. Because for almost everyone who comes here, Palermo is nothing like what you expect.

A BRIEF HISTORY OF PALERMO

Like most anywhere on Sicily (or in Italy, for that matter), Palermo's roots go back several millennia. The city's modern name is derived from "Panormus," from the Greek for "all port," but it was the Phoenicians who first exploited this fine natural harbor in the 8th century B.C. From then on, the city would go through a couple of different names—Ziz and Paleopolis—before settling on Palermo and earn the dubious distinction of being the most-conquered city in world history.

Palermo reached its heyday in the 9th and 10th centuries A.D., when it flourished under Arab rule. In 973 it was famously described as the "city of 300 mosques." During this period and for the next century, when it was reclaimed by the Normans, Palermo was considered one of the grandest cities in Europe. Much of the architecture you see today, from smooth pink domes to Gothic spires to Byzantine basilicas, are remnants of this era.

Even during the Norman occupation, Palermo remained a bridge between East and West—look closely at the great Catholic buildings here, like the city's

Palermo

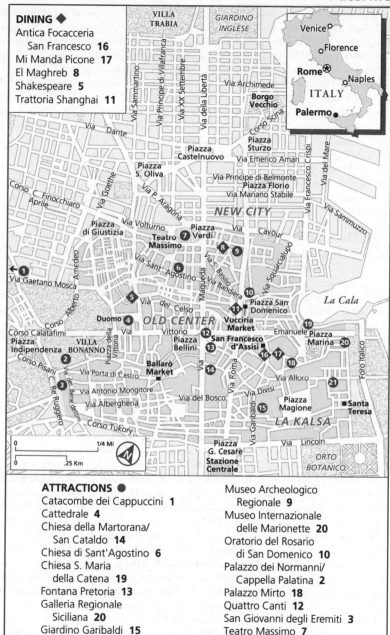

DINING ◆
Antica Focacceria
  San Francesco **16**
Mi Manda Picone **17**
El Maghreb **8**
Shakespeare **5**
Trattoria Shanghai **11**

VILLA TRABIA
GIARDINO INGLESE

Via Sammartino
Via Principe di Villafranca
Via XX Settembre
Via della Libertà
Via Archimede
BORGO VECCHIO
Corso Scinà

Via Dante

Piazza Castelnuovo
Piazza S. Oliva

Piazza Sturzo
Via Emerico Amari
Via Principe di Belmonte
Piazza Florio
Via Mariano Stabile

Via Francesco Crispi
Via del Mare
Via Sammuzzo

Corso C. Finocchiaro Aprile

Via Goethe
Via P. Aragona
Via Volturno

Piazza di Giustizia
Teatro Massimo
Piazza Verdi

NEW CITY
Via Cavour

Via Squarcialupo

Via Sant' Agostino

Corso Alberto Amedeo
Via Gaetano Mosca

Via del Celso

Via S. Basilio
Via Bandiera
Maqueda

Piazza San Domenico
Vucciria Market

La Cala

Duomo
Corso Calatafimi
Piazza Indipendenza
VILLA BONANNO
Via della Vittoria
Vittorio
Piazza Bellini
OLD CENTER
Piazza della Vittoria
Emanuele
San Francesco d'Assisi
Piazza Marina
Foro Italico

Corso Pisani
Via Porta di Castro
Ballarò Market
Via Roma
Via Alloro

Corso Re Ruggero
Via del Bene detini
Via Antonio Mongitore
Via Alberghria
Via del Bosco
Via Divisi
Via Garibaldi

Corso Tukory
Piazza Magione
Santa Teresa
LA KALSA

0   1/4 Mi
0   .25 Km

Piazza G. Cesare
Stazione Centrale
Via Lincoln
ORTO BOTANICO

ATTRACTIONS ●
Catacombe dei Cappuccini **1**
Cattedrale **4**
Chiesa della Martorana/
  San Cataldo **14**
Chiesa di Sant'Agostino **6**
Chiesa S. Maria
  della Catena **19**
Fontana Pretoria **13**
Galleria Regionale
  Siciliana **20**
Giardino Garibaldi **15**

Museo Archeologico
  Regionale **9**
Museo Internazionale
  delle Marionette **20**
Oratorio del Rosario
  di San Domenico **10**
Palazzo dei Normanni/
  Cappella Palatina **2**
Palazzo Mirto **18**
Quattro Canti **12**
San Giovanni degli Eremiti **3**
Teatro Massimo **7**

Venice
Florence
Rome
Naples
ITALY
Palermo

massive cathedral, and you'll notice that the columns are inscribed with verses from the Koran. The city was and is multicultural, not only in its eclectic architecture but in its sultry charm. Over the centuries, various rulers tried to impose logic on the city plan, building arrow-straight streets (like Via Vittorio Emanuele and Via Maqueda, which intersect at the heart of the city—the Quattro Canti—dividing it into four distinct districts), but Palermo couldn't be tamed, as you'll see when you wander along the narrow, meandering back streets. Here you'll come upon tiny shops selling exotic textiles and ebony statues alongside conventional Italian pottery, and stumble on small ethnic restaurants abutting traditional Italian *trattorie*. Over the years, Palermo has been inhabited by Jewish merchants, Turkish and Syrian craftsmen, Persian artists, Spanish royalty, and Mafia dons—and each faction has left its mark. A more contemporary symbol of Palermo's diversity and tolerance is a place in the northern part of the city where three streets form a triangle: They're called Via Martin Luther King, Via Isaac Rabin, and Via Anwar Sadat.

LAY OF THE LAND

You're most likely to arrive by air at the Falcone e Borsellino Airport, 31km (19 miles) west of the city center; by sea at the main Port of Palermo, just minutes outside the city center; or by rail at the main train station, Palermo Centrale, on Piazza Giulio Cesare, just south of the heart of historical Palermo. For the most part, you'll want to spend your time in the historical center with its web of narrow, winding streets, parsed into quadrants by two pencil-straight thoroughfares, Via Vittorio Emanuele and Via Maqueda. These streets intersect at Palermo's core, the Quattro Canti (Four Corners). "New" Palermo is to the north of the old city, on either side of Viale della Libertà. There aren't as many sights here, per se, but you'll get your share of wonderful local flavor if you spend some time on these streets and duck into neighborhood shops and restaurants.

The Quattro Canti (again, where Via Vittorio Emanuele and Via Maqueda meet) is the best point of reference for exploring the city. Spreading back from each corner of the intersection are the four distinct districts of historical Palermo: Albergheria, Il Capo, Vucciria, and La Kalsa. It makes the most sense to attack these districts individually, devoting a half-day or so to each, time permitting.

For free maps and other handy visitor information, stop by one of the tourist board "info points," green kiosks, brimming with brochures—there's one at the airport, one at the main train station, and one at Piazza Castelnuovo. On the tourist board's website, www.palermotourism.com, you can download brochures and an informative city map. A final word about Palermo maps: Make sure you remember that the water is on the east side of the city, so it should be on the right side as you look at your map. The tourist board map is printed with west at the top (water at the bottom), and if you're at all sensitive to the movement of the sun, you'll get hopelessly disoriented, which is already easy to do in Palermo!

ALBERGHERIA (SOUTHWEST QUADRANT)

The heart of Norman-influenced Palermo and the most multicultural section of the city is Albergheria. The streets here are lined with ethnic restaurants that offer some of the best alternatives to Italian cuisine in the country.

As you wander around, you can't really miss the hubbub of activity around the **Ballarò market** ✪✪, which stretches from Piazza del Carmine north along Piazza Ballarò, and you wouldn't want to! Of Palermo's historic markets, this is the most authentic one—far more real Palermitans shop here than at Vucciria (see below). Spend a good half-hour (you could easily devote more time) navigating the open-air stalls of everything from fresh octopus, to bulk Eastern spices, to household objects, and let the orchestra of howling hawkers wash over you. Without even trying, you'll be making eye contact with jovial men and women who will try to sell you—fully aware that you're a tourist—several pounds of swordfish, and the fish is so fresh and glistening that you'll be mighty tempted. Like so many of Palermo's markets, Ballarò is thronged with people, some unsavory types among them, so keep a firm hand and keen eye on your valuables.

Five minutes' walk west of the market, along Via Porta di Castro, is ground zero for Palermo sightseeing: the **Palazzo Reale,** or **Palazzo dei Normanni** ✪✪ (Piazza Indipendenza 1; ☎ 091-7051111; www.ars.sicilia.it; Mon–Tues and Sat 8:30am–noon and 2–5pm, Sun 8:30am–2pm; 5€, or 6€ for the palace and the Cappella Palatina) is a complex of palaces built by Arabs in the 9th century (its current Arab-Norman facade was last reworked in the 17th c.). The main palace is now the seat of the Sicilian parliament. Its halls are closed to the public during parliamentary sessions, primarily Tuesday through Thursday. When it's open, you can wander (accompanied by a "guide" who probably speaks little English—oh, well) through the smaller reception rooms to the massive main hall with its ornate, gilded ceiling. The Royal Apartments are not always open to the public except for the Byzantine Sala dei Venti. If they are open, be sure to follow the signs to the Sala di Ruggero II, which was King Ruggero's rapturously lovely bedroom, encrusted with mosaics of colorful peacocks and amorous leopards, and nearly as beautiful as the Cappella Palatina (see below). Outside, walled ornate gardens, called the Parco d'Orleans, have been planted over the centuries with African kapok trees, exotic rare orchids, and imported banyan trees.

Inside the Palazzo dei Normanni is the one must-see sight of Palermo, the **Cappella Palatina** ✪✪✪ (in the Palazzo dei Normanni; ☎ 091-7054879; Mon–Sat 9am–noon and 2–5pm, Sun 8:30am–2pm; 4€ for the chapel only, 6€ for the chapel and Palazzo dei Normanni), with long lines to prove it. The interior of the small chapel, built by the Norman King Roger II when he ruled Sicily in 1130, is an explosion of precious gems and shiny mosaics covering every square inch of space. Tiny marble tiles are inlaid with gold leaf or painted to look like lapis and designed to depict stories from the Old Testament and Sicilian history. The gold and silver backing of the tiles makes them glitter. The facial expressions are more realistic and emotionally compelling than one would expect from mosaics, which may be why art historians agree that they're among the finest in the world. Other notable works of art in the chapel include the exquisite mosaic-encrusted throne in the nave and the traditionally Islamic *muqarna* design on the ceiling, created by North African artisans in the 12th century (a surprising element in a Christian chapel).

To the south of the Palazzo dei Normanni is the **Chiesa di San Giovanni degli Eremiti** ✪✪ (Via dei Benedettini; ☎ 091-6515019; 6€; Mon–Sat 9am–7pm, Sun and holidays 9am–1pm), home to the five red Arab-Fatimite domes featured on

Crypt of the Living Dead

Italy's most ghoulish sight is a short walk west of the Royal Palace, but squeamish types will want to give the **Catacombe dei Cappuccini** ✫✫✫ (Via Cappuccini 1; ☎ 091-212117; Mon–Sat 9am–noon and 3–5pm; 2€) a very wide berth. No horror movie or haunted house can compete with this crypt filled with thousands of bodies, dressed from head to toe, and suspended by hooks on the walls.

Your visit to the crypt begins with an elderly monk who gestures solemnly toward the cool and dark stairway that leads to the crypt. Inside, it feels more like walking onto the set for *Night of the Living Dead*—or a really great Halloween party—than entering a sacred site. The facial expressions of the dead are still eerily discernible: some are calm, some seem pained, and most look they are about to reach out and grab you. The whole point of the crypt, caretakers here say, is to remind the living of the inevitability of death.

The crypt dates back to 1599, when local priests mummified a holy monk and exposed his primitively preserved dead body for all to see. The effect was so profound on the public that in time, regular Palermitans wanted themselves and their relatives "remembered" the same way. Soon there were hundreds of corpses. Some of the deceased actually wrote wills, in which they indicated the clothes in which they wanted to be displayed. Some asked to have their clothes changed from time to time by the crypt's caretakers (church attire on Sun, of course). To keep things organized down here, the priests didn't stash the bodies willy-nilly but divided them into men, women, virgins, children, priests, monks, and a somewhat random category called "professionals," which includes an American and some writers and lawyers.

If you're keeping a scrapbook of your travels (or want to send hate mail to anyone), souvenir postcards of your favorite corpses are conveniently sold at the crypt's gift shop.

so many postcards of Palermo. The frescoes inside the church itself are seriously worn, so head straight for the lush green cloister and lose yourself in the heady aromas of jasmine, orange, and pomegranate. One of the finest oases in Palermo, the garden belonged to the Benedictine convent that once occupied this church. From here you can study the intricate weave of Norman and Arab architecture. For many, this church represents the harmonious blending of cultures, which is, of course, the basis of Sicilian history.

IL CAPO (NORTHWEST QUADRANT)

The labyrinth of streets that makes up the Il Capo district—across Via Vittorio Emanuele from Albergheria—is home to some of Palermo's most imposing attractions. The main **cathedral** ✫✫✫ (Via Vittorio Emanuele; ☎ 091-334376;

www.cattedrale.palermo.it; free; Mon–Sat 7am–7pm, Sun 8:30am–1:30pm and 4–7pm) sprawls over a flat, palm-tree-lined square that seems out of place among the tightly clenched apartment blocks that surround it. The cathedral has undergone many metamorphoses over the centuries. It was built by Archbishop Gualtiero Offamilio in 1184 on the site of a crumbling basilica, and transformed into a mosque during a period of Arab control. It was restored again to a Christian church by the Normans. Each transformation left architectural additions: The twin towers were added in the 14th century, the three-arched portico made its appearance in the 15th century, and the towering, somewhat ugly baroque cupola was the "fault" of architect Ferdinando Fuga in the 18th century. As with many of Palermo's great churches, the inside is relatively barren. But the tombs of famous Norman rulers, including Roger II and Frederick II, are worth a peek.

The **Capo market** ✗, which extends from Porta Carini down Via di Sant'Agostino, is another primo place to soak up the sights and sounds of Palermitan daily life at its liveliest. In the midst of the market scene is the **Chiesa di Sant'Agostino** (Via Sant'Agostino; Mon–Sat 7am–noon and 4–5:30pm, Sun 7am–noon), a classic Gothic church complete with a rare-for-Sicily 14th-century rose window. In the 15th century, the side portal, which is now a defining feature, was hastily added. Many of Palermo's churches are austere shells tucked inside lavish exteriors, but the artwork inside Sant'Agostino is an explosion of fussy baroque stuccoes. It's a popular wedding spot, especially on Saturday around lunchtime, when multiple wedding parties chat and men in sunglasses scurry about, changing flowers between ceremonies.

VUCCIRIA (NORTHEAST QUADRANT)

The liveliest of Palermo's districts is the once-downtrodden Vucciria (from the French *boucherie,* or "butcher shop"), which has transformed itself in recent years from the center of Palermo's poverty and crime to a quaint, offbeat village with a crop of new boutiques and some of Palermo's best museums. The souklike **Mercato Vucciria** ✗✗ is the city's largest and most colorful market (although more touristy than the Ballarò market; p. 583), and the best place to sink your teeth into some Palermitan street food specialties (see "Street Eats" on p. 591). One of the main thoroughfares here, Via Argenteria, is filled with "unofficial" restaurants that residents operate out of their ground-floor apartments.

Top on the list of sights to see in the Vucciria is the wonderful **Museo Archeologico Regionale** ✗✗✗ (Piazza Olivella 24; ☎ 091-6116805; 6€; Tues–Sat 8:30am–6:45pm, Sun–Mon and holidays 8:30am–1:45pm), a world-class showcase of Sicilian antiquities—Etruscan, Roman, and everything in between. The museum contains over 10,000 Etruscan artifacts, making it one of the largest such collections anywhere, as well as 5th-century Phoenician sarcophagi, Greek carvings, bronze statues, and the world's largest collection of ancient ship anchors. The museum is straightforward to navigate, with exhibits on either side of a lush, tranquil cloister. The highlights of the collection, housed on the ground floor, are the sculptures, or Metopes—all of them unearthed at the seven Greek temples of Selinunte (p. 613)—including Hercules entangled with an Amazon, and Perseus beheading the Gorgon. You'll definitely want to check these out if you have visited Selinunte or plan on visiting the temples later in your visit. Off the main exhibit room is a tiny room lined with 19 lions' heads that were spouts for a massive fountain (59 lion heads in all) from the Templo della Vittoria in Selinunte. The halls upstairs are lined with Etruscan vases and mirrors, and other treasures.

Palermo's churches are largely used by the island's devout, who frown upon visitors entering during Mass. When Mass is not going on, be sure to take an unobtrusive peek through the front door of the **Chiesa di San Domenico** (Piazza San Domenico; ☎ 091-5844872; free; Mon–Fri 9–11:30am, Sat–Sun 5–7pm), with its monumental baroque facade and high bell towers. It was built in 1640, and its facade was added more than a century later. Inside are the tombs of Sicilian nobility and high-ranking politicians like former Prime Minister Francesco Crispi, making it comparable to the Pantheon in Rome in terms of cultural and historic significance. The inner church is inlaid with marble designed by famous marble craftsman Antonello Gagini and members of the Gagini school. Also don't miss the **Oratorio del Rosario di San Domenico** ✪✪ (Via dei Bambinai 2; Mon–Fri 9am–1pm, Sat 2–5:30pm) and the **Oratorio del Rosario di Santa Cita** ✪✪ (Via Valverde 3; Mon–Fri 9am–1pm and 3–6pm, Sat 9am–1pm), which sit just behind the church. Inside these marble chapels is some of Palermo's finest stuccowork, done by Giacomo Serpotta, who labored from 1686 to 1718 to carve the dozens of cherubim who frolic on the altars, their faces eerily lifelike. The Oratorio del Rosario di Santa Cita was damaged by heavy bombing during World War II, and major works of art have not yet been restored. Miraculously, these little angels survived, and are worth seeing. The oratories are sometimes not open at the posted times, but ask inside the church and the custodian will open the door for you. In the Oratorio del Rosario di San Domenico, check out the columns to the right of the altar. The lizard is meant to depict strength and courage. Above the altar is a cupola painted with gawking knights, noble ladies, and young boys who seem to be peering down as you stare up.

LA KALSA (SOUTHEAST QUADRANT)

The oldest district of Palermo was on the blacklist of most visitors for decades. The Kalsa was heavily damaged by air bombardment on May 9, 1943, and an astonishing number of buildings—even entire blocks—still bear the scars of that destruction. Plagued by poverty and its natural consequences, crime and corruption, the state of affairs in the Kalsa even earned the pity of Mother Theresa, who set up a mission here. Today, thanks to ongoing building restoration and a burgeoning art scene, the Kalsa is one of the bright spots of Palermo (it's my favorite part of the old city for authentic discovery) and home to some of its most compelling museums and churches. Though this neighborhood is on the up and up, locals don't advise walking alone through the quieter streets after dark, but that's no reason not to be here in the evening at one of its myriad restaurants; just plan to take a cab or walk in a large group.

Give yourself a few daylight hours and start a thorough exploration of this district at Piazza Bellini and the adjacent churches of La Martorana and San Cataldo. Raised one story above street level and separated by lush palm trees, these two holy places have teetered between Christian and Muslim worship for centuries. **La Martorana** ✪✪ (Piazza Bellini 2; ☎ 091-6161692; free; Mon–Sat 9:30am–1pm and 3:30–6:30pm, Sun 8:30am–1pm), also known as the Chiesa dell'Ammiraglio, was built by the Syrian Emir George of Antioch in the 12th century as a mosque, though it was never used as one. (The Greeks took over shortly after its construction and used it as a church, but keen eyesight—or better yet, good binoculars—will help you see the Arabic lettering repeating "Allah" around the base of the cupola). The interior is striking for its blue-and-gold-toned mosaics, also from the 12th century and believed to be the work of the same artists who decorated the Cappella Palatina (p. 583). The glittering scenes depict George of Antioch hiding from the Virgin Mary, and local honcho Roger II with a crown reportedly given to him by Christ. Try to visit La Martorana in the morning for the best light. In 1433, the church became a Benedictine convent, and the good, if short-sighted, sisters reworked it by destroying the Norman apse, adding some flowery baroque design to the facade and replacing many of the mosaics with now-faded frescoes. In the 1930s, the church was returned to the Greek Orthodox community of Palermo, which still celebrates the Greek Mass here. A bonus to visiting this church is the sense of cultural understanding and acceptance this church seems to invite, as visitors of varying religions come to pray.

Adjacent to La Martorana is the rustic church of **San Cataldo** ✪✪ (Piazza Bellini; ☎ 091-6161692; 1€ donation; Tues–Fri 9am–5pm, Sat–Sun 9am–1pm; obtain a key from the sacristan at La Martorana), an intimate structure topped with three classic red Arab-Norman "golf-ball" domes. The interior of the church has wonderful pointed arches in exposed masonry and is completely devoid of decoration except for its wrought-iron cross. It's also completely lit by candles (the church was never wired for electricity) and the flickering lights against the worn wooden benches and brick arches give it a deeply serene, spiritual aspect that's quite moving. If you're lucky, you'll visit San Cataldo when one of the local clergy is humming prayers.

Farther into the winding web of streets in the Kalsa is Sicily's most impressive art museum, and one of the finest collections in Italy, the **Galleria Regionale Siciliana–Palazzo Abatellis** ✪✪✪ (Via Alloro 4; ☎ 091-6230011; 6€; daily 9am–1pm, Tues–Thurs 2:30–7pm). The setting couldn't be more ideal: The 15th-century Palazzo Abatellis is a superb example of Catalonian-Gothic architecture—all Spanish-style mullioned windows and narrowing towers. Though it was nearly destroyed by bombs in World War II, it was tastefully restored in 1954 and has housed this collection of sculpture and paintings, dating from the Middle Ages through the 18th century, ever since. The inner courtyard is lined with rows of marble sculptures from the Romanesque era through the 16th century. A closed hall surrounding the courtyard houses wooden sculptures from the 12th to the 16th centuries and delicate stone statues from the 14th and 15th centuries. The museum's prize work of art is the intricately detailed bust of *Eleonora of Aragon,* created by Francesco Laurana in 1471 and widely considered to be his masterpiece. Farther along, the mural-size *Triumph of Death* fresco—painted in the 15th century by an unknown artist, or, some believe, a collection of artists—depicts Death as a fiendish fellow on horseback, shooting arrows at the local youth, who dodge them and dart away. On the mezzanine you can sit and ponder this depiction of death on a lone bench that hangs perilously close to the railing-free edge.

If you've got kids in tow, don't miss the **Museo Internazionale delle Marionette** ✪✪ 🧒 (Piazzetta Niscemi 5/Via Butera 1; ☎ 091-328060; www. museomarionettepalermo.it; adults 5€, children 3€; daily 9am–1pm, Mon–Fri 3:30–6:30pm), which celebrates the art of puppetry, as much a part of the Sicilian life as sunshine. Here you'll find over 3,000 puppets ranging from traditional Italian puppets from the theaters of Naples and Catania, to a small collection of international puppets from China, India, Turkey, and Africa. Every Friday afternoon the curators hold a show (check the website for schedules).

Just down the street from the puppet museum is the **Giardino Garibaldi park** ✪✪ (Piazza Marina; free; daily 24 hr.), and inside it, Palermo's oldest tree, a 150-year-old tangled *ficus magnolioides* that reaches 25m (82 ft.). This garden, which looks like it could be in the American Deep South, is a calm oasis in the middle of an often overwhelmingly hectic city and a great spot for a picnic lunch. The benches stay cool under the shade of the tree, even in the most grueling heat.

Not far from here, past some rather derelict blocks (where you might happen to glimpse a chicken coop fashioned out of an old bombed-out building), lies one of Palermo's most romantic and breathtaking sights. In fact, walking into the skeletal church of **Santa Maria dello Spasimo** ✪✪✪ (Via dello Spasimo; ☎ 091-6161486; free; daily 24 hr.) is what I like to call a "moment." The church's ruined appearance is not the result of World War II bombing, but the fact that the grand plans for the church were never completed, and over the centuries, it fell into disrepair. All that remains of this 16th-century construction are the walls, the apse, and some brick vaults overhead that have a gorgeous, Gothic ribcage look to them. The painting that Raphael did for this church in the early 1500s, *Lo Spasimo di Sicilia,* today hangs in the Prado in Madrid. Two mature trees now grow out of the wood-floored nave, past the brick vaults into the Palermitan sky, and concerts are often held here on summer nights. Santa Maria dello Spasimo is an incredible example of all the beauty in imperfection that you can find in Palermo. Raphael would have loved it.

The "New" City

Around Piazza Verdi (Teatro Massimo) and points north is where the "new Palermo" begins. Here, stately Art Nouveau apartment buildings and theaters, like the Teatro Massimo and Teatro Politeama, replace the cramped and often unkempt blocks of the *centro storico*. Via Principe di Belmonte is a pedestrian-only street with smart shops and cafes, and a fun place to watch well-dressed Palermitans gather to see and be seen on weekends. Viale della Libertà runs north from Piazza Castelnuovo and is the most glamorous part of the city, lined with Art Nouveau villas and pretty public parks, like the **Giardino Inglese** ✪✪ and the Villa Trabia, which are perfect places to escape the mayhem of Palermo.

Contrary to what some guides say, the newer parts of Palermo are not without local flavor. I especially recommend going for a stroll around the **Borgo Vecchio market** ✪✪ (between Corso Scinà and Via Carini). This is old-school Palermo at its finest—residents hang out on lawn chairs in front of their apartments and let their pets run amok. Last time I was here, I had a close encounter with an ornery goose named Candy.

A Beach Day at Mondello

If you're visiting Palermo when it's warm, and especially if you have the kids in tow, consider an excursion to the city's favorite beach, **Mondello** ✪✪ 🧒 (take bus no. 806 from the Politeama theater, about 30 min.; 1.50€). The crescent-shaped bay here has calm, shallow water and is immensely popular with Palermitan families. (From their antics, it's clear that Sicilian family dynamics are responsible for the way Italians have been stereotyped in the U.S.!) The pier in the center of the beach has a wonderful peach-colored Art Nouveau clubhouse on it, completing the charming old-world bathing scene. The tiny town itself has several casual restaurants as well as carnival games and rides. Mondello's proximity to the city and the frequency of bus connections makes even a half-day trip here doable.

ACCOMMODATIONS, BOTH STANDARD & NOT

The historical center is the most enjoyable place to stay in Palermo. Many of the city's best-priced hotels are right around Via Roma, between the train station and the Quattro Canti. Giorgio's House and Casa Giuditta are two spots in particular that will give you a better taste of local flavor than a standard hotel.

€   Like many other cities in Italy, Palermo also has a growing list of self-catering apartments available as vacation rentals. **PoliteamAffitti** (Corso Domenico Scinà 27; ☎ 091-7434797 or 340-5210329; www.politeamaffitti.com) offers 10 spacious and homey apartments (in the same building) of various layouts (penthouses with sloping ceilings, duplexes with loft bedrooms) that can sleep from three to seven people. The units are decorated with the verve of a Sicilian housewife—a more-is-more aesthetic with bright and clashing upholstery, little throw rugs and wall hangings everywhere, unexpected furniture placement—which just adds to the authenticity and lovability of these Palermo accommodations. Double-occupancy rates start at 60€ per day or 300€ per week. These apartments are great solutions for families, and you can shop for food and wine at the wonderful Borgo Vecchio market, just up the street, which is open every day.

€   Staying at **Giorgio's House** ✦✦ (Via A. Mongitore; ☎ 091-525057; www. giorgioshouse.com; cash only) is like finding that long-lost Sicilian cousin we all wish we had—and in crazy Palermo, crashing at your *cugino siciliano*'s place is a huge boon. Giorgio will take care of everything, from picking you up at the airport to planning your itinerary. He'll take you around the city or highlight your map so you can do it yourself. There are only three rooms for rent here, each of which is impeccably clean with large comfortable beds and luxurious bedding, so book as soon as you know your dates. Prices are 29€ per person for a double room for up to 2 nights, and 26€ a person for 3 nights or more. Giorgio will also organize windsurfing courses, sailing courses, wine tastings, and nightlife outings for those who have the energy. Nothing you suggest is beyond this Sicilian's reach. This is truly living like a local.

€€   Tucked behind the church of Santa Teresa in the Kalsa district, **Casa Giuditta** ✦✦ (Via Savona 10; ☎ 328-2250788; www.casagiuditta.com; MC, V) is another dream spot in Palermo. Though it's technically a bed-and-breakfast, the "rooms" here are actually self-catering apartments that give the comfy feeling of being not in a bland vacation rental, but in someone's private home. All units have kitchens, washing machines (no dryer, so you'll hang your clothes on a line *alla palermitana*), and A/C, though you might not even need it with the tile floors, thick stone walls, and relative lack of sunlight (the only downside here, but typical of the Kalsa) keeping things blessedly cool. Casa Giuditta's double-occupancy apartments go for 78€ per night, while larger units suitable for families are about 115€, but they give discounts for stays longer than 7 days. Unlike most self-catering apartments, these feel like a sort of community (there's a front desk, and your neighbors will be travelers just like you), which lends the place a wonderful intimacy that you'll remember long after you've left.

€€   In the heart of the Kalsa, and only a 5-minute walk from the train station, **Il Giardino dell'Alloro** ✪ (Vicolo San Carlo 8, corner of Via Alloro; ☎ 091-6176904; www.giardinodellalloro.it; MC, V) is a cozy bed-and-breakfast with temporary installations by local Palermitan artists in the guest rooms (100€ for a double) and common areas. The "laurel garden" in the name refers to a sunny courtyard where guests can hang out, and where breakfast is served in warm weather. All rooms have such mod-cons as Internet connections, A/C, and LCD TVs, though the overall feel of the place is a bit bohemian.

€€   A longtime favorite of budget travelers in Palermo, the **Hotel Ambasciatori** ✪✪ (Via Roma 111; ☎ 091-6166881; www.ambasciatorihotelpalermo.com; AE, MC, V) has surprisingly spacious and well-appointed rooms, considering the price tag—doubles start at 78€ from Nov to June and at 95€ from July to Oct. For carpet this new and paint this fresh (with minibar and A/C), you'd expect to pay at least twice that. The Ambasciatori's biggest asset is its rooftop terrace, with great views over the nearby mountains and the wonderfully cluttered skyline of Palermo. The more basic "Dependance" side of the property has rooms for about 10€ less than the regular hotel.

€€   You can get away with paying less than 100€ for a hotel room in Palermo, so staying at the **Hotel Tonic** ✪ (Via Mariano Stabile 126; ☎ 091-581754; www.hoteltonic.com; AE, MC, V) can be considered a splurge. I list it because it has a sense of style that gives it a much more pricey feel. The rooms (100€ for a double) are elegantly appointed with antique furniture, rich bed linens, velvet curtains, and ample pillows. Unusual for Italy, the rooms are spacious, with enormous beds and lots of floor space. All units come with phone, safe, and wet bar. You won't get the personal service offered at Giuditta or Giorgio's, but this is the best choice for those who prefer a more anonymous hotel setting at a very reasonable price.

DINING FOR ALL TASTES

Dining establishments are more diverse in Palermo than in any other city in Italy, and it's difficult to dine poorly here—even the street food is top quality. But instead of eating on the main thoroughfares, where restaurants tend to cater to group tourists, try delving deep into the back streets, where you'll find tiny trattorie with uniquely Sicilian fare. Trattoria Shanghai (below) is one of many places in the Vucciria district where you actually eat in someone's home—it's just one of the few with a phone number and a tax ID. All around the city, but especially in the Vucciria and Kalsa districts, wherever you see more than a single family's

Street Eats

Forget the Arab-Norman-Byzantine churches! It's in the street-food *(cibo di strada)* stalls of Palermo that you'll really begin to feel the city's Eastern influences. If you are steely of stomach, definitely try out some of the traditional foods cooked and sold in markets like Vucciria and Ballarò. Slaughterhouse leftovers play a starring role on the "menu" at these stands, so you might be better off not asking what's in them (or reading any further in this paragraph, for that matter). These nondescript meats will surely tempt you with their aromas, but I feel it's only fair to disclose that *stigghiola* is essentially barbecued goat intestines, and that the *pane con milza* sandwich consists of chopped stewed spleen in a roll of bread with cheese on top. Real Palermitans go crazy for this stuff, and you'll earn major cred if you step up to the challenge. (Bonus points for ordering *babaluci,* baby snails with olive oil, garlic, and fennel.) On the less daring side, *sfincione* is a typical Palermitan pizza with tomatoes, anchovies, onion, and grated cheese. Craving stadium food? Try some *pane con salsiccia,* an herby Sicilian riff on bratwurst. If you are vegetarian, try a delicious (and protein-filled) *pane e panelle* (chickpea fritter sandwich). Least bizarre of all, *arancini* are another typical Sicilian snack and easy to eat on the go. These deep-fried rice balls with mozzarella or meat inside will cost you about 1€ each. The best *arancini* in town are at Antico Caffè Spinnato (below).

worth of tables set up inside a ground-floor apartment, and there are good smells issuing from it, don't be shy about asking *"Si può mangiare?"* ("Can you eat here?").

€   If you need a caffeine jolt or have any interest in knowing what the best *cassata* in Palermo tastes like, go to **Antico Caffé Spinnato** ✪✪ (Via Principe di Belmonte 107/115; (☎ 091-329229; www.spinnato.it; daily 7am–2am; MC, V). This handsome bar and cafe, situated on the only pedestrian street in the city, won Gambero Rosso's prestigious "Best Bar in Italy" award in 2005 and 2006 for its excellent coffee and pastries. On weekends, you'll have to muscle your way through the chic, Gucci-bag-toting crowd to get to the counter, but it's worth it.

€   In a stately palazzo in the Kalsa district, the beloved **Antica Focacceria San Francesco** ✪✪ (Via Alessandro Paternostro 58; (☎ 091-320264; www.afsf.it; Wed–Mon 9am–4pm and 5:30pm–midnight; MC, V) is unlike any place you've ever eaten in Italy. Is it a takeout joint? A fancy restaurant? A men's club? Well, this historic spot that attracts everyone from tourists to bridge-playing old-timer locals is all of the above. The cheapest way to eat here is to grab a tray and assemble a combo plate (6€–12€, includes ¼ liter of wine and a dessert) from the counter display on the left—there are mini-pizzas, lasagna, swordfish roulades, and the incredibly yummy *panelle* (discs of fried chickpea mash). Next, go see the guys in back for your *vino* or soft drink. Behind the counter in the center of the down-stairs area is an enormous black cauldron where a grim-faced man churns and stews bits of spleen for the *pane con milza* sandwiches. He who stops to load his plate here is either a full-blooded Palermitan or a tourist with nerves of steel—or Anthony Bourdain. Grab a table downstairs or upstairs, and enjoy your meal. You can go back for seconds (you'll just pay again), but whatever you do, leave room for your *cannolo!* (It's included in the price of your combo meal, and one of the best examples of this treat in Sicily.) You can also eat alfresco in the fancier "restau-rant" on the pretty square across the street, where there's a different menu (pasta dishes from 8€ and *secondi* from 12€). Cafeteria-style or formal table service, the food here is strictly authentic *palermitano*.

€   One of the most unique dining experiences you can have in Palermo is on the balcony of the **Trattoria Shanghai** ✭✭ (Vicolo dei Mezzani 34; ☎ 091-5897025; Mon–Sat 12:30–2:30pm and 7:30–10:30pm; cash only). This is not a Chinese restaurant; the owner gave his restaurant this name because of the exotic view you get, over the Vucciria market, when you eat here. Getting to the restaurant is half the adventure. You'll enter through the door of a typical historical Palermo apartment building and follow the signs upstairs. There you'll go into the tiny apartment-cum-restaurant. The owner and his children will probably be sitting watching TV in the kitchen and will barely look up to greet you before nodding or pointing to a table (it's a bit odd—and you may feel as though you're crashing someone's mealtime rather than going to a restaurant—but the cooking more than makes up for it). Choose a seat on the balcony overlooking the Vucciria mar-ket; depending on the crowds and availability, what you order is often lifted before your eyes in a tattered wicker basket from the vegetable stand below. A simple and filling plate of sardine and tomato pasta costs just 5€; other pastas and vegetable dishes, just as fresh and delicious, range from 5€ to 7€. You'll want to order mul-tiple courses just to stay and enjoy the Palermo life below.

€   African cuisines are popular in Palermo. For authentic Tunisian dishes, head to one of the city's oldest eateries, **El-Maghreb** (Via Bara all'Olivella 75; no phone; daily noon–10pm). Here you can enjoy *shawarma* and kabobs for 4€ to the sound of Arabic music. The ambience is rustic, with whitewashed walls and wrought-iron tables, and the atmosphere is casual and friendly.

€€   Next door to the Antica Focacceria San Francesco, **Mi Manda Picone** ✭ (Via Alessandro Paternostro 59; ☎ 091-6160660; Mon–Sat 7pm–1am; MC, V) is an atmospheric wine bar/restaurant with exposed stone vaults and wood beams where you can make a lighter (and less classically Sicilian) meal of *antipasti* (8€–12€), meat or fish dishes (8€–14€), generous cheese and cured meat plates (12€–14€), and wines by the glass. The place is popular with young and hip Palermitans, who often come here in large and friendly groups.

€€   A splurge in Palermo means spending 10€ to 12€ on a plate of pasta, and if you're in the mood for "going all out," head straight to **Shakespeare & Co.** ✭ (Salita Artale 5; ☎ 091-7495205), in the shadow of the cathedral. The food here tastes as though it's worth much more than you're paying, with healthy portions of seafood (try the seafood packet in phyllo pastry) for just 11€. This is where trendy professional Palermitans come for a night out, so you'll get a good glimpse of local life.

THE OTHER PALERMO

Straight back toward the harbor from the San Domenico church is the cacophonous, crowded, exhilarating morning market, **Mercato Vucciria** (p. 585), which is best known for its swaying carcasses of meat hanging from the awnings over a fog of dry ice; and its live seafood "demonstrations," in which the fishmonger ends up swallowing some sort of squirmy, live sea creature as the gathering crowd gasps in disgust. How entertaining is this? Look up and you'll see the elderly Palermo residents hanging perilously out their windows to watch the morning spectacle as if it were a television sitcom.

Here, among the stalls and decaying buildings, you'll get an idea of the local Palermo palate and how it differs from others across the country. Almost every stand sells hot peppers, exotic spices, and other condiments that you won't find in mainland Italian cuisine. You'll also see couscous instead of pasta, Asian rice, and oddly shaped imported vegetables. Don't be shy about asking questions. The vendors will welcome you and explain the produce and how to prepare it. You'll likely be offered wedges of ripe fruit or chunks of raw vegetables dipped in open jars of hot peppery confections if you feign even the slightest interest. The seafood dealers will dish out cooked mussels and clams on request, and the butchers always seem to have some cured meat to nibble on. Never mind if you don't understand them, their gestures will generally get the point across, and you'll come away feeling like a local—and satisfied enough to skip lunch.

If you'd actually like to do something productive and educational with all that market going, consider signing up for the **Market Cooking Class with Mamma Lucia and Vincenzo** (at Ristorante Cin Cin, Via Manin 22; ☎ 091-6124095; clemente.vincenzo@gmail.com). The 5-hour, 150€-per-person culinary adventure begins at 9am with a visit to one of the major street markets (Vucciria, Il Capo, or Borgo Vecchio), where Mamma Lucia and Vincenzo (who couldn't look more stereotypically Sicilian if you plucked them out of central casting) will teach you how to shop for calves' feet at the butcher's stall, how to spot a good swordfish at the fishmonger's, and all about the subtleties of Sicilian vegetables at the endless produce stands. As with the entire Palermitan culinary scene, this is not for the squeamish. It's a hands-on experience that will involve unfamiliar meats and getting intimate with octopus tentacles and the like back in the kitchen (the course borrows the professional kitchen of Ristorante Cin Cin). Donning kitschy aprons emblazoned with the monuments of Sicily, you'll prepare a feast of *antipasti,* pasta, and fish, and scarf it down around a convivial table with wine and *digestivi.*

NIGHTLIFE

If you have energy to hit the town after traipsing through Palermo all day, well, more power to you. Around Piazza Olivella (between Via Maqueda and Via Roma, south of Teatro Massimo), there are a handful of small and cozy small places where you can go for a relaxed *aperitivo* or for after-dinner cocktails and live music.

Corleone: Real-Life Hometown of Sicilian Godfathers

Just 60km (38 miles) out of Palermo, toward the center of the island, is the famous Mafia haven of Corleone. Seeing the sheer number of construction cranes that dot the city sky, it's not hard to believe that organized crime is still an integral part of everyday life here. Many of the city center's buildings are under scaffolding, which in Sicily usually means that money is being laundered through bogus construction contracts. But you aren't here to linger; you're here to visit the Mafia museum, officially called the **Centro Internazionale Documentazione sulle Mafie e sul Movimento Antimafia** (Palazzo Provenzano, Via Orfanotrofio; ☎ 091-8463655; free; Mon–Sat 9am–1pm and 3–7pm, Sun 9am–1pm), which is a serious look at Italy's fight against organized crime. There are reams of court documents, displays of bullets from famous hits, and an uncomfortable number of bloody pictures of arrests, murders, and maimings. It's worth coming here to understand Italy's struggle to stamp out the Mafia. The fact that this museum even exists in what is widely known as the heart of Mafia country is a testament to the fact that the struggle is getting results. At the time of this writing, the Mafia museum was under a veil of scaffolding, too. To reach Corleone, take an AST bus (1 hr. 45 min., 7€ round-trip) from behind Palermo's central train station.

One of the best hangouts in Palermo (with cute bartenders, to boot) is **I Grilli** ✪✪ (Largo Cavalieri di Malta 11, next to the church of San Domenico; ☎ 091-6111243; Tues–Sun until 3am). They have a pretty good *aperitivo* buffet with different kind of pizza pieces. After dinner, the DJ plays house music and on Fridays and Saturdays there's live jazz music.

An easy place to wile away an evening is **Cortile Patania** ✪ (Via G. Patania 34, Piazza Olivella; ☎ 091-7434772; Tues–Sun until 3am), which has comfy sofas around the tables, even board games to play. The hip factor is not high, but then again, you probably won't have the energy to act cool anyway! On Wednesdays, a vegetarian buffet is served from 8pm; on Thursdays they have live jazz after dinner; and on Sundays, they serve American brunch starting at noon.

Along the promenade between the Kalsa and the waterfront, **Kursaal Kalhesa** (Foro Italico [Umberto I] 21; ☎ 091-6162111; www.kursaalkalhesa.it; Tues–Sat 11:30am–1:30am, Sun 6:30pm–1:30am) is a wine bar and restaurant, book shop, and coffee shop, with a garden area outside. During the evening, the garden fills up with young intellectuals who use literature conversations as an excuse to drink wine. The innovative space has some very impressive architecture.

A SIDE TRIP FROM PALERMO

Just 8km (5 miles) from the city center is the day-trip destination to end all day-trip destinations, the magnificent **Cattedrale di Monreale** (Piazza Duomo,

Monreale; ☎ 091-6404413; free, recommended audioguide 4€; daily 8am–6pm), one of the most spectacularly mosaiced churches in Christendom. You thought St. Mark's in Venice was over the top? Wait until you enter this giant complex, the last of the Norman Sicilian cathedrals—an amalgam of different styles, with elements from Muslim, Byzantine, and Romanesque architecture added over the years. Inside, a whopping 6,340 sq. m (68,243 sq. ft.) of gold mosaics are plastered over every conceivable space, from the arched apse ceiling to the sanctuary aisles. Of special note are the luminous scenes from the Old Testament over the nave, and the Christ Pantocrator, in the main apse, whose eyes seem to follow you as you roam the church. The artists were Venetians and Sicilians who were perfecting mosaic techniques during the 12th and 13th century; in certain areas, the work gets a more experimental edge to it. The complex also houses a lovely and contemplative Benedictine cloister set with 228 twisted columns inlaid with mosaics.

CEFALÙ

The second city of the northern coast, Cefalù, earned fame (and more tourism) when director Giuseppe Tornatore chose this picturesque beach town as the location for his film *Cinema Paradiso*. Cefalù is dominated by an enormous promontory, La Rocca, at whose feet medieval buildings are scattered along a ladder of streets that provide incidental glimpses of the sea. The beach in town is soft and sandy, though not particularly deep, and the water is clean. Except for July and August, when Cefalù swells to the gills with British and German sun seekers, this is a quiet town, so if you like tranquillity, base yourself here for a few days.

It's enough to spend your time here just wandering around the historical city center, dipping into the main monasteries built by Frederick II and Roger II, or gazing at the impressive but ungainly **Duomo di Cefalù** ✪ (Piazza del Duomo; ☎ 0921-922021; free; daily 8am–noon and 3:30–7pm), with its two towers that seem to converge at the top (an optical illusion, of course). The church was built by Roger II, supposedly to fulfill an impulsive promise he made to God when his ship was caught in a storm off the coast. The interior of the church has an 1150 mosaic of an emotional Christ holding a Bible. Behind the church is the massive Rocca, which you climb by a winding staircase called the Salita Saraceno.

ACCOMMODATIONS, BOTH STANDARD & NOT

Staying in Cefalù can be pricey because of growing interest in this coastal town, but there are still a few options if you book early. You can also check out listings for holiday apartments (in town, minimum stay of 3 nights) and villas (just outside town, minimum stay of 1 week) on www.cefalu.it. Holiday apartments are the only way to stay in the historical center of Cefalù; hotels and most other accommodations options are in the modern part of the city (closer to the beach). Note that prices skyrocket—as much as 100%—in the month of August. Just down the street from the Duomo, the **Casa del Duomo** (Via lo Duca 27; ☎ 368-7868771; www.cefalumare.it; MC, V) has two self-catering apartments that start at 50€ per day based on double occupancy. The units are simple but spacious, and the location, in the heart of the *centro storico*, is one that few visitors to Cefalù are fortunate enough to enjoy.

€€   In a modern palazzina near the beach, the sunny **Villa Gaia** ✿✿ (Via V. Pintorno; ☎ 0921-420992; www.villagaiahotel.it; MC, V) offers good-size double rooms for 140€ during the summer months, 98€ off season—and a lot of bang for the buck. The rooms are clean and cozier than what you normally find in seaside inns, with large beds. Many have sea views, a few even have private balconies with lounge chairs. Bathrooms feature newfangled shower stalls with electronic controls for various kinds of water massage (such contraptions are a growing trend in Sicily). The suites are a bargain at 120€ to 150€. Even though the hotel is close to the city center, most rooms are in the back, so street noise is minimal. This is a hotel that fills up seasons ahead by returning customers, so book as far in advance as you can.

€€   Another good-value hotel, though not as charming as the Villa Gaia, is the reliable old **Astro Hotel** ✿ 🔵 (Via Nino Martoglio 10; ☎ 0921-421639; www. astrohotel.it; MC, V; closed Nov and first 2 weeks of Dec), where decor is that classic European brand of 1960s beach-utilitarian. It's clean, the rooms are ample, and the bathrooms are large by Italian hotel standards. A single room starts at 60€, doubles at 110€, though they soar to twice that in August. A bonus is the different types of beds, especially if you're traveling with kids. Ask for cots, baby beds, or whatever you need, and the staff members are likely to come through.

DINING FOR ALL TASTES

Dining well in Cefalù takes a bit of work. Increasingly, restaurants here cater to tourists, with raised prices and lowered quality, but there are a few holdouts from a time when quality was all that mattered.

€   Of all the restaurants on the main square, Piazza del Duomo, the only one offering good value is the **Ostaria del Duomo** ✿ (Via Seminario 5; ☎ 0921-421838; www.ostariadelduomo.it; daily noon–3pm and 7–10:30pm; MC, V). Expect very filling plates of traditional Sicilian cuisine, mainly seafood-based (though there are plenty of "turf" options, too), for under 10€. The fettuccine with prawns is fantastic. They have an extensive wine list, even by the glass, and the view of both the imposing cathedral and the *passeggiata* (evening stroll) complete the dining experience.

€€   Another good bet is **Al Gabbiano** ✿ (Lungomare G. Giardina; ☎ 0921-421495; Thurs–Tues noon–3pm and 7pm–midnight; MC, V), on the waterfront. Dining here, while gentle sea breezes blow and waves lap at the shore, is definitely a romantic experience. The specialties are seafood—I like the swordfish rolls for 11€, but pastas are also available and a bargain at 7€.

AEOLIAN ISLANDS ✿✿✿

Wildly diverse and seductively appealing for anyone in search of an island getaway, Sicily's Aeolian islands are among the best offbeat escapes in the Mediterranean. The tiny islands are the peaks of a 3,000m (9,840-ft.) volcanic mountain range that was formed more than a million years ago. Today two of the islands, Vulcano and Stromboli, still smolder and sizzle, but the rest are largely dormant. In the warmer months, hydrofoils and ferries leave from Milazzo (the principal port for reaching the islands), Palermo, and Messina and hop from island to island. You can also reach the Aeolians from Naples by ferry or hydrofoil. The main island is Lipari and almost all ferries from Sicilian ports stop here first (boats originating in Naples usually stop at Stromboli first, since it's the closest island to Naples). **Siremar** (☎ 090-9283242; www.siremar.it), **SNAV** (☎ 090-www.snav.it), and **Ustica Lines** (☎ 090-9287821; www.usticalines.it) all operate interisland ferries and hydrofoils. In high season, hydrofoils run about three times as often as ferries, but hydrofoils do not run year-round or when seas are rough.

The table below shows travel times to the Aeolians and ticket prices. Routes are mostly linear (Filicudi is the one island off the arc), so travel time between two islands is usually just the difference between the respective travel times to those islands from Milazzo. So, between Lipari and Stromboli, it's 4 hours by ferry or 1 hour, 55 minutes by hydrofoil.

Ferry & Hydrofoil Travel Times from Milazzo to the Aeolian Islands

Island	Ferry	Hydrofoil
Vulcano	1 hr. 30 min., 8.80€	40 min., 14€
Lipari	2 hr., 9.30€	55 min., 14€
Salina	3 hr. 20 min., 11€	1 hr. 30 min., 16€
Panarea	4 hr. 35 min., 11€	2 hr., 16€
Filicudi	5 hr., 14€	2 hr. 30 min., 21€
Stromboli	6 hr., 13€	2 hr. 50 min., 20€

LAY OF THE LAND

For most purposes, I recommend that you base yourself in **Lipari,** as it offers the widest range of rooms and apartments. As the capital of the Aeolians, it also has the most to see and the most frequent connections for exploring the other islands. The Citadel is the focal point in the only real "town" in the Aeolians. Start at Via del Concordato, with its 17th-century Cattedrale di San Bartolomeo and its 12th-century Benedictine cloister. Then head straight for the archaeological dig, which is a quarry for the nearby **Museo Archeologico Eoliano** (Via del Castello; ☎ 090-9880174; 4.50€; daily 9am–1:30pm and 3–7pm). You can easily spend a few hours poking around the vases, sculpture, and other ancient artifacts in the two buildings that make up this museum. German and Italian tourists come here for the clear waters, the snorkeling, the scuba diving, and its beaches. The most popular beaches are at Canneto, a 20-minute walk north of the town, and Spiaggia Bianca, a bit farther north. This second beach was named for its white sands, an anomaly on the islands, whose sands are mostly black.

Tiny **Panarea** is the most glamorous of the Aeolians, complete with boho-chic boutiques, Greek-style whitewashed villas, and very expensive restaurants. Until a few years ago, Panarea was a fairly well-kept secret, but now it's been a bit overrun by young people who seem to want to turn it into Ibiza. Still, it's worth at least a day trip to check out the scene. Sleek yachts in the harbor and around the island's pretty coves cater to movie stars and wannabes. Paparazzi speedboats circle the island like pesky mosquitoes. There's a fascinating 23-hut Bronze Age Village on the southern shore, but most of the best artifacts are on display at the Archaeological Museum in Lipari. The island is busy in August, and then sinks into a heavy lethargy for the rest of the year.

Unlike Vulcano and Lipari, **Salina** is wooded and speaks to visitors who love the outdoors; hikes take you to the volcanic peaks of Fossa delle Felci and Madonna Del Terzito. Religious pilgrims trek through the valley between the two during the mid-August Feast of the Assumption (which can be a reason to stay away at this time). The island produces vegetables, citrus, and Malvasia wine and has some wonderful little hotels. It's also where the film *Il Postino* was shot. If you're a nature lover (and don't need any nightlife because there is none here), I recommend staying in Salina as opposed to Lipari.

Stromboli is best at night, when the fireworks from the very active volcano light up the night sky and make the water look like a blazing pool. Almost everything on this island revolves around the volcanic activity. There are a handful of tour operators who specialize in guided visits to the volcano. The most experienced and entertaining group of guides are at **Magmatrek** (Via Vittorio Emanuele; ☎ 090/986-5768; www.magmatrek.it), whose 5-hour evening trek is the gold standard in Stromboli ascents. The tours depart daily at 4pm from March to June, when conditions are safe, and cost 25€ per person.

Vulcano, the archipelago's second largest island after Lipari, is worthwhile for its live volcanoes and inexpensive spa treatments. The Fossa di Vulcano crater is a steamy reminder that this island is very much alive. Sulfur bath treatments are synonymous with Vulcano for Italians who summer on Sicily; the mud here is widely felt to be therapeutic. Access to the public mud baths is 1.50€, which includes entrance to the steaming pools and beach. Hotels along the coast offer treatments, including massage and shower starting at around 35€, but the accommodations themselves aren't much to write home about. You may not want to stay overnight anyway: The smell of sulfur is overpowering after a few hours.

Filicudi and **Alicudi,** two small, isolated islands, are also good bets, like Salina, for nature lovers. They're also great for tent campers and those who don't need amenities. If camping is not for you, Filicudi is a fine place to visit for an afternoon hike or for an overnight at the chic La Canna hotel; just take a ferry from one of the other islands.

ACCOMMODATIONS, BOTH STANDARD & NOT

You can spend a lot of money to sleep on the Aeolian islands, but because it can take a couple of hours to get here from the mainland, a day trip really isn't advisable. The widest range of accommodations are on Lipari.

€–€€€   If you have the time, and you're with the family or a larger group, consider staying awhile in the Aeolians at a vacation rental. There are some fantastic (and affordable) villas available for rent through **Eoliando** (☎ 090-9814948; www.eoliando.it). For example, the Villa Rinella on Salina has two bedrooms (sleeps four), two full bathrooms, a washing machine, a full kitchen, and a gorgeous panoramic terrace (the better to enjoy all those home-cooked meals) and costs just 525€ per week in the warm months of June and September. Most villas require a weeklong stay, which is the perfect amount of time for relaxing, exploring your own island, and ferrying around to sample the other islands.

€   For a great value on Lipari, get in touch with longtime expat **Diana Brown** ★★ (Vico Himera 3; ☎ 090-9812584; www.dianabrown.it; MC, V). She offers homey, island-style double rooms starting at 40€ and self-catering mini-apartments with kitchenettes starting at 40€ per person. This is a great base for all your Aeolian exploration as it's just 5 minutes from the ferry and hydrofoil port. You can also have your laundry done here and generally avail of the extraordinary helpfulness of the staff. Even when her B&B is full, she'll go out of her way to help you find something else.

€€€   On Stromboli, my favorite place to stay is **La Locanda del Barbablu** (Via Vittorio Emanuele 17–19; ☎ 090-986118; www.barbablu.it; MC, V; closed Nov–Feb). The hodgepodge furnishings at "Bluebeard's Inn" may strike you as odd, but when you consider that this historic structure was once a bona fide mariner's hostel, that narrow bunk bed in the corner of room no. 5 that looks like it was salvaged from a shipwreck makes more sense. All rooms (starting at 120€) have beds on the floor, too—and views, whether of the sea, the summit of the volcano, or the town, from a small private terrace.

€€–€€€   One of the only year-round hotels in the Aeolians is also one of the nicest: **Filicudi's La Canna** ★★ (Via Rosa 43; ☎ 090-9889956; www.lacanna hotel.it; AE, MC, V). For how much comfort and style this place offers, it's also a relative bargain (64€ Oct–May, 90€ June and Sept, 100€ July, and 140€ Aug). The low-slung, whitewashed hotel is laid out on sloping gardens with splendid views of Salina. Some rooms even have their own ample private terraces, with chairs and tables, with the same views. Sun worshippers will love the large pool and wide-open, chaise-filled deck. The only drawback is its secluded location on Filicudi, so you might want to stay here just a night or two.

Around the Aeolians by Scooter or Boat

Most of the islands have strict rules regarding who's allowed to bring cars, so it's best not to bother. To get around the islands, you can either walk, take a local bus, or rent a scooter for about 25€ to 30€ per day, with discounts for longer rentals. You can also completely forgo the land exploration and rent a small motorboat (a rubber *gommone*, 50€ for a half-day) to explore the perimeter of your particular island. This is the most joyous way to see the Aeolians, if you ask me. No experience is necessary (the seas here are calm), and these easy-to-maneuver boats will allow you to access hidden coves that can't be reached by land. Bring a picnic, drop anchor, and go for a swim whenever you like. It's pure Mediterranean fabulousness! For both scooters and boats, rental outfits are conveniently located near where the ferries and hydrofoils dock on each of the islands.

TAORMINA

Taormina is a resort town in every sense of the word: It's drop-dead gorgeous and laced with wonderfully decadent romantic hotels and restaurants, giving it a general feel of luxury. But Taormina exists solely for the droves of northern European and American tourists who flock here, and therefore has little to do with the rest of Sicily. Don't come to Taormina expecting to have it to yourself, or to have many authentic Sicilian encounters; still, its jaw-dropping setting and some truly lovely hotels make it a worthwhile stop for a night or two. It's also an excellent base for a visit to Mt. Etna.

Taormina's main sightseeing attraction is the **Teatro Greco Romano** ✪✪✪ (Via Teatro Greco; ☎ 0942-232220; adults 6€, seniors and students 3€; summer daily 9am–7pm, Nov–Mar until 4:30pm). This marvelous ruin, which overlooks both Mt. Etna and the Ionian Sea, was originally built by the Greeks in the 3rd century B.C., and the Romans embellished it in the 1st century A.D. Woody Allen even chose the Greco-Roman theater as the set for his Chorus in *Mighty Aphrodite.* In summer, don't miss a chance to see an opera production here.

The rest of Taormina can be enjoyed by simply walking along the main streets, which are lined with gift shops and descending shaded stairways just to see where they lead. You can see Mt. Etna from many vistas, and there are churches like the baroque Chiesa San Giuseppe and the 13th-century cathedral that are worth a look. A 12th-century clock tower at the entrance of the Borgo Medioevale marks the entrance to the city's old town. For even better views of the seaside below, climb the Monte Tauro above Taormina town and gaze out over the Saracen castle ruins.

It's important to note that Taormina itself is not on the water but hundreds of meters above it. Handy public transportation makes it easy to reach the nearby beaches and waste a glorious day or two hanging out on the pebbly sand and swimming in the cerulean water. There's a cable car *(funivia)* that connects Taormina town with the beaches of Mazzarò directly below, and buses depart the main bus station of Taormina for Letojanni and Giardini-Naxos, the other popular beach destinations in the vicinity.

ACCOMMODATIONS, BOTH STANDARD & NOT

Staying in Taormina is generally not cheap, especially when you consider the inflated restaurant prices. A few nicely priced hotels are available, but it's essential to book early because these are the fastest to go. Even if your hotel advertises Wi-Fi, don't count on it. Taormina's aerielike position means that it has to communicate with Catania for Internet connections, and these are often interrupted by the scirocco winds. Oh, and don't be jealous of the snobby types staying at the superfancy San Domenico and Grand Hotel Timeo—they're paying upwards of $800 per night to sit around, look stuffy, and wait for something fabulous to happen (and argue with supercilious desk staff when it doesn't). You can save considerable money in Taormina by booking a B&B or vacation rental, but the minimum stay is usually 3 nights (and 1 week in high season), which may be more time than you want to spend here. You'll find B&B listings for Taormina at www.bed-and-breakfast-sicily.it, and vacation rentals at www.case-vacanza-sicilia.it, but be sure that you look for "Taormina center" in the description, as some of these properties are located away from town, and will be quite inconvenient if you don't have a car.

€€   One of the nicer B&B choices here, near the southern end of Corso Umberto, is the **Villa Floresta** ✪ (Via Damiano Rosso 1; ☎ 0942-620184; www.villafloresta.it; MC, V), where basic but character-filled rooms with private bathrooms run between 60€ and 85€; some even have balconies with splendid views over the sea. The building is a government-protected 13th-century heritage site, with a courtyard that seems unchanged in at least 700 years!

€€   **Hotel La Campanella** ✪ (Via Circonvallazione 3; ☎ 0942-23381; cash only) is a great choice if you're fit—there are over 100 steps from the street to the entrance of this tiny 12-room hotel, and at this price, just 80€ for a double, you'll have to lug your bags up yourself. The rooms are simple but clean, and you can enjoy breakfast and a drink on the hotel's lush rooftop garden with views of the sea. The center of town is about 10 minutes away on foot, but the walk is picturesque, passing through a residential district.

€€   The budget-friendly **Hotel Condor** ✪ (Via Dietro Cappuccini 25; ☎ 0942-23124; cash only) is basic, but a gem for the value and convenient location it offers in overpriced Taormina. It's about a 5-minute walk from Corso Umberto on a flat, quiet street on the more modern north end of town, where the tourist throngs dwindle and you might actually meet some real Taorminese! Spread out over four floors, the 12 rooms have large beds, and many have spacious bathrooms and gorgeous sea views, too. Doubles start at 78€. The hotel also has a delicious restaurant with its own *nonna* (grandma) behind the stove. The Condor is harder to get into than La Campanella because returning guests tend to book months in advance, but it's worth the effort.

€€€   The lovely **Villa Schuler** ✪✪ (Via Roma, Piazzetta Bastione; ☎ 0942-23481; www.villaschuler.com; AE, MC, V; closed mid-Nov to Feb) is old-fashioned European resort style at its classiest. Run by soft-spoken Gerhard Schuler, this salmon-colored palazzo below the hubbub of Corso Umberto has enormous, airy rooms, many with small private balconies overlooking the sea and the plunging, eucalyptus-filled hillside. The least expensive doubles (128€) face the garden, while seaview doubles range from 152€ to 182€. Bathrooms are large and well equipped, and those with bathtubs have the most excellent Jacuzzis I've experienced in Sicily. Breakfast is served in the terrace below the hotel building, among fragrant Mediterranean flowers. Upon check-in, all guests will find a complimentary bottle of Nero d'Avola (a Sicilian red wine) in their room. On every level, service is fantastically helpful and gracious. Staying at this gentle place gives you a sense of what it might have been like in Taormina a century ago.

€€€–€€€€   High above Taormina town, **Villa Ducale** ✪✪✪ (Via Leonardo da Vinci 60; ☎ 0942-28153; www.villaducale.com; AE, MC, V) may be one of the finest hotels in all of Sicily. Its serene and panoramic location, far from the chaos of Corso Umberto, and casual rustic layout make you wonder why anyone would stay down in Taormina proper. (The hotel's frequently running free shuttle van makes access to the town a non-issue.) It is a bit of a splurge (doubles run from 120€–260€ depending on the season) but the homey and service-oriented Villa Ducale really is worth it. Guest rooms have tons of Sicilian character, with just the right amount of kitsch, color, and tile or stone to warm them up, and in the techy bathrooms you'll find Etro toiletries and shower stalls with electronically programmable jets. All rooms have a large furnished terrace for Etna- and sea-gazing Common areas include a pretty terrace where breakfast and an evening *aperitivo* buffet are served.

DINING FOR ALL TASTES

Unfortunately, the majority of restaurants in Taormina are in the business of fleecing tourists. It's not that the food is all terrible or horribly overpriced, it's just that you can find much better, for much less, on most of the rest of Sicily, so meal tabs tend to sting here. The restaurants listed below are places where locals actually eat, but you might also do well picking up sandwiches from a local deli or some lasagna from a *tavola calda* (hot-food cafe)—and saving a bundle of money—every other meal or so.

€   Right off the main bus terminus, **Aucello Cateno's Rosticceria** ✮ (Via Cappuccini 8; ☎ 0942-623672; hours vary; cash only) has hot and ready-to-eat savory dishes such as roast chicken, cannelloni, lasagna, and *arancini* (Sicilian rice balls), and nothing's over 5€. There's a certain *simpatia* that develops between you and the owners here after a few visits—you're getting respect for being a savvy traveler and not falling for Taormina's tourist-trap "real" restaurants.

€–€€   About halfway down the "strip" of Corso Umberto, there's an Irish pub called **O'Seven** (Largo La Farina 6; ☎ 0942-24980; Tues–Sun noon–2am; MC, V; closed Jan 6–Feb 1). This a huge and cozy place, with multiple big-screen TVs tuned to various sporting events, where you can relax with a beer and a panino (from 4.50€, and they even have burgers). It isn't the least bit Sicilian, but it's a comfortable and low-key place for a quick meal.

€€–€€€   With a large back garden and fantastic seafood, **Licchio's** ✮✮ (Via C. Patricio 10; ☎ 0942-625327; Fri–Wed 7:45–11:30pm; MC, V) is the locals' favorite for dinner out. The vast menu starts with classic Sicilian and Mediterranean fare and then ventures into more creative territory (like delicious tuna burgers topped with sun-dried tomato salsa). Among the *antipasti* (6.50€–13€), sample the amazing fish carpaccios—the *cernia* (grouper) is served with a mustard-carrot sauce that perfectly complements the butteriness of the fish. Pastas (7€–16€) are rigorously homemade and paired only with what's in season. Waitstaff is young and hip but respectful of older clients. My only complaint would be about the lighting, which could be taken down a few watts, yet somehow the surgical brightness of it makes Licchio's seem all that more authentic.

€€–€€€   Around the corner from Licchio's, a slightly more elegant place to eat a less seafood-focused dinner is **L'Arco dei Cappuccini** ✮✮ (Via Cappuccini 1; ☎ 0942-24892; Thurs–Tues 7:45–11:30pm; AE, MC, V). The menu is more regional Italian than Sicilian, but it's sure to satisfy whatever you're craving, whether it's a hearty plate of Roman-style *spaghetti alla carbonara* (8€) or Sicilian *penne alla Norma* (8€), or a northern Italian dish like eggplant *alla parmigiana* (9€). On a recent visit, needing a break from seafood, I ordered the *filetto ai*

Shopping on Sicily

Taormina, Palermo, and Siracusa all boast chichi fashion boutiques, but shopping is not typically part of the Sicilian experience (unlike, say, in Rome, Florence, and Milan). Focus your purchases on artisanal foods, which can be packaged and easily put in suitcases for friends back home. Other souvenirs representing the soul of the island are colorful pottery, handmade puppets, and jewelry. The three-legged Trinacria, often reproduced in the form of an inexpensive terra-cotta wall-hanging, is said to represent the three points of Sicily. In Siracusa, you can buy items made of papyrus, which grows along the banks of the Ciane and Anapo rivers nearby.

funghi porcini dell'Etna (beef filet with porcini mushrooms gathered from the slopes of Mt. Etna, 15€), which was perfectly cooked, tender, and bursting with fresh and earthy flavor. If you want seafood, there's plenty of that on the menu, but at a higher price, with fish entrees ranging from 13€ to 20€. The wine list here will impress serious oenophiles.

CATANIA

Catania is a working-class town that relies far too heavily on Mt. Etna tourism. It just doesn't have the same sort of wonderful chaos as Palermo, nor does it possess the warm charm of Siracusa. You should only swing through Catania for a coffee break on your way up or down Mt. Etna, or if you're going to or coming from Fontanarossa Airport. Spend the night elsewhere.

DINING FOR ALL TASTES

However, good meals in Catania are easy to come by and inexpensive. Fresh seafood is standard in most restaurants and street snacks range from *crispelle* (fritters made with either anchovies or ricotta cheese) to *arancini di riso* (round rice balls in a light batter). And desserts in Catania are worth skipping lunch for. Most famous is Olivette di Sant'Agata, named for the patron saint who has protected this city against Mt. Etna's wrath for centuries. It's a scrumptious layered cake with almond paste, identifiable by its green coloring.

€   If you're planning to dine in Catania, try the tiny **Pesce Cotto** ✪ (Via S. Sofia 103b; ☎ 095-515959), but go early or book ahead because this perfect little trattoria has only three tables. The eatery survives on a substantial takeout business, which is also a viable option. You can't choose your meal, though, because you'll be served exactly what the chef is making that day. You can eat in the restaurant, with wine, for less than 10€.

€   A reliable choice for lunch or dinner is one of Catania's oldest restaurants, **Turi Finocchiaro** ✪ (Via E. Reina 13; ☎ 095-7153573; www.turifinocchiaro.it; Thurs–Tues 7:30–11:30pm, Sun 12:30–3pm; MC, V). The *antipasti* selection, displayed on a massive table near the entrance, is really enough for lunch. For bigger appetites, the seafood dishes are fresh and cost around 10€ for ample portions.

€ For late-night snacks and bar food, try **Guliven's** ✿ (Via Crociferi 69; ☎ 095-311192; daily noon–3pm and 7:30pm–midnight; MC, V), which offers the type of memorable experience you hope for. The outdoor tables butt up against the steps to the nearby church, on which live music, poetry readings, and other events are held throughout the year. The specialties here are dinner salads, cheese-and-salami plates, and stuffed sandwiches served with cold white wine.

MT. ETNA

You must go through at least the outskirts of Catania to see Sicily's best natural disaster in waiting, **Mt. Etna** ✿✿✿ (get latest information from Parco Naturale dell'Etna, Via Etna 107, Nicolosi, ☎ 095-821111, daily 9am–2pm and 4–7pm, www.parcoetna.ct.it; or from the Linguaglossa tourist office, Piazza Annunziata 5, ☎ 095-647352, daily 9am–3pm, www.prolocolinguaglossa.it). At 3,324m (10,903 ft.), Mt. Etna is the largest volcano in Europe, a giant in comparison to its mainland cousin, the 1,281m (4,202 ft.) Mt. Vesuvius near Naples. A visit to the summit is thrilling and unforgettable, one of Sicily's must-dos.

No matter what, you should always check with the authorities before starting up the peak. As recently as 2001, the monster showered the densely inhabited city of Catania with ash, and lava seeped within kilometers of the tiny village of Nicolosi—where residents brought out their trusty relics of Sant'Agata to ward off the volcano's wrath (Sant'Agata has been called on to protect this tiny village for centuries). Again in 2002, the mountain stirred, this time from the northern flanks, and hot lava wiped out a stylish ski resort and much of a lush pine forest. Mt. Etna has four summit craters and 200 cones (major and secondary). No one is allowed all the way up to the summit craters, but many of the nearby cones (about 300–400m/1,000–1,300 ft. lower) are approachable by guided tour. It's strongly recommended that you not try to explore the cones on your own. The expert source for up-to-date information on volcanic activity is the National Institute of Geophysics and Vulcanology (www.ct.ingv.it), and you can always ask the staff at your hotel if they've heard anything about Etna on the news lately—locals are usually tuned in to this kind of information.

Conditions at the summit area are extremely windy, which is exciting but not recommended for anyone with a heart or respiratory condition or balance problems. The lava near the cones is hot and slippery, and while the park officials will gladly sell you a ticket to the highest point, they don't check your footwear or give much in the way of eruption advice. There is, however, a tiny disclaimer on your ticket that releases them from responsibility should an eruption occur and you're not wearing sturdy shoes. You can rent hiking boots at the cable car station above Rifugio La Sapienza.

SIRACUSA

Sure, it's one of the most historically significant places in Sicily—in its prime, this ancient city took on both Carthage and Rome—but Siracusa is above all a delight, filled with baroque splendor and enough ancient attractions to keep you busy and

Visiting the Volcano

If you have a car, you can easily drive to the highest points on Mt. Etna that are accessible by regular vehicle. You can drive up the wooded northern slope of Etna and park at Rifugio Linguaglossa, then make your way to about 3,000m (9,840 ft.)—300m (1,000 ft.) below the summit—by special all-terrain vehicles. However, I'm partial to driving up the southern side and parking at Rifugio La Sapienza because the approach is filled with the barren lava rock of recent eruptions, reminding you of just what kind of mountain you're ascending, and because there's an exciting gondola (www.funiviaetna.com; daily 9am–5pm) from Rifugio La Sapienza that takes you to a higher staging area, where all-terrain vehicles then take you to the Torre Filosofo area, where there are some steaming cones.

The AST bus from Catania's main bus station will also get you there. The bus departs at 8:15am daily and arrives at Rifugio La Sapienza at 10:15am, and returning leaves Rifugio La Sapienza at 4:30pm, arriving in Catania at 6:30pm. The cost is 8€ round-trip (bus only).

The combined ticket for the funivia and all-terrain vehicles is 46€. If you're fit, you can even climb the 350m (1,150 ft.) from the upper gondola station to the crater area on foot and save 20€, but the footing here is an unfriendly mixture of loose pumice . . . and ladybugs. Believe it or not, Mt. Etna is home to millions of ladybugs *(coccinelle),* most of them dead—and you will no doubt crunch several as you walk around! At the crater area, there are some grizzled old *guide alpine* (mountain guides) who speak no English but are nevertheless colorful characters (who smoke cigarettes the entire time—at 3,000m/10,000 ft.!).

If you prefer not to go it alone on Mt. Etna, the following recommended tour companies will organize everything for you:

Centro Ippico Amico del Cavallo (Via A. Gramsci 27, Misterbianco; ☎ 095-461-882) offers horse rides through the farmland surrounding the volcano (7-hr. return) plus additional treks for 2 or 5 days.

Ferrovia Circumetna (Via Caronda 352a, Catania; ☎ 095-541250; www.circumetnea.it) has day treks that include transport from Catania for around 25€.

Natura e Turismo (Via R. Quartararo 11, Catania; ☎ 095-911505) offers expert treks around the craters with a volcanologist. Prices vary greatly depending on who is available and the size of your group.

happy for several days. Try to spend at least a few nights. In this laid-back seaside town, there are great restaurants and bars, and good shopping—and a sunny vibe that gets more addictive the more time you spend here. Siracusa is eminently tourist-friendly (with facilities like Internet points and laundromats that are cheaper and more accessible than other cities in Sicily) but not touristy, and in warm weather, you can reach lovely beaches within a 15-minute drive.

When the Greeks ruled Sicily, Siracusa was the most important coastal city on the island. Over the centuries, Siracusa produced some of Sicily's most creative thinkers, from the Greek poet Epicharmus to the physicist and mathematician Archimedes, to the winner of the 1959 Nobel Prize for Literature, Salvatore Quasimodo. The modern parts of Siracusa are sunny and friendly, but what visitors flock here for is the historic island of Ortygia, one of my favorite places on earth. Ortygia, the Old City, has been inhabited for thousands of years. The Duomo is here, as well as many ancient ruins, small crafts shops, boutiques, and charming, family-run restaurants. And, of course, there's the sea slapping relentlessly against the shore.

ACCOMMODATIONS, BOTH STANDARD & NOT

Siracusa has plenty of nifty little places to stay, so there's really no need to settle for the bland chain hotels in the modern part of town. The cheapest of the cheap are found near the train station, but for just a few euros more (and with some advance planning) you can stay on Ortygia—and it makes a world of difference being based here. In the summer, a number of Siracusan families convert their homes into makeshift B&Bs. Start with **www.sleepinsicily.it**, which offers rooms in the heart of Ortygia and villas in rural areas just outside of Siracusa (not bad if you have a car) for anywhere from 30€ to 52€ per person a night. Some of these private B&Bs are actually quite hotel-like in their ambience (for all the good and bad that implies), others have more character and the list is sure to expand in coming seasons, as almost all of Ortygia was a work site when I last visited. The back streets were thick with plaster dust as all the old baroque palazzi were being restored, with a good number of them I'm assuming to be converted to B&Bs and vacation rentals. Of those that I did see, I was impressed by how spotlessly clean and comfortable they were, with invariably friendly hosts.

€€   If you can't score a private B&B (see above), your pick on Ortygia should be the **Approdo delle Sirene** ✮✮✮ (Riva Garibaldi 15; ☎ 0931-24857; www.apprododellesirene.com; AE, MC, V), a fantastic and friendly new bed-and-breakfast along the waterfront (to the right as soon as you cross the bridge onto the island). The "Mermaid's Landing" is run by a charming and energetic mother and son, Fiora and Friedrich, who left Rome years ago for the laid-back shores of Siracusa. The place has a sort of contemporary-nautical vibe, with dark-wood floors, white cabinetry, and colorful striped linens. Rooms (100€ for a Standard double; 125€ with a view of the water) are spacious, airy, and immaculate, and all have their own private, well-equipped bathrooms. Fairly impressive for a B&B, all rooms also have A/C, TVs, phones, and minibars. This is also the only place I've ever stayed in Italy that advertises propertywide Wi-Fi where the Wi-Fi actually works everywhere, all the time, and there's no charge for it! Breakfast is included in the rate and served on the sunny panoramic terrace, and Fiora will even prepare a wonderful Sicilian dinner for you upon request. They also arrange canoe rentals and other excursions on the water (including scuba tours) and have bikes available for guests at no extra charge. There's a 2-night minimum stay requirement in June and August, but trust me, you'll want to stay at least that long here.

€€   In a light blue building on the quieter "back" (eastern) side of Ortygia, the **Hotel Gutkowski** ★ (Lungomare Vittorini 26; ☎ 0931-465861; www.guthotel.it; AE, MC, V) offers a modern, minimalist decor that may strike you as a little out of sync with this ancient town, but it sure is soothing. Water pressure is a bit of a problem here, and the bathrooms are tiny, even by Italian standards. Never mind—doubles are a reasonable 100€, and the rooms, though somewhat bare, are large. There's also a small roof terrace and a wine bar in the hotel, and they offer informal cooking classes and wine tastings on request.

€€€   A favorite hotel for return visitors is **Domus Mariae** ★★ (Via V. Veneto 76; ☎ 0931-24854; www.sistemia.it/domusmariae; MC, V), a converted convent attached to a working convent (which rents out rooms as well, when the hotel is full) on the eastern side of Ortygia. Domus Mariae is known for its impeccable, friendly service, perhaps because it's run by nuns who seem to live vicariously through their visitors, always curious about the day's excursions and genuinely pleased to meet new people. The rooms are large, especially considering the locale in the center of Ortygia, with comfortable furnishings. You can almost always get a sea view if you book ahead, and you can just as easily save 30€ per night if you forfeit the view. Double rooms start at 105€ without a view, 135€ with a view. The one oddity here: Rooms are cleaned only every other day.

DINING FOR ALL TASTES
€   Less than a minute's walk from Piazza del Duomo, the sleek indoor/outdoor wine bar **San Rocco** (Piazzetta San Rocco 3/5; ☎ 333-9854177; daily 5pm–1am) has a swell *aperitivo* spread (thick cuts of *salame* and mountains of couscous) and a young, hip atmosphere. The later it gets, the louder the Timbaland remixes blare, making this one of the better options for nightlife.

€€   In the words of Enzo Italia, proprietor of **Enoteca Solaria** ★★ (Via Roma 86; ☎ 0931-463007; www.enotecasolaria.com; Tues–Sat 5–11pm; MC, V), "a dinner without wine is like a day without sun." This is the most prestigious wine shop in Siracusa, so if you are not going to drink wine, pick somewhere else to eat. The meal is secondary to the wine but well made. A steak with salad is 9€, plates with ham and cheese 5€, all types of bruschettas are just 1.50€. A bottle of wine, which Enzo will select for you and have strong opinions about, costs from 10€ to 15€. It's worth knowing that Enzo is an ex-hippie and anarchist, so conservative Americans who don't welcome political debate may not feel comfortable here!

€€€   Arguably the finest restaurant in Siracusa is **Giovanni Guarneri's Don Camillo** ★★★ (Via Maestranza 96; ☎ 0931-67133; www.ristorantedoncamillo siracusa.it; Mon–Sat 12:30–3pm and 7:30–11pm; AE, MC, V; reservations recommended). It's the kind of place where long after you've eaten there, you'll remember exactly how every course looked, smelled, and tasted. Everything is elegantly presented and simply exquisite. For an *antipasto,* try the gorgeous marinated raw shrimp with pachino tomatoes, olive oil, and pepper (14€). You'll never be able to look at shrimp cocktail again. The restaurant's pasta specialty is the *spaghetti delle sirene* (15€), with shrimp and sea urchin (common in Sicily), a lovely dish with little mild orange bits of urchin at the height of freshness. The dining room, with exposed vaults of local limestone and antique bookcases and hutches, is slightly more formal than most restaurants on Ortygia, but don't let that keep you away—it's not a stuffy place.

WHY YOU'RE HERE: THE TOP SIGHTS & ATTRACTIONS

I suggest that you start on Ortygia and just walk around—it doesn't matter where. Whether you take the wide Corso Matteotti to the heart of Ortygia or meander along the web of tiny piazzas and side streets, you won't get lost, and without even trying, you'll likely see all the major sights, including the **Piazza del Duomo** ★★★. When I was planning my first visit to Siracusa several years ago, friends told me this was one of the most beautiful squares in all of Italy. I had seen a lot of piazzas in Italy, and I had my doubts that this could top them. But when I saw Siracusa's Piazza del Duomo in person, I had to agree. Its theatrical baroque perfection—honey-tinged stone, paving of white limestone, and continuous flow of lively people—seems to be the creation of Franco Zeffirelli or some other great set designer. At some point during your visit, sit down at one of the cafes here and watch the daily pageant go by. Dominating the square is the **Duomo (Cathedral)** ★★ (daily 8am–noon and 4–7pm), the former Greek Temple of Athena, with its 5th-century Doric columns providing the main support and needed balance against the gaudy baroque shell. The main altar is another surviving remnant from the Greeks, who first settled this island. The original temple was topped with a shiny golden statue of Athena that was visible from the sea and beckoned sailors to the island. (The smaller church on the square, behind a palm-treed courtyard, is the requisite church dedicated to Siracusa's patron saint, **Santa Lucia,** who was born here in the 3rd century A.D.) The striking **Palazzo Beneventano del Bosco** ★★ on the northwest side of the square is more theatrical perfection, with 12 convex, wrought-iron balconies on the main facade. Also on Piazza del Duomo and recently opened to the public (though hours are currently erratic) is an entrance to **Hypogeum** ★★ (look for the small door along the southeast side of the square; no phone; 3€; usually Tues–Sun 9am–1pm and 4–8pm), a network of underground chambers and corridors dug in World War II so that Siracusani could seek shelter here during air raids.

Along the west side of Ortygia, overlooking the harbor, you'll stumble upon the railings surrounding the sunken **Fonte Aretusa** ★★, an incredibly lovely (and rare) freshwater fountain that once served as the city's main water supply. During the summer, migratory ducks paddle around the fountain, and there's a dense clump of wispy papyrus growing in the middle of it. Smart cafes line the sidewalks above the Fonte Aretusa, where teens gather until late in the evening.

Deeper into the heart of the town, you'll come to **Piazza Archimede,** with a fountain that seems to draw the crowds for the evening passeggiata. Walking to the boardwalk that skirts the island, you'll pass the former **Jewish Ghetto** and the recently unearthed **Jewish Miqwe** (Via G.B. Alagona 52; ☎ 0931-22255; 5€; daily 10am–7pm), consisting of three freshwater pools used for ritual bathing, and a private pool for the rabbi. Near Piazza Pancali, back toward the bridges that connect Ortygia to modern Siracusa, are the ruins of the 6th-century-B.C. **Temple of Apollo** ★ (no access), the oldest Doric temple in Sicily.

I also highly recommend taking a **boat tour** ✦✦ around Ortygia. Several companies offer these excursions at comparable prices—just head down to the port (on the west side of Ortygia) and you'll see all the brightly colored signs advertising "island tours" or similar. The tour costs 8€ and lasts about 2 hours. Try to go at sunset if your schedule permits it. Many of these outfits also offer trips up the nearby rivers Ciane and Anapo, where dense papyrus grows. It's wonderfully atmospheric, like being on a miniature Nile cruise! You can also access these rivers yourself by taking Via Elorina (SS115) a kilometer or so south of town. Park at the bridge that crosses the Anapo and Ciane and you'll often find typical little rowboats waiting for passengers.

Attractions Elsewhere in Siracusa

There is plenty to do in Siracusa outside the old town of Ortygia, starting with what is unquestionably one of the finest archaeological museums in Italy, the **Museo Archeologico Regionale "Paolo Orsi"** ✦✦ (Via Cadorna; ☎ 0931-464022; 6€, or 9€ when combined with Parco Archeologico della Neapolis, below; Tues–Sat 9am–2pm). Sector A of the museum offers insight into the island's Stone Age and Bronze Age cultures, with rare prehistoric tools on display. Sector B focuses on the Greek and Roman settlements in the Siracusa area. The museum's most important possession is here: the headless Venus Landolina, from the Hellenistic period in the 2nd century B.C. The last sector is primarily home to artifacts found in eastern Sicily, including sculptures found near Agrigento.

The nearby **Parco Archeologico della Neapolis** ✦✦✦ (Via del Teatro; ☎ 0931-66206; 4.50€, or 6€ when combined with Museo Archeologico; daily 9am–2pm) is an excellent accompaniment to the museum. Pick up a map with your ticket because this is a working excavation in a constant state of evolution. Don't miss the **Latomia del Paradiso (Quarry of Paradise)** on the north side of the park. The Greeks used this lush and primeval-feeling garden area as a prison work camp, forcing penitents to mine limestone blocks. At the center is a manmade grotto called the **Orecchio di Dionisio.** Twenty-three meters (75 ft.) high and 65m (213 ft.) deep, it was used for theatrical performances after the prison closed down. Nearby is the **Grotta dei Cordari,** a pillar-supported cave where rope was manufactured. In the park you'll find the gigantic **Teatro Greco (Greek Theater),** one of the greatest ancient theaters, which could seat 16,000 people. The Italian Institute for Drama presents plays here in the summer in even-numbered years. Across the park is the **Anfiteatro Romano (Roman Amphitheater),** which is Italy's third largest (after the Colosseum in Rome and the amphitheater in Santa Maria Capua Vetere, near Naples). During the 2nd century A.D., gladiators fought to the death here, and mock sea battles were staged for the people of Siracusa and surrounding villages.

A DAY AT THE BEACH NEAR SIRACUSA

Just 30 minutes by bus or car from Siracusa is the beachside community of **Fontane Bianche.** The wide and soft sand beach and quiet and clean waters here make for a nifty half- or full-day getaway from the sightseeing grind. Entrance at any of the *stabilimenti* (beach clubs) is 5€, which gets you a beach chair and umbrella. By car, take Via Elorina, which becomes Rte. 115, toward Cassibile, and follow the signs to Fontane Bianche. In summer, there are also frequent buses from Siracusa's main bus terminal to the beach.

RAGUSA ★★

The province of Ragusa is rich in history and largely untouched by the outside world. Most Sicilians believe it is the most authentic of Italy's provinces, thanks to the absence of foreign invasions in modern times. Sicilian poet Gesualdo Bufalino appropriately calls it *"un'isola nell'isola"* (an island within the island). Virtually no tourists come here, and for me to urge you to start the trend seems almost sacrilegious. But it's such a wonderfully intriguing place, where unmarked roads wind through hills swathed in cascading vineyards and orchards. Small towns like Modica magically appear in the valleys. There is very much a *cultura contadina,* or peasant culture, here, which I hope will not soon succumb to the pressures of modernity. This is primarily a wine- and beef-producing area with pockets of oil production. Its asphalt is so durable that it's exported to weather-challenged countries like England.

Start in the provincial capital of Ragusa. Originally a Norman fortress, it grew to become one of the most important Hellenistic cities of the 5th through the 1st centuries B.C. Then an earthquake in 1693 destroyed much of this island and reduced the thriving city of Ragusa to rubble. Surviving businessmen built a new city, Ragusa Alta, on the top of the hill rather than along its flanks, but die-hard Ragusans refused to accept this new location and rebuilt a baroque version of ancient Ragusa exactly where it had been: clinging to the hillside. Today the ornate town at the base of the hill is known as Ragusa Bassa, or simply as Ibla (meaning "old"), and is unique on the island for its dazzling display of hillside architecture. It's hard to imagine churches built in a more precarious setting.

The two Ragusas coexisted separately until 1926, when they were officially joined as one municipality. Ragusa Alta has some baroque churches that are worth a peek, but your real gratification will come from spending a few hours wandering through the medieval streets of Ibla, below. The largest church, Basilica di San Giorgio, on Piazza Duomo, is so ominously top-heavy that it's a bit unnerving to stand near it. Midway up the massive steps, look directly up at the statues, which give the impression of movement—a trick that the famous architect Rosario Gagliardi repeated across this province in the many churches he designed, including the modest church of San Giuseppe.

Ragusa's whimsy continues all along its quaint streets. The Palazzo Arezzo, just off the Piazza Duomo, is covered with hedgehog sculptures. Nearby, at the Circolo di Conversazione, is the old haunt of Ragusa nobility, who came here to gain inspiration from the statues—of Michelangelo, Galileo, Dante, and Bellini—that still grace the somewhat faded interior.

As rich as the physical attributes of Ragusa seem, it's the people who make this place so special. There is still a sense of nobility among those who live in Ibla. If you take a leisurely lunch or morning coffee in the main Piazza Duomo square, you're likely to see working-class men kissing their superiors' hands when they greet them. The people here are welcoming to strangers and will go to great lengths to explain what's worth seeing in their town. There's a gracious friendliness here that could soon be spoiled by mass tourism, but for now few tour buses intrude on the quiet, and you should come and enjoy the tranquillity while it lasts.

From Ragusa (or Siracusa, above) try to make a side trip to Modica, which is a stunningly situated town that seems to spill into the valley from the top of two high hills. A monstrous auto bridge cuts the valley view in half from below, but does save hours in driving time by going over the valley rather than around it. Like Ragusa, Modica is divided into upper and lower sections and has been a victim of natural disasters for centuries. You may not want to base yourself here, but do stop by to see the glorious baroque **Chiesa di San Giorgio** in Modica Alta that sits atop a 250-step stairway. Modica was known as the Venice of the south until a devastating flood in 1902 wiped out the canals. The rivers have now been diverted and the gaps filled with cobblestone streets, perfect for walking.

ACCOMMODATIONS & DINING

€ A spartan place to sleep—though it's great if you have kids—is the tiny **Le Fiorere** ★ kids (Via Maria Paternò Arezzo 104, corner of Piazza Duomo; ☎ 0932-621530; www.bblefioriere.it; MC, V), which has two mini-apartments with stoves and fridges for just 65€ low season, 80€ high season, including breakfast and parking. The rooms are not swank, but they're the next best thing to living in a Ragusa apartment. The owners even bring up morning breakfast from the coffee bar below.

€€ **Il Barocco** ★★ (Via Orfanotrofio 29; ☎ 0932-663105; www.ilbarocco.it; Thurs–Tues 12:30–3pm and 7:30–10:30pm; MC, V) is a one-stop hotel and restaurant that has evolved from a four-room bed-and-breakfast, and that has handled basically all the city's visitors for decades. They offer lovely double rooms with original antiques, large bathrooms, and sweeping views of the town or valley below from 100€. A suite costs from 120€. The restaurant (☎ 0932-652397) is a true find, offering authentic southern Sicilian cuisine like vermicelli with *seppie* (cuttlefish) and creative seafood dishes based on the season, most under 12€ a plate. There is even an ice-cream parlor with freshly made flavors based only on seasonal fruits.

€€–€€€ The finest restaurant in Ibla is **Il Duomo** (Via Bocchieri 31; ☎ 0932-651265; Tues–Sat 12:30–3pm and 7:30–11:30pm, Sun 12:30–3pm; www.ristorante duomo.it; AE, MC, V), just a block from the cathedral in the old town. Try the bread homemade from local wheat, and dip it in some of the 20-odd types of olive oil. Menus change with the seasons, and main courses range from 9€ to 16€. Also near the cathedral is **La Bettola** (Largo Camerina 7; ☎ 0932-653377), with its kitschy, 1940s prewar decor. My favorite dishes here are the homemade penne and the herb-infused chicken breast.

CENTRAL SICILY

One sight in particular deserves your attention in this region. **Villa Romana del Casale** ★★★ (near Piazza Armerina; ☎ 0935-680036; www.villaromanadel casale.it; adults 6€, seniors and students 3€; daily 8am–6:30pm), along the road from Palermo to either Siracusa or Agrigento, is widely considered to be the most significant Roman site on the island for its magnificent, gory, dramatic, and delightful (oh, and amazingly well-preserved) mosaics. The villa was built in the early 4th century, probably by Maximianus Herculeus, who ruled with Diocletian from A.D. 286 to 305. It was abandoned over time, ravaged by wars, and then buried under many feet of mud in a torrential storm in the 12th century. It remained covered for more than 700 years. Only in the 1950s did true excavation begin, and it still continues in various parts of the villa. The compound consists of some 40 rooms, most of which are still set with original mosaics. Don't attempt this site without one of the official maps—the catwalklike routes are constantly changing and very disorienting. A major restoration is underway at the site and is scheduled to wrap up by early 2009, at which time accessibility and visibility should be greatly improved. The most important mosaics, in the *palestra,* portray scenes from the Circus Maximus in Rome. These are the only ones of their kind in Italy. Farther along the eastern part of the villa is a great corridor with a mosaic hunting scene, *Ambulacro della Scena della Grande Caccia,* depicting African animals brought to Rome for battles with gladiators. In the **Sala delle Dieci Ragazze** (aka the Sala delle Ragazze in Bikini) are the oft-photographed bikini-clad women (note the physiques of these ladies and the jam-jar barbells they're lifting). If it's open, also try to get a glimpse of the elliptical courtyard.

AGRIGENTO

You must fit a trip to the phenomenal Greek ruins of Agrigento's Valley of the Temples into your Sicilian agenda. But you should not stay there overnight. Much of the area is marred with unfinished shells of buildings that are built quickly at night before local authorities can stop them. Known as *abusivismi,* they are built without permits, often, it is said, for the financial benefit of organized-crime syndicates, and many end up being abandoned. Many of them are plainly visible from the **Valley of the Temples** ✹✹✹ (Archaeological Park, Via dei Templi entrance indicated by signposts; 6€; western zone daily 8:30am–7:30pm, eastern zone daily 8:30am–10pm). Founded a century after Selinunte (p. 613), Agrigento followed much the same arc—slowly growing to prosperity, expanding its population, investing in its temples—until its run-ins with the ferocious Carthaginians. The city became a colony of Carthage until 210 B.C., when it fell into Roman hands.

GETTING THERE

Agrigento is an easy day trip from Palermo on the northern coast or from Siracusa on the southern coast. Cuffaro runs buses from Palermo to Agrigento every few hours; the 2-hour trip costs 7.20€ round-trip. Check the seasonal schedule at any tabacchi. Try to avoid buses on Sundays, when schedules rarely apply. Trains are more reliable but also more expensive (7.45€ one-way), departing for the 2-hour trip from Palermo's central station every 2 hours. From Siracusa, consider taking a chartered excursion booked through Sicily's tourism bureau (www.compagnia sicilianaturismo.it). These van tours shuttle small groups to a site for around 40€. I recommend them because they streamline the process of getting there from farther-flung places like Siracusa. This is especially important when you're there in the summer and the last thing you want to deal with after a sweaty day in Agrigento is slow and multiple means of transportation back to your base. Here's what I mean: If you take the train from Siracusa you must first travel to Catania and then switch to Agrigento; the trip can take 4 to 6 hours each way. In your own car, the drive from Palermo takes about 2½ hours.

TOURING THE RUINS

The archaeological park and museum, which lie in the plain below the town, are all you really need to visit on this part of the southern coast. It can be uncomfortably hot here in summer, so to beat the heat start in the western zone in the early morning, break up the day with a leisurely lunch and a visit to the museum, and then head to the eastern zone, which is open until 10pm. Better yet, come in the off season. In the late winter, from February to early April, the whole valley is covered with almond blossoms.

The western zone is dominated by the **Temple of Zeus,** which was never completed, thanks to a Carthaginian battle and a subsequent earthquake. Had it been finished, it would have been the largest temple ever built, with 20m-high (66-ft.) Doric columns. Here you'll find the famous 8m-tall (26-ft.) telamon (Atlas), meant to support the structure. The nearby **Temple of Dioscuri (Temple of Castor and Pollux)** is composed of fragments from different buildings. At various times it honored Castor and Pollux (twin sons of Leda); Demeter (Ceres), the goddess of marriage; and Persephone, the personification of spring. Across the Via dei Templi is the eastern zone of the archaeological park. This is a far more complex area, home to the oldest and most impressive of the temples. The first temple to your right after the entrance is the **Temple of Hercules,** which was built in the 6th century B.C. to honor, yes, Hercules. At one time it ranked in size with the Temple of Zeus; today only eight pillars are standing. As you wander through the site, peek out at the distant sea, a reminder that these temples stood as a beacon to sailors and shone brightly through the day under the brutal Sicilian sun, the gold decorations no doubt adding to the sparkle. The next large temple is the nearly intact **Temple of Concord,** with its 34 columns. In the 4th century A.D. it was consecrated as a basilica, which saved it from abandonment. The original intent of this temple is a mystery; it was only named the Temple of Concord in 1748, when it was restored to the state that you see today.

The last of the major temples in the eastern zone is the **Temple of Hera,** which was used for sacrificial offerings (the red is not remnant blood, though, but the scars of fires during various wars).

The **Museo Archeologico** (Via dei Templi; ☎ 0922-40111; adults 6€, students and seniors 3€; Mon 9am–1:30pm, Tues–Sat 9am–6pm) is a comprehensive museum with very detailed explanations in both Italian and English of the many artifacts unearthed in this area. Of note are the prehistoric findings from the area and a plan of the ancient city of Akragas (the old Greek name for Agrigento). The prize piece is the red ceramic krater from 490 B.C. that was used to mix wine and water. Many similar kraters were illegally excavated from ruins in this area and sold to American museums. This museum also has a full telamon (an architectural support in the form of a man—the male version of a caryatid) and several telamon heads similar to the one found above in the Temple of Zeus.

SELINUNTE

Like so many of the ancient ruins you see across Italy, Selinunte reminds me of how fleeting empires can be, and how even the most magnificent buildings and cities decay and disappear. One of the mightiest and most powerful of the Greek outposts, Selinunte was founded in the 7th century B.C. by immigrants from Syracuse who thrived in this coastal locale, building temple after temple as a thank

Selinunte

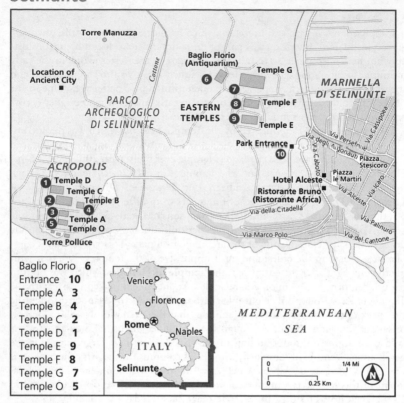

Map labels (clockwise / by area):

Torre Manuzza

Location of Ancient City

Baglio Florio (Antiquarium) — 6

Temple G — 7

PARCO ARCHEOLOGICO DI SELINUNTE

Cortone

MARINELLA DI SELINUNTE

EASTERN TEMPLES

Temple F — 8

Temple E — 9

Park Entrance — 10

Via degli Argonauti · Via Cassiopea · Via Persefne · Via Caboto

Piazza Stesicoro

Piazza le Martiri

ACROPOLIS

Temple D — 1

Temple C — 2

Temple B

Temple A — 4

Temple O — 5

Hotel Alceste

Ristorante Bruno (Ristorante Africa)

Via della Citadella

Via Alceste · Via Icaro · Via Palinuro

Torre Polluce

Via Marco Polo · Via del Cantone

Legend:

Baglio Florio	6
Entrance	10
Temple A	3
Temple B	4
Temple C	2
Temple D	1
Temple E	9
Temple F	8
Temple G	7
Temple O	5

Venice · Florence · Rome · Naples · ITALY · Selinunte

MEDITERRANEAN SEA

0 — 1/4 Mi
0 — 0.25 Km

you to the gods for their generosity. The statues and friezes they created for these temples now fill the museums in Palermo; once you've seen them, you'll want to journey to their source. At the height of its glory, the ancient city had some 100,000 residents. The death blow came in 250 B.C., when Carthage pillaged Selinunte, not once but twice. It was forgotten until the 16th century, when Sicilians started to settle this area once again.

Getting There

Selinunte is 122km (76 miles) southwest of Palermo and 113km (70 miles) west of Agrigento. If you're driving from Palermo or Agrigento, allow at least 2 hours. The easiest way to get there without your own wheels is by train to Castelvetrano. Shuttle buses for 2.50€ (get your ticket first in the tabacchi inside the train station) run half-hourly from the train station to the site.

Touring the Ruins

Approaching this archaeological grave land, most are overwhelmed by its haunting desolation. The ruins of the once-mighty temples, most of them built in the 5th century B.C., lie in vulnerable heaps along the cliff tops above the sea. They fell in stages, as mighty earthquakes shook this region.

The site has two main areas: the **Acropolis and the Eastern Temples** ★★ 😊 (☎ 0924-46251; 5€; Mon–Sat 9am to 1 hr. before sunset, Sun 9am–noon and 3–7pm). In the Acropolis the temples are brilliantly named A, B, C, D, E, F, G, and O. Ask for the free site map at the ticket stand (they won't offer it unless you ask). The oldest is **Temple C,** dedicated to Apollo, which was built in the mid–6th century B.C. Many of the exhibits in Palermo's archaeological museum (p. 585) were unearthed at Temple C, including the Gorgon mask. The next oldest is believed to be **Temple D,** which was built in the late 6th century B.C. and dedicated to Neptune. The Eastern Temples area of the site, dominated by **Temple G,** is a short walk up a gravel road. Most endearing of all these temples is Temple E, partly because it was so completely reconstructed in the 1950s, and partly because of the way the columns reflect the sun and cast shadows on the plateau. These are magical ruins, which invite you to wander around for hours. They're also especially child-friendly, with bathrooms, refreshment stands, and lots of wide-open spaces.

WESTERN SICILY: TRAPANI PROVINCE

This is the heart of what was historically Muslim Sicily and, surprisingly, the home of the famously sweet Sicilian Marsala wine. Unfortunately, it's become touristy and expensive in recent years, but the byproduct is a full agenda of community activities, mostly centered in the provincial capital of Trapani. During the summer

Erice: Honeymooner Heaven

The city of Trapani is not the province's favorite city. That honor goes to tiny Erice, dramatically perched high in the mountains (at 743m/2,437 ft.) and known for its Carthaginian walls, still covered with Punic etchings and symbols, and the lovely 14th-century Duomo, Chiesa Matrice, at its heart. The city was founded by early Mediterranean settlers called the Elymians, who worshipped the goddess of fertility (Astarte to the Elymians, Aphrodite to the Greeks, and Venus to the Romans). Early Elymian art depicts her annual winter departure with a random escort to her shrine in what is now El Kef, in Tunisia. When she returned, springtime began in Sicily. Superstitious Sicilians, who wish to honor the goddess of fertility, honeymoon here even today. Many couples who are hoping to begin a family book a room in one of the small pensioni that line the narrow cobblestone streets. Romans even practiced a form of holy prostitution in Erice by keeping women of the night (and day) in the city temple to service the local men.

Erice is also deliciously famous for its sweet cakes. They are replicated all across the island, but none are as wonderfully decadent as the originals here. If you'd like your own romantic tryst, try the reasonably priced **Edelweiss** (Cortile Padre Vincenzo; ☎ 0923-869158; no website; MC, V), where rooms start at 82€ per double, per night. I'd add that because the town gets overrun with tour buses during the daytime, an overnight stay is key to discovering its charms.

there are outdoor plays, concerts, and fairs almost every weekend. This area makes a fun-filled day trip from Palermo, but staying here isn't recommended unless you're willing to spend a lot for very little. The region around Trapani is one of Sicily's richest, producing coral, tuna, and salt. Don't even bother looking at Trapani until you get past the concrete jungle on the outskirts and dive into the old historical center, which is a fine mess of tangled streets that intersect with Via Garibaldi and the Corso Vittorio Emanuele. Once here, don't miss the **Cattedrale di San Lorenzo** (Corso Vittorio Emanuele; ☎ 0923-432111), styled in classic 18th-century baroque.

EGADI ISLANDS

To round out your visit to Sicily, consider a quick jaunt to the islands of the Egadi archipelago. Ferries run from Trapani and Marsala, take about 10 to 20 minutes, and cost between 4€ and 7€, depending on the season.

Levanzo is best known for its Grotta del Genovese with its cave etchings of bison and deer—animals one doesn't automatically associate with Sicily. Visiting the caves is an adventure unto itself because you must first locate the custodian, Signor Natale Castiglione, who will either be at his souvenir shop just behind the port or at ☎ 339-7418800 (ncasti@tin.it). For 6€ (by foot) or 12€ (by boat), he'll take you deep into the caves. You can try to find the caves yourself, but they're not well marked and the trek with Mr. Castiglione is far more colorful.

For a taste of island wildlife, pick up a local hiking map. This is also a good island for swimming, sunbathing, or fishing (contact the San Giuseppe Association at ☎ 0923-923290).

15 The Essentials of Planning

by Keith Bain

PLANNING CAN MAKE OR BREAK A TRIP, ESPECIALLY WHEN IT COMES TO pricey Italy. In the pages that follow, I'll cover all the essential information, from when to go, to where to book, to what travelers with special needs—families, people with disabilities, and others—need to know before they hop on the plane.

In addition to this book, the Italian Government Tourist Board operates a better-than-expected website (www.italiantourism.com) with masses of resources—addresses, travel articles, information about latest events and festivities—that will get you excited about your trip. The massive Italian-based travel agency www.itwg.com can also be quite a good resource to troll for deals. And www.ultimateitaly.com carries information about just about every aspect of life, culture, and travel in Italy.

WHEN TO VISIT

Spring and fall (Apr to early June and Sept–Oct), are the best times to visit Italy. Temperatures are lovely, crowds are fewer, and the country is open for business. Late June through August, tourists overrun the country, the sun is blazing, and 90% of the country is on vacation in August (mostly at the same beach), with many hotels, restaurants, and some sights closed. November through March is the cheapest time to visit, with most hotels charging off-season rates and airfares being significantly less expensive. But, like in August, many locals take vacation during this time, which means a shortage of good restaurant and hotel options, and limited hours at sights.

Italy's Major Festivals

You may want to gear your visit to one of the following special celebrations. Yes, prices for hotels will be at their peak during these times, but the excitement of seeing these events may well make the splurge a worthy one.

March/April

Ravello Music Festival (Mar to early Aug and Sept to early Nov): A world-famous music event is set in this cliff-hugging Amalfi town—the stage juts out from a cliff high above the sea, making the setting every bit as spectacular as the lineup.

Easter Holiday Celebrations: Virtually every city in Italy has a series of traditional celebrations during Holy Week. The Vatican is obviously at the center of things, with the pope leading a procession across Rome. On Easter Sunday he blesses the huge crowds from his balcony at St. Peter's. Florence and Orvieto have similar celebrations, known as **Scoppio del Carro (Explosion of the Cart),** on Easter Sunday, during which a mechanical dove drops from a wire to ignite a cart full of fireworks, while oxen pull the cart in a procession around town to the Duomo.

Maggio Musicale Fiorentino (until June): Opera, ballet, and modern music are presented in major Florence theaters and free on the piazzas.

May

Maggio dei Monumenti: Naples's Monument of May celebrations feature concerts in the piazzas, exhibitions and fairs everywhere, and palazzi open for the public to admire.

Corso dei Ceri (Race of the Saints' Candles): On May 15, Gubbio becomes a mob scene for this race of three 9m-tall (30-ft.) shrines up the streets and the mountain above the town.

June

Festival di Ravenna (mid-June to July): Ravenna hosts a world-renowned classical-music festival, with ballet and opera performances also on the roster.

Calcio in Costume (late June): Florence stages a series of medieval rugby matches with players in traditional costume, with the finals around June 24.

Spoleto Festival (until July): An annual music-and-arts festival featuring some of the top performers in the world (in Spoleto, of course).

Festa di San Pietro: In honor of St. Peter's feast day, Rome holds a series of ceremonies around St. Peter's Basilica toward the end of the month.

Giostra del Saracino: Mid-June jousting matches are staged in Arezzo's main square, with processions of costumed characters across town.

July

Shakespeare Festival: Verona hosts a series of plays, ballets, and music related to Shakespeare.

Il Palio (through Aug): Siena's major event is a crazy bareback horse race around the central piazza. Neighborhoods hold parties in support of their team during this 2-month time period. The races take place July 2 and August 16.

Umbria Jazz: Perugia's annual world-class jazz festival attracts top names to every venue in the city in mid-July.

Festa del Redentore: Venice celebrates the town's freedom from the plague in 1578. The third weekend in July is marked with fireworks, boating events, and other festivities.

Festa International di Musica Antica: Italy's largest Renaissance and baroque music festival is held in Urbino.

August

Venice International Film Festival (late Aug to early Sept): This is akin to France's Cannes Film Festival.

September

Regata Storica: Venice's annual gondola and boat festival, with processions through the canals and races on the first Sunday in September.

Festa dell Uva: Chianti's annual grape harvest and wine-swilling festival happens in Impruneta, the last Sunday in September, with historical processions and plenty of tastings. Also check out the Chianti Classico festival the second Sunday of the month, in Greve.

December

Christmas Festivities: Major celebrations in cities across Italy are highlighted by the pope's blessing Christmas Day in St. Peter's Square, and by the display of the Virgin's girdle in Prato.

ENTRY REQUIREMENTS

If you're traveling to Italy you must have a valid passport that expires at least 6 months later than the scheduled end of their visit. If you are going to be in Italy for more than 3 months, or are planning to take up studies or a job while you're in the country, you'll need to get a permit to stay (permesso di soggiorno),

The Climate at a Glance

Italy has hot, dry summers, with temperatures reaching the 90s (30s Celsius) and higher from Florence southward, and unless you get up into the Alps, the northern towns don't get a whole lot cooler. In winter, northern regions of Italy have rain and some snow, but from central Italy on south it usually doesn't get much cooler than the 50s (10s Celsius), though some winter nights will require a jacket, and occasionally snow will fall in a central Italy hill town.

Italy's Average Daily Temperature & Monthly Rainfall

Rome	Jan	Feb	Mar	Apr	May	June	July	Aug	Sept	Oct	Nov	Dec
Temp. (°F)	49	52	57	62	72	82	87	86	73	65	56	47
Temp. (°C)	9	11	14	17	22	28	31	30	23	18	13	8
Rainfall (in.)	2.3	1.5	2.9	3.0	2.8	2.9	1.5	1.9	2.8	2.6	3.0	2.1

Florence	Jan	Feb	Mar	Apr	May	June	July	Aug	Sept	Oct	Nov	Dec
Temp. (°F)	45	47	50	60	67	76	77	70	64	63	55	46
Temp. (°C)	7	8	10	16	19	24	25	21	18	17	13	8
Rainfall (in.)	3	3.3	3.7	2.7	2.2	1.4	1.4	2.7	3.2	4.9	3.8	2.9

Naples	Jan	Feb	Mar	Apr	May	June	July	Aug	Sept	Oct	Nov	Dec
Temp. (°F)	50	54	58	63	70	78	83	85	75	66	60	52
Temp. (°C)	10	12	14	17	21	26	28	29	24	19	16	11
Rainfall (in.)	4.7	4	3	3.8	2.4	.8	.8	2.6	3.5	5.8	5.1	3.7

which can be arranged once you're in the country, usually from a local police station.

For Residents of the U.S.: Whether you're applying in person or by mail, you can download passport applications from the **U.S. State Department** website at http://travel.state.gov. For general information, call the **National Passport Information Center** (☎ 877-4872778).

For Residents of Australia: You can pick up an application from your local post office or any branch of Passports Australia, but you must schedule an interview at the passport office to present your application materials. Call the **Australian Passport Information Service** (☎ 131-232), or visit the government website at www.passports.gov.au.

For Residents of Canada: Passport applications are available at travel agencies throughout Canada or from the central **Passport Office** (Department of Foreign Affairs and International Trade, Ottawa, ON K1A 0G3; ☎ 800-5676868; www.ppt. gc.ca). *Note:* Canadian children who travel must have their own passport. However, if you hold a valid Canadian passport issued before December 11,

2001, that bears the name of your child, the passport remains valid for you and your child until it expires.

For Residents of Ireland: You can apply for a 10-year passport by sending an application to either of the country's two **Passport Offices** (P.O. Box 9718, Co. Dublin; ☎ 01-6711633; or 1A South Mall, Cork; ☎ 021-4944700; http://foreign affairs.gov.ie). Children ages 3 to 17 must obtain a 25€, 5-year passport; under-3s get a 15€, 3-year passport. You can generate application forms online or get them at most main post offices.

For Residents of New Zealand: You can pick up a passport application at any **New Zealand Passports Office** (☎ 0800-225050 in New Zealand; or 04-4748100) or download it from www.passports.govt.nz.

For Residents of the U.K.: To pick up an application for a standard 10-year passport (5-year passport for children under 16), visit your nearest passport office, major post office, or travel agency, or contact the **United Kingdom Passport Service** (☎ 0870-5210410; www.ukpa.gov.uk).

GETTING THE BEST AIRFARE TO ITALY

High season on most airlines' routes to Italy is usually from June to September. This is the most expensive and crowded time to travel. **Shoulder season** is April to May, early September to October, and December 15 to December 24. **Low season** is November 1 to December 14 and December 25 to March 31.

FROM NORTH AMERICA   Fares to Italy are constantly changing, but you can expect to pay somewhere in the range of $498 to $800 for a round-trip ticket from New York to Rome in coach class in any but the summer months; a fair summer average fare in 2008 is $1,210. Rates from other major East Coast airports (Philadelphia; Boston; Washington, D. C.) won't be much higher. Next in the price pantheon are the other major international hubs, such as Chicago (where you'll add $100–$200 to these rates) or Los Angeles (I've seen prices go for just $100–$300 more from there, as well). Rates really rise when you're flying in from smaller gateways (such as Louisville, Billings, Madison, or Oklahoma City). In such cases, you may want to find the cheapest airfare into New York City and then add on the cheapest airfare from there to Italy (or if you're really a cost cutter, from there to London, which is the cheapest European hub, and then another flight into Rome).

Choosing the right airline can be a good way to save. **British Airways** (☎ 800-AIRWAYS; www.britishairways.com), **Virgin Atlantic Airways** (☎ 800-8215438; www.virgin-atlantic.com), **Air France** (☎ 800-2372747; www.airfrance. com), **Northwest/KLM** (☎ 800-2252525; www.nwa.com), and **Lufthansa** (☎ 800-6453880; www.lufthansa-usa.com) offer some attractive deals for anyone interested in combining a trip to Italy with a stopover in, say, Britain, Paris, Amsterdam, or Germany. Sometimes your best-value deal might be to fly to London with either British Airways or Virgin Atlantic (or any of the North American airlines), and then catch a no-frills/budget flight (with EasyJet or Ryanair, for example) to Italy. See "From the United Kingdom" (below) for more details on this method.

Another budget option concerns a new player on the market, **Eurofly** (www.euroflyusa.com), which flies only from New York City, but often has fares so low (in spring of 2008, it was selling New York–Rome for just $399 *including* the $300 fuel surcharge), it may well be worth your while to fly into the Big Apple on another carrier and then hop your transatlantic flight from there. It flies into numerous cities in Italy. Be sure to check out its rates before booking (it's also a good source for air-hotel packages).

FROM THE UNITED KINGDOM   I now have two favorite sources for inexpensive airfares from the U.K. to, well, really any place on the continent of Europe (and that includes Italy). LowCostAirlines.org maintains up-to-the-minute listings of no-frills carriers throughout Europe. Even more helpful is the brand-new aggregator site Momondo.com, a Danish search engine that collects data from some 600 carriers worldwide, making it the most complete search around. I've found fares on this site—legitimate, inexpensive ones—that I haven't found anywhere else. Search here if you want to hop a jet from the U.K.

British newspapers and some magazines (*Time Out,* for instance) are good resources for classified ads touting slashed fares to Italy. You'll usually see **Trailfinders** (☎ 0845/058-5858; www.trailfinders.com) listed there; it consolidates bulk ticket purchases and then passes the savings on to its consumers. It offers access to tickets on such carriers as SAS, British Airways, and KLM.

The best thing about flying in from the U.K. is the abundance of no-frills or budget airline flights—top deals are available from **Ryanair** (www.ryanair.com), **EasyJet** (www.easyjet.com), and **bmibaby** (www.bmibaby.com); there are flights to many more destinations—including some "smaller" cities—than you might find with the major airlines, and at rates so low they'll make your head spin. Usually the lowest rates go to those who book well in advance (so do your homework as soon as you know you're going). Just be aware of all the rules pertaining to these flights (only available online); for example; you can't change your flight dates, and may have to pay a small surcharge for each piece of check-in luggage. Also, no-frills means no free beverages or food on board. If you're flying into the U.K. from somewhere else, be aware that you may need to change airports within London, since the low-cost carriers invariably fly from Gatwick, Stansted, or Luton airports rather than Heathrow, where most international flight arrive.

OTHER METHODS FOR SAVING ON AIR

Beyond the suggestions listed above, here are some additional ways to keep your airfare costs down:

- Passengers who **fly midweek** or during less trafficked hours may pay a fraction of the full fare. If your schedule is flexible, say so, and ask if you can secure a cheaper fare by changing your plans.
- **Search the Internet** for cheap fares (see "Surfing for Airfares," below).
- If you're using London as a hub and you're planning to travel around Italy, consider searching for two sets of one-way tickets arriving and departing from different airports that are closer to where you want to be at the start and end of your journey. Many travelers find themselves wasting time and money returning to a point of arrival in order to make an outbound connection.

Traditionally, one-way flights have always been more expensive, but with the low-cost airlines and certain online fares offered by the larger airlines (including British Airways, in many instances), this is not actually the case. So you could easily fly from London to Rome (or Naples), and then at the end of your trip, depart from Venice or Milan, or whatever city you've chosen as your final port of call in Italy.

♦ **Consider booking through a consolidator: STA Travel** (www.statravel. com; p. 631) has been the world's lead consolidator for students since purchasing Council Travel, but their fares are competitive for travelers of all ages. **Flights.com** (www.flights.com) often has excellent fares to Europe. A company simply called **Airline Consolidator** (www.airlineconsolidator.com) can also be a good source. *Note:* Always compare the rates found through these sites with the ones obtained directly from the airline. There's no guarantee that their fares will be lower, and sometimes the change penalties they add on are even more draconian than those of the airlines.

♦ **Join frequent-flier clubs.** Frequent-flier membership doesn't cost a cent, but it does entitle you to rack up mileage toward free flights. And you don't have to fly to earn points; frequent-flier credit cards can earn you thousands of miles for doing your everyday shopping. With more than 70 mileage awards programs on the market, consumers have never had more options, but the system has never been more complicated—what with more and more mileage holders competing for the same number of seats, and airlines frequently changing their policies. So research the various programs thoroughly; an excellent source of advice is Tim Winship's column on SmarterTravel.com. Access to Winship's advice is free.

PACKAGES VS. INDEPENDENT TRAVEL

The major Italian cities, in particular Rome and Florence, are some of the top destinations in the world for travel packages—by which I mean travel products that bundle together airfare, hotel, and sometimes car at one reasonable price. Why? Because these überdeveloped destinations have hundreds of hotel rooms that need to be filled year-round. Though the cheapest of these packages traditionally use mainstream, somewhat dull hotels, booking a travel package can result in big savings—in some cases costing $100 a day or less for airfare and hotel (not including taxes or security fees). No, you won't have the choicest of lodgings, but you will get a clean, convenient place to stay (always with private bathroom), perfect for those simply using their hotel as a place to crash after long days of viewing art and eating pasta.

Go-Today.com is the first site you should check. It serves every gateway in the United States, and offers a number of well-priced options that include weeklong stays in one city, air/car-rental packages allowing you to tour the countryside, and deals allowing you to stay in a couple of cities (Rome and Paris or Rome-Florence-Venice are two of their most popular offerings). Deals are phenomenal in the off season (as little as $889 round-trip with airfare from New York to Italy and then touring Rome, Florence, and Venice—with train travel and hotels included—for 9 nights per person sharing; single rates are more expensive) but obviously less attractive in summer. Be sure to total all the costs—including additional airport taxes and security fees—when you're shopping around.

Surfing for Airfares

By far the best way to search for airfares to Italy is to use the "aggregator" websites, so named because they don't sell travel, but simply aggregate information on what the other sites are offering (they then get a commission from these sites if you make a booking via their search). Because they usually take you directly to the airlines' websites, you bypass the fees charged by such online travel agencies as **Expedia, Travelocity,** and **Orbitz** (also, the aggregators don't allow companies to pay for placement, yielding a more logical search). Best of all, if one of the big three named above is having a special on airfares to Italy, that will come up in an aggregator search. The top four aggregators right now are **Kayak** (www.kayak.com), **Momondo** (www.momondo.com), **Sidestep** (www.sidestep.com), and **FareCompare** (www.farecompare.com). Of those, Momondo may have the edge as it now searches over 600 airlines and travel agencies worldwide. FareCompare and Sidestep, however, have a nifty tool that allows travelers to see fares by the month, allowing them to choose the cheapest months and days to travel. If you can be flexible on your dates of travel, I highly recommend **CheapFlights.com,** which works with small discounters, allowing them to post their lowest fares online with no dates attached (you then contact the site in question directly to book travel). Each of the smaller sites searched by CheapFlights.com has different business deals with the airlines and may offer different fares on the same flights, so it's wise to shop around.

Gate 1 Travel (☎ 800-6823333; www.gate1travel.com) is Go-Today.com's fiercest competitor and often matches its rates (occasionally undercutting them). It, too, offers many permutations on the standard air/hotel package: air/car, air/train, and hotel/tour guide/bus, among others. Nonpeak season 8-day packages in Tuscany, for example, including a four-star hotel accommodations and airfare, with all transfers, some meals, and a guide, start at $1,499 per person sharing, which is quite good considering that's what many plane tickets go for.

1-800-FlyEurope (☎ 800-3593876; www.1800flyeurope.com) is the best place to go for airfare/car-rental deals. Three more packagers to keep in mind (though they rarely beat the three above): **TourCrafters** (☎ 800-6212259; www.tourcrafters.com), **Italiatour** (www.italiatour.com)—great because it specializes in Italian destinations—and **EuropeASAP** (www.europeasap.com), which also dishes up good fly-and-drive specials.

A few other things to keep in mind when booking a package:

- Prices are always based on double occupancy, so these might not be good deals for solo travelers.
- Be sure to crunch numbers before booking: Look at the seasonal airfare to Italy at the time you'll be going (do a search on an aggregator site; see "Surfing for Airfares," above) and then subtract that to find out how much

Untours

As the name implies, **Untours** (☎ 888-8686871 or 610-5655242 from outside the U.S.; www.untours.com) is an alternative-travel company that specializes in booking airfare and 2-week stays at a local apartment, farmhouse, or cottage. Unlike standard apartment rental companies, they have a representative on-site who Untours participants can seek out should they need help booking sightseeing tours or dealing with a problem in the apartment. They have a near cultlike following from customers who enjoy a more concentrated, local oriented vacation rather than a city-a-day-type tour. Untours books locations around Venice, Rome, Sicily, and Tuscany (including Florence), and Umbria.

---

you're paying for the specific hotel room. If you can do better, book separately.

- Packages are usually only good for the major cities: Rome, Florence, Venice, sometimes Milan, and sometimes the ski resort areas. If you're hoping to go to Ravenna or Perugia, this method probably won't work for you (though there are fly/drives that may make sense, as car rental in Italy is the priciest in western Europe).

- **Read the fine print.** Sometimes cancellation policies on packages are ugly. Consider getting travel insurance if you book a package but never buy it from the packager (if the company goes belly up, you lose all your money).

- Finally, look for **hidden expenses.** Ask whether airport departure fees and taxes, or fuel surcharges, for example, are included in the total cost. Particularly with security fees after the September 11, 2001, terrorist attacks, these charges can add up in a hurry to the $250-plus range if you're going through multiple airports. Italian **car rentals** also can add a nearly **20% tax** on top of an already high rate. On a positive note, many places offer a **hidden savings**—a good 10% or more if you pay for the package with cash.

TRAVEL INSURANCE—DO YOU NEED IT?

Check your existing insurance policies and credit card coverage before you buy travel insurance. You may already be covered for lost luggage, canceled tickets, or medical expenses.

The cost of travel insurance varies widely, depending on the price and length of your trip, your age and health, and the type of trip you're taking, but expect to pay between 5% and 8% of the vacation itself. You can get estimates from various providers through **InsureMyTrip.com.** Several reliable insurers with far-reaching benefits and a range of insurance options—from trip cancellation to medical coverage—are: **Access America** (☎ 800-2848300; www.accessamerica.com), **AIG Travel Guard** (☎ 800/826-4919; www.travelguard.com), **Travel Insured International** (☎ 800/243-3174; www.travelinsured.com), and **Travelex Insurance Services** (☎ 888/457-4602; www.travelex-insurance.com).

TRIP-CANCELLATION INSURANCE Trip-cancellation insurance will help retrieve your money if you have to back out of a trip or depart early, or if your travel supplier goes bankrupt. Permissible reasons for trip cancellation can range from sickness to natural disasters to the State Department declaring a destination unsafe for travel. Today, there are even insurance policies that allow travelers to cancel without giving reason, but these tend to be much more expensive than standard policies. For more information, contact one of the recommended insurers above.

MEDICAL INSURANCE For travel overseas, most health plans (including Medicare and Medicaid) do not provide coverage, and the ones that do often require you to pay for services upfront, and reimburse you only after you return home. Even if your plan does cover overseas treatment, most out-of-country hospitals make you pay your bills upfront, and send you a refund only after you've returned home and filed the necessary paperwork with your insurance company. In addition to those insurers listed above, additional medical insurance can be obtained from **MEDEX Assistance** (☎ 800/732-5309; www.medexassist.com) or **Travel Assistance International** (☎ 800/821-2828 or 800/777-8710; www.travelassistance.com).

LOST-LUGGAGE INSURANCE On international flights (including U.S. portions of international trips), baggage coverage is limited to approximately $9.05 per pound, up to approximately $635 per checked bag. Travelers who have had luggage lost or stolen through baggage handler incompetence almost always get a bad deal when it comes time to be compensated. If you plan to check items more valuable than what's covered by the standard liability (never a good idea), see if your homeowner's policy covers your valuables, or get baggage insurance as part of your comprehensive travel-insurance package from one of the insurers recommended above. Don't buy insurance at the airport, where it's usually overpriced. Be sure to take any valuables or irreplaceable items with you in your carry-on luggage because many valuables (including books, money, jewelry, business papers, and electronics) aren't covered by airline policies. Most airlines require that you report delayed, damaged, or lost baggage within 4 hours of arrival. The airlines are required to deliver luggage, once found, directly to your house or destination free of charge.

GETTING AROUND

AIR TRAVEL WITHIN ITALY

It's unlikely that you'll need to fly within Italy, given the relatively compact size of the country and the ease of getting around by train. It's always useful to consider the time you spend getting to airports, checking in, waiting to board, waiting for take off, and then waiting again on the other side before obtaining transport from the airport into your destination city; oftentimes, you end up wasting precious time (and money) that a train trip would have spared you. The only time you may well want to consider using air transport is for trips between the far south (say Puglia) and the north (Liguria, or Venice, perhaps), or to get to Sicily (especially if you're not keen on water travel). Before plunging into the overpriced world of

Alitalia, consider Italy's no-frills airlines, Air Italy (www.airitaly.it) and myair (www.myair.com), which both offer exceptional ticket prices and feature regular deals on their websites. These are also viable options if you're continuing to destinations elsewhere in Europe; also worth comparing is Wind Jet (www.volawind jet.it).

TRAINS

You can plan all train travel within Italy by using www.trenitalia.com. Once you've registered with the site, you can make online purchases of any and all train tickets, which you collect from machines at the station on the day of travel; just follow the collection instructions clearly, since these differ according to station of origin and type of train. It's a good idea to shop around on this site, comparing prices for journeys at different times. You'll need to balance your desire for low price with the amount of time you're prepared to spend traveling. Usually the quicker the trip, the higher the ticket price will be.

RENTAL CARS

Italy has the most expensive car-rental rates in Europe, partially because by law you must purchase more insurance there than in other countries. But there are ways to get a good deal. I've always found that **AutoEurope** (☎ 888-2235555; www.auto europe.com) significantly undercuts the prices of the major international car-rental agencies, sometimes by as much as 30% (a recent search for prices in Rome and Florence came up with specials as low as $36 per day, based on a 7-day rental period, and excluding taxes and other surcharges). I would suggest pricing its vehicles before looking at the other sites.

Travelers should also remember that smaller cars are not only less expensive, but they'll also be cheaper to gas up (gasoline is heavily taxed and therefore quite expensive throughout Europe) and easier to drive in the narrow cobblestone streets of Italy's ancient cities. Keep in mind, too, that manual transmission vehicles are significantly less expensive than those with automatic transmission.

SAVING MONEY ON ACCOMMODATIONS

Throughout this guide, you'll find information on alternative accommodations—B&Bs, monasteries and convents that accept guests, apartment rentals, and even the occasional hostel (which will usually have basic private rooms). A number of Italian hoteliers (especially smaller ones) will also give discounts for longer stays, cash payments, and even the presentation of this book.

Here are three more general money-saving tips:

SURF THE WEB   Don't forget to check the hotel's website: Sometimes you'll find discounts there that the reservationist may forget to tell you about if you use the phone. Then compare those prices with those offered by online booking services. Such sites as **Venere.com, Sidestep, Hotels.com,** and **Quikbook** can be very helpful for zeroing in on "distressed merchandise": hotel rooms that have gone unsold and are therefore available at a discount. For last-minute travel, you can also find very good deals on the British site **LateRooms.** Look at all your options before booking, especially if you're considering a multinight stay (some hotels give discounts for those, but only to customers booking direct). Whenever booking via the Web, be sure to **get a confirmation number** and **make a printout** of any online booking transaction.

In the opaque website category, **Priceline** (www.priceline.com) is an excellent option, though in general it's much better at getting five-star lodging for three-star prices than at finding anything at the bottom of the scale, and you need to check the details on their listings quite carefully because they often get the location muddled, for example. Before booking on Priceline head to www.biddingfor travel.com, the website where users of Priceline spill the beans on how much they paid and what they got (it's an extraordinarily useful site). For both Priceline and its competitor Hotwire, you pay upfront before knowing what hotel you've gotten, and the fee is nonrefundable. One thing you should bear in mind is that these sites don't really work for smaller destinations, and they overlook all the interesting, intimate, and "local" establishments.

If you have a specific hotel in mind, be sure to check the big three on the Web: **Travelocity** (www.travelocity.com), **Expedia** (www.expedia.com), and **Orbitz** (www.orbitz.com). These monolithic sites offer a variety their competitors can't match, and while their lowest prices usually aren't quite as low, for midrange and luxury hotels they tend to be quite competitive.

LOOK INTO *AGRITURISMO*   This is the Italian government's "farm stay" program, and all lodgings covered by it must derive at least half their revenues from farm products. Whether that's always the case is up in the air (there are a good number of hotels that plant a few olive trees out back and call themselves *agriturismi;* over 2,500 establishments are certified as *agriturismi* in Tuscany alone). But in many cases your stay will be an idyllic adventure, your lodging a 400-year-old stone farmhouse surrounded by vineyards.

So how do you make a selection? We've included a number of *agriturismo* options in this book. Or turn to the feds. The government has created a rating system, with one to five ears of corn (no, really) ranking the facilities, amenities, and rooms for each establishment. Decide what you're looking for in a "farm holiday," whether it be a rustic horse-riding ranch (Rendola Riding; p. 191) or a full-service hotel with swimming pool (Le Silve Hotel; p. 211). This book includes many *agriturismo* options; you may also want to also look at the following two sites for additional information:

- ◆ **www.agriturismo.regione.toscana.it**: A helpful, government-run site focused on rural accommodations and farm stays in Tuscany with a searchable database by subregion.
- ◆ **www.agriturismo.com**: A privately run site with direct links to a number of "farms," including places in Puglia, Liguria, the Veneto, and Sicily. Look out for last-minute offers posted on this site.

CONSIDER A HOME EXCHANGE   House swapping is becoming a more popular and viable means of travel; you stay in their place, they stay in yours, and you both get an authentic and personal view of the area, the opposite of the escapist retreat that many hotels offer. Many people simply do this informally, staying at the homes of friends or friends of friends. If you don't know anyone in

Italy, though, try **HomeLink International** (www.homelink.org), the oldest home-swapping organization, founded in 1952, with over 13,000 listings worldwide ($110 for a yearly membership). You'll find numerous homeowners across Italy specifically requesting exchanges with the owners in the United States. **HomeExchange.com** ($100 for 17,000 listings) is the same website that enabled Cameron Diaz and Kate Winslet to swap homes and alter the course of their lives in the 2006 film *The Holiday* (although you're unlikely to meet Jack Black or Jude Law in your swapped-out home in Italy). **InterVac** (www.intervac.com; $95 for over 20,000 listings in 50 countries) is also reliable.

MONEY MATTERS

Italy is fully integrated into the euro system, and ATMs (known as *bancomat* in Italy) are readily available; they typically accept all cards bearing Visa, Eurocard/MasterCard, Maestro, and Cirrus symbols. Best of all, the rate of exchange at ATMs always beats that of the exchange bureaus targeting tourists. However, you may have to contend with hefty user fees, sometimes as much as $8 per transaction, but sometimes free (look for a bank with a "refund all fees" policy; many credit unions also charge low fees for usage abroad). It's good to have backup in case a machine eats your card, your wallet gets stolen, or the like. Either bring an alternate ATM card, or bring two or three traveler's checks. Traveler's checks can be more hassle than they're worth, but they do offer the security of being replaced if they're stolen.

Credit cards are another safe way to carry money. They provide an excellent rate of exchange and a convenient record of all your expenses. But try to never use them for cash advances, which carry a very high interest rate. Keep in mind that many banks now assess a 1% to 3% "transaction fee" on all charges you incur abroad (whether you're using the local currency or U.S. dollars). To report a stolen or lost **American Express** card, call ☎ 800/864046; for **MasterCard,** ☎ 800/870866; for **Visa,** ☎ 800/819014.

Credit cards are widely accepted for accommodations and restaurant payments; Visa and MasterCard have far deeper reach than American Express or Discover due to the high charges levied by the latter two companies. It's a good idea to carry more than one card, just in case one is not accepted or if there's a problem with the terminal that links one of your cards to the authorizing institution. Many smaller hotels and B&Bs are loath to accept cards and would prefer you pay with cash; they'll usually offer a discount for cash payments.

HEALTH & SAFETY

Tourism is big business for Italy, so the authorities do their best to ensure that **heavily touristed areas are safe** at any time day or night, meaning violent crime against tourists is exceedingly rare. That being said, tourists are a target for petty theft, from pickpocketing to the theft of goods left in rental cars. Never carry large amounts of money on your person, keep your passport in a safe at your hotel, and consider using a money belt to better hide your money. Fanny packs are the worst place to keep money or valuables; they're easily opened and mark you as a tourist. Do not leave bags next to tables or chairs in restaurants and cafes, and—even worse—don't hang them over the backs of chairs. Be vigilant about bags hanging loosely over shoulders, and make sure that bags are zipped or clipped shut after you retrieve something.

As for health dangers, traveling through Italy in the heat of summer brings on the threat of **heatstroke** or **sunstroke,** particularly for those determined to see a number of sights in a single day. A couple of basic rules:

* **Relax:** Unless you're a guidebook writer on deadline, you don't have rush to cover every sight in town.
* **Stay hydrated:** Keep a bottle of water with you, and replenish as the day goes on. *A note on water:* Italian tap water is perfectly safe to drink, which means it is unnecessary to buy bottled water (an expensive and environmentally questionable indulgence)—rather keep a reusable bottle with you and refill this whenever the opportunity presents itself.
* **Stay covered:** Wear a cap, sunglasses, and sunscreen to escape the blazing sun; carry a parasol or umbrella if you'd prefer a sense of being in the shade. Take some breaks in the shade, and take some breaks in the middle of the day—this is what the Italians do, and they've been living here for a couple of thousand years, so they should know.

SPECIALIZED TRAVEL RESOURCES

FOR FAMILIES

Italy is an extremely family-friendly country. Children are given free or highly discounted admission to almost all attractions. It's not at all unusual to see children out with their parents for a night at a *trattoria;* there are playgrounds and parks in every city and small town; and the Italians simply love kids, meaning that if your baby starts to squall in a museum or restaurant, you won't get the evil looks you might in other countries. (In fact, you're more likely to get offers of help.) Of course, you're going to want to make sure that you approach the vacation in a sensible way: Mix and match museum days with days spent simply kicking back at the local park, and skip the wine tastings in favor of a bike ride or a paddle on a nearby river. There's lots in Italy to keep the kids involved.

What isn't always easy is finding hotel lodgings with enough space to squeeze in an extra bed or two, plus all those extra bags; you'll really battle to cope with the average bathroom size, particularly when you need to assist kids. Always inquire about such matters when making a reservation and be specific about the amount of space you need if you feel that it's likely to be an issue. Better still, go for apartment rentals wherever possible; you'll find solutions discussed throughout this book.

FOR TRAVELERS WITH DISABILITIES

Italy isn't the most convenient country for travelers with disabilities, with narrow sidewalks, uneven cobblestone streets, and historical-preservation laws that prevent certain old buildings from becoming barrier-free. But many museums and churches have been adding ramps and elevators to increase accessibility. The newer transit lines also have increased space and usability for those with disabilities.

In general, most disabilities shouldn't stop anyone from traveling. There are more options and resources out there than ever before. Many travel agencies offer customized tours and itineraries for travelers with disabilities. A company called **Accessible Journeys** (☎ 800/846-4537 or 610/521-0339; www.disabilitytravel. com) caters specifically to slow walkers and wheelchair travelers and their families and friends. To find other such U.S.-based operations, consult with **SATH (Society for Accessible Travel & Hospitality)** (☎ 212/447-7284; www.sath.org; annual membership fees: $49 adults, $29 students and seniors aged 63-plus), which offers a wealth of travel resources for all types of disabilities and informed recommendations on destinations, access guides, travel agents, tour operators, vehicle rentals, and companion services. The **American Foundation for the Blind (AFB)** (☎ 800/232-5463; www.afb.org), is a helpful referral resource for the blind or visually impaired that includes information on traveling with Seeing Eye dogs. And **MossRehab** (www.mossresourcenet.org) provides a library of accessible-travel resources online.

Italy-specific resources for travelers with disabilities include **Italia Per Tutti (Italy for All)** (www.italiapertutti.it); the website asks you what region you're visiting and what service you require (accommodation, dining, transport, or other), and then spits out recommendations based on elected accessibility criteria (from allergies through reduced mobility, blindness, impaired hearing, and more); it also searches for options that can cater to specific special needs. Within Italy, you may want to contact **SuperAbile** (call center ☎ 800-810810; www.superabile.it), an organization with extensive info on places (accommodations and restaurants, in particular) that cater to people with disabilities; the website is only in Italian.

FOR SENIOR TRAVELERS

Many Italian museums, and some bus and rail lines, offer reduced rates to seniors 65 or older (some have 60-plus discounts). To fish for discounts, mention that you're a senior: *un anciano* (for men) or *una anciana* (for women).

A number of reliable agencies and organizations target the 50-plus market. Boston-based **Elderhostel** (☎ 800/454-5768; www.elderhostel.org) arranges study programs for seniors 55 and over (and a spouse or companion of any age) in more than 90 countries, including Italy. Most courses last 2 to 4 weeks, and many include airfare, accommodations in university dormitories or modest inns, meals, and tuition. Award-winning **Grand Circle Travel** (☎ 800/959-0405; www.gct.com), in business since 1958, is one of the leaders in the field and consequently has greater buying power than many of its competitors. All its trips feature easygoing itineraries, perfect for older travelers or travelers with disabilities, and decently priced tours (in 2008, a 14-day, all-inclusive guided tour of Tuscan towns—with airfare—costs $2,995). Its "Discovery Series" events bring travelers into contact with locals with events such as cooking classes, visits with schoolchildren, and meals in private homes.

Recommended publications offering travel resources and discounts for seniors include the quarterly magazine *Travel 50 & Beyond* (www.travel50andbeyond. com); *Travel Unlimited: Uncommon Adventures for the Mature Traveler* (Avalon); *101 Tips for Mature Travelers*, available from Grand Circle Travel (see above); and *Unbelievably Good Deals and Great Adventures That You Absolutely Can't Get Unless You're Over 50* (McGraw-Hill), by Joann Rattner Heilman.

FOR GAY & LESBIAN TRAVELERS

While Italy is a traditional Catholic country in many respects, it has become more tolerant of homosexuality in recent years. That being said, aside from a few larger cities like Florence and Rome, there isn't much of a gay "scene." Or, rather, you need to put in a little effort to discover where the scene is happening. But Italy does have a national support group, **ARCI-Gay/Lesbica** (www.arcigay.it), headquartered in Bologna with "political and recreational" offices in cities across the country offering information and welfare services; there are over 150,000 members.

The **International Gay and Lesbian Travel Association (IGLTA)** (☎ 800/448-8550 or 954/776-2626; www.iglta.org) is the trade association for the gay-and-lesbian travel industry, and offers an online directory of friendly travel businesses; go to their website and click on "Members." **Gay.com Travel** (☎ 800/929-2268 or 415/644-8044; www.gay.com/travel), is an excellent online successor to the popular *Out & About* print magazine.

The following travel guides are available at many bookstores, or you can order them from any online bookseller: *Frommer's Gay & Lesbian Europe* (www.frommers.com), an excellent travel resource to the top European cities and resorts; *Spartacus International Gay Guide* (Bruno Gmünder Verlag; www.spartacusworld.com/gayguide; $32.95/£19.95/28.95€) and *Odysseus: The International Gay Travel Planner* (Odysseus Enterprises Ltd.; www.odyusa.com), both good, annual, English-language guidebooks focused on gay men; and the **Damron guides** (www.damron.com), with separate, annual books for gay men and lesbians (online subscription is available for $31.95 a year).

FOR STUDENTS

Arm yourself with an **International Student Identity Card (ISIC),** which offers substantial savings on rail passes, plane tickets, and entrance fees. It also provides you with basic health and life insurance and a 24-hour help line. The card is available for $22 from **STA Travel** (☎ 800/781-4040; www.sta.com or www.statravel.com), the biggest student travel agency in the world. If you're no longer a student but are still under 26, you can get an **International Youth Travel Card (IYTC)** for the same price from the same people, which entitles you to many discounts. **Travel CUTS** (☎ 800/667-2887 or 416/614-2887; www.travelcuts.com) offers similar services for both Canadians and U.S. residents. Irish students may prefer to turn to **USIT** (☎ 01-6021906; www.usitnow.ie), an Ireland-based specialist in student, youth, and independent travel. Australian and U.K. students should consider deals and offers presented by **Student Flights** (www.studentflights.com), a division of Flight Centre; they organize good deals on air travel, working holidays, and student cards.

Many museums and cultural attractions throughout Italy offer substantial discounts to students—as long as you are simply carrying your valid student identity card. In some instances, these discounts will only be available to E.U. citizens; in other situations, you'll get the discount simply for being under a certain age (which may vary from place to place). Always ask if there is a youth or student discount.

RECOMMENDED READING

Beyond this guidebook, you can increase your enjoyment of Italy immensely by doing some reading before you arrive. Here are some of my recommendations for fun, informative reads.

NONFICTION

To learn more about Renaissance-era Florence, pick up a copy of *Brunelleschi's Dome,* by Ross King, an entertaining account of the creation of the dome of the Duomo in Florence in the 15th century. It's a must-read before climbing to the top. *April Blood,* by Lauro Martines, is another page turner about the Pazzi family's plot against the Medicis in Florence in 1478. For a straight historical text, try Harry Hearder's *Italy, A Short History.*

The first of two wonderful biographical approaches to Italy is Norman Lewis's *Naples '44: An Intelligence Officer in the Italian Labyrinth;* one of my all-time favorites, it's the story of a British soldier getting his first taste of Italian culture during the chaos of World War II. The second is *Pietro's Book* by Jenny Bawtree, the biography of a Tuscan farmer that gives a much better feeling for the hard countryside life than do the slew of the "Oh, it's so tough to build a vacation home" books on the market. If that's what you want, you'll get it in *Under a Tuscan Sun* (Frances Mayes), in which the writer shares her sensual experience of moving to and living in Tuscany.

A couple of older Italy travelogues still have entertainment value as well as valuable insights about the country. Mary McCarthy's 1956 *The Stones of Florence/Venice Observed* offers such sharp commentary it seems like it was written last year, not 50 years ago. And Mark Twain's 1878 *Innocents Abroad* is still a hilarious read, especially the chapters where he torments tour guides, complains incessantly, and rewrites history.

For an insight on contemporary Italian culture, try Tobias Jones's *The Dark Heart of Italy* (2003), which skewers Italian politics, the Mafia, and the Red Brigade, with scathing criticism of Silvio Berlusconi's "might makes right" regime. A lighter modern tale is told by Joe McGinnis in his book *The Miracle of Castel Di Sangro.* An account of a year with a small-town soccer team, it takes you into the heart of Italian *calcio* mania. For a look at contemporary Venetian society, read Michael Berendt's *The City of Falling Angels,* highlighting eccentricities and quirks of life in a city that distinguishes itself from—and above—all others.

A collection of Italy travel stories makes a good companion for a trip around Italy. Try *Travelers' Tales Italy,* edited by Anne Calcagno, which has 30 thematically organized stories about travelers' experiences across the country; also see *Travelers' Tales Tuscany* for stories focused there. *Tuscany in Mind,* edited by Alice Powers, is another nice compilation with 20 famous authors, from Dickens to Twain. For a women's take on the country, read *Italy, A Love Story,* edited by Camille Cusamano, in which two dozen women write about how their lives have been shaped by their experiences in Italy.

FICTION

The definitive Renaissance classic is Dante's *Divine Comedy (Inferno, Purgatory, Paradise)*—the epic poem that practically created the Italian language also has biting political commentary, with Dante's enemies ending up in various levels of hell. The Penguin Classics edition translated by Mark Mura has good commentary (essential for understanding all the obscure references) and cool maps of hell from prior editions. Boccaccio's *The Decameron,* also from the 14th century, is a bawdy collection of stories taking place at the time of the Black Death. If you can get through the archaic writing, it's a good read.

Historical fiction is a fun way to learn about the old days without reading a dry textbook. Written in 1960, Giuseppe di Lampedusa's *The Leopard,* recounts the last days of a fading aristocracy in Sicily counterbalanced with the political life of Italy in the 1860s. If you want more literature set in Sicily, look out for any of the novels of Leonardo Sciascia. Irving Stone's *The Agony and the Ecstasy* (1961) adds drama and intrigue to the life and times of Michelangelo. In *The Name of the Rose,* postmodern philosopher and novelist Umberto Eco uses the framework of a murder mystery taking place in a 14th-century Italian abbey to debate the essence of literature, history, and religion. Get a softer take on Naples in *Falling Palace: A Romance of Naples* (Dan Hofstadter), and an intriguing historical look at that city with Vesuvius firmly in the near background in Susan Sontag's brilliant *The Volcano Lover.*

ITALY ON THE BIG SCREEN

The influential Italian Neo-Realist movement—which sought to erase the superficiality of the silver screen's interpretation of life into fantasy—includes films that take a raw look at Italian social reality during some of the more turbulent periods of the last century; there's none finer than Vittorio De Sica's *Bicycle Thieves* (1947), regarded as one of the most important films ever made. Roberto Rossellini's *Rome, Open City* (1945) is in a similar vein, incorporating actual documentary footage of the time. A better bet, by far, is to spend a night with a handful of films by Federico Fellini, arguably Italy's greatest filmmaker; they provide colorful (and oftentimes hallucinatory) insight into the Italian psyche. Fellini's classics are near-surreal works of dreamlike storytelling; they include *8½* (1963) and *La Dolce Vita* (1968), but my favorite has got to be his ode to teenage memories in a tiny, idiosyncratic village of the 1930s—*Amarcord* (roughly "I Remember," 1974) is an exuberant celebration of life in Italy, and plays out in Rimini (where Fellini was born) where the grip of Fascism is humorously satirized.

The ABCs of Italy

Area Codes The international country code for Italy is **39;** you'll need to dial this after entering the international access code from wherever you're calling, and then dial the city code (for example **06** for Rome and **55** for Florence), which is now built into every number. To make international calls from within Italy, first dial 00, followed by the country code (U.S. and Canada are 1, U.K. is 44, Ireland is 353, Australia is 61, New Zealand is 64), destination area code, and then the specific number you are trying to reach; for some countries (like the U.K. and Ireland) you must omit the zero at the start of the area code. When calling within Italy, always include the three- or four-digit area code before dialing the required landline number, even if you are calling from the same area. Mobile phone numbers in Italy begin with 3.

Business Hours Shops almost all close for afternoon *siesta,* which may stretch from 1 to 4pm (or later), but seems to vary with the whims of individual storeowners. When shops reopen (which they need not necessarily do should someone not be feeling quite up to it), they stay open until around 8pm. Sunday is a well-observed day of rest for most businesses. Cities that are entirely sustained by tourism (like Venice) tend not to subscribe to this national cultural policy, and you may be able to shop throughout the afternoon and even on Sunday. Banks are usually open Monday through Friday from 8:20am until 1:20pm and then from 2:45 to 3:45pm. They will be shut on all public holidays, and when there's a holiday coming up (that is, on the following day) you'll likely find them closed in the afternoon.

Drinking Laws The legal age for the purchase and consumption of alcohol is 16. From the age of 16 you can drink wine and beer in a bar or pub, although you're not legally entitled to order spirits until you're 18.

Electricity Italian electrics work on 220 volts AC (50 cycles) that is standard in Europe, Australia, and New Zealand. If your small appliances use 110 or 120 volts (if you're North American, in other words), be sure to buy an adaptor and voltage converter before you leave home if you can find one, or pick one up when you arrive. You'll need a two-pin plug adapter, too, easily available in Italy.

Embassies Embassies are in Rome: **United States** (Via Vittorio Veneto 119/A; ☎ 06-46741; http://rome.us embassy.gov); **Australia** (Via Alessandria 215; ☎ 06-852721; www.italy.embassy. gov.au); **Canada** (Via Giovanni Battista De Rossi 27; ☎ 06-854441; www. dfait-maeci.gc.ca/canada-europa/italy/ ambassador_ita-en.asp); **Ireland** (Piazza di Campitelli 3; ☎ 06-6979121); **New Zealand** (Via Zara 28; ☎ 06-4417171;

www.nzembassy.com); **United Kingdom** (Via XX Settembre 80a; ☎ 06-42200001; www.britishembassy.gov.uk).

Emergencies Call ☎ **112** for the *carabinieri* (military police), or ☎ **113** for the *polizia.* To report a fire call ☎ **115**, and to get an ambulance call ☎ **118.** If you have a medical emergency that does not require an ambulance, you should be able to walk into the nearest hospital emergency room, called *pronto soccorso.* If your car breaks down, you can contact **Italy's Automobile Club** at ☎ **803-116.**

Smoking You may find it hard to believe but there are actually laws in Italy prohibiting smoking in public spaces, including bars and restaurants and on public transport (and anywhere where the VIETATO FUMARE [NO SMOKING] sign is displayed). These rules tend to be disobeyed with alarming regularity, but not to the extent that you'll be offended.

Telephone My advice is to bring a cellphone (as long as it's a GSM phone that operates on 900, 1800, or 1900 bands) with you and then purchase a local SIM card upon arrival in Italy; I use Tim, which supposedly has the best coverage and service. Just go into the first shop you see that sells mobile phones or similar technology and they'll either be able to help you or point to the nearest mobile phone operator. Once you've bought the SIM card, be sure to get it activated. For international visitors these can be the least expensive way to call home. You can also have the phone with you wherever you go, so it's ideal if you need to call for directions or assistance. Try to have the numbers of places where you intend to stay on you all the time so you'll always have a "friendly" local whom you can call when you're in a tight spot. Pay phones are temperamental and inconvenient; you'll pay .10€ for a basic local call—almost all public phones require you to have purchased a prepaid phone card (from a *tabacchi*), although some accept credit cards and some still take coins. You can also get special phone cards for international calls (again, from a tabacchi) which can be used in pay phones as well as private phones and work with units that are deducted as you talk. Reverse-charge calls are made by dialing ☎ 170; this will connect you with one of Italy's international operators.

Time Italy is an hour ahead of GMT, which means when it's noon in London, it's 1pm in Rome. Italy is 6 hours ahead of New York. Daylight saving moves clocks an hour ahead at the start of spring, and an hour back in autumn.

16 Italy: A Closer Look

THE CUISINE OF ITALY
by Bill Fink

Anyone looking for the quintessential Italian meal is likely to be disappointed. Why? Because there's no such thing.

To be sure, there's plenty of Tuscan fare. And Neapolitan specialties are available across the land. But Italian cuisine? You may as well request "Earth Cuisine" or "The Table of the Northern Hemisphere."

Like the history of the Italian provinces that spawned it, Italian cuisine has a highly regionalized, even localized, character. And these distinctions are serious. Ranging from the selection of the ingredients to the method of preparation to the ceremony of the meal, Italian dining could be considered the second major religion of Italy (after Roman Catholicism, and slightly ahead of soccer). Here's a quick review of Italy's regional specialties, moving from north to south.

Northern Italian cuisine has a strong flavor of the French, German, and Austrian traditions. **Piedmont,** to the northeast, serves Swiss-like *fonduta* (fondue), a concoction of melted cheese mixed with butter, milk, and egg yolks. *Bagna cauda* is a vegetable-dipping variation made with the addition of olive oil, garlic, and anchovies. Just west of Piedmont, in **Lombardy,** the locals like their *cotoletta alla milanese,* veal cutlets in egg and olive-oil batter. It took a while for Marco Polo's pasta to make it up to these parts, so polenta (cornmeal) and risotto (rice) often serve as the starches for a meal. **Trentino** carries on the Austrian-German traditions of its neighbors to the north, with heavier meat-and-potato dishes, along with an endless selection of strudels.

Venice, as befits its maritime tradition, features seafood, and grilled fish is often served with the regional red radicchio. Don't leave town without sampling *sarde in soar* (marinated sardines) and nibbling on *ciccheti,* the Venetian equivalent of aperitif snacks, served smorgasbord-style at bars throughout the city and best enjoyed with a glass of *prosecco* or *spritz* (a uniquely Venetian concoction usually consisting of *prosecco* and Campari). And in the Veneto region, surrounding Venice, you'll regularly find horse meat in everything from stews to pizza toppings. **Liguria,** on the opposite northern coast, boasts menus full of seafood, including a spicy *burrida* fish stew resembling French bouillabaisse, but it's the world famous pesto that originated here that you simply have to try, preferably with *trofie,* the local pasta.

When pressed, many Italians outside the **Emilia-Romagna** region of Bologna, Ravenna, Parma, and Ferrara grudgingly admit that this area may have the best Italian cuisine; certainly, items like spaghetti *alla bolognese* (with meat sauce) will instantly appeal to visiting tourists. Most permutations of pasta shapes came from this region: *tagliatelle* (long strips of macaroni), *cappelletti* (little, hat-shaped pasta), *tortellini* (small dough squares stuffed with meats), and lasagna (layered squares of pasta mixed with layers of meat or vegetables). *Parmigiano* cheese, of course, comes from Parma, which is also known for its hams.

The tables of **Tuscany,** which is south of Emilia-Romagna, will always await you with a bottle of the region's fine olive oils (although sometimes less responsible eateries will "forget" to leave a bottle on a tourist's table—some locals think their expensive specialty will be wasted on a foreign palate, so request it if you don't see it). Tuscan dishes are characterized by hearty peasant fare, meats, and pastas with tomato-based sauces. Florence is famous for its *bistecca alla fiorentina,* a thick steak of Chianina beef charcoal-grilled to juicy perfection.

Umbria, still farther south, is a center for truffles; be sure to sample some shavings of the local fungi on your pasta when in season. Game dishes such as hare, wild boar *(cingiale),* and venison dot the menus of many Umbrian kitchens.

Rome, the largest and most central Italian city, offers the best chance for a one-stop experience of the country's cuisines. Located near the sea, Rome offers many seafood specialties, including dishes like *scampia alla griglia* (grilled prawns), *zuppa di pesce* (fish stew with white wine and spices), and *fritto di scampi e calimaretti* (fried squid and prawns). Characteristic pastas include the stuffed, tube-shaped cannelloni and the potato-flour dumplings of *gnocchi alla romana* (covered in meat sauce and cheese). Try the *saltimbocca alla romana* (thin-sliced veal and ham with cheese and sage) or *carciofi alla romana* (artichokes cooked in white wine with mint, garlic, and other herbs).

Southern Italian cuisine is well represented by the foods of **Naples,** which include thin-base pizzas, clam sauce pastas, and mozzarella cheeses. Across Italy, locals will point you to the nearest Neapolitan restaurant to find the best pizza in town, so don't miss a chance to try some in this center of the pizza universe. Fresh fried fish in Naples is also a standard dish. Just off the coast of Naples, the isle of Capri is home to the famous Caprese salad, made with the best buffalo mozzarella in the country. On the other side of southern Italy, **Puglia** features fare heavy on vegetables and seafood, as well as such specialties as orecchiette ("little ear" pasta), with sautéed local greens. The region also boasts an abundance of local cheeses.

The hot hills of **Sicily** have spawned a strong-tasting, often spicy, cuisine. *Maccheroni con le sarde* is a traditional Sicilian spaghetti with sardines and olive oil flavored with pine nuts, fennel, and other spices. At smaller coastal towns, order fish fresh off the boat; swordfish is quite popular and tasty. *Involtini siciliani* are bread-covered meat rolls stuffed with egg, ham, and cheese. Sicily is also famous for its desserts. Its *cannoli* pastries, stuffed with ricotta or chocolate, and its *gelati* ice creams are considered some of the best in Italy.

THE CHOICE OF RESTAURANTS

So where to go? The major categories of Italian restaurants are the bar, the *trattoria,* the osteria, and the *ristorante.* An Italian bar is more of a cafe (not to be confused with a pub) that serves coffee, sodas, and sometimes ice cream and snacks. Stop at a bar for a quick panino and a drink. But be careful: The prices usually double if you sit at one of their tables; if you're counting euros, it's best to either chow down at the bar or wander off to eat in the shade.

The differences between osterias, *trattorie,* and *ristoranti* are less distinct than they once were. Traditionally, an osteria was a rustic and rudimentary open kitchen in which travelers could grab a plate of pasta and a glass of wine. A trattoria represented a step up the food chain, so to speak, offering multicourse meals with a selection of wine in a traditional setting. And a ristorante had a formal atmosphere, with linen tablecloths, wine lists, professional waitstaff, and a bit of ceremony in the presentation. But now ristoranti have added the word "osteria" or "trattoria" to their titles to seem more authentic, while the osterias and trattorie have been passing themselves off as ristoranti in an effort to jack up prices. Regardless, the quality of food can be first class at any of these; try them all and reach your own conclusions.

Finally, remember to factor in the *coperto* charge, aka *pan e coperto* (bread and cover) into the cost of your meal. This initial expense ranges from 1€ to 4€ at many places. Look at the menu displayed at the door, where the charge is often disclosed (along with a service charge of up to 15%), or else you'll be surprised to find yourself paying double for that cheap snack of pasta and tap water. Unless it's a particularly famous restaurant, try to avoid any place with more than a 2€ coperto.

A BRIEF HISTORY OF ITALY
by Reid Bramblett

One of the major reasons to come to Italy is to look at, live in, and walk through more than 2,000 years of vivid history. In a sense, the entire nation is a huge, open-air museum. You can hardly kick a soccer ball in Italy without hitting some kind of historical structure, from Roman amphitheaters to Renaissance statues.

The following history of Italy focuses on major dates and associated sights of interest to travelers. For a more detailed history, check out some of the books in the "Recommended Reading" section of chapter 15.

PRE-ROMAN TIMES

As many statues (and AS Roma soccer logos) commemorate, Rome was founded in 730 B.C. by the brothers Romulus and Remus. According to legend, a she-wolf discovered the brothers in the woods and suckled them to good health. Remus's son Senius went on to found Siena, where additional statues can be seen.

If you're not buying that story, a slightly more reliable one has Etruscan tribes unifying across north-central Italy in the 8th century B.C. to create the first statelike entity on "the boot." The Etruscans defeated Latin tribes and made Rome their capital about 600 B.C.

The Etruscans continued to be a strong presence in trade, war, culture, and shipping, until first losing in Greek naval wars in the 4th century B.C. and then becoming subjugated and fully absorbed into the Roman Empire by the 2nd century B.C.

SIGHTS Etruscan ruins dot the country, with their largest concentration in Volterra, in Tuscany, and the

Dateline

800 B.C. Etruscan tribes begin to consolidate control of north-central Italy, creating Italy's first nation-state.

510 B.C. Roman Republic is established.

250 B.C. Roman and other forces defeat the Etruscans, marking the beginning of the Roman Empire.

50 B.C. Rome rules all of Mediterranean Europe.

45 B.C. Julius Caesar becomes ruler of Rome.

44 B.C. Caesar is assassinated.

27 B.C. Caesar Augustus becomes emperor, marking the beginning of Pax Romana and the Golden Age of Rome.

necropolis southeast of Tarquina. Many Roman walls, wells, and roads across north-central Italy are based on Etruscan foundations. Etruscan tomb relics and tablets can be seen in many museums across Italy, including the Museo Nazionale di Villa Giulia in Rome.

THE ROMAN EMPIRE

The Roman Republic began in 510 B.C. when Latin tribes evicted the Etruscans from Rome. Through a combination of alliances, colonization, and efficient infrastructure-building, Roman armies expanded throughout Italy—building roads, aqueducts, and walled cities as they went. With Rome's triumph in the Punic Wars, and with the destruction of Carthage in the 3rd century B.C., Rome became the greatest power in the Mediterranean region.

The generals and armies of Rome expanded across Mediterranean Europe through the 1st century B.C. Julius Caesar conquered most of what is now France to the Rhine River and invaded Britain. Pompey led armies to the east, conquering what is now Syria and Asia Minor. In 60 B.C., Caesar, Pompey, and Marcus Crassus (a leader in Rome) allied to create the First Triumvirate to rule the empire. Following Crassius's death in battle, a civil war broke out between Caesar and Pompey. Caesar defeated Pompey's armies in 45 B.C. and returned to Rome a hero. He seized power to effectively become dictator of the Roman Empire, which now stretched from the Atlantic Ocean to the Black Sea.

Julius Caesar ruled for 1 short year. In 44 B.C., he was assassinated by senators eager to re-establish the Republic. Mark Antony (Caesar's top general) briefly shared power with Caesar's adopted son Octavian and Marcus Lepidus in the Second Triumvirate from 43 to 32 B.C. Naturally, they couldn't get along, either, and another civil war broke out. Antony fled to Egypt, hiding out with his mistress, Cleopatra, until they both committed suicide as Octavian's armies and navies swept through the region.

The Golden Age

The rule of Octavian (now known as Caesar Augustus) from 27 B.C. to A.D. 14 launched the "Golden Age of Rome" and the 200 years of the Pax Romana, during which the Roman armies kept Europe and the Middle East free from any major wars. Art, architecture, and commerce flourished during the time, with the major structures being built, including the Roman Forum, Colosseum, and Pantheon, as well as the Roman roads crisscrossing Europe.

A.D. 40 Emperor Caligula declares himself a god and names his horse to the senate.

300s Rome's decline is scored with corrupt emperors, collapsing regimes, and armies losing control.

Early 400s Rome is sacked by barbarian hordes.

800 Charlemagne is declared Holy Roman emperor, and his armies control most of Italy.

1200 Rise of power of Italian city-states like Florence, Genoa, and Venice.

1348 The Black Death/bubonic plague sweeps through Italy, killing a third to half of all inhabitants.

1401 Giotto completes Florence's Baptistery doors, making a convenient mark for the start of the Renaissance.

1498 Leonardo da Vinci paints *The Last Supper*.

1508–12 Michelangelo paints the Sistine Chapel.

1527 Charles V of France conquers Rome and becomes Holy Roman emperor.

1602 Galileo Galilei is among the first to use a telescope to study the stars and planets, collecting data to help prove a sun-centered solar system.

Not that all was quiet in Rome during the Golden Age. Succession battles raged following the death of emperors (rarely from natural causes). The Emperor Caligula famously married his sister, named his horse to the senate, had himself declared a god, and generally turned Rome into his personal nuthouse until he was assassinated in A.D. 41. Revolts in Palestine and the rise of Christianity (and its subsequent persecution) created continuous unrest throughout the realm.

The Fall

By the beginning of the 3rd century, the Roman Empire was wracked with civil wars, barbarian invasions, and domestic unrest. Following the death of Marcus Aurelius, in 180, the empire began its slow but steady decline. During the next 73 years, 23 different emperors "ruled" the empire. In 306, Constantine became the first Christian emperor, relocating the capital from Rome to Constantinople (now Istanbul). In 395, the empire formally split between the western section in Rome and the eastern section in Constantinople.

The barbarian hordes reached the gates of Rome in 410, with the Visigoths being the first to sack the city. Attila the Hun swept through Italy in the 450s, and the Vandals made a name for themselves with a savage destruction of Rome in 455. Competing groups battled for control for the next 100 years, leaving Rome a depopulated, crumbling husk of a city to begin the Dark Ages.

SIGHTS   Virtually every construction in Italy has some foundation in the Roman era. Rome obviously has the bulk of the sights, with the Colosseum, Pantheon, and Forum being three of the top attractions. Roman amphitheaters cover the country, from Verona to Gubbio to Arezzo, and they continue to host performances. The National Archaeological Museum in Naples houses many relics from all eras of the Roman Empire.

DARK AGES TO EARLY MIDDLE AGES (A.D. 475–1000)

As my grade-school history teacher liked to say, the Dark Ages was the era in which "the light of civilization was nearly extinguished." Competing tribal armies fought across Italy, with the Goths and Lombards carving out areas of control. For their own survival, the popes became temporal power brokers as they allied with warlords to protect the Christian realm. Pope Leo III crowned Charlemagne emperor in 800, and the Christian king became a papal ally. After the era of Charlemagne came the Holy Roman Empire—the largest power base of the time. Battles between northern European forces, the Lombards, Normans, and various local groups created the decentralized, highly divided environment in which the Italian city-states arose in the Middle Ages.

SIGHTS   With one of the leading tribes of the time called the Vandals, it's no wonder there aren't too many historical relics from this era. Byzantine-styled religious relics (Ravenna is a center for this) and paintings are the bulk of art from this era.

MEDIEVAL ITALY (A.D. 1000 TO 14TH C.)

With the continual sweeps of competing armies through Italy, only the strongest, most self-sufficient Italian cities survived. The Middle Ages featured the rise of city-states including Venice, Genoa, and Pisa, with merchant fleets driving their economic growth. This era spawned the first of the merchant banks, whose money sponsored the armies and fortifications necessary to survive external attack. The era also featured the growth of the guild system, with artisans banding together to create cohesive economic and political groups within the cities. The crusades and pilgrim routes brought a number of travelers through the cities of northern and central Italy, further enriching the cities with trade. But southern Italy didn't experience the same economic progress, owing to Norman conquests and an extended period of feudalistic torpor.

As Italian city-states began to protect themselves from external invaders, they fell prey to internal strife. The rivalry between the Holy Roman Empire and papal forces created a multicentury family feud throughout Italy. While ostensibly a battle between the temporal powers of the empire and the spiritual powers of the pope, it was essentially a fight between two groups who wanted to be in charge. The "team" names were the Ghibellines (the "whites": pro-Emperor, feudalistic) and the Guelphs (the "blacks": pro-Pope, merchant-class). The struggle between these groups involved such luminaries as Dante and Machiavelli, both of whom were exiled from their hometowns for supporting the wrong team.

The second major internal disruption of the period came from the Black Death of 1348. Fleas carrying the bubonic plague bacteria arrived on the backs of rats riding trade ships from Asia. Between a third and half of the population of Italy died during a 6-month period. Crowded cities with little sanitation suffered the worst, and many never fully recovered.

1994 Billionaire Silvio Berlusconi is elected prime minister as part of "clean government" campaign.

1995 Berlusconi resigns as coalition dissolves and corruption trials loom.

2001 Berlusconi is re-elected prime minister with a huge majority vote.

2002 Euro is introduced as the currency of Italy.

2004 Berlusconi transfers $400,000 to judge's bank account.

2004 Judges dismiss all corruption charges against Berlusconi.

2005 New corruption charges are introduced against Berlusconi.

2006 Romano Prodi is elected prime minister, but heads a coalition government.

2007 Police shoot dead an innocent soccer fan, causing nationwide riots and protests.

2008 Silvio Berlusconi is elected prime minister for the third time.

Venice, Siena, San Gimignano, and Orvieto are among those almost frozen in time, with their 14th-century art and architecture, which is what makes them a boon for tourists.

SIGHTS   Pisa, Venice, Genoa, and Siena reached their apogee during this period. See the Romanesque architecture of Pisa, the Gothic cathedrals of Milan and Siena, and the Middle Eastern–influenced architecture and art of Venice. In Venice and Perugia are guildhalls from this period. Ruined medieval fortifications dot the countryside across northern and central Italy.

THE RENAISSANCE (LATE 14TH TO LATE 16TH C.)

The Renaissance, meaning "rebirth," signaled a second coming of the humanistic focus of the Greco-Roman classical period, as Italian thinkers started to study the works of that era. Michelangelo, da Vinci, Dante, Petrarch, and Galileo are just a few of the famed figures of this period. The unofficial beginning of the Renaissance might be 1401, with Giotto's famous carved doors of Florence's Baptistery. Florence itself is practically synonymous with the Renaissance; the entire city is a living reminder of the art, architecture, and politics of the time.

Politically, the Renaissance was the time of the Medicis, a power-hungry family of bankers and textile merchants based in Florence. The family first leveraged their finances to control local, and then regional, government, sponsoring and banking politicians and their armies. Soon, the Medicis took direct control of the city, essentially making themselves dictators, while installing their relatives as popes (Leo X and Clement VII) to expand their control nationwide. Lorenzo de' Medici (1449–92) is most tightly associated with the Renaissance, being a patron of Michelangelo and a Renaissance man himself: He had a career in art, politics, banking, hunting, and horsemanship.

As the era moved to the late 1500s, the Medicis, and others like them, tried to carry on their family fortunes through hereditary rule, rather than through legitimate business or political skill. Power-grabbing battles between (and inside) cities made them vulnerable to foreign invasion. When the king of Spain, Charles V, sacked Rome in 1527, it marked the beginning of the end of Italy's reign as the economic, political, and cultural center of Europe.

SIGHTS   Along with the Roman Era, the Renaissance is Italy's richest source for sights. Florence is practically a one-stop shop, with the city chock-full of artwork and buildings dating from the era, including the Uffizi Galleries, Michelangelo's *David* in the Accademia, and Brunelleschi's dome on the Cathedral. Rome's Sistine Chapel, da Vinci's *Last Supper* in Milan, and the National Gallery in Perugia are also emblematic of the progression of the arts through this period.

DARK AGES, PART II, AKA THE COUNTER-REFORMATION (1500–1850)

With the end of the reign of the powerful merchant families, the Roman Catholic Church once again became the most powerful Italian political, social, and military force. And as during the Church's first reign in the early Middle Ages, Italy became a feudalistic, static region. The Church led the Counter-Reformation to fight the Protestant movement and the teachings of Martin Luther. While some reforms were introduced to rein in corrupt clergy, and a new generation of churches was built, Italy suffered through the Inquisition, autocratic rule, and a medieval mentality which put it at the mercy of northern European rivals progressing economically, militarily, and artistically.

For a couple of hundred years Italy became a plaything for Spanish, French, and Austrian invaders whose armies conquered wide swaths of the country, sacking towns and ensuring continued misery for the citizens of the countryside. Napoleon declared himself emperor over the Kingdom of Italy in 1804, famously grabbing the crown from the Pope, whom he commanded to come to France for the ceremony. When Napoleon hit his Waterloo in 1815, Austrian overlords moved in to fill the power vacuum.

SIGHTS   This period is noted for elaborate baroque and rococo art, embodied by Rome's Spanish Steps and Trevi Fountain, the entire Sicilian town of Noto, and the churches of Lecce, as well as many older churches across Italy remodeled during this period at the behest of the counter-reforming Church.

ITALIAN UNIFICATION (LATE 19TH C.)

Despite its long history, Italy is a young country—its myriad cities and provinces unified in 1861. Italian unification is the story of the heart (Joseph Mazzini), the head (Camilo Cavour), and the sword (Giuseppe Garibaldi). Mazzini led some of the revolutionary activities sweeping Europe in 1848, writing and publicizing his radical and romantic plans for the unification of Italy. Cavour, a career politician and prime minister of Sardinia in 1852, picked up on Mazzini's passionate writings but modified them into a more practical plan, particularly in the face of the reactionary Church powers. Garibaldi, an Italian exile fresh from struggle for independence in Uruguay, led a military movement across Italy. Garibaldi's squadrons of armed "Red Shirts" coordinated with (or were manipulated by) Cavour's political element to unify nearly all of Italy outside of Rome and Venice (which were added after the Franco-Prussian war of 1870). The Vatican condemned the republic and remained in a cold war with it until a formal independence agreement was crafted in 1929.

SIGHTS   Garibaldi statues fill town squares across Italy, the most notable of which stands in front of an epic mountain view in Todi, Umbria. Piazza della Repubblica in Florence, with its triumphal arch, commemorates the brief period in which Florence served as capital of the new republic. The late 19th century featured many neoclassical monuments, particularly in areas under Napoleonic influence (such as Lucca's main square).

20TH-CENTURY ITALY

During World War I, Italy fought on the side of the Allies, having conducted a secret treaty in London that awarded Italy the Trentino, the south Tyrol, Trieste, and some Dalmatian Islands as an incentive for victory. For the most part, Italians weren't enthusiastic about the war and became less so after suffering large casualties on the northern front. Following the war, Italy suffered from the inflation and unemployment rampant throughout Europe in the 1920s.

Benito Mussolini took control of Italy with his Brown Shirt squads in the 1920s. Through ruthless executions and purges, he solidified his power, joining into an alliance with Hitler on the eve of World War II. His plan for a new Roman Empire extended to conquests over two nearly defenseless targets: the farmers of primitive Albania and the poison gas–aided victory over the tribes of Ethiopia. While many Italians embraced Mussolini as a newfound symbol of national pride, an equal number took part in the anti-Fascist, Partisan movement. The Allies invaded Sicily in 1943, and the Italian army surrendered about a minute later, but remaining German troops and Italian Fascists fought rear-guard actions through the country until 1945. The Partisans caught up to Mussolini in 1945 and strung his naked body (and that of his mistress) upside down from a gas station roof.

Postwar Italy provided a replay of prewar politics, with Fascist- and communist-dominated parties fighting for control of the country, struggles that continue to the present day. Following World War II, the U.S. Marshall Plan channeled huge sums of money to anti-communist elements in Italy. While this led many die-hard Fascists right back into the government, it also stimulated a rapid industrialization program that improved the standard of living across the country.

Since then, the saying is that there have been 50 changes of government in the 50 years after the war, but most of these were really different permutations of the same ruling party and shifting coalition partners. In the 1970s, a low-level civil war nearly arose, with communist Red Brigade terrorists kidnapping and killing politicians, and Fascist power brokers staging civilian bombings and arrests. Beginning in 1999, Silvio Berlusconi's coalition government (including neo-Fascist and racist groups) imposed some level of stability in the country, despite a series of corruption scandals. Because Berlusconi owns or controls seven of eight TV stations in the country, as well as Italy's largest publishing company, it's not surprising that many of these scandals didn't get much play in the local press. In April 2008, Berlusconi was re-elected prime minister after a 2-year hiatus out of office.

Index

660 Index